Characters in
CHILDREN'S
LITERATURE

Characters in CHILDREN'S LITERATURE

Raymond E. Jones

GALE

DETROIT · NEW YORK · TORONTO · LONDON

Gale Research Staff

Kevin S. Hile, *Senior Editor*
Joyce Nakamura, *Managing Editor*

Copyeditors: Diane Andreassi, Laurie Hillstrom, Marijke Rijsberman,
Doug Smith, and Michaela Swart Wilson
Proofreaders: Sharon R. Gunton, Janet L. Hile, Melissa Hill, Motoko
Fujishiro Huthwaite, and Crystal Towns

Mary Beth Trimper, *Production Director*
Evi Seoud, *Assistant Production Manager*
Shanna Heilveil, *Production Assistant*
Susan M. Trosky, *Permissions Manager*
Maria L. Franklin, *Permissions Specialist*

Michele Lonoconus, *Permissions Associate*
Cynthia Baldwin, *Product Design Manager*
Tracey Rowens, *Senior Art Director*
Randy Bassett, *Image Database Supervisor*
Mikal Ansari and Robert Duncan, *Imaging Specialists*

∞™ This book is printed on acid-free paper that meets the minimum requirements
of American National Standard for Information Services—Permanence Paper
for Printed Library Materials, ANSI Z39.48-1984.

Library of Congress Cataloging-in-Publication Data

Jones, Raymond E.
   Characters in children's literature / Raymond E. Jones
   p.   cm.
   Includes bibliographical references and index.
   ISBN 0-7876-0400-3 (alk. paper)
1. Children's literature—Stories, plots, etc. 2. Characters and characteristics in
literature. 3. Children's literature—Book reviews. 4. Children—Books and reading.
I. Title.
Z1037.A1J78   1997
[PN1009.A1]
809.3'0083—dc21   97-4999
                                                                           CIP

10 9 8 7 6 5 4 3 2 1
Printed in the United States of America

Contents

Contents

Preface

Introduction

Characters are the life-force of children's fiction. They perform actions, evoke emotions, and generate themes, making children's fiction entertaining, moving, memorable, and meaningful. Whether we encounter them first in childhood, when we are most impressionable, or in adulthood, when nostalgia may make especially appealing their energy, optimism, and apparent simplicity, the characters from children's literature usually become a vital part of our imaginations. Whatever their form—human, animal, or toy—these characters are so animated and idiosyncratic, so full of fun, and so charged with basic meaning that they live even outside the books that introduce them. Alice and Peter Pan, for example, are familiar figures of popular culture, known even to those who have never read the classics that recount their adventures.

The characters in children's literature support what Henry James once noted about characters in adult fiction. In "The Art of Fiction" James asked, "What is character but the determination of incident? What is incident but the illustration of character?" Because children's literature is concrete, event and character are inseparable, especially in works for younger audiences. In other words, character is action. Characters may have thoughts, dreams, and conversations, but they repeatedly define their identities, reveal their values, and establish their significance through physical action. The journeys that are such a prominent feature of children's stories are, for example, concrete expressions of inward development. In moving from one location to another, characters signal changes in maturation, self-worth, understanding, spiritual values, or social status. Readers who travel with these characters will pass through many imaginative realms, will experience exciting and trying adventures, and will face significant questions about identity and values. Above all, they will meet personalities who will give immediate pleasure and will linger in memory, where they will continue to amuse and inspire.

Scope of This Work

Characters in Children's Literature (CCL) is aimed primarily at teachers and librarians who work with children, but it is also designed as an aid for scholars of literature and popular culture, for post-secondary educators training librarians and teachers, and for students who wish to learn more about children's literature. It therefore offers critical introductions to more than 1700 characters from 230 works of fiction. These works originate primarily in the United States, Great Britain, Australia, and Canada, but a few were published in other countries and were translated into English. Over 100 illustrations from children's books have been reproduced within these pages to add visual context to these fictional works.

The selected titles come from both the 19th and 20th centuries and include titles that are historically important, titles that are important from a literary and educational perspective because they are frequently taught in school, titles that are culturally important because they should be part of everyone's intellectual equipment, and titles that are important because they are popular—that is, children read them voluntarily.

This work does not include characters from nursery rhymes, folktales, fairy tales, legends, and myths. Although such characters should be part of every child's listening and reading experience, they are so numerous and appear in so many variant tellings that to include them within this book would adversely affect both the quality and the number of discussions of characters from other sources.

Advisory Board

The final list of authors and works for *CCL* was compiled with the indispensable advice of an international advisory board, the members of which are listed below. Their understanding of the needs of librarians, teachers, students, and scholars, as well as those of the ultimate beneficiaries of any understanding of children's books, the children themselves, ensured that the entries would be most relevant to this book's intended audience.

Jonathan Betz-Zall, Children's Librarian for the Sno-Isle Regional Library System in Edmonds, Washington, and book reviewer

Kay Cuthrell, Youth Services Librarian, Southfield Public Library, Southfield, Michigan

Christine Francis, Assistant Professor of English, Central Connecticut State University, New Britain, Connecticut; author of essays, reviews, and teacher's literature guides; member of the Committee on Notable Trade Books, NCTE

Karen Nelson Hoyle, Professor and curator of the Children's Literature Research Collections, University of Minnesota Libraries, Minneapolis; author of reference books; former president of the Children's Literature Association; former member of the Newbery Award Committee; former chairperson of the Caldecott Award Committee

Anita Moss, Professor of English, University of North Carolina at Charlotte; editor of *Children's Literature in Education;* author of numerous articles and reviews; and winner of the Children's Literature Association Award in Criticism, 1982

Jon C. Stott, Professor of English, University of Alberta, Edmonton; first president of the Children's Literature Association; Senior Consultant to the Joseph Campbell Foundation Project on Mythology; author of numerous books and articles on children's literature

Constance Vidor, Library Media Specialist, Baltimore County Public Schools; author of articles and reviews of children's books

Organization

The entries are arranged alphabetically by author. Each entry begins with the author's name, birth and death dates, nationality, and principal occupations. Authors are listed according to the names by which they are best known to readers. If an author writes under a pseudonym, his or her legal name (or other variant name) is also provided for reference purposes. When an author entry contains more than one title, these titles are arranged chronologically. (Works in a series are arranged chronologically under the series heading and the series heading is placed according to the date of the first published title in that series.) Title headings include the full title (including a foreign-language title where required), the genre, and the date of publication. Because illustrators are indispensable contributors to children's picture books, their names are also provided whenever the illustrator is someone other than the author.

The essay on each title begins with a brief plot synopsis and analysis of themes so that readers will have a context for understanding the characters, who, as noted above, establish their identities through action. Subsequent parts of the essay analyze major characters in some depth and minor characters at a length commensurate with their importance. (For ease of use, character names appear in boldface the first time they are mentioned in the text.) These character discussions are critical: they explicate characters' contributions to conflicts and themes, evaluate their effectiveness in communicating themes, and occasionally evaluate their aesthetic contributions.

Each essay concludes with a list of works for further reading. This list is highly selective, focusing on standard reference works, such as those published by Gale Research (including *Something about the Author, Children's Literature Review, Dictionary of Literary Biography, Contemporary Authors, Something about the Author Autobiography Series, Twentieth-Century Children's Authors, Contemporary Literary Criticism,* and

Twentieth-Century Literary Criticism), or on titles of wide appeal that can be found in any large metropolitan library. These secondary works contain further bibliographic information so that readers can locate the scholarly articles and books that have shaped the author's understanding of children's literature over the years. (Dashes at the beginning of citations indicate a repetition of author information.)

Sequels, Series, Trilogies, and Other Related Works

In the world of children's literature, many characters reappear in sequels, series, and trilogies. In order to avoid duplication of discussions in the character essays, these works have been organized in the following manner:

For Sequels:

In cases where major characters in a book appear in one or more sequels that are given equal coverage, a single character essay has been written to avoid duplication of information. Each plot summary concludes with the line "See below for character descriptions" to notify the user that there is no separate character essay for that particular book.

For Series, Trilogies, and Tetralogies:

Some series in children's literature, such as the "Hardy Boys" books, contain too many books to be covered adequately within *CCL*. In these cases, a general discussion of the series is provided, or, as with the "Encyclopedia Brown" books, one representative title has been selected to help illustrate the major characters in the series.

Trilogies, tetralogies, and limited series are also special cases. In some entries, such as with the "Frances the Badger" books by Russell Hoban, only some books have been selected to represent the entire series as per recommendations from the advisory board. In instances where it has been deemed important to do so, all the books in a series have been included. Plot synopses for these books have been grouped together under one title (for example, Lloyd Alexander's "The Prydain Chroni-

cles"). For ease of reference, each title in the series is set in boldface within the combined plot summary.

For Other Related Works:

There are a number of instances in which characters appearing in one book are featured in other works not discussed in detail in *CCL*, either because the characters do not change significantly in subsequent books by the author or because the book in which they are discussed has been deemed to be the most important work in the series. For reference purposes, however, the author, when necessary, has added at the end of each plot summary a list of titles in which the characters also appear.

Character and Title Index

Characters in Children's Literature (*CCL*) has been released simultaneously with its companion book, *Characters in Young Adult Literature* (*CYAL*). Because these books together cover a broad spectrum of children's and young adult literature, two genres which are closely related though not identical, characters and titles from both *CCL* and *CYAL* have been indexed together here. Fewer than five percent of the characters appear in both books.

It was the goal of the author and editor to index character names in such a way as to make them easily accessible to users of this book. For this reason, characters have been indexed alphabetically by their first names. Thus, the hero of Stevenson's *Treasure Island* is listed as "Jim Hawkins," not "Hawkins, Jim." Also, if a character is known by more than one name—for example, "Mr. Black" is also "Jack Field" in Leon Garfield's *Smith*—both are boldfaced in the characters discussion, and both are included in the index. Characters who are commonly known by a rank or other title (for example, Mr., Ms., Captain, or Reverend) are listed alphabetically by that title. Captain Hoseason, who appears in Stevenson's *Kidnapped*, for example, is thus indexed under "Captain."

In children's literature, many characters are also given generic names, such as "mother" or "narrator." In these instances, the title of the novel in which they appear is provided in parentheses after the character's name. For example, a narrator might be indexed as "narrator (*Miss Rumphius*)." Characters who appear in unrelated stories (for example, King Arthur appears in several books by different authors), or who are identified by only a common first name, such as Mary or John, will be treated similarly in instances where a neglect to do so might cause confusion.

A few characters, such as "Long John Silver" and "Little Bear," present problems. Generally, these have been indexed by using the epithet as the first name, but two entries have been provided for some characters who might otherwise be difficult to locate. Stevenson's one-legged pirate is thus indexed as both "Long John Silver" and "John Silver, Long."

Acknowledgments

Many people, including my students over the years, have made incidental contributions to this book, but I wish to signal the special contributions of a few. First, I wish to thank Leah Knight, New Product Development Editor at Gale Research, for her initial faith in me and the project: without her urging, I would have never undertaken it. I also want to thank Kevin S. Hile, my editor, who has shown patient professionalism and kindness throughout the preparation of the manuscript. I'm going to miss our long-distance telephone conversations. I also wish to express gratitude to the University of Alberta, which granted me a six-month leave so that I could research and write the initial portions of this book. I owe a huge debt of gratitude to Jon C. Stott, one of the pioneers in the serious study of children's literature. He first recruited me to teach children's literature, and he guided me during my first shaky steps in the classroom. Since then, I have benefited from his advice, wisdom, and friendship. Finally, I must thank my family: Maryam, my wife, was, as always, encouraging, understanding, and good-humored, even when I seemed to be visiting the Land of the Wild Things too often; Mark and Sara, whose bedtimes first gave me excuses for exploring children's books, continually urged me to explore the interests they helped to foster, helping me to gain fresh perspectives on familiar titles.

We Welcome Your Suggestions

To offer comments or suggestions about *Characters in Children's Literature*, write to: The Editor, *Characters in Children's Literature*, Gale Research, 835 Penobscot Bldg., 645 Griswold St., Detroit, MI 48226-4094.

Acknowledgments

Page 1—Illustration by Pat Marriott. From *The Wolves of Willoughby Chase*, by Joan Aiken. Jonathan Cape, 1962. Illustrations copyright © 1962 by Jonathan Cape Limited. All rights reserved. Reproduced by permission. **Page 17**—Illustration by James Marshall. From *Miss Nelson Is Missing*, by Harry Allard. Houghton Mifflin Company, 1977. Illustrations copyright © 1977 by James Marshall. All rights reserved. Reproduced by permission of Houghton Mifflin Company. **Page 19**—Illustration by Edward Ardizzone. From *Little Tim and the Brave Sea Captain*, by Edward Ardizzone. Oxford University Press, 1936. **Page 29**—Illustration by W. W. Denslow. From *The Wonderful Wizard of Oz*, by L. Frank Baum. George M. Hill Company, 1900. **Page 35**—Illustration by Edward Gorey. From *The House with a Clock in Its Walls*, by John Bellairs. The Dial Press, 1973. Pictures copyright © 1973 by Edward Gorey. All rights reserved. Used by permission of the publisher, E. P. Dutton, an imprint of New American Library, a division of Penguin USA. **Page 37**—Illustration by Ludwig Bemelmans. From *Madeline*, by Ludwig Bemelmans. The Viking Press, 1939. Copyright © 1939 by Ludwig Bemelmans. Renewed 1967 by Madeleine Bemelmans and Barbara Bemelmans Marciano. Used by permission of Viking Penguin, a division of Penguin USA. **Page 39**—Illustration by William Nicholson. From *The Velveteen Rabbit*, by Margery Williams. G. H. Doran, 1922. **Page 43**—Illustration by Roy Doty. From *Tales of a Fourth Grade Nothing*, by Judy Blume. Dutton Children's Books, 1972. Illustrations copyright © 1972 by E. P. Dutton, Inc. All rights reserved. Used by permission of the publisher, E. P. Dutton, an imprint of New American Library, a division of Penguin USA. **Page 45**—Illustration by Peggy Fortnum. From *A Bear Called Paddington*, by Michael Bond. Houghton Mifflin Company, 1960. Copyright © 1958 by Michael Bond. All rights reserved. **Page 47**—Deeter, Catherine, illustrator. From a cover of *The Children of Green Knowe*, by Lucy M. Boston. Harcourt Brace Jovanovich, Publishers, 1989. Copyright © 1955, renewed 1983 by Lucy M. Boston. Reproduced by permission of Catherine Deeter. **Page 51**—Illustration by Trina Schart Hyman. From *Caddie Woodlawn*, by Carol Ryrie Brink. Simon & Schuster Books for Young Readers, 1973. Copyright © 1973 by Simon & Schuster, Inc. All rights reserved. Reproduced by permission. **Page 53**—Illustration by Kurt Wiese. From *Freddy the Detective*, by Walter R. Brooks. Knopf, 1932. Copyright © 1932 by Walter R. Brooks. **Page 56**—Illustration by Anthony Browne. From *Gorilla*, by Anthony Browne. Knopf, 1983. Copyright © 1983 by Anthony Browne. Reproduced by permission of Alfred A. Knopf, Inc. **Page 57**—Illustration by Jerry Lazare. From *Queenie Peavy*, by Robert Burch. The Viking Press, 1966. Copyright © 1966 Robert Burch. All rights reserved. Used by permission of Viking Penguin, a division of Penguin USA. **Page 61**—Illustration by Tasha Tudor. From *A Little Princess*, by Frances Hodgson Burnett. J. B. Lippincott Company, 1963. Illustrations copyright © 1963, renewed 1991 by Tasha Tudor. Reproduced by permission. **Page 69**—Illustration by Virginia Lee Burton. From *Mike Mulligan and His Steam Shovel*, by Virginia Lee Burton. Houghton Mifflin, 1939. Copyright © 1939, renewed 1967 by Virginia Lee Demetrios. All rights reserved. Reproduced by permission of Houghton Mifflin Company. **Page 72**—Illustration by Ted CoConis. From *The Summer of the Swans*, by Betsy Byars. Viking, 1970. Copyright © Betsy Byars, 1970. All rights reserved. Used by permission of Viking Penguin, a division of

Acknowledgments

Penguin USA. **Page 74**—Illustration by Robert Henneberger. From *The Wonderful Flight to the Mushroom Planet*, by Eleanor Cameron. Little, Brown, 1954. Copyright © 1954 by Eleanor Cameron. **Page 76**—Illustration by John Tenniel. From *Alice's Adventures in Wonderland*, by Lewis Carroll. Macmillan and Co., 1866. **Page 86**—Illustration by Louis Darling. From *Ramona the Pest*, by Beverly Cleary. William Morrow, 1968. Copyright © 1968 by Beverly Cleary. All rights reserved. Reproduced by permission of William Morrow and Company, Inc. **Page 93**—Illustration by Attilio Mussino. From *The Adventures of Pinocchio*, by C. Collodi. Translated by Carol Della Chiesa. Macmillan Publishing Co., 1969. Reproduced with permission of Macmillan Publishing Company, a division of Simon & Schuster, Inc. **Page 100**—Illustration by Barbara Cooney. From *Miss Rumphius*, by Barbara Cooney. Viking Penguin Inc., 1982. Copyright © Barbara Cooney Porter, 1982. All rights reserved. Used by permission of Viking Penguin, a division of Penguin USA. **Page 101**—Wiesner, David, illustrator. From a cover of *The Dark Is Rising*, by Susan Cooper. Collier Books, 1986. Cover illustration copyright © 1986 by David Wiesner. Reproduced with permission of Macmillan Publishing Company, a division of Simon & Schuster, Inc. **Page 111**—Illustration by Trina Schart Hyman. From a jacket of *Ordinary Jack*, by Helen Cresswell. Macmillan Publishing Co., 1977. Copyright © 1977 Helen Cresswell. All rights reserved. Reproduced by permission of Macmillan Publishing Company, a division of Simon & Schuster, Inc. **Page 113**—Illustration by James Spanfeller. From *Dorp Dead*, by Julia Cunningham. Knopf, 1987. Text copyright © 1965, by Julia Cunningham. Reproduced by permission of Alfred A. Knopf, Inc. **Page 121**—Illustration by Quentin Blake. From *The BFG*, by Roald Dahl. Jonathan Cape, 1982. Illustrations copyright © Quentin Blake, 1982. All rights reserved. Reproduced by permission of Jonathan Cape Ltd. **Page 125**—Illustration by Jean de Brunhoff. From *Histoire de Babar, le petit elephant*, by Jean de Brunhoff. Le Jardin Des Modes, n.d. Reproduced by permission. **Page 127**—illustration by Maurice Sendak. From *The House of Sixty Fathers*, by Meindert DeJong. Harper & Row, Publishers, 1956. Copyright © 1956, renewed 1984 by Meindert DeJong. All rights reserved. Reproduced by permission of HarperCollins Publishers, Inc. **Page 130**—Illustration by Tomie de Paola. From *Strega Nona*, by Tomie de Paola. Aladdin Paperbacks, 1975. Copyright © 1975 by Tomie de Paola. All rights reserved. Reproduced with permission of Macmillan Publishing Company, a division of Simon & Schuster, Inc. **Page 133**—Illustration by Paul Galdone. *From Hans Brinker; or, the Silver Skates*, by Mary Mapes Dodge. Nelson Doubleday, 1954. Copyright © 1954 by Nelson Doubleday, Inc. **Page 135**—Illustration by William Pene du Bois. From *The Twenty-One Balloons*, by William Pene du Bois. Viking Penguin, 1947. Copyright © 1947, renewed 1975 by William Pene du Bois. All rights reserved. Used by permission of Viking Penguin, a division of Penguin USA. **Page 138**—Illustration by N. M. Bodeck. From *Half Magic*, by Edward Wager. Harcourt Brace & Company, 1954. Copyright © 1954, by Harcourt Brace & Company. Renewed 1982 by Jane Eager. Reproduced by permission of the publisher. **Page 141**—Illustration by Louis Slobodkin. From *The Moffats*, by Eleanor Estes. Harcourt, Brace, and Co., 1941. Copyright © 1941, renewed 1968 by Eleanor Estes. Reproduced by permission of Harcourt Brace & Company. **Page 143**—Illustration by Keith Ward. From *The Black Stallion*, by Walter Farley. Random House, 1941. Copyright © 1941, renewed 1968, by Walter Farley. Reproduced by permission of Random House, Inc. **Page 145**—Illustration by Louise Fitzhugh. From *Harriet the Spy*, by Louise Fitzhugh. HarperCollins Publishers, 1964. Copyright © 1964 by Louise Fitzhugh. Renewed 1992 by Lois Anne Morehead and E. Seward Stevens. All rights reserved. Reproduced by permission of HarperCollins Publishers, Inc. **Page 151**—Illustration by Peter Sis. From *The Whipping Boy*, by Sid Fleischman. Greenwillow Books, 1986. Illustrations copyright © 1986 by Peter Sis. All rights reserved. Reproduced by permission of William Morrow and Company, Inc. **Page 155**—Illustration by Don Freeman. From *Corduroy*, by Don Freeman. The Viking Press, 1968. Copyright © Don Freeman, 1968. All rights reserved. Used by permission of Viking Penguin, a division of Penguin USA. **Page 168**—Illustration by Tasha Tudor. From *The Doll's House*, by Rumer

Godden. The Viking Press, 1962. Copyright © 1947, renewed 1962 by Rumer Godden. All rights reserved. Used by permission of Viking Penguin, a division of Penguin USA. **Page 172**—Illustration by Ernest H. Shepard. From *The Wind in the Willows*, by Kenneth Grahame. Copyright © 1933 Charles Scribner's Sons. Renewed 1961 Ernest H. Shepard. All rights reserved. Reproduced with permission of Macmillan Publishing Company, a division of Simon & Schuster, Inc. **Page 177**—Cover of *M. C. Higgins, the Great*, by Virginia Hamilton. Macmillan, 1974. Copyright © 1974 by Virginia Hamilton. All rights reserved. Reproduced by permission of Jerry Pickney. **Page 179**—Illustration by Garth Williams. From *Bedtime for Frances*, by Russell C. Hoban. Harper & Row, Publishers, Inc., 1960. Illustrations copyright © 1960, renewed 1988 by Garth Williams. Reproduced by permission of HarperCollins Publishers, Inc. **Page 191**—Illustration by Shirley Hughes. From *Dogger*, by Shirley Hughes. Lothrop, Lee & Shepard, 1988. Copyright © 1988 by Shirley Hughes. All rights reserved. Reproduced by permission of Lothrop, Lee & Shepard, a division of William Morrow and Company, Inc. **Page 195**—Illustration by Pat Hutchins. From *Rosie's Walk*, by Pat Hutchins. Macmillan, 1968. Copyright © Patricia Hutchins 1968. All rights reserved. Reproduced with permission of Macmillan Publishing Company, a division of Simon & Schuster, Inc. **Page 199**—Illustration by Maurice Sendak. From *The Bat-Poet*, by Randall Jarrell. The Macmillan Company, 1963. Copyright © The Macmillan Company 1963, 1964. Renewed 1992 by Mary Von Schrader Jarrell. All rights reserved. Reproduced by permission. **Page 201**—Illustration by Jules Feiffer. From *The Phantom Tollbooth*, by Norman Juster. Epstein & Carroll Associates, Inc., 1961. Illustrations copyright © 1961, 1989 by Jules Feiffer. All rights reserved. Reproduced by permission of Random House, Inc. **Page 205**—Illustration by Ezra Jack Keats. From *Peter's Chair*, by Ezra Jack Keats. Harper Trophy, 1967. Copyright © 1967 by Ezra Jack Keats. All rights reserved. Reproduced by permission of HarperCollins Publishers, Inc. **Page 214**—Illustration by Fritz Eichenberg. From *The Jungle Book*, by Rudyard Kipling. Grosset & Dunlap, 1950. Copyright © 1950, by Grosset & Dunlap, Inc. **Page 221**—

Illustration by E. L. Konigsburg. From *From the Mixed-up Files of Mrs. Basil E. Frankweiler*, by E. L. Konigsburg. Atheneum, 1967. Copyright © 1967 by E. L. Konigsburg. All rights reserved. Reproduced with permission of Atheneum Publishers, a division of Simon & Schuster, Inc. **Page 224**—Cover from *This Can't Be Happening at Macdonald Hall!* by Gordon Korman. Scholastic Inc., 1978. Copyright © 1978 by Gordon Korman. All rights reserved. Reproduced by permission. **Page 226**—Illustration by Jose Aruego. From *Leo the Late Bloomer*, by Robert Kraus. Windmill Books, 1971. Illustrations copyright © 1971 by Jose Aruego. All rights reserved. Reproduced by permission. **Page 229**—Illustration by Symeon Shimin. From *Onion John*, by Joseph Krumgold. Thomas Y. Crowell Company, 1959. Copyright © 1959 by Joseph Krumgold. All rights reserved. **Page 232**—Illustration by Robert Lawson. From *Rabbit Hill*, by Robert Lawson. Viking Press, Inc., 1944. Copyright © 1944 by Robert Lawson. Copyright renewed 1972 by John W. Boyd. Used by permission of Viking Penguin, a division of Penguin USA. **Page 235**—Illustration by Robert Lawson. From *The Story of Ferdinand the Bull*, by Munro Leaf. The Viking Press, 1936. Copyright © 1936 by Munro Leaf and Robert Lawson. Copyright © renewed 1964 by Munro Leaf and John W. Boyd. Used by permission of Viking Penguin, a division of Penguin USA. **Page 240**—Illustration by Michael Hague. From *The Lion, the Witch, and the Wardrobe*, by C. S. Lewis. Macmillan Publishing Company, 1983. Copyright © 1981 Macmillan Publishing Company. All rights reserved. Reproduced by the permission. **Page 257**—Illustration by Louis S. Glanzman. From *Pippi Longstocking*, by Astrid Lindgren. Translated by Florence Lamborn. Puffin Books, 1977. Reproduced by permission. **Page 259**—Illustration by Leo Lionni. From *Frederick*, by Leo Lionni. Pantheon, 1967. Copyright © 1967, by Leo Lionni. All rights reserved. Reproduced by permission of Random House, Inc. **Page 261**—Illustration by Anthony Maitland. From *The Ghost of Thomas Kempe*, by Penelope Lively. E. P. Dutton, 1973. Illustrations copyright © 1973 by William Heinemann Ltd. All rights reserved. Used by permission of the publisher, E. P. Dutton, an imprint of New American Library, a division of Penguin

USA. **Page 263**—Illustration by Arnold Lobel. From *Frog and Toad Are Friends*, by Arnold Lobel. Harper & Row, Publishers, 1970. Copyright © 1970 by Arnold Lobel. All rights reserved. Reproduced by HarperCollins Publishers, Inc. **Page 267**—Illustration by Diane DeGroat. From a jacket of *Anastasia Krupnik*, by Lois Lowry. Houghton Mifflin Company, 1979. Copyright © 1979 by Lois Lowry. All rights reserved. Reproduced by permission of Houghton Mifflin Company. **Page 280**—Illustration by Marcia Sewall. From a cover of *Sarah, Plain and Tall*, by Patricia MacLachlan. Harper & Row, Publishers, 1985. Cover art copyright © 1985 by Marcia Sewall. Cover copyright © 1985 by HarperCollins, Publishers, Inc. Reproduced by permission of HarperCollins Publishers, Inc. **Page 283**—Illustration by Michele Chessare. From a jacket of *The Haunting*, by Margaret Mahy. Margaret K. McElderry Books, 1982. Copyright © 1982 by Margaret Mahy. All rights reserved. Reproduced with the permission of Margaret K. McElderry Books, an imprint of Simon & Schuster, Inc. **Page 285**—Illustration by Mercer Mayer. From *There's a Nightmare in My Closet*, by Mercer Mayer. Dial Books for Young Readers, 1968. Copyright © 1968 by Mercer Mayer. All rights reserved. Reproduced by permission of the publisher, Dial Books for Young Readers. **Page 287**—Illustration by Robert McCloskey. From *Homer Price*, by Robert McCloskey. The Viking Press, 1943. Copyright © 1943 by Robert McCloskey, renewed 1971. Used by permission of Viking Penguin, a division of Penguin USA. **Page 290**—Illustration by Rachel Isadora. From *Flossie & the Fox*, by Patricia C. McKissack. Dial Books for Young Readers, 1986. Copyright © 1986 by Mercer Mayer. All rights reserved. Reproduced by permission of the publisher, Dial Books for Young Readers. **Page 291**—Illustration by Ernest H. Shepard. From *The House at Pooh Corner*, by A. A. Milne. E. P. Dutton, 1928. Copyright © 1928 by E. P. Dutton & Co., Inc. Renewed, 1956, by A. A. Milne. All rights reserved. Used by permission of the publisher, E. P. Dutton, an imprint of New American Library, a division of Penguin USA. **Page 295**—Illustration by Maurice Sendak. From *Little Bear*, by Else Holmelund Minarik. HarperTrophy, 1957. Illustrations copyright © 1957, renewed 1985 by Maurice Sendak. All rights reserved. Reproduced by HarperCollins Publishers, Inc. **Page 297**—Illustration by Ernest H. Shepard. From *The Cuckoo Clock*, by Mrs. Molesworth. J. M. Dent & Sons Ltd., 1954. Reproduced by permission of the publisher. **Page 299**—Illustration by Jody Lee. From *Anne of Green Gables*, by L. M. Montgomery. Grosset & Dunlap, Publishers, 1983. Illustrations copyright © 1983 by Jody Lee. All rights reserved. Reproduced by permission of The Putnam & Grosset Group. **Page 302**—Illustration by Michael Martchenko. From *The Paper Bag Princess*, by Robert N. Munsch. Annick Press Ltd., 1980. Art copyright © 1980 Michael Martchenko. All rights reserved. Reproduced by permission. **Page 313**—Illustration by Evaline Ness. From *Sam, Bangs & Moonshine*, by Evaline Ness. Henry Holt, 1966. Copyright © 1966 by Evaline Ness. Reproduced by permission of Henry Holt and Company. **Page 318**—Illustration by Beth Krush and Joe Krush. From *The Borrowers*, by Mary Norton. Harcourt Brace, 1953. Copyright © 1953 by Mary Norton. Renewed, 1981, by Mary Norton, Beth Krush and Joe Krush. Reproduced by permission Harcourt Brace & Company. **Page 322**—Illustration by Zena Bernstein. From *Mrs. Frisby and the Rats of NIMH*, by Robert C. O'Brien. Aladdin Paperbacks, 1975. Copyright © 1971 by Robert C. O'Brien. All rights reserved. Reproduced with permission of Macmillan Publishing Company, a division of Simon & Schuster, Inc. **Page 327**—Illustration by Fritz Siebel. From *Amelia Bedelia*, by Peggy Parish. HarperCollins, 1992. Revised illustrations copyright © 1992 by the Estate of Fritz Siebel. All rights reserved. Reproduced by HarperCollins Publishers, Inc. **Page 329**—Illustration by Donna Diamond. From *Bridge to Terabithia*, by Katherine Paterson. HarperCollins Publishers, 1977. Copyright © 1977 by Katherine Paterson. All rights reserved. Reproduced by HarperCollins Publishers, Inc. **Page 343**—Illustration by Charles C. Gehm. From *Soup*, by Robert Newton Peck. Knopf, 1974. Copyright © 1974 by Robert Newton Peck. All rights reserved. Reproduced by permission of Alfred A. Knopf, Inc. **Page 351**—Illustration by Beatrix Potter. From *The Tale of Jemima Puddle-Duck*, by Beatrix Potter. Frederick Warne & Co., Inc., 1908. Copyright © 1908, renewed 1936 by Frederick Warne & Co. All rights reserved. **Page 353**— Illustration by Arthur Ransome. From *Swallows and Amazons*, by Arthur Ransome. Jonathan Cape, 1953. Reproduced by permission of Jonathan Cape Ltd. **Page 359**—Illustration by Brock Cole. From *The Indian in the Cupboard*, by Lynne Reid Banks. Avon Books, 1981. Illustrations copyright © 1981 by Brock Cole. All rights reserved. Reproduced by permission. **Page 362**—Illustration by H. A. Rey. From *Curious George*, by H. A. Rey. Houghton Mifflin, 1941. Copyright © 1941, renewed 1969 by Margaret Rey. All rights reserved. Reproduced by permission of Houghton Mifflin Company. **Page 363**—Illustration by Fritz Wegner. From *Jacob Two-Two Meets the Hooded Fang*, by Mordecai Richler. McClelland & Stewart Ltd., 1975. Illustrations copyright © 1975 by Alfred A. Knopf, Inc. **Page 365**—Illustration by Dave Henderson. From a cover of *Freaky Friday*, by Mary Rodgers. HarperTrophy, 1991. Cover art copyright © 1991 by Dave Henderson. Cover copyright © 1991 by HarperCollins Publishers, Inc. Reproduced by permission of HarperCollins Publishers, Inc. **Page 368**— Illustration by Richard Doyle. *From The King of the Golden River; or, the Black Brothers*, by John Ruskin. Lee and Shepard, Publishers, 1889. **Page 370**—Illustration by Rene Ade. From a jacket of *Missing May*, by Cynthia Rylant. Orchard Books, 1992. Jacket painting copyright © 1992 by Rene Ade. Reproduced by permission Orchard Books, New York. **Page 373**—Illustration by Antoine de Saint-Exupery. From *The Little Prince*, by Antoine de Saint-Exupery. Translated by Katherine Woods. Harcourt Brace & Company, 1943. Copyright © 1943, renewed 1971 by Harcourt Brace & Company. Reproduced by permission of the publisher. **Page 375**—Illustration by Garth Williams. From *The Cricket in Times Square*, by George Selden. Ariel Books, 1960. Copyright © 1960 by George Selden Thompson and Garth Williams. All rights reserved. **Page 377**—Illustration by Maurice Sendak. From *Where the Wild Things Are*, by Maurice Sendak. Harper & Row, Publishers, 1963. Copyright © 1963 by Maurice Sendak. **Page 381**—Illustration by Dr. Seuss. From *Horton Hears a Who*, by Dr. Seuss. Random House, Inc., 1954. Copyright © 1954, renewed 1982 by Dr. Seuss. Reproduced by per-

mission. **Page 389**—Illustration by Alton Raible. From *The Egypt Game*, by Zilpha Keatley Snyder. Atheneum, 1967. Copyright © 1967 by Zilpha Keatley Snyder. All rights reserved. Reproduced by permission of Atheneum Publishers, Inc., a division of Simon & Schuster, Inc. **Page 397**—Illustration by Sperry Armstrong. From *Call It Courage*, by Armstrong Sperry. Macmillan Publishing, 1940. Copyright © 1940 by Macmillan Publishing Company. Renewed 1968 by Sperry Armstrong. All rights reserved. Reproduced with permission of Macmillan Publishing Company, a division of Simon & Schuster, Inc. **Page 403**—Illustration by Jessie Willcox Smith. From Heidi, by Johanna Spyri. McKay, 1922. **Page 407**—Illustration by William Steig. From *Abel's Island*, by William Steig. Farrar, Straus and Giroux, 1976. Copyright © 1976 by William Steig. All rights reserved. Reproduced by permission of Farrar, Straus and Giroux, Inc. **Page 413**—Illustration by Lynd Ward. From *Kidnapped*, by Robert Louis Stevenson. Grosset & Dunlap, 1948. Copyright © 1948, by Grosset & Dunlap, Inc. Renewed 1976 by Lynd Ward. Reproduced by permission. **Page 423**—Illustration by Mary Shepard. From *Mary Poppins*, by P. L. Travers. Reynal & Hitchcock, 1934. **Page 428**—Illustration by C. Walter Hodges. From *The Adventures of Tom Sawyer*, by Mark Twain. J. M. Dent & Sons Ltd., 1955. Reproduced by permission of the publisher. **Page 432**—Illustration by Chris Van Allsburg. From *Jumanji*, by Chris Van Allsburg. Houghton Mifflin Company, 1981. Copyright © 1981 by Chris Van Allsburg. All rights reserved. Reproduced by permission of Houghton Mifflin Company. **Page 435**—Illustration by Bernard Waber. From *Ira Sleeps Over*, by Bernard Waber. Houghton Mifflin Company, 1972. Copyright © 1972 by Bernard Waber. All rights reserved. Reproduced by permission of Houghton Mifflin Company. **Page 436**—Illustration by Lynd Ward. From *The Biggest Bear*, by Lynd Ward. Houghton Mifflin Company, 1952. Copyright © 1952, renewed 1980 by Lynd Ward. All rights reserved. Reproduced by permission of Houghton Mifflin Company. **Page 439**— Illustration by Garth Williams. From *Charlotte's Web*, by E. B. White. Harper Trophy, 1952. Copyright © 1952 by E. B. White. All rights reserved. **Page 447**—Illustration by Helen Mason Grose.

Acknowledgments

From *Rebecca of Sunnybrook Farm*, by Kate Douglas Wiggin. Houghton Mifflin Company, 1925. **Page 451**—Illustration by Garth Williams. From *Little House on the Prairie*, by Laura Ingalls Wilder. Revised edition. Harper, 1953. Pictures copyright © 1953 by Garth Williams. All rights reserved. **Page 462**—Illustration by Steve Brennan. From a cover of *Shadow of a Bull*, by Maia Wojciechowska. Aladdin Books, 1992. Cover illustration copyright © 1992 by Steve Brennan. Reproduced by permission of the illustrator. **Page 467**—Illustration by Lynd Ward. From *The Swiss Family Robinson*, by Johann Wyss. Edited by William H. G. Kingston. Grosset & Dunlap, 1949. Copyright © 1949, by Grosset & Dunlap, Inc. Renewed 1977 by Lynd Ward. Reproduced by permission. **Page 469**—Illustration by Taro Yashima. From *Crow Boy*, by Taro Yashima. The Viking Press, 1955. Copyright © 1955 by Mitsu and Taro Yashima. Renewed by Taro Yashima, 1983. Used by permission of Viking Penguin, a division of Penguin USA. **Page 471**—Illustration by Bruce Degan. From *Commander Toad in Space*, by Jane Yolen. Coward, McCann & Geoghegan, 1980. Illustrations copyright © 1980 by Bruce Degan. All rights reserved. Reproduced by permission of Coward, McCann & Geoghegan, Inc.

Characters in
CHILDREN'S
LITERATURE

Joan Aiken

1924-, English author

The Wolves of Willoughby Chase

(gothic novel, 1962)

PLOT: According to Aiken, this melodramatic novel is "a sort of pastiche of all the Victorian tales about poor little orphans who were in the power of frightful villains." Sir Willoughby Green must take the sickly Lady Sophia Green on a recuperative voyage. His lawyer, Abednego Gripe, sends Miss Letitia Slighcarp to teach Sir Willoughby's daughter, Bonnie, and her orphaned cousin, Sylvia Green. Sylvia leaves elderly Aunt Jane in London and sets out by train for Willoughby Chase. When Josiah Grimshaw, a passenger, is apparently knocked unconscious, Sylvia has him brought to the house. Later, wolves chase Bonnie and Sylvia, who seek refuge in the cave where a boy named Simon lives. When Simon escorts them home, they see Grimshaw and Miss Slighcarp plotting to take over Willoughby Chase. Miss Slighcarp wears Lady Green's clothes, forges a will, fires the servants, and locks Bonnie in a cupboard. Two loyal servants, Miss Pattern, who hides in the house, and James, the footman, remain to serve Bonnie secretly.

Miss Slighcarp, having intercepted a note asking for help, tells Bonnie that her parents are dead and takes the girls to Mrs. Brisket's charity school. Mrs. Brisket works her pupils and nearly starves them. Diana, her daughter, increases their misery by making them serve her. Eventually, Simon helps the disguised Bonnie and Sylvia escape to London. There they find Aunt Jane to be seriously ill. Dr.

An illustration by Patricia Eleanor Howard of the evil governess Miss Letitia Slighcarp from **The Wolves of Willoughby Chase**

Gabriel Field tends her and also helps them to subdue Grimshaw, who breaks into the house that night. Learning that Grimshaw is a forger, Dr. Field gets Gripe and two policemen to come with him and the girls to Willoughby Chase. Hiding in a secret passage, the policemen overhear enough to arrest Miss Slighcarp and Mrs. Brisket. At this point, Sir Willoughby and the recovered Lady Green return. Dr. Field agrees to have Simon educated as a painter, and Sir Willoughby agrees to have Aunt Jane set up a school for Mrs. Brisket's orphans.

The loosely connected "Wolves" series includes Black Hearts at Battersea *(1964),* Nightbirds on Nantucket *(1966),* The Whispering Mountain *(1968),* The Cuckoo Tree *(1971),* The Stolen Lake *(1981),* Dido and Pa *(1986), and* Is Underground *(1993).*

CHARACTERS: Because, as Aiken has said, "The book was based on exaggeration," the characters are flat, being examples of extreme vice or virtue. **Bonnie Green**, the spunky heroine, is a small, slender, rosy-cheeked girl with masses of black hair. Robust, she is good at skating and shooting. Bonnie has a fiery temper. When she observes Miss Slighcarp hitting a maid, for example, she throws a jug of water on her. Later, she refuses to be silent, ordering Miss Slighcarp to remove her mother's clothes. At Mrs. Brisket's house, Bonnie throws gravy at a cook who hits her. Bonnie's indomitable spirit enables her to comfort Sylvia, to steal eggs for needed sustenance, and to plot an escape. Kind-hearted and generous, she nurses Sylvia, who becomes ill, and gives the orphans Mrs. Brisket's cheese basket, leaving Mrs. Brisket ample payment so that the other children will not be punished after her escape. Once her home is restored, she exhibits enthusiastic kindness by suggesting that her father have Aunt Jane supervise a school for Mrs. Brisket's orphans.

Sylvia Green, Bonnie's orphaned cousin, is a delicate blond who is thoughtful and obedient. Although hungry during her train journey, she follows Aunt Jane's instructions about lady-like behavior and refrains from eating in the presence of Grimshaw. Sylvia is observant, prudent, and quick-witted. She warns Bonnie about getting trapped in a secret passage and distracts Miss Slighcarp when Bonnie makes a noise that would reveal that she is hiding in it. Loving and kind-hearted, she worries that Bonnie will get into trouble for showing her kindness at Mrs. Brisket's. After their escape, Sylvia lovingly tends to the ill Aunt Jane.

Miss Letitia Slighcarp is the quintessential evil governess. (She introduces herself as Bonnie's fourth cousin, once removed, but Lady Green calls her Sir Willoughby's cousin.) Her spiteful looks and comments indicate that she is a domineering woman unwilling to tolerate exuberant children. Thin and immensely tall, Miss Slighcarp wears a gray wig to cover her bald head. She is quick-tempered and cruel. Thus, she viciously hits a maid for touching personal papers, and she locks Bonnie in a dark cupboard when Bonnie opposes her. Later, she locks orphans in the dungeons below Willoughby Chase. Worst of all, she tries to kill Bonnie's parents by ensuring that they set sail on a decrepit ship. Miss Slighcarp is avaricious and selfish. She burns Sir Willoughby's papers, obtains a forged will that bequeaths everything to her, and sells everything, including the children's toys. She dresses in Lady Green's finest gowns and, although insisting that the children eat plain fare, indulges herself in champagne and delicacies. **Josiah Grimshaw** is skilled as a forger and uses his ability to assist Miss Slighcarp in plundering Sir Willoughby's estate. He is friendly to Sylvia on the train, but he is a bully willing to intimidate Aunt Jane.

Mrs. Gertrude Brisket, who runs the charity school, is a tall, massive, yellow-eyed woman with a bad temper; she covers her big-knuckled hands with rings and dresses smartly, but she is plainly cruel. Although paid to care for orphans in her school, she puts them to work to earn her money. Lacking enough beds, she forces the children to sleep in shifts. She further robs them of their identities by chopping off their hair, refusing to let them talk to each other, and calling them by number instead of name. Mrs. Brisket, who reads aloud from the Bible while the children work, is a hypocrite. When the inspector comes, she forces the orphans to pretend that they are learning lessons. She maintains control through fear and starvation. Although she dines handsomely at the head table, she feeds the orphans small quantities of unpalatable food. Taking advantage of this, she turns them against each other by giving bits of cheese to any who report infractions. **Diana Brisket**, her fifteen-year-old daughter, is a tall, thin, pale girl who walks with a slouch. Always insolent, she forces the orphans to mend her clothes and secretly steals from her mother. Although friendless after her mother's arrest, she improves morally because of Aunt Jane's example.

Unlike the villains, the good characters like children. **Sir Willoughby Green**, Bonnie's father, is elegant and jovial. He is benign and indulges Bonnie's high spirits. **Lady Sophia Green**, his seriously ill wife, is a dark-eyed, sad woman. But she is kind and thoughtful, arranging before her departure to have Pattern prepare flattering clothes for Sylvia. Her trip transforms her into a bright, beautiful woman. **Aunt Jane**, Sir Willoughby's frail, elderly sister, is prim and proper. She insists that Sylvia always behave like a lady and willingly sacrifices her few possessions so that Sylvia may be properly attired. Proudly averse to charity, she hides her poverty and nearly dies of malnutrition. **Miss Pattern**, Bonnie's maid, and **James**, the footman, are ideal, loyal servants. When Miss Slighcarp dismisses the servants, both stay on so that they can secretly serve Bonnie and Sylvia. Pattern hides in the house, but James, wisely understanding Miss Slighcarp, pretends to be evil so that she will retain him. Although only a child himself, **Simon** has an adult role as a helper and protector. Presumed to be an orphan who has left a cruel master, Simon dwells in a cave and lives on chestnuts and the proceeds from the geese he raises. He is brave, using his bow and arrows to protect Bonnie and Sylvia from wolves, and resourceful in helping them to escape from Mrs. Brisket's school. **Dr. Gabriel Field**, in spite of his brusque manner, is kind. He tends to Aunt Jane and helps the girls. A painter himself, he recognizes Simon's talent and generously pays for his education as an artist. He is also moral and energetic, going to Gripe to learn about Grimshaw and summoning the police to put an end to Miss Slighcarp's plot. **Abednego Gripe**, Sir Willoughby's lawyer, is a thin, gray-haired, agitated man. He functions as a red herring; because he arranged for Miss Slighcarp to be a governess and because Grimshaw visited his offices before going to Aunt Jane's, he first seems party to the conspiracy. Actually, he earlier fired Grimshaw as a forger; entirely innocent of the plot, he helps to expose it.

Further Reading

Authors and Artists for Young Adults. Vol. 1. Detroit: Gale Research, 1989.

Berger, Laura Standley, ed. *Twentieth-Century Young Adult Writers.* 1st ed. Detroit: St. James, 1994.

Children's Literature Review. Vols. 1, 19. Detroit: Gale Research, 1976, 1990.

Collier, Laurie, and Joyce Nakamura, eds. *Major Authors and Illustrators for Children and Young Adults.* Detroit: Gale Research, 1993.

Contemporary Authors New Revision Series. Vol. 34. Detroit: Gale Research, 1992.

Contemporary Literary Criticism. Vol. 35. Detroit: Gale Research, 1985.

De Montreville, Doris, and Donna Hill, eds. *Third Book of Junior Authors.* New York: H. W. Wilson, 1972.

Hunt, Caroline C., ed. *British Children's Writers since 1960: First Series.* Vol. 161 of *Dictionary of Literary Biography.* Detroit: Gale Research, 1996.

Something about the Author. Vols. 2, 30, 73. Detroit: Gale Research, 1971, 1983, 1993.

Something about the Author Autobiography Series. Vol. 1. Detroit: Gale Research, 1986.

Louisa May Alcott

1832-1888, American author

Little Women; or, Meg, Jo, Beth and Amy

(novel, 1868)

PLOT: The loosely connected episodes of *Little Women* celebrate home life and domestic virtues by tracing the struggles of four sisters who mature into good little women. Meg, Jo, Beth, and Amy March begin this struggle after receiving a letter from their father, a Union chaplain in the Civil War. Following his advice, they begin imitating the protagonist in John Bunyan's *Pilgrim's Progress* by shouldering the burden of their personal flaws. In subsequent episodes, the sisters receive lessons about character. On Christmas Day, Marmee, their mother, teaches them about charity by having them donate their breakfasts to a poor German family. Hearing of the sacrifice, Mr. James Laurence, their wealthy neighbor, sends them treats. Jo later meets Mr. Laurence's grandson, Laurie, at a party and charitably informs his grandfather that Laurie needs companionship. Consequently, both Laurie and his grandfather befriend Jo. Mr. Laurence even arranges for shy Beth to play his piano in private and gives her a cabinet piano. Frivolous Amy endures humiliation when the teacher punishes her for bringing pickled limes to school. When Jo refuses to let her come to the theater, Amy vindictively burns the fairy tales Jo has written. Having vowed never to forgive Amy, Jo is tempted to leave when Amy falls through the ice while skating. After Laurie rescues Amy, Mrs. March teaches the penitent Jo to control her anger. Meg herself learns a lesson about vanity when she spends a week at wealthy Annie Moffat's house. Jealous of the other girls, Meg dresses and behaves inappropriately, but she later confesses her foolishness to Marmee.

In spite of their efforts to be good, the girls complain about their poverty and endless chores. When Marmee retires to her room and leaves the chores to them, however, the ensuing disasters teach the girls to value work. Later, their example as members of their own Busy Bee Society leads Laurie to vow that he will stop rebelling against his grandfather. Jo carries over her industry into writing, placing some stories for publication. When a telegram comes urging Mrs. March to go to her husband, Jo even sells her hair to raise money. After Marmee leaves with John Brooke, Laurie's tutor and Meg's secret admirer, the girls fend for themselves. Unfortunately, the other sisters fail to relieve the exhausted Beth, who becomes seriously ill while caring for the dying baby of the poor German family. Before Jo can decide to send for her mother, Laurie does so. Under her mother's care, Beth recovers, and the other girls continue to develop. Amy, having been previously sent to stay at Aunt March's to avoid the illness, endeavors to be good in order to inherit Aunt March's turquoise ring. She becomes such a model of good behavior that Aunt March allows her to have the ring. After Marmee appropriately reprimands Laurie for sending a letter to Meg and signing it with Mr. Brooke's name, Jo makes peace between the angry Mr. Laurence and Laurie. At Christmas, Mr. March returns. During the happy family celebra-

tions, Aunt March orders Meg not to marry John Brooke. Determined to have her own way, however, Meg accepts John's proposal.

In the sequel, Good Wives *(1869), in recent editions usually bound together with the first part, Beth dies, but the others complete their progress: Meg marries John Brooke, Amy marries Laurie, and Jo marries Professor Fritz Bhaer. Other volumes about the March family are* Little Men *(1873) and* Jo's Boys and How They Turned Out *(1886).*

CHARACTERS: The first characters in American fiction for children to have realistic mixtures of virtues and flaws, the March girls are closely based on Alcott's own family. The oldest sister, sixteen-year-old **Meg** (**Margaret**, named after her mother) is based on Anna Alcott. She is a pretty girl with large eyes, brown hair, a sweet mouth, and white hands, of which she is vain. She supports the family by working as a governess. Her flaws are laziness and vanity, but she learns the value of work when Marmee deliberately leaves the management of the house to the girls. As a Pilgrim, she wanders into her Vanity Fair when, envious of wealthier girls, she wears a daring gown, talks flirtatiously, and drinks champagne. After both Laurie and an elderly officer express disapproval, she feels foolish that she abandoned her own character. Thereafter, she confesses to her mother and redoubles her efforts not to be dissatisfied or vain. Meg is the first of the girls to fall in love. When Aunt March orders her not to marry John Brooke, Meg shows a disdain for the wealth she once coveted, declaring that she will choose her own husband, even if he is poor.

Fifteen-year-old **Jo** (**Josephine**), a bookworm with talent as both an actress and a writer, is based on Louisa May Alcott herself. Disappointed that she is a girl and therefore has limited freedom and opportunities, Jo affects boyish behavior, such as walking with her hands behind her and whistling. Jo does not care much for girls or their gossip, and she takes little interest in her appearance or clothing. She has big hands and feet, sharp gray eyes, and thick chestnut hair that she regards as her one beautiful feature. Jo ultimately sacrifices her hair when she sells it to provide money for her sick father. Her gesture has no practical consequences because her father returns with her money, but it shows a determination to humble her pride, display Christian charity, and become a good Pilgrim. As a Pilgrim, Jo's major burden is her quick temper. Jo wrestles with her anger, which is compared to Bunyan's monster Apollyon, when she is tempted to leave Amy, who has fallen through the ice. Meg resists temptation and, by following Marmee's example, learns to control the monster. Although Jo eventually loses some of her rough wildness, she is always confident and forthcoming when she feels she is right. Thus, Jo confronts Mr. Laurence and gets him to settle his differences with Laurie. Furthermore, although ambitious to write something of enduring value, she is pragmatic and determined when seeking publication of her formulaic fiction. Jo ultimately becomes more womanly than boyish, but she remains the most independent and memorable of the sisters.

Beth (Elizabeth), based on Alcott's sister of the same name who died as a result of scarlet fever, is thirteen. Her shy manner, timid voice, and peaceful expression lead her father to call her "Little Tranquillity." Her shyness makes her incapable of going to school or meeting people; her kind and nurturing qualities are evident in the care she bestows upon her dolls. She later shows the same tender consideration for the dying German baby. Always concerned about others, Beth never speaks angry words. A talented musician, she temporarily overcomes her shyness when Mr. Laurence allows her to play the piano in private and she directly expresses her gratitude.

Amy, based on May Alcott, is a conceited twelve-year-old. She has blue eyes, curly yellow hair, and a flat nose, which she feels is a flaw. Amy, who is called "Little Raphael," is a talented artist who dreams of doing great work. She is pretentious, but her frequent malapropisms make her seem comical and innocent. As a Pilgrim, Amy enters Bunyan's "Valley of Humiliation" in the pickled lime episode. Spitefully excluding one girl from sharing in the treats, she is betrayed by that girl and publicly punished by the teacher. Consequently, Amy loses her limes and endures the public humiliation of being feruled. Nevertheless, Amy remains vindictive and spoiled. Thus, when her crying and screaming do not change Jo's mind about letting her come to the theater, she burns the only copy of the fairy tales Jo has written. Her punishment and humiliation for this nasty act come when she surreptitiously follows Jo on a skating trip and falls through the ice. When she goes to stay with Aunt March, Amy seems superficial because she determines to become good merely to inherit Aunt March's turquoise ring. Nevertheless, Amy recognizes her vanity and sincerely tries to control it.

Marmee (Mrs. Margaret March) is the ideal mother. A tall, noble-looking woman, she has a cheerful voice and friendly demeanor that conveys her willingness to help others. She encourages her daughters in this charitable outlook, convincing them to donate their Christmas breakfasts to a poor family. Marmee is equally charitable at home. She is a confidant to her daughters, always listening and never raising her voice when they confess their lapses. She constantly offers advice, but it is so sound that her girls willingly follow it. She is also a model of practical wisdom, which she demonstrates when she leaves so that her girls can learn for themselves the necessity of fulfilling domestic duties. Marmee claims that she once had a temper that she now controls, but she displays no flaws during the course of the novel. Her husband, **Mr. March**, a chaplain with the Union Army, is even more unrealistic and idealized. Inspired by Bronson Alcott, the author's father, Mr. March is a charitable man who lost his property by helping a friend and thus plunged his family into genteel poverty. He appears only at the end of the novel, but throughout he is a force inspiring the girls to follow Christian conduct. Wealthy, elderly **Aunt March** is a foil to Mr. March. Afflicted with a physical lameness that suggests a spiritual deformity, she lacks both the love and spirituality of her relatives. Although she listens to daily readings from dry religious books, she is a materialist. Thus, she threatens to disinherit Meg, who she claims has a duty of making a rich match. Unlike Marmee, who inspires people to goodness,

Aunt March fails to get her way because her domineering manner provokes opposition.

Laurie Laurence (Theodore, also called **Teddy)** is nearly sixteen when the novel opens. An orphan who was born in Italy, he is a fun-loving and handsome boy. He has curly black hair, brown skin, and large black eyes. Laurie has good manners, but he can at times be inconsiderate, as when he pretends that the notes he sends to Meg are actually from John Brooke. Laurie, who longs to be a famous musician in spite of his grandfather's opposition to such a career, can be stubborn. He has, however, a good heart, which is evident in the way he follows advice from both Marmee and Jo. The elderly **Mr. James Laurence**, Laurie's grandfather, is a tall, bald man who has a stern mouth and gruff voice. He is exceedingly proud and stubborn. When his son defied him by marrying an Italian musician, he never again spoke to him. Mr. Laurence similarly imposes his will on Laurie, discouraging his love of music and insisting that he attend college. Nevertheless, as his eyes indicate, Mr. Laurence is basically kind. He sends treats to the March girls, ensures that Beth has a piano to play, and gives book-loving Jo the run of his library. Furthermore, he is susceptible to Jo's youthful charms. Following her advice, he apologizes to Laurie for ever doubting him and thereby reestablishes his relationship with his grandson.

Further Reading

Berger, Laura Standley, ed. *Twentieth-Century Children's Writers*. 4th ed. Detroit: St. James, 1995.

Bingham, Jane M., ed. *Writers for Children: Critical Studies of Major Authors since the Seventeenth Century*. New York: Scribner's, 1988.

Burke, Kathleen. *Louisa May Alcott*. New York: Chelsea House, 1988.

Children's Literature Review. Vol. 1. Detroit: Gale Research, 1976.

Collier, Laurie, and Joyce Nakamura, eds. *Major Authors and Illustrators for Children and Young Adults*. Detroit: Gale Research, 1993.

Elbert, Sarah. *A Hunger for Home: Louisa May Alcott and* Little Women. Philadelphia: Temple University Press, 1984.

Estes, Glenn E., ed. *American Writers for Children before 1900*. Vol. 42 of *Dictionary of Literary Biography*. Detroit: Gale Research, 1985.

Johnston, Norma. *Louisa May: The World and Works of Louisa May Alcott*. New York: Four Winds Press, 1991.

MacDonald, Ruth K. *Louisa May Alcott*. Boston: Twayne, 1983.

Meigs, Cornelia. *Invincible Louisa: The Story of the Author of* Little Women. Boston: Little, Brown, 1968.

Myerson, Joel, ed. *The American Renaissance in New England*. Vol. 1 of *Dictionary of Literary Biography*. Detroit: Gale Research, 1978.

Payne, Alma J. *Louisa May Alcott: A Reference Guide*. Boston: G. K. Hall, 1980.

Riley, Sam G., ed. *American Magazine Journalists, 1850-1900*. Vol. 79 of *Dictionary of Literary Biography*. Detroit: Gale Research, 1988.

Saxton, Martha. *Louisa May: A Modern Biography of Louisa May Alcott*. Boston: Houghton Mifflin, 1977.

Yesterday's Authors of Books for Children. Vol. 1. Detroit: Gale Research, 1977.

Lloyd Alexander

1924-, American author

The Prydain Chronicles

(fantasy series, 1964-1968)

PLOT: "The Prydain Chronicles" form a *bildungsroman*, or story of apprenticeship. Taran, the central character, has adventures that enable him to grow up, to understand himself and his values, and to find a meaningful personal and social identity. In **The Book of Three** (1964), Taran, Assistant Pig-Keeper at Caer Dallben, home of the enchanter Dallben, finds his life dull. Longing to be a hero, Taran impetuously tries to make a sword after the farmer Coll refuses to show him how. Shortly afterwards, Hen Wen, the oracular pig, escapes from her pen. While searching for her, Taran encounters the evil Horned King. Prince Gwydion rescues Taran and takes up the search for Hen Wen. Gurgi, a half-human creature, soon joins them.

After losing Hen Wen's trail, Gwydion decides that they must warn the people of Caer Dathyl that the Cauldron-Born, the invincible warriors of Arawn Death-Lord of Annuvin, are going to attack. The Cauldron-Born capture the Taran, Gurgi, and

Gwydion, however, and take them to Spiral Castle. Separating him from Gwydion, the evil Queen Achren throws Taran into her dungeons. Eilonwy, a young princess, frees Taran and then takes Dyrnwyn, a magical sword, from a burial mound. She leads Taran to Fflewddur Fflam, whom she has also released, along with Melyngar, Gwydion's horse. Gurgi, who escaped capture, then rejoins Taran. Because Spiral Castle collapses immediately after their escape, Taran believes that Gwydion is dead, so he takes up the quest of warning Caer Dathyl and becomes the group's leader.

During their trek, Gurgi is injured, but Taran refuses to desert him. Melyngar then leads them to the hidden valley of Medwyn, who heals Gurgi and counsels Taran. Resuming the quest, Taran crosses a black lake, which sucks them into the underground kingdom of the King Eiddileg of the Fair Folk. After Gurgi discovers that Eiddileg has also captured Hen Wen, the king returns the pig and sends the dwarf Doli with them as a guide. The party soon finds a wounded gwythaint, a deadly bird from Annuvin. Taran insists that they nurse it; the gwythaint then escapes, and Hen Wen also runs away.

Taran now realizes that the Horned King is ahead of them and makes a desperate effort to warn Caer Dathyl. When the Horned King attacks him, Taran tries to draw Dyrnwyn, but he is knocked down by a powerful lightning bolt. Gwydion, informed of Taran's whereabouts by the healed gwythaint, arrives and destroys the Horned King by using his secret name. Later, Gwydion gives gifts to everyone, granting Taran the gift of returning home. Once there, Taran humbly confesses to Dallben that he succeeded only through mistakes. Dallben, noting that Taran kept the group together, thereby helping to recover Hen Wen and to warn Caer Dathyl, suggests that Taran has matured.

The Black Cauldron (1965) combines an external battle against the forces of evil and an internal struggle with egotism. The external struggle involves efforts to destroy the Black Crochan, or Black Cauldron, which produces the deathless Cauldron-Born warriors of Annuvin. Among those undertaking the quest is arrogant Prince Ellydyr, who verbally and physically humiliates Taran. His behavior generates the internal conflict, which tests Taran's pride and sense of identity and teaches him about sacrifice and tolerance. During the journey to Annuvin, Ellydyr argues with Taran, accidentally pushing him over a cliff. In an amazing display of strength, he then rescues Taran and his horse.

At the gates of Annuvin, Taran, Ellydyr, and Adaon, whose brooch gives him visions of the future, act as rear guard. Doli, who is able to make himself invisible, Fflewddur Fflam, Coll, and Gwydion try to recover the cauldron while King Morgant creates a distraction. During the night, Eilonwy and Gurgi join Taran's group. Fflewddur Fflam and Doli soon bring news that the cauldron is not in Annuvin and that Gwydion wants them to go to Caer Cadarn, King Smoit's stronghold. They are attacked by the Huntsmen of Annuvin, who grow stronger whenever one of their number is killed, and Ellydyr saves Taran's life. Pursued, they seek refuge with Gwystyl of the Fair Folk. From him and his crow, Kaw, they learn that Orddu, Orwen, and Orgoch have the cauldron in the Marshes of Morva. Taran, told by Adaon to choose their course, decides to seek the cauldron.

Wanting honor for himself, Ellydyr sets off alone to find the cauldron. When Huntsmen then attack the others, Fflewddur and Doli lead the Huntsmen away, but Adaon is killed and Doli does not return. Taran, to whom Adaon gave his brooch, now has dreams and visions that guide him to the cottage of Orddu, Orwen, and Orgach. Although he values the wisdom it gives him, Taran trades the brooch for the cauldron. While he is struggling to bring it back, it becomes lodged among river rocks. Ellydyr, stumbling upon them, forces them to agree to say that he alone recovered the cauldron. After trying to kill Taran, Ellydyr sets off with the cauldron. Taran and his group soon meet King Morgant, who has turned evil. Having captured Ellydyr and the cauldron, Morgant threatens to turn Taran's companions into Cauldron-Born at dawn unless Taran agrees to serve him. The invisible Doli now returns, freeing Taran and, at Taran's orders, Ellydyr. Ellydyr, knowing that the only way to destroy the cauldron is for a person to sacrifice his life by getting in it, heroically leaps into the cauldron, which shatters. Gwydion and King Smoit then arrive, and Smoit kills King

Morgant. Having faced evil and his own destructive pride, Taran returns to his duties as Assistant Pig-Keeper.

The Castle of Llyr (1966) addresses Taran's growing awareness of his feelings for Eilonwy, but questions of identity and worth remain central. When Dallben decides that Eilonwy must be trained as a lady, he sends her to King Rhuddlum and Queen Teleria on the Isle of Mona. Taran, Gurgi, and Kaw accompany her on the ship. On Mona, Taran finds Fflewddur Fflam living in the stables because he has run afoul of Magg, the Chief Steward. He also meets Prince Gwydion, disguised as a shoemaker. Gwydion warns Taran that Eilonwy is in great danger from Achren, who survived the collapse of Spiral Castle. The next day, Magg abducts Eilonwy. King Rhuddlum sends out a search party, but he has Taran vow to protect his bumbling son, Prince Rhun, to whom he has betrothed Eilonwy.

During the search, Rhun becomes lost. Taran, Gurgi, and Fflewddur find him in a cottage. They also discover a blank book, which Rhun takes, and some papers indicating that Glew turned a mountain cat, Llyan, into a giant. Llyan soon appears, but he is so charmed by Fflewddur's music that the party escapes. Resuming their search for Eilonwy, they discover her "bauble." Rhun soon falls into a pit, which collapses on the party when they try to rescue him, trapping them in a cavern. Glew, who has used a potion to transform himself into a giant, now imprisons them, intending to kill one of them so that he can create a potion to return to his proper size. Discovering that one of their party can escape if they form a human ladder, Taran sends Rhun to freedom. Rhun soon returns, however, using Eilonwy's bauble to blind Glew.

After escaping, Taran realizes that Eilonwy's bauble reveals spells written in the supposedly blank book Rhun took from the cottage. Having been informed by Kaw that Eilonwy is at Caer Colur, Eilonwy's ancestral home, they sail there with Gwydion. Taran locates Eilonwy, but she doesn't recognize him because Achren has bewitched her. Threatening to kill Eilonwy, Achren forces the companions to give her the book of spells and the Golden Pelidryn, Eilonwy's bauble. She then orders Eilonwy

to cast a spell. As Eilonwy does so, the book and then the castle begin burning. Magg, Achren's henchman, floods the castle, which crumbles, washing everyone into the sea. Llyan saves everyone, including a now powerless Achren. Eilonwy indicates that she will never marry Prince Rhun. She then gives Taran an ancient battle horn, the only thing remaining of Caer Colur, as a pledge of her continuing friendship.

The prefatory Author's Note describes *Taran Wanderer* (1967) as "more essentially heroic" than the previous volumes because Taran, searching for his identity, encounters "a merciless opponent: the truth about himself." Taran, feeling that he must know who he is in order to wed Eilonwy, receives permission from Dallben to search for his parents. Accompanied by Gurgi, he travels to the Marshes of Morva, but Orddu, Orwen, and Orgoch tell him only to go to the Mirror of Llunet in the Llawgadarn Mountains. On the way, when Lord Goryon's men steal Taran's horse, the farmer Aeddan comes to his aid. Aeddan and his wife give Taran their dead son's coat, symbolically offering themselves as parents, but Taran continues his quest. He tricks Goryon the Valorous into returning his horse and then dines with the stingy Gast the Generous. Joined by Fflewddur, who rides Llyan, Taran and Gurgi visit King Smoit. After Taran saves Smoit's life and settles a long-standing feud between Goryon and Gast, Smoit offers to adopt Taran. Taran refuses, insisting that he must learn who he is.

Taran next shows humanity, wisdom, and generosity in a complex encounter with the evil wizard Morda. This adventure begins when Kaw the crow leads Taran to discover a box containing a bone fragment and Llyan finds Doli, who has been transformed into a frog by Morda. Morda captures the companions and transforms Fflewddur into a hare and Gurgi into a mouse. Taran, however, breaks the bone fragment, which holds Morda's life, destroying the wizard and ending his spells. Although Taran considers trading Morda's magical blue jewel to the hags for information about his birth, he overcomes temptation and gives it to Doli, whose people originally owned it. Shortly afterwards, Taran's party encounters another arrogant villain, the outlaw Dorath, who treacherously takes Taran's sword.

Taran's hopes that he was nobly born are dashed when a poor shepherd named Craddoc claims to be Taran's father. Although Craddoc confesses his lie when he falls from a cliff, Taran summons the aid of the Fair Folk by using the final magical call in his hunting horn. Craddoc dies, however, and in the spring, Taran begins his quest anew. Entering the Free Commots, he meets Llonio, who professes to rely on luck for his living. Taran then apprentices himself to Hevvyd the Smith, Dwyrach Weaver-Woman, and Annlaw Clay-Shaper, thereby learning that he is unsuited to follow their crafts. On an errand for Annlaw, Taran helps Llassar, a shepherd boy, and his village defend against a raid by Dorath and his outlaws. Taran then goes to the Mirror of Llunet. He glances into the pool of water before Dorath stamps his foot and destroys it. During the subsequent fight, the sword Taran made while working for Hevvyd remains true, but Dorath's stolen sword breaks. Dorath escapes, however, because Taran tends to the wounded Gurgi. Taran has, however, succeed in his quest: his momentary glance into the pool makes him realize that he is Taran, that he is a man like any other, and that manhood is earned, not given.

The High King (1968), winner of the Newbery Medal, concludes the series with both heroic battles against evil and personal choices about identity. Arawn, disguised as Taran, attacks Gwydion and steals the sword Dyrnwyn. Determined to recover the sword, Gwydion sets out with Taran, Gurgi, Coll, Eilonwy, Fflewddur Fflam, King Rhun, and the former giant Glew. Gwydion, Taran, Coll, and Gurgi go to King Smoit's castle, where Magg, now Arawn's liegeman, imprisons them with Smoit. Fflewddur discovers what has happened, so the companions attack, using smoke and fire bombs that Gwystyl provides. King Rhun, while tricking the guards into thinking that he heads an army, is killed, but Gwydion and the others are rescued.

Gwydion now sends Taran into the Free Commots, where Hevvyd, Llassar, and Llonio (who dies in battle) are among those who join the new war leader. Later, Taran is summoned to Caer Dathyl, where Gwydion, Math the High King, and Taliesin the Chief Bard await reinforcements from King Pryderi. Pryderi,

however, has joined Arawn and demands their surrender. During the subsequent battle, the Cauldron-Born kill the High King and capture Caer Dathyl. Gwydion then devises a new plan: while he goes by sea to attack Annuvin, Taran is to delay the return of the Cauldron-Born. Coll is killed during a harrying raid; later, Eilonwy and Gurgi are among the missing. Doli and the Fair Folk join Taran and lead him through some tunnels, but Glew, while greedily gathering jewels, causes a cave-in. Forced to emerge, Taran sees a brilliant light: Eilonwy, whom Medwyn's wolves have rescued from Dorath, uses her magic bauble to warn him about nearby Huntsmen. Taran then goes above the Huntsmen's camp and melts a frozen lake, which pours down on the camp.

While Taran heads towards Annuvin, Pryderi threatens Dallben but dies when he touches the wizard's *Book of Three*. After Taran rescues Queen Achren, who is dying in the frozen wilderness, Fflewddur burns his harp, which magically warms them all night. Achren then guides Taran's party into Annuvin. Near the summit of Dragon Mountain, Taran falls. The gwythaint he saved as a fledgling rescues him, but the Cauldron-Born come after him. In desperation, Taran begins throwing rocks and uncovers Dyrnwyn. Drawing the flaming sword, he slashes at the Cauldron-Born warrior, who dies, as do the rest of his kind. When Gwydion then demands the sword, Taran realizes that he is facing a disguised Arawn. Magg then tries to put on Arawn's crown, but it kills him. Soon after, Arawn assumes the shape of a serpent and kills Achren, but Taran slays him with the sword. Gwydion, Dallben, Fflewddur, and Gurgi then leave for the Summer Land, a place of eternal happiness. Taran and Eilonwy, however, decide to remain mortals. They marry, and Taran becomes the new High King.

Two picture books illustrated by Eveline Ness, Coll and His White Pig *(1965) and* The Truthful Harp *(1967), are also about Prydain.* The Foundling and Other Tales *(1973) contains six stories about events preceding those described in the Chronicles.*

CHARACTERS: Although some characters have their origin in the Welsh *Mabinogian,* Alexander has modified them and surrounded them with unique and colorful characters of his own invention. With the exception of Taran, the prominent recurring characters display a dominant comic trait, usually signaled by a repeated phrase in their speeches. These characters provide comic relief, but many critics complain that the contemporary tone of their speeches and the endless repetition of their eccentricities makes it difficult to accept them as actors in a heroic battle of good against evil.

Taran, Assistant Pig-Keeper at Caer Dallben, is an orphan and thus an appropriate figure for combining mythological fantasy and contemporary democratic themes. That is, Taran is both the conventional hero who fulfills a prophetic destiny and the focus for the theme that individual identity and worth depend on deeds, not birth. Taran, who entertains a secret hope that he has noble blood, is initially a naive and impatient boy. Bored with his menial work tending the oracular pig, he despairingly believes that he can never achieve a meaningful identity because he lacks both social status and opportunities for physical action. At the same time, he is eager to show that he possesses the valor conventionally associated with nobility. His failure to make a serviceable sword, however, symbolizes that he is not yet a man and shows that he must acquire knowledge and patience before he can achieve a substantial identity. Because he is naive, Taran judges things by appearance, refusing to believe that the plainly dressed man who rescues him from the Horned King is the noble Gwydion or that a bald man like Coll could be a hero.

Furthermore, Taran is unaware of his own limitations and of the need to cultivate abilities. He nearly drowns while crossing a river, for example, because he foolishly assumes that he will be able to swim as soon as he tries. During the course of his quests to find Hen Wen and to warn Caer Dathyl about the Cauldron-Born, Taran develops into a leader. He also learns to be part of a group, giving and accepting help. He thus refuses to abandon the wounded Gurgi, whom he originally viewed as a pathetic coward, and he comes to appreciate the company of brave companions. Finally, Taran accepts responsibility for his errors and gains the humility to recognize that his successes depend on mistakes, not exceptional ability.

In his subsequent adventures, Taran is sometimes rash, but he gradually tempers his egotism, putting the interests of Prydain or his companions ahead of his own. Resisting temptations to personal power, he makes significant sacrifices, trading the brooch that made him wise for the Black Crochan, agreeing to give Ellydyr credit for finding the Cauldron, and keeping his promise to King Rhuddlum that he will protect Prince Rhun, whom he believes will one day have the hand of Eilonwy. Taran's growth is particularly evident in *Taran Wanderer*. Seeking to learn who he is by discovering his parents, Taran displays the qualities of a good leader by creating peace between Goryon and Gast. Later, when Craddoc claims to be his father, Taran sinks to his lowest point of self-esteem, giving up his dreams of greatness and of marrying Eilonwy. After Craddoc reveals his deception and Taran proves his innate nobility by rescuing him, Taran exhibits new-found maturity. First, he accepts that heroism takes many forms and that the common folk display heroism in their daily struggles to make a living. Second, he decides that his pride should not come from his birth but from what he is inside. By apprenticing himself to the smith, weaver, and potter, he learns about his own abilities, limitations, and desires. He is thus able to accept the vision in the Mirror of Llunet: "Now I know who I am: myself and none other."

Ironically, once Taran humbly accepts that he is like other men, he establishes his superiority. In *The High King*, he proves that he is a brave and a gifted leader after Gwydion makes him a war leader and the people of the Free Commots rally to join him. He also displays the compassion characteristic of his actions throughout when he rescues Achren. Taran, who once scorned help, then discovers the sword Dyrnwyn only because the gwythaint he saved during the quest for the Cauldron rescues him. Taran makes victory possible by using it to slay the deathless Cauldron-Born, but he ensures victory by demonstrating the wisdom he originally lacked. Taran, who once was fooled by the plain appearance of Gwydion has the wit to penetrate the disguise when Arawn assumes the appearance of Gwydion and therefore refuses to surrender the magic sword. Taran is then able to slay Arawn.

The significant point, however, is that Taran is able to wield the sword that nearly destroyed him earlier. Consequently, although Taran may lack noble birth, he has something more important than heroism: "noble worth." He continues to display this worth, rejecting eternal happiness in the Summer Lands because he feels a responsibility to Prydain and because he has learned that true heroism involves striving for others, not for oneself. Just when he accepts that he can be happy as Assistant Pig-Keeper, however, Taran learns that his sacrifice has made him a worthy High King.

In his progress from boy to man and from pig-keeper to king, Taran rises because of his merit, not his birth, and he learns to appreciate the needs of others, not simply the rights of privilege. Taran, who is never physically described, thus becomes a figure in a democratic myth, overcoming the challenges and questions of identity that everyone faces. As Alexander says in the note that opens the first volume, "we are all Assistant Pig-Keepers at heart."

Eilonwy, Princess of the House of Llyr, is a year or two younger than Taran but just as tall. Eilonwy has a delicate, elfin face, blue eyes, and long, reddish-gold hair. She always carries a "bauble," a golden globe that magically lights up. Eilonwy plays the traditional roles of both love interest for the hero and damsel who sometimes needs rescuing, but she is far from conventional. In fact, she adds a distinctly modern and feminist tone to the novels. A fiercely independent orphan, she resents the family tradition that would make her become an enchantress, and she resists being educated to behave as a young lady. Eilonwy also resents Taran's assumptions that she is a little girl whom he can order about. Eager to be part of the adventures, she sometimes endangers Taran, as she does when she sneaks away from Caer Dallben to join the party searching for the Cauldron. At other times, however, she proves her bravery, as she does when she dons armor to fight with Taran's troops in the final battles.

Taran thinks of Eilonwy as scatterbrained because she chatters constantly, fills her speeches with similes, and can't stop talking to Taran in spite of frequent angry threats that she will. For her part, Eilonwy frequently punctures Taran's pride by noting that it does not require intelligence to be an Assistant Pig-Keeper. That, however, is only one side of the prickly relationship that develops between them. Eilonwy also encourages Taran with advice and praise, noting how often he surprises her with his accomplishments. Although Eilonwy is sometimes foolishly independent, she is usually bright, perceptive, and practical. She is the one, for example, who frees Taran from Achren and who realizes that Gwydion is in trouble when Magg captures him. Eilonwy also makes wise, thematically important pronouncements. When Taran becomes jealous of Prince Rhun, for instance, she tells him that if a pig-keeper and prince each do their best, there is no difference between them. Eilonwy's maturation is as meaningful as Taran's. Eilonwy cries out against a destiny that would force her to go to the Summer Land and thereby earns the right to choose her destiny. Some feminists may decry her choice as a loss of independence, but by giving up magic and immortality for marriage to Taran, Eilonwy indicates that she has matured as a woman and that she values human relationships more than social status or tradition.

Fflewddur Fflam, who has given up kingship of a small northern realm to wander as a lowly bard, contrasts with Taran because he has overcome his concern with social status. Fflewddur is tall and lanky, has a long, pointed nose, and a shock of spiky yellow hair. Fflewddur is not officially a bard, having failed to master the traditional lore, but Taliesin gave him a special harp that almost plays itself. Whenever Fflewddur lies or, as he prefers to say, "colors the truth," the harp's strings break. Because he has the heart of a bard and therefore likes to entertain others with colorful stories, the strings frequently snap. Fflewddur, then, presents a comical side of Taran's dilemma, for he, like the pig-keeper, must learn to face the truth about his life. Fflewddur is also characterized by his repeated references to the qualities a Fflam possesses. Although a predominantly comic character, Fflewddur is a brave and accomplished fighter. His finest moment, however, is when he sacrifices his beloved harp to make a life-saving fire that saves the party during the march to Annuvin. As one of the Sons of Don, Fflewddur must voyage to the Summer Land, where he will become a true bard under Taliesin's instruction.

Gurgi, Taran's constant and faithful companion, is the most original and memorable comic character in the Chronicles. Part animal and part human, Gurgi is covered by matted fur and has long, skinny arms and flexible feet. Gurgi speaks of himself in the third person and fills his speeches with such rhyming expressions as "munchings and crunchings." Gurgi initially seems base and nasty, jumping down from a tree to strangle Taran. He also seems to be a coward, running away and hiding from danger in the early adventures. Even though Gurgi punctuates his speeches with praise of his own bravery and cleverness, he obviously lacks self-worth: he whines about his "poor tender head," he repeatedly notes that he lacks wisdom, and he excessively praises Taran and his companions. As Taliesin points out, however, Gurgi is wrong to think that he lacks wisdom because he possesses "the wisdom of a good and kindly heart." Thus, he remains loyally, even sentimentally, devoted to Taran. Furthermore, once Taran accepts him, Gurgi masters his fears enough to fight bravely in some skirmishes and to act as flag bearer in the final battles. Gurgi makes important contributions to the quests by being lucky and sharp-sighted: he finds Hen Wen, the Cauldron, and the secrets of various trades that Arawn had stolen and hidden in a coffer in Annuvin. He is also a helper, using the gift Gwydion gave him after the first quest, a magic wallet that is never empty, to feed his companions, and saving the life of the greedy Glew by pulling him away from the fires in Annuvin's treasure room. His most important contribution, however, is in developing Taran's character. Gurgi's devotion teaches Taran not to judge others by appearances, and Gurgi's plea to be killed when he is wounded tests Taran's compassion, causing him to act on his concern for others.

The two men who raise Taran are mentors. The wizard **Dallben** is the archetypal wise old man. He announces the thematic purpose of the journeys that dominate the series when he says that one often learns more by seeking than by finding answers.

Dallben himself knows much, but says little. Three hundred and seventy-nine years old, Dallben has a long beard and spends his time "meditating," a task so difficult that he can perform it only by lying down and closing his eyes. Although he thus seems comical, he is a serious character in the final volume. In it, he appears as a weary, care-worn man, but he is also a powerful one. Although forbidden to use his powers to kill others, he protects himself by blowing gales with his breath, causing earthquakes by pounding his staff, and weaving fire with his hands. Dallben frequently consults *The Book of Three* for prophecies, but he finally declares that a man's deeds, not prophecies, shape a man's destiny, thus articulating the major theme of the series. **Coll**, a bald, stocky, and powerful farmer, contributes to the theme of appearances in the first volume because Taran is shocked to learn that a bald man can be a hero. (Years earlier, Coll had rescued Hen Wen from Annuvin.) Coll is brave in battle, saving Taran's life and dying while single-handedly opposing the Cauldron-Born. By repeatedly placing more value on growing turnips than on destroying others, however, Coll embodies values that Taran matures into appreciating. Coll is also a mentor, telling Taran that the foundations of learning are "see much, study much, suffer much."

Three other mentors teach Taran. **Prince Gwydion** is a warrior and a magician based on a figure in the *Mabinogian*. He is tall, with a lined, weather-beaten face, shaggy, wolfish gray hair, and penetrating green eyes. Gwydion is essentially static, representing the ideal of the hero to which Taran aspires. Gwydion announces the appearance-reality theme in the first adventure when Taran refuses to believe that someone coarsely dressed could be a legendary hero. Gwydion tells Taran that clothes don't make a prince and a sword doesn't make a hero. Gwydion continues to act as Taran's mentor, telling him that he is a fool if he doesn't fear the forces of evil and insisting that he must accept responsibility for his faults. Gwydion's heroism in resisting the tortures of Achren, his unwavering opposition to evil, and his pointed advice turn Taran into a wise leader. Acknowledging Taran's maturity, Gwydion elevates the pig-keeper to the status of war leader. **Medwyn**, a huge, muscular man, with long white hair and a beard hanging to his waist, wears a coarse brown robe and has a narrow gold band set with a single blue jewel on his forehead. Medwyn is an animal protector who lives in a valley humans normally can't find. Seeing the weathered remains of an ancient ship, Taran asks if Medwyn is Nevvid Nav Neivion, a Noah-like person who took two of every animal aboard a ship when waters flooded Prydain. Medwyn cuts him off, however, claiming only that he is Medwyn. In *The Book of Three*, Medwyn is a helper, healing Gurgi from a potentially fatal wound. He is also a counselor. His advice about respecting all living creatures inspires Taran to be kind to the gwythaint who later saves his life. His statement that Taran should neither refuse to give help nor refuse to accept it warns the proud Taran away from foolish and ineffective solitary heroism. In the final volume, Medwyn orders all the animals to turn against Arawn's forces. **Adaon**, son of the Chief Bard Taliesin, exemplifies wise nobility. A tall man with straight black hair and deep gray eyes, he is gentle, observant, and wise. He carries herbs to heal bodies, and he offers advice to heal minds. His brooch gives him insight and visions of the future. He thus tells Taran about the "black beast" that controls Ellydyr, preparing Taran to feel compassion later. More significantly, Adaon foresees his own death, so he lets Taran decide their course so that he will not make a selfish decision. Adaon sacrifices himself, putting his body in front of a dagger hurled at Taran. The brooch he bequeaths to Taran represents the wisdom of age. Using it, Taran gains compassionate understanding of Ellydyr and the insight to guide his party safely to the Cauldron.

Two lords adopt patently false identities, testing Taran's wisdom in the process. **Goryon the Valorous**, a burly lord with a dark beard flecked with gray, is a loud bully. When he realizes that moral claims hold no weight with Goryon, Taran tricks the overly proud lord into returning his horse by offering it as a gift from a pig-boy. **Gast the Generous** is even more inappropriately named. Wearing numerous rings, silver armbands, and costly but food-splattered clothing, Gast brags of his wealth and generosity, but he is actually a glutton who gives little to his guests and doesn't properly value what he does own. Taran, who can appreciate a simple wine bowl, has greater natural taste and appears more innately aristocratic than Gast. Together, Gast and Goryon show that an extreme concern for honor is foolish and that a humble farmer like Aeddan, who grows things and supports life, does more valuable work.

Others try to offer Taran a home and an identity. The red-bearded **King Smoit**, who sits on a throne carved in the shape of a bear, is a gigantic, loud man with a thick neck, battle-scarred face, nose battered to his cheekbones, heavy forehead, and fierce, tangled eyebrows. A volatile man, he takes great pleasure in eating and fighting. He tells Taran that a king's strength lies in the will of those he rules, but he tries to bludgeon Gast and Goryon into submission. Impressed by Taran's display of kingly wisdom in creating peace, Smoit offers to adopt him. **Aeddan**, a weather-beaten, sinewy farmer with uncropped gray hair, shows his goodness and sense of fair play by helping Taran when Goryon's men steal his horse. He provides Taran with the first example of ordinary, nonmilitary bravery by scratching out a living on a poor farm. Aeddan symbolically offers to adopt Taran by offering him both a place on the farm and his dead son's coat. Although Taran learns to respect and admire the farmer, he refuses. **Craddoc**, an old shepherd, severely tests Taran's moral and psychological merit. Hobbling on a crutch because of his lame right leg, Craddoc is a tall, broad-shouldered man with gray hair and a gray beard. Lonely and needing help in tending his sheep, he falsely claims to be Taran's father. Taran stays with him out of a sense of duty and because he feels that his dreams of marrying Eilonwy have been crushed. Taran redeems himself from pettiness by overcoming the temptation to let Craddoc die after the wounded old man confesses his lie.

The people whom Taran encounters in the Free Commots represent various philosophies of life. **Llonio** is so thin and sticklike that he resembles a crane or a stork. He has lank hair and blue eyes, and he wears ill-fitting patchwork clothes. An affable, optimistic man, he supports his family by scavenging. Although he professes to believe that life depends on luck, he later tells Taran that his extraordinary luck is actually a matter of recognizing opportunities and of having the wits to use whatever he acquires. **Hevvyd the Smith** is a gruff, bearded, barrel-chested, man with a loud, gravelly voice. He becomes a mentor by teaching Taran that life is a forge in which one is tempered. In addition to learning humility and patience from Hevvyd, Taran learns to make a sword, thus succeeding in a manly task at which he failed in the opening scene of the Chronicles.

Dwyrach Weaver-Woman is a bent and bony woman with withered, wrinkled cheeks and long white hair. Her work exhausts Taran as much as Hevvyd's did because he lacks skill, but Dwyrach remains spry at the end of the day. Sharp-tongued and demanding, she teaches Taran to weave his own cloak. In doing so, she gives him a graphic lesson of her belief that life is a loom because all things must be done strand by strand. **Annlaw Clay-Shaper** is the prototypical artist, a man who has merged so fully and joyfully into his craft that he can't separate himself from it. He is famous, but he lives and dresses simply because he delights in his craft, not the wealth he could gain from it. When he is at his potter's wheel, this old man with the close-cropped, iron-gray hair and beard is as powerful as Hevvyd and more intricate than Dwyrach. Annlaw doesn't claim that life is a potter's wheel, but clay is a traditional symbol of humans. He offers a valuable comparison between skill, which is increased by use, and the heart, which also renews itself. Taran's experiences with Annlaw also teach him that desire is not sufficient to create a new identity because, although he loves the work, he learns that he lacks the true gift for it. **Llassar**, a young shepherd, exhibits the same mixture of fear and bravado that Taran had when he first set out. Llassar fights bravely against Dorath and joins Taran's troops to fight Arawn. For Taran, Llassar represents both the heroism of daily toil and the contentment with one's place that Taran has not yet learned.

Three of the Fair Folk are notable, with two of them appearing in more than one volume. **King Eiddileg**, a plump dwarf with a bristling yellow beard, dresses in garish red and green and wears numerous rings. Ruler of the underground kingdom of the Fair Folk, he is cantankerous, resentful of humans, and somewhat devious, not revealing that he has captured Hen Wen because he has not been directly asked about her. When his honor is questioned, however, Eiddileg helps Taran. **Doli**, a red-haired dwarf with red eyes who is nearly as broad as he is tall, uses his ability to turn invisible to help Taran. Doli appears to be ill-tempered and angry, perpetually grumbling and complaining about everything, but he is both kind and brave, thus contributing to the appearance versus reality theme. Doli also contributes to the comedy. When Taran first meets him, Doli holds his breath until he is blue in a vain effort to become invisible, a traditional ability in his family. After Gwydion gives him the power of invisibility, Doli repeatedly complains that his ears ring with the sound of bees and hornets whenever he uses it. **Gwystyl** is deliberately deceptive. Resembling sticks with cobwebs on top because he is extremely thin and has sparse, stringy hair, he adopts an attitude of perpetual gloom. Although he operates a secret way station near Annuvin, he seems reluctant to offer Taran assistance. Actually, Gwystyl is a shrewd servant of the Fair Folk, and he bravely uses his ability to mislead others into thinking that he is of negligible importance, to aid in the battle against evil. Although appearing reluctant to do so, he helps by sending Taran to the three hags for information about the Cauldron, and he provides the smoke and fire bombs for the assault on Smoit's captured castle.

Prince Rhun is a foil who illuminates Taran's maturity. About Taran's age, he has a round face, blue eyes, and straw-colored hair. Well-meaning but hapless, Rhun constantly falls into water or has other accidents. Nevertheless, Rhun is cheerful, habitually greeting everyone with ''Hullo, hullo,'' but he is not witless, as he seems at first. He understands, for example, that he is not really in charge of the party searching for Eilonwy. After becoming **King Rhun**, he is no longer feckless, having learned from his failures to plan carefully and intelligently. He becomes a hero, sacrificing his life while playing a clever ruse that turns the tide of battle during the rescue of those Magg imprisoned in Smoit's castle.

The evil characters represent the shadowy side of Taran's longing for high status, and most of them ironically become subject to the very power that they believe they can control. **Prince Ellydyr**, the youngest son of Pen-Llarcau and Taran's rival in *The Black Cauldron*, is a tragically ironic villain. Having inherited only his title and his sword, Ellydyr is so obsessed with winning honor and glory that he behaves despicably and dishonorably. He is also a cautionary figure who shows the destructive side of qualities that Taran possesses. Quick-tempered and easily offended, Ellydyr is ruled by his pride, the "black beast" that Adaon envisions as riding him. A few years older than Taran, Ellydyr has tawny hair, deep-set, dark eyes, and a pale, arrogant face. He consistently behaves in rude, spiteful, and unwise ways. For example, contemptuously insisting that the "pig-boy" should ride at the rear of the procession, he jostles Taran, knocking him over a cliff. After using his amazing strength to save Taran, he contemptuously dismisses Taran's awe-struck gratitude. He also insults Taran after saving him from the Huntsmen, indicating that he puts no value on Taran's life. In his quest for solitary glory, Ellydyr is both selfish and mad. He thus begins valuing reputation over deeds, as he shows by insisting that he be credited with finding the cauldron. Lacking integrity himself, Ellydyr assumes that Taran will betray him, so he tries to murder Taran to ensure his silence. Ellydyr redeems himself and gains genuine honor, however, when he sacrifices himself by jumping into the Crochan to destroy it.

Two other villains also undergo transformations. **Achren** is beautiful, yet evil. She has a youthful appearance, long, silver tresses, cold eyes, and a deathly pale complexion. Long ago, when she was Queen of Prydain, she chose Arawn as her consort, teaching him magical powers. After he rid himself of her, she vowed revenge. She is cruel, visiting unspeakable tortures on Gwydion in a vain attempt to get him to side with her against Arawn. Later, she casts a spell on Eilonwy to gain the book and bauble that would increase her magical power. Eilonwy's destruction of the book, however, causes Achren to lose all her power. Taking up residence at Caer Dallben, Achren seems reformed, serving Dallben

faithfully, but she nurses her anger. Rescued by Taran after Magg's troops and the gwythaints attack her, Achren leads Taran into Annuvin. Then, in an act of revenge in which she dies, she points out that Arawn has transformed himself into a serpent. **Glew** is a little person inside, but he turned himself into a giant and became trapped in a cave, where Taran tumbled in on him. A grotesque being three times Taran's height, Glew has flabby arms, moss-covered knees, a lumpy nose, and flapping ears. His hair and beard are covered with mold and toadstools. Glew calls himself a king, complains of his situation, and tries to kill one of Taran's companions so that he can make a restorative magical brew. After Dallben restores him to his proper size, Glew irritates everyone by constantly talking about what he would do if he were still a giant. Selfishness personified, Glew endangers others by his greedy concern with gathering wealth. Glew improves slightly after Gurgi saves him in Annuvin, telling the truth about the rescue and giving Taran a jewel.

Most of the villains, however, are permanently corrupted. **King Morgant** of Madoc takes the opposite course of Prince Ellydyr, throwing away the honor of a blameless life by finally succumbing to the temptations of power. Dark, with a falconlike nose and keen, heavy-lidded eyes, Morgant is noted as an icy, fearless warrior, second only to Gwydion in prowess. He prides himself on his understanding of others, recognizing that Taran has good mettle. His offer to make Taran his war leader is thus a temptation that tests Taran's moral worth. At the same time, Morgant reveals his own madness. Resenting that he has served those whom he believes to be inferior, he is so completely devoid of compassion that he is willing to destroy anyone to wield power. Tall, golden-haired **King Pryderi**, the most powerful lord in Prydain, exhibits a similar arrogance and illustrates the idea that good can't come from evil. Pryderi arrogantly assumes that he can use Arawn to bring peace and then overthrow him to become absolute ruler himself. Pryderi is Arawn's dupe, however, when he attacks Dallben. Ironically, Pryderi fulfills Dallben's prophecy that he is marked for death in *The Book of Three*, by touching the forbidden book. **Morda** the wizard has a hairless skull, gaunt, clay-colored face, cold, lidless eyes, and a mouth that resembles a livid scar stitched with wrinkles. He embodies in extreme form Taran's concern with a superior identity, becoming evil because of his excessive pride. From Eilonwy's dying mother, Morda acquired a jewel that gave him power and long life. Holding humanity in contempt and dismissing moral concepts as mere toys, he came to believe that it was his destiny to be the master of all humans. Morda concentrated his soul in his little finger, which he then chopped off and hid. As a result, Morda could not be killed by ordinary means, as Taran discovers when he pierces Morda with his sword. Morda's apparent invulnerability tests Taran, who figures out that Morda has failed to cast a spell on him because he is carrying the bone, a part of Morda himself. Ironically, Morda plays a role in his own death: Taran is unable to break the bone, but it snaps when the preternaturally powerful Morda tries to grab it from him. **Dorath**, a foil to Taran, is the leader of a gang of mercenaries and outlaws; he insists that power comes from brute force: "Dorath is king wherever he rides." As a demonic parody of nobility, Dorath neither looks nor behaves like royalty. Always dressed in muddy clothes, the heavy-faced Dorath has a stubbly beard, long, tangled, yellowish hair, and cold-blue eyes. Dorath lacks honor and cheats during his fight for Taran's sword by drawing a concealed knife. Furthermore, he is about to defile Eilonwy when one of Medwyn's wolves kills him.

Magg, King Rhuddlum's elegantly dressed and efficient Chief Steward, is a skinny, spiderlike man who constantly spins nefarious plots. At first, he works for Achren, kidnapping Eilonwy because he has been promised that he will become a king. Later, he puts himself in the service of Arawn, who has promised that he will inherit the Death-Lord's iron crown. The lust for power drives the arrogant Magg into madness. During the final battle, he proclaims himself the King of Annuvin, but when he puts on the iron crown, it turns white hot and kills him. **The Horned King**, Arawn's war leader, is the most obvious representative of evil in *The Book of Three*. He is a gigantic man with crimson-stained arms, a crimson cloak, and a mask made from the skull and antlers of a stag. The Horned King's attack reveals Taran's bravery. The Horned King's destruction, which occurs because Gwydion speaks his secret name, establishes that knowledge, more than physical power, is necessary to defeat evil. **Arawn** Death-Lord, King of Annuvin, represents the idea that evil takes many forms because he is a shape shifter who can't leave his kingdom in his own form. Once the consort of Achren, he dethroned her after she had taught him magic powers. Pitiless, he has made gwythaints into vicious killers and he has transformed many dead into the merciless and invincible Cauldron-Born. He attracts the arrogant and greedy to his service with promises of power and status. His shape shifting challenges Taran's wits, showing that heroism requires more than strength.

Fitting outside of good and evil are **Orddu**, **Orwen**, and **Orgoch**, who are reminiscent of the mythological Fates, especially because they weave a tapestry of Taran's life. Appearing as either old hags or beautiful women, they articulate important themes about personal identity and freedom. By telling Taran to pick any parents, they suggest that he is free to establish his own identity. By asking him if he is brave enough to scratch for worms, they foreshadow Taran's discovery of the heroism of daily toil. Finally, by showing him the tapestry in his dream, they insist that the individual, not fate, determines one's course in life. Although they wear the same stained, shapeless robes, have the same lumpy, round faces, and confuse themselves and others by constantly exchanging identities, the three hags of the Marshes of Morva are distinguishable. Orddu does most of the talking; Orwen wears a necklace of milky stones; Orgoch, who makes the most threats, keeps her face concealed with her hood.

Three animals have recurring roles. **Hen Wen**, a white pig, has oracular powers. Her capture by the forces of Annuvin establishes the heroism of Coll, who once rescued her, and her flight from Caer Dallben initiates the adventures that test Taran's wisdom and courage. **Kaw**, the talking crow that Gwystyl gives to Taran, is a conventional bird helper, providing information and warnings to the heroes. **Llyan**, a golden-tawny mountain cat that Glew transformed into a giant, is as tall as a horse. She loves Fflewddur's music, the only thing that tames and calms her. Fflewddur eventually rides her instead of a horse.

Further Reading

Authors and Artists for Young Adults. Vol. 1. Detroit: Gale Research, 1989.

Children's Literature Review. Vols. 1, 5. Detroit: Gale Research, 1976, 1983.

Collier, Laurie, and Joyce Nakamura, eds. *Major Authors and Illustrators for Children and Young Adults.* Detroit: Gale Research, 1993.

Contemporary Authors New Revision Series. Vol. 38. Detroit: Gale Research, 1993.

Contemporary Literary Criticism. Vol. 35. Detroit: Gale Research, 1985.

De Montreville, Doris, and Donna Hill, eds. *Third Book of Junior Authors.* New York: H. W. Wilson, 1972.

Estes, Glenn E., ed. *American Writers for Children since 1960: Fiction.* Vol. 52 of *Dictionary of Literary Biography.* Detroit: Gale Research, 1986.

May, Jill P. *Lloyd Alexander.* Boston: Twayne, 1991.

Something about the Author. Vols. 3, 49, 81. Detroit: Gale Research, 1972, 1988, 1995.

Something about the Author Autobiography Series. Vol. 19. Detroit: Gale Research, 1995.

Stott, Jon. C. "Alexander's Chronicles of Prydain: The Nature of Beginnings." In *Touchstones: Reflections on the Best in Children's Literature.* Vol. 1. Edited by Perry Nodelman. West Lafayette, IN: Children's Literature Association, 1985.

Harry Allard

1928-, American academic, author, and translator

Miss Nelson Is Missing!

(picture book, 1977; illustrated by James Marshall)

PLOT: Understandably a favorite with teachers, this comical story presents a new twist on the old theme

In this illustration by James Marshall from **Miss Nelson Is Missing!**, *Miss Nelson's scary disguise frightens away her students.*

that people do not appreciate what they have until they lose it. Room 207 is the worst-behaved class in the school. The children throw spitballs and paper airplanes, are rude during story hour, and refuse to do their lessons. Miss Nelson, their teacher, decides that something must be done. The next morning, Miss Viola Swamp, an ugly woman in a black dress, takes over the class. She bosses the children, cancels story hour, and makes them work hard. The plot thus turns on the idea that Miss Nelson must be missing before she can be missed. Some children now go to the police station, but Detective McSmogg is no help in finding Miss Nelson. Others go to her house, but they run away when they see Miss Viola Swamp coming up the street. Just when the children are about to give up hope of her return, Miss Nelson comes back. The children, who now behave properly, admit that they have missed her and ask Miss Nelson where she has been, but she says only that it is her little secret. When Miss Nelson asks why the children are now so good, they tell her that that is *their* little secret. The story concludes with a twist when, that night, Miss Nelson hangs her coat in her closet next to an ugly black dress. In an epilogue, readers learn that Detective McSmogg is now looking for Miss Viola Swamp.

Miss Nelson Is Back *(1982) and* Miss Nelson Has a Field Day *(1985) are sequels.*

CHARACTERS: The central character fits into a tradition of "split" heroes, characters with two identities. Miss Nelson is more like such split heroes as Clark Kent/Superman, who chooses an alternate identity, than she is like Dr. Jekyll/Mr. Hyde, who has an alternate identity beyond personal control. Nevertheless, this gently ironic story suggests that circumstances do change personalities. James Marshall has indicated that he partially based Viola Swamp on his second-grade teacher, who laughed at his early attempts to be creative.

Miss Nelson is pictured as the epitome of gentleness, a blonde woman who wears a pink dress and speaks in a sweet voice. She is clearly shocked and dismayed by the antics of her class. Although she appears ineffective, Miss Nelson obviously has an excellent understanding of children. She knows that they have typecast her and will never change unless she shocks them into appreciating her. A dedicated teacher, Miss Nelson does not give up on the class but resorts to imaginative deception. She returns under her own identity only when the children are ready to let her be herself. When she does return, she shows wit and consideration, retaining the secret of her alternate identity so that she can use it again if necessary, yet she allows the children to save face and feel important by letting them keep their "little secret" about the reason for their improved behavior.

Miss Viola Swamp is an identity created to meet the demands of a particular circumstance. To the children, she looks and acts like a witch. Viola Swamp is physically the opposite of Miss Nelson: she is dressed in an ugly black dress, wears hideous green-striped stockings, and has frizzy black hair, a long nose, and a pointed chin. She even seems to be wearing black lipstick. She is also the opposite in

classroom manner. She is a rigid disciplinarian who is completely lacking in sympathy for the children. She eliminates the things that they may enjoy, such as story hour, and piles on the homework. She does not allow talking. Miss Viola Swamp thus represents the dark or shadowy side that every good teacher normally suppresses.

Further Reading

Berger, Laura Standley, ed. *Twentieth-Century Children's Writers.* 4th ed. Detroit: St. James, 1995.

Children's Literature Review. Vol. 21. Detroit: Gale Research, 1990.

Crawford, Elizabeth D., and Doris De Montreville, eds. *Fourth Book of Junior Authors.* New York: H. W. Wilson, 1978.

Estes, Glenn E., ed. *American Writers for Children since 1960: Poets, Illustrators, and Nonfiction Authors.* Vol. 61 of *Dictionary of Literary Biography.* Detroit: Gale Research, 1987.

Something about the Author. Vols. 6, 51, 75. Detroit: Gale Research, 1974, 1988, 1994.

Edward Ardizzone

1900-1979, English artist, illustrator, and author

Little Tim and the Brave Sea Captain
(picture book, 1936; revised edition, 1955)

PLOT: Although its settings and characters are realistic, *Little Tim and the Brave Sea Captain* is a fantasy that expresses a child's desire for adventure. Little Tim lives by the sea and wants to be a sailor. His parents laugh at his ambition, saying that he can't go to sea until he is grown up. Saddened, Tim determines that he will run away. He gets his chance to go on a sea voyage when an old boatman asks him to come along on a visit to a steamer. Tim hides on the steamer, and the boatman forgets about him. Once the ship is at sea, Tim shows himself to the captain, who becomes furious and puts the stowaway to work scrubbing decks. Soon Tim is working as a cabin boy and becomes well liked. During a storm, Tim becomes seasick and takes to his bunk. Because he is so small, the sailors do not notice him and therefore leave him behind when they abandon

Ardizzone's illustration of Little Tim and the Captain.

ship. But Tim finds the captain still on the bridge. Together, they bravely await death, but fortunately they are rescued just before the steamer sinks. When Tim finally returns home, the captain tells his parents how brave their son was, and they agree to let him go on the captain's next voyage.

Ardizzone published ten sequels: Tim and Lucy Go to Sea *(1938; revised 1958),* Tim to the Rescue *(1949),* Tim and Charlotte *(1951),* Tim in Danger *(1953),* Tim All Alone *(1956),* Tim's Friend Towser *(1962),* Tim and Ginger *(1965),* Tim to the Lighthouse *(1968),* Tim's Last Voyage *(1972), and* Ship's Cook Ginger *(1977).*

CHARACTERS: Describing how he creates picture books, Ardizzone once said, "Characters have to be created pictorially because there is no space to do so verbally in the text." The pictures in *Little Tim and*

the Brave Sea Captain define the visual identity of the characters, as well as suggesting their moods.

Little Tim is a blond-haired child who is always dressed in a long-sleeved red sweater and knee-length navy shorts. His age is not given, but Tim must be five or six because he appears to be much smaller than he is in the next volume in the series, *Tim and Lucy Go to Sea,* in which he is seven. Tim is a bright child, astonishing his parents with his ability to identify ships. He is also friendly, readily becoming close to an old sea captain and the old boatman. The illustrations also suggest that Tim is not the type to hide his emotions. After his parents laugh at him, he is pictured from behind with his hands clasped behind his back and head bowed in dejection. (Ardizzone felt that character's backs could be exceptionally expressive.) On the facing page, the adventurous Tim reveals his joy over the invitation to visit the steamer: both hands are in the air, and he is dancing or jumping on one foot.

When the steamer captain makes him work, Tim cries oversized tears. Nevertheless, he perseveres and completes his tasks. When he becomes a cabin boy, Tim is energetic, courteous, and dutiful. He cries after he is left on board the sinking ship, but he quickly shows that he can be brave when the captain asks him to dry his eyes. Significantly, he holds hands with the captain, getting reassurance from a father substitute. Although Tim does not think once about his parents when he is at sea, he shows that he can be a loving and thoughtful son by sending them a telegram after he is rescued. Furthermore, he eagerly runs into his mother's arms when he returns home.

The brave captain is pictured as the archetypal seaman. Formally attired in a uniform and cap, he has white hair and a full white beard. Although he is furious when Tim is brought to him, the amused reaction of the sailor who found Tim suggests that the captain is playing a role to teach Tim a lesson. Whatever his initial feelings, the captain comes to appreciate Tim's usefulness as a cabin boy. When the ship is sinking, he adopts a no-nonsense attitude, not hiding the fact that they are "bound for Davey Jones's locker." He does, however, hold Tim's hand, and he sets an example of bravery in the face of death. When he visits Tim's parents, the captain becomes an agent of wish fulfillment. By testifying to Tim's bravery, the captain compels his parents, who had earlier laughed at their son's desire to be a sailor, to recognize his abilities and to let him follow his dream.

Further Reading

Ardizzone, Edward. *The Young Ardizzone: An Autobiographical Fragment.* London: Studio Vista, 1970.

Berger, Laura Standley, ed. *Twentieth-Century Children's Writers,* 4th ed. Detroit: St. James, 1995.

Bingham, Jane M., ed. *Writers for Children: Critical Studies of Major Authors since the Seventeenth Century.* New York: Scribner's, 1988.

Children's Literature Review. Vol. 3. Detroit: Gale Research, 1978.

Collier, Laurie, and Joyce Nakamura, eds. *Major Authors and Illustrators for Children and Young Adults.* Detroit: Gale Research, 1993.

Contemporary Authors New Revision Series. Vol. 8. Detroit: Gale Research, 1983.

Fuller, Muriel, ed. *More Junior Authors.* New York: H. W. Wilson, 1963.

Something about the Author. Vols. 1, 28. Detroit: Gale Research, 1971, 1982.

White, Gabriel. *Edward Ardizzone: Artist and Illustrator.* London: Bodley Head, 1979.

Wintle, Justin, and Emma Fisher. *The Pied Pipers: Interviews with the Influential Creators of Children's Literature.* New York: Paddington Press, 1974.

William H. Armstrong

1914-, American teacher and author

Sounder

(novel, 1969)

PLOT: A grim novel about racism, *Sounder* focuses on a nameless family of African American sharecroppers. The father loves to hunt with Sounder, his great coon dog, but game is scarce. To feed his family, he steals some ham and sausages. The sheriff and two deputies arrest him. When Sounder tries to defend his master, one deputy shoots him, and the wounded dog wanders away. Later, the mother sends the boy to the jail with a cake. A red-faced, bullnecked jailer smashes the cake and laughs at the father, who tells the boy not to come again. Left alone, the mother supports her children by shelling walnuts and doing laundry. Months later, Sounder returns, crippled, mutilated, and whining, instead of barking. Each year after finishing his summer farm work, the boy sets out to find his father, who has been sentenced to a chain gang. One year, while examining inmates in a prison camp, he puts his hands on the fence. A guard smashes his fingers with a pipe and then howls with glee.

On his way home, the boy, who has always wanted to read, finds a book. Shortly afterwards, an elderly black teacher tends his wounded fingers and befriends him. When the mother hears that the teacher will teach the boy to read, she calls it a sign from the Lord and sends the boy to live with him. During the summer, when the boy is back, his father returns, having been released from prison because an explosion crippled him. As in days past, Sounder greets the father with a magnificent bark. The father soon dies while hunting with Sounder. Shortly afterwards, Sounder also dies. The boy, coming home from school, knows that Sounder will live on in his memory.

CHARACTERS: Critics who have cited as evidence of condescending racism the namelessness of the black family have not appreciated Armstrong's attempt to universalize his characters by leaving out details. Furthermore, they have failed to note that the white characters are both nameless and cruel.

The boy, who is not described physically, develops from a child to a young man. At first, he is timid, feeling lonely because of fear. He finds security only in his father's strong presence and his mother's stories. Curious and intelligent, he is determined to read because he believes that reading stories would prevent loneliness. The boy is also observant and compassionate. He notices his mother's worry and tries not to distress her. After his father is arrested, he becomes hard-working and resolute, taking on a man's duties. As he grows older, the boy remains loyal, setting out every autumn to find his father. His journeys reveal the brave and hopeful spirit encouraged by his mother's stories about the travels of biblical figures. His journeys also test him, forcing him to endure the taunts of the bullnecked jailer and the physical abuse of the camp guard who smashes his fingers. Although the boy indulges in fantasies of violent revenge on both occasions, he is practical and conceals his feelings. He establishes superiority, for instance, by walking away from the camp guard in silent, dignified defiance. Although he begins his journeys convinced that worthy efforts always succeed, the boy does not succumb to despair when he fails to find his father. The boy is similarly resolute in his quest to improve himself by learning to read. Education increases his understanding, but he stays

humble and considerate, refusing to correct his mother when she misinterprets the origin of the term "dog days." When he grows into a man, he preserves these experiences as the history about which the author claims to be reporting.

The fate of **Sounder** foreshadows the father's and symbolizes the treatment accorded Southern blacks. A mixture of bulldog and Georgia redbone hound, Sounder is a large coon dog whose name comes from his loud, melodic voice. Sounder is shot because his intense loyalty makes him jump at the wagon carrying away his master. Having lost an eye and part of an ear, as well as use of one leg, the emaciated Sounder returns home months later, but he is dispirited and whines instead of barking. With the return of the father, Sounder's bark returns, symbolizing the triumph of endurance, loyalty, and love. Because Sounder is about the same age as the boy, his death symbolizes the end of the boy's childhood.

The father is a strong man who loves hunting with Sounder and who knows the ways of nature. He is devoted to his family and steals only when he becomes desperate. His unjustly long imprisonment breaks him, however. Crippled and deformed on one side because of an explosion, he illustrates the inhumane results of racism. **The mother**, as her singing of the spiritual about walking the lonesome valley alone indicates, is resigned to a life of suffering. Still, she never complains. A hard worker, she shells walnuts every night to earn money. She is also a good storyteller, reciting biblical tales that shape the boy's imagination. The mother has one idiosyncrasy: when worried, she sucks in her lips and hums instead of singing. Although she is initially fatalistic, telling her boy that he must learn to lose after the wounded Sounder disappears, she is not defeated by life. She views the teacher's offer to educate her son as a sign from the Lord and urges him to accept it. **The teacher** is a lean, elderly man with snow-white hair, mellow eyes, and a gentle voice. A man of learning, wisdom, and compassion, he uses a story to gain the boy's friendship. Understanding the boy's hunger for knowledge from the book he carries, the teacher generously offers to educate him, thereby giving him hope for the future.

The white characters are cruel authority figures. **The sheriff** and his **two deputies** are barely distinguishable. They are insulting and violent, callously abusing their prisoner. **The red-faced, bullnecked jailer** has repulsive physical features which parallel his moral ugliness. He maliciously smashes the cake that the boy brings to his father, arrogantly makes the boy pick up the crumbs, and cruelly laughs when the father says that he will soon be home. **The camp guard** is equally repulsive. His cap has created a white strip between his sunburned face and brown hair. He is wantonly cruel, sneaking up on the boy to smash his fingers. The guard reveals his base character by swinging his arms in "apelike gyrations of glee." He thus establishes that, although the white authorities treat black men and dogs alike, they are the real animals.

Further Reading

Children's Literature Review. Vol. 1. Detroit: Gale Research, 1976.

Collier, Laurie, and Joyce Nakamura, eds. *Major Authors and Illustrators for Children and Young Adults.* Detroit: Gale Research, 1993.

Contemporary Authors New Revision Series. Vol. 9. Detroit: Gale Research, 1983.

De Montreville, Doris, and Donna Hill, eds. *Third Book of Junior Authors.* New York: H. W. Wilson, 1972.

Something about the Author. Vol. 4. Detroit: Gale Research, 1973.

Something about the Author Autobiography Series. Vol. 7. Detroit: Gale Research, 1989.

Natalie Babbitt

1932-, American author and illustrator

Tuck Everlasting

(fantasy, 1975)

PLOT: Using the wheel as a recurring symbol, *Tuck Everlasting* celebrates the cycle of life and concludes that death is necessary for human happiness. Winnie (Winifred) Foster lives near Treegap in an overly protective home. She often thinks of running away, but she never does. In August 1880, she goes into the woods to learn what made the music she had heard the previous night. Winnie discovers Jesse Tuck, a teenage boy, drinking from a spring at the base of a tree. Although it is hot, Jesse refuses to let her drink. Shortly afterwards, his mother, Mae Tuck, and his brother, Miles, arrive. They kidnap Winnie and, to reassure her that she will be safe, they tell her their sad story. Eighty seven years earlier, the family had been heading west to find land for a farm when they drank from the spring at the base of the tree. Years later, they learned that they had become immortal and impervious to injury. Because they did not age, people suspected them of witchcraft and they had to move away. Since then they have never been able to stay very long in any one place.

When they arrive with Winnie at the Tuck household, Mae's husband, Angus Tuck, tries to convince Winnie that death is natural and necessary. He tells her that she should neither tell anyone about the spring nor drink from it. Jesse, however, secretly tells her that she should wait until she is seventeen, drink from the spring, and then marry him.

Meanwhile, a man wearing a yellow suit has heard stories about a family that never ages and has become obsessed with finding them. By coincidence, he sees the Tucks taking Winnie away from the woods, follows them, and hears their story. Then he goes off to tell Winnie's parents where she is in exchange for the deed to the woods where the spring is located. This accomplished, he returns to the Tucks and informs them that he will sell the water to those who can afford it. He offers them a job to demonstrate the truth of his claims about the water. When they refuse to be medicine show freaks, the man in the yellow suit starts to drag Winnie away, saying that he will make her drink the water and display its effectiveness. Angry, Mae Tuck hits him on the head with a shotgun.

The Treegap constable has witnessed the entire episode and arrests Mae. He takes Winnie home and drags Mae off to jail. The man in the yellow suit dies from his injury, and Winnie realizes that the Tucks' secret will come out if Mae is sentenced to hang. Having come to love the Tucks as friends and having been changed by her experience with them, Winnie volunteers to help Mae escape. When the Tucks break Mae out of jail during the night, Winnie climbs into the cell and covers herself on the cot so that Mae will have time to get away before her escape is detected. Later, instead of drinking a bottle of the special spring water that Jesse has given her, she pours it over her favorite toad.

In an epilogue set in 1950, Angus and Mae Tuck come back to the greatly changed town of Treegap. They discover that the wood has been bulldozed. In the cemetery, Angus finds a tombstone that indicates that Winnie became a wife and mother and died two years before this visit. On the way out of town, Angus moves a strangely unfrightened toad from the middle of the highway.

CHARACTERS: Although they are portrayed in considerable detail, the characters in *Tuck Everlasting* are reminiscent of folktale characters, representing basic attitudes to moral and existential problems. Ten-year-old **Winnie Foster** (Winnie is short for Winifred) changes as a result of her experience with the Tucks. In the beginning, she is an overly protected child living in isolation in a "touch-me-not cottage." Although she is rankled by the restrictions imposed on her, she does little more to establish her independence than think of running away. The messy house of Angus and Mae Tuck introduces her to a more comfortable way of living. Winnie thinks that the Tucks might be crazy, but she comes to love them as friends. When she sees that their secret is in danger, she loses her timidity and does what she thinks is right. She sneaks out of her house at midnight, knowing that her parents would never permit her to help the Tucks. She takes Winnie's place in jail, violating the law by helping a murderer escape. Winnie's active heroism ends her isolation. Children who once considered her too prissy and clean to be a real friend become attracted to her as a romantic figure.

Winnie wanted to do something that made a difference in the world. She accomplishes this goal by preserving the secret of the spring and thus sparing many people the misery that the Tucks endure. She also achieves it by making a more personal decision. Although early on she tells Angus

Tuck that she doesn't want to die, she chooses to be mortal in the end. By resisting the temptation to drink the water, she overcomes her fear of death and her juvenile infatuation with the handsome Jesse and his offer of eternal fun. Her tombstone says that she was born in 1870 and died in 1948, but it also testifies that she entered lovingly into the human community to become Winifred Foster Jackson, "Dear Wife, Dear Mother."

The members of the Tuck family are fixed at different stages of the human cycle. All lead lives of isolation, being compelled to move periodically so that their neighbors don't become inquisitive about their unchanging appearance. None has any education. The elder Tucks lack both ambition and imagination, living in an untidy house and making money by selling handicrafts. **Angus Tuck**, the father, is a huge man with baggy pants, but he is no rustic clown. He has a face creased with melancholy and rarely smiles, except when dreaming about death. He is at the stage of life when death becomes appreciated as a release from the weariness of life. The most philosophic Tuck, he voices the novel's theme. According to Angus, life means movement, growth, and change—life requires death. He describes life as a wheel and says he would gladly get back on it to die.

Mae Tuck, his wife, who is described as a "great potato of a woman," has brown eyes set in a round face. She sometimes forgets their condition and at other times wonders why it happened to them. Uncertain whether they have received a curse or a blessing, she stoically endures, insisting that one must take what life deals out. As a result, she still looks forward to reunions with her children every ten years. Mae shows a motherly concern for Winnie and protects her from the man in the yellow suit. Significantly, Mae swings the shotgun around her head "like a wheel" before striking the man. This image suggests that she preserves the natural order from which she has been excluded. Her role as an agent of the natural order eases her guilt and justifies the fact that she literally gets away with murder.

Miles Tuck, the older son, is stuck at the age of twenty-two. A broad-shouldered, muscular man, he has knuckles and nails blackened from his work as a blacksmith. Miles is bitter about his lot because it has cost him his wife and children. Nevertheless, he is sympathetic when Winnie indicates her fears of death. He rejects both his father's melancholy retreat from life and his brother's selfish concern with pleasure. Instead, he says that people must do something useful and that he will do something important some day. **Jesse Tuck**, forever seventeen years old, is a thin, handsome boy with a thick mop of curly brown hair. A youthful hedonist, he says that the purpose of life is to enjoy oneself. Unlike his parents and brother, who want to convince Winnie that drinking the water would make her unhappy, he actively tries to get her to drink so that she can marry him.

The man in the yellow suit is remarkably tall and has a thin beard and gray hair. His courteous manners lead people to give him information to help him on his quest, but he never reveals any information about himself until he thinks that he has achieved his goal. He is mastered by his quest, however, admitting to the Tucks that the idea of people never aging "took possession" of him. At first, he sought philosophic and scientific solutions to the dilemma of mortality by studying at the university. As his jaunty yellow suit suggests, however, he is neither an intellectual nor a scientist. Rather, he is a salesman, an entrepreneur without a conscience, who believes that money is the measure of human worth. Caring nothing for the philosophic implications of immortality, he wants only to profit financially from the water. He is an arrogant, class-conscious man who claims that ignorant people like the Tucks are unworthy of immortality. He would preserve the water for himself and for those who show that they "deserve" it by paying handsomely. Selfish and materialistic, he lacks respect for the feelings and rights of others. He extorts the deed to the woods from the Foster family in return for the information about Winnie, yet he himself later tries to kidnap her. Even worse, he intends to force her to drink the water so that he can exploit her immortality as an advertisement.

The Treegap constable is a fat, talkative man who wheezes when he speaks. Unlike Winnie, who

decides that situations sometimes require breaking the rules, he follows the letter of the law. Thus, he decides that Mae Tuck should hang and that Winnie is a criminal accomplice in Mae's escape.

Further Reading

Berger, Laura Standley, ed. *Twentieth-Century Children's Writers.* 4th ed. Detroit: St. James, 1995.

Children's Literature Review. Vol. 2. Detroit: Gale Research, 1976.

Collier, Laurie, and Joyce Nakamura, eds. *Major Authors and Illustrators for Children and Young Adults.* Detroit: Gale Research, 1993.

Contemporary Authors New Revision Series. Vol. 38. Detroit: Gale Research, 1993.

De Montreville, Doris, and Elizabeth D. Crawford, eds. *Fourth Book of Junior Authors.* New York: H. W. Wilson, 1978.

Estes, Glenn E., ed. *American Writers for Children since 1960: Fiction.* Vol. 52 of *Dictionary of Literary Biography.* Detroit: Gale Research, 1986.

Levy, Michael M. *Natalie Babbitt.* Boston: Twayne, 1991.

Something about the Author. Vols. 6, 68. Detroit: Gale Research, 1974, 1992.

Something about the Author Autobiography Series. Vol. 5. Detroit: Gale Research, 1988.

J. M. Barrie

1860-1937, Scottish journalist, novelist, and playwright

Peter and Wendy

(fantasy, 1911; republished as Peter Pan and Wendy, *1921)*

PLOT: *Peter and Wendy* is based on *Peter Pan; or, The Boy Who Wouldn't Grow Up,* a three-act play produced in 1904 and constantly modified until it was published as a five-act play in 1928. A mixture of childish wish-fulfillment, maudlin sentimentality, and wry adult humor, it celebrates the empowering world of the imagination while presenting childhood as a self-centered stage that children must leave in order to form meaningful relationships.

Mr. and Mrs. George Darling engage Nana, a Newfoundland dog, as nurse for their children, Wendy, John, and Michael. One night, after Mr.

Darling pours his medicine into Nana's dish because he is afraid to take it himself, he chains Nana outside. Because of this, Nana loses her respect for him. While Mr. and Mrs. Darling attend a party, Peter Pan and Tinker Bell enter the nursery. Wendy sews on Peter's shadow, which Nana bit off earlier, and Peter then convinces the children to fly to Neverland. Nana warns the Darlings, but they are too late to stop their children. During the flight to the island, Tinker Bell becomes jealous of Wendy. She therefore tells the Lost Boys of Neverland—Tootles, Nibs, Slightly, Curly, and the Twins—that Peter wants them to shoot "the Wendy." Tootles shoots, but his arrow strikes a button Peter gave Wendy. Wendy and Peter then become the mother and father of the boys.

Subsequent episodes satirize adventure stories or domestic life. The adventures deal with Peter's conflict with Captain Hook. Some time ago, Peter cut off Hook's arm and threw it to a crocodile. Liking the taste, the crocodile pursues Hook, but it always signals its approach because it also swallowed a loudly ticking clock. The first major adventure occurs on Marooners' Rock. When two of Captain Hook's pirates, Smee and Starkey, try to maroon the Indian princess Tiger Lily, Peter imitates Hook and orders her release. Shortly afterwards, Hook appears. After humiliating him by calling him a "codfish," Peter fights Hook, who bites him before escaping. Peter saves Wendy and then bravely awaits death, but the Never bird lets him use her nest as a boat.

Although Wendy, Peter, and their children subsequently enjoy domestic tranquility, Wendy decides to leave Neverland when Peter reveals that he feels like her devoted son. At this moment, Hook surprises Tiger Lily's friends, who are guarding Peter's underground home, and captures Wendy and the boys. Hook then descends to the house and puts poison in Peter's pretend medicine. Tinker Bell prevents Peter from drinking it, however, by flying between the glass and his lips. In turn, Peter saves her by getting all children who believe in fairies to clap. Peter then heads for Hook's ship, unconsciously imitating the crocodile's clock, which has finally stopped. As Hook prepares to make Wendy watch

the boys walk the plank, he hears the ticking and crouches in terror. Peter is then able to climb aboard and begin killing the pirates. Hook, who is obsessed with the importance of gentlemanly behavior, then happily enters the crocodile's gaping jaws after making Peter kick him in a display of bad form. Afterwards, Peter dresses and acts like Hook.

Wendy, John, and Michael now reenter their nursery, where Mrs. Darling lovingly accepts them. Mr. Darling, who has stayed in Nana's kennel ever since the children left, eventually agrees to keep the lost boys. The final chapter, which contains material staged only once, indicates that Peter often forgets to return for Wendy, who promises to do his spring housecleaning. Eventually, she becomes a real mother, and Peter goes off with her daughter, Jane. Subsequently, each new generation goes off with Peter because children are "gay and innocent and heartless."

CHARACTERS: Peter Pan first appeared in *The Little White Bird* (1902); the relevant chapters were published separately as *Peter Pan in Kensington Gardens* (1906). In his first incarnation, Peter was a baby who, at the age of one week, flew from his parents' window to Kensington Park, where fairies accepted him as a "Betwixt-and-Between," neither human nor bird. Named after Peter Llewelyn Davies and the god Pan, Peter played the pan pipes and rode a goat. In *Peter and Wendy*, Peter claims to have run away on the day he was born because he did not want to become a man. He is not a baby, although he still has his first teeth. A lovely boy dressed in skeleton leaves, Peter occasionally plays the pipes, but the goat is not mentioned.

Peter gives himself symbolic meaning: "I'm youth, I'm joy." A comic version of the archetypal hero, he projects every child's dream of triumphing over adults. Nevertheless, Peter's character has a profoundly negative cast because he lacks the deepest human emotions and values. A thoughtless child, Peter can't distinguish between reality and make-believe. More seriously, he never remembers anything or anyone, forgetting Wendy, Tinker Bell, and even Captain Hook. His negative qualities are apparent in Peter's relationships. Peter, who signals his presence by crowing with self-satisfaction, is cocky and conceited. When he frightens Hook, for example, he praises his own cleverness, forgetting that he imitated the crocodile unconsciously. Although he performs heroic deeds, Peter is interested in his reputation and in clever plans, not saving lives. He therefore endangers himself and Wendy on Marooners' Rock by unnecessarily revealing his identity. His childishness then proves nearly fatal: Peter becomes dazed when Hook bites him because, lacking memory, he responds as if he were encountering unfairness for the first time. Although he later kills Hook, Peter has no moral understanding. He thus becomes Captain Pan and behaves like Hook: he smokes two cigars, holds his finger like a hook, and treats his crew like dogs.

Peter's relationship with Wendy emphasizes emotional limitations. He treats Wendy with patriarchal deference and turns fatherhood into an adventure. However, Peter rejects the adult role of lover that Tinker Bell, Tiger Lily, and Wendy obviously want him to adopt. By getting Wendy to acknowledge that he is only a pretend father and by insisting that his feelings for Wendy are those of a devoted son, Peter frees himself from family life and the procreative cycle of nature. Ironically, this freedom condemns him to endlessly repeated adventures with a changing cast of children he can never remember. Peter Pan offers ordinary children the chance of escape and imaginative fulfillment in Neverland, but Peter himself can never be fulfilled because he can never change.

Captain James Hook is a romantic villain. A handsome man with blue eyes, a dark complexion, a black voice, and hair hanging in black curls, he dresses dashingly in clothes from the period of Charles II. His exceptional manliness is symbolized by the two cigars he smokes at once. The hook on his right arm is, of course, the feature that gave him his name. Under another name, Hook attended Eton—in the play his final words are "Floreat Etona"—and then became the only pirate whom Barbecue (Robert Louis Stevenson's Long John Silver) feared. Hook is diabolically clever. In an episode satirizing romantic fiction, he unscrupulously launches a surprise attack instead of waiting for the Piccaninny tribe to kill him at dawn. He then deceitfully lures the children from their haven by sounding the Piccaninny tom-toms. Viciously pragmatic, Hook bites Peter at Marooners' Rock and basely resorts to poison because Peter's cockiness angers him. Perhaps his foulest deed, however, is attempting to make Wendy watch while the boys walk the plank, an act signalling his hostility to the world of love and family that is forever barred to him.

Although normally brave, Hook fears the crocodile. He also finds offensive his own blood, which is a peculiar color that Barrie does not describe. Hook is cruel, but not entirely evil. He loves flowers and music. He is deeply disturbed that no children love him. He also has a fragile sense of identity: his spirit breaks after Peter calls him a "codfish." Hook is, in fact, obsessed with another sign of acceptance and belonging, the public school concept of good form. Worried that he is too self-conscious for good form, Hook goes to his death happy after he lures Peter into the bad form of kicking him.

Although Hook may represent age defeated by youth, psychological critics also see him as a dream projection of the father because on stage one actor traditionally plays both Hook and Mr. Darling. Certainly, Hook's obsession with status and good form parallels Mr. Darling's concern with respect and admiration. Furthermore, some critics interpret Hook's hostility to Peter as an oedipal conflict between the son (Peter), the mother (Wendy), and the father (Hook). Regardless, Hook is paradoxical: he is brave, cowardly, gallant, cruel, flashy, pragmatic, status-conscious, and base.

In contrast to Hook, **George Darling** is comically ridiculous and unromantic. He won his wife by taking a cab so that he would arrive at her house before any other suitors. He has carefully calculated the cost before deciding whether to keep each new baby. To maintain social appearances, he engages a dog as nurse. Mr. Darling worries about being admired, yet he does nothing to earn respect. Emotionally childish, he throws a tantrum when he can't tie his own tie, and he shows cowardice by pouring his medicine into Nana's dish instead of drinking it.

When he realizes that Nana does not admire him, he becomes petty and banishes her, an act symbolizing his failure to be a protective father. His later attempt to punish himself by literally staying in the doghouse ironically gives him pleasure because it earns him attention and admiration. Mr. Darling longs for recognition: once the lost boys assure him that he is not a cipher, he adopts them.

Mrs. Darling is mysterious, a woman with a mind like a series of nesting boxes and a mouth with one kiss that nobody but Peter can get. The kiss may symbolize a mother's deep love for childish innocence, but Mrs. Darling initially represents repressive motherhood. While they sleep, she tidies her children's minds. Mrs. Darling is a protective parent, but she is so indulgent that she does not want to deprive her callous children of any pleasure that they may have by being absent or by surprising her. Furthermore, although Mrs. Darling insists that her daughter needs a mother, she allows Wendy to visit Peter for spring housecleaning. Strangely, the kind and caring Mrs. Darling suffers a disturbing fate: after Wendy grows up, Mrs. Darling is "dead and forgotten."

Wendy Darling—Barrie coined her given name because a small acquaintance called him her "fwendy"—is a conventionally domesticated girl. Sentimental, she looks on Peter as a "tragedy" because he has no mother. Skilful and resourceful, she sews on his shadow. She goes to Neverland because Peter tempts her with the opportunity of darning clothes and tucking in children at night, acts that at the time the novel was written were standard signs of female competence. In fact, Freudian critics see the arrow that Tootles fires as a phallic symbol that turns Wendy into a mother who instantly acquires children. Regardless, Wendy declares that she is a "motherly person" and shows tenderness for her children. Sometimes Wendy's attitudes satirize rule-governed mothers: she objects to the pirates because their ship is dirty, and she is constantly concerned that the children are awake beyond their bedtime. Wendy has one heroic moment, becoming the emblem of imperial motherhood when she urges the captured boys to "die like English gentlemen." Most significantly, Wendy contrasts with Peter. Her longing for Peter as a husband and her attraction to the dashing Hook are signs of an awakening sexuality forever beyond Peter. By consciously deciding to grow up, she abandons childish selfishness to form the loving relationships open to an actual mother.

Domestic bliss tempts Wendy, but exciting adventures lure her brothers. **John Darling**, who wears a hat, is the older and braver brother. He sensibly chooses tea over unnecessary danger, but he demonstrates bravery and loyalty by choosing to walk the plank instead of denouncing the king. **Michael Darling** is most notable for playing the role of Wendy's baby in Neverland, but he also refuses to denounce the king. **The lost boys**, children who went to Neverland after falling out of their prams, wear round, furry bearskins because Peter refuses to allow them to look like him. **Tootles**, the kindest and humblest, has a melancholy look because he is absent whenever adventures occur. Barrie repeatedly calls him silly, but Tootles bravely offers to let Peter kill him after he shoots Wendy, and he magnificently defends Wendy when the others talk of forcing her to stay in Neverland. Finally, Tootles is prudent: he avoids annoying Hook by claiming that his mother will not allow him to join the pirates. **Slightly** (in the play he says his name is Slightly Soiled because those words were written on his pinafore) is the most conceited. He falsely claims to remember things from the time before he was lost. Addicted to drinking water, Slightly has swelled out. Instead of reducing himself, Slightly enlarged his personal entrance to Peter's underground home, thereby making it big enough for Hook to use when he attempts to poison Peter. The other lost boys are insignificant: **Nibs** is called gay and debonair; **Curly** is called "a pickle," that is, a mischievous boy; and **the Twins**, not allowed to know more about themselves than Peter does, are always vague about their separate identities.

Tinker Bell, whose name indicates that she mends pots and pans, is a tiny fairy. Plump and womanly, Tinker Bell frequently calls Peter a "silly ass" because he is unaware of her strong feelings for him. Tinker Bell is coarse: she swears when she is annoyed and claims that she glories in being abandoned. Absurdly feeling that she is in a love triangle with Peter and Wendy, she jealously pulls Wendy's hair, and she tricks Tootles into shooting Wendy. Tinker Bell is noble, however, when she drinks the poison intended for her beloved Peter. **Tiger Lily**, the beautiful warrior daughter of the chief of the Piccaninny tribe, faces death stoically at Marooner's Rock. After Peter saves her, she becomes devoted to him, protecting his home while inspiring Wendy's jealous prejudice against the tribe. Two of Hook's pirates warrant mention. **Starkey**, once an usher in a public school, is dainty in his ways of killing. After Hook dies, he becomes a nurse to the Piccaninnies. **Smee**, the Irish bosun, is pleasant and stupid. Industrious and obliging, he frequently works at the sewing machine. Smee habitually wipes his glasses instead of his knife after killing a person. Although he says horrid things and hits them with the palm of his hand—not his fist—children love him because he is pathetically unaware of his good form. After Hook's death, Smee claims to be the only pirate whom Hook feared. Finally, three animals have brief, symbolical roles. **Nana**, a Newfoundland dog, provides social satire because the Darlings engage her as a nurse to keep up appearances. As a nurse, Nana is the mother's surrogate, carefully tending to the children's needs. As a dog, she symbolizes the instinctual tendency to protect children: she is the one who grabs Peter's shadow, and she is the one who knows that he has come into the nursery while the Darlings are absent. **The Never bird**, which saves Peter by giving him her nest as a boat, represents the compassion of mothers, who sacrifice themselves for children. **The crocodile** with the ticking clock quite clearly represents Hook's fate, or mortality: when the clock runs down, Hook is out of time.

Further Reading

Asquith, Cynthia. *Portrait of Barrie*. New York: Dutton, 1955.

Birkin, Andrew. *J. M. Barrie and the Lost Boys*. London: Constable, 1979.

Children's Literature Review. Vol. 16. Detroit: Gale Research, 1989.

Collier, Laurie, and Joyce Nakamura, eds. *Major Authors and Illustrators for Children and Young Adults*. Detroit: Gale Research, 1993.

Contemporary Authors. Vol. 136. Detroit: Gale Research, 1992.

Geduld, Harry M. *Sir James Barrie*. New York: Twayne, 1971.

Green, Roger Lancelyn. *Fifty Years of Peter Pan*. London: P. Davies, 1954.

————. *J. M. Barrie*. London: Bodley Head, 1960.

Ormond, Leonee. *J. M. Barrie*. Edinburgh: Scottish Academic Press, 1987.

Rose, Jacqueline. *The Case of Peter Pan; or, The Impossibility of Children's Fiction*. London: Macmillan, 1984.

Twentieth-Century Literary Criticism. Vol. 2. Detroit: Gale Research, 1979.

Weintraub, Stanley, ed. *Modern British Dramatists, 1900-1945, Part 1*. Vol. 10 of *Dictionary of Literary Biography*. Detroit: Gale Research, 1982.

Yesterday's Authors of Books for Children. Vol. 1. Detroit: Gale Research, 1977.

Zaidman, Laura M., ed. *British Children's Writers 1880-1914*. Vol. 141 of *Dictionary of Literary Biography*. Detroit: Gale Research, 1994.

L. Frank Baum

1856-1919, American businessman, salesman, and author

The Wonderful Wizard of Oz

(fantasy, 1900; republished as The New Wizard of Oz, *1903)*

PLOT: This "modernized fairy tale," as Baum called it, revolves around three separate quest journeys. Although the plot is haphazard, these quests add novelty to the time-tested themes of identity and belonging.

When a cyclone strikes the Kansas farm of Uncle Henry and Aunt Em, Dorothy and her dog, Toto, are whirled away in the farmhouse to the colorful Land of Oz. The house lands on the wicked Witch of the East, whose death frees the blue-clad Munchkins. Neither the Munchkins nor their friend the good Witch of the North can tell Dorothy how to return to Kansas. Therefore, Dorothy begins her first quest, a journey along the yellow brick road to the Emerald City to get the help of the Wizard of Oz. Before

Dorothy leaves, she is given the dead witch's enchanted silver slippers and a protective kiss on her forehead.

Three characters, each with his own request for the Wizard, join Dorothy. The straw-stuffed Scarecrow wants a brain; the Tin Woodman, who was Nick Chopper before being enchanted by a witch, wants a heart; and the Cowardly Lion wants courage. Their journey involves many dangers: they leap over a chasm on the Lion's back; they escape from the fierce Kalidahs (who have the heads of tigers on the bodies of bears); they get a stork to rescue the Scarecrow when he becomes stranded in a river; and they escape the deadly fumes of a poppy field with the aid of the Queen of Mice and her subjects.

Once they arrive at the Emerald City, they are given a new quest. The Wizard of Oz, who appears in a different shape to each member of the party, insists that they earn their reward. He promises to grant their wishes if they kill the wicked Witch of the West. The one-eyed witch sees them as they approach her country and tries to destroy them by sending out wolves, crows, and bees. When each attack fails, she puts on her Golden Cap and orders the winged monkeys to destroy the Scarecrow and Tin Woodman, to cage the Lion, and to bring Dorothy to her as a slave. The witch then tries to starve the Lion, but Dorothy secretly feeds it. She gets one of Dorothy's silver slippers, but Dorothy throws water on her before she can retrieve the other, and the wicked witch dissolves.

Dorothy then rescues the Lion. The yellow-clad Winkies, freed by the death of the witch, gratefully restore to Dorothy the Tin Woodman and the Scarecrow. Using the Golden Cap, Dorothy commands the winged monkeys to fly the party back to the Emerald City. When they finally get an audience with the Wizard, Toto knocks over a screen and they discover that he is actually a little old man. Although the Wizard admits that he is a humbug, the others demand their rewards. He therefore makes them happy by filling the head of the Scarecrow with bran and pins, putting an embroidered heart inside the Tin Woodman, and giving the Cowardly Lion a bottle of liquid "courage" to drink. The Wizard, who is really a circus performer from Omaha, offers to take

W. W. Denslow created this illustration of Dorothy and her friends from The Wonderful Wizard of Oz.

Dorothy home in a hot air balloon, but he leaves her behind when she searches for Toto.

Dorothy then begins her third quest journey. She and her companions set out to ask Glinda, the good Witch of the South, to help Dorothy cross the desert surrounding Oz. Along the way, they escape from trees that try to grab them, cross over a land where everything is made of china, and pass through a wood where the Lion kills a giant spider-like creature. When they can find no way past the Hammer-Heads, short armless creatures who attack them with heads balanced on extending necks, they call upon the winged monkeys, who fly them to the land of the red-clad Quadlings. Glinda offers to help in return for the Golden Cap. She uses it to make the Scarecrow the ruler of the Emerald City, the Tin Woodman the ruler of the Winkies, and the Lion the ruler of the forest where he killed the spider. Having thus exhausted her three wishes, she frees the winged monkeys by giving them the cap. As for Dorothy, Glinda reveals that she can make her own way back by using her silver shoes. Dorothy and Toto thus return to the welcoming arms of Aunt Em.

Baum published thirteen sequels, and Ruth Plumly Thompson continued the Oz series after Baum's death, producing twenty books. Several other authors have also added titles to the series.

CHARACTERS: Although some of the characters were inspired by the European fairy tales Baum hoped to replace, others are so novel that they have given *The Wizard of Oz* the reputation of being the first distinctly American contribution to the genre.

Dorothy (her full name is given as Dorothy Gale in *Ozma of Oz*, 1907) is an orphan. Although the Munchkins honor her as a witch because she accidentally killed the Witch of the East, Dorothy considers herself "only an ordinary little girl." Nevertheless, she is remarkable because she liberates or improves nearly everyone who comes into contact with her. She does so partly because she has a sensitive heart. She lets the Scarecrow accompany her because she feels sorry for him, and she aids the Tin Woodman because his sad voice moves her. She also refrains from taking some china people home with her once she realizes that doing so would make them unhappy.

Although Dorothy is a loving child and prefers her gray Kansas home to the beauties of the Land of Oz, she is not the conventionally sentimental Romantic child. Rather, she is a sturdy and determined modern girl. Sometimes she becomes frightened, but she is generally brave, and she never loses her composure. For example, she quickly gets over her fright when the house is picked up by the cyclone and goes to sleep while it flies through the air. Dorothy's bravery complements her loving nature. When the Cowardly Lion first appears, Dorothy does not think about her own danger. To prevent the Lion from biting Toto, she strikes it hard on the nose. Dorothy also has an indomitable spirit. She suffers disappointment, such as when she learns that the Wizard is a fraud, and endures hardship, such as when the Witch of the West makes her a kitchen slave, but she never cries. Furthermore, she bluntly and unhesitatingly expresses her opinions, telling the Lion that he is a coward and the Wizard that he is a humbug. Dorothy is not stubbornly hard, however, and forgives both the Lion and the Wizard for their actions because she does not think that either is really evil.

Dorothy rids the Land of Oz of its evil witches, but she is not actually heroic. She can take no credit for her house falling on the first witch, nor is she truly responsible for destroying the Witch of the West, since she did not anticipate the consequences of throwing water on the witch. In her one deliberate opposition to evil, she is the stereotypical nurturing female: she sneaks food to the starving Lion. Throughout, Dorothy clearly depends more upon luck than wit or skill.

Nevertheless, her actions are symbolically appropriate. The good, modern American girl replaces the representatives of Old World evil and gives freedom to its enslaved subjects. It is notable that Dorothy, who has been careful to wash herself at every opportunity during her adventure, acts as the ultimate good housekeeper and washes away the evil witch. Adding to the symbolic appropriateness is the fact that the silver shoes "fitted her as well as if they had been made for her" and the Golden Cap "fitted her exactly." These items clearly belong to Dorothy. They represent powers she did not previously know that she possessed but which become hers because she rids the world of wickedness. By understanding these items, she symbolically gains self-knowledge, which is the key to her success. She uses the magic objects to benefit both herself and others. In the end, knowledge gives her independence. She does not require the help she sought during her journey because she uses her silver shoes to return home.

Dorothy's companions provide object lessons in the power of positive thinking. **The Scarecrow** is a true grotesque. His head is a small sack stuffed with straw on which a face has been painted. The ears are crooked and one blue eye is larger than the other. He is dressed in the faded blue clothing typical of the land of the Munchkins. The Scarecrow considers himself a failure because he does not succeed in keeping the crows away from the crops. Although he fears only fire, he is of little use in physical encounters. He is always falling into holes in the road and getting knocked over by those who attack the party.

In spite of his belief that he lacks brains, the Scarecrow is actually something of an intellectual who provides solutions to many problems. For example, he is the one who suggests building a bridge to cross a chasm and then chopping it to destroy the pursuing Kalidahs. The Scarecrow has confused intelligence with knowledge. As the Wizard tells him, all he really needs is more experience to gain more knowledge. Nevertheless, because he insists that his happiness depends on receiving a brain, the Wizard gives him "bran-new" brains filled with pins to make him feel sharp. Thus made content, he is ready to succeed the wise Wizard as ruler of the Emerald City.

The Tin Woodman is a valiant fighter whose ax frequently destroys enemies, but he is also an innocent unaware of his own qualities. He was once a flesh-and-blood woodchopper named **Nick Chopper**. He loved a Munchkin girl, but an old lady kept him from marrying her by having the Witch of the East put a curse on his ax. He then chopped himself to pieces, replacing each part with tin. Although the Tin Woodman desires a heart because he says that the heart brings happiness, he is already extremely sentimental. For example, when he accidentally steps on a beetle, he cries until the tears rust his jaw shut. He becomes satisfied with himself when the Wizard gives him an embroidered heart, but he forgets that he wanted the heart so that he could love the Munchkin girl. Instead of seeking her out, he becomes ruler of the Winkies in the West.

The Cowardly Lion believes that he lacks courage, but he has confused fear with cowardice. At every instance along the way, he demonstrates true courage. When the Kalidahs attack, for example, he is frightened but prepares to fight them to the death. After the Wizard gives him a liquid that he says becomes courage once swallowed, the Lion is tricked into believing in himself. He willingly makes a deal with the tigers, who agree to let him become their king if he kills the giant spider. The Lion proves that courage does not imply foolishness when he attacks the monster while it sleeps.

As a purely American element in the fairy tale, **the Wizard of Oz** shows the power of advertising and technological tricks. A little old man who is bald and has a wrinkled face, the Wizard is actually a circus balloonist who was born in Omaha. (In *Dorothy and the Wizard of Oz*, 1908, he reveals that his name is Oscar Zoroaster Phadrig Isaac Norman Henkle Emmanuel Ambroise Diggs: O.Z.P.I.N.H.E.A.D.) Because he descended from the clouds when his balloon was accidentally blown to the Land of Oz, people assumed he was a great wizard. Being an opportunistic man, he ordered them to build the Emerald City and became their leader. The Wizard cheerfully admits that he is a "humbug" whose power depends upon illusion. (One of his tricks is to make his subjects wear green glasses so that they think that the Emerald City is more magnificent than it truly is.) Furthermore, he creates an air of mystery by refusing to let himself be seen. When Dorothy and her companions receive an audience with him, the Wizard uses ventriloquism and stage tricks to make them think that he can change shape. Although the Wizard claims to be a bad wizard but a good man, Dorothy's companions believe that he is indeed a good wizard. Each attributes his happiness to the Wizard instead of Dorothy, whose acts have done more to help them than the Wizard. The Wizard voluntarily leaves Oz in his balloon because he is lonely and tired of his trickery.

Those with true supernatural power play minor roles. **The Witch of the North** is a little old lady who walks stiffly. Her hair is nearly completely white and her face is very wrinkled. She is a helper figure who plants a protective kiss on Dorothy. **Glinda, the Witch of the South**, is another helper. Although old, she appears young and beautiful with flowing red hair and blue eyes. As Dorothy exclaims, she is as good as she is beautiful. She fulfills the desires of each of the companions by having them taken to a place where each will be a ruler. She also liberates the winged monkeys. Finally, she becomes the traditional wise woman helper by giving Dorothy the knowledge of how to use the silver shoes.

In contrast, **the Witch of the West** is as evil as she is ugly. She possesses only one eye, but it is as powerful as a telescope. She is so wicked that her blood has dried up. She enslaves the Winkies, tries three times to kill Dorothy and her friends, attempts to starve the Lion into submission, and makes a servant of Dorothy. Strangely, for one so evil, she is afraid of the dark and can't steal the silver shoes while Dorothy sleeps. Her greatest fear, however, is of water, a conventional symbol of both life and purity. It ultimately dissolves her.

Three characters from Kansas play small roles. **Toto**, Dorothy's little black dog, stands apart from the grayness of Kansas. He is an external sign of her vibrant spirit, making her laugh in spite of her grim surroundings. He leads her to knowledge when he knocks over the screen concealing the Wizard. Toto also reveals Dorothy's loyalty: she bravely faces the Lion to protect him, and she misses her ride in the Wizard's balloon because she will not leave without him. **Uncle Henry** is a grim man with a long, gray beard. Years of hard work have left him a humorless man who seldom speaks and never laughs. **Aunt Em**, his wife, has also been defeated by the harsh life on the Kansas prairie. Her eyes, cheeks, and lips have become as gray as the landscape. Thin and gaunt, she never smiles, and she screams whenever she hears Dorothy's merry voice. Together, this couple symbolizes what would happen to Dorothy if she did not have the opportunity to escape into the colorful Land of Oz.

Further Reading

Baum, Frank Joslyn, and Russell P. MacFall. *To Please a Child: A Biography of L. Frank Baum, Royal Historian of Oz*. Chicago: Reilly & Lee, 1961.

Baum, L. Frank. *The Annotated Wizard of Oz*. Edited by Michael Patrick Hearn. New York: Clarkson N. Potter, 1973.

Berger, Laura Standley, ed. *Twentieth-Century Children's Writers*. 4th ed. Detroit: St. James, 1995.

Bingham, Jane M., ed. *Writers for Children: Critical Studies of Major Authors since the Seventeenth Century*. New York: Scribner's, 1988.

Carpenter, Angelica Shirley. *L. Frank Baum, Royal Historian of Oz*. Minneapolis: Lerner Publications, 1992.

Cech, John, ed. *American Writers for Children 1900-1960*. Vol. 22 of *Dictionary of Literary Biography*. Detroit: Gale Research, 1983.

Children's Literature Review. Vol. 15. Detroit: Gale Research, 1988.

Collier, Laurie, and Joyce Nakamura, eds. *Major Authors and Illustrators for Children and Young Adults*. Detroit: Gale Research, 1993.

Contemporary Authors. Vol. 133. Detroit: Gale Research, 1991.

De Montreville, Doris, and Donna Hill, eds. *Third Book of Junior Authors*. New York: H. W. Wilson, 1972.

Greene, David L. *The Oz Scrapbook*. New York: Random House, 1977.

Moore, Raylyn. *Wonderful Wizard, Marvelous Land*. Bowling Green, OH: Bowling Green University Popular Press, 1974.

Something about the Author. Vol. 18. Detroit: Gale Research, 1988.

Nina Bawden

1925-, English author

Carrie's War

(novel, 1973)

PLOT: During a visit to Wales, a widow tells her three children about events that occurred thirty years earlier during World War II. Evacuated from London to Wales, Carrie (Caroline) Wendy Willow and her brother, Nick (Nicholas) Peter Willow, are billeted with a grocer named Samuel Isaac Evans and his sister Louisa. Auntie Lou, as the children call her, is intimidated by her miserly, bullying brother. Carrie pities Mr. Evans. Nick, on the other hand, doesn't like the grocer because Mr. Evans caught him stealing biscuits. On his birthday, Nick is polite and restrained when he thanks Mr. Evans for his present, but he is warm and demonstrative in thanking Auntie Lou.

At Christmas, Mr. Evans sends the children to Druid's Bottom to get a goose from his estranged, dying sister, Mrs. Dilys Gotobed. Once there, the children become friends with Hepzibah Green (the woman who takes care of Mrs. Gotobed), Mr. Johnny Gotobed (a simpleminded man with a speech impediment), and another evacuee named Alfred Sandwich. Hepzibah tells Nick and Carrie the legend of a skull that is supposed to bring ruin if it is removed from the house.

During another visit, Mrs. Gotobed gives Carrie a message to deliver to Mr. Evans after her death; Auntie Lou secretly begins dating Major Cass Harper; and Frederick, Mr. Evans's son, comes home on leave from the army. Frederick helps with the haying, but he teases Mr. Johnny, who stabs at him with a pitchfork. Shortly after this incident, Mrs. Gotobed dies.

When Carrie tells Mr. Evans that his sister had said that she hadn't forgotten that he was her own flesh and blood but that she owed more to strangers, his subsequent anger puzzles her. After Mr. Evans gets control of his sister's house, he evicts Hepzibah. Alfred says that Mr. Evans probably stole Mrs. Gotobed's will to avoid the obligation of giving Hepzibah free rent. Later, Alfred declares that Mr. Evans stole from Mrs. Gotobed's effects the ring that he had given Carrie as a farewell present. In anger, Carrie throws the skull into the horse pond.

That night, Mr. Evans learns that Auntie Lou has eloped with Major Harper, and Carrie receives proof that Mr. Evans did not steal the will or the ring. The next morning, Carrie sees Druid's Bottom burning as she leaves. She believes that she has killed her friends by throwing away the skull. Thirty years later, however, her children find that Hepzibah and Mr. Johnny are still living in the burned house, that Mr. Johnny caused the fire by playing with matches, and that Alfred still visits them.

Carrie and her family also appear in Rebel on a Rock *(1978).*

CHARACTERS: In the frame story, **Carrie Wendy Willow**, a widowed mother of three children and a gifted storyteller, is torn between a need to face the past and a desire to flee from it. In the flashback story she tells, Carrie is a green-eyed girl of eleven sent to live with strangers. She is mature and responsible in watching over her brother, although greed and insensitivity annoy her. She also displays mixed attitudes toward adults. Carrie is impatient with the weakness of Auntie Lou, but she pities her because she is bullied. Similarly, Carrie despises the bullying of Mr. Evans, but she feels compassion for him, too, because Nick hates him and she knows that he has had a hard life. Consequently, Carrie is polite and respectful to Mr. Evans.

Carrie is both perceptive and naive. Realizing that Mr. Evans becomes upset and jealous whenever someone else makes the children happy, Carrie prudently tempers her expressions of pleasure whenever she returns from visiting Hepzibah. Later, however, she fails to realize that Mrs. Gotobed's message to Mr. Evans will not comfort him. She is therefore surprised by his anger and vindictiveness. Because she maintained a sympathetic demeanor earlier, however, Mr. Evans confides that his sister had left a photograph and the ring that he gave to Carrie. Relieved to learn that he is not a thief, Carrie sees his pathetic isolation. She fails, however, to understand herself as thoroughly. For thirty years, Carrie feels guilt for throwing away the skull. Because she makes no inquiries about the fire, she believes that she killed her friends. When her children rush to tell her that Hepzibah is alive, she is walking to Druid's Bottom, finally ready to learn the truth and to be freed from her irrational guilt.

Nick Peter Willow, who is nearly ten when he and his sister are evacuated, is never beset by doubts or mixed feelings. A greedy boy who is always stuffing himself with food, he can't control his appetite and steals biscuits from Mr. Evans. Nick tends to get overexcited. Each new pleasure he experiences becomes his newest "best thing." Furthermore, his feelings for people are always intense. He thus becomes very close to Auntie Lou, sharing her secret about the elopement, and to Hepzibah, climbing onto her lap while she tells stories. He feels hatred for Mr. Evans, however, and is disgusted by Carrie's expressions of sympathy. Nick is cagey and manipulative because he does not fear people. For example, he immediately shakes hands with Mr. Johnny. More significantly, Nick finds Mr. Evans ridiculous because of his ill-fitting false teeth. Nick also knows how to manipulate the grocer, avoiding a beating after stealing biscuits by threatening to tell everyone that he stole because he was hungry. Nick is forceful and loyal: Carrie sends away Major Harper, but Nick insists on telling Auntie Lou about the Major's visit, even if Mr. Evans learns about it and makes Louisa suffer later.

Samuel Isaac Evans is easy to loathe and pity. Physically unattractive, he is tall and thin, has bulging eyes and spiky, protruding nostril hairs, and wears poorly fitting false teeth that click when he talks. His personality is even more repulsive. Mr. Evans is miserly, puritanical, and dictatorial. Emotionally scarred by the mine accident that killed his father, he endured years of suffering and frugality, which made him cold and mean. Thus, when Dilys married the son of the mine owner, he stopped talking to her. His greed, however, dominates his life. For example, he forces his sister and the children to use the outdoor privy instead of the upstairs bathroom in order to save wear on the carpet. He himself, however, uses the indoor bathroom because he doesn't want to compromise his dignity as a town councilor. Mr. Evans also practices a stern, narrow, and joyless religion in which his meanness is a virtue. He is most disgusting, however, because his is a loud bully who humiliates the timid Louisa. Whenever he is upset, he explodes in fits of short-lived temper. Only Nick's threats to expose his nasty habits bring him under control.

Although Mr. Evans is rude, abusive, and domineering—traits that naturally lead Alfred Sandwich to suspect that he stole the will and the ring—he is also pitiful. Mr. Evans is capable of kindness, such as when he gives the children farewell gifts, but he can't express his emotions, and his manner makes others unable to feel deep gratitude for him. Mr. Evans is most pitiful, however, because he is unloved and lonely. Resentment cuts him off from Dilys, and his bullying alienates Louisa. Ironically, he pretends to console himself with the very cheapness that drove Louisa away. Unaware that Frederick has decided not to work in the store, he claims his son will receive more because there will be one less mouth to feed.

Mr. Evans's younger sister, **Louisa Evans**, whose need for loving relationships is apparent in her desire to be called **Auntie Lou**, is timid and weak. A small woman not much taller than the young Carrie, she caters to her domineering brother's needs, taking his abuse and sacrificing her own comforts. Because she doesn't share his strict religious views or his bias against Americans, she is hurt when Mr. Evans forbids her to go to dances at the American base. She finally asserts her independence and

secures her happiness by eloping with Major Harper. **Mrs. Dilys Gotobed**, Mr. Evans's older sister, is willful and stubborn. Estranged from her brother because of her marriage, she is too proud to patch up their relationship after she becomes a poor widow. Her spite is evident in her message to her brother, but her charitable feelings come to naught because she forgets to make a will that would grant Hepzibah free rent. **Frederick Evans**, Samuel's son, is a broad, beefy, enormously strong man. He shows his stupidity and nastiness by teasing Mr. Johnny. By indicating to Mrs. Gotobed that he has no intention of taking over his father's store, Frederick makes Mr. Evans's nastiness seem pathetic and futile.

Hepzibah Green, who cares for Mrs. Gotobed, is a tall woman with a freckled face, copper hair, and lovely teeth with a gap between the front two. A good storyteller, she is reputed to be a witch who knows how to use healing herbs. She is a kind and understanding woman who shows her loving nature by caring for Mr. Johnny and by constantly offering the children food. Even after Carrie delivers Mrs. Gotobed's message, which leads to her eviction, Hepzibah is kind and refuses to blame her. Thirty years later, she shows her understanding by telling Carrie's children that Carrie will come to the burned cottage. **Mr. Johnny Gotobed**, a small, simpleminded man who is unable to talk, reveals the moral and psychological qualities of others by the way they treat him. Hepzibah calls **Alfred Sandwich**, "Mr. Head," in contrast to Carrie, who is "Miss Heart." Alfred loves to read and does advanced work at school. A tall boy a couple of years older than Carrie, he teases her about her emotional judgment of Mr. Evans, offering an alternative to the conclusion that Mr. Evans is a thief. Alfred has a crush on Carrie and kisses her before she leaves. But he is too shy and stubborn to write first, so he loses contact after she leaves. (In *Rebel on a Rock*, he is Carrie's second husband.) **Major Cass Harper**, a tall, polite American soldier with a soft drawl, provides an escape for Louisa, eventually eloping with her.

Further Reading

Berger, Laura Standley, ed. *Twentieth-Century Young Adult Writers.* 1st ed. Detroit: St. James, 1994.

Children's Literature Review. Vol. 2. Detroit: Gale Research, 1976.

Collier, Laurie, and Joyce Nakamura, eds. *Major Authors and Illustrators for Children and Young Adults.* Detroit: Gale Research, 1993.

Contemporary Authors New Revision Series. Vol. 29. Detroit: Gale Research, 1990.

De Montreville, Doris, and Elizabeth D. Crawford, eds. *Fourth Book of Junior Authors.* New York: H. W. Wilson, 1978.

Hunt, Caroline C., ed. *British Children's Writers since 1960: First Series.* Vol. 161 of *Dictionary of Literary Biography.* Detroit: Gale Research, 1996.

Rees, David. "Making the Children Stretch: Nina Bawden." In *The Marble in the Water: Essays on Contemporary Writers of Fiction for Children and Young Adults.* Boston: Horn Book, 1980.

Something about the Author. Vol. 72. Detroit: Gale Research, 1993.

Something about the Author Autobiography Series. Vol. 16. Detroit: Gale Research, 1993.

Townsend, John Rowe. "Nina Bawden." In *A Sounding of Storytellers: New and Revised Essays on Contemporary Writers for Children.* New York: J. B. Lippincott, 1979.

John Bellairs

1938-1991, American teacher and author

The House with a Clock in Its Walls

(fantasy, 1973)

PLOT: In this gothic adventure, a battle against evil magic enables a frightened boy to demonstrate bravery and gain self-acceptance. When his parents are killed in an accident, ten-year-old Lewis Barnavelt is sent to New Zebedee, Michigan, to live with his uncle, Jonathan van Olden Barnavelt. Lewis learns that Jonathan and Mrs. Florence Zimmermann, a neighbor, are wizards. He also learns that Jonathan's mansion was previously owned by evil wizards, Isaac Izard and his wife, Selenna. For some reason, Isaac hid a clock within its walls. Jonathan hears it constantly, though he can't find it.

Lewis becomes best friends with the popular Tarby Corrigan. In an effort to cement their friendship, he invites Tarby to watch Jonathan eclipse the

Lewis, his uncle, and Mrs. Zimmerman listen to clock noises in this illustration by Edward Gorey from **The House with a Clock in Its Walls.**

moon. Because Tarby later insists that he was hypnotized and that the eclipse wasn't real, Lewis boasts that he will raise the dead on Halloween. On the appointed night, the boys go to the cemetery. Lewis uses a spell copied from one of his uncle's books and raises Selenna Izard from her tomb. Lewis is afraid to tell his uncle what he has done, even after a number of strange occurrences. He finally tells Jonathan the truth after he is threatened for watching Hammerhandle, a hobo, move Mrs. O'Meagher's belongings into the house across the street. His uncle's uncharacteristic anger convinces Lewis that something is seriously wrong.

Lewis begins to understand the situation only after he discovers Isaac Izard's notes. Secretly listening while Jonathan and Mrs. Zimmermann discuss the notes, Lewis realizes that Isaac Izard created a clock that will end the world, that he hid it in the mansion, that Mrs. O'Meagher is really Selenna, and that she has come back to set off the clock. When the frightened Tarby refuses to help him, Lewis confronts Selenna alone. Fortunately, Mrs. Zimmermann shows up and defeats Selenna. At Jonathan's suggestion, Lewis then devises a magic ritual that enables them to discover the clock. Suddenly, however, Selenna Izard is behind them and the ghost of Isaac Izard is ahead. A spell freezes the adults, but Lewis smashes the clock. The ghost of Isaac Izard disappears, and Selenna Izard dissolves. Afterward, Lewis accepts the fact that Tarby will never be his friend. He is happy, though, because he has learned that he is brave and he has met a girl who shares his interest in military history.

Sequels are The Figure in the Shadows *(1973) and* The Letter, the Witch, and the Ring *(1976).*

CHARACTERS: The characters function as figures in a problem novel about a child's feelings of rejection and as moral types in a supernatural battle against evil. **Lewis Barnavelt**, a ten-year-old orphan, comes to understand and accept himself because of encounters with the supernatural. As the prayers he recites on his way to New Zebedee indicate, Lewis feels insignificant and alone. He craves acceptance, but other children reject him because he is fat and incompetent at sports. Consequently, he becomes so desperate to keep Tarby's friendship that he foolishly boasts that he can raise the dead. To avoid complete rejection following a failure even to attempt the spell, Lewis disobeys his uncle's commands and secretly studies magic. Although Lewis in some ways resembles the sorcerer's apprentice in the old folktale, he plays a vital role in ending the disaster that follows his disobedience.

Once he realizes that Tarby, whom he thought to be a daredevil, has been frightened by the experience at the tomb, he learns to rely on himself more. Lewis, who has cried on several earlier occasions, shows newfound bravery by confronting the evil Mrs. Izard alone. Lewis also shows his fun-loving attachment to life by devising a comical magic ritual to oppose the life-hating rationality of the Izards. When Mrs. Izard appears after the discovery of the clock, Lewis proves himself to be quick-witted and brave. An avid reader of history, he recognizes that Mrs. Izard is using a "Hand of Glory" to numb the adults, and he therefore avoids looking directly at it. He then heroically destroys the clock and the evil forces behind it. By doing so, Lewis also destroys his sense of inadequacy. He thus comes to understand that he has been truly brave and that he need not worry about Tarby's lost friendship.

Jonathan van Olden Barnavelt, Lewis's uncle, is a pot-bellied wizard who has a bushy red beard streaked with gray. A kind and jovial man, he engages in friendly insults with Mrs. Zimmermann, whom he calls such epithets as "Hag Face" and "Frumpy." Jonathan modestly calls himself "pretty much of a parlor magician," but he can eclipse the moon and create the illusion that Lewis has gone back in time to observe famous battles. Nevertheless, his major contribution to the fight against evil is not magic but insight. He intuits that only playful irrationality can defeat the relentless, life-despising logic of the Izards. **Mrs. Florence Zimmermann**, his neighbor, friend, and cook, is a much more serious and powerful wizard than Jonathan. She has earned the degree of *Doctor Magicorum Artium* from the University of Göttingen in Germany. The gray-haired Mrs. Zimmermann always wears purple. Most of the decorations in her house are also purple. Mrs. Zimmermann returns Jonathan's affectionate banter, calling him "Brush Mush" and "Weird Beard." Although she rescues Lewis from Mrs. Izard, her most important function is to make Lewis realize his own qualities. Twice she praises him, making him understand that his moral actions, not Tarby's showing off, constitute true bravery.

Tarby Corrigan serves as a foil to Lewis. Unlike Lewis, he is a popular and accomplished athlete. Tarby's inadequacies, however, help to emphasize Lewis's genuine virtues. Thus, Tarby sneers about magic, which Lewis knows to be real, and he mocks Jonathan, whom Lewis respects and defends. Although Tarby has a reputation as a daredevil because he rides his bike through bonfires and hangs from trees by his knees, he is not actually as brave as Lewis. Tarby has nightmares after going to the cemetery and never again associates with Lewis. Tarby's fear, however, makes Lewis feel strong.

There are three evil characters in the book. **Selenna Izard**, a witch who reappears as Mrs. O'Meagher, is the most powerful. Her spectacles appear as two freezing circles of gray light. The grayness suggests the joylessness that has compelled her to try to destroy all life in order to usher in future life. **Isaac Izard**, the wizard who devised the clock, is as evil and sorrowful as his wife, but he appears only as a feeble ghost. **Hammerhandle**, a mean hobo reputed to be able to tell the future, has been given his nickname because he makes and sells handles for various tools. He becomes Mrs. Izard's servant and then her victim: needing the hand of a hanged man to make a Hand of Glory, Selenna apparently kills him.

Further Reading

Collier, Laurie, and Joyce Nakamura, eds. *Major Authors and Illustrators for Children and Young Adults.* Detroit: Gale Research, 1993.

Contemporary Authors New Revision Series. Vol. 24. Detroit: Gale Research, 1988.

Holtze, Sally Holmes, ed. *Fifth Book of Junior Authors and Illustrators.* New York: H. W. Wilson, 1983.

Something about the Author. Vols. 2, 68. Detroit: Gale Research, 1971, 1992.

Ludwig Bemelmans

1898-1962, American author, illustrator, and artist

Madeline

(picture book, 1939)

PLOT: The first part of this rhymed tale presents a group of twelve girls who live in a convent school in an old house in Paris. Whether eating, brushing their teeth, sleeping, or taking walks, they live "in two straight lines" under the watchful eye of Miss Clavel. The smallest girl, Madeline, is not as timid as the others and frequently frightens Miss Clavel. One night, Miss Clavel is awakened by Madeline's crying. She phones the doctor, who immediately takes Madeline to the hospital to have her appendix removed. The second part of the story focuses on the girls without Madeline. Accompanied by Miss Clavel,

Little Madeline shows off her operation scar to her envious schoolmates in Bemelmans's illustration from Madeline.

they solemnly visit Madeline in the hospital. They are surprised to discover that Madeline's father has sent her candy and toys. They are most startled, however, to see the scar on Madeline's stomach. That night Miss Clavel again wakens to crying. The remaining eleven girls jealously want to have their appendixes out, too. Smiling, Miss Clavel orders them back to sleep.

Bemelmans published four more books about Madeline: Madeline's Rescue (1953), Madeline and the Bad Hat (1956), Madeline and the Gypsies (1959), and Madeline in London (1962). Madeline's Christmas, a tale originally published in a magazine, was issued posthumously in 1985 with artwork enlarged and recolored by Jody Wheeler.

CHARACTERS: Like other series characters, Madeline and Miss Clavel become more substantial with each book. In the first volume, the pictures make a larger contribution to characterization than the text does. **Madeline** and her story were inspired by Bemelmans's memories of his time in a French hospital where, while recuperating from a bicycling accident, he met a little girl who proudly displayed the scar from her recent appendectomy. Named after his wife, she first appeared as Madeleine, a minor character in *The Golden Basket* (1936). She is described there as having "copper-red" hair and blue eyes, details in accord with her presentation in the colored pictures of *Madeline*.

Madeline's age is never given, but she is the smallest of the twelve girls. Although her life is rigidly regulated by the two lines in which the convent girls do everything, Madeline is a spirited individualist. For example, when mice come into the kitchen, the picture shows the rest of the girls hovering in a group in the background while Madeline, the only one unafraid, crawls toward the mice as if trying to make them into pets. Similarly, the picture of a trip to the zoo shows the girls near the tiger's cage clinging in fear to Miss Clavel. Madeline stands apart, eyes closed, hands behind her back, her body arrogantly tilted toward the roaring tiger, to whom she calmly says, "Pooh-pooh." Madeline's adventurous spirit is also evident when she breaks ranks and walks along the ledge of a bridge, an act that demonstrates her unique ability to frighten Miss Clavel. Perhaps Madeline's most engaging trait, however, is her ability to turn trouble into triumph, as she does when she proudly displays the scar that once again makes her different from the other girls.

Miss Clavel is a sympathetic nurse to the children. Pictures show her sharing the children's joy when they skate and their tears of sorrow when Madeline is rushed to the hospital. She is considerate when they visit the hospital, breaking up the bouquet that she purchases so that each girl has a flower for Madeline. Miss Clavel is stiff in the pictures and prim enough that she always dons her habit before rushing to an emergency. The exaggerated tilt of her body when she runs "fast / and faster" to the children's room shows, however, that she cares deeply about them. Furthermore, Miss Clavel's smile when the other girls cry that they want to have their appendixes removed indicates a kind and understanding disposition.

Further Reading

Berger, Laura Standley, ed. *Twentieth-Century Children's Writers*. 4th ed. Detroit: St. James, 1995.

Bingham, Jane M., ed. *Writers for Children: Critical Studies of Major Authors since the Seventeenth Century*. New York: Scribner's, 1988.

Cech, John, ed. *American Writers for Children 1900-1960*. Vol. 22 of *Dictionary of Literary Biography*. Detroit: Gale Research, 1983.

Children's Literature Review. Vol. 6. Detroit: Gale Research, 1984.

Collier, Laurie, and Joyce Nakamura, eds. *Major Authors and Illustrators for Children and Young Adults*. Detroit: Gale Research, 1993.

Contemporary Authors. Vols. 73-76. Detroit: Gale Research, 1978.

Fuller, Muriel, ed. *More Junior Authors*. New York: H. W. Wilson, 1963.

Something about the Author. Vol. 15. Detroit: Gale Research, 1979.

Margery Williams Bianco

(wrote as Margery Williams before 1925)

1881-1944, English author

The Velveteen Rabbit; or, How Toys Become Real

(fantasy novella, 1922; illustrated by William Nicholson)

PLOT: The plot of this sentimental story has two parts. In the first, the Velveteen Rabbit learns what it means to become Real through a child's love. Given to the Boy as a Christmas gift, the Velveteen Rabbit is forgotten after two hours of play. In the toy cupboard, where he is stored, only the Skin Horse is kind to the Rabbit. The Skin Horse tells him that love makes a toy Real. He also says that the process is gradual and that the toy must become physically shabby. The Rabbit's own transformation begins when the Boy starts sleeping with him. The Boy loves the Rabbit and takes him everywhere. During one outing, the Rabbit sees wild rabbits. Although the now-shabby toy knows that he is Real, he envies the other rabbits' ability to jump about freely.

An illustration by William Nicholson of Margery Williams's Velveteen Rabbit and the real rabbits he longs to join.

The second part of the story presents a metamorphosis that creates some thematic confusion. After the Boy becomes ill, the doctor orders the Rabbit burned because it is "a mass of scarlet fever germs." Taken away in a sack, the Rabbit cries a real tear. A flower grows where the tear falls, and the nursery magic Fairy appears in the center of the flower. She takes the Rabbit to the wild rabbits, telling them that he will live with them "for ever and ever." She then kisses the Rabbit, who discovers that he suddenly has hind legs and can jump like the others. (The book doesn't explain how this mortal rabbit will now be able to live forever.) The following spring, the Boy sees a rabbit that looks like his lost toy, but he never learns that it is really his former beloved Velveteen Rabbit.

CHARACTERS: The characters belong to both fairy tale and toy fantasy traditions. Because of plotting weaknesses, however, they lack the symbolic significance usually associated with fairy tale characters. **The Velveteen Rabbit** passes through three stages.

In each, he has a different physical appearance and sense of identity. In the first two stages, his feeling of inferiority requires that he advance to the next to feel accepted and happy. In the beginning, the Rabbit looks splendid. He has a spotted brown-and-white coat, thread whiskers, and pink sateen lining in his ears. But he feels inferior to mechanical toys because he is stuffed with sawdust. Although he has feelings and can talk, he is not Real. When the Rabbit is granted his wish to be Real, his appearance changes. Because of the rough handling he receives while the Boy plays with him, the Rabbit becomes shabby, but he is not worried because he is Real. Aside from his general happiness, however, it is not clear how he is different from what he was before. His feelings of inferiority in this stage resurface when he sees the wild rabbits.

His final transformation by the fairy is troublesome. First, it comes after he sheds a tear of despair because being Real has led only to his being discarded. This tear makes the transformation a sentimental plot device instead of a symbol of personal development. Second, the transformation into a real rabbit ends his loneliness but evades the issue of mortality. One would expect that a wild rabbit would be more subject to mortality than a toy. However, by saying that he will live forever, the Fairy removes the Rabbit from the cycle of nature. This statement prevents the reader from thinking that the Rabbit may one day look on his life as a wild rabbit with the same regret with which he looked upon his life as a toy.

The Skin Horse plays the fairy tale role of the wise helper, telling the Rabbit both about being Real and about the insignificance of appearances. The Skin Horse himself shows signs that love has made him Real. His brown coat contains bald patches, and most of his tail hairs are missing. The oldest of the toys, he has gained wisdom by watching boastful mechanical toys break before they are loved enough to become Real.

The nursery magic Fairy is a *deus ex machina* (a convenient plot device) who exploits sentimentality. Appearing in the middle of a flower blossom that springs from the Rabbit's tear, she wears a dress of pearl and dewdrops, and she has flowers in her hair and around her neck. Her face resembles a perfect flower. This magical helper says that she turns Real toys into beings who are Real to everyone. It is not clear why a fairy of nursery magic is identified with flowers. Perhaps the flower symbolizes both feelings and transformation. In any case, her reassurances and kisses provide a happy ending by bringing the Rabbit to life.

The Boy is both rough with his Rabbit and kind to it, taking it everywhere and building nests for it. He shows the fickleness of childhood by forgetting the Rabbit immediately after getting it for Christmas and, permanently, after his illness.

Further Reading

Berger, Laura Standley, ed. *Twentieth-Century Children's Writers*. 4th ed. Detroit: St. James, 1995.

Children's Literature Review. Vol. 19. Detroit: Gale Research, 1990.

Collier, Laurie, and Joyce Nakamura, eds. *Major Authors and Illustrators for Children and Young Adults*. Detroit: Gale Research, 1993.

Contemporary Authors. Vol. 109. Detroit: Gale Research, 1983.

Kunitz, Stanley J., and Howard Haycraft, eds. *The Junior Book of Authors*. 2nd ed. New York: H. W. Wilson, 1951.

Something about the Author. Vol. 15. Detroit: Gale Research, 1979.

Judy Blume

1938-, American author

Are You There God? It's Me, Margaret
(novel, 1970)

PLOT: *Are You There God? It's Me, Margaret.* (Blume insists the period is part of the title) is a first-person narrative that reveals the biological, social, and religious anxieties of an eleven-year-old girl. Tension comes from the narrator's fears that she may not be normal: that is, like all of her friends. Margaret Ann Simon's social anxieties are partially the result of moving from New York City to Farbrook, New Jersey. Margaret believes that her parents want to keep her away from Sylvia Simon, her paternal grandmother. Sylvia, however, soon visits and later arranges for Margaret to accompany her regularly to Lincoln Center. Margaret and her new friend, Nancy Wheeler, are in a class taught by Miles J. Benedict, Jr. Although the students play tricks on him, the new teacher soon gains control. After school, Margaret, Nancy, Gretchen Potter, and Janie Loomis hold meetings of the secret PTS (Pre-Teen Sensations) Club. They agree to go without socks, wear bras, keep a "Boy Book" listing who they like, and tell each other when they get their periods. Margaret worries her breasts aren't growing and she won't get her period when the others do.

As well as worrying about her physical development, Margaret worries about religion. Her father was born Jewish and her mother Christian, but they have left it to her to choose her own religion. When

Mr. Benedict assigns a personal project, Margaret chooses religion as her subject. She hopes to learn enough that she will know which religion to join. Margaret goes to temple with Sylvia but insists to her excited grandmother that she is not Jewish. She also goes to different churches with Janie and Nancy. Although she secretly talks to God when she's alone, Margaret doesn't feel Him at any of these institutions.

Margaret's development includes a number of discoveries. At a party she plays a game that teaches her what it feels like to kiss boys. She discovers that Nancy has lied to her about having had her period. Nevertheless, when Margaret becomes angry with Laura Danker, she repeats Nancy's stories about Laura going behind the A & P with boys. When Laura denies these stories, Margaret follows Laura to a Catholic church. Margaret enters a confessional and quickly tells the priest that she is sorry. Margaret's most traumatic moment, however, comes when her mother's estranged parents visit. Mr. and Mrs. Hutchins insist that Margaret is a Christian, but her parents deny this. Margaret herself angrily says she is nothing and decides never to talk to God again. Instead of turning in a lengthy report on her religion project, Margaret writes a short letter to Mr. Benedict explaining her problem. Shortly afterward, she gets her first period and gratefully resumes her conversations with God.

CHARACTERS: Reviewers have criticized the characters as stereotypical and shallow, but many readers have indicated that the central character accurately reflects their anxieties about growing up. **Margaret Ann Simon** turns twelve during the course of the novel. She is a secretive girl, seldom telling her parents about her worries and never telling them that she talks to God. What Margaret wants most out of life is to be like the other girls, to belong. Her concern about developing breasts and her fear of being the last to get her period indicate her desire to be like everyone else, which she defines as being normal. This wish is reflected in her actions. She goes without socks, even though she gets blisters, to be like the other PTS Club members. She

repeatedly lists the handsomest boy first in her Boy Book because she is afraid to admit that she likes someone the others don't. Her quest for a religion also suggests a social rather than a spiritual need. Because she has no religion, Margaret thinks of herself as "nothing" and feels excluded because she can't join either the Y or the Jewish Center like the others. In fact, her private conversations with God never go beyond concerns with belonging. For example, she makes a deal with God to do household chores if He will make her breasts grow, and she resumes talking to God to thank Him for giving her a period.

Margaret is sometimes comically innocent, such as when she does Nancy's bust-developing exercises, or when she buys sanitary napkins and is surprised that the male clerk doesn't think her purchase is unusual. More often, her naivete impedes her growth or causes pain. For example, she believes Nancy is more observant and knowledgeable than she is. Even after she discovers that Nancy has lied about her period, Margaret confronts Laura Danker (as well as a boy she blames) for spreading stories about Laura. These episodes are painful lessons that Nancy is not an authority, and Margaret apologizes to both Laura and God. Nevertheless, Margaret does not face all of her problems. She prides herself on her ability to raise her right eyebrow and thereby distract people whenever she can't think of anything to say. Characteristically, she runs away from her teacher after submitting a letter about her religion project. Unbelievably, Margaret makes no further mention of this episode, an omission supporting the view of those critics who claim the novel is superficial in its resolutions.

Two of Margaret's classmates develop significantly as characters. **Nancy Wheeler** is a taller girl with a turned-up nose and the kind of bouncy hair that Margaret wants. Nancy presents herself as an authority on sexual matters, claiming that boys are only interested in dirty books, that the teacher can't resist looking at Laura Danker, and that her brother and his friend go behind the A & P with Laura. Nancy craves attention. Disappointed that she is not the first to get her period, she lies about having it. When the PTS Club members all buy bras, she announces that hers is larger and if they want to get out of "baby bras" they must do exercises. Nancy becomes pathetic when Margaret learns she has lied about her period. Instead of being calm and knowledgeable, Nancy is frightened by the very experience she desired.

Margaret longs for physical development that will make her "normal," and **Laura Danker** is an object lesson in what happens when one is different. So tall that Margaret at first mistakes her as a teacher, Laura has had to wear a bra since the fourth grade. Consequently, she has endured stares and crude comments. When she reveals her pain, Laura forces the self-centered Margaret, at least temporarily, to consider the feelings of others.

The most thoroughly developed adult in the story is **Sylvia Simon**, Margaret's sixty-year-old paternal grandmother. Sylvia approaches the Jewish grandmother stereotype with her questions about Jewish boyfriends, her belief in the supremacy of New York deli food, and her knitting of sweaters with custom labels. Sylvia is, however, the adult most sympathetic to Margaret. Friendly and considerate, she takes Margaret to cultural affairs at Lincoln Center and conspires against the arbitrary rules Margaret's parents set by telling her to remove her boots during performances. Although Sylvia is eager for Margaret to accept Judaism, she does not force her to make a decision. In contrast, Margaret's maternal grandparents, **Mr.** and **Mrs. Hutchins**, exemplify bigotry. Unlike Sylvia, who changes her hair color monthly and wears stylish clothes, they look and behave like old people. As the huge cross Mrs. Hutchins wears around her neck indicates, the Christian religion dominates their lives. They cut all contact with their daughter after she married a Jew. Still intolerant years later, they abruptly end their visit of reconciliation, declaring that Margaret is a Christian because her mother was raised as one.

Although mentioned frequently, Margaret's parents play a minor role. Her father, **Herb Simon**, is a stereotypically inept father who injures himself the first time he tries to mow a lawn. Raised as a Jew but married to a Christian, he is liberal in his religious attitudes and insists that Margaret choose her own

religion. **Barbara Simon**, Margaret's mother, who places little value on religion in a young person's life, supports her husband. Because she has a sentimental attachment to family, she writes a Christmas card that initiates her parents' disastrous visit.

The only other adult of consequence is **Miles J. Benedict, Jr.**, a twenty-four-year-old graduate of Columbia Teachers College. Initially, he appears uncertain, coughing nervously when he speaks. He loses his cough and proves that appearances are deceptive by gaining firm control of the class when the students play tricks on him. Margaret is impressed by his respectful attitude (he says "please" when asking students to study). He seems understanding and sympathetic, but Margaret doesn't indicate that he influences her in any way.

Tales of a Fourth Grade Nothing
(novel, 1972)

PLOT: In a series of ten loosely connected episodes, this first-person narrative provides a slapstick look at the problems of living with an unruly younger sibling. At a birthday party, Peter Warren Hatcher wins a turtle that he names Dribble. His mother doesn't like turtles, but Peter's biggest problem is keeping it away from his two-and-a-half-year-old brother. Farley Drexel Hatcher, called "Fudge" by everyone, is hard to live with. When Mr. and Mrs. Yarby, the owners of the Juicy-O company, visit, Fudge creates a costly stir. He brings Dribble to the table, scares Mrs. Yarby by wearing a gorilla mask, and decorates their suitcase with green stamps. Mr. Yarby is so upset that he cancels his account with the advertising agency represented by Fudge's father, Warren Hatcher. On another occasion, Fudge stubbornly refuses to eat for several days. His father, having warned him to eat or wear his food, pours cereal on his head, and Fudge resumes eating. Fudge's next adventure leads to personal injury. Fudge climbs a jungle gym when Sheila Tubman, Jimmy Fargo, and Peter, who were supposed to watch him, begin horsing around. Pretending to be a bird, Fudge falls off and knocks his front teeth out. Mrs. Hatcher is angry at Peter, but she apologizes the next day.

Peter is constantly pressed into service to help his parents manage Fudge. At his brother's third birthday, Peter entertains the children. Ralph throws up, Sam cries at everything, and Jennie bites Peter and later "makes a tinkle" on the floor. When Fudge refuses to open his mouth at the dentist's, Peter is enlisted to trick him, just as he is when Fudge refuses to wear new shoes. Fudge's desire to imitate Peter causes Peter serious trouble when Fudge scribbles all over a poster for a school project that Peter, Jimmy, and Sheila are working on. When Fudge enters Peter's bedroom and uses Peter's belongings to paint himself and to chop off his hair, their parents finally give Peter a chain for his door. Although Peter is jealous of the attention Fudge receives, he tricks him into making a television commercial for Mr. George Vincent. When their father takes them to the movies, Fudge disappears. The movie is stopped, and Peter has to search for Fudge. Peter laughs about Fudge thinking he could touch the bears on the screen and about Fudge's appetite for his father's awful omelet. He finds nothing funny, however, when Fudge eats Dribble. In fact, Peter becomes so angry that he wishes Fudge had never been born. What especially upsets Peter is that everyone worries about Fudge and no one expresses concern that his turtle is dead. When Fudge is released from the hospital, however, his parents give Peter a dog, one that will grow too big for Fudge to eat.

Superfudge *(1980) is a sequel to* Tales of a Fourth Grade Nothing.

CHARACTERS: Because this book depends upon episodes of broad physical comedy, most of the characters are caricatures. Nine-year-old **Peter Warren Hatcher** is often jealous of his little brother. Peter is particularly resentful because, unlike Fudge, whom people fuss over, he always behaves well. When Mr. and Mrs. Yarby give him a picture-

Peter's little brother, Fudge, acts like a brat again in **Blume's** Tales of a Fourth Grade Nothing, *illustrated by* **Roy Doty.**

book dictionary suitable for smaller children, for example, he hides his disappointment and politely thanks them. Peter also resents being forced to care for Fudge because he feels his parents ignore him. Actually, his parents show appreciation for his efforts. His mother, for example, laughs with him after the party, and his father laughs with him after they throw out the omelet that Fudge likes. Clearly, they regard him as mature, even though he doesn't always realize it. When taking care of Fudge, Peter is patient and considerate, going along with efforts to trick Fudge even when he feels slightly embarrassed. Furthermore, although Fudge constantly annoys him and destroys his property, Peter never hits him.

Farley Drexel Hatcher, known to all as **Fudge**, is a comic stereotype common in movies and television shows: the obnoxious brat. Stubbornly persistent in his troublemaking, Fudge is adept at throwing tantrums and frustrates all attempts to be controlled by force or persuasion. The only thing that works is trickery. He admires his older brother so much that he will do anything to be like him. At the dentist's office, for example, he opens his mouth only after the dentist says that he can't possibly open as well as Peter does. Although many readers find his antics funny, others consider him to be a gross caricature of a child in the "terrible twos." The other children at Fudge's party are similar caricatures. In order to make Fudge seem uniquely colorful and lovable, however, each has only one typifying bad behavior: Fat **Ralph** eats so much he throws up; **Sam** is so timid he screams in fright at everything; and **Jennie** enforces her will by biting anyone who opposes her.

Mrs. Hatcher, Peter's mother, is exceptionally patient with the wayward Fudge. An ideal parent, she never raises her voice, and she loses her composure only when Fudge falls from the jungle gym. Even then, she is careful to apologize to Peter afterwards for blaming him for the accident. Although she fawns over Fudge and makes Peter look after him, she does not, as Peter charges, ignore Peter. She respects Peter as a mature child and, when she has time, as she does after the birthday party, she puts her arm around him while they silently share their feelings. **Warren Hatcher**, Peter's father, is also tolerant. He doesn't complain, for example, when Fudge's antics cause Mr. Yarby to cancel business with his advertising company. Nevertheless, he is less patient than his wife. When Fudge refuses to eat after receiving a warning, Mr. Hatcher carries out his threat and makes Fudge wear his food by pouring it on his head. Mr. Hatcher realizes that force won't always work, however, and when Fudge refuses to ride a bike during the filming of a commercial, he gets Peter to trick him. Like his wife, Mr. Hatcher shares his feelings with Peter, joining him in laughing about Fudge after the omelet incident.

The other adults are not as tolerant as Fudge's parents. **Mr. Yarby**, the owner of the Juicy-O drink company, praises Fudge when he first sees him, but he soon begins talking about the need for "old-fashioned good manners." He cancels his account with Peter's father because of Fudge's misdeeds. **Mr. George Vincent**, the president of the Toddle-

Bike company, is a similar caricature of the bullying businessman. Like Mr. Yarby, he initially finds Fudge irresistible. When Fudge refuses to cooperate in the commercial, however, he threatens to remove his business from Mr. Hatcher's company.

Peter's friends are not extensively developed, but **Sheila Tubman**, the central character of *Otherwise Known as Sheila the Great* (1972), is given some personality. She is somewhat immature, as she demonstrates by finding "cooties" on the boys and thereby neglecting her job of watching Fudge. She is also bossy. When she, Jimmy, and Peter are assigned a project together, she dictates what each will do. Finally, she is sneaky. Although the others make it clear that no one should take individual credit for their project, she puts her name on the cover as the one who did the handwriting.

Further Reading

Authors and Artists for Young Adults. Vol. 3. Detroit: Gale Research, 1990.

Berger, Laura Standley, ed. *Twentieth-Century Children's Writers*. 4th ed. Detroit: St. James, 1995.

Children's Literature Review. Vols. 2, 15. Detroit: Gale Research, 1976, 1988.

Collier, Laurie, and Joyce Nakamura, eds. *Major Authors and Illustrators for Children and Young Adults*. Detroit: Gale Research, 1993.

Contemporary Authors New Revision Series. Vol. 37. Detroit: Gale Research, 1992.

Contemporary Literary Criticism. Vols. 12, 30. Detroit: Gale Research, 1987, 1993.

De Montreville, Doris, and Elizabeth D. Crawford, eds. *Fourth Book of Junior Authors*. New York: H. W. Wilson, 1978.

Estes, Glenn E., ed. *American Writers for Children since 1960: Fiction*. Vol. 52 of *Dictionary of Literary Biography*. Detroit: Gale Research, 1986.

Lee, Betsy. *Judy Blume's Story*. Minneapolis: Dillon Press, 1981.

Rees, David. "Not Even for a One Night Stand: Judy Blume." In *The Marble in the Water: Essays on Contemporary Writers of Fiction for Children and Young Adults*. Boston: Horn Book, 1980.

Something about the Author. Vols. 2, 31, 79. Detroit: Gale Research, 1971, 1983, 1995.

Weidt, Maryann N. *Presenting Judy Blume*. Boston: Twayne, 1990.

Wintle, Justin, and Emma Fisher. *The Pied Pipers: Interviews with the Influential Creators of Children's Literature*. New York: Paddington Press, 1974.

Michael Bond

1926-, English author

A Bear Called Paddington

(animal fantasy, 1958)

PLOT: *A Bear Called Paddington* consists of independent episodes linked by the character of Paddington, a talking bear, whose initiation into the customs, pastimes, and daily routines of English life produces a series of comical disasters. Paddington is introduced to the story sitting, deserted and lost, on a suitcase in London's Paddington Station. A London couple, Henry and Mary Brown, find him and insist that he stay with them a while. The hungry bear, whom they name after the station, immediately makes a mess of the cream-and-jam cakes Mr. Brown buys him. In spite of his clumsiness, Mrs. Bird, the Browns' housekeeper, allows the Browns and their children, Judy and Jonathan, to make Paddington a member of the family. Because he is not used to English customs, however, Paddington makes more messy mistakes. First, he draws a shaving cream map on the bathroom floor, and then he lets the tub flood the bathroom. On a shopping trip the next day, Paddington becomes separated from Mrs. Brown and Judy in the London Underground. He is nearly arrested for pushing the emergency button of an escalator. At a department store, he knocks over a window display, but his bumbling efforts to restore it draw a large crowd. The manager rewards him with a large jar of his favorite food, marmalade, and so, characteristically, Paddington's adventure unexpectedly turns from disaster into fortune.

Paddington learns to shop for Mrs. Bird and makes friends with the merchants. His best friend, Mr. Gruber the antique dealer, shows him that some paintings conceal works by old masters. After Paddington cleans a painting in the Brown household and discovers that the canvas beneath is blank, he repaints the picture. The resulting abstract wins Mr. Brown first prize in a contest. Similarly positive

results occur when Paddington goes to the theater. He creates several noisy scenes that upset the lead actor and weaken his delivery. Paddington saves the play, however, after he goes backstage to urge the play's villain to change his ways. In response, the actors make him their prompter.

Paddington's next adventure occurs at the seashore. Falling asleep on the sand after building a sand castle, he must save himself at high tide by paddling around in his sand bucket. Finally, Paddington performs magic tricks at his birthday party. Unfortunately, he has neglected to read carefully the directions in his magic kit. In one trick, he smashes the watch of Mr. Curry, a mean, uninvited guest, and, of course, he is unable to put the pieces together again. Mr. Gruber then helps Paddington by pulling a valuable coin from his own ear and giving it as a present. Similar misadventures enliven the approximately seventy-five additional works featuring Paddington. Besides sequels, these include picture, activity, concept, and pop-up books.

CHARACTERS: Books in the Paddington series can all be read independently. The characters do not grow or develop markedly from one volume to another, and the first book sketches the basic traits the major characters display throughout.

Michael Bond's prose and Peggy Fortnum's drawings have made the character of **Paddington Brown** one of the most recognizable and beloved in twentieth-century children's literature. A small honey-brown bear with black ears and round eyes, Paddington is perennially young, his exact age a mystery. Paddington looks and sometimes acts like a bear, as when he gets on the table to eat, but for the most part he behaves like a human child. He is often proud of very simple accomplishments, such as surviving on marmalade during his trip to England.

Paddington is attached to his possessions. Although he will wear other hats, he insists on keeping his large, floppy bush hat. He also insists on carrying a suitcase, which contains his pictures and most recent acquisitions, such as his breakfast bacon. Most notably, Paddington is prone to misadventures. As he says, "Things are always happening to me. I'm that sort of bear." One reason is that he is from Darkest Peru and does not know the ways of English middle-class life; another is that he is somewhat literal-minded; a third is that he is a small creature in a large world. These three factors, combined with his single-minded pursuit of any idea that catches his imagination, result in one comical mistake after another. Paddington is so good-natured, polite, and friendly, however, that most people like him and willingly help him out of his scrapes. Paddington can also display adult competence. He successfully stowed away on a boat in order to emigrate to England, for example. He also strikes excellent bargains with merchants because he likes value for his money. Whenever people anger or displease him, he makes them uncomfortable by using the powerful stare that his Aunt Lucy taught him.

Next to Paddington, the minor characters are bland. The Brown family is entirely vapid. **Henry Brown** is described as a fat man with a big mustache and glasses. Although he is called jolly, he shows few signs of hilarity. Rather, he seems to be a good-hearted man who is controlled by his family. Still, he is a good father. He treats Paddington as one of his own children and never becomes angry when Paddington causes trouble. His plump wife, **Mary Brown**, exercises her control over him merely by altering her tone. Although she is snobbishly concerned about Paddington's frumpy wardrobe, she is a kind and generous woman. It is she, after all, who immediately reaches out to Paddington at the station. **Judy Brown**, their daughter, and **Jonathan Brown**, their son, accept Paddington as something of a younger brother. Neither is highly individualized, but Judy does show wit in making the Underground inspector drop charges against Paddington because he is a bear and not a person; Jonathan's most distinguishing trait is his constant use of the word "Crikey."

The characters outside the immediate family are more distinctive. Bond has said that he included **Mrs. Bird**, the housekeeper, because she could be sterner than the "soft touch" Browns. Her appearance does not suggest much sternness. The gray-haired Mrs. Bird is "a stout, motherly lady," whose eyes twinkle kindly. The Browns respect her and defer to her because, according to Judy, she "knows everything about everything." With Paddington, Mrs. Bird acts as a nanny. She accepts him as a favored child and spoils him with his favorite foods. She is quick in realizing that Paddington has talent, however, and she turns her shopping over to him because he strikes better bargains than anyone she has met. **Mr. Gruber**, the antique dealer, is Paddington's closest friend outside the family, perhaps because he too is a foreigner. Mr. Gruber always addresses Paddington as "Mr. Brown," a habit that makes Paddington feel important. He respects Paddington as an adult and introduces him to new ideas and experiences. In *A Bear Called Paddington* he teaches him about old masters. In later books, he takes him to a band concert, an auction, and a wax museum. In all cases, he is kind. At Paddington's birthday, for example, he helps Paddington to save face as a magician by pulling a coin out of his own ear.

The closest thing to a villain in the series is **Mr. Curry**, whose role is that of foil to Paddington, taking some of the bear's traits to an extreme while being his opposite in other things. Paddington expects his money's worth, whereas Mr. Curry is tight-fisted, coming to Paddington's party uninvited to get free tea, for instance. Paddington is naturally curious, but Mr. Curry is a busybody who pokes his nose into other people's business. Paddington is friendly and likable, but Mr. Curry criticizes and complains all the time. Paddington prides himself on being a truthful bear, but Mr. Curry is dishonest, lying about the value of the watch that Paddington smashes. In every book, the haughty Mr. Curry gets his just deserts, experiencing some embarrassment that ruins his dignity.

Further Reading

Berger, Laura Standley, ed. *Twentieth-Century Children's Writers.* 4th ed. Detroit: St. James, 1995.

Children's Literature Review. Vol. 1. Detroit: Gale Research, 1976.

Collier, Laurie, and Joyce Nakamura, eds. *Major Authors and Illustrators for Children and Young Adults.* Detroit: Gale Research, 1993.

De Montreville, Doris, and Donna Hill, eds. *Third Book of Junior Authors.* New York: H. W. Wilson, 1972.

Something about the Author. Vols. 6, 58. Detroit: Gale Research, 1974, 1990.

Something about the Author Autobiography Series. Vol. 3. Detroit: Gale Research, 1987.

Lucy M. Boston

1892-1990, English author

The Children of Green Knowe

(fantasy, 1954)

PLOT: *The Children of Green Knowe* is a fantasy of wish fulfillment: a lonely boy discovers both a true home and the continuity with the past that gives him a sense of family. The novel opens with one of a number of echoes of Frances Hodgson Burnett's *The Secret Garden.* Like Mary Lennox in that story, seven-year-old Toseland takes a rainy journey on a train toward an ancient manor that will soon become home. Toseland's father and stepmother live in Burma, and they have decided to send their son to spend Christmas with great-grandmother Linnet Oldknow at Green Noah, a manor once called Green

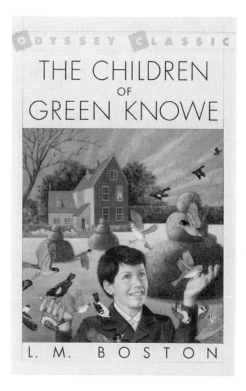

Tolly discovers his true home in Boston's The Children of Green Knowe.

Knowe. Alone and lonely, Toseland wishes for a family, especially brothers and sisters. After the train journey, Mr. Boggis, whose family has served at Green Knowe for generations, rows him to the house, which looks like an ark in a flood.

The process of renewal this image symbolizes begins immediately. Granny Oldknow, seeing that Toseland resembles his grandfather, greets him by saying, "So you've come back!" She also gives him his grandfather's nickname, Tolly, connecting him to his family's past. In exploring the manor, Tolly notices a picture of some seventeenth-century ancestors: Toby, Alexander, Linnet, their mother, and their grandmother. Tolly pretends that they are his brothers and sister, something Granny Oldknow herself had done as a child. As he discovers objects represented in the painting or otherwise connected to the children's lives, Tolly gains a stronger sense of their presence. At first, he hears only mysterious whispering and laughing. After he rescues Neptune, a carp supposedly once Toby's pet, he feels that the children are playing hide-and-seek with him. He can't find them, but a twig forming the letter T is mysteriously placed on his head. On the fourth day, Tolly catches a glimpse of Linnet and Alexander in the mirror. Later, in another echo of *The Secret Garden*, a chaffinch that he has encouraged to live in Linnet's bird cage leads him to a long-lost key. It opens a wooden chest in which Tolly finds a sword, a flute, and other objects depicted in the painting. Afterwards, a marble rolls across the floor, dominoes fall by themselves, and someone puts hands over Tolly's eyes.

Tolly finally meets the three children after a snowstorm. Led by the sound of Alexander's flute, he finds them sheltered beneath a tree with a variety of animals. No one speaks, and when a peacock screams, they vanish. When he returns home, Tolly plays Alexander's flute, which he found in the chest. Listening to Tolly, Granny Oldknow suggests that Alexander has given him the flute. The next day, Tolly again meets the children, who tell him about their deaths and warn him about Green Noah, a topiary figure in the garden. When Tolly sees this figure the following day, he runs from it in fear. Safely in the house, he reads an article that explains the figure's history as an object cursed by Old Petronella, a gypsy woman.

When Tolly next comes across Green Noah, he taunts it with a rhyme Linnet taught him. That night, Tolly becomes lost while going to the barn. Lightning flashes, and he sees Green Noah coming toward him. The voices of Toby, Alexander, and Linnet call out for help from St. Christopher, whose statue is also in the garden, and a bolt of lightning completely destroys the topiary figure. Granny Oldknow then announces that they will plant a new Noah and have the priest bless it. In the morning, Tolly buys a gift for Granny Oldknow and acquires presents for his ancestors and the animals of Green Knowe. At midnight mass, Tolly dozes and sees his ancestors enter the church. On Christmas morning, he finds Toby's jacket in his room, puts it on, and rushes to the stable. There he gets his long-held wish of seeing Feste, Toby's fierce horse, about whom Granny

Oldknow has told stories. During Christmas day, he gains a living friend, Boggis's grandson, Percy, and he is given a dog that resembles the one in the portrait.

Sequels are The Chimneys of Green Knowe *(1958; U.S. title* Treasure of Green Knowe*),* A Stranger at Green Knowe *(1961),* An Enemy at Green Knowe *(1964), and* The Stones of Green Knowe *(1976).*

CHARACTERS: Lucy Boston was devoted to the Manor, a twelfth-century house in Hemingford Grey that she purchased in 1939. It inspired Green Knowe, which is almost a character in itself in this pastoral fantasy. The simultaneous existence of characters from the past and present at Green Knowe suggests that time, normally an enemy in pastorals, need not always be destructive.

Toseland, who is nicknamed **Tolly**, is a seven-year-old orphan in all but fact. He is extremely lonely because his father and stepmother, a woman he hardly knows, live in Burma. Tolly is clearly a dreamer with an active imagination. His experiences at Green Knowe, whether actual or imagined, symbolize his discovery of his past and, hence, of himself. Two patterns reinforce his development. First, numerous references to mirrors, doubles, and shadows suggest that Tolly is engaged in an exploration of his unconscious. Second, Tolly's constant discovery of objects from his past, especially those depicted in the painting of his ancestors, is a correlative for his discovery of the continuing force of the past in his life. His ultimate discovery, meeting his dead ancestors, marks a conscious recognition of his heritage. For example, Alexander's announcement that he has given his flute to Tolly and Tolly's later feelings that the flute is playing itself are poetic explanations for his previously unknown musical talent.

Tolly's growing understanding of the past is connected to his developing kindness. Under Granny Oldknow's direction, he learns to feed the birds and then other animals. He saves Toby's fish, and he makes his room into a haven for the birds when the melting snow freezes into ice. He also encourages the chaffinch to live in Linnet's cage in his room. These actions unite him with his ancestors as a part of the pastoral world of Green Knowe. Tolly shows his kindness to people by willingly giving an old collar depicted in the ancestral portrait to Granny Oldknow and by thinking hard before choosing the perfect Christmas gift for her. Tolly's growing understanding also makes him aware of sorrow and evil. He comes to an acceptance of death when he learns his ancestors died centuries ago in a plague. He also comes to an understanding that evil is a powerful force that should not be trifled with when he foolishly imperils himself by taunting Green Noah. At the same time, however, the intercession of his ancestors teaches him the value of family. Ultimately, Tolly gains the warmth of family and friends, and he develops a new confidence in himself.

Granny Linnet Oldknow, Tolly's great-grandmother, remains enigmatic. As her surname suggests, Granny Oldknow is a wise old woman who knows all about the past. She passes along her knowledge of family history through stories that engage Tolly's imagination. Like Tolly, she was an orphan in the house. Although bent with age and heavily wrinkled, she has a merry, conspiratorial smile that indicates she has not forgotten what it was like to be a lonely child. An effective teacher, she allows Tolly to make his own discoveries and refuses to impose an interpretation on events. She does not, for example, directly answer Tolly when he asks whether his ancestors actually attended midnight mass. Because she allows Tolly's imagination to run free, he is able to meet his ancestors; in this way, Granny Oldknow both preserves and renews the past. In a similar vein, she decides to replant Noah, along with his wife, but wisely has the new tree blessed; and she also gives Tolly a dog that resembles the one in the portrait.

Tolly's three seventeenth-century ancestors are helper figures. In particular, they reward Tolly for his kindness by calling upon St. Christopher to protect him from Green Noah. **Toby Oldknow** (Toby is short for Toseland) is a fourteen-year-old boy whose portrait portrays him wearing a sword and petting a deer. He thus demonstrates that strength and gentleness can exist together. He also exhibits the pastoral harmony with nature because his fish comes to him when he calls it in Latin. Granny Oldknow's story about his daring ride to fetch a doctor for his sick sister illustrates Toby's courage and love for family, as well as the special bond between animals and people. **Alexander Oldknow**, his younger brother, is pictured with a book and a flute. His ability to charm birds with his flute is reminiscent of Dickon Sowerby's similar talent in *The Secret Garden*. Granny Oldknow's story of his triumphant musical performance before the king is a tale of wishes realized that illustrates how people must be prepared to seize opportunities and to make their talents known. **Linnet Oldknow**, their little sister, is shown with the bird cage in Tolly's room and a chaffinch, much like the one that befriends Tolly. Linnet is full of high spirits and is always laughing. Granny Oldknow's tale of Linnet's Christmas Eve vision of the St. Christopher statue suggest goodness is an active force in the pastoral world. **Mr. Boggis**, the servant, is a comical rustic figure with a bald white head and red face. He is a great tease, suggesting to Tolly he will have to swim to the house during the flood. A member of the family that has served at Green Knowe for generations, he is another sign of pastoral continuity.

Further Reading

Berger, Laura Standley, ed. *Twentieth-Century Children's Writers*. 4th ed. Detroit: St. James, 1995.

Children's Literature Review. Vol. 3. Detroit: Gale Research, 1978.

Collier, Laurie, and Joyce Nakamura, eds. *Major Authors and Illustrators for Children and Young Adults*. Detroit: Gale Research, 1993.

Contemporary Authors. Vols. 73-76. Detroit: Gale Research, 1978.

De Montreville, Doris, and Donna Hill, eds. *Third Book of Junior Authors*. New York: H. W. Wilson, 1972.

Rose, Jasper. *Lucy Boston*. New York: Walk, 1966.

Something about the Author. Vol. 19. Detroit: Gale Research, 1980.

Wintle, Justin, and Emma Fisher. *The Pied Pipers: Interviews with the Influential Creators of Children's Literature*. New York: Paddington Press, 1974.

Carol Ryrie Brink

1895-1981, American author

Caddie Woodlawn

(historical novel, 1935)

PLOT: Inspired by the reminiscences of the author's grandmother, this episodic Newbery Medal winner illustrates the central character's belief that "life is just a lot of everyday adventures," while also exploring issues of racism, sex roles, and democratic values. Caddie (Caroline Augusta) Woodlawn lives in Wisconsin with her pioneer parents, Johnny and Harriet, and her six siblings, Clara, Tom, Warren, Hetty (Henrietta), Minnie, and baby Joe. Caddie constantly plays with Tom and Warren, to her mother's chagrin, especially when the Circuit Rider, Mr. Tanner, sees Caddie dirty and disheveled. Caddie's father, however, encourages her wild ways. In the fall, Uncle Edmund visits and plays a practical joke, paying Caddie a silver dollar in penance. He saddens Caddie by taking away her dog, Nero, for training and then by writing that it has run away.

During the winter, Caddie attends school, falls through the ice while skating, learns to repair clocks, and protects Tom from teasing by ensuring that no one learns that he sent Katie Hyman a fancy valentine. When rumors of an imminent Indian attack lead the settlers to gather at her house, Caddie overhears a plot to kill Indian John and his people, so she rides to warn the Indians. Her father, however, calms the settlers and reaffirms peace with the Indians. Afterwards, Indian John asks Caddie to care for his wounded dog and to hold his scalp belt because his people are leaving. When the departure of their mother makes three half-breed children of Sam Hankinson miserable, Caddie spends her dollar buying them candy, combs, and handkerchiefs. After publicly exhibiting the scalp belt, Tom and Caddie give the sick Katie Hyman a private viewing. On the last day of school, the stage-struck Warren recites an embarrassing version of his speech, and Tom, Caddie, and Warren narrowly escape death when lightning strikes a tree under which they had sought shelter moments earlier.

The final episodes involve significant changes. Alerted by Indian John's dog, Obediah Jones becomes a hero, defending the school against a prairie fire. When her pretentious cousin, Annabelle Grey, visits from Boston, Caddie joins Tom in playing a series of practical jokes on her. Mrs. Woodlawn punishes Caddie for failing to be a lady, and after listening to her father, Caddie overcomes her fear of growing up. The next day, she lets Annabelle teach her a quilting stitch. Implausibly, Johnny Woodlawn learns that he can be an English lord if he renounces America forever. The family votes, however, to remain in America. Indian John then returns, and Caddie gives him the scalp belt and sends the dog after him. When Nero also returns, the contented Caddie thinks of the changes she has gone through.

CHARACTERS: In her author's note, Brink says that, although she invented episodes, she tried "to keep the real background and the characters of the real people always in mind." During the course of a year, **Caddie Woodlawn** (her full name is Caroline Augusta Woodlawn) changes from a carefree tomboy to a responsible young woman. Eleven years old when the novel opens, Caddie has red-gold ringlets and is brown and strong because her father has let her run wild for seven years. Caddie enjoys playing with her brothers, but she occasionally feels uncomfortable that she is not a lady. Her daring and willfulness sometimes lead to trouble, as when she foolishly skates on black ice and falls through. At other times she is spirited and unyielding: Caddie boldly says that she will beat Uncle Edmund home on her raft and then refuses to be bribed into silence when he plays the practical joke of loosening her raft's logs. Furthermore, when Obediah refuses to take his feet off a friend's desk, she hits him. Caddie is curious and clever, happily learning the unfeminine task of repairing clocks. She is also sensitive. She is thus saddened by the wholesale capture of pigeons. More significantly, she protects Tom from teasing by cleverly deflecting the talkative Hetty's suspicions that he is the purchaser of the fancy valentine, and she cheers the Hankinson children by spending all of her money on them. Caddie differs from most of the settlers in that she has no prejudices against Indians. Consequently, she makes a cold and dangerous ride to warn the Indians of danger. Caddie begins to take pleasure in conventionally female activities, such as stitching, but her true maturity comes when she accepts that being a lady is not a matter of fashion but of character. She demonstrates the compassionate character of a woman when she suddenly understands that Hetty is a tattletale because she is lonely and when she orders Indian John's dog, who is attached to her, to return to his master. Twelve years old at the end, an age traditionally assigned to social transitions, Caddie ably embodies the sturdy and optimistic spirit of the American pioneering woman.

Johnny Woodlawn, Caddie's father, is descended from British nobility, but he is fiercely democratic, believing that what one earns oneself is more valuable than what one is given. He shows his democratic fervor by allowing his family to vote on whether they remain in America or accept the English title he has been offered. (Although the scene stirs patriotism, it lacks authenticity because lordships can't be bequeathed or given conditionally.) Johnny is, however, superior to his neighbors because he lacks their prejudice against the Indians. As a result, he is able to stop his neighbors from plotting murder and to ensure peace. In his domestic life, Johnny is also iconoclastic, insisting that it will be beneficial to Caddie's health if she runs wild with the boys. His climactic speech to Caddie, in which he separates the spheres of men and women, has disturbed some feminists, but it accords females a valuable role within an historically restrictive society. Furthermore, he rejects the notion that a lady is defined by fashion and manners. Instead, he calls on Caddie to be "a woman with a wise and understanding heart, healthy in body and honest in mind." By doing so, he makes Caddie's maturity represent the development of a moral character. His wife, **Harriet Woodlawn**, who looks back nostalgically on her life in Boston society, creates domestic conflict by trying to make Caddie conform to conventional notions of ladylike behavior. When Caddie disappoints her by teasing Annabelle, she therefore punishes Caddie

Caddie confronts the bully Obadiah in an illustration by Trina Schart Hyman from Caddie Woodlawn.

for violating a lady's proper duty of showing hospitality to a guest.

Caddie's red-headed siblings have limited roles. **Clara**, the oldest, contrasts with Caddie because she is a conventional girl who does domestic chores. Clara is the only one who votes to go to England, but she immediately changes her mind. **Tom**, the one with the darkest hair, is two years older than Caddie. He is resourceful, as he shows by earning money for a valentine and by suggesting that Caddie charge children to see the scalp belt. Tom is also an accomplished storyteller who invents wild tales that entertain his siblings. In love with Katie Hyman, Tom shows consideration by insisting that she must not be the only one who has not seen the scalp belt. Tom has a manly sense of responsibility: he tells the teacher that he is responsible for Warren's embarrassing recital, and he accepts the justice of a thrashing for teasing Annabelle. Carrot-topped **Warren**, who is two years younger than Caddie, is always present, but he is most notable when, because of stage fright, he remembers only the comic version of the simple piece he is to recite. **Hetty** (short for Henrietta) is a seven-year-old who is always an outsider because she has no siblings close to her in age. A notorious tattletale, she reports everything that Tom, Caddie, and Warren do. **Minnie** and baby **Joe** play no role in these "everyday adventures."

Two relatives, however, cause such adventures. **Uncle Edmund**, Mrs. Woodlawn's brother and an irresponsible practical joker, humiliates Caddie by untying the logs on the raft she is using to race against him. After she falls into the water, he tries to bribe her into silence by offering the silver dollar he bet on the race. **Annabelle Grey**, Caddie's cousin from Boston, is a foil. She has many accomplishments, but embodies a superficial definition of a lady. Obsessed with fashion, she prides herself on having more buttons on her dress than her friends do. Her superior airs anger her rustic cousins, but Annabelle displays surprising pluck when they prey on her naivete: she doesn't cry when she is knocked from a horse or mobbed by sheep eager for the salt she holds. She cries only when Caddie puts an egg down her blouse and the egg cracks during a somersault. Unlike Caddie, who values her American heritage, Annabelle has a mindless admiration for status, becoming thrilled with the notion that her cousins will be English nobility.

His broken English and stoic attitude make **Indian John** a stereotype of the Native American. His tender concern for Caddie and his insistence that he and his people are friendly, however, humanize him. These qualities also establish his superiority to the frightened settlers, who condemn the Indians as savages. **Obediah Jones**, a hulking bully, shows that circumstances create character when he becomes a hero by directing the fight against the prairie fire, thereby saving the very school in which he suffered humiliation. **Miss Parker**, the teacher, a small woman with great courage, controls her school by standing up to Obediah. Children obey her out of fear, but she is compassionate and understanding.

Further Reading

Berger, Laura Standley, ed. *Twentieth-Century Children's Writers*. 4th ed. Detroit: St. James, 1995.

Children's Literature Review. Vol. 30. Detroit: Gale Research, 1993.

Collier, Laurie, and Joyce Nakamura, eds. *Major Authors and Illustrators for Children and Young Adults*. Detroit: Gale Research, 1993.

Contemporary Authors New Revision Series. Vol. 3. Detroit: Gale Research, 1981.

Kunitz, Stanley J., and Howard Haycraft, eds. *The Junior Book of Authors*. 2nd ed. New York: H. W. Wilson, 1951.

Something about the Author. Vols. 1, 31. Detroit: Gale Research, 1971, 1983.

Walter R. Brooks

1886-1958, American editor and author

Freddy the Detective

(animal fantasy, 1932)

PLOT: The detective work of Freddy the pig connects the episodes in this story. Freddy's career begins when Jinx the cat and two ducks, Alice and Emma, tell him about the theft of a toy train. Freddy discovers that the rats, led by Simon and his sons, Zeke and Ezra, have stolen it to use as armor during their grain thefts. When Freddy fails to get the rats out of the train, he tries to prove that he is a real detective by searching for Egbert, a missing rabbit. Freddy questions and then sends home a young rabbit, not realizing that he has found Egbert. Continuing the search, he comes across the cabin of Red and Looey, two robbers who chase him, causing him to get lost in the woods.

Freddy soon proves competent, however. He catches Ferdinand the crow stealing Prinny the dog's dinner. After Mrs. Wiggins the cow gives Freddy the idea, he and Jinx use a pulley to upset the train and capture Ezra. Charles the rooster, the elected judge, is roused from bed in spite of the objections of Henrietta, his domineering wife, and sentences Ezra to the barnyard jail. Freddy's case load increases, so Freddy makes Mrs. Wiggins his partner. He is dismayed to learn, however, that the crime spree is the result of animals, including Charles the judge, wanting to go to jail to have fun. Serious

Freddy the detective and friends as illustrated by Kurt Wiese.

cases, though, demand attention. First, Freddy tries to prove that Jinx is innocent of killing a crow. Second, after a visit from the sheriff and Mr. Boner, a city detective, Freddy decides to capture Red and Looey. Disguised as a human, he joins them and foils a robbery. He then uses a fake treasure map to lure them into Mr. Bean's barn, where the animals capture them. Mr. Boner tries to take credit for the capture, but Mr. Bean has Peter the bear chase him away. At Jinx's trial, Freddy proves that Simon framed Jinx. He orders Simon tried for lying, but the rats flee into the woods. Jinx and Freddy, needing a change, set out on the open road.

Freddy the Detective *is the third of twenty-five Freddy books.*

CHARACTERS: The first of the series in which Freddy emerges as a central and distinct character, this novel contains a large cast of characters with small roles. Animal characters understand humans, but they talk only to each other.

Brooks said that "Pigs in general are not built for the heroic role." **Freddy** is not, however, a common pig. A unique, engaging mixture of qualities, Freddy is good-hearted but pragmatic. He sympathizes with the plight of the rats, whom everyone else despises, because he understands what it must be like to be an outcast. At the same time, he criticizes those who are sentimental about

the prisoners in the jail. Like traditional heroes, Freddy is a superior creature. Unusually intelligent, Freddy can read and write. He also uses his reading to good purpose, learning from Sherlock Holmes how to notice and interpret clues. As well as being smart, Freddy is resourceful and cunning, getting Eeny the mouse to gather evidence. Furthermore, knowing that Simon will lie during Jinx's trial, Freddy shrewdly offers protection as long as Simon does not commit a crime. Freddy displays the traditional heroic confidence, announcing beforehand that he will prove Jinx innocent. Because he values his reputation, he tries to prove himself after his initial failure with the rats. Later, unwilling to let the sheriff steal the glory, Freddy captures the robbers himself. By donning a disguise and giving the robbers a fake treasure map, he shows another side of his heroism: Freddy becomes an archetypal trickster.

In spite of his superior abilities, Freddy is sometimes a comical bumbler. He becomes so absorbed with acting like a detective when he questions Egbert that he fails to realize that he has found the rabbit for whom he is searching. Later, when lost in the woods, he doesn't realize that he is following his own footprints. When disguised as a man, Freddy foils the bank robbery only because he is awkward: he falls from a ladder he is using to enter the bank and thereby alerts the guards. Such comical failures prevent Freddy from being grandly heroic, but they make him engaging. Freddy combines the joyous innocence of childhood and the shrewd wisdom of adulthood. Freddy's world is dated, but he lives on as one of the most memorable characters in animal fantasy.

Jinx, the black cat, is sarcastic but loyal, deferring to Freddy's judgment. He has a volatile temper and talks fiercely but is actually insecure and constantly worries about his fate should Mr. Bean discover that he failed to prevent the rats from entering the house. **Mrs. Wiggins** is a cow who helps Freddy and becomes his partner. She has common sense, though she acts foolishly when she tramples the cornfield while practicing the detective skill of shadowing. Later, however, humble Mrs. Wiggins, although denying that she has ideas, figures out how to get the train away from the rats. **Charles** the rooster is an absurd, self-centered orator who delights in pompous phrases. Although he craves status and therefore gets himself elected judge, he is so restricted at home that he sentences himself to jail so that he can have a good time. Charles is henpecked by his domineering wife, **Henrietta**, who forbids him to make speeches and controls his actions. Henrietta is a comical hypocrite. She often denounces Charles for acting ridiculous, but she lavishly praises him when he is missing. Henrietta is also a social climber: she basks in her husband's status, opposing efforts to remove him from office.

The major antagonist is **Simon**, the leader of the rats. He makes speeches about the rats' right to live, but, as his beady black eyes and oily smile suggest, Simon is evil. Devoid of integrity, he breaks a promise and moves into the barn. He steals the train and uses it to steal grain. Simon is arrogant, taunting Freddy and Jinx with a song; he is also clever, as his use of the train and his vicious plot to frame Jinx demonstrate. But his pride leads to his downfall. Adopting an air of mock humility, he is so contemptuous that he fails to realize that he forfeits protection by lying in court. He then shows cowardice by fleeing into the woods. His sons are similar to him. **Zeke** is arrogant and selfish, angrily asking what the animals have done for the rats. **Ezra** is meek and

submissive once he loses the protection of the train. The chief human antagonists, the robbers **Red** and **Looey**, are caricatures who always wear their masks. Red, the larger one, is a magnificent driver. Looey knits mufflers and worries about Red being warm enough during their nocturnal robberies. They appear especially foolish because of their contests: Red plays the harmonium and Looey sings, each racing to see who can finish a song first. Their greed and stupidity are evident in their belief in Freddy's fake map. **Mr. Montague Boner**, a city detective, is also an antagonist. A cross-looking, hard-faced man with a cigar stub in his mouth, he has contempt for the animals and country life in general. Selfish and dishonest, Mr. Boner tries to claim the reward and fame for the capture of the robbers.

Incidental but notable roles are played by animals and humans. **The Sheriff** is a foil to Mr. Boner. He looks like a bumpkin because of his tuft of thin gray whiskers, but he is wise enough to see that the animals are remarkable and deserve respect. **Mr. Bean**, a farmer unfazed by his remarkable animals, comically insists on maintaining the farm's routine, even if robbers are lurking about. His strong sense of fair play makes him summon Peter when Mr. Boner takes credit for capturing the robbers. In this episode, **Peter** the bear serves as a convenient plot device to preserve Freddy's reputation. Throughout, he is a challenge to Charles because Freddy threatens to make Peter the judge if Charles behaves foolishly. **Eeny** the mouse is industrious and intelligent, assisting Freddy by carefully gathering evidence. **Ferdinand** (also called **Ferdy**) the crow steals Prinny's dinner, but he is more jokester than criminal. He prosecutes Jinx, showing cleverness by avoiding the facts of the case. Timid **Alice** and stubborn **Emma**, white ducks, are foils to clever Freddy: they can't understand explanations of anything that they do not already know.

Further Reading

Berger, Laura Standley, ed. *Twentieth-Century Children's Writers*. 4th ed. Detroit: St. James, 1995.

Contemporary Authors. Vol. 111. Detroit: Gale Research, 1984.

Kunitz, Stanley J., and Howard Haycraft, eds. *The Junior Book of Authors*. 2nd ed. New York: H. W. Wilson, 1951.

Sale, Roger. "Two Pigs." In *Fairy Tales and After: From Snow White to E. B. White.* Cambridge, MA: Harvard University Press, 1978.

Something about the Author. Vol. 17. Detroit: Gale Research, 1979.

Anthony Browne

1946-, English picture book author and illustrator

Gorilla

(picture book, 1983)

PLOT: The dream fantasy in *Gorilla* reveals a child's feelings of neglect and her need for a relationship with her father. Hannah loves gorillas, but she has never seen one in person because her father is always too busy to take her to the zoo. The night before her birthday, Hannah wakes up to find a parcel at the foot of her bed. She has asked for a gorilla, but the parcel contains only a toy one. Disappointed, Hannah throws it into the corner. During the night, it grows into a huge living gorilla. Donning her father's hat and coat, the gorilla takes Hannah to the zoo, a movie, and a restaurant. When Hannah awakens in the morning, she finds the toy gorilla in her bed. She rushes downstairs, where her father invites her to go to the zoo. Happily, Hannah goes off with him.

CHARACTERS: The spare text is less important in developing the interior life of the characters than the color, details, and repeated elements of the elaborate pictures. Ultimately, these pictures imply, rather than show, the climactic moment of character transformation.

Hannah apparently lives alone with her father. Picture details suggest she is a loving child who finds life lonely and unsatisfying. In the first large picture, for example, Hannah wears red, a warm color, but everything else is blue, an emotionally cold color. Furthermore, the checkerboard patterns on the towel, dishes, walls, and floor are in perfect alignment, thereby suggesting a rigid, orderly, sterile existence. This and other pictures, however, also reveal that Hannah uses her rich imagination to compensate for her loneliness. Thus, the facing pages of her father's newspaper contain numerous photographs of gorillas. Significantly, she watches television alone in a completely bare room, suggesting the emptiness of her home life. The partially darkened walls, though, contain outlines of various African animals that again suggest that she employs her imagination to transform her boring life. Hannah's dream ultimately helps her to cope with her loneliness. The dominant yellow color of the picture in which she awakens to find the gorilla in her bed suggests that she has learned to be happy with even a token of her father's love.

The **gorilla** is a dream figure who embodies Hannah's concept of the ideal father. Tellingly, he is huge, but Hannah's father's hat and coat are a "perfect fit." Throughout the story Hannah hugs him because, unlike her father, the gorilla satisfies her emotional needs. He does this first, of course, by taking her to see the gorillas at the zoo, but, more importantly, he does it by paying attention to her. The picture of Hannah and the gorilla at the restaurant contrasts with the earlier scene of her at breakfast with her father. First, the significantly narrower table brings the two physically closer; second, the gorilla, unlike the father, looks directly at Hannah; third, this table is a jumble of delicious foods, whereas the earlier table was mostly bare and orderly; and finally, the dominant yellow and red colors suggest warmth and happiness.

Hannah's **father** is a man who initially ignores his daughter. He is pictured as putting a newspaper between them or as having his back turned to her. Her feeling that he is unresponsive is symbolized by his cold blue clothing. Ironically, the father is the one who changes as the result of Hannah's dream. The text does not say so, and the pictures do not

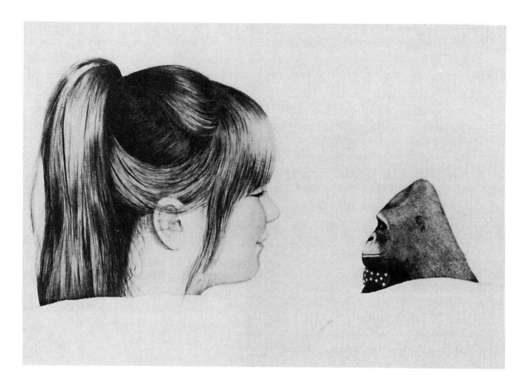

A little girl's toy gorilla comes to life in Browne's self-illustrated picture book.

show it, but the father must have come into Hannah's room during the night and placed the toy back in her bed. He must have finally understood the depth of Hannah's frustrated desires, and that is why he invites her to the zoo. His change of heart is symbolized by the wearing of a red sweater, which matches Hannah's red robe. That he now makes Hannah happy by living up to her desire for contact is evident in the final picture. It repeats with slight variation an earlier one in which the gorilla took the girl to the zoo. In both, the adult figure wears the same hat and coat, and an affectionate Hannah holds his hand.

Further Reading

Berger, Laura Standley, ed. *Twentieth-Century Children's Writers*. 4th ed. Detroit: St. James, 1995.

Children's Literature Review. Vol. 19. Detroit: Gale Research, 1990.

Holtze, Sally Holmes, ed. *Sixth Book of Junior Authors and Illustrators*. New York: H. W. Wilson, 1989.

Something about the Author. Vols. 45, 61. Detroit: Gale Research, 1986, 1990.

Robert Burch

1925-, American author

Queenie Peavy

(novel, 1966)

PLOT: Set in rural Depression-era Georgia, this novel focuses on the title character's transition from troublesome tomboy to self-respecting adolescent. Thirteen-year-old Queenie Peavy, whose father is in prison, is always in trouble. She spits tobacco juice in Judge Lewis's courtroom, and she throws a rock to scare little Tilly Evans, who is taunting her with a chant about her father. At school, Queenie endures constant teasing about her father, especially from Cravey Mason. Queenie gets even by rigging a log so that Cravey will fall from it. When Cravey breaks his leg, Principal Hanley warns Queenie that he may have to expel her. She promises to apologize to Cravey, but he mocks her, so she threatens him instead. On the way home, Persimmon Gibbs invites her to smoke some cigarettes. The next day, Persimmon claims that Queenie threw rocks and broke the windows in a church. After learning of the accusation, Queenie keeps her word and apologizes to Cravey, but he taunts her, saying that she is going to a reformatory. Shortly afterwards, Martha Mullins (called "Little Mother") faints, and Queenie accompanies her to Doctor Palmer's office, where she helps the doctor treat an injured child.

Queenie thinks that her troubles are over when her father is paroled. But her black neighbor, Elgin Corry forbids his children, Dover and Avis, to go to Queenie's house anymore. Furthermore, her father ignores Queenie, leaving her in a ditch when he hitches a ride on a log truck. Believing that she will soon be sent to the reformatory, Queenie decides to pretend that her father's arrival has changed her. She becomes cooperative at school, nominating Cravey for a committee and singing solo at assembly. At home, the sight of her father's gun makes her cry because she now realizes that he doesn't care for his family. The next day, Mr. Hanley clears Queenie of the vandalism charge by revealing that Persimmon, egged on by Cravey, broke the church windows. That night, Mrs. Peavy announces that she has obtained a better paying job and that Queenie's father threatened some people with his pistol and was sent back to prison. Queenie shows a genuine change in character by resisting an urge to throw stones at the church window. In the end, she happily accepts an invitation to a school party and a sleepover at Little Mother's house.

CHARACTERS: Thirteen-year-old **Queenie Peavy** has formed a tough shell to protect herself from pain, appearing as a tough-talking, tobacco-chewing eighth-grade tomboy. Angered and alienated by being teased about her father, she is given to hostile outbursts. For example, she declares to the principal that she doesn't care about anything. Queenie is also impulsive and clever. She exacts revenge by rigging a log to fall and then daring Cravey to walk on it.

Jerry Lazare's illustration of Burch's troublesome tomboy, Queenie Peavy.

Although she didn't intend for him to get hurt, she threatens to break his other leg when he later taunts her. Her one source of pride is her deadly aim in throwing rocks, but Queenie has other virtues. She is a bright and dedicated student who always does her homework. Her stories and songs with Dover and Avis Corry show that she has a sense of humor and can be gentle; she demonstrates maturity and composure while helping the doctor; she is also responsible at home and does the chores, such as milking and churning. Queenie's integrity and goodwill are evident when she tries to keep her word by apologizing to Cravey, when she resists an urge to hurt him by insulting his father, and when she offers to help Cravey and Persimmon earn money to pay for the windows they broke.

Queenie's major flaw is her naivete. She clings to a childish belief that her father is not responsible for his crime and that his presence will transform her life and allow her to become good. By pretending to be a model student, however, she actually changes.

She receives such pleasure from doing well and being appreciated, and she realizes that she is hurting herself by her bad behavior. The sight of her father's pistol, though, provides the major epiphany: she tearfully realizes that he doesn't care about his family and is responsible for his crimes, and she therefore no longer uses him to excuse her own misconduct. Accepting that she will live under the shadow of the jail and that those who taunt her express their own crudeness, Queenie learns to think before acting. As a result, she begins to adapt and get along with others, becoming part of the school's social life.

Two authority figures express the theme of personal responsibility in the advice they offer Queenie. **Mr. Hanley**, the principal, is a kind and patient man who tries to help Queenie in spite of her off-putting manner. Unlike other adults, he believes her when she professes innocence to the charge of vandalism, and he therefore investigates until he identifies the real culprits. In his role as wise counselor, he tells Queenie that people who tease her are only showing their own flaws. She tries to take his lesson to heart, refraining from teasing Cravey about his father out of respect for Cravey's feelings. Mr. Hanley also reiterates the theme after Queenie reforms, telling her that it is up to her whether she leads a decent and happy life. **Judge Lewis** foreshadows Queenie's own understanding of her father's true character when he tells her that people are responsible for their own conduct. He also points out that living in the shadow of the jail—that is, with the taunting that comes when a family member is in prison—can make one give up on life. He thus warns Queenie not to let others control how she feels and behaves.

Martha Mullins, called **Little Mother** because she is always trying to make things run smoothly, is a foil to the hostile and aggressive Queenie. Martha thus shows tolerance and understanding by quickly brushing aside Cravey's comments when he mocks her. She also contrasts with Queenie because she doesn't (as she herself points out) feel the need for foolish pride. Because she is hungry, she has no qualms about eating the sweet potato that Cravey threw away. Martha is, however, too saintly to be plausible. She sacrifices her own food so that her six brothers and sisters will have enough to eat and consequently becomes malnourished. **Cravey Mason**, a boy better at sports than school work, illustrates Mr. Hanley's idea that taunting is a reflection of inner weakness. An arrogant bully, Cravey ruthlessly teases both Queenie and Martha. When Queenie's act of vengeance leads him to break his leg, he becomes even nastier, deliberately trying to hurt her by having her sent to a reformatory for a crime she did not commit. **Persimmon Gibbs**, a seventh-grader, is a coward who is bullied into blaming Queenie for the vandalism he committed. Mr. Hanley forces him to accept responsibility for his actions.

Mr. Peavy, Queenie's father, is rude, selfish, and mean-spirited. After his release from prison, he does not give Queenie the affection and attention she craves. When he hitches a ride, he doesn't even notice that she falls into a ditch to avoid being hit by the log truck. Vindictive, he violates parole by using a pistol to threaten those who testified against him. **Mrs. Peavy** is a hardworking woman who never condemns her husband in Queenie's presence. She advocates responsibility by stressing the need for Queenie to do her chores. **Elgin Corry**, the Peavys' black neighbor, is a foil to Mr. Peavy. Industrious and cheerful, he is a successful farmer who lives in a neat, well-kept brick house. As a father, he cares for and protects his children, forbidding them to go to Queenie's house once her father is released from prison. Eight-year-old **Dover Corry** and his five-year-old sister, **Avis**, idolize Queenie and delight in sneaking up on her and singing with her. Their relationship with Queenie reveals her sense of humor and her kindness.

Further Reading

Berger, Laura Standley, ed. *Twentieth-Century Young Adult Writers.* 1st ed. Detroit: St. James, 1994.

Collier, Laurie, and Joyce Nakamura, eds. *Major Authors and Illustrators for Children and Young Adults.* Detroit: Gale Research, 1993.

Contemporary Authors New Revision Series. Vol. 17. Detroit: Gale Research, 1986.

De Montreville, Doris, and Donna Hill, eds. *Third Book of Junior Authors.* New York: H. W. Wilson, 1972.

Estes, Glenn E., ed. *American Writers for Children since 1960: Fiction*. Vol. 52 of *Dictionary of Literary Biography*. Detroit: Gale Research, 1986.

Something about the Author. Vols. 1, 74. Detroit: Gale Research, 1971, 1993.

Frances Hodgson Burnett

1849-1924, English-American novelist and playwright

Little Lord Fauntleroy

(novel, 1886)

PLOT: Although it devotes most of its attention to the period during which the hero is wealthy, *Little Lord Fauntleroy* is a variation of the Cinderella story. The fairy-tale plot shows the value of combining American egalitarianism with British respect for tradition. Cedric Errol, a remarkably beautiful boy, grows up in poverty. His father, the youngest son of John Arthur Molynuex Errol, Earl of Dorincourt, has been cut off from his family because he married an American. After Cedric's father dies, his mother raises him in the back streets of New York. There, Cedric becomes friends with a grocer, Mr. Hobbs, who hates the British nobility, and a bootblack named Dick Tipton. Cedric's poverty ends when Mr. Havisham, the earl's solicitor, informs him that he is now Lord Fauntleroy and therefore next in line to be earl. Before leaving for England, little Fauntleroy is generous with the money put at his disposal. He pays the bills of a sick man, provides for the comfort of an old apple seller, buys out Dick's partner so that Dick can be independent, and gives a gold watch to Mr. Hobbs.

Once in England, Fauntleroy gradually transforms his selfish and bitter grandfather. Unaware that the old man hates his mother and has a reputation for selfishness, Fauntleroy believes the earl is good and generous. He even attributes his own acts of generosity to the earl. For his part, the anti-American earl is pleased by his grandson's appearance, manners, and courage. On their first meeting, for example, Fauntleroy suggests that the gout-stricken earl lean on his shoulder on the way into dinner. The earl tests the boy by leaning on him heavily, but Fauntleroy neither complains nor gives up. The earl becomes both proud and fond of Fauntleroy. Because he now has feelings for another person, the earl consequently becomes healthier in body and mind.

At this point in the story, a vulgar American woman claims that her son is the rightful Lord Fauntleroy. The earl is furious, but Fauntleroy is unconcerned. He is even willing to go to work in Mr. Hobbs's store. Implausibly, the woman turns out to be the wife of Dick Tipton's brother. Dick and Mr. Hobbs read the story in an American paper and inform the earl of the truth, after which they go to England to expose the fraud. The earl subsequently sends Dick to university, while Mr. Hobbs sets up a store near the earl's castle.

CHARACTERS: Probably because of his appearance, **Cedric Errol, Little Lord Fauntleroy,** has an undeserved reputation with readers as an angelic sissy. A beautiful seven-year-old boy with curly golden hair that falls in lovelocks on his shoulders, Cedric wears a black velvet suit with knickerbockers and a lace Vandyke collar. Both Reginald Birch's original illustrations (modeled after photographs of Burnett's son, Vivian) and the practice of having girls portray him in stage and movie versions might have contributed to the idea that Cedric is effeminate. In fact, in Hodgson's text Cedric is completely boyish. Athletic, he wins a race against other street boys in New York. He is also brave, enduring his grandfather's weight when he leans on him and showing no fear around his grandfather's hound or horses.

Cedric's innate "nobility" is wedded to an inveterate and sincere charm, which springs from his thoroughly egalitarian outlook on other people. He not only looks like a lord but acts the way an ideal lord should, too. He is devoted to his family. He always thinks of his mother, whom he cloyingly calls "Dearest," and he is eager to assume the best about the earl. Furthermore, he is naturally charitable. He uses his money to help those in need and suggests that bad conditions on the earl's estate be improved. In addition, Cedric has a charmingly social personality. He makes intelligent observations and puts all those who hear him completely at ease. He considers his lowly American acquaintances to be as worthy of friendship as the noble earl. When he thinks that he is no longer a lord, he has no regret for his loss of status or wealth. Instead, he shows an American determination to provide for his family, even if he has to work in a grocery store.

Although Cedric is not perfect, his faults are minor ones that add to his charm. For example, he mispronounces big words and misspells most. Cedric's blend of aristocratic and democratic virtues is ultimately a moral influence that makes the earl a better person. For this reason, Cedric is a perfect example of a popular nineteenth-century type: the innocent child who charms and then transforms a cynical and disillusioned adult. Cedric himself is remarkably static, remaining the same whether poor or wealthy.

Whereas Cedric represents the highest concept of nobility, **John Arthur Molynuex Errol, Earl of Dorincourt**, is nobility's worst realization. A rather stern-looking man with shaggy white hair and eyebrows, an aquiline nose, and fierce eyes, the earl is selfish and proud. Absorbed in his own pleasures, he is a failed patriarch. He has neglected his children and has been callously cruel to his tenants. His moral infirmity is suggested by his physical disability, a crippling gout. The earl initially despises Americans, especially Cedric's mother. Nevertheless, Cedric's innocent respect for the earl, the child's devotion to his "Dearest," and his bravery in supporting the earl and in riding a horse transform the old man. He grows fonder of Cedric and begins thinking more about others, while his health improves. Eventually, he even makes friends with Cedric's mother.

Cedric's **mother** contrasts with the earl, who is a failure as a parent. She is an ideal mother who is determined to do what is best for her son. Thus, she refuses to tell Cedric that the earl hates her. She knows that doing so would turn the boy forever against his grandfather. She also demonstrates that Americans have their own form of nobility when she refuses to take money from the earl. Before they go

to England, **Mr. Havisham**, the earl's old solicitor and a bachelor with a keen respect for an old family name, establishes that both mother and son are virtuous and will not be an immediate disgrace to the title. Havisham never informs Cedric that the money he gives away to others was intended to bribe him into liking the earl.

Fat, bald **Mr. Hobbs**, the grocer, hates all things aristocratic. Mr. Hobbs is not very intelligent, but he is a kindly father figure to young Cedric. Just as the elitist earl comes to respect republican openness, Mr. Hobbs comes to respect aristocratic stability and tradition. Therefore, he decides to remain in England. **Dick Tipton**, the bootblack, is an enterprising American boy who needs only a fair chance to succeed. Immensely loyal to Cedric, he exposes the fraudulent claimant to the earl. The fact that he attends an English university establishes the idea that social station does not limit intelligence.

A Little Princess
(novel, 1905)

PLOT: An expanded version of an earlier novel, *Sara Crewe; or, What Happened at Miss Minchin's* (1888), *A Little Princess* is another reversal-of-fortune story. The familiar riches-to-rags-to-riches plot illustrates that nobility is a quality of character independent of material wealth. Before returning to India, the wealthy Captain Ralph Crewe places his motherless daughter in a London boarding school, Miss Maria Minchin's Select Seminary for Young Ladies. Seven-year-old Sara Crewe becomes the star pupil, paraded in front of visiting parents because of her fine clothes and her intellectual accomplishments. Sara, a gifted storyteller, is popular with most of the girls. She "adopts" Lottie Legh, a four-year-old whose mother has died, thereby stopping the little girl's frequent tantrums; she also befriends the intellectually dull Ermengarde St. John and Becky, the illiterate chamber maid. Lavinia Herbert, the school's oldest student, is the only one unmoved by Sara's kindness. Jealous of Sara's popularity and active imagination, she derisively calls her Princess Sara.

On Sara's eleventh birthday, Miss Minchin receives word that Captain Crewe lost his fortune and is dead. Miss Minchin therefore decides to send the now penniless Sara to live in the garret with Becky. Poorly fed and clothed, Sara becomes the school's drudge as well as a teacher of younger students. No matter how much she is abused, however, Sara maintains the calm and dignified manner of a true princess. Sara's attitude enrages Miss Minchin and spurs her on to further humiliations. Lottie and Ermengarde make secret visits, but Sara's main solace is her imagination. Through it, Sara transforms the privation she and Becky endure into something romantic.

Sara's fortunes begin to change when the ailing Mr. Tom Carrisford moves next door. His Indian servant, Ram Dass, witnesses Sara's deprivation through a skylight. He sees Miss Minchin, tipped off by Lavinia, discovering Ermengarde when she brings food to Sara and Becky. The furious Miss Minchin decrees that Sara will go without food the next day. Ram Dass, acting on his employer's wishes, secretly brings food, blankets, books, and coal for a fire into Sara's garret. Later, Sara returns an escaped monkey to Ram Dass. Mr. Carrisford learns her identity and reveals that he is her father's business partner. He has been searching for her to tell her that her father's fortune was not lost. Mr. Carrisford takes Sara into his house and begins recovering, now that he has done his duty. Sara soon learns that her example of kindness during her poverty has affected others. For example, she has inspired a baker to take in a street urchin. Miss Minchin returns to her school, where her younger sister, Amelia, finally stands up to her.

CHARACTERS: The evil people in this story are concerned only with money and appearances; the good ones value character more than social status. In both wealth and poverty, **Sara Crewe** supports the novel's theme that true royalty is a matter of

Little Sara meets the villainous Miss Maria Minchin in this illustration by Tasha Tudor from Burnett's **A Little Princess.**

character, not status. Sara is seven when she first comes to Miss Minchin's seminary, eleven when she loses her fortune, and about seventeen when she regains it. Although wealthy and intelligent, Sara is completely without vanity. For one thing, she mistakenly thinks of herself as ugly. Although she is not beautiful, Sara does have a distinctive charm. Slim and tall, she has heavy black hair, large greenish gray eyes, long lashes, and an intense yet attractive face. Most people who see her sense her kindness and friendliness. Sara's understanding that her wealth and intelligence are accidents of birth also prevents her from becoming vain or arrogant.

Sara loves books and willingly continues her studies even after she becomes a servant. Gifted with a powerful imagination, she uses her ability as a storyteller to entertain others and to make her own drab existence tolerable. One of Sara's favorite "pretends" is that she is a princess, and she always acts as if she actually were one. Thus, when Miss Minchin abuses her, Sara refrains from talking back. Instead, she fantasizes that she is sparing Miss Minchin from execution by not exercising her powers as a princess. More importantly, Sara shows that she is a true princess by always being kind to others. Her natural charity prompts her to show kindness to Ermengarde, who is often ridiculed. She adopts Lottie, who feels sorry for herself because she has no mother. And she offers stories to Becky, who is eager for any scrap of romance. Her concern for others leads Sara to give buns to a poor girl even though she herself is hungry. Sara is similarly kind once her fortune is restored. She takes Becky as her servant, and she sets up an account so that a baker can feed hungry children.

Miss Maria Minchin shows that respectable people can be villains. A tall, ugly woman with cold, fishy eyes, she is completely mercenary. She is obsequious to Sara's father and makes Sara into a show pupil in order to create the false impression that Sara has acquired her learning at the school. When Sara becomes poor, however, Miss Minchin sees her only as an economic drain and turns brutally hard-hearted. Miss Minchin is not particularly intelligent. She develops a deep grudge against Sara because the child can speak French and she can't. Furthermore, she is unable to understand Sara's restraint whenever she is abused. Miss Minchin has a fierce temper, and, unlike Sara, she is unable to control it. Ironically, Miss Minchin's lack of charity costs her financially. She not only loses her show pupil, but she lives in dread that the story of her cruelty will become public and cause other students to leave. Furthermore, Miss Minchin's actions diminish her power. At first, she completely controls her fat, dumpy younger sister, **Amelia Minchin**. Amelia never disobeys an order, even when she disagrees with it. In the end, however, Amelia becomes hysterical and correctly points out that Maria's cruelty has been ruinous. In doing so, she suggests that Miss Minchin will never again be able to make the better-natured Amelia subservient.

The girls in the school play minor but necessary roles. **Lavinia Herbert** is a foil to Sara. Lavinia is a pretty thirteen-year-old when Sara first arrives. (It is

never explained why she is still present ten years later.) Unlike the helpful Sara, she is domineering with the little children, insisting on her own way. Furthermore, she is accustomed to assuming grand airs. The best-dressed person in the school until Sara's arrival, she becomes vicious and spiteful. She mocks Sara's imaginative play and tries to make "Princess Sara" a term of derision. She also delights in Sara's humiliation, and she deliberately increases Sara's sufferings by informing Miss Minchin of Ermengarde's secret visits. **Ermengarde St. John,** a fat, good-natured girl about the same age as Sara, is "the monumental dunce of the school." Her slowness points up Sara's intellectual gifts. Her association with Sara also illustrates Sara's character as a true princess: although Ermengarde's slowness tries Sara's patience, Sara is never rude to her. Similarly, **Lottie Legh** is a plot vehicle that allows Sara to exhibit her mature understanding of others and her innate kindness. Lottie, who is four years old when Sara arrives, responds to Sara's warmth and sympathy. She is bewitched by Sara's stories and "adopts" her as her mother. **Becky**, the dirty, stunted young maid, elicits yet another side of Sara's compassionate nature. Becky speaks with a decidedly lower-class accent, and she does not seem very intelligent. In spite of their differences of class, Sara is sympathetic enough to sense Becky's hunger for romance and feed it with stories. Sara again proves herself a princess when she is forced to share Becky's life of drudgery. She never treats Becky as anything but a friend, thereby winning the rewards of loyalty.

Two men play small, somewhat mechanical roles in reestablishing Sara to a life of wealth. **Mr. Tom Carrisford** was Captain Crewe's great friend and business partner. A man of rigid conscience, he is ill because he feels he behaved villainously with Captain Crewe. He shows his true goodness by showering Sara with material comforts even before he learns her identity. Whereas Sara shows the power of mind and imagination to triumph over adversity, Mr. Carrisford shows that a mind ill at ease can cause its own problems. Once he learns that he has found Sara and that she willingly accepts him as a friend, he begins to recover from his lingering illness. **Ram**

Dass, his secretary, is an Indian of sharp perceptions. He knows that he needs to distract his employer to help him recover; he also knows from looking at her that Sara is a sensitive soul suffering adversity. It is he who devises the scheme to smuggle comforts into Sara's room, thereby adding magic to what he considers a life of deprivation. By doing so, he shows that Sara is not alone in responding to inner character instead of superficial status.

The Secret Garden

(novel, 1911)

PLOT: When cholera strikes her home in India, Mary Lennox's self-indulgent parents and their Indian servants forget all about her. Possibly because she is left alone, Mary is the only one who survives the epidemic. A sickly, unpleasant child, Mary is sent to England to live at Misselthwaite Manor, the ancient Yorkshire home of her uncle, Archibald Craven. At first, this new home is not much better than the one in India. Mr. Craven still mourns the accidental death of his wife ten years earlier and completely ignores Mary. The housekeeper, Mrs. Medlock, warns Mary to stay out of people's way. Mary herself is unhappy with her new situation. She hates the windy Yorkshire moors; she is annoyed that Martha Sowerby, the servant who cares for her, expects her to dress herself; and she is lonely, having neither companions nor activities to occupy her time. The only things that arouse her interest are Martha's stories of her own family and of a garden that Mr. Craven shut up when his wife died. Mary decides to find and enter this secret garden.

The subsequent action develops two parallel quests involving the discovery of a secret. In each case, discovery leads to changes that demonstrate the value of healthy interests and the power of positive thinking. The first quest, the search for the garden, changes Mary significantly. Because the exercise of skipping rope while she searches makes her eat properly, Mary becomes healthier in both body and mind. Furthermore, although she has never liked anyone before, Mary soon makes friends with a gardener, Ben Weatherstaff, and with a robin whom Ben has befriended. By observing this robin, Mary locates the secret garden and finds the buried key to its door. Eventually, Mary discovers the door itself hidden behind a curtain of vines. After she enters this secret garden, Mary decides to make it bloom again. She obtains Mr. Craven's permission to use any unwanted land for a garden. He does not realize that she intends to restore his wife's beloved garden, and Mary does not risk rejection of her plans by telling him her secret. She begins weeding the garden, but she is unable to achieve her goal alone. Therefore, she enlists the help of Martha's brother, Dickon Sowerby, who knows all about animals and plants. Together, they bring the neglected garden back to life. As they do so, Mary herself changes, becoming an attractive and pleasant child.

The second quest parallels Mary's discovery of the garden and her attempts to restore it. One night Mary discovers another secret at Misselthwaite Manor. Hearing cries, Mary explores the house, just as she had explored the gardens. She discovers that Mr. Craven has a son whom the servants are not allowed to mention. Colin, a strange, sickly boy, fears that he will become a hunchback like his father and will die young. Consequently, he refuses to leave his room or even to try to walk. He frequently throws violent tantrums. The household staff, the hired nurse, and even his physician, Dr. Craven, can't control him. Unlike the adults, Mary does not let Colin intimidate her. Instead, she begins to change him by raising his curiosity about the secret garden. Eventually, Mary has Dickon take Colin to the garden, where he joins the others in their work to restore it. The set of exercises Colin follows, the work in the garden, the fresh air, and his newfound positive thinking make Colin as physically and emotionally healthy as Mary. But Colin wants to surprise his father with the changes in his health, so he pretends that he is still sick. He and Mary refuse most of the meals they are sent and live on food supplied by Susan Sowerby.

The conclusion of the novel has disappointed many readers because it ignores Mary. While touring Europe, Mr. Craven has a dream in which his wife says that she is in the garden. Because he also receives a letter from Susan Sowerby urging his return, he heads home. When he arrives at Misselthwaite Manor, he discovers the transformation of both the secret garden and his son. Delighted by what he sees, he fulfills Colin's deepest wish by proudly accepting his son.

CHARACTERS: *The Secret Garden* is a story of transformation with fairy-tale qualities. Two sickly, unattractive, and unlikable children become healthy, attractive, and lovable. The parallels between the major characters are most important, but the minor characters establish themes about the power of nature and of positive thinking in developing mental and physical health.

Born and raised in India, **Mary Lennox** has been constantly sick because of the climate. As a consequence, she is "the most disagreeable-looking child ever seen." She is thin, with lank yellow hair, a sallow complexion, and a sour expression on her face. Her personality is as unattractive as her appearance, for she is "as tyrannical and selfish a little pig as ever lived." Neglect is the root of Mary's emotional troubles. Her father is too busy or too ill to pay attention to her; her beautiful, vain mother never wanted a child at all and completely ignores her. After her parents die, Mary temporarily stays with some children who call her "Mistress Mary Quite Contrary" because she rudely refuses to play with them. Mary has never played with others and does not know how. Moreover, she is not accustomed to thinking about the feelings of others, so she does not realize that she is disagreeable. Without knowing it, Mary is a lonely child who has never felt loved.

Mary's story is not a typical tale of maturation: she becomes younger instead of older. Mary, that is, recovers the childhood she could not have in India. The removal of her black mourning clothes at Misselthwaite Manor symbolically marks Mary's rebirth. She begins to take an interest in others, including Martha, Martha's mother (before even meeting her), Dickon, Ben Weatherstaff, and a robin.

These friendships and her improving physical health renew her. Both Mrs. Medlock and Ben Weatherstaff, for example, at first describe her as an old woman, but both later see her transformation into a pretty little girl. The most powerful cause of this change, however, is Mary's attachment to the secret garden. When she was in India, Mary pretended to plant gardens, thereby showing a frustrated love of beauty and a desire to nurture. The secret garden in England is more revealing of her character because it is linked symbolically to Mary. It has been shut up for ten years, and she is ten years old; like her, it has been neglected and blossoms when given the proper attention. In making the garden bloom, then, Mary makes her own character bloom.

At the same time that she restores this garden, Mary revives Colin, who is also ten years old. She first discovers him because of the curiosity and love of secrets that led her to discover the garden. Ironically, her lack of sensitivity, which makes most people dislike her, is beneficial with Colin. Because she obstinately refuses to do what he wants as long as he throws tantrums, she controls him as no adult can. Mary transforms Colin into a healthy boy, but she also benefits from her relationship with him. In sharing her secret about the garden with a boy whose very existence has been a secret, Mary ends both her selfishness and her loneliness.

Colin Craven is in many ways Mary's night-world twin. He resembles Mary because he is sickly and contrary. Although not initially ugly, he has agate-gray eyes that are too large for his delicate, ivory-colored face. Like Mary, he is a victim of parental neglect. After Colin's mother died, his father abandoned him to the care of servants. Colin fears that he is going to become a hunchback and will die young. Symbolically, he is already spiritually dead because he does not exist for most of the world. He refuses to let people see him or talk about him. He remains in a darkened room, lying in what seems a deathbed, refusing to go outside. Colin resorts to violent temper tantrums when he does not get his way or when he has great fears of dying. As a result, he is not only physically weak but emotionally isolated. None of the servants like him. He himself likes no one and even keeps a picture of his mother covered with a curtain because he hates her for dying and thus abandoning him.

Like Mary, Colin is linked to the garden because he, too, has been shut up for ten years. Colin supposedly has a better imagination than Mary because he has spent much of his time reading. He certainly has a more developed pride in his identity. In fact, Mary thinks of him as a rajah because he constantly gives orders and expects unquestioning obedience. Because Mary makes him interested in the garden, Colin believes that its "magic" will enable him to live and be healthy. Colin thinks of this magic as a force within nature, but the novel indicates that a positive outlook on life is equally responsible for creating it.

In some ways, Colin resembles Mary. She recovers a lost childhood, and he becomes a "real boy." But Colin also develops maturity and forcefulness. After he enters the garden, Colin takes charge. He demands that everyone keep his recovery secret, he leads the others in exercises, he forces them to follow a "scientific experiment" of positive thinking, and he commands them to listen to his lectures about his experiment. Colin also proudly insists on his identity, denying Ben Weatherstaff's description of him as a cripple. His primary aim is to please his father. Ironically, when they meet at the end of the novel, his father does not immediately recognize the tall, handsome boy who runs into him outside the garden. Once Colin reveals himself, however, his father lovingly accepts him. Colin changes from a boy whose existence is a secret into "Master Colin," the publicly acknowledged heir of Misselthwaite.

A number of minor characters aid in the restoration of Mary and the garden. **Martha Sowerby** is an untrained Yorkshire rustic who refuses to be subservient. A lively, talkative girl from a family of twelve children, Martha begins Mary's transformation. Because Martha forces her to brush her own hair and to dress herself, Mary becomes self-reliant. Martha broadens Mary's sympathies by telling stories of her brother Dickon and of her loving mother. She also makes Mary less contrary by forcing her to play

outside, which helps her to become healthier. **Dickon Sowerby**, Martha's twelve-year-old brother, plays a more active role. A funny-looking boy with rust-colored hair, a turned-up nose, and large eyes, he is constantly accompanied by a fox cub and a crow. Pan-like, Dickon plays the pipes and charms animals. He instructs Mary in the art of gardening and also helps her pique Colin's interest in the garden—and, hence, in life—by bringing his animals into Colin's room. **Ben Weatherstaff**, the gardener, resembles Mary in that he is both surly and lonely. Because he speaks bluntly about Mary's appearance and character, he makes her consider her own behavior. In spite of his crustiness, however, Ben is kind. His friendship with the robin demonstrates his closeness to nature, and his secret pruning of the roses in the closed garden shows his sentimental attachment to the late Mrs. Craven. Although he forms a friendship with Mary, Ben is first and foremost a good servant. He helps to restore the garden because Colin, the future master of Misselthwaite, commands his obedience. **The robin**, although initially Ben's friend, also plays a role in Mary's development. It takes an immediate liking to her, thereby suggesting that she possesses an innate goodness. The bird illustrates the power of intuitive insight when it leads Mary directly to the buried key to the garden's door. Mary thinks of the robin as a person, and toward the end of the novel Burnett anthropomorphizes it by reporting events in the garden from its viewpoint.

Not surprisingly, parental figures are thematically important in this story about neglected children. **Archibald Craven** is the failed father. His high, crooked shoulders make him a hunchback. A constant expression of misery prevents his face from being handsome. He is so attached to his late wife that he turns his back on life, frequently abandoning both his son and Misselthwaite. Mr. Craven's experiences parallel both Mary's and Colin's. Like them, his venture into nature leads to a rebirth in the Tyrol, where the sight of the aptly named forget-me-nots brings back memories and revives positive thoughts that reawaken him to life. The process continues when he has a dream vision of his wife. In this dream, **Lilias Craven** tells her husband that she is in the garden. In this way, she symbolically directs him to their son, who has just decided that he will live. Lilias is the voice of spiritual understanding in this dream. She forces her husband to turn away from gloomy thoughts and back to involvement in life.

Susan Sowerby, the living ideal of motherhood, also acts as a life-affirming force in the story. When Susan writes to Mr. Craven and urges him to return, her words have force because she has a reputation for common sense and for knowing what children need. In fact, Susan Sowerby is more an emotional and moral force in the novel than she is an actual character. Martha and Dickon, for example, constantly quote her, and everyone recognizes her as a sound source of wisdom about children. A mother of twelve, Mrs. Sowerby knows that children need both affection and exercise. Although poor, she spends money on a skipping rope so that Mary can get exercise, and she provides Colin and Mary with food so that they can keep Colin's recovery a secret. A comfortable woman with remarkable blue eyes, Martha Sowerby wears a blue cloak when she enters the garden near the end of the novel. Her physical appearance and her arrival during the singing of the Doxology suggest that she is indeed a saint.

The other minor characters initially seem repressive and unsympathetic, but they, too, become more likable after Mary and Colin change. **Mrs. Sarah Ann Medlock**, the housekeeper, is a stout woman with very red cheeks. She does not want to have much to do with Mary, whose arrival threatens her own comfortable routine at Misselthwaite. Mrs. Medlock is blunt with Mary, showing little understanding of her physical and emotional needs, but her attitude softens once Mary ceases to be contrary. The professional **nurse** who tends Colin is also harsh at the beginning. A big, unattractive woman who can't stand invalids, her apparent callousness benefits Colin, just as Mary's lack of sensitivity does. She resents Colin's tantrums, which rob her of sleep, so she does not oppose Mary's request to spend time with Colin. The nurse is instrumental in making the doctor allow the children to go outside alone. Know-

ing that the novelty is helping Colin, she threatens to resign if she has to go with him. **Dr. Craven**, Archibald's cousin, is a somewhat puzzling character. Colin believes that the doctor wants him to die because he would then inherit Misselthwaite. This certainly creates sympathy for Colin, who seems to have been abandoned by all adults who should care for him. As the narrator points out, however, the doctor is not unscrupulous. The thought crosses his mind that Colin's recovery will mean that, after enduring so much abuse from the boy, he will lose a chance at the inheritance. Nevertheless, he does not stand in the way of Colin's health. He does not actively promote the boy's recovery only because at first Colin will not follow his directions and later because Colin does not let the doctor in on his secret.

Further Reading

Berger, Laura Standley, ed. *Twentieth-Century Children's Writers*. 4th ed. Detroit: St. James, 1995.

Bingham, Jane M., ed. *Writers for Children: Critical Studies of Major Authors Since the Seventeenth Century*. New York: Scribner's, 1988.

Bixler, Phyllis. *Frances Hodgson Burnett*. Boston: Twayne, 1984.

Carpenter, Angelica Shirley. *Frances Hodgson Burnett: Beyond the Secret Garden*. Minneapolis: Lerner Publications, 1990.

Children's Literature Review. Vol. 24. Detroit: Gale Research, 1992.

Collier, Laurie, and Joyce Nakamura, eds. *Major Authors and Illustrators for Children and Young Adults*. Detroit: Gale Research, 1993.

Laski, Marghanita. *Mrs. Ewing, Mrs. Molesworth, and Mrs. Hodgson Burnett*. London: A. Barker, 1950.

Murray, Heather. "Frances Hodgson Burnett's *The Secret Garden*: The Organ(ic)ized World." In *Touchstones: Reflections on the Best in Children's Literature*. Vol. 1. Edited by Perry Nodelman. West Lafayette, IN: Children's Literature Association, 1985.

Thwaite, Ann. *Waiting for the Party: The Life of Francis Hodgson Burnett, 1849-1924*. New York: Scribner's, 1974.

Yesterday's Authors of Books for Children. Vol. 2. Detroit: Gale Research, 1977.

Zaidman, Laura M., ed. *British Children's Writers 1880-1914*. Vol. 141 of *Dictionary of Literary Biography*. Detroit: Gale Research, 1994.

Sheila Burnford

1918-1984, Canadian author

The Incredible Journey

(novel, 1961)

PLOT: *The Incredible Journey* is a wilderness survival novel in which three animals experience adventures that test their friendship and determination. John Longridge, a writer living in remote northern Ontario, has been looking after three pets while their owners are in England. Three weeks before the Hunter family is to return, Longridge goes hunting, leaving instructions for the animals' care. That day, however, Luath, a Labrador retriever, decides to lead Bodger, a bull terrier, and Tao, a Siamese cat, back home, which is more than two hundred and fifty miles away. The three pets suffer privation and hardship. When old Bodger collapses from hunger and fatigue, a bear cub rakes him with its claws. Jumping on the cub's back, Tao rescues Bodger and, aided by Luath, frightens the mother bear. Tao then catches food for Bodger, but the starving Luath must learn to catch frogs and rabbits himself.

Although some humans shoot at the animals, others help. Ojibway Indians feed Bodger and Tao, but Luath remains warily apart. Mad old Jeremy Aubyn takes them into his cabin and eats while they watch. In an implausible coincidence, a beaver dam breaks while the animals are crossing a river, and Tao is washed downstream. A Finnish family—Reino Nurmi, his wife, and his daughter, Helvi—save Tao, but he leaves them when he recovers. A lynx then stalks him, but, implausibly again, a boy shoots the lynx. Meanwhile, Bodger fights a farmer's collie to protect the chicken-stealing Luath, and Luath then receives a mouth full of quills while attacking a porcupine. After Tao rejoins the dogs, James Mackenzie and his wife, Nell, take the dogs into their home, feeding and nursing them. Mackenzie locks the dogs in his barn, but Tao frees them by lifting the latch. Their journey concludes with a touching reunion. The Hunter family and Longridge are at their summer cabin when Luath comes to Professor

Jim Hunter, his master, and Tao comes to nine-year-old Elizabeth Hunter. Twelve-year-old Peter Hunter, having sadly resigned himself to the death of Bodger, is overjoyed when his old dog finally arrives.

CHARACTERS: Burnford, who modeled the protagonists after her own pets, said that she was fascinated by the "individual and original communication" between animals living harmoniously together. In showing the mutual understanding and concern of the three animals, however, Burnford makes their emotions seem human. **Luath** is a large, young, red-gold Labrador retriever. A one-man dog who pines for his master, Luath, instinctively knowing that he must head west, sets out for home. Luath is a good leader because he is loyal to his companions. He thus protects Bodger by walking on his blind left side, and he does not desert him when the old dog collapses. Luath is also brave, joining Tao in facing down the bear, and considerate, licking Bodger's wounds and putting leaves on them. Luath suffers more than the others because, trained to retrieve without harming game, he must face starvation before he overcomes his instinct against killing. Ironically, this instinct is his salvation. When James Mackenzie shoots a duck, Luath automatically retrieves it, allowing Mackenzie the opportunity to remove the porcupine quills that have festered in Luath's mouth and have prevented him from eating.

Bodger (his registered name is Ch. Boroughcastle Brigadier of Doune) is an old white English bull terrier who walks with a peculiar nautical roll. Blind in the left eye, he has poor vision. The journey is hard on him, but he bravely persists until he collapses. Bodger, whose ears and body show old battle scars, enjoys fighting, as he shows when he saves Luath from the farmer's collie. He is, however, also a docile family pet who misses the children. Bodger, who loves human attention, shows his pleasant disposition by wagging his tail and by comically displaying his friendly but hideous grin when he begs for food. **Tao**, Bodger's devoted friend, is a slender, wheat-colored Siamese cat. He seems selfish and aloof at first, refusing to share the food he kills. He is, however, as altruistic as the others. He bravely defends Bodger by jumping on the cub and by frightening its mother, and he saves the old dog's life by sharing his food with him. Tao is devoted to humans as long as he needs them. Deaf after being saved from the river, he follows the Nurmi family everywhere. Once his hearing is restored, though, he leaves. Tao has one special talent: he can lift latches and turn door handles. He uses this ability to release his friends from the Mackenzie barn.

John Longridge, a tall bachelor of about forty, is a writer. A kind man worried that he has hurt the Hunter family by losing their pets, he does everything possible to find the animals. **Jim Hunter**, an English professor, trained Luath since puppyhood to hunt with him, earning the dog's devotion. **Elizabeth Hunter**, his nine-year-old daughter, never loses her optimistic faith that Tao will survive. **Peter Hunter**, who turns twelve on the day the animals return, is the opposite, being pessimistically certain that his beloved Bodger is dead. **Jeremy Aubyn**, a mad old hermit, is used to reveal the gentle nature of the hungry animals: when Jeremy eats in front of them, they politely watch without making a move for his food. The Nurmis, a Finnish family, are their first major helpers. **Reino Nurmi**, a loving father, saves Tao for his daughter's sake and then allows her to keep him as a pet. Reino is the first to realize that the cat is deaf, thus providing readers with an understanding of why Tao stays and why he leaves. Ten-year-old **Helvi Nurmi**, by reading to her parents at night, provides historical and legendary information about Siamese cats. A lonely girl, she experiences through Tao the love and joy that pets bring. Elderly **James Mackenzie** and his wife, **Nell Mackenzie**, are models of loving kindness. Having raised eight children, they are used to dogs and like them. Nell finds Bodger amusing and, shocked that anyone would abandon their pets, is willing to adopt both dogs. James understands dogs, immediately bringing Luath under control when he finds him. He shows his kindness to animals by removing the quills from Luath's mouth and his consideration for humans by trying to find the dogs' owner. He emphasizes the main theme by telling his wife that nothing will keep the dogs on their farm if they are heading somewhere with a purpose.

Further Reading

Berger, Laura Standley, ed. *Twentieth-Century Children's Writers*. 4th ed. Detroit: St. James, 1995.

Children's Literature Review. Vol. 2. Detroit: Gale Research, 1976.

Collier, Laurie, and Joyce Nakamura, eds. *Major Authors and Illustrators for Children and Young Adults*. Detroit: Gale Research, 1993.

Contemporary Authors New Revision Series. Vol. 1. Detroit: Gale Research, 1981.

De Montreville, Doris, and Elizabeth D. Crawford, eds. *Fourth Book of Junior Authors*. New York: H. W. Wilson, 1978.

Something about the Author. Vol. 3. Detroit: Gale Research, 1972.

Virginia Lee Burton

1909-1968, American author and illustrator

Mike Mulligan and His Steam Shovel

(picture book, 1939)

PLOT: *Mike Mulligan and His Steam Shovel* fits into the American tradition of tall tales. Nevertheless, it has a serious theme that celebrates loyalty and continuity. Mike Mulligan loves and takes excellent care of his steam shovel, Mary Anne, and he repeatedly boasts of her abilities. For years, Mike and Mary Anne are among those who build canals for boats, mountain cuts for trains, roadways for automobiles, landing fields for airplanes, and cellars for skyscrapers. Eventually, however, gasoline, electric, and diesel shovels end the call for steam shovels.

Mike and Mary Anne are sad. When Mike Mulligan hears that the people of Popperville want to build a new town hall, he promises Henry B. Swap, a selectman, that they will dig the cellar in a day or forfeit Mike's pay. A little boy in green overalls, hearing from Mike that he and Mary Anne work faster and better when someone watches, gets people to come to the site. Consequently, Mike and Mary

Mike Mulligan and his steam shovel, as illustrated by Burton for her picture book.

Anne complete the job in time. Because Mike did not provide a way for Mary Anne to get out of the hole, however, Henry B. Swap declares that Mike will not be paid. The little boy then suggests the perfect solution: the hall is built around Mary Anne, who becomes its furnace, and Mike is hired as the janitor.

CHARACTERS: The characters have symbolic value in the development of the theme. **Mike Mulligan** shows his tall-tale heritage by continually boasting that Mary Anne can dig as much in a day as a hundred men can dig in a week, even though he is not certain that she can. He is not conceited, however. His boasting reflects pride in Mary Anne and their accomplishments in building important elements of American civilization. A smart worker, he keeps Mary Anne in such good condition that she never grows old. Mike is also faithful to Mary Anne and

Mike Mulligan and his steam shovel, as illustrated by Burton for her picture book.

refuses to scrap her, even though all the other steam shovels have been discarded. By preserving Mary Anne, Mike Mulligan symbolically indicates that the values of the past do not necessarily become obsolete. Striking up his deal in Popperville, Mike shows initiative, tests the truth of his own faith in Mary Anne, and proves the worth of preserving the past.

Mike Mulligan's role is inseparable from that of **Mary Anne**, his red steam shovel. Although she never speaks or thinks, Mary Anne is clearly personified. In the illustrations, Burton places eyes on Mary Anne's bucket and makes its hinged opening a mouth. Mary Anne symbolizes the work ethic of the early years of the twentieth century. The fact that she and Mike work even harder when watched indicates their desire to please, but it also symbolizes the idea that effective action requires appreciation. By digging the cellar in a single day, Mary Anne reaffirms Mike's faith in the ways of the past and ensures that his boasting is heroic, not foolish. When she becomes a furnace, Mary Anne becomes the warm heart of the small community, indicating that the values of the past live there.

Two of the spectators speak and play important roles in the plot. The unnamed **little boy,** pictured in green overalls, represents both youthful faith and ingenuity. After he hears that Mike and Mary Anne work better when people watch, he shows wit by quickly gathering a crowd. He embodies the idea that even young people can appreciate the values of the past and thereby ensure their effectiveness. Fittingly, he has the presence of mind to see that Mary Anne should be the heart of the community. **Henry B. Swap**, the selectman, is a caricature of the shrewd New Englander. He has a characteristically mean grin when he thinks that he can get Mike Mulligan and Mary Anne to work for nothing. After hearing the little boy's proposal, however, he is not quite so mean. He recognizes that Mary Anne will continue to benefit the town. After the town hall is built, he spends his time in the cellar, listening to Mike's stories, all the time smiling in a way that is not unkind. Continuing contact with values from the past, in other words, humanizes him.

The Little House

(picture book, 1942)

PLOT: Even more forcefully than *Mike Mulligan and His Steam Shovel*, *The Little House* celebrates traditional American values. The first section of the plot presents a pastoral world. A man builds the Little House far out in the country, declaring that "This Little House shall never be sold for gold or silver and she will live to see our great-great-grandchildren's great-great-grandchildren living in her." In one of the night scenes that signals meditation throughout the book, the Little House wonders about the city, but she lives happily for many years, watching the activities that accompany the changing

of the seasons. In the lengthy middle section, the Little House loses her idyllic life. A road is built next to her, and soon a city springs up in the countryside. Abandoned by her owners, she becomes worn, chipped, sad, and lonely. In the third section, the fortunes of the Little House change on an archetypally appropriate spring morning. The great-great-granddaughter of the builder notices the Little House. She discovers that the Little House is still sound and has her moved to the country, where she is put upon a hill that resembles the one on which she was originally built. Having experienced depersonalization in the city, she is now completely content with rural life. Happy once again, the Little House dismisses all thoughts of the city.

CHARACTERS: *The Little House* succeeds in making an inanimate object both a living central character and a symbol for a way of life. **The Little House,** representing an idealized version of the rural American past, is personified in the pictures. Her windows form eyes, and the porch steps bend in a gentle smile. Drawn without a single straight line, she fits harmoniously into the curves of the rural world illustrated in the book. As a house, she herself is fixed and static, yet she exists in the midst of two kinds of change. In the pastoral opening section, she patiently and contentedly watches the natural changes of the seasons. Although years pass, this rural world remains predictable and basically unaltered. The Little House thus symbolizes the happiness of family life lived in harmony with nature. In the middle section, the Little House enters a world of rapid urbanization brought on by technology. At first, the Little House, like the America she represents, is fascinated by the city and wonders what it is like to live there. Ironically, once the city is built around her, the Little House becomes lonely. For one thing, crowds rush by without looking at her. For another, no one lives in her, indicating that what she represents is no longer valued. Neglected, the Little House becomes shabby, with boarded windows and dull, chipped paint. Beneath her shabby appearance, however, she is still sound, just as the values she symbolizes are supposed to be. In the final section, the sad house becomes happy again as she moves to a rural area resembling her starting point. This physical journey symbolizes a return to the past that critics have called naive. Regardless, the story is satisfying because the Little House is a character, not merely a symbol for a conservative ideal.

Further Reading

Berger, Laura Standley, ed. *Twentieth-Century Children's Writers*. 4th ed. Detroit: St. James, 1995.

Bingham, Jane M., ed. *Writers for Children: Critical Studies of Major Authors since the Seventeenth Century*. New York: Scribner's, 1988.

Cech, John, ed. *American Writers for Children 1900-1960*. Vol. 22 of *Dictionary of Literary Biography*. Detroit: Gale Research, 1983.

Children's Literature Review. Vol. 11. Detroit: Gale Research, 1986.

Haycraft, Howard, and Stanley J. Kunitz, eds. *The Junior Book of Authors*. 2nd ed. New York: H. W. Wilson, 1951.

Something about the Author. Vol. 2. Detroit: Gale Research, 1971.

Stott, Jon C., and Teresa Krier. "The Little House: Technological Change and Fundamental Verities." In *Touchstones: Reflections on the Best in Children's Literature*. Vol. 3, *Picture Books*. Edited by Perry Nodelman. West Lafayette, IN: Children's Literature Association, 1989.

Betsy Byars

1928-, American author

The Summer of the Swans

(novel, 1970)

PLOT: This brief Newbery Medal winner spans two days, during which a family crisis matures fourteen-year-old Sara Godfrey and brings her to a better understanding of herself and others. Sara, who lives in a small West Virginia town, is unhappy. She hates her appearance and is jealous of her beautiful sister, Wanda. She resents that Aunt Willie (Willamina) Godfrey, who has cared for her since the death of her mother six years earlier, makes her spend so much time with Charlie, her brain-damaged brother.

One day, Wanda's boyfriend, Frank, comes by on his scooter. After cleverly demonstrating to Aunt Willie that Wanda will be safe riding it, he and Wanda go to the lake to watch some swans. When Sara decides to go, Aunt Willie makes her take Charlie along. Once they see the swans, Sara must force the fascinated Charlie to leave. That night, Charlie wanders away. The next morning, Sara realizes that Charlie may have gone to see the swans. When her search for him at the lake is unsuccessful, the frantic Aunt Willie calls the police. Sara then sets out with Mary Weicek to search the woods and hills. Sara rejects the help of Joe Melby, whom she accuses of having once stolen Charlie's watch.

After Mary establishes Joe's innocence, Sara apologizes and lets him join the search. While searching, Mary talks about going to a party that night. When Joe finds Charlie's slipper, Mary leaves to inform the search party. Eventually, Sara finds Charlie in a ravine. Joe then asks Sara to come to the party with him. When she gets home, Sara receives a call from her father, who says that since Charlie has been found he won't be coming home until the weekend. The novel concludes with Sara feeling that she has gained a greater understanding of life.

CHARACTERS: The shifting point of view enables readers to sympathize with and understand both Sara and Charlie. **Sara Godfrey** is miserable because she defines herself as inconsequential: "I'm not anything." Sara considers herself unattractive because she has big feet, skinny legs, and a crooked nose. In spite of her aunt's and her sister's claims to the contrary, Sara believes that looks are important. She thus envies Wanda, whom she considers to be beautiful. Her appearance is not all that is bothering Sara, however. She resents Aunt Willie because she thinks she is loud and insensitive. She also feels

Sara and Charlie Godfrey, in an illustration by Ted CoConis from The Summer of the Swans *by Betsy Byars.*

burdened by having to pay constant attention to Charlie. To make matters worse, Sara has wild mood swings. Behind all of these problems is one more: she constantly thinks of her joyless father, who is working in Ohio and seldom comes home.

Charlie's disappearance transforms Sara. Her attitude begins to change when she admits she has been mistaken in blaming Joe for stealing Charlie's watch. Previously, she was proud of doggedly hanging on to grudges against those who picked on Charlie. After learning of Joe's innocence, she gains the courage to humble herself by apologizing. When Sara finds Charlie, her joy makes her realize he is not a burden but someone whom she loves and values. When Joe asks her out, she thinks of the swans and believes she is really not so ugly and need not be lonely. After her father's call, however, Sara reaches her moment of greatest understanding. She

has stepped out of the shadows and sees that life offers her unlimited challenges and possibilities. At the same time, she realizes the difficulties Charlie faces and the hopeless resignation her father feels.

Charlie, Sara's retarded ten-year-old brother, has not spoken since two diseases damaged his brain when he was three. Because the narrative is partly from his viewpoint, it is clear Charlie needs the security of routine because he is easily confused, and the reader also sees how much he loves the beauty of the swans. **Wanda**, Sara's nineteen-year-old sister, keeps Sara's problems in perspective by treating them with a mixture of wit and seriousness. Although she is pretty, she insists that looks are not important. She also reassures Sara that she will eventually find someone who likes her. **Aunt Willie Godfrey** (Willie is short for Willamina) has taken care of the children during the six years since their mother died. She is overly protective of Wanda, refusing to let her ride a scooter until Frank shows her it is safe. She annoys Sara by being loud and seemingly insensitive to her needs and problems. Aunt Willie becomes nearly hysterical when Charlie wanders away, thus emphasizing Sara's calm and understanding approach to the search. **Mr. Godfrey**, Sara's father, is absent, but Sara thinks of him as someone who has changed from a lighthearted man to a sad and gloomy one since her mother's death. Mr. Godfrey alienates his daughter by seldom coming home and by ignoring the children when he does. Nevertheless, she shows her maturity when her resentment turns into an understanding of how life has defeated him.

Two of Sara's friends have brief roles. **Mary Weicek** provides Sara with an example of immature and self-centered narcissism. Although her hair is in curlers in preparation for a party, Mary joins the search for Charlie. She spends all her time, however, indicating that she won't let the search interfere with her pleasure. Mary also has an important expository role by telling Sara that Joe did not steal Charlie's watch. **Joe Melby** reveals Sara's limited understanding of others when she falsely accuses him of stealing Charlie's watch. Joe is an honest boy who returned the watch after other boys took it in order to tease Charlie. Joe's character contrasts with Sara's in that he does not hold a grudge, a trait he demonstrates when he joins the search in spite of Sara's insults. By asking Sara to the party, he shows that she has matured into a graceful swan.

Further Reading

Berger, Laura Standley, ed. *Twentieth-Century Young Adult Writers*. 1st ed. Detroit: St. James, 1994.

Children's Literature Review. Vols. 1, 16. Detroit: Gale Research, 1976, 1989.

Collier, Laurie, and Joyce Nakamura, eds. *Major Authors and Illustrators for Children and Young Adults*. Detroit: Gale Research, 1993.

Contemporary Literary Criticism. Vol. 35. Detroit: Gale Research, 1985.

De Montreville, Doris, and Donna Hill, eds. *Third Book of Junior Authors*. New York: H. W. Wilson, 1972.

Estes, Glenn E., ed. *American Writers for Children since 1960: Fiction*. Vol. 52 of *Dictionary of Literary Biography*. Detroit: Gale Research, 1986.

Rees, David. "Little Bit of Ivory: Betsy Byars." In *Painted Desert, Green Shade: Essays on Contemporary Writers of Fiction for Children and Young Adults*. Boston: Horn Book, 1984.

Something about the Author. Vols. 4, 46, 80. Detroit: Gale Research, 1973, 1987, 1995.

Something about the Author Autobiography Series. Vol. 1. Detroit: Gale Research, 1986.

Eleanor Cameron

1912-1996, American librarian and author

The Wonderful Flight to the Mushroom Planet

(science fantasy, 1954)

PLOT: Inspired by her son's request for a book in which he and his friend would have an adventure on a small planet, Cameron wrote this novel, which combines fantasy and science fiction. When Tyco M. Bass advertises for a spaceship built by a boy, Dr. Topman suspects a joke. Nevertheless, it becomes the archetypal call to heroic adventure for his son, David, and his friend, Chuck Masterton, who build a spaceship and take it to Mr. Bass. A member of a race of Mushroom People, Mr. Bass has used a special telescope filter to discover his home, a satellite he calls Basidium-X. Sensing that the Basidiumites are in trouble, he sends David and Chuck, who take a hen as a mascot, to help them and to bring back air from Basidium-X.

On Basidium two Wise Men named Mebe and Oru tell the boys that the Mushroom People are dying because the magic plant upon which they depend no longer grows. Unable to save their people, Mebe and Oru have been condemned to death for their failure. The boys then accompany the Great Ta, the king, to the pool where the magic plant grew. Smelling the water, David realizes that the Mushroom People need sulfur and saves them by teaching them to hard-boil the hen's eggs. The grateful Ta spares his Wise Men and gives the boys a necklace of stones.

Back on Earth, the boys can't prove that their adventure was not a dream because they lose Ta's

The Great Ta says farewell to the children in an illustration by Robert Henneberger from Cameron's **The Wonderful Flight to the Mushroom Planet.**

necklace when a storm wrecks their spaceship. They therefore decide to take Mrs. Topman and Chuck's grandfather, Cap'n Tom, to see Mr. Bass. Chuck gets out of the car, however, and the others learn that a wind blew Mr. Bass away. They find Mr. Bass's will, which leaves his house to the boys and asks them to start an astronomy club, warning them to keep the telescope filter and Ta's necklace safe. Chuck arrives with the necklace, which he found on the beach. The novel ends with the boys using the filter to look at Basidium.

Sequels are Stowaway to the Mushroom Planet *(1956),* Mr. Bass's Planetoid *(1958),* A Mystery for Mr. Bass *(1960), and* Time and Mr. Bass *(1967).*

CHARACTERS: Only sketched in this first installment, the recurring characters become more complex over the course of the series. **David Topman**, a tall, quick, ordinary boy between eight and eleven years of age with freckles and sun-bleached, brown hair, becomes heroic by refusing to doubt or despair. Although he longs to replace the imaginary space flights he takes every night with a real adventure, David is pragmatic. He thus wishes for a small planet that a boy could explore in a couple of days. David, who delights in making plans, carefully drawing his spaceship before building it. Nevertheless, he is not always thorough: he forgets to bring a canning jar to gather air on Basidium-X, he nearly forgets about the need to bring a mascot, and he forgets Ta's necklace in the spaceship. David is trusting, following Mr. Bass's instructions and admonitions; he is bright, recognizing that hard-boiled eggs can provide the Mushroom People with sulfur; and he is good-hearted. He helps the Mushroom People and saves Mebe and Oru from execution. Furthermore, he keeps Basidium a secret because he fears that Earth people would commercialize it, thereby destroying the happiness of its primitive people.

Chuck Masterton, David's friend, shares his love of adventure but contrasts him in other ways. Short, square, with brown skin and dark hair, he is always hungry. Whereas David likes to make plans, Chuck is impetuous. Although he later forgets about using it, Chuck is quick-witted enough to realize that his sugar jar can be used to gather Basidium air. Chuck seems less sensitive than David because he is fascinated by the idea of Basidium-X becoming a tourist attraction, but he agrees that the Mushroom People would suffer. Chuck can be stubborn, but his stubbornness can be a virtue: by refusing to give up, he finds Ta's necklace, which was lost after the storm wrecked their spaceship.

Tyco M. Bass of 5 Thallo Street tests and helps the boys. Realizing that children can perform heroic deeds because they lack adult skepticism, he calls David to adventure through an advertisement that inspires David to build his spaceship. He thereby grants David his wish for a real adventure and helps him develop confidence and compassion. A little old man no taller than the boys, Mr. Bass is a descendant of the Mushroom People of Basidium-X. Thousands of years old, he has a huge, round, pale head topped by a few thin locks of hair, enormous round eyes, thin arms, and weblike hands. He grows and sells mushrooms for a living, but his passion is outer space. He paints elaborate pictures of it and spends his time in his personal observatory. A brilliant and intuitive inventor—his tinkering transforms the boys' homemade spaceship into a real one—Mr. Bass can't duplicate his inventions because he does not record his procedures. Sensitive and caring, as he shows by his efforts to save Basidium-X, Mr. Bass can read thoughts. Apparently, he also projects them, because Mrs. Topman and Cap'n Tom surprisingly allow the boys to fly into space. Mr. Bass also senses a coming change in his life. Appropriately for a person identified with spores, he blows away to begin a new life elsewhere.

David's father, **Dr. Frank Topman**, has knowledge about space and therefore voices conventional scientific doubts. By denying the possibility of a small planet and by suggesting that Mr. Bass's advertisement is a joke, he tests David's faith in Mr. Bass. Although Dr. Topman encourages David's ambition to be a spaceman, he is a protective father and tries to check out Mr. Bass before David delivers his finished ship. **Mrs. Anabelle Topman**, David's mother, also represents adult doubts. She humors her son, asking him about his adventures on Basidium, which she considers to have occurred in dreams. Such doubts dismay David and inspire Chuck to seek physical proof of their adventure. **Cap'n Tom Masterton**, Chuck's grandfather, indulges the boys by providing material for building their spaceship. Although he believes in flying saucers, he apparently equates the boys' story with the yarns he tells about his life at sea. Nevertheless, Cap'n Tom is practical and thorough, deciding that the boys need a lawyer after Mr. Bass bequeaths them his house. **Mebe** and **Oru**, the Wise Men of Basidium-X, take a simple delight in reciting the history they have recorded. Lacking an understanding of scientific methods of analysis, they are unable to save their planet. **The Great Ta**, ruler of Basidium-X, is imperial in bearing and fearless in attitude. Open to new methods and ideas, he possesses the wisdom that his counselors lack. Although harsh in condemning them, he is essentially kind, as he shows when he grants David's request and pardons Mebe and Oru.

Further Reading

Berger, Laura Standley, ed. *Twentieth-Century Young Adult Writers.* 1st ed. Detroit: St. James, 1994.

Cameron, Eleanor. *The Seed and the Vision: On the Writing and Appreciation of Children's Books.* New York: Dutton Children's Books, 1993.

Children's Literature Review. Vol. 1. Detroit: Gale Research, 1976.

Collier, Laurie, and Joyce Nakamura, eds. *Major Authors and Illustrators for Children and Young Adults.* Detroit: Gale Research, 1993.

Contemporary Authors New Revision Series. Vol. 22. Detroit: Gale Research, 1988.

De Montreville, Doris, and Donna Hill, eds. *Third Book of Junior Authors.* New York: H. W. Wilson, 1972.

Estes, Glenn E., ed. *American Writers for Children since 1960: Fiction.* Vol. 52 of *Dictionary of Literary Biography.* Detroit: Gale Research, 1986.

Something about the Author. Vols. 1, 25. Detroit: Gale Research, 1971, 1981.

Something about the Author Autobiography Series. Vol. 10. Detroit: Gale Research, 1990.

Lewis Carroll

(pen name for Charles Lutwidge Dodgson)

1832-1898, English mathematician, novelist, and nonsense poet

Alice's Adventures in Wonderland

(dream fantasy, 1865)

PLOT: Bored with the book her sister is reading, Alice notices a peculiar White Rabbit who exclaims that he is late and then takes a watch from his waistcoat pocket before dashing off. Curious, Alice follows the rabbit down a hole. After falling an enormous distance, she discovers a number of doors. The smallest door leads into a beautiful garden that Alice longs to enter. Too big to get in, Alice drinks from a bottle marked "Drink Me." She becomes small, but, having left the key to the garden's door on a table, she is still unable to get in. Next, she grows to nine feet by eating some cake. Big enough to get the key, she is again too big for the doorway. Upset by her failure, Alice begins to cry. She nearly drowns in her own tears, for she has been using a fan that makes her shrink to less than two feet.

The famous mad tea party scene from Alice's Adventures in Wonderland, *as illustrated by the also quite famous John Tenniel.*

Although Alice continues her quest to enter the beautiful garden, *Alice's Adventures in Wonderland* does not have a strong, unified plot. Instead, it consists of a series of episodes in which Alice meets strange and comical creatures. These meetings provide the opportunity for numerous nonsense jokes that mock ordinary life and logic. Many contain parodies of famous poems of the day, for, in trying to show off what she knows, the confused Alice mangles every poem she recites. Alice's first encounter is with the Mouse, the Dodo, and other birds nearly drowned by her tears. She listens to a boring lesson (the driest one the Mouse knows) and runs in a "caucus-race" to get dry. Afterwards, she unintentionally scares these creatures away by talking about her cat's ability to catch mice and birds. Next, the White Rabbit, who confuses her with his servant, sends Alice to his house to fetch his gloves and a fan. There, she drinks from an unlabeled bottle and grows so large that she completely fills the house.

The Rabbit and his friends try various means to get her out, but Alice leaves only after they throw pebbles that turn into magic cakes. She eats one and shrinks again.

Alice now meets the hookah-smoking Caterpillar, who gives her advice about controlling her size, and a Pigeon, who argues that if girls eat eggs, they must be serpents. When Alice arrives at the house of the Duchess, she makes herself nine inches tall to avoid frightening its inhabitants. Once inside, she nurses a crying baby, who is being treated very roughly by the Duchess and her cook. The baby soon turns into a pig, however, so Alice releases it. Heading through the woods, she again encounters the Duchess's Cheshire Cat, whom she had met in the house. The Cheshire Cat gives her directions and then vanishes slowly, his grin being the last part to disappear. Following the directions, Alice comes upon an outdoor tea party, which she joins after making herself two feet tall. Alice finds the party to be quite mad, for those attending—the March Hare, the Mad Hatter, and the Dormouse—declare that, because it is always teatime and they have no time to clean up, they must move from place to place around a large table.

At the end of the seventh chapter, Alice completes her quest: she finds the key to the door, becomes small, and enters the garden. She is immediately disappointed, however, for she learns that the roses in the garden have been painted red. Furthermore, the creatures in the garden are not people but playing cards. The bullying Queen of Hearts forces Alice to play a croquet game in which everyone uses flamingoes for mallets. The Queen then takes Alice to the Gryphon. The Gryphon, in turn, introduces Alice to the Mock Turtle, who tells the pun-filled history of his education. Finally, the Gryphon takes Alice to the trial of the Knave of Hearts, who is accused of stealing the Queen's tarts. Upset by the absurdity of the trial, in which the Queen demands the sentence before the verdict, Alice grows increasingly bigger. Finally, she brushes aside the King and Queen as nothing but playing cards. At this point, Alice wakes up, her whole adventure having been a dream.

CHARACTERS: *Alice's Adventures in Wonderland* is celebrated as the first children's book to make entertainment, not instruction, its main focus, and its characters are among the most memorable in literature. Because the book recounts a dream, all of the characters exist in Alice's imagination. They reflect her confusion about growing up and about the rules that govern her waking world.

Alice is based on Alice Liddell, the second daughter of the Dean of Christ Church, where Carroll was a lecturer in mathematics. Carroll told her and her two sisters the original version of the story during a boating excursion on July 4, 1862. Although Alice Liddell was ten at the time of the trip, the character in the book is seven, and Carroll attached a picture of Alice Liddell at age seven to the hand-written version he presented to her. In the published version, Alice is curious and impulsive, jumping down the rabbit hole without even considering how she will get out. Her desire to enter the beautiful garden, a conventional symbol of edenic

innocence, suggests that she longs for the childhood idealized by sentimental Victorians. Alice is, however, initially too large to enter the garden, a fact that suggests both that she is too big for such a childhood and that she literally cannot be herself if she is to have such childhood experiences. Indeed, much of the first part of the story focuses on questions of Alice's identity. Alice, whose habit of talking to herself as if she were two people implies that she is caught between two stages of development: she is confused by her rapid changes in size and by her inability to repeat what she has been taught. She herself states the theme: "Who in the world am I? Ah, *that's* the great puzzle!" Alice will not, however, accept just any solution to this puzzle: she does not want to be like her waking-world friend Mabel, who lacks both Alice's material advantages (a good house, many toys) and her intelligence. Determined to find a suitable identity, she declares that she will not leave the rabbit hole until she is somebody she likes.

Alice begins as a conventionally polite child, whose life has been governed by clear rules. She is concerned with adult approval, and for this reason she practices curtseying while falling and decides not to ask for directions in case she appears ignorant. She is so completely absorbed in her own interests that she constantly frightens or offends others, as when she tells the mouse that her cat is a good mouser. Alice can, however, be extremely considerate. She always apologizes for her misdemeanors, and she makes herself smaller before entering the Duchess's house because she doesn't want to frighten anyone. She conceals the fact from the sentimental Mock Turtle that she eats lobsters. Although at first she silently endures rudeness, she does not always remain so timid. During the trial, for instance, she dismisses the Queen's statements as nonsense and says that she doesn't care about the court, who are only a pack of cards. In acting with adult assertiveness, Alice, who has been repeatedly ordered around by the creatures of Wonderland, finally exerts power over them and thereby ends her dream.

Alice develops some maturity, learning how to control her height and how to stop the Queen's outbursts. As she struggles to understand herself, however, she also provides unintentional comic criticism of ordinary logic and of Victorian society. Her confusion about mathematics, geography, measurement, time, and language shows how meaningless most of her schooling has been. When she is falling, for example, she considers her latitude and longitude, terms she does not understand but which she likes because of their sound. Furthermore, her distorted recitation of poems, in which injustice, violence, and death are prominent, mocks the sentimental platitudes she is taught in the waking world. In the end, however, Alice needs the logical order and rule-governed world mocked in Wonderland, for she can survive only by having a firm identity. The fact that during the trial she grows to her normal size without eating or drinking anything indicates that she is now pleased with her identity as Alice and is ready to return to the world above.

The numerous minor characters appear in satirical set pieces that mock logic, rules, and Victorian etiquette. The **White Rabbit**, who carries a watch and wears a waistcoat, is a jab at the arrogant obtuseness of the upper classes in that he does not recognize that Alice is not his maid. Although he is foolish in proposing to burn his house to evict Alice and timid in his fear of both Alice and the Queen, he represents conventional logic at the trial, forcing the King to follow normal trial procedures. The short-tempered and frightened **Mouse** provides a lesson in relativity, for he fears the cat and the dog that Alice treasures. Some of his companions in the pool of tears are based on members of the original story-telling excursion: the kindly **Dodo**, who insists that everyone in the caucus race receive prizes, is the author who stammered his name ("Do-Do-Dodgson"); the **Duck** is the Reverend Robinson Duckworth, who shared rowing duties on the trip; the **Lory** is Lorina Liddle, Alice's older sister; and the **Eaglet** is her younger sister, Edith.

The three-inch tall, hookah-smoking **Caterpillar**, who reads Alice's mind to give her useful information about controlling her size with a mushroom, is a mocking portrait of self-important adults who treat children rudely. The Caterpillar asks Alice *who* she is, but the hysterical **Pigeon**, who insists that anything that eats eggs is a serpent, challenges Alice's assumptions by asking *what* she is. The **Duchess**, whom John Tenniel, the original illustrator, patterned after a painting of a fourteenth-century duchess reputed to be the ugliest woman in Europe, is probably the most effective satiric portrait of adulthood. She mistreats her baby, insisting that it is deliberately bad, repeatedly tacks on inappropriate morals to every statement she makes, and displays some ignorance, for she thinks that mustard is a bird. Her pet, the **Cheshire Cat**, on the other hand, may use comically questionable logic, but he does understand that everything in Wonderland is irrational, including Alice. His most memorable trait, however, is his ability to make his body vanish separately from his grin, a quality that shows the illogical separation of attributes from the objects that create them. More craziness is evident in the **Mad Hatter** (hatters supposedly became insane from sniffing the mercury fumes used in their trade) and the **March Hare** (during the March mating season, hares run about wildly). Their bewildering behavior at the tea party—at which they make a mess of the table—pokes fun at adults, whom children probably imagine as being arbitrary and above the rules that bind the young. They also subvert the logic of time keeping, for they are permanently stuck at six o'clock, teatime, and measure time in days, instead of hours. When they try to stuff the sleepy **Dormouse** (a hibernating nocturnal rodent that many Victorian children kept as a pet) into a teapot, their behavior points a finger at the cruelty and insensitivity with which adults often treat children. The most memorable adult, however, is the **Queen of Hearts**, who, in spite of belonging to a suit that would suggest love and compassion, is so completely incapable of controlling her temper that she orders the head of anyone who offends her to be chopped off. In spite of her thundering voice, the Queen is mostly powerless, for no executions are ever carried out, and Alice is able to silence her by saying that she spouts nonsense. The **King of Hearts** is a silly hen-pecked husband, for he is quiet during the Queen's explosions of temper, and he has no idea how to run a trial. Nevertheless, he is kind, quietly pardoning everyone the Queen condemns as he follows behind her.

Although most of the characters Alice encounters are rude and argumentative, the **Gryphon**, a mythological monster with a lion's body and the head and wings of an eagle, and the sobbing **Mock Turtle**, a creature with a turtle's body and a calf's head (mock turtle soup was made from veal), are gentle and excessively sentimental. Their pun-filled discussion of the Mock Turtle's schooling challenges Alice's complacency about her own education and is one of the book's comic masterpieces.

Through the Looking-Glass

(dream fantasy, 1871)

PLOT: Like *Alice in Wonderland, Through the Looking-Glass* is, as Carroll himself said, "made up almost wholly of bits and scraps." These bits and scraps fit neatly into a narrative pattern based on a chess game whose structure emphasizes the theme of personal identity: beginning as a lowly pawn, Alice crosses the board to become a queen. Frequent play with issues of language and meaning further enrich the episodic structure of the book.

Alice's adventures begin more deliberately than in the previous book. Playing indoors in the late fall with two kittens, Alice pretends that the mirror over the fireplace is gauze and that she can pass through it. Soon (obviously asleep) she does just that. In the room on the other side of the mirror, she discovers that the chess pieces can talk. Too large to be seen by the pieces, she moves them about, and when the White King tries to write she guides his pen. She also reads a mirror book containing the famous nonsense poem "Jabberwocky." Going outside, she discovers a garden full of rude, talking flowers. Alice soon learns the major rule of travel in this mirror land: to get to one place, she must go in the opposite direction. After doing so, she joins the Red Queen on a hill. Below them, hedges and streams divide the countryside into a chessboard. The Red Queen lets Alice join the game as one of the White Queen's pawns and gives her instructions on how to become a queen herself.

Alice's subsequent movement from square to square on the chessboard leads her into encounters with pieces on adjacent squares and with other creatures who inhabit the different regions. When Alice begins the pawn's conventional two-square opening move, she finds herself inexplicably in a railway carriage. She and a Gnat, who had been whispering in her ear, fall out when the train leaps to the second square. They talk about this land's strange insects, such as the Bread-and-butter-fly, which lives on weak tea with cream. Alice next enters a wood in which things have no names. Both she and a Fawn she hugs close forget their names. When they leave the woods, however, the Fawn remembers. Realizing that Alice is a human, it runs away in fear. Alice finds comfort in remembering her name and determines not to forget it. Her next encounter is with Tweedledee and Tweedledum, twins governed by the words in a nursery rhyme. In accordance with the rhyme, they continually battle each other over a damaged rattle. This episode also includes the nonsense poem "The Walrus and the Carpenter." Furthermore, it introduces the disturbing notion that Alice might only exist in the dreams of the sleeping White King. Alice's last encounter in this square is with the White Queen, who explains the problems of living backwards. Alice kindly fixes the disheveled White Queen's shawl and hair.

Moving forward into the next square, Alice finds herself in a shop run by an old Sheep. After a strange incident in which Alice rows the Sheep in a boat, she finds herself back in the shop. She tries to buy an egg that gets farther away the closer she gets to it. Puzzled, she crosses into Humpty Dumpty's square. He sits precariously on a wall, trusting that the King will send all his horses and men to pick up the pieces if he falls. Alice, aware of the nursery rhyme, knows that his confidence is foolish, but she says nothing. Humpty Dumpty then engages Alice in a lengthy discussion of the meaning of words. After Alice leaves, she hears the crash of his fall. Alice next meets two more creatures governed by a nursery rhyme, the Lion and the Unicorn. As in the rhyme, they fight over a crown. The Unicorn brings up questions of identity because it has always considered children to be "fabulous monsters." It finally agrees to believe in Alice if she will believe in him. A large group now assembles. It includes the royal messengers Haigha (pictured as the White Rabbit) and Hatta (the Mad Hatter). Alice serves them cake, passing it around first and cutting it afterwards. Terrified by the sound of drums, Alice runs into the next square. Here she meets the White Knight, who keeps falling off his horse. Alice helps him up and recites a long song named "The Aged Aged Man" but called "The Haddock's Eyes." This episode satirizes the arbitrary connection between names and things.

When the White Knight rides off, Alice crosses over to the eighth square. She discovers a crown on her head and realizes that she has become a queen. Positioned between the Red Queen and the White Queen, Alice endures an examination of her right to the title. When her examiners fall asleep, Alice enters a castle through an arch labeled "Queen Alice." Within is a strange banquet at which the food talks. As events become more chaotic, Alice grabs the Red Queen (capturing her in the chess game and thereby checkmating the Red King). The dream ends with Alice holding a kitten instead of a chess piece and with the problem of whether she or the Red King dreamed the whole adventure.

CHARACTERS: The chess game structure suggests the view that life is predetermined. The nursery rhyme characters and others who debate issues of language and meaning intensify this darkly philosophic undercurrent without destroying the fun on the surface of the adventure.

Alice indicates that she is "seven and a half, exactly." In the six months since her previous adventure, she has matured somewhat. For instance, she remembers perfectly all the nursery rhymes she recites. Nevertheless, Alice is still attempting to define herself. For one thing, she seeks power. At the beginning, for example, she is pleased to think that she can avoid adult control by entering the Looking-Glass House. Once there, she can warm herself by the fire and no adult will be able to pass through the

mirror to scold her away. Furthermore, Alice's desire to join the game symbolizes a longing to enter the mysterious world of adult purposefulness. Although willing to be a pawn, she really wants to be a queen, the most powerful piece in chess. Unlike the pawn, which is limited to childlike single square moves, a queen can range freely over the entire board.

Alice is still kind and curious in this book, but she is far more competent in dealing with the foolish adults she meets. She is almost maternal in the attentions she bestows on the White Queen and the White Knight. She also plays the role of the tolerant parent when she tries to embarrass the Tweedle twins into giving up their fighting. Nevertheless, Alice is always ready to argue with others. She is firmly committed to the rules of the waking world and quickly challenges all inversions of them. When told that she is part of the Red King's dream, for example, she is angry. She insists on her own reality and her imaginative power as a dreamer. She even threatens to wake the Red King to find out who is in control. At the banquet, she finally loses patience when the food comes alive and everything loses even a semblance of stable identity. Declaring that she can't stand the chaos, she ends the dream and reasserts the comforting rules of the waking world. After waking, however, Alice considers whether she or the Red King was the dreamer, a sign that she is still bothered by the puzzling nature of language and reality.

As in the previous book, the minor characters are dream projections. They appear in set pieces that reveal Alice's concerns about the connections between language and reality. Carroll described the **Red Queen** as "the concentrated essence of all governesses!" She repeatedly instructs Alice in the rules of etiquette, and she examines her at the end to see whether she is worthy of progressing from pawn to queen. Nevertheless, the Red Queen is the most considerate and helpful character Alice meets. She allows Alice to join the chess game, and she accurately maps out the course Alice must take to become a queen herself. The **White Queen**, on the other hand, is completely incompetent. Carroll called her "gentle, stupid, fat and pale." In a mirror reversal of roles, Alice is the adult and the Queen is a child who needs to be dressed and combed. The White Queen has, however, an important philosophic role. She insists that she lives backwards. This causes Alice to think about the nature of justice because she is told that in the Queen's world the punishment quite properly precedes the crime. The **White King** is also an incompetent adult. His major symbolic function is to suggest how writing has a life of its own and never quite captures what one intends. Thus, when he wishes to record his feelings, Alice, an invisible muse in this episode, guides his pen and makes him write something he didn't even know. The most incompetent and comical of the chess pieces, though, is the **White Knight**. In keeping with the chess knight's peculiar L-shaped move, the White Knight periodically falls off one side or another of his horse. The Knight himself has shaggy hair and large mild eyes set in a gentle face. As most commentators point out, he resembles Carroll. Strengthening the resemblance is the Knight's fondness for peculiar inventions, something that also delighted Carroll. In any case, Alice finds the White Knight to be the most memorable character of her adventures and remembers him with fondness years later.

Alice also encounters characters who are not chess pieces. Most of these nonsensically mock her assumptions about language and reality. The **Gnat** introduces the theme by talking about strange insects whose names dictate their identities. Although he is a guide and warns Alice about the woods where things have no names, he is the least significant of the characters she encounters. He appropriately sighs himself away. The **Fawn**, in contrast, appears much more briefly, but it has a significant thematic role. In the woods, when it knows neither its own nor Alice's identity, it illustrates the harmony of a mythic realm where humans and animals are equal. But the Fawn runs away when it recovers its memory. The Fawn's actions suggest that language and names, not innate qualities, create divisions in the real world. **Tweedledee** and **Tweedledum**, the two fat twins who remind Alice of schoolboys, insist on their individuality but are obviously identical to each other. Each hugs the other and each, mirror-like, offers to shake with a different hand. They illustrate

the theme of determinism by constantly fighting in accordance with the words of a nursery rhyme. Their most important role, however, is in challenging Alice's sense of individuality by suggesting that she exists only in the Red King's dream. **Humpty Dumpty** has an even more inflated sense of his importance than the Tweedle twins do. Like theirs, his life is predetermined, for he is condemned to repeat the actions of a nursery rhyme. Still, Humpty Dumpty is arrogant and boasts of meeting the King. Like the most pretentious of aristocrats, he offers a single finger for Alice to shake. Such gestures make Humpty Dumpty a cautionary figure. As Martin Gardner has pointed out, Humpty Dumpty's pride precedes his great fall. The last of the characters illustrating determinism are the **Lion** and the **Unicorn**. The Unicorn is particularly important because he again brings up the question of Alice's identity. By suggesting that he and Alice believe in each other, the Unicorn advances the notion that reality and existence are matters of convention and belief.

Further Reading

Bingham, Jane M., ed. *Writers for Children: Critical Studies of Major Authors since the Seventeenth Century.* New York: Scribner's, 1988.

Blake, Kathleen. *Play, Games, and Sport: The Literary Works of Lewis Carroll.* Ithaca, NY: Cornell University Press, 1974.

Carroll, Lewis. *The Annotated Alice: Alice's Adventures in Wonderland and Through the Looking-Glass.* Edited by Martin Gardner. New York: Clarkson N. Potter, 1960.

———. *Alice in Wonderland.* Edited by Donald J. Gray. New York: Norton Critical Edition, 1971.

Children's Literature Review. Vols. 2, 18. Detroit: Gale Research, 1976, 1989.

Clark, Anne. *Lewis Carroll: A Biography.* New York: Shocken, 1979.

Clark, Beverly Lyon. "Lewis Carroll's *Alice* Books: The Wonder of Wonderland." In *Touchstones: Reflections on the Best in Children's Literature.* Vol. 1. Edited by Perry Nodelman. West Lafayette, IN: Children's Literature Association, 1985.

Fredeman, William E., and Ira B. Nadel, eds. *Victorian Novelists after 1885.* Vol. 18 of *Dictionary of Literary Biography.* Detroit: Gale Research, 1983.

Guiliano, Edward, and James R. Kincaid, eds. *Soaring with the Dodo: Essays on Lewis Carroll's Life and Art.* Charlottesville: University Press of Virginia, 1982.

Kelly, Richard. *Lewis Carroll.* Rev. ed. Boston: Twayne, 1990.

Phillips, Robert, ed. *Aspects of Alice: Lewis Carroll's Dreamchild as Seen through the Critics' Looking-Glasses, 1865-1971.* New York: Vanguard, 1971.

Rackin, Donald. *Alice's Adventures in Wonderland and Through the Looking-Glass: Nonsense, Sense, and Meaning.* Boston: Twayne, 1991.

Sale, Roger. "Lewis Carroll." In *Fairy Tales and After: From Snow White to E. B. White.* Cambridge, MA: Harvard University Press, 1978.

Yesterday's Authors of Books for Children. Vol. 2. Detroit: Gale Research, 1978.

John Christopher

(pen name for Samuel Youd)

1922-, English author

The White Mountains

(science fiction, 1967)

PLOT: Set in a time after aliens have conquered and enslaved Earth, *The White Mountains* uses a quest to introduce questions about what makes human life meaningful. Thirteen-year-old Will Parker is nervous about the Capping he must undergo at fourteen. Capping, the fixing of a metal plate to a person's head, will make him an adult who willingly serves the Tripods, the great metal machines that rule the planet. When his cousin Jack Leeper undergoes Capping, Will is dismayed because Jack loses his youthful yearning and becomes complacent. Shortly afterwards, Will meets Ozymandias, who pretends to be a mad Vagrant, one of those for whom Capping has failed. He gives Will a map to guide him to the White Mountains, where uncapped people are preparing to fight the Tripods. When Will sets out from home, however, his cousin Henry Parker insists on joining him. Will lets him come, even though he hates Henry.

Their journey is filled with trouble and danger. Will, for example, twists his ankle when Henry, hearing the noise of sheep, has them run from supposed pursuers. At a seaport, a sailor tries to kidnap them, but Captain Curtis rescues the boys and takes them to France on his boat. When French villagers then imprison Will and Henry, Jean-Paul, a boy they call Beanpole, frees them and insists on coming along. After passing through a ruined city, where they obtain grenades, Will becomes ill, which causes them to be captured. Taken to a castle, Will becomes a favorite of the Comtesse de la Tour Rouge and her daughter, Eloise. Will discovers that Eloise has been Capped, but after the Comtesse offers to make him a knight, he decides to stay and be Capped himself. Will therefore tells Henry and Beanpole to escape without him. When he discovers that Eloise will be leaving to serve the Tripods, however, Will flees. A Tripod captures him, but Will later wakes up with no memory of how he escaped.

After Will catches up to Henry and Beanpole, they notice that a Tripod is following them and discover a metal disc implanted under Will's arm. Beanpole removes the disc, but the Tripod locates them anyway. Although they lob grenades at the machine as Beanpole suggests, it does no damage. When the Tripod grabs Will, however, Will throws a grenade inside it, "killing" the Tripod. Jean-Paul then puts herbs on Will's wound and locates a hiding place, where they spend several days avoiding detection by Tripods. Eventually, the boys join the freedom fighters in the White Mountains.

The Tripods series continues with The City of Gold and Lead *(1967) and* The Pool of Fire *(1968). When the* Tripods Came *(1988) is a prequel.*

CHARACTERS: Will Parker, the narrator, is an observant, thoughtful, and rebellious thirteen-year-old. Although his parents forbid him to associate with Vagrants, he secretly meets Ozymandias because he is attracted to those who do not conform. Will, who believes that human life can't be valuable unless one possesses an inquiring mind, sees those who are Capped as lacking this essential element of humanity. Nevertheless, he is tempted by the

Comtesse's offer of status and comfort. Enjoying his life of privilege and seeing the absence of doubt as a positive result of Capping, he comes to think that assured happiness is more important than independence. In addition, because he loves Eloise and resents the deepening friendship between Henry and Beanpole as something that isolates him, Will is able to suppress all qualms about being loyal to his companions and to those who helped him escape from home. The information that Eloise is being sent away finally shocks him into understanding that even the privileged are mindless slaves. When he rejoins his companions, he is therefore ashamed of himself. Subsequently, Will shows bravery and loyalty, offering to go alone so that he can lure the Tripods away from the others. When Jean-Paul says that would be impractical, he then readily endures the painful removal of the homing device planted in his arm. Although he "kills" the Tripod with a grenade, enabling success in their quest, his act establishes only that he has the luck of a hero. Will develops other heroic qualities in the later volumes.

Will's companions are sketched rather than fully characterized. **Henry Parker**, Will's cousin, is taller and heavier than Will even though he is a month younger. He has always disliked Will. His presence on the journey therefore tests Will's self-restraint and ability to cooperate, especially after Henry excites Will's jealousy by becoming close to Jean-Paul. Henry is loyal to Will, however, and does not desert him when Will becomes ill. Nevertheless, Henry is a pragmatist and accepts the idea of leaving Will on both occasions when Will suggests the idea in the castle. Henry is clever in understanding Will's desire to remain with Eloise and to become a knight, and he is suspicious about Will's loyalty afterwards. **Jean-Paul**, a French boy called "**Beanpole**" by his companions, is a tall, thin orphan. Tremendously clever, he has shaped two unequal lenses into a pair of glasses and has taught himself English from a book. He is also very knowledgeable and resourceful, as he later shows when he finds plants to heal the wound in Will's arm. More curious about technology than people, Jean-Paul discovers how grenades work. Because he is spirited as well as intelligent, he plays a vital role in the boys' journey. He shows that

it is impractical for Will to sacrifice himself by going off alone and therefore operates to remove the disc in Will's arm. When the Tripod comes, he suggests that they attack it with grenades, leading to Will's lucky demolition of the machine. Afterwards, he finds a hiding place when the others have given over to despair.

Will has two uncapped helpers. **Ozymandias**, a powerfully built man in his thirties, has red hair and beard. He feigns madness in order to recruit people to the cause of freedom. He encourages Will by giving him a map and telling him about Captain Curtis. **Captain Curtis** is a tall, swarthy seafarer with a black beard and long, thin-lipped face. A commanding and self-possessed man, he stops another sailor from kidnapping the boys merely by ordering him to release them. He then helps the boys on their journey by taking them to France. Will's cousin **Jack Leeper**, who is a year older than Will, is a cautionary figure. Before his Capping, he is skeptical about its benefits and longs for freedom; afterwards, he is complacent, obedient, and satisfied. Two aristocrats show another side of slavery that temporarily fools Will. **The Comtesse de la Tour Rouge** lost none of her kindness and compassion after being Capped, leading Will to see Capping in a more positive light. Her daughter, **Eloise**, is a pretty girl with a small oval face, ivory skin, and brown eyes. She is as kind as her mother and doesn't report Will after he removes her turban and sees her Capped head, an act that her class considers offensive. The fact that she is perfectly happy to be leaving her parents forever to serve the Tripods makes Will realize that mindless happiness is appalling.

Further Reading

Berger, Laura Standley, ed. *Twentieth-Century Young Adult Writers*. Detroit: St. James, 1994.

Children's Literature Review. Vol. 2. Detroit: Gale Research, 1976.

Collier, Laurie, and Joyce Nakamura, eds. *Major Authors and Illustrators for Children and Young Adults*. Detroit: Gale Research, 1993.

Contemporary Authors New Revision Series. Vol. 37. Detroit: Gale Research, 1992.

De Montreville, Doris, and Elizabeth D. Crawford, eds. *Fourth Book of Junior Authors*. New York: H. W. Wilson, 1978.

Something about the Author. Vols. 30, 47. Detroit: Gale Research, 1983, 1987.

Beverly Cleary

1916-, American author

Henry Huggins

(novel, 1950)

PLOT: This book contains six loosely connected but independent episodes. In the first episode, Henry Huggins's monotonous routine changes when he finds a skinny dog. Henry's mother gives him permission to keep Ribsy, as he names the dog, if he can find a way to bring him home on the bus. After several failed attempts to get on the bus with the dog, Henry wraps Ribsy as a parcel. Ribsy breaks loose, however, and causes havoc on the bus. Henry and Ribsy are kicked off of the bus, but the police, sent by Henry's worried mother, drive them home with sirens blaring. In the next episode, Henry buys guppies. They breed so quickly that he is soon using every jar in the house to hold the offspring. He eventually sells all his guppies and uses the money to buy an aquarium and heater. His father then buys him a catfish, which will not breed in captivity.

The next complication in Henry's life occurs when he accidentally throws Scooter McCarthy's new football into the window of a passing car. To earn the money to buy a replacement, Henry digs for worms for Mr. Grumbie. He works late, collecting over a thousand worms, but he still does not have enough. His mother and father help him gather the last couple of hundred worms. The next day, a man returns the ball that Henry had thrown into his car, and Henry realizes that now both he and Scooter will have footballs.

The fourth adventure focuses on Glenwood School. When Henry is chosen to play the role of a little boy in the Christmas operetta, everyone teases

him. Henry is embarrassed to appear on stage in pajamas, and he dreads being kissed by the girl playing his mother. His schemes to avoid playing the role fail, but Ribsy inadvertently provides a solution when he spills green paint all over Henry. Henry is delighted to be given the more acceptable role of the Green Elf.

The last two chapters highlight Henry's relationship with Ribsy. In the first, Henry enters Ribsy in a dog show with comical results. He tries to cover up the dirt on Ribsy with talcum powder in order to make him look presentable, but instead it turns Ribsy pink. Ribsy subsequently misbehaves and entangles Henry in his leash, but he nevertheless ends up winning the prize for "most unusual" dog. In the final episode, the children on Klickitat Street realize how much Ribsy means to them when a boy claims that Ribsy is actually Dizzy, his lost dog. Scooter devises a test in which Ribsy, after several comical delays, chooses Henry as his master. The cheering children forget their previous quarreling and play together.

There are five subsequent volumes to Henry Huggins: Henry and Beezus *(1952),* Henry and Ribsy *(1954),* Henry and the Paper Route *(1957),* Henry and the Clubhouse *(1962), and* Ribsy *(1964).*

CHARACTERS: *Henry Huggins* introduces several residents of Klickitat Street, notably Beezus and Ramona Quimby, who become important in Cleary's later books. In this novel, however, they do not have important roles. Because this book emphasizes slapstick action, only the title character is developed to a significant degree.

Henry Huggins is an ordinary boy to whom slightly extraordinary things happen. A third-grader with hair like a scrubbing brush, Henry does not create mischief himself but nevertheless always ends up in the midst of chaos—often because of his dog. Henry does not possess exceptional intelligence, but he is determined to find solutions to his problems. To bring Ribsy home on the bus, for example, Henry wraps up his dog like a package to overcome transit regulations. When his sense of responsibility compels him to replace Scooter's football, Henry comes up with a plan to gather more than a thousand worms in a single night at the park. Of course, Henry does not always succeed. As the shortest student in his class, he hates being teased about playing the little boy in the Christmas operetta. He tries and fails to get out of the role and then tries to make others respect it. Before Ribsy saves him, he shows his characteristic determination by deciding to endure the humiliation of playing the part.

Henry loves animals, as he demonstrates by adopting Ribsy and raising the guppies. He is a responsible boy who properly cares for his ever-increasing guppy population, even though his duties prevent him from playing with the other children. Another of Henry's notable traits is his loyalty to his dog. He believes Ribsy is worthy of a trophy, and he lovingly defends him against all criticism. Henry sometimes teases girls by calling them names, but he remains popular because he is never truly mean.

Ribsy, who received his name because he was so skinny that his ribs showed, is the perfect companion for Henry. He is not "any special kind of dog," except in Henry's loving eyes. Neither big nor small, he is a motley white, brown, black, and yellow mongrel. Ribsy does not always behave himself, but he is always loving, friendly, and loyal, although he takes his time about finally choosing Henry as his master.

Henry's mother and father are idealized middle-class parents. **Mrs. Huggins** is understanding whenever Henry takes up a new interest. She is kind, never becomes angry, and willingly helps Henry by pitching in to gather worms. Her one idiosyncrasy is her habit of correcting Henry's grammar. **Mr. Huggins** is a perfect father who never loses his temper. He supports his son by gathering worms, by driving him to the pet store, and by buying him a catfish.

Only one of Henry's friends achieves individuality in this book. Fifth-grader **Scooter McCarthy** can be a bully, such as when he threatens Henry by giving him a deadline for buying a new football. He shows disdain when he calls Ribsy "only a mutt,"

and arrogant foolishness when he crashes while showing off by riding his bike with no hands. Nevertheless, Scooter values justice and sets up a fair contest for Ribsy to choose his own master. In the end, he is as delighted as the others by Ribsy's decision to choose Henry.

Beezus and Ramona

(novel, 1955)

PLOT: Featuring two characters from the Henry Huggins books, this novel focuses on an older child's feelings about her younger sister. Nine-year-old Beezus (Beatrice) Quimby finds four-year-old Ramona Geraldine Quimby "just plain exasperating." Ramona frequently causes trouble. For example, when Beezus grows tired of rereading the same story over and over to Ramona, she takes her to the library for a new book. Before they return it, Ramona scribbles her "name" in crayon on every page, insisting that the book is now hers. The librarian who makes them buy the book wisely tells Ramona that it belongs to Beezus. Beezus, who now feels in control, agrees to read the book when they get home. Later, Beezus feels inferior when she goes to her weekly art class. Ramona is always praised for her imagination, but Beezus is unable to produce a good painting. After Ramona embarrasses her by disrupting the class, Beezus paints a picture of Ramona's invisible pet lizard. When the teacher praises it, Beezus understands that she too has an imagination.

Beezus gradually comes to a better understanding of both her sister and her own feelings. One day, for example, Ramona is particularly naughty. She deliberately knocks over the game of checkers Henry Huggins and Beezus are playing, throws a tantrum, and punishes Ribsy for taking a cookie by shutting him in the bathroom. Mrs. Quimby must rescue the dog by using a nail file to unlock the door. Ramona is not at all sorry, and Beezus realizes that she does not like Ramona. She feels guilty, however, because she believes that sisters should like each other. On another occasion, Ramona hides from

Cleary

Ramona being herself in Cleary's **Ramona the Pest,** *illustrated by Louis Darling.*

Beezus, who finds her in the basement, where she is taking one bite out of every apple because she believes the first bite is the best. Following the advice of her aunt, Beatrice Ann Haswell, Beezus and her parents ignore Ramona. Ramona then behaves for the rest of the day. Beezus thus understands how Ramona only acts badly because she craves attention.

At times, Beezus sympathizes with Ramona. One rainy day, Howie Kemp and some other children show up unexpectedly for a party. Beezus and Mrs. Quimby make the party a success by entertaining the guests with a parade and food, but Ramona throws cookies and has a tantrum. When Ramona reveals that she invited the children because she knew that she would be refused a party if she asked, Beezus understands her view. At the same time, however, Beezus identifies with the adults, agreeing with her mother that all they can do is wait for Ramona to grow up.

Beezus learns her greatest lesson on her tenth birthday. After Ramona ruins one cake by putting egg shells in the batter and another by putting her doll into the oven with it, Beezus becomes angry but soon after feels like a terrible person for not loving Ramona. She wants to be as loving as her mother and Aunt Beatrice. When Aunt Beatrice reveals that

she was once a naughty younger sister like Ramona, however, Beezus accepts the idea that she does not have to love Ramona all the time.

See below for character descriptions.

Ramona the Pest

(novel, 1968)

PLOT: Set a year after *Beezus and Ramona,* this novel about acceptance focuses on Ramona's feelings and relationships. Ramona is excited to start kindergarten, but a series of misunderstandings cause her some problems. For example, when her teacher Miss Binney tells her to sit in her seat "for the present," Ramona believes that she is going to receive a gift but is disappointed to later learn that "present" means "now." Because others do not understand her intentions, Ramona often gets into trouble. She is fascinated by her classmate Susan's curls, for example, and can't resist "boinging" them—an act Susan considers hair-pulling. After Ramona is made to sit on a bench for her punishment, she tries to show Miss Binney that she is the best rester in the class by gently snoring. Soon the entire class is loudly snoring, too.

In spite of these early misunderstandings, Ramona comes to love Miss Binney. She enjoys doing seat work and learns to print her name, turning the Q in Quimby into a picture of a cat. Ramona's only problem comes after she lends Howie Kemp an old stuffed rabbit for show and tell. Miss Binney gives the bunny a ribbon, which Howie and Ramona fight over. Howie finally gives Ramona the ribbon when she agrees to let him convert her tricycle into a two-wheeler.

Ramona's troubles soon become more dramatic. When a substitute teacher takes over the class, she feels betrayed by Miss Binney and runs away and hides. After Ramona is found, Beezus takes her to see the principal, who understands Ramona's feelings and reassures her by introducing her to the new teacher. When Ramona finally gets a new pair of red girls' boots to replace Howie's brown hand-me-downs, she endures the humiliation of becoming stuck in some mud. Ramona is grateful that Miss Binney does not scold her. She is even more grateful to Henry Huggins, who rescues her, and declares that she will marry Henry.

Ramona's self-confidence is tested in the next episode. Dressed as the "baddest witch" for the school's Halloween parade, Ramona becomes frightened when no one recognizes her behind her mask. She hastily reasserts her identity by carrying a sign bearing her name. Ramona's most trying adventure, however, comes after she loses a tooth—a symbol that she is growing up. She gives the tooth to Miss Binney for safekeeping. Feeling excited, she "boings" Susan's hair. After Miss Binney tells her not to pull anyone's hair again, Ramona forgets almost immediately because Susan calls her a pest. When Miss Binney asks Ramona if she thinks she can stop pulling Susan's hair, she truthfully says "No." Ramona is then sent home until she can behave, and she decides that her teacher no longer loves her. Mrs. Quimby tries but can't convince Ramona to return to school. Several days later, Howie brings a letter from Miss Binney that changes Ramona's mind. In the note, which has Ramona's tooth taped to it, Miss Binney asks when she is returning and, best of all, makes a Q like a cat. Thus reassured that her teacher understands and likes her, Ramona decides to return to school.

See below for character descriptions.

Ramona Quimby, Age Eight

(novel, 1981)

PLOT: The sixth Ramona book, *Ramona Quimby, Age Eight*, concentrates on Ramona's reactions to significant changes in her life. When she must go by bus to a new school, Ramona is not sure that she likes Mrs. Whaley, her third-grade teacher. She also has mixed feelings about Danny, a mischievous classmate she calls "Yard Ape." Because her parents both work and her father attends college, Ramona begrudgingly goes every day after school to Howie Kemp's house, where she has to be nice to bossy four-year-old Willa Jean. At first Ramona avoids

playing with Willa Jean by insisting that she must do Sustained Silent Reading, though Willa Jean eventually figures out the ploy.

Things do not go well at school, either. When Ramona follows a fad by cracking an egg on her head, she winds up being embarrassed because her mother has mistakenly given her a raw egg rather than a hard-boiled one. Ramona is too angry to forgive her apologetic mother for the mistake with the eggs. When dinner that night turns out to be tongue, she joins Beezus in complaining. Forced to make the next evening's dinner themselves, the sisters improvise but make a mess of the kitchen. Their parents, pleased with the dinner, offer to wash the dishes. The girls hastily vanish before their parents can enter the kitchen.

While cleaning up in the office at school one day, Ramona is deeply hurt when she overhears Mrs. Whaley call her a "show-off" and a "nuisance." Ramona comes to dread school, and she decides to prove Mrs. Whaley wrong. She truly believes she is a "supernuisance," however, when she throws up in class. Staying at home because of her illness, she wallows in self-pity. When she returns to school, Ramona must deliver a report that "sells" a book to the class. She bases her report on a television commercial for cat food. Although Ramona giggles and blurts out an unscripted conclusion, Mrs. Whaley praises her highly. Ramona, still wearing the cat mask she used while delivering her report, then confronts Mrs. Whaley with what she overheard. Reassured that she has misunderstood, Ramona comes out from behind her mask to talk honestly to the teacher.

Ramona comes to a further understanding of herself on a rainy Sunday. The entire family is in an irritable mood, so Mr. Quimby orders everyone to be pleasant and then takes them to a restaurant, where the family relaxes and has a good time. When they get ready to leave, they discover that an old man has already paid their bill because he thought they were a nice family. On the drive home, the Quimbys decide that they are indeed nice, although not all of the time. Ramona, who does think that she is always nice, realizes that she and other people may sometimes have their niceness "curdled" on the outside.

Pleased to be part of a "sticking-together family," Ramona becomes determined to get along with Willa Jean and Mrs. Whaley.

Other volumes in the Ramona series are Ramona the Brave *(1975),* Ramona and Her Father *(1977),* Ramona and Her Mother *(1979), and* Ramona Forever *(1984).*

CHARACTERS: Four-year-old **Ramona Geraldine Quimby** is the focus of every episode of *Beezus and Ramona*. Ramona is self-centered and demanding. She deliberately enters Beezus's art class, which she is forbidden to do, and she takes a boy's lollipop simply because she wants it. She is domineering and persistent in getting her own way. For example, she insists that Beezus repeatedly read the same story and add sound effects, and she deliberately spoils her sister's game of checkers with Henry so that Beezus will play with her. When punished or frustrated, Ramona resorts to throwing tantrums.

Some aspects of Ramona's personality make her engaging, however, such as her belief that Bendix is the most beautiful name in the world for a doll, her habit of leading the invisible lizard by a string, and her insistence that her eyes are brown and white. The logic behind such actions as inviting the children over or taking only first bites from the apples is comically understandable. Her belief that she is unfairly excluded because she is little is also evident in episodes like the one in which Beezus tries to make her leave the art class. Because the point of view is Beezus's, however, the reader sees that Ramona really is a pest.

By presenting events from Ramona's point of view, *Ramona the Pest* creates tension between Ramona's feelings and the perceptions others have of her. Now five years old, Ramona is as exasperatingly stubborn as she was in *Beezus and Ramona*, but the change in point of view prevents her from appearing as obnoxious. Although others still consider her a pest, Ramona thinks that bigger people are unfair to her. She believes that she must make her characteristic noisy fusses because she is the youngest person in the house and on the block. Fussing is her way of demanding attention and respect.

Although she is bright and lively, Ramona is also amusingly naive. She thus misunderstands the teacher's meaning of "for the present" and thinks the song about the "dawnzer lee light" describes a lamp. Ramona also becomes fixated on ideas. Having short, straight, brown hair herself, for example, she is fascinated by Susan's long curls. Ramona is even more attracted to the curls because they remind her of the "boinging" sound of springs in cartoons. Ramona is alert to anything unfair, but she is also scrupulously honest. Thus, when she thinks about Susan's annoying habit of always trying to seem bigger than she is, Ramona truthfully admits that she will not be able to resist pulling her hair.

Ramona's major concerns by this second book in the series are with her identity and her relationships with others. She feels that she is special and lovable, but she can be overly sentimental. For example, she feels indulgently sorry for herself when she hides because of the substitute teacher. Ramona needs to be noticed to feel that she is important. For that reason, she becomes scared when nobody recognizes her in her witch costume. By carrying a sign with her name on it, she assures herself that everyone will know her and that she will thus continue to be a special individual. Ramona is sensitive to others' attitudes, which explains why she dislikes Susan for committing the schoolyard crime of "acting big." But Ramona worries most especially that Miss Binney will not love her. When she feels loved, Ramona loves school and learning. She therefore eagerly returns when Miss Binney's letter—though it does not use the extravagant terms Ramona had hoped for—shows that the teacher both understands and likes her.

Because Ramona is older than she was in early volumes of the series, in *Ramona Quimby, Age Eight* she perceives more complexity in both herself and others. Ramona feels the burdens of being the youngest member of her family. In particular, she resents the unfairness of having to entertain Willa Jean just because she's younger than Beezus. She demonstrates her imagination and wit by making Willa Jean believe that Sustained Silent Reading is an important piece of homework; she shows even more creativity by using a television commercial as the basis of her book report. The focus in the novel, however, is Ramona's understanding of her mixed feelings about others. With the mischievous Danny, for example, she is angry when he steals her eraser, fierce in trading insults, and grateful when he shows sympathy. Consequently, she comes to like him. She also has mixed feelings about Mrs. Whaley because she does not always understand her teacher's attitudes. When Ramona believes that Mrs. Whaley thinks she is a nuisance, she angrily asserts her independent identity by refusing to write a cursive Q. She also stops volunteering answers in class. Significantly, the masked Ramona hides behind an identity that has earned Mrs. Whaley's respect when she confronts the teacher. Once she is reassured that Mrs. Whaley does like her, Ramona assumes her true character by removing her mask. She then admits that she does sometimes show off.

Ramona's relationship with her family reflects her changing perceptions. Although she resents the fact that Beezus uses junior high school homework to avoid playing with Willa Jean, she feels close to her sister when they cook a meal together. Ramona likes her father, but his drawings force her to recognize that he is not as accomplished as she thought when she was younger. She resents her mother's constant reminders to behave and is unforgiving when she makes the mistake with the eggs. Ramona often feels sorry for herself and believes that both parents lack adequate sympathy for her when she is sick. She herself gains sympathy for them, however, when she learns how really hard it is to prepare a meal. In the end, Ramona accepts that her family is not always nice. More importantly, she realizes that she is not perfect, either—that her own niceness can sometimes become "curdled." Consequently, she shows maturity by accepting her family and by determining to do her best in contributing to it.

Although Ramona creates both the comedy and the conflict in *Beezus and Ramona*, the story is told from Beezus's point of view, which makes her character the focus of the reader's sympathy. **Beezus Quimby** (Beezus is short for Beatrice) is an average nine-year-old who is both embarrassed by and jealous of her flamboyant little sister. Beezus is a responsible child who often takes care of Ramona. She is good-natured and resourceful, for example, when she organizes the entertainment for Ramona's party. Nevertheless, she is often embarrassed by her sister's antics: when Ramona dons homemade rabbit ears for their trip to the library, for instance, Beezus lingers behind, hoping people will not know they are together. When some ladies stop them, however, Beezus is somewhat jealous that they praise Ramona's looks.

Beezus is also envious when people compliment Ramona on her imagination. She slowly comes to realize that the attention showered on younger children does not make older ones less talented or likable. She gains some insight into her own worth when she paints her clever picture of Ramona's invisible lizard, which she depicts as a dragon with a lollipop spine. Though Beezus sometimes feels sorry for herself and thinks that her situation is unfair, she does occasionally assert herself. For example, she refuses to read the newly purchased library book if Ramona throws a tantrum. She also refuses to play tiddlywinks after Ramona spoils her day with Henry.

Beezus eventually gains a more complete understanding of relationships. At first she is confused because she does not like Ramona. Her confusion intensifies when she simultaneously sympathizes with Ramona for not wanting to ask for a party while accepting her mother's view that growing up will eventually change her sister. Beezus later gets a direct lesson in the changes that growing up can bring when she learns that her mother and Aunt Beatrice were not always so loving. She then realizes that relationships can't always be ideal and that she does not have to love Ramona at every moment. Ironically, her understanding that Ramona is not always lovable makes her more capable of tolerating her sister.

By the second book, *Ramona the Pest*, Beezus is attending junior high school, but she still causes nearly as much friction in the family as Ramona because she wants more freedom. When she sleeps over at a friend's house, for example, she is so tired that she fights at home. With the sixth installment of the series, Beezus plays a distinctly minor role. Her growing maturity is still evident, however: even though she continues to find Ramona annoying, she defends her when outsiders criticize her.

The important adult characters in the Ramona books include parents, family, and teachers. **Mrs. (Dorothy) Quimby** is Beezus and Ramona's harried but understanding mother. She tolerates Ramona's naughtiness, but she is firm in making her go to her room whenever she throws a tantrum. Although she does not always understand Beezus's frustrations in caring for Ramona, Mrs. Quimby tries to be sympathetic. Often tired because of her job, the housework, and mounting bills, Mrs. Quimby still manages to be reassuring to her children. She is nevertheless wise enough to point out that even parents are not nice all the time. Mrs. Quimby is somewhat flawed in that she often gives in to her daughter, but she is concerned enough to meet with Miss Binney and to try to reassure Ramona that she is loved. **Mr. (Bob) Quimby**, the girls' father, is aging, as his thinning hair indicates, but he is still lively and humorous. He is also ambitious, but he places family before career. In *Ramona Quimby, Age Eight*, he understands that his family needs relief from their intense budgeting and decides to take everyone to the restaurant.

Aunt Beatrice Ann Haswell, Mrs. Quimby's younger sister, is a teacher who figures prominently in the first book. She takes on the role of the wise woman who understands children. For example, she advises the family that Ramona is seeking attention by being naughty. When she arrives for Beezus's birthday, she shows understanding by bringing a small gift for Ramona. Most significantly, she helps Beezus cope with her feelings by offering herself as an example of the naughty child who turned into a loving and lovable adult.

The most important secondary character in *Ramona the Pest* is Ramona's teacher, **Miss Binney**. A first-time teacher, she learns after the embarrassing confusion over the word "present" that she must choose her words carefully. Although she does not always understand Ramona's intentions—she doesn't realize, for example, that Ramona snores to show that she is a good rester—Miss Binney is sensitive to her students. She ensures that children do not laugh at Ramona's choice of Chevrolet for her doll's name.

By sending the tooth to Ramona and drawing the Q as a cat, Miss Binney shows that she respects Ramona's desire to be an individual. Another teacher character is **Mrs. Whaley**, who appears in *Ramona Quimby, Age Eight*. Although her casual manner confuses Ramona, Mrs. Whaley is a sympathetic teacher. She helps Ramona gain understanding by getting her to admit that she sometimes shows off.

There are also several important children characters in the Ramona stories besides Ramona and her sister. **Howie Kemp** first appears in *Beezus and Ramona* as the noisiest boy at Ramona's nursery school—nearly as rambunctious as Ramona herself. He is just as insistent on getting his own way, and he and Ramona frequently fight. His presence suggests that Ramona may be exceptionally imaginative, but she is not unusual in her naughtiness. In *Ramona the Pest* Howie is a sturdy blond boy, who has a history of fighting with Ramona. His lack of enthusiasm for school makes Ramona's love of it more dramatic. **Susan**, who appears in the second book, also serves as a contrast to Ramona. A big girl with curly hair, she angers Ramona, who respects honesty, because she is always trying to be a mother figure and act like a big shot.

In *Ramona Quimby, Age Eight* Ramona gets a taste of her own medicine from four-year-old **Willa Jean Kemp**, who acts just like Ramona did at her age by constantly demanding her own way. Through her, Ramona experiences the frustrations Beezus once felt, although she is not conscious of the similarity. Also in this book, Ramona is tormented by **Danny**, whom Ramona calls "Yard Ape." Danny seems like an obnoxious brat when he steals Ramona's eraser, but he later reveals himself to be a lively and sympathetic boy.

Dear Mr. Henshaw

(novel, 1983)

PLOT: This Newbery Medal winner consists of the letters and diary entries of Leigh Marcus Botts. When he was in the second grade, Leigh began writing to Boyd Henshaw, author of his favorite book, *Ways to Amuse a Dog*. Forced to write a report in the sixth grade, Leigh sends a list of questions to Mr. Henshaw, but he becomes angry when Mr. Henshaw replies with his own questions. Bonnie Botts, Leigh's mother, forces her son to write another letter to the author. In his letter, Leigh reveals that he lives with his divorced mother and misses both his father, Bill, a long-distance trucker, and their dog, Bandit. Having moved to a new city, Leigh has no friends and thinks that no one notices him. He is also angry that someone is stealing the special treats put in his lunch by the caterer for whom his mother works part time. His one bright spot comes when Mr. Fridley, the school custodian, notices Leigh and asks him to raise the flag each morning.

Following Mr. Henshaw's advice, Leigh begins to keep a diary. His entries, addressed to "Mr. Pretend Henshaw," express his frustrations at home. Leigh's father, for example, does not visit at Christmas, although he has another trucker deliver a present. Later, his father promises to call but forgets. When Leigh telephones him, he learns that Bandit is lost. Furthermore, hearing a boy in the background say that his mother is ready to go out, Leigh realizes that his father, in spite of his claims, was not going to call that night. After talking to his mother while they eat chicken and watch the ocean, Leigh comes to accept that he is not responsible for his parents' divorce. He also realizes that he can't hate his father.

At school, meanwhile, Leigh is happy when the librarian notices him and lends him Mr. Henshaw's latest book. For the most part, however, he is angry about the thefts of his lunch. In frustration, Leigh starts to drop-kick someone else's lunch, but Mr. Fridley stops him. After walking among trees harboring monarch butterflies, Leigh is symbolically lifted in spirit. He decides to follow Mr. Fridley's earlier advice and make a burglar alarm for his lunch box. Because no one tries to steal his lunch the next day, Leigh himself sets off the alarm. The resulting chaos leads students and teachers alike to notice him and admire his ingenuity. He then becomes friends with Barry, who even invites Leigh for dinner one night.

Although he ends the thefts and gains a friend, Leigh struggles with another problem—writing a story for a contest. He abandons a symbolic piece about a trucker made of wax and writes a description of a grape-hauling trip he took with his father. His piece earns an honorable mention. But when the winning poem turns out to have been copied, Leigh is allowed to attend the prize lunch with a famous children's writer. She makes him feel special by calling him an author and praising his originality. When his father finally does visit, he tries to leave Bandit with Leigh. Leigh demonstrates forgiveness by telling his father to keep Bandit so that he will not be lonely. Leigh also shows maturity by accepting that his parents will never reunite. Nevertheless, he also realizes that his father's visit is a sign of continuing love.

The sequel, Strider, *was published in 1991.*

CHARACTERS: Although the characters fit patterns common in adolescent problem novels, they are not simply types. Cleary's realism and humor combine to make the narration vividly alive. Consequently, all of the characters Leigh describes gain believable complexity.

During the course of the novel, **Leigh Marcus Botts** learns to value himself and to accept his parents' divorce. He initially feels insignificant, however, calling himself "just a plain boy" and the "mediumest boy in the class." Leigh tries to fit in at his new school by refraining from telling the teacher about the lunch bag thefts so that he will not be called a "snitch," and by playing soccer after school even though he does not like the game. Nevertheless, he has no friends and longs for someone to invite him over after school. Leigh also feels insignificant because his father calls him "kid" and never says that he misses him. Leigh resents that his busy mother does not have time to prepare the kind of meals she cooked before the divorce. For all of these reasons, Leigh is angry, resentful, and lonely. His way of finding stability and comfort is to reread *Ways to Amuse a Dog* over and over and to write to Mr. Henshaw. Although Leigh's letters and his diary obviously put Mr. Henshaw in the role of Leigh's absent father, the very act of writing develops

Leigh's understanding of himself. Significantly, Leigh stops addressing his diary entries to Mr. Henshaw once he realizes that he can't hate his father.

As Leigh's wishes are fulfilled, he becomes more mature. Adults are the first to grant Lee's wish to be noticed. By recognizing his individuality, Mr. Fridley and the librarian provide Leigh with evidence that he is not as insignificant as he had imagined. He must accept the responsibility of ending his own loneliness, however, because he creates the alarm that makes everyone notice him. Leigh subsequently has another wish fulfilled when Barry, impressed by Leigh's knowledge and ingenuity, invites him home after school. He also he gets his wish of meeting a famous writer, and she gives him further confidence by praising his writing.

When his long-held wish for a visit from his father finally happens, Leigh shows maturity. Having earlier understood that the divorce was not his fault, he now also accepts the fact that his parents will never reunite. More importantly, Leigh—who once hoped that his father would drive him to school so that he would be noticed—no longer relies on his father to solve his problems. Leigh now sees his father realistically for the first time. Having grown himself, Leigh first notices that his father is not as tall as he once thought and that he is seriously flawed and will always be unreliable. The greatest sign of Leigh's newfound maturity, however, is that complex motives and emotions no longer confuse or anger him. He knows that his father's job brought him near, for example, but Leigh also knows that love made his father actually come to the house. No longer doubting his father's love, Leigh can think of him and be both sad and relieved.

Although Leigh's parents are divorced, neither tries to turn Leigh against the other. **Bonnie Botts**, his mother, is considerate and understanding when Leigh feels depressed. She is careful to reassure him that he is not responsible for the divorce. She also insists that Leigh's father is not totally at fault, explaining that she married young and changed, whereas her husband did not. In the end, she is strong and honest, clearly telling Billy that a reconciliation is impossible. **Billy Botts**, Leigh's father, is a carefree man in love with the highway and his own

freedom. Leigh frequently mentions his father's habit of playing video games, an indication that Bonnie is correct when she says her ex-husband never grew up. Billy has good intentions, but he does not always act on them. Unable to communicate easily himself, he fails to understand Leigh's anger at being called "kid." Nevertheless, it is clear that he loves Leigh when he sends him a Christmas present, sends him money as an apology for losing Bandit, and, after finding the dog, tries to leave Bandit with Leigh.

Two characters act almost as substitute fathers to Leigh. The first, **Boyd Henshaw**, never actually appears in the story, but Leigh's letters and diary entries give him an active role in the novel. A children's author who specializes in books about animals, Mr. Henshaw expresses many of the ideas Cleary developed after her readers began inundating her with mail. Cleary expresses her belief that children need to recognize that authors have a limited amount of time, for example, through Mr. Henshaw's comical remark that his favorite animal is the purple monster who eats children who send authors questions instead of doing research in the library. The list of questions Mr. Henshaw sends to Leigh is something Cleary daydreamed about doing herself. Mr. Henshaw's books comfort Leigh, but Mr. Henshaw himself is the wise adult who provides him with sound advice about writing. **Mr. Fridley**, the custodian, is also a wise adult. He seems to know everything that goes on in the school, and his involvement with Leigh contrasts with the neglect of Leigh's father. Mr. Fridley not only notices Leigh, but makes him feel important by having him raise the flag. Whereas Mr. Henshaw gives advice about writing, Mr. Fridley advises Leigh about life. He thus tells Leigh that his angry attitude prevents people from becoming his friends. Finally, Mr. Fridley shows concern, and simultaneously indicates that Leigh is not insignificant, when he prevents Leigh from kicking a lunch and thus getting into trouble.

Further Reading

Authors and Artists for Young Adults. Vol. 6. Detroit: Gale Research, 1991.

Berger, Laura Standley, ed. *Twentieth-Century Children's Writers.* 4th ed. Detroit: St. James, 1995.

Children's Literature Review. Vols. 2, 8. Detroit: Gale Research, 1976, 1985.

Cleary, Beverly. *A Girl from Yamhill: A Memoir*. New York: Morrow, 1988.

Collier, Laurie, and Joyce Nakamura, eds. *Major Authors and Illustrators for Children and Young Adults*. Detroit: Gale Research, 1993.

Contemporary Authors New Revision Series. Vol. 36. Detroit: Gale Research, 1992.

Estes, Glenn E., ed. *American Writers for Children since 1960: Fiction*. Vol. 52 of *Dictionary of Literary Biography*. Detroit: Gale Research, 1986.

Pflieger, Pat. *Beverly Cleary*. Boston: Twayne, 1991.

Something about the Author. Vols. 2, 43, 79. Detroit: Gale Research, 1971, 1986, 1995.

C. Collodi

(pen name for Carlo Lorenzini)

1826-1890, Italian soldier, journalist, civil servant, and author

The Adventures of Pinocchio

(fantasy, 1883; published in Italy as Le avventure di Pinocchio*)*

PLOT: *Pinocchio* has been attacked by critics because of its inconsistencies, violence, and repetitious episodes. It is celebrated more frequently, however, as a fanciful blend of folklore and mythology that avoids the extreme didacticism common in the children's books of its era. The major theme of its transformation plot is the maturing identity of the central character, who develops from mischievous boy to model adolescent.

Mastro Cherry, a carpenter, gives a piece of talking wood to Mastro Geppetto. Geppetto, who wants to earn money, carves it into a marionette named Pinocchio. As soon as he is completed, Pinocchio becomes mischievous and races out the door. Geppetto tries to bring the puppet home, but he is arrested and thrown in jail. Pinocchio then returns to Geppetto's house, where the Talking Cricket warns him that his naughty ways will lead to trouble. In a fit of anger, Pinocchio kills Talking Cricket with a mallet. When Geppetto returns from prison the next day, he finds Pinocchio has fallen

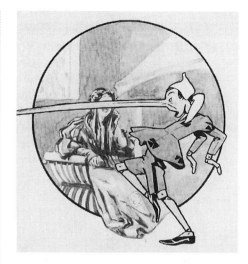

Pinocchio receives a punishment for lying in this illustration by Attilio Mussino from Collodi's moralistic story.

asleep near the fire and burned off his feet. He gives the hungry Pinocchio his own breakfast, makes him new feet, and clothes him. He then sells his coat to buy Pinocchio a primer for school. Although Pinocchio promises to attend school regularly, he trades the primer for a ticket to a marionette show. During the performance, Harlequin and the other puppets recognize him and forget about their show. Fire-eater, the showman, angrily threatens the puppets. He relents, however, after Pinocchio offers to be burned instead of Harlequin. Fire-eater then sends Pinocchio back to Geppetto with five gold pieces.

On the way home, Pinocchio meets Fox and Cat, who convince him that they know a place where buried gold grows into trees of money. After a meal at an inn, Fox and Cat set out ahead of the sleeping Pinocchio. In spite of warnings by the ghost of Talking Cricket, Pinocchio pursues them and is beset upon by assassins. When they learn he has the gold coins in his mouth, the assassins hang him from a tree. A blue-haired child, a fairy who earlier told Pinocchio she was dead, rescues him. She brings in three doctors (one of whom is Talking Cricket) to examine him. Although he promises to take his medicine if given sugar, Pinocchio repeatedly breaks his promise until the sight of undertakers coming for him scares him. Pinocchio then lies to the Fairy about his money, causing his nose to grow. After the Fairy shortens his nose, Pinocchio sets out to find Geppetto. Unfortunately, he again meets Fox and Cat, who convince him to bury his money. When Pinocchio discovers that his money has been stolen, he complains to a gorilla judge, who sentences him to prison. Upon Pinocchio's release, a farmer catches him stealing grapes and makes him act as a watch-dog. Pinocchio faithfully catches some thieves and earns his release.

Pinocchio now discovers the blue-haired child is dead. A pigeon flies him to the seashore to meet Geppetto. After vainly trying to catch up with Geppetto, who has sailed away in a boat, Pinocchio again encounters the Blue-Haired Fairy, who is now a woman. He promises to be good and study because he wants to become a real boy. Although he keeps his promise at first, he is eventually lured away by bad companions to see a shark. When one of them is wounded in a fight, however, Pinocchio is arrested. He escapes, but he saves Alidoro, a pursuing police dog, from drowning. Afterwards, he is caught by the Green Fisherman, who wants to fry him. Rescued by Alidoro, Pinocchio returns to the Fairy's house. The servant Snail makes him wait hours for admission. Pinocchio is good and studious for a year, so the Fairy says he will be turned into a boy the next day. That night, however, Pinocchio is tempted by his friend Lampwick to run away to the Land of the Toys. After five months without responsibilities, Pinocchio and Lampwick become donkeys. The coach driver who brought him to the Land of Toys sells Pinocchio to a circus. The donkey Pinocchio becomes lame, however, so he is sold. The buyer, who wants to make a drum from his skin, tries to drown him, but the Fairy rescues him again by sending fish to eat away the donkey skin and make Pinocchio a puppet again. Pinocchio then escapes, only to be swallowed by the terrible shark known as "The Attila of the Sea." Inside the shark, Pinocchio discovers Geppetto and leads him out through the shark's mouth. Tunny Fish, which followed them out of the shark's belly, carries them to shore. Pinocchio takes Geppetto to a cottage, where Talking Cricket again gives him advice. Pinocchio reforms, taking care of Geppetto, working hard to earn food, and

studying. Finally, Snail tells Pinocchio the Fairy is dying in the hospital. Pinocchio sends Snail back to her with all of his money. That night the Fairy appears in a dream and forgives Pinocchio for his failures. He awakens to find himself a real boy and lives happily after.

CHARACTERS: Adaptations, especially the Disney animated version, have altered perceptions of the characters. The characters in the novel show a greater mixture of traits than they possess in such versions. **Pinocchio** (whose name means "eye of pine" or "pine knot" in Tuscan) undergoes a physical transformation that symbolizes a moral transformation. Physically, he begins as a block of wood, becomes a boy-like puppet, and is finally changed into a real boy. Morally, he begins as naughty and selfish and becomes good, studious, and generous. When he is unshaped wood, a condition symbolizing the unformed identity of infancy, Pinocchio shows a disregard for others by causing Mastro Cherry and Mastro Geppetto to fight. As Geppetto carves each of his features, a stage symbolizing the development of awareness in early boyhood, Pinocchio becomes increasingly mischievous. He turns each new feature against his father, using his mouth to laugh at Geppetto, his hands to snatch his wig, and his feet to kick him in the nose. Self-absorbed, Pinocchio lacks gratitude for Geppetto's sacrifices of his breakfast and his coat. Pinocchio is not evil, however, and he repeatedly feels guilty for his misdeeds and promises to study and behave. His problem is that he is thoughtless, a point brought out by numerous references to his wooden head. He therefore does not appreciate the need to behave, to study, and to work. Lacking foresight, he wants immediate pleasure. For instance, on the way to his first day of school, he sells his book in spite of Geppetto's sacrifice to obtain it and his own desire to learn to read. Even in this episode, however, signs of Pinocchio's basic good-ness are evident. He is noble, for example, when he insists that he will not let Harlequin die in his place. Nevertheless, Pinocchio continues to suffer because he stubbornly refuses to heed the advice of such wise elders as Talking Cricket and the Fairy. Furthermore, because he is ignorant and gullible, he strays when returning to Geppetto and falls victim to the temptations of easy riches offered by Fox and Cat.

Pinocchio's suffering takes him through a series of symbolic identity changes and deaths. After his initial construction, he burns off his feet, a symbol of laziness destroying one's abilities. Later, after the Fairy saves him from hanging, Pinocchio nearly dies because he foolishly resists taking unpleasant medicine, a situation that symbolizes his repeated refusals to heed advice he does not like. As his adventures continue, Pinocchio repeatedly is likened to lesser life forms. Thus, after stealing grapes, he becomes a watchdog; although he previously shirked his responsibilities, he honestly and faithfully serves as a dog and earns another chance at being a boy. When he later skips school to look at the shark, he is reduced to the level of a fish by the Green Fisherman, who tries to cook him. Pinocchio's most visible transformation, however, occurs just when he is about to be changed into a real boy. Lured away to the Land of Toys by the promise of freedom from work and study, he physically becomes the donkey that he is intellectually and temperamentally. Once released from his donkey form, Pinocchio undergoes yet another symbolic death when the shark swallows him. His love for Geppetto, his good sense, and his optimism, however, save him and his father. He emerges from the shark as one who knows how to express love and who values work and study. Significantly, he listens to advice from Talking Cricket. In a scene echoing both Geppetto's sale of his coat, and therefore symbolizing adult compassion and sacrifice, Pinocchio later gives up his clothes money to help the hospitalized Fairy. By doing so, he reveals that he is a morally responsible young adult. As a reward, the Fairy transforms his body, making him in fact the good boy he has become by learning to work, study, and care about others.

Geppetto is an extremely poor, little old man nicknamed Polendina (cornmeal mush) because of his yellow wig. The short-tempered Geppetto resents the nickname and quickly gets into a fight when he thinks Mastro Cherry has used it. Although Geppetto has mercenary motives in creating Pinocchio, love for his "child" soon makes him forget his plans.

Indeed, Geppetto is generally a kind and patient father. After his release from prison, for example, he is understandably angry with Pinocchio, but his anger quickly turns to pity when he sees the puppet's burned feet. As a father, Geppetto willingly makes sacrifices, giving up his food and his warm coat so his son won't be hungry and can go to school. At the same time, Geppetto has enough wisdom to know Pinocchio, like all children, tends to make promises whenever he wants something. When Pinocchio disappears, Geppetto shows the depth of his love by searching relentlessly. His imprisonment for two years in the stomach of the shark symbolizes the death of Geppetto's hope for his son. He is literally and symbolically reborn by the return of Pinocchio, who leads him from the shark's belly and restores him to health. In the end, he achieves happiness because his child has grown into a good boy.

The Talking Cricket is a didactic device. Having lived for more than a hundred years, he symbolizes the wisdom of age. He is also the voice of conscience. A patient teacher who is unperturbed by Pinocchio's rudeness, he voices the moralistic message of the novel when he tells Pinocchio his carefree ways will lead to grief. He also foreshadows Pinocchio's fate when he warns him that his neglect of school will make him a donkey. By killing Talking Cricket, Pinocchio symbolically stifles his own conscience. Even after his death, however, Talking Cricket continues to offer advice. He thus appears as a ghost to warn Pinocchio about Fox and Cat. In one of the novel's many inconsistencies, Talking Cricket is alive later. He appears as a doctor who refuses to diagnose Pinocchio's physical state but identifies his moral condition by defining him as a rogue. At the end of the novel, he again appears as owner of the cottage to which Pinocchio takes the ailing Geppetto. This time he is a device for displaying the changes in Pinocchio, who willing admits his earlier misbehavior and shows concern for Geppetto's welfare. Talking Cricket also gives a final lesson about the value of compassion.

The Blue-Haired Fairy appears in a number of forms. She is a blue-haired child who speaks without moving her lips, a little woman, a beautiful woman who observes Pinocchio's performance as a donkey, a blue-haired goat that tries to save him from the shark, and a figure in a dream. The Fairy augments the didactic functions of Talking Cricket, constantly urging Pinocchio to be good and studious so he can become a real boy. She even tries to teach him a lesson by having his nose grow when he lies to her. She also serves as a *deus ex machina*, whose blue hair may symbolize a heavenly nature. In spite of her initial appearance as a child, she has lived for a thousand years and has control over the creatures of nature. She is thus able to command birds to save Pinocchio from hanging and fishes to save him from drowning when he is a donkey.

The Fairy's changing appearance and her deaths may reflect Pinocchio's changing needs. She is a child who is dead to him until he learns the true evil of the assassins. Then she becomes a living child whom Pinocchio regards as almost a sister. Later, when he needs love and nurturing so that he can become an obedient and studious child, he thinks of her as almost a mother. After each of his failures to be good, he seeks her out as the forgiving mother whom he tries to please. Like Talking Cricket, her final function is to complete the identity theme by revealing the genuine changes in Pinocchio, who willingly gives up his hard-earned money when he hears she is ill. Unlike Cricket, however, she has power to change things. She therefore reconciles appearance and reality by physically changing Pinocchio into the real boy he has become emotionally, intellectually, and morally. **Snail**, the Fairy's maidservant, punishes the impatient Pinocchio by making him wait outside for hours while she makes her way from the top of the Fairy's house to the door. Later, she is the messenger who tests Pinocchio by telling him that the Fairy is impoverished and dying. She also supports the motif of appearance and reality because she begins running once Pinocchio shows his generosity by giving her money for the Fairy.

More than forty characters play minor roles, but only a few are notable. **Fire-eater**, the showman, is part of the novel's appearance-and-reality motif. A tall, ugly man with a long black beard that reaches the ground, a mouth like an oven, and fiery red eyes, he frightens all who see him. Fire-eater can be cruel, such as when he orders the puppets to be burned to

cook his mutton, but he has a good heart. He has the odd habit of sneezing whenever he feels pity for another, and Pinocchio makes him sneeze when he tells Fire-eater tales of his hardships and when he nobly protects Harlequin. Fire-eater thus begins as a villain but becomes a benefactor when he learns more about Pinocchio's character. The **coach driver** who takes Pinocchio to the Land of Toys contrasts with Fire-eater. A small man who is broader than he is tall, the driver is soft and pleasant, immediately pleasing the boys he lures away. Within this facade, however, he is completely heartless, never showing pity for those whom he victimizes.

Even more deceptive to Pinocchio are the Fox and the Cat. **Fox**, in keeping with the folktale tradition of foxes as tricksters, pretends to be lame. He is actually a wily, observant, and cruel thief who even becomes an assassin in his efforts to rob Pinocchio. Fox is a cautionary figure, showing what happens to those who refuse to work honestly. Eventually, he must even sell his tail to buy food. **Cat**, who follows Fox and has a tendency to repeat everything Fox says, also suffers an ironic fate: pretending to be blind as a way to trick others, he later loses his sight in reality. He is also maimed when Pinocchio bites off his paw during his struggle with the assassins. Fox and Cat initially reveal Pinocchio's naivete. They are devices for measuring Pinocchio's growth. He is initially gullible in believing they will make him rich, but he rejects their pleas for pity at the end because he now knows them to be scoundrels.

Romeo, the friend whom Pinocchio loves best, is nicknamed **Lampwick** because he is long and thin. Lampwick is the laziest and most mischievous boy at school. He is the one who lures Pinocchio to the Land of Toys. He then becomes a cautionary figure whose fate contrasts with Pinocchio's. Lacking the saving love of the motherly Fairy, Lampwick remains a donkey and is worked to death by a farmer. **Alidoro**, the police dog, reveals Pinocchio's good heart when the escaping puppet saves him from drowning. Later, Alidoro repays the deed by rescuing Pinocchio from the Green Fisherman. By doing so, he illustrates the message that Talking Cricket later propounds: We should treat others kindly so we may be treated kindly when we have need. The **Green Fisherman** has green skin and eyes, green leaves for hair, and a long green beard that reaches to the ground. He contributes to the identity theme by judging Pinocchio entirely by circumstances: because he found Pinocchio in a fish net, he insists on treating Pinocchio as if he were a fish.

Further Reading

Bingham, Jane M., ed. *Writers for Children: Critical Studies of Major Authors since the Seventeenth Century*. New York: Charles Scribner's Sons, 1988.

Children's Literature Review. Vol. 5. Detroit: Gale Research, 1983, 1983.

Collier, Laurie, and Joyce Nakamura, eds. *Major Authors and Illustrators for Children and Young Adults*. Detroit: Gale Research, 1993.

Kunitz, Stanley J., and Howard Haycraft, eds. *The Junior Book of Authors*. 2nd ed. New York: H. W. Wilson, 1951.

Something about the Author. Vol. 29. Detroit: Gale Research, 1982.

Wunderlich, Richard, and Thomas J. Morrisey. "Carlo Collodi's *The Adventures of Pinocchio*: A Classic Book of Choices." In *Touchstones: Reflections on the Best in Children's Literature*. Vol. 1. Edited by Perry Nodelman, pp. 53-64. West Lafayette, IN: Children's Literature Association, 1985.

Susan Coolidge

(pen name of Sarah Chauncy Woolsey)

1835-1905, American author

What Katy Did

(novel, 1872)

PLOT: Probably inspired by Louisa May Alcott's *Little Women*, *What Katy Did* is an episodic family story about the taming of a girl's wild spirit. Katy, the eldest child of Dr. Carr, has three sisters, Clover, Elsie, and Joanna (called John or Johnnie). She also has two brothers, Dorry and Phil. Because Katy's mother is dead, Aunt Izzie Carr manages the house. The early chapters focus on the troublesome Katy's disorderly fun and her relationships with her siblings and friends. Katy, her best friend, Cecy Hall, and Clover attend Mrs. Knight's school. One day,

Katy gets into trouble by inventing the Game of Rivers, in which the children run around in a raucous, furniture-spilling frenzy. At home, Katy produces her own religious newspaper, for which she writes romantic stories.

One night when Aunt Izzie is out, Katy, her siblings, and Cecy play Kikeri, a wild, forbidden game. Upset that Katy disobeyed Aunt Izzie, Dr. Carr tells her that she must begin assuming her late mother's role with the children. He also expresses displeasure when he overhears the pretentious Imogen Clark, whom Katy invited for a visit, telling ridiculous lies. Later, Katy becomes friends with Cousin Helen, an invalid who stays with the family awhile.

Katy's rebelliousness eventually leads to disaster. After Aunt Izzie forbids her to use a swing without explaining that it needs repairs, Katy defiantly plays on it, falls, and injures her spine. Confined to bed, Katy becomes despondent. Cousin Helen, however, tells Katy about "The School of Pain," inspiring her to become neat, cheerful, and considerate. At Christmas, Katy gets Aunt Izzie to purchase thoughtful gifts for the others. She is delighted when the stockings are hung in her room and when the others give her presents. On Valentine's Day, Katy enlists Cecy's help to arrange a party for her siblings. That autumn, Aunt Izzie dies of typhoid fever, and Katy takes over management of the house. Although she makes mistakes, Katy eventually learns how to run things smoothly. Two years later, Katy has two visitors who highlight the changes in her character. Katy thus wonders why she ever liked Imogen Clark, but she insists that everyone treat fat, talkative Mrs. Worrett, one of Aunt Izzie's friends, kindly. Miraculously, Katy eventually regains use of her legs. In another visit, Cousin Helen praises her as the center and sun of the family.

Sequels are What Katy Did at School *(1873),* What Katy Did Next *(1886),* Clover *(1888), and* In the High Valley *(1890).*

CHARACTERS: *What Katy Did* has remained in print because its characters capture the fun, friendship, and mischief of ordinary children. **Katy Carr** is a tall, awkward, spirited, imaginative, and tomboyish twelve-year-old. She is messy, constantly tearing her dresses in rough play, and lacks all interest in being called "good." Katy is fond of reading and telling stories, and she likes to write romances for a religious paper that she publishes for her family. An open and accepting girl, Katy has always made friends with all sorts of people. Naive romanticism clouds her judgment, however, when she befriends Imogen, whose absurd stories lead Katy to see her as a true romantic heroine. Katy is a natural leader in the family and at school: she organizes expeditions and entertainments for her siblings, and she invents the Game of Rivers for her schoolmates. At all times, Katy has integrity. When her thoughtless and wild play causes trouble, as it does when the noisy Game of Rivers attracts a crowd outside the school, she courageously admits responsibility. After Dr. Carr reprimands her for playing Kikeri and reminds her that her dead mother asked her to be a mother to her siblings, Katy tries to be more thoughtful.

Katy hopes to do something grand in life, but like many supposedly naughty children in didactic literature, she suffers for her rebellious personality. Upset after accidentally breaking a gift from Cousin Helen and angrily pushing Elsie, Katy deliberately disobeys Aunt Izzie by going on the swing. After she becomes paralyzed, Katy descends into self-pity and slovenliness, neglecting her appearance and her surroundings. Inspired by the beloved Cousin Helen's tutoring about "The School of Pain," Katy begins to care for her own appearance again, makes her room neat and attractive, takes charge of her own education, and constantly thinks of ways to please others. She thus arranges a Valentine party and Christmas gifts for her siblings, and she becomes especially attentive to Elsie, whom she previously excluded from her activities. After taking over management of the house, Katy occasionally goes to comical extremes in planning meals, but she eventually displays mature competence and earns the respect of family and servants alike. Four years after the accident, Katy's growth in character is apparent when she has two visitors. She tolerates Imogen, questioning afterwards why she liked her, and when

Mrs. Worrett stops by, Katy is kind and considerate to the old, somewhat ridiculous woman. Katy is rewarded for her saintly reformation: she becomes the center of the loving family and then recovers full use of her legs. Unfortunately, the reformed, ladylike Katy is so wooden that most readers will long for the unkempt tomboy.

Plump **Clover**, Katy's sister, who is ten when the novel opens, is staid and conventional, but she looks up to Katy as one of the wisest people in the world. Clover has straight, light-brown hair that she wears in pigtails. Because she spends every Saturday night in uncomfortable, tightly pinned curling papers, she despises fashionable curls. Clover's short-sightedness makes her blue eyes seem tear-filled, but she is jolly, loving, and lovable. A born peacemaker, she stops fights between the siblings. Wavy-haired **Elsie**, a thin, brown eight-year-old with beautiful dark eyes, is the odd child out in the family. Deeply hurt that Katy, Clover, and Cecy exclude her from their games, she spitefully spoils their game of post office by finding their secret mailboxes. Elsie is, however, forgiving and generous. After Katy falls, Elsie gives Katy her most prized possessions, thereby unintentionally teaching Katy a dramatic lesson in kindness. **Dorry**, a pudgy six-year-old boy with a rather solemn face, is a glutton and becomes upset if he is kept waiting for food. Whereas Dorry seems like a girl in boy's clothing, five-year-old **Joanna** seems like a boy in a frock (and she is always called **John** or **Johnnie**). A square child with big eyes and a wide mouth, she seems perpetually ready to laugh. Pretty four-year-old **Phil** enjoys being with his brother and sisters. He shows how inappropriate stories affect children. When Cousin Helen tells a story about robbers, Phil is warlike, declaring that they couldn't frighten him. But he becomes comically pathetic that night, crying because he believes that robbers are under his bed.

Dr. Carr is a kind, busy man with bright eyes and a good sense of humor. Wanting hardy and bold children, he encourages them to engage in vigorous and rough play. He is otherwise conventional, acting as a moral guide who draws the line when Katy becomes too rough or inconsiderate. He thus bans Kikeri and reminds Katy of her mother's wish that she raise her siblings. In contrast, **Aunt Izzie Carr**, his sister and housekeeper, embodies a stern, conventional attitude to children. A petite, sharp-faced, neat, old-looking woman, she expects children to be obedient, gentle, and tidy. Her belief that children owe adults unquestioning obedience leads her to forbid Katy to use the swing without telling her that it is unsafe. She is thus an example of the ineffectiveness of old-fashioned child-rearing habits. Nevertheless, given the opportunity—as she is after Katy's accident—Aunt Izzie shows that she has a warm heart. **Cousin Helen**, the most important adult, is also the most unconvincing and wooden of the characters. A saintly invalid, the neat and lively Helen turns her room into an attractive gathering place and becomes the center of the children's lives, delighting them with her imaginative games and stories. After Katy's accident, Helen becomes her mentor, telling her that "The School of Pain" can teach her patience, cheerfulness, helpfulness, and neatness. As a consequence, Katy ceases to be filled with self-pity and becomes nearly as saintly as Helen.

Cecy Hall, who lives next door, contrasts with Katy, being neat, clean, and prim. Cecy spends so much time with Katy and Clover that she is almost one of the Carr family. She shows her good heart by helping Katy to arrange the Valentine surprise party. **Imogen Clark** (her real name is Elizabeth) is a foil. Like Katy, she is a bright girl who loves novels and likes to tell stories. Imogen's head has been turned by fiction, however, so she presents as truth the patently absurd stories that she tells about a brigand. Imogen dresses inappropriately and pretentiously, and she rejects healthy play outdoors. Four years after Katy's accident, Imogen shows that she has not matured. Dressed in fashionable but cheap clothes, she persists in telling stories about the brigand, and she is so self-absorbed that she neglects to inquire about Katy's health. She thus contrasts with the sensitive and modest Katy, who realizes how foolish she was to like someone so vain and superficial.

Further Reading

Berger, Laura Standley, ed. *Twentieth-Century Children's Writers*. 4th ed. Detroit: St. James, 1995.

Contemporary Authors. Vol. 115. Detroit: Gale Research, 1985.

Estes, Glenn E., ed. *American Writers for Children before 1900*. Vol. 42 of *Dictionary of Literary Biography*. Detroit: Gale Research, 1985.

Barbara Cooney

1917-1994, American author and illustrator

Miss Rumphius

(picture book, 1982)

PLOT: Narrated by the great-niece of the title character, *Miss Rumphius* honors continuity, but it also celebrates the individualism necessary to fulfill the legacy of goals and ideals. When Alice Rumphius was a girl, her grandfather, an artist, inspired her with stories of his travels. Alice said that she, too, would go to faraway places when she grew up and live by the sea when she grew old. Her grandfather said, however, that she must also make the world more beautiful. Alice agreed, but she did not know what she could do. After she grew up and became Miss Rumphius, she worked as a librarian in a city far from the sea. Eventually, she traveled to tropical islands, mountains, jungles, and deserts, everywhere making friends she would not forget. One day, she hurt her back getting off a camel and decided to make her home by the sea. Miss Rumphius then puzzled about her third promise, how to make the world more beautiful. After recovering from a lengthy illness, she discovered some lupines growing from seeds the wind scattered from her garden. Miss Rumphius began scattering seeds wherever she walked. Soon, she achieved her goal because the countryside was beautifully covered with lupines. Now old and known as the Lupine Lady, Miss Rumphius entertains her great niece with stories of faraway places. The narrator says that she, too, will travel to faraway places and then live by the sea. Miss Rumphius tells her, however, that she must also do something to make the world more beautiful. The

Miss Rumphius gives lupines to the world in Cooney's illustration for her picture book.

narrator agrees, although she does not know yet what she will do.

CHARACTERS: The story spans five generations, but skips over the parents of both Miss Rumphius and the narrator, thus emphasizing the role of the elderly as voices of wisdom. Each of the three generations portrayed shares a delight in adventure, a close connection to the landscape, and an idealistic commitment to making the world better. Alice's **grandfather**, a well-traveled nineteenth-century immigrant, is an artist who makes figureheads, carves wooden Indians, and paints pictures. His loving warmth, evident when he puts Alice on his knee to tell her stories, inspires her love for travel and for a home by the sea. When he tells Alice that

she must also do something to make the world more beautiful, however, his artistic credo becomes the ethical teaching of an archetypal wise old man. His simple statement proclaims that one must not live selfishly but must in some way create beauty.

Miss Alice Rumphius helped her grandfather by painting in the clouds on some of his pictures, but she does not become an artist. Nevertheless, she has an artistic temperament, and as Barbara Cooney has said, she "has *real* soul." Miss Rumphius is a determined woman. When she works as a librarian, she reads about faraway places, and she visits a conservatory that is like a tropical isle. But Miss Rumphius does not settle for substitutes. Courageous, daring, and independent, she actually travels to distant places. In fact, her skirts, which begin at pre-World War I length and become shorter, suggest that she travels for decades. In each place, she makes friends whom she remembers, indicating that she is sociable and loving. After she hurts her back and moves to a house by the sea, thus completing her second goal, Miss Rumphius shows her idealism by puzzling about improving an already beautiful world. When she realizes that she can add beauty by scattering lupine seeds, she becomes an eccentric to some, who call her "That Crazy Old Lady." Nevertheless, she persists and achieves her quest when beautiful lupines grow everywhere. Her victory is signaled by her new public identity: everyone now calls her the Lupine Lady.

Even as an old, white-haired woman, Miss Rumphius continues to contribute to the world. In a scene paralleling the earlier one with her grandfather, she becomes the archetypal wise old woman: she passes on his legacy by inspiring her great-niece with the same goals of traveling, living by the sea, and, most importantly, of doing something that adds beauty to the world. **The narrator** is a young girl who is attentive to and proud of her great-aunt. By adopting the three goals that shaped her great-aunt's life, she shows the continuity of values. Because, like the young Alice Rumphius before her, she does not know what she will do to add beauty to the world, she demonstrates that each generation must find its own way of achieving the ideals bequeathed by the past.

Further Reading

Children's Literature Review. Vol. 23. Detroit: Gale Research, 1991.

Collier, Laurie, and Joyce Nakamura, eds. *Major Authors and Illustrators for Children and Young Adults.* Detroit: Gale Research, 1993.

Contemporary Authors New Revision Series. Vol. 37. Detroit: Gale Research, 1992.

Something about the Author. Vols. 6, 59. Detroit: Gale Research, 1974, 1990.

Susan Cooper

1935-, English author

The Dark Is Rising Sequence

(fantasy series, 1965-75)

PLOT: Cooper has said that the "underlying theme" of her fantasy sequence is "the ancient problem of

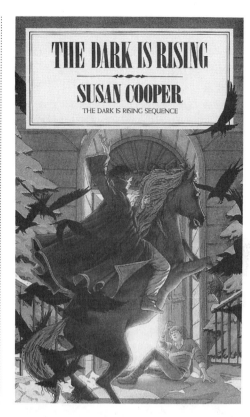

"The ancient problem of the duality of human nature" is addressed in Cooper's well-known fantasy sequence, of which this is the second installment.

the duality of human nature." Begun as an entry in a contest honoring E. Nesbit, ***Over Sea, Under Stone*** (1965) is more holiday adventure than fantasy, but it introduces motifs important in subsequent volumes: deceptive appearances, Celtic legend, magical artifacts, and the continuing struggle between good and evil. The setting is Trewissick in Cornwall, England. Dr. Dick Drew, his wife, Ellen, and their children, Simon, Barney (Barnabas), and Jane are vacationing in a house rented by Gumerry, Great-Uncle Merriman "Merry" Lyon. While exploring the house, the children discover an old map. That evening, Norman Withers and his sister, Polly, invite everyone to spend the following day on their yacht. Jane declines, deciding to talk to the vicar who wrote a guidebook with a map of the local coastline. At the vicarage, Mr. Hastings tells her that the author is dead and then questions her closely about maps.

After someone then ransacks the Drew house, the children confide in Merry. Examining their map, he explains that it leads to a grail depicting King Arthur's life that is vital in the battle between good and evil.

Once Barney notices that their map is a perspective drawing, the children realize that they must line up shadows with topographical features to find the treasure. As they do so, Miss Withers sees them and orders Bill Hoover, a young bully, to take their map, but Simon flees with it. The next night, while Merry, Jane, and Simon investigate topographical features under moonlight, Barney finds the housekeeper, Mrs. (Molly) Palk, searching his room. The next day, Mrs. Palk gives Merry a false message to get him out of the way. Consequently, the children are unprotected, and Norman and Polly Withers, costumed for the Trewissick Carnival, kidnap Barney when he is separated from the others. Hastings puts Barney under a trance, but the howling of Rufus, a dog who has befriended the children, breaks it, and Barney escapes. The three Drews now go to a cave (accessible because of an extraordinarily low tide) where Barney recovers the grail and a lead tube holding an ancient document. Hastings and his servants find them and demand the grail. Merry drives them away, but the map and the lead tube are lost in the sea. The Drew children donate the grail to the British Museum.

In *The Dark Is Rising* (1973), the battle between the Light and the Dark moves in and out of historical and magical times. Will Stanton, youngest child of Roger and Alice Stanton, has eight siblings: Stephen, Max, Robin, Paul, James, Gwen, Barbara, and Mary. On Midwinter's Eve, the day before his eleventh birthday, Farmer (Frank) Dawson gives Will an iron ornament shaped like a cross within a circle. On his birthday, Will finds himself in the past, where John Wayland Smith (an incarnation of the smith of the gods) defends him against the Black Rider. Passing through two doors in the Chiltern Hills, Will enters a great hall, where he meets the Lady and Merriman Lyon. They tell him that he is the last of the Old Ones, a race of immortals, and that he must acquire six signs of power, the first of which, the Sign of Iron, Dawson gave him. Back in his time, Will obtains the Sign of Bronze from the Walker, a

tramp, but needs the help of Merriman when Dawson's milkmaid, Maggie Barnes, casts a spell on him.

On Christmas Eve, Will goes to the manor to sing for the mistress Miss Greythorne. Transported to another time, he acquires the Sign of Wood. Merriman, aided by his liegeman, Hawkin (the Walker), also produces the Book of Grammarye, from which Will learns his powers. Merriman then destroys the book, shocking Hawkin. Will immediately finds himself at the manor in 1875, where Hawkin is betraying Merriman to Maggie Barnes. On Christmas Day, the Rider, calling himself Mr. Mitothin, delivers a gift to the Drew house and takes a strand of Mary's hair. At church Will acquires the Sign of Stone, but he needs the help of the Dawson, Dawson's farmhand, Old George Smith, and the Old Ones to withstand a stormy assault by the Dark. Because unprecedented amounts of snow and cold temperatures now grip England, Merriman convinces Will to bring the Walker, whom Will found unconscious in the snow, to the manor, where the villagers are gathering. Will acquires the Sign of Fire and then confronts the Walker, who is aiding the Dark, which is freezing the manor with the ice candles of winter. Will, ordering the Walker to be sedated, turns the candles to the service of the Light. As the snow now turns to rain, the Dark causes Will's mother to fall, knocking herself unconscious, and his sister, Mary, to wander off. Will rescues Mary from the Black Rider and acquires the Sign of Water from the body of a king on an ancient ship. Accompanied by Farmer Dawson, he then places a mask on the head of Herne the Hunter, who drives the Rider away. As he leaves, however, the Rider dumps Hawkin from his horse. Lying with a broken back, Hawkin is reconciled with Merriman and dies. John Smith then joins the symbols of power together. Before Will returns to his family, Miss Greythorne, now recognized as the Lady, gives him a flute for Paul and a silver hunting horn for himself.

The Greenwitch (1974) begins with the theft of the Celtic grail from the British Museum. To recover it, Great-Uncle Merry asks Simon, Jane, and Barney to return to Trewissick, where Will Stanton is also visiting. Barney goes to the beach to draw and sees a dark-haired man painting a garish abstract. The man steals Barney's own drawing and kidnaps Rufus, Captain Toms's dog. A note warns the Captain to stay away from the making of the Greenwitch. Jane joins the village women in their annual weaving of the Greenwitch, an effigy formed from branches that brings good fishing and bountiful harvests. Before the men push the Greenwitch into the sea (a ceremony that is believed to improve the fishing and harvests), Jane wishes that it could be happy. Later, the children stumble upon Rufus being chased by the dark-haired artist. The man starts to cast a spell, but Merry, Will, and Captain Toms appear in a blaze of light to drive him away. That night, Jane dreams that the Greenwitch is jealously guarding the lead tube lost during the grail adventure.

The next day, Barney and Simon again encounter the dark-haired painter. He gives them drinks and shows them the grail. He then mixes oil and water inside it, getting Barney to describe the scenes they form. Barney receives his stolen drawing and forgets everything after sipping from his drink (which contains a potion), but Simon, who only pretended to taste his drink, tells Merry about the encounter. Merry and Will, realizing that they must immediately seek help from Tethys, dive into the sea. After they give Barney's drawing to Tethys, the White Lady, she allows them to ask the Greenwitch for the lead tube. Meanwhile, the dark-haired man makes a painting that summons the Greenwitch. It refuses his commands to surrender the lead tube and spreads through the village like smoke, bringing past horrors to life. After Merry, Will, and Captain Toms arrive and remind the Greenwitch of Jane's kind wish, a crowd from the village's past forces the dark-haired painter onto a ghostly ship that takes him away. Meanwhile, the Greenwitch appears to Jane in another dream and gives Jane the lead tube. The next day, the children locate the grail in a gypsy caravan. The manuscript inside the tube enables Merry, Will, and Captain Toms to read the inscription on the grail and to gain knowledge for their battle against the Dark. Finally, Will presents Jane with an engraved gold strip to throw into the sea as a gift for the Greenwitch.

In **The Grey King** (1975), Will goes to Wales to recuperate from hepatitis. He meets an albino boy named Bran Davies. Merriman has instructed Bran to help Will in his quest to acquire a harp that will wake the Six Sleepers. Caradog Prichard, claiming that Cafall, Bran's dog, is a sheep killer, now threatens to shoot it. Shortly afterwards, Will is helping John Rowlands when something attacks a sheep. Will soon learns that the Grey King, a lord of the Dark, is making foxes attack the sheep. A fire now traps Will, Bran, and Cafall on the mountain, where foxes surround them. To escape, Will casts a spell and enters a great hall in the mountain, where three Lords of the High Magic test Bran and Will with riddles. Having answered them correctly, Will receives a golden harp. When Will, Bran, and Cafall exit the mountain, Cafall chases a gray fox. Unable to see the fox, everyone believes that Cafall is attacking the sheep, and Caradog Prichard kills him.

Rowlands now tells Will that Gwen, Bran's mother, brought her baby to Owen Davies and disappeared shortly after Prichard tried to assault her. Afterwards, while retrieving his harp, Will needs a spell to control the angry Prichard. Heading home, Will sees a fox change to resemble Rowlands's dog, Pen. A misty presence, the Grey King, then orders him to abandon his quest. Because Prichard is trying to kill Pen, Will and Rowlands take him to Idris Jones. After Rowlands and Jones leave for town, Bran arrives to warn that Prichard is coming. Will, Bran, and the dog therefore take refuge in a deserted cottage. The Grey King flattens Pen to the floor, so Will leaves to get the harp to break the spell. During his absence, Owen Davies arrives, tells Bran that he and Gwen lived there, and shows him the note Gwen left. Feeling new power, Bran speaks words that break the spell, and then he leaves with his father. As Will returns to meet them, Prichard grabs him. Will creates a huge wave to terrify Prichard, but Prichard gives himself to the Dark and counters Will's spell. Will then plays the harp, awakening the Sleepers, six riders who salute Bran. Enraged, Prichard throws the harp into the lake and then tries to kill Pen. When John Rowlands tackles him, Prichard collapses into madness. Will thus realizes that Bran is the Pendragon, son of Arthur and Guinevere (Gwen), who had Merriman take him to the future because she feared that Arthur might not accept him as his own.

Silver on the Tree (1975) concludes the sequence with a chaotic melange of bizarre adventures in various settings and time periods. It begins with bullies taunting a Sikh boy, supposedly evidence of the malignancy of the rising Dark. Will and Merriman then relive their hiding of the Signs in Roman Britain in order to retrieve them at the modern excavation of Caerleon. The action shifts to Wales, where the vacationing Drew children meet Will and Bran. The Lady appears to Jane and gives her a message. The monstrous "afanc" demands that Jane tell it what the Lady said, but Bran commands the creature to leave. Because of the message, Will and Bran go to the Lost Land. The Drews, after meeting John Rowlands and his wife, Blodwen, find themselves in the time of John's grandfather, Captain Evan Rowlands. When Caradog Lewis, a sawyer working for the Dark, beats Evan, Simon tries to help, but Merriman must rescue him, thereby missing his chance to go to the Lost Land.

Meanwhile, in the Lost Land, Will and Bran are seeking the crystal sword. The bard Gwion, also known as Taliesin, guides them, and the Black Rider, the White Rider, and other riders of the Dark hound them. Will and Bran pass a test by finding their way through a maze of mirrors, and then they head towards the crystal palace. A giant horse skeleton attacks them, but they find refuge in a cottage with a hawthorn on its roof. The hawthorn's flowers fall on the horse and destroy it. After Will blows his horn to stop a spinning wheel blocking the entrance, he and Bran enter the palace, where King Gwyddno Garanhir, maker of the sword, gives the weapon to Bran. In revenge, the Dark destroys the Lost Land with a flood. Will and Bran escape to their own time and meet the Drews, but the White Rider snatches Barney, forcing them to go to the time of Owain Glyndwr to rescue him.

The scene now shifts to a train, which the major characters eventually board. During the journey, Blodwen Rowlands, revealed to be an agent of the Dark, transforms into the White Rider and gallops off. The train becomes a boat, with the Lady at its prow. Arthur, in another boat, asks Bran to join him after his quest, but the Black Rider challenges Bran's right to participate. Asked to judge the case, John Rowlands dismisses the pleas of Blodwen and gives Bran the right to continue. The Drews, Will, Merriman, and Bran then hold the signs of power and form a circle around an oak with budding silver mistletoe, which Bran is to cut with the crystal sword. Herne appears with the Sleepers, and the Black and White Riders lunge at the tree. To enable Bran to use both hands, John Rowlands takes his place in the circle. Bran cuts the mistletoe, ending the rising of the Dark. Afterwards, the Lady has John Rowlands forget his wife's betrayal, Bran chooses to remain in the twentieth century, and Merriman makes the Drew children forget their adventures.

CHARACTERS: Because the immortal beings in Cooper's books are there to fulfill predetermined destinies, there is no opportunity for conventional heroism. The immortals therefore become one-dimensional figures, while the major mortal characters do not learn and grow by participating in moral battles because they lose all memory of their experiences.

The parents of the Drew children are **Dr. Dick Drew**, an affable man who loves to fish, and **Ellen Drew**, a painter. Throughout the books, they remain unaware of their children's adventures. **Simon Drew**, the oldest of the children, is filled with self-importance. He longs to lead his siblings and verges on the obnoxious when he is correct or understands something more quickly than they do. He is logical and observant, figuring out how to align topographical features during the search for the grail. He is also brave and quick-witted, seizing the map and running when Polly Withers tries to take it, throwing the grail to Uncle Merry when Hastings tries to take it from Barney, and jumping on Caradog Lewis to protect Evan Rowlands. Simon is particularly astute when he refrains from drinking an orange beverage that the black-haired artist gives him, thereby escaping a spell. Simon, like his siblings, resents the presence of Will on the second trip to Trewissick, but he eventually comes to like and support Will.

Jane Drew, Simon's sister who wears her hair in a ponytail, is intuitive. She immediately dislikes Norman Withers, and she distrusts Mrs. Palk. Her sense of cold uneasiness makes her refrain from telling too much to Mr. Hastings. She is, however, naive, neglecting to tell Merry about her visit to the vicarage because she does not think that it is important. Because she is compassionate and feels sorry for the Greenwitch, the Greenwitch is drawn to her in her dreams, revealing the existence of the lead tube and then actually delivering it to her. Similarly, the Lady chooses her as the medium for delivering a message. Although the afanc terrifies Jane, she bravely resists it and has enough wit not to forget the message she was given.

Barney Drew (Barney is short for Barnabas), the youngest in his family, is a fair-haired boy with an extensive knowledge of Arthurian lore. Consequently, he regards the search for the grail as a personal quest. Barney is perceptive and artistic. By closing his eyes, he visualizes the landscape and thereby understands that the grail map is a perspective drawing. Barney also has wit: he tries to deceive Miss Withers when she asks about maps, and he feigns ignorance when Mr. Hastings questions him. And Barney is noble and dedicated: he risks his life by crawling beneath rocks blocking the passage in the grail cave, and he refuses, even when threatened with death, to give information to Owain Glyndwr in case Owain serves the Dark. He possesses the common sense and self-control to resist Hastings's intimidation and does not foolishly surrender the grail. By his second visit to Trewissick, Barney has begun to express his artistry through drawings. Although Barney is immature at times (he feels hostility to Will before knowing anything about him) he gradually matures and accepts the need to cooperate with others.

Will Stanton, a round-faced boy with blue-gray eyes and brown hair, is the seventh son of a seventh son (the first Stanton child died in infancy). On his eleventh birthday, Will undergoes a rebirth, awakening to his true identity as the last of the Old Ones, immortals destined to serve the Light. Specifically, Will is the Sign-seeker, who must gather the magical items that prophecies say are to be used against the Dark. Will instantly acquires immense power and knowledge: he can travel through time and communicate telepathically in Old Speech. At first, Will is torn between his boyish emotions and the dispassionate understanding of an Old One. For example, when the Lady and Merriman are teaching him about his identity, he breaks the magic circle because the Dark makes him think that his mother is begging to enter the hall. Such human moments, however, are infrequent. As an immortal, Will is immune to harm. Furthermore, he does not expend much effort in gathering the signs, doing little more than follow instructions. Will does not need to grow as a person, and his adventures do not significantly test him. For example, he has previously learned the answers to the riddles he is asked inside the mountain from the Book of Grammarye. Will almost sleepwalks through his adventures, coming through them primarily by remembering some preordained solutions. His one moment of grandeur comes when he refuses to trade the signs for Mary's safety, an act of cold defiance reminiscent of Merriman's treatment of Hawkin. When Will is secondary, he is a device for character revelation. His presence thus tests the sympathy and insight of both the Drew children and John Rowlands.

The rest of the Stantons are minor characters. **Roger Stanton**, a round, chubby-faced jeweler, is a family man so stubbornly proud of his abilities to protect and support his family that he must be tricked into going to the manor during the snowstorm. A man without racial prejudice, he contrasts with the father of one of the bullies who taunted the Sikh boy. **Alice Stanton**, his wife, is a broadbeamed, red-faced, motherly woman. They have five sons and three daughters, not counting Will or the first son they lost. **Stephen**, a lieutenant in the Royal Navy, is attached to Will and sends him the mask that becomes Herne's head. He stops a bully from attacking the Sikh boy, thereby showing that his father has raised him to be moral and sensitive. **Max**, an art student in London, is the biggest member of the family. Mechanically minded **Robin** hides his love of music because he doesn't want to appear enthusiastic about something as "ladylike" as carol singing. His twin, **Paul**, the family genius, who wears horn-rimmed glasses, plays the flute and seems more sensitive to strange occurrences than the other family members. **James** loves to tease his siblings, but he is fair-minded. **Gwen**, the eldest sister, helps with the cooking. Sixteen-year-old **Barbara** adopts a superior tone when talking to James. Like James, plump fourteen-year-old **Mary** loves to tease. The Dark uses her concern for her family to trick her into leaving the house, but the Light clouds her memory so that she remembers only a horse ride.

Bran Davies, whose given name means "crow," is the "raven boy" mentioned in the poem that guides Will's quest. Bran, an albino, has white hair and skin, and he often wears dark glasses to protect his strange tawny-golden eyes. Used to being an alien among the dark-haired Welsh, he discovers that he is really the son of King Arthur and Guinevere. His mother, fearing that Arthur would not accept that Bran was his son, enlisted Merriman's aid and brought him into the twentieth century, where Owen Davies raised him. Bran is sometimes bitter about his suffering and contemptuous of the English. When he begins to intuit his special identity, he changes, becoming more authoritative. He is particularly forceful in dismissing the afanc. Although he accompanies Will on many adventures and cuts the mistletoe which ends the rising of the Dark, Bran is one-dimensional. At the end of the series, however, he gains complexity. Accepting that human ties are more important than a heroic destiny, he decides not to join Arthur at the back of the North Wind. Instead, he chooses to return to the mundane world to become an ordinary human boy with no recollection of his heroic ancestry but with the love of adopted father and friends. **Owen Davies**, who adopted Bran, is ordinary, except that he has no laughter in him. Gwen's disappearance devastated him, but Owen raised Bran as his own. Irrationally, he feels as guilty as a man who had fathered an illegitimate child. Therefore, he plunged himself into a stern, penitential religion. He reconciles with Bran after revealing how devoted he was to Gwen.

The one character who appears in every volume is **Professor Merriman Lyon** of Oxford University. The Drew children call him **Great-Uncle Merry** or, more affectionately, **Gumerry**, but he is not related

to them. Merriman is actually the first and oldest of the Old Ones, and his name, as Barney Drew perceives, indicates his archetypal identity: Merry Lion, Merlion, Merlin. He thus shows due reverence whenever King Arthur appears. In appearance, Merriman resembles the archetypal wizard, being tall and straight with thick, wild, white hair, a hawk's curved nose, and deep-set eyes. In the first and third books, he is an avuncular advisor and protector. With his vast knowledge, he helps the Drew children to understand their map. He later warns them not to judge Will before knowing him. He keeps his promise that no harm will come to them by arriving in the nick of time to save Simon from Bill Hoover, by rescuing the three children after they recover the grail, and by chasing away the painter when the Drews find Rufus. He takes an active role in bargaining with the Greenwitch, but it is Jane's human sympathy, not his magical power, that causes the Greenwitch to surrender the lead tube. In the final volume, Merriman saves Simon from drowning, thereby losing the opportunity to enter the Lost Land. Because he is an Old One who places the cause of the Light above the concerns of any individual, Merriman does not appreciate human emotions. As a result, he shows little regard for Hawkin's feelings, using him without understanding how much he is hurting him. After the defeat of the Dark, Merriman indicates that he will never appear again.

The Lady is a small, fine-boned, fragile old woman who wears a great rose-colored ring and leans on a stick. She is present on two occasions when Will must place candles in special holders to drive back the Dark. Each one seems to exhaust her, but she appears during two Hunting of the Wren rituals, one on the day after Christmas and the other on Twelfth Night. Because she takes the place of the dead wren and seems to be resurrected in these ceremonies, she may symbolize the reviving year or life. In the final volume, she is a misty figure who helps the Light by giving an important message to Jane. Identifying Jane with Juno, Roman protectoress of females, she says that they are alike. In any case, her power as part of the High Magic seems absolute: both the Light and the Dark are bound by her decisions.

Several Old Ones aid Will. **Miss Greythorne** appears in the modern world as the imperious mistress of the manor. Thin-faced and bright-eyed, with her gray hair always piled in a knot, she has not walked since she was injured in a fall from a horse as a young woman, but she refuses to be seen in a wheelchair. Will also sees her as a charming younger woman at the manor in 1875. In the first instance, she helps him get the Sign of Wood, and in the second, she provides the opportunity for him to study the Book of Grammarye. **Farmer Frank Dawson**, who has a weathered face and dark eyes, gives Will the Sign of Iron. He protects Will during the early stages of his awakening. **John Wayland Smith**, an English incarnation of the Scandinavian Volund, or smith of the gods, protects Will during his first meeting with the Rider, and he joins all of the signs at the end of Will's quest. **Old George Smith**, Dawson's farmhand, becomes a guide and tutor, leading Will to Herne. **Captain Toms**, an elderly man with a short gray beard, walks with a stick because he has gout. He aids Merry and Will in opposing the dark-haired artist and in dealing with the Greenwitch.

John Rowlands, who is honored as the best man around with sheep and a person with encyclopedic knowledge, is not big, but he exudes strength. On several occasions, he is a brave, quick-thinking helper, stopping Caradog Prichard from killing Pen and taking Bran's place in the circle around the tree. Sensitive and intelligent, John senses that Will has power, and he finds it unseemly. His most important function, therefore, is to represent human values and emotions in a world of moral absolutes. Calling those of the Light fanatics because they place absolute good above mercy and charity, he declares that he would put human beings above principles. When asked to judge Bran, he thus decides that, since Bran's failure to speak the language of the past would isolate him and since he has formed loving bonds in the present, Bran truly belongs in the present. Although deeply hurt because the Light exposed Blodwen's evil nature and ruined his happiness, he has the strength to resist false emotional appeals. Insisting that humans have free will, he therefore dismisses Blodwen's claim that she has been possessed by the Dark. Ironically, however, John becomes incapable of choosing his own future. Faced with the choice of remembering that Blodwen was of the Dark or of forgetting her role and living in sadness at her death in the mortal realm, he has the Lady choose for him. Protectively, she makes him forget the evil.

Some figures from myth and history also appear. **Herne the Hunter**, the legendary stag-headed hunter of Windsor forest, traditionally identified as a bringer of death, conveniently wraps things up in *The Dark Is Rising*. He disposes of the Dark, but it is unclear why he hunts the Dark and why the immortal Rider should fear him. In the final volume, he joins the six Sleepers and drives the Dark completely outside of time. **Tethys**, the Greek goddess of the sea, is called the **White Lady**. Because she is the sea itself, Merry and Will cannot see her. As a major force of the Wild Magic (nature itself) she does not participate in the battles of the force of High Magic, the Light and the Dark. Flattery, in the form of the gift of Barney's drawing, does make her give the Light a chance to negotiate with the Greenwitch.

Gwion, also known as **Taliesin**, the magical bard of Welsh myth, is a small man with a strong-featured face, curly gray hair, and a curly gray beard that has a dark stripe down its center. He takes the place of Merriman in the Lost Land, being guide and advisor during the quest for the crystal sword. A renegade in his own land because he chooses to help the Light instead of remaining neutral, he is a devoted servant to King Gwyddno Garanhir, proving his loyalty by remaining when the destructive floods start. **King Gwyddno Garanhir**, maker of the crystal sword, is a symbol of artistic despair. Having made the sword for the Light, he feared that he would never again do anything of worth. In despair, he locks himself in his crystal palace with the sword. He has dreamed about Bran as the one who would deliver him; Bran fulfills that prophesied role and releases him from despair. **Owain Glyndwr** (Owen Glendower, who revolted against Henry IV in 1400) is a good leader who fights the Dark in the form of the English oppression of the Welsh people. **King Arthur**, a semi-divine authority figure, is the first and greatest of the fighters against the Dark. He has blue eyes set in a sunburned face, gray-streak brown hair, and a gray beard. Apparently connected to the High Magic, he appears as one of the lords asking Will and Bran riddles. His most notable appearance is at the end of the series, when he offers to take Bran back of the North Wind. When Bran later decides to remain an anonymous mortal, Arthur smiles on his son with pride and then ferries the Lady away.

Although it seems mythological, Cooper invented **the Greenwitch**, a figure woven from branches: hazel for the frame, hawthorn for the body, and rowan for the head. Made by women, it is a fertility symbol that is pushed into the sea to ensure good fishing and fruitful harvests. Once made, it becomes sentient, feeling loneliness and sadness. It also becomes possessive, delighting in having a secret—the lead tube—that it can withhold from humans. Although belonging to the Wild Magic of nature, the Greenwitch becomes an agent of retributive justice. It turns the ambitious artist into a scapegoat who is removed to the outer edges of Time, and then, moved by Jane's unselfish wish for its happiness, it gives Jane the lead tube.

The Black Rider is the major antagonist and representative of the Dark. He is a tall man with longish, red-brown hair. He wears a long black cloak and rides a black steed with fiery eyes. He is arrogant and domineering. He also appears as **Mr. Mitothin**, using Mr. Stanton's invitation to enter the house, acquiring an ornament and a strand of Mary's hair that he later uses in a magic spell to trap Mary. Although the Rider is impressive in appearance and is certainly vicious in throwing down the Walker, he is actually an ineffective villain. He fails to harm Mary or to do much of the damage he so frequently threatens. He seems most dangerous when he cunningly asks that Rowlands decide whether Bran can continue, but his callous dismissal of Rowlands's questions about human concerns dictates his own defeat. Furthermore, he is easily beaten, simply fleeing when Herne arrives.

Blodwen Rowlands is both the friendly wife of John Rowlands and **the White Rider**, the white-hooded Lord of the Dark who takes Barney into the past, where he risks being executed as a spy. Unfortunately, as a human she does nothing overt to serve the Dark. (Jane senses, however, that her knitting needles are saying, ''into the dark,'' a spell that is ludicrous at best.) Because Blodwen appears only as a pleasant woman with a soft, melodious voice until she is exposed, her duplicity has little dramatic force. After John dismisses her claim that she was possessed, however, she says, in the voice of the White Rider, that he was always a fool, showing that she never genuinely loved him.

The Grey King, identified in local legend with the mist on the mountain, is supposed to be the most dangerous of the Lords of the Dark. Through warestones (tiny stones that are placed in various locations) the Grey King is able to keep tabs on his enemies and to exert some power over them. He appears to Will in an unearthly shape as a huge figure of mist, warning him to abandon his quest. **The afanc**, a gigantic creature with an iridescent-green body and fish-white belly, has a long neck, a fringy mane, and a small, pointed head with hornlike antennae and black teeth. The Dark uses it to send threats into Jane's mind. When it finally speaks itself, it has a cold, high, thin voice. Although terrifying in appearance, it actually has no power, and Bran contemptuously sends it away.

Duplicity is central to many who serve the Dark. **Mr. Hastings**, whom Uncle Merry has known under various names, is the chief agent of evil in the first volume. Tall, dark, and forbidding, he has thick black eyebrows that grow together in the middle. He has a deep, cold voice that he makes silky and gentle while persuading others. When he can't persuade, he resorts to hypnotic mind control or violence. He is deceitful, letting Jane think that he is a vicar and telling Barney that Merry is concerned only about his own scientific reputation. **Mrs. (Molly) Palk**, a large, red-faced village woman hired to be the Drews' housekeeper, at first appears to be the very embodiment of domestic virtue and concern. She seems to be always beaming, singing hymns, and offering food. When Barney becomes sunburned, she appears protectively maternal, refusing to let him go out at night with the others. In fact, she is related to Bill Hoover and has a reputation for doing anything for extra money. In league with the evil forces led by Mr. Hastings, she tries to search Barney's room for the map, and she tells a deliberate lie to get him out of town during the Carnival. **Norman Withers**, who claims to be an antique dealer, is a tanned, dark-haired man with flashing white teeth and an old-fashioned way of talking. He disguises the fact that he is a servant of evil, appearing in immaculate white flannels at the Drew house and in the white robes of a sheik during the Carnival, where he kidnaps Barney. **Polly Withers**, supposedly his sister, is equally deceptive in appearance. A slim, pretty girl with twinkling eyes and black curls, she temporarily reveals her true nature when she tries to take the map from the children: rage contorts her face until it is neither pretty nor young. During the carnival, she dons the costume of a black cat, perhaps symbolizing that she is the familiar or servant of the black wizard Mr. Hastings. **Bill Hoover**, a tall, dark-haired boy with a short, thick neck and curiously flat face, is a lower-class bully. Obviously enamored of Polly Withers, he does her bidding.

Maggie Barnes, Farmer Dawson's apple-cheeked milkmaid, is another innocent-appearing servant of the Dark. She acts like a witch, casting a spell on Will to steal his signs and going into the past to tempt Hawkin into betraying Merriman. The nameless **dark-haired artist** has dark eyes and a white face. His wild abstract painting expresses his demented moral state; his absurd kidnapping of Rufus makes the forces of the Dark seem ridiculous. He has powers, casting a spell over Barney, but his clumsy methods enable Simon to fake a trance. Painting with mad concentration, the dark-haired artist is also able to turn his painting into a light-emitting spell that summons the Greenwitch. His ambition is to acquire Things of Power so that he can bribe his masters into making him a lord of the Dark. The Greenwitch, however, makes him a scapegoat for the past sins of the community, and the artist is taken in a flying ship to the outer edges of Time.

Caradog Prichard, a thick-set, chunky man with thinning red hair and a sneering, malevolent grin, is patently nasty. Because Gwen was an unmarried woman with a child, he assumed that she would submit to him and then tried to rape her when she resisted his advances. After being stopped, he resents Owen Davies, with whom Gwen stayed, and Bran, her son. He is used by the Dark to create turmoil, especially through his hot-headed insistence on shooting the dogs for killing sheep. In the end, the Dark uses him as a shield while trying to prevent Will from waking the Sleepers. When the Dark fails, he collapses into insanity. Red-haired **Caradog Lewis**, who physically and temperamentally resembles Prichard, is evidently his ancestor. A sawyer who serves the Dark by making ships that sink, he is warned by Merriman that the Dark will vengefully destroy any of his ancestors over whom it gains power.

The most complex and interesting character in the entire sequence has a dual identity as Hawkin and the Walker. After his parents died, **Hawkin**, who comes from the thirteenth century, was raised as Merriman's son and liegeman. A small, energetic, cheerful, and friendly young man who is childishly fond of his dapper green velvet coat, he is proud to be granted the privilege of moving through time to serve Merriman. He seems so happy and nonchalant about this service that he even instructs Will on the intricacies of time travel. Hawkin does not, however, fully appreciate the risk he runs. To protect the Book of Grammarye from the Dark, Merriman has arranged for it to be removed from its hiding place in a clock only if he is touching Hawkin. Furthermore, if while doing so Merriman touches the clock's pendulum, Hawkin will die. When Merriman removes the book, Hawkin is shocked by both the reality of his peril and the callous disregard for his life that Merriman displays. Lacking a sign that his beloved master loves him in return, Hawkin is filled with horror, outrage, and hatred. He thus changes from faithful servant to evil betrayer, plotting with Maggie Barnes against the Light. Consequently, the Light punishes him, stripping him of his proud identity to transform him into **the Walker**, a nameless, penitential figure reminiscent of the Wandering Jew or the Ancient Mariner. A dirty, shambling tramp with greasy gray hair and a wizened but crafty face, the Walker has wandered for centuries carrying the Sign of Bronze. After Will relieves him of his burden, however, the Walker retains his bitterness. Accepting the promises of the Dark that he will wear Will's signs and be the new Sign-Seeker, he betrays a second time, calling the Dark to bring coldness to the manor. The Old Ones stop this second betrayal only by sedating his bitter, mortal mind, rendering him unconscious. The pathos of his situation, of course, is that the Dark has no more concern for his feelings as an individual mortal than the Light does. When he has no more use for him, the Rider throws down the Walker, breaking his back. After Merriman then assures the Walker that he had the freedom to rest if he had only chosen it instead of a second betrayal, the Walker is reconciled to Merriman, calling him "Master" and then dying. His body is taken back to the thirteenth century for burial.

Further Reading

Authors and Artists for Young Adults. Vol. 13. Detroit: Gale Research, 1994.

Berger, Laura Standley, ed. *Twentieth-Century Young Adult Writers.* 1st ed. Detroit: St. James, 1994.

Children's Literature Review. Vol. 4. Detroit: Gale Research, 1982.

Collier, Laurie, and Joyce Nakamura, eds. *Major Authors and Illustrators for Children and Young Adults.* Detroit: Gale Research, 1993.

Contemporary Authors New Revision Series. Vol. 37. Detroit: Gale Research, 1992.

De Montreville, Doris, and Elizabeth D. Crawford, eds. *Fourth Book of Junior Authors.* New York: H. W. Wilson, 1978.

Rees, David. "The Dark Is Risible." In *What Do Draculas Do?: Essays on Contemporary Writers of Fiction for Children and Young Adults.* Metuchen, N.J.: Scarecrow Press, 1990.

Hunt, Caroline C., ed. *British Children's Writers since 1960: First Series.* Vol. 161 of *Dictionary of Literary Biography.* Detroit: Gale Research, 1996.

Something about the Author. Vols. 4, 64. Detroit: Gale Research, 1973, 1991.

Something about the Author Autobiography Series. Vol. 6. Detroit: Gale Research, 1988.

Helen Cresswell

1934-, English author

Ordinary Jack

(novel, 1977)

PLOT: The quest for a meaningful identity is a dominant theme in many children's books, but in *Ordinary Jack* it is primarily a device to launch slapstick pandemonium. Jack Bagthorpe's family is brilliant. His parents, Henry and Laura Bagthorpe, and his siblings, William, Tess, and Rosie, each excel in several activities. Jack, who does not excel in anything, longs to be an equal. The chaos that punctuates his attempts to achieve his wish begins at Grandma's birthday party, attended by Grandma, Grandpa (Alfred), Aunt Celia and Uncle (Russell) Parker, their four-year-old daughter, Daisy, and the Bagthorpes. Zero, Jack's dog, is under the table, where Daisy is playing with firecrackers. Frightened by a noise, Zero rushes out, pulling down the tablecloth and lighted birthday cake, which causes the fireworks to explode and sets fire to the Bagthorpe home. The next day, Uncle Parker decides to help Jack by making everyone think that Jack is a prophet. While Jack writes what he is to do in a notebook, Daisy, who has become fascinated by flames, again sets fire to the Parker house.

Following Uncle Parker's instructions, Jack creates mysterious impressions. Mrs. Fosdyke, the au pair, doesn't notice, but Grandma does, falling off her chair while Rosie is painting her portrait. Jack then pretends to have a vision in which he sees a "Lavender Man Bearing Tidings." After another chaotic meal, during which Mr. Bagthorpe breaks his arm while trying to stand on his head, Uncle Parker arrives wearing a lavender suit and announces that the Bagthorpe's new au pair, Atlanta, will soon arrive from Denmark. Because Jack's vision came true, the family is wary of him. Mr. Bagthorpe—after finding Jack on his hands and knees with a stick in his mouth teaching Zero to fetch—even declares that Jack is mad. Uncle Parker now tells Jack to have a vision of a giant bubble and brown bears. This vision comes true during Rosie's outdoor birthday, when a hot-air balloon carrying two bears appears. Mr. Bagthorpe shows that the bears are costumed men and exposes the plot by producing Jack's notebook. At that moment, Daisy sets another fire, saving Jack from punishment. Later, the other Bagthorpes are grateful to Jack: they can now tease Mr. Bagthorpe, who has always condemned comic books, because he found the notebook while secretly reading Jack's comics. Judged as imaginative and mischievous, Jack is happy that, at least for awhile, the others accept him as an equal.

The Bagthorpe Saga continues with Absolute Zero *(1978),* Bagthorpes Unlimited *(1978),* Bagthorpes v. the World *(1979),* Bagthorpes Abroad *(1984),* Bagthorpes Haunted *(1985),* Bagthorpes Liberated *(1989),* Bagthorpes Triangle *(1992), and* Bagthorpes Besieged *(1995).*

CHARACTERS: Eleven-year-old **Jack Matthew Bagthorpe** feels ordinary in a family of geniuses. Although he has no outstanding athletic, intellectual, or artistic abilities, Jack possesses something the rest of his egotistical family lacks: sensitivity. Jack is particularly sensitive to Zero's feelings. Probably because of the condescension he himself has received, Jack feels that he must build Zero's confidence by constantly praising him. Furthermore, Jack takes the time to teach the dog (whom everyone else dismisses as unteachable) how to fetch. In doing so, Jack shows patience and ingenuity. Furthermore, he unconsciously establishes that those who appear to lack talent may develop and shine under the right circumstances.

Jack's sensitivity also appears during his plot. After causing a few disasters, he is careful not to distress people unnecessarily. Jack is persistent and dedicated, following Uncle Parker's instructions and carefully recording each stage of the plot in his notebook. Seeing him in a new light, his family accepts him—at least temporarily—as an equal. More importantly, because of the attention he has received, Jack gains confidence in himself and feels special.

In keeping with the zany plot, the others characters are comical eccentrics. To use their favorite expression, the Bagthorpes have "more than one

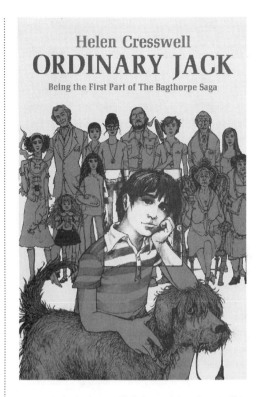

Jack tries to prove he's as special as the rest of his family in Cresswell's premier Bagthorpe book.

string to their bows." Although they are geniuses, they become foolish because they are tricked by Jack's visions. **Mr. Henry Bagthorpe**, Jack's father, is talkative, impatient, intemperate, and domineering. He can be especially categorical in his pronouncements when he knows nothing about a subject. Always shouting, he signals the oncoming of his frequent outbursts of anger by inserting long pauses between his words. Mr. Bagthorpe is full of contradictions. Although proud of his family, he ignores Jack. He despises technology, yet he makes his living by writing television scripts; he presents himself as a writer of great genius, yet he steals dialogue from Uncle Parker; he condemns comic books, but he locks himself away for an afternoon reading Jack's; he mocks Zero as incompetent, yet he himself can't properly operate a tape recorder. The exposure of his hypocrisy in reading comics has the beneficial effect of making him quieter. **Mrs. Laura Bagthorpe**, Jack's mother, is a juvenile court magistrate and, under the name Stella Bright, the author of a newspaper advice column. She remains calm in the face of her husband's outbursts, but she shows motherly concern when Jack has visions, constantly checking to see if he is ill. **William**, their oldest child, claims five strings to his bow: electronics, tennis, mathematics, drums, and darts. He tries to make himself important by claiming that he is in ham radio contact with an anonymous man who is a pirate. Love-struck, he becomes foolish when he tries to make the Danish au pair notice him. Thirteen-year-old **Tess** plays the piano and oboe, reads Voltaire in the original French for pleasure, has a black belt in judo, and is learning to speak Danish. Eight-year-old **Rosie** plays the violin, is good at mathematics, and excels at portrait painting. She also brags about being able to beat Jack at swimming. Because she likes to keep records of things, she collects the autographs of the firemen who put out the blaze at their house, and she photographs the food served at her birthday. She becomes quite upset and worried about disasters when Jack has visions. Seventy-five-year-old **Grandma Bagthorpe**, a loud, talkative woman, loves to argue. She obsessively talks about portents of death and her dead cat, a vicious beast she praises as a gentle and loving pet. Eighty-five-year-old **Grandpa (Alfred) Bagthorpe** wears a hearing aid, but he has S.D. (Selective Deafness): he can hear the birds early in the morning, but he tunes out everything his wife or the argumentative Bagthorpes say.

Six-foot-four **Uncle (Randall) Parker** is a foil to the demonstrative and self-centered Mr. Bagthorpe. He genuinely cares about Jack, and he is protective of his overly sensitive wife. Uncle Parker uses his own brand of genius to turn Jack into a prophet. Uncle Parker also provides editorial comment, calling attention-seeking a blight on the Bagthorpe family. He is himself, however, an eccentric. He is a notoriously bad driver, frightening pedestrians and his passengers. He cultivates mystery by refusing to explain how he makes his living doing something at home for a few hours a day. He is concerned with health, exercising every morning, although he lounges around drinking gin in the afternoons. Uncle Parker's attacks on the pretentious Bagthorpes are hypo-

critical, for even though he claims that he does not watch television, Jack knows that he does. Furthermore, he is attracted to dubious intellectual trends. He therefore agrees that the way to cure Daisy is through saturation, letting her set as many fires as she wishes. **Aunt Celia**, his wife, shares the Bagthorpe tendency to excel in several areas, being a potter and a poet. Exceptionally high-strung, she becomes hysterical when she receives strange telephone calls. (Actually, they come from Jack who, fearing that he will expose the plot, hangs up when Uncle Parker doesn't answer.) Four-year-old **Daisy**, their daughter, is a genius who can read, but she is also a pyromaniac, causing repeated disasters by setting fires.

Mrs. Fosdyke, the Bagthorpe's au pair, can look busy without doing much. She refuses to live with the family because the Bagthorpe house is so chaotic, but she delights in entertaining her friends at the pub with stories about her employers. Her inclination to consider the family's property her own generates comedy because she seems more concerned than the Bagthorpes when the house catches fire. Mrs. Fosdyke is also comical because of her vanity, which leads her to make attractive food for the party after learning that Rosie will photograph it. **Zero**, Jack's honey-colored mutt, received his name from Mr. Bagthorpe, who declared that the dog was worth less than nothing. Zero creates comedy after he learns to fetch by repeatedly running off with the microphone to Mr. Bagthorpe's tape recorder. But his primary function is to reveal the arrogance of Mr. Bagthorpe and the contrasting sensitivity and concern of Jack.

Further Reading

Berger, Laura Standley, ed. *Twentieth-Century Children's Writers*. 4th ed. Detroit: St. James, 1995.

Children's Literature Review. Vol. 18. Detroit: Gale Research, 1989.

Collier, Laurie, and Joyce Nakamura, eds. *Major Authors and Illustrators for Children and Young Adults*. Detroit: Gale Research, 1993.

Contemporary Authors New Revision Series. Vol. 37. Detroit: Gale Research, 1992.

De Montreville, Doris, and Elizabeth D. Crawford, eds. *Fourth Book of Junior Authors*. New York: H. W. Wilson, 1978.

Hunt, Caroline C., ed. *British Children's Writers since 1960: First Series*. Vol. 161 of *Dictionary of Literary Biography*. Detroit: Gale Research, 1996.

Rees, David. "Persons from Porlock." In *What Do Draculas Do?: Essays on Contemporary Writers of Fiction for Children and Young Adults*. Metuchen, NJ: Scarecrow Press, 1990.

Something about the Author. Vols. 1, 48, 79. Detroit: Gale Research, 1971, 1987, 1995.

Julia Cunningham

1916-, American author

Dorp Dead

(novel, 1965)

PLOT: The portraits of grim and uncaring adults who abuse helpless children have made *Dorp Dead* highly controversial. Nevertheless, this symbolic story affirms the need for love and individuality. The plot turns on the ironic significance of its major settings. After his grandmother's death, Gilly Ground, the narrator, is sent to Mrs. Heister's orphanage. Driven crazy by bell-bonging routines, Gilly seeks refuge in a crumbling tower that he imaginatively turns into his "kingdom." Here he meets a mysterious Hunter, whom Gilly briefly imagines is his father. Gilly stays away so long, however, that Mrs. Heister sends him to live with the eccentric ladder maker, Kobalt. Although the routines in Kobalt's clock-filled house are more rigid than in the orphanage, Gilly is pleased. He finds protection in his quiet and orderly life as a "royal" prisoner. Gilly does not immediately see that he is losing all identity and significance.

Gilly's life changes again shortly after he makes another visit to his tower. He meets the Hunter, who asks if Gilly is "bewitched" and gives him an envelope containing his name. Returning to Kobalt's, Gilly loses his complacency after he discovers Kobalt beats his dog, Mash, to teach it to die. Gilly then deliberately angers Kobalt by rearranging ladders. He finally rejects his new home when he discovers that Kobalt has built a new cage like the one that

*Gilly flees to a stone tower to hide from the abusive Kobalt in Cunningham's controversial **Dorp Dead**, illustrated by James Spanfeller.*

once held Mash, but it is just the right size for Gilly. Having sprained his ankle during the discovery and believing that Kobalt has already killed Mash, Gilly realizes his life is in danger, so he flees to his tower. Instead of being a safe retreat, however, the tower becomes a prison, where Gilly is vulnerable to attack by the hammer-wielding Kobalt. Fortunately, Kobalt did not succeed in killing Mash, and the dog suddenly appears and attacks Kobalt. After Gilly, who has never learned to spell properly, scratches "Dorp Dead" on Kobalt's door, he and Mash go to live with the Hunter.

CHARACTERS: The indeterminate setting and the strange action make the stylized characters seem like actors in a symbolic contemporary fairy tale. **Gilly Ground** (Gilly is short for Gillford) is eleven years old when he tells the story, but he is ten when he goes to Mrs. Heister's orphanage. He has roughly cut, brown hair, green eyes, and what he calls a "foxy" face because of its narrow chin. Although he declares that he is "ferociously intelligent," he refuses to learn to spell in order to maintain a separate identity from others. Gilly is, in fact, intensely alienated. He resents his grandmother for dying and leaving him alone; and he resents Mrs. Heister because she has no concern for him as anything other than another mouth to feed. He retreats to the tower because it gives him a sense of importance. In the tower he pretends that he has a kingdom and a home. Gilly is willing at first to give up his meager independence for the security Kobalt provides. He likes Kobalt's home because it offers refuge from the incessant bells of the orphanage. Gilly is not, however, completely resistant to feelings. He tries to make friends with Mash and to give the dog a sense of worth. When his awakened curiosity leads him to find the cage Kobalt has built, he is wise enough to know that he must flee, especially because his injury makes him vulnerable to immediate attack. In the end, Gilly discovers that he must be himself if he is to have a meaningful life, so he rejects the false security of this previous refuge to become a family member in the Hunter's house. There, he declares, he no longer hides his brilliance.

In this story of wish fulfillment in which an orphan gains a place in a family, Gilly's name may be symbolic. "Gilly" is a variant of a Scots word for the attendant of a chieftain or hunter. Gilly Ground finds himself only after he rejects being Kobalt's slave and willingly attends the Hunter as a family member.

The novel has two "villains." **Mrs. Heister**, superintendent of the village Home for Children, lets her duties squeeze out her humanity. A "big, over-stuffed woman," she has a passion for bells, which symbolize her commitment to routine. She is so concerned with running her institution efficiently that she does not recognize the orphans as individuals.

A more conventional villain is **Kobalt**, the cruel and eccentric ladder maker. Like Gilly, he bears a symbolic name. It is a variant of "kobold," a type of demon that inhabits mines. Significantly, this evil man shows "subterranean relish" when he hears that Gilly has hurt his ankle, and he threatens Gilly by declaring, "I will have you under the earth sooner or later!" Even Kobalt's appearance equips him for the symbolic role of demon: he is a very short but heavily muscled man. On another level, Kobalt represents the illusion of order. He keeps a neat and clean house in which everything has its assigned place and role. Kobalt boasts that he lives "in lanes of time," and he places five clocks in every room. It is clear, however, that he is a prisoner of routine. He does not know how to make his life genuinely meaningful. His ordered life excludes kindness and love, as Gilly discovers when he can find no place in his room to put his grandmother's picture. Instead of sharing his life with others, this selfish man needs to dominate them, something that emotionally destroys them and ultimately may lead to physical death.

The novel balances these villains with two protectors. The first is **Mash**, Kobalt's dog. A bony, drab-colored animal, he symbolizes the effects of emotional abuse. Kobalt mistreats him, making him feel inferior. Gilly, relying on his knowledge of how orphans respond to kindness, treats Mash with respect in order to make him feel more important. Mash thus shows how love can change lives. He changes from a passive victim (who is mashed by Kobalt's brutality) into an active rescuer (who mashes Kobalt when he tries to kill Gilly).

The most enigmatic character in the novel is **the Hunter**. Clothed entirely in black, he carries a gun with no bullets because he hunts only "to see." He also makes Gilly see the truth about himself, suggesting that Gilly has become bewitched by contenting himself with the routines in Kobalt's house. Hunters are commonly father figures in folk tales, and this one literally takes on that role in the novel. Some critics have surmised that the nameless Hunter is Christ, a suggestion that Cunningham has met by saying that the Hunter represents someone who gives our lives "strength and meaning." The Hunter also represents adult goodness in a novel dominated by callous people: he accepts Gilly as an individual and offers help.

Further Reading

Berger, Laura Standley, ed. *Twentieth-Century Children's Writers*. 4th ed. Detroit: St. James, 1995.

Contemporary Literary Criticism. Vol. 12. Detroit: Gale Research, 1980.

Cunningham, Julia. "Dear Characters." *Horn Book Magazine* 43 (April 1967): 233-34.

Collier, Laurie, and Joyce Nakamura, eds. *Major Authors and Illustrators for Children and Young Adults.* Detroit: Gale Research, 1993.

De Montreville, Doris, and Donna Hill, eds. *Third Book of Junior Authors.* New York: H. W. Wilson, 1972.

Something about the Author. Vols. 1, 26. Detroit: Gale Research, 1971, 1982.

Something about the Author Autobiography Series. Vol. 2. Detroit: Gale Research, 1986.

Roald Dahl

1916-1990, English author

James and the Giant Peach

(fantasy, 1961)

PLOT: Like a fairy tale, this story presents a journey from loneliness and abject misery to love and happiness. James Henry Trotter is orphaned at age four when an escaped rhinoceros eats his parents. Sent to the south of England to live with Aunt Sponge and Aunt Spiker in a ramshackle house on top of a desolate hill, he is miserable for the next three years. His cruel aunts beat him, overwork him, deny him friends, and forbid him to leave the hill. One day an old man in a green suit gives James a bag of strange green objects. He tells James that they are magical and will end his sorrow and dejection if he drinks a potion made from them. James accidentally spills the magical green items, which proceed to wiggle into the earth at the base of a tree. The tree soon sprouts an enormous peach, and his aunts charge admission to see this wonder. When they send James to clean the litter left by the paying visitors, he discovers a hole at the bottom of the peach. Crawling inside, he enters a chamber in its pit and meets seven giant insects: the Ladybug, the Centipede, the Old-Green-Grasshopper, the Earthworm, the Spider, the Silkworm, and the Glow-worm.

The next morning, the Centipede bites the stem holding the peach to the tree, causing the peach to roll down the hill and kill the two aunts. It eventually lands in the ocean. When sharks attack the peach, James devises a plan to save the insects and becomes their undisputed leader. Using threads spun by the Silkworm and the Spider, James ties the peach to seagulls, who lift it into the air. The overjoyed Centipede falls from the peach into the ocean, however, and James must rescue it. Later, the Centipede mocks some Cloud-Men, who hurl hailstones. Shortly thereafter, the peach smashes into a rainbow being painted by other Cloud-Men. One tries to climb down to the peach, but James orders the Centipede to cut the string on which the Cloud-Man is descending. In anger, a Cloud-Man dumps purple paint onto the Centipede, but a torrent of water emptied from a cloud washes off the color. Over New York City, a plane cuts the threads attaching the peach to the seagulls, and it falls safely onto a spike atop the Empire State Building. After James makes a speech that calms the frightened New Yorkers, they hold a parade in celebration, during which children eat the entire peach. The whole group lives happily afterwards. The once-lonely James now makes his home in the peach stone in Central Park and entertains many friends with his fantastic story.

CHARACTERS: Dahl made the supporting characters giant insects because he wanted to do something different and felt that they would be "amusing or interesting if one gave them character." The main human character, seven-year-old **James Henry Trotter**, resembles a conventional folktale hero. Never given a physical description, he is defined completely by his actions. James undertakes a journey of wish fulfillment: he begins in lonely isolation, becomes central to a select group of friends, and winds up famous and well-loved. Although he was happy when his parents were alive, James, like many folktale heroes, experiences misery as an orphan. Deprived of all that he desires, such as friends and trips beyond his aunts' garden, he is mistreated, like a male Cinderella, and must perform domestic chores. James's fortunes change, however, once he crawls into the peach. Just as the descent into monster-filled caves marks the symbolic rebirth of heroes in myth and folklore, James's entry into the peach signals a similar transformation.

Subsequent adventures develop his previously hidden qualities. When at first James exhibits fear, the Centipede makes him a servant, just as his aunts did. When the sharks attack, however, and James cleverly proves his ability to avert potential tragedy, he becomes the acknowledged captain of the floating peach, earning everyone's admiration and trust. James displays ingenuity by utilizing the seagulls to fly with the peach. Thereafter, whenever trouble strikes, the group turns to him for a solution. He has the quick wit, for example, to order the Centipede to cut the string on which the angry Cloud-Man is descending.

James also demonstrates a hero's physical courage and loyalty when he lowers himself to the ocean to rescue the Centipede. Finally, although he feared verbally opposing his aunts, James develops a talent for using language persuasively during his journey. He thus delivers a witty rhyming speech that makes the New Yorkers cheer his unusual companions. He further demonstrates this eloquence by entertaining his numerous visitors and by writing his story. (The last sentence reveals that he is the novel's third-person narrator.)

Dahl gives four of the insects colorful personalities. The **Centipede**, like the other insects, is the size of a large dog because he has eaten the magic green objects. Although he knows that he has only forty feet, he repeatedly claims that he has one hundred. He is fond of wearing boots, but ties them with such intricate knots that he requires help removing them. Proud to be a pest, the Centipede loves fun, has a gift for composing and singing rhyming songs, and delights in teasing the Earthworm. He lacks restraint, however, and provokes the Cloud-Men with insults. Furthermore, his uninhibited joy at escaping the sharks, expressed in a wild dance, nearly kills him when he falls from the peach. He achieves happiness when he is put in charge of sales for a boot and shoe manufacturer. The **Earthworm**, who constantly bickers with the Centipede, is a pessimist. Although he boasts that farmers love him for his contributions to soil enrichment, he finds his great-

est happiness in complaining. He allows James to use him as bait to lure the seagulls, despite his fear of them. Ironically, the blind worm ends up in television commercials for cosmetics because his skin is pink and smooth. The class-conscious **Ladybug** (called the **Ladybird** in the British edition), proud that she is useful in controlling pests, points out that the manners of ladybugs with fewer than nine spots are inferior. Nevertheless, the Ladybug is kind and gentle, behaving almost like a mother to James. Before the peach starts rolling, for example, she offers to protect him under her wing. Because she is afraid of fire, she finds happiness by marrying the head of the New York fire department. The **Old-Green-Grasshopper** occasionally plays the role of the wise old man of folktales. He notices that James has yet to wonder about many things and explains some unusual traits of insects. Like the others, this "short-horned" grasshopper is proud of a unique attribute—his ability to play music by using his leg as a bow across his wing. He becomes an admired member of the New York Symphony. The other three insects play primarily supporting roles. The **Spider** and the **Silkworm** provide the means for James to display his ingenuity when he turns their string-making abilities into a device for survival. They learn to spin nylon thread and open a factory, producing rope for tightrope walkers. The least significant character, the **Glow-worm** provides light in the peach stone during the journey and later lights up the lamp in the Statue of Liberty.

Although they appear only briefly, the cruel aunts are vivid grotesques reminiscent of the wicked stepmothers in folktales. They differ only in physical appearance. **Aunt Sponge** is short and enormously fat. Her body resembles a white, soggy, overboiled cabbage, and she has a flabby white face in which are set small piggy eyes and a sunken mouth. **Aunt Spiker**, in contrast, is a tall, skinny woman who wears steel-rimmed glasses clipped to her nose. She has a screeching voice, and she shoots little flecks of spittle from her mouth whenever she is angry or excited. Their inability to love and to provide a true home is symbolized by their ramshackle house: isolated atop a hill, it has a scraggly garden in which nothing grows. Hard-hearted and cruel, the aunts beat James, and they refuse to address him by his name, calling him instead such insults as "disgusting little beast." Although ugly, both are vain, and they taunt each other about their appearances. Both are also greedy and try to become rich by charging admission to see the peach. They die in a classic scene of poetic retribution: James, the child they abused so mercilessly, is not only responsible for the growth of the peach but is also inside the giant fruit when it crushes them.

Charlie and the Chocolate Factory

(fantasy, 1964; revised edition, 1973)

PLOT: Although this fantasy is highly popular with children, some adult critics have attacked it as shallow, tasteless, violent, and racist. Defenders have praised it, however, as a witty satire of cautionary tales—stories in which terrible calamities befall naughty children.

Poor Charlie Bucket lives in a small house with six adults. His paternal grandparents, Grandpa Joe and Grandma Josephine, and his maternal grandparents, Grandpa George and Grandma Georgina, have been bedridden together in the only bed they own for twenty years. Charlie's mother cares for them. The family is starving because Charlie's father has lost his job at a toothpaste factory. The family's fortune changes, however, after Willy Wonka, an eccentric chocolate maker, announces a contest. He offers a tour of his secret factory and a lifetime supply of candy to the five children and their chaperons who find golden tickets hidden in his chocolate bars. Charlie is despondent that his family can't afford money for more than one candy bar, yet the day before the contest ends, Charlie finds a dollar, spends some of it on chocolate bars, and miraculously discovers the final golden ticket.

The next day, Charlie and Grandpa Joe join the other winners for their tour. Willy Wonka himself leads them into a series of fantastic underground rooms and tells them about his workers, the Oompa-Loompas. During the tour, the other children frequently disobey Willy Wonka's rules and suffer fitting punishments. In the Chocolate Room, the enormously fat Augustus Gloop greedily drinks from a river of chocolate after Willy Wonka admonishes the visitors to avoid contaminating the purity of the river. He is sucked away by the pipes that deliver the chocolate to other parts of the factory. In the Inventing Room, Willy Wonka shows the group a gum that tastes like a complete meal when chewed. Despite warnings that the process has not been perfected, the gum-loving Violet Beauregarde grabs a piece and begins chewing. She soon turns into an enormous blueberry and is carried away by the Oompa-Loompas. When Willy Wonka shows the room in which squirrels crack walnuts, the rich and spoiled Veruca Salt tries to grab a squirrel as a pet, but instead the animals throw her and her parents down a garbage shoot. When Willy Wonka demonstrates a camera that can transport candy to a television screen, the video-loving Mike Teavee deliberately ignores Wonka's warnings and darts in front of the camera, which reduces him in size and inserts him in the television screen. When he is taken out, Mike is only one inch tall. Willy Wonka then reveals to Charlie, the only remaining golden ticket holder, that he has won the entire factory. Using his glass elevator, Willy Wonka flies Charlie and Grandpa Joe home, gathers the rest of Charlie's family, and flies them back to live in the factory.

The sequel, Charlie and the Great Glass Elevator, *was published in 1972.*

CHARACTERS: Like characters in traditional cautionary tales, most of these are one-dimensional representatives of a single vice or virtue. **Charlie Bucket** is the only bland character in the book, representing the ideal good boy. He is polite and considerate, especially to his grandparents. When the family faces starvation, he refuses the extra food his mother tries to slip to him. As a consequence, he becomes thin and his pinched face turns frighteningly white. Charlie's one idiosyncrasy is his love of chocolate, yet unlike the other children in the book, Charlie has self-control. He is given only one chocolate bar a year on his birthday, but he makes it last a month.

The other prize-winning children are unlikable satirical characters, identified primarily by a single controlling passion. **Augustus Gloop** is a glutton. A grotesquely fat nine-year-old boy, Gloop has a face like a ball of dough with greedy eyes that resemble small currants. His selfish behavior causes the pollution of the river of chocolate. His trip to the chocolate factory ultimately alters his physical appearance: squeezed by the chocolate pipe, he emerges thin as straw. **Veruca Salt** is a selfish and spoiled rich girl. (Willy Wonka emphasizes her unpleasant disposition when he delightedly points out that a "veruca" is a plantars wart.) She coerces her weak parents into giving her everything she wants by throwing tantrums that can last for hours. When she insisted on winning a golden ticket, her father obliged by buying millions of chocolate bars and having his factory workers open them until a ticket appeared. Veruca demands everything that she sees and never accepts a refusal. Appropriately, she is thrown into a garbage chute when she disobeys Mr. Wonka by trying to seize a squirrel. She and her parents are still covered with refuse when they go home. **Violet Beauregarde** is a habitual gum chewer. She has been chewing the same piece of gum for three months, storing it at night on a bedpost and sticking it behind her ear for meals. Violet selfishly grabs an experimental gum in the Chocolate Factory and turns into a rotund blueberry when the dessert portion of the treat malfunctions. Her first name achieves special significance because her skin remains purple after she returns to her regular size and shape. **Mike Teavee** represents the mindless and lazy child addicted to television. He wears eight toy pistols, which he shoots off during television shows. Lacking interest in all other pursuits, he becomes angry when reporters interrupt him during a television program. During the tour, Mike's all-consuming obsession with TV leads to his size reduction to television-screen proportions. The Oompa-Loompas try to stretch him back to his normal size, but he ends up ten feet tall. Willy

Wonka cheerfully predicts that basketball teams will recruit him.

The only member of his family who is individualized is **Grandpa Joe**, Charlie's paternal grandfather. The eldest of the grandparents at ninety-six-and-a-half years, Grandpa Joe is delicate and weak. Like the other grandparents, he has been completely bedridden for twenty years. Grandpa Joe's one delight is his grandson. He generously spends a dime that he has kept hidden to buy a chocolate bar, giving Charlie a chance at winning the tour. When Charlie eventually does win with the dollar he found, Grandpa Joe is rejuvenated by joy and leaps out of bed. During the visit to the factory, he seems somewhat frightened that he will be left behind and clings to Charlie's hand. Nevertheless, Grandpa Joe shows more wit than the parents accompanying the rest of the children. He recognizes the misbehavior of the other children and defends Willy Wonka's sanity when the other adults criticize the candymaker's unusual and peculiar actions.

Willy Wonka is an eccentric creator of chocolate treats. His strange inventions generate much of the humor in the book. This small, green-eyed man with the neatly trimmed black goatee sports a plum-colored velvet tailcoat, bottle-green trousers, gray gloves, and a black top hat. He carries a gold-topped cane and moves in a rapid, spasmodic manner. His entire appearance suggests fun and amusement. In fact, his merry laughter, especially after each naughty child meets with a punishment, leads the adults to believe that he is crazy. Willy Wonka seems to delight in absolute justice because each of the victims deserves his or her fate. Impatient at interruptions, he insists on being in complete control of every situation. Critics who attack the book consider him to be an insensitive racist colonialist, charging that he cruelly fired his other workers so that he could exploit the cheap labor provided by the Oompa-Loompas. (Willy Wonka himself, of course, believes that he is saving the Oompa-Loompas from starvation.) Furthermore, critics allege, Wonka is callously negligent because he tests various inventions on Oompa-Loompas, with some disastrous consequences. They also describe Willy Wonka as an "ageist" in his disregard for the fears of the parent and grandparent chaperons. In some instances, however, he exhibits sensitivity, such as when he notices that Charlie appears to be starving and offers him a drink of the very chocolate that led to disaster for Augustus Gloop.

The **Oompa-Loompas** from Loompaland were originally described as pygmies with pure black skin and fuzzy hair who love dancing and singing. Dahl denied that he was racist in his portrayal, but he sympathized with those hurt by the description. In the revised version, they have rosy-white skin and golden-brown hair. In both versions, the men wear deerskins, the women wear leaves, and the children are naked. The Oompa-Loompas act as a chorus, singing a rhymed song which points out the moral of the child's fate following each disaster.

Fantastic Mr. Fox

(animal fantasy, 1970)

PLOT: This talking animal fantasy describes a conflict between Mr. Fox and three nasty farmers named Boggis, Bunce, and Bean. Because Mr. Fox routinely raids their farms to feed his wife and four children, the angry farmers decide to kill him. Farmer Bean leads the others to Mr. Fox's hole, where they hope to shoot him when he emerges. Although the ambush fails to kill Mr. Fox, the farmers do shoot off his tail. Farmer Bean then urges his companions to dig up the family of foxes. Mr. Fox's family, however, burrows deeper below ground. Frustrated by their inability to reach the foxes, Farmer Bean then suggests that they use mechanical shovels. While Mr. Fox and his family desperately dig even deeper, the three farmers reduce a hill to a big crater. Enraged when they still fail to reach the fox, the three farmers vow to remain at the hole until they catch him.

Confined to the burrow, the foxes become weak from starvation, but Mrs. Fox refuses to let her husband leave. Mr. Fox therefore devises a plan that allows him to save his family and yet remain underground. With the help of his four children, he digs a hole to Farmer Boggis's chicken house, where he

steals three chickens. Aided by Mr. Badger, Mr. Fox then digs his tunnel to Farmer Bunce's storehouse, where he appropriates some choice supplies, and to Farmer Bean's cellar, where he pilfers some cider. In each case, he conceals any signs of his entry. He then returns home, where he has invited the families of Badger, Mole, Rabbit, and Weasel to a feast, and everyone joins Mrs. Fox in praising her clever husband. Mr. Fox then announces that, because of the tunnels, none of the animals will ever have to risk going above ground again. Unaware of the feasting below, the three farmers continue their futile vigil at the hole's entrance.

CHARACTERS: Because Mr. Fox is dedicated to his family and the farmers are repulsive in physical appearances and manners, the reader sympathizes with the animals during the tense conflict. Although critics have compared him to the medieval Reynard, **Mr. Fox** is more than a stereotypical trickster. He is conventionally clever and exercises caution in avoiding capture by carefully approaching the farms with the wind blowing toward him. He further displays ingenuity by digging the tunnels to the three farms, by ensuring that he doesn't take too much food to be readily noticed, and by concealing all signs of his entry. Such cleverness warrants his wife's praise. What separates Mr. Fox from the archetypal prankster, however, is his love of family and his generosity with others. When Mr. Badger asks him if he isn't bothered by stealing, he points out that he does not physically attack the farmers, as they do him. He further queries whether Badger knows anyone who would not steal chickens to feed his starving children. In spite of this attitude, Mr. Fox is not amoral. He readily accepts blame for bringing starvation to Badger and the other digging animals. He atones for this by inviting them to a feast and by generously providing for their safety and prosperity in the future. In addition to his cunning behavior, Mr. Fox is an ideal family man and a considerate leader of society. **Mrs. Fox** is a cautious and loving wife. She sensibly points out that the farmers are trying to lure

Mr. Fox out of the hole and therefore advises him not to try to snatch food from them. Her major plot function, however, is to describe Mr. Fox's cleverness by exclaiming after each of his exploits that he is fantastic.

The appearance and habits of the three nasty farmers make them unsympathetic characters. Unlike the moderate Mr. Fox, who provides a varied diet for his family, all three farmers gluttonously consume the same menu every day. Hatred motivates their actions, a contrast from Mr. Fox's genuine love for his family and their well-being. An enormously fat poultry farmer, **Farmer Boggis** eats three chickens smothered in dumplings every day at every meal. **Farmer Bunce** is a pot-bellied dwarf who raises ducks and geese. He eats goose livers stuffed into doughnuts, a diet that upsets his stomach and gives him a foul temper. **Farmer Bean**, who raises turkeys and grows apples, is the most elaborately individualized character. A thin man who drinks gallons of cider instead of eating food, his scarlet gums appear more prominent than his teeth. The disgustingly dirty Farmer Bean never takes a bath or washes; consequently, his ears are "clogged with all kinds of muck and wax and bits of chewing gum and dead flies," rendering him somewhat deaf. Furthermore, he completely lacks manners: whenever he talks, he "delicately" picks his nose, and he drinks freely, but he never offers his flask to his partners. Farmer Bean insults his companions, calling Bunce a "miserable midget" when he attempts to persuade him to enter the hole. A liar as well, Bean pretends that he has already considered the possibility when Boggis accuses him of failing to foresee that the fox could dig right through a hill. He then arranges to have the hill surrounded. Farmer Bean's intense hatred, which drives him nearly insane, contributes to the dramatic excitement of Dahl's plot. At the same time, the farmer's hatred reveals the extent of the foolish nature of this supposedly clever man and his companions. Farmer Bean fails to realize that the vow to remain at the hole until he catches the fox ensures Mr. Fox's survival: with the farms unprotected, Mr. Fox has an easier job of stealing whatever food he wants while remaining concealed underground indefinitely.

The BFG
(fantasy, 1982)

PLOT: This humorous fantasy twists folktale conventions by creating unlikely heroes from a giant and his captive. When Sophie the orphan sees the BFG, the Big Friendly Giant, blowing dreams into children's heads, he kidnaps her so that she can't reveal his existence to others. He takes her to Giant Country, where he lives with nine other giants. While the other giants eat "human beans," the BFG assures Sophie that his diet consists of a fizzy drink called frobscottle and foul-tasting snozzcumbers, the only vegetable that grows there. The BFG hides Sophie when one of the giants, Bloodbottler, searches his cave for humans. Later, the BFG endures abuse from Fleshlumpeater, but he manages to smuggle Sophie to Dream Country to show her how he catches dreams.

Sophie turns from victim to hero after she learns that the nine nasty giants plan to go to England to eat little boys and girls. She devises a plan to save them using the BFG's special abilities. They journey to England, where the giant blows a dream about his child-eating counterparts into the Queen's mind. When the Queen awakens, she discovers Sophie, who introduces her to the BFG. After the Queen has her butler, Mr. Tibbs, feed him, the BFG advises her that she can capture the giants while they sleep. She therefore orders the Head of the Air Force and the Head of the Army to follow the BFG and Sophie to the unmapped land of the giants. They manage to tie up eight giants before Fleshlumpeater awakens. The BFG heroically rushes at him to stop him from consuming a soldier, but Fleshlumpeater brushes him aside. Sophie then stabs him with the pin of a brooch. Thinking quickly, the BFG convinces Fleshlumpeater that he has been bitten by a snake and thereby fools him into being tied up. Helicopters fly the giants back to England, where they are put in a deep pit and fed snozzcumbers. The Queen rewards the BFG by building him a huge house and proclaiming him the Royal Dream Blower. The recipient of a house next door to the BFG teaches him how to speak and write properly. He is then revealed to be the author of the book.

CHARACTERS: Sophie and the BFG resemble the somewhat one-dimensional characters typical of folktales, but coarse humor and language play transform them into a unique pair of unlikely heroes. The **BFG**, or **Big Friendly Giant**, was introduced in stories told by the father character in Dahl's *Danny, the Champion of the World* (1975). The BFG, a small giant at only twenty-four feet tall, has a wrinkly face, flashing eyes, a sharp nose, and huge swivelling ears. He depends on his acutely sensitive hearing both to avoid detection and to catch the dreams he blows into children's sleep. The BFG wears a black cloak that conceals him in the dark and carries a suitcase full of bottled dreams and a trumpet with which he blows the dreams into children. He glides effortlessly when he moves, and he can run so quickly that helicopters can barely keep pace with him.

The BFG has two conventional plot functions. He is, first of all, a folkloric *pourquoi* character; that is, he provides a fanciful explanation of the origin— the "why"—of human dreams. Second, the BFG is an unlikely hero. Different from the other giants, he is physically smaller, morally superior, and more intelligent than his "friends"; he refuses to eat children and must therefore subsist on a diet of the foul snozzcumbers. He philosophically points out to Sophie that giants, unlike humans, do not kill each other. Despite his strong convictions, which cause the others to ridicule and beat him, the BFG holds fast to his beliefs and hides Sophie while Bloodbottler searches his cave for a "human bean." He exhibits bravery by rushing at Fleshlumpeater, but the BFG succeeds in capturing the giant only when he employs guile and cunning. Having the wit to recognize the nasty giant's cowardice, the BFG cleverly scares Fleshlumpeater into assuming a position that leads to his uncomplicated capture.

The BFG also provides the comic center to the novel. The humor results from the BFG's equal position as an outsider with both the humans and

An illustration of the BFG by Quentin Blake for Dahl's story about a not-so-mean giant.

the giants. He seems, in fact, something like an overgrown child. He delights in the flatulence, which he calls "whizzpopping," that results from drinking frobscottle; he considers whizzpopping normal and acceptable, so he even demonstrates it for the Queen. Such coarse behavior reflects Dahl's belief that "children regard bodily function as being both mysterious and funny." What makes the BFG comically memorable, however, is his language. Self-educated from a book he found, the BFG has a habit of tangling up words. His language contains nonsense, puns, spoonerisms, and other forms of word play. The BFG speaks of Sophie's talk as "interesting babblement," but warns her not to "gobblefunk around with words," admitting that his own words get "squiff-squiddled around." He worries that he will become so thin that he is all "skin and groans," talks about searching every "crook and nanny," calls Charles Dickens "Dahl's Chickens," devises a plan that requires an attack on the giants while they are "snozzling" (sleeping), and scares Fleshlumpeater by mentioning poisonous "vindshield vipers." A measure of the BFG's intelligence and talent is that he writes the very novel that enables readers to hear the comic speech he once used.

Sophie is an orphan who wears steel-rimmed glasses with very thick lenses. Her development as an unlikely heroine follows a familiar pattern, beginning unhappily in an orphanage, where she receives cruel treatment. Her experiences in the dangerous Giant Country educate her to the evils in the world. They also provide her with the opportunity to demonstrate her innate bravery, intelligence, and compassion. Although frightened when Bloodbottler searches the cave, Sophie has the presence of mind to remain silent and hide in a snozzcumber. Later, she displays courage by stabbing Fleshlumpeater in the ankle with her brooch. She reveals her cleverness by devising the plan to plant the nightmare about child-eating giants into the Queen of England. Her compassion is evident in her concern to protect children from the giants and her love for the BFG, whom she teaches to speak, read, and write properly. By the end of the book, Sophie has matured from a dependent orphan to a confident woman. She has a house of her own—a conventional symbol for maturity—and a family, in the form of the BFG.

Two of the nine flesh-eating giants are fully developed and individualized characters. Like the other giants, the fifty-foot **Bloodbottler** is primitive in both appearance and nature. Wearing only a dirty piece of cloth around his waist, he has reddish-brown skin with black hair on his chest, arms, and stomach. Beneath his long, tangled hair, his "squashy-looking" face has a small, flat nose, tiny black eyes, and a huge mouth. Craggy yellow teeth stick out between lips that resemble purple frankfurters, and repugnant rivers of spittle pour down his chin. This foul-tempered and abusive villain possesses no redeeming qualities. **Fleshlumpeater**, the biggest and nastiest of the giants, eats children as if they were popcorn. Although he resembles Bloodbottler, Sophie notices that his tongue is jet black. Fleshlumpeater bullies the BFG by calling him names and by initiating a game in which all the giants throw the BFG into the air. Nevertheless, the cowardly Fleshlumpeater panics when he believes that a snake has bitten him. His stupidity, a typical trait of folktale giants, also renders him vulnerable

to his ultimate destruction. When the BFG convinces him that Sophie's brooch is the snake's teeth, Fleshlumpeater then foolishly closes his eyes and puts his hands and legs together, thereby essentially effecting his own capture.

The human characters play small roles in humor development and plot resolution. The **Queen of England** is an elegant, tactful, and sensible woman. After recovering from the initial shock of seeing Sophie sitting on her windowsill, she behaves with dignity and restraint, even after meeting the BFG. Still, she demonstrates her affinity with common humanity when she can't suppress a smile as the BFG demonstrates whizzpopping. Most notable as a kind and compassionate ruler, the Queen worries that children are being eaten and makes plans to capture the giants. Insisting that it would be wrong to kill them, she instead imprisons them in a pit. **Mr. Tibbs**, the Queen's butler, is a comic celebration of the stereotypically unflappable British butler. In preparing a meal for the BFG, he ingeniously devises a seating arrangement and serving plan. The **Head of the Air Force** and the **Head of the Army** are both satiric portraits of self-important authority figures. They accentuate the bravery of Sophie and the BFG because both are concerned with making a personal retreat when they encounter Fleshlumpeater. Although they have no real role in defeating the giants, they consider themselves worthy of medals.

Further Reading

Baldwin, Dean, ed. *British Short-Fiction Writers, 1945-1980.* Vol. 139 of *Dictionary of Literary Biography.* Detroit: Gale Research, 1994.

Berger, Laura Standley, ed. *Twentieth-Century Young Adult Writers.* 1st ed. Detroit: St. James, 1994.

Children's Literature Review. Vols, 1, 7. Detroit: Gale Research, 1976, 1984.

Collier, Laurie, and Joyce Nakamura, eds. *Major Authors and Illustrators for Children and Young Adults.* Detroit: Gale Research, 1993.

Contemporary Authors New Revision Series. Vol. 37. Detroit: Gale Research, 1992.

Contemporary Literary Criticism. Vols., 1, 6, 18, 79. Detroit: Gale Research, 1973, 1976, 1981, 1994.

Dahl, Roald. *Boy: Tales of Childhood.* New York: Farrar, Straus & Giroux, 1984.

———. *Going Solo.* New York: Farrar, Straus & Giroux, 1986.

————. *My Year.* London: Jonathan Cape, 1993.

De Montreville, Doris, and Donna Hill, eds. *Third Book of Junior Authors.* New York: H. W. Wilson, 1972.

Powling, Chris. *Roald Dahl.* London: Hamilton, 1983.

Rees, David. "Dahl's Chickens." In *What Do Draculas Do?: Essays on Contemporary Writers of Fiction for Children and Young Adults.* Metuchen, N.J.: Scarecrow Press, 1990.

Something about the Author. Vols. 1, 26, 73. Detroit: Gale Research. 1971, 1982, 1993.

Tresglown, Jeremy. *Roald Dahl: A Biography.* London: Faber & Faber, 1994.

West, Mark I. *Roald Dahl.* New York: Twayne, 1992.

Wintle, Justin, and Emma Fisher. *The Pied Pipers: Interviews with the Influential Creators of Children's Literature.* New York: Paddington Press, 1974.

Paula Danziger

1944-, American author

The Cat Ate My Gymsuit

(novel, 1974)

PLOT: This novel, which Danziger has called her "angriest and most autobiographical book," is about acceptance and self-respect. Overweight thirteen-year-old Marcy Lewis is miserable. Martin Lewis, her father, constantly yells at her, while Lily Lewis, her mother, takes tranquilizers and has crying spells. Although Marcy loves Stuart, her four-year-old brother, she doesn't like it when he demands that Marcy play with him and Wolf, his teddy bear. At school, Marcy is bored and quiet; embarrassed by her weight, she makes up excuses to avoid gym class.

Marcy changes when Ms. Barbara Finney becomes her new English teacher. Ms. Finney interests the class in writing and reading. She also starts Smedley, a club aimed at helping the students find out about themselves. When Mr. Frank Stone, the principal, removes Ms. Finney from the school because of her unconventional teaching methods and her refusal to recite the Pledge of Allegiance, Marcy speaks out. Soon she and her friends, Nancy Sheridan and Joel Anderson, organize a protest. The angry principal suspends the students, and

the school board cancels classes until after Ms. Finney's hearing.

Although Marcy's social life improves—she has her first date when Joel takes her to Nancy's party—her home life remains stormy. Unlike Joel's father, who supports his son, Marcy's father forbids her involvement in the protest. Marcy's mother, however, begins to change. She tries to get along with her daughter and writes to the newspaper in support of Ms. Finney. On the night of the hearing, Marcy's father sabotages the car to prevent his wife and daughter from attending, but they make other arrangements. The board reinstates Ms. Finney, who immediately resigns, declaring that she can't be an effective teacher when so many oppose her. Joel feels betrayed, but his father and Marcy help him to understand. In the following month, Marcy's mother enrolls in college, while Marcy begins to lose weight and starts to see a psychologist. She also gets a sign of coming adolescence: her first pimple.

There's a Bat in Bunk Five (1980) is a sequel.

CHARACTERS: Some critics have complained that Danziger's characters are one-dimensional stereotypes. As the novel's popularity suggests, however, many young readers recognize in these characters both themselves and adults they know.

Marcy Lewis is an overweight and acutely self-conscious thirteen-year-old in the ninth grade. Low self-esteem makes her think of herself as a blimp with wire-frame glasses and mousy brown hair. Marcy is physically awkward, and she is so embarrassed by her body that she refuses to undress for gym class. Consequently, she creates ridiculous excuses to avoid participating. Because she is shy and afraid of being hurt, she often keeps to herself.

Marcy begins to feel better about herself once Ms. Finney arrives. She gains some self-esteem when she discovers that Nancy and Joel like her in spite of her appearance. She also courageously opposes Mr. Stone and becomes a leader in the student protest. She continues to be torn by conflicting desires, however. Marcy wants to be an individual, for example, and therefore resents her mother's efforts to make her look like everyone else. Nevertheless, she drinks beer at Nancy's party because she does not want to appear different. But as she gains confidence in her identity, Marcy begins to influence others: she helps her mother to become independent, and she helps Joel to accept Ms. Finney's resignation. Although Marcy does not resolve all her problems—she continues to hate her intolerant father—she achieves greater self-acceptance, loses weight, and starts seeing a psychologist. Furthermore, although she previously dreaded acne, she shows a good-humored ability to deal with the normal problems of adolescence by naming her first pimple Agnes.

Martin Lewis, Marcy's father, is intolerant and paternalistic. His constant yelling and ever-present smelly cigar make him obnoxious. Mr. Lewis insists on conformity and despises "radicals" and their "bleeding-heart causes." A self-centered man who professes that his motto is "watch out for yourself," he has no respect for others. Thus, although he does not want to talk to his family, he insists that his wife and daughter do what he wants. When his daughter fails to behave as he wishes, he yells and then blames her for making her mother cry. His only sign of affection is providing money for shopping trips after his violent explosions. When his wife begins to resist his dictatorial ways, Mr. Lewis becomes childishly vengeful: he removes a part from the car so that his wife can't drive it to Ms. Finney's hearing.

Lily Lewis, Marcy's mother, undergoes as profound a change as her daughter. She begins the story as a worried woman who copes with stress by taking tranquilizers and crying. Although she is not as abusive as her husband, she hurts Marcy by constantly commenting on her appearance and by trying to make her look like the other children. Mrs. Lewis tries to make Marcy understand and accept her father. Ironically, Marcy eventually teaches her mother to be a liberated individual instead. Mrs. Lewis thus becomes sensitive to her daughter's feelings, defies her husband, and returns to school.

Stuart Lewis, Marcy's four-year-old brother, strengthens the contrast between Marcy and her father. Mr. Lewis berates Stuart for always carrying Wolf, his teddy bear, but Marcy cares for, talks to,

and loves Stuart. Because Stuart is too young to share the hatred that Marcy feels for their father, his presence supports Marcy's belief that adolescence brings with it a painful awareness of problems.

Two educators play contrasting roles. **Ms. Barbara Finney** is a young, progressive English teacher. She values communication as the basis for self-understanding. Ms. Finney creatively involves her students and makes them eager to read and write. She also respects them, listens to them, and makes them feel important. Because she dresses unconventionally, employs unusual teaching methods, and refuses to recite the Pledge of Allegiance, the principal considers her a radical. Actually, Ms. Finney is idealistic. She does not recite the Pledge because she believes that America does not yet offer liberty and justice for all. Nevertheless, she considers herself a good American and cares about her country and its people. Knowing that she can't be an effective teacher after dividing community opinion, she shows her dedication to good education by resigning. On the other hand, **Mr. Frank Stone**, the appropriately named principal, is a blunt and rigid reactionary. He resembles Mr. Lewis in his intolerant and domineering personality: unlike Ms. Finney, he does not listen to or try to understand the students. Marcy and her friends therefore see him as making school numbingly dull.

Marcy's friend, **Joel Anderson**, the smartest boy in the class, pulls her out of her shell and later benefits from Marcy's understanding. Joel, who has the self-confidence that Marcy lacks, likes her and insists that appearances are irrelevant. Like Marcy, however, Joel shows that middle-class children also have problems. He is particularly upset that his mother left his father. He provides an opportunity for Marcy to show her growth in confidence and understanding: when Ms. Finney resigns, Joel bitterly equates her with his mother, but Marcy pushes him toward a more mature acceptance. **Mr. Anderson**, Joel's father, contrasts with Marcy's father, providing a positive example of parenthood that Marcy's mother soon follows. A lawyer with a social conscience and a member of the school board, Mr. Anderson accepts and supports his son's decisions. He also listens to him and tries to understand his feelings. Another friend of Marcy's, the beautiful **Nancy Sheridan**, also provides opportunities for Marcy to grow. Early in their friendship, Marcy sees herself as Beast beside Beauty, and she thinks that Nancy's mother has forced her to be kind. However, Marcy later learns that Nancy likes her because of her personality and feels close enough to be honest with her.

Further Reading

Authors and Artists for Young Adults. Vol. 4. Detroit: Gale Research, 1990.

Berger, Laura Standley, ed. *Twentieth-Century Young Adult Writers*. 1st ed. Detroit: St. James, 1994.

Children's Literature Review. Vol. 20. Detroit: Gale Research, 1990.

Collier, Laurie, and Joyce Nakamura, eds. *Major Authors and Illustrators for Children and Young Adults*. Detroit: Gale Research, 1993.

Contemporary Authors New Revision Series. Vol. 37. Detroit: Gale Research, 1992.

Contemporary Literary Criticism. Vol. 21. Detroit: Gale Research, 1982.

Holtze, Sally Holmes, ed. *Fifth Book of Junior Authors and Illustrators*. New York: H. W. Wilson, 1983.

Something about the Author. Vols. 30, 36, 63. Detroit: Gale Research, 1983, 1984, 1991.

Jean de Brunhoff

1899-1937, French artist, illustrator, and author

The Story of Babar, the Little Elephant

(picture book, 1931; English translation, 1933;
published in France as Histoire de Babar, le petit
elephant*)*

PLOT: *The Story of Babar, the Little Elephant* began as a tale de Brunhoff's wife told to their children. In its expanded, published form, it has become one of the world's best-loved picture books for small children. It also initiated a series that made its central character one of the most recognizable in juvenile literature.

très content
de ses achats
et satisfait
de son élégance,
Babar va
chez le photographe.

De Brunhoff did his own illustrations for the original **Histoire de Babar, le petit elephant.**

The simple plot of *Babar* traces a circular journey, during which the central character grows up from a baby to a respected adult. The story opens with Babar's birth. He is loved by his mother and enjoys a happy childhood. One day, however, a "wicked hunter" kills his mother. The frightened Babar flees to a city, where a rich Old Lady gives him money to buy clothes. Babar goes to a department store, where he repeatedly rides the elevator before buying a green suit. Babar then goes to live with the Old Lady, eating and exercising with her. He drives a car on outings, studies under a learned professor, and entertains the Old Lady's guests with stories about the jungle. Occasionally he has sad memories of his former life.

Two years later, Babar's cousins Arthur and Celeste arrive in the city. Babar buys them clothes and gives them cakes to eat. When Arthur and Celeste's mothers come to fetch them, Babar decides to return with them to the jungle. That very day, the elephant King eats a bad mushroom and dies. When Babar arrives, the elephants admire his car and clothes, and Old Cornelius suggests that they make Babar the new king. Babar accepts on the condition that Celeste, to whom he is engaged, becomes his queen. Babar makes Cornelius a general, and then everyone celebrates the wedding and coronation. Afterwards, King Babar and Queen Celeste set out in a yellow balloon to seek further adventures.

Jean de Brunhoff produced five sequels, two of which were posthumously published: The Travels of Babar *(1932; English translation, 1934),* Babar the King *(1932; English translation, 1935),* Babar's ABC *(1936; English translation, 1937),* Babar at Home *(1938; English translation, 1938), and* Babar and Father Christmas *(1941; English translation published first, 1940). Laurent de Brunhoff continued the series after his father's death and has published more than thirty Babar books.*

CHARACTERS: As the first book in a series, *Babar* introduces characters who become substantial only through the accumulated episodes of later adventures. **Babar the Elephant** develops through a variety of experiences. He enjoys a happy infancy and a joyous childhood that poignantly contrast with the sad death of his mother. He is then pictured crying overly large tears that foreshadow the sensitive nature he displays as an adult, when thoughts of his mother again make him cry. When Babar goes to the city, he immediately admires fine clothes, showing that he has an innate sense of sophistication. Once he gets the green suit—which he is never parted from again—he ceases to walk on all fours and stands upright like a human. (Much of his unique appeal is in the pictures of a large clothed elephant performing normal human actions.) Babar matures as he becomes more human. Before buying his suit, for example, he acted like a small child by riding the elevator ten times. Afterwards, he follows a serious routine. He shows his diligence and intelligence by being a good student, and he demonstrates social skills by elegantly leaning against the mantle while he converses with the Old Lady's dinner guests. Babar is also affectionate, joyfully greeting Arthur and Celeste and kissing the Old Lady farewell when he leaves her.

Babar's most notable traits in later books are hinted at in this first one. He is generous, and he values family life. He buys Arthur and Celeste clothes, treats them to cakes, accompanies them back to the

jungle, and insists that he will be king only if Celeste is queen. He shows signs of being a benevolent and wise leader when he makes Cornelius a general. Various critics have seen political messages in Babar's actions, which can be interpreted as supporting colonialist policies: Babar and his people become better once they wear clothes and adopt "civilized" habits. In this first book, however, Babar undergoes a more universal maturation process. His development toward maturity culminates in the conventional fairy tale symbol of adult competence and independence: kingship.

The **Old Lady** is the only human character of continuing importance in the series. A rich woman, she uses her wealth to bring happiness to others. Her basic goodness is also evident in her fondness for elephants and in her sympathetic understanding of Babar's longing for a suit. She becomes a mother figure. She gives Babar a home that provides the material well-being and social opportunities necessary for him to develop into a good adult. Other characters are sketched in only the barest outline. **Cornelius**, the oldest elephant, demonstrates that he has the wisdom that conventionally goes with age by suggesting that Babar should be king. **Celeste**, Babar's cousin and wife, shows a love of adventure by running to the city. She will later prove to be a good wife and gentle mother.

Further Reading

Bingham, Jane M., ed. *Writers for Children: Critical Studies of Major Authors since the Seventeenth Century.* New York: Charles Scribner's Sons, 1988.

Children's Literature Review. Vol. 4. Detroit: Gale Research, 1982.

Collier, Laurie, and Joyce Nakamura, eds. *Major Authors and Illustrators for Children and Young Adults.* Detroit: Gale Research, 1993.

Contemporary Authors. Vol. 137. Detroit: Gale Research, 1992.

Hildebrand, Ann Meinzen. *Jean and Laurent de Brunhoff: The Legacy of Babar.* New York: Twayne, 1991.

Kunitz, Stanley J., and Howard Haycraft, eds. *The Junior Book of Authors.* 2nd ed. New York: H. W. Wilson, 1951.

Something about the Author. Vol. 24. Detroit: Gale Research, 1981.

Weber, Nicholas Fox. *The Art of Babar: The Work of Jean and Laurent de Brunhoff*. New York: Abrams, 1989.

Meindert DeJong

1906-1991, American author

The House of Sixty Fathers

(novel, 1956)

PLOT: Now regarded as a classic war novel, *The House of Sixty Fathers* was not published until fifteen years after it was written because editors thought that its scenes of violence and deprivation would be too disturbing for young readers. Structured around the journeys of a Chinese boy during World War II, the novel contains themes of endurance and compassion. When the Japanese attack his village, Tien Pao, his father (Tien Hsu), his mother (Yin), and his baby sister (Beauty-of-the-Republic) flee in a sampan to Hengyang. Left alone while his parents seek work, Tien Pao ferries an American airman, Lieutenant Hamsun, across the dangerous, rain-swollen river. The next day, the sampan loses its mooring and Tien Pao is swept past the Japanese lines. After beaching the sampan and releasing his pet ducklings, Tien Pao sets out with his pig, Glory-of-the-Republic, to rejoin his parents.

Tien Pao's journey presents scenes of both horror and human kindness. Encountering children eating grass and mud, Tien Pao hides his pig but gives a boy the last of his rice. Afterwards, he hides in caves during the day to assure his pig's survival and eats leaves to avoid starvation. After the Japanese shoot down a fighter, Tien Pao shouts a warning to save the American pilot (improbably, it is Lieutenant Hamsun) from a Japanese soldier. A Chinese guerilla leader then aids them, sending Hamsun back to the American airfield and leading Tien Pao to a toothless crone, who gives him two bowls of rice. Disguised, Tien Pao follows the guerilla

Tien Pao and his pig go on a harrowing journey in war-torn China in DeJong's **The House of Sixty Fathers,** *illustrated by Maurice Sendak.*

past Japanese soldiers. The guerilla's wife, Yin, bathes Tien Pao, tends to his wounds, and stops her husband from using the pig to lure Japanese soldiers into ambush. At Hengyang, now under attack, the guerilla leaves Tien Pao, who can't find his parents. A crazy old woman tries to steal his pig but then buys him passage on a train. A soldier forces others to make room for Tien Pao, but the boy and his pig later fall off the freight car.

Tien Pao then watches for his parents among the refugees streaming along the tracks. After he faints, two American airmen take him to their base, where Master Sergeant Wilson and his squadron adopt Tien Pao, becoming his sixty fathers. While continuing to watch for his parents, Tien Pao takes pity on a starving old man, giving the poor man money that he received from the Americans. Afterwards, Tien Pao asks Lieutenant Hamsun to fly over the stream of refugees. As they return from this unsuccessful attempt to locate his parents, Tien Pao glimpses his mother working at the airfield. He and his family are joyfully reunited.

CHARACTERS: Presented from Tien Pao's viewpoint, the characters are developed only to the extent that he understands them. **Tien Pao** is an innocent Chinese boy who knows nothing about life beyond his village. Having never before seen Americans, for example, he fears that blond Lieutenant Hamsun is a golden river god. Before his experiences test him, Tien Pao is unremarkable. He is bright enough to overcome boredom and loneliness on the sampan by inventing games and by talking to his pets. He chafes under his parents' rules, but he violates his father's injunction against taking the sampan from shore only because a neighbor convinces him that he would please his parents by earning money and preventing their starvation.

After he is swept downriver, Tien Pao shows intelligence, resourcefulness, tenacity, kindness, and understandable selfishness. Determined to rejoin his parents, Tien Pao wisely follows the river, locates caves where he and his pig sleep safely during the day, and eats leaves to delay starvation. By observing the downed airman, Tien Pao learns to resist the urge to run in panic. Consequently, he avoids capture and his compassionate concern enables him to shout a warning to Hamsun. Tien Pao is horrified by destruction and killing, but his sensitive nature is also apparent when he releases his ducklings, when he gives the grass-eating boy the last of his rice, and when he gives the old man money for food. Tien Pao is not, however, improbably virtuous. Although he feels sorry for the starving people he meets, he has greater concern for his pig because it is his friend and comforter. He repeatedly begs people not to harm it, even though the pig could become food to save lives or a lure to destroy the enemy. Nevertheless, he feels guilty about his selfish attachment, and this guilt partly motivates his acts of charity. Tien Pao's profound need for his family enables him to endure extreme physical and emotional hardships. His reunion with his parents is improbable, but it is poetically fitting that a boy who faced deprivation and despair, yet always showed kindness and bravery, should receive love and security.

Tien Pao's **father (Tien Hsu)** is brave and resourceful in saving his family. He is uncompromising when his son frightens him by taking the sampan out and refuses to listen to his excuses. Tender, compassionate, and more understanding, Tien Pao's

mother (Yin) is an ideal parent. She is frightened by his disobedience, but she listens sympathetically to his explanations. **Lieutenant Hamsun**, the blond American airman, establishes Tien Pao's naivete when the boy mistakes him for a god. After his crash, he provides an opportunity for a display of Tien Pao's courage and resourcefulness. Kind and generous, Hamsun flies the plane over the crowd of refugees to satisfy the boy's need to exhaust every possibility to locate his parents. Green-eyed, redheaded **Master Sergeant Wilson**, who seems as hairy as an ape to Tien Pao, shows the dangers of judging from appearances. He is a kind and solicitous representative of the sixty fathers who adopt Tien Pao and bring him into their house (their barracks) after learning that he saved Hamsun. The Chinese **guerrilla**, a tall, bearded man, has a similar function. Tien Pao mistakes him for a bandit, and the Japanese, fooled by his disguise, mistake him for a farmer. Although fierce and clever, the guerrilla shows fatherly understanding with Tien Pao, sparing the pig after his wife intervenes. **Yin**, the guerilla's wife, has the same name as Tien Pao's mother, a coincidence underlining her maternal role. Like Tien Pao's mother, she tends to Tien Pao's physical and emotional needs. After Tien Pao confides his deep need for the pig, the sympathetic Yin convinces her husband to spare the pig.

The withered, toothless **crone**, who gives Tien Pao a second bowl of rice to sustain him on his arduous journey, earns Tien Pao's love. Her cruel fate—the Japanese burn her hut while she is inside—emphasizes the sacrifices people make during war. The **crazy old woman** shows rapacity and kindness. Abandoned during the panic to flee Hengyang, she is a self-centered opportunist who tries to steal Tien Pao's pig. Needing the comfort of companionship, however, she buys his passage to safety, ironically failing to escape herself. A similar mixture is evident in the **Chinese soldier**, who is kind when he bullies the passengers into making room for Tien Pao and indifferent when Tien Pao falls from the train.

Further Reading

Berger, Laura Standley, ed. *Twentieth-Century Children's Writers*. 4th ed. Detroit: St. James, 1995.

Children's Literature Review. Vol. 1. Detroit: Gale Research, 1976.

Collier, Laurie, and Joyce Nakamura, eds. *Major Authors and Illustrators for Children and Young Adults.* Detroit: Gale Research, 1993.

Contemporary Authors New Revision Series. Vol. 36. Detroit: Gale Research, 1992.

Estes, Glenn E., ed. *American Writers for Children since 1960: Fiction.* Vol. 52 of *Dictionary of Literary Biography.* Detroit: Gale Research, 1986.

Fuller, Muriel, ed. *More Junior Authors.* New York: H. W. Wilson, 1963.

Something about the Author. Vol. 2. Detroit: Gale Research, 1971.

Tomie dePaola

1934-, American artist, author, illustrator, and teacher

Strega Nona: An Old Tale

(picture book, 1975)

PLOT: Strega Nona, a witch living in Calabria, hires Big Anthony to help her around the house and garden. She warns him, however, that he must never touch her pasta pot. One day, Big Anthony overhears Strega Nona singing a spell that causes the pot to fill with pasta. Unfortunately, he does not see her complete the spell by blowing three kisses to the pasta pot. When Big Anthony tells about the magic pot, people laugh at him. Angry, he vows that he will someday demonstrate his magical knowledge. He receives his chance two days later, when Strega Nona goes away. Big Anthony utters the spell and invites everyone to Strega Nona's house for pasta. The townspeople treat Big Anthony like a hero and eat their fill, but when he utters the words to stop the pot from cooking, he fails to blow the required three kisses and the pot keeps cooking. Pasta fills the house and begins overflowing into the town. Just in time, Strega Nona arrives and stops the pot from cooking. The angry townsfolk want to hang Big Anthony, but Strega Nona instead makes him eat all the pasta so that she can sleep in her own bed that night.

Sequels are Big Anthony and the Magic Ring *(1979),* Strega Nona's Magic Lessons *(1982),* Merry Christmas, Strega Nona *(1986), and* Strega Nona Meets Her Match *(1993).*

CHARACTERS: Although its subtitle suggests otherwise, *Strega Nona: An Old Tale* is an original tale, based upon a traditional story about a magic porridge pot. The characters resemble conventional folktale types, but at the same time they are also original creations.

Strega Nona ("Grandma Witch") is an old witch who has genuine powers. Although the people whisper about her, even the priest and nuns seek her help. Not at all a wicked witch, Strega Nona performs only good deeds, such as curing headaches, banishing warts, and finding husbands for young maidens. She is the conventional Wise Woman whose power depends upon her knowledge, and she is kind, too. She does not become angry after Big Anthony deliberately disobeys her; instead, her considerable wit permits her to save him from the angry townsfolk. Ever practical, she both punishes Big Anthony and solves the problem of cleaning up the mess he caused by making him eat the pasta he conjured up.

Big Anthony is the conventional big, stupid man found in many folktales. Ironically, although he is hired to help Strega Nona, he ends up needing her help. He possesses two major flaws: he doesn't pay attention, and he can't control his anger when the townspeople laugh at him. Combined, these flaws render him a bumbling fool. His inattention makes him miss the crucial gesture of kissing that terminates Strega Nona's spell, and his anger at the townspeople's skepticism of his magic claims compels him to violate Strega Nona's orders to leave the pot alone. His lack of attention also emerges later in the story when he becomes so preoccupied with listening to compliments that he does not see the pasta flowing out of the house.

De Paola's illustration of Strega Nona, a witch whose character is based on a traditional story.

Further Reading

Berger, Laura Standley, ed. *Twentieth-Century Children's Writers.* 4th ed. Detroit: St. James, 1995.

Children's Literature Review. Vols. 4, 24. Detroit: Gale Research, 1982, 1992.

Contemporary Authors New Revision Series. Vol. 37. Detroit: Gale Research, 1992.

Estes, Glenn E., ed. *American Writers for Children since 1960: Poets, Illustrators, and Nonfiction Authors.* Vol. 61 of *Dictionary of Literary Biography.* Detroit: Gale Research, 1987.

Holtze, Sally Holmes, ed. *Fifth Book of Junior Authors and Illustrators.* New York: H. W. Wilson, 1983.

Something about the Author. Vols. 11, 59. Detroit: Gale Research, 1977, 1990.

Something about the Author Autobiography Series. Vol. 15. Detroit: Gale Research, 1993.

Franklin W. Dixon

(house pseudonym used by the Edward Stratemeyer Syndicate)

"The Hardy Boys"

(mystery series, 1927–)

PLOT: Literary critics, teachers, and librarians have repeatedly condemned the Hardy Boys action-adventure series because the novels are formulaic in plot and characterization. The Stratemeyer Syndicate contracted ghostwriters to produce the books from plot outlines and then the manuscripts were edited to ensure uniformity of style. Because of this assembly-line approach, Leslie McFarlane (1902-1977), who wrote twenty of the first twenty-five volumes, dubbed the Syndicate's owner, Edward Stratemeyer (1862-1930), the "Henry Ford of fiction for boys and girls." However little adults think of these books, they have become the most successful fiction series ever produced because they satisfy young readers who are looking for fast-paced action and comfortably familiar characters. Launched in 1927 with *The Tower Treasure*, the series has undergone changes with the passage of time. The original books were revised in 1959 and shortened significantly. Offensive material, especially racial and ethnic stereotypes, was removed, and references to boats, cars, planes, leisure activities, and clothing were updated. A parallel series for slightly older readers, "The Hardy Boys Casefiles," was begun in 1987.

Frank and Joe Hardy live with their father, Fenton, a wealthy world-famous detective, and mother, Laura, in Bayport, a small Atlantic coast city on Barmet Bay. A typical mystery begins in one of three ways: the brothers have an unusual experience, such as nearly being forced over a cliff by a speeding car—the first episode in their first adventure—or they notice a suspicious character, or their father asks them to help with one of his cases. Shortly after taking on a case, the brothers often receive warnings to stay uninvolved, which they always ignore. Through a lucky sighting of a suspicious character (almost always a dark foreign-appearing man in the early books) or through a hunch, Frank and Joe gain clues to the identity of the villains. Needing more evidence, they begin to pursue their suspects, but stumble into danger that either ends in a fight, escape from capture, or both. Frank and Joe then apprehend or trap the villains until the police can take them away. They return the stolen property to its rightful owners, and for their efforts they receive a substantial cash reward and gratifying fame.

CHARACTERS: The Hardy brothers differ from each other primarily in appearance. **Frank Hardy** is a tall, dark-haired sixteen-year-old (eighteen in later books) who is sometimes described as the sharp-witted leader in their adventures. **Joe Hardy** is a blue-eyed fifteen-year-old (seventeen in later books) who has curly blonde hair. He is sometimes described as the impetuous one. He is slightly awkward around girls, often mumbling in the presence of his girlfriend, Iola Morton. The Hardy Boys are in high school, but they have an exceptional amount of freedom. Both parents allow them to enter dangerous situations. Because their father is wealthy, they live in a big house and move among the richest social classes. They are always properly attired. What makes them especially appealing is the technology at their command: they own motorcycles, a roadster, and a motorboat called *The Sleuth*. The Hardy Boys can deduce facts and often must piece together several related puzzles to solve a crime, but they frequently rely on hunches that lead them to important clues or to the villains themselves. Both Frank and Joe are brave and capable fighters. Because the police often are unresponsive or inept, Frank and Joe may prevent them from interfering with their investigations by withholding information or by misleading them.

Frank and Joe undertake most of their adventures alone, but minor characters appear in the background. **Fenton Hardy**, their father, is a world-famous detective who sometimes enlists their aid, especially when he has to be on one of his frequent trips from home. A former New York policeman, he is friendly with the police and uses his connections with them to help solve cases. **Laura Hardy**, their mother, is a pretty woman who remains apart from the mysteries to attend to domestic matters. She is a stereotypical wife, leaving decisions about the boys' safety up to her husband.

Frank and Joe have several friends who can sometimes provide information or spy for them: chubby **Chet Morton**, who has an insatiable appetite; muscular **Biff Hooper**, who is a skilled boxer; and **Tony Prito**, who is the son of an Italian contractor. Because of Stratemeyer's strictures, the wholesome relationships between Frank and Joe and their girlfriends, **Callie Shaw** and **Iola Morton** respectively, are devoid of conventional romantic elements. Finally, in the original editions, Frank and Joe compete with—and use information from—Bayport's notoriously incompetent police: **Chief Collig**, a stubborn and dim man; **Officer Con Riley**, a cowardly fool who runs from snowball-throwing children and who is so unobservant that a pickpocket lifts his handcuffs; and private detective **Oscar Smuff**, who is eager to beat Fenton and his sons to the solution, but who is not skillful in interrogating suspects or in figuring out clues.

Further Reading

Billman, Carol. *The Secret of the Stratemeyer Syndicate: Nancy Drew, the Hardy Boys, and the Million Dollar Fiction Factory*. New York: Ungar, 1986.

Collier, Laurie, and Joyce Nakamura, eds. *Major Authors and Illustrators for Children and Young Adults*. Detroit: Gale Research, 1993.

Contemporary Authors New Revision Series. Vol. 27. Detroit: Gale Research, 1989.

Johnson, Deidre. *Edward Stratemeyer and the Stratemeyer Syndicate*. New York: Twayne, 1993,

McFarlane, Leslie. *Ghost of the Hardy Boys*. New York: Two Continents, 1976.

Something about the Author. Vols. 1, 67. Detroit: Gale Research, 1971, 1992.

Mary Mapes Dodge

1831-1905, American editor and author

Hans Brinker; or, The Silver Skates

(novel, 1865)

PLOT: *Hans Brinker* combines a family story with information about the geography, history, customs, and art of Holland. Set in Broek, near Amsterdam, it focuses on the fortitude of Hans Brinker, a boy who never lets troubles defeat him. The first part of the novel centers upon the Brinker family. Hans and his sister, Gretel, work hard to help support their family. Ten years earlier their father, Raff Brinker, had been injured working on the dikes. He became an invalid, and since then his wife, Meitje, and their children have struggled in poverty. When Hans tells Dr. Gerard Boekman, a famous surgeon, about his father, the surgeon agrees to examine Raff soon. Meanwhile, the wealthy van Gleck family announces a race, with the prize to be silver skates. Hans and Gretel have unsuitable wooden skates, but they acquire steel ones after Hilda van Gleck and Peter van Holp separately buy carved chains from Hans. Not everyone is happy to have the poor Brinkers join the race: Carl Schummel, Rychie Korbes, and Katrinka Flack are particularly vocal in their opposition.

The central section of the novel describes a skating journey undertaken by Peter, Carl, Ludwig van Holp, Jacob Poot, Lambert van Mounen, and his English cousin, Ben Dobbs. This journey is primarily an opportunity for presenting much of the novel's educational material, including the famous story of the boy who saved his town by sticking his finger in the dike. It also contains three notable episodes. In the first, Peter loses his purse, which contains the entire group's money. Hans finds it and returns it to Peter. In the second, plump Jacob Poot collapses from exhaustion and has to be prevented from falling asleep in the cold. In the third, a knife-wielding thief tries to rob the sleeping boys. Carl runs away while Peter and the others subdue the thief.

The last part of the novel returns to the story of the Brinkers and includes a subplot involving Dr.

Boekman, whose son, Laurens, disappeared ten years earlier. The surgeon operates on Raff and restores his faculties. Raff then remembers that he buried the family's money before he was injured, but Hans is unable to find it. Desperate, Hans decides to sell his skates. Instead, his friend Annie Bouman gives him money, pretending it has come from a buyer. Annie then plays a game of fairy godmother and unwittingly gives Hans a clue that enables him to locate his father's money.

The now-happy Brinker family then provides information to Dr. Boekman. On the night of his accident, Raff had helped a man who thought he had accidentally killed a patient. The man turns out to be Laurens, who gave Raff his watch and a message for his father. Unfortunately, Raff can't remember the message. Things work out for the doctor, however, after the big skating race. Hans sacrifices his own chances by giving Peter a replacement for a broken strap, and Peter wins the boys' race. Gretel wins the girls' race, and the case for her silver skates contains the address of the doctor's son, who made it. After he and Laurens are reunited, Dr. Boekman agrees to put Hans through university. A final chapter looks ahead to the future, when Hans becomes a famous doctor.

CHARACTERS: Numerous parallels and contrasts add thematic interest to characters who are fundamentally conventional types. Fifteen-year-old **Hans Brinker** is the ideal son. A sturdy boy with square shoulders, bushy yellow hair, and honest blue eyes, he obeys and respects his mother. Hans is completely unselfish and endures hardships because he puts his family's needs ahead of his own. He is thus willing to sell his new steel skates to buy rich food for his father's recovery. Hans is a slow, steady worker who excels at both school and manual labor. A talented carver, he makes wooden skates for himself and Gretel, as well as wooden chains and fancy trimming for the van Holp residence.

Hans is described as having "a true Dutch horror of tears, or of emotion of any kind." Consequently, he refuses to show disappointment or give in to despair when he fails to obtain work. Instead, he whistles bravely and sets out to do whatever he can to earn money. As well as being resolute, Hans is proud. He refuses the charity Hilda offers and the reward Peter tries to tender for finding his purse. Hans also demonstrates that nobility of character is independent of social station. He thus approaches Dr. Boekman because his conscience will not let him rest when he has a chance to help his family. Hans also willingly surrenders his chance to win the skates so that Peter can triumph. Finally, he expresses admiration for the surgeon's art because it requires wisdom and "a reverence for God's work." Not surprisingly, Hans marries Annie Bouman and becomes a famous surgeon himself.

Hans's sister, **Gretel Brinker** is a lithe, blue-eyed, twelve-year-old with golden tresses. She dreads books, but she is a hard worker. She is more emotionally demonstrative than Hans, sometimes shedding tears in his presence. Nevertheless, she is similarly proud, denying to Hilda that she is freezing in her thin clothing. Furthermore, when it is decided that Hans will go to the university, Gretel decides to apply herself to her studies so that she will not be an embarrassment to him. Gretel sometimes feels excluded because she is a girl, such as when Dr. Boekman sends her away during the operation to avoid the possibility of her screaming and fainting. Nevertheless, she dreams of accomplishment and realizes her dream by winning the silver skates.

Mrs. Meitje Brinker (née Klenck) is a devoted wife and mother. She serves as an example of Dutch industriousness, insisting that both she and Gretel occupy themselves with work while she tells a story about St. Nicholas. She is a loving and faithful wife, tending her husband through ten long years of poverty, even when he became abusive. Furthermore, in spite of dire need, she has the integrity to resist selling the watch he entrusted to her before his accident. Although once a loving husband and father, **Raff Brinker** forgets his former life and becomes violent following his injury on the job. After the operation, he is again an example of the cheerful and honest family man.

Like Raff Brinker, **Dr. Gerard Boekman**, Holland's most famous surgeon, is changed by circum-

Paul Galdone's illustration of Hans and Gretel Brinker from the classic story by Mary Mapes Dodge.

stances and later restored to his true self. After the disappearance of his son, Laurens, Dr. Boekman—with his thin, lank, unsmiling face—became known as the crossest man in Holland. In spite of his reputation, his dispassionate discussion of medical cases, and his nervousness around women, which makes him speak roughly to Gretel—he is actually kind-hearted. He responds generously to Hans, who reminds him of Laurens, takes no fee for performing the operation on Raff, and gives his patient the fine foods necessary for his recovery. The cares melt from his face and he becomes his old self when Laurens returns. He shows his loving and generous nature by symbolically adopting Hans and sending him to the university.

Three young people demonstrate heroic compassion. **Peter van Holp**, the seventeen-year-old "captain" of the skating journey, resembles Hans in being an ideal boy. Peter does not, like some of the other wealthy children, shun Hans. One sign of his own merit is that he admires Hans for his honesty, pride, and dedication to family. Peter is charitable without being condescending: he buys a chain from Hans and arranges work for him. Peter is also like Hans in facing trouble: when he loses his purse, he insists that the group should display fortitude. Peter himself is brave and composed when he captures the robber. Later, he demonstrates Christian charity by insisting that the robber is his brother and that altered circumstances might have made any of the rich boys turn to crime.

Hilda van Gleck, the fourteen-year-old daughter of a rich burgomaster, is Peter's female counterpart. Physically and morally, she is of greater stature than the other girls. She feels sympathy for the Brinkers, but she recognizes that an offer of charity would wound Hans's pride. Therefore, she buys his wooden chain so that he can have money for steel skates. She similarly feels angry at herself for embarrassing Gretel by mentioning her thin clothing. Hilda becomes a hero when she prevents Gretel, who has been expelled from the house during the operation, from falling asleep in the snow. She later marries Peter.

Annie Bouman, a peasant girl, is the only other person not afraid to show friendship for the Brinkers. She pretends to buy Hans's skates so that he can obtain money quickly while retaining his pride. Her importance to Hans is underlined by the fact that, by pretending to be his fairy godmother, she inspires the fairy tale reversal of fortunes that occurs when he digs up the money. Fittingly, she later marries Hans.

Two characters are major antagonists to the Brinkers. **Carl Schummel** contrasts with Peter. Carl is a snob who lacks compassion and tries to make everyone despise the poor Brinkers. He is frequently bitter and insolent, such as when he complains about Peter losing the purse. A bully to smaller boys, he proves to be a coward when he sees the thief. Carl is a cautionary figure: lacking friends because of his cold attitude, he becomes a menial bookkeeper after his father suffers a financial reversal. **Rychie Korbes**, the proud daughter of the leading man of Amsterdam, shows that beauty is often superficial. Haughty and uncharitable, she does not consider poor Gretel

to be a human being and is not concerned with the sufferings of the poor. She therefore bitterly opposes Gretel's entry into the race. Strangely, Rychie later undergoes a transformation, deepening her sympathies to become an author.

Four other young people are prominent enough to warrant mention. **Jacob Poot** is a genial boy whose stoutness makes him tire before the others do. When he tries to sleep outside during the skating journey, he provides an opportunity for Peter to display his qualities as a leader. **Ben Dobbs**, Jacob's English cousin, and **Lambert van Mounen**, the only boy who speaks English, are devices for introducing educational discussions. Ben often has a greater knowledge of Dutch history than his hosts. Nevertheless, he can't accept the Dutch custom of men wearing hats in church and thus shows the need for being sympathetic to other cultures. **Katrinka Flack** is a merry coquette. She opposes the Brinkers, but only because Rychie is the first to speak to her about them. Although beautiful and lively, she has no moral depth. The fact that she never marries symbolically underlines her selfish frivolity.

Further Reading

Berger, Laura Standley, ed. *Twentieth-Century Children's Writers*. 4th ed. Detroit: St. James, 1995.

Bingham, Jane M., ed. *Writers for Children: Critical Studies of Major Authors since the Seventeenth Century*. New York: Charles Scribner's Sons, 1988.

Collier, Laurie, and Joyce Nakamura, eds. *Major Authors and Illustrators for Children and Young Adults*. Detroit: Gale Research, 1993.

Contemporary Authors. Vol. 137. Detroit: Gale Research, 1992.

Estes, Glenn E., ed. *American Writers for Children before 1900*. Vol. 42 of *Dictionary of Literary Biography*. Detroit: Gale Research, 1985.

Gannon, Susan R. *Mary Mapes Dodge*. New York: Twayne, 1992.

Griswold, Jerry. "Sunny Land, Angry Waters: *Hans Brinker.*" In *Audacious Kids: Coming of Age in America's Classic Children's Books*. New York: Oxford University Press, 1992.

Howard, Alice Barrett. *Mary Mapes Dodge of St. Nicholas*. New York: J. Messner, 1943.

Riley, Sam G., ed. *American Magazine Journalists, 1850-1900*. Vol. 79 of *Dictionary of Literary Biography*. Detroit: Gale Research, 1988.

Something about the Author. Vol. 21. Detroit: Gale Research, 1980.

William Pène du Bois

1916-1993, American illustrator and author

The Twenty-One Balloons

(novel, 1947)

PLOT: A spoof of stories about utopian societies, this Newbery Medal winner is filled with descriptions of amusing gadgets. It ballasts its comedy, however, with mild satire. In 1883, Professor William Waterman Sherman, a retired school teacher and avid balloonist, is rescued in the Atlantic ocean. Ill and exhausted, the Professor insists that the Western American Explorers' Club in his home of San Francisco must be the first to hear his adventures. When he arrives home aboard the Presidential train, a huge crowd honors the Professor for cutting in half the record of traveling around the world in eighty days.

Lying in a bed and attended by the mayor, a doctor, and nurses, the Professor tells his story. Seven days after he left San Francisco, a gull punctured his balloon. He was therefore forced to land on the volcanic island of Krakatoa. Mr. F, a resident of the supposedly uninhabited island, befriended him, provided him with elegant clothes, showed him the island's fabulous diamond mines, and introduced him to a wealthy society. The residents of Krakatoa financed a life of leisure by discreetly selling diamonds. They lived in elaborate houses, had a government based on gourmet cooking, and spent their time in creative pastimes. The Professor was delighted by their inventions, especially a Balloon Merry-Go-Round. Soon, however, the volcano erupted. The residents escaped on a platform suspended from twenty balloons. The Krakatoans eventually used parachutes to jump to land below. Lacking a parachute, the Professor was

Professor Sherman is rescued from the doomed island of Krakatoa in this illustration by du Bois for his adventure spoof.

forced to crash-land the platform in the Atlantic, where he was rescued. At the end of this speech, the Professor rises from his bed, which he has not needed, and indicates that he will sell his diamond cuff links to finance another attempt at his original quest: spending a peaceful year aloft in a balloon.

CHARACTERS: Character is secondary to descriptions of a fantastic way of life, but the Professor, who narrates most of the book, is a vivid presence. **Professor William Waterman Sherman** is a sixty-six-year-old arithmetic teacher who has grown exceedingly tired after forty years of instructing unruly boys. Consequently, the Professor dreams of spending a blissful year in solitary peace by floating in a balloon. After his plans go awry, he demonstrates extreme loyalty. He even refuses to tell his story to the President, insisting that protocol requires that he tell his adventures first to the Western Explorers' Club. The Professor, in fact, understands his new notoriety. He tells the mayor and doctor that he is amused that two men whom he could never have seen before his adventure are now his eager servants. Although he attributes this reversal to ballooning, he clearly appreciates that his status literally depends on the winds of chance.

The Professor is careful, courageous, and quick-witted during both his trip to and his escape from the island. He realizes, for example, that he must cast off even his clothing to ensure that his damaged balloon safely reaches Krakatoa. The Professor initially displays greed by grabbing as many diamonds as he can carry. Once he understands that their value depends on their scarcity, however, he feels foolish and concentrates on the fruits of wealth, rather than the acquisition of it. The Professor is adaptable. He is proud of quickly becoming accustomed to the shaking ground of Krakatoa, and he easily fits into its routine of leisure and amusement. The Professor is a charming, entertaining speaker. He recounts with ease both what he saw and what Mr. F told him. He also takes pleasure in entertaining the residents of Krakatoa with stories about San Francisco. Nevertheless, he has few qualms about deceiving others when his own interests are at stake. He therefore lies to the Krakatoans about his profession so that they will not ask him to teach their children. Although fully recovered, he delivers his San Francisco speech from bed simply because he considers it foolish to miss an opportunity for personal comfort. Such acts may suggest that the Professor is a humbug, but his offer to sell the diamond cuff links that he wore in Krakatoa establishes his honesty. The Professor is ultimately an eccentric whose devotion to the idea of escaping civilization for a year of solitary comfort makes him an amiable critic of greed, numbing routine, and arbitrary status.

Mr. F represents all the islanders and functions as a guide. A man wholly devoted to the concept of civilized living, he is always aristocratically attired in a perfectly tailored morning suit of tropical white. Mr. F explains to the Professor the history and customs of the Krakatoans, and he demonstrates the fantastic gadgets that make island life easy and enjoyable. Like the other islanders, Mr. F came from San Francisco and adopted a new identity on the island. His name represents the elegance of France. He thus lives in a house that showcases French architecture and interior decoration. When his monthly turn to feed all the other families comes around, he serves French cuisine. Mr. F is amused by the Professor's greedy hoarding of diamonds, but he is honest enough to admit that the islanders themselves went through a period of intensely selfish greed. He demonstrates that wealth has not made him selfish when he voluntarily remains with the Professor aboard the escape platform until the last possible moment.

Further Reading

Berger, Laura Standley, ed. *Twentieth-Century Children's Writers*. 4th ed. Detroit: St. James, 1995.

Children's Literature Review. Vol. 1. Detroit: Gale Research, 1976.

Kunitz, Stanley J., and Howard Haycraft, eds. *The Junior Book of Authors*. 2nd ed. New York: H. W. Wilson, 1951.

Something about the Author. Vols. 4, 68, 74. Detroit: Gale Research, 1973, 1992, 1993.

Roger Duvoisin

1904-1980, American illustrator and author

Petunia

(picture book, 1950)

PLOT: When she finds a book, Petunia the goose remembers Mr. Pumpkin telling his son that "He who owns and loves Books is wise." Taking the book everywhere, Petunia is convinced that she is now wise. Seeing her neck stretched in pride, the other animals ask for her advice and opinions. Petunia's responses, however, create problems. She makes King the rooster fearful about shaking his comb when she says that it is plastic. She worries Ida the hen by telling her that she has more than the nine chicks she should have. She injures Noisy the dog by setting a fire in a rabbit hole when he becomes stuck in it. She tells Straw that he must have all his teeth removed to end his toothache, making the frightened horse run away to suffer in silence. She also injures a number of animals who fall when they take her advice about standing on top of each other to reach a kitten in a tree. Her worst error, however, is telling the farmyard animals that a box of firecrackers contains candies. When they go to eat them, the firecrackers explode, injuring Petunia and her friends. Humbled, Petunia now notices that the book contains writing. She understands that she must learn to read the book, not just carry it around, if she is to be wise.

Other books in the series are Petunia and the Song *(1951);* Petunia's Christmas *(1952);* Petunia Takes a Trip *(1953);* Petunia, Beware! *(1958);* Petunia, I Love You *(1965); and* Petunia's Treasure *(1975).*

CHARACTERS: In the tradition of animal fables, the Petunia books are didactic, using animals as representatives of the human world and thereby fulfilling what Duvoisin called "that little sneaking desire to teach and to moralize." Noisy the dog, King the rooster, and Charles the gander (he appears in *Petunia's Christmas*, in which Petunia rescues and marries him) are recurring characters, but they exist only as occasions for conflict or as symbols of its resolution by accepting Petunia after her errors.

Petunia is an archetypal silly goose. She thus fails to understand that to become wise she must fully understand the contents of the book, not merely possess it. Her unwarranted pride in her wisdom intensifies her silliness. Concerned with her reputation, Petunia assumes an air of superiority while delivering foolish advice and opinions. On each occasion, Petunia becomes more conceited, her pride leading her to stretch her neck further and further. Duvoisin brilliantly conveys Petunia's absurd distortion of her identity by drawing her with her neck stretched so far that her head cannot fit on the page. Petunia becomes so proud that she will not admit that she does not know how to count the chicks or how to read the words on the box of firecrackers. She becomes so self-absorbed that she

does not see that her silliness causes grief—the narrator ends each episode by calling the animals who listen to her "poor." Petunia's pride precedes her fall; after the explosion, her bandages are external signs of her wounded pride. Although her neck snaps back to its former proportions, Petunia is different. She realizes that she must work to acquire wisdom, that she must learn to read so that she can keep the book in her mind and heart. Furthermore, her experience makes her less selfish. Whereas she first wanted to impress her friends, she now wants wisdom so that she can help to make them happy.

Further Reading

Children's Literature Review. Vol. 23. Detroit: Gale Research, 1991.

Collier, Laurie, and Joyce Nakamura, eds. *Major Authors and Illustrators for Children and Young Adults.* Detroit: Gale Research, 1993.

Contemporary Authors New Revision Series. Vol. 11. Detroit: Gale Research, 1984.

Estes, Glenn E., ed. *American Writers for Children since 1960: Poets, Illustrators, and Nonfiction Authors.* Vol. 61 of *Dictionary of Literary Biography.* Detroit: Gale Research, 1987.

Kunitz, Stanley J., and Howard Haycraft, eds. *The Junior Book of Authors.* 2nd ed. New York: H. W. Wilson, 1951.

Something about the Author. Vols. 2, 30. Detroit: Gale Research, 1971, 1983.

Edward Eager

1911-1964, American playwright, lyricist, and author

Half Magic

(fantasy, 1954)

PLOT: Although obviously an imitation of E. Nesbit's fantasies, *Half Magic* succeeds as a witty comedy about troublesome magical wishes. Set in the 1920s, it focuses on four children—Jane, Mark, Katherine, and Martha—who live with their widowed mother, Alison. After Jane finds a nickel, strange events occur whenever the children express a wish because the nickel is actually a magical talisman that grants half of what one wishes. When Jane is bored and

Little Katherine and her siblings journey to King Arthur's world in one of the adventures from Half Magic, *illustrated by N. M. Bodecker.*

wishes that there would be a fire, for example, a playhouse immediately burns. That night, during a visit to some relatives, her mother wishes she were home and finds herself in the country, where Mr. Hugo Smith sees her and gives her a ride home. Jane, realizing that her mother has borrowed the nickel, reclaims it. Before she can explain matters to her siblings, Martha accidentally wishes the cat into half-talking, and Mark, getting half his wish that they were all on a desert island, transports them to the desert. Achmed, a caravan driver, captures them, but Mark uses the charm to provide Achmed with a wife, children, and young camels. Mark then makes a wish to return home with his siblings.

When Katherine receives a turn to wish, she transports them into King Arthur's day. After Sir Launcelot expresses resentment that they used magic to rescue him from Morgan Le Fay's dungeon, Katherine uses the charm to defeat him in a joust. Merlin makes everyone forget this humiliation, casts a spell preventing further time and space travel, and sends the children home. Next, at a movie theater, Martha causes a panic when she wishes she wasn't there and becomes as transparent as a ghost. She flees to Mr. Smith's bookstore, where the others find her and some robbers try to steal the charm. Mark uses it to capture them, but their mother faints because she can't believe what she sees. Because Mr.

Smith and the mother become close, Jane now wishes to belong to another family, becoming the prissy Iphigenia, nicknamed Comfort. Mr. Smith uses the talisman to restore her identity. The children now try to convince their mother that she isn't mad and therefore can marry Mr. Smith. Their new wishes comically complicate matters, however, until Mr. Smith uses the charm. The mother then accepts Mr. Smith's proposal, and the adults forget about the charm. Jane, granted one last wish, dreams that her father approves the marriage. The children, knowing that they have exhausted their wishes, leave the coin where a little girl immediately discovers its magic.

CHARACTERS: Eager's children, who read Nesbit's books and long for the magical adventures they narrate, resemble Nesbit's characters in their banter, rivalry, and hatred of unfairness and slyness. **Jane**, the oldest, is forceful, argumentative, careful, and clever. When she first detects that her wishes come strangely true, she becomes unhappy and refuses to wish again until she understands the rules of the magic. Jane is clever, deducing that the coin's magic requires that they wish for twice as much as they want. The only one of the children who remembers their late father, Jane becomes resentful when she thinks that Mr. Smith is trying to replace him. By wishing to belong to another family, Jane engages in a battle between heredity and environment. Although remaining herself deep within, Jane becomes the prissy Iphigenia (known as Comfort) the product of a home in which children are not properly valued. After being restored to her true family, Jane gains new appreciation for her home and becomes kinder and more even-tempered. Jane's final wish, which makes her father half present to reassure her that he approves of the marriage and his family's happiness, marks a symbolic advance in her maturity. Jane is at peace knowing that life can continue happily without denying the past.

Eleven-year-old **Mark** has contempt for girls, yet he eagerly shares their adventures. A rationalist who doesn't believe in magic, Mark insists that they test Jane's belief that they have participated in magic, and he skeptically dismisses Martha's claim that the cat is talking. Once he realizes that he is involved in magic, however, Mark cleverly learns to double whatever he desires when making a wish. Mark is thoughtful and has moral scruples. He notes, for example, that people once were unfair to natives and that, therefore, the coin could have been stolen from Achmed's people. His wit and sensitivity combine when he uses the coin to grant Achmed his heart's desire, transforming the Arab from someone sinister into a man pleased with his fortune.

Nine-year-old **Katherine** is a poetry-loving, docile child. Feeling neglected because she is the middle girl, she repeatedly boasts that she is her mother's comfort, much to the annoyance of the others. Her romantic sensibility is most evident in her wish that the children go back to Arthur's day and do a good deed. Because she is emotional, Katherine sometimes forgets to control the magic properly. When she becomes angry with Morgan Le Fay, for example, she forgets to double her wish, making the evil enchantress jump into a puddle instead of a lake. Katherine also misinterprets the effect of her magical actions. Believing that she could do a good deed by humbling the arrogant Launcelot, she defeats him in a joust. Afterwards, she tearfully accepts responsibility, when her good intentions actually discredit the Round Table. Katherine's romantic naivete leads to a similar but more comical misjudgment in her own time. Trying to prove the existence of magic by giving her mother what she most desires, Katherine transforms her into a circus bareback rider, thereby confusing her mother even more.

Martha, the youngest, is a difficult child because she is sometimes a willful baby, but sometimes she is as mature as the others. Martha loses self-control when she becomes "half there" in the theater, wildly crying and causing a panic. At other times, however, she shows remarkable sensitivity and insight. When the others note that the coin has made them happy, for instance, she points out that their mother is sad. When the coin no longer grants wishes, she suggests that it may work for others, inspiring the idea of passing on the magic.

Because she can't accept the reality of magical experiences and believes that she is mad, the children's **mother**, **Alison**, is comical. Once Mr. Smith utters a wish that enables her to accept her sanity, however, she becomes a serious character. She reveals that her heart's desire depends on love, not magic: she wishes to marry Mr. Smith, to have her children love him, to be able to quit her job to care for the children, and to be able to have the children spend the summer in the country at a lake. Although all of these wishes are attainable without magical intervention, Jane unselfishly wishes that her mother receive her heart's desire. Ironically, the mother not only gets all of her expressed wishes, but she also gets an unexpressed one: Mr. Smith's beard, which she does not like, disappears. **Mr. Hugo Smith**, a small gentleman with a pointed beard is a special kind of adult: he understands and amuses children, but he never ceases to be an adult. Mr. Smith becomes a helper when he rescues Jane from her role as Iphigenia. In the climactic scene, when everyone is trying to convince the mother that magic is real, he seems comically ineffective, failing to stop the children from making inappropriate wishes. When he finally asserts himself, he wisely wishes that the mother become herself and not have fears of madness, enabling her to accept his loving marriage proposal.

Four adults distant in space or time contribute to character-revealing adventures. **Achmed**, the caravan driver, initially appears as an offensive stereotype of the sly Arab. Grabbing the children for ransom, he falsely claims that the magic coin is his. After Mark gives him his heart's desire, however, Achmed is transformed into a happy and loving man, a transformation that suggests, perhaps, that only poverty and loneliness made him evil. **Sir Launcelot** annoys Katherine by displaying an arrogant self-assurance and a close-minded refusal to see the children as anything other than fiends or witches. He is insulted that she uses magic to release him from the dungeons and insists that they allow him to fight his enemies by himself. After Katherine shames him, Launcelot nobly undertakes a quest to restore his honor. **Merlin** the magician is the archetypal wise old man. Noting that no good can come from altering the pattern of history, he tells Katherine that her ill-conceived attempt to perform a good deed by humbling Launcelot actually caused evil. He therefore limits the children's magic to their own time and place. Merlin also indicates, however, that Katherine has performed a good deed by assuring him that the values he helped to originate with the Round Table have continued into the future. **Morgan Le Fay** is a conventional villain, but she becomes comically absurd when Katherine magically dumps her into a puddle, where she becomes stuck in the mud.

Further Reading

Berger, Laura Standley, ed. *Twentieth-Century Children's Writers.* 4th ed. Detroit: St. James, 1995.

Cech, John, ed. *American Writers for Children 1900-1960.* Vol. 22 of *Dictionary of Literary Biography.* Detroit: Gale Research, 1983.

Collier, Laurie, and Joyce Nakamura, eds. *Major Authors and Illustrators for Children and Young Adults.* Detroit: Gale Research, 1993.

Contemporary Authors. Vols. 73-76. Detroit: Gale Research, 1978.

Fuller, Muriel, ed. *More Junior Authors.* New York: H. W. Wilson, 1963.

Something about the Author. Vol. 17. Detroit: Gale Research, 1979.

Eleanor Estes

1906-1988, American librarian and author

The Moffats

(novel, 1941)

PLOT: This celebration of family life is set in Cranbury (a fictional version of the author's home town of West Haven, Connecticut) shortly before World War I. It explores themes of family unity, security, and change.

Mrs. Moffat (Mama), a widowed dressmaker, and her four children—Sylvie, Joe, Jane, and Rufus—live in a yellow house at 27 New Dollar Street. The unconnected episodes/chapters begin with the sale of the house by its owner, Dr. Witty, and end a year later when the Moffats move out. In the first major episode, Peter Frost tells Jane that she will be arrested for imitating the peculiar walk of Mr. Pennypepper, the new school superintendent. When she subsequently sees Chief Mulligan, she hides in fear inside a bread box at Mr. Brooney's store, where she becomes trapped when Mrs. Shoemaker sits on it. After Chief Mulligan discovers her, he eases Jane's anxiety, and the two become friends. In the next episode, Mr. Pennypepper tells Rufus to watch Hughie Pudge on the day they start school. When Hughie leaves the classroom, Rufus attempts to bring him back, but Hughie resists. Rufus follows Hughie into a boxcar, in which they take an unexpected train ride. When they return, Hughie decides to attend school so that he can become an engineer. Joe, Jane, and Rufus share the next adventure, in which they drive a wagon for Captain Rowley of the Salvation Army while he sleeps in back. Unknown to them, he inadvertently falls out and is caught outside in a rainstorm. Another adventure finds Sylvie leading her siblings in a Halloween plot to frighten the obnoxious Peter Frost with a pumpkin ghost placed in their attic.

In the next episodes, clumsy Joe becomes the star of Miss Chichester's recital when a dog joins him in dancing the sailor's hornpipe, and Mama tells stories about her life to Rufus when he is quarantined with scarlet fever. During the winter, Joe goes to buy coal but loses the family's last five dollars. After a desperate search, he finds that he left the money at home. When the weather turns warm, Jane feels guilty after buying an ice cream cone for herself—breaking the family's unwritten rule about sharing. When the siblings later offer her their cat's kittens, she is happy to get her choice, though she does not believe that she deserves it because of her selfishness with the ice cream. Jane next shows her wit in chasing away Letitia Murdock, who is often at their house because her parents are thinking of buying it. After pretending to hypnotize Joe into acting like a frisky dog, Jane threatens to turn Letitia into a cat. The children are amused observers in the next episode, in which McCann, and old motorman, drives his trolley directly toward one driven by young O'Brien to resolve an argument. In the final chapter, the Murdocks have purchased the yellow house, and the Moffats are both sad and excited to be moving out. Jane is especially happy when Nancy Stokes, her new neighbor, offers to become her best friend.

Sequels are The Middle Moffat *(1942),* Rufus M. *(1943), and* The Moffat Museum *(1983).*

CHARACTERS: The novel provides few physical details, so minor characters are rather thinly developed, but the three youngest Moffats come alive because their feelings and responses are central to a number of episodes.

Ten-year-old **Jane** (often called **Janey**) is a keen observer who meditates on things. She watches her mother peel apples and wonders if she will ever be as skilled. She delights in viewing all of New Dollar Street from the yellow house. The sensitive Jane transforms her dull and dilapidated reality into something better: she makes the yellow house seem brighter and the new house more inviting by looking at them upside-down between her legs. Furthermore, she is able to cope with difficulties—such as when she is trapped in the bread box—by dreaming that she is a princess with golden curls. Despite her romantic nature, Jane recognizes the difference between dreams and reality. While she dreams of dancing gracefully and being the center of admiration, she knows that in dancing class she is awkward and that, without her customary pigtails, her hair would look ridiculous. Although Jane is compassionate and loving, she is not perfect. She has great trouble memorizing her catechism lessons and spends money on herself instead of buying a family treat. She is careful never to walk on Chief Mulligan's lawn or to make a noise near his house because she is afraid of being arrested. Consequently, she panics when Peter Frost threatens to tell the Chief that she is imitating the superintendent. Nevertheless, Jane learns to cope with new and sometimes confusing situations. She shows great wit by pretending to be a hypnotist, which scares Letitia away. At the end of the book, Jane's purpose serves to define and focus the author's theme: Jane realizes that although life's changes often bring sorrow, such as leaving the

An illustration by Louis Slobodkin of Estes's Moffat family.

yellow house, change can also bring happiness and joy, such as having a best friend for the first time.

The other Moffats play lesser roles. Adventurous twelve-year-old **Joe** decides that they should drive Captain Rowley's wagon instead of going to Sunday School. He is, however, usually a responsible boy, which he demonstrates when he admits to losing the coal money. He loves his mother and feels miserable that his carelessness results in extra work for her. Once he finds the money, he shows consideration by immediately going out into the bitter weather to get the coal. Joe, who hates taking dancing lessons and can never remember the steps, is the center of a comic set piece. Expecting only to be an usher and page turner for the pianist at the dance recital, he is called upon to perform in another boy's absence. A dancing dog saves the day for the embarrassed Joe, but he is too shy to ask Miss Chichester for the ten cents she promised to give him if the recital turned out well. Five-and-a-half-year-old **Rufus** has an astonishing memory and knows the catechism lessons that Jane can't remember. He eagerly looks forward to school and takes his responsibility seriously when Mr. Pennypepper asks him to supervise Hughie Pudge at school. During the subsequent adventure, he remains calm. Seventeen-year-old

Sylvie, a graceful dancer and church chorister, is the least prominent of the children. She organizes the children's revenge on Peter Frost with the same efficiency that she displays when she takes over household management while her mother tends to the sick Rufus. During this time, she entertains the younger children by singing and telling stories. Sylvie wears her hair up like an adult on moving day. She symbolically indicates that the family will convey past joys to a new setting when she brings plant sprigs from the yellow house for transplanting at their new one. **Mrs. Moffat**, who is always called **Mama**, is a widowed dressmaker who shows resourcefulness and determination in supporting her children. Although a constant presence, she is central only when she entertains the ailing Rufus with stories about her childhood in New York. Mama believes in propriety and respectability, despite the family's poverty. Thus, she never leaves the house without putting on gloves and a hat, and she sews for Miss Chichester in exchange for the dancing lessons that she feels are social necessities for her children. When Joe confesses to losing the money for coal, the loving and understanding Mama doesn't scold him. Instead, she declares that they must accept the situation and earns the money by working through the night.

Four neighborhood children play important roles in at least one episode each. **Peter Frost** is an obnoxious boy who deliberately uses the loud siren on his bicycle to startle Rufus, causing him to fall into a mud puddle; he falsely and maliciously tells Jane that he will have Chief Mulligan arrest her; and he always pulls Sylvie's curls and dips Jane's braids into ink wells. Peter displays insufferable arrogance when he comes to the Moffat's on Halloween, but he turns pitifully frightened at their prank and later becomes less obnoxious. **Hughie Pudge**'s character contrasts with the bright and eager Rufus. He is a year late in starting school because he refused to attend the year before. Hughie comes to value school only when he learns that he will have to study in order to be a motorman. **Letitia Murdock** is an annoyingly persistent girl. At the dance recital, she repeatedly threatens to be sick. When her parents consider buying the yellow house, she constantly visits, rudely banging on the doors and peering through the windows. She also inconsiderately refuses to share her candy and treats. Letitia is so obstinate and insensitive that Jane must frighten her away to get rid of her. In contrast, **Nancy Stokes** is open and accepting. A ten-year-old girl with golden curls, she lives next door to Jane's new house. She exchanges dreams with Jane and offers to be her best friend.

A number of adults play small roles and develop the sense of community throughout the book. **Chief Mulligan** initially appears as a frightening figure to Jane, but his jolly laughter convinces her of his good nature. He educates Jane by explaining that policemen serve to protect, not scare, people. **Mr. Pennypepper**, the school superintendent, has a peculiar rocking, but nonetheless dignified, gait. He tilts back his small head, nods from side to side, and sticks out his stomach. He seems to understand and like children, exhibiting gentle firmness in persuading Hughie to attend school. **Mr. Brooney**, the friendly owner of the delicatessen, gives Jane a lollipop but says that he'll never give away his secret potato salad recipe. His love of idle conversation forces Jane to remain concealed in the bread box while he talks to **Mrs. Shoemaker**, who sits on the box so Jane can't get out. But Mr. Brooney's concern for keeping an accurate inventory leads to Jane's discovery. **Miss Chichester**, the dance teacher, is concerned with appearances. She commissions clothes from Mrs. Moffat, but she is unable to pay and, in a barter transaction, gives the children free lessons. Although she praises Joe after his impromptu dance with the dog, she doesn't mention the ten cents she had promised to pay him. **Captain Rowley**, a loud-snoring member of the Salvation Army, sleeps so soundly that only a drum can awaken him. Two trolley motormen are prominent in a comic episode which stresses respect for authority. **McCann**, an old man with a walrus mustache, takes his job seriously. Tired of a younger man's failure to follow rules and to show consideration for others by alternating runs on the single-track line, he drives his trolley into a head-on confrontation. **O'Brien**, the young motorman, is a picture of youthful impudence: he wears his hat tilted back and slouches in his seat. Although he knows himself to be complete- ly in the wrong, he insults McCann, but subsequent- ly backs down when he realizes that the crowd is against him.

This illustration by Keith Ward depicts Alec and Black escaping from the sinking ship in Farley's **The Black Stallion.**

Further Reading

Berger, Laura Standley, ed. *Twentieth-Century Child- ren's Writers.* 4th ed. Detroit: St. James, 1995.

Cech, John, ed. *American Writers for Children 1900- 1960.* Vol. 22 of *Dictionary of Literary Biography.* Detroit: Gale Research, 1983.

Children's Literature Review. Vol. 2. Detroit: Gale Research, 1976.

Collier, Laurie, and Joyce Nakamura, eds. *Major Authors and Illustrators for Children and Young Adults.* Detroit: Gale Research, 1993.

Contemporary Authors New Revision Series. Vol. 20. Detroit: Gale Research, 1987.

Kunitz, Stanley J., and Howard Haycraft, eds. *The Junior Book of Authors.* 2nd ed. New York: H. W. Wilson, 1951.

Smith, Louisa. "Eleanor Estes' *The Moffats:* Through Colored Glass." In *Touchstones: Reflections on the Best in Children's Literature.* Vol. 1. Edited by Perry Nodelman. West Lafayette, IN: Children's Literature Association, 1985.

Something about the Author. Vol. 7. Detroit: Gale Research, 1975.

Walter Farley

1915-1989, American writer

The Black Stallion

(novel, 1941)

PLOT: This quick-paced horse story offers the gratification of fairy tales: the humble hero gets his deepest wishes, and the outsider triumphs over those with fame and status. The first part of the novel is an island survival story. While sailing home from India, Alexander (Alec) Ramsay, Jr., becomes fascinated by a wild black stallion loaded on board at an Arabian port. Although the stallion kicks violent- ly whenever anyone approaches, Alec begins leaving sugar for the Black. When a storm strikes, Alec releases the horse just before the ship sinks. The Black swims to a small island, pulling Alec along by a

rope. Violently dragged ashore, Alec manages to cut himself free. Over the next couple of weeks, he struggles to survive, but he also develops a close relationship with the Black. Alec shares food with him, and the Black saves him from a snake; he also learns to call the Black and to ride him. When another storm blows fire onto his shelter, a passing ship discovers Alec. After he figures out how to load the Black on board, he sails to Rio de Janeiro. The Black fights another stallion on the dock, but Alec gets him on a ship and home to New York.

The story now focuses on training and racing horses. Receiving permission from his father and his mother, Belle, to keep the horse, Alec boards it with Henry Dailey, a retired jockey and trainer. The Black does run away once, but it becomes calmer, especial- ly in the presence of Napoleon, an old workhorse. With Henry's help, Alec trains the Black for racing, even though it lacks thoroughbred registration. Henry even arranges for the Black to practice at night at Belmont. After Jim Neville, a famous sports columnist, witnesses one of these secret sessions, he writes a column about a mystery horse that can beat the fastest thoroughbreds. As a result, the Black is invited to run in a match race against Cyclone and Sun Raider. Just before the start of the race, Sun Raider kicks the Black, making his leg bleed. Alec begins dismounting to examine the leg, but the race starts. The Black takes off, with Alec barely hanging on. Overtaking his thoroughbred rivals, the Black sets a world record in winning the race.

CHARACTERS: The relationship between the Black and Alec has captured the imagination of animal-loving readers, but Farley does not create full-blooded characters. Most of the secondary characters, from crewmen on the ship to attendants at the race track, are merely props who confirm the size, wildness, and speed of the Black.

Alec Ramsay, Jr., (Alec is short for Alexander) demonstrates the respect and understanding that may develop between animals and humans. A red-haired, freckle-faced youth, Alec is intelligent and generally sensible. He remembers to put on his life belt during the storm; he recalls that he has a knife and cuts the rope before the Black drags him along the island; he figures out how to build a shelter; he remembers that dried sea moss is edible. Nevertheless, Alec is one-dimensional. His passion for horses dominates everything. It prompts Alec to show kindness to the Black, as he does when he feeds him sugar. As a result, Alec conquers the Black, making it come when he whistles and riding it. Alec's passion makes him loyal. He thus decides that he would starve on the island rather than kill the Black for food. It also makes him brave. He swims under the Black's slashing hooves to fasten a sling because he does not want to leave it behind on the island. Furthermore, the horse brings out Alec's patience. He thus devotes all of his free time to caring for the Black. Finally, it makes him sneaky: he goes out at night without informing his parents. Alec undergoes little change. A natural horseman, he becomes better with practice and learns to control the Black, but he remains a boy thrilled by its speed and power.

The Black shows wildness, beauty, and a strange love for Alec. A glistening black stallion, his gigantic size indicates that he is not a pure Arabian. He has a long, slender neck; a small, savage head; and a flowing mane that is like a crest. He signals Alec with a peculiar whistling sound. Violent with men and stallions, he is gentle around old Napoleon, who no longer represents a challenge, and Alec, who shows him kindness. The Black is loyal and brave, as he shows when he saves Alec from the poisonous snake while they are on the island. He also possesses such astonishing power and speed that Alec nearly passes out when riding him. Furthermore, even when wounded and not given a fair start, he outraces the best thoroughbreds. Such implausible feats make the Black mythic. His imaginative appeal to young readers, however, probably lies in the fact that the Black is never completely tamed, yet he truly belongs to one boy, Alec. **Napoleon**, an old gray workhorse stabled at Henry's house, brings out the gentle side of the Black, showing that he is not entirely a savage loner.

Henry Dailey is Alec's mentor and friend. A short, chunky man with small gray eyes and large shoulders and hands, Henry is a retired jockey and trainer. Although he acts with good intentions, Henry is sly. Thus, he arranges to have the Black train at Belmont during the middle of the night. Furthermore, he keeps his wife and Alec's parents ignorant of what he is doing. Because he shares Alec's passion for horses and racing, he functions as a substitute father. He can do so because Alec's real father, **Alexander Ramsay, Sr.**, remains ignorant of his son's activities. A tall, thin man, he is kind in allowing his son to keep a horse. He shows parental concern by making Alec write his exams before going to the match race. The fact that he would allow a boy who had never ridden in a race to enter this one is completely improbable, but it supports the fairy tale tenor of the book. **Belle Ramsay**, Alec's short, plump mother, adds comedy. She is so completely ignorant of racing and her son's activities that she attends the match race without knowing that her son will be riding in it. **Jim Neville**, the sports broadcaster and columnist, serves as a convenient plot device. This tall, broad-shouldered, graying man developed the idea of a match race between the country's two best thoroughbreds. His authoritative declaration that the Black could beat both horses allows the Black to race even though he lacks the necessary thoroughbred registration.

Further Reading

Berger, Laura Standley, ed. *Twentieth-Century Young Adult Writers*. 1st ed. Detroit: St. James, 1994.

Cech, John, ed. *American Writers for Children 1900-1960*. Vol. 22 of *Dictionary of Literary Biography*. Detroit: Gale Research, 1983.

Collier, Laurie, and Joyce Nakamura, eds. *Major Authors and Illustrators for Children and Young Adults*. Detroit: Gale Research, 1993.

Contemporary Authors New Revision Series. Vol. 29. Detroit: Gale Research, 1990.

Contemporary Literary Criticism. Vol. 17. Detroit: Gale Research, 1981.

Kunitz, Stanley J., and Howard Haycraft, eds. *The Junior Book of Authors*. 2nd ed. New York: H. W. Wilson, 1951.

Something about the Author. Vols. 2, 43. Detroit: Gale Research, 1971, 1986.

Louise Fitzhugh

1928-1974, American author and illustrator

Harriet the Spy

(novel, 1964)

PLOT: A controversial novel, especially because an adult tells a child to lie, *Harriet the Spy* combines scenes of social criticism with a story of psychological development. Uniting these two elements are themes about loving others, maintaining individuality, and understanding and being accepted by others.

Harriet M. Welsch wants to be a writer. She records all of her thoughts in a notebook that she carries everywhere. One day, Ole Golly, her nurse, takes Harriet and her friend Sport to visit Ole Golly's mother in order to provide an example of a person with no outside interests. Harriet has already been learning about the world, however, by spying on people. Every day after her milk and cake, Harriet dons her special spy outfit and secretly observes

The ever-snooping Harriet, as drawn by Fitzhugh for Harriet the Spy.

people. The newest person on Harriet's route is Mrs. Agatha K. Plumber. Harriet sneaks into her house and hears her claim that the secret of life is staying in bed. Harriet also spies on the Dei Santi family, who run a grocery store. She is especially interested in how Mama, Papa, and Bruno, their oldest son, respond to Fabio, a younger son who always wants to borrow the family truck. At the same time, Harriet spies on their delivery boy, Little Joe Curry, who is always stealing food. Another stop on Harriet's route is the home of the Robinsons, a couple who never talk when alone but always show off their possessions to visitors. Her favorite person on the spy route is Harrison Withers, an old bird cage maker who owns twenty-six cats. When Harriet discovers that her nurse has a boyfriend, she even spies on Ole Golly and George Waldenstein, a grocery delivery man, when they are on a date.

At school, Harriet's best friends are Janie Gibbs, a girl whose ambition is to blow up the world, and Sport, who acts as housekeeper for his writer father.

The most powerful student in the class, however, is Marion Hawthorne. She and Rachel Hennessey intimidate Beth Ellen Hansen and other students into voting for Marion to be class president. Harriet's life follows a rigid routine until Ole Golly and Mr. Waldenstein take her with them on a date while her parents are out. They return late, and Mrs. Welsch fires the nurse. Saying that she is getting married and would be leaving in any case, Ole Golly departs the next day. Harriet continues with her routines, eating a tomato sandwich every day for lunch and following her spy route. But one day she is caught spying on Mrs. Plumber. Shortly afterwards, she drops her notebook during a game. After reading it, the other children become angry. They are cruel to her in school, spilling ink on her and stealing her tomato sandwich. They also form the Spy Catcher Club, the chief purpose of which is to exclude Harriet. Led by a student Harriet calls "The Boy with the Purple Socks," the club members parade past Harriet and stick their tongues out at her.

Harriet now becomes increasingly estranged from people. Harry Welsch, her father, tries to join her in pretending to be an onion for the school pageant, but he and Mrs. Welsch become distressed when they notice that Harriet frequently stops to write in her notebook. Because she devotes all her time to writing in her book, her parents forbid her to take it to school. Harriet subsequently loses all interest in life. Soon, she acts as mean as she feels: she trips Pinky Whitehead, pinches Carrie Andrews, throws a paper wad at Sport, throws a pencil at Beth Ellen Hansen's face, hurts Rachel by saying her absent father doesn't love her, puts a frog in Marion's desk, chops off some of Laura Peters's hair, stomps her feet to make the cook's cake fall, and throws a shoe at her father when he tries to find out what is wrong. At night Harriet cries for Ole Golly. Her worried parents take her to a psychologist, Dr. Wagner. Following his advice, Mr. and Mrs. Welsch arrange with the school to have Harriet made editor of the sixth grade page of the newspaper. They also get Ole Golly to write a letter to Harriet. Ole Golly tells Harriet to apologize and then to lie to those she hurt in her writing. Harriet eventually issues a retraction in the school newspaper.

The conclusion wraps up the loose ends of all the plotlines. Mrs. Plumber, who had been ordered to bed for life by her doctor, is told that the diagnosis was wrong, and so she plunges into a vigorous round of activities. Fabio has had an accident with the truck, but his parents are forgiving when he explains that he needed it because he was working as a salesman. Harrison Withers, whose cats were taken away by the health department, learns to be content with just a single cat. Of those on the spy route, only the Robinsons, who have ordered a huge statue of a baby, remain unchanged. The Spy Catcher Club dissolves when Marion tries to turn it into an exclusive bridge club for herself, Rachel, Laura, and Carrie. Led by Sport and Janie, Beth Ellen and the others quit. Harriet herself also changes, developing more compassion. In the final scene, she imagines herself as both Sport and Janie. In turn, they show acceptance by patiently waiting while she makes an entry in her notebook. The three become friends again.

Harriet also appears in The Long Secret *(1965).*

CHARACTERS: *Harriet the Spy* has an unusually large number of sharply delineated characters, many of them eccentric. Most make only brief appearances, but all contribute to the humor and social criticism in the book.

Eleven-year-old **Harriet M. Welsch** has no middle name, but she insists on using an initial, presumably because many writers do. The imaginative Harriet is rigid and dictatorial. She demands that Sport follow her directions in playing the game of Town. Harriet also loves to do everything in the same way every day: at meals she waits to be reminded to drink her milk; at school she always has a tomato sandwich for lunch; after school she has cake and milk; and every night in bed she reads by flashlight until Ole Golly takes it away. The two most unusual elements in Harriet's routine, however, are connected to her quest for knowledge. Having been told by Ole Golly that a writer should write everything down, Harriet records all her thoughts in a notebook. In order to know more about people for her writing, she develops the spy route. Harriet always dresses the same when spying, wearing old blue jeans her mother has forbidden her to wear, an old dark-blue sweatshirt, blue sneakers with holes in the toes, and black-rimmed spectacles with no glass in them. She also wears a tool belt with hooks for holding cases for her notebook and pens, a water canteen, a flashlight, and a boy scout knife. Although her mother is bemused by her behavior, Harriet insists that what she does is work, not play, because it is necessary for her chosen profession.

Harriet is intelligent and inquisitive, but she lacks compassion. When Ole Golly cites a passage by nineteenth-century Russian novelist Fyodor Dostoyevsky about how one must love something before one can understand it, Harriet seizes on the idea of knowing everything and ignores the message about love. Thus, while Harriet's notebook entries are truthful records of her thoughts, they show no sympathy for others. Harriet is not deliberately cruel—she does not intend for others to see her book. Nevertheless, because she can't understand other people's feelings, Harriet is slow to change after her classmates read her book. Once they ostracize her and her parents try to take away her notebook, she begins to feel an emptiness in her life. Deprived of the opportunity to express herself and having lost her friends and Ole Golly, the lonely Harriet is filled with hatred. Forgetting Ole Golly's message about love, she becomes destructive, attacking her classmates and even her own father.

After Ole Golly sends her a letter, Harriet realizes that she can't cling to the past and changes her ways. Harriet does not, however, undergo a dramatic reversal of character. She does not, that is, stop being a girl who loves herself and appreciates her own talent. Instead, Harriet learns how to maintain her individuality and still be a part of the community. The change begins when Harriet follows Ole Golly's advice to apply her talent. Harriet publishes her work, ending her isolation by communicating with others. Although her newspaper columns are as judgmental as her notebook entries, Harriet tactfully avoids writing about her classmates. She also displays her newly developed pragmatism by following Ole Golly's advice about lying: to end the pain her classmates feel, she publishes a retraction of her

notebook comments. Accompanying these outward changes is an internal one. Harriet becomes less emotionally rigid and slightly more empathetic by imagining herself as both Janie and Sport.

Although Harriet's nurse's name is **Catherine Golly**, Harriet thinks of her as **Ole Golly**, a name that suggests her role as the voice of wisdom. Ole Golly is an eccentric in appearance and habit. A fairly unattractive woman with a big nose, she wears only two sets of clothing, one for indoors and a billowing pile of tweed for outdoors. Her sometimes comical habit of quoting famous authors occasionally frustrates Harriet, but it makes Ole Golly an authority figure who gives meaningful advice. Ole Golly has, in fact, more influence on Harriet than her parents do. For example, they consider Ole Golly "magic" because she convinces Harriet to take dancing lessons. Ole Golly's real magic, however, is her ability to understand others: she succeeds where Harriet's parents failed because she treats Harriet's ambitions seriously. She thus points out that a female spy would have to know how to dance in order to avoid discovery. In most cases, Ole Golly is a patient instructor who lets Harriet discover things for herself.

Ole Golly is responsible for developing Harriet's curiosity because she has told her to try to view life from different perspectives so that she won't have to live like her parents. The advice obviously comes from Ole Golly's own experience with her simple-minded mother. Her own actions show that change is an inevitable part of life and that one must sometimes act differently around other people. Harriet is surprised, for example, when Ole Golly behaves differently around Mr. Waldenstein than she does around her parents and when she claims that a dinner of German food—which she does not like—was good. As a voice of wisdom, Ole Golly is often profoundly idealistic. She voices a major theme when she quotes Dostoyevsky to advise Harriet that she must feel love for all of creation. She tells Harriet on another occasion that love makes the world a bigger place. Ole Golly can, however, also be practical. In her letter, she ends Harriet's lonely depression by telling Harriet that she doesn't miss her, that she no longer needs her, and that she should get on with her life. Ole Golly's most controversial piece of advice, however, is that Harriet should lie to get her friends back. By thus placing people's feelings ahead of rigid adherence to a moral rule, Ole Golly emphasizes her point that writing exists to add love to the world, not to hurt others.

Harriet has important contacts with several other adults. Ole Golly presents her mother, **Mrs. Golly**, to warn Harriet against mindless routine and selfishness. Mrs. Golly is an enormously fat and simpleminded woman who has no interests. Her stagnation makes her daughter an effective example of someone who has seen more of the world so that she didn't have to live like her parents. But on another level, Mrs. Golly's role as a cautionary figure is not entirely successful because she doesn't appear to be capable of changing her own life. In contrast, **Mr. George Waldenstein**, Ole Golly's suitor, has shown that one can change for the better. Mr. Waldenstein is a rotund, cheerful man with a little black mustache. He is a grocery delivery man who is a comical figure when he uses his delivery bike to take Ole Golly and Harriet to the movies. Nevertheless, he also plays a serious role. He was once a successful jeweler, but his life gave him no joy. He therefore gave his wife all of his money, abandoned his routine, and started over again. Consequently, he rediscovered joy by learning about the truly valuable things in life, one of which is love, which leads him to propose to Ole Golly.

Although they begin as parents who seem oblivious to their child because they are always hiding behind their newspapers, Harriet's mother and father develop an appreciation for her talents and her needs. **Mrs. Welsch** doesn't really understand her daughter. She herself likes math, for example, and when she helps Harriet with homework she becomes so absorbed that she doesn't notice that Harriet is writing in her notebook. Unlike Ole Golly, who treats Harriet with complete seriousness, Mrs. Welsch is somewhat condescending because she finds Harriet amusing when she asks questions about falling in love. In her wild mood swings, Mrs. Welsch resembles Mama Dei Santi. She becomes hysterical when Harriet is out late and fires Ole Golly, but immediately says that Ole Golly can't leave when the nurse announces that she will depart in the morning. **Mr.**

Harry Welsch is a pressured television executive who delights in calling everyone a "fink." Although he frequently rants about his job, he is calmer than his wife and seems to have a sense of humor. He joins Harriet on the floor, for example, to practice being an onion. Nevertheless, he is equally out of touch with his daughter and is hurt when Harriet suddenly writes in her notebook. In spite of their initial lack of understanding, the Welsches are concerned parents who seek out professional advice and dutifully follow it. That advice comes from **Dr. Wagner**, a psychologist. He is an exceptionally tall man who has bright-red hair around a bald pate, yellow teeth, a strange nose, and big glasses. In spite of his odd appearance and what Harriet takes to be his foolish addiction to children's toys, Dr. Wagner is sensitive and perceptive. He realizes that Harriet needs her notebook to communicate, and he suggests ways of releasing her creative energy.

Harriet's classmates tend to be either eccentrics or conformists. **Simon Rocque**, better known as **Sport**, is Harriet's best friend. He aspires to be a baseball player and has no interest in anything to do with writing. Forced to clean and cook for his absentminded and irresponsible writer father, he is arrogant about his knowledge of money and financial matters. He is, however, an understanding boy. He rejects Marion's snobbish attempt to form an exclusive bridge club, but he accepts Harriet's need to write in her notebook. **Janie Gibbs**, Harriet's best friend after Sport, is a plain, freckled, and intensely shy girl who always walks with her head turned so that she doesn't have to see anyone. Janie is deeply disturbed. She calls her family the "Rat Pack," and she spends all of her time with a chemistry set. Her ambition is to blow up the world. The leader of the conformists is **Marion Hawthorne**. Marion is bossy, acting like a teacher at every chance and intimidating students into voting her way during elections. Her major role is to show what happens when people don't follow Ole Golly's advice to see how others live and develop love. Smug and self-important, Marion wants to form an exclusive club to keep out those she thinks are inferior. By rejecting others and by wasting her time in afternoon bridge games, she shows that she will grow up to be exactly like her mother. **Rachel Hennessey** is always with Marion and does everything she does. Her one act of individuality is cruel: she deliberately spills ink on Harriet and then feigns concern. **Carrie Andrews** and **Laura Peters**, the other two who remain in the bridge club are nonentities who lack any distinguishing traits. **Peter Matthews** is called **The Boy with the Purple Socks** because he is so boring that no one remembers his name. His idiosyncratic attire suggests the need for acceptance and security: he was once lost at the circus and his mother said she could find him if he had purple socks.

Two other students also seem to belong to the conformists, but each reveals to Harriet a surprising depth of character. **Pinky Whitehead** is a thin, pale, and weak boy who looks like a glass of milk. Harriet is often disgusted by his appearance. Pinky shows that everyone is capable of change because he goes against Marion and votes for Harriet as editor. **Beth Ellen Hansen**, who comes to school in a limousine, shows a similar change. The prettiest girl in school, she is timid and always looks as if she might cry. She proves that she is not necessarily a mouse when she finally stands up to Marion and Rachel by leaving their club. Her story is developed more fully in *The Long Secret*.

The people on Harriet's spy route provide social and psychological criticism. **Mrs. Agatha K. Plumber** is a strange, theatrical divorcée who spends all of her time talking on the telephone. Mrs. Plumber looks ancient to Harriet, but she is only forty years old. She is foolishly wasting her life after claiming that the secret of life is staying in bed. If Harriet is correct in assuming that the doctor tricks Mrs. Plumber into reassuming an active life, her transformation shows that lying can actually benefit people. The Dei Santi family bring out differences in attitudes between generations. **Papa Dei Santi**, who started the business with only a pushcart, is a hard-working man who suspects the worst when one of his sons seems to lack his drive. Nevertheless, he becomes a proud and accepting father when he learns that Fabio has displayed manly independence. **Mama Dei Santi** is an overly emotional, almost hysterical woman, a parody of the earth mother type. She loves her children, but she lashes out at Fabio for scaring her

with the accident. Although she is at first violent when she discovers that her delivery boy steals from her, she becomes tender and generous when she learns that he gives food to hungry children. **Bruno Dei Santi**, the oldest child, is a burly man who accepts that Fabio is different from him and his father. He supports his brother even when he thinks that Fabio wants to borrow the truck just to have fun. Eighteen-year-old **Fabio Dei Santi** is a tall, thin, gloomy-looking boy who illustrates the need for determination and individuality in order to achieve happiness. Although he appears to reject his parents' values, he simply wants to find his own way in life. **Little Joe Curry**, the Dei Santis' delivery boy, is always eating. He is an opportunist who steals, but he is also generous in providing other children with food. **The Robinsons** (her first name is Grace; his is never given) satirize the consumer culture. They never talk or even read when alone, yet they think that their lives are perfect. In fact, they live for the times when they can show guests their latest material acquisitions. Their pride in their purchase of an enormous statue of a baby symbolizes that the childless Robinsons are emotionally sterile and loveless. The one person on her route for whom Harriet has any sympathy is **Harrison Withers**. An elderly maker of bird cages who loves cats, Harrison Withers is an individualist. After the health department removes his twenty-six cats, he impresses Harriet with his individualism by getting a new cat.

Further Reading

Berger, Laura Standley, ed. *Twentieth-Century Children's Writers*. 4th ed. Detroit: St. James, 1995.

Bosmaijian, Hamida. "Louise Fitzhugh's *Harriet the Spy: Nonsense and Sense*." In *Touchstones: Reflections on the Best in Children's Literature*. Vol. 1. Edited by Perry Nodelman, pp. 71-82. West Lafayette, IN: Children's Literature Association, 1985.

Children's Literature Review. Vol. 1. Detroit: Gale Research, 1976.

Collier, Laurie, and Joyce Nakamura, eds. *Major Authors and Illustrators for Children and Young Adults*. Detroit: Gale Research, 1993.

Contemporary Authors New Revision Series. Vol. 34. Detroit: Gale Research, 1992.

De Montreville, Doris, and Donna Hill, eds. *Third Book of Junior Authors*. New York: H. W. Wilson, 1972.

Estes, Glenn E., ed. *American Writers for Children since 1960: Fiction.* Vol. 52 of *Dictionary of Literary Biography.* Detroit: Gale Research, 1986.

Something about the Author. Vols. 1, 45. Detroit: Gale Research, 1971, 1986.

Wolf, Virginia L. *Louise Fitzhugh.* New York: Twayne, 1991.

Sid Fleischman

1920-, American novelist

The Whipping Boy

(novel, 1986)

PLOT: The twists and turns of plot in this rollicking Newbery Medal winner lead two young boys to dramatically change their understanding of themselves and others. Prince Horace is so naughty and annoying that he is known as Prince Brat. Because it is illegal to spank a prince, his whipping boy, Jemmy, receives punishment in his place. Jemmy, an orphan, dreams of escaping back to his life as a rat catcher. Prince Brat, who finds court life boring, also wants to escape and orders Jemmy to accompany him.

Lost in a fog, they are captured by two notorious highwaymen, Hold-Your-Nose Billy and Cutwater. Seeing a chance to save the Prince while escaping himself, Jemmy convinces the highwaymen that he is the Prince and his companion is his whipping boy. Prince Brat refuses to go along with Jemmy's plan, however, and betrays him, but when Jemmy escapes the Prince follows. When the opportunity comes, Jemmy is unable to leave the Prince behind, so he gets them a ride in the coach of Captain Harry Nips, a potato seller. The highwaymen stop the coach and discover the hiding boys. Still believing Jemmy's story about their identities, Billy whips the Prince. Fortunately, Betsy and her dancing bear, Petunia, arrive to frighten away the villains.

The adventures that follow bring new understanding to both Jemmy and the Prince. Jemmy, the Prince, Betsy, Petunia, and Harry Nips travel together to a fair. There the Prince learns that the common people hate him and dread the day he will become king. Shortly afterwards, the villains again discover them. Jemmy and the Prince seek refuge in the sewers, where the Prince fools the highwaymen into going down the wrong tunnel. Attacked by hordes of rats, the outlaws seek safety by stowing away on a convict ship. The Prince goes home, where he ensures that Betsy and Captain Nips receive a reward for his return. He also promises to behave. Jemmy, who realizes that he loves the knowledge he has acquired at court, discovers that he has also acquired a friend.

CHARACTERS: The minor characters are painted with broad, colorful strokes, but the limited third-person point of view maintains the focus on Jemmy. The story, that is, presents only Jemmy's thoughts, thereby making his reactions the most important element of the narrative.

Jemmy, the orphan son of a rat catcher, is proud and brave. He maintains his dignity and frustrates the Prince by refusing to yell whenever he is whipped. Jemmy is also intelligent, having learned to read and write during the Prince's lessons. In spite of his intelligence and his wit in devising escape plans, however, Jemmy does not truly understand either the Prince or himself. He views the Prince's inability to read and his stubborn insistence on his royal identity as signs of stupidity. Jemmy is also puzzled by his own concern for the Prince's safety. A kind and considerate person, he comes to appreciate how boring the Prince's narrow life at court is. After the Prince silently endures a whipping and displays bravery in the sewers, however, Jemmy realizes the full truth: their adventures together have transformed his former tormentor into a friend. Consequently, Jemmy trusts the Prince who once betrayed him. Jemmy's final taste of self-understanding comes with his realization that he loves the books and the knowledge he has acquired at court. Mature enough to realize that he can never again be satisfied with his former life of ignorance, he understands that the castle he once wanted to escape is indeed a true home.

Prince Horace, fittingly known to all his subjects as **Prince Brat**, is mischievous because he is bored. His refusal to learn to read and write also makes him appear stupid, as do his constant rejections of Jemmy's plans to help him escape. The truth is that the haughty Prince, lacking any purpose in life, demands his own way, even if that means betraying Jemmy to stop him from leaving. The turning point in the Prince's development comes when he endures a whipping and, like Jemmy, refuses to cry out. He thereby shows both bravery and respect for the boy he has formerly humiliated. His moment of greatest understanding, however, comes when he accepts that his behavior has made his people hate him. Humbled by this knowledge, he is able to admit to Jemmy in the sewers that he is afraid and he admires Jemmy's bravery. The full extent of his transformation is evident in his final actions. The once impractical Prince saves Jemmy and himself by fooling the thieves. Furthermore, the once selfish Prince displays generosity by arranging for Harry Nips and Betsy to get a reward. Finally, the Prince promises to behave and to apply himself to his lessons, which indicates a mature sense of princely responsibility. More importantly, his promise marks a moment of friendship, because it ensures that Jemmy will never again endure a whipping.

The two villains form a stark contrast to the two heroes. **Hold-Your-Nose Billy** is a notorious highwayman whose deeds are celebrated in ballads. A large, hairy man, he earned his nickname from his habit of eating vast quantities of garlic. Billy is both brutal and stupid, being constantly fooled by Jemmy's stories. **Cutwater**, Hold-Your-Nose Billy's skinny companion, is a follower who is equally stupid. Their climactic act of foolishness, stowing away on a convict ship, brings a fitting punishment to both.

The other minor characters show the goodness and generosity of the common people. **Betsy**, who

*Prince Horace and Jemmy try to escape Hold-Your-Nose Billy and Cutwater in this illustration by Peter Sis from Fleischman's **The Whipping Boy.***

travels with her dancing bear, **Petunia**, has a kind heart that prompts her to intervene when Billy whips the Prince. **Captain Harry Nips,** the Hot-Potato Man, has poor eyesight, which leads him into constant wrecks with his coach. Nevertheless, he is sharp sighted enough to see goodness in the poorly dressed Jemmy. He also displays friendship and generosity by feeding Jemmy and the Prince.

Further Reading

Berger, Laura Standley, ed. *Twentieth-Century Children's Writers.* 4th ed. Detroit: St. James, 1995.

Children's Literature Review. Vols. 1, 15. Detroit: Gale Research, 1976, 1988.

Collier, Laurie, and Joyce Nakamura, eds. *Major Authors and Illustrators for Children and Young Adults.* Detroit: Gale Research, 1993.

De Montreville, Doris, and Donna Hill, eds. *Third Book of Junior Authors.* New York: H. W. Wilson, 1972.

Something about the Author. Vols. 8, 59. Detroit: Gale Research, 1976, 1990.

Paula Fox

1923-, American author

The Slave Dancer

(historical novel, 1973)

PLOT: This controversial Newbery Medal winner is set in 1840 and graphically portrays the horrors of the illegal slave trade. Its thirteen-year-old narrator endures an initiation into evil that transforms him into a wiser but sadder man. Jessie Bollier lives with his seamstress mother and sister, Betty, in New Orleans. Needing light so that she can work late, his mother sends him to borrow candles from crochety Aunt Agatha. On the way home, Jessie is kidnapped by Claudius Sharkey and Clay Purvis, who have heard him play his fife. They take him to their ship, *The Moonlight*, to be a slave dancer, a boy who plays music to exercise the slaves. Jessie becomes an unwilling member of the crew, which includes: Captain Cawthorne, a cruel man who bites Jessie's ear and renames him Bollweevil; Nicholas Spark, the first mate, who is a mindless and sinister shadow of the captain; and Ned Grimes, the carpenter who pretends to be beyond the evil of the trade. Another crewman, Benjamin Stout, tries to befriend the boy, but Jessie finds himself more attracted to Purvis. During the voyage to Africa, Stout blames Purvis for emptying his sea chest. Later, Stout steals an egg and blames Purvis, whom Cawthorne has whipped. When they reach Africa, sailor Seth Smith explains the trade and Jessie's role in keeping the slaves healthy.

After the slaves are loaded on board and the ship begins its journey to Cuba, Jessie is forced to play while the slaves dance. After he sees Stout throw a feverish woman overboard, Jessie starts to hate the slaves and he throws down his fife. Cawthorne has Stout whip him for his disobedience. The horrors mount as fever kills both slaves and crew members alike, including Ned Grimes. Spark shoots a slave who attacked him and the angry captain punishes Spark by having him thrown overboard. Stout, who assumes the post of first mate, now becomes hostile to Jessie. He throws Jessie's fife down the slave hold to make him retrieve it.

Once off the coast of Cuba, Stout incorrectly identifies a pursuing ship, and *The Moonlight* is forced to flee. As a storm builds, reflecting the moral chaos on the ship, Cawthorne orders the slaves thrown overboard. Jessie hides in the hold with Ras, a slave his own age. When they emerge, the crew is dead. They escape from the sinking ship and reach land, where an escaped slave named Daniel sends Ras north to freedom and Jessie south to his home. After reuniting with his mother, Jessie becomes an apothecary and moves his family north. Forever changed by his experience, Jessie can no longer bear the sound of music because of the memories it brings back.

CHARACTERS: This novel clearly depicts the defenders of slavery as evil, but it has been criticized for portraying the slaves as passive and pathetic. Actually, Fox shows them as understandably dazed and confused. She also shows that they had little chance to rebel because of the overwhelming forces opposing them. Furthermore, this argument against the book is contradicted by the fact that the two blacks Jessie comes to know are portrayed as dignified individuals.

Thirteen-year-old **Jessie Bollier** loses his innocence when he participates in the horrors of slavery. At first, he is a curious and slightly rebellious boy who, in spite of his mother's prohibitions, frequents the slave market and other dangerous areas. Jessie dreams of becoming a wealthy chandler and indulging in the luxuries that slavery creates, but his vision of life changes after he is kidnapped. On board *The Moonlight*, Jessie shows that he is a sensitive and capable judge of character. Intelligent and observant, he sees through the hypocrisies of both Grimes and Stout. He realizes, too, that Purvis considers compassion for slaves to be an insult to his indentured Irish parents.

In the beginning, Jessie sympathizes with the slaves, probably because his mother is originally from Massachusetts. He loses his original identity, however, once he is reduced to being Bollweevil the slave dancer. He then starts to hate the slaves for their filth and degradation. Jessie is saved from becoming as callous as the rest of the crew, however, when the captain has him whipped. The pain restores his identity and his sense of humanity because he is able to identify with Ras and his sufferings. Jessie demonstrates his humanity, as well as his presence of mind, by taking Ras into the hold when the men begin throwing the slaves overboard. This descent represents a symbolic death, and his emergence and ultimate reunion with his mother is like being reborn. But Jessie does not simply resume his old life. He is now opposed to slavery and the society built on it. Thus, he pursues a career as an apothecary, a profession associated with healing others, and moves his family to the North, for which he fights during the Civil War. Jessie's moral salvation costs him dearly. During the voyage, he realized that the world was not as promising as he once thought and that *The Moonlight* was merely a microcosm of its evils. Returned to land, he no longer plays or listens to music. For Jessie, music is no longer an innocent pleasure but a reminder of human perversity and suffering.

The stench of *The Moonlight* symbolizes the moral decay of its crew. **Captain Cawthorne**, its master, is cruel and greedy. Cawthorne bites Jessie's ear to make him listen before speaking; he has Purvis whipped, primarily to reassert his position of command. He seems somewhat mad, changing moods according to the weather and refusing to trim his sails even if it means endangering the ship. The captain takes a perverse delight in terrifying others and in asserting his superiority. Thus, he rewards Jessie when he fails to guess the contents of a costume trunk, pointedly saying that he would have received nothing if he had guessed correctly. Furthermore, although Cawthorne strictly rations his crew's food and drink, he indulges himself and even keeps hens to provide him with fresh eggs. Cawthorne is obsessed with profit from what he calls his "God-granted trade" in slaves. Completely devoid of compassion, he orders dying slaves thrown overboard to save money. Cawthorne also becomes furious when Spark eats into his profits by unnecessarily killing a slave, for which offense he has his first mate bound and thrown overboard. Similarly, when Stout misidentifies the pursuing ship, he angrily declares that Stout has murdered him and has all the slaves thrown overboard.

Nicholas Spark, the first mate, is the brainless shadow of his captain. Because he serves Cawthorne, he terrifies Jessie. Spark's most significant role is to show the depth of Cawthorne's cruel passions following the shooting of the slave. Old **Ned Grimes**, the philosophical carpenter, illustrates the hypocrisy of many in the slave trade. He talks as if he were not involved in the creation of human suffering and says his heart is not in the trade, but, as Jessie notices, Ned is not averse to sharing in the profits. Nevertheless, Ned contributes to the moral theme by offering a view of money that contrasts with Cawthorne's. When he is dying of fever, Ned tells Jessie that death, not gold, is the wages of sin. **Seth Smith** expresses the sailors' contempt for blacks and denounces Stout for his underhanded treatment of Purvis. His major function, however, is expository: he explains the details of the slave trade to Jessie, providing readers with crucial background information.

The most prominent crew members, however, are two men who try to befriend Jessie. **Clay Purvis**, a big-jawed sailor, enthusiastically defends the slave trade. As Jessie realizes, however, Purvis justifies his role by pointing to the suffering of his Irish parents. Purvis somehow regards any show of sympathy for the black slaves as an affront to his ancestors, who endured hardships when they emigrated. Nevertheless, when he contracts the fever, he vows never to sail on a slaver again. In spite of his moral blindness to the evils of slavery, Purvis is kind to and protective of Jessie, although he does hit Jessie across the back when Jessie whines about wanting something more to drink during a period of intense rationing. The act is not cruel, however, and it makes Jessie feel better because it ends his hysterical fear. Although Purvis is stoical when he himself is whipped after being falsely accused of stealing an egg, he does not want Jessie to suffer unnecessarily. Thus, after Jessie expresses his fear of Stout, Purvis vows that he will not let Stout beat him.

Tall, heavy-limbed **Benjamin Stout** is mild in manner but thoroughly evil in his actions. Stout, whom Purvis contemptuously calls Saint Stout, constantly reads the Bible. He tries to befriend Jessie, surreptitiously offering him bread when he first arrives and warning him about the captain and mate. He also warns Jessie that he will be initiated into a knowledge of evil when he says that Jessie might as well witness the world's cruelties because they will happen whether or not he sees them. Stout himself is, however, one of the worst people Jessie encounters. He is wantonly cruel, telling Jessie that sailors kill rats out of necessity but insects for pleasure. He also uses his ability to speak the slaves' language to indulge his nefarious whims, such as taunting and perhaps molesting a woman he later throws overboard. Equally malicious with the crew, Stout actually is the one who steals the egg, framing Purvis, possibly in revenge for emptying his trunk. Stout eventually becomes synonymous with the wickedness aboard the ship. Thus, when Jessie says that he hates the ship, Stout declares that Jessie must necessarily hate him. Stout then begins to exact revenge: he steals Jessie's fife and forces him to descend into the slave hold to retrieve it. Although he is devious, Stout is not clever. The men know of his plots, and Cawthorne berates him for his foolishness in wrongly identifying the pursuing ship. Stout dies in the storm entangled in a "web of rope" that ironically symbolizes his web of deceit.

Only two blacks are seen as individuals in the novel. **Ras**, a thirteen-year-old slave, insists on his dignity by refusing to dance until he is struck and then deliberately making eye contact with Jessie. He displays understandable fear during the storm, but he bravely enters the water when the ship is sinking. Jessie, who has himself been kidnapped, learns greater sympathy for others because he identifies with Ras and becomes almost like a brother to him. **Daniel**, the escaped slave who helps them when they reach land, is a wise and compassionate man. He not only arranges for Ras to escape north to freedom, but he recognizes that he can trust Jessie enough to give him directions home. Jessie sees Daniel as a father figure and longs for a display of affection. Daniel is affectionate with Ras, but he is only understanding toward Jessie.

Jessie's family is important in the frame story to his initiation adventure. Jessie's **mother**, a hard-working widow originally from Massachusetts, may have inspired his original sympathy for the slave. She manages to keep her family happy in spite of her poverty. No matter how tough things are, she finds blessings and declares their life preferable to conditions elsewhere. **Aunt Agatha** is a neat and bossy woman who seems to dislike Jessie. She announces an important element of the maturation theme—his need to examine issues seriously—when she asks Jessie who will teach him to think. Jessie's disappearance shocks her into showing affection. Although she once declared that he couldn't benefit from schooling, she has a friend arrange his apprenticeship to an apothecary.

Further Reading

Authors and Artists for Young Adults. Vol. 3. Detroit: Gale Research, 1990.

Berger, Laura Standley, ed. *Twentieth-Century Young Adult Writers.* 1st ed. Detroit: St. James, 1994.

Children's Literature Review. Vol. 1. Detroit: Gale Research, 1976.

Collier, Laurie, and Joyce Nakamura, eds. *Major Authors and Illustrators for Children and Young Adults.* Detroit: Gale Research, 1993.

Contemporary Authors New Revision Series. Vol. 36. Detroit: Gale Research, 1992.

Contemporary Literary Criticism. Vols. 2, 8. Detroit: Gale Research, 1974, 1978.

De Montreville, Doris, and Elizabeth D. Crawford, eds. *Fourth Book of Junior Authors.* New York: H. W. Wilson, 1978.

Estes, Glenn E., ed. *American Writers for Children since 1960: Fiction.* Vol. 52 of *Dictionary of Literary Biography.* Detroit: Gale Research, 1986.

Rees, David. "'The Color of Saying': Paula Fox." In *The Marble in the Water: Essays on Contemporary Writers of Fiction for Children and Young Adults.* Boston: Horn Book, 1980.

Something about the Author. Vols. 17, 60. Detroit: Gale Research, 1979, 1990.

Don Freeman

1908-1978, American musician, artist, illustrator, and
author

Corduroy

(picture book, 1968)

PLOT: This toy fantasy presents two linked stories
of wish fulfillment. Corduroy, a stuffed bear who
lives in the toy department of a big store, longs for
someone to take him home. Lisa wants to buy him,
but her mother, who has spent too much money
already, refuses. She also points out to Lisa that the
bear does not seem new because he has a button
missing from the shoulder strap of his green overalls. That night, Corduroy goes through the store to

*A slightly defective toy bear finds love from a little girl
who sees he is special in Freeman's self-illustrated
book, Corduroy.*

find his lost button. During his search, he fulfills
many wishes he has had. By riding the escalator, he
achieves the wish to climb a mountain; by going to
the furniture department, he realizes his wish to live
in a palace; and he climbs onto a bed to fulfill his
wish of sleeping in one.

Unfortunately, Corduroy knocks over a lamp
while pulling a button from the mattress. The noise
alerts a night watchman, who returns him to the toy
department. The next morning, Lisa gets her first
wish when she buys Corduroy with her own money.
In Lisa's modest room, where a bed just his size
awaits him, Corduroy achieves his wish for a home.
After Lisa sews a button on Corduroy's overalls,

both indicate that they have received one more wish: to have a friend.

A Pocket for Corduroy *(1978) is the sequel.*

CHARACTERS: Although Corduroy moves about the store, he speaks only to Lisa, suggesting that the child's imagination brings him to life. **Corduroy** is pictured as a rather ordinary toy bear; only his green overalls make him distinctive. His desire to be purchased shows his initial loneliness. He becomes self-aware after Lisa's mother points out that he does not look new. His subsequent search for his missing button shows that he is respectable and wants to be appealing. This quest enables him to appreciate the simple but important facets of life. Thus, although Lisa's room is not a palace, Corduroy finds that it is perfect for him because it is a genuine home where everything is adapted to his needs. The once lonely bear is therefore able to achieve his ultimate wish of having a true friend.

Like Corduroy, who represents her feelings, **Lisa** moves from loneliness to the happiness of friendship. Only the pictures indicate that Lisa is an African American girl. Kind and loving, she is attracted to Corduroy in spite of his shop-worn appearance. She shows determination by using her own savings to purchase him and consideration by sewing on a button to make him more comfortable. By setting up a bed just Corduroy's size, Lisa establishes the theme that happiness depends on belonging and being loved, not on grand surroundings.

Further Reading

Berger, Laura Standley, ed. *Twentieth-Century Children's Writers.* 4th ed. Detroit: St. James, 1995.

Collier, Laurie, and Joyce Nakamura, eds. *Major Authors and Illustrators for Children and Young Adults.* Detroit: Gale Research, 1993.

Contemporary Authors. Vols. 77-80. Detroit: Gale Research, 1979.

Contemporary Authors New Revision Series. Vol. 44. Detroit: Gale Research, 1994.

Children's Literature Review. Vol. 30. Detroit: Gale Research, 1993.

Fuller, Muriel, ed. *More Junior Authors.* New York: H. W. Wilson, 1963.

Something about the Author. Vol. 17. Detroit: Gale Research, 1979.

Leon Garfield

1921-, English author

Smith

(novel, 1967)

PLOT: A colorful depiction of eighteenth-century London's underworld, *Smith* is both a mystery and a novel of development. After he steals a document, Smith, a young pickpocket often called Smut, witnesses two men murder his victim, Mr. Field. He also hears a third man order them to search for the document. Smith decides that the document is valuable and that he must learn to read if he is to profit from it. Before he can do so, however, the murderers locate him. The escaping Smith knocks over Mr. Mansfield, a blind magistrate, whom he then leads home. Mr. Mansfield gives him a position, and Miss Mansfield, his daughter, teaches him to read. After he is stripped of his rags and bathed, however, Smith discovers that the document is missing. Meg, the scullery maid, has put it on the magistrate's desk. When Smith tries to retrieve it, Miss Mansfield catches him. Therefore, when attorney Thomas Billing says that he saw Smith murder Mr. Field, the Mansfields believe him.

Billing visits Smith daily in prison, offering freedom in exchange for the document. Smith also has visits from his sisters, Miss Bridget and Miss Fanny, his friend and idol, the highwayman Lord Tom, and from Meg, who tells him that the magistrate has the document. Mr. Mansfield himself informs Smith that he will deliver it to a lawyer. Smith, following Billing's plan, tries to escape through an air shaft. The assassins are waiting for him, so Smith escapes by hiding under Miss Bridget's dress. He and Lord Tom then set out to rob the magistrate of the document. When he sees Lord Tom talking to the murderers, however, Smith realizes that he has been betrayed. He therefore pulls the magistrate from his carriage and leads him through a snow-storm. They take shelter in the house of Charlie Parkin, where Mr. Mansfield protects the boy by lying about Smith's name.

After reading the document, Smith accompanies the magistrate to Mr. Field's house. They overhear Billing discussing Field's murder with Mr. Black, the wooden-legged man who ordered the body searched. Mr. Black is actually Jack Field, the murdered man's long-missing son. Discovering the magistrate and Smith, Billing orders the murderers to kill them. But Lord Tom shoots one murderer before both he and Jack Field are killed. The document leads to the discovery of a buried fortune, and Smith receives a handsome share that he uses to set up his sisters in a house. He himself goes to live with the Mansfields. Ironically, Billing, having made a deal to escape the gallows, is murdered in prison by an old man, a prisoner who once befriended Smith and who turns out to be the father of Mr. Jones, the hangman.

CHARACTERS: The vivid characters display the deceptive appearances and moral ambivalence typically at the center of Garfield's novels. **Smith**, called **Smut** by some, is a twelve-year-old pickpocket who undergoes a process of education. A dirty, dark-haired, sharp-featured boy possessing remarkable speed, Smith seems devoid of moral values. He not only steals for a living, but he dreams of becoming a highwayman like his idol, Lord Tom. Nevertheless, Smith possesses a good heart. The pity he feels when he knocks over the blind magistrate thus causes him to lead the man home. In the bathing scene, in which the rotting layers of his clothes are peeled off and he is cleaned until he becomes a "ghost of his former self," Smith is reborn. Clean and happy with the new respect he has acquired, he learns to read. Once Billing charges him with murder and the Mansfields refuse to believe him when he professes his innocence, however, Smith reverts to his former character. Sent to the symbolic hell of Newgate, he becomes dead to the outside world and is filled with hatred for both Mansfields. He also exhibits his former shrewdness. Thus, to deceive Billing into thinking that he possesses the document, he feigns

happiness when Meg tells him that the magistrate has it.

After his escape from prison, Smith becomes physically and morally heroic. Receiving another blow to his faith in human nature when he discovers that Lord Tom is planning to betray him, Smith saves the magistrate from being robbed. While leading him through the snowy night, Smith is tempted to desert the magistrate, whom he fears will turn him in to the authorities at the first opportunity. Nevertheless, professing to be "only" a human being, Smith overcomes temptation and leads the magistrate to safety. By doing so, he gives the stern magistrate a lesson in compassion that awakens the older man's heart. Although Smith later experiences a temporary bout of treasure lust, he finds something far more valuable on his journey. After the noble death of Lord Tom, Smith abandons his dream of being a highwayman and finds true friendship with the magistrate.

The Justice of the Peace, **Mr. Mansfield**, is a huge man who has been blind for twelve years, the exact length of Smith's life. He lost his sight while rescuing his daughter from a fire that claimed his wife's life. Since that time, he has been the very emblem of blind justice, declaring that to him "devils and angels are one." Mr. Mansfield, who thinks of justice as the only fixed thing in his dark world, immediately accepts the idea of Smith's guilt in the murder. Later, he insists that duty compels him to deliver the document without knowing its contents. Smith's refusal to desert him in the snowstorm, however, teaches the magistrate to see with his heart. He therefore lies when Parkin asks for his companion's name and later insists that Smith read the document before they deliver it. A final sign of his transformation into a kind and compassionate man comes when, guided by Smith, he gratefully shakes the hand of the dying Lord Tom.

Lord Tom, a highwayman who always wears green, is both a villain and a hero. A flamboyant man given to telling romantic stories, Lord Tom is Smith's idol. He falls from his pedestal, however, when he betrays Smith by conspiring with the murderers. Nevertheless, he later redeems himself and becomes truly a romantic hero by protecting Smith from the murderers. **Mr. Thomas Billing**, a handsome attorney who is about thirty years of age, has rosy cheeks, a dark mustache, and eyes that shine with shrewdness and wit. Although he is in love with Miss Mansfield, he is otherwise lacking in feeling. A callous man who sets up the murder of Mr. Field, betrays Smith during the prison escape, and orders the murder of Smith and the magistrate, he repeatedly refuses to accept responsibility for his evil deeds. Instead, he blames the world for his depravity. Fittingly, he is killed after accepting the supposed friendship of the hangman's father. **Jack Field**, the wooden-legged villain Billing calls **Mr. Black**, disappeared twelve years earlier—once again the length of Smith's life—and evidently took up a disreputable lifestyle. Spurred on by Billing, he participates in the murder of his own father. Heavy-handed symbolism reveals his character: he sits upon his favorite spot in the churchyard, a statue of a black angel. **Charlie Parkin**, the constable who saves the lives of Smith and the magistrate by giving them shelter, provides an object lesson in narrow concepts of justice. Parkin writes down each deed he does so that he can charge the parish for it. Recognizing his own adherence to the cold letter of the law in Parkin's behavior, Mr. Mansfield finally listens to his heart, protecting Smith by lying to the constable. The imprisoned **old man**, the father of Mr. Jones, the hangman, is an ironic agent of justice. He is cynically delighted to hear about scoundrelly behavior, yet he is protective of Smith, subtly warning him not to reveal too much to Billing. He helps Smith to escape, and he kills Billing, who used a technicality to avoid the gallows.

Most of the female characters do not display the mixture of qualities found in the males. The exception is **Miss Mansfield**, who speaks respectfully to her father, but who makes faces that suggest deep frustration over attending to him. Although she and her father call each other saints and each praises the other for the kindness shown to Smith, Miss Mansfield is more compassionate. She gives Smith another chance when she finds him searching the magistrate's papers, and she believes in him once he goes to prison. **Meg**, the Mansfield's scullery maid with lobster-red arms, constantly rails against brains as the cause of most troubles. While she herself has an ample heart, her lack of intelligence makes her ineffective in helping Smith. **Miss Bridget**, the older of Smith's sisters, is stern and practical. She shows wit by concealing Smith beneath the hoop of her skirt during his escape. In contrast, nineteen-year-old **Miss Fanny**, Smith's other sister, is silly and sentimentally romantic. She is foolishly talkative during Smith's escape and hopelessly smitten with Lord Tom.

Further Reading

Authors and Artists for Young Adults. Vol. 8. Detroit: Gale Research, 1992.

Berger, Laura Standley, ed. *Twentieth-Century Young Adult Writers.* 1st ed. Detroit: St. James, 1994.

Children's Literature Review. Vol. 21. Detroit: Gale Research, 1990.

Collier, Laurie, and Joyce Nakamura, eds. *Major Authors and Illustrators for Children and Young Adults.* Detroit: Gale Research, 1993.

Contemporary Authors New Revision Series. Vol. 41. Detroit: Gale Research, 1993.

Contemporary Literary Criticism. Vol. 12. Detroit: Gale Research, 1980.

De Montreville, Doris, and Elizabeth D. Crawford, eds. *Fourth Book of Junior Authors.* New York: H. W. Wilson, 1978.

Hunt, Caroline C., ed. *British Children's Writers since 1960, First Series.* Vol. 161 of *Dictionary of Literary Biography.* Detroit: Gale Research, 1996.

Something about the Author. Vols. 1, 32, 76. Detroit: Gale Research, 1971, 1983, 1994.

Alan Garner

1934-, English author

The Owl Service

(fantasy, 1967)

PLOT: *The Owl Service* is set in a Welsh valley where variations of a legendary event recur periodically. In the Welsh legend, which is included in the medieval collection *The Mabinogian,* Gwydion creates a bride of flowers for his kinsman Lleu Llaw Gyffes. Blodeuwedd, as the bride is called, falls in love with Gronw Pebyr and betrays her husband, telling Gronw the secret of how to kill Lleu. Gronw kills Lleu, who then becomes an eagle. After Gwydion restores Lleu to his own shape, Lleu kills Gronw, and Gwydion transforms Blodeuwedd into an owl. In recent times, another trio reenacted this drama: Huw Halfbacon caused the death of Bertram, with whom his lover, Nancy, was flirting. As the novel opens, the ancient passions seize three adolescents: Gwyn, Nancy's son; Alison, who is related to Bertram; and Alison's stepbrother, Roger Bradley.

Alison and Roger are vacationing in Wales with Clive, his father, and Margaret, her mother, who have been recently married. Nancy is their cook, and Huw is their gardener. Discovering an old set of decorated plates, Alison traces their design onto paper, rearranging it into an owl. The design on the plate disappears, as does the paper owl. Shortly afterwards, Gwyn finds a medieval painting of Blodeuwedd beneath crumbling pebbledash. (It soon disappears.) Events quickly become ominous: Alison's book flies through the air, attacking Gwyn; Gwyn finds Alison obsessively making paper owls; and Alison and Gwyn simultaneously see a reflection of Blodeuwedd's face in a pool.

Becoming fond of Alison, Gwyn tells her about Huw's tragic past. He also tells her that Nancy wants him to work in a shop, but that he has higher ambitions and has purchased elocution records to improve his chances in life. Alison's family has contempt for the Welsh. As Alison tells Gwyn that Margaret won't let her talk to him, Roger comes by and taunts Gwyn about his records.

When Nancy then announces that she is taking Gwyn out of school, he runs away, but a sow forces him to spend a night in a tree. Huw then tells him that he is Gwyn's father and that Gwyn must suffer for his people. That day, Roger opens a sealed room containing Bertram's motorcycle, a stuffed owl, and Alison's paper owls. Nancy destroys the owl. As a storm rages, Nancy and Gwyn leave in a taxi, but fallen trees block their way. Meanwhile, Alison falls unconscious, feathers gather around her, and her

face shows owl scratches. Huw tells Gwyn to save Alison by comforting her, but Gwyn instead hurls insults at Roger. When Huw explains that Gwyn is too hurt to make Alison into flowers, Roger becomes the hero, telling Alison that she is flowers, not owls. The marks on Alison's face disappear, and the air becomes filled with petals.

CHARACTERS: Insistent parallels between the modern and mythic worlds, coupled with an absence of physical description, make the characters represent grand passions. Dialogue, the only device distinguishing characters, makes them ordinary, even banal, twentieth-century individuals. Although most critics praise Garner's technique, some feel that the connection between mythic passion and adolescent anxieties is strained and that the dialogue is confusing.

Gwyn is the center of related conflicts involving family, class, and nationality. He comes from the working class, but he wants to be more than a shop assistant, the height of his mother's ambition for him. Indeed, Nancy's domineering selfishness makes him hate her. He denounces her as a cow before his friends, he spitefully corrects her grammar, and he contemptuously puts owl droppings in her purse. Gwyn is intelligent, and he is determined to succeed, even if he has to go to night school. He realizes, however, that intelligence and talent are not enough in a society as conscious of nationality as it is of class. To change his Welsh accent, he has purchased a set of elocution recordings; pathetically, he does not own a record player. Although Gwyn knows that his heritage is an economic liability, he is intuitively attached to Welsh culture. He feels at home within a week of his arrival in the valley because he has paid close attention to Nancy's stories about her life there. Furthermore, Gwyn resents the disdain the English express for the Welsh. When Roger calls him a Welsh oaf and accuses him of scraping off the picture of Blodeuwedd, Gwyn shows his resentment by adopting the role of a violent, thick-headed servant.

Within the mythic pattern, Gwyn is Lleu to Alison's Blodeuwedd and Roger's Gronw. Gwyn, for example, obviously loves Alison, sending her notes, constantly seeking her out, and protecting her from her mounting fears. Like Lleu, who told Blodeuwedd the secret of how he could be killed, Gwyn tells Alison a secret, his purchase of elocution records. He subsequently suffers betrayal when she tells Roger, who then taunts Gwyn. Gwyn, in a way, dies from this. Like Lleu, however, Gwyn is reborn. Huw, like Gwydion in Welsh lore, brings Gwyn down from the tree where the sow has chased him and reveals his new identity. Gwyn's tragedy is that, although he is a Welsh lord because Huw is his father, he fails in his duty. Selfishly concerned with his own pain, he continues the mythic cycle of betrayal and anger. Just as Lleu threw his spear at Gronw, he hurls insults at Roger. By trying to "kill" Roger instead of comforting Alison, he sees her as an owl, a betrayer, instead of a flower, a beautiful girl who did not intend to hurt him. Placing his own feelings above his duty to protect others, he repeats the myth. However understandable such bitterness is in an ordinary adolescent, it signals that Gwyn has failed to be a true lord and has become merely the vassal of his passions.

Roger Bradley, who reenacts Gronw's role, is a snobbish English boy. For much of the novel, he seems incapable of escaping prejudices. He dismisses Gwyn as an intelligent Welsh lout, calls him a "Welsh oaf," claims that Gwyn has a chip on his shoulder, and declares that it is shameful for a boy to cry when he sees Gwyn in tears after arguing with Nancy. Finding nothing wrong with being destined to enter his father's business, Roger does not appreciate Gwyn's ambition or the obstacles he faces. Throughout most of the novel, then, Roger is a foil to Gwyn. Many critics therefore feel that his heroism is an unwarranted plot twist. Roger is obnoxious, but his sudden sensitivity does have a basis in other traits. First, he has an artistic temperament, evident in his passion for photography. Second, he feels deep pain that his mother deserted her family. Third, he is honest, gallant, and caring when he tells Gwyn that Alison did not laugh at him, accepts full responsibility for hurting him, and begs him to help her. Even after he realizes that Alison has told Gwyn his secret about his mother's desertion, Roger refuses to see her as cruel, a hunting owl. Instead, under-

standing what Gwyn will not—Huw's cryptic warnings that perceptions control Alison's identity—he asks Alison to display her inner beauty, her flowery nature. By doing so, he ceases to be Gronw, and Gwyn's vengeful blow does not metaphorically kill him. Instead of fatalistically accepting his role in an ancient pattern, as the self-absorbed Gwyn does, the independent Roger ruptures the pattern for the sake of another.

Alison, Roger's stepsister, is a weak person overcome by outside forces that may represent her insecurity. At times, she is sensitive and perceptive. She cleverly recognizes that the flowery design on the plates can be rearranged to form owls. She can also be charming and thoughtful, as when she reassures Gwyn that she likes his accent and values his individuality. Alison lacks a firm sense of identity, however, behaving one way with Gwyn and another with her mother. Thus, she can be extraordinarily shallow, giving in to her mother's threats to remove her from the choir and to cancel her tennis club subscription unless she stops talking to Gwyn. Furthermore, although she doesn't intend to hurt Gwyn, Alison is dense and patronizing in telling Roger his secret. The sensitive and cruel sides of Alison's nature are represented by flowers and owls, respectively. In spite of her role in unleashing violent passions, however, Alison is not a schemer like Blodeuwedd. Indeed, Garner's declaration that the novel is "a ghost story" enables us to see her as possessed by the evil Blodeuwedd. This possession accounts for Alison's feeling of dislocation—she becomes confused about past and present—and for her mistaking Blodeuwedd's face for her own reflection. Although her betrayals of Gwyn and Roger suggest adolescent thoughtlessness, she is not responsible if Blodeuwedd possesses her. Alison is a conventionally passive female whose identity depends on the perception of males. She becomes flowers rather than an owl because Roger perceives her as such; she does not choose her identity herself.

Huw Halfbacon, known as both Huw Hannerhob and Huw the Flitch, appears to the English as a half-wit Welsh gardener. To the Welsh, however, he is a lord, a nobleman descended from Gwydion. Huw lives in mythic time, past and present being indistinguishable to him. He even declares that he performed the deeds of mythic personages. As an archetypal wise old man, Huw is Gwyn's mentor, his true father, and he teaches Gwyn about the legend, its recurrence, and his duty to protect others from pain. He also tells Gwyn, "She wants to be flowers, but you make her owls." This cryptic statement simultaneously assigns responsibility to Gwyn for what happens to Alison and offers him the hope that he can alter the course of events by willing Alison/Blodeuwedd to become flowers. Huw himself is caught up in the mythic pattern. In the present, he is Gwydion, bringing Gwyn/Lleu down from a tree to assume his true identity. In the past, he was Lleu, the betrayed lover. After seeing Nancy, his beloved, riding with Bertram, he removed the brakes from Bertram's motorcycle, a vengeful act that led to Bertram's death and Nancy's subsequent domineering cruelty. **Nancy**, Gwyn's mother, is ignorant, selfish, and bitter, an example of the owl nature that may consume Alison. Hoping to improve her lot by marrying the wealthy Bertram, she betrayed Huw. Bertram's death embittered her. She resents Alison, who has inherited Bertram's house from her father, and she has contempt for Mr. Bradley, who lacks the qualities a true gentleman possesses. Nancy thus dominates her employers, constantly threatening to leave and thereby exacting more money from Mr. Bradley. Nancy also inflicts her bitterness on Gwyn, declaring that she will pull him out of school in spite of his desire to continue. Her fate is ambiguous: she disappears in the mist after Gwyn refuses to accompany her further.

Clive Bradley speaks in the cheery, mindless clichés commonly associated with the most feckless English gentry. In spite of his self-assured dismissal of the Welsh as unrefined, he himself is devoid of taste, regarding imitation paneling as tasteful and purchasing a "Kelticraft" owl made in England under the mistaken impression that it is a fitting Welsh souvenir for Alison. Furthermore, Nancy delights in exposing his social clumsiness by serving peaches, which he fails to eat properly. Ironically, Clive's constant efforts to avoid conflict merely make matter worse. **Margaret**, his wife and the mother of Alison, does not appear in the novel, but she is a

force with whom everyone must reckon. A domineering person and a bigot, she demands that Alison stop seeing Gwyn. She also dominates her husband, who is constantly paying off Nancy so that Margaret won't be distressed by unpleasantness.

Further Reading

Berger, Laura Standley, ed. *Twentieth-Century Young Adult Writers.* 1st ed. Detroit: St. James, 1994.

Children's Literature Review. Vol. 20. Detroit: Gale Research, 1990.

Collier, Laurie, and Joyce Nakamura, eds. *Major Authors and Illustrators for Children and Young Adults.* Detroit: Gale Research, 1993.

Contemporary Authors New Revision Series. Vol. 15. Detroit: Gale Research, 1985.

Contemporary Literary Criticism. Vol. 17. Detroit: Gale Research, 1981.

De Montreville, Doris, and Donna Hill, eds. *Third Book of Junior Authors.* New York: H. W. Wilson, 1972.

Hunt, Caroline C., ed. *British Children's Writers since 1960: First Series.* Vol. 161 of *Dictionary of Literary Biography.* Detroit: Gale Research, 1996.

Philip, Neil. *A Fine Anger: A Critical Introduction to the Work of Alan Garner.* New York: Philomel, 1981.

Rees, David. "Hanging in Their True Shapes: Alan Garner." In *The Marble in the Water: Essays on Contemporary Writers of Fiction for Children and Young Adults.* Boston: Horn Book, 1980.

Something about the Author. Vols. 18, 69. Detroit: Gale Research, 1980, 1992.

Townsend, John Rowe. "Alan Garner." In *A Sounding of Storytellers: New and Revised Essays on Contemporary Writers for Children.* New York: J. B. Lippincott, 1979.

Jean Craighead George

1919-, American novelist

My Side of the Mountain
(novel, 1959)

PLOT: George has called this first-person account of a teenage boy's life alone in the wilderness a "documentary novel." It combines elements of a survival story with a nonfiction guide to the wilderness.

Young Sam Gribley leaves his New York City home in May, intending to live in the wilderness on ancestral property in the Catskills. With the help of an old man who shows him how to make fire and a librarian, Miss Turner, who provides maps, Sam builds a home inside a hemlock tree deep in the woods. Sam soon makes a number of animal friends: Frightful, a baby falcon he trains as a hunter; the Baron, a noisy weasel he finds in a box trap; and Jessie Coon James, a thieving raccoon. Sam also encounters people: during berry season, old Mrs. Thomas Fielder forces him to pick strawberries with her; and when a poacher shoots a deer, Sam steals the carcass. His most significant meeting, however, is with a lost college English teacher, whom he calls Bando. After staying a week, Bando promises to return at Christmas.

The novel records in detail Sam's efforts to catch and prepare food, make a shelter and new clothing, and learn the ways of the wild. His most dramatic lesson occurs when he spreads food around to give the animals a Halloween party. Raccoons invade his storehouse of nuts, and a skunk sprays him. Sam has a steadily growing number of visitors, including some hunters from whom Sam steals deer for food. When Christmas arrives, Sam's father and Bando visit, and Bando tells Sam that newspapers are circulating stories about a Wild Boy. In the spring, Matt Spell, a teenager hoping to write about this Wild Boy, encounters Sam. He promises not to write the story if he can stay during vacation. Aaron, a songwriter, visits a couple of times, and Tom Sidler, a boy from town, becomes a frequent guest. When photographers and reporters finally discover Sam, he believes that his experiment is over. To his surprise, however, his mother, father, four brothers, and four sisters arrive to make their home with him.

CHARACTERS: The protagonist is often little more than a vehicle to communicate lessons about the wilderness. **Sam Gribley** is a determined teenager

unhappy with life in the big city. Although no one believes him when he says that he is going to live in the woods, he carries out his plan. Intelligent but naive, he makes mistakes lighting a fire, heating his shelter, and catching food. Nevertheless, he does not succumb to these frustrations. He patiently devotes himself to tasks until he achieves his goals. Sam is smart enough to combine book knowledge, observation, and experience to survive. Unlike most people, Sam appreciates and respects nature. He begins to understand himself more, too, even questioning whether he wants to be found so that he can have more human contact. However, the novel implies that Sam is searching for a lost ideal in his retreat, a way of life that is no longer viable. Aptly, Bando calls the boy "Thoreau."

Bando, as Sam calls the college English teacher he befriends, gives intellectual respectability to Sam's adventure. Calling him Thoreau, he links Sam to the great 19th-century philosopher and naturalist, Henry David Thoreau, who left civilization to live at Walden Pond. Bando's expressions of envy suggest that a simple life close to nature is still an American ideal. But when he brings Sam newspaper stories about the Wild Boy, he does more than expose the flaws of the press. The newspaper stories form the basis of the book's argument that Americans have lost respect for individuality: "you can't live in America today and be quietly different."

Matt Spell, the teenager hoping that the newspaper will publish his story about Sam, is naive about nature. He is not stupid, however, and he easily sees that Sam is trying to fool him by denying that he is the Wild Boy. The fact that Matt wants to spend time in the woods with Sam suggests that those who are properly introduced to nature find it appealing. Much the same is true of **Tom Sidler**, whom Sam calls Mr. Jacket because of his fancy leather jacket. He seems sarcastic and dismissive when he first meets Sam, but he becomes a regular visitor. Significantly, he first asks his mother for permission. Unlike Sam, he does not need to break the rules to experience nature. **Aaron**, the songwriter, appears primarily to show that experience in nature can be artistically stimulating. Finally, **Mr. Gribley**, Sam's father and a dock worker who longs to go to sea, denies his family's history as people of the land. Sam's success teaches him that he can find happiness living close to the land. Mr. Gribley shows that one is never too old to learn about oneself or to make a meaningful change, but his failure to search for his son for nearly eight months makes him completely unbelievable.

Julie of the Wolves

(novel, 1972)

PLOT: *Julie of the Wolves* is divided into three sections, the middle one being a long flashback. In the opening section, the title heroine is referred to by her Eskimo name, Miyax. Lost on the Alaskan tundra, with no food and few supplies, Miyax must communicate with a group of wolves to survive. Her father, Kapugen, once told her that wolves had saved him when he was starving, but he did not tell her how he communicated with them. By carefully observing the wolves and by remembering her father's advice, Miyax gradually comes to understand the wolves. First, she notices that each wolf is different, and she names the ones that stand out from the pack the most. Amaroq is the male leader; Kapu, named after her father, is the leader of the pups, and Jello is a cowardly wolf living on the edge of the pack. Next, Miyax learns wolf "language." She stays on all fours so that she does not appear threatening and strokes Amaroq beneath the chin. He sprays her, and she becomes one of the pack. Finally, when she realizes that she can dominate Jello, she clamps his nose as a signal to say that she is his boss. Kapu later helps her by making Jello regurgitate his food, saving her from starvation.

As she struggles to survive, Miyax changes. She begins to appreciate ancient Eskimo customs, realizing that they aid her survival. She also learns to read signs in nature and determines the way she must travel to reach Point Hope, her destination. Her relationship with the wolves also changes. Amaroq invites her to the den, and he allows her to walk on

two feet, permitting her to be herself. Jello, having been driven out of the community, threatens her survival, however. He digs up her buried cache of food, and she must chase him away. The first part ends with Miyax realizing that winter is on the way and that the wolves have left her alone.

The second section recounts Miyax's life before her journey. When Miyax was four years old, her mother died. She and her father lived at a seal camp on Nunivak Island. Kapugen maintained the ancient ways of his people and taught Miyax to live in harmony with her environment. Government regulations forced Kapugen to enlist in the army and Miyax to enroll in a school. She went to her Aunt Martha in Mekoryuk, where she assumed the white name of Julie Edwards. There she learned that her father had been killed in a kayak accident. She rejected the old Eskimo ways and began longing to go to San Francisco, where she had been invited to come to by her pen pal, Amy. At the age of thirteen, Julie moved to Barrow to live with her father's friend, Naka, and, in accordance with the old ways, to marry Naka's son, Daniel. Naka is an alcoholic, however, and Daniel is retarded. When Daniel attacked her in an attempt to consummate their ceremonial marriage, Julie fled. Again taking on the name of Miyax, she started to cross the tundra for Point Hope, where she hoped to catch a boat to San Francisco. The flashback ends there, having brought her to the novel's beginning, with Miyax lost on the tundra and dependent on the wolves.

In the third part, Miyax, having developed confidence in her abilities, continues alone toward Point Hope. The wolves help her again, killing Jello after he steals her pack and saving her from a grizzly bear. For the most part, however, her survival depends on her own skill. Just when Miyax comes across oil drums and other litter that signals that she is approaching civilization, a plane appears. Hunters in the plane shoot and kill Amaroq. Horrified, Miyax rejects San Francisco and the civilization it represents. From an Eskimo hunter and his wife she hears that Kapugen is alive and in Kangik, so Miyax goes to meet him. She hopes that they will again follow the old ways together. When she arrives in Kangik, however, Miyax discovers that her father has mar-

George

ried a white woman and is a pilot, possibly the one who flew the hunters who killed Amaroq. She runs away to live in the wilderness, but the death of a golden plover she had rescued and named Tornait persuades her that the old life is gone, and she heads back to her father's house.

Julie *(1994) is a sequel.*

CHARACTERS: For much of the novel, *Julie of the Wolves* is a wilderness survival story that presents only one human character. With the exception of Julie's father, the other humans are incidental. In spite of its limited cast of significant characters, the novel develops a moving theme about the relationship between humans and nature and about the differences between the ancient Eskimo ways and those of modern technological society.

Julie Edwards Miyax Kapugen is, as her double name suggests, split between two cultures. As Miyax, she is "a classic Eskimo beauty." Her physique (small bones, wiry muscles, short limbs, round face, and small nose) is perfectly suited to her harsh environment. Miyax is a child who thinks of her father as perfect. As a result, she loves and admires all things traditional. At school in Mekoryuk, she becomes Julie and is embarrassed by the old ways. She symbolically marks this change in identity by throwing away her *i'noGo tied,* the traditional totemic spirit she wears around her neck. As Julie, she admires *gussak* (white) ways and does not appreciate her own attractiveness. She is even delighted that starvation on the tundra begins to give her *gussak* features. Occasionally she appreciates Eskimo ways, such as when she participates in the ceremony of the sunrise. Mostly, however, she dreams about belonging to white culture, symbolized by the pink room waiting in Amy's house in San Francisco. Furthermore, she accepts a traditional symbolic marriage, primarily so that she can move from a dreary home to a larger, more Americanized settlement.

Even though Miyax thinks that she has driven the memory of her father from her heart, his advice—

the advice of a traditional Eskimo—guides her in difficult times. He has told her that when she is afraid she should change what she is doing. Therefore, when Daniel attacks her, she leaves. She continues to follow her father's advice when she becomes Miyax on the tundra. Nevertheless, she also displays qualities very much her own, such as patience, intense powers of observation, and sharp intelligence in understanding wolf habits. As Miyax, she also comes to a richer appreciation of the culture that Julie rejected. She realizes that dancing is an important survival tactic that warms the dancer. By becoming a "wolf girl" to ensure her survival, she also comes to appreciate the Eskimo idea that humans are not superior to animals and cannot wantonly destroy them. Later, after the hunters kill Amaroq, she rejects the white culture she once thought superior to her own because of its lack of respect for nature.

Although Miyax's journey is a symbolic initiation into the ways of her people, it is also a journey of maturation. Miyax must finally make a sad, but mature decision. When she discovers that her father is alive and has adopted white ways, she rejects him. With the death of the bird Tornait, whose name means "spirit of the birds," however, Miyax realizes the futility of her plans. She can't go to San Francisco, which represents the horror of the technology that is destroying the wilderness, and she can't remain on the tundra because the old ways, as Tornait's death symbolically attests, are dead. She therefore accepts her father in spite of his shortcomings and accepts that she must again become Julie.

Kapugen, known as **Charlie Edwards** among the whites, is both a mythic figure and a fallible human. When Miyax was young, he was an accomplished hunter and maintained a close relationship to nature. He was also the voice of traditional wisdom. He celebrated Eskimo life, telling Miyax, "We live as no other people can, for we truly understand the earth." He expressed this understanding by following the old rituals and by teaching her that people are not superior to animals. He told her, for example, that wolves are "gentle brothers." Throughout the novel, Miyax follows his advice, which enables her to befriend the wolves and to

survive. At the end, however, she realizes that Kapugen is not the mythic Wise Old Man but an Americanized Eskimo who has succumbed to the *gussak* values he once criticized as arrogant. When he speaks of himself as being rich, for example, he no longer means that he has spiritual qualities. Instead, he means that he has acquired material possessions. The most frightful sign of change, however, is that he is a pilot who lets hunters shoot wolves from his plane. Kapugen thus represents the loss of traditional Eskimo culture.

Although wolves are not anthropomorphized, they have distinct identities as ''gentle brothers'' who deserve respect. **Amaroq**, the leader, resembles Kapugen the hunter. He possesses the qualities that Eskimos identify as signs of wealth: intelligence, fearlessness, and love. When Miyax pats his chin, he responds instinctively with love. He is intelligent because he realizes that Miyax can't change her ways and allows her to walk on two feet. He also seems to understand her need for food, and he protects her from other animals. **Kapu**, whom Miyax names after her father, is the fearless, smart, and ''wealthy'' leader of the pups. He takes over the leadership of the pack after Amaroq is killed. **Jello**, in contrast, has an appropriate *gussak* name. Poor in spirit, he is a slippery coward who demonstrates that not all wolves are good. He nearly kills Miyax by stealing her food and the backpack containing her needles, knife, and boots. Eventually, however, the wolves kill him because wolf society has no place for those who will not contribute.

Further Reading

Authors and Artists for Young Adults. Vol. 8. Detroit: Gale Research, 1992.

Berger, Laura Standley, ed. *Twentieth-Century Young Adult Writers.* 1st ed. Detroit: St. James, 1994.

Children's Literature Review. Vol. 1. Detroit: Gale Research, 1976.

Collier, Laurie, and Joyce Nakamura, eds. *Major Authors and Illustrators for Children and Young Adults.* Detroit: Gale Research, 1993.

Estes, Glenn E., ed. *American Writers for Children since 1960: Fiction.* Vol. 52 of *Dictionary of Literary Biography.* Detroit: Gale Research, 1986.

Fuller, Muriel, ed. *More Junior Authors.* New York: H. W. Wilson, 1963.

Something about the Author. Vols. 2, 68. Detroit: Gale Research, 1971, 1992.

Fred Gipson

1908-1973, American writer

Old Yeller

(novel, 1956)

PLOT: This coming-of-age story is set in Texas during the late 1860s. Before leaving on a cattle drive, Papa asks Travis Coates to be the man of the house. Papa promises to bring Travis a horse if he does the farmwork and cares for his mother and his brother, Little Arliss. Shortly afterwards, a stray dog steals meat from the cabin, and Little Arliss claims it as his pet. Travis dislikes Old Yeller, as the dog is called. Old Yeller plays with Arliss in the drinking water, comes at Travis when he gets angry with Arliss, and runs away instead of helping Travis control two fighting bulls that threaten the cabin. But Travis changes his opinion when Old Yeller protects Mama and Arliss by fighting a bear. Realizing now that he loves Arliss and Old Yeller, Travis takes them squirrel hunting. He also has Yeller sleep with him and Arliss after Bud Searcy visits with his granddaughter, Lisbeth, who tells Travis that Old Yeller has been stealing from the neighbors. Old Yeller stops stealing and earns his keep by catching predators and herding a heifer for milking.

Darker events now test Travis. Burn Sanderson comes to claim Old Yeller. Although he trades the dog for a meal, he warns Travis of a plague of hydrophobia. Travis continues working with Old Yeller, who helps him to mark and castrate wild hogs. When they go after a second bunch, however, Travis falls, and Old Yeller is severely gored defending him from the hogs. Although wounded himself, Travis gets Mama to come and bring Old Yeller home to nurse him. Lisbeth, who previously brought Travis one of Old Yeller's pups, comes to help. Rabid animals soon appear around the cabin. In an episode paralleling the bear's attack, a rabid wolf attacks Mama and Lisbeth; Old Yeller again fights the attacker. After Travis kills the wolf, however, he protects his family by shooting Old Yeller, who, because he was bitten, may have contracted rabies. When Papa returns with a horse for Travis, he tells his son that a man shouldn't dwell on the bad things in life because he will miss what is good. Travis remains sad, however, until he sees Arliss and Old Yeller's puppy playing together in the drinking water. Laughing at the sight, he decides to take both of them hunting.

Savage Sam (1962) *is a sequel.*

CHARACTERS: The focus is on the development of Travis, who narrates events that had profoundly changed him many years earlier. Old Yeller, like most of the human characters, tests and reveals the narrator's qualities.

Travis Coates, the fourteen-year-old narrator, matures into a man who can cope with the unpredictable events of life. Travis is eager to prove that he can be a man. He therefore refuses to cry when his father leaves, and he does the farm work before his mother has to tell him. Nevertheless, his resentment when his mother and brother don't accord him the unquestioned authority of a man shows that Travis is still a boy. He thus loses his temper when Little Arliss doesn't obey him, is upset that Mama supports Arliss in their battles, and becomes childishly sneaky by trying to trick Old Yeller into stealing more meat so that he can banish him. Travis starts to mature after the bear attack, which causes him to understand himself better because it teaches him that he loves Arliss. Subsequently, Travis also becomes attached to Old Yeller. When the dog saves him from the hogs, he shows his loyalty by valiantly insisting that Mama save the dog. Travis lacks, however, the ability to handle sorrow and loss. He desires a horse, for instance, because he has not yet come to terms with the death of his first dog. After he kills Old Yeller, an act of mature responsibility, he finds no joy in the horse, nor can he accept the pup as a replacement. Even his father's advice about dwelling on the positive doesn't help. Travis matures only when he himself understands the continuity of life, a

continuity evident when the pup displays Old Yeller's characteristics and habits. By laughing at Arliss and the pup as they play in the drinking water, Travis shows that he has learned to be a man by enjoying, as his father said he should, life's good times. Finally, by deciding to take Arliss and the pup hunting, Travis signals his desire to participate in and extend these good moments.

Old Yeller is a large, slick-haired dog whose name suggests both his dingy yellow color and his peculiar bark, which resembles a yell. Old Yeller is physically ugly: he has a stump for a tail and has had one ear chewed off. He is also a clever, thieving rascal. He figures out how to steal meat hanging at the cabin, and he repeatedly steals from the neighbors. For the most part, however, his cleverness makes him an asset. He learns how to distract squirrels during a hunt, how to herd a heifer, and how to lure the wild hogs into a position that enables Travis to mark them. Old Yeller is friendly and loving, taking immediately to Travis and Little Arliss. His most notable traits, however, are his fierce loyalty and bravery. Travis mistakes him for a coward when Old Yeller flees while the bulls are fighting. Actually, Old Yeller is understandably avoiding the boy who previously abused him. Old Yeller soon proves Travis wrong when he fights a bear, cleverly ensuring that Arliss and Mama are safe before abandoning the fight. Similarly, he fights the wild hogs to save Travis. Most importantly, even though he has not fully recovered from the hog attack, he defends Mama and Lisbeth from the rabid wolf. Old Yeller is not only central to the novel's drama; he is also central to one of its themes. In spite of his heroism, Old Yeller poses a threat to the family because the rabid wolf bit him. By shooting Old Yeller, Travis learns that the responsibilities of a man are not always pleasant or fair.

Papa, a tall, straight, handsome man with drooping black mustaches, expresses mature wisdom. He establishes the quest for manhood by telling Travis to be the man while he is away. When he returns, he pronounces the theme, stating that a man must accept that life is not always fair and must, if he is to prevent it from becoming all bad, focus on the good parts. **Mama** is a loving, hard-working, and clever woman. When Travis and Old Yeller are wounded by the hogs, she figures out how to transport the dog home, and she dutifully nurses both her son and the dog. Although she cries after the wolf bites Old Yeller, she is not soft: her firm commitment to protecting her family gives Travis the strength to shoot his dog. Although his main function is to test Travis's maturity, five-year-old **Little Arliss** adds humor because he is as wild and untamed as the Texas frontier. Willful and boisterous, Arliss tests Travis through his constant disobedience. He regularly takes his clothes off, for instance, to play in the drinking water. Arliss also shows the strength of the bond between a boy and a dog when he defends his Old Yeller by throwing rocks at both Travis and Burn Sanderson.

Shiftless **Bud Searcy**, a red-faced man with a bulging middle, provides a negative example of manhood. A man who carelessly spits tobacco juice everywhere and hangs around waiting for invitations to dinner, he talks about a man's responsibilities but never fulfills them. **Lisbeth**, his eleven-year-old granddaughter, is a white-haired girl with penetrating brown eyes. She is kind, warning Travis that Old Yeller is a thief but promising not to tell anyone. Travis's self-absorption becomes apparent when she offers him one of Yeller's pups and he dismisses the gift by saying that Arliss could have it. **Burn Sanderson**, a slim, polite, young man, who comes to claim Old Yeller, makes the Coates family realize how much they love the dog. Sanderson shows understanding and kindness by trading Old Yeller for a meal. Sanderson's major role, though, is to foreshadow the ending: he warns Travis that a man must shoot any animal suspected of having hydrophobia if he is to protect his family.

Further Reading

Berger, Laura Standley, ed. *Twentieth-Century Young Adult Writers*. 1st ed. Detroit: St. James, 1994.

Collier, Laurie, and Joyce Nakamura, eds. *Major Authors and Illustrators for Children and Young Adults*. Detroit: Gale Research, 1993.

Contemporary Authors New Revision Series. Vol. 3. Detroit: Gale Research, 1981.

De Montreville, Doris, and Donna Hill, eds. *Third Book of Junior Authors*. New York: H. W. Wilson, 1972.

Something about the Author. Vol. 2. Detroit: Gale Research, 1971.

Rumer Godden

1907-, English author

The Dolls' House

(novel, 1947)

PLOT: In this popular story, relationships between children and dolls and between the dolls themselves contrast love with selfishness and hatred. Emily and Charlotte Dane have created a family of dolls. Mr. Plantagenet is the father; Birdie, a celluloid doll, is the mother; Tottie, a wooden farthing doll, is the daughter; and Apple, a tiny plush doll, is the son. They have a dog named Darner. Because the dolls live in a cramped shoe box, Tottie encourages them to wish for a house. Soon afterwards, Emily and Charlotte are given their late great-aunt's dolls' house, which they clean and restore. Meanwhile, their friend Mrs. Innisfree places Tottie in a doll exhibition. Because the sisters change their minds about accepting payment for displaying their doll, Mrs. Innisfree later pays to restore the tattered dolls' house furniture.

At the exhibition, Tottie is sad until the Queen offers to purchase her and she learns that she is not, as she feared, for sale. Nevertheless, Tottie is distressed to meet Marchpane, an elegant doll who once lived with her. Marchpane, who has been cleaned and restored, despises children and is contemptuous of Tottie. After the exhibition, Tottie returns to her happy family life. At Christmas, she is pleased when each doll receives the gift she had wished for it. Tottie is worried, however, because Emily and Charlotte are given Marchpane. In spite of Charlotte's protests, Emily soon makes Marchpane the mistress of the house and insists that Apple is her child and the others are her servants. The doll family is miserable. Shortly afterwards, Marchpane watches while Apple is singed by a birthday candle; Birdie saves him, but her celluloid body ignites, and the fire consumes her. The sisters blame Marchpane

Godden's dolls, illustrated here by Tasha Tudor, are brought to life through the imaginations of the children who play with them.

and donate her to a museum. The dolls do not forget Birdie, but they try to be happy.

CHARACTERS: The dolls can't move by themselves or talk to humans. Limited to expressing desires by wishing, these dolls actually represent the imaginations of the children whose play brings them to life. **Tottie Plantagenet**, being made of good wood, is solid and natural. Tottie is a small, neatly jointed, Dutch farthing doll who has a round head with glossy painted hair and blue painted eyes. Although made a child in the Plantagenet family, Tottie is over a hundred years old. Furthermore, her memory gives her an excellent understanding of the world. She thus convinces Mr. Plantagenet that sometimes bad fortune can't be avoided and that he must try to be happy even without Birdie. Tottie also insists that dolls can improve their lots by wishing until the girls who play with them respond. She is generous, wishing for a house and Christmas presents for her family. Tottie, having been in the same family for generations, is hurt when she believes that she is being sold. She becomes happy again, however, after the Queen, whose offer reflects Tottie's value as an emotional treasure, is told that Tottie is not for sale. Tottie then becomes a moral leader. Comforted by the knowledge that wood is strong and neither cheap nor shoddy, she maintains her self-esteem when Marchpane insults her. She also continues to believe that Emily will eventually see Marchpane for what she truly is. Furthermore, Tottie keeps up the family's spirits by insisting that the dolls can fight Marchpane's hatred by continuing to wish. Tottie's power is finally evident when Charlotte echoes her thoughts with the suggestion that she and Emily donate Marchpane to a museum.

Marchpane is physically, psychologically, and morally the opposite of Tottie. Marchpane is expensive: her body is sawdust-filled kid, her head is china, she has real yellow hair, and her china eyes open and shut. Appropriately named after a sweet, sticky icing, Marchpane soon becomes tiresome because her conceited head has room only for thoughts of herself. Valuing appearances alone, the elegantly beautiful Marchpane rejects the idea of children playing with her. Although she believes that she is a superior creature, her decision actually reduces her to a mere object instead of a living toy. Marchpane is not just conceited, arrogant, and selfish. She exudes the nasty odor of cleaning fluids, symbolizing that she is morally foul. Cold, jealous, and vengeful, Marchpane reduces the Plantagenets' happy home to a mere house. Her malevolence becomes obvious even to Emily when she sits and smiles instead of trying to save Apple. Ironically, Marchpane obtains her greatest wish. She is locked in a glass museum case to be admired for her beauty but never brought to life through loving play.

Tottie's family is a mixed group. **Mr. Plantagenet** is timid because previous owners abused him. A delicate doll with a china face on which some boys have drawn an indelible mustache, he has brown glass eyes and real brown hair. Mr. Plantagenet delights in being the traditional male head of the home. He thus cherishes a Christmas carol blessing the master of the house. Mr. Plantagenet seems simple compared to Tottie, but he makes overt the theme that love is essential to identity when he declares that, because she does not like children, Marchpane is a thing, not a doll. **Birdie Plantagenet**, who began life in a party favor, is always happy. A cheap celluloid doll with fluffy yellow cotton hair, she is not quite right in the head, which rattles with beads and confuses her thoughts. In keeping with her name, Birdie loves birds and feathers. Furthermore, she is so flighty that she can't distinguish what is real from what isn't. Nevertheless, she understands what love is and she fulfills the role of heroic motherhood by sacrificing herself for her child. **Apple Plantagenet**, who is the size of Emily's thumb, is a plump, pink-brown plush doll. His sewn-in dimples, brown darning-wool hair, and tiny garments make him loveable to dolls and humans alike. Apple is naughty and delights in somersaulting down the stairs. Because he likes those who indulge him, he disobediently persists in seeing Marchpane, thereby revealing Marchpane's hatred and Birdie's love. **Darner**, the Plantagenets' dog, is named after his darning needle backbone. He is covered with grimy clipped wool over pipe-cleaner legs. He tells the others that Marchpane is dangerous by growling with his warning, "Prrick."

To a considerable degree, the dolls express the characters of the girls who play with them. **Emily Dane**, the older sister, comes up with the most ideas and is more insistent in carrying them out. Emily is initially responsive to Tottie, feeling the doll's reproach when Tottie believes that she has been sold. Emily is too easily impressed by appearances, however, and succumbs to Marchpane's superficial charms. In a sense, Marchpane reflects the darker side of Emily's character. Emily uses Marchpane to dominate her sister, selfishly dictating every facet of their doll games that the girls once shared. Charlotte finally convinces Emily to change her mind. By rejecting Marchpane, Emily resumes her generous and loving relationship with her sister. Although **Charlotte** is shy and awkward, she is more sensitive than Emily. Consequently, she remains faithful to Tottie and the Plantagenets, who represent the joy of loving relationships. Because Charlotte is weak and indecisive she fails to stop Emily from calling Marchpane their best doll and from turning the Plantagenets into servants. After Birdie's sacrifice, though, Charlotte forcefully points out that Marchpane did not move to help, thus convincing Emily that Marchpane is evil. Furthermore, Charlotte voices the idea (supposedly originating with

Tottie) of donating Marchpane to a museum. By leading instead of following, she reestablishes with Emily the loving relationship that they symbolize by giving their dolls happy lives. Their friend, **Mrs. Innisfree**, whom Charlotte perceptively likens to Tottie, represents tradition. A kind and understanding woman, she has the dolls' furniture restored. By thus teaching the sisters to appreciate Victorian craftsmanship, she shows them how to respect the solid values of the past.

Further Reading

Authors and Artists for Young Adults. Vol. 6. Detroit: Gale Research, 1991.

Berger, Laura Standley, ed. *Twentieth-Century Children's Writers.* 4th ed. Detroit: St. James, 1995.

Children's Literature Review. Vol. 20. Detroit: Gale Research, 1990.

Collier, Laurie, and Joyce Nakamura, eds. *Major Authors and Illustrators for Children and Young Adults.* Detroit: Gale Research, 1993.

Contemporary Authors New Revision Series. Vol. 36. Detroit: Gale Research, 1992.

Contemporary Literary Criticism. Vol. 53. Detroit: Gale Research, 1989.

Fuller, Muriel, ed. *More Junior Authors.* New York: H. W. Wilson, 1963.

Hunt, Caroline C., ed. *British Children's Writers since 1960: First Series.* Vol. 161 of *Dictionary of Literary Biography.* Detroit: Gale Research, 1996.

Something about the Author. Vols. 3, 36. Detroit: Gale Research, 1972, 1984.

Something about the Author Autobiography Series. Vol. 12. Detroit: Gale Research, 1991.

Kenneth Grahame

1859-1932, English banker and writer

The Wind in the Willows
(animal fantasy, 1908)

PLOT: Grahame began *The Wind in the Willows* as a bedtime story for his four-year-old son, Alistair.

He later expanded the story in a series of letters when Alistair was vacationing at the seaside. The published version combines the rollicking adventures of the original bedtime story with quieter scenes that convey a nostalgic longing for pastoral life. Grahame must have had these scenes in mind when he wrote to Teddy Roosevelt that his book was "an expression of the very simplest joys of life as lived by the simplest beings."

The plot contrasts the journeys of Mole and Toad to convey related themes: the value of home, the joys of freedom, and the benefits and responsibilities of friendship. Fed up with spring housecleaning, Mole deserts his underground home and journeys to the River Bank. He moves in with Water Rat, who introduces him to leisurely pleasures, especially "messing about" with boats. Rat also introduces Mole to the wealthy Toad of Toad Hall. Toad, who constantly takes up new fads, convinces Rat and Mole to join him in his latest enthusiasm, traveling in a gypsy caravan. Their journey ends when a speeding motor car frightens their horse, which backs into a ditch and smashes the caravan. Far from being upset, Toad develops a new passion for automobiles.

During the winter, Mole sets out alone to explore the Wild Wood, a dangerous area beyond the River Bank. He becomes lost, but Rat finds him. When a sudden snowstorm threatens both, they take refuge in the home of Badger. Later, Mole is seized by an irresistible urge to visit his own abandoned home. Rat accompanies him and shares his hospitality while a group of caroling field mice entertain them.

At this point, chapters alternate between Toad's adventures and the pastoral experiences of the other animals. With the arrival of summer, Badger enlists the help of Rat and Mole. Together, they try to convince Toad—who by this time has wrecked a number of automobiles—that he must become more responsible and must no longer embarrass his friends. When this fails, they lock Toad in his room. Toad tricks Rat, however, and escapes through a window, steals a car, and proceeds to wreck it. He is consequently sentenced to twenty years in jail. While Toad suffers in the Wide World, the human realm beyond the Wild Wood, Rat and Mole have a mystical experience that reveals the basic goodness of the river world Toad has deserted. Rat and Mole search for Portly, the missing son of their friend Otter. On their journey they hear music played by Pan (who is also called the Friend and Helper) which fills them with ecstasy. The music guides them to Portly, whom the Friend has kept safe on an island. Mole and Rat return Portly to his parents, but the Friend removes the memory of their mystical experience so that they won't become discontented with their normal lives.

Meanwhile, the jailed Toad overcomes his initial despair and gets the jailer's daughter to help him escape. Disguised as a washerwoman, he convinces a railway engine driver to take him on board. The police chase the train, but Toad escapes and tries to make his way home. Meanwhile, Rat becomes enchanted by the idea of travel after listening to the tales of a Sea Rat. Mole physically restrains him and ends this obsession by getting Rat to resume his poetry writing.

Toad has further adventures on his journey home. He rides on a barge, but a woman throws him off when the disguised Toad is unable to wash clothes. Toad steals the barge horse, but soon sells it to a gypsy for money and food. As he walks along, the very car he stole earlier comes by, and because he is still in his washerwoman disguise, the occupants offer him a ride. Toad takes over the driving and becomes so intoxicated with power and speed that he removes his disguise. In the ensuing fight for the wheel, the car crashes. Toad, chased by the chauffeur and two policemen, escapes by plunging into the river. He surfaces at Rat's house, where he discovers that ferrets, stoats, and weasels have taken over Toad Hall. In spite of Toad's foolish disregard of them, his friends come to his aid. Mole, disguised in Toad's washerwoman clothes, scouts out the enemy and makes them think that a large force is on the way. As a result, Badger, Mole, Rat, and Toad easily recapture Toad's home from the frightened trespassers. Toad seems to have learned nothing from his experiences: he intends to be the center of attention at the ensuing victory banquet by making speeches and singing songs celebrating himself. When his friends forbid him to carry out his plans, Toad sings his victory song alone in his room. At the banquet itself, he surprises everyone. Instead of being conceited, he appears as a modest, well-behaved, and reformed Toad.

CHARACTERS: The anthropomorphized characters exhibit few of the traits of realistic animals. Grahame does not attempt to preserve even the relative scale of his characters: Toad, for example, is able to drive the same car that humans do. By making the central characters bachelors and by giving no major roles to females, Grahame depicts a life of gentlemanly leisure, free from the cares of work, family, and sex.

Some critics view **Mole** as Grahame's alter ego. By abandoning the drudgery of housework, he achieves the freedom that Grahame, who hated his job at the bank, longed to have. In his underground home, Mole is cut off from nature: the change of seasons means only more drudgery. When spring's "spirit of divine discontent and longing" finally calls him to the bright world above, however, Mole is symbolically reborn. Like a child, he must learn new things, such as how to row a boat and how to enjoy himself at a picnic. At times, his naivete is dangerous. His foolish decision to explore the Wild Woods nearly costs him his life. Generally, though, Mole is a creature of common sense, and he becomes increasingly competent. He displays wit and courage when he visits Toad Hall wearing Toad's washerwoman disguise. His clever taunts are instrumental in securing victory for the four friends. During the battle, he is brave and efficient.

Mole's role in developing the theme of home is complex. Although he learns to appreciate the joys of life on the river, he is later seized by an urge to return to his neat little home. Mole realizes, however, that both this home and the life it once offered are too limited. Still, he recognizes "the special value of some such anchorage in one's existence." Mole, in other words, needs to maintain a connection to his origins, but he also needs a life that offers more opportunities. Understanding the value of the freedom and friendship offered by his new home, he

tries to prevent Toad and Rat from leaving the River Bank. Mole accepts the obligations of friendship and physically prevents Rat from harming himself by abandoning his home and friends. When he distracts Rat by getting him to write poetry, he shows exceptional thoughtfulness: Mole himself does not appreciate poetry, but he is alert to his friend's love for it. Similarly, Mole shows friendship to Toad, both in trying to cure of him of his obsession with cars and in joining the party of "heroes" that recaptures Toad Hall.

Whereas Mole throws off drudgery and becomes "emancipated," **Toad of Toad Hall** is "mastered" by his passions. The wealthy Toad lives in his family's ancestral house that, unlike the houses of the other animals, is human in its external architecture. Conceited and self-satisfied, Toad does not realize that his ever-changing fads are foolish. He calls each new fad "the real thing" or "real life." Significantly, Toad's whims all involve forms of transportation—boats, a gypsy wagon, and motor cars—indicating that he does not properly appreciate his home or the River Bank. Furthermore, Toad's obsession with cars inevitably leads to wrecks, symbolizing the destruction that technology causes to the pastoral world.

Toad is self-centered and does not realize that he takes advantage of his friends. During the gypsy caravan trip, for example, he is completely unaware that Rat and Mole do all of the work. Clearly, Toad is immature. He even plays as a child would. When Badger and the others lock him in his room to force him out of his passion for cars, he lines up the chairs to pretend that he is driving. Although his immaturity is comical, it is also dangerous, since he can't imagine a car ride ending in anything other than a crash. Toad is good natured and agrees temporarily with the opinions of others, but his passions always regain control of him. Thus, he steals a car to gratify his urge for destructive speed, and he removes his disguise, inviting recapture, to satisfy his desire to be recognized. Toad's lack of control is also evident in his extreme shifts in emotion. He experiences manic glee when he is driving a car or escaping from the police. At such times he makes up songs celebrating his own heroism and intelligence. When he believes

Mole and Rat, in a classic illustration by Ernest H. Shepard, enjoy gentlemanly pleasures on the water in Grahame's classic, The Wind in the Willows.

he is going to be caught, however, he plunges into deep despair, berating himself for his foolishness. But his sorrow is never long lived: Toad lacks the intelligence and maturity to retain a serious thought.

Toad's most notable trait, after his obsession with motor cars, is his conceit. He has an invincible sense of social superiority, and he thinks of himself as dashingly handsome. In prison, for example, he believes that the jailer's daughter is falling in love with him. In fact, she is interested in animals as pets. Convinced that he can do anything, he brags about his ability to wash on the barge. When he bungles the job, the bargewoman tosses him overboard because, of course, he is only a toad, an estimation of his station in life that Toad never comes to appreciate. During his trip home, his bragging, combined with his outlandish disguise, highlights his role as a parody of the romantic hero. Unlike Mole, Rat, and Badger, who are truly heroic, Toad thinks only of appearances. He is not vicious, and he genuinely likes his friends, but he is simply incapable of putting

his own interests aside for long. For this reason, most commentators do not believe it when he apparently reforms his ways: they see him at the banquet as only playing the new game of modest Toad. Nevertheless, the childish, adventurous Toad is the novel's most engaging character.

The **Water Rat** exemplifies friendship. He loves his world of water, boats, and leisure, and he willingly shares it. When Mole arrives, Rat becomes a teacher, introducing his new friend to boating. He remains good natured after Mole foolishly upsets the boat. Rat again displays friendship when he searches for the missing Mole in the Wild Wood, a place he does not like. Rat is sensitive to the feelings of others and acts accordingly. For example, when Mole—too loyal to leave Rat—begins crying because he longs to return to his tiny house, Rat accompanies him. Furthermore, Rat, understanding his friend's emotional needs, praises Mole's rather dreary home. Rat also takes care of everyone during the visit of the caroling field mice and ensures that Mole has no anxieties. He demonstrates a similar commitment to Toad. He knows that Toad is not very smart and is conceited, but he also appreciates that Toad can be generous and kind. Out of concern, Rat suggests to Badger that the friends save Toad from his obsessions.

Rat's contribution to the theme of home is almost as complex as Mole's. The Sea Rat's alluring stories of travel take possession of him, just as a fascination with motor cars possesses Toad. Rat's desires are not as foolish as Toad's, but giving in to them would be destructive: Rat would lose his life of leisure and his friends. Mole therefore does the duty of a friend. He restrains Rat in a scene that some critics have compared to the episode in the *Odyssey* in which Ulysses blocks the ears of his sailors so they don't hear the alluring but fatal call of the Sirens. Encouraging Rat to write poetry, he steers him to a more acceptable preoccupation that strengthens Rat's imaginative connection with his world and makes him content with it.

Badger lives in the Wild Woods in an underground home that was once a human city. A solitary being who hates society, Badger has rough manners. He does not, for example, value conventional table etiquette. Although blunt and forceful, Badger has the reputation of being kind hearted. Nevertheless, many animals fear him; certainly, none would anger him by hurting one of his friends. Although Badger is generally tolerant of the animals in the Wild Woods, he is gruffly paternalistic with Toad. A friend of Toad's late father, Badger worries that Toad is squandering his inheritance, physically endangering himself, and embarrassing his friends. Because he is a true friend, he limits Toad's independence in a bid to make Toad aware of his social responsibilities. By using his abilities as a fierce fighter in the military expedition on Toad Hall, Badger also restores the social and moral order of the community. Not infatuated with the new, Badger supports tradition and continuity. The novel suggests he is right in thinking that badgers, with their appreciation for traditional ways of life, will endure longer than humans.

Further Reading

Chalmers, Patrick R. *Kenneth Grahame: Life, Letters and Unpublished Work.* London: Methuen, 1933.

Children's Literature Review. Vol. 5. Detroit: Gale Research, 1983.

Collier, Laurie, and Joyce Nakamura, eds. *Major Authors and Illustrators for Children and Young Adults.* Detroit: Gale Research, 1993.

Graham, Eleanor. *Kenneth Grahame.* New York: H. Z. Walck, 1963.

Grahame, Kenneth. *My Dearest Mouse: "The Wind in the Willows" Letters.* London: Pavilion, 1988.

———. *Paths to the River: The Origins of* The Wind in the Willows. London: Souvenir Press, 1983.

Green, Peter. *Beyond the Wild Wood: The World of Kenneth Grahame, Author of* The Wind in the Willows. Exeter, Devon, England: Webb & Bower, 1982.

———. *Kenneth Grahame: A Biography.* Cleveland, OH: World Publishing Company, 1959.

———. *Kenneth Grahame, 1859-1932: A Study of His Life, Work, and Times.* London: Murray, 1959.

Kuznets, Lois R. *Kenneth Grahame.* Boston: Twayne, 1987.

Yesterday's Authors of Books for Children. Vol. 1. Detroit: Gale Research, 1977.

Zaidman, Laura M., ed. *British Children's Writers 1880-1914.* Vol. 141 of *Dictionary of Literary Biography.* Detroit: Gale Research, 1994.

Constance C. Greene

1924-, American author

A Girl Called Al

(novel, 1969)

PLOT: This episodic novel focuses on the pains and joys of relationships. The major relationship is between the nameless narrator and Al, who hates being called Alexandra. Al is a self-professed nonconformist. At school, for example, she vainly tries to get the principal to let her take shop instead of sewing. A second relationship involves Mr. Richards, the assistant superintendent of the apartment building where the narrator lives. A kind man, he gives the girls food, listens to them, and helps them make a bookshelf. Al also becomes friends with Mr. Keough, her seventh grade teacher. He shows her respect by calling her Al and not Alexandra, and so she feels guilty when she hurts his feelings by imitating him one day.

Al, whose divorced mother frequently leaves her by herself, becomes a regular visitor at the narrator's apartment. She likes the narrator's mother and her good-humored father. For her part, the narrator insists that her mother stop prejudging Al's mother and invite her for tea. Shortly after this tea, Al reveals one day that her mother is dating Herbert Smith. As weeks pass, Al gains weight. Her mother shows no sympathy, and a classmate chants insults, but Mr. Richards tactfully serves carrots instead of sugar-covered bread when the girls visit. Conflict enters the friendship when the narrator says that fathers have a special feeling for their daughters. After that remark, Al, who longs for a visit from her father, stops seeing the narrator. When the narrator's brother, Teddy, her mother, and her father mention Al's absence, the narrator decides to apologize.

Al changes in subsequent episodes. She enjoys dinner with Herbert Smith and her mother after Mr. Richards gives her an article on pollution so that she will have something to talk about. She starts to lose weight, gives up expecting a visit from her father, and buys clothes for herself for the first time. When the girls discover that Mr. Richards has had a heart attack, Al's mother finally shows sympathy by staying home with her daughter. That week, the girls visit Mr. Richards in the hospital and overhear him agree that they could be called his granddaughters. He dies that night. In the following weeks, Al loses more weight, agrees to replace her pigtails with a more becoming hairstyle, and looks forward to vacationing with her mother. The narrator turns her thoughts to the future, resolving never to forget Mr. Richards.

CHARACTERS: The two girls come alive because of their contrasting personalities and family situations. **Al**, short for **Alexandra**, is overweight, wears glasses, walks stiffly, and seldom smiles. She is a year older than the narrator, but is also in the seventh grade, having been set back a year. Al notes that she has a high I.Q. but does not use it to its full potential. Although she sometimes confuses words, such as when she refers to Mrs. Keough needing an opera-

tion for "ball stones," her intelligence is evident in her acute observations. She notices, for example, that Mr. Keough always pulls his ear when he doesn't know what to say next. Al is especially proud of being a nonconformist. Thus, while all the other girls wear their hair straight, she has pigtails that stand out as if they were starched. Having lived in a number of places, including Los Angeles, she is blasé about moviemaking and Disneyland, subjects that the narrator finds fascinating. Although she does not say so, Al has been deeply hurt by her parents' divorce. She loves her father and longs for him to visit; she respects but does not love her mother as much. Al is lonely and keeps on the lights and television for company when her mother is absent. She is also bitter, at first refusing to have dinner with Herbert Smith, and she gains weight in order to humiliate her clothes-conscious mother.

Al gets along with people despite her habit of being too blunt. She tells Mr. Keough, for example, that his tie does nothing for him. She forms a particularly meaningful relationship with Mr. Richards with whom she sympathizes because he has no family. Her identification with him is so complete that at one point she even narrows her eyes until they are slits like his. Over the course of the story, Al matures and changes her attitude to others and to herself. Encouraged by Mr. Richards, who gives her an article on pollution so that she can make conversation, she finally accepts a dinner invitation from Herbert Smith and enjoys the meal. She gives up on the idea of her father visiting her and becomes sorry for him because he is missing out on the growth of his only daughter. She asserts her independence by buying her own clothes and shows pride by losing weight and adopting a better hair style. Al also becomes more accepting of her mother and looks forward to a vacation with her.

The narrator (Greene once admitted that not naming her was a mistake) serves as a contrast to Al. She is skinny and has straight hair. Because her parents do not have much money, she has never been on a plane or lived in any other place. Unlike Al, she does have a loving, caring family. She is, however, in awe of Al's flamboyance and experience. Greene has indicated that the narrator's role is that of a "straight man," whose relative lack of sophistication highlights Al's character. Nevertheless, the naive narrator has an engaging personality. She is observant and inquisitive. She notes, for example, that although her mother uses lotion, her father doesn't react to it the way men do on television commercials. The narrator is also sensitive and feels sorry when she realizes that she has hurt Al's feelings. Once her mother prompts her by suggesting that Al is lonely, she shows integrity and concern by apologizing. The narrator does not change as dramatically as Al, but she learns to be silent when she isn't sure of what to say. Moreover, she achieves insight into the power of relationships and the sadness of change. She thus vows that she will never forget Mr. Richards, but she regrets that he will not see whether she will become, as he predicted, "stunning."

Mr. Richards, the assistant superintendent of the apartment building, is a retired bartender who is about seventy years old. An eccentric who always has a toothpick in his mouth, he shines his kitchen floor by skating over it with rags on his feet. He was divorced when quite young and has no contact with his daughter or his grandchildren. Although he lives alone, he is a loving man, as is suggested by his tattoo that says "Home Sweet Home." Mr. Richards gives the girls sweets, makes them laugh, and is a good listener who never interrupts. He promotes their self-esteem by predicting that they will grow up to be stunning women. The narrator finds him "refreshing" because he is an adult who always keeps his word. Thus, he follows through on his offer to teach both girls how to make a bookshelf. He is sensitive to the girls' feelings, giving the nervous Al an article on pollution so that she will have something to say to Herbert Smith. Mr. Richards symbolically adopts the girls, emphasizing their importance to him when he indicates that they could be his granddaughters. Although Greene has said that Mr. Richards is "a sweetie" and that having him die was her greatest mistake as a writer, his death underscores the importance of loving relationships and the inevitability of change. **Mr. Keough**, the seventh grade teacher who also has some influence on the girls, is poorly realized. He is friendly and understanding, the only teacher who calls Al "Al." He is hurt when Al imitates him, but he doesn't hold a grudge. It is unclear why the predictable Mr. Keough suddenly wears a new tie.

Al's **mother** is a negligent parent who frequently leaves her daughter alone. She wears heavy eye makeup and long artificial fingernails, dresses in lounging pajamas, and pretentiously "takes a tub" instead of a bath. Because she works as a clothes buyer, she is sensitive to fashion. She is insensitive to her daughter's feelings, however, when Al gets fat. She takes her to a doctor, but she says that fat people have no excuse for their problem. But once Mr. Richards has his heart attack, she changes. She stays home that night and she later plans a vacation with Al. The narrator's **mother** contrasts with Al's mother because she is a concerned and attentive parent. She immediately dislikes Al's mother because of her flashiness. Nevertheless she invites her to tea after the narrator points out that she is guilty of judging by first impressions. The narrator appreciates her mother because she is consistent in the way she treats her children. The narrator's mother becomes the voice of wisdom when she suggests that Al's freedom from parental rules may actually make her lonely. She thus forces the narrator to see Al in a new light and, consequently, to apologize for hurting her feelings. The narrator's **father** is a balding man who is not very tall. He is attentive to his daughter's needs and thus contrasts with Al's absent father. He is a joker who always pretends to forget his daughter's age on her birthday or Al's name when she visits. When he suggests that an elderly man shouldn't shovel wet snow, he becomes a device for foreshadowing Mr. Richards's death. **Teddy**, the narrator's nine-year-old brother, brings out a sense of rivalry because she feels that her mother favors him. He shocks her into realizing that Al is establishing new relationships after being hurt by the narrator.

Further Reading

Authors and Artists for Young Adults. Vol. 7. Detroit: Gale Research, 1992.

Berger, Laura Standley, ed. *Twentieth-Century Children's Writers.* 4th ed. Detroit: St. James, 1995.

Collier, Laurie, and Joyce Nakamura, eds. *Major Authors and Illustrators for Children and Young Adults.* Detroit: Gale Research, 1993.

Contemporary Authors New Revision Series. Vol. 38. Detroit: Gale Research, 1993.

De Montreville, Doris, and Elizabeth D. Crawford, eds. *Fourth Book of Junior Authors.* New York: H. W. Wilson, 1978.

Something about the Author. Vols. 11, 72. Detroit: Gale Research, 1977, 1993.

Something about the Author Autobiography Series. Vol. 11. Detroit: Gale Research.

Virginia Hamilton

1936-, American author

M. C. Higgins the Great

(novel, 1974)

PLOT: Winner of both the Newbery Medal and the National Book Award, *M. C. Higgins the Great* develops themes associated with growing up: the conflict between independence and loyalty to one's family, the acceptance of differences, the disappointments of first love, and the choice of responsible actions over naive dreams. Mayo Cornelius Higgins, called M. C., lives on Sarah's Mountain below a spoil heap, a mound of uprooted trees, dirt, and refuse left by a strip mining company. M. C. fears that the spoil heap will slide down the mountain and kill his family, but he can't convince his father, Jones, to move. M. C. therefore hopes that the "dude," who is coming to record his mother's voice, will make her a singing star, and the family will have to leave. After secretly meeting Ben Killburn, whose family is considered "witchy" because of their unusual appearance, M. C. notices a strange girl walking the hills. He climbs atop a forty-foot pole in his yard—a prize his father gave him for swimming across the Ohio River—and watches while his siblings, Lennie Pool, Harper, and Macie Pearl, swim in a pond. M. C. then meets the dude, James K. Lewis, and arranges for him to return that evening. At lunch, M. C.'s teasing turns a playful fight with Jones into a serious contest. That afternoon, M. C. tracks the girl, jumps on her, and kisses her. During the struggle, he pricks her with his knife, and she flees in terror.

As he gains understanding, M. C. matures. First, he sees his home in a new light when Banina, his mother, explains that the pole and the junk in their yard mark the spots from which Jones removed the gravestones of his ancestors. Banina then sings for James Lewis. The next morning, M. C. discovers Lurhetta Outlaw, the girl he attacked, camping at the pond. She challenges M. C. to take her through an underwater tunnel he has discovered. Once in the water, M. C. realizes that Lurhetta can't swim, but he gets her through the tunnel safely. When he takes her home for lunch, Lurhetta is appalled at the superstitious hostility Jones directs at the Killburn men when they deliver ice. She then challenges M. C. to visit the Killburn compound. During this visit, M. C. talks to Ben's mother, Viola, and remembers that he spent his happiest days there. M. C. then has two disappointments: James Lewis tells M. C. that he can't sell Banina's voice, and Lurhetta goes away, leaving behind only her knife. M. C. then gets "a perfect idea." Using the knife to dig, he begins making a wall to stop the spoil heap. Insisting to Jones that he will choose his own friends, he defiantly invites Ben to help him. Jones then offers M. C. a shovel and gives him Great-grandmother Sarah's gravestone to add to the wall.

CHARACTERS: The characters are African Americans who represent various attitudes to change and differences. Over two days, **Mayo Cornelius Higgins**, called **M. C.**, grows up, asserting his independence while maintaining family ties. A thirteen-year-old with oak-brown skin, M. C. is tall, muscular, athletic, and graceful. He is proud of his physical accomplishments: he has shown bravery and strength by swimming the Ohio River, and he alone can climb his prize, a forty-foot pole. This pole, the one thing that makes him feel peaceful, is fitted with a bicycle seat and pedals so that he can "ride" it. Because it enables him to be alone, to do something no one else can do, and to gain a unique knowledge of the country, the pole symbolizes M. C.'s aloof individuality, proud masculinity, and sense of superiority.

M. C. initially is naive, arrogant, and aggressive. Highly imaginative, he has visions, daydreams, and nightmares in which the spoil heap destroys his family. Because his father seems oblivious to the danger, M. C. feels constrained and expresses frustration in several ways. First, he daydreams about supplanting his father by leading the family to safety. Second, he entertains the naive hope that James Lewis will replace his father by making Banina a star, and the family will leave with her. Finally, he expresses his rivalry physically. Playfully fighting with his father, he becomes cocky and rudely taunts Jones about his declining powers. After Jones jumps on him, the resentful M. C. denies entertaining the conceited thought that he was "M. C. Higgins, the Great." Nevertheless, he displays the same aggression and conceit with Lurhetta. In an episode that parallels his fight with Jones, he again loses control in what begins as a playful encounter, kissing her and then wounding her with the knife. Later, he childishly introduces himself to Lurhetta as M. C., the Great, an arrogant act that nearly costs them their lives when she challenges him to prove his boast.

M. C. changes dramatically because of Lurhetta, gaining knowledge, humility, and independence. When he saves her in the tunnel, he shows that he can exercise the self-control he previously lacked. He also learns that, instead of acting rashly, he must ask questions and carefully consider his actions. After Lurhetta challenges him to go to the Killburns, he is humbled by new knowledge: he sees that he has accepted his father's bigotry; he sees that the ropes connecting the Killburn buildings inspired his own idea for a bridge, an idea he had the conceit to think was original; and he realizes that the despised Killburns provided him with his happiest times. Because Lurhetta leaves without saying good-bye, M. C. also learns that love is not always reciprocated. Her gift of the knife, however, inspires him to turn his aggression into positive actions by transforming her weapon into a tool. When he begins digging the wall with it, M. C. simultaneously defies tradition by asserting his independence from its prejudices by inviting Ben's help, and he affirms tradition by trying to preserve his ancestral home, his inheritance. This wall may not stop the spoil heap, and M. C. will probably have to leave to learn more about himself, but his act reveals maturity, independence,

Hamilton's 1974 novel won both the Newbery Medal and the National Book Award.

and love of family. By choosing to act instead of depending on others, by challenging his father's prejudices, and by secretly deciding to throw his knife if Jones attacks Ben, M. C. acts responsibly as an individual, a son, and a friend. He truly becomes M. C. Higgins, the Great.

Jones Higgins, M. C.'s father, has mixed feelings about his son. A good family man, he loves M. C., is proud of him, and respects his understanding, almost believing that he has "second sight." Nevertheless, Jones, a powerfully built man with a broad chest, narrow hips, and muscular legs, feels threatened by him. Resenting his son's teasing about his declining powers, he becomes more violent than he intended when he reasserts his superiority. Jones has a deep feeling for the mountain and its history: he erects the pole to mark the ancestral graveyard should the spoil heap fall. He stubbornly refuses, however, to leave. Although Jones values tradition as the source of his identity, as he shows with the pole and in his stories about Great-grandmother Sarah, tradition is not entirely good. Because he clings to the traditional superstitions about the Killburns, he is callous and cruel. Jones changes, however, after M. C. declares his friendship with Ben. Instead of again violently asserting his will, Jones proudly accepts his son's independence, symbolically turning over guardianship of the past by contributing Sarah's gravestone to the wall.

Banina Higgins, M. C.'s mother, is straight and proud in posture. She is tall and attractive, with a soft mouth, high cheekbones, skin tanned reddish from the sun, and short brown hair with red streaks. Possessing a remarkable singing voice, she represents the culture inspired by the hills. She sings yodels to announce her arrival, traditional songs to entertain, and rounds to strengthen family bonds. Her major role is that of counselor. She helps M. C. to understand Jones and begins his transformation by telling him that the pole is a marker for the dead. M. C.'s brothers, nine-year-old **Harper Higgins** and ten-year-old **Lennie Pool Higgins**, are background characters who establish the loving warmth of the Higgins family. M. C.'s sister, eight-year-old **Macie Pearl Higgins** has a more fully developed personality. She is obedient, sweet-voiced, fun-loving, talkative, and brash with strangers. Macie deeply misses her mother during the day and gives Lurhetta a lesson in hill etiquette by objecting to a question about her mother's job.

Gray-haired, with a creased face the color of barn-dried walnuts, **James K. Lewis** is called **the dude** because of his fancy clothing: soft leather shoes, a suede jacket, and a wide-brimmed suede hat. An outsider, Lewis contributes to the conflict between Jones and M. C. by validating the boy's fear that the spoil heap is sliding. He also offers the false hope that Banina will become a singing star. A collector, like his father before him—and thus part of his own tradition—he apologizes that he can't make Banina a star, noting that she would have to change and that her music depends on the hills. He thus pushes M. C. from a naive dependence on others towards independent action.

Older than M. C., **Lurhetta Outlaw** is more independent and knowledgeable. Having only a mother and having earned her own money since she was fourteen, Lurhetta travels where she wishes. Perhaps because of M. C.'s assault, she behaves foolishly. Childishly intent on ensuring that he isn't the only one who has gone through the underwater tunnel, she doesn't tell him that she can't swim and nearly drowns. She thus gives him his first chance to show greatness. A perceptive outsider, Lurhetta announces the theme of accepting differences. Appalled by the way Jones treats the Killburn men, she condemns superstitious intolerance, citing it as an indefensible inheritance. By challenging M. C. to prove that he isn't superstitious, she changes him, making him see that he must not accept without question everything that he is told. She herself gains from her experiences: she accepts herself more fully by ceasing to be embarrassed by her surname, she learns about love of place, and experiences some of the joys of family life.

The Killburns, an extended family of vegetarians, are feared as "witchy": they have pale yellow skin, twelve fingers, twelve toes, and red hair. They live communally, men and women dressing alike in overalls. **Ben Killburn**, who is the same age but only half the size of M. C., is kind and helpful. Aware of the traditional animosity, he accepts that he must never touch M. C. He proves to be just like any other boy, however, when he proudly struts around to show his home to his friends. **Viola Killburn**, Ben's mother, has the reputation of being a magic healer. Easy to talk to, surrounded by babies, and always ready with food and refreshments, she is an ideal nurturer. **Mr. Killburn**, the iceman, is sarcastic and delights in making M. C. uncomfortable. A snake handler who believes in the power of magic, he tries to heal the land by laying his hands on the wounds left by the mining company.

Further Reading

Authors and Artists for Young Adults. Vol. 2. Detroit: Gale Research, 1989.

Berger, Laura Standley, ed. *Twentieth-Century Young Adult Writers.* 1st ed. Detroit: St. James, 1994.

Contemporary Authors New Revision Series. Vol. 37. Detroit: Gale Research, 1992.

Collier, Laurie, and Joyce Nakamura, eds. *Major Authors and Illustrators for Children and Young Adults.* Detroit: Gale Research, 1993.

Contemporary Literary Criticism. Vol. 26. Detroit: Gale Research, 1983.

Children's Literature Review. Vols. 1, 11. Detroit: Gale Research, 1976, 1986.

Davis, Thadious M., and Trudier Harris, eds. *Afro-American Writers after 1955.* Vol. 33 of *Dictionary of Literary Biography.* Detroit: Gale Research, 1984.

De Montreville, Doris, and Elizabeth D. Crawford, eds. *Fourth Book of Junior Authors.* New York: H. W. Wilson, 1978.

Estes, Glenn E., ed. *American Writers for Children since 1960: Fiction.* Vol. 52 of *Dictionary of Literary Biography.* Detroit: Gale Research, 1986.

Mikkelsen, Nina. *Virginia Hamilton.* New York: Twayne, 1994.

Rees, David. "Long Ride Through a Painted Desert: Virginia Hamilton." In *Painted Desert, Green Shade: Essays on Contemporary Writers of Fiction for Children and Young Adults.* Boston: Horn Book, 1984.

Something about the Author. Vols. 4, 56, 79. Detroit: Gale Research, 1973, 1989, 1995.

Townsend, John Rowe. "Virginia Hamilton." In *A Sounding of Storytellers: New and Revised Essays on Contemporary Writers for Children.* New York: J. B. Lippincott, 1979.

Russell Hoban

1925-, American artist, illustrator, copywriter, art director, and author

Frances the Badger Series

(picture books, 1960-1970)

PLOT: The first book about Frances, ***Bedtime for Frances*** (1960; illustrated by Garth Williams), is about bedtime fears. It begins with Frances making requests in order to delay the inevitable. Mother and Father indulge her, giving her a glass of milk, a piggyback ride, her teddy bear and doll, and additional kisses. Unable to sleep, however, Frances sings a song that convinces her that a tiger is in her room. She tells her parents, but Father satisfies her that the tiger won't hurt her. Back in her room, Frances mistakes a coat for a giant. Again Father reassures her, giving her a piece of cake. Frances returns to her room but worries that something will come out of the crack in the ceiling. Once more,

Garth Williams illustrated the first of the Frances the badger books.

Father persuades her that she is safe. Sleepy Father is less sympathetic when Frances awakens him to say that the curtains are moving: he warns her that she will get a spanking if she doesn't go to sleep. When a moth bangs against her window, therefore, Frances resists her urge to tell her parents. Because the thumping of the moth against the window reminds her of the sound of a spanking, Frances becomes tired and falls asleep.

In ***A Baby Sister for Frances*** (1964; illustrated by Lillian Hoban) Frances feels neglected after the arrival of Gloria, her baby sister. Frances sits beneath the kitchen sink and sings, but no one notices her until she marches around making more noise. Her parents then indulge Frances. Mother asks her to help put Gloria to sleep, Father raises her allowance because she is a big sister, and at bedtime both parents bring her all of her favorite possessions, including her tricycle and sled. In the morning, however, Frances discovers that Mother has not had time to iron her blue dress or to buy raisins for her cereal. Therefore, she decides to run away. Frances packs up her things and goes beneath the dining-room table. Mother and Father, sitting in the living room, talk about how much they miss Frances and how essential she is to the family. Finally, Frances makes a pretend telephone call to her parents, announcing that she is returning because everybody misses her. To celebrate her return, Mother bakes a chocolate cake.

The gently humorous ***Bread and Jam for Frances*** (1964; illustrated by Lillian Hoban) looks at children's eating obsessions. At breakfast, Father, Mother, and baby Gloria enjoy soft-boiled eggs. Frances, singing a song expressing dislike for eggs, eats bread and jam instead. At dinner, Frances insists that she doesn't need to try new foods because she is always pleased with bread and jam. The next morning, Mother serves poached eggs, but she gives Frances bread and jam. At school, Frances discovers that Mother has packed her a lunch of bread and jam. Mother gives Frances a bread and jam snack after school and serves her the same thing for dinner. Seeing everyone else enjoying spaghetti and meatballs, Frances cries and asks for them too. Ironically, Frances says that Mother won't know what Frances likes unless she tries to give her new dishes to eat. The next day at school, Frances eats an elaborate and varied lunch. Her friend Albert, whom she imitates by eating a bit of everything in turn, announces the theme that it is nice that there are different kinds of meals to enjoy.

Best Friends for Frances (1969; illustrated by Lillian Hoban) is the most complex story of the series. It uses parallel situations to teach lessons in acceptance and friendship. When Gloria asks Frances to play ball, Frances refuses, saying that Gloria is too little. Leaving the crying Gloria, Frances asks Albert to play ball. Albert, however, tells her that it is his "wandering day" and refuses to let her accompany him because she doesn't know his methods. The next day, Frances again asks Albert to play ball, but Albert is playing a no-girls game with Harold. Frances goes home and announces that she and Gloria will be best friends. Pulling a wagon containing a well-packed picnic hamper and carrying a sign announcing "Best Friends Outing: No Boys," they pass Albert's house. Albert, obviously attracted by their hamper, asks if he can join them. Frances sarcastically refuses him, but Gloria says that Albert

can be a best friend and can teach her to catch snakes. After Albert promises that there will be no more no-girls baseball, Frances agrees. The three friends have a good time, and Albert eats an enormous quantity of food. The next day, Albert brings Frances some daisies, declaring that he is her best boyfriend. Fearing that Frances will no longer be her best friend, Gloria cries. Frances soothes Gloria by sharing her flowers. Albert, Harold, Frances, and Gloria then play ball together.

The other two books in the "Frances the Badger" series, both illustrated by Lillian Hoban, are ***A Birthday for Frances*** (1968), in which Frances overcomes both sibling rivalry and selfishness when she gives her sister a birthday present, and ***A Bargain for Frances*** (1970), which tells how Frances outwits Thelma, who has cheated her out of a new tea set. Afterwards, Frances convinces Thelma that being friends is more important than being wary of each other.

CHARACTERS: Only the drawings indicate that Frances is a badger. In all respects, Frances behaves like a human child experiencing the small but disturbing problems of growing up. **Frances** is a warm and friendly badger who is memorable because she expresses her feelings and copes with trying situations by singing rhyming songs. In the early books, Frances is insecure and seeks assurance that she is safe or that she is a valuable member of the family. Frances is wary of change, whether in the form of a new sister or a new meal. With the arrival of Gloria, for instance, Frances feels neglected, makes noise to be noticed, and surrounds herself with her possessions to maintain stability. She seems comical when she runs away by sitting under the table, but her gesture expresses a serious concern about her place in the home. Similarly, Frances's stubborn insistence on eating only bread and jam is an effort to maintain reassuring stability.

Some of Frances's problem are self-imposed. For example, her active imagination frightens her by transforming a hanging coat into a giant. Because Frances understands that actions have consequences—

such as a spanking if she again awakens her parents—she learns to control her fears. In the final three books, Frances is concerned with relationships. Frances has a typical older child's contempt for the incompetence of smaller children until she is the victim of similar prejudice against girls. Consequently, she becomes more tolerant and befriends her little sister. Later, Frances even shows mature consideration by sharing her daisies so that the sobbing Gloria will not feel left out. Even though her other friends sometimes hurt her and she exacts some revenge, Frances values friendship. Thus, although she initially suspects that Albert's appetite motivates his desire, Frances overcomes her wounded pride and gives Albert, as she later does Thelma, the chance to be a good friend.

Father is an indulgent and understanding middle-class parent. In the first book, he is the one who gives Frances the piggyback ride, her toys, and the piece of cake. He shows tact and wit in helping Frances conquer her fears. He does not, for example, deny the reality of the tigers or giants in her bedroom; instead, he convinces Frances that any tigers in her room are harmless. Father's patience does have limits, however, as he shows when he threatens Frances with a spanking to get her to go to sleep. After the third book, Father no longer plays a role. **Mother** is a background figure in the first book, but in the second she is as important as her husband. She shows understanding of Frances's feelings, praising her and letting her know that she is loved. Mother's major role is in *Bread and Jam for Frances*, in which she unobtrusively teaches Frances an important lesson. Instead of lecturing her daughter or forcing her to eat new foods, Mother indulges Frances, allowing her to discover for herself the value of a varied diet.

Gloria, Frances's little sister, is both vulnerable and surprisingly competent. She frequently cries because she feels excluded. Nevertheless, Gloria is more capable than Frances first thinks. Gloria can catch a ball if it is thrown from close by, and she can catch frogs, something Frances can't do. Gloria is also generous and open. She is the first to accept Albert as a best friend, and she convinces Frances that they can all get along. **Albert**, Frances's friend,

has an enormous appetite. He plays a vital role in dramatizing the theme of two books in which he appears. In *Bread and Jam for Frances*, Albert voices the theme that variety is nice. In *Best Friends for Frances*, he is instrumental in showing Frances how unfair she herself has been. Albert, that is, parallels Frances, who rejects Gloria for alleged incompetence. Although food inspires his change of heart, Albert keeps his word about not excluding girls. Indeed, he shows that boys can be friends with girls and that children of different ages and abilities can be friends when he and Harold play ball with Frances and Gloria.

The Mouse and His Child

(toy fantasy, 1967)

PLOT: Critics have questioned whether this violent, intellectually complex fantasy is a children's book. Its quest patterns, however, affirm themes common in children's literature: the need for a home and a satisfying identity. The mouse and his child are a single wind-up toy connected at the hands so that the mice face each other. The child longs to live in a dollhouse with a mechanical elephant and a performing seal. The toy mice are sold, however, and on their fifth Christmas, the child cries at the sight of a dollhouse. The cat notices and knocks over a vase that smashes the mice. A tramp finds them, repairs them, and winds them up, saying, "Be tramps."

Opposing quests now develop. The mice seek family and home, while the villain, Manny Rat, relentlessly tries to destroy them. Manny becomes angry after a bluejay reports that the mice, whom he had enslaved, have escaped. Frog, a charlatan who mysteriously becomes a real fortune teller, saves them by outwitting Manny. Frog and the toy mice, however, are captured by some shrews, who are killed by some weasels, who are killed by an owl. The owl's mate carries off Frog. The mouse and his child next join Mr. and Mrs. Crow's Caws of Art, a theatrical troop performing *The Last Visible Dog*, an absurd drama. When Manny sneaks up during a production, the mice escape by making the audience attack him as the play's villain.

Because the mice want to be self-winding, Euterpe, the repertory parrot, takes them to Muskrat, a theoretician. To prove that he is practical, however, Muskrat turns them into a tree-chopping machine. Manny again finds them, but the tree they are chopping falls and flings them into a stream. They end up in the mud at the bottom of a pond. There, in a thematically central scene, they meet C. Serpentina, a snapping turtle and author of *The Last Visible Dog.* Staring at the play's inspiration, infinitely regressing dogs pictured on the label of a can of Bonzo Dog Food, the child realizes that "nothing" is beyond the last visible dog. After Miss Mudd, an insect, peels off the label, however, the child sees his own reflection beyond nothing. He decides to think for himself to get out of the pond. Therefore, he gets Miss Mudd to loop a string over a branch, tying one end to them and the other to a good luck coin. A passing bass takes this lure and yanks them onto shore. A marsh hawk seizes them but drops them into a dump because they are inedible. Fortunately, Frog, having escaped from the owl, gets a bittern to help him follow the hawk. The performing seal and the kingfisher also follow. At the dump, Frog repairs the smashed father and son, making them separate toys.

The mouse, his child, and their friends, attack the dollhouse. The mouse, transformed into a mechanical catapult, defeats Manny by knocking out his teeth with the lucky coin. The mouse then marries the elephant, the seal becomes the child's sister, and they all live in the restored dollhouse. Apparently reformed, Manny makes them self-winding. But he also plots revenge, which the elephant inadvertently foils during housecleaning. Although accidentally electrocuted as a result, Manny survives. Truly reformed this time, he is welcomed into the house, which becomes a hotel. At Christmas, the tramp appears and says, "Be happy."

CHARACTERS: Because this picaresque fantasy develops its theme in set pieces, it contains a large number of significant characters. Hoban connected many to an identity theme, explaining, "they found out what they were and it wasn't enough, so they found out how to be more."

The tin wind-up **mouse and his child** become more by breaking the clockwork rules against talking and crying. Joined by their hands, they begin as facing parts of one toy. The father, who contains the motor, originally dances in a circle, throwing his son into the air. His circular movement symbolizes their meaningless existence. After the tramp repairs them, their movement in a straight line literally and symbolically allows them to get somewhere.

The child's innocent questions and dreams give meaning to their wanderings and inspire the father to action. One of his first questions, "*What* are we, Papa?" initiates the identity theme. Ironically, the child's crying, which leads to their destruction, frees them from the meaningless circles of their dance. Thematically, this crying suggests that emotions are prerequisites to a meaningful identity. The child's innate desire for love and family—he wants the elephant for a mother and the seal for a sister, and he calls their helpers uncles—also gives meaning to their sufferings by becoming the goal of their wanderings.

The child depends on his father, who pushes him backwards and therefore sees where they are going. A change occurs, though, when they are stuck in the mud. Only the child sees the pictures on the Bonzo Dog Food can. Submerged in water, a symbol of the unconscious, he becomes mature and contemplative. He rejects, however, C. Serpentina's assertion that nothing is the ultimate truth. He himself discovers another truth when he sees his reflection for the first time. No longer defining himself through his father, he becomes an existential hero. Taking responsibility for his fate, he devises the plan that extricates them from the mud. Ultimately, his actions lead to the "shattering fall" prophesied by Frog. This shattering in the dump, like their destruction by the vase, reshapes their identities: the child, separated from the father, achieves independence.

The father also articulates an existential theme. When the Caws of Art audience laughs at their real problems, he declares that he and his child are ridiculous because they can't control their lives. He therefore decides to become self-winding, a symbol of human autonomy, and to acquire territory, a sign of significant identity. After the "shattering fall," the father redefines himself. No longer a mere toy, he accepts his son's dreams as his goals. He then undergoes mechanical transformations, as when Frog replaces his arms with tin donkey's legs to make him a deadly catapult. These changes symbolize his new ability to adapt. After Manny makes him self-winding, the father accepts that autonomy is not absolute and that he needs friends to rewind him occasionally. He also forms a community by turning their home into a hotel. Thus, he becomes capable of finding happiness.

Manny Rat pursues an evil quest of destruction but turns into the father's benefactor. Manny, wearing a greasy scrap of silk paisley as a dressing gown, reeks evil: he smells of darkness and rot. Manny rules the dump through physical force: his yellow teeth are the longest, strongest, and sharpest. He also possesses mechanical ingenuity and makes toys into slaves. Because their escape mocks his identity as a ruler in absolute control, Manny obsessively pursues the toy mice. His attempts to destroy them test the mice and their helpers, but his repeated failures add comedy. In spite of his fatalistic belief in Frog's prophecy about his fall, which comes true when Sirius, the Dog Star, rises, Manny fights on. After he loses his teeth in the battle and becomes physically powerless, however, he changes. Wearing the clean sackcloth of a penitent, he fulfills the father's wish by making him self-winding. Ironically, his success makes Manny acutely aware of his previous defeat, so he again becomes evil. Although he is apparently killed when his plot to burn the house goes awry, Manny revives. Symbolically, he is reborn by the child's praise of "Uncle Manny," who sacrificed himself to give them electric lights. No longer filled with darkness, Manny truly reforms and becomes a teacher who shares his mechanical knowledge with the young.

The child also adopts other helpers as "uncles." **Uncle Frog** adds an enigmatic counterbalance to the themes of identity and freedom. Frog, who wears an old glove, is a fraudulent fortune teller. He has keen powers of observation that enable him to satisfy customers. When he tells the fortunes of the toy mice and Manny, however, some mysterious force masters him, and he becomes a prophet. Frog's inability to utter intended lies and the fact that his cryptic prophecies come true suggests that fate governs lives. The difference between such fate and determinism, however, remains elusive. Frog changes in another way, too. He is willing to betray the mice when Manny catches them, but, after he involuntarily prophesies Manny's downfall, he becomes a true helper. He himself seems to be blessed by fate, escaping the owl because it grabbed him by his glove. He returns to become crucial to Manny's overthrow, using his mechanical ability to repair the toy mice and to alter the father for the attack.

The elephant learns humility. In the toy store, she is the voice of determinism, pompously declaring that "One does what one is wound to do." Dressed in a purple headcloth, she erroneously considers herself a permanent resident and feels superior to the "transient elements." After she is sold and then discarded, she realizes her folly. Although she deteriorates, she maintains her dignity, refusing to speak when Manny makes her a slave. Some feminist critics have complained that the elephant, who marries the father, is a stereotype of the homemaking female. Her obsession with tidiness is crucial to the plot, however, because she unwittingly foils Manny's plan for revenge. The performing **seal**, who becomes the child's sister, does not play a significant role, but her wanderings and physical changes parallel those of the toy mice, suggesting that loneliness and suffering are universal.

Muskrat, a theoretical thinker, reduces knowledge to mathematical formulations: "Why times How equals What." Muskrat wants recognition, so his pride is wounded when he learns that everyone laughs at him as useless. Although he subsequently applies himself to the practical problem of chopping a tree, he fails to understand practical morality. He places his own goals ahead of the more pressing needs of the mice and reduces them to meaningless objects, symbolized by their going around in circles again to chop his tree. Ironically, Muskrat is killed by a tree felled by beavers restoring the lodge that his tree destroyed.

C. Serpentina, a morose snapping turtle with a big appetite, writes absurdist dramas resembling those of Samuel Beckett. Basing his existential philosophy on a dog food can at the bottom of a pool, he argues that striving for goals is pointless because all places are one and that "Nothing is the ultimate truth." He exhibits a fatalistic satisfaction with his conclusions, but the child challenges his intellectual authority. **Miss Mudd**, an ugly insect, does not accept her appearance as her true identity because she feels clean and beautiful inside. Inspired by the child's rebellion, she becomes a helper, tearing off the label, polishing the coin, and rigging the lure. Her appearance finally agrees with her nature when she becomes a shining dragonfly. The **marsh hawk** proclaims a Darwinian view of existence, in which the balance of nature is a "beautiful pyramid" that has the hawk on top and his food beneath. Ironically, his vision lacks room for mechanical mice, so he drops them, unwittingly creating the "shattering fall" of Frog's prophecy.

Mr. and Mrs. Crow, leaders of the Caws of Art, satirize artistic pretensions. Mr. Crow enthusiastically stages C. Serpentina's play even though he doesn't understand it. Although she is not certain that staging the play is a good idea, Mrs. Crow joins her husband in condemning the unappreciative audience as hayseeds. **Euterpe**, once a pet named Polly, is a frowsy repertory parrot who wears several dolls' sweaters and a muffler. She blandly sees Manny's pursuit of the mice as an image of life, but she helps by taking them to Muskrat.

The bittern uses his abilities to hammer to help the mice in the assault on Manny. Originally concerned only about his privacy, he ends his isolation because he becomes emotionally attached to the toy mice. **The kingfisher**, who befriends the seal, adds irony by catching the bass that took the good luck coin. He also helps to overthrow Manny and becomes chef in the hotel. The **bluejay** reporter has three functions. He satirizes the sensationalistic tabloid press with his headlines. He influences the action: Manny pursues the mice because the bluejay announces their escape, and he informs readers about undramatized events, such as Muskrat's death. Several critics see **the tramp**, whose appearances at Christmas frame the narrative, as a symbolic author. He shares an author's godlike ability of setting his creations on the road to adventures, and he concludes their sufferings, commanding, "Be happy."

Further Reading

Berger, Laura Standley, ed. *Twentieth-Century Children's Writers*. 4th ed. Detroit: St. James, 1995.

Children's Literature Review. Vol. 3. Detroit: Gale Research, 1978.

Collier, Laurie, and Joyce Nakamura, eds. *Major Authors and Illustrators for Children and Young Adults*. Detroit: Gale Research, 1993.

Contemporary Authors New Revision Series. Vol. 37. Detroit: Gale Research, 1992.

Contemporary Literary Criticism. Vols. 7, 25. Detroit: Gale Research, 1984, 1992.

De Montreville, Doris, and Donna Hill, eds. *Third Book of Junior Authors*. New York: H. W. Wilson, 1972.

Estes, Glenn E., ed. *American Writers for Children since 1960: Fiction*. Vol. 52 of *Dictionary of Literary Biography*. Detroit: Gale Research, 1986.

Something about the Author. Vols. 1, 40, 78. Detroit: Gale Research, 1971, 1985, 1994.

Mary Hoffman

1945-, British journalist and author

Amazing Grace

(picture book, 1991; illustrated by Caroline Binch)

PLOT: This realistic story traces a girl's success in overcoming sexist and racist preconceptions. Grace loves stories. She acts them out, always giving herself the most exciting parts. When her teacher announces that the class will perform *Peter Pan*, Grace therefore wants the title role. Some classmates, however, say that Grace can't have the role because she is a girl and because Peter Pan isn't black. Grace is sad, but Ma tells her that she can be

Peter Pan if she wants. On Saturday, Nana takes Grace to see a performance of *Romeo and Juliet* starring a black ballerina. Grace dances in her room afterwards, inspired with the idea that she can be anything that she wants. At the audition, Grace impresses everyone and wins the part. The play is successful, and Grace is amazing. When Grace happily says that she feels as if she could fly home, Ma says that Grace probably could, and Nana says that Grace can do anything if she puts her mind to it.

The sequel is Boundless Grace *(1995; British title,* Grace and Family*).*

CHARACTERS: Adult characters denounce sexist and racist stereotypes while encouraging the self-esteem of the central character in this tale. **Grace** is a thin, imaginative, and intelligent black girl who illustrates the power of positive thinking. She loves stories, especially fairy tales, and her powerful imagination is evident in her habit of dressing in costumes to act out stories. This habit also indicates that Grace does not feel limited by gender or race. In fact, Grace shows a healthy self-respect and ambition when she keeps her hand up after other children tell her that she is not right for the role of Peter Pan. Nevertheless, Grace is sensitive, and their comments sadden her. Because she is intelligent, however, Grace learns from and is inspired by the success of the black ballerina. She immerses herself in the role of Peter Pan, learning the lines and actions so well that she impresses even those who criticized her desire to have the lead role.

The adults in Grace's family clarify the themes about gender and race. **Ma** criticizes sexist assumptions, insisting that a girl can be Peter Pan if she wants to. Because Ma becomes angry when Grace brings up the issue, **Nana** teaches Grace that race is not a limitation on accomplishment. An archetypal wise grandmother, Nana understands Grace's passion for spectacle and therefore teaches her by taking her to the ballet. Nana also gives voice to the theme, twice insisting that Grace can be whatever she wants.

Further Reading

Contemporary Authors. Vol. 131. Detroit: Gale Research, 1991.

Something about the Author. Vol. 59. Detroit: Gale Research, 1990.

James Houston

1921-, Canadian Arctic administrator, designer, artist, and author

Frozen Fire: A Tale of Courage

(novel, 1977)

PLOT: *Frozen Fire* presents the themes of courage, inner strength, and loyalty traditionally found in wilderness survival adventures. It also treats the importance of respecting cultural differences. Thirteen-year-old Matthew Morgan accompanies Ross Morgan, his geologist father, to Frobisher in the Canadian Arctic. There, Matt becomes friends with Kayak, an Eskimo boy his age. Mr. Morgan, convinced that he knows where to find a huge copper deposit, sets out in a helicopter piloted by his Australian friend, Charlie. When a storm arises and they do not return, authorities launch an air search. But fog grounds the search aircraft, so Kayak and Matt depart by snowmobile. Their rescue attempt turns into a disaster that tests both boys' courage and resourcefulness. They lose all their fuel, suffer through a blizzard in a shelter Kayak builds, spend a day walking in a circle, and lose all of their equipment when Kayak falls into a crevasse.

A wild man, a strange Eskimo who wears watches without hands and lives underground with his wife, saves them. He offers them gifts, including a plastic bow and arrows, caribou meat, and a snow knife, and he gives them directions home. On the way, Matt breaks the bow when he tries to shoot an owl. The incident leads him to discover gold nuggets. Matt packs his bags full of gold, but Kayak, contemptuous of what he calls "white man's madness," takes only a flintstone. Eventually, Matthew can't carry his heavy load of gold any longer and is forced to dump it. He and Kayak then find themselves on a floating ice pan. A polar bear climbs on, kills a seal, and then departs. Kayak despairs that they will never get home alive, but Matt urges him to build a shelter. After doing so, Kayak warms them with a lamp stove made from the seal's heart and lighted using his flintstone.

The knowledge shared between their two different cultures leads to the boys' rescue. Matt uses a mirror he removed from their snowmobile to signal a passing plane, and Kayak draws a circle around their shelter with seal's blood that enables Charlie's helicopter to locate them. When they are returned to Frobisher, Matt is reunited with his father, who had heroically rescued Charlie after their helicopter crashed. His father informs Matt that they are going to stay in Frobisher. Matt, who now feels at home and among friends, decides that his discovery of the gold will remain a secret for now.

Sequels are Black Diamonds: A Search for Arctic Treasure *(1982) and* Ice Swords: An Undersea Adventure *(1985).*

CHARACTERS: In addition to showing how circumstances test inner resources, the major characters demonstrate the wisdom of respecting the traditional culture of the Eskimos. His Arctic adventure enables **Matthew Morgan** to discover who he is and where he belongs. A tall, slim, gray-eyed thirteen-year-old with sandy hair, Matt has lived in a variety of places, none of which feels like a true home. His friendship with Kayak, who calls him a brother, changes him and his feelings. Matt initially represents white culture. He is a bright boy who has acquired his knowledge of the land only by studying geology books. Nevertheless, Matt is so brave during the blizzard that Kayak praises him as being like an Eskimo, "a real man." He also exhibits loyalty and courage by pulling Kayak from the crevasse. Matt's subsequent behavior shows, however, that he does not yet fully belong in the unforgiving world of the Arctic wilderness. When he discovers gold and completes a quest that his father had repeatedly failed, Matt fails to understand that the acquisition of wealth, a sign of success in white society, can be foolish and perilous in the Arctic. Carrying the gold

drains Matt's strength, and the gold itself, unlike Kayak's flintstone, does not contribute to their survival effort. When he abandons the gold, Matt maturely demonstrates both acceptance of their urgent predicament and respect for their harsh environment. He encourages the despondent Kayak to build a shelter on the ice pan. Although he has had persistent nightmares about encountering a polar bear, he maintains self-control when actually confronted with one. Furthermore, he displays resourcefulness in using a mirror to signal a passing plane. The most significant change, however, is his decision to conceal his discovery of the gold. Feeling at home in Frobisher, Matt now understands that happiness and contentment must come from within, and that material wealth does not guarantee personal and emotional satisfaction.

Kayak, who is Matt's age, represents Eskimo culture. Kayak disdains the white man's values and actions and considers the knowledge of Afghanistan that Matt demonstrates in school irrelevant to his life. He also sees the destructiveness of his own culture in the actions of an uncle whose alcoholism makes him unfit to live in the traditional way and equally incapable of living among the whites. Kayak uses traditional knowledge to save their lives. He builds shelters, erects markers so that they do not walk in circles, makes a lamp stove from a frozen seal heart, and uses the seal's blood to mark their location. Kayak teaches a particularly significant lesson when he proves to Matt that, in the Arctic, a flintstone has much more value than gold. Although Kayak's role in the book serves to criticize whites who do not understand the severity of the Arctic environment, his character has broader and more complex implications. Kayak survives because of both traditional culture and the white man's technology: Matt uses the mirror to signal an airplane, and Charlie takes them from the ice pan with his helicopter. Nevertheless, Kayak represents a traditional society that respects nature and values human relationships. He quickly accepts Matthew as a brother and assures him that, should Matt's father not survive, he will be a member of Kayak's family.

Ross Morgan, Matthew's father, is a geologist and teacher. His comment to Matt that in the Arctic a man can call his soul his own heralds one of Houston's themes. Nevertheless, his obsession to discover mineral wealth and stake a claim before anyone else causes him to risk his life—and Charlie's—by deceiving Charlie into filing a false flight plan. Ross Morgan ultimately exhibits physical heroism by seeking help for Charlie after they crash and moral responsibility by deciding to accept employment that will enable him and Matt to stay in Frobisher.

Charlie is a short, gregarious Australian helicopter pilot with a thick neck and shoulders, fiery red hair, freckles, and a ready smile. Charlie's fun-loving conversation forces Ross Morgan to hide their true destination from him until they are in the air. Charlie contributes to the author's ecological message by praising traditional Eskimo ways and by proclaiming that white people must change some of their foolishly careless and wasteful behaviors. The **wild man** is an improbable helper who has the symbolic function of showing the relative value of white and Eskimo culture in the north. A shaggy-haired Eskimo who lives apart from all communities, he wears a half dozen watches without hands on each arm to indicate his contempt for the white man's artificial sense of time. Like typical folktale helpers, he provides important and significant gifts to the other characters. The plastic bow and arrows, which break when Matt uses them, illustrate that some white man's effects are the junk he calls them. In contrast, the meat and snow knife establish the usefulness of Eskimo culture. His third gift, directions for the way home, reveals the wisdom of a man who understands the land and represents the practical geographic knowledge that Matt lacks.

Further Reading

Berger, Laura Standley, ed. *Twentieth-Century Young Adult Writers.* 1st ed. Detroit: St. James, 1994.

Children's Literature Review. Vol. 3. Detroit: Gale Research, 1978.

Major Authors and Illustrators for Children and Young Adults. Detroit: Gale Research, 1993.

Contemporary Authors New Revision Series. Vol. 38. Detroit: Gale Research, 1993.

Something about the Author. Vols. 13, 74. Detroit: Gale Research, 1978, 1993.

Something about the Author Autobiography Series. Vol. 17. Detroit: Gale Research, 1994.

James Howe
1946-, American actor, director, and author

Bunnicula: A Rabbit-Tale of Mystery
(fantasy, 1979; written with wife, Deborah Howe)

PLOT: This slapstick story is written by Harold, the mongrel pet of a family he calls the Monroes. One night, Mr. Robert Monroe, Mrs. Monroe, Pete, and Toby come home with a tiny rabbit in a shoe box filled with dirt. Because they found it in a theater showing *Dracula*, Mrs. Monroe names it Bunnicula. Chester the cat becomes suspicious because a mysterious note found with the rabbit is written in a dialect used in Transylvania. Furthermore, Bunnicula sleeps all day, mysteriously gets out of his cage at night, and sucks the juices from vegetables, turning them white. Chester's reading convinces him that Bunnicula is a vampire, so he tries to get rid of the rabbit. First, he mimes a warning about vampires, biting Harold on the neck, but Mrs. Monroe thinks that Chester wants to be petted. Next, Chester puts on a garlic pendant and scatters garlic about the house, thereby confining Bunnicula to his cage. This plan to starve Bunnicula goes awry, however, when Mrs. Monroe bathes Chester to get rid of the smell. Having read that the way to destroy a vampire is to drive a sharp stake into his heart, Chester takes a steak from the kitchen and tries to pound it into Bunnicula's chest. When the Monroes catch him in the act, Chester throws water, hoping to dissolve the vampire. Exasperated by his behavior, Mrs. Monroe puts Chester outside and gives the ruined steak to Harold.

A few days later, Harold discovers that Chester, again wearing garlic, has been stealing Bunnicula's food and is blocking off the kitchen. Unable to get the Monroes to see that the rabbit is starving, Harold takes Bunnicula from his cage and puts him next to the salad bowl. Chester jumps at Bunnicula but ends up on his back in the salad bowl. Rushing into the room, the Monroes discover that Bunnicula is not well. They take him to a veterinarian. Afterwards, Bunnicula eats only a liquid diet, so the Monroes discover no more white vegetables. Harold and

Bunnicula also become good friends; because of his strange behavior, Chester is sent to a cat psychiatrist.

Sequels are Howliday Inn *(1982),* The Celery Stalks at Midnight *(1983),* Nighty-Nightmare *(1987),* Return to Howliday Inn *(1992), and* Rabbit-Cadabra! *(1993).*

CHARACTERS: The two main animals read, write, and talk to each other, but they do not talk to humans. **Harold**, the narrator, is a sad-eyed, droopy-eared mongrel. Because he has Russian wolfhound ancestry, he recognizes that a strange note found with Bunnicula is written in an obscure dialect of the Carpathian Mountain region. Harold is not scholarly, however, and he has trouble understanding many English words. Harold is an unlikely hero. He loves comfort and food, making it a point to sleep in Toby's room on Fridays when Toby has chocolate cupcakes. Because he is compassionate and comes to like Bunnicula, Harold becomes heroic, trying to save the rabbit when Chester starves it.

Chester, an intelligent cat, loves to read. He can explain big words to Harold, and he can satisfy his curiosity and suspicions through research about vampires. He is observant, logical, and persistent, figuring out what Bunnicula is doing in the kitchen and making repeated efforts to stop him. Chester insists that he is saving the Monroes, but he seems, especially in comparison to the tender-hearted Harold, to be cold and cruel. Although he tries to be a hero, he becomes a comical character: each of his plans goes awry, and the Monroes become increasingly convinced that something is wrong with him. In the end, he becomes a vehicle for satirizing popular psychology: after reading *Finding Yourself by Screaming a Lot*, he goes to the basement and screams.

Bunnicula, a tiny black-and-white rabbit, seems to be a vampire. He was found in a box of dirt with a note written in a Transylvanian dialect; he sleeps all day; he turns vegetables white by sucking the juice from them; and, according to Chester, he has fangs. Unlike the other animals, he does not speak. His role is to reveal, by the contrasting treatment they give him, the characters of Harold and Chester.

The human characters, whose surname Harold invents to protect them, have limited roles. **Mr. Robert Monroe** is an English professor. **Mrs. Monroe**, his wife, is a lawyer. She generates comedy by repeatedly misunderstanding Chester and performing acts, such as kissing his nose or washing him, that he considers objectionable. The Monroe children constantly bicker. Ten-year-old **Pete** is obsessed with his status as the older boy and suggests that he will be traumatized if his parents permit his brother to name the rabbit. Eight-year-old **Toby** teases Harold, but unlike Pete, he shares his food. Harold rewards Toby by sleeping with him.

Further Reading

Berger, Laura Standley, ed. *Twentieth-Century Children's Writers*. 4th ed. Detroit: St. James, 1995.

Children's Literature Review. Vol. 9. Detroit: Gale Research, 1985.

Collier, Laurie, and Joyce Nakamura, eds. *Major Authors and Illustrators for Children and Young Adults*. Detroit: Gale Research, 1993.

Contemporary Authors New Revision Series. Vol. 46. Detroit: Gale Research, 1995.

Holtze, Sally Holmes, ed *Sixth Book of Junior Authors and Illustrators*. New York: H. W. Wilson, 1989.

Something about the Author. Vols. 29, 71. Detroit: Gale Research, 1982, 1993.

Monica Hughes

1925-, Canadian novelist

The Keeper of the Isis Light

(science fiction, 1980)

PLOT: Monica Hughes wrote *The Keeper of the Isis Light* after reading a newspaper article about a boy named David, who had to be isolated in a bubble because he had an immune deficiency. She has said that she intended the novel to explore the difference between being alone and being lonely. Even more dramatic, however, are themes of prejudice, maturation, and self-acceptance.

Olwen Pendennis is an orphan whose Earth parents have been killed by a radiation storm on the planet Isis. She has been raised alone by the robot, Guardian. To protect her from the planet's ultraviolet radiation, Guardian has surgically and genetically altered Olwen. When the novel opens, Olwen is preparing to celebrate her birthday: she is ten on Isis but sixteen in Earth terms. She learns on this day that a group of settlers from Earth is about to arrive. As keeper of the planet's signal, it is her duty to greet the settlers. Guardian insists, however, that she wear a suit and mask that completely cover her while she does so, claiming this measure is necessary to protect her from germs.

Among the eighty settlers Captain Tryon brings to Isis on the spaceship Pegasus II is Mark London, a boy who becomes friendly with Olwen. She soon falls in love with him. One day, however, Mark comes unannounced to Olwen's home and climbs to the mesa above it. From this vantage point, he sees Olwen without her usual suit and mask. When she turns around, Mark falls from the cliff in horrified shock: Olwen has the color and features of a lizard. A few days later, Olwen—again without her mask—is playing with her pet hairy dragon, Hobbit. Some of the settlers are frightened by the beast and kill it. One settler even aims his gun at Olwen. Angrily, Olwen storms into the settlement, where everyone except Jody, a little East African boy, is frightened by her appearance.

Olwen then enters a new phase of her development, becoming fully aware of herself. Guardian restores her memory, which he had wiped away so that she would not be lonely for her parents. He also provides a mirror so that Olwen can see what she looks like for the first time in her life. Despite her appearance, Olwen is pleased with herself because her body is functional: she is able to go into all areas of Isis, whereas the settlers can't. Still, she vows never again to go among the settlers. Olwen then decides to journey to an unexplored area of upper Isis. During her trip, she suddenly experiences a peculiar restless feeling. Looking about, she realizes that a cosmic storm is coming. She takes refuge in a cave, where she also protects a baby hairy dragon, whom she names Little Hobbit.

In the final stage of her maturation, Olwen, who has previously obeyed Guardian, takes full control of her life. Returning from her journey, she realizes that she can sense the coming of another storm. When Guardian informs her that little Jody is lost, she brushes aside his objections and sets out in the storm to find him. She rescues Jody from a sinkhole and returns him to his family. Afterwards, Captain Tryon offers to take her to Earth to be surgically restored. Although she had once thought of undergoing the operation to enable Mark to love her, Olwen rejects his offer. During their discussion, however, Captain Tryon calls Guardian a robot. Although Olwen had previously considered him a person, her new understanding does not alter her love for Guardian.

Olwen makes one more major decision in the novel. Mark, who previously rejected Olwen as hideous, now professes his love for her inner self. Olwen gently rejects him, however, because she has decided that they share nothing in common and that she values her freedom to move anywhere on the planet. Together with Guardian, she sets out to establish a new home in the wilderness. Although she will be alone there, she will feel useful as she issues early warnings to the settlers about approaching storms.

The story continues in two sequels, The Guardian of Isis *(1981) and* The Isis Pedlar *(1982).*

CHARACTERS: In this novel, Hughes carefully controls point of view in order to develop readers' attitudes toward the characters. Despite foreshadowing, therefore, readers do not discover the fact of Olwen's inhuman appearance until after Mark and the villagers see her. In this way, Hughes insures that readers identify with Olwen as a person before they confront the prejudices of the Earth settlers and the issues raised by prejudice.

Although she has thick red hair, **Olwen Pendennis** is otherwise reptilian in appearance: her skin is a thick bronzy green; a bony lump shades her blue eyes, which are protected by nictitating membranes; and she has wide nostrils and a large rib cage to enable her to breathe in the thin atmosphere. In other words, she is perfectly adapted for survival on Isis. In spite of her appearance, Olwen is entirely human in her feelings. The dual methods used to calculate Olwen's age—which make her ten on Isis but sixteen in Earth years—symbolize her position between child and woman.

At first, Olwen is childishly selfish, unwilling to share her planet with anyone. Later, when she meets Mark, she falls in love and develops into an adolescent. Olwen experiences loneliness for the first time after Mark falls and the settlers shoot Hobbit. She becomes full of bitterness and rejects all involvement with society. Her trip into the wilderness, however, marks a symbolic rebirth. In the womb-like cave, her ability to love returns: she actually prays for the safety of the settlers, and she saves a small hairy dragon from the storm. Consequently, Olwen recants her vow to have nothing more to do with the settlers. Filled with a moral but irrational bravery, she risks her life to save Jody. In this feat, she is aided by her newly awakened sympathetic imagination, which lets her picture herself as Jody. When she pulls the boy from the sinkhole, she becomes a nurturing woman who places the well-being of others ahead of her own desires.

Olwen's appearance supports the theme of prejudice in the novel. The settlers reject her as a monster, and at first Olwen entertains a typically adolescent notion of conformity when she considers an operation that will make her look more like Mark. In rejecting Captain Tryon's offer of surgical restoration and the shallow judgments it represents, however, she displays a mature acceptance of herself. Olwen comes to consider herself beautiful because her body is functional. She is free to go anywhere on the planet, something the Earth settlers can't do. Eventually, she becomes so close to nature that she is able to sense approaching storms. Nevertheless, Olwen's decision to withdraw from society is tinged with ironic pathos. Having learned to love another, Olwen now feels loneliness. When Guardian says that he can never be lonely, however, Olwen does not envy him. Instead, she says, "Poor Guardian." Olwen thus expresses a belief that suffering is worthwhile if it develops human emotions and sympathies.

Guardian, the gleaming metallic robot who raised Olwen, represents pure rationality. Acting as both mother and father, Guardian has done everything logical to ensure Olwen's physical and emotional well-being. He physically altered her to protect her from the environment and to give her freedom of movement. Although he wisely teaches Olwen that beauty results from the union of form and function, he fails to anticipate the extreme emotional reactions of humans to her appearance. As a consequence, his rational approach causes problems. For example, his decision to make Olwen wear a mask when meeting the settlers ultimately creates unnecessary pain. If he had warned both the settlers and Olwen, he might have spared her grief.

In the end, the novel implies that emotions are superior to Guardian's rigid rationality. Thus, Olwen "feels" a storm sooner than his scientific instruments can detect it. Also, Guardian does not understand why Olwen would risk her life to save a settler. In fact, he advises against a rescue attempt. The mature Olwen eventually realizes that Guardian is not, as she once thought, perfect. Always loyal, however, Guardian relinquishes his role as parent and becomes the ideal servant to Olwen.

The book's minor characters represent different perceptions. **Mark London** is a seventeen-year-old who is governed by appearances. When he falls in love with Olwen, he literally falls in love with a mask. This, Hughes has said, is a common enough problem with teenage romances. When Mark sees Olwen without her mask, his physical fall from the cliff symbolizes a moral and emotional fall. He admits that Olwen shared thoughts and feelings with him, but he bitterly accuses her of deceiving him by hiding the "main fact" of her appearance. Mark does develop some maturity later, however, when he offers to resume his relationship with Olwen.

Captain Jonas Tryon adds complexity to the theme of perceptions. He thinks Olwen is beautiful when he considers her an alien and revolting when he sees her as human. Furthermore, he is the one who points out that Guardian is "only" a robot, something Olwen never previously noticed. Although he is kind when he offers to take Olwen to Earth for an operation, he nevertheless reflects the settlers' ethnocentric belief in the rightness of their own appearance.

On the other hand, **Jody N'Kumo** (his family name is given in the sequel) shows that prejudices are learned. A nine-year-old (five on Isis) from East Africa, he is the youngest colonist. Because of his age and, perhaps, his status as a minority among the settlers, he is the only one who is not frightened by Olwen. He sees her simply as the "funny lady." His symbolic delivery from the sinkhole offers hope for a future in which character, not appearance, will matter.

Further Reading

Berger, Laura Standley, ed. *Twentieth-Century Young Adult Writers*. 1st ed. Detroit: St. James, 1994.

Children's Literature Review. Vol. 9. Detroit: Gale Research, 1985.

Holtze, Sally Holmes, ed. *Sixth Book of Junior Authors and Illustrators*. New York: H. W. Wilson, 1989.

Jones, Raymond E. "'True Myth': Female Archetypes in *The Keeper of the Isis Light*." In *Science Fiction and the Young Reader*. Edited by C. W. Sullivan III, pp. 169-78. Westport, CT: Greenwood, 1993.

Something about the Author. Vols. 15, 70. Detroit: Gale Research, 1979, 1993.

Something about the Author Autobiography Series. Vol. 11. Detroit: Gale Research, 1991.

Shirley Hughes

1929-, English author and illustrator

Dogger

(picture book, 1977; published in the United States as Dave and Dog, 1978)

PLOT: Dave is very fond of Dogger, an old and worn stuffed toy. He takes it everywhere and sleeps with it. One day, Dave and his Mum go with Joe, the baby, to school to meet his big sister, Bella. They notice people preparing for a Summer Fair, and Dave pushes Dogger up to the fence to show him what is

Dave sleeps with Dogger as Bella does somersaults in Hughes's illustration from her picture book, Dogger.

going on. Just then, Bella rushes out of school, and an ice-cream van comes around the corner. Dave's Mum gives them money, and they have ice cream. At bedtime, Dave asks for Dogger, but no one can find him. Although Bella lends him a teddy, Dave keeps waking up because he misses Dogger. The next day, the family goes to the School Summer Fair. Bella wins a three-legged race and a giant teddy bear in a raffle. Dave discovers Dogger for sale in one of the stalls. The lady in charge does not listen to his explanations, and Dave does not have enough money to buy Dogger back, so he rushes off to find his parents. Ready to cry because he can't find them, he notices Bella. She hurries back to the stall with him, but they arrive too late: a little girl has already purchased Dogger and refuses to sell him to Dave. Both the girl and Dave cry, but Bella saves the day by trading her giant teddy for Dogger. Dave gratefully hugs her. That night, Bella responds to Dave's questions about missing the big teddy. She says she will not miss it because it would crowd her out of her bed.

CHARACTERS: Pictures provide all of the physical descriptions of the characters, and the text explains their feelings. As well as showing the deep attachment children can have to special toys, this simple story presents a realistic portrait of sibling relationships.

Dave is a blond preschooler whose deep attachment to Dogger provides the emotional center of the plot; pictures suggest that Dogger is his only playmate. Dave acts out the role of a caring but more powerful person with Dogger, giving him rides, wrapping him in a blanket to keep him warm, and bathing him. Understandably, Dave is not always attentive. The pictures show that Dave must have left Dogger at the fence when he was distracted by the ice cream van. At the Summer Fair, the saddened Dave resents Bella: she gains a new teddy while he endures the loss of his special toy. Dave also discovers his own powerlessness when the stall lady will not pay attention to him. His need overcomes his temporary dislike of Bella, and he seeks her aid. Dave is properly grateful for the return of Dogger. His real sign of growth in understanding comes, however, when he shows concern for his sister's feelings by asking if she will miss her giant teddy.

Bella, who appears to be several years older than Dave, is at the thematic center of the plot. She is competent in everything she does, something that upsets Dave, who obviously feels incompetent in losing Dogger. She reveals a sympathetic and generous heart when she notices that the little girl is attracted to her giant teddy and offers to trade it for Dogger. Bella has seven teddies, but she is aware that Dave likes only Dogger, making the toy irreplaceable. When she reassures Dave that she will not miss the giant teddy, Bella shows she is rich in more than teddies: she is a mature, unselfish, and loving sister.

Further Reading

Berger, Laura Standley, ed. *Twentieth-Century Children's Writers*. 4th ed. Detroit: St. James, 1995.

Children's Literature Review. Vol. 15. Detroit: Gale Research, 1988.

Holtze, Sally Holmes, ed. *Fifth Book of Junior Authors and Illustrators*. New York: H. W. Wilson, 1983.

Something about the Author. Vols. 16, 70. Detroit: Gale Research, 1979, 1993.

Mollie Hunter

1922-, Scottish author

The Walking Stones

(fantasy, 1970; published in England as The Bodach*)*

PLOT: In *The Walking Stones*, a conflict between representatives of technological change and traditional values leads a boy to discover his own powers and his future identity. Donald Campbell, son of Ian and Kitty, is a friend of the Bodach, an elderly storyteller with second sight. One night, the Bodach has a vision of three visitors who bear the same name. The next night, three men named Rory Mackenzie come to the Campbells' house. Distinguished by their hair color only, they are Rory Ban (Rory the Fair), a forester; Rory Rudh (Red Rory), an engineer; and Rory Dubh (Black Rory), boss of a dam project that will flood the glen when it is completed. The Bodach proclaims, however, that they will not flood the glen until he gives them leave. With the arrival of Big Callum Mor and the Tigers, the construction workers, Donald becomes filled with dam fever, even forgetting his imaginary friend, Bocca. Eventually, the Campbells move to town, but the Bodach refuses to leave his doomed home.

Two years later, the Bodach prevents Black Rory from flooding the glen by suddenly appearing below the completed dam and mysteriously disappearing whenever the police approach him. Actually the Bodach has created a Co-Walker, an image who can't be captured because he exists in his mind. His purpose, he tells Donald, is to delay the flooding until he can see thirteen ancient stones walk, as they do every hundred years. Shortly afterwards, however, the Bodach saves Donald from the Washer of the Forge, but is himself doomed by her deadly touch. The Bodach therefore gives Donald the gift of second sight and his magical possessions. Because the Bodach becomes mortally ill, Donald prevents the flooding by having Bocca, *his* Co-Walker, appear beneath the dam to lead Big Callum on a merry chase. Taking the Bodach's staff, Donald then watches the ancient stones walk. At sunrise, Donald leaps into their center and feels a temporary influx of understanding. He then sees the Bodach's Co-Walker depart, a sign that the Bodach is dead. Donald knows that the stones will soon be covered by water, but he consoles himself with the knowledge that the magic and the Bodach's stories will continue.

CHARACTERS: The two central characters represent imaginative power and respect for the old knowledge that technology is destroying. **The Bodach** (Gaelic for "old man") has no name because he represents the archetypal wise old man. Physically, he resembles a traditional wizard: he is tall, and he has shoulder-length silky white hair, a long white beard, faded blue eyes that reveal a kind nature, and strong features, including an eaglelike nose. In fact, he possesses magical powers, including second sight, which allows him to see the future. In addition, he has rare knowledge of the Otherworld, and he is a born storyteller who preserves Highland lore. The dam builders, the government officials who attempt to move him, and even Mr. and Mrs. Campbell believe that he is mad for declaring that the flooding will not go ahead without his permission. Actually, his declaration is an heroic boast, the proclamation legendary heroes typically make before undertaking tasks. He lives up to his boast, showing wit and power by sending his Co-Walker—a double projected from his mind—to make fools of those trying to flood the glen.

The Bodach's purpose in stopping the flooding may seem selfish: he wants to see a rare event, the walking of the stones, and to gain the knowledge of ancient priests by standing in the center of the stone circle at sunrise. Unquestionably, he desires personal fulfillment. Nevertheless, as he makes clear after heroically saving Donald from the Washer at the Ford, the Bodach is most concerned with preserving the old knowledge that the dam will destroy. Therefore, he asks Donald to take his place. A good teacher, the Bodach first makes his student understand his own powers by revealing that Bocca is Donald's Co-Walker, not a lonely boy's imaginary friend. Then he increases Donald's powers, passing on the gift of the second sight and his magical possessions. By doing so, the Bodach teaches Don-

ald to understand himself, and he ensures that Donald will appreciate and preserve the old stories and the magic.

Through the help of the Bodach, **Donald Campbell** matures to fully understand himself. In the beginning, Donald is unaware of his situation and character. He does not, for example, realize that the Bodach is his master and is teaching him through the stories that Donald loves. Donald also does not understand his own innate power. He has created Bocca, a companion who appears whenever he thinks of him. He insists that Bocca is real, but once the dam builders come, Donald succumbs to the allure of technology and forgets Bocca, thereby ignoring his imaginative power. When Bocca one day reappears—mist traps Donald on a mountain, so he passes time by thinking of him—Donald decides that his father was right, that Bocca is only imaginary. He soon learns otherwise. An observant boy, Donald asks the Bodach, who he learns is his Co-Walker, why he did not carry his staff when he appeared beneath the dam to stop the flooding. After the Bodach saves his life, twelve-year-old Donald undergoes a symbolic rite of passage. He is given the gift of second sight and two magical items: a book and a rope. Donald then shows mature control over his imagination—perhaps he symbolizes the artist as hero—by sending Bocca to prevent Rory Dubh from flooding the glen. Afterwards, Donald completes his symbolic journey into manhood by taking the Bodach's magical staff. Donald shows integrity and bravery by keeping his promise to the Bodach, watching the walking stones and then entering their circle to acquire a temporary flash of understanding. Having completed the Bodach's quest, Donald has a new identity as master. He becomes an adult who must preserve the Bodach's stories, seek more walking stones, and eventually pass on the gift of second sight.

With one exception, the minor characters, who represent elements of modern society, are foils to the Bodach. The exception is **Rory Ban Mackenzie** (Rory the Fair), the golden-haired forester hired by the dam builders. He has an instinctive appreciation of the Bodach. Significantly, he is associated more with nature than technology, and he is kind to the animals being displaced by dam construction. He becomes a helper, pointing out to Donald that the Bodach is a teacher of rare wisdom and that the Bodach has a good heart. **Ian Campbell**, Donald's father, is a shepherd who has faith in second sight, but he regards the Bodach as crazy for insisting that he can prevent the flooding of the glen. Unlike the Bodach, he willingly gives up his home for a modern house in the village and a new job. Furthermore, he tells his son that acknowledging that Bocca is only imaginary is a sign of manhood, whereas the Bodach teaches Donald that Bocca is real as long as he accepts him as real. **Kitty Campbell**, Donald's mother, is a pretty woman who calls the idea of second sight superstitious rubbish. Although she also thinks that the Bodach is not really sane, she is humane and kind, vigorously opposing Rory Dubh's callous attitude toward the Bodach.

Stern, unsmiling **Rory Dubh Mackenzie (Black Rory)**, the black-haired man who designed the dam and chose its site, is the chief representative of technology. As the Bodach's second sight indicates, he represents death to the glen and to the stones, repositories of ancient wisdom. A cruel man who is unwilling to let an individual get in the way of technological progress, he is willing to drown the Bodach in order to save face at the dam's opening ceremonies. **Rory Rudh Mackenzie (Red Rory)** is an engineer with flaming red hair. He may be responsible for the compromise that allows the dam's opening ceremonies to go ahead without drowning the Bodach, a compromise that shows that love of technology need not mean a lack of respect for human life. **Big Callum Mor**, chief of the Tigers—the construction workers building the dam—fascinates the town boys, and even Donald, because, like the Bodach, he tells stories. Although his stories about dam building celebrate technological power, he appears foolish because he fails to catch Bocca.

Further Reading

Authors and Artists for Young Adults. Vol. 13. Detroit: Gale Research, 1994.

Berger, Laura Standley, ed. *Twentieth-Century Young Adult Writers.* 1st ed. Detroit: St. James, 1994.

Children's Literature Review. Vol. 25. Detroit: Gale Research, 1992.

Collier, Laurie, and Joyce Nakamura, eds. *Major Authors and Illustrators for Children and Young Adults.* Detroit: Gale Research, 1993.

Contemporary Authors New Revision Series. Vol. 37. Detroit: Gale Research, 1992.

Contemporary Literary Criticism. Vol. 21. Detroit: Gale Research, 1982.

De Montreville, Doris, and Donna Hill, eds. *Third Book of Junior Authors.* New York: H. W. Wilson, 1972.

Hunt, Caroline C., ed. *British Children's Writers since 1960: First Series.* Vol. 161 of *Dictionary of Literary Biography.* Detroit: Gale Research, 1996.

Something about the Author. Vol. 54. Detroit: Gale Research, 1989.

Something about the Author Autobiography Series. Vol. 7. Detroit: Gale Research, 1989.

Pat Hutchins

1942-, English picture book author and illustrator

Rosie's Walk

(picture book, 1968)

PLOT: *Rosie's Walk* consists of two simultaneous stories. The first—a single, thirty-two word sentence—is so uneventful and bland that it hardly qualifies as a story at all. Quite simply, the text says that Rosie the hen goes for a walk and returns in time for dinner. Her journey takes her by a pond, a haystack, a mill, a fence, and some beehives. The only textual interest lies in the fact that Rosie passes each of these obstacles in a different way. Thus, she goes "around the pond" but "over the haystack" and "under the beehives."

The second story, however, rendered entirely in pictures, makes *Rosie's Walk* a genuine classic of ironic humor. These pictures reveal that a fox has been stalking Rosie. Every time he tries to pounce on the hen, he has an accident. He lands on a rake that flips up and smacks him in the face; he leaps too far and splashes into the pond; he jumps too hard and sinks into the haystack. In one instance, Rosie unwittingly causes the accident: while in a mill, she trips on a rope that releases a bag suspended in the air, completely covering the fox in flour. The climac-

The fox pursues an oblivious Rosie in Hutchins's comical illustration for Rosie's Walk.

tic events in this slapstick series occur when the fox lands in a wagon after he bounds over the fence. The wagon rolls downhill and smashes into the beehives. When last seen, the fox is heading over the hill, chased by an angry swarm of bees.

CHARACTERS: The two-dimensional pictures are the perfect medium for the flat characters. **Rosie the hen** is completely oblivious to her environment. No matter what happens, her posture remains the same: she keeps her head pointed up and her eyes half closed. Her lack of observation comically contrasts with that of all the background characters who definitely notice the fox. The frogs, for example, anticipate the fox landing in the water and leap away. Like these animals, the reader knows what the naive Rosie does not. She is satisfied with the simple events of her walk, culminating in her evening meal; the reader realizes that she has unwittingly taken part in a grand adventure, several times narrowly escaping disaster.

The **fox** is a parody of folktale foxes. Instead of exhibiting the slyness traditionally attributed to his species, he is a bumbling fool who repeatedly fails in his attempts to catch Rosie. His ineptitude, coupled with his pathetic persistence, ironically transforms him from a predator to a victim. What makes his fate so laughable, though, is that he succeeds in one element of his plot: Rosie remains as ignorant of his presence at the end as she would have been up until the moment of a successful attack.

Further Reading

Berger, Laura Standley, ed. *Twentieth-Century Children's Writers.* 4th ed. Detroit: St. James, 1995.

Children's Literature Review. Vol. 20. Detroit: Gale Research, 1990.

Crawford, Elizabeth D., and Doris De Montreville, eds. *Fourth Book of Junior Authors.* New York: H. W. Wilson, 1978.

Something about the Author. Vols. 15, 70. Detroit: Gale Research, 1979, 1993.

Tove Jansson

1914-, Finnish artist, illustrator, and author

Finn Family Moomintroll

(fantasy, 1948; English translation, 1950; published in Finland as Trollkarlens hatt*)*

PLOT: Scenes of family solidarity and episodes of magical adventure achieve Jansson's professed goal of describing both security and excitement. After their winter hibernation, Moomintroll, Sniff, and Snufkin discover the Hobgoblin's hat. At Moominpappa's suggestion, they use it for a wastepaper basket, but the eggshells Moomintroll throws into it become clouds that the youngsters ride. Later, Moomintroll hides under the hat and is transformed into an unrecognizable creature. To test the hat's magic, Moomintroll and the Snork use it to transform the Ant-lion into a small hedgehog. Moominpappa and Moominmamma, deciding that the hat is dangerous, roll it into the river, which becomes raspberry juice. Moomintroll and Snufkin secretly retrieve the hat and hide it in a cave. Muskrat, who makes the cave his retreat, places his false teeth in the hat and receives a terrible but unspecified shock.

The next adventures occur during an outing on the Hattifatteners' Lonely Island. While searching for botanical specimens, the Hemulen encounters the Hattifatteners and takes their barometer. During a storm that night, the Hattifatteners retrieve the barometer, but they brush against the Snork Maiden, burning off her hair. The next day, after everyone gathers treasures washed up by the storm, the family returns home. Shortly afterwards, Moominmamma throws a plant into the hat, which she is again using as a wastepaper basket, and a jungle grows around the house. When Moomintroll and the others arrive with a giant fish that the Snork has caught, they go through the jungle, leaving the unhappy Hemulen in the rain with the fish.

The final adventures contrast possessiveness to generosity. They begin with the arrival of Thingumy and Bob, who carry the King's Ruby in a suitcase. When the ground-freezing Groke tries to reclaim the Ruby, Moominmamma convinces her to accept the hat instead. Later, Thingumy and Bob take Moominmamma's purse to sleep in. When Moominmamma promises to throw a party if the purse is found, Thingumy and Bob return it. During this party, the Hobgoblin arrives and tries to convince Thingumy and Bob to trade the Ruby. When he fails, he cheers himself up by granting everyone a wish. The climax comes when Thingumy and Bob wish for a gem just like the King's Ruby and present it to the grateful Hobgoblin.

The Moomin series includes Comet in Moominland *(English translation, 1951),* The Exploits of Moominpappa *(English translation, 1952),* Moominsummer Madness *(English translation, 1955),* Moominland Midwinter *(English translation, 1958),* Tales from Moomin Valley *(English translation, 1963),* Moominpappa at Sea *(English translation, 1965), and* Moominvalley in November *(English translation, 1971).*

CHARACTERS: The bizarre characters depend on Jansson's drawings for their physical substance. **Moomintroll,** who looks like a chubby, friendly hippopotamus, has short legs, little ears, and a small tail. The quintessential child, the inquisitive Moomintroll seeks adventures outside the home yet needs his mother's comfort and reassurance. Moomintroll is intelligent, figuring out how the hat works. He is also sociable and considerate. Fond of the Snork Maiden, he consoles her when her hair is burned off. He is even more deeply attached to Snufkin, sleeping with him during hibernation and exploring springtime wonders with him afterwards. Two episodes suggest that Moomintroll is maturing.

First, when he hides the hat in the cave, he recognizes that he is doing something that, for the first time in his life, he must keep secret from his parents. Secondly, when the Hobgoblin transforms his sadness at Snufkin's departure into expectancy, Moomintroll learns, albeit symbolically, to cope with his emotions.

Moominmamma is the ideal mother. She warmly accepts new people into the house and makes them happy and comfortable. On three occasions, she demonstrates a profound understanding of her child's needs. When the hat changes Moomintroll into an unrecognizable creature, she looks into his frightened eyes and reassures him that she will always know him. When they are on the Hattifattener's island, she knows that he wants to explore and tells him that he can help her by doing so. Finally, when the Hobgoblin offers to grant her wish, she asks him to take away the sadness that Moomintroll feels over Snufkin's departure. She is equally clever in understanding others. She gets rid of the Groke, for example, by offering her the hat in exchange for the ruby. Although Moominmamma is the stable and loving center of the home, she is comical in one respect: she feels incapable of accomplishing anything unless she has her purse. **Moominpappa** is kind-hearted but self-centered. Although he builds things for the house and gives directions during the adventure to the island, his major occupation is writing his memoirs.

Snufkin, Moomintroll's closest friend, is a free-spirited wanderer who loves to be alone and to see things beyond the Moomins' ideal home. Nevertheless, Snufkin is a model of contentment. Unable to understand why everyone else needs to possess things, he is satisfied with wearing old clothes and is attached to only one material object, his beloved harmonica. Snufkin loves adventures and interesting complications. He is, for example, the one who suggests the trip to the mountains that leads to the discovery of the magical hat. Furthermore, when the Hemulen complains about his troubles with the Hattifatteners, Snufkin contentedly notes that life is not peaceful.

In contrast with Snufkin, a number of characters are obsessed with possessions. **The Hemulen** has a long face, large, round eyes, and a fringe of long hair around his balding pate. Like all of his kind, he wears a dress. The Hemulen is materialistic and unimaginative. Able to find purpose in his life only by collecting things, he is melancholy when he completes his stamp collection. After he decides to collect plants, the Hemulen becomes a satiric example of the dispassionate scientist; absorbed with labelling specimens and counting their stamens, he is unaware that flowers are beautiful. The Hemulen is also foolish because of his cowardly panic during his encounter with the Hattifatteners and because of his stubborn petulance when he takes their barometer. **The Hattifatteners**, pale creatures who can neither hear nor speak and who are nearly blind, are obsessed with their barometer. Able to recharge themselves during lightning storms, the Hattifatteners are dangerous, as they show when they accidentally burn the Snork Maiden's fringe. **Thingumy** and **Bob**, a pair of tiny creatures, are amusing because they speak in spoonerisms. Filled with desire, they take what they want, whether it is the King's Ruby, which they carry in a suitcase, or Moominmamma's purse, which they use as a bed. Although materialistic, they are capable of sympathy, as they show when they use their wish to provide the Hobgoblin with a ruby. **The Groke**, a hairy creature with large round eyes, represents the monstrous side of materialism. She longs for the King's Ruby. The cold-hearted nature of her acquisitiveness is suggested by the fact that she turns everything cold, freezing whatever she touches. In contrast, **the Hobgoblin**, who also desires the King's Ruby, is filled with humane warmth. A bearded magician with red eyes, the Hobgoblin rides a black panther and changes his shape at will. Although powerful, he is moral and therefore can't steal the ruby. Furthermore, he is not vindictive when denied his own desire; instead, he grants others their wishes. Ironically, his generosity earns him his heart's desire when Thingumy and Bob wish for a ruby just like their own.

Sniff, who looks like a big-eared, long-tailed mouse in the drawings, is the comical baby of the amorphous Moomin family. He is timid, being the first to express fear about transforming the Ant-lion. He is also self-centered, suggesting that the boat on which they sail to the island should be named the *Sniff.* Feeling insulted by Thingumy and Bob, he vindictively requests that he be their prosecutor at a trial. **The Snork Maiden**, who is romantically interested in Moomintroll, resembles him except that she has a fluffy fringe of hair. She plays adventurous games with the others, but she is stereotypically female in her vanity, which she exhibits both after the Hattifatteners burn her fringe and when she foolishly wishes for the Hobgoblin to give her eyes like those on a ship's wooden figure. Her brother, **the Snork**, has a minor role. His most significant action demonstrates the triumph of family love over selfishness: he uses his wish to have the Hobgoblin restore his sister to her former appearance. **Muskrat**, a self-professed philosopher who studies a book titled *The Uselessness of Everything*, is ridiculously obsessed with his dignity. After his hammock breaks and tumbles him to the ground, he foolishly decides to withdraw from the world because he is unwilling to risk any situations that would allow young people to laugh at him.

Further Reading

Children's Literature Review. Vol. 2. Detroit: Gale Research, 1976.

Collier, Laurie, and Joyce Nakamura, eds. *Major Authors and Illustrators for Children and Young Adults*. Detroit: Gale Research, 1993.

Contemporary Authors New Revision Series. Vol. 38. Detroit: Gale Research, 1993.

De Montreville, Doris, and Donna Hill, eds. *Third Book of Junior Authors*. New York: H. W. Wilson, 1972.

Jones, W. Glyn. *Tove Jansson*. Boston: Twayne, 1984.

Something about the Author. Vols. 3, 41. Detroit: Gale Research, 1972, 1985.

Randall Jarrell

1914-1965, American poet, fiction author, and academic

The Bat-Poet

(animal fantasy, 1964; illustrated by Maurice Sendak)

PLOT: This animal fantasy is an extended parable about the poet, his craft, and his audience. When a group of bats moves from the porch roof to the barn, a little brown one stays outside. Unaccustomed to sleeping alone, he begins to awaken during the day. The songs of the mockingbird deeply impress him, but the bat can't get the other bats to stay awake to listen to them. The little bat tries to sing like the mockingbird but is unsuccessful. He then uses words to capture what he sees and feels. When he recites a poem about the daytime to the other bats, however, they criticize it. Hurt by this rejection, the bat-poet tries to get the mockingbird to be his audience. The mockingbird at first misunderstands the bat-poet's hesitant request and repeatedly sings his own most recent composition. When he finally listens to the bat-poet's poem about an owl, he praises only its technique. Again disappointed with his audience, the bat-poet searches for a better listener. The chipmunk, who shivers at the owl poem, proves to be more responsive. The bat-poet then composes the chipmunk's "portrait in verse." Encouraged by the appreciative chipmunk, the bat-poet next tries to compose a poem about the cardinal. He finds himself unable to produce the poem, but he soon composes one about the mockingbird. Although the chipmunk is impressed by this verse portrait, the mockingbird becomes angry when he hears it and claims that the bat-poet simply doesn't understand the sensitive mockingbird. The bat-poet next turns to his own life for his subject and makes a poem about a baby bat and its mother. The poem is so successful that the chipmunk forgets that it is a poem. The bat-poet decides that his fellow bats will appreciate this poem too and flies into the barn. As soon as he snuggles up to them in their winter hibernation, however, he begins to forget his poem. The story ends in a disappointing and inconclusive way with the forgetful bat yawning and snuggling closer to the others.

CHARACTERS: The animals represent poets and their audience but also symbolize specific people in Jarrell's life. **The bat-poet** represents the poet in general and, according to a key supplied by Jarrell's wife, Mary Jarrell, both Jarrell and his friend Bob Watson. The bat-poet is notably different from his companions. Physically he is different because he is a lighter brown; emotionally he is different because he is willing to experience what they reject. He not only stays alone on the porch but also learns to see during the daytime. Symbolically, his actions suggest that the poet is one who is willing to see that which is too painful or too difficult for others to see.

The bat-poet is shy and sensitive. He is hurt when the other bats criticize his vision of the bright day and when the mockingbird focuses on the technical features of his poem. The bat-poet does come to appreciate the technical elements of poetry, however, and talks about them after he recites his poem about the mockingbird. Nevertheless, the bat-poet's failure to compose a poem about the cardinal demonstrates that poetry is a mysterious art and that poems can't be summoned on command. The bat-poet's fate is ambiguous. His sleepy forgetfulness when he rejoins the others in the barn might represent the tragedy of a loss of distinctive individuality: the poet abandons his career to enjoy the comforts of social acceptance. On the other hand, it might only represent a temporary delay in acceptance: the poet must wait until his audience is awake enough to appreciate what he has done. In either case, the bat-poet is one of the most accessible portraits of the poetic temperament available to children.

The mockingbird is a conceited, self-satisfied, and accomplished poet whose songs symbolize high art. According to Mary Jarrell, he represents the poets Robert Frost and Robert Lowell. Overbearingly conceited, the mockingbird cuts off the shy bat-poet because he assumes that he wants another performance of his songs. As an established poet, the mockingbird is intimidating when he finally does pay attention to the young bat-poet. The mockingbird adopts a formal "listening expression" to hear the poem and follows it with a pompous lecture on technical devices. If his response here suggests an absence of emotional appreciation, his anger when he suspects criticism of himself suggests hypersensitivity. Significantly, he curtly notes that he did not even notice the technique of the poem about him. The mockingbird's haughty conceit shows that great talent does not necessarily imply sensitivity to others or the ability to see oneself as others do.

A bat represents the frustrations of the poet in Jarrell's
The Bat-Poet, *illustrated by Maurice Sendak.*

The chipmunk, on the other hand, is an appreciative audience. Mary Jarrell has identified the chipmunk as being a combination of Jarrell's editor, Michael di Capua, and herself. Like them, the chipmunk listens attentively, responds appropriately, and gives encouragement to the poet. The chipmunk understands better than the poet how audiences will react. He warns the bat-poet, for example, that the mockingbird will not like his verse portrait. The chipmunk's major role, however, is to express meaningful responses to poems. He doesn't talk about the poem's techniques but about his feelings. He even likes a poem that makes him shiver. His highest praise comes when he tells the bat-poet that he forgot that the poem about a mother and baby bat was a poem at all.

Further Reading

Berger, Laura Standley, ed. *Twentieth-Century Children's Writers.* 4th ed. Detroit: St. James, 1995.

Children's Literature Review. Vol. 6. Detroit: Gale Research, 1984.

Collier, Laurie, and Joyce Nakamura, eds. *Major Authors and Illustrators for Children and Young Adults.* Detroit: Gale Research, 1993.

Contemporary Authors New Revision Series. Vol. 34. Detroit: Gale Research, 1992.

Contemporary Literary Criticism. Vols. 1, 2, 6, 9, 13, 49. Detroit: Gale Research, 1973, 1974, 1976, 1978, 1980, 1988.

De Montreville, Doris, and Donna Hill, eds. *Third Book of Junior Authors*. New York: H. W. Wilson, 1972.

Estes, Glenn E., ed. *American Writers for Children since 1960: Fiction*. Vol. 52 of *Dictionary of Literary Biography*. Detroit: Gale Research, 1986.

Griswold, Jerome. *The Children's Books of Randall Jarrell*. Athens: University of Georgia Press, 1988.

Quartermain, Peter, ed. *American Poets, 1880-1945*. Vol. 48 of *Dictionary of Literary Biography*. Detroit: Gale Research, 1986.

Something about the Author. Vol. 7. Detroit: Gale Research, 1975.

Norton Juster

1929-, American architect, educator, and author

The Phantom Tollbooth

(fantasy, 1961)

PLOT: Reminiscent of *Alice in Wonderland* in its humorous wordplay and bizarre characters, *The Phantom Tollbooth* is a comic allegory about the importance of learning. Milo, a boy bored with everything, receives a mysterious gift, a small turnpike tollbooth. After assembling it, he drives past it in his small electric car and finds himself in the Land Beyond. Bored and inattentive, Milo makes a wrong turn into the Doldrums, where Tock, the watchdog, prevents him from joining the apathetic Lethargarians. By thinking hard, Milo leaves the Doldrums and, accompanied by Tock, goes to Dictionopolis. In the market, where letters are sold, Milo witnesses an argument between the Spelling Bee and the Humbug. Officer Shrift blames Milo and throws him into a dungeon. There he meets Faintly Macabre, whom Milo promises to release from imprisonment by bringing the exiled princesses Rhyme and Reason back to the Kingdom of Wisdom. Letting himself out of the dungeon, Milo dines with King Azaz the Unabridged, who says that Milo must get the King's brother, the Mathemagician, to agree to the rescue of the princesses. Azaz then gives Milo a box of all the words he knows, and he "volunteers" the Humbug as Milo's guide.

On their journey, Milo, Tock, and the Humbug meet Alec Bings, a boy who floats in the air. He gives Milo a telescope that sees through things. After conducting the symphony of Chroma the Great, which brings color to the world, and meeting the noisy Kakofonous A. Dischord, Doctor of Dissonance, and his servant, the awful Dynne, Milo and his companions enter a valley that lacks all sounds. Although Milo defies the Soundkeeper by restoring sound to the valley, she gives him a gift of beautiful sounds. When the companions finally arrive in Digitopolis, the Dodecahedron guides them to a number mine, where they meet the Mathemagician. After a dinner of subtraction stew that only makes him hungrier, Milo tricks the Mathemagician into letting him seek Rhyme and Reason. The Mathemagician gives him a miniature staff, a pencil with which he can do calculations.

The companions now enter the Mountains of Ignorance, where they encounter several demons: the Everpresent Wordsnatcher, the Terrible Trivium, the demon of insincerity, the Gelatinous Giant, and the Senses Taker. Through luck, wit, and the use of his gifts, Milo gets past them and enters the Castle in the Air, where the princesses are held. He then brings Rhyme and Reason back to the Kingdom of Wisdom. The massed armies of Azaz and the Mathemagician meet them and drive the pursuing demons back into Ignorance. Milo, having accomplished a task the two kings knew was impossible, is honored as a hero. After Milo returns home, the tollbooth disappears, but Milo realizes that his room contains so many interesting things that he has no time to return to the Land Beyond.

CHARACTERS: The characters are as important for generating puns, wordplay, and logical jokes as they are for their allegorical meanings. **Milo** is a boy who doesn't know what to do with himself because he has no interest in anything. Although he is never anxious about being anywhere, he always hurries, keeping his head down and never noticing anything around him. Milo considers learning the biggest waste of time because he sees no use for it. His allegorical pilgrimage in the Land Beyond thus becomes a "Learner's Progress." By completing a quest, Milo realizes that he doesn't know much and that learning and the judicious application of knowledge are important. Milo's initial situation in the Land Beyond symbolizes his condition in his own world. Bored and inattentive, he enters the Doldrums, where he becomes sleepy and incapable of laughter. Only the arrival of Tock, who teaches him that he must think in order to get out of the Doldrums, saves Milo from becoming terminally lethargic. Because he has begun thinking, Milo becomes interested in things, such as the letters for sale in the Dictionopolis market. He is still naive, however, because he is attracted to words he doesn't understand. Nevertheless, his education has begun. He thus understands by talking to the courtiers, who provide multiple synonyms for everything they say, that good communication depends on the words one chooses and not on how many words one says. Milo changes more after he is imprisoned: he feels compassion for Faintly Macabre and unselfishly vows to get her released. As a result, he gains a purpose, something he formerly lacked.

Milo's subsequent journeys employ traditional quest elements: he receives various helping objects; he undertakes a long and perilous journey; he overcomes obstacles because of luck, bravery, and wit; and he succeeds in a quest that benefits the community. His quest also transforms him by forcing him to be observant; by providing him with a new understanding of words, sound, color, and logic; and by making him aware of himself and his surroundings. Milo's success shows that people can accomplish many things if they do not know that their tasks are supposed to be impossible. Having learned to take an interest in things, to appreciate his resources for success, and to understand his need for knowledge, Milo looks at the toys, books, and other things in his room as new and interesting. Actually, only his vision is new: Milo has transformed into a boy eager and willing to explore life.

Tock, the watchdog, has a normal dog's head, feet, and tail, but his body is a ticking alarm clock. Given the duty of seeing that no one wastes time, Tock chases away the Lethargarians and helps Milo by making him understand that he can escape the

Milo, Tock, and the Humbug meet the Princess of Sweet Rhyme and the Princess of Pure Reason in an illustration by Jules Feiffer from Juster's The Phantom Tollbooth.

Doldrums only by thinking. Tock is the voice of wisdom when he tells Milo that words confuse only when many are used to say little. He also functions as a *deus ex machina*, conveniently coming to Milo's aid. Because "time flies," he is able to fly through the air, carrying everyone from the Castle in the Air to safety. Another of Milo's friends, **The Humbug**, is a large, nattily dressed, beetlelike insect. He wears a lavish coat, striped pants, checked vest, spats, and a derby hat. As his name indicates, the Humbug is a braggart who knows very little, talks loudly, and agrees with even contradictory opinions. The Humbug is a foil to Milo, who must learn to use words wisely and to know what he is talking about. Milo comes to like the Humbug, who adds comedy to several scenes.

The two arguing rulers represent, respectively, Art and Science. **King Azaz the Unabridged** is the ruler of Dictionopolis, the source of all words. He is a large man who has piercing eyes, a long gray beard, and a huge stomach, the product of constantly eating his own words. He wears a small crown and a robe decorated with the letters of the alphabet. Azaz helps Milo by sending along the Humbug as a guide, by giving him a gift of words, by withholding from him the information that the quest is impossible, and by driving away the pursuing demons. His brother, **the Mathemagician** rules Digitopolis, where numbers are mined. He wears a robe covered with mathematical equations and a tall, pointed cap. He carries a staff that has a pencil point at one end and an eraser at the other. He eats subtraction stew: the more one eats of it, the hungrier one becomes. He loves mathematical logic, but he is irrationally stubborn. He therefore represents a test for Milo, who displays wit by making the Mathemagician see that he and his brother agree in their disagreement. Like his brother, he is a helper, withholding the impossible nature of the quest and giving Milo a pencil to do calculations. The **Princess of Sweet Rhyme** and the **Princess of Pure Reason**, idealized representatives of Art and Science respectively, have been exiled from the Kingdom of Wisdom because they believe that words and numbers are equally important. When they are absent, nothing goes right. Together, they express the major themes, telling Milo that he must not fear mistakes, that learning is important, that he must learn how to apply his knowledge, and that all actions have consequences.

The **Lethargarians** in the Doldrums are small creatures who resemble each other and who take on the color of any nearby object. They are cautionary figures: because they do not think, laugh, or take an interest in anything, they are sleepy time-wasters with no individual identity. **The Spelling Bee** illustrates the power of education: once an ordinary bee, education made him twice Milo's size. The Spelling Bee shows his knowledge by spelling the most important word in every sentence. As his appearance indicates, **Officer Shrift**, who is two feet tall and almost twice as wide, gives "short shrift" to justice. Policeman, judge, and jailer, he sentences Milo to six million years in prison for being around when the Spelling Bee and the Humbug fought. **Faintly Macabre**, the not-so-wicked Which, was once in charge of choosing which words would be used, but she became so miserly that people became silent. She inspires interest and compassion in Milo, who determines to release her. She also gives him the quest of releasing Rhyme and Reason, providing the background information about their exile and the benefits of their return to Wisdom.

Once his journey begins, Milo meets characters who expand his awareness. **Alec Bings** floats in the air because people in his family begin with their heads at the height they will be when they are adults and grow downward until their feet touch ground. Alec thus represents an adult viewpoint, something Milo has never adopted. Able to see through things, Alec gives Milo a telescope that will permit him to do the same. **Chroma the Great**, a gaunt man with a long, pointed nose and long, pointed chin, is a conductor whose orchestra creates color. His symphonies sharpen Milo's aesthetic appreciation. Milo's attempt to conduct the orchestra himself shows that many activities are more difficult than they seem. **Kakofonous A. Dischord**, (the "A" stands for "As Loud as Possible") is a specialist in noise, a Doctor of Dissonance. He wears a long white coat and has a stethoscope around his neck and a mirror on his forehead. His ears are as large as his head, and he roars all of his statements. His servant, the awful **Dynne**, emerges from a bottle as a thick bluish smog with yellow eyes and a frowning mouth. He gathers noises for the doctor's medicines. He is also addicted to puns: an orphan raised without benefit of a governess, he declares that "No nurse is good nurse." By contrast, Milo's trip to **the Soundkeeper** makes him appreciate both silence and noise. The Soundkeeper, a talkative woman who collects all the sounds ever made, has deprived the valley of sound because the people merely turn it into ugly noise. Milo establishes his concern for others and his wit by smuggling a sound out of her fortress. The Soundkeeper helps Milo by giving him a package of sounds. **The Dodecahedron**, who is constructed of carefully labeled lines and angles, wears a handsome beret on his twelve-sided head, each surface of which contains a different face. Milo's guide in Digitopolis, he stresses accurate calculation of problems whether or not the problems make sense.

In the Mountains of Ignorance, Milo faces obstacles before he reaches the Castle in the Air. The first is a nuisance, not a true demon. **The Everpresent Wordsnatcher** is a large, unkempt, dirty bird with a sharp beak. He belongs in Context but is out of it because he finds it unpleasant. He confuses Milo by taking words out his mouth. The Humbug claims credit for driving him off, but it is not clear that he actually did so. Milo gets past the actual demons only by using his gifts of calculation, sight, words, and sound. **The Terrible Trivium** is an elegantly dressed man whose face has no features and thus can show no emotions. The demon of petty tasks and worthless jobs, he calls himself a monster of habit. He distracts the companions from their quest by getting them to move sand with tweezers, empty a well with an eyedropper, and dig a hole with a needle. Milo breaks the spell of habit by using the Mathemagician's wand to calculate that the tasks are worthless. **The demon of insincerity** claims to be the long-nosed, green-eyed, curly haired, wide-mouthed, thick-necked, broad-shouldered, round-bodied, short-armed, bowlegged, big-footed monster. By promising to help Milo and his companions, he lures them into a deep pit. The encounter establishes Milo's ability to look closely, something he never did in his own world. Using his telescope, Milo sees that the monster is a small furry creature with a sheepish grin; once revealed, it leaves in tears. **The Gelatinous Giant**, who takes whatever shape he is near, is incredibly large and has long, unkempt hair and bulging eyes. He is ferocious because he is afraid to make a decision, and he can't swallow ideas because they give him indigestion. Milo escapes from him by saying that Azaz's box of words contains all the ideas in the world. The final demon, **the Senses Taker**, is a little, round, ink-stained man with thick glasses. He steals their sense of purpose, sense of duty, and sense of proportion by putting the questers into trances in which they see delightful illusions. Milo, for example, has a vision of a circus. Milo escapes because of heroic luck: the Soundkeeper's package of sounds falls, spilling out laughter. This laughter, which prevents the Senses Taker from taking their sense of humor, frees the companions from his power.

Further Reading

Berger, Laura Standley, ed. *Twentieth-Century Young Adult Writers*. 1st ed. Detroit: St. James, 1994.

Collier, Laurie, and Joyce Nakamura, eds. *Major Authors and Illustrators for Children and Young Adults*. Detroit: Gale Research, 1993.

Contemporary Authors New Revision Series. Vol. 44. Detroit: Gale Research, 1994.

De Montreville, Doris, and Elizabeth D. Crawford, eds. *Fourth Book of Junior Authors*. New York: H. W. Wilson, 1978.

Something about the Author. Vol. 3. Detroit: Gale Research, 1972.

Ezra Jack Keats

(born Jacob Katz)

1916-1983, American author and illustrator of picture books

The Snowy Day

(picture book, 1962)

PLOT: Keats has said that he wanted *The Snowy Day* "to be a chunk of life" that would express "the joy of being alive" and "awareness." Keats realizes both thematic goals by combining a simple text and colorful collages to communicate the sensory pleasures of an ordinary day of playing in the snow.

The action covers a twenty-four hour period. Peter awakens to discover a huge snowfall. Outside he becomes aware of the sound of his feet crunching in the snow and of the various footprints and tracks he can leave. A stick becomes a toy for making lines and banging snow from a tree, right on top of his head. Because Peter is too small to join the big boys in a snowball fight, he plays alone. He makes a snowman and snow angels. Pretending to be an explorer, he climbs a snow mound and slides down. Peter then puts a snowball in his pocket and goes inside to tell his mother about his adventures. After his bath, he is saddened that his snowball is no longer in his pocket. That night he dreams that the sun has melted all the snow. In the morning, however, he discovers that the snow is still there and that more is falling. Joyfully, he and his friend from across the hall go out to play together in the snow.

See below for character descriptions.

Whistle for Willie

(picture book, 1964)

PLOT: In this simple story, the text reports the facts of Peter's repeated failures to whistle. The bright collages add to the emotional component. Together, they establish the events as important in the development of the central character's self-esteem.

The story begins with Peter's desire to whistle. When a bigger boy whistles, his dog comes to him. Peter tries, but he can't whistle. In frustration, he spins around to make himself dizzy. Spying his dog, Willie, Peter hides in a box and tries to attract his attention by whistling, but he fails again. He then draws chalk lines all the way to his door, where he once more fails to whistle. Inside, he puts on his father's hat to look older, but he still can't whistle. Pretending to be his father, he goes outside to look for Peter and Willie. Just after he discovers that he can't get away from his shadow, he sees Willie coming towards him. He gets into the box again and this time blows a real whistle. When Willie responds by running straight to him, his mother and father are proud of Peter's accomplishment. They signal their belief in his growth and his competence by sending him on an errand. Peter, accompanied by Willie, whistles all the way.

See below for character descriptions.

Peter's Chair

(picture book, 1967)

PLOT: The third volume of Peter's adventures introduces the related themes of growth and sibling rivalry. When the story begins, Peter is building a tower of blocks. It tumbles, foreshadowing the collapse of the life Peter has known. Thus, his mother tells him to play more quietly because they have a new baby in the house. Peter then notices that his old crib has been painted pink. When his father asks if he would like to help to paint his sister's high chair, Peter whispers that it is his high chair.

Looking around, Peter sees that his cot is now pink, but his old chair has not yet been painted. Taking the chair, a toy crocodile, and a baby picture of himself, Peter decides to run away. He arranges these possessions in front of his house. When he tries to sit in the chair, however, he discovers that he is too big for it. His mother soon calls him to lunch, but Peter pretends not to hear. Deciding to trick his mother, he places his shoes at the bottom of the curtain. His mother, thinking that he is hiding behind it, pulls back the curtain, but Peter jumps out from behind a chest. He then goes to lunch and sits in "a grown-up chair." After lunch, Peter and his father act on Peter's suggestion that they paint the little chair for his sister.

Although he becomes less prominent as he gets older, Peter also appears in A Letter to Amy *(1968);* Goggles! *(1969);* Hi, Cat! *(1970);* Apt. 3 *(1971); and* Pet Show! *(1972)*

CHARACTERS: In this series of picture books, each story concentrates on Peter's shifting sense of identity. *The Snowy Day* was the first full-color picture book to use an African American as the central character. While admitting that various ethnic groups have experiences unique to themselves, Keats insisted that he aimed for something universal: "The experiences in my books are those which all people share." Only the pictures indicate that **Peter** is an African American. In the first book, he is a preschooler who seems to be experiencing his first major snowfall. Peter keenly senses the environment around him, happily enjoying its sights and sounds. He is creative in making use of the stick and in building the snowman. Still, Peter is anxious about two things. One is that he must play alone because he is too small to join the snowball fight. At first, Peter compensates by building imaginary playmates: the snowman and the angels. The next day, however, he demonstrates social growth when he invites a friend to join him before he goes outside. Peter's other concern is his fear that the snow and, hence, his happiness will not last. He naively tries to preserve

Peter helps his dad paint the chair in Keats's self-illustrated picture book, Peter's Chair.

his pleasure by bringing a snowball inside. His subsequent fear that the outside snow will melt, just as his snowball did, implies frustrated desires and an incomplete understanding of nature. Whether Peter fully understands it or not, the abundant new snow that greets him when he awakens indicates that nature is not governed by his moods. More significantly, Peter's joyous expression shows that he now realizes that his pleasure will last more than a single day.

As in *The Snowy Day*, Peter is the only major character in *Whistle for Willie*. The expressionistic collages here use a variety of devices, including placement of secondary characters to convey Peter's desires and his feelings about himself. Peter is slightly older than he was in *The Snowy Day*. The opening picture shows that he is sad because he cannot whistle; at the far left of the illustration, he

leans on a lamp post, his head and eyes down. The massive brick wall dominating the picture suggests that Peter feels insignificant. Peter evidently identifies whistling with being grown up and with companionship. Each time he fails to achieve his goal, he resorts to a different emotionally revealing activity. After he fails to imitate the big boy calling his dog, for example, he whirls himself into dizziness. This is a little child's way of escaping the truth. The next time, he draws lines on the sidewalk, an attempt to make his mark in another way and, thus, to be noticed. Putting on his father's hat is a futile attempt to develop an older identity instantly, and his attempt to run away from his shadow, his final childish activity, is a symbolic effort to leave behind his identity.

When Peter jumps up and lands on his shadow, he symbolically accepts that he must be himself. Peter is admirably persistent in trying to whistle. His feelings of joy when he succeeds are first indicated by color and character position. When he successfully whistles, that is, his dog is facing him and is on a warm red-colored block similar to the one that he is on. During his earlier failure, Willie was not looking at him, and they were on differently shaded, emotionally cold, blue blocks. Perspective is the second expressionistic device communicating Peter's emotions. When he whistles for his proud parents, his head is in the foreground and occupies all of the left page. Perspective serves as a metaphor: Peter has a big head because he is so proud of his accomplishment. The happy Peter now enters a new stage of development. Whistling gives him the companionship of his dog and the respect of his parents, signaled by his mother's trust in sending him on an errand.

In *Peter's Chair*, Peter is jealous of his baby sister because he thinks that she threatens his identity and his place in the house. His insistence that the high chair is his shows he has not yet accepted the idea that he is no longer the baby of the family. By running away, he indicates that his house is not a home to him anymore: he does not feel that he has a secure place there. The fact that he takes a picture of himself as a baby also suggests that he is trying to hang on to an identity that he has outgrown. He recognizes his growth and his changed identity, however, when he tries to sit in his small chair. The trick he subsequently plays on his mother reveals two other ways that Peter has grown. First, he now understands the difference between appearance and reality. Thus, while he may appear to be losing the objects that formerly identified him, the truth is he now exists in a different place. The second development the trick reveals is that Peter is now secure enough of himself to play tricks with his identity. The jealous little Peter vanishes behind the curtain; a new, confident, less childish Peter jumps up from behind the chest. He appropriately signals this new identity by sitting in a "grown-up" chair and by suggesting he and his father paint the small chair, which he now willingly passes on to his sister.

Further Reading

Berger, Laura Standley, ed. *Twentieth-Century Children's Writers.* 4th ed. Detroit: St. James, 1995.

Children's Literature Review. Vols. 1, 35. Detroit: Gale Research, 1976, 1995.

Collier, Laurie, and Joyce Nakamura, eds. *Major Authors and Illustrators for Children and Young Adults.* Detroit: Gale Research, 1993.

Estes, Glenn E., ed. *American Writers for Children since 1960: Poets, Illustrators, and Nonfiction Authors.* Vol. 61 of *Dictionary of Literary Biography.* Detroit: Gale Research, 1987.

Fuller, Muriel, ed. *More Junior Authors.* New York: H. W. Wilson, 1963.

Marantz, Kenneth A. "Ezra Jack Keats' *The Snowy Day:* The Wisdom of a Pure Heart." In *Touchstones: Reflections on the Best in Children's Literature.* Vol. 3, *Picture Books.* Edited by Perry Nodelman, pp. 70-73. West Lafayette, IN: Children's Literature Association, 1989.

Something about the Author. Vols. 14, 57. Detroit: Gale Research, 1978, 1989.

Carolyn Keene

(house pseudonym used by the Edward Stratemeyer Syndicate)

"Nancy Drew"

(mystery series, 1930–)

PLOT: Like the Hardy Boys, Nancy Drew was the invention of Edward Stratemeyer (1862-1930), who commissioned ghostwriters to produce the books. Two of the important early contributors to the series were Mildred Augustine Wirt Benson (1905-) and Stratemeyer's daughter, Harriet Stratemeyer Adams (1892-1982). Like all series books from the Stratemeyer Syndicate fiction factory, the Nancy Drew books were edited to minimize stylistic variation. For years, Stratemeyer's daughter, Alice Adams, claimed to be the original Carolyn Keene, but Mildred A. Wirt, later Mildred Wirt Benson, actually wrote twenty-two of the first twenty-five volumes. From the first volume, *The Secret of the Old Clock* (1930), Nancy Drew proved as popular with girls as the Hardy Boys were with boys. The Nancy Drew books have undergone significant changes over the years: beginning in 1959, all titles published before 1957 were rewritten and shortened to update them and to remove inappropriate racial and ethnic comments. A parallel series for adolescent readers, "The Nancy Drew Files," began in 1986.

Nancy Drew lives in a large brick house in River Heights, a midwestern city (it somehow creeps closer to New York in later volumes). Her father, Carson Drew, is a wealthy and famous lawyer. Mrs. Drew died when Nancy was three. Their housekeeper is Mrs. Hannah Gruen. Typical Nancy Drew mysteries combine detection with hints of gothic melodrama because the settings are often old mansions with secret passages or other exotic locations. The plots usually require her to recover a stolen heirloom or to prevent someone from being swindled out of an inheritance. Nancy typically becomes involved either because the case connects to one her father has undertaken or because she is hired by those who know of her skill. Despite warnings to mind her own business, she doggedly insists on visiting crime scenes. As a result, she is frequently knocked unconscious, and she, her father, her friends, or a client may be held prisoner. Once she escapes or is rescued by friends or the police, Nancy quickly establishes the identity of the villains, who tend to make immediate confessions. She always refuses cash rewards, but she does accept mementos of her victories.

CHARACTERS: Because the books have changed with the times and because early titles have been rewritten, the characters are not entirely fixed in appearance or personality. **Nancy Drew** is an idealized character. A pretty, blue-eyed sixteen-year-old (eighteen in later books), with curly golden hair (it becomes titian), Nancy is competent at whatever she does, from dancing to riding to painting to arranging flowers. She is also brilliant. Although she does not go to school, she has the intellectual discipline to acquire an astonishing amount of knowledge about a wide range of topics. Nancy is independent, dashing about in her blue roadster. She is comfortable socially, possessing superb manners and natural courtesy. Always well dressed, she is dignified and easily mingles with wealthy people around the country. Her status as an "amateur sleuth" who always refuses to accept payment for her services probably reflects her class consciousness. Nancy becomes involved in cases because she is outraged that an injustice has been perpetrated or a worthy but vulnerable person has been victimized. Once she undertakes a case, she is not easily intimidated, always ignoring the messages that tell her to quit her investigation. She is extremely perceptive and can tell a person's moral character from his or her appearance and manners. She also notices the smallest clues and can locate even the most cleverly concealed trap doors and secret passages. She is resourceful, breaking into locked rooms or cabinets to examine documents. Brave and level-headed, she never succumbs to fears of the supernatural because she perceives the human agents creating every supposed haunting. Finally, she possesses one quality that ensures success. Nancy is extraordinarily lucky, always being in a place where she will overhear an important conversation or will otherwise obtain a significant clue.

Nancy's father, **Carson Drew**, is a former district attorney who has become a wealthy and famous lawyer specializing in criminal and mystery cases. A tall, dignified man who wears horn-rimmed glasses, smokes cigars, and carries a cane, he has immense respect for Nancy. He therefore allows her to sit in during discussions with clients. He provides her with information and advice about her cases, and he refers cases to her. During the course of the series, **Mrs. Hannah Gruen**, the Drews' plump, elderly housekeeper, develops into someone who is almost part of the family. She is sometimes comical in her worrying, but her concern for Nancy provides a gauge to measure Nancy's bravery and independence.

Two friends who assist Nancy represent extremes of female identity. **George Fayne** is tomboyish. Slender and athletic, she has short brown hair and wears tailored clothes. George is blunt and impetuous, but her strength and fearlessness make her a useful companion. George's first cousin, **Bess Marvin**, is a stereotype of extreme femininity. Plump and always thinking about food, blonde-haired Bess wears frilly clothes and is timid. Nancy's boyfriend,

Ned Nickerson, the tall, handsome star quarterback at Emerson College, lends an occasional hand, especially when a situation requires masculine muscle.

Further Reading

Billman, Carol. *The Secret of the Stratemeyer Syndicate: Nancy Drew, the Hardy Boys, and the Million Dollar Fiction Factory*. New York: Ungar, 1986.

Collier, Laurie, and Joyce Nakamura, eds. *Major Authors and Illustrators for Children and Young Adults*. Detroit: Gale Research, 1993.

Contemporary Authors New Revision Series. Vol. 27. Detroit: Gale Research, 1989.

Johnson, Deidre. *Edward Stratemeyer and the Stratemeyer Syndicate*. New York: Twayne, 1993.

Plunkett-Powell, Karen. *The Nancy Drew Scrapbook*. New York: St. Martin's Press, 1993.

Something about the Author. Vol. 65. Detroit: Gale Research, 1991.

Charles Kingsley

1819-1875, English clergyman, professor, and author

The Water-Babies: A Fairy Tale for a Land-Baby

(fantasy, 1863)

PLOT: *The Water-Babies* attempts to reconcile the opposition between religion and science that had developed in Victorian England, especially after the publication of Darwin's *Origin of Species* (1859). Kingsley's narrator thus declares that the story's "doctrine" is "that your soul makes your body, just as a snail makes his shell." The plot supports this theme through a quest journey, during which the protagonist undergoes external changes that symbolize internal development. Numerous satiric asides develop additional themes, but they treat subjects far beyond a child's knowledge.

On the way to sweep the chimneys of Harthover Place, Tom and his brutal master, Mr. Thomas Grimes, meet a mysterious Irish lady. She warns them that those who wish to be clean will be clean and those who wish to be foul will be foul, and then she disappears. While sweeping, Tom mistakenly descends into the white bedroom of Ellie, Sir John Harthover's daughter. Seeing himself in a mirror, Tom understands for the first time that he is dirty. Ellie awakens and screams in fear. Tom then flees out the window, escaping to a school taught by an old lady. Because he is ill, she feeds him and puts him to bed. Hearing church bells and filled with an urge to be clean, Tom gets up, goes to a nearby stream, disrobes, and becomes a water-baby.

While swimming toward the ocean, Tom sees Mr. Grimes, who is poaching, get into a fight and fall into a river. Frightened of Grimes, Tom hurries to the sea. By coincidence, Ellie and Professor Ptthmllnsprts are at the seashore arguing about the existence of water-babies. The professor accidentally catches Tom, who bites him and escapes. Looking to see what has become of Tom, Ellie falls into the water and hits her head. She is put to bed, but the fairies bring her wings, and she flies away. After his escape, Tom saves a lobster caught in a trap; suddenly able to see other water-babies, he goes to their home on St. Brandan's Isle. Two fairies then direct his development. Mrs. Bedonebyasyoudid punishes him when he misbehaves and rewards him when he is good; Mrs. Doasyouwouldbedoneby cuddles him when he needs affection. Eventually, Tom steals the candy Mrs. Bedonebyasyoudid uses as rewards, his body grows prickles, and Tom confesses his greed. The fairies bring Ellie to teach him, and his prickles vanish.

Tom then becomes curious about where Ellie goes every Sunday. The fairies tell him that he can't see it until he sees Mr. Grimes at the Other-end-of-Nowhere. To give him courage to undertake a distasteful quest, Mrs. Bedonebyasyoudid reads the history of the Doasyoulikes, who became extinct. Tom makes a lengthy journey to Mother Carey, who tells him how to find Grimes. After encountering many foolish creatures, Tom locates Grimes, who is stuck in a chimney as punishment for his sins. Seeing Tom and hearing how the schoolteacher (Grimes's mother) helped Tom, Grimes repents. He is released and sent to sweep the crater of Mt. Etna. Tom and Ellie are now reunited. They see that Mother Carey, the fairies, and the Irish woman are one person, and then they reenter the world as adults.

CHARACTERS: Ten-year-old **Tom** the chimney sweeper illustrates Kingsley's contention that spirit controls matter. With one parent dead and the other exiled to Botany Bay, Tom has had no education. He can't read or write, he knows nothing of cleanliness, and he is ignorant of God and Christ. Not surprisingly, he is a cunning little criminal who has been jailed a couple of times. Furthermore, because he is mistreated, he believes that hunger and violence are normal in life. In fact, his ambition is to become a master so that he can abuse apprentices the way Grimes abuses him. His soot-blackened body thus symbolizes the dirty condition of his soul. Until he sees himself in a mirror, however, Tom is ignorant of his condition.

After this shock of self-knowledge, Tom is ready to become physically and spiritually clean. His body therefore dies in this world: Sir John finds Tom's dirty body in the stream and declares that he has drowned. Actually, Tom has been reborn in the water—symbol of both baptism and life—as a four-inch-long water-baby who has gills that look like a lace frill. Clean for the first time and unable to remember the life that made him dirty, he must develop a new identity. Tom is not, however, immediately saintly. Lacking sympathy for other creatures, he torments a caddis, a trout, and a larva. But he begins to change, becoming kind to others so he can have company, only after the ugly larva transforms into a dragonfly (a process analogous to Tom's own change). He then shows his new-found consideration by warning a salmon about the presence of a vicious otter. More significantly, he shows consideration by rescuing his friend the lobster from a trap. Having risked himself for the sake of another, Tom gains spiritual understanding, symbolized by his ability to see other water-babies.

Although his spirit is growing stronger, Tom still takes some steps back morally. When he arrives on St. Brandan's Isle, he returns to his cruel ways, putting a stone in a sea anemone. As a consequence, Mrs. Bedonebyasyoudid puts a stone in Tom's mouth. Even after he learns justice from her and charity

from Mrs. Doasyouwouldbedoneby, his childish selfishness persists, leading him to steal candy. As a consequence, he develops a prickly skin that symbolizes his prickly heart. He therefore must pursue a solitary, unselfish quest to become an adult. Tom's journey to see Grimes leads him to Mother Carey, from whom he learns self-reliance. Finally, he sees Grimes, whose condition moves Tom to pity. Having overcome selfishness and vindictiveness, Tom becomes the agent of moral growth for another person. He thus truly becomes an adult and earns the right to reenter the human world as an important man. Before he does so, however, he receives a fleeting vision of the unity of the spiritual world, and those who helped his soul mature are seen as a single person.

The Queen of the fairies is a helper who assumes different guises. She first appears as a poor, tall, handsome **Irish woman**, who has bright, gray eyes and black hair. In this form, she is a prophet, warning both Tom and Grimes that they will become what they wish, that their spirits, in other words, control their bodies. She is also a caring person, showing kindness by commanding the fairies to protect Tom after he enters the stream. By forbidding them to talk to him, she allows Tom the freedom to learn from his experiences. As **Mrs. Bedonebyasyoudid**, the Queen is an ugly woman with a big hooked nose who wears large green spectacles and carries a birch-rod. She represents retributive justice, teaching Tom morality by punishing him and rewarding him. When Tom steals, she becomes a model of the wise parent, remaining quiet so that she doesn't drive him into naughtiness or lying. Finally, she is a wise teacher, using the history of the Doasyoulikes (who devolved from humans to apes and then became extinct) to show that complacency and laziness are ruinous. As **Mrs. Doasyouwouldbedoneby**, she is beautiful beyond description. She represents consoling love, cuddling the babies and making them feel secure and happy. As **Mother Carey**, she is like an iceberg, a white marble lady on a marble throne. Symbol of the creative spiritual force operating within nature, she allows things to make themselves, never interfering with the process. She is also a wise tutor who advises Tom to rely on his dog (perhaps a symbol of spiritual instinct) to lead the way to Grimes. Finally, she is the ineffable mystery of spirit: Tom, who has understood things while looking into her eyes, finds her eyes too blinding to understand who she truly is.

For many critics, **Thomas Grimes**, Tom's master, is an element in a social crusade against child labor and cruelty. Certainly, Grimes is a cruel man who beats and starves Tom. He is fond of drink, and he detests washing, a symbol of his spiritual dirtiness. He is most important, however, for his theological role. His redemption, after Tom shows him kindness and brings back memories of his mother, illustrates Kingsley's conviction that it is never too late to repent and be saved. **Professor Ptthmllnsprts** is a satiric portrait of dogmatic scientists and educators, especially those of the rationalist school who refuse to believe what they can't prove with the senses. The professor is so vain that he becomes a hypocrite: he refuses to admit that he was wrong about water-babies even after he sees Tom. He goes mad, writing a book contrary to all of his old opinions. As a result, he is cured of pride, vanity, and willful blindness, becoming sadder but wiser. **Ellie**, the daughter of Sir John Harthover, is both physically and spiritually a foil to Tom. Physically, she is a white-skinned, golden-haired beauty who contrasts with the dirty chimney sweep. Spiritually, she needs no reformation. She knows about Christ and can teach Tom kindness and honesty. Because the narrator claims that only princesses marry in fairy tales, she does not marry Tom, but she does become his adult friend and takes him home on Sundays.

Further Reading

Bingham, Jane M., ed. *Writers for Children: Critical Studies of Major Authors Since the Seventeenth Century.* New York: Scribner, 1988.

Fredeman, William E., and Ira B. Nadel, eds. *Victorian Poets Before 1850.* Vol. 32 of *Dictionary of Literary Biography.* Detroit: Gale Research, 1984.

Nadel, Ira B., and William E. Fredeman, eds. *Victorian Novelists before 1885.* Vol. 21 of *Dictionary of Literary Biography.* Detroit: Gale Research, 1983.

Uffleman, Larry K. *Charles Kingsley.* Boston: Twayne, 1979.

Yesterday's Authors of Books for Children. Vol. 2. Detroit: Gale Research, 1978.

Dick King-Smith

1922-, English farmer, teacher, and author

Babe: The Gallant Pig

(animal fantasy, 1985; published in England as The Sheep-Pig, *1983)*

PLOT: Without becoming either sentimental or didactic, this engaging fantasy about unlikely dreams coming true demonstrates the power of politeness and the deceptive nature of appearances. When Farmer Hogget wins a baby pig at the fair, Mrs. Hogget thinks that it will provide lovely hams at Christmas. Fly, the sheepdog, feels an instant attachment to the pig, and soon regrets telling her four pups that pigs are stupid. Fly becomes a foster mother to Babe, as she calls the pig, and Babe calls her Mum. After Fly's pups are sold, Babe announces that he wants to be a sheep-pig. Fly tries to teach him how to dominate animals, but Babe has little success. One day, however, he talks to Ma, a sick ewe being treated in the barn, and understands that the sheep become confused by rudeness but willingly respond to polite requests.

Babe soon tests his new knowledge. One day when Mr. and Mrs. Hogget are off to market with Fly, sheep rustlers arrive. Babe politely asks the sheep not to go with the thieves. Stunned by his politeness, the sheep hesitate and then run away when the rustlers' dogs go after Babe. Because Babe foiled the robbery, Mrs. Hogget declares that Babe will never be butchered. After this incident, Farmer Hogget notices that the sheep are reluctant to obey Fly, so he turns the work over to Babe. When Babe fights off two dogs that kill Ma, however, Farmer Hogget sees blood on the pig and decides to shoot him. Just in time, the police telephone with a warning about sheep-killing dogs in the area. In the meantime, Fly politely asks the sheep about the incident and learns that Babe is a hero. Farmer Hogget now begins training Babe for the Grand Challenge Sheep Dog Trials. Fly helps by learning from the sheep a password that will make even strange sheep listen to Babe. On the day of the trials, the crowd laughs, but Babe uses the password and politely asks the sheep to go through the gates. They comply, allowing Babe and Farmer Hogget to win the trial with a perfect score.

CHARACTERS: Sharp dialogue and brief revelatory actions bring the comical characters to life. **Babe**, so named because that is the name his mother called all her piglets, is a Large White of unusual intelligence, compassion, and politeness. Babe instinctively understands character. At the fair, he squeals when picked up, but he does not squeal when kind Farmer Hogget holds him to estimate his weight. On the farm, Babe immediately likes Fly and readily accepts her as his Mum. Kind and considerate, Babe can't dominate animals the way sheep dogs do. Nevertheless, he longs to herd sheep and to be a sheep-pig. Although Babe learns the rudiments of the craft from Fly, he succeeds because he lacks prejudice. Consequently, he does what Fly has never done: he listens to Ma and understands the sheep's view of matters. Babe first applies his knowledge when he saves the sheep from the rustlers. Although he doesn't know it, his quick wit and bravery also save his own life because the grateful Mrs. Hogget no longer wants to butcher him. Afterwards, Babe becomes doglike. Having first assured himself that he is not hurting Fly's feelings, he takes over Fly's duties, succeeding because he always asks the sheep to do what he wants them to do. He also begins to enter the house, where he is treated in the same way that Fly is; he even eats dog food. In addition to being clever and considerate, Babe is disciplined and brave. When Fly tells him that he can't succeed as a sheep-pig unless he is faster, Babe willingly undertakes a regimen of unpiglike exercise and dieting to become quick and hard-muscled. His physical conditioning subsequently helps him when he bravely attacks the dogs that kill Ma. Brave in deed and polished in manners, Babe is, as the subtitle of the American edition says, a gallant pig.

Fly, a black-and-white collie, is a helper within the fairy-tale-like plot. She teaches Babe the skills of the sheepdog, she gets him to exercise and diet so that he will be agile in the trials, and she learns the password that enables Babe to gain the cooperation of the sheep in the trial. From the beginning, Fly is a good mother. She reassures her own pups about their safety and patiently teaches them their craft. The tender-hearted Fly also feels maternal affection for the unhappy Babe. After becoming Babe's foster mother, Fly protects his innocence by stopping her own pups whenever they are about to reveal the pig's destiny as Christmas ham. Fly is also a foil to Babe. Believing that sheep are stupid, Fly has contempt for them and insists that the only way to herd them is to dominate them with rude and aggressive behavior. She even laughs when Babe mentions asking, instead of telling, the sheep to do something. Consequently, Fly doesn't hear what the sheep say and doesn't understand them. Nevertheless, Fly changes, thereby reinforcing the theme of the power of politeness. After Ma is killed, she is so desperate to reassure herself that Babe has not turned killer that she politely asks the sheep about the incident. Later, when she worries that the strange sheep in the trial will not give Babe a chance to request their cooperation, she again politely requests assistance, thus learning the password that enables Babe to succeed. **Ma**, the ewe, provides a comical balance to the self-assurance and arrogance Fly displays. By contradicting Fly, Ma becomes a helper. She thus insists that sheep are not stupid but only easily confused by rudeness. By reassuring Babe that sheep will happily comply with polite requests, she gives Babe the knowledge that indirectly saves his life and that enables him to succeed in his unlikely dream of being a sheep-pig.

Farmer Hogget, a long-legged, tall, thin man with a brown face, is very laconic, wasting neither words nor movement. He rapidly becomes attached to Babe, whom he simply calls Pig, but he is unable to tell his wife that he thinks it would be a pity to butcher the pig. An observant and understanding man, he realizes that Babe has better rapport with the sheep than Fly and therefore lets him take over Fly's duties. Characteristically, he does not inform his wife of this fact. Farmer Hogget contributes to the theme of deceptive appearances when he rashly assumes that Babe has killed Ma and therefore decides to shoot him. After he learns the truth, however, he becomes more confident in Babe than ever. By taking Babe to the trials—by this time he thinks of the pig as a dog—he contributes to the theme that ability, not appearance or other people's expectations, is the most important factor in achieving success. His patience and faith are rewarded when Babe wins the trial for him. **Mrs. Hogget** is a foil to her husband, contrasting with him physically and temperamentally. A woman with a "comfortable" red face, she comes close to understanding what is going on around her, but she always dismisses her speculations as ridiculous. Consequently, she does not appreciate Babe until he saves the sheep from the rustlers. She then declares that they will not butcher Babe, being unaware that her husband has long opposed the idea. Mrs. Hogget most obviously differs from her quiet husband in being talkative. Sometimes this trait generates humor, as when she is so long-winded during her telephone call to the police that the rustlers escape. At other times, it creates comic irony, as when, on the day of the trial, she says that the way her husband has cleaned up the pig, one would think that he was entering it in the trial.

Further Reading

Berger, Laura Standley, ed. *Twentieth-Century Children's Writers*. 4th ed. Detroit: St. James, 1995.

Collier, Laurie, and Joyce Nakamura, eds. *Major Authors and Illustrators for Children and Young Adults*. Detroit: Gale Research, 1993.

Contemporary Authors New Revision Series. Vol. 22. Detroit: Gale Research, 1988.

Holtze, Sally Holmes, ed *Sixth Book of Junior Authors and Illustrators*. New York: H. W. Wilson, 1989.

Something about the Author. Vols. 38, 47, 80. Detroit: Gale Research, 1985, 1987, 1995.

Rudyard Kipling

1865-1936, English author

The Jungle Books

(animal fantasy series, 1894, 1895)

PLOT: *The Jungle Book* (1894) contains three stories about Mowgli, an Indian boy raised by wolves.

In "Mowgli's Brothers," Mowgli the Frog, as he is called, comes to the cave of Mother Wolf (Raksha) and Father Wolf after a tiger attacks his parents. The tiger, Shere Khan, directed to the cave by Tabaqui the jackal, demands Mowgli as his prey, but the wolves refuse him. Later, when none of the wolves support Mowgli's entry into the Pack, Baloo, the bear who teaches the Law of the Jungle, speaks for Mowgli, and Bagheera the panther buys Mowgli's membership with a freshly killed bull. Years later, Shere Khan incites the young wolves into demanding Mowgli's blood, but Mowgli drives them away with fire. After ordering the wolves to spare Akela, even though their aged leader has missed a kill, Mowgli tearfully leaves the jungle. In "Kaa's Hunting," an earlier adventure, the Bandar-log (monkeys) kidnap Mowgli and hold him prisoner in the Cold Lairs, a deserted city. After Baloo, Bagheera, and Kaa the python rescue Mowgli, Kaa dances hypnotically before eating the monkeys. "Tiger, Tiger" picks up the threads of the first tale. Mowgli lives in a village with Messua, whose child was taken by a tiger years earlier. Learning that Shere Khan is planning to kill him, Mowgli, aided by Akela and Mowgli's wolf brothers, traps Shere Khan between two buffalo herds, which crush the tiger. Buldeo the hunter, eager to claim a bounty, demands the tiger's skin, but Akela pins him down. Buldeo then convinces the villagers that Mowgli is a demon, and they throw stones at Mowgli. Rejected by animals and men, Mowgli decides to hunt alone in the jungle.

Two stories are about animal heroes. In "The White Seal," Kotick sees some men killing his fellow seals, so he searches for an island where men never go. Eventually, some sea cows lead him through an underwater tunnel to the perfect sanctuary. Kotick then fights the other seals so that they will follow him. "Rikki-tikki-tavi" overlays an account of mongoose behavior with mythic patterns. After a flood washes Rikki-tikki-tavi out of his home, an English family revives the mongoose. When Rikki-tikki then encounters the cobra Nag, only the warning of Darzee the tailor bird saves him from being struck from behind by Nagaina, Nag's wife. Shortly afterwards, Rikki-tikki saves Teddy, the English child, from a poisonous snake. That night, Rikki-tikki learns from Chuchundra the muskrat that the cobras are planning to kill the English family. Rikki-tikki kills Nag, has Darzee's wife lure Nagaina from her eggs, and destroys all but one. Using it to lure Nagaina away from Teddy, he pursues her down her hole. Although Darzee sings his death song, Rikki-tikki emerges victorious.

In "Toomai of the Elephants," Petersen Sahib hears of Little Toomai's bravery in the elephant stockades and jokingly tells him that he can be an elephant tamer once he sees the elephants dance. That night, Little Toomai is on Kala Nag (Black Snake) when it heads into the jungle to dance with other elephants. Afterwards, Machua Appa changes the boy's name to Toomai of the Elephants. "Her Majesty's Servants" advances Kipling's belief in the virtue of unquestioning obedience. In a conversation, an old breech-piece mule (Billy), a cavalry horse, a young mule, a baggage camel, two gun-bullocks, and Two Tails the elephant describe their military duties.

The Second Jungle Book (1895) contains five Mowgli stories. In "How Fear Came," Mowgli listens while Hathi the elephant narrates a *pourquoi* myth about the jungle's fall from innocence and the reasons animals fear men. "Letting in the Jungle" is a revenge tale. Learning that Buldeo has convinced the villagers to burn Messua and her husband as witches, Mowgli saves them and then calls on Hathi and other animals to make the village uninhabitable. In "The King's Ankus" Mowgli learns the deadly power of greed after accompanying Kaa to visit White Hood, a cobra guarding the treasure beneath the Cold Lairs. Mowgli takes a richly decorated ankus, or elephant-goad, but he throws it away because Bagheera convinces him that it will bring death. After he and Bagheera discover the bodies of men who have killed each other for the ankus, Mowgli returns it to White Hood. Mowgli is the heroic savior of the Pack in "Red Dog." With Kaa's help, Mowgli lures an invading army of dholes (wild dogs) into chasing him past the rock hives of the Little People, the bees. The Pack kills the surviving dholes, but Akela dies in the battle. "The Spring Running," which is set in the mating season, when the animals are busy dancing and do not obey

Mowgli's summons, focuses on Mowgli's need for human companionship. Feverish and confused, Mowgli visits the widowed Messua, who regards him as a god, and then goes to the Council Rock one last time. After Baloo and Kaa indicate that it is time for him to live with men, Bagheera pays a bull to free Mowgli from all debts to the jungle.

In the best of the remaining tales, "The Miracle of Purun Bhagat," Purun Dass, an internationally honored Prime Minister becomes Purun Bhagat, a Sunnyasi, or holy man. One night, during a heavy rain, animals alert him to the fact that the mountain is about to collapse. After warning the villagers below, he dies. "The Undertakers" is an ironic tale in which a crocodile, Mugger of Mugger-Ghaut, reminisces with the Adjutant-crane and a Jackal. Mugger regrets that, years earlier, he missed when he snapped at the hand of an English boy. That boy, now a man, shoots and kills him. "Quiquern" is an Eskimo survival story. During a time of starvation, Kotuko, having heard a spirit voice, sets out to find food. A vision of a Quiquern—a two-headed, eight-legged dog—leads him and the girl accompanying him safely from the cracking ice floes. The vision is only a mirage created by two of Kotuko's runaway dogs, but it helps Kotuko to find seals and to save his people from starvation.

CHARACTERS: Mowgli the Frog may be, as some critics argue, a symbol of imperialism because he is the intelligent and powerful stranger who dominates the native inhabitants of a foreign region. Mowgli, torn between his biological heritage as a human and his social identity as the adopted cub, also illustrates themes about identity and belonging. Mowgli at first regards himself as a wolf cub, and he hunts and eats like a wolf. Furthermore, Baloo's formal instructions about the Law and various Calls prepare him to live like an animal. Because he is human, however, Mowgli is innately superior to his animal brothers. As a toddler, he has no fear: he laughs when he first sees Father Wolf, and he shoves the cubs aside to suckle with Mother Wolf. His human intelligence enables him to maintain this superiority. He uses fire, which the animals fear, to dominate Shere

Baloo, Mowgli, Bagheera, and Kaa, as illustrated by Fritz Eichenberg for Kipling's **The Jungle Book.**

Khan, and he plays clever tricks to destroy both Shere Khan and the dholes. At the Cold Lairs, Mowgli shows his difference from animals when he alone is unaware of Kaa's hypnotic spell. The implication is that his humanity keeps him ignorant of destructive animal impulses. Mowgli's superiority is most evident, however, in his eyes: none of the animals can withstand his stare. This stare and his knowledge of animal Calls make Mowgli the acknowledged Master of the Jungle.

At various times, both animals and humans challenge Mowgli's identity. Shere Khan and the young wolves insist that Mowgli is a human who has no place among them. The tears that Mowgli subsequently sheds do more than indicate his love of the jungle. They redefine Mowgli, making him, as Bagheera notes, a man forever cut off from the jungle he enjoyed so passionately when he was a cub. Ironically, however, Mowgli's jungle training makes him superior to and incapable of fitting in with humans. Mowgli understands the need to kill for food, for example, but the greed that leads men to murder for the ankus strikes him as sheer madness. Mowgli's knowledge of jungle animals also frees him from superstition. Having laughed at Buldeo's stories, he does not understand why the villagers insist that his own command of the animals makes him a sorcerer or demon.

Mowgli is a hero, the lone leader who uses his powers to help others. Fiercely loyal, he defends Akela from the Pack and Messua from the villagers. When the dholes invade, he courageously risks his life to save the Pack that rejected him. In this episode, Mowgli ignores past grievances, but he is often vengeful, fierce, and unforgiving, as he shows when he destroys the village and when he kills Shere Khan. Modern sensibilities regard such vengeance as a failing, but Kipling honors it as part of the Law of the Jungle, a means for preserving peace. Ultimately, the Law requires Mowgli to acknowledge the feelings that determine his identity. During mating season, Mowgli's feverish unrest signals his need for human companionship. By leaving the jungle, Mowgli finally accepts his difference, defining himself irrevocably as a man. "In the Rukh," published in *Many Inventions* (1893), describes Mowgli's later life as a forest ranger.

The animals in the Mowgli stories speak in an elevated language that gives them a mythic dimension. **Baloo**, a sleepy brown bear, hits Mowgli to make him learn the Law, but he is a kind, loving teacher, and he is proud of his best pupil. Baloo is the first to speak on behalf of Mowgli at the Council, and he is the one who suggests that they enlist Kaa's aid when the monkeys kidnap Mowgli. He reaffirms Mowgli's humanity at the end. **Bagheera** the black panther becomes Mowgli's closest friend and advisor after he buys Mowgli's membership in the wolf Pack with a freshly killed bull. Bagheera cares for Mowgli because their histories are parallel. Bagheera was born in captivity in the King's Palace at Oodeypore, but he broke the lock on his cage and escaped to the jungle. Bagheera refuses to flatter or to display false modesty. He is cunning, bold, and reckless, but the other animals fear him because he knows men and their ways. Bagheera applies this knowledge when he advises Mowgli to use fire against the wolves. Loyal as well as wise, Bagheera reminds Mowgli to save Akela from death because Akela always acted as a friend. As well as being a counselor, Bagheera is a physical helper, coming to Mowgli's aid when he is captured and playing a vital role in rescuing Messua. Because he knows and loves Mowgli, Bagheera anticipates his objections to leaving the jungle and frees him from all debts with a bull. **Kaa** is a thirty-foot rock python whose powerful coils strangle enemies but gently cradle his beloved Mowgli. With the lawless monkeys, Kaa is a wily trickster: he traps his prey by assuming the appearance of a branch or a stump. Filled with a deep understanding of animal behavior, he hypnotizes those who look into his face, making them easy victims of the Dance of the Hunger of Kaa.

Mother Wolf (**Raksha**, or the Demon), who adopts Mowgli and comes to love him more than her own offspring, is fierce as well as loving. She foreshadows Mowgli's greatness by prophesying that he will one day kill Shere Khan. In Kipling's imperialist vision, she is the native who comes to love the superior outsider she nurses. **Father Wolf** is less fierce than his wife, but he loves Mowgli and tries to make him one of the Pack. **Akela**, the great gray Lone Wolf, leads the Pack by cunning and strength. He displays nobility when the wolves want to kill Mowgli: he promises that, if they spare Mowgli, he will not resist when it is his own time to be killed. Akela loses his leadership after missing a kill, but he grows white with age because Mowgli has ordered that he be spared. Akela is killed while bravely fighting to protect the Pack from the dholes. **Hathi** the wild elephant is called Master of the Jungle, a title Mowgli later earns. Hathi knows the Law and proclaims a water truce, he teaches wisdom by telling the story about the origin of fear, he grants Mowgli power by teaching him Master-words that control animals, and he helps him by destroying the village.

Shere Khan, a ten-foot tiger, was born lame in one foot, a physical infirmity symbolizing moral weakness. Mowgli's archenemy, Shere Khan represents lawlessness: he violates the Law by hunting outside of his own region and by killing men. In contrast with Mowgli, he is an evil leader: he destroys the unity of the Pack by turning the younger wolves against Mowgli and Akela. Shere Khan is devious, vicious, and vengeful, but he is also cowardly and incompetent. He fails to claim Mowgli at Council because Bagheera has a greater knowledge of the Law. He fails to lead the wolves against Mowgli because he fears both Mowgli's eyes and the fire that Mowgli uses to singe him. And he later fails to kill Mowgli because, after he foolishly boasts of his intentions, Mowgli's friends alert him. Mowgli, possessing superior understanding, knows when Shere Khan is most vulnerable and easily outwits him. **Tabaqui** the Dish-licker is a jackal, the most despised animal in the jungle because he is prone to madness. A mischievous trickster, he deliberately breaks rules of hospitality and leads Shere Khan to Mowgli.

Two human characters have major roles in *The Jungle Books*. **Buldeo**, the village hunter, represents the worst elements of humans. Superstitious and vain, he invents ridiculous stories to excuse his own incompetence as a hunter. Greedy, he tries to take the tiger skin away from Mowgli. Vengeful, he tries to kill both Mowgli and Messua, who had given Mowgli shelter. **Messua**, the village woman with whom Mowgli lives, represents the good side of humanity. Having lost her child, called Nathoo, years earlier to a tiger, she may be Mowgli's actual mother. Regardless, she parallels Mother Wolf because she gives Mowgli shelter and comes to love him as her own son. Messua's troubles provide an opportunity for Mowgli to display a heroic concern for humans equal to that he shows for animals. Her feeling that the adolescent Mowgli is a god underscores the fact that he is as superior to men as he is to animals.

Characters in the non-Mowgli stories support Ernest Thompson Seton's statement that Kipling's tales are not realistic animal tales but "wonderful, beautiful fairy tales." In "The White Seal," the white fur that makes **Kotick** different from the other seals is the sign of even greater internal differences. More curious than others, he follows the men who herd and then kill the young seals. Horrified by the killing, he unselfishly dedicates himself to changing conditions. Kotick intelligently seeks advice, but his heroism lies in his unflagging quest for a new home. Kotick establishes his superiority by courageously fighting the seals who mock him. Having compelled obedience, he shows that he is a good and wise leader by taking the seals to safety.

Rikki-tikki-tavi, the hero of the story of the same name, is a small mongoose whose pink eyes blaze red when he is angry. His adventures follow a mythic pattern, symbolic deaths marking his transformation to a hero. His first transformation occurs because of the flood. Teddy says that Rikki-tikki is dead, but the adults revive him. Reborn, Rikki-tikki gains self-confidence after escaping Nagaina's blow from behind and then proves his value by saving Teddy from the small snake. Knowing that a full mongoose would not be fast enough to kill Nag, he wisely refrains from eating this snake. Rikki-tikki is patient and brave in stalking and killing Nag. He is cunning when he destroys Nagaina's eggs, saving one to lure her away from Teddy. His pursuit down Nagaina's hole resembles the mythic hero's journey to the underworld. Darzee sings his death song, but Rikki-tikki-tavi, having defeated evil, is symbolically reborn as the hero. **Nag**, the five-foot black cobra, represents evil: he eats fledgling birds, and he attacks humans. His fear of the mongoose foreshadows Rikki-tikki's heroism. **Nagaina**, Nag's mate, is more evil than her husband. She attacks Rikki-tikki from behind, and she urges Nag to kill the humans so that the snakes can rule the garden. Vindictive after her husband is killed, she taunts Teddy while preparing to make a lethal strike. Her one redeeming value is her maternal concern for her eggs. **Darzee** the tailor bird is an easily flustered fool who sings aloud whatever he thinks. He underscores Rikki-tikki's archetypal heroism by singing his death song. In contrast, **Darzee's wife** is sensible and brave. She is the clever trickster who lures Nagaina away from her eggs so that Rikki-tikki can destroy them. **Chuchundra** the muskrat is a helper because he informs Rikki-tikki of the snakes' plans to kill the family. His excessive timidity accentuates Rikki-tikki's bravery.

A brave boy, as he shows by rushing into the stockade to help a man taming wild elephants in "Toomai of the Elephants," ten-year-old **Little Toomai** expresses his longing for adventure by banging a drum. Little Toomai accomplishes the seemingly impossible when he becomes the first person to see the elephants dancing. His night-time journey aboard Kala Nag symbolizes a discovery of unconscious qualities. When the elephants amplify the longing expressed by his drum with the jungle-destroying thumping of their dance, Little Toomai discovers his own wild energy. Renamed **Toomai of the Elephants**, the name of his great-grandfather who was Kala Nag's original mahout (keeper), the boy is transformed into a man who will accomplish great things and will command the respect of men and animals. **Kala Nag**, which means **Black Snake**, is a huge government elephant who is nearly seventy years old. A powerful fighter used to tame wild elephants, Kala Nag has been gentle and obedient to four generations of Toomai's family. This tamed wild animal is the medium through which Little Toomai discovers his own suppressed wild nature.

Like all of the animals in "Her Majesty's Servants," **Billy**, the old breech-piece mule, is essentially a soldier who is proud of his military role. Although his experience makes him calmer than the other animals, he becomes furious when reminded that his father was a donkey. **The young mule**, a new recruit, lacks Billy's knowledge and calmness. His role is to initiate the theme of obedience by asking why the animals take part in wars. The **cavalry horse**, "Number Fifteen, E Troop, Ninth Lancers—Dick Cunliffe's horse," shows how intimately animals identify with their masters. Fierce and proud, he provides a description of cavalry charges. Because he has bad dreams and becomes nervous, the **baggage-camel**, who charges madly around the camp, earns the contempt of other animals. Nevertheless, he proudly describes how camels lie down in battle to provide a protective square for their soldiers. The two **gun-bullocks** who drag the heavy guns are slow and stubborn, insisting that their way is the only way to fight. **Two Tails** the elephant says that his intelligence, which makes him able to envision what will happen, is the reason he is a coward in battle.

Purun Dass, a Brahmin, or upper caste Indian, exhibits the highest ideals of two societies in "The Miracle of Purun Bhagat." In his youth, he exemplifies the British ideal of public service. Close-mouthed and diplomatic, he affects Western social reforms, such as the building of schools for girls. After charming sophisticated London and receiving his nation's highest honors, he fulfills the Indian ideal of contemplation by becoming **Purun Bhagat**, a wandering mendicant, or begging monk. Patient and ungrasping, he inspires the trust of the animals, who warn him of danger. In his final act, he reconciles his identities. Becoming Purun Dass, western man of action, he warns the villagers; afterwards, as Purun Bhagat, Indian man of contemplation, he assumes the cross-legged posture of Enlightenment and dies.

All of the animals in "The Undertakers" are thoroughly unpleasant predators. His continuing desire for a taste of an English boy's hand makes the **Mugger of Mugger-Ghaut**, an ancient, blunt-nosed, twenty-four-foot crocodile, particularly repugnant. This wily, patient trickster's memories of the people he has eaten provide a glimpse of Indian life and history. The **Jackal**, a notorious coward, is obsequious, and he bemoans that he is universally despised. The **Adjutant-crane**, who is respected by humans because he is a first-class scavenger, is an ugly and cowardly bird. His excellent memory stimulates the Mugger's reminiscences.

Kotuko, an Eskimo hunter in "Quiquern," is a conventional survival hero and lacks individuality. As a boy, he longs to be a man. As a man, he becomes the greatest of his people, saving them from starvation. His vision of the Quiquern, even though Kipling provides a logical explanation, underscores Kotuko's status as mythic hero.

Just So Stories for Little Children
(humorous myths, 1902)

PLOT: These twelve stories are primarily mock *pourquoi* myths, humorous explanations of the origins of such things as animals' features or human culture. In "How the Whale Got His Throat," the 'Stute Fish realizes that the Whale has eaten every fish but him, so he suggests that the Whale try eating Man. The Whale swallows a shipwrecked Mariner, who makes such a sickening ruckus that the Whale takes him home. Before leaving the Whale's belly, the Mariner lodges a grating, fashioned from his raft and suspenders, in the Whale's throat so that it can eat only small fish. "How the Camel Got His Hump" is a cautionary tale. On successive days, Horse, Dog, and Ox ask the Camel to help with the work, but he refuses, saying only "Humph." Although the Djinn in charge of All Deserts warns him, the Camel says "Humph" to him, too. The Camel's back then swells into a "humph" (now called a hump to spare his feelings), enabling him to work for three days without eating. In "How the Rhinoceros Got His Skin," the Rhinoceros chases a Parsee up a tree and eats his cake. During a heat wave, the rhinoceros takes off his skin and bathes in the sea. The Parsee fills the skin with cake crumbs and burned currants. When the Rhinoceros puts it on, he is so uncomfortable that he tugs, scratches, and pulls it out of shape. Every rhinoceros now has a bad temper and wears a skin with great folds. "How the Leopard Got His Spots" explains protective coloration. After Giraffe and Zebra leave the High Veldt, the Ethiopian and the Leopard can find no game. Baviaan advises the Leopard to go into other spots and the Ethiopian to change. After they see how successfully the Giraffe and the Zebra blend into the forest, the Ethiopian changes his skin to black and puts tiny finger marks on the Leopard.

"The Elephant's Child" is about curiosity and its rewards. Whenever the Elephant's Child asks puzzling questions, the adults spank him. When he wants to know what the Crocodile eats for dinner, the Kolokolo Bird advises him to go to the "great gray-green Limpopo River." There, the Child asks the Crocodile, who answers by grabbing his nose and trying to eat him. The Bi-Colored-Python-Rock-Snake aids the Child in pulling free. The Child's nose is permanently stretched into a trunk, but he learns that it is useful, especially in spanking adults. All the elephants then have their noses stretched into trunks. In "The Sing-Song of Old Man Kangaroo," Kangaroo annoys the gods, asking to be made different from other animals and to be popular and run after. Big God Nqong grants his wish, setting Yellow-Dog Dingo chasing him until Old Man Kangaroo begins hopping and his legs and tail change shape. In "The Beginning of Armadillos" Painted Panther becomes so confused about the identities of Stickly-Prickly Hedgehog and Slow-Solid Tortoise that both escape from him. They then practice each other's survival tactics, becoming so like each other that they form a new species called Armadillo.

"How the First Letter was Written" is a tale of comical mix-ups. When her father breaks his spear, Taffimai Metallumai, known as Taffy, solicits a stranger to deliver a letter asking her mother to send another spear. The stranger, seeing the pictures that Taffy draws, thinks that her father is a king under attack. When he delivers the picture, Taffy's mother thinks that the stranger has killed her husband, but everything is resolved happily. In the tedious sequel,

"How the Alphabet Was Made," Taffy and her father invent a system of representing sounds through stylized pictures.

Pau Amma, "The Crab that Played with the Sea," sneaks away when the Eldest Magician teaches the animals to play. He creates tides when he feeds. The Eldest Magician shrinks this giant crab; Man gives him the gift of living on land or in water; the Man's daughter gives him scissors for claws. The Fisherman of the Moon, obeying the Magician's orders, creates daily tides so that the Man won't have to paddle hard going home each day. In "The Cat that Walked by Himself," the Woman tames Wild Dog, Wild Horse, and Wild Cow, but has no need for Cat. She agrees, however, that if she praises him three times he can enter the cave, sit by the fire, and drink warm milk. By calming her baby, by making it laugh and sleep, and by eating a mouse, the Cat makes the Woman praise him three times. Because he insists that he walks alone and all places are alike to him, however, the Cat earns the perpetual enmity of the Man and the Dog. In "The Butterfly That Stamped" Suleiman-bin-Daoud is distressed by the arguments of his nine hundred and ninety-nine wives. One day he hears a butterfly boast that one stamp of his foot would make the palace vanish. Balkis, Suleiman-bin-Daoud's wise and loving wife, tells the butterfly's wife to order the butterfly to stamp. When the butterfly stamps, Suleiman-bin-Daoud magically makes his palace disappear. The argumentative butterfly wife becomes pleasant to her husband, and Balkis reveals that she provoked the butterfly wife so that Suleiman-bin-Daoud would do something that would control his own argumentative wives.

CHARACTERS: (Character names that appear only in the glosses to Kipling's drawings are cited in parentheses.) The animal characters are humorous types whose adventures account for their descendants' appearance and behavior. **The Whale** (Smiler) represents uncontrolled appetite. The grating punishes him for his greed by ensuring that he can eat only very small fish. He is comical when he arrives at the Mariner's home and announces stations as if he were a train. The **'Stute Fish** (Pringle) is truly astute, saving himself by directing the Whale to other prey. After playing his trick, the 'Stute Fish fearfully hides under the Doorsills of the Equator, but a gloss indicates that he and the Whale later became friends. **The Mariner** (Henry Albert Bivvens, A.B.) seems like a little boy because his mother permits him to paddle his feet in the ocean, but he is clearly "a man of infinite-resource-and-sagacity." He not only makes the Whale so uncomfortable that it becomes his servant and takes him home, but by ingeniously lodging the grating in its throat, he also ensures that it will never again swallow a man. The lazy and inconsiderate **Camel** receives poetic justice for his arrogant and contemptuous "humph" because the hump that forms on his once elegant back enables him to do more work than he could otherwise have done.

The **Rhinoceros** (Strorks) begins as a smooth-skinned animal without manners. He is bad when he eats the Parsee's cake. His punishment, which makes him perpetually uncomfortable, humorously accounts for both the baggy skin of the rhinoceros and its bad temper. The **Parsee** (Pestonjee Bomonjee) wears only a hat that reflects the sun's rays "in more-than-oriental splendor" and eats only cake. Unaffected himself by the terrible heat, he gleefully devises an excruciating punishment for the rude Rhinoceros. **Baviaan**, the dog-headed Baboon who is the Wisest Animal in All South Africa, is a helper figure whose cryptic advice tests the wit of those he counsels. **The Ethiopian** (Sambo) begins as a grayish-brownish-yellowish man. He is a good hunter and is wiser than Leopard because he is the first to figure out Baviaan's advice. He possesses magic powers because he can change his skin color. Like his companion, who ironically illustrates that an Ethiopian did change his skin, **the Leopard** (Spot) mocks a popular saying of the day, "a Leopard can't change its spots." The Leopard is notable for his vanity, insisting that he won't look like Zebra or Giraffe.

The **Elephant's Child** represents the essence of childhood. He is always polite, but his "'satiable curiosity," evident in his constant stream of questions, frustrates adults. When he sets out to learn what the Crocodile eats, the innocent Child bravely embarks on a quest for knowledge. His naivete nearly destroys him, however, because, unaware that the Crocodile wants to eat him, he gets too close. His transformed nose becomes an appropriate reward for curiosity, or nosiness. His trunk helps him to eat and be comfortable. Knowing that he is now superior to other elephants, he indulges in every child's fantasy of retribution: he spanks the adults who once spanked him. **The Crocodile** is a wily trickster. He appears to be a log, and he weeps crocodile tears (a phrase indicating his great insincerity) when he identifies himself to the Child. Although he offers to do what no other adult has done, to satisfy the Child's insatiable curiosity, the knowledge he offers is deadly because he wants to show what he eats by eating the Child. **The Bi-Colored-Python-Rock-Snake**, who speaks in a humorously pompous manner, begins as another of those who spank the Child, but he becomes his most important helper. He physically aids the Child in the tugging match. Afterwards, he points out the advantages of the Child's altered condition and advises him, even suggesting that he spank the adults.

Old Man Kangaroo is inordinately proud. A gray woolly animal with four small feet, he foolishly wishes to be different from other animals and to be popular and run after. Instead of being changed through magic, as he anticipated, he endures a painful chase, during which his hind legs become strong and his tail becomes a balancing device. His story illustrates the idea that animals adapt to survive. **Painted Panther** is naive and slow-witted. Unable to identify either Hedgehog or Tortoise, this predator falls prey to their clever deceptions. **Stickly-Prickly Hedgehog** is a trickster who confuses Panther by twisting words and who escapes by making Panther touch his prickly quills. **Slow-Solid Tortoise** is also a trickster, playing a brilliant game of reverse psychology. By telling Panther that he will escape if he enters the water, he leads Panther to believe that he is lying. Through diligent effort, Hedgehog and Tortoise alter themselves into Armadillos, ensuring their safety even after Panther learns to distinguish a Hedgehog from a Tortoise.

Taffimai Metallumai (which means "Small-person-without-any-manners-who-ought-to-be-spanked"), called **Taffy**, is a Neolithic girl, but her habits of speech and her love of drawing are those of a modern child. Taffy is resourceful, determined, and clever in thinking of the idea of sending messages, but she is not a skillful artist, so her comically ambiguous first letter proves that words communicate better than pictures. She shows even more cleverness in coming up with the idea of representing sounds through pictures.

Pau Amma, the King Crab, stretches from Sarawak to Pahan, and he is taller than the smoke of three mountains. Impatient, inconsiderate, and selfish, he sneaks away before the Magician teaches him the proper way to play. He is filled with self-importance when he learns that he makes the oceans rise and fall. The Eldest Magician fittingly punishes his childishness and arrogance by making him small and by making his shell soft once a year. Because the Magician, the Man, and his daughter accept blame for allowing the Crab to create mischief, they grant gifts that enable him to survive: the ability to hide, the ability to live on land and in water, and the use of scissors for claws. **The Eldest Magician** is a mythic creator and a kindly parent figure. He punishes the Crab, but he is kind in allowing protective gifts. He also is kind in ordering the Fisherman of the Moon to create the tides that make it easier for the Man to paddle.

The Cat is a clever trickster when he bargains with the Woman. Wise and patient, he earns his first praise by remaining out of Woman's sight when he calms the baby. He uses his special talents of purring and catching mice to earn the next two words of praise, thus claiming a right to the domestic comforts of a cave, a place by the fire, and warm milk. Cat remains aloof, however, insisting that he walks alone and that all places are alike to him. His repeated statements of his proud independence are foolish, however, because they anger the Man and the Dog. Ironically, Man and the Dog limit Cat's domestic comfort by requiring that he always catch mice and treat babies kindly, and they qualify his freedom to go alone by insisting that they will throw things at him and chase him. **The Woman** is a magician. Her magic singing, which lures the wild animals to her cave, symbolizes the attractive power of the comfort-

able domestic life that she creates. Wise about what makes others happy, the Woman is also a trickster who offers what the wild animals desire in exchange for their service to her family. The Woman also shows her concern for others by insisting that Cat also strike bargains with Man and Dog.

In "The Butterfly That Stamped," **Suleiman-bin-Daoud**—Solomon son of David—is a ruler so wise that he understands everything, even insects. He is humble and becomes ashamed when he does anything out of pride or anger. Consequently, he can't use his magic powers to control his nine hundred and ninety-nine-argumentative wives. Suleiman-bin-Daoud has a sense of humor, and he delights in the butterfly's boast and in tricking the butterfly's wife into believing that her husband is powerful. Ironically, the wise ruler does not know that his first wife, **Queen Balkis the Most Beautiful**, is an even more accomplished trickster. Balkis is truly wise, understanding both men and women. Because she loves her husband and wants him to be happy, Balkis tricks the butterfly's wife into demanding that the butterfly stamp, and she tricks her husband into thinking that he is the one playing a trick that amuses him and helps the butterfly. Actually, her trick is an expression of love that makes Suleiman-bin-Daoud do what fear of shame earlier prevented: take control of his unruly wives.

Further Reading

Berger, Laura Standley, ed. *Twentieth-Century Children's Writers*. 4th ed. Detroit: St. James, 1995.

Bingham, Jane M., ed. *Writers for Children: Critical Studies of Major Authors since the Seventeenth Century*. New York: Scribner's, 1988.

Collier, Laurie, and Joyce Nakamura, eds. *Major Authors and Illustrators for Children and Young Adults*. Detroit: Gale Research, 1993.

Contemporary Authors New Revision Series. Vol. 33. Detroit: Gale Research, 1991.

Green, Roger Lancelyn. *Kipling and the Children*. London: Elek, 1965.

Sale, Roger. "Kipling's Boys." In *Fairy Tales and After: From Snow White to E. B. White*. Cambridge, MA: Harvard University Press, 1978.

Tompkins, J. M. S. *The Art of Rudyard Kipling*. London: Methuen, 1959.

Yesterday's Authors of Books for Children. Vol. 2. Detroit: Gale Research, 1978.

Zaidman, Laura M., ed. *British Children's Writers 1880-1914*. Vol. 141 of *Dictionary of Literary Biography*. Detroit: Gale Research, 1994.

E. L. Konigsburg

1930-, American author and illustrator

From the Mixed-Up Files of Mrs. Basil E. Frankweiler

(novel, 1967)

PLOT: Mrs. Basil E. Frankweiler, a rich widow, narrates this Newbery Medal winner in a letter to Saxonberg, her lawyer. Recounting the adventures of his grandchildren, she focuses on themes of identity.

Bored and feeling unappreciated, Claudia Kincaid decides to run away to teach her family a lesson in "Claudia appreciation." She plans carefully, enlisting her brother Jamie in the scheme because he has money. On a Wednesday, which is music lesson day, they leave home carrying instrument cases packed with clothes. After hiding on the school bus when the other students get off, they take a train to New York. They then walk to the Metropolitan Museum of Art because Jamie, who is rather tight with his cash, won't let Claudia spend money on a taxi. Following Claudia's plan, they successfully hide in the museum after it closes. By the time they go to sleep in an elegant sixteenth-century bed, they have stopped their former bickering and have begun to feel like a team.

The next day, Claudia tries to make their stay more productive by learning all about the museum. Upon seeing a small statue of an angel, however, Claudia is seized with the idea of proving that Michelangelo made it. On Saturday, Jamie and Claudia do their laundry and then do research on Michelangelo at the library. That night, pretending to be Sir James and Lady Claudia, they bathe in the museum's fountain. Claudia feels clean and elegant, whereas Jamie delights in the coins he collects. On Sunday, they find that the statue has been moved, but an impression of Michelangelo's mark remains on the velvet cover of its pedestal. Later, they are nearly

Konigsburg's illustration of Claudia, Jamie, and Mrs. Frankweiler in From the Mixed-Up Files of Mrs. Basil E. Frankweiler.

discovered when Jamie's class visits the museum. Claudia, hoping to be a hero, takes advantage of the situation, however, by having Jamie deliver a letter in which they outline their discovery. While waiting for a reply, they visit the United Nations building, where Claudia briefly considers wearing a sari as a way of appearing unique. When the children finally receive a reply to their letter, Claudia is crushed because the museum already knows about Michelangelo's mark. Both children then do something uncharacteristic. Claudia acts on a hunch, proposing a visit to Mrs. Frankweiler, who sold the statue, and Jamie buys train tickets without asking the price. They take the final leg of the journey in a taxi, and Jamie doesn't even protest the extra expense.

When they meet Mrs. Frankweiler, Jamie unwittingly reveals where they have been while Claudia is taking a bath. Nevertheless, Mrs. Frankweiler makes a deal. In return for information about their adventure, she gives them one hour to discover the statue's secret in her eccentric filing system. The children follow Claudia's planned approach to the search, but fail. Claudia then follows a hunch and finds Michelangelo's drawing of the statue. She weeps with joy. To preserve the secret, Mrs. Frankweiler tells the children that she will bequeath to them the drawing, provided they do not reveal its existence while she is alive. On the way home, Claudia and Jamie decide to adopt Mrs. Frankweiler as a grandmother because they realize she has unfulfilled maternal needs.

CHARACTERS: The narrator does not appear until the final two chapters, but she provides the key to interpreting the other characters. **Claudia Kincaid**, a pretty brunette, is one month under twelve years of age. As the oldest child and only girl in her family, Claudia feels the injustice of doing chores that her three brothers avoid. She is also bored with being a straight-"A" student and with the monotony of family life. Because she is a child of the affluent suburbs who loves beauty and elegance, Claudia does not care for uncomfortable adventures. Consequently, she runs away to the elegant Metropolitan Museum of Art when she decides to teach a lesson in "Claudia appreciation."

Claudia's main concern is her identity. Although she pretends to be the elegant Lady Claudia, she still plans their daily activities and insists on doing the laundry and bathing. She never feels homesick because she is well-adjusted and able to manage well on her own. Nevertheless, Claudia changes over the course of the story. First, the cautious Claudia bonds with the more adventurous Jamie so that, as she had planned, they complement each other. Claudia doesn't stop arguing with him, nor does she resist correcting his grammar to assert her superiority, but she does get along much better as the tale progresses. Second, Claudia changes her goals. Her quest to discover the origin of the Angel—she thinks that she resembles it—becomes a quest for self-knowledge. Claudia believes that discovering the statue's origin will make her a hero. She is,

however, naive in believing that she can learn enough about Michelangelo in an afternoon to teach museum experts.

Claudia realizes that she doesn't want to return home unless she can discover a way to assert her uniqueness. She eventually rejects superficial differences, such as changing clothes and wearing a sari, because she wants to change what is inside. She begins this change when she expresses her previously repressed creativity by taking her first unplanned action: the visit to Mrs. Frankweiler. During her subsequent interview with the widow, Claudia learns that running away did not change her deeply because she followed a routine, just as if she were at home. Claudia thus realizes that she can't run away from herself. Nevertheless, possessing Mrs. Frankweiler's secret does have an effect on her. After she discovers the statue's origin by following inspiration instead of careful plans, Claudia realizes that being a hero to oneself—experiencing self-assurance—is what makes her a true individual. No longer needing public recognition to feel special, she can return home contented.

Jamie Kincaid (whose given name is James) is nine. Claudia includes him in her adventure because he is a tightwad who has plenty of money. Jamie obtained most of it by cheating at cards, but he cheats because he loves to make all his activities as complicated as possible, not out of avarice. Jamie's penny-pinching habits prevent the luxury-loving Claudia from wasting their money and prematurely ending the adventure. In spite of his financial acumen, Jamie sometimes acts like a little boy. For example, he nearly reveals their presence to his class because he is angry that Claudia silences him by putting her hand over his mouth. More significantly, he takes away Claudia's bargaining tool when he accidentally reveals to Mrs. Frankweiler that they had stayed in the museum. Nevertheless, Jamie can be quick witted: when a janitor sees him in a washroom and asks where he came from, Jamie quickly responds that his mother told him that he came from heaven. He is the one who brings up the issue of homesickness, and he decides that they are too sure of themselves to feel it. Jamie does not change dramatically, but he does develop sympathy for others. When Claudia suggests that they visit Mrs. Frankweiler, Jamie buys the train ticket without asking the price, something he would never have done before. Furthermore, he doesn't say a word when Claudia spends the last of their money on a taxi ride. Finally, Jamie enthusiastically supports the idea of secretly adopting the lonely Mrs. Frankweiler as their grandmother.

Eighty-two-year-old **Mrs. Basil E. Frankweiler**, the narrator, is a wealthy widow and a reclusive eccentric. Wearing baroque pearls and a white lab coat, she conducts research that consists of reading newspapers and filing away items of interest in her numerous filing cabinets. Some critics see her only as a *deus ex machina* who provides a solution to Claudia's quest for the statue's secret. Others, however, suggest that she is a narrative device that generates ironic humor and clarifies the theme in ways that a child could not. Mrs. Frankweiler is also the archetypal wise old woman. She can interpret Claudia's actions and understand her character because they share many traits. Both, for example, love elegance, cleanliness, and comfort. As a wise woman, Mrs. Frankweiler knows that outward displays are not the key to individuality. She therefore gives Claudia the opportunity to discover and keep an important secret, something that can make her different on the inside.

Saxonberg, Mrs. Frankweiler's lawyer and the grandfather of Claudia and Jamie, never appears in the story, but he acts as a buffer between the reader and the narrator. Mrs. Frankweiler explicates one theme by suggesting that Saxonberg's interest in finances and family is unnecessarily narrow. When she urges him to go to the museum, she simultaneously urges the readers (the actual recipients of her words) to extend their interests and feelings.

Further Reading

Authors and Artists for Young Adults. Vol. 3. Detroit: Gale Research, 1990.

Berger, Laura Standley, ed. *Twentieth-Century Children's Writers*. 4th ed. Detroit: St. James, 1995.

Children's Literature Review. Vol. 1. Detroit: Gale Research, 1976.

Collier, Laurie, and Joyce Nakamura, eds. *Major Authors and Illustrators for Children and Young Adults*. Detroit: Gale Research, 1993.

Contemporary Authors New Revision Series. Vol. 39. Detroit: Gale Research, 1993.

De Montreville, Doris, and Donna Hill, eds. *Third Book of Junior Authors*. New York: H. W. Wilson, 1972.

Estes, Glenn E., ed. *American Writers for Children since 1960: Fiction*. Vol. 52 of *Dictionary of Literary Biography*. Detroit: Gale Research, 1986.

Hanks, Dorrel Thomas. *E. L. Konigsburg*. New York: Twayne, 1992.

Rees, David. "Your Arcan Novelist: E. L. Konigsburg." In *The Marble in the Water: Essays on Contemporary Writers of Fiction for Children and Young Adults*. Boston: Horn Book, 1980.

Something about the Author. Vol. 48. Detroit: Gale Research, 1987.

Gordon Korman

1963-, Canadian author

This Can't Be Happening at Macdonald Hall!

(novel, 1977)

PLOT: Comic-book slapstick punctuates every episode of this boarding school story. At Macdonald Hall, roommates Bruno Walton and Boots (Melvin) O'Neal have a well-deserved reputation as troublemakers. They fly the Malbonian flag on the school's flagpole, kidnap the mascot of a rival hockey team, and substitute the song "The Strip" for the national anthem. The headmaster, Mr. William Sturgeon, known as The Fish, therefore forbids them to see each other. Bruno moves in with Elmer Drimsdale, a boy obsessed with science projects, and Boots moves in with George Wexford-Smyth III, a rich hypochondriac. Bruno and Boots decide to make their new roommates complain about them so that The Fish will again let them room together. Bruno therefore frees Elmer's ant colony, and Boots uses George's rare stamps on a letter. The Fish orders restitution. Next, Bruno frightens Elmer with a borrowed pet skunk; Boots prints a phony newspaper article,

Bruno and Boots create all sorts of mayhem in Korman's first installment of their adventures, published in 1977.

paints spots on a sleeping George, and convinces him that he has a deadly disease. The Fish suspends their privileges.

Boots now decides to reverse their course and make Elmer and George look bad. Helped by Diane Grant and Cathy Burton, they frame Elmer and George as the perpetrators of a chaotic panty raid at Miss Scrimmage's Finishing School for Young Ladies. Mr. Sturgeon pretends to expel Elmer and George, forcing Bruno and Boots to confess. He orders them to repair Miss Scrimmage's damaged flower beds. Diane, Cathy, and the girls do the work. When Bruno and Boots then go to Mr. Sturgeon's house to report the job finished, Mildred Sturgeon becomes angry at her husband for making the boys work so hard. Bruno's next plan has them becoming good students, but Mr. Sturgeon attributes their scholastic success to the influence of their current roommates. That night, they rescue Francisco Diaz, the son of the Malbonian ambassador, from a bal-

loon that drifted into a tree. Chaos follows their heroism: Elmer declares that U.F.O.s have landed and Miss Scrimmage fires a shotgun blast, bringing the balloon's basket down on Elmer. Afterwards, Bruno, Boots, and Elmer receive medals, and a board member grants Bruno the reward of rooming with Boots.

Other "Bruno and Boots" novels are Go Jump in the Pool! *(1979)*, Beware the Fish! *(1980)*, The War with Mr. Wizzle *(1982)*, The Zucchini Warriors *(1988)*, and Macdonald Hall Goes Hollywood *(1991)*.

CHARACTERS: The characters are broadly sketched and tend to be eccentric. **Bruno Walton**, the more daring and mischievous of the protagonists, originates most of their capers. Although cool in plotting and executing his plans, he is impatient to see results, and he loves to witness the chaos he has caused. Bruno is casual about rules, believing that he creates his own privileges. He therefore repeatedly sneaks out of his room after lights-out. Bruno also lacks discipline, except in devising plots: he regularly sleeps in instead of eating breakfast, and he is frequently late for class. Bruno is sarcastic and flippant: when Elmer says that he is an entomologist, for instance, Bruno says that he always suspected that he was buggy. In spite of his contempt for authority and the inherent cruelty of some of his jokes, Bruno is honest: he immediately confesses his guilt when he thinks that Elmer is being expelled. He can also be sensitive. To prevent Elmer from becoming a laughing stock after the U.F.O. incident, he gets the Ambassador to give Elmer a medal. For the most part, however, Bruno is a clever opportunist. When the board chairman thinks of rewarding the students for the rescue, Bruno gets Elmer to ask for a new telescope and he himself asks to room with Boots.

Boots O'Neal (his real name is **Melvin**), Bruno's blonde companion, is much like him. Clever and capable of being a good student, Boots can devise ingenious plans, but he is nervous about their success and needs Bruno's constant reassurance. Boots is a skillful hockey player and captain of the team. Boots is popular, but he despises his given name and those, such as George, who use it. In spite of the cruelty of some tricks and his willingness to deceive authority figures, he is also essentially honest: he immediately confesses when he thinks that George is being expelled.

As far as the students are concerned, the headmaster, **Mr. William Sturgeon** (nicknamed "**The Fish**"), has no sense of humor. Whenever Bruno and Boots play a trick, they see stern disapproval in the headmaster's steely gray eyes. Behind closed doors, however, Mr. Sturgeon delights in triumphing over rival headmasters and in outwitting his mischievous charges. He basks in his hockey team's victory, for example, telling the opposing headmaster that his boys did not steal the mascot, even though he knows the truth. In dealing with Bruno and Boots, Mr. Sturgeon is no fool: when they frame Elmer and George, he outwits them, forcing them to confess. Mr. Sturgeon is, however, comical at home, where his wife, **Mildred Sturgeon**, rules. A tender-hearted woman easily taken in by Bruno and Boots, she makes her husband treat them more leniently.

Two eccentric students also figure prominently. **Elmer Drimsdale**, a tall, skinny boy with thick glasses and a crewcut, is obsessed by science, repeatedly claiming that every kind of science is his life. He has ants in a glass case, goldfish in the bathtub, and plants in the dresser. Although scientifically clever, he is emotionally immature, declaring girls are "icky." Improbably for one so intelligent and knowledgeable, Elmer becomes a bumbling fool who mistakes a balloon for a spaceship carrying aliens. Wealthy **George Wexford-Smyth III** is obsessed with money; he has a teletype in his room and avidly follows the stock market. He is also a hypochondriac who has a bathroom full of medicines and insists on disinfecting the entire room every day. Arrogant and pretentious, he scorns nicknames as vulgar, calling Boots by his given name. George becomes ludicrous when he believes that he has contracted a potentially fatal disease.

Two girls attending Miss Scrimmage's school have minor roles. **Diane Grant**, Bruno's favorite, lends him the pet skunk and lets him into the school so that he can stage the fake panty raid. **Cathy Burton** (her surname appears in a later volume), her

roommate and Boots's friend, sounds the fire alarm to create as much confusion as possible. After doing the boys' work for them, both girls offer Bruno and Boots wise advice about making Mr. Sturgeon feel guilty about the work they have done. **Miss Scrimmage**, their headmistress, is an absurdly comic foil to the cool Mr. Sturgeon: she panics at every disturbance, and her shotgun blasts away with comically destructive results.

Further Reading

Authors and Artists for Young Adults. Vol. 10. Detroit: Gale Research, 1993.

Berger, Laura Standley, ed. *Twentieth-Century Children's Writers.* 4th ed. Detroit: St. James, 1995.

Children's Literature Review. Vol. 25. Detroit: Gale Research, 1992.

Collier, Laurie, and Joyce Nakamura, eds. *Major Authors and Illustrators for Children and Young Adults.* Detroit: Gale Research, 1993.

Contemporary Authors New Revision Series. Vol. 34. Detroit: Gale Research, 1992.

Something about the Author. Vols. 41, 49, 81. Detroit: Gale Research, 1985, 1988, 1995.

Stott, Jon C., and Raymond E. Jones. *Canadian Books for Children: A Guide to Authors and Illustrators.* Toronto: Harcourt Brace Jovanovich Canada, 1988.

Robert Kraus

1925-, American cartoonist, illustrator, author, and publisher

Leo the Late Bloomer

(picture book, 1971; illustrated by José Aruego)

PLOT: A common problem, a child's comparatively slow development of skills, forms the theme of this simple, reassuring book. Leo the tiger is incompetent: unlike the other animals, he can't read, write, draw, or speak. He also makes a mess when he eats. Leo's mother reassures his worried father that Leo is merely a late bloomer. When Leo's father takes to watching for signs that Leo is blooming, his mother suggests patience. Although the father stops watch-

Leo finally does bloom in the conclusion of Kraus's Leo the Late Bloomer, *illustrated by José Aruego.*

ing, Leo still doesn't bloom. One day, in his own time, Leo blooms. Able to read, write, draw, and eat neatly, Leo proudly talks, telling his parents, "I made it!"

Leo the Late Bloomer Takes a Bath *(1981) is a sequel.*

CHARACTERS: Leo the tiger symbolizes the child who has lagged behind others in some or all phases of his physical and intellectual development. His pictorial placement on the page conveys his consequent feelings of inadequacy. In the initial descriptions of Leo's incompetence, he appears at the bottom of each page, with the competent animals physically above him to suggest their superiority. Even when he is with his parents, Leo seems sad: he appears on a page opposite them, lying with his back to them. After Leo's father ceases to watch him, Leo sometimes appears at the top of the page, but he is not central in any picture. When he finally blooms, however, Leo is pictured as much larger than he was in previous illustrations, suggesting a growth in his

confidence. He is also the central object on the page, indicating his new sense of self-worth. The fact that Leo blooms when the flowers bloom reinforces the idea that his development occurs at a natural time for him personally. His confidence and popularity are evident in subsequent pictures, several of which show Leo to be the center of attention while he accomplishes a formerly impossible task. Most significantly, the final picture contrasts with the earlier one of Leo with his parents. Whereas Leo formerly had his back to them, indicating shame and low self-esteem, he later cuddles with his mother while his father lovingly leans over them. Combined with his declaration of "I made it!" the last illustration indicates a triumphant sense of achievement and belonging.

Leo's loving parents represent contrasting attitudes. Leo's **father** is a worrier. He notices that his son is different and suspects a problem. Although his wife assures him that Leo will develop, the father remains anxious, closely observing his son for signs of normality. When advised that he is harming his son, he stops watching so closely. The picture in which he surreptitiously looks at his son from behind his chair suggests, however, that he remains uneasy. Leo's **mother** is a patient and wise woman. She understands that development differs with each person, that patience is necessary, and that anxious parents can retard normal development. By counseling her husband to have patience, she helps Leo to develop. As her loving embrace at the end indicates, she is proud of her son, who has confirmed her faith in his abilities.

Further Reading

Berger, Laura Standley, ed. *Twentieth-Century Children's Writers.* 4th ed. Detroit: St. James, 1995.

Collier, Laurie, and Joyce Nakamura, eds. *Major Authors and Illustrators for Children and Young Adults.* Detroit: Gale Research, 1993.

Contemporary Authors. Vols. 33-36. Detroit: Gale Research, 1978.

De Montreville, Doris, and Donna Hill, eds. *Third Book of Junior Authors.* New York: H. W. Wilson, 1972.

Something about the Author. Vols. 4, 65. Detroit: Gale Research, 1973, 1991.

Something about the Author Autobiography Series. Vol. 11. Detroit: Gale Research, 1991.

Joseph Krumgold

1908-1980, American novelist, screenwriter, director, and
producer

And Now Miguel

(novel, 1953)

PLOT: This Newbery Medal winner is a coming-of-age story. Its first-person narrator gains a satisfying identity as a part of the group and learns a lesson about his place in the universe. Miguel Chavez lives on a sheep farm near Taos, New Mexico, where he dreams of going with the men when they take the sheep into the Mountains of the Sangre de Cristo. Miguel even lies to Faustina and Pedro, his little sister and brother, by claiming that he has a plan that will enable him to go. During lambing, Miguel works at the important job of branding sheep. He feels that he is showing his grandfather (Padre de Chavez), his father, his older brothers (Blasito, known as Young Blas, and Gabriel), and his uncles Eli and Bonifacio that he can work like a man. Nevertheless, he knows that he must do something more before his father, Old Blas, will say he is ready to go to the mountains. Miguel's opportunity comes when he goes alone to rescue some stray sheep. Although the men praise his work, his father tells him that he is still not ready.

The disappointed Miguel then prays to San Ysidro to help arrange matters for him. Shortly afterwards, his father begins involving him in decisions about the upcoming shearing, and Miguel believes his prayers are being answered. When the Marquez brothers come for the shearing, Miguel works hard. Juan (Johnny) Marquez praises Miguel and even suggests that he eat dinner with the men. Miguel's father agrees. The next day, however, while helping Uncle Eli to stack fleeces, Miguel falls into the bag. His father accuses Miguel of playing games, crushing Miguel's hopes of joining the men's ranks. Nevertheless, he gets his wish when Gabriel receives a draft notice. Believing that his prayer to San Ysidro has harmed Gabriel, Miguel is miserable, but

Gabriel eases his brother's guilt by telling him that he is also at fault because he wished to see the ocean. After arguing about why San Ysidro won't fix matters, the two reconcile. Miguel shows his maturity by indicating that he will abandon selfish requests and will pray next year for things to work out as the saint desires. The next day, Miguel, now officially one of the Chavez men, journeys to the mountains.

CHARACTERS: Miguel, the narrator, is so obsessed with his position that his narrative brings to life only those people who directly affect his sense of identity. In his longing to go to the mountains so that he can become a man, twelve-year-old **Miguel Chavez** achieves social and spiritual maturity by the story's conclusion. Because manhood in his traditional culture depends upon the recognition and acceptance of other males, Miguel feels that he must constantly prove himself, especially to his father. To do so, however, he must fit in as part of the group while still calling attention to himself as an important individual. Miguel fits in as a tireless worker at important jobs during lambing and shearing. Consequently, the men temporarily recognize him as worthy of dining with them. Miguel also demonstrates his worth in a more dramatic fashion when he goes alone after the stray lambs. To make this a hard deed worthy of being a rite of passage, he even leaves a stone in his shoe. In spite of his physical efforts, Miguel has weaknesses that make it difficult for him to change his father's mind. He dreams about how conversations will go, but he is unable to express his complex feelings and ideas clearly. Miguel's reactions are also sometimes inappropriate. He is embarrassed and becomes silent after he falls into the fleece bag, so his father accuses him of playing. He also makes people repeat their words of praise, a habit that, ironically, makes him look childish and uncertain at the very moment that people are accepting him as a man.

Krumgold has said that Miguel "must learn that the rewards of maturity come through believing in a wisdom far more universal than his own." At first,

Miguel is completely absorbed with his own identity. After he lies to the younger children, he does everything possible to earn the respect of the adults. When he fails to achieve his goal through his own efforts, he adds a spiritual element to his plan. Although he is sometimes pragmatic, such as when he thinks that some people get more out of a fiesta than prayer, he prays that San Ysidro will arrange matters so that he can go to the mountains. When Miguel later realizes that he will go only because Gabriel can't, he gains a more mature perspective both psychologically and spiritually. He feels guilty that his prayer, an expression of a selfish wish, may cause Gabriel harm. Next, he realizes that human wisdom alone can't conceive of all the consequences of a wish. Finally, he displays spiritual maturity by promising that in the future he will not pray for selfish reasons but only for what the saint believes to be right. At this point, the self-absorbed boy becomes a man. The social change to manhood is signaled by his journey to the mountain. The psychological change, however, is underlined by the fact that Miguel delays the customary carving of his own name on a mountain tree. Instead, he keeps his promise to his absent brother and finishes carving the name of Gabriel's girlfriend.

Psychologically, Miguel stands somewhere between his two brothers. On one extreme is nineteen-year-old **Gabriel Chavez**, who easily gets everything he wants. Gabriel is a star athlete, an accomplished dancer, and the president of the Future Farmers. As well as being a role model, Gabriel promotes Miguel's spiritual maturity by discussing the consequences of prayers and wishes. Gabriel forces Miguel to think for himself and to recognize the selfishness of his prayers. Gabriel is important to the spiritual theme because he connects Miguel's future prayers to the words of "The Lord's Prayer": "thy will be done." At the other extreme, is seven-year-old **Pedro Chavez**. Unlike Miguel, Pedro is satisfied with whatever he has. He is also content to sit and watch, instead of joining in with the work. For Miguel, he represents a childish absence of ambition and longing. As a person in his own right, Pedro admires Miguel for his supposed plan and teases him when he learns the truth. Three-year-old **Faustina Chavez**, the youngest in the family, is the only prominent female. Her habit of making up words comes to represent the childishness of imposing without understanding a personal interpretation of the world.

Adult males are understandably important to the story, serving as Miguel's role models. **Old Blas**, Miguel's father, is a quiet, inarticulate man who has trouble understanding his son's feelings because he believes Miguel is always trying to do two things at once. For example, he can't understand why Miguel needs to be recognized for doing jobs that the men do automatically. He also fails to see that Miguel is not playing a game when he falls into the bag of fleeces. Although he plays the role of an antagonist, Old Blas is not cruel. He is kind when he makes Miguel feel important by giving him significant tasks. Old Blas comes into opposition with Miguel because he places the welfare of the group ahead of any individual's desires. **Grandfather**, known as **Padre de Chavez** (Father of the Chavez's), is almost eighty. Although he no longer goes to the mountains, nothing on the farm is done without his help. Grandfather introduces the spiritual themes. He says that, even though he has worked hard for the family, God is responsible for their well-being. Furthermore, he views the life of the shepherd in moral terms, saying that it is a sin to let living things die. These views contrast with those of the two uncles. **Uncle Bonifacio**, a man who smiles but never laughs, pragmatically attributes the family's success to the wisdom of grandfather in obtaining a grazing permit. Bonifacio's description of the beauties of life in the mountains whets Miguel's desire to go there. **Uncle Eli** is a foil who provokes grandfather's spiritual explanations when he declares that the work of a shepherd is only a job and that the life or death of sheep has only economic significance. Miguel's oldest brother, **Blasito Chavez**, often called **Young Blas**, is the least prominent male. He is the first to praise Miguel when he returns with the stray sheep and therefore indicates that the men recognize Miguel's abilities. **Juan Marquez** (sometimes called Johnny), an itinerant sheep shearer, is the only important outsider. He contrasts with Old Blas in his easy, good-natured recognition of Miguel.

Instead of blandly accepting that Miguel is doing a necessary job, he praises his work and suggests that Miguel join the men at the table. He is, therefore, the first one to acknowledge formally that Miguel is a man.

Onion John

(novel, 1959)

PLOT: Like his first novel, Krumgold's second Newbery Medal winner is a coming-of-age story. Its first-person narrator becomes mature and independent, and his father learns to respect his son's individuality. Following a baseball game in which he both commits a major error and hits the winning run, Andrew J. Rusch, Jr., becomes friends with eccentric Onion John Claiblin. To his surprise, Andy discovers that he can understand John's peculiar way of talking. Andy and Eechee (Dick) Ries help John with a rain procession to end a drought in Serenity, New Jersey, but John insists that they made a mistake in the ceremony. Although Andy's father argues against superstition, Andy believes in John because it rains after John's second ceremony. When Halloween comes, Andy invites Onion John to a party with Eechee, Bo Hemmendinger, and Bitsy Schwarz. The group becomes so intrigued with John's ceremonies for warding off spirits and making gold that the boys fail to meet their fathers at a banquet. Afterward, Andy realizes that his father is opposed to his friendship with Onion John.

Nevertheless, Andy's father soon insists that he is also John's friend. After seeing the decrepit state of John's house, he even arranges for the entire town to join together to build John a house in a single day. Although he tries to act in the "civilized" manner that Andy's father expects, John insists that a curse is on the house and that only a special ceremony can prevent disaster. Before he has the chance to perform it, however, he accidentally burns down the house. While John is hospitalized, Andy's father decides that the town should rebuild the house. He also reveals that, in spite of Andy's opposition, he

In an illustration by Symeon Shimin, Onion John says good-bye to Andrew in the conclusion of Krumgold's Newbery Medal winner.

has arranged a summer job for him. Mrs. Rusch tries to make Andy understand that his father is trying to make his own frustrated dreams come true through his son, but Andy decides to run away. Therefore, when he learns that John has escaped from the hospital, Andy finds him and convinces him that they both must leave Serenity. That night, however, John tells Andy that he is going away alone because Andy has grown up. At the insistence of Andy's mother, Mr. Rusch then agrees that his son can decide his own future. He also supports Ernie Miller, the newspaper editor, when he argues that the town should not force its will on John by rebuilding the house. Weeks later, during the town's fish drive, Andy tells his father that he wants to be like him. While they talk, smoke from a fire John has lit to drive away evil spirits blows toward Serenity.

CHARACTERS: The characters establish differing ideas about the value of independence and personal identity, culminating in a vision of the ideal relationship between father and son. **Onion John Claiblin** is a six-foot-three immigrant whose nickname comes from his habit of eating onions the way most people eat apples. His surname, which the town learns twenty years after his arrival, only approximates his actual name and was given to him by immigration authorities. John is an eccentric. He has a mustache and wears two coats, heavy sneakers, and a pointed knitted hat. He always carries a bulging burlap bag and a spade. He performs odd jobs for the same fee that was the standard when he first arrived in America and prowls the town dump for useful items. John lives in a one-room house he built from stones. It contains four bathtubs, none used for bathing, and a picture of Saint Stepan, below which candles constantly burn. John has a great knowledge of the history of superstitions and believes in magic and spirits. He therefore follows some odd practices, including tying stones around an apple tree to shame it into growing bigger apples, performing a ceremony in which he symbolically dies in order to bring rain, and trying to make gold. John's speech is so peculiar that no one, except Andy, understands him.

When Mr. Rusch arranges for a new house, Onion John tries to fit in by acting like everyone else. He even refuses an onion for breakfast. After he accidentally burns down his house, however, he decides that he can't change who he is. When Andy convinces him that the town will force him to accept a new house, Onion John agrees that he must leave Serenity, even though he is happy there. He will not take Andy with him, however, because he realizes that Andy has lost his belief in magical rites. Onion John refuses to be patronized by those who think they know what is best for him and heroically insists on determining his own identity. He thereby inspires Andy's parents to allow their son to decide his own future. Ironically, John fumigates the town at just the moment that Andy and his father honestly confront each other.

Andrew J. Rusch, Jr., who goes by **Andy**, is the narrator and is central to the identity theme, which he introduces when he fails to recognize himself in a newspaper picture. Although he subsequently devel-

ops a public identity as a star baseball player, Andy is a friend to Onion John and a reincarnation of the dreams his father once had for himself. John first thinks of Andy as a magician because he is the only one who can understand his speech. Andy is kind to John, going along with his magical rituals because he believes that they can do no harm and will make John happy. When the rituals apparently get some results, however, Andy comes to believe in them. While he likes John, Andy admires his father and plans on working in the hardware store with him. Still, Andy feels torn between John and his father. He wants to be close to both, but he opposes his father because he believes that John has a right to refuse another house. When his father insists on the new house and also his own plans for his son, however, Andy asserts his identity by trying to run away. Although the act seems one of childish desperation, it leads to personal growth because Andy is committed to the truth. (Earlier, he corrected a newspaper reporter, saying that not he but his father was John's best friend.) He also got John to agree to let him come with him by confessing that he wants to run away for his own reasons, not John's. Therefore, when John questions him to show why they can't run away together, Andy admits that he considers John's magic ways to be foolish. In doing so, he acknowledges that he has grown, that he accepts his father's "sensible" view of the world. Nevertheless, Andy still doesn't accept his father's plans for him to become an engineer. During the fish drive, he therefore becomes an ideal son by telling his father how much he admires and wants to be like him.

Andrew J. Rusch, Sr., Andy's father, considers himself a failure even though he owns a hardware store and is president of the Serenity Rotary Club. Having failed to become an engineer, he tries to make his son follow his dream. For much of the story, he represents the voice of scientific reason and opposes John's magic and superstition. In a sense, he enters into competition with John for the affection and respect of his son. Although John accepts Mr. Rusch as his best friend, Mr. Rusch is actually patronizing: he humors John about his attempts at goldmaking and about other beliefs. He doesn't do so to be cruel but because he honestly believes people should help to direct the lives of those who are less capable. He thus insists on building John a "civilized" house and on changing him so that he fits into the twentieth-century community. Similarly, Mr. Rusch tells his son that he should study science and arranges a job for him that will advance his scientific prospects. Mr. Rusch gives up trying to push Andy into the future, however, after seeing himself through John's eyes as a man who would banish his son to the moon. He then shows pragmatism, courage, and wisdom by changing his mind about building John a new house and forcing Andy into a career he might not want. Ironically, his son then provides him with a new identity as an ideal father: Andy calls him a great man and indicates that he wants to be like the man his father is now, not the man he failed to become.

Three minor characters are significant to the story. **Mrs. Rusch**, Andy's mother, provides the background information about her husband's failed dreams. She thereby enables both Andy and the reader to sympathize with him. Mrs. Rusch becomes forceful when Andy tries to run away. She quietly insists that Andy will choose his own course and, therefore, gets her husband to accept Andy's independence. **Eechee Ries** (whose real name is Dick), Andy's friend and teammate, is a talkative boy who habitually spreads news all over town. When he shows no interest in telling others that John left because both Andy and his father said that fumigating was foolish, he forces Andy and his father to overcome their guilt and accept each other. **Ernie Miller**, editor of the *Lamp*, Serenity's newspaper, initiates the identity theme because his paper doesn't print pictures in which the people are recognizable. He opposes Mr. Rusch by arguing that the town should not force its values on John by rebuilding his house. His argument is that no one should, even out of kindness, ignore another's rights. When Andy agrees with him and realizes that, for the first time in his life, he is not on his father's side, he has taken an important step toward growing up.

Further Reading

Berger, Laura Standley, ed. *Twentieth-Century Young Adult Writers.* 1st ed. Detroit: St. James, 1994.

Collier, Laurie, and Joyce Nakamura, eds. *Major Authors and Illustrators for Children and Young Adults.* Detroit: Gale Research, 1993.

Contemporary Authors New Revision Series. Vol. 7. Detroit: Gale Research, 1982.

Contemporary Literary Criticism. Vol. 12. Detroit: Gale Research, 1980.

Fuller, Muriel, ed. *More Junior Authors.* New York: H. W. Wilson, 1963.

Something about the Author. Vols. 1, 48. Detroit: Gale Research, 1971, 1987.

Robert Lawson

1892-1957, American artist, illustrator, and author

Rabbit Hill

(animal fantasy, 1944)

PLOT: This Newbery Medal winner celebrates cooperation among living creatures. The animals on Rabbit Hill in rural Connecticut are elated by news that New Folks are moving into the old house. The animals, who have known only hard times for several years, hope that these Folks will plant a garden. Mother Rabbit, however, also worries about new dangers. Father Rabbit suggests that they invite lonely Uncle Analdus for a visit because he might give them advice, so they send their son, Little Georgie, to get him. Although Little Georgie becomes so absorbed in making up a song that he is almost caught by a hound, he brings the elderly bachelor to Rabbit Hill. Along the way, animals and humans alike unwittingly testify to the unity of life by humming Little Georgie's song about the coming of New Folks.

When the Folks arrive, Father Rabbit declares them to be gentlefolk because they slammed on their brakes when he jumped in front of their car. Gray Fox praises the Man because he remained calm

Lawson illustrated his Rabbit Hill, *about country animals who learn to get along with the New Folks.*

when Fox came upon him unexpectedly. Porkey the Woodchuck praises the Lady for throwing a rock at a dog that had cornered him. Phewie the Skunk is pleased with the abundance of uncovered "garbidge." Willie Fieldmouse learns their kindness firsthand when the Folk rescue him from drowning in the rain barrel. Tim McGrath and Louie Kernstawk, however, don't understand why their employers don't trap or poison the animals, especially after Mole ruins the newly prepared lawn.

Trouble comes shortly after the animals divide up rights to the crops in the garden. Little Georgie is hit by a car, the Man and Lady take him away, and the animals grieve his loss. When the animals learn that Little Georgie is alive, Uncle Analdus angrily claims that the Folk are torturing him and using him as a hostage to protect the garden. On Midsummer's Eve, however, Little Georgie, his broken leg mended, rejoins the animals. The animals discover that the Folks have built a statue of St. Francis of Assisi with the inscription "There is enough for all." Fresh vegetables on a ledge in front of it provide the

animals with a feast. After Red Buck leads them in a solemn procession around the garden, he declares that it is forbidden ground. Later, Tim McGrath and Louie Kernstawk are unable to understand why the unprotected garden of the Folks thrives, whereas predators attack other gardens.

CHARACTERS: Few of the many animal characters are developed in depth, but all successfully combine natural and human traits. **Little Georgie Rabbit** is the most beloved animal on Rabbit Hill. He is cheerful and enthusiastic, traits he reveals by composing a song celebrating the arrival of New Folks. He therefore contrasts with both his mother and Uncle Analdus. His circular journey to fetch Uncle Analdus is a quest that tests his competence. He nearly fails when boredom makes him forget the survival lessons his father has taught him, but he is mature enough to eventually recall what he learned, and his extraordinary physical abilities also help him survive. Thus, he leaps a brook that not even his father could jump. After he recovers from his injuries from the car, Little Georgie becomes the agent for revealing the genuine goodness of the Folks, whom some of the animals regard with suspicion. **Father Rabbit** speaks with a pompous eloquence that comes from his background as a Southern Gentleman. Although he bores others by repeatedly talking about Bluegrass Country until he is stopped, he is no fool. When beckoned by business, such as instructing his son in how to undertake a journey safely, he has no time for social conversations. He is wise and considerate, as he shows when instructing his son and when trying to convince Porkey to move out of his home near the house. **Mother Rabbit (Molly)** is defined by a single characteristic: she worries excessively. **Uncle Analdus** adds humor and, by negative example, illustrates the need for cooperation and trust. An elderly and messy bachelor who reeks, possibly from tobacco, he seems at first to be a wise elder. He thus teaches Little Georgie tricks in survival, and he points out to the other animals that Mr. Muldoon, the cat owned by the Folks, is so old that he poses absolutely no threat to them. Later, however, he is an obstacle to harmony because his pessimism about the Folks turns into distrust, obstinacy, and bitterness. Uncle Analdus thus creates conflict when he convinces many animals that the Folks are evil and turns them against both the Folks and those who don't share his judgment.

Two characters have a touching, symbiotic relationship. In digging his tunnels, **Mole** provides Willie Fieldmouse with easy access to roots. Mole, who deeply loves Willie, is so enraged when he believes that the humans have harmed his friend that he destroys their lawn, ironically revealing the tolerance of the Man. **Willie Fieldmouse** pays back the blind Mole by acting as his eyes. He also spies on the Folks and reports what he learns. Willie is generous and grateful. After the Folks save him, he tries unsuccessfully to get the animals to reserve part of the garden for the house. On Midsummer's Eve, the ecstatic Willie again acts as eyes, describing for both the Mole and the reader the statue of Saint Francis and its inscription.

Porkey the Woodchuck is a stubborn creature of limited understanding. Although warned by Father Rabbit that his home is unsafe, he insists that he will never move. His stubbornness ironically reveals the kindness of the Man, who refuses to destroy Porkey's home in a wall or to allow him to be killed. Porkey nevertheless represents the rift between animals and people because he speaks for the animals who refuse to allot the Folks a share during division of the garden. **Phewie the Skunk** is a comical contrast to the gentlemanly Father Rabbit. Thus, he speaks in a lower-class manner about his passion for "garbidge." From his perspective, the Folks are not gentle people because they protect animals but because they make their garbage accessible. His friend **Gray Fox**, the only other meat-eating animal, supports the positive estimation of the Folks by reporting how the Man calmly accepted his presence. **Red Buck** brings out the nobility within the animals. Realizing that the Folks have provided them with food, he returns the favor by getting the animals to leave the garden alone.

The Folks are idealized respecters of nature. **The Man** is a genial intellectual. He remains unfazed by Mole's attack on his lawn. He is so concerned about the small animals that he even erects a sign warning drivers about them. Although the workmen consider him to be crazy, the Man shows a deep understanding of nature's ways: by providing for the animals, he ensures that they have no need to attack his garden. **The Lady** is similarly respectful of nature. She competently protects Porkey by throwing a stone at an attacking dog. She nurses both Willie and Little Georgie, and she makes sure that her cat, Mr. Muldoon, doesn't attack Willie. The locals comically contrast with the New Folks. **Tim McGrath**, the man who tends to the fields, lawn, and gardens, is an anti-intellectual who believes that books rot the mind. He can't understand why the Man won't permit him to trap or poison Mole. He is also incapable, however, of understanding why the garden of the Folks is untouched, whereas his suffers from constant raids. **Louie Kernstawk**, the mason, also does not understand why the Man would leave unrestored a section of a wall that houses Porkey. Nevertheless, he is neither as anti-intellectual as Tim nor as ready to believe that the Folks have a good garden because of beginner's luck.

Further Reading

Berger, Laura Standley, ed. *Twentieth-Century Children's Writers*. 4th ed. Detroit: St. James, 1995.

Bingham, Jane M., ed. *Writers for Children: Critical Studies of Major Authors since the Seventeenth Century*. New York: Charles Scribner's Sons, 1988.

Cech, John, ed. *American Writers for Children 1900-1960*. Vol. 22 of *Dictionary of Literary Biography*. Detroit: Gale Research, 1983.

Children's Literature Review. Vol. 2. Detroit: Gale Research, 1976.

Collier, Laurie, and Joyce Nakamura, eds. *Major Authors and Illustrators for Children and Young Adults*. Detroit: Gale Research, 1993.

Contemporary Authors. Vol. 137. Detroit: Gale Research, 1992.

Haycraft, Howard, and Stanley J. Kunitz, eds. *The Junior Book of Authors*. 2nd ed. New York: H. W. Wilson, 1951.

Jones, Helene L. *Robert Lawson: Illustrator*. Boston: Little, Brown, 1972.

Something about the Author. Vol. 20. Detroit: Gale Research.

Yesterday's Authors of Books for Children. Vol. 2. Detroit: Gale Research, 1978.

Munro Leaf

1905-1976, American author and illustrator

The Story of Ferdinand the Bull

(picture book, 1936; illustrated by Robert Lawson)

PLOT: A study of a determined individualist, *The Story of Ferdinand the Bull* follows the ironic non-adventures of its title character. At the beginning of the story, Ferdinand is a young bull who would rather smell the flowers or quietly sit in the shade of a cork tree than run about or butt heads with other bulls. Ferdinand's mother, reassured that he is not lonely, allows him to be happy in his gentle solitude. Years pass, and Ferdinand grows up big and strong. One day, men come to select bulls for the fights in Madrid. All the bulls except Ferdinand clamor to be chosen, so they run, snort, and butt heads to create a fierce impression. Ferdinand, however, retires to his cork tree, where, unfortunately, he sits on a bumblebee, which stings him. The startled Ferdinand jumps, snorts, and butts the ground as if crazy. The men, admiring his ferocity, choose him to fight in the ring. In Madrid, the Banderilleros, the Picadores, and the Matador tremble at the sight of Ferdinand the Fierce. When he enters the bull ring, though, Ferdinand sits down to smell the flowers in the ladies' hair. Nothing induces him to battle, so the angry bullfighters send him home, where he happily resumes sitting under his favorite cork tree, quietly enjoying the flowers.

CHARACTERS: The development of Ferdinand's character depends on irony: the reader understands elements of Ferdinand's behavior that the men do not realize. **Ferdinand the Bull** differs from other bulls in his environment. Lawson's pictures of him as a youngster establish Ferdinand's dreamy-eyed appreciation of beauty as he inspects a butterfly or lies amid the flowers. The silhouettes of Ferdinand sitting in a nearly human position beneath his favorite cork tree provide a memorable contrast with the conventional young bulls, who rush about and engage in much more aggressive activities. When Ferdinand become a full-grown bull, his large, muscular body belies his gentle nature. While the men from Madrid are too far away to see the bee that stings Ferdinand into temporarily acting so fiercely, Lawson's illustration clearly shows Ferdinand in the foreground with a distinctly startled expression. The men in the background jump with delight, however, because they think they have found the ferocious competitor they seek.

From the point at which Ferdinand reaches maturity until his entrance into the bull ring, Lawson places buzzards in the picture. These somber symbols remind the reader that an early death is the inevitable end for a fighting bull. We are told that the Banderilleros and Picadores are supposed to stick the bull with their weapons to incite him to fight. Although there are no pictures to illustrate this, it is reasonable to assume from the text, which states that Ferdinand "wouldn't fight and be fierce no matter what they did," that they do stick him. The bull who was driven crazy when surprised by a bee thus bravely and quietly endures deliberate tortures to remain true to his character. By smelling the flowers and refusing to fight, Ferdinand saves his life and preserves his integrity. Munro Leaf said, "The bee became a mechanical device for the book to have a plot," but it also functions as an important device for appreciating Ferdinand's brave steadfastness of character. Whether he represents the artist, the pacifist, or simply the person who is different from the crowd, Ferdinand shows that happiness comes only by remaining true to one's self.

Ferdinand's **mother** is a foil to the men from Madrid and the Matador. As a good parent, she worries that her son is not associating with the other bulls, but after talking to him she understands that he is not lonely and lets him live the life he chooses. On the other hand, the **Matador**, the most important of the men from Madrid, most obviously represents their limitations. He is proud man, but he is frightened by the sight of Ferdinand, because he does not realize the bull's true nature. The flowers thrown by the women and the flowers stitched on his cape ironically connect him to Ferdinand, yet unlike Ferdinand, who embraces life, the Matador lives to deal out death. He loses his identity and exits the arena in shame when Ferdinand refuses to be bullied into fighting.

Further Reading

Berger, Laura Standley, ed. *Twentieth-Century Children's Writer's.* 4th ed. Detroit: St. James, 1995.

Children's Literature Review. Vol. 25. Detroit: Gale Research, 1992.

An illustration by Robert Lawson of Ferdinand from **The Story of Ferdinand the Bull.**

Haycraft, Howard, and Stanley J. Kunitz, eds. *The Junior Book of Authors.* 2nd ed. New York: H. W. Wilson, 1951.

Something about the Author. Vol. 20. Detroit: Gale Research, 1980.

Madeleine L'Engle

1918-, American novelist

A Wrinkle in Time

(science fiction/fantasy novel, 1962)

PLOT: Winner of the 1963 Newbery Medal, *A Wrinkle in Time* is a complex quest novel that combines elements from science fiction, fantasy, family problem novels, the Bible, and mythology. Despite the novel's intellectual complexity, its plot is relatively simple. Meg Murry and her companions attempt to rescue her father, who is a prisoner on another planet. Each of the planets Meg visits during her quest marks a stage in her personal development.

At the beginning of the novel, Meg Murry is dissatisfied. Her twin brothers, Sandy and Dennys, happily fit into the community, but Meg and Charles Wallace, her youngest brother, are outsiders. Both are brilliant, but Charles Wallace has a reputation for being a moron, while Meg has difficulty in school, where she constantly fights with other children. Furthermore, Meg's mother is a beautiful scientist, but Meg feels ugly and hates being different. At the heart of her problems is the absence of her father, who has mysteriously disappeared. Meg's only friend is Calvin O'Keefe, a star basketball player who gets along with others by hiding his intelligence.

Meg's adventures begin with the arrival of three old ladies who are actually supernatural beings in disguise. Mrs. Whatsit, Mrs. Who, and Mrs. Which "tesser" (a form of travel that wrinkles space and time) Meg, Charles Wallace, and Calvin into space to find Meg's father. They stop on the planet Uriel, where Mrs. Whatsit transforms herself into a creature resembling a centaur and shows them a black cloud circling Earth. Meg then understands that her quest involves a battle between good and evil. After narrowly avoiding accidental destruction on a two-dimensional planet, they arrive at a gray planet in Orion's Belt. In the cave of the Happy Medium, Meg stares into a crystal ball and receives a further vision of the black cloud and of Mrs. Whatsit, in the form of a star, giving up her life to push back the darkness. Meg also shows significant growth and compassion when, following a vision of Calvin's loveless home, she comforts Calvin by holding his hand.

Meg confronts evil directly on Camazotz, a planet of extreme conformity. The three helpers do not accompany Meg, Charles Wallace, and Calvin, but they give them "gifts" of advice and a pair of special glasses to help them. The children locate the building where Meg's father is held, but Charles Wallace falls under the hypnotic spell of the Man with Red Eyes, the spokesperson for the planet's evil ruler, IT. Nevertheless, Meg uses her special glasses

and frees her father from a transparent column. To save themselves from Charles Wallace's fate, Meg, her father, and Calvin hastily tesser to another planet.

They arrive on the spring-like planet of Ixchel. Meg is cold and paralyzed, a condition symbolizing emotional and spiritual death. Aunt Beast, a loving creature without eyes, treats Meg as an infant and nurses her back to physical and spiritual health. Meg is thus symbolically reborn as a person who understands and accepts herself. As a result, Meg is no longer angry that her father couldn't make everything instantly better. She also appreciates her own individuality, which caused her so much pain on Earth. Armed with her new self-knowledge, she agrees to go alone to Camazotz to rescue Charles Wallace. When she finally confronts IT, a disembodied brain, Meg realizes that she possesses one strength that IT lacks: love. By concentrating on her love, she breaks the spell holding Charles Wallace. Along with Calvin and their father, the siblings tesser back to Earth for a joyful reunion with their mother.

Other books in the "Time Fantasy" series are A Wind in the Door *(1973),* A Swiftly Tilting Planet *(1978),* A House Like a Lotus *(1984),* Many Waters *(1986), and* An Acceptable Time *(1989).*

CHARACTERS: The majority of the characters in *A Wrinkle in Time* are highly unusual or eccentric. These characters symbolize sophisticated ideas about conformity and individuality, appearance and reality, dependence and personal responsibility, logic and love.

Meg Murry (Meg is short for Margaret) develops from a self-centered and alienated adolescent into a person who respects herself and loves others. Meg initially thinks of herself as a "monster" because she has braces on her teeth, thick glasses, and unruly mouse-brown hair. Although she is very bright, Meg is failing at school. She is rude to her teachers and constantly fights with classmates who make comments about her family. Meg hates herself for being an "oddball" and wishes to be a different person. She believes that only the return of her father can make things better. Meg's mother, however, tells her that the solution is for her to "plow through some more time." Meg's lengthy adventures enable her to do so without growing older. Tessering leads Meg to numerous experiences that help her to mature, while permitting Meg to return to Earth at about the same time as she left.

Meg's adventures make her self-reliant, allow her to appreciate her individuality, and give her emotional and spiritual strength. At first Meg is excessively dependent on others, frequently attempting to hold hands. She depends on her father so much that she becomes filled with resentment when he fails to solve their problems. Before she can be independent, Meg has to understand herself and others. From Meg's initial judgment of her own reflection in the mirror as that of a monster, references to seeing and glasses symbolize Meg's need to replace superficial vision with genuine insight. When she arrives on Ixchel, she is like a frozen stone statue, a condition symbolizing emotional coldness. After she is emotionally and spiritually reborn through the love of Aunt Beast, she accepts herself as a loving individual. She shows mature insight when she agrees to rescue her brother: "I see, see, I understand, it has to be me. There isn't anyone else." Although Meg confronts IT alone, her three helpers give her words of encouragement that suggest that Meg needs the "theological" virtues of faith, hope, and charity. Because Meg must puzzle out the meaning of their words, these gifts test and develop her maturity. Meg succeeds when she realizes that her unique strength—which conformity would suppress—is her ability to love. In asserting her individuality and her spiritual insight, Meg becomes the archetypal nurturing female hero. Without resorting to violence, she had freed her father; now she delivers her brother, bringing him back to life through her love. Meg begins the novel consumed by self-hatred, but she grows into a character who loves both herself and others.

Whereas Meg represents the power of the heart, **Charles Wallace**, her five-year-old brother, repre-

sents the limitations of intellect. Charles Wallace is a "sport," a person significantly different from other humans. He can communicate without words and sense what other people are feeling. Although he is a genius, Charles Wallace hides the truth about himself to get along with others, but because he did not speak until he was almost four, people call him a moron. Charles Wallace has significant faults. When he is upset, he becomes indignant. On Camazotz, he shows his immaturity when he resorts to violence for the first time in his life after the Man with the Red Eyes makes him angry. Most significantly, Charles Wallace is full of intellectual arrogance. He believes that he can deliberately go into IT's mind and return unharmed. After he fails, Charles Wallace has glazed eyes that symbolize his lack of spiritual insight. His actions suggest that mindless conformity destroys the ability to love and that intelligence alone is not enough to secure individuality.

The other members of Meg's family have only minor roles. **Sandy** and **Dennys**, her ten-year-old twin brothers, seem frustratingly average to Meg. They get along with everyone, leading Meg to believe that differences cause problems. Their most important thematic role is to suggest that Meg will not be fulfilled until she finds a "happy medium." **Mrs. Murry**, Meg's mother, is a scientist. Her extraordinary beauty makes Meg unhappy with her own plainness. Mrs. Murry conceals her sadness and anxiety from her children, thus contributing to the theme of deceptive appearances. Meg discovers the truth only when she looks into the Happy Medium's crystal ball and sees her mother crying. Like Meg, **Mr. Murry** wears thick glasses, but he does not lack insight. A scientist with several doctoral degrees, he teaches Meg valuable lessons. First, by admitting that he is fallible, he helps Meg recognize that parents can't solve every problem. Next, by using phrases from the Bible that speak of being sent for a purpose, he indicates that true heroism sometimes requires setting aside individual goals.

Meg's friend, fourteen-year-old **Calvin O'Keefe**, resembles Charles Wallace. He is a sport who senses unspoken things, and he hides his true brilliance. Instead, he uses his skills as a basketball player to make people accept him. Calvin is tall and skinny, with orange hair, freckles, and oddly blue eyes. His ill-fitting, frayed clothing indicates poverty. Known as a skillful communicator, Calvin often cites such authorities as Lincoln, Roosevelt, and the Bible. Calvin's most important contribution to the novel's theme comes when he tells Meg that she does not realize how lucky she is to have a loving family. Abused and neglected by his alcoholic mother, Calvin declares that the love in the Murry household has made him feel as though he were born again. His speech foreshadows Meg's need to be reborn through love and her success in using love to save Charles Wallace.

Meg has four nonhuman helpers. Three appear to her as eccentric old ladies but perform the roles of spiritual guides, or of guardian angels and messengers of God. Like helper figures in fairy tales, these ladies bestow useful gifts and then withdraw so that the heroine can accomplish the final task alone. Their strange names suggest that their major role is to make Meg ask fundamental questions. **Mrs. Whatsit** wears strange clothes that make her gender difficult to guess. Because she resembles a bag lady, she illustrates that appearances are not an accurate guide to identity. This point becomes most obvious later when Mrs. Whatsit transforms herself into a creature resembling a centaur, and then the Happy Medium shows Meg a vision of Mrs. Whatsit as an exploding star. **Mrs. Who** wears owl-like glasses and is fond of quoting the Bible and famous authors, especially when giving advice. She represents insight and the voice of wisdom. **Mrs. Which** makes a visual pun on her name when she first appears looking like a witch from *Macbeth*. Her strange, slurring speech forces Meg and the reader to pay close attention to her words, which contain commands or advice about the choices Meg must make to be successful in her mission. **Aunt Beast**, the fourth helper, is a "monster" who inhabits the planet Ixchel. She is a tall, gray creature with four arms that have waving tentacles on their ends. Her face has indentations instead of prominent features and tentacles where one would expect hair and ears. Most significantly, Aunt Beast lacks eyes. The sym-

bolism is obvious. Aunt Beast quotes 2 Corinthians 4:18, explaining that creatures on Ixchel concentrate on unseen things because these are eternal. Aunt Beast thus indicates that Meg, who considers herself a monster, should ignore trivial things, such as her appearance, and instead concentrate on spiritual values. Because she herself demonstrates spiritual values in her actions, Aunt Beast is the perfect surrogate mother. She revives Meg, who is frozen by hatred, and fills her with the warmth of love.

The Man with the Red Eyes continues the motif of vision. His eyes have a strange reddish glow. He speaks with a kind voice while trying to enslave the children, but he does not move his lips. These details suggest that he is a hollow puppet who can't see or speak for himself. In fact, **IT**, the feared ruler of Camazotz, actually provides the words for the Man. A quivering, pulsating, disembodied brain, IT symbolizes the cruelty of the mind when it is separated from the heart. Appropriately, IT resides in a skull-like domed building and uses the building's powerful rhythms to make people abandon the rhythm of their own thoughts. IT rules a nightmare version of the world of conformity that Meg had desired on Earth. IT promises Meg that conformity will remove the burden of responsibility and give her the peace she seeks. The citizens of Camazotz Meg encounters, however, display fear, not happiness. Furthermore, when Charles Wallace succumbs to IT, he ceases to care for other members of his family. Because IT lacks a heart, IT and those IT controls are incapable of loving anyone. By resisting IT and saving Charles Wallace, Meg asserts her individuality and demonstrates that the heart is more powerful than the mind.

Further Reading

Authors and Artists for Young Adults. Vol. 1. Detroit: Gale Research, 1989.

Berger, Laura Standley, ed. *Twentieth-Century Young Adult Writers*. 1st ed. Detroit: St. James, 1994.

Blackburn, William. "*A Wrinkle in Time:* Seeking the Original Face." In *Touchstones: Reflections on the*

Best in Children's Literature. Vol. 1. Edited by Perry Nodelman, pp. 123-31. West Lafayette, IN: Children's Literature Association, 1985.

Children's Literature Review. Vols. 1, 14. Detroit: Gale Research, 1976, 1988.

Collier, Laurie, and Joyce Nakamura, eds. *Major Authors and Illustrators for Children and Young Adults.* Detroit: Gale Research, 1993.

Contemporary Literary Criticism. Vol. 12. Detroit: Gale Research, 1980.

Estes, Glenn E., ed. *American Writers for Children since 1960: Fiction.* Vol. 52 of *Dictionary of Literary Biography.* Detroit: Gale Research, 1986.

Fuller, Muriel, ed. *More Junior Authors.* New York: H. W. Wilson, 1963.

Gonzales, Doreen. *Madeleine L'Engle: Author of* A Wrinkle in Time. New York: Dillon Press, 1991.

Something about the Author. Vols. 1, 27, 75. Detroit: Gale Research, 1971, 1982, 1994.

Something about the Author Autobiography Series. Vol. 15. Detroit: Gale Research, 1993.

C. S. Lewis

1898-1963, English academic and author

The Chronicles of Narnia

(fantasy series, 1950-1956)

PLOT: *The Lion, the Witch and the Wardrobe* (1950), the first volume of the "Chronicles of Narnia," combines elements of fairy tales, heroic fantasy, talking beast tales, and allegory to illustrate the scheme of salvation through Christ's death and resurrection. During World War II, siblings Peter, Susan, Edmund, and Lucy are evacuated to an elderly professor's house. While exploring, Lucy enters a wardrobe and finds herself in Narnia, where it is always winter but never Christmas. Mr. Tumnus, a faun, invites her to tea, intending to turn her over to the evil White Witch, but he is unable to betray his guest. When Lucy returns home, the others don't believe her story. Edmund, however, later follows Lucy into Narnia, where he meets the White Witch. She feeds him Turkish Delight and promises to make him king if he will bring his brother and sisters to her. Returning with Lucy, Edmund lies, saying

that Narnia is only pretend. The truth comes out, though, when all four children pass through the wardrobe into Narnia. After discovering that Mr. Tumnus has been arrested and his house wrecked, they encounter Mr. Beaver, who takes them to his home, where Mrs. Beaver feeds them. Afterwards, Mr. Beaver tells them that Aslan, the great Lion, is coming and that Jadis, the White Witch, will be destroyed once the Sons of Adam and Daughters of Eve sit on the four thrones at Cair Paravel. During this story, Edmund sneaks away to Jadis's castle.

Realizing that Edmund is a traitor, the Beavers and the children set out to meet Aslan. After spending the night in a hole, they learn that Christmas has come. Father Christmas then distributes gifts and provides morning tea. In contrast, the Witch feeds Edmund stale bread and water, instead of the Turkish Delight she promised. She then sends the head of her Secret Police, Fenris Ulf, to kill the Beavers and the children. Following behind him, Jadis must abandon her sleigh because Aslan's arrival has brought spring, which melts the snow. Learning that Peter has killed Fenris Ulf, she then prepares to kill Edmund, but a party sent by Aslan rescues him. Citing the law of Deep Magic, Jadis demands the blood of Edmund the traitor. Aslan talks to her, however, and she renounces her claim. After a sad night, Aslan goes to the Stone Table with Susan and Lucy, who have followed him, until he tells them to stop and hide. Unseen, they watch the Witch's helpers tie him, muzzle him, shave off his mane, and taunt him. Jadis then kills Aslan.

After the Witch and her followers leave, the heartbroken girls tend to Aslan's corpse and, when they turn away to go, hear the deafening sound of the Stone Table cracking in two. In the early morning light, they discover Aslan is alive. Citing the Deeper Magic, he tells Susan and Lucy that when a willing victim who has committed no treachery is killed in a traitor's stead, death itself starts to work backwards. Aslan then goes to the Witch's castle, restores Mr. Tumnus and the others whom she turned into statues, and leads them into battle, during which Aslan kills Jadis. Afterwards, Peter,

The children rule over Narnia from the throne at Cair Paravel in a scene illustrated by Michael Hague for Lewis's **The Lion, the Witch and the Wardrobe.**

Susan, Edmund, and Lucy are crowned rulers of Narnia. Years later, while pursuing a White Stag, they pass through the wardrobe, returning to their own world at about the same time they had originally left. Though they had grown to maturity while in Narnia, they return to being children again when they arive home.

The first of a trilogy focusing on Caspian, **Prince Caspian: The Return to Narnia** (1951) is not allegorical. But the story does extend the theme of faith or belief introduced in the previous book. A year after their first adventures, magic pulls Peter, Susan, Edmund, and Lucy back to Narnia. About a thousand years have passed since they ruled. After they save Trumpkin, a Red Dwarf, from execution, he tells them of Miraz, the Telmarine ruler of Narnia, who denies stories about the Old Narnia when Peter, Susan, Lucy, and Edmund reigned. Miraz decided to kill Prince Caspian, his nephew and heir, after Queen Prunaprismia gave birth to a son. However, Caspian's half-dwarf tutor, Doctor Cornelius, helped the prince to escape. Caspian was knocked off his horse and taken in by the talking badger named Trufflehunter and the dwarfs Trumpkin and Nikabrik. Trufflehunter enlisted into Caspian's service many talking beasts. When Doctor Cornelius joined Caspian, he had him move his troops to Aslan's How, the ancient site of the Stone Table. Losing in battle to Miraz, Caspian sent Trumpkin to Cair Paravel and blew Susan's magic horn, hoping to summon the ancient rulers back to Narnia.

After making Trumpkin believe in their identities, the children set out to join Caspian. Lucy sees Aslan beckoning them to climb a cliff, but the others don't, so Peter leads them in a different direction. Attacked, they retreat. Aslan then privately tells Lucy that she must follow him, even if she comes alone. Gradually, the others see Aslan, but Trumpkin believes only after Aslan shakes him. When they complete their journey, Aslan sends the three males into Aslan's How. They overhear Nikabrik suggest that Caspian use black magic to ask the White Witch for help. In a brief fight, Nikabrik and his companions, a hag and a werewolf, are killed. Peter then challenges Miraz to single combat. Miraz, duped by Lord Glozelle and Lord Sopespian into accepting, trips during the duel, and Glozelle kills him. In the ensuing battle, Miraz's army is defeated. Meanwhile, Aslan leads a joyous procession that includes Bacchus and the Awakened Trees (in their shapes as Dryads, Hamadryads, and Silvans). Once Caspian is crowned king, Aslan builds a doorway. Through it, the Telmarines, originally from the same world as the children, return to a remote island. After Aslan tells Peter and Susan that they are too old to return to Narnia, the children pass through this doorway and onto the railway platform where their adventure started.

In *The Voyage of the "Dawn Treader"* (1952), the second volume of the Caspian trilogy, a voyage to the end of the world symbolizes an inward journey to mystical vision. Edmund and Susan Pevensie are staying with Aunt Alberta, Uncle Harold, and their obnoxious cousin, Eustace Clarence Scrubb. One day, the children are pulled into a picture and onto King Caspian's vessel, *Dawn Treader*. Caspian is trying to discover the fates of seven exiled lords. Reepicheep the mouse is seeking the "Utter East" promised to him in a rhyme. Eustace complains constantly and causes trouble by swinging Reepicheep by the tail, apologizing only to avoid a duel.

In the Lone Islands, the slaver Pug captures Caspian, Reepicheep, and the children. Lord Bern, one of the seven lords, purchases Caspian and helps him to overthrow Gumpas, the corrupt governor. After the *Dawn Treader* resumes sailing, Reepicheep catches Eustace stealing rationed water. When the ship next lands, Eustace bitterly goes off alone, watches a dragon die, falls asleep on its treasure, and awakens as a dragon himself. This physical change initiates a character transformation: Eustace feels lonely for the first time and also helps the crew to obtain provisions. Aslan finally restores Eustace by ripping the dragon skin from him and immersing him in a well. Because an arm-ring convinces the adventurers that Lord Octesian, another of the seven missing lords, was transformed into a dragon or killed by it, they leave Dragon Island without touching its treasure.

After escaping a sea serpent, Caspian's party lands on an island where a pool transforms everything to gold. At its bottom is Lord Restimar, now a gold statue. Overcome with lust for riches, Caspian threatens Edmund, but Aslan appears and growls disapproval. Naming the island Deathwater, Caspian flees it. When they arrive on the island of the magician Coriakin, its invisible inhabitants threaten the landing party. Lucy therefore agrees to read a spell which makes visible a race of one-legged, stupid dwarfs called Dufflepuds. The next adventure is psychologically symbolic. The ship enters a dark cloud in which the adventurers rescue Lord Rhoop, who is fleeing an island where dreams come horrifyingly true. Guided by Aslan, who takes the shape of an albatross, the *Dawn Treader* leaves this place of despair and reenters the light. On the next island, Caspian finds the Lords Revilian, Argoz, and Mavramorn sleeping deeply at Aslan's Table. Attended by the transformed star Ramandu and his daughter, Caspian's company dines. Leaving behind only the hesitant Pittencream, Caspian sails to the Silver Sea to undo the spell that is upon the sleeping lords. At the end of the world, Aslan convinces the reluctant Caspian to return to Narnia. Reepicheek completes his quest, going over a wave into Aslan's country. Edmund, Lucy, and Eustace also leave the ship. They meet Aslan, who appears as a lamb and then as a lion. After telling Lucy and Edmund that they will not return to Narnia, Aslan sends the children back to their world.

The Silver Chair (1953) closes the Caspian trilogy. Its quest plot and the motif of appearance versus reality develop themes about faith, temptation, and salvation. Fleeing from bullies at Experiment House, Jill Pole and Eustace Scrubb pass through a door and onto a mountain in Aslan's Land. Eustace falls, but Aslan blows him safely to Narnia. Aslan then gives Jill a quest to find the missing Prince Rilian, four signs to help her, and a warning not to trust appearances. After Aslan blows Jill into Narnia, Jill realizes that they missed the first sign: Eustace did not recognize and greet the elderly Caspian, who was setting out to find Rilian. That night, Glimfeather the Owl takes them to a parliament of owls, at which the children learn that Prince Rilian was lured away by a woman dressed in green. Glimfeather then takes them to Puddleglum, a Marshwiggle, who is to accompany them.

On their way to the ruined city of giants, the second sign, they encounter a silent knight in black armor and a woman, who calls herself the Lady of the Green Kirtle. She advises them to tell the gentle giants of Harfang that they were sent for the autumn feast. Cold and hungry, the children ignore Puddleglum's cautionary advice and rush to the giants' castle. From a window, they realize that they passed over the ruined city, the second sign, and nearly missed the third sign: a huge inscription reading "UNDER ME." When Jill then discovers that the giants intend to eat them, they escape into a tunnel beneath the ruined city. Silent Earthmen take them to an underground castle, where a handsome man, the knight in black armor, tells them that he must be bound to a silver chair every night because he turns into a serpent. When he calls out Aslan's name, the fourth sign, they realize that he is Prince Rilian. They break his bonds, freeing him from enchantment, and Rilian destroys the silver chair.

The Queen of the Underland, the Lady of the Green Kirtle, tries to re-enchant Rilian because she plans to marry him and set him up as a puppet king in Narnia. Clouding their minds with scented smoke and music, she claims that the sun and Aslan are

merely tales. When Puddleglum stamps on the fire producing the smoke and insists that he prefers such tales to her reality, the minds of the others become clear. The witch then turns into a serpent, but they slay it. Immediately, her world collapses. Rilian and his rescuers escape to Narnia, where Rilian is reunited with Caspian, who dies. Aslan then takes Jill and Eustace to his land. With blood from his paw, he brings Caspian to life as a young man. Aslan, Caspian, Eustace, and Jill return to Experiment House, where they frighten the bullies and the Head.

Set during the Golden Age when Peter was High King, ***The Horse and His Boy*** (1954) is the only volume of the "Chronicles" that does not bring characters from the ordinary world to Narnia. In this adventure, several quests for freedom support a theme about true identity. When Shasta overhears Arsheesh bargaining to sell him to a Calormen Tarkaan, or lord, he learns that he is not the fisherman's son and decides to escape to Narnia with the Tarkaan's talking horse, Bree. While trying to outrun some lions, Bree and Shasta meet Hwin, a talking mare, and Aravis Tarkheena, a girl escaping a forced marriage. When the group reaches the Calormene capital of Tashbaan, visiting Narnians mistake Shasta for Prince Corin of Archenland and take him to their residence. There, Shasta overhears Tumnus devise an escape for King Edmund and Queen Susan, who wishes to avoid marrying Prince Rabadash. After the real Corin appears, Shasta goes to the Tombs of the Ancient Kings, where he is to rejoin his companions. That night, a large cat protects Shasta from wild animals and comforts him.

Meanwhile, Aravis and her friend Lasaraleen overhear Rabadash, the Tisroc, and Aravis's suitor (Ahoshta) plot to capture Archenland and Narnia. When Aravis rejoins Shasta and the horses, they decide to set out across the desert to warn the Archenlanders. During the journey, a lion chases the horses and scratches Aravis; Bree panics, but Shasta tries to protect Aravis. The Hermit of the Southern March then tends to Aravis and the horses, but he sends Shasta on foot to warn the king. Shasta finds King Lune, but becomes separated from him in a fog. That night, Aslan accompanies Shasta and explains the roles he has played throughout Shasta's life. In the morning, Shasta realizes that Aslan has led him safely into Narnia. Hearing his story, some Narnians send for help. King Edmund, Queen Lucy, Prince Corin, and a Narnian army soon arrive. Although forbidden to do so, Prince Corin and Shasta take part in the battle, during which Rabadash is captured. After the battle, Aslan appears to Hwin and Bree, who is humbled by the sight of the Lion. King Lune reveals that Shasta is really Prince Cor, Corin's elder twin, who was kidnapped when he was an infant. Prince Rabadash refuses the merciful conditions offered by the victors, so Aslan turns him into a donkey. Aravis marries Cor, who eventually becomes king of Archenland.

Although *The Magician's Nephew* (1955) was the sixth book in the series to be published, this poetic creation myth is chronologically set at the beginning of "The Chronicles of Narnia." Its quest adventure contrasts selfishness with charitable concern. Digory Kirke and his mortally ill mother, Mabel, are staying with Uncle Andrew and Aunt Lettie Ketterly. While exploring a passageway, Digory and Polly Plummer, his neighbor, mistakenly enter Uncle Andrew's study. Andrew, a magician, tricks Polly into touching a magic ring that transports her to another world. Eager to learn about it, Andrew compels Digory to bring Polly back. Digory joins Polly in the Wood between the Worlds. After ensuring that they can use the rings to return home, Digory convinces Polly to explore other worlds. They go to the ruins of Charn, where they find a room of immobile people. Digory, tempted by a sign promising an explanation, rings a bell that awakens Jadis, the queen who destroyed Charn. Digory and Polly unintentionally transport Jadis to the Wood and then to Andrew's study. Jadis creates havoc in London, wrecking a cab. Digory and Polly use their magic rings to take her away, but they also accidentally carry off Uncle Andrew, a cabby named Frank, and his horse, Strawberry. The children try to go to Charn, but they enter a new world instead.

Here, the group observes Aslan singing Narnia into existence. Filled with hatred, Jadis throws a lamppost at Aslan and flees. Uninjured, Aslan turns some animals, including Strawberry, who is renamed Fledge, into talking beasts. After bringing

Nellie, the cabby's wife, from London, Aslan makes them King Frank and Queen Helen. Meanwhile, the animals, unable to communicate with Andrew, plant him like a tree; when they later realize that he is alive, they confine him to a cage. Digory, after asking Aslan for a cure for his mother, undertakes a quest to undo the harm he has caused. Riding Fledge, who has been transformed into a flying horse, Digory, accompanied by Polly, goes to a garden for a silver apple. Jadis tempts him, suggesting that he use the apple to cure his mother, but Digory resists and returns to Aslan. Aslan has Digory throw the apple, which grows into a tree that will protect Narnia from the witch. Aslan then gives Digory an apple to cure his mother and sends Digory, Polly, and Andrew home. In later years, the core of the apple grows into a tree, and Digory uses its wood to build the wardrobe through which the Pevensie children pass into Narnia in *The Lion, the Witch and the Wardrobe*.

The Last Battle (1956), the final volume of the "Chronicles," symbolically presents Christian eschatology, the study of final things. The motif of disguise is central to a theme about true faith and the last judgment. Forcing Puzzle the donkey to disguise himself as Aslan, Shift the talking ape tells everyone that Aslan wants them to work for the Calormenes. Tirian, king of Narnia, hears about Aslan's return. Roonwit the Centaur warns him that the stars indicate trouble and that he must be wary, but Tirian acts rashly. He and Jewel the Unicorn kill two Calormenes who are whipping some talking horses. Feeling dishonored, Tirian surrenders to Shift and the Calormenes. Tied to a tree, Tirian has a vision of seven friends of Narnia. Two of them, Eustace Scrubb and Jill Pole, appear and release him. Disguised as Calormenes, these three head to the stable housing the false Aslan. Tirian frees the captured Jewel, and Jill leads Puzzle away.

Tirian and his companions now attack some Calormene soldiers who are leading dwarfs into slavery. Griffle, the dwarf leader, refuses to join Tirian, proclaiming that dwarfs will no longer be fooled. Only Poggin the dwarf joins Tirian. Soon Tirian's group sees Tash, the Calormene god, heading towards the stable. Learning that the Calormenes have captured Cair Paravel and killed Roonwit, Tirian heads to the stable, where he sees Shift, Rishda Tarkaan, and Ginger the cat plotting. Shift, declaring that Tash and Aslan are one, invites everyone to enter the stable to meet "Tashlan." Ginger volunteers but rushes out in horror. Emeth, a Calormene soldier, enters next; he is thrown out dead. When Rishda tries to force others into the stable so that he can burn it as an offering to Tash, Tirian throws Shift into the stable and then attacks. During the battle, Griffle and his dwarfs attack both sides. Seeing that he is losing, Tirian pulls Rishda into the stable with him.

Inside, the seven friends of Narnia—Digory Kirke, Polly Plummer, Eustace, Jill, Peter, Edmund, and Lucy (Susan is no longer a friend because she has rejected Narnia as a childish fancy)—suddenly appear. They order Tash, who has grabbed Rishda, to depart. Tirian then notices that he is no longer inside a stable, but he can't convince the dwarfs that they are not confined in darkness. Even Aslan can't make them see the truth. Aslan then awakens Father Time, who sounds a trumpet, bringing an end to Narnia. Everyone comes to the stable door for judgment. Finally, Peter locks the door with a golden key, and the group moves further into the world on their side of the door, meeting other characters from the history of Narnia. Subsequent discussions reveal that the Pevensies and their friends were killed in a railway accident in their world and will live forever with Aslan.

CHARACTERS: Although the "Chronicles" illustrate the Christian scheme of salvation and dramatize virtues such as faith, Lewis insisted that he was writing "supposals," not allegories. For Lewis, allegory personified ideas and therefore relied on unreal characters; supposals, on the other hand, transferred spiritual facts to a setting in which the characters were real and followed logical courses of action. Inspiration for these characters came from the Bible, folklore and fairy tales, Greek epics and mythology, and the family stories of E. Nesbit.

Folktale and biblical elements combine in the portrait of **Aslan**, a huge, golden lion who is the King of Beasts and the son of the Emperor-beyond-the-sea. He is obviously a symbolic representation of Jesus Christ, who is called the Lion of Judah in Revelations 5:5. Aslan's name (apparently derived from the Turkish word for "lion") fills the good with joy and the evil with horror. Those who meet him can't look directly into his eyes, and they feel awe or fear until he calms them with his deep voice. As Mr. Beaver points out, Aslan is not safe, but he is good. He has powerful paws, but he can velvet them to romp like a kitten with the children. A rich smell hangs over Aslan's hair.

The major events of Aslan's story in *The Lion, the Witch and the Wardrobe* parallel Christ's passion and crucifixion. Like Christ, Aslan becomes sad and has a dinner suggestive of the Last Supper. Afterwards, he walks alone in the woods, as Christ walked in Gethsemane. Like Christ, he expresses a desire for company. During this walk, Aslan stumbles, just as Christ stumbled on the way to Calvary. At the Stone Table, he is shaved and taunted as "Puss," humiliations that are reminiscent of the stripping of Christ and the mocking of him as King of the Jews. Even the White Witch's taunt that he should despair and die echoes Christ's agonized call in Matthew 27:46, "My God, my God, why hast thou forsaken me?" Of course, the major parallel is that, like Christ, Aslan, who knows of the Deeper Magic that makes death run backwards, rises from the dead. The subsequent breaking of the Stone Table symbolizes that Aslan, like Christ, ends the old law and brings a new one. Aslan's journey to the White Witch's castle resembles the harrowing of hell, Christ's descent to the underworld to rescue the souls of the good. Aslan then gives new life to the statues by breathing on them, an act that may symbolize the coming of the Holy Spirit. Finally, Aslan mysteriously provides a feast, an event recalling Christ's feeding of the multitudes with loaves and fishes.

In the final two books of the "Chronicles," Aslan's deeds parallel events described in Genesis and Revelations, respectively. In *The Magician's Nephew*, he sings into creation Narnia's plants and animals. He thus contrasts with Jadis, whose words destroyed her world. Aslan shows his goodness by giving animals the power of speech, by appointing Frank and Helen as rulers, by ensuring that Polly forgives Digory, by giving Digory the chance to redeem himself, and by protecting Narnia from the Witch. In *The Last Battle*, Aslan enacts scenes from Revelations when he brings Narnia to an end and has everyone pass before him in judgment. Significantly, both books establish the paradox of limited omnipotence: Aslan can't save those who refuse faith and salvation. Thus, in *The Magician's Nephew*, he can't "unfrighten" Andrew, who is incapable of hearing the Lion, and in *The Last Battle*, he can't save the dwarfs, who refuse to see him. He does, however, save Emeth, who believes in Tash, because all good deeds are done because of Aslan.

In other books, suggestive imagery and biblical parallels establish Aslan's divinity. In *The Voyage of the "Dawn Treader,"* light repeatedly bathes Aslan, whether he appears as a dreamlike vision or a cross-shaped albatross. When Aslan appears to the voyagers as a radiant lamb, a conventional representation of Jesus Christ, his invitation to the children to a breakfast of fish echoes the resurrected Christ's invitation to Peter (John 21:12). Similarly, the scene in *The Silver Chair* in which he forces Jill to pass near him to drink from a stream echoes John 7:37 to indicate that Jill needs the refreshing courage of faith. Aslan also symbolically illustrates the power of Christ's blood to bring eternal life when blood from his paw washes over the corpse of Caspian, bringing him to life and restoring him as a young man. Aslan then shows his concern for this world by returning to Experiment House to frighten the bullies by showing his back (see Exodus 33:23). In *The Voyage of the "Dawn Treader,"* Aslan promises to negate death by linking the children's world to his, calling himself a bridge builder, a medieval title applied to Christ. In *The Horse and His Boy*, Aslan answers the question of who he is by replying three times, "Myself." His answer echoes God's response to Moses, "I am that I am" (Exodus 3:14), while the repetition suggests the Christian trinity.

Some critics object that Aslan evokes the awe of Old Testament divinity by correcting, chastising, and punishing, but lacks Christ's compassion and humility. Aslan does, however, show sympathy with Edmund, Eustace, Reepicheep, Emeth, and even Rabadash. Furthermore, throughout the series, Aslan is a helper and protector. He saves Edmund by taking his place on the Stone Table. He restores Eustace by ripping away his dragon shape, the symbol of sin. He aids the crew of the *Dawn Treader* several times, as when he assumes the shape of the albatross to lead them from the cloud. He saves Lucy from temptations offered by the book of spells. In *The Horse and His Boy*, he guides, protects, and teaches. He unites Shasta and Aravis by sounding like two lions and thus driving their horses together. In the shape of a cat, he protects Shasta from jackals at the Tombs and comforts him in his loneliness. Later, he scratches Aravis, helping her to become sensitive to the feelings of others.

The young heroes were obviously inspired by those in the family stories of E. Nesbit. Once in Narnia, however, these Sons of Adam and Daughters of Eve, as they are called, become characters of high fantasy, a genre combining elements from fairy tales, medieval romances, and epics. Through their journeys, these children discover identities that were not evident in the mundane world. With the exception of Susan Pevensie, they become the **seven Friends of Narnia** who respond to Tirian's call for help in *The Last Battle*. In their own world, the seven die in a railway accident.

Thirteen-year-old **Peter Pevensie** (the surname first appears in *The Voyage of the "Dawn Treader"*) is significant in only the first two volumes. Although he doesn't believe Lucy's stories, he is kind and protective, criticizing Edmund for jeering at her. Once he enters Narnia, Peter becomes a chivalric hero. He shows integrity and humility by apologizing to Lucy and by having her lead the party to Mr. Tumnus's house. Peter undergoes a symbolic death and rebirth when he spends the night in the hole and emerges on Christmas day. Father Christmas acknowledges Peter's heroic identity by giving him a shield and sword, adult tools, not children's toys. After meeting Aslan, Peter proves his moral worth and courage. He accepts responsibility, confessing that his own anger may have pushed Edmund into treachery. He later kills Fenris Ulf, earning heroic status by becoming Sir Peter Fenris-Bane (Wolf's-Bane in British editions). Peter's greatest deeds, however, are leading the army after Aslan is killed and engaging Jadis in hand-to-hand combat. Crowned High King of Narnia, Peter becomes a great warrior, a tall, deep-chested man known as King Peter the Magnificent.

In *Prince Caspian*, Peter is again heroic. He attacks Nikabrik and his foul companions, and he fights Miraz in single combat. His most important role, however, is in developing tension between reason and faith. Peter tends to be logical. He deduces, for example, that they are in the ancient ruins of Cair Paravel, that challenging Miraz will buy his troops valuable time, and that he must lead the children home through Aslan's door to reassure the fearful Telmarines that it is safe. Peter's rationality, however, has a negative side. His initial failure to see Aslan reflects a lack of faith. Instead of accepting Lucy's word that Aslan wants them to climb up, Peter leads the party down, symbolically a negative spiritual direction. Once Peter regains his faith, however, he also sees Aslan.

The fate of twelve-year-old **Susan Pevensie** suggests that not all who are called find salvation. Susan is initially no more flawed than the others. She acts older than her age, but she is not arrogant or dishonest, just practical and maternal. She suggests, for example, that they wear fur coats to protect themselves from the cold on their first trip to Narnia, and, in *Prince Caspian*, she makes the children carry their shoes when they explore the seashore in bare feet. She is petty, however, saying "I told you so" when things go wrong. Susan is also timid, a trait especially evident when she meets Aslan and when the Stone Table cracks. Susan's fears have spiritual consequences. After she sees Aslan in *Prince Caspian*, she admits that she believed "deep down inside" that he was present but didn't openly believe because she was afraid of the woods. Therefore, when the children meet Aslan, she hangs back with Trumpkin, another doubter. Aslan makes her braver by breathing on her, a symbol of the spirit entering into her.

Susan does not remain true because she is superficial. In Narnia, Susan becomes Queen Susan the Gentle, a tall, beautiful woman with long black hair. She has numerous suitors but is attracted to the handsome, courteous, and evil Rabadash. Lewis's biases clearly limit Susan's role in the battles against evil. Declaring his disgust at the idea of females fighting in the war against Jadis, he allows Susan only to blow the horn that warns Peter of the presence of Fenris Ulf. Although a superb archer, she is absent when the Narnians fight Rabadash. *The Voyage of the "Dawn Treader"* indicates that in her own world she does poorly in school and ceases to be a friend of Narnia. She is not present for judgment in *The Last Battle*, but the novel allows a vague hope that she may reform.

In the first volume, ten-year-old **Edmund Pevensie** changes from a Judas-like traitor to King Edmund the Just. Initially, Edmund contrasts with Lucy. Whereas she wisely keeps the wardrobe door open, he foolishly closes it. Whereas she is truthful, he lies about visiting Narnia. Whereas she embodies faith, he casts doubts and demands evidence, pointing out, for example, that the children don't know that the Beavers are friends. Unlike Lucy, Edmund, who attends a bad school, is spiteful, vowing to avenge the tongue lashing Peter gives him. Edmund succumbs to evil when the White Witch feeds him Turkish Delight, a symbol of sin because it is sweet, isn't filling, and can be deadly. After eating it, Edmund reveals his spiritual corruption: he feels horror at hearing Aslan's name, he suppresses his feelings that the Witch is evil, and he mocks Aslan by drawing a mustache on a stone lion in the Witch's courtyard. Edmund changes when Jadis turns some Christmas revelers into stone. Feeling sorry for them, he becomes less selfish and more compassionate. After his rescue from Jadis, Edmund apologizes for his treachery, demonstrating that sinners can change. He then proves his worth in the battle, displaying wit and bravery by breaking the Witch's wand.

Subsequent volumes present Edmund as grave, serious, and mostly just. In *Prince Caspian*, he represents obedient faith by gallantly supporting Lucy, although he himself does not see Aslan.

Mindful of his own treachery, Edmund repeatedly shows compassion. In *The Horse and His Boy*, others argue that Rabadash should be executed, but he advocates Christian charity. Furthermore, on the voyage of the *Dawn Treader*, he comforts the "undragoned" Eustace by telling him how he, too, was a traitor saved by Aslan. During this voyage, Edmund reveals other qualities. He is noble, telling Caspian that the king can't desert his people to go to the end of the world. A reader of detective fiction, Edmund is also logical, reasoning that Lord Restimar dived into the pool that turned him to gold. Edmund allows his skepticism to resurface when he asks Ramandu's daughter how he can know that she is a friend. Finally, Edmund's curiosity becomes important when Aslan gives Lucy and him the quest of finding Aslan's name in their world. Edmund, having glimpsed Aslan's land, thus represents the visionary who must find spiritual meaning in the ordinary world.

Lucy Pevensie grows up to be the "gay and golden-haired" Queen Lucy the Valiant, but she is a timid eight-year-old when she enters the wardrobe. It is symbolically appropriate that the youngest child discovers Narnia because she is the most innocent and the most open to the spiritual vision entrance to Narnia represents. In keeping with this vision motif, Lucy is the first to notice that Edmund has vanished from the Beavers' house and that the mice are gnawing the cords binding Aslan. In *Prince Caspian*, only Lucy sees Aslan beckoning them to follow. Her vision also tests her because she is unwilling to lie about her experiences simply to get along with the others. In the second volume, though, she is not spiritually strong enough to leave them. After repenting, however, she receives strength by burying her face in Aslan's mane. Her subsequent brave display of faith, in which she declares that she will follow Aslan, even if she goes alone, inspires the others to follow her.

Throughout, Lucy is compassionate and forgiving. She demonstrates a Christian ideal by forgiving Mr. Tumnus and Peter. Lucy is forbidden to fight against Jadis, but she uses the cordial Father Christmas gave her to heal Edmund. Concerned only about her brother, she grows in compassion once Aslan points out that others will die unless she helps.

She needs no prompting to nurse and console Eustace before and after he becomes a dragon. Lucy also feels compassion for the Dufflepuds, courageously agreeing to make them visible and restoring their self-worth by convincing them that they are not ugly. In *The Horse and His Boy*, she suggests that Rabadash be offered a second chance, and she pities him when he foolishly rejects the offer. In *The Last Battle*, Lucy asks Aslan to do something for the unbelieving dwarfs.

Lucy undergoes her greatest trial helping the Dufflepuds. Her ascent to the room with the book symbolizes entry into her unconscious, where her flaws, such as jealousy of Susan's beauty, test her. With Aslan's help, she overcomes vanity and does not recite a spell to make herself beautiful. Lucy fails, though, to respect others. She utters a spell that gives her a vision of some girls talking about her, misjudges the situation, and, as Aslan says, loses a potentially valuable friendship. Nevertheless, spiritually refreshed, she again becomes a person of faith. When Caspian's ship enters the black cloud, a symbol of despair, Lucy prays for Aslan's help and is rewarded: the albatross that guides the ship tells her alone, in Aslan's voice, to have courage.

Eustace Clarence Scrubb, the cousin of the Pevensies, is a puny bully in *The Voyage of the "Dawn Treader."* An only child raised in a modern way—he calls his parents by their first names—he lacks a healthy imagination and values only those books that present facts. In Narnia, he complains constantly, threatens to contact the British Consul, and disparages the ship as inferior to modern vessels. He also fails to see himself and his situation truly. Although the sea is normal, for example, he records in his diary that it is stormy. Resentful of Reepicheep's directness, Eustace childishly gets even by swinging him by the tail and then apologizes only to escape a duel. Eustace does not recognize his worthlessness even when no one on the Lone Islands will accept him for free as a slave. Furthermore, he tries to steal rationed water because he convinces himself that his need is greater than that of others.

Eustace's transformation into a dragon symbolizes the triumph of selfishness. At first, Eustace is overjoyed by thoughts of exacting revenge on his companions. Gradually, however, he realizes that his loneliness makes him a monster. Eustace subsequently helps the others by bringing food, finding a tree suitable for a mast, and making fire. Ultimately, in a symbolic conversion suggesting that Christ alone can transform a person, Aslan rips off the dragon skin and drops Eustace into a well, symbol of baptism, where he again becomes a boy. The once cowardly Eustace shows physical bravery by slashing at the sea serpent and psychological bravery by agreeing to spend the night at the table of the sleeping lords. With his role as antagonist ended, Eustace becomes a narrative device, asking questions that allow exposition and explanation.

In *The Silver Chair*, Eustace is still pompous, easily angered, and occasionally resentful, as when he mutters that he is not responsible for missing the first sign. He is, however, loyal to Aslan and Narnia. For example, he warns Jill against trying black magic to enter Narnia. Still, Eustace is fooled by appearances. Feeling that Puddleglum is always wrong, he ignores his advice and accepts the illusory comfort offered by the giants of Harfang. Eustace also shows his former skepticism when he declares that Rilian used only the *words* of the final sign. Eustace finally takes responsibility: using Jill's Christian name for the first time, he apologizes for being difficult.

In *The Silver Chair*, **Jill Pole** is a coward who cries and hides from bullies at school. Her journey into Narnia forces her to be brave and to see clearly. After Aslan rescues the petrified Jill on the mountain, he begins her transformation by making her have enough courage to pass near him for a drink. Aslan further tests Jill by giving her the quest and the signs. Ironically, Jill's desire for comfort and her fear of suffering increase her misery and danger. Believing the giants of Harfang will provide a warm haven, for example, she forgets Aslan's instructions and fails to recognize the ruined city. After Aslan strengthens her by appearing in a dream, Jill displays courage and wit, fooling the giants by appearing to be an innocent child. Her subsequent journey underground is a symbolic rebirth journey or voyage to the unconscious. During it, the claustrophobic Jill confronts her fears and passes tests of perception

and wit. Thus, Jill sees that something is wrong with Rilian and overcomes her indecision when he calls out Aslan's name. Her decision to free the bound prince, even if it means death, is brave and motivates the others. After the witch is destroyed, Jill shows that she has changed. Calling Eustace by his Christian name for the first time, she accepts responsibility for her faults and apologizes for constantly quarreling. Thereafter, she is brave, getting horses and overcoming her fear of the dark tunnels. She displays the same courage in her own world, chasing the bullies at Experiment House. In *The Last Battle*, Jill takes childish delight in disguising herself, but she shows maturity in bringing Puzzle from the stable and compassion in begging Tirian to spare him.

In the first volume, **Digory Kirke** is the wise, shaggy-haired, and nameless **Professor**. He suggests, by establishing the possible truth of Lucy's story, that logic need not deny the world of faith represented by Narnia. *The Magician's Nephew*, however, reveals that Digory previously went to Narnia. The journey changed him from a grubby, self-pitying boy to a brave child able to overcome personal desires and to do his moral duty. Digory, who cries helplessly because his father is in India and his mother is dying, develops courage by trying to rescue Polly. Digory is already insightful and intelligent. Realizing that fairy tales are true, for example, he predicts that Andrew will pay for his selfishness and evil. Digory's desire to know everything, however, becomes a spiritual weakness: curious about Charn, he wakes Jadis. When Polly opposes him, he charges that girls lack the desire for significant knowledge. This intellectual arrogance makes Digory look like Andrew, whose words he uses during this argument. Arrogance also makes Digory see Jadis as regally beautiful, brave, and strong. Lacking moral strength, Digory displays inappropriate compassion: when Jadis is unable to breathe in the Wood between the Worlds, he hesitates to leave her behind even though he knows that she intends to conquer his world.

Digory changes by humbling himself, apologizing for freeing Jadis and indicating his need for Polly's help. He then replaces his selfish quest for knowledge with a quest to cure his mother. After

Digory accepts responsibility for bringing the Witch into Narnia, he becomes a model of faith. Putting aside personal desires, he undertakes the redemptive quest for the apple. In a scene reversing Adam and Eve's fall, Digory passes a test of faith by resisting the temptation to eat the forbidden fruit. He does waver when the Witch tempts him with the "terrible choice" of saving his mother or serving Aslan. When Jadis suggests that he desert Polly, however, Digory sees that she is evil and rejects her offers. Ironically, his moral triumphs bring success to the quest he abandoned in despair: Aslan gives him an apple that cures his mother. Fittingly, Digory becomes a wise professor who cites Plato's concept of a world of shadows to explain the new Narnia existing beyond the old one.

Polly Plummer, Digory's compassionate neighbor in *The Magician's Nephew*, befriends him because he is lonely and aids him because she understands his concern for his mother. Polly's feelings are a moral barometer. Her fear when Andrew locks the door of his study, for example, indicates the presence of evil. Polly's vanity, however, blunts her perceptions. She falls for Andrew's trick when he calls her attractive and offers her a beautiful magic ring. Similarly, Polly, who immediately dislikes Charn, remains there because Digory wounds her pride by questioning her courage. Once Polly is in Narnia, her joy signals the presence of goodness. Furthermore, unlike Andrew and Jadis, she does not fear Aslan's approach.

The observant Polly provides insight into other characters. She thus tells Digory that he is like Andrew, and Andrew that he is like Jadis. Most significantly, Polly is a foil whose pragmatism and caution emphasize Digory's rashness. Before exploring other worlds, for example, Polly demands that they test their ability to return. Polly advises against ringing the bell that awakens Jadis. She also recognizes that Jadis is evil, displaying the moral insight that Digory lacks. Furthermore, unlike Digory, Polly bluntly calls the Witch's explanations "bosh." Polly's moral firmness in urging Digory to abandon Jadis establishes his hesitancy as a flaw. Polly also exposes Digory's sexist arrogance, and her demand for an apology pushes him toward spiritual maturity.

The other high fantasy heroes are not Sons of Adam or Daughters of Eve, though **Caspian**, as a Telmarine, is descended from human pirates. Caspian's love for the stories of Old Narnia and belief in Aslan signal his imaginative and spiritual potential. In *Prince Caspian*, his adventures initiate him into knowledge of himself and his world. The hardships he endures in opposing Miraz toughen him and give him a kinglier appearance. Caspian passes a test of humility when he tells Aslan that he doesn't feel sufficient to take up the kingship of Narnia. Aslan therefore rewards him with the knowledge that his human lineage makes it right for him to ascend the throne.

After ruling three years, sixteen-year-old King Caspian the Tenth sets out on the *Dawn Treader* to find seven missing lords. Caspian shows intelligence, bravery, and a finely developed sense of justice in overthrowing Gumpas and ending the slave trade. Having been enslaved because he was foolishly adventurous, however, Caspian becomes too cautious. Reepicheep therefore must provoke him into confronting the invisible Dufflepuds. When they approach the dark cloud, Caspian avoids responsibility by leaving to Lucy the decision about advancing. On two occasions, Caspian's flaws become dangerous. Consumed by greed on Deathwater Island, he threatens Edmund. Fired by a sense of adventure at the end of the world, he prepares to abandon his quest in order to accompany Reepicheep. On both occasions, visions of Aslan restore Caspian's sense of duty. Thereafter, he completes his quest and keeps his word by returning to marry Ramandu's daughter. In *The Silver Chair*, Caspian is a frail old man who illustrates the concept of immortality: he dies, but Aslan's blood restores him to life as the handsome man of his youth.

Shasta is actually **Prince Cor** of Archenland, and his discovery of his true identity is the central theme of *The Horse and His Boy*. Shasta has the mysterious origins of mythic heroes: kidnapped by his father's enemies, he was found and raised by Arsheesh. Shasta is sensitive, a sign of his royal blood. He is uneasy, for example, because he doesn't love Arsheesh. After learning that Arsheesh is not his father, Shasta exclaims, "Why, I might be anyone!" He then undertakes adventures that make him worthy of the noble identity hinted by his interest in the free north, his qualms about stealing food, and his determination in remounting his horse after each fall.

Shasta's journey also exposes his ignorance of himself and others. For example, he initially dismisses Aravis as "only a girl." When Edmund and Susan mistake him for Corin, Shasta conceals the truth because he doesn't understand that humane, free people wouldn't kill him. Furthermore, he doesn't recognize his similarity to Corin because he has never seen himself in a mirror, a symbolic indication that he lacks self-reflection. Although he embarrassingly puts on airs with Aravis, Shasta becomes princely after the cat comforts him near the Tombs. Having confronted terror—although he boasted that he wouldn't have fear—he becomes truly brave. Thus, when the lion scratches Aravis, he defends her. Later, although fatigued, he sets out on foot to warn King Lune, thereby fulfilling his prophesied destiny of saving his country. His heroic endurance leads to understanding. When he despairs that he has lost King Lune in the fog, Aslan reveals that he has always guided his destiny. After Shasta learns his identity, he marries Aravis, symbolically confirming his maturity.

Aravis, a Tarkheena, or noblewoman, possesses intelligence, polished manners, and an accomplished way of telling stories. She is proud, however, and must learn humility and consideration. She does so after playing a number of roles. When her stepmother maliciously tries to make her marry Ahoshta, Aravis attempts suicide. After Hwin talks her out of her despair, Aravis cleverly acts as a dutiful daughter, but then devises an elaborate plan and escapes by assuming the role of a boy. The haughty Aravis descends in status by assuming the role of a slave girl in Tashbaan, but she rises in moral understanding. She thus rejects Lasaraleen's claim that status, wealth, and power are the most important attributes of a husband. Instead, she develops appreciation for Shasta and life as a "nobody" in Narnia. Courageous and determined, Aravis forces Lasaraleen to help her escape and then initiates the quest to warn King Lune of the plot she overheard. After the lion scratches her, Aravis sees Shasta's courage and humbly apologizes for her shameful arrogance. Aravis then receives another painful lesson: Aslan reveals that he gave her ten scratches so that she could know the pain of her slave, who was whipped ten times after Aravis drugged her. By recognizing the value of those beneath her in station, Aravis becomes worthy of being the princess bride of Cor.

Prince Corin of Archenland, Cor's younger twin, is adventurous and argumentative. He fights a boy who maligns Queen Susan, and he gives Shasta a dark look for suggesting that he would lie about the mix-up in their identities. Later, he disobeys orders against entering battle, but he proves himself a brave and competent warrior. The fun-loving Corin is pleased when he learns that he won't have to be king. His father, **King Lune** of Archenland, is a fat, apple-cheeked man whose jolly and humane nature contrasts with that of the fat Tisroc.

Prince Rilian is the son of King Caspian and Ramandu's daughter. In *The Silver Chair*, the witch, appearing as a beautiful woman, lures him into slavery. His enchantment may symbolize the enslavement of revenge because his vow to avenge his mother's death leads him to the witch. Many critics, however, see the enchantment as symbolizing the enslavement of romantic love. Attracted by physical beauty, Rilian ceases to be himself and to value spiritual love. In the upper world, therefore, he is the silent black knight who lacks an identifying crest on his shield. Underground, he is foolish and leads an inverted life: he sits in a throne that enslaves him, he calls the evil witch divine, and he looks forward to obeying the witch once he rules Narnia. Once the enchantment ends, Rilian becomes himself. Significantly, his shield bears the crest of Aslan, who sent his rescuers.

Tirian, the last king of Narnia, is between twenty and twenty-five years old. He is a hard-muscled, blue-eyed man with a scanty beard. Although fearless and honest, he is an ineffective king. He is unaware, for example, that the Calormenes are enslaving talking animals and are chopping down the trees that give life to the dryads. He is also rash: he ignores Roonwit's warnings and does not wait for help before investigating reports about the chopping of the woods. After his overwhelming anger makes him kill the Calormenes who are whipping the talking animals, he compounds his fault by ignoring his responsibilities as a ruler. Feeling that he has not been honorable, he surrenders to Narnia's enemies. Tied to a tree, Tirian moves from despair to hope after he selflessly calls out to Aslan to let him be killed but to help his people. Afterwards, he is kind in releasing Jewel and brave in fighting against overwhelming odds. Tirian's passage through the stable door symbolizes his death. Inside, he undergoes physical and spiritual transformations. Made clean and bright, he sees the true Narnia and feels the joy of knowing the real Aslan.

The high fantasy tradition also supplies magical villains. **Jadis, the White Witch**, is the self-proclaimed Queen of Narnia. She is extremely tall and has a wintry white face and red lips. Descended from Adam's first wife, the jinn Lilith, and a giant, she is devoid of human blood. In *The Magician's Nephew*, which recounts her early history, she is **Queen of Charn**. She believes that she is a superior being, that people exist to do her will, and that she is free from all rules. At first, Jadis seems comically ridiculous, holding Jill's hair to leave Charn and standing on the roof of a London cab as though it were a chariot. Nevertheless, Jadis is selfish, violent, and evil. Unlike Aslan, who creates Narnia by singing, she destroys Charn by speaking the Deplorable Word when she realizes that she can't rule it. In London, she throws Aunt Letty across the room, and in Narnia, she hurls a lamppost bar at Aslan. Satanlike, she tempts Digory to eat an apple, but, ignoring the rules posted at the garden, she also eats one herself to gain unwearying strength and endless days. As a result, her face turns as white as salt, symbolizing her sterility, and she condemns herself to perpetual misery.

In *The Lion, the Witch and the Wardrobe*, Jadis dresses in white fur, wears a golden crown, and carries a golden wand. Her actions symbolize her cold, unloving character: she turns Narnia into a land of death by creating a perpetual winter, and she turns her enemies into stone. Unlike the good characters, who provide abundant, nourishing meals, Jadis enslaves Edmund by feeding him enchanted Turkish Delight, a symbol of the unsatisfying nature of sin, and later feeds him only stale bread and water. Jadis is arrogant and treacherous. Before sacrificing Aslan, she boasts that she has tricked him and will kill Edmund afterwards. Although Jadis insists on her rights under the law of Deep Magic, she is ignorant of Deeper Magic. Consequently, the resurrected Aslan, symbol of divine goodness, fittingly slays her.

Andrew Ketterly, Digory's uncle in *The Magician's Nephew*, is an evil, arrogant, and vain magician. Tall and thin, with a pointed nose, bright eyes, and tousled gray hair, the self-centered Andrew has no concern for the subjects of his experiments. Completely unscrupulous, he even tries to abandon the others on Narnia. Like Jadis, the "dreadfully practical" Andrew arrogantly proclaims himself free from common rules because he follows "a high and lonely destiny." Andrew is a contemptible coward who grovels before Jadis, but he is also a comically ridiculous tippler who imagines that Jadis will fall in love with him. Andrew is most ridiculous, however, because of his limited comprehension. Hatred and fear make him hear a roar when Aslan sings and dangerous growls when the animals talk. His willful deafness indicates a spiritual decline, a point symbolized when the talking animals mistake him for a tree and then a strange beast, whom they name Brandy because he constantly calls for alcohol. Andrew gives up magic, but he remains foolishly in awe of Jadis.

The Queen of the Underland, also known as **the Lady of the Green Kirtle**, is central to the appearance-versus-reality theme in *The Silver Chair*. She appears in two forms. She is a giant serpent that is "green as poison" when she kills Rilian's mother. This form symbolically connects her to Satan. She later appears as a tall, beautiful lady in a thin garment that is also "green as poison," a form symbolizing temptation and deception. Thus, she lures Rilian with her beauty and keeps him enchanted by lying about the silver chair. Using the sensual aids of sweet smoke and music to cloud the minds of Rilian and his rescuers, she also tries to convince them that the upper world and Aslan do not exist. She is defeated because Puddleglum, who represents faith, insists that a false world created by wishes is preferable to her joyless one. Failing in her intellectual deceptions, she resorts to physical force, transforming into the serpent, but Rilian and Puddleglum kill her.

Not all high fantasy villains are magical. In *Prince Caspian,* the Telmarines, descendants of human pirates who found a way into Narnia, represent both the limits of rationality and self-serving treachery. **King Miraz,** Caspian's evil uncle, is an extreme rationalist who calls the stories of Old Narnia fairy tales. A usurper who killed Caspian's father to become king, he decides to murder Caspian, his declared heir, after Queen Prunaprismia gives him a son. **Lord Glozelle,** his evil advisor, cleverly exploits the king's foolish vanity, implying that only a coward would refuse Peter's challenge to single combat. Bitter because Miraz called him a coward, Glozelle treacherously stabs the king. In *The Voyage of the "Dawn Treader,"* His Sufficiency, **Gumpas,** Governor of the Lone Islands, is a bilious, corrupt bureaucrat whose materialism makes him defend slavery as economically essential to progress. His overthrow allows Caspian to demonstrate true leadership. **Pittencream,** a crewman who hesitates when Caspian calls for volunteers to sail to the end of the world, illustrates the religious theme that not all who are called will be chosen.

The villains in *The Horse and His Boy* are Calormenes, dark-skinned southern people who wear turbans and resemble medieval Arabs. They demonstrate the cruelty and follies of an autocratic society. **Ahoshta,** a base-born Calormene who becomes Grand Vizier, is Aravis's suitor. A sixty-year-old hunchback with an ape-like face, he cringes and fawns while listening to Rabadash's plot, but he treacherously hopes to turn the Tisroc against Rabadash. **The Tisroc of Calormen** is an old, enormously fat man, who wears a pointed hat and elaborate, bejewelled robes. Although he speaks with a cool, placid voice, he is exceptionally cruel, executing a cook for giving him mild indigestion. **Rabadash,** eldest son of the Tisroc and heir to the throne, is a tall man with flashing eyes and teeth. While courting Queen Susan in Narnia, he appears meek and courteous, but he is devious and rash.

After Susan rejects him, he exacts revenge by attacking Archenland and Narnia. Captured, he foolishly calls Aslan a demon, refuses honorable conditions for his release, and vows vengeance. Aslan appropriately transforms Rabadash, whose greatest fear is looking ridiculous, into a donkey. Restored in front of his own people, Rabadash is unable to wage further wars because he will become a donkey if he ventures more than ten miles from the temple of Tash. Publicly, he therefore becomes Rabadash the Peacemaker; secretly, people call him Rabadash the Ridiculous. **Lasaraleen** (whose name comes from an old Scots word for *leisure*) is an idle, gossiping, vain, and silly Tarkheena who talks but doesn't listen, and who shows her materialism by encouraging Aravis to marry Ahoshta because of his wealth and high status. *The Last Battle* presents contrasting Calormene Tarkaans. **Rishda** is a greedy, deceitful tyrant. He tells Shift that he bravely captured Tirian, who surrendered to him. Rishda doesn't believe in Tash, but when strange lights and noises come from the stable, he placates Tash by burning Narnians. Fittingly, Tash carries him off. The racism evident in the presentation of such evil, dark-skinned Calormenes is eased somewhat by the portrait of **Emeth.** A brave and dignified believer in Tash, who contrasts with the atheistic Rishda, Emeth is admitted to the New Narnia because he feels love when he sees Aslan. Aslan's assurance that Emeth performed his good deeds for him, not Tash, symbolically indicates that one need not be a Christian to be saved.

Invented creatures are a staple of high fantasy. In the "Chronicles," the most unusual is **Puddleglum,** the Marsh-wiggle, a wise guide and the true hero of the quest in *The Silver Chair.* Puddleglum has long arms and legs, webbed hands and feet, a long, thin face, a sharp nose, a muddy complexion, and flat locks of greenish-gray hair covering his large ears. He wears earth-colored clothes and a wide-brimmed pointed hat. His apparent pessimism leads him to suggest repeatedly that the worst will happen. Actually, Puddleglum is cautious and reasonable: he suggests that Jill constantly recite the signs, he warns the others not to reveal their quest to the Lady of the Green Kirtle, and he is suspicious when the giants are called gentle. Ironically, when Jill and

Eustace despair underground, Puddleglum becomes optimistic because they are following Aslan's signs. Puddleglum is physically heroic when he defies pain to stomp out the fire clouding the questers' minds. He becomes spiritually heroic by opposing the witch's cynical reasoning, declaring that a dream of Aslan is superior to her reality. Puddleglum thus stands for faith. Nevertheless, Puddleglum becomes comical again because, after Jill kisses him, he has the vanity to think he is good-looking.

Of the characters inspired by mythology, the first to appear is **Mr. Tumnus** the faun, who has the body of a goat below his waist and that of a man above it. First appearing in *The Lion, the Witch and the Wardrobe*, he has reddish skin, a short pointed beard, curly hair, and two horns. Tumnus introduces the deception and food motifs by luring Lucy for tea. Tumnus's generous meal, however, establishes his goodness. He thus abandons his plot to turn Lucy over to the Witch. In *The Horse and His Boy*, Tumnus is a wise, elderly courtier. As a figure from popular mythology, **Father Christmas** weakens the heroic nature of the opening volume. Furthermore, because Christ is unknown in Narnia, he confuses the symbolic theology that makes Aslan the savior. He is a helper, distributing gifts that enable the children to fulfill their royal destinies. Like other good characters, he provides a cheerful meal. Most importantly, by bringing Christmas he restores the natural order. In *The Magician's Nephew*, **Frank** the cabby becomes **King Frank**, first monarch of Narnia. He is brave, risking blows from Jadis to calm his horse, and pious, immediately singing a hymn when he believes that the Wood is the site of an afterlife. Frank is loving, wanting his wife with him, and humble, protesting that he lacks the education to be a ruler. Accepting the kingship of Narnia, he becomes a symbol of the biblical Adam. **Nellie**, his loving wife, has a kind and honest face. As **Queen Helen**, she parallels Eve.

Characters derived from mythology also appear in *The Last Battle*. **Tash**, god of the Calormenes, shows that evil is real. A demon with a human shape but vulture's head, Tash has four arms and fingers that end in talons. Tash floats over the ground, giving off a deathly smell and wilting the grass

beneath him. Cruel and bloodthirsty, he is the opposite of Aslan. **Roonwit the Centaur** is a wise adviser who warns Tirian about impending disaster and the need to control his temper. He foreshadows the end of Narnia and indicates that noble death is a treasure. Tirian's best friend, **Jewel the Unicorn**, represents faith because he refuses to accept the false Aslan.

Magical figures in *The Voyage of the "Dawn Treader"* have mythological overtones. **Coriakin**, an old, barefooted magician with a waist-length white beard and white hair, wears a red robe, has a chaplet of oak leaves on his head, and carries a curiously carved staff. Once a star, he was put in charge of the Dufflepuds as punishment for an unnamed offense. They call him cruel, but he is kind and patient. **Ramandu**, who presides over Aslan's Table, appears to be an old man, but he is a star at rest. Each day he and his daughter sing a welcoming to the rising sun and then a bird places a fire berry in his mouth, which renews him. His role is that of mentor: He tells Caspian how to end the spell keeping the lords asleep. In *The Horse and His Boy*, the 109-year-old **Hermit of the Southern March**, who wears a robe the color of autumn leaves, is a kind healer, tending to Aravis and the horses, and a wise adviser, sending Shasta to find King Lune.

The most significant folkloric characters are dwarfs. In *Prince Caspian*, **Trumpkin** is a Red Dwarf. About three feet high, stocky, and deep-chested, he has an immense red beard and whiskers, a beaklike nose, and twinkling black eyes. He is characterized by a verbal idiosyncrasy, alliterative expletives such as "horns and halibuts." Trumpkin is good, brave, and obedient, but he needs direct proof before he will believe that the children are ancient royalty. Aslan has to shake him before he will accept the reality of the King of Beasts. In *The Silver Chair*, he is the old, nearly deaf Lord Regent of Narnia, who, by forbidding their quest, represents the earthly authority that Jill and Eustace must ignore to answer their spiritual call. **Nikabrik**, a Black Dwarf, displays consuming anger and hatred. He proposes, for example, that the others kill Caspian when they find him unconscious. Nikabrik is devoid of faith, declaring that he will believe in either Aslan or the White Witch if that person opposes the Telmarines. His hatred destroys him. He brings a hag and a werewolf to summon the Witch through black magic, but when Caspian resists, the enraged Nikabrik attacks him and is killed. **Doctor Cornelius**, Caspian's tutor, is a half-dwarf who keeps his ancestry a secret from the Telmarines. A small, fat man with a long, pointed silver beard and a wrinkled brown face, he is a fairy-tale wise old man, instructing Caspian in the true history of Narnia.

Dwarfs contribute to the theme of faith in *The Last Battle*. After Shift fools him, cynical **Griffle**, chief of the black dwarfs, refuses to believe that Aslan exists. Selfishly declaring that the dwarfs will look out only for dwarfs, he fights against both sides during the last battle. **Diggle** illustrates the limitations of an intellect that refuses to allow faith. He insists that the dwarfs are in the dark in the stable and therefore can't see the New Narnia around him. Because **Poggin** joins Tirian and believes in Aslan, he shows that only their personal decisions prevent dwarfs from being saved.

The most unusual dwarfs are in *The Voyage of the "Dawn Treader."* The invisible **Dufflepuds** were **Duffers**, a group of common, although stupid, dwarfs. Because they were disobedient, Coriakin changed them into **Monopods**, three-foot tall creatures with one thick central leg and an enormous foot that they use as an umbrella while sleeping. Feeling ugly, the Monopods uttered the spell of invisibility, an act suggesting their inability to face truth. After they become visible again, the Dufflepuds comically use their feet as pontoons.

The talking animals of Narnia have their ancestry in folktales, where talking beasts are substitutes for humans. In *The Horse and His Boy*, **Bree** (short for **Breehy-hinny-brinny-hoohy-hah**), a dappled horse with a flowing mane and tail, must learn humility. Boastful and haughty, Bree worries that such animal habits as rolling on the ground are inappropriate for a talking horse. After he flees from the lion, the humiliated Bree learns that he is

"nobody special." Bree, who arrogantly declares that Aslan is only metaphorically a lion, takes on the role of doubting Thomas when Aslan appears (see John 20:26-29). After Aslan invites Bree to touch and smell him, Bree admits his foolishness, although he still remains vain about his tail and mane. Shy, quiet, and gentle, the talking mare **Hwin** feels the stings when Bree arrogantly rejects her ideas. Wise and pragmatic, she suggests entering Tashbaan in disguise. Hwin's common sense is evident in her declaration that she will roll on the ground whether talking horses do so or not. Instead of running away when Aslan appears, as Bree does, she moves toward him, showing the spiritual maturity that earns Aslan's promise, "Joy shall be yours."

In *The Last Battle*, **Shift**, an old, ugly, wrinkled ape, believes in neither Aslan nor Tash. Shift lives by deception: he turns Puzzle into his servant by claiming to be a friend and the Narnians into slaves by disguising Puzzle as Aslan. He declares that freedom means doing what he says and that Aslan and Tash are the same. Shift becomes a drunkard, dresses in an ill-fitting red coat and paper crown, calls himself Lord Shift, and proclaims that he is a wise man, not an ape. Appropriately, Tash carries him off. **Ginger**, a huge, clever, and conniving tomcat who joins Shift's plot, becomes so terrified at the sight of the real Tash that he changes from a talking to a dumb animal. **Puzzle** the donkey is a dupe. Shift makes him a servant and forces him to play the role of Aslan, but Puzzle never complains because he feels lucky to have a clever friend. Because Puzzle is not evil, he enters the New Narnia and is transformed to his true self, a beautiful gray donkey with an honest face, the first animal called to Aslan's side.

In keeping with his romantic disposition, **Reepicheep**, the "gay and martial" mouse, wears a crimson feather in a gold band around his head. In *Prince Caspian*, the brave and ferocious Reepicheep loses a tail in battle and apologizes for coming before Aslan without "the honor and glory of a Mouse." Amused by Reepicheep's vanity, Aslan restores the tail, which becomes instrumental in revealing Reepicheep's chivalric and honorable qualities in *The Voyage of the "Dawn Treader."* After Eustace swings Reepicheep by his tail, the mouse slaps Eustace with the flat of his sword instead of piercing him. Always adventurous, Reepicheep urges Caspian to sail into the dark cloud and to stand against the invisible Dufflepuds. Nevertheless, Reepicheep understands the limits of force getting the crew to push, not fight, the sea serpent coiling itself around the ship. Reepicheep represents faith in Providence, being steadfast in his belief in a prophecy that he will find what he seeks in the Utter East. His faith and persistence in seeking his destiny are rewarded by an ecstatic vision of Aslan's country before he goes over the world's end.

Most talking animals are helpers. In *The Lion, the Witch and the Wardrobe*, **Mr. Beaver**, an industrious, modest animal, provides the children with basic information about Narnia's history, and he guides them to Aslan. **Mrs. Beaver**, his wife, is a good housekeeper, as her devotion to her sewing machine suggests. She possesses practical wisdom: while everyone else panics after Edmund goes to the White Witch, she calmly packs food for their journey. In *Prince Caspian*, **Trufflehunter** the badger represents tenacious faith. The first Old Narnian to accept Caspian as king, he recruits others to Caspian's cause and defends Aslan against the sneers or doubts of others. **Glimfeather**, a huge white Owl, helps the questers in *The Silver Chair* by flying them to the parliament of owls, where they receive necessary information. Glimfeather fills his speech with words that rhyme with his call, "Tu-Whoo." In *The Magician's Nephew*, Aslan twice transforms **Strawberry**, a tired London cab-horse. He first turns him into a talking horse renamed **Fledge**. Later, Aslan makes him the first flying horse. Fledge helps Digory by carrying him during his quest for the apple. But not all helpers are good. In *The Lion, the Witch and the Wardrobe*, **Fenris Ulf** (called **Maugrim** in British and recent American editions), the head of Jadis's Secret Police, is a vicious wolf whose obedience in carrying out the Witch's commands emphasizes her evil.

Finally, two humans deserve mention. **Aunt Letty Ketterley** (Letty is short for Letitia), Andrew's unmarried sister in *The Magician's Nephew*, is firm, but kind. The sober and morally upright Letty adds comedy when she boldly confronts Jadis, whom she considers an inebriated "hussy." In *The Silver Chair*, the unnamed **Head of Experiment House**, who favors the school's bullies because she finds them psychologically interesting, satirizes modern educators. After being removed as Head, she enters parliament.

Further Reading

Authors and Artists for Young Adults. Vol. 3. Detroit: Gale Research, 1990.

Berger, Laura Standley, ed. *Twentieth-Century Children's Writers.* 4th ed. Detroit: St. James, 1995.

Beum, Robert, ed. *Modern British Essayist, First Series.* Vol. 100 of *Dictionary of Literary Biography.* Detroit: Gale Research, 1990.

Bingham, Jane M., ed. *Writers for Children: Critical Studies of Major Authors since the Seventeenth Century.* New York: Scribner's, 1988.

Children's Literature Review. Vols. 3, 27. Detroit: Gale Research, 1978, 1992.

Christopher, Joe R. *C. S. Lewis.* Boston: Twayne, 1987.

Collier, Laurie, and Joyce Nakamura, eds. *Major Authors and Illustrators for Children and Young Adults.* Detroit: Gale Research, 1993.

Contemporary Authors New Revision Series. Vol. 33. Detroit: Gale Research, 1991.

Contemporary Literary Criticism. Vols. 1, 3, 6, 14, 27. Detroit: Gale Research, 1973, 1975, 1976, 1980, 1984.

Ford, Paul F. *Companion to Narnia.* San Francisco: Harper & Row, 1980.

Fuller, Muriel, ed. *More Junior Authors.* New York: H. W. Wilson, 1963.

Glover, Donald E. *C. S. Lewis: The Art of Enchantment.* Athens, OH: Ohio University Press, 1981.

Green, Roger Lancelyn, and Walter Hooper. *C. S. Lewis: A Biography.* New York: Harcourt, Brace, Jovanovich, 1974.

Hooper, Walter. *Past Watchful Dragons: The Narnian Chronicles of C. S. Lewis.* New York: Collier, 1979.

Manlove, C. N. *"The Chronicles of Narnia": The Patterning of a Fantastic World.* New York: Twayne, 1993.

Oldsey, Bernard, ed. *British Novelists, 1930-1959. Part I: A-L.* Vol. 15 of *Dictionary of Literary Biography.* Detroit: Gale Research, 1983.

Something about the Author. Vol. 13. Detroit: Gale Research, 1978.

Astrid Lindgren

1907-, Swedish author

Pippi Longstocking

(novel, 1945)

PLOT: In eleven independent episodes, Pippi Longstocking comically violates rules of conventional behavior. The strange-looking Pippi is an orphan who lives in a house called Villa Villekula with her monkey, Mr. Nilsson, and a white horse that she keeps on the porch. She befriends her neighbors, Tommy and Annika Settergren, whom she teaches to be Thing-finders and then shows them how to have fun with whatever they find. She also demonstrates her extraordinary strength when she protects a boy from a gang of bullies by putting their leader in a tree. Later, when policemen come to take her to an orphanage, Pippi taunts them by playing tag and then picks them up by their belts. This quickly persuades them that she is able to live on her own.

When Pippi goes to school, she talks so much and behaves so badly that the teacher informs her that she won't be allowed to return. In the following adventures, Pippi shows Tommy and Annika how to have fun inside a hollow tree trunk; takes them on a picnic, during which she protects Tommy from an enraged bull by breaking off its horns and then riding it; goes with them to the circus, where she wins money by defeating the strong man; and forces two tramps who try to steal her gold to dance the schottische, before she sends them on their way with a gold coin that she says they have earned.

Pippi uses crayons for makeup in an effort to be stylish when she goes to Mrs. Settergren's coffee party. Again she behaves badly—eating all the cakes and telling fantastic stories—so Mrs. Settergren tells her that she must never come again. In the following episode, Pippi proves superior to the adults: she demonstrates her intelligence and resourcefulness by figuring out how she can reach a burning building and then heroically saving two children trapped in it. In the final episode, Pippi invites Tommy and Annika to her birthday party. She gives them gifts, frightens them with lies about an attic full of ghosts, shoots a hole in the ceiling, and sends them home with some pistols, asking them if they, too, are going to be pirates when they grow up.

The sequels are Pippi Goes on Board *(1956) and* Pippi in the South Seas *(1957).*

CHARACTERS: Pippi is the only well-developed character. Her friends and the adults whom she frustrates are two-dimensional figures who serve only to illuminate her unconventional personality. **Pippi Longstocking**, who insists that her name is really **Pippilotta Delicatessa Windowshade Mackrelmint Efraim's Daughter Longstocking**, is a nine-year-old orphan. She says that her mother, who died when Pippi was young, is an angel in heaven, and she believes that her sea captain father, who was washed overboard and lost, managed to swim ashore and become king of an island populated by cannibals. Pippi is remarkable in appearance. She wears her carrot-colored hair in two braids that stick straight out from her head. She has a freckled nose that resembles a small potato, a wide mouth, and strong teeth. When she was making the blue dress that she wears, Pippi ran out of material, so she completed it by randomly sewing on pieces of red cloth. Pippi wears long stockings, one black and one brown, and black shoes that are exactly twice the length of her feet. She has a suitcase full of gold, and she frequently lets Mr. Nilsson, the monkey given to her by her father, ride on her shoulder.

Even more remarkable than her appearance is Pippi's behavior and personality. Independent, unpredictable, unconventional, wealthy, imaginative, strong, and daring, Pippi is a projection of every child's innermost wish: she is self-sufficient and ignores adult rules. Pippi, who claims to be the strongest girl in the world, gets her way, for example, because she out-muscles the policemen who try to put her in an orphanage. She is so powerful, in fact, that she keeps her horse on the porch and lifts him down when she wants to ride. Although her conversation is often sprinkled with nonsense, Pippi is very witty, which she shows by humiliating the policemen by tricking them into playing a game of tag. More impressively, she proves her intelligence at the house fire. Instead of despairing as the adults do, she turns simple objects into a bridge and rescues the children. Pippi never displays conventional manners. She sleeps with her feet on a pillow and her head under the covers; she loves to walk in gutters and washes her hair in a pool. At Mrs. Settergren's coffee party, she eats all the cakes and dips her face into a pie. Prone to lying—as she cheerfully confesses—she delights in telling fantastic stories.

Although she triumphs over the adults, Pippi sometimes is very childish. She lacks artistic taste, which is evident when she applies so much crayon to her eyes that, instead of appearing stylish, she looks scary. Furthermore, Pippi seems incapable of learning conventional school subjects and consequently can't count properly and is not very good at writing. Nevertheless, Pippi possesses some notable virtues. She believes in fairness and humiliates bullies; she is ingenious in turning ordinary chores into fun (she puts brushes on her feet, for example, and skates with them when she washes the floor). Pippi is also generous, freely passing out gifts from a seemingly endless supply in her chest of drawers. Devoid of the vulnerability conventionally associated with girls, Pippi is memorable because she lives up to her reassuring boast, "I'll always come out on top."

Pippi's neighbors serve as contrasts with her because they are conventionally good, well-raised, obedient children who play together nicely. **Tommy Settergren** never bites his nails and does exactly what his mother tells him to do. He is slightly braver

Louis S. Glanzman's illustration of the remarkable Pippi Longstocking.

than his sister. When he goes to Pippi's birthday, for example, he is willing to see the ghosts upstairs, especially because he thinks no ghost would dare hurt Pippi. **Annika Settergren** never fusses when she doesn't get her own way and always keeps her clothes neat. She is a conventionally timid girl who is afraid of going down the hollow tree and fears the ghosts in the attic. For Tommy and Annika, Pippi provides a temporary escape from the regulations of middle-class life.

Further Reading

Collier, Laurie, and Joyce Nakamura, eds. *Major Authors and Illustrators for Children and Young Adults.* Detroit: Gale Research, 1993.

Contemporary Authors New Revision Series. Vol. 39. Detroit: Gale Research, 1993.

Cott, Jonathan. "The Happy Childhoods of Pippi Longstocking and Astrid Lindgren." In *Pipers at the Gates of Dawn: The Wisdom of Children's Literature.* New York: Random House, 1983.

Children's Literature Review. Vol. 1. Detroit: Gale Research, 1976.

Fuller, Muriel, ed. *More Junior Authors.* New York: H. W. Wilson, 1963.

Hurwitz, Johanna. *Astrid Lindgren: Storyteller to the World.* New York: Viking Kestrel, 1989.

Something about the Author. Vols. 2, 38. Detroit: Gale Research, 1971, 1985.

Leo Lionni

1910-, American commercial designer, painter, editor, author, and illustrator

Swimmy

(picture book, 1963)

PLOT: This simple story celebrates both individuality and cooperation. Swimmy is a small black fish living in a school of red fish. When a hungry tuna begins eating the little fish, only Swimmy escapes. Scared and sad, Swimmy journeys on alone. Seeing such marvels as a medusa, a lobster, strange fish, seaweeds, a long eel, and sea anemones, he becomes happy again. Eventually, he comes across a school of fish like his own hiding in the rocks and weeds. He invites the fish to see the wonders he has encountered. But, fearing that they will be eaten by a big fish, they refuse. Swimmy comes up with a solution by teaching them to swim close together so that they look like a giant fish in which he forms the eye. The fish then swim out and chase away the big fish.

CHARACTERS: Lionni has said that his "characters are humans in disguise." By representing his characters as animals, he is able to isolate human situations and "to bring them to a clean, uncluttered, symbolic pitch *outside* of ourselves." **Swimmy** is an individual who clearly stands out on the page. His brothers and sisters are drawn in red outline only, whereas his black form is filled in completely. This graphic difference emphasizes his individuality and suggests that he has more substance than they do. But this substance is not immediately apparent. Swimmy survives the attack by the tuna merely because he has superior physical abilities: he swims faster than the others. He begins to develop other qualities only during his solitary journey. At first he is understandably scared and sad, but the marvels he sees make him happy again. Some critics have criticized the similes describing these marvels. They have noted, for example, that a description of the sea anemones as "pink palm trees swaying in the wind" is inappropriate because it doesn't describe something a fish would know. Nevertheless, the story clearly indicates that Swimmy discovers beauty, which makes him appreciate life. Because he wants the new school to share his joy—to "SEE"—he reveals more of his character. He demonstrates that he is both intelligent and resourceful by organizing the fish so that each has a role that contributes to the group's survival. His own role, that of the eye, is singularly appropriate. First, it makes use of his individuality as a black fish in a school of red ones. Second, the external eye symbolizes the insight he displays by developing a plan that succeeds by fooling the eyes of his enemies. Finally, it suggests that Swimmy may be more than a wise political leader. Lionni has said that the artist has a specific function: "he is the eye—not the body." Organizing the many fish to look like a giant fish is an act of artistic creation. Swimmy is thus the artist whose own vision enables him to show society how it can survive.

Frederick

(picture book, 1967)

PLOT: This variant of Aesop's "The Ants and the Grasshopper" celebrates the spiritual contributions that the artist makes to his community. While the other field mice busily work to store food for winter, Frederick appears to do nothing. When the others question him, he insists that he is working, storing sun rays, colors, and words for the winter. During the first part of the winter, the mice are happy eating and telling stories. Once most of the food is gone, however, they are cold and no longer feel like

"Frederick, why don't you work?" they asked.
"I *do* work," said Frederick.
"I gather sun rays for the cold dark winter days."

Frederick the mouse gathers "sun rays for the cold dark winter days" in Lionni's self-illustrated picture book.

chatting. Finally, they ask Frederick for his supplies. He comforts them by making them feel the sun, cheers them by making them see colors, and entertains them by telling a rhymed myth about the seasons. The mice applaud and exclaim that Frederick is a poet. The blushing Frederick shyly says, "I know it."

CHARACTERS: By making Frederick graphically identical to the other mice, Lionni forces the reader to appreciate his hero's differences in character. **Frederick** is the archetypal poet. During busy times, his community does not appreciate him. Lionni suggests Frederick's social isolation by physically separating him from the other mice. In all of the pictures showing the preparations for winter, Frederick is apart from the others, usually with his back to them. Nevertheless, Frederick remains confident of his identity and the importance of his own art. Thus, he insists that he *is* doing work and that his fellow mice will one day appreciate it. When winter comes and the mice finally call on Frederick to produce his supplies, the pictures indicate his changed status. Instead of being in the lower left-hand corner of the picture where he has been through most of the story, Frederick is shown on a rock above the other mice. This elevated physical position symbolizes his superior social and spiritual importance once he contributes the gift of his imagination. Frederick's imaginative powers have disappointed some critics because they are undistinguished. In addition, his mythic poem preserves rhyme at the expense of grammar. Pictorially, however, the effects of his gifts are impressive because Lionni brightens the cold gray with warm yellow when Frederick talks about the sun and enlivens it with many other colors when Frederick speaks of nature. Although everyone applauds Frederick, he remains engaging and lovable because he is shy. His final line is a variation of an old saying: whenever someone would accidentally rhyme words, children once would chant, "He's a poet, and he doesn't know it." Unlike his surprised audience, however, Frederick has known all along that he is a poet. He needed only the opportunity to use his talents. When he did, he also showed that filling one's imagination is as important as filling one's stomach.

Further Reading

Berger, Laura Standley, ed. *Twentieth-Century Children's Writers*. 4th ed. Detroit: St. James, 1995.

Children's Literature Review. Vol. 7. Detroit: Gale Research, 1984.

Collier, Laurie, and Joyce Nakamura, eds. *Major Authors and Illustrators for Children and Young Adults*. Detroit: Gale Research, 1993.

Contemporary Authors New Revision Series. Vol. 38. Detroit: Gale Research, 1993.

De Montreville, Doris, and Donna Hill, eds. *Third Book of Junior Authors*. New York: H. W. Wilson, 1972.

Estes, Glenn E., ed. *American Writers for Children since 1960: Poets, Illustrators, and Nonfiction Authors*. Vol. 61 of *Dictionary of Literary Biography*. Detroit: Gale Research, 1987.

Something about the Author. Vols. 8, 72. Detroit: Gale Research, 1976, 1993.

Penelope Lively

1933-, English author

The Ghost of Thomas Kempe

(fantasy, 1973)

PLOT: This Carnegie Medal winner focuses on ten-year-old James Harrison's growing awareness of ideas that dominate Lively's novels: the significance of place and the continuity of time. While renovating East End Cottage in the village of Ledsham, workers accidentally break a bottle, thereby releasing a trapped poltergeist. Mr. and Mrs. Harrison and their two children, James and Helen, move into the cottage, and the poltergeist begins to make noise and to damage items. Able to write messages on mirrors and in James's notebook, the poltergeist reveals that he is Thomas Kempe. Kempe, an apothecary and sorcerer who lived in the cottage during the reign of James I, wants to reestablish himself and to make James his apprentice. Kempe advertises his services by placing signs in the village. Whenever James resists his orders, Kempe angrily destroys things. Mr. and Mrs. Harrison don't believe in ghosts, so they punish the normally mischievous James whenever something is damaged or the ghost creates trouble, as he does when he pulls the chair out from under the visiting vicar. Simon, a school chum, offers good advice, but he can't believe in the ghost either.

Hearing from his talkative neighbor, Mrs. Verity, that Bert Ellison is an exorcist, James seeks his help. Bert fails, however, to trap the poltergeist in a bottle. When James discovers the diary of Miss Fanny Spence, who lived in the cottage in 1856, he understands why. Miss Spence recorded that during a visit by Arnold Luckett, a ten-year-old boy who resembles James, Kempe had created problems and that they had managed to confine him to a bottle. Using a different method, Bert again fails because Mrs. Verity interrupts the exorcism. After writing that he doesn't understand modern ways, Kempe maliciously burns the cottage of Mrs. Verity, whom he accuses of being a witch. Realizing that the poltergeist is asking for help to go away, James and Bert locate his tomb and send him to his final rest.

CHARACTERS: The characters come from two periods in the past and from three generations in the present. They contrast in their flexibility and willingness to accept the unconventional. **James Harrison**, a ten-year-old with freckles and thick butter-colored hair, is, as he himself admits, normally mischievous. He is given, for example, to unmercifully teasing his sister. Nevertheless, he is merely being playful, not bad. In fact, James can be methodical and serious. For instance, he records the day's events and his aspirations in a notebook. Furthermore, when Kempe's writing appears James investigates all possibilities before concluding that he has no choice except to believe in ghosts. James also turns his natural fondness for digging into an investigative tool, unearthing Kempe's spectacles and pipe and Miss Spence's diary. This diary expands James's understanding, emotionally connecting him to Arnold Luckett as a friend to whom he can tell his problems. Because of the actual Kempe and the imagined Arnold, James learns about various phases of the past. His connection to Arnold also helps him to accept the limitations of Simon, who disappoints and angers him because of his refusal to believe in the existence of Kempe. Because James is logical, he realizes that Kempe is stuck in the mental habits of his own time. Because he is resourceful, James also seeks the aid of Bert Ellison, and his sensitivity leads him to realize that Kempe needs his help. By helping Kempe to find peace, James symbolically rejects the most insidious elements of the past. He also gains a mature sense of himself as existing in the midst of time, which stretches from the remote past to the unknown future.

Thomas Kempe, a poltergeist, was an apothecary and sorcerer who lived in East End Cottage during the reign of James I. Kempe is evident only because he creates cold drafts and noise, and because he writes messages all over the village. Arrogant and willful, Kempe tolerates no opposition. Thus, he destroys the television because he considers weather forecasting his rightful role, and he pulls the chair out from under the vicar because he doesn't like priests. Similarly, he demands that James serve as his apprentice and destroys items in the house until James agrees. Kempe illustrates the mental and moral limitations of his time. He thus insists that Mrs. Verity is a witch and burns her cottage. At the end, however, he is pathetic, wearily admitting that he doesn't understand the present and begging for help to return to his rest. By subtly resisting Kempe and by helping him to find peace, James symbolically rejects the most insidious and bigoted elements of the past.

Mrs. Harrison, James's mother, represents the inflexible habits and attitudes of adults. A pragmatic woman whose knowledge of her son's past behavior makes her unwilling to believe that he is not responsible for the damage that Kempe makes, she punishes him for each fresh disaster. **Mr. Harrison** is less obtrusive, but he shares his wife's attitudes.

Antony Maitland's illustration of James Harrison from Lively's **The Ghost of Thomas Kempe.**

Helen, James's little sister, affects a feminine elegance but takes all arguments so seriously that she pursues them to the bitter end. Consequently, she provokes James's naughty streak, which, in turn, makes his parents blame him for Kempe's destructive deeds.

Simon, a short, stumpy boy who wears enormously thick, round glasses, is, as his name suggests, a doubter. A cheerful and engaging boy, his honest admission of his inability to believe in ghosts makes it difficult for James to prolong his anger when Simon doubts him. Although Simon believes James is responsible for Kempe's mischief, he offers good advice, such as suggesting that they research the topic of ghosts. **Arnold Luckett**, who appears only through his Aunt Fanny's diary entries and James's imagined conversations with him, suggests the continuity of past and present because he resembles James. Like James, he was ten years old and suspected of doing mischief himself when Kempe tormented him. Arnold also represents the possibilities of the future because Mrs. Verity remembers him as being the elderly benefactor of the school when she was a child. **Miss Fanny Spence**, Arnold's fun-loving spinster aunt, also only appears through the diary. Unlike James's parents, she is flexible, comes to believe in the poltergeist, and helps Arnold to confine it. **Mrs. Verity**, an elderly widow, is a busybody who knows and tells all the village news. She brings out the viciousness in Kempe, who attacks her as a witch, and the kindness of the Harrisons, who realize that she is lonely. She provides guidance to James by telling him about exorcism and connects the past to the present by telling him about the elderly Arnold Luckett. **Bert Ellison** is a heavy-built, slightly balding builder and exorcist. He plays the role of the wise adult, a kind and understanding man who seriously considers James's account of the poltergeist. Bert is ultimately responsible for ending the haunting because he has the knowledge and the courage to get the poltergeist to reenter his tomb.

Further Reading

Berger, Laura Standley, ed. *Twentieth-Century Children's Writers*. 4th ed. Detroit: St. James, 1995.

Children's Literature Review. Vol. 7. Detroit: Gale Research, 1984.

Collier, Laurie, and Joyce Nakamura, eds. *Major Authors and Illustrators for Children and Young Adults*. Detroit: Gale Research, 1993.

Contemporary Authors New Revision Series. Vol. 29. Detroit: Gale Research, 1990.

Contemporary Literary Criticism. Vols. 32, 50. Detroit: Gale Research, 1985, 1988.

De Montreville, Doris, and Elizabeth D. Crawford, eds. *Fourth Book of Junior Authors*. New York: H. W. Wilson, 1978.

Hunt, Caroline C., ed. *British Children's Writers since 1960: First Series*. Vol. 161 of *Dictionary of Literary Biography*. Detroit: Gale Research, 1996.

Rees, David. "Time Present and Time Past: Penelope Lively." In *The Marble in the Water: Essays on Contemporary Writers of Fiction for Children and Young Adults*. Boston: Horn Book, 1980, pp. 185-98.

Something about the Author. Vols. 7, 60. Detroit: Gale Research, 1975, 1990.

Arnold Lobel

1933-1987, American author and illustrator

Frog and Toad Are Friends

(beginning reader stories, 1970)

PLOT: As the title of this book for beginning readers indicates, the theme of its five brief tales is the friendship between the title characters. In "Spring," Frog fools the hibernating Toad into joining him in the April sunshine by tearing off the calendar pages to indicate that it is now May. In "The Story," Toad stands on his head, pours water on himself, and bangs his head against a wall in a vain effort to think of a story to entertain his bedridden friend. Seeing how terrible Toad looks as a result of his efforts, Frog gets out of bed and tells him a story about Toad's efforts to tell a story. In the third episode, Frog helps Toad look for a button that has fallen off his jacket. They find all kinds of buttons, but none belong to Toad. When Toad discovers his button at home, he sews on his jacket all the buttons they had found and gives it to Frog. "A Swim" is a bit of a joke about logical expectations. When Frog and Toad go swimming, Toad insists that Frog not look at him because he looks funny in his bathing suit. A tortoise, some lizards, a snake, two dragonflies, and a field mouse all refuse to leave the pond until they see Toad's bathing suit. When Toad finally gets out of the water, everyone, including Frog, laughs because Toad looks so funny. Toad says, "Of course I do," and he goes home. The final story, "The Letter," is comical yet moving. Toad is sad because he never gets any mail, so Frog runs home, writes a letter expressing his happiness with their friendship, and gives it to a snail to deliver. He then runs to Toad's house and rouses Toad from bed to await the letter. They wait for four days before the snail delivers it.

See below for character descriptions.

Frog and Toad Together

(beginning reader stories, 1972)

PLOT: This sequel expands the characterization established in *Frog and Toad Are Friends*. In the opening story, Toad faithfully follows a list of his day's activities until the wind blows the list away. He then insists that, without his list, he must sit and do nothing. When Frog says that it is time for sleep, Toad remembers that sleep was the last thing on his list. He writes it down in the dirt, crosses it out, and goes to sleep. In "The Garden," Toad wishes for a garden like Frog's. Frog gives Toad some seeds, but when they don't grow instantly, Toad begins yelling at them. Frog tells him that he is frightening the seeds and should leave them alone for a few days. Toad gets up in the middle of the night, however, to calm his seeds by reading them a story. Over the next few days, he sings to them, reads them poems, and plays music for them. Exhausted, he falls asleep. Frog awakens him to look at the plants which are now growing in his garden. The delighted Toad confesses that Frog was right in saying that gardening was hard work. In "Cookies," Toad shares some freshly baked cookies with Frog. They find themselves unable to stop eating, so Frog tries to help their willpower by suggesting numerous ways to hide the cookies from sight. Toad, however, repeatedly notes that they can always get to the cookies, no matter how well wrapped or stored they are. Frog finally throws them to the birds. The saddened Toad, rejecting this example of willpower, goes home to bake a cake. "Dragons and Giants" is the most heavily ironic story in the book. After reading a story about people who fight dragons and giants, Frog and Toad wonder whether they are very brave. During a walk to test their courage, Frog and Toad are frightened by a snake, an avalanche, and a hawk. Toad Runs home, jumps into bed, and pulls the covers over his head, while Frog jumps into the cupboard and closes the door. They happily feel brave together. In the final story, Toad dreams that he is a famous performer and that Frog watches him from the audience. After each of Toad's performances, Frog becomes progressively smaller. When

Lobel's illustration of good friends Frog and Toad from **Frog and Toad Are Friends.**

Frog completely shrinks away, Toad, fearing that he will be lonely, stops his performance. He awakens to the presence of a full-sized Frog, and they go out together.

Frog and Toad All Year (1976) *is the final installment of the series.*

CHARACTERS: Arnold Lobel said that characters who live for children "are so clearly defined that they seem to be alive even when the child is not reading the book. They seem to have a life outside of that book." Through his pictures, which provide all of the physical descriptions and nuances of personality, Lobel has succeeded in creating such memorable characters in Frog and Toad.

Lobel claimed that "Frog and Toad are really two aspects of myself." If so, **Toad**, whom he called "a neurotic," is the innocent and childish side of his adult personality. Toad is impatient, for example, and becomes upset when the seeds fail to grow instantly. Toad is also easily fooled, such as when Frog convinces him to come out and play by changing the calendar. Toad governs his life by a comically consistent logic, accepting that it must be May if the calendar says so, or that he cannot act without following a list once he has made it. In the cookie episode, he applies solid reasoning so consistently that he misses the point behind placing the cookies inconveniently out of reach. Nevertheless, his logic does provide him with a distinct outlook on the world. He knows that he looks funny in his bathing suit, and he realizes that Frog's display of willpower in throwing away the cookies deprives them both of pleasure. Toad is not particularly smart and often seems ridiculous. For example, he tortures himself trying to think of a story to entertain Frog and finally must be put to bed himself.

Toad greatly values his friend Frog, as he demonstrates by giving him the jacket covered with buttons. His dream of being the world's greatest performer may reveal a sense of inferiority. Toad, however, rejects the egotism that diminishes his friend by ending his dream. He awakens to confirm that friendship is the most important thing in his life.

Frog is more mature and responsible than Toad. He is nurturing when he gets out of the bed, puts Toad in it, and tells him a story. He is understanding when he tries to control Toad's impatience over the seeds by explaining things in a way that Toad can grasp. Frog can, however, sometimes look ridiculous himself. For example, he displays adult willpower in the cookie episode only by completely removing the temptation of the cookies. In the episode in which they test their bravery, he and Toad are both scared, but they keep up appearances by crying out that they are not frightened. Even in the midst of hiding, they each accept that the other one is brave. Frog is most notable, though, as a dedicated friend. He chases after Toad's lost list and searches for his lost button. Frog is sensitive to his friend's moods. He thus writes a letter to give his sad friend the thrill of receiving mail. His actions border on absurdity because he entrusts the letter to a snail for delivery and must reveal its contents long before it arrives, but they also constitute a superb celebration of friendship.

Further Reading

Berger, Laura Standley, ed. *Twentieth-Century Children's Writers*. 4th ed. Detroit: St. James, 1995.

Children's Literature Review. Vol. 5. Detroit: Gale Research, 1983.

Collier, Laurie, and Joyce Nakamura, eds. *Major Authors and Illustrators for Children and Young Adults*. Detroit: Gale Research, 1993.

De Montreville, Doris, and Donna Hill, eds. *Third Book of Junior Authors*. New York: H. W. Wilson, 1972.

Estes, Glenn E., ed. *American Writers for Children since 1960: Poets, Illustrators, and Nonfiction Authors*. Vol. 61 of *Dictionary of Literary Biography*. Detroit: Gale Research, 1987.

Shannon, George. *Arnold Lobel*. Boston: Twayne, 1989.

Something about the Author. Vols. 6, 55. Detroit: Gale Research, 1974, 1989.

Hugh Lofting

1886-1947, English-American prospector, surveyor, civil engineer, and author

The Story of Dr. Dolittle, Being the History of His Peculiar Life and Astonishing Adventures in Foreign Parts

(fantasy, 1920)

PLOT: Fast-paced, discrete adventures reveal the compassion of Dr. John Dolittle. Because he has numerous pets, all his human patients desert him. But his parrot, Polynesia, teaches him to speak to the animals, and Dr. Dolittle becomes a successful animal doctor. Consequently, more animals join his household. He rescues Chee-Chee the monkey from an abusive organ grinder, and a crocodile, whose tooth he cures, stays but frightens pet owners. Sarah Dolittle, his sister and housekeeper, can't tolerate these new conditions, so she leaves the impoverished doctor. Because of his fame, however, Dolittle is asked to cure the dying monkeys of Africa. Borrowing a ship, he sails with Polynesia, the crocodile, Chee-Chee, Jip the dog, Too-Too the owl, Gub-Gub the pig, and Dab-Dab the duck. After a shipwreck, the doctor and his animals are imprisoned by the King of the Jolliginki. Polynesia tricks the superstitious King into releasing the doctor, who escapes over a bridge of living apes. Dolittle then treats the sick monkeys. The proud Leader of the Lions at first refuses to help, but changes his mind when the Lioness discovers that a cub is ill.

After leaving the monkeys, who send the two-headed pushmi-pullyu with him, Dr. Dolittle is again captured by the King of the Jolliginki. Polynesia now tricks Prince Bumpo. As part of the escape plan, Dr. Dolittle whitens Bumpo's face in exchange for a ship. Chee-Chee, Polynesia, and the crocodile remain in Africa, but the rest set sail. When Ben Ali and his Barbary pirates approach, thousands of swallows pull Dolittle's ship into an island bay. While the doctor explores the land, the pirates board his ship. Dr. Dolittle takes over their ship and then, when his original ship sinks, saves the pirates from sharks after they promise to become birdseed farmers. On board the pirate ship, he discovers a captured boy. Jip the dog, using his keen sense of smell, helps Dr. Dolittle to rescue the boy's uncle, who was abandoned on a deserted island. He and Jip receive rewards for taking the man and boy home. Dr. Dolittle then exhibits the pushmi-pullyu at English fairs. Having earned enough money to pay his debts, the doctor reestablishes his comfortable home.

Lofting wrote a total of twelve Doctor Dolittle books, three of which were published posthumously. Doctor Dolittle's Treasury *(1967), offers a selection of previously published adventures.*

CHARACTERS: Because modern readers object to racist elements in some portraits, this novel now appears in an edited version. The title character, **John Dolittle, M.D.**, of Puddleby-on-the-Marsh, is both comical and profound. He is also not entirely practical. For example, he fails to discourage animals, such as the crocodile, from staying with him. Finding money a nuisance, he twice becomes impoverished. Still, he is eternally optimistic, correctly assuming that a sailor will lend a boat and that the grocer will wait for payment. Nevertheless, Dolittle is also morally responsible, exhibiting the pushmi-pullyu primarily to repay his helpers. Clever Dr. Dolittle is memorable because he understands and speaks animal languages, but his unique talent is more notable for the use he makes of it. From the beginning, Dolittle is obviously kind and compassionate, qualities signaled by the fact that children and animals follow him. After he learns animal languages, he listens to the animals to heal their pains, not to make his fortune. Compassion and

wisdom characterize all his actions. Although he punches the organ grinder, he does so only to rescue Chee-Chee, and he pays for the monkey. When Dolittle learns that African monkeys are dying, he immediately resolves to cure them. Later, he refuses to sell the pushmi-pullyu because he insists that it must remain free. Dolittle even spares Ben Ali, but only after he ensures that the pirate will become a birdseed farmer. Dr. Dolittle is often a wise teacher. He thus warns the Lion that those who are too proud to help others may not receive help themselves. More significantly, he opposes the animals who criticize Prince Bumpo's appearance. Dr. Dolittle insists that the Prince has a good heart and that "handsome is as handsome does." Ironically, this phrase is applicable to his own character. Although Lofting notes only that Dolittle is strong, but not tall, and that he wears a high hat, the illustrations present him as a dumpy, balding man with a large nose. (Later illustrations make him seem less grotesque.) Nevertheless, he is handsome in all of his compassionate deeds.

The portraits of Africans reveal the racism of Lofting's time. The **King of the Jolliginki** is understandably hostile to white men because they have mined his land for gold and killed the elephants for their tusks. Polynesia preys on his superstitious gullibility by convincing him that she is the invisible John Dolittle who must be released if the King is to avoid the mumps. Most critics find the portrait of **Prince Bumpo**, a reader of romantic fairy tales, the book's most objectionable feature. He believes that Polynesia is a fairy. In order to win the hand of Sleeping Beauty, whom he previously frightened with his black face, he begs the doctor to make his face white. Although the animals have contempt for Bumpo, calling him stupid and ugly, Dr. Dolittle praises his sound heart. The only other notable human is **Ben Ali, the Barbary Dragon**. A bloodthirsty pirate, Ben Ali benefits from the doctor's merciful optimism. Dolittle spares him from the sharks but ensures that he lacks further opportunity to commit evil. Ben Ali consequently supports the natural world by growing birdseed.

The animals speak, but some of their characteristics are conventional animal traits. **Polynesia** is a wise, loquacious parrot who is 182 or 183 years old. Because she knows human and animal languages, she can teach Dr. Dolittle to understand animals. Contemptuous of human ignorance, she delights in her own knowledge, defining such things as "bunk," "life line," and "ruse." Her pedantry is more overtly comic when she insists, for example, that one rings a ship's bell regularly to know the time. Polynesia is a gifted mimic who fools the King and Prince Bumpo with her voices. Unfortunately, Polynesia, who was born in Africa, expresses contempt for Africans in such racist terms that modern audiences will be more repelled by her statements than impressed by her cleverness. **Chee-Chee** the monkey (whose name means "ginger" in monkey language) enables Dr. Dolittle to show forceful concern for animals when he punches the organ grinder who abused the monkey. Chee-Chee, an excellent guide, hides the group after they escape from the King of the Jolliginki. He adds to our understanding of Dolittle's integrity when he explains to the monkeys that the doctor is determined to leave in order to pay his debts.

Jip the dog resents feeling inferior. He therefore boasts that, in spite of the eagles' claim that no one can find the uncle captured by pirates, his sensitive nose will enable him to succeed. Because he succeeds, his boasting is heroic, not foolish. Afterwards, Jip tries to appear modest, even though he is immensely proud. He becomes comical, however, because once in Puddleby he immediately shows a conceited collie the golden collar he was given as a reward. Because **Too-Too**, a conventionally wise owl, is good at arithmetic he is more aware than Dolittle of the doctor's finances. His most impressive feat is to understand situations simply by listening to sounds that others can't hear. In later books, **Gub-Gub** the baby pig is notable for his greed, which is evident only briefly here. Timid and fearful, Gub-Gub weeps in prison and at the bridge of apes, thus emphasizing by contrast the bravery and calmness of Polynesia, Chee-Chee, and Dr. Dolittle. **Dab-Dab** the duck has a minor role, retrieving the doctor's hat after the shipwreck and reporting on the elegance of the pirate ship. The **crocodile**, who stays after Dr. Dolittle cures his toothache, shows animal loyalty and affection; he even promises not to eat the fish in the doctor's pond. **The Leader of the Lions** provides an occasion for a moral lesson because his pride makes him refuse to help Dr. Dolittle care for the monkeys. **The Lioness** represents courtesy and pragmatism. She respects Dolittle and realizes that her own cub will need medical help, so she forces the Lion to help. The **pushmi-pullyu**, a shy two-headed animal with sharp horns on each head, is descended from the last of the Unicorns. By agreeing, in spite of its timidity, to be exhibited at fairs, it shows the animal kingdom's respect for Dr. Dolittle.

Further Reading

Berger, Laura Standley, ed. *Twentieth-Century Children's Writers.* 4th ed. Detroit: St. James, 1995.

Bingham, Jane M., ed. *Writers for Children: Critical Studies of Major Authors since the Seventeenth Century.* New York: Scribner's, 1988.

Children's Literature Review. Vol. 19. Detroit: Gale Research, 1990.

Collier, Laurie, and Joyce Nakamura, eds. *Major Authors and Illustrators for Children and Young Adults.* Detroit: Gale Research, 1993.

Contemporary Authors. Vol. 137. Detroit: Gale Research, 1992.

Hettinga, Donald R., and Gary D. Schmidt, eds. *British Children's Writers, 1914-1960.* Vol. 160 of *Dictionary of Literary Biography.* Detroit: Gale Research, 1996.

Kunitz, Stanley J., and Howard Haycraft, eds. *The Junior Book of Authors.* 2nd ed. New York: H. W. Wilson, 1951.

Schmidt, Gary D. *Hugh Lofting.* New York: Twayne, 1992.

Something about the Author. Vol. 15. Detroit: Gale Research, 1979.

Lois Lowry

1937-, American author and photographer

The Anastasia Series

(novels, 1979-1991)

PLOT: The first novel in this series, ***Anastasia Krupnik*** (1979), humorously explores a ten-year-old girl's changing perceptions. Anastasia Krupnik is the daughter of Dr. Myron Krupnik, an English professor, and Katherine Krupnik, a painter. Anastasia records the things she loves and hates in her green notebook, revising entries as her experiences broaden. She puts Mr. Belden at the drugstore on her list of people she hates because he has embarrassed her and adds Mrs. Westvessel, her fourth grade teacher, after she gives Anastasia an "F" on a writing assignment because her poem didn't rhyme. She also hates her parents when she finds out that they are going to have a baby. Hurt that she wasn't consulted, Anastasia packs to move away. She agrees to stay, however, after her father gives her the right to name the baby anything she wants.

As she learns more, Anastasia changes her opinions. Because she hates her name, she decides to become a Catholic when Jennifer MacCauley tells her that Catholics can give themselves an extra name. She changes her mind about converting, however, when Jennifer says that Anastasia must repent for her sins, such as wishing for Mrs. Westvessel to have bad luck. After her father tells her about Anastasia, the daughter of Czar Nicholas II of Russia, she decides she likes her name after all. Another change comes when Anastasia falls in love with Washburn Cummings, a sixth-grade black boy with a high Afro. To attract him, Anastasia tries to give herself an equivalent hairdo. After Washburn laughs at her new hair, she places him on her hate list.

Aside from the upcoming birth of the baby, Anastasia is most disturbed by her senile grandmother. She gradually understands that she doesn't hate her grandmother, only the fact that she is old. When Anastasia attends one of her father's poetry classes, she also realizes that her grandmother has what the poet William Wordsworth called the "inward eye"—memories that keep her happy. After she gets her parents to tell about their early love affairs, Anastasia delights her grandmother by asking her about her deceased husband. Grandmother dies shortly afterward, and Anastasia realizes that she is developing memories of her own. That same day, her mother gives birth to the baby. Anastasia then revises her hate list, removing Mrs. Westvessel, who makes a sympathetic telephone call to her, and Mr. Belden, who gives her a chocolate cigar. She removes babies and, instead of naming her brother One-Ball Reilly, she names him Sam, in honor of her

Spunky and rebellious Anastasia Krupnik is introduced to readers in Lowry's 1979 novel.

grandmother's husband. By the end of the novel, Anastasia has removed everything from her hate list, except liver.

The second Anastasia book, **Anastasia Again!** (1981), bases its comedy on numerous premature assumptions. When her parents decide to move, Anastasia is sure that the family doesn't belong in the suburbs. Her parents promise, however, that they won't move until they find a house that has qualities that they all want. Anastasia, believing that her requirements will prevent the move, therefore insists that she wants a house with a tower. Although their real estate agent wrongly assumes that they are unhappy, the entire family is delighted by the house she shows them: it has a study for Myron, a studio for Katherine, and a tower for Anastasia. Before she moves away, Anastasia goes bike riding with Robert Giannini, a boy she previously hated. Because of Anastasia's awkwardness in talking to boys, Robert misunderstands her and thinks that her precocious brother, Sam, has a physical handicap. Anastasia also bids farewell to Jenny MacCauley, but both promise to keep in touch.

Once in her new house, Anastasia and Sam visit Gertrude Stein, an elderly neighbor whom Sam describes as a witch. The reclusive Mrs. Stein immediately likes Sam, but says she doesn't like older children. Nevertheless, Anastasia makes friends with her after she buys her a goldfish and begins fixing her hair every day. Anastasia also becomes friends with Steve Harvey, the first boy she finds her age who is taller than she is. A series of premature assumptions create the comic conclusion. Anastasia forgets that she has invited both Robert and Jenny (whom she assumes are fast friends) to ride over on Saturday. (She mistakenly assumes that they are fast friends because Jenny, who really can't stand Robert, went to a movie with him.) Consequently, in her eagerness to introduce the lonely Mrs. Stein to others, she invites the people at the Senior Center to visit. Katherine Krupnik assumes that her daughter has invited a gang of young people. To make matters worse, Anastasia must turn down an invitation to join Steve's family for a Saturday picnic.

On the fateful Saturday, the Krupniks send Mrs. Stein to the beauty parlor. The children and the seniors arrive, and Jenny is embarrassed by Robert's presence, but everyone gets along well. When Gertrude returns wearing a hat because she thinks she looks ugly, the seniors convince her to join the party. Steve and his family, who have canceled their outing because of rain, also show up. Gertrude overcomes her fear of life and indicates that she will seek further social outings, and Anastasia adds to Gertrude's happiness by showing her some writing on the wallpaper of Anastasia's room: it is a message of love from Gertrude's former neighbor. Robert leaves knowing that Sam is not handicapped, but he now assumes that Sam is emotionally disturbed because he "flashed" the guests. Anastasia, who had assumed that writing a novel would be easy once she had a title, quickly concludes her novel about "The Mystery of Saying Good-Bye" to join Steve on the tennis courts.

Other books in the Anastasia series include: Anastasia at Your Service *(1982);* Anastasia, Ask Your Analyst *(1984);* Anastasia on Her Own *(1985);* Anastasia Has the Answers *(1986);* Anastasia's Chosen Career *(1987); and* Anastasia at This Address *(1991).*

CHARACTERS: Only the central character changes, but her altered perceptions present different views of each minor character. **Anastasia Krupnik**, a spunky and often rebellious ten-year-old, wears glasses with large, owl-like lenses. She has hair the color of a Hubbard squash and fourteen freckles across her nose. Anastasia, who calls herself "mercurial," records words, beginnings of poems, and lists in her green notebook to analyze her constantly changing feelings. In doing so, she is always honest because lying gives her a stomachache. Anastasia's major concern is with defining her identity. She hates her name, for example, because she can't make a nickname ending in "i" and is therefore the only girl excluded from the "*i* Club." Furthermore, Anastasia believes that the other children never elect her class secretary because they can't spell her name. The idea of a new name (and of wearing a "wedding" dress for Holy Communion) makes Catholicism temporarily attractive, but her characteristic honesty in refusing to say she is sorry about having bad thoughts about Mrs. Westvessel prevents her from converting. Because Anastasia wants to be interesting and special, she even grasps at the idea that she is the czar's daughter. At other times, however, she has difficulty appreciating her individuality. She feels dumb, for example, because she is the only one who likes cold spinach sandwiches. When she learns that she is going to have a brother, she therefore feels further isolated and determines to give him a nasty name.

Although Anastasia is disturbed by her changing feelings—she removes almost everything from the hate list—the changes indicate that she is bright and sensitive. Both qualities are notably evident in her responses to poetry. She loves words and writes a fine poem, even though Mrs. Westvessel's reaction makes her doubt her ability. She also understands Wordsworth better than her father's university students do. Realizing that her grandmother can be happy with the "inward eye" of memory, Anastasia thereby overcomes her uneasiness about the elderly. She then shows compassion and respect by getting her grandmother to talk about the past. Anastasia's sensitivity is also evident when Mrs. Westvessel calls. Forced to think of her teacher as a woman with a first name and her own personal sorrows, Anastasia no longer hates her. The final sign of Anastasia's growing maturity comes when she realizes that she no longer hates babies. She therefore offers to change her brother's wet diapers occasionally and abandons the idea of vengefully naming him One-Ball Reilly. In naming him Sam, Anastasia honors her grandmother's love for her husband and shows that she has developed a highly sensitive "inward eye."

In keeping with the major motif of *Anastasia Again!*, the characters are revealed primarily through the premature assumptions that they make. Spunky, opinionated Anastasia is now ten. Although she no longer makes lists, she still uses her notebook to sort out her life. Her concern for finding words that accurately describe situations and her writing of a mystery novel are attempts to understand things that bother or confuse her. Part of her trouble is that Anastasia makes assumptions about herself. Because she is taller than all the boys in her class and has skinny legs and oily hair, she believes that she is unattractive and will remain so. After hearing that Mrs. Stein married because she was a desperate spinster, Anastasia even assumes that she will eventually have to marry Robert Giannini because he will be the only man interested in her. Another part of her trouble is that she is afraid that she won't make new friends. Consequently, she clings to her false assumptions about the suburbs as a way of protecting herself from the pain of change.

Anastasia's conversational awkwardness causes others to make faulty assumptions, but she displays maturity and sensitivity. Once her mother explains why Gertrude behaves as she does, Anastasia insists on becoming Gertrude's friend. She is blunt when talking to Gertrude, but she kindly volunteers to fix the elderly woman's hair. She understands Gertrude's fears, so she makes the beauty shop appointment without consulting her and cleverly arranges the seniors' surprise visit. Anastasia is also kind and sensitive when she shows Gertrude the writing on the wallpaper: by doing so she gives the old lady something joyful to remember that, combined with her new appearance, makes her confident about rejoining society. Ultimately, Anastasia notices her likeness to Gertrude because she, too, feels better about herself after fixing her troublesome hair. Anastasia therefore happily enters into the suburban social world that she once assumed she would hate.

Anastasia's father, **Dr. Myron Krupnik**, is a six-foot-four-inch Harvard English professor and poet. He is bald, has a beard the color of a Hubbard squash, and wears glasses. As a modern parent, Dr. Krupnik has such an open and honest relationship with his daughter that he is able to talk about the love affair he had before he met his wife. He is also kind and understanding. For example, he changes the "F" on Anastasia's poem into the word "Fabulous." He is perceptive in recognizing that Anastasia feels excluded from the family and therefore gives her the responsibility of naming her brother. He also is wise in leading Anastasia to discover for herself her feelings about Wordsworth and her grandmother. In *Anastasia Again!* Dr. Krupnik has his moments of bad temper, but he is fundamentally a supportive parent. He introduces the theme of premature assumptions by pointing out early that Anastasia has no basis for her opinions. He also introduces the theme of accuracy by demanding that Anastasia use a word other than *weird* to describe situations. He demonstrates his respect for his daughter by insisting that she help choose their new house and by treating seriously her request for a house with a tower.

Anastasia most frequently thinks of **Katherine Krupnik**, her thirty-five-year-old mother, in terms of the smells that define her roles: turpentine because she is a painter, vanilla and brown sugar because she is a mother, and perfume because she is a wife and lover. Mrs. Krupnik is not as prominent in shaping her daughter's attitudes as her husband, but she humors Anastasia without being condescending. She is also open, displaying a range of adult emotions in front of her daughter. Thus, she tells Anastasia about a love affair she had before she met her husband, explains why she is in love with her husband, and becomes obviously jealous at the mention of her husband's previous relationships. In *Anastasia Again!* Anastasia's mother endears herself to her daughter because she is understanding and never laughs at her problems. When Anastasia tells her about Robert's premature assumption about Sam, for example, Katherine explains that she herself once caused even more embarrassing assumptions. Katherine is patient and wise: she explains why Gertrude behaves in a gruff way and thereby helps Anastasia to understand both Gertrude and herself.

Sam Krupnik, Anastasia's two-and-half-year-old brother, is verbally precocious, but he is still a baby and needs a security blanket to comfort him. Because Gertrude responds favorably to him, he is a device for showing that she is a kind person. He also adds comedy to situations, such as when he remembers what Anastasia told him about flashers and so he gleefully flashes the guests at the party.

Anastasia's paternal **grandmother** plays a crucial role in making Anastasia deal with ambivalent feelings. Grandmother is a ninety-two-year-old woman with scabby wrinkles at the sides of her mouth. She annoys Anastasia, who is uncomfortable around old people, by spilling food, talking with her mouth full, and being forgetful. Nevertheless, this senile woman leads Anastasia to important discoveries. Gray-haired Grandmother lives in the past when Sam, her loving husband, called her "Ruthie with the red, red hair." Anastasia learns that, although she can feel the pathos of her grandmother's isolation, her grandmother is happy because she escapes into memories. Anastasia also appreciates her grandmother's love for her husband, which she lovingly honors by naming her brother Sam.

Minor characters in *Anastasia Krupnik* reveal changes in Anastasia's maturing feelings. **Mrs. Dorothy Westvessel**, Anastasia's fourth grade teacher, contrasts with her grandmother. Mrs. Westvessel has a wrinkly face, brown spots on her hands, and a faint gray mustache. She wears stockings with seams and shoes that lace at the side. Although she appears

old, she doesn't act it; she even dances a jig in class. Mrs. Westvessel presents Anastasia with contradictory feelings. Anastasia's father uses her as an example of a person who doesn't understand poetry after she gives Anastasia's poem an "F." Although she is puzzled by the poem, Mrs. Westvessel actually fails Anastasia for not listening to instructions that required a poem with rhyme and capital letters. She clearly shows concern and compassion when she calls Anastasia after her grandmother's death, thereby teaching her that others can understand and sympathize with her. **Mr. Belden**, who runs the drugstore, at first appears to be an insensitive adult. He humiliates Anastasia in front of the boys and annoys her by calling her "girlie." Anastasia appreciates another side of his character when he is polite and gives her a chocolate cigar after her brother is born.

Some of Anastasia's friends in *Anastasia Krupnik* serve as influences on her, too. **Jennifer MacCauley** has attributes that Anastasia admires: curly hair, a broken tooth, and more Barbie clothes than any other girl in the fourth grade. Jennifer has a confused notion of her Catholic religion. Nevertheless, she creates a way of gauging Anastasia's emotional growth. When she tells Anastasia that good Catholics must be sorry for wishing ill on others, Anastasia rejects the idea of becoming a Catholic. Later Anastasia shows she has changed by being sorry for wishing that Mrs. Westvessel would get pimples. **Washburn Cummings** is an African-American boy in the sixth grade. He is the same height as Anastasia, but he has a towering Afro into which he tucks his comb. Washburn is rebellious, displaying an obscene tee shirt in class after he is told to go home. He attracts Anastasia because of his style. Anastasia, who tries to bounce an imaginary basketball and wiggle her hips in the same cocky way that he does, learns that she must be herself when he laughs at her attempt at an Afro.

In *Anastasia Again!* **Mrs. Gertrude Stein** is an elderly woman whose ugly face and unkempt hair gives her a witchlike appearance. Actually, she is a frightened woman whose arthritic hands prevent her from taking care of her hair. She married because she didn't want to be an old maid, but her husband left her after only three years. Forty years later, she is a lonely recluse. Although she assumes that she doesn't like either older children or other adults, Gertrude comes to value Anastasia's friendship and, because of her, learns that she can be happy again with other adults. **Robert Giannini** is an eccentric boy who carries a briefcase everywhere so that he has a place for the junk he collects. He speaks with a squeaky, girlish voice that annoys Anastasia. He demands so many trivial details during a telephone conversation that Anastasia thinks of him as the "Detail Freak." Robert is the only character who lives up to Anastasia's assumptions. Some of the seniors find Robert interesting, but Jenny and Anastasia, who have both spent time with him, decide that he is an embarrassing jerk. **Jenny MacCauley**, Anastasia's best friend in Cambridge, temporarily replaces her with Robert as a friend, but she becomes embarrassed by his clothing and his obsession with details. **Steve Harvey**, Anastasia's suburban friend, is taller than she is, thereby destroying her assumption that her height will guarantee loneliness. He and his talented family destroy Anastasia's preconceptions about the tackiness of suburban life, just as she and her family destroy his assumptions that people from Cambridge are intellectuals who always drink rose-hip tea.

Number the Stars

(novel, 1989)

PLOT: Set in 1943 during the Nazi occupation, this Newbery Medal winner celebrates the humanity and courage of the Danish people who saved almost all of the Jews living in Denmark. Annemarie Johansen is terribly frightened when German soldiers stop her, her sister, Kirsti, and her Jewish friend, Ellen Rosen, while they are running home from school. The experience makes her doubt her own courage. Later, when her parents learn that the Germans are going to round up Jews for relocation, they hide the Rosen family. Peter Neilsen was engaged to Lise,

Annemarie's sister, when she died three years earlier. He takes Ellen's parents to a safe place to hide, while the Johansens keep Ellen with them. That night, German soldiers come to their apartment, and Annemarie rips off Ellen's Star of David chain so they won't see it. Mr. Johansen shows the soldiers a baby picture of Lise to persuade them that the dark-haired Ellen is really their daughter. The next day, Mrs. Johansen takes the three children to the coast to Uncle Henrik, a fisherman.

During the visit, her mother and uncle stage a funeral for Great-Aunt Birte, a person whom Annemarie knows did not exist. (Her uncle warns her that too much knowledge can be dangerous.) That night, Ellen's parents join a group watching over the coffin. Annemarie keeps her wits when German soldiers demand to know who has died. Inge, her mother, then prevents them from opening the coffin by claiming that Great-Aunt Birte died of typhus. After clothing the Jewish "mourners" with supplies hidden in the coffin, Peter Nielsen and Inge lead separate groups to Uncle Henrik's boat so he can smuggle them to freedom in Sweden. Early in the morning, however, Annemarie makes two discoveries. First, her mother has broken her ankle while returning from the boat. Second, Mr. Rosen has dropped a package that Henrik needs. Annemarie volunteers to deliver the package, which is hidden in a lunch basket. German soldiers with guard dogs stop her and open the package, but they allow Annemarie, who puts on an act that she is a very silly girl who knows nothing, to proceed. Afterward, she learns that she delivered a handkerchief soaked with a chemical that blunts a dog's sense of smell and that Henrik used it to stop the Germans from discovering the Rosens. The novel concludes with the Johansens preparing for the return of the Rosens at the end of the war. Annemarie, who knows that Peter Nielsen has been executed, now learns the truth about her sister: like Peter, Lise was a member of the Resistance and was killed by the Germans.

CHARACTERS: This is a third-person narrative told from Annemarie's viewpoint. Consequently, characters are revealed only to the degree that they contribute to her development. **Annemarie Johansen** demonstrates that even ordinary people are capable of heroic courage. A lanky ten-year-old with long, silvery-blond hair, Annemarie doubts that she is brave enough to die for anyone because she was so frightened when soldiers detained her. She naively assumes, however, that she is an ordinary person and that bravery is necessary only in fairy tales. But circumstances eventually prove her wrong. She shows great presence of mind, for example, when she tears off Ellen's Star of David before the German officer can see it. When she realizes that her mother is lying about Great-Aunt Birte, Annemarie enters the adult world of understanding. She also demonstrates mature competence by keeping her wits when the officer asks her who is in the coffin. That night she approaches despair while thinking that God could not number the stars because the universe is too big and cruel. Annemarie herself, however, shows that compassion and goodness still exist.

After Annemarie has a hero's traditional luck in finding the dropped package, she courageously volunteers to deliver it, succeeding because of her physical and intellectual abilities. First, Annemarie uses her talent as a swift runner who has won school races to reach the boat before it sails. Second, she shows her intelligence and powers of observation, as well as her acting talent: while the Germans examine her basket, she behaves just as Kirsti did earlier when the soldiers stopped them on the street. As she later learns, her ignorance of the true nature of the package also helps by preventing her from mistakenly revealing its nature. Annemarie, who told herself a fairy tale during her quest to help her keep calm, does not realize that she has been as brave as any fairy-tale hero. Uncle Henrik, too, explains that, although she was frightened, she was truly brave because she forgot about the danger she was in and concentrated solely on her duty.

Inge Johansen, Annemarie's mother, is an emotionally strong woman. After the Germans visit the family's apartment, she agrees that they must get Ellen out of Copenhagen. Although her husband wants to accompany them, she convinces him that she and the children would be safer alone. Mrs.

Johansen displays heroic ingenuity when she tells the lie about Great-Aunt Birte dying of typhus, thereby preventing the Germans from discovering that the coffin actually contains supplies. She also shows love and courage after she breaks her ankle. Knowing that Annemarie would be worried, she crawls for hours to be with her again. **Mr. Johansen** plays a lesser role, but he also shows compassion, courage, and cleverness. He not only takes in Ellen and helps her parents to escape, but he cleverly pulls out a baby picture of his deceased daughter, Lise, to prove that one of his children could have dark hair. Only at the end of the novel does it become clear that he and his wife avoided talking about Lise in order to protect their other children from knowing too much. **Kirsti Johansen** is a stubborn five-year-old with short, tangled curls. Because the Germans have been in Copenhagen for as long as she can remember, she does not feel quite the same fear that Annemarie does. Kirsti's main function is to create tension and suspense: because Kirsti is so young, Annemarie worries that she will say something that will expose Ellen Rosen's Jewish identity to the soldiers. **Uncle Henrik**, Mrs. Johansen's brother, is a bachelor fisherman who lives in a dirty and messy house on the coast. He demonstrates the bravery and ingenuity of the Danes who risked their lives by smuggling Jews to Sweden. He also functions as a wise old man. He foreshadows Annemarie's development by assuring her that she would be brave if the occasion required her to be. A practical man, he also explains to Annemarie why ignorance promotes safety. Finally, he makes the theme explicit when he explains to Annemarie and, by extension, to the reader that bravery means performing one's duty in spite of being afraid.

Red-headed **Peter Nielsen** embodies the courage and idealism that Annemarie thought belonged only to heroes in fairy tales. Once a fun-loving boy, he becomes more somber after the Germans kill his fiancée. Nevertheless, he risks his life by working with the Resistance and by helping Jews to escape. He becomes a heroic victim when the Nazis execute him. **Ellen Rosen**, Annemarie's stocky, dark-haired Jewish friend, is imaginative and can make any game more fun. She brings out the best qualities in

Annemarie, who protects her by removing her Star of David and by not telling her the truth about Great-Aunt Birte. **Sophy Rosen**, Ellen's mother, is a cautious and protective woman. **Mr. Rosen**, her father, is a dedicated teacher who becomes a plot device: when he accidentally drops the package, he creates the situation that tests Annemarie's bravery.

Further Reading

Authors and Artists for Young Adults. Vol. 5. Detroit: Gale Research, 1991.

Berger, Laura Standley, ed. *Twentieth-Century Young Adult Writers*. 1st ed. Detroit: St. James, 1994.

Children's Literature Review. Vol. 6. Detroit: Gale Research, 1984.

Collier, Laurie, and Joyce Nakamura, eds. *Major Authors and Illustrators for Children and Young Adults*. Detroit: Gale Research, 1993.

Contemporary Authors New Revision Series. Vol. 43. Detroit: Gale Research, 1994.

Estes, Glenn E., ed. *American Writers for Children since 1960: Fiction*. Vol. 52 of *Dictionary of Literary Biography*. Detroit: Gale Research, 1986.

Holtze, Sally Holmes, ed. *Fifth Book of Junior Authors and Illustrators*. New York: H. W. Wilson, 1983.

Something about the Author. Vols. 23, 70. Detroit: Gale Research, 1981, 1993.

Something about the Author Autobiography Series. Vol. 3. Detroit: Gale Research, 1986.

George MacDonald

1824-1905, Scottish minister, academic, and author

At the Back of the North Wind

(fantasy, 1871)

PLOT: Part symbolic fantasy and part realistic fiction, this novel is about spiritual maturation and the acceptance of death. Little Diamond, son of Joseph the coachman, is awakened by North Wind, who appears in the form of a beautiful lady. Instructed to go outside, Diamond obeys but can't find her. On another night, Diamond accompanies North Wind on her rounds. She turns into a wolf to scare a drunken nurse and then has Diamond ride in her hair while she sweeps away London's smells. North Wind leaves when Diamond helps Nanny, a crossing-sweeper being buffeted by the winds. Because Sal, Nancy's gin-drinking grandmother, locks them out, Nanny and Diamond spend the night wandering. On her next visit, North Wind tests Diamond's courage by taking him to a ledge high up in a cathedral. While she then goes off to sink a ship, Diamond falls asleep and dreams that the apostles are talking to him. Later, Diamond's mother, Martha, sends him away for his health. North Wind takes him to the country at her back. When he returns, Martha tells Diamond that he has been deathly ill.

At this point in the story, fantasy elements give way to realism. The Colemans, Joseph's employers, lose their fortune, forcing Joseph to move his family and become a cabman. Diamond makes many friends and learns to drive a cab. When he hears a drunken cabman beating his wife, Diamond enters their rooms and calms their baby. His saintly disposition improves the cabman's character. Diamond also helps Nanny: he saves her from bullies and gets wealthy Mr. Raymond to put her in the hospital after she becomes ill. When Joseph becomes ill, Diamond drives his cab to support the family. One day, a shabby gentleman chases away some boys trying to rob Diamond. Recognizing that the man is Mr. Evans, the long absent fiancé of Miss Coleman, Diamond takes him to the Colemans' new home. Mr. Raymond, who must go abroad, then arranges for Joseph to take in Nanny and care for his horse, Ruby. The arrangement costs Joseph, especially after Ruby injures himself and can't earn his keep. (Diamond overhears Ruby telling Old Diamond, the horse, that he is an angel horse testing Joseph.) Mr. Raymond finally returns and invites Joseph to move to the country as his coachman. Diamond, Mr. Raymond's page, arranges a position for Nanny's crippled friend, Jim. Nanny and Jim continue to mock Diamond as a simpleton, "God's baby." The narrator now reveals that he met Diamond, who was again seeing North Wind. She takes Diamond to his original residence, but Diamond realizes that it is no longer home.

Shortly afterwards, when Diamond is found dead, the narrator says that Diamond has gone back of the North Wind.

CHARACTERS: North Wind, the only fantasy character, assumes many forms. She first appears as a lady who grows into a giant with flowing hair that waves across the sky and surrounds her moonlike face. Later, she is a young girl, a wolf, a spider, a weasel, a cat, and winds varying from breezes to gales. She also has multiple roles. In keeping with the archetypal symbolism of wind, she is a spiritual force, the servant of a baby who is clearly Christ. In addition, North Wind is a mother figure who comforts and reassures Diamond. She is a mentor speaking, as MacDonald's wise characters typically do, in paradoxes that her student does not fully grasp. North Wind also has physically active roles. She is an agent of retribution, assuming the form of the wolf to punish a drunken nurse for her dereliction. She is bad fortune, evil chance, or ruin, as she shows when she sinks the ship that kills innocent passengers and ruins the Colemans. She insists, however, that she does good, not evil. By sinking the ship, for example, she saves Mr. Coleman from dishonest speculations and makes Mr. Evans recognize that he loves Miss Coleman. North Wind is also death, a symbolic function particularly evident when she becomes a gigantic sphinx-like being through whose cold center Diamond must pass to reach the country at her back. By taking Diamond to the "picture" of this country, she gives him a vision of heavenly bliss that alters his life. She thus symbolically teaches him that death, the journey to the real country at her back, is nothing to fear.

Little Diamond, named after his father's horse, is good from the beginning, but he develops a higher innocence that other people regard as simplemindedness. Diamond's development occurs in three stages. In the first, North Wind tests and educates him. Diamond learns immediate and unquestioning obedience because North Wind leaves when he takes too long to go outside. Later, he learns that he must

not rely on appearances because she takes many forms. He also learns intellectual humility, accepting that she is good although she does cruel things. Furthermore, Diamond develops courage, losing all fear after North Wind places him on the ledge of the cathedral and then blows in his face, an act symbolizing a gift of spiritual power. Having acquired faith that she will not harm him, Diamond is rewarded with a dream vision in which false apostles make him recognize that the institutional church is materialistic. This stage culminates with Diamond's visit to the country at the back of the North Wind. Because Diamond undergoes a symbolic death, losing consciousness as he passes through the burning coldness of the North Wind and appearing to be on the point of death in his own room, his journey denotes a rebirth. Receiving a spiritual vision of a country that is the picture of the true country back of the North Wind (that is, heaven), he is reborn as "God's baby." The change in character is evident afterwards because he composes and sings verses, imaginative activities inspired by the poem of the river in that country.

In the second stage, Diamond matures and ministers to the mundane world. At home, he helps his mother with the children, and he assumes adult responsibility by earning money when his father is ill. Outside the home, he is a model Christian, refusing to cheat, lie, or misrepresent things. His meek, innocent, and optimistic demeanor makes the cabmen control their vulgarity. More importantly, Diamond is an angelic deliverer. He reforms the drunken cabman. He also saves Miss Coleman from misery and sickness by bringing Mr. Evans to her. Diamond shows courage by gallantly defending Nanny against thugs and by taking a dangerous journey to the social underworld to visit her when she is ill. He then shows cleverness, saving her life by getting Mr. Raymond's help. Far from having "a tile loose," as Nanny claims, Diamond is saintly, even Christ-like.

In the final stage, Diamond moves to the country, where nature reinvigorates his spiritual vision. Living in a tower, MacDonald's architectural symbol of spirituality, he again meets North Wind. She allows him to recognize that his first home isn't home any longer and that he can't return to childhood. In fact, Diamond is so spiritual that Earth is no longer his home: he thus completes his development by moving to the true country at the back of the North Wind.

Joseph, Diamond's father, is an upright, honest coachman and a proud, patient father. Like Job in the Bible, he is faithful when Mr. Raymond tests his character by boarding Ruby with him. **Martha**, Diamond's mother, is a loving woman who worries about her son's deteriorating physical health. **Old Diamond**, Joseph's horse, is a faithful animal who represents the dutiful and respectful servant. **Ruby**, Mr. Raymond's horse, at first advocates taking advantage of others whenever one can, yet he finally declares that he is an angel horse sent to test Joseph's goodness by adding to his troubles. **Nanny**, the little crossing-sweeper, underlines one mystery of human existence: not everyone receives equal treatment. Nanny, an orphan raised by a cruel, gin-drinking grandmother, does not have Diamond's spiritual resources. When she becomes ill, she does receive a spiritual vision and becomes a better person, but she is too prosaic to see that dreams are truth. Rational and skeptical, she patronizingly insists that Diamond is a half-wit. **Jim**, her crippled friend, is improved by meeting Diamond, but he lacks gratitude and supports Nanny's assessment.

Mr. Raymond, a tall, wealthy gentleman, is a *deus ex machina*, helping to resolve the plot. A kind man, he saves Nanny by having her hospitalized. He also improves the life of Joseph and his family by offering Joseph a position at his country estate. As a poet, Mr. Raymond has superior understanding and recognizes that Diamond, far from being a half-wit, is actually a genius in his spiritual understanding. **The narrator**, a tutor who also recognizes Diamond's spiritual genius, renders Diamond's childish record of his experiences into comprehensible form. A confidant, the narrator is the only adult who understands that Diamond finally entered the country at the back of the North Wind. **Mr. Evans**, who survives the wreck of the ship, demonstrates positive benefits of adversity. He is a crass materialist who delayed his marriage to Miss Coleman because he wanted to give her a fine house, but he learns the meaning of love because of the shipwreck. Humbled, he returns for forgiveness. **Miss Coleman**, his sickly fiancée, becomes worse when she believes that Mr. Evans is dead because she has nothing useful to do. She and her parents share the blame for her empty life, a lesson they learn when the shipwreck destroys their way of life.

The Princess Books

(fantasy series, 1872, 1883)

PLOT: The symbolic "Princess Books" support MacDonald's contention that "A genuine work of art must mean many things." They have received widely varying interpretations, but critics agree that their themes concern faith, intellectual knowledge, change, and salvation.

The Princess and the Goblin (1872) focuses on the conflict between evil goblins and humans. While exploring her castle, Princess Irene discovers an old lady, her great-great-grandmother Irene, in a tower. The princess tells her nurse, Lootie, about the meeting, but Lootie doesn't believe her. Later, Lootie and Irene are frightened by goblins and become lost on the mountain. Curdie, a miner and son of Peter Peterson, scares away the goblins. Soon afterwards, Curdie finds the goblins' home and overhears a plot against the miners. That winter, Irene rediscovers her grandmother, who heals her inflamed thumb. On the night appointed for a return visit, Irene flees outside in panic when she sees a long-legged cat. Seeing a light in the tower, however, Irene gains the courage to go back. Her grandmother then gives Irene a ring. In times of danger, Irene is to follow an invisible thread attached to the ring.

Meanwhile, Curdie, marking his trail with a ball of string, explores the goblins' realm. He overhears the goblin king and queen arguing about kidnapping Irene as a bride for Prince Harelip. The goblin queen, who wears granite shoes, captures Curdie and imprisons him in a hole, where she hopes to starve him to death. Irene, wakened by a noise, follows her thread into the caves. She releases Curdie and takes him to the tower. Irene then talks to her grandmother, but Curdie sees and hears nothing. After Curdie leaves, the grandmother bathes Irene. Thinking that Irene fooled him, Curdie is angry, but his mother (Joan) suggests that some people see what others can't. Curdie soon learns what it means to be doubted. Shot while patrolling the castle grounds, he tells his story about the goblins, but Lootie and the soldiers don't believe him, especially after his wound makes him delirious. After the goblins break into the castle's wine cellar, the grandmother appears in a dream and heals Curdie. He then leads the attack against the goblins, preventing Harelip from carrying off Lootie. When the battle ends, Curdie feels the invisible thread and follows it home, where he finds Irene. The next day, Irene's King-papa agrees that she must keep an earlier promise and kiss Curdie. During a subsequent banquet, Curdie realizes that the goblins are flooding the mines. He evacuates the castle, saving everyone. Although the King offers him a position, Curdie decides to stay with his parents and asks only for a warm petticoat for his mother.

Set a year later, ***The Princess and Curdie*** (1883) begins when Curdie wantonly shoots a white pigeon. He goes to the tower, where the grandmother heals the pigeon and then warns Curdie against laughing about her. At work, Curdie remains silent when the miners joke about Old Mother Wotherwop. After the others leave, a light guides Peter and Curdie to a young lady. She gives Peter a stone and tells Curdie that he has royal blood. Admitting that she is actually Irene's grandmother, she says that she will appear in many forms. She appears to be even younger the next night, when she has Curdie put his hands into a fire made of roses. Curdie thereby gains the power to know people's inner natures by touching their hands. As instructed, Curdie tells Peter that his stone will indicate whether Curdie is safe, and then he departs for the King's court.

Lina, an ugly beast, joins Curdie, protecting him from attacking birds and subjugating other beasts in the forest. In Gwyntystorm, home of the court, Lina kills two butcher's dogs that attack Curdie. After spending the night in the cottage of old Derba, Curdie is arrested and imprisoned. Lina finds him

and helps him to escape into a cellar, where Curdie observes a butler drawing wine. Realizing that he is in the palace, Curdie finds the King's chamber, where Princess Irene reveals that her father is ill. Secretly observing Dr. Kelman, Curdie concludes that the doctor is giving the King drugged wine. Curdie fetches good wine and bread, enabling the King to recover sufficiently to refuse the Lord Chamberlain's request to sign a document.

After getting an honest maid to warn that retribution is at hand, Curdie has Lina and her subjugated beasts drive out of Gwyntystorm the carousing servants and the seven officials conspiring against the King. The deposed Lord Chancellor, however, convinces a neighboring army to attack. Before the attack, the grandmother places the King in a fire of roses, restoring his health. Sir Bronzebeard, the loyal colonel who had also been drugged by the conspirators, joins the King, Curdie, Lina, and the animals in attacking the enemy. Peter, alerted by the stone, joins them and stops a soldier from killing the faithful maid, who is actually the grandmother. She summons thousands of birds and defeats the enemy. The conspirators are then appropriately punished, and the good are rewarded. When she reaches age, Irene marries Curdie, who is now Prince Conrad. After Irene's father dies, they rule the kingdom. Dying childless, they are forgotten, and Gwyntystorm eventually collapses.

CHARACTERS: Most of the characters have symbolic attributes, but they also function as fairy-tale figures. **Princess Irene** is a fair and pretty eight-year-old whose blue eyes each contain a melted star. In MacDonald's symbolism, a princess represents the ideal attainable by every good girl. Polite, considerate, and truthful, Irene honorably insists on keeping promises and therefore kisses Curdie for saving her. Irene undergoes a process of maturation: repeatedly becoming lost, she finds herself through faith. Irene's discovery of her grandmother symbolizes spiritual vision. Her maturation requires that she accept such spiritual visions, even when they are contrary to commonplace logic. Significantly, Irene afterwards fails when she deliberately seeks her grandmother. Instead of going up to the tower—a movement suggesting spiritual elevation—she goes down to the kitchen, suggesting a descent into rationality and the world of the senses. She must therefore learn that spiritual truth is given, not discovered through conscious seeking. Once she enters the spiritual world symbolized by the tower, however, she finds that it is restorative: the grandmother heals Irene's inflamed thumb.

Although given faith, Irene must pass tests to preserve it because conversations with rationalists make her doubt her own experiences. Irene must therefore overcome irrational fears (represented by the long-legged cat) in order to see the grandmother again. The faith that she confirms is symbolized by the invisible thread, which she, unlike Curdie, can feel. By using it as a guide, she saves Curdie from death and leads him through a river (symbol of life) to the upper world. As a reward, the grandmother gives Irene a bath. A symbol of baptism, it makes her feel as if she were made new, an indication that she is now "twice born." In the sequel, Irene is only a figure of the dutiful and loving daughter, sacrificing her own sleep to watch over her sick father.

In the first volume, **Curdie**, who is nearly thirteen, is both helper and hero. Brave and witty, Curdie saves Irene and Lootie by singing rhymes that infuriate the goblins. He similarly fends off the goblins after they imprison him. His talent may therefore symbolize the artist's control over the unconscious or the passions. As a hero, Curdie saves the castle, leading the attack against the goblin invaders and then evacuating it before the goblins can flood it. From the beginning, Curdie is morally upright. He thus rebukes Lootie for failing in her duty to protect Irene. He is also gallant, promising to return for Irene's kiss. In addition, he is a loving and dutiful son who works overtime so that he can purchase a warm petticoat for his mother and who remains with his parents instead of going away with the king.

Curdie's most notable function, however, is that of foil to Irene. A representative of rationality, Curdie explores the goblins' cave by marking his trail with a ball of string, a logical device paralleling the invisible thread of faith guiding Irene. Unable to accept what his senses do not confirm, Curdie can't comprehend what Irene perceives through faith. Thus, Curdie refuses to believe that Irene has a thread. Furthermore, lacking the spiritual vision to see and hear the grandmother, he thinks that Irene is mocking him. Suffering, however, transforms Curdie. After being wounded and ridiculed for his tales about the goblins, Curdie becomes sensitive, although not to the same degree as Irene. Thus, he then sees the grandmother, but only in a dream. Nevertheless, even this spiritual vision heals him and enables him to feel the invisible thread, signaling his acquisition of faith. What is more, after apologizing to Irene, Curdie shows moral growth: he refrains from judging those who did not believe his warnings about the goblins.

In the sequel, Curdie must show that he is a true prince because he has become complacent and now doubts his spiritual experiences. When he shoots the pigeon, Curdie suffers a fortunate fall, a sin that shocks him into recognizing his spiritual decline and that invites the grandmother's mystical intervention. Although Curdie now sees the grandmother, she tests his perception by appearing in many forms, forcing him to judge those he meets by character and deeds, not appearance. The magical gift he receives, the ability to determine by touching a hand whether a person is truly a human or a beast, symbolizes new spiritual and psychological awareness.

During his classic fairy-tale journey from home to the palace, Curdie grows in bravery and understanding. He recognizes the crass commercialism and selfishness in Gwyntystorm, he understands the duplicitous conspirators, and he sees the depredations of the servants. Becoming a force of moral and social order, he drives out evil and restores Gwyntystorm to its rightful ruler. His maturity and moral certainty earn him a new name and status: Curdie becomes Prince Conrad and eventually rules the kingdom.

Grandmother Irene, the great-great-grandmother of Princess Irene, says that she is a queen, but she is called the old princess in the second book. She appears in many guises, from a crone to a beautiful young woman. Most frequently she is an old woman with a spinning wheel, an image of fate.

In spite of her age, her skin is smooth, making her seem beyond the reach of time. She is also an archetypal wise old woman. Frequently expressing herself in paradoxes, she instructs both Irene and Curdie. At times, the symbols associated with her suggest religious meanings. She thus talks about approaching two thousand years of age (a length identified with the Christian era) and she washes Irene's feet, which is reminiscent of the act Christ performed for the apostles. When she bathes Irene, she performs a baptismal ritual. Furthermore, she is identified with white birds, conventional symbols of the Holy Spirit. The grandmother's rooms in the tower are larger than logic permits and have impossible views of the heavens. Because MacDonald typically uses architecture to symbolize human faculties, the grandmother's lodgings may thus symbolize spiritual understanding or imagination.

Although it is impossible to pin a single meaning on the grandmother, her role is simple: she is a magical helper or fairy godmother. She thus heals Irene when her thumb is inflamed and Curdie when he is wounded by the arrow. During the battle in Gwyntystorm, she directs the birds who defeat the attacking army. Furthermore, she performs magical rituals that renew those who are good: she uses a fire of roses (an image combining symbols of love and purification) to liberate Lina, to renew the King, and to grant Curdie magical knowledge through touch; she uses her mystical tub to bathe and renew Irene. She also provides magical help, giving Irene the ring and invisible thread, and shining a moonlike light or sending bird messengers to guide people to safety. The grandmother frequently tests people before helping them, but she is a nurturing, reassuring presence who aids those who believe or are capable of changing their conduct.

Because his home is built on a rock, suggesting the idea of Peter and the rock upon which the Church is built, **Peter Peterson**, Curdie's father, is connected to the idea of religious legitimacy. A poor man and an honest worker, he is a loving father and a model of proper behavior. When the grandmother's stone calls him to action, he shows fatherly concern by immediately leaving home. During the battle, he is a hero, saving the grandmother, who is disguised as the maid. **Joan Peterson**, Curdie's mother, has coarse and rough hands because of hard work, but she is a true lady inside. An earthly parallel to the ethereal wise grandmother, she is a loving woman who listens to her son and offers sage advice about his conduct. She supports the theme of faith by encouraging Curdie to believe Irene, noting that some people see what others can't. Irene's **King-papa** is taller than his subordinates, an indication of his superiority. He has a beard that comes to his waist, blue eyes, and an eagle-like nose. He represents legitimate authority. In the sequel, after he is poisoned by the conspirators (possibly a symbol of succumbing to deadly sins) he comes to his senses with the help of good wine and bread, symbols of the Eucharist, but he still needs to suffer in the grandmother's rose flame in order to be renewed. He then restores order and punishes sinners.

The elderly **Derba** is yet another earthly parallel to Irene's grandmother. She shows Christian charity by taking in Curdie when everyone else refuses him shelter. A nurturing, caring woman, she becomes the King's chatelaine (the mistress of the castle), bringing order and honesty to his household and healthfulness to his meals. **Lina**, apparently a human who has sinned, is a child beneath her grotesque body: her body is short, but she has long legs like those of an elephant, a tail twice the length and thickness of her body, a head that is a cross between that of a polar bear and that of a snake, a long neck, and teeth like a fringe of icicles. She redeems herself by being a faithful helper to Curdie. She shows him how to escape from the vault, she punishes Dr. Kelman, and she leads the animals against the servants and the attacking army. Afterwards, she enters the fire of roses and dissolves in smoke. **Sir Bronzebeard**, the King's colonel of the guard, is a loyal subject who is also drugged by the conspirators. Healed during the night by the grandmother, he is brave during the battle and is rewarded with the title of duke.

Lootie, Irene's nurse, represents the limitations of ordinary intellect. She can't believe Irene's truthful accounts, calling them nonsense. Her rudeness accentuates Irene's qualities as a true princess. Lootie's spiteful denunciation of Curdie causes others to ignore his warnings about the goblins. She is properly humiliated when Harelip kidnaps her, an act that shows that she is almost suitable as a bride for the goblins, the symbols of close-minded rationality.

Because of intellectual pride and selfishness, the **goblins** have devolved, losing their humanlike appearance to become grotesque monsters. They have soft-soled feet (possibly, as one of Curdie's songs suggests, because they lack souls). The goblins also have hard heads, symbolizing their intellectual arrogance. They thus ridicule humans for depending on the sun, whereas they provide their own lights (light is an archetypal symbol of knowledge). Their fear of poetry, furthermore, suggests a rejection of higher creative faculties. **The goblin king** is a foil to Irene's King-papa, being vindictive and selfish. **The goblin queen** has egg-shaped eyes that sit vertically instead of horizontally in her head. When she laughs, her mouth stretches to her ears, which are in the middle of her cheeks. Her personality is as ugly as her appearance. A liar and a hypocrite, she denies that her stone shoes conceal the fact that she has six toes on each foot. The goblin queen contrasts with the grandmother and Joan Peterson, both nurturing mother figures. She thus jealously opposes her stepson's plans to marry the beautiful Irene, and she decides on starving the captured Curdie. As a suitor to Irene, **Harelip**, the goblin crown prince, is a comical foil to Curdie. His misshapen mouth underlines the fact that he can't speak the creative rhymes and the truths that Curdie utters. His foolishness is apparent when, unable to find Irene, he tries to carry off Lootie for his bride.

Only two of the seven people who conspire against the King in Gwyntystorm are individualized. **The Lord Chamberlain**, as Curdie discovers by touching his hand, is devolving into a bird of prey. His appearance supports this characterization: lean, long, and yellow-skinned, he has a small, bald head with tufts of hair at the back and the ears; a thin, hooked noose; loose skin beneath the chin and on the throat; tiny, glittering black eyes; an exceptionally small mouth; and long, skinny fingers. He tries to deceive the King into signing a will that would enable the conspirators to seize power. As punish-

ment for his rapacity, he is tied to the leg-serpent, an animal representing his natural enemy in the wild. **Dr. Kelman**, the King's physician, is a little round man who is devolving into a serpent. He even utters an involuntary hiss of hatred while he is attending the King. Although snakes are associated with the caduceus, the symbol of medicine, Dr. Kelman has perverted his calling to become one who sickens his patients instead of helping them. Fittingly, Lina crushes his leg so that he can't walk.

Further Reading

Berger, Laura Standley, ed. *Twentieth-Century Children's Writers*. 4th ed. Detroit: St. James, 1995.

Bingham, Jane M., ed. *Writers for Children: Critical Studies of Major Authors Since the Seventeenth Century*. New York: Scribner, 1988.

Collier, Laurie, and Joyce Nakamura, eds. *Major Authors and Illustrators for Children and Young Adults*. Detroit: Gale Research, 1993.

Contemporary Authors. Vol. 137. Detroit: Gale Research, 1992.

McGillis, Roderick, ed. *For the Childlike: George MacDonald's Fantasies for Children*. West Lafayette, IN: Children's Literature Association, 1992.

MacDonald, Greville. *George MacDonald and His Wife*. London: Allen & Unwin, 1924.

Nadel, Ira B., and William E. Fredeman, eds. *Victorian Novelists After 1885*. Vol. 18 of *Dictionary of Literary Biography*. Detroit: Gale Research, 1983.

Reis, Richard H. *George MacDonald*. New York: Twayne, 1972.

Something about the Author. Vol. 33. Detroit: Gale Research, 1983.

Twentieth-Century Literary Criticism. Vol. 9. Detroit: Gale Research, 1983.

Patricia MacLachlan

1938-, American novelist

Sarah, Plain and Tall

(novel, 1985)

PLOT: Patricia MacLachlan has said that "basically character and plot amount to the same thing. One grows from the other." The two are certainly closely tied together in her Newbery Medal-winning nov-

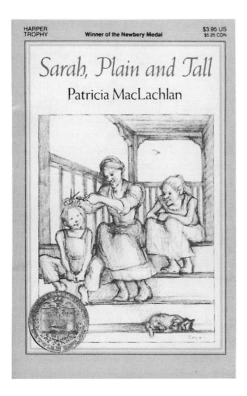

HARPER TROPHY · Winner of the Newbery Medal · $3.95 US $5.25 CDN

Sarah, Plain and Tall
Patricia MacLachlan

Sarah, with Caleb and Anna, from the cover of MacLachlan's Newbery Medal-winning novel.

el, *Sarah, Plain and Tall*. Based on a story MacLachlan's mother told her about a mail-order bride, this spare, poetic account of life on a pioneer farm does not contain much dramatic action. It is, however, filled with emotional tension.

The novel's major themes concern family relationships and the need to belong. The story is narrated by Anna, the daughter of Jacob Witting. Papa, as she calls him, is a widower. As winter comes to a close, he tells Anna and her brother, Caleb, that he has received a response to his newspaper advertisement for a new wife. The children are excited about the possibility of having a new mother. They are also nervous that Sarah Elisabeth Wheaton from Maine may not want to come to their isolated farm on the Great Plains. After they exchange letters with her, however, she agrees to a one-month trial visit.

Sarah arrives in the spring, the symbolic season of changes, and immediately fills a void in the family. Papa, who stopped singing when his wife died,

begins to sing again. The children constantly worry, however, that Sarah will miss her home by the sea and not want to stay with them. Caleb is especially sensitive, studying every action and word. He is encouraged by little things, such as when Sarah calls the hay pile on which they slide "our dune."

Sarah learns to plow, and she teaches the children how to swim in the cow pond. She seems cheerful until their neighbors Matthew and Maggie visit. Sarah's eyes fill with tears when she talks about Maine, which makes the children worry. Later, Sarah puts on Jacob's overalls and insists that she must learn to ride a horse and drive a wagon. She also insists on helping Jacob repair the roof to prepare for a coming storm. After this violent storm passes, Sarah helps Jacob replant the fields. When she insists on driving to town alone, the children fear that she will never come back. But she returns that evening, having purchased blue, gray, and green pencils so that she can add the colors of the sea to drawings of her new prairie home. The novel closes with Anna's joyful anticipation of the coming year, during which Sarah will be with them as their mother.

CHARACTERS: In her Newbery acceptance speech, MacLachlan said the characters in her novel grew from "what my mother used to call the heroics of a common life." The characters are ordinary people who not only endure but triumph over hardships and doubts.

Sarah Elisabeth Wheaton is not physically attractive. As she herself says, she is "plain and tall," and she has large hands roughened by years of hard work. She possesses, however, an engaging character. She is a generous person who is aware of her position in the world and the needs of those around her. She leaves Maine because she realizes that she will be in the way after her brother marries. At times, Sarah is unconventionally lively. She joyfully slides down the hay pile, and she coaxes the children, who have never been swimming, to plunge into the cow pond with her. Sarah continually displays her sensitive nature. She cries when she discovers a dead lamb, and she makes pets of the chickens that the neighbors bring her for eating. It is little wonder that the dogs are first to love her. Sarah also delights in nature, eagerly learning the names of new plants and flowers; she shows sensitivity by shedding tears when she thinks about all the people in Maine whom she misses.

By simply being herself, Sarah subtly alters those around her. Even Jacob throws his hair to the birds for use in their nests after she explains the custom. Sarah is most notable, however, for her practical qualities. She is a hard worker and is competent in many things. She dries flowers, makes good meals, sings, draws pictures, cuts hair, plows, repairs a roof, and drives a wagon alone. This last action is the most important sign of her independent spirit. This spirit is evident earlier, however, when she wears overalls despite Jacob's objections and when she insists that they repair the roof together. At such times, her independence emphasizes her differences as an outsider. When she drives the wagon alone, however, she shows that although she values her independence, she also wants to belong. (Driving is a skill that was common among the women of the plains, but not among the women of Maine.) By purchasing colored pencils, she is able to make drawings that preserve what she loves of her Maine home while committing herself fully to a new one.

The other characters do not have as much depth as Sarah. They primarily serve to demonstrate the effects of her personality. **Papa Jacob Witting** is a loving and attentive father. He is also a lonely man, as evidenced by the fact that he quit singing after his wife died. A hard worker himself, he initiates Sarah into the demands of prairie life by teaching her to plow. Jacob seems somewhat conservative, objecting to Sarah's decision to wear overalls, but he is not inflexible or stodgy. For example, he is the one who first demonstrates that a hay mound makes a good dune for sliding. When he begins using Sarah's expressions in conversation, he shows a willingness to reach out to her. He secretly throws hair out for the nesting birds, showing that she has made him more sensitive to nature. When he brings Sarah the first summer roses, he expresses through his actions the love that he is too shy to express in words.

His son, **Caleb**, is a talkative, inquisitive child. By constantly demanding that his sister tell him the story of his birth, Caleb reveals a need to define himself and an intense desire for a mother's love. Because Caleb is acutely observant, his questions and statements become primary devices for understanding the adults. He is the one who reveals Papa's sadness by asking whether Papa sang with their mother. He also notes every phrase Sarah uses and tries to decide whether she will stay or not. By worrying about Sarah's intentions, he adds emotional drama to the novel. His sister, **Anna**, is the narrator, but she is not as vividly present as the others. She obviously has the patience of an adult. She has played a large role in raising Caleb, because their mother died the day after he was born, and she also does much of the domestic work. Nevertheless, she longs for a mother, and her fears that Sarah will leave combine with Caleb's to bring suspense to the story.

The neighbors appear only briefly, but the wife plays an important role. **Maggie**, herself a mail-order bride from Tennessee, shows Sarah that an arranged marriage can be happy. She is also a voice of practical wisdom. She understands that Sarah is lonely and tells her that one always misses things wherever one goes. Maggie then advises Sarah on how to overcome her loneliness and sense of isolation. She urges Sarah to plant a garden on the prairie like the one she had tended in Maine, and she insists that Sarah learn to drive a wagon, although she had always walked in Maine. **Matthew**, Maggie's husband, demonstrates the generosity of prairie people when he brings horses to help Jacob plow. When he admits to Sarah that Maggie is occasionally lonely, he gives Sarah a role outside her new family. Sarah and Maggie are part of a community and must support each other emotionally.

Further Reading

Berger, Laura Standley, ed. *Twentieth-Century Children's Writers*. 4th ed. Detroit: St. James, 1995.

Children's Literature Review. Vol. 14. Detroit: Gale Research, 1988.

Collier, Laurie, and Joyce Nakamura, eds. *Major Authors and Illustrators for Children and Young Adults*. Detroit: Gale Research, 1993.

Holtze, Sally Holmes, ed. *Sixth Book of Junior Authors and Illustrators*. New York: H. W. Wilson, 1989.

Something about the Author. Vol. 62. Detroit: Gale Research, 1991.

Margaret Mahy

1936-, New Zealand librarian and author

The Haunting

(fantasy, 1982)

PLOT: An elegant twist makes *The Haunting* more than a tense supernatural thriller. With its ironic conclusion, it advances themes about deceptive appearances, true identity, and self-acceptance. Eight-year-old Barney Palmer is haunted by a strange boy who says that Barnaby is dead, a statement that Barney believes is an announcement of his own death. He soon learns, however, that his Great-uncle Barnaby Scholar has just died. Barney is afraid to tell his beloved stepmother, Claire, about the haunting because she is pregnant and his own mother died in childbirth. Fearing their reactions, he also keeps the secret from his father, John, and his sisters, talkative Tabitha and silent Troy. Matters change when the Palmer family makes a sympathy visit to the Scholar household. Writing suddenly appears on the pages of a book Barney is examining. Tabitha sees it and begins talking about magic. Everyone seems to ignore her, but nasty Great-granny Scholar proclaims that Barney is unreliable.

Later, the haunting presence says that it is coming for Barney because he is a Scholar magician. Becoming sicker with worry, Barney finally confides in Tabitha. She goes to Great-uncle Guy, a pediatrician, who tells her that male members of the Scholar family often inherit magical power. His brother Cole was a magician, but he never got along with his mother and ran away. His mother claimed that Cole died soon after, but Cole kept in touch with the recently deceased Great-uncle Barnaby. Barney and Tabitha now understand that Cole is haunting Barney because he wants a companion to replace the deceased Barnaby. Great-uncle Cole soon enters the

Palmer house to take Barney away. Claire objects, but Cole creates a nightmare vision to show that she can't stop him. Great-granny Scholar then arrives and denounces Cole, who fears her. In a surprising turn of events, however, Troy announces that she, not Barney, is the magician. She also reveals that Great-granny hates Cole because she once used her own magical powers to burn her sister's hair. Great-granny afterwards hid her guilt by claiming that only male Scholars were magicians. Great-granny leaves after telling Troy that she never wants to see her again. Troy knows that her revelation also puts a barrier between herself and her father, but she is happy to assert her identity and to be friends with Cole, who is not evil, only lonely.

CHARACTERS: The ending of this story is a powerful surprise because the focus is on the younger Palmer children until the climax. **Barney Palmer** is a sensitive, loving eight-year-old. Worried about upsetting his pregnant stepmother and thus causing her death in childbirth, he gallantly maintains the secret of his haunting, even though it begins to make him sick. Barney advances the identity theme by stubbornly telling the haunting voice that he is an ordinary boy and not a magician. Furthermore, after Troy's revelation, he tells Claire that he doesn't want to perform magic. Barney shows, however, that an ordinary boy can have significant depth. He is thus self-sacrificing, bravely offering to go away if Cole won't hurt anyone. **Tabitha Palmer**, a round-faced, plump girl who doesn't worry about being fat, is the comic center of the novel and is a foil to her siblings. Tabitha is talkative, conceited, and eager to be the center of attention. The self-proclaimed family novelist, she carries a notebook everywhere and records what people say and feel so that she can incorporate their experiences into her novel. Tabitha is comically naive in her feeling that Barney's experiences are wasted on him because he is ordinary and she is a novelist who could appreciate them. She becomes a helper by going to Great-uncle Guy and finding out about Cole. She also makes an ironic contribution to the identity theme, discovering that she, who prided herself on being the unusual and talented member of the family, is the most ordinary one of all. **Troy Palmer** is central to the themes of deceptive appearances and of identity. A silent, thin, knobbly thirteen-year-old with a long nose and a black cloud of hair, she seems perpetually scornful and constantly isolates herself in her room. She is, however, kind and sensitive. Long aware of her magic powers, she used them after her mother's death to provide the lonely Barney with imaginary friends until Claire arrived. She also uses them to summon her father when Cole comes for Barney. When Great-granny Scholar and Cole argue, she reveals her true identity as a magician, exposing Great-granny's evil nature and deceptions at the same time. She then shows self-acceptance by deciding that she will no longer conceal her powers, even though they separate her from her father.

Claire Palmer is the reverse of the stereotypical fairy-tale stepmother: she is a loving woman who accepts and cares about her stepchildren as if they were her own. She thus shows great concern for Barney when he is haunted and tries to stop Cole from taking him away. Her husband, **John Palmer**, a tall, bald man, was filled with so much grief after his wife's death that Barney is still uncertain of his love. He is a good and protective father, but he becomes distant from Troy after her transformation, a feeling that may symbolize a father's inability to accept his daughter's movement from childhood to independent adolescence. Great-uncle **Cole Scholar**, a man of about fifty with golden, owl-like eyes, contributes to the theme of deceptive appearances. Reputedly dead, he has kept in touch with his favorite brother, the only person with whom he has been able to share his feelings. He seems evil when he haunts Barney and tries to take him away. In fact, he is simply lonely and fears that the Great-granny may crush Barney's magical talents. Ironically, he is mistaken about Barney, showing that his power is limited. His relationship with Troy offers him an opportunity to develop the humanity suppressed by long years of exile. **Great-granny Scholar**, his mother, is a nasty eighty-eight-year-old woman, the only true villain in the novel. Because she misused her own magical powers, she became fearful of magic, misrepresenting it as a talent only males

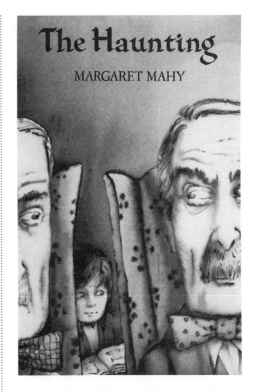

Eight-year-old Barney Palmer keeps secret from his family the ghost he has seen of a young boy in Mahy's 1982 supernatural thriller.

could possess and driving away her own magically gifted son. Great-granny is a cautionary figure, illustrating the consequences of suppressing one's true identity. As Troy explains, when Great-granny crushed the magic out of her life, she also crushed good things, killing what made her special. Because she denied her own identity and knew what she had lost, she became filled with hatred for those who possessed the gifts she suppressed. In contrast, Great-uncle **Guy Scholar**, a tall, bent pediatrician, shows the kindness and acceptance of the other members of the Scholar family, helping Tabitha to understand Cole's history.

Further Reading

Authors and Artists for Young Adults. Vol. 8. Detroit: Gale Research, 1992.

Berger, Laura Standley, ed. *Twentieth-Century Young Adult Writers*. 1st ed. Detroit: St. James, 1994.

Children's Literature Review. Vol. 7. Detroit: Gale Research, 1984.

Collier, Laurie, and Joyce Nakamura, eds. *Major Authors and Illustrators for Children and Young Adults.* Detroit: Gale Research, 1993.

De Montreville, Doris, and Elizabeth D. Crawford, eds. *Fourth Book of Junior Authors.* New York: H. W. Wilson, 1978.

Contemporary Authors New Revision Series. Vol. 38. Detroit: Gale Research, 1993.

Something about the Author. Vols. 14, 69. Detroit: Gale Research, 1978, 1992.

Mercer Mayer

1943-, American picture book artist and author

There's a Nightmare in My Closet

(picture book, 1968)

PLOT: Obviously inspired by Maurice Sendak's *Where the Wild Things Are* (1963), this picture book similarly portrays internal fears as monsters. The unnamed narrator is a little boy who recounts how he once was afraid of the nightmare that lived in his closet. Every night, he closes the closet door and, too afraid to turn around and look, gets into bed. One night, he faces his nightmare. When it comes out of the closet, he turns on the light and threatens that, if it doesn't go away, he will shoot it with his pop-gun. The narrator shoots the nightmare, which begins to cry. Although the angry narrator orders it to stop crying because it may wake the boy's mother and father, the nightmare persists. The boy then drags it by the hand, tucks it into his bed, closes the closet door, and gets into bed himself. He realizes that another nightmare may be in the closet, but he says that his bed isn't big enough for three. In the final wordless picture, he and his nightmare are contentedly asleep while another nightmare watches from the closet.

CHARACTERS: The narrator is the only real character. His nightmares are devices for making visible his struggle with his emotions. **The narrator**, a small boy dressed in one-piece pajamas, learns to confront and accept his fears. The double-page spreads that begin the book illustrate his feelings of smallness by emphasizing the largeness of the room. They also suggest that he believes that only physical force, something that adults possess in abundance, can overcome the nightmare. Thus, he lies in bed with a pop-gun and toy cannon. A general's helmet and toy soldiers are on the floor. Significantly, on the night that he decides to confront the nightmare, he puts on the helmet, symbolizing a decision to take charge of the situation. He also brings the toy soldiers into bed, suggesting that he doesn't feel completely vulnerable. When he turns on the light, a conventional symbol for gaining knowledge, he begins a transformation. The single-page pictures, in which the background disappears, focus attention on his mastery of his emotions. At first, he persists in trying to use force against the monster, shooting it before it can decide whether or not to leave. Once it cries, however, the narrator realizes that the nightmare is easy to defeat, that it is not as powerful as he once thought. Because of this new understanding, he overcomes his anger and takes off his helmet, thereby renouncing violence as the proper way to handle emotions. When he then asks the nightmare to be quiet so that it won't wake his parents, he obviously realizes how disturbing he himself has been to them. He therefore demonstrates the same sympathy his parents have shown him and puts the nightmare to bed. By doing so, he accommodates his fears: he knows that he can't destroy them, but he also knows that he can live safely with them. The final double-spread pictures, which echo those of the beginning, thus emphasize his mastery of his emotional environment.

The nightmare is a huge, ugly, spotted beast. It has three toes on each foot and three fingers on each hand. It has an enormous mouth, but only two blunt teeth. These are visible even when its mouth is closed because it has an overbite. It also has large eyes that clearly convey its sadness and fear. In spite of its intimidating size, it is a comical creature. It behaves like a very small child, crying when it is afraid. The nightmare is thus a device that allows the narrator to understand how he himself appears to his parents. It also permits him to realize that, through understanding, he can overcome even great fears.

Further Reading

Children's Literature Review. Vol. 11. Detroit: Gale Research, 1986.

Collier, Laurie, and Joyce Nakamura, eds. *Major Authors and Illustrators for Children and Young Adults*. Detroit: Gale Research, 1993.

Contemporary Authors New Revision Series. Vol. 38. Detroit: Gale Research, 1993.

De Montreville, Doris, and Elizabeth D. Crawford, eds. *Fourth Book of Junior Authors*. New York: H. W. Wilson, 1978.

Estes, Glenn E., ed. *American Writers for Children since 1960: Poets, Illustrators, and Nonfiction Authors*. Vol. 61 of *Dictionary of Literary Biography*. Detroit: Gale Research, 1987.

Something about the Author. Vols. 16, 32, 73. Detroit: Gale Research, 1979, 1983, 1993.

Robert McCloskey

1914-, American artist, illustrator, and author

Make Way for Ducklings

(picture book, 1941)

PLOT: The plot of this Caldecott Medal winner consists of two journeys. In the first, Mr. and Mrs. Mallard search for a safe place to live. Mrs. Mallard rejects each of Mr. Mallard's suggestions until they come to an island in the Boston Public Garden. Delighted that people on the Swan Boat feed them peanuts, Mrs. Mallard decides that they have at last found a safe home to raise ducklings. When a boy on a bicycle nearly runs her over, however, she decides that the pond is unsafe for babies. After resuming their search, they find an island on the Charles River, where Mrs. Mallard builds a nest and hatches eight ducklings.

The second journey is a dangerous trip back to the Public Garden. Mr. Mallard leaves his family to explore the river, promising to meet them in one week on the island in the Public Garden. After Mrs.

The not-so-scary-after-all nightmare, as illustrated by Mayer, from There's a Nightmare in My Closet.

Mallard teaches Jack, Kack, Lack, Mack, Nack, Oack, Pack, and Quack to swim, dive, and follow her in a line, she sets out for the meeting. The ducklings are unable to cross a busy street, until Michael the policeman stops traffic for them. He then has other policemen stop traffic farther along the ducks' route. After thanking the policemen, Mrs. Mallard and her ducklings join Mr. Mallard. The ducklings like the island so much that the Mallards make it their home.

CHARACTERS: McCloskey has said that his drawings are not entirely accurate representations of mallards because the birds he used as models "were largely puddleduck." Few readers have objected, however, because McCloskey's drawings make his simple characters interesting and amusing.

Mrs. Mallard is careful and conscientious. Her major concern is the safety of her family. She repeatedly rejects the nesting sights her husband suggests because she does not want to raise her family where there might be foxes and turtles. When she realizes that the Public Gardens is not as safe as she originally thought, she insists on searching further. Mrs. Mallard is also conscientious and competent after she becomes a mother. She alone teaches her ducklings the skills they need to survive and to be safe. In addition, she succeeds in making them polite and respectful: the ducklings join her in thanking the policemen who help them across the streets. Mrs. Mallard is not, however, completely idealized. Her very need of help spotlights two negative elements of her character. First, when she is unable to cross the street because of the heavy traffic, she foolishly expresses her frustration in a display of quacking. Second, as McCloskey's brilliant drawing shows, Mrs. Mallard becomes haughty, comically expressing scorn for the automobiles that Michael stops. **Mr. Mallard**, her husband, lacks his wife's understanding and must have the dangers of each situation pointed out to him. Furthermore, he foolishly thinks that the Swan Boat is a living bird. It is not clear why Mr. Mallard feels that he must leave his family to explore the river. The fact that he keeps his word and meets his family in the Public Garden shows that he is devoted to them. McCloskey's drawings make **the ducklings**, who appear in a variety of poses, seem like rambunctious children on a kindergarten outing. Only **Quack**, the last in line, has a unique and consistently recognizable personality. He is the tardy one, frequently shown as running at full speed to catch up to the others.

Michael, a portly policeman, is an essential helper. He demonstrates his kindness by feeding the ducks and by helping them across the street. Because McCloskey uses what he called a "duck's-eye view," Michael is, in keeping with his importance to the ducks, appropriately huge in all the drawings. Michael is, however, also a caricature. Whereas the ducks are relatively realistic, Michael is definitely cartoonish, and his reactions, such as his frantic call for other policemen to help, are exaggerated. Consequently, he adds a comic note to the theme of the search for a safe home.

Homer Price

(stories, 1943)

PLOT: Six loosely connected stories present a comical, affectionate look at a midwestern town. In the first, Homer uses his pet skunk, Aroma, to capture four robbers when the sheriff is too slow in coming to arrest them. In the next, Homer goes with Freddy and his little brother, Louis, to meet their favorite movie hero, the Super-Duper. After Homer and the boys rescue the inept Super-Duper from a car crash, Freddy and his brother lose respect for their hero. "The Doughnuts" twists the familiar tale of the sorcerer's apprentice. Uncle Ulysses leaves Homer in charge of his diner, asking him to make a batch of doughnuts while he's gone. Wealthy Miss Naomi Enders, who insists that Homer use her recipe, helps him to mix the batter, but she accidentally drops her diamond bracelet into it. Once Homer starts the new doughnut machine, he is unable to stop it. Thousands of doughnuts soon fill the diner. Homer then ingeniously aids both Miss Enders and his Uncle. By turning the search for the bracelet into a contest, he sells most of the doughnuts before a customer finds the bracelet.

Homer is not the central character in the final three stories. In "Mystery Yarn" the sheriff and Homer's Uncle Telemachus enter a contest at the fair, agreeing that the owner of the shorter ball of string will leave the other free to court Miss Terwilliger. Miss Terwilliger, however, enters and wins the contest by secretly unraveling her knitted dress. Afterwards, Miss Terwilliger chooses to marry Uncle Telemachus. Homer is more prominent in "Nothing New Under the Sun (Hardly)." When the unkempt Michael Murphy arrives in town, the sheriff convinces everyone that he is like Rip Van Winkle because he has separated himself from society for thirty years. After Mr. Murphy is hired to rid the town of mice, the librarian suggests that Murphy is more like the Pied Piper of Hamlin. Panicking because all the children follow Murphy out of town, the sheriff orders Murphy to let them go. Puzzled, Murphy releases the captured mice. Homer then explains to the sheriff that the children were deaf to adult commands because he had—following the example of Homer's Ulysses, who saved his crew from the dangerous song of the sirens—taken the precaution of having a doctor put cotton in their ears. Homer recedes into the background of the satirical "Wheels of Progress." Uncle Ulysses convinces Miss Enders to build a suburb of mass-produced homes. Once the elegant old homestead that had been located in the new development is removed, however, the residents can't distinguish their identical homes because the streets lack signs. Homer and Freddy discover that Dulcey Dooner, the man hired to put up street signs, is drunk on cough medicine he discovered while digging a hole. Although Dulcey puts up the signs the next day, the old homestead is restored as a precautionary measure.

Centerburg Tales *(1951) is a sequel.*

CHARACTERS: The text records the characters' words and actions, but McCloskey's illustrations convey their physical appearance and suggest their personalities. **Homer Price** (the surname, which does not appear in the text, was suggested by the publisher for marketing purposes) is pictured as a thin boy with a brush cut. Homer is not sloppy, but his shirt tends to come untucked and his shirt cuffs are frequently undone. His bedroom has the homey clutter typical of boys with wide interests. Homer, for example, builds radios for a hobby. The text establishes Homer as a friendly, good-natured boy who readily helps his parents at their tourist camp. He also helps his relatives without complaint, even when Uncle Ulysses takes advantage of him by leaving him in charge of the diner. Homer is intelligent and creative. He devises the contest that simultaneously recovers the bracelet and disposes of the doughnuts. He captures the robbers because he is observant in realizing who the men are and quick-witted in using their fear of his pet skunk. (A way with animals is also a conventional sign of goodness in children's books.) His powers of observation make him superior to both other children and adults. He notices, for example, that the stories about Super-Duper follow a formula. Consequently, unlike the hero-worshipping Freddy, he is cynical about Super-Duper and is the first to notice that the man who plays the role is incompetent and vulnerable. Homer is also one of the few males who perceives how Miss Terwilliger wins the string contest. Evidently, he has the tact never to mention what he saw. Homer also realizes before the adults

Homer Price and the doughnut machine in a scene from McCloskey's Homer Price, *illustrated by the author.*

do that Michael Murphy is a Pied Piper figure and takes appropriate measures in case Murphy can lure children as well as mice.

Uncle Ulysses, who is always pictured wearing a chef's hat, apron, polka-dotted shirt, and bow tie, has a decided weakness for labor-saving devices. His obsession with machinery comes partly from his desire to avoid work (Aunt Agnes, his wife, frequently finds him gossiping in the barber shop). Uncle Ulysses' behavior helps McCloskey satirize progress for the sake of progress. He is proud of his machines, but neither his toaster nor his doughnut maker works properly. He also champions the virtues of mass production, inspiring the construction of a community of houses so identical that the residents can't find their own homes.

The sheriff is pictured as an older man who wears glasses on the end of his nose and has a bushy, droopy mustache. He adds a comic element with his habitual spoonerisms, which suggest that he is a bungler. He is attached to his Saturday-night ritual of a haircut, checkers, and gossip at the barber shop. Consequently, he puts off arresting the robbers for so long that Homer must capture them. The sheriff's rival for the hand of Miss Terwilliger, **Uncle Telemachus**, is bald and middle-aged. He is obsessed with string collecting and is proud that he has wound his ball of string more tightly than the sheriff has. Comical irony develops when he proposes the bet with the sheriff to win Miss Terwilliger's hand. He is blind to the fact that Miss Terwilliger maintains control over her own life by tricking her suitors. **Miss Terwilliger** is a clever woman with two notable talents: knitting and cooking fried chicken. She has worn the same knitted blue dress for years, carefully shortening or lengthening the hem to keep it in fashion. Like her suitors, she is an eccentric. She has collected so much string that she must have the wall of her house removed to get the ball out. Like Penelope in the *Odyssey*, Miss Terwilliger tricks her suitors by unraveling a garment. Her trick asserts a woman's right to control her own destiny by choosing a husband herself.

The wealthy **Miss Naomi Enders** seems bossy and oblivious to the rights of others when she makes Homer use her recipe for doughnuts. She does, however, have a social conscience. She creates a community where deserving people can have homes at reasonable rents. Her major role is to show the confusion that occurs when traditional values, symbolized by her family homestead, are removed. Moving the homestead back to the center of the community symbolizes a restoration of the values that allow people to find their way in life. **Michael Murphy** has long hair and a long beard. He wears a long, old-fashioned coat and is unkempt because he retired from the world for thirty years, during which time he invented a humane mousetrap. As well as generating humor with the chaos that follows his efforts to rid Centerburg of mice, this shy man reveals the limitations of those who meet him. Thus, the barber judges him solely by his hair, and the shoe repairman by his feet. **Dulcey Dooner** is a caricature used to satirize labor unions. The sole member of the Street Sign Putter-Uppers Union, he threatens to strike unless he is hired at a high rate to put in new posts (although they are already in place).

He becomes drunk on cough medicine, suggesting that the unionized worker is not dedicated to his job.

Blueberries for Sal
(picture book, 1948)

PLOT: Little Sal and her mother go to Blueberry Hill to gather berries for the winter. Little Sal eats what she collects; whenever she takes berries from her mother's pail, her mother sends her away. Little Sal then happily sits in a patch and eats. Meanwhile, Little Bear and his mother are on the other side of the hill, eating berries so that they will grow fat for the winter. Little Sal soon wanders away. She mistakes some crows for her mother and eventually ends up near Little Bear's mother. Little Bear also wanders away, and, after mistaking partridges for his mother, he ends up near Little Sal's mother. Neither mother looks back, so neither is aware that the one behind her is not her child. When Little Bear's mother hears the sound of Little Sal's pail, however, she discovers the child, carefully backs away, and goes in search of her cub. At the same time, Little Bear eats so many berries from the pail held by Little Sal's mother that she discovers him. She slowly backs away and searches for her daughter. Both mothers discover their offspring and go home down opposite sides of the hill. The endpapers show Little Sal and her mother canning their blueberries.

CHARACTERS: Parallel scenes in the text and pictures (both presented in a blue that emphasizes the blueberries as a linking device) suggest the unity of living things. **Little Sal**, whose picture is based on McCloskey's daughter Sarah (Sally), is a small child with unruly hair and an overall strap that refuses to stay in place. She is more interested in eating than in gathering supplies for the winter. As a small girl, she conveniently lacks coordination (she tries to pick one berry from her mother's pail but ends up with a handful). Little Sal also tires quickly, and soon sits down to eat. The drawings show that Little Sal is fascinated by all that she sees, including the crows and the mother bear. She is too small to realize her danger when she is near the bear, to worry when she is alone, or to concentrate on the task at hand, either when she is picking or canning. Little Sal's journey is, nonetheless, one of discovery that ends happily in a scene of domestic security. **Little Sal's mother** is based on McCloskey's wife. She tries to turn the trip into an educational experience by telling Little Sal that they are gathering food for the winter. She becomes so absorbed in her work that she loses track of her daughter and does not turn around when she feels someone touching her pail. When she sees Little Bear, she keeps her head and backs away. She displays adult competence when she discovers her daughter because of the sound of berries hitting the bottom of the empty pail (earlier, Little Sal had mistaken the sounds of crows and of the bear for her mother). The mother ends up doing all of the picking and all of the work in preserving the berries.

The only major difference between **Little Bear** and Little Sal is that he is *supposed* to eat the berries because that is how he stores food. Like his human counterpart, Little Bear sits in a patch to eat, mistakes the sound of birds and of the other mother for his own, and is discovered while eating the berries. He is similarly uncoordinated: he tries to eat a few berries from the mother's bucket but ends up eating a mouthful. **Little Bear's mother** resembles the human mother, especially because she is anthropomorphized by her speech: she is also teaching her child about the necessity of getting food for the winter. Similarly, she becomes absorbed in her task and loses sight of her offspring. Just as the human mother was shy of the cub, the bear is shy of the small child and carefully backs away; like the human mother, she hears sounds that lead her to her child.

Further Reading

Berger, Laura Standley, ed. *Twentieth-Century Children's Writers*. 4th ed. Detroit: St. James, 1995.

Cech, John, ed. *American Writers for Children 1900-1960*. Vol. 22 of *Dictionary of Literary Biography*. Detroit: Gale Research, 1983.

Children's Literature Review. Vol. 7. Detroit: Gale Research, 1984.

Collier, Laurie, and Joyce Nakamura, eds. *Major Authors and Illustrators for Children and Young Adults*. Detroit: Gale Research, 1993.

Contemporary Authors New Revision Series. Vol. 47. Detroit: Gale Research, 1995.

Kunitz, Stanley J., and Howard Haycraft, eds. *The Junior Book of Authors*. 2nd ed. New York: H. W. Wilson, 1951.

Manna, Anthony. "Robert McCloskey's *Make Way for Ducklings*: The Art of Regional Storytelling." In *Touchstones: Reflections on the Best in Children's Literature*, Vol. 3: *Picture Books*. Edited by Perry Nodelman, pp. 90-100. West Lafayette, IN: Children's Literature Association, 1989.

Schmidt, Gary D. *Robert McCloskey*. Boston: Twayne, 1990.

Something about the Author. Vols. 2, 39. Detroit: Gale Research, 1971, 1985.

Patricia C. McKissack

1944-, American journalist, scriptwriter, and author

Flossie and the Fox

(picture book, 1986; illustrated by Rachel Isadora)

PLOT: This ironic trickster tale is based on one McKissack's grandfather told to her. As in many African American tales, the meaning extends beyond the plot. In this case, the characters and events form a humorous fable about blacks outwitting the whites who would victimize them. The plot employs a quest. Big Mama sends Flossie Finley to take eggs to Miz Viola, whose chickens have been troubled by a sly fox. She warns Flossie that the fox will do anything to get eggs. But when Flossie meets a creature who introduces himself as a fox, Flossie says that she doesn't believe him. Eager to prove his identity and to frighten her, the fox follows Flossie through the woods and repeatedly points to his appearance to prove his identity. Unconvinced, Flossie calls him a rabbit because he has luxurious fur, a rat because he has a pointed nose, and a squirrel because he has a bushy tail. Finally, when she sights Miz Viola's cabin, Flossie points out that the hounds are com-

Flossie and the fox in an illustration by Rachel Isadora from McKissack's 1986 book.

ing. As the exasperated fox runs away, he brags that he can outsmart them because he is a fox. Flossie says that she knows he is. Having outwitted him, she takes the eggs to Miz Viola.

CHARACTERS: Dialect is a major characterizing device. Although not essential, Rachel Isadora's pictures enhance the distinctive personalities of the characters. **Flossie Finley** is an unlikely hero. Not only is she a small, bright-eyed girl, as the pictures show, but she is also without significant formal education, as her rural dialect suggests. Furthermore, throughout most of the tale she seems polite but stubbornly ignorant. Flossie, however, deliberately plays a role. She thus demonstrates the survival tactics African Americans had to employ during the nineteenth and early twentieth centuries. Flossie is actually brave, observant, and clever. Noticing that he does not take his eyes off her basket, Flossie obviously remembers Big Mama's warning that a fox loves eggs. She thus distracts him by denying that he is a fox. Flossie, of course, knows his identity. By accusing him of trying to fool her, Flossie exploits his conceit, making him waste his time. Flossie thus

shows that she is both a hero, succeeding in her quest of safely delivering the eggs, and a far smarter trickster than the fox.

The fox, who speaks in a formal, somewhat pompous manner that contrasts with Flossie's rural dialect, obviously represents pretentious whites. He begins as a predator but, because of his vanity, unwittingly becomes a victim. The fox, that is, becomes so absorbed in insisting on his own identity that he fails to appreciate Flossie's. Unable to see that she is playing a role, he becomes flustered, pathetically pleading and whining for recognition. By forgetting about Flossie's eggs while he does so, he ironically establishes that she is the better trickster and that he is actually a fool. **Big Mama**, Flossie's grandmother, is a wise helper. Her warnings about the fox enable Flossie to survive. Her statement that "a fox be just a fox" gives Flossy courage and focuses the reader's attention on the tale's identity motif.

Further Reading

Children's Literature Review. Vol. 23. Detroit: Gale Research, 1991.

Collier, Laurie, and Joyce Nakamura, eds. *Major Authors and Illustrators for Children and Young Adults.* Detroit: Gale Research, 1993.

Contemporary Authors New Revision Series. Vol. 38. Detroit: Gale Research, 1993.

Something about the Author. Vols. 51, 73. Detroit: Gale Research, 1988, 1993.

A. A. Milne

1882-1956, English playwright and author

The Pooh Books

(toy fantasies, 1926, 1928; illustrated by Ernest H. Shepard)

PLOT: Both Pooh books contain discrete humorous episodes with themes about companionship, acceptance, and enjoying the adventure of daily life. *Winnie-the-Pooh* (1926) is a frame tale: a father tells his son, Christopher Robin, tales about the boy and his toys, especially his teddy, Edward Bear, renamed

Winnie-the-Pooh. In the first tale, Christopher Robin helps when Pooh, in an unsuccessful attempt to get honey, tries to fool the bees into thinking that he is a black cloud. In the next, Pooh eats too much, becomes stuck in Rabbit's door, and must lose weight before Christopher Robin can free him. Later, Pooh and Piglet track Woozles, only to discover that they have been following their own footprints. Pooh proves useful when Eeyore the donkey loses his tail: he discovers that Owl has inadvertently taken the tail to use as a bell rope. In the next episode, the frightened Piglet mistakes Pooh, whose head is stuck in a honey pot, for a Heffalump. Following that, Piglet and Pooh ruin their birthday gifts for Eeyore, but he is happy with Piglet's burst balloon because he can put it in the "useful" empty honey pot that Pooh gives him.

In the only episode with overt antagonism, Rabbit attempts to force Kanga and Roo to move away by getting Piglet and Pooh to help him kidnap Roo. Kanga, discovering that Piglet has replaced Roo in her pouch, pretends that she thinks he is Roo and treats him very roughly. Christopher Robin, who comes to announce that Rabbit and Roo are friends, plays along with Kanga's joke. During an "expotition" to find the North Pole, Pooh uses a pole to rescue Roo, who has fallen into the water. Christopher Robin then declares that Pooh has found the North Pole. When rains flood his home, Pooh escapes by floating on an empty honey jar. He then suggests that Christopher Robin can rescue

Kanga, Tigger, Rabbit, Eeyore, Owl, Pooh, and Piglet in a classic Ernest H. Shepard illustration from Milne's **The House at Pooh Corner.**

Piglet by using an umbrella as a boat. In the final tale, Christopher Robin gives a party for Pooh. Eeyore, thinking it is for him, makes a speech. Christopher Robin interrupts and presents Pooh with a special pencil case. The concluding frame has Christopher Robin dragging his toy bear behind him as he heads upstairs for his bath.

The House at Pooh Corner (1928) does not use the frame. A comical mistake highlights the first tale: Pooh and Piglet build a new house for Eeyore only to learn that they have disassembled and rebuilt his original house. A new character, Tigger, then learns that, contrary to his claims, he doesn't like honey, acorns, or thistles. His favorite food is actually Roo's medicinal extract of malt. Next, Piglet and Pooh search for one of Rabbit's relatives, Small (Very Small Beetle), and separately fall into their Heffalump trap. After dreaming about being brave, Piglet discovers Small on Pooh's back. The following story is pure slapstick: having bragged to Roo about his abilities, Tigger climbs a tree, is unable to climb down, and falls on top of Eeyore. A transitional chapter foreshadows Christopher Robin's departure from the fantasy world. When Rabbit finds Christopher Robin's note, "GON OUT, BACKSON. BISY, BACKSON," Owl tells him that the boy is with a Backson. Meanwhile, Piglet picks flowers for Eeyore, who is disgusted when Rabbit knows that Christopher Robin has arranged sticks to form the letter "A." Finally, Christopher Robin leaves a new note, "GONE AWAY. BACK SOON," thereby indicating that he is learning to spell at school.

Tigger is important in the next two episodes. First, during a game of Poohsticks, which involves watching sticks float under a bridge, Pooh, Piglet, Rabbit, and Roo notice Eeyore floating below. Pooh drops a big stone, "hooshing" Eeyore to shore. Afterwards, Eeyore reveals that he fell into the river because Tigger startled him. In the next episode, therefore, Rabbit decides that Tigger is so bouncy that he, Pooh, and Piglet must calm him by losing him in the woods. Ironically, Tigger immediately goes home, but the others become lost. Pooh and Piglet stumble on Christopher Robin, who must find Rabbit. Piglet displays his worth in the next two tales. When he and Pooh visit Owl one windy day, Piglet does a grand deed. After the tree supporting Owl's house falls, Piglet overcomes his fear, squeezes out of the damaged house, and goes to Christopher Robin for help. When Eeyore then offers Owl a house, unaware that it is Piglet's, Piglet nobly agrees that Owl should live there. Pooh then suggests that Piglet move in with him. The book concludes touchingly with Christopher Robin attempting to explain to Pooh why he is leaving the enchanted places of childhood.

CHARACTERS: Milne has indicated that he based the fantasy characters, with the exception of Rabbit and Owl, on toys owned by his son. Each is distinguished by a dominant trait. The central character was originally a teddy bear named **Edward Bear**, but he became **Winnie-the-Pooh**, called **Pooh**, because he wanted a more exciting name. According to the introduction to *When We Were Very Young* (1924), Christopher Robin named a swan Pooh because he could pretend that he was only saying "Pooh" if the swan failed to come when he called it. The swan left, so the name became available. In *Winnie-the-Pooh*, the narrator says that "Winnie" came from a black bear in the London zoo. (It was called Winnie because it was the mascot of a Canadian army regiment from Winnipeg.)

Pooh appears in two guises. In the frame, he is a toy whose head is banged on the stairs when Christopher Robin carries him. In the tales, he is a portly bear who lives alone under a sign with the name of Sanders. Pooh is silly, creative, egotistical, humble, sociable, and loyal. Pooh is most obviously characterized, however, by his appetite. Always ready for "a little something," Pooh lives in a house in which the clock is stuck at five to eleven, nearly snack time. Pooh's appetite makes him comical and ridiculous, as when he eats so much that he gets stuck in Rabbit's door or when he gets his head stuck in a honey jar. Because he sociably visits others, his appetite also tests their generosity. Although Pooh cannot control this appetite, as he shows by eating the honey he intends to give to Eeyore as a birthday present, he is not selfish. For instance, he offers to share his breakfast when Tigger claims that honey is his favorite food. Of course, he is not so generous that he isn't relieved when Tigger discovers that he doesn't like honey.

As Pooh humbly describes himself, he is a "Bear of Very Little Brain": he can't tell left from right, he can't read or write, and he has trouble understanding explanations. Furthermore, he seems ludicrous when he disguises himself as a cloud to fool the bees and when he goes around in circles thinking that he is following the tracks of a Woozle. Although he often merits Christopher Robin's affectionate description as a "Silly Old Bear," Pooh is not predominantly silly. For one thing, he solves problems that defeat others. He is the one who realizes that Owl has used Eeyore's tail as a bell rope, that he can use a pole to rescue Roo, and that Christopher Robin can turn his umbrella into a boat to rescue Piglet. For another, he is creative, inventing poems and songs, or "hums." Pooh is self-centered in his belief that bees make honey for him to eat, and he uses songs to express egotistical self-satisfaction, but Pooh is generous and considerate. He thus suggests building a house for Eeyore and giving him presents to cheer him up on his birthday. Concerned about others, Pooh makes Piglet feel important by writing a poem that celebrates the heroism he displayed when Owl's house was damaged. Finally, Pooh has the wit and generosity to suggest that Piglet move in with him after Piglet nobly allows Owl to have his house. Winnie-the-Pooh may seem like a Bear with Very Little Brain, but he deepens into a bear with a very large heart.

The dominant characteristic of Pooh's closest friend, **Piglet**, is timidity. Thinking of himself as a "Very Small Animal," tiny, pink Piglet constantly worries about his safety. As he does when tracking Woozles, he often runs away when he believes danger is at hand. At the same time, he is ashamed and frequently tries to disguise his timidity. Piglet seems selfish when he tries to be the first to give Eeyore a present even though Pooh came up with the idea, but he is usually kind and generous, as he shows when he picks flowers for Eeyore. Two episodes strengthen Piglet's character. When Owl's house topples, Piglet, realizing that his friends depend upon him, overcomes his fears. Ironically, Piglet becomes a hero because his smallness, the basis for his timidity, turns into an asset: he is the only one able to squeeze out of the house. Afterwards, Piglet honestly admits that, contrary to the claim in Pooh's poem, he felt fear. When Pooh assures him that he "blinched" inside only, Piglet feels truly brave. In the second episode, Piglet behaves nobly by refusing to embarrass Eeyore, who has unwittingly given Piglet's house to Owl. As a result, Piglet receives his wish of having a companion, for Pooh invites him to live with him.

Appropriately, **Eeyore** the Old Gray Donkey lives in the Gloomy Place. Ostentatiously morose, Eeyore constantly predicts that things will go wrong, assumes that the world is conspiring against him, and asserts that no one treats him respectfully. Eeyore's self-pity and sarcasm create humor and expose the limitations of other characters or their plans. They are also clever devices of manipulation. On his birthday, for example, Eeyore sarcastically tells Pooh to look at all his presents; once he understands the joke, Pooh generously arranges presents for Eeyore. Eeyore gloomily suggests that he is of no consequence, but he is actually egotistical. He assumes, for example, that Christopher Robin has thrown a party for him, not Pooh, and makes an embarrassingly incoherent speech. Although usually gloomy, Eeyore can be happy, as he

shows when he plays with his birthday presents. In spite of his biting sarcasm, Eeyore cares for his friends. After Rabbit suggests that he must make more of an effort to reach out, he therefore finds a home for Owl. Because he has previously remained aloof, he doesn't realize that he has given away Piglet's home; Piglet's silence suggests that Eeyore's friends respect him and want him to be happy.

Owl is pretentious, aggrandizing himself by telling convoluted stories and by using long words that obscure his meaning. Although he glories in a reputation for wisdom because he can spell Tuesday, he is a charlatan. Unable to write properly—he spells his own name WOL—he writes an unintelligible birthday message only after carefully ascertaining that Pooh won't be able to read it. Similarly, he tricks Rabbit into revealing what Christopher Robin's note says. Equally full of himself, **Rabbit** has contempt for the intelligence of others. The bossy Rabbit therefore tries to control them by making lists and initiating plots. Impulsively hating change, he plots to get rid of Kanga and Roo, but he then learns that he likes Roo. In spite of his superior airs and his intelligence, evident in his ability to read and write, Rabbit turns into a buffoon because he overestimates himself; ironically, he becomes lost when he tries to lose Tigger.

The infantile **Tigger** is comically devoid of self-knowledge: he repeatedly claims that various foods are his favorites, yet he dislikes them once he tastes them. He appears even more ridiculous when he brags about his abilities and then fails at the simplest of these feats by becoming stuck in a tree. He is most notable, however, for his unbridled energy. He is so "bouncy" that he is unintentionally dangerous, startling Eeyore into falling into the river. **Kanga**, the only female, is an obsessively overprotective mother. She is aggressively cruel when she plays her joke on Piglet, teaching him a lesson by washing him roughly in cold water and by giving him foul medicine. She is kind, however, with Tigger, adopting him because she recognizes that, in spite of his great size, he has as much need of kindness as her child does. Her child, **Roo**, is naive, energetic, and self-centered. When he falls in the water, for example, he shouts at his rescuers to look at him because he is swimming.

Roo understands that his mother's "maybe" actually means "no," so he sometimes rebels, as when he deliberately falls into the water while playing Poohsticks.

Christopher Robin first appeared in the poems of *When We Were Very Young*. Although named after the author's son, Christopher Robin is a composite formed from Milne's own memories, his ideas of childhood in general, and his son's life. Like Pooh, Christopher Robin appears in two guises. In the frame, he is a naive and awe-struck boy, asking for the stories so that Pooh can remember them. He also seems insecure, wondering if he gave Eeyore a present or if his pencil case is as good as Pooh's. Finally, he seems a bit careless, dragging the teddy behind him so that its head bangs on the stairs. In the tales, Christopher Robin sometimes displays childish ignorance and incompetence. For example, he sets out for the North Pole, although he doesn't know what it is, and then he declares that Pooh has found it. Childishness incompetence is also evident in his poor spelling, in his attempts to conceal his ignorance from the others, and in his inability to put on his boots by himself. For the most part, however, Christopher Robin is a surrogate for adults. He is concerned about the animals, offers them unconditional love, and extricates them from their difficulties. During the second volume, he changes, not only learning to spell but also realizing that he will no longer be able to maintain his enchanted world as he grows older. **The father** who narrates the stories strikes some critics as an intrusive and condescending figure who pitches jokes over the head of his ostensible listener and satirizes him in the tales. Although the stories are supposed to reflect Christopher Robin's imagination, they are thus clearly products of an adult intelligence. The father does show concern by reassuring his child about his role in the stories.

Further Reading

Berger, Laura Standley, ed. *Twentieth-Century Children's Writers*. 4th ed. Detroit: St. James, 1995.

Bingham, Jane M., ed. *Writers for Children: Critical Studies of Major Authors since the Seventeenth Century*. New York: Scribner's, 1988.

Children's Literature Review. Vols. 1, 26. Detroit: Gale Research, 1976, 1992.

Collier, Laurie, and Joyce Nakamura, eds. *Major Authors and Illustrators for Children and Young Adults*. Detroit: Gale Research, 1993.

Connolly, Paula T. *"Winnie-the-Pooh" and "The House at Pooh Corner": Recovering Arcadia*. New York: Twayne, 1995.

Contemporary Authors. Vol. 133. Detroit: Gale Research, 1991.

Crews, Frederick C. *The Pooh Perplex, a Freshman Casebook*. New York: Dutton, 1965.

Hettinga, Donald R., and Gary D. Schmidt, eds. *British Children's Writers, 1914-1960*. Vol. 160 of *Dictionary of Literary Biography*. Detroit: Gale Research, 1996.

Kunitz, Stanley J., and Howard Haycraft, eds. *The Junior Book of Authors*. 2nd ed. New York: H. W. Wilson, 1951.

Milne, A. A. *Autobiography*. New York: Dutton, 1939.

Milne, Christopher. *The Enchanted Places*. London: Eyre Methuen, 1974.

Shepard, Ernest H. *The Pooh Sketchbook*. New York: E. P. Dutton, 1984.

Swann, Thomas Burnett. *A. A. Milne*. New York: Twayne, 1971.

Thwaite, Ann. *A. A. Milne: The Man behind Winnie-the-Pooh*. New York: Random House, 1990.

Yesterday's Authors of Books for Children. Vol. 1. Detroit: Gale Research, 1977.

Wilson, Anita. "Milne's Pooh Books: The Benevolent Forest." In *Touchstones: Reflections on the Best in Children's Literature*, Vol. 1. Edited by Perry Nodelman. West Lafayette, IN: Children's Literature Association, 1985.

Else Holmelund Minarik

1920-, American author

Little Bear

(beginning reader stories, 1957; illustrated by Maurice Sendak)

PLOT: Maurice Sendak, the book's illustrator, seems correct in asserting that the text of *Little Bear*

presents "the ideal dream of an ideal childhood." The four easy-to-read stories are simple anecdotes that focus on the loving home life of its central character. In the first episode, Little Bear repeatedly tells Mother Bear that he is cold. In turn, she gives him a hat, coat, and snowpants. When he comes back from outside claiming that he is still cold, she offers him a fur coat. She then removes the hat, coat, and snowpants, and Little Bear plays outside, snug and warm in only his natural fur. Little Bear worries that Mother Bear has forgotten his birthday in "Birthday Soup." He therefore cooks up some soup to feed his visiting friends. Just as they sit down to eat, however, Mother Bear arrives with a birthday cake. In "Little Bear Goes to the Moon," Mother Bear joins Little Bear's imaginary game, which begins when Little Bear puts on a homemade space helmet and jumps from a tree in order to fly to the moon. He comes back to his house, where his mother goes along with the game by pretending to be a moon mother. The game ends when Little Bear tells his mother to stop fooling around. In the final story, "Little Bear's Wish," Mother Bear discovers that her son is still awake, dreaming of impossible wishes. She grants his final wish and tells him a story about himself that summarizes the events in the previous three stories.

Sequels are Father Bear Comes Home *(1959),* Little Bear's Friend *(1960),* Little Bear's Visit *(1961), and* A Kiss for Little Bear *(1968).*

CHARACTERS: Although the characters are animals, their animal characteristics play a role only in the first tale. **Little Bear** is an imaginative and loving child. His creativity is evident in the list of impossible wishes he tells to his mother, but it is most prominent when he tries to fly to the moon. He is able to pretend that he has a space helmet (the pictures reveal it to be a cardboard box with wires) and that a familiar setting is actually the moon. Little Bear knows when to draw the line between imagination and reality, however, as he shows when he tells

Little Bear and Mother Bear, as illustrated by Maurice Sendak for Minarik's picture book.

his mother to stop pretending that she is a moon mother. Throughout, Little Bear craves the attention of his mother and accepts unquestioningly whatever she tells him. For example, he is warm playing outside after she gives him a fur coat by taking off his other clothing. Always affectionate and obedient, Little Bear is the ideal child.

Sendak said that he drew **Mother Bear** "to be an image of warmth and strength—nothing less than motherhood itself." Therefore, he pictured her in voluminous Victorian skirts to give her substance. Mother Bear is the loving and understanding center of her son's world. She is patient when he requests more clothes and knows how to make him happy. When he is anxious, she reassures him, telling him, for instance, that she will never forget his birthday. She delights in her son's imagination and joins in to make his games fun for him. She is the ideal mother because, as Little Bear tells her in the final story, "You always make me happy."

Further Reading

Berger, Laura Standley, ed. *Twentieth-Century Children's Writers.* 4th ed. Detroit: St. James, 1995.

Children's Literature Review. Vol. 33. Detroit: Gale Research, 1994.

Collier, Laurie, and Joyce Nakamura, eds. *Major Authors and Illustrators for Children and Young Adults.* Detroit: Gale Research, 1993.

Contemporary Authors. Vols. 73-76. Detroit: Gale Research, 1978.

Something about the Author. Vol. 15. Detroit: Gale Research, 1979.

Mrs. Molesworth

(Mary Louisa Molesworth)

1839-1921, English author

The Cuckoo Clock

(fantasy, 1877; originally published under the pen name of Ennis Graham)

PLOT: In this mildly didactic fantasy, a lonely girl learns patience and eventually acquires a friend with whom she can share imaginative games. Griselda, sent to live with her staid great-aunts, Miss Grizzel and Miss Tabitha, finds life tedious. Fond of moralizing, Aunt Grizzel tells Griselda that the cuckoo clock can teach her punctuality and faithful discharge of duties. When Griselda, upset because she has trouble doing her lessons, thinks that the cuckoo is mocking her, she throws a book at it. Afterwards, for the first time in fifty years, the cuckoo fails to announce the hour. The aunts are upset, and their servant, Dorcas, tells Griselda that the clock, which has always brought good luck, may be a fairy clock. When Griselda then asks the cuckoo for forgiveness, it comes alive and invites her inside the clock. Although it says that she has much to learn, it also admits that she needs amusement. Therefore, it takes her dancing in the Land of Nodding Mandarins, where the people resemble the figures in the aunts' Chinese cabinet. The next morning, Griselda finds a tiny shoe in her bed; Dorcas says that she must have taken it from the cabinet, but Griselda regards it as proof that she did not dream her adventure.

When Griselda becomes ill, the cuckoo entertains her by showing her "pictures" from the life of Sybilla, her grandmother and the clock's first owner. Later, the cuckoo appears as a bird that Griselda rescues from the cold. It then takes her to Butterfly Land to see the butterflies painting flowers. Eventually, it introduces her to five-year-old Master Phil, who also needs a friend. Aunt Grizzel, however, punishes Griselda for associating with a stranger, but Dorcas urges the aunt to make inquiries about him. The cuckoo then takes Griselda to the dark side of the moon. The next day, Griselda applies herself faithfully to her lessons and receives permission to play with Master Phil. She and Phil become lost in the woods while searching for fairy land, but the cuckoo leads them to Phil's home, where his long-absent mother awaits him. That night, in a dream, the cuckoo bids farewell to Griselda, saying that she no longer needs help.

CHARACTERS: The book's appeal lies primarily in the colorful fantasy scenes, but the two central figures have distinctive, relatively complex personalities. **Griselda**, a little girl with gray eyes and curly brown hair, is appropriately dressed in gray when she arrives at the house of her great-aunts: her life there is a dull, monotonous affair devoid of the proper amusements to make schoolwork tolerable. Although usually polite, Griselda succumbs to ill temper because her life is an unrelieved round of duties. Consequently, when the cuckoo seems to echo Grizzel's moralizing about doing one's duty, the exasperated Griselda hurls a book at it. Similarly, her ill temper makes her ask permission to play with Phil in such an obnoxious way that she ensures Aunt Grizzel's refusal. Less seriously, Griselda becomes annoyed with the cuckoo, begging it to refrain from repeatedly telling her how much she has yet to learn. Whether dreams or not, Griselda's adventures provide a necessary escape from tedium and indirectly teach her self-control. She thus learns obedience when the cuckoo insists that she must stop dancing with the nodding mandarins. She learns to appreciate her elders when she sees scenes from their past. She learns trust when the cuckoo, having tested her compassion by appearing as a shivering bird, asks her to cling to its back so that it can fly her to Phil's house. Gradually coming to see that life can be easier and more pleasant if she does her duty, Griselda applies herself to her lessons, thereby making admirable intellectual progress for the first time. Griselda does not find her way to fairy land, but she acquires a friend who is willing to search with her. Able to balance schoolwork with enjoyable play and companionship, she no longer needs to escape into fantasy worlds.

Whether it is genuinely a magical creature or only a figure in fanciful dreams, **the cuckoo** enables Griselda to endure tedium and loneliness. The cuckoo is a droll, sometimes irritable teacher and helper. For example, when it resumes sounding the hours after Griselda apologizes for throwing the book at it, it responds to her question about whether it is back for good by teasing that it is certainly not there for evil. It also notes with exasperating regularity that Griselda has much to learn. Furthermore, when Griselda has trouble understanding how she can enter the clock or ride on its back, given the difference in their sizes, it repeatedly snaps that she is failing to understand that time and sizes are merely fancies. It also tests her compassion by appearing as a bird in need of help, and her trust by ordering her to get on its back even though she is much larger than it is. Finally, the cuckoo insists to Griselda that there are many things that she is not supposed to understand. Although it echoes Aunt Grizzel's instructions, the cuckoo differs in one major respect: it admits that children need meaningful amusements. Consequently, it takes Griselda to magical realms where she sees beauty and is the center of attention, thereby refreshing her and giving her the enthusiasm to face the next day in good spirits. Its departure signals the end of her loneliness, the end of her need for nightly escapes from oppressive reality.

Aunt Grizzel, Griselda's great aunt, is a staid woman who doesn't fully understand what children need. She thus forbids Griselda to touch the mandarins in the China cabinet and believes that she should be sufficiently amused by solitary walks on the terrace. Miss Grizzel also turns even simple things into lessons, noting that the clock can teach punctuality and faithful fulfillment of duties. Although stiff and proper, she is not cruel or insensitive. In spite of her suspicion that all boys are rude and naughty, she makes an effort to assure herself that Master Phil is respectable and then permits Griselda to play with him.

Griselda travels to the Land of Nodding Mandarins in this illustration by Ernest H. Shepard for Molesworth's
The Cuckoo Clock.

Aunt Tabitha is a comic character who merely repeats everything her sister says. **Dorcas**, the elderly servant, is a kind and considerate woman. She introduces the possibility of magic by suggesting that the clock is a fairy clock. She also acts as a helper. Obviously moved by Griselda's essential goodness, she gets Aunt Grizzel to make inquiries about the suitability of Master Phil as a playmate. Five-year-old **Master Phil** is a kindred spirit to Griselda, a person to whom the cuckoo also speaks, probably because he is just as lonely as Griselda is. He believes in fairies and thinks that he may have found his way into fairy land, which seems likely when he appears wearing wings during Griselda's trip to the dark side of the moon. Phil supplies Griselda's need for a playmate and reveals her kindness because she is willing to teach him to read.

Further Reading

Berger, Laura Standley, ed. *Twentieth-Century Children's Writers*. 4th ed. Detroit: St. James, 1995.

Bingham, Jane M., ed. *Writers for Children: Critical Studies of Major Authors since the Seventeenth Century*. New York: Scribner, 1988.

Green, Roger Lancelyn. *Mrs. Molesworth.* London: H. Z. Walck, 1964.

Thesing, William B., ed. *British Short-Fiction Writers, 1880-1914: The Realist Tradition.* Vol. 135 of *Dictionary of Literary Biography.* Detroit: Gale Research, 1994.

L. M. Montgomery

1874-1942, Canadian novelist

Anne of Green Gables

(novel, 1908)

PLOT: *Anne of Green Gables* is an episodic orphan story obviously inspired by Kate Douglas Wiggin's *Rebecca of Sunnybrook Farm.* In tracing the maturation of the central character over approximately five years, its comic events develop themes of wish fulfillment and belonging.

The first eight chapters establish Anne Shirley, an orphan from Nova Scotia, as a resident of Green Gables, the Prince Edward Island home of elderly Matthew Cuthbert and his sister, Marilla. Having sent for a boy to help with the farm work, Matthew is surprised to find instead a red-haired girl waiting for him at the railway station. During the ride to Green Gables, the talkative Anne is excited because she has always wanted a "really truly home." She also expresses seemingly impossible desires to be divinely beautiful, dazzlingly clever, and angelically good. Her spirited conversation and her joyful appreciation of nature charm the shy bachelor. When Marilla objects to taking in a girl, Matthew insists that they might do the child good. Anne's interesting conversations soon win over Marilla as well.

The major episodes consist of amusing "mistakes" that Anne makes as she matures. Most involve breaches of propriety, but Anne is never truly naughty. Anne's mistakes begin when Mrs. Rachel Lynde says that Anne is homely and has hair the color of carrots. Anne becomes angry, insults Mrs. Lynde, and then turns her forced apology into a pleasurable drama. Next, Anne scandalizes Marilla by attending Sunday school with flowers in her hat.

More serious mistakes follow. Anne falsely confesses to losing a brooch because Marilla will not allow her to attend a picnic until she does so. When Gilbert Blythe calls her "carrots," Anne smashes a slate over his head and declares that she will never forgive him. She stubbornly maintains her grudge for years. Another mistake occurs when Anne unwittingly gets her friend Diana Barry drunk on alcoholic cordial. Mrs. Barry forbids Anne to see Diana again and only relents after Anne saves her baby from a nearly fatal attack of croup. Readmitted to the Barry house, Anne becomes friends with a visiting aunt, Josephine Barry, after accidentally jumping on her in bed. Anne also becomes friends with another woman through a mistake: she accidentally puts liniment in a cake she bakes to impress the new minister and his wife. Mrs. Allan, the minister's wife, helps her to overcome her humiliation.

Many of Anne's mistakes mock romantic fiction and ideas. For example, Anne frightens herself by imagining that the woods are haunted. Later, she defends her honor by accepting a dare to walk a ridge pole. She falls off, breaking her ankle. This episode teaches her that fainting—a staple of romantic stories—is not romantic at all. In perhaps the most famous episode of the book, Anne tries to make herself a raven-haired beauty like those in romance novels, but the dye turns her hair green. Finally, while role playing the romantic death of a maiden, Anne nearly drowns in a sinking boat. Forced to cling awkwardly to a bridge pile, she is rescued by Gilbert Blythe. Humiliated, Anne stubbornly refuses Gilbert's offer of friendship.

Although the novel focuses on Anne's innocent errors, it also recounts her effect on others and her triumphs at school. Most notable are the changes Anne brings about in Matthew, who is shy around most women but quite attached to Anne. Matthew endures a number of embarrassments in order to buy Anne a dress with stylish puffed sleeves so that she can be like her friends. At school, Anne blossoms when a new teacher, Miss Stacy, encourages her writing. Spurred by a rivalry with Gilbert Blythe, Anne wins a college scholarship and achieves her wish to be clever. At college, she achieves another wish: her hated red hair turns almost auburn, and

Anne develops a reputation as a beauty. She also wins another prize as an outstanding student.

By the book's final chapters, Anne is a mature young woman. She achieves her most impossible wish—to be angelically good—when she makes two morally responsible choices. First, after Matthew dies, Anne saves Green Gables by taking a teaching position instead of returning to college. Second, Anne makes peace with Gilbert Blythe, who has given up his own teaching position at a nearby school so that Anne can have it.

The story of Anne and her family continues in nine sequels: Anne of Avonlea *(1909),* Chronicles of Avonlea *(1912),* Anne of the Island *(1915),* Anne's House of Dreams *(1917),* Rainbow Valley *(1917),* Further Chronicles of Avonlea *(1920),* Rilla of Ingleside *(1921),* Anne of Ingleside *(1921), and* Anne of Windy Poplars *(1930).*

CHARACTERS: The novel focuses upon Anne's personal growth and her struggles toward maturity. In addition, the interactions between the spirited Anne and more conventional characters criticize rigid, puritanical attitudes toward raising children.

In the beginning of the novel, **Anne Shirley** is called a "freckled witch." By the end, however, Marilla calls her a "blessed girl." These terms mark the extremes of Anne's development. Initially, Anne seems disruptive and naughty, but later she is almost a saint. When Anne arrives at Green Gables, her attitudes shock the conventional and pious Marilla. Anne wears flowers to church, for example, and she displays what Marilla considers a sinful preoccupation with her appearance. Because adults have forced Anne into a life of drudgery, she has never experienced religion as a positive force. Indeed, her only solace has come from the romantic stories she devours. Such stories do not, however, help Anne to accept herself. A thin eleven-year-old with a large mouth, pointed chin, and eyes that change from gray to green depending on the light, Anne is unhappy that she does not resemble fictional heroines. What distresses Anne most are her decidedly unromantic freckles and red hair (both archetypal signs of a witch). Anne shocks Marilla by declaring

Anne shows her spunk in facing the busybody Mrs. Rachel Lynde in this illustration by Jody Lee from Montgomery's **Anne of Green Gables.**

that she stopped caring about God when she learned that He had deliberately made her hair red. Anne's persistent concern with her appearance culminates in her attempt to dye her hair, an act that Marilla considers wicked. Anne is more obviously naughty when her temper explodes, as it does in the incidents with Mrs. Lynde and Gilbert Blythe. Moreover, she displays a stubborn lack of charity when she has been hurt. She apologizes to Mrs. Lynde only after Matthew requests that she do so as a special favor to him, and she maintains her grudge against Gilbert long after she gets over being called "carrots."

For the most part, Anne's naughtiness is merely the innocent expression of a lively spirit and imagination. Her mistakes are results of immaturity—such as when she accepts a dare to walk on the roof—or of domestic incompetence—such as when she puts liniment in the cake. She never has evil intentions. Even her supposed impiety is innocent: Anne would rather feel a prayer than recite meaningless words. Furthermore, although Anne tends to hold grudges, she does not hesitate to rescue Mrs. Barry's baby, even though Mrs. Barry has been unfair in claiming that Anne deliberately made Diana drunk. Nevertheless, Anne is disruptive. Marilla correctly recognizes that the talkative Anne is "casting a spell" over Matthew. Anne does the same with Marilla and Josephine Barry, making all of these elderly people more sensitive. Indeed, Anne needs people and displays a "genius for friendship." During her lonely days as an orphan, she used her imagination to transform an echo and a reflection into friends. When she comes to Avonlea, she searches out "kindred spirits" with whom she can share her love of nature and beauty. Although she is more intelligent and more talented than her friends, Anne is never conceited.

Mark Twain called Anne "the dearest, and most loveable child in fiction since the immortal Alice." The secret of Anne's appeal may lie in her statement that "There's such a lot of different Annes in me. . . . If I was just the one Anne it would be ever so much more comfortable, but then it wouldn't be half so interesting." As Anne grows up, the various Annes merge. She stops using big words, gives up on romantic stories, and learns to control her temper. Anne becomes a veritable saint, even performing a kind of miracle by giving Marilla new life. Unfortunately, the comically odd girl who was the perfect vehicle for satirizing puritanical religion and staid social routines ends up being sentimental, socialized, and comparatively dull.

Matthew Cuthbert, an elderly bachelor who has long gray hair and a full brown beard, is the first of Anne's kindred spirits. Matthew represents a humane approach to child raising. Always kind, he considers Anne's welfare above all else. He insists on keeping the orphan because he believes that he and his sister can do her some good. Although he seldom talks, he is free and generous with his praise for Anne. His gentle persuasion works with Anne, whereas Marilla's threats fail. Matthew is responsible for saving Anne from a life of misery, and he also benefits from his contact with her. Her presence awakens him to life and new interests. The most comical evidence of this comes after Matthew realizes that Anne is the only girl wearing a dress without puffed sleeves. Shy and habitually frightened of all things female, the embarrassed Matthew buys unneeded supplies instead of cloth to make Anne a new dress. Determined to please Anne, however, he finally gets up the courage to enlist Mrs. Lynde's help in making the dress.

Described as a tall, thin woman with angles and no curves, **Marilla Cuthbert** possesses a correspondingly rigid character. Her emotional life is nearly as sterile as her "painfully clean" house. Although she occasionally shows a sense of humor, she is generally efficient, practical, and puritanical. She thus objects to fashionable puffed sleeves as vanities and insists upon dressing Anne in plain, serviceable clothes. She also objects to Anne reading and writing stories, which she views as a waste of time. A more serious problem is Marilla's inability to express her love for Anne. She withholds affection in part because she is afraid it will make Anne vain. Thus Matthew tells Anne that he is proud of her after her recital at a concert, but Marilla remains silent. A more basic reason for Marilla's silence is that she is repressed and does not know how to express her emotions. Her puritan conscience also makes her worry that a deep attachment to a fellow mortal is sinful. Consequently, Marilla is stiff toward other people, so Anne is unaware that she has brought out a "throb of the maternity" that the spinster has missed. Marilla does, however, benefit from Anne's presence as much as Matthew does, and she finally tells Anne that she loves her as her own flesh and blood.

Anne has significant contact with a number of women in the community. **Mrs. Rachel Lynde** is the target of satire. Mrs. Lynde is an overweight busybody, the "all-seeing eye" of Avonlea. Socially, she is a conservative who objects to both female teachers and higher education for girls. Religiously, she is a puritan who believes in the wickedness of infants. She says that Anne is full of original sin. Mrs. Lynde also turns every occasion into a moral lecture. After Anne falls from the roof, for example, she says that she hopes the experience will make her a better girl. Intolerant of faults in others, Mrs. Lynde is unaware of her own. Although she calls Anne homely, she is not intentionally cruel. Rather, she prides herself on speaking her mind, and she is completely unaware that children have feelings, too. **Mrs. Allan**, the minister's wife, represents the opposite attitudes. She is exceptionally tolerant and gives positive examples instead of negative lectures. She lets Anne know that naughtiness is not the same as sinfulness, pointing out that she herself was sometimes a very naughty child. She also helps Anne see the joyful side of religion. **Miss Stacy**, Anne's new teacher, has a similar role. Unlike Anne's first teacher, she shows kindness and sympathy, thereby inspiring Anne to do her best. **Miss Josephine Barry**, an aunt of Diana Barry's father, represents all those whom Anne touches. She is a prim, rigid, wealthy, and domineering seventy-year-old woman whose temper is well known. Her conversations with Anne, however, oil her "rusty" imagination. As a result, Miss Barry becomes pleasant and rediscovers the joys long absent from her life.

Of the children who associate with Anne, only two are prominent. **Diana Barry** lives in the house nearest Green Gables and fulfills Anne's wish for a "bosom friend." The contrast between Anne and Diana emphasizes Anne's virtues. A pretty, dark-haired girl with a ready laugh, Diana lacks Anne's imagination. Nevertheless, she eagerly joins in Anne's games and rituals. Diana's upbringing also puts Anne's domestic life into perspective. Mrs. Barry believes the worst of Anne after Diana becomes drunk. She forbids Anne to see Diana again. By contrast, Marilla appreciates Anne's innocence and comes to her defense. Because Diana's conservative family does not believe in sending girls to college, they also emphasize Anne's good fortune in belonging to a family that encourages her intellectual abilities. **Gilbert Blythe** provokes the worst and best in Anne. A handsome, roguish boy with curly brown hair and a teasing smile, he calls Anne "carrots" so that she will look at him. His taunt causes Anne to explode in anger and to develop a lingering grudge. More positively, Gilbert is a good student and inspires in Anne a rivalry that encourages her academic excellence. As he matures, Gilbert becomes the noble beau. Even though Anne refuses his friendship when he rescues her, he is selfless later when he gives up his teaching position so that she can have it.

Further Reading

Authors and Artists for Young Adults. Vol. 12. Detroit: Gale Research, 1994.

Berger, Laura Standley, ed. *Twentieth-Century Children's Writers.* 4th ed. Detroit: St. James, 1995.

Children's Literature Review. Vol. 8. Detroit: Gale Research, 1985.

Collier, Laurie, and Joyce Nakamura, eds. *Major Authors and Illustrators for Children and Young Adults.* Detroit: Gale Research, 1993.

Reimer, Mavis, ed. *Such a Simple Little Tale: Critical Responses to L. M. Montgomery's* Anne of Green Gables. Metuchen, NJ: Children's Literature Association and Scarecrow Press, 1992.

Ridley, Hilda M. *The Story of L. M. Montgomery.* Toronto: Ryerson Press, 1956.

Rubio, Mary. "L. M. Montgomery's *Anne of Green Gables:* The Architect of Adolescence." In *Touchstones: Reflections on the Best in Children's Literature,* Vol. 1. Edited by Perry Nodelman, pp. 173-87. West Lafayette, IN: Children's Literature Association, 1985.

Sorfleet, Robert John, ed. *L. M. Montgomery: An Assessment.* Guelph, Ontario: Canadian Children's Press, 1976.

Yesterday's Authors of Books for Children. Vol. 1. Detroit: Gale Research, 1977.

Robert Munsch

1945-, Canadian storyteller and author

The Paper Bag Princess

(picture book, 1980; illustrated by Michael Martchenko)

PLOT: This feminist parody of traditional dragon stories establishes that clothes make neither the man nor the woman. When a dragon smashes the castle and carries off Prince Ronald, Princess Elizabeth decides to rescue her fiancé. Putting on a paper bag because the dragon has burned her clothes, she follows a trail of destruction to the dragon's cave. She knocks on the door, but the dragon tells her to come back the next day. Princess Elizabeth knocks a second time. Before the dragon can again slam the door, she begins tricking him. First, she asks him about his fiery breath. The dragon repeatedly shows off, burning up forests until he has no fire left. Next,

Princess Elizabeth finally sees Prince Ronald for the shallow boy he is in Munsch's satirical tale, illustrated by Michael Martchenko.

she asks him about his speed, twice getting him to fly around the world. The exhausted dragon then falls asleep. When Princess Elizabeth opens the cave door, Prince Ronald calls her a mess and orders her to come back when she is dressed like a real princess. Princess Elizabeth tells Ronald that, although he looks like a real prince, he is really a "bum," and she decides not to marry him.

CHARACTERS: The characters are parodic variations on traditional types. Michael Martchenko's drawings flesh them out, providing anachronisms that intensify their comic meaning. **Princess Elizabeth** is a trickster hero who learns the difference between appearance and reality. In doing so, she proves her identity as a true princess. At first, Elizabeth is a conventionally beautiful, blond princess who loves the conventionally handsome, blond prince. Her true character emerges, however, after the dragon burns her expensive clothes. As the picture of her clenching her teeth and tightening her fists indicates, she is angry that the dragon has taken away her fiancé. She is also practical, putting on a paper bag because she can find nothing else to wear. Brave and determined, Elizabeth follows the dragon

and does not give up when it first slams the door. Unlike traditional male heroes, Elizabeth uses wit and intelligence to defeat the dragon. She thus makes this vain male dragon exhaust himself in an attempt to earn the admiration of a female. Cautious and practical, Elizabeth enters the dragon's cave only after yelling in his ear to ensure that he is unconscious. When Ronald then rejects her, she shows she can be perceptive, too. By calling him a bum, she indicates that she has freed herself from the conventional attitudes that Ronald represents. Knowing that identity is a matter of character, not appearance, Elizabeth shows her new-found independence by happily skipping alone into the sunset.

Prince Ronald represents the vain and superficial male who does not understand that he can't accurately judge females by their appearance. His anachronistic attire (he wears a tennis sweater and carries a racquet, while also wearing tights and medieval long-toed slippers) suggests that his attitudes are not necessarily those of the past. Ronald fails to see that Elizabeth's bravery, not expensive clothing, is the sign of her identity as a true princess. Consequently, Ronald is a foil: unlike Elizabeth, he has a royal appearance but a base character. **The dragon** is a symbol as well as a character. In traditional stories, capture by a dragon often symbolizes entrapment by a weakness that prevents full human growth. Here the dragon projects Ronald's vanity. Elizabeth's triumph over him also symbolizes her triumph over her own vanity. As a character, the dragon reinforces this symbolism. He is arrogant, telling Elizabeth that he is too busy to see her. He is also, like Ronald, self-destructively vain. Unlike the subtle and wise dragons in traditional stories, he is foolish. He thus sends Elizabeth away instead of capturing her. Furthermore, he exhausts himself in order to earn Elizabeth's praise for his displays of power and speed.

Further Reading

Berger, Laura Standley, ed. *Twentieth-Century Children's Writers.* 4th ed. Detroit: St. James, 1995.

Children's Literature Review. Vol. 19. Detroit: Gale Research, 1990.

Collier, Laurie, and Joyce Nakamura, eds. *Major Authors and Illustrators for Children and Young Adults.* Detroit: Gale Research, 1993.

Contemporary Authors New Revision Series. Vol. 37. Detroit: Gale Research, 1992.

Something about the Author. Vols. 48, 50, 83. Detroit: Gale Research, 1987, 1988, 1996.

E. Nesbit

1858-1924, English author

The Story of the Treasure Seekers

(novel, 1899)

PLOT: *The Story of the Treasure Seekers* is a family story extolling imagination and generosity. Because Mr. Richard Bastable's partner cheated him, his six motherless children endure hard times. The attempts of Dora, Oswald, Dicky, Alice, Noel, and Horace Octavius (called H. O.) to restore the family fortune repeatedly fail. When they dig for treasure, their tunnel falls on Albert-next-door Morrison, whose uncle rescues him and then notices two half-crowns in their pit. Albert's uncle again rescues them when Oswald, playing detective, falls and knocks himself unconscious. On the train, they meet a new benefactor: Mrs. Leslie. A poet, Mrs. Leslie gives Oswald and Noel money and her card, which Noel uses to gain admittance to a newspaper editor who buys his poems. Noel acts on his other plan of marrying a princess when he proposes to a real princess in the park. Next, H. O. has them become bandits, but they anger Albert's uncle by holding Albert for ransom.

After editing their own paper and trying to borrow money from Mr. Rosenbaum to start a business, the children next try Oswald's idea of setting their dog upon Lord Tottenham in order to rescue him from danger. Lord Tottenham threatens to take Noel to the police, but Alice gets him to accept their apologies. The next scheme also backfires. They try to sell hideously sweetened sherry to various people, including a teetotalling minister, Mr. Mallow. Next, so that they can invent a money-making medicine, Dicky tries to catch a cold. Instead, Noel gets sick. Because their father is away, Alice telegraphs Albert's uncle for help, and he chastises the children for their foolishness. Oswald then sells some flowers Mrs. Leslie has given to Noel and repays the telegraph company for the bad coin Alice used to send the telegram.

The children have a complex adventure when Oswald captures a robber, who captures another robber. The second robber escapes, and the first confesses that he is really their father's friend, Mr. Foulkes. Alice, using a divining rod, then discovers a coin under the floorboards of the nursery, and they use it to buy food. After they hear their Indian Uncle complaining about the dinner their father served, the children, believing that their uncle is poor, invite him to share their feast. The Indian Uncle joins in their games and is touched when they try to give him money. Actually wealthy, their Indian Uncle soon showers them with gifts. He also invites them to a Christmas dinner attended by most of their earlier benefactors and announces that they and their father will now live with him.

Sequels are The Wouldbegoods *(1901) and* The New Treasure Seekers *(1904).*

CHARACTERS: Because their mother is dead and their father distracted by business worries, the children have an unusual degree of freedom to indulge their imaginative plans. **Dora Bastable**, the oldest child, is caught between childhood desires and adult responsibilities. On one hand, Dora insists that they first try digging for treasure because people in books always find it. On the other, she has a smothering sense of propriety and offers adult objections to many of their plans. As she finally reveals, Dora does so because she labors under the painful and alienating burden of her mother's deathbed instructions that she should care for her siblings and teach them to be good.

Oswald Bastable, the twelve-year-old narrator, generates irony because he is unaware of the true meaning of what he describes. For example, when Dora sees nothing on the spot where Albert's uncle found a coin, Oswald praises his uncle's eyesight instead of concluding that he planted the coins in the pit. Similarly, Oswald believes that when his father laughs after tasting the sugared sherry it indicates that it is a fine wine. A continuing irony concerns Oswald's attempt to keep the narrator's identity a secret. He identifies himself almost immediately by slipping into the first person when describing a kick that Oswald aimed at Noel. He makes similar lapses throughout the story. Still, Oswald is a skilful narrator. Well-read (he mentions Rudyard Kipling, Arthur Conan Doyle, and Charles Dickens), he knows what children like to read and therefore focuses on events rather than descriptions.

As a character in his own right, Oswald is imaginative but comically naive about the difference between life and fiction. Romantic stories have convinced him, for example, that he will become wealthy by rescuing a rich man from danger. Oswald is full of himself, ironically expressing his sense of superiority by claiming that he knows that it is not through his own merit that he is cleverer than some people. He also frequently praises his own qualities, such as his thoughtfulness and firmness. Nevertheless, Oswald is not obnoxiously arrogant because he is honest enough to present contradicting opinions about himself. For instance, he says that during their encounter with Lord Tottenham everyone cried, except Oswald, but he notes that the others say Oswald also cried.

Oswald is adventurous and has contempt for girls, but he can be sensitive. Once he learns why Dora is so concerned with correct behavior, he consoles her. He is melodramatic about his nobility in sacrificing family pride by selling flowers, but he gallantly eases Alice's guilt by earning the money to replace the bad coin she used for the telegram. Indeed, Oswald tries to be a gentleman in more than manners. He thus accepts responsibility whenever he realizes that he has been at fault. Furthermore, he is scrupulously honest. Therefore, he confesses that he really did not behave bravely when he burst upon "the robber" because he thought that he would be confronting a cat. A far from simple character, Oswald is one of Nesbit's finest creations.

Dicky, the next oldest, plans before acting and never reveals ideas before completing them. Because he likes to have things settled, his father has nicknamed him "the Definite Article." Dicky, who is

good at sums, is relatively more practical than his siblings. Attracted to businesses, he suggests that they get a loan to buy a business and that they answer the advertisement that leads to them selling sherry on commission. He also points out that medicines are profitable. Dicky seems less sophisticated, however, when he comically insists that he should catch the cold and test their medicine because he originated the idea.

Ten-year-old **Noel** is sickly, but he never complains about his health. He is also a poet, whose writings add humor. When he discovers that he hasn't written enough poems to fill a book, Noel gladly sells them to the newspaper editor, not realizing that the editor is patronizing him. Noel's plan to gain wealth by marrying a princess shows that fairy tales have influenced his thoughts. His improbable meeting with a real princess indicates that commoners may have advantages of freedom and imagination. His twin sister, **Alice**, is a spirited girl who has had her hair cut short so that she can play boys' parts in their games. Although tough, she can be sensitive, as she shows when she becomes worried about Noel's health and wires Albert's uncle. Alice is also considerate: she doesn't tell Oswald that she used a bad coin to pay for the telegram because she doesn't want him to stop her or to share her guilt. Alice loves ritual, turning the divining rod treasure hunt into a mystical rite. Kind and generous, she suggests inviting the Indian Uncle to share their dinner. Because she is open to others, she then gives him the choice of having a staid, adult dinner or an exciting play dinner. Although he is eight years old, **Horace Octavius**, called **H. O.**, can't yet tell time, probably because his father's financial troubles have limited his schooling. Not as aware of manners as the others, he tends to say exactly what he thinks. An exuberant child, he says that even if it is wrong, it would be fun to pretend that they were bandits. **Mr. Richard (Dick) Bastable**, their father, is plagued by business worries. He asks his children to consult him about their business ventures and he shows that they sometimes amuse him, but he is weak and ineffective because of his frequent absences.

Albert Morrison, usually called **Albert-next-door**, contrasts with the Bastables. A tidy child who wears frilly collars and velvet knickerbockers, Albert is a sissy. He complains and cries whenever the Bastables make him part of their games. As Oswald indicates, Albert lacks the imagination to join into games because he doesn't like reading. Three adults possess the childish enthusiasm that Albert lacks. **Albert's uncle**, a writer, understands childhood and knows how to join in games by speaking as heroes do in books. He enjoys the imaginative Bastables and adds to their fun by surreptitiously planting money in their treasure pit. His major role is that of benevolent adult helper: a surrogate for their absent father, he extricates them from difficulties and provides advice to both. **The Indian Uncle** is a staple figure of Victorian fiction: the formidable adult warmed into generosity by the innocence of children. His innate goodness first appears when he plays at the children's dinner, jubilantly slaying a pudding as if it were a boar. After the children, who believe he is poor, insist that he take their remaining money, he solves the financial problems the children could not.

The Indian Uncle invites three people to the Christmas party because they were the children's benefactors. **Mr. Foulkes** becomes a benefactor when he lets his childish imagination loose and plays along after Oswald mistakes him for a robber. Obviously one who understands and sympathizes with children, he entertains the Bastables by inventing romantic tales about his life as a pirate. **Mrs. Leslie**, the leading female poet of the day, is a benefactor drawn to Oswald and Noel because their references to Kipling suggest that they are imaginative. She kindly gives them a way of meeting an editor, and she later sends flowers to Noel. **Lord Tottenham**, an eccentric old man known as the Mad Protectionist, becomes a benefactor when he refrains from taking Noel to the police after the children set their dog on him. His act of kindness is inspired by the children's tears and by Alice's touching statement of contrition.

Two benefactors are ambiguous. **Mr. Rosenbaum**, the money lender whom the children naively consider to be a Generous Benefactor, offers to lend them a pound, but suddenly decides to charge sixty percent interest. Although Oswald is not clear about the episode, Mr. Rosenbaum appar-

ently eases their father's mind by then offering an extension on his debts. Although **the editor** of the *Daily Recorder* buys Noel's poems, he patronizes the children and uses them both for information about Lord Tottenham and for material for his own writing. **Mr. Mallow**, the teetotalling minister, is the only completely negative character. He cribs his sermons and is abusively intolerant when the children try to sell him sherry.

The Five Children Books
(fantasy series, 1902-1906)

PLOT: The episodes in the first two volumes are variations on the idea that wishes can create comic incongruities or discord. ***The Five Children and It*** (1902) introduces Cyril, Anthea, Robert, Jane, and their baby brother, called the Lamb, who are spending the summer in the country. The children discover the Psammead, a sand fairy who grants three wishes a day, each lasting until sunset. These wishes, however, complicate life. When the children wish to be beautiful, they become unrecognizable, and Martha, their housekeeper, refuses to let them in. Wishing that the servants won't notice doesn't solve their problems. When they wish for wealth, they can't spend their strange coins, and they are arrested on suspicion of theft. Even accidental wishes prove troublesome. When Robert, angry that they must care for the baby, wishes that everybody would want the Lamb, Lady Chittenden kidnaps the baby and then gypsies claim him. After Anthea wishes for wings, the children take food from a vicarage, fall asleep, and become stranded on a church tower when their wings disappear at sunset.

Romantic wishes go awry after the children wish that they were in a besieged castle; only sunset saves them from the attacking army of Wulfric de Talbot. Later, when a baker's boy beats him, Robert bitterly wishes he were bigger and becomes eleven feet tall. Robert scares the baker's boy and then becomes an exhibit at a fair; when he returns to his normal size, the children use a clever ruse to help him escape from the greedy showman. After Cyril arranges for them to receive wishes without being near the Psammead, he angrily wishes that the Lamb would grow up: the baby suddenly becomes a vain and obnoxious dandy. Cyril's next unwitting wish, for small Red Indians, proves dangerous. The children escape death only because the Psammead hears the angry Indians wishing they were in their native forests. The final episode is complex. After Jane dreamily wishes that her mother had some jewels stolen from Lady Chittenden, Anthea saves the day through a series of wishes that undo the robbery and prevent her mother from being angry at Martha, whose fiancé had helped her clean the windows. In return for these wishes, the children agree never to ask for another wish and never to tell about the Psammead.

In *The Phoenix and the Carpet* (1904), the children find an egg rolled up in a carpet. The Phoenix hatches from the egg and reveals that the carpet is magical. Flying to France on the carpet, the children discover buried treasure but can't return with it because they have exhausted their limit of three wishes in a day. The Phoenix rescues them by going to the Psammead and wishing them home. Next, the children decide to cure the Lamb's whooping-cough by taking him to a tropical island. They take along their troublesome cook, leaving her to become queen of the cannibals. They then fly to India to obtain items for a church bazaar. When someone accidentally sells their carpet to cantankerous Mrs. Biddle, Anthea wishes that the woman had an angelic temper, and they retrieve the carpet. The vain Phoenix now demands to go to his "temple," the offices of the Phoenix Fire Insurance company. Fortunately, the businessmen assume that they dreamed his visit. The children then return to France for the treasure. Learning, however, that it should belong to the impoverished old Manon and her nephew, Henri, who are about to lose their ancestral estate, they give the fortune to them.

A connected series of events follows. The carpet brings one hundred and ninety-nine Persian cats, some muskrats, and a cow into the children's house. That night, Jane catches a burglar and convinces him to reform. When the burglar is then arrested for stealing cats that the children gave him, they rescue him from jail and fly him to the tropical island. They also bring the Reverend Septimus Blenkinsop to the island to marry the burglar and the cook. Later, Robert and Jane again meet Reverend Blenkinsop when, having fallen from the flying carpet, they enter his house. The Phoenix becomes more active in the final adventures. First, he rescues the Lamb after the carpet, obeying his baby talk, whisks him away. Then he sets a theater on fire to make it fitting as his temple. When he subsequently decides to depart, the relieved children use the carpet to send his egg to a place where it will not hatch for two thousand years. They prepare a pyre. Afterwards, the children and their parents receive gifts, produced by the last wish the Phoenix made of the Psammead.

Organized around a quest plot, *The Story of the Amulet* (1906) contains themes about social justice and the nature of time. While both parents and the Lamb are abroad, Cyril, Anthea, Robert, and Jane stay with old Nurse in London. Finding the Psammead offered for sale as a monkey, they buy him and a curio, which is actually half of a magical Egyptian amulet that can take them into the past. The Psammead says that if they recover the other half, which was long ago destroyed, the amulet will grant their hearts' desire: the safe return of their parents. The children therefore embark on a series of dangerous journeys.

They locate the amulet in an Egyptian village in the year 6000 B.C., but attacking soldiers force them to flee without it. In Babylon, the Queen, angered by Robert's rash demand for the amulet, throws him, Cyril, and Anthea into her dungeons. Following the advice of the magically summoned Nisroch, they rejoin Jane and the Psammead. The Queen has wished to see their home, however, so she appears in London, where she causes havoc and death until a clerk wishes that everything was a dream. Next, the children take Jimmy, the learned gentleman upstairs, to Atlantis. Convinced that he is dreaming, Jimmy insists on seeing the city destroyed and must be forced to return. Shortly afterwards, the children find Imogen, a London street orphan. Again accompanied by Jimmy, they take her to Britain in the year 55 B.C., where a British queen, mistaking Imogen for her missing child, takes her in. They also cross the English Channel to meet Julius Caesar.

Becoming more methodical, the children go to ancient Egypt, where Rekh-mara, a priest, takes them to the Pharaoh, who imprisons them. After escaping, the children go to the future, hoping they will remember finding the amulet in the past. Instead, they discover a utopian society and learn, by talking to a boy temporarily expelled from school and his mother, that their own society is barbarous. The children next go to ancient Tyre, where Rekh-mara is a slave wearing an identical half-amulet. Like the children, Rekh-mara uses the amulet to escape from a sinking ship. Rekh-mara then appears in London. Agreeing to be partners with them, he and the children go to Egypt during the dawn of belief and retrieve the amulet. Everyone now receives his heart's desire: the children learn that their parents are arriving; the souls of the learned gentleman and Rekh-mara merge into one; and the grateful Psammead is wished safely into the past.

CHARACTERS: The series depends on comical incongruities and exciting events, but the central characters come alive as bright but otherwise unexceptional children. They frequently argue, yet they care about and support each other. They are honest and upright, insisting on fair play and opposing sneakiness or lying. Although occasionally annoyed by the need to care for the Lamb, the older children deeply love him.

The eldest, **Cyril**, nicknamed **Squirrel**, tends to be logical and practical. He thus figures out that their besieged castle is superimposed on their ordinary house, thereby enabling them to solve the problem of eating, and he suggests that they take modern items when they journey into the past so that they can win over the people. He also engineers Robert's escape from the fair because he realizes that the showman and his wife are guarding against the departure of a giant, not a normal-sized child. Cyril's practicality brings him into conflict with Anthea, who advocates rigid adherence to rules. When the children have wings and become hungry,

for example, he pompously equates himself with great generals and declares that, like soldiers at war, they have a right to take the provisions that people have been too frightened to sell them. Responding to Anthea's objections that taking food is wrong, he insists that their need is more important. Nevertheless, Cyril has a conscience and reluctantly agrees to leave some money in payment.

Although Cyril advises the others to be wise in making wishes, he plays a major role in showing the irony inherent in literally receiving one's wishes. Thinking himself crafty in asking that the children be granted wishes even when the Psammead is not present, he foolishly ignores the warnings that trouble will follow. Cyril thus loses his temper and unintentionally turns the Lamb into a grown man and, without realizing that he has done so, causes Red Indians to appear. Cyril occasionally expresses boyish contempt for girls, but he can be a thoughtful and protective gentleman. He thus avoids frightening Jane when they are trapped in the French treasure tower. Furthermore, he respects his sisters, listens to their ideas, and apologizes when he misbehaves.

The next in age, **Anthea**, called **Panther**, is the most prominent throughout the series. Anthea is sometimes obstinate because she wants to finish what she starts. She is also thoughtful, privately seeking advice from the Psammead when she sees the disastrous results of their initial wishes. Anthea subsequently suggests that the children take turns wishing, and she shows her own romantic and poetic sensibility by wishing for wings. More notably, Anthea is considerate and caring, responding to the feelings and needs of others. She thus is the only one who remembers to tell the Psammead that she hopes his sore whisker will get better. She is also the one who most often calls for peace when the siblings quarrel. Worried about the learned gentleman, she takes him his meals. At Christmas, she suggests that they use the carpet to perform good deeds. Her compassion is dramatically evident in two episodes. When she realizes that Cyril has wished for Red Indians, she devises a clever plan to get Martha to remove the Lamb from potential danger. Only after succeeding does she break down into tears. In the second episode, she, unlike Robert, looks beyond the dirty Imogen's hostility to see her deep need. By then insisting that they help Imogen, Anthea becomes instrumental in providing her with a loving home in the past.

Anthea has the most highly developed conscience of the children, as she shows when she insists that it is wrong to take food from the vicar's house. Her conscience won't allow her to disobey her mother in any way and compels her to tell her mother the truth about their experiences. Thus, even though she knows she won't be believed, Anthea tells her mother about taking the cook to sunny shores. Although most often connected to feelings and moral issues, Anthea is ingeniously pragmatic when she resolves all the difficulties at the end of *The Five Children and It*, Like the biblical Jacob wrestling for a blessing, she refuses to release the Psammead until he grants the wish that the jewel robbery never occurred and that her mother doesn't remember being angry with Martha. Aware of the Psammead's needs, she secures his cooperation by offering never to ask for another wish—not a great sacrifice given the way the children's wishes have turned out—and by agreeing never to talk about him.

Robert, often called **Bobs**, is brave, as he demonstrates by defying the attackers and by rallying the children in their besieged castle. He is also honorable, and he is presented as an example of British manliness when he refuses to beat the baker's boy once he becomes much bigger. Because he believes in doing one's duty, he shows his contempt for the servants who left the house without permission by booby-trapping the door on the night after the episode involving the cats and the burglar. Robert shares the family's penchant for honesty and earns the Phoenix's trust and respect when he admits that he hatched its egg by accident. A sensible and occasionally thoughtful boy, Robert is able to learn from experience. Because the children were lost in the dark when they found the treasure in the French tower, he afterwards takes along candles and matches when they go on magic carpet trips. Robert enjoys being important and delights in lighting matches to show his powers to

the Babylonian Queen. He lacks restraint, however, and becomes carried away with himself. Shaking off Anthea's sensitive remarks about good manners, he rashly demands that the Queen give him the amulet, thereby ending up in her dungeons.

Jane, the next youngest, is often a conventional character: the loving and innocent child who melts the hearts of adults. She appears in this role after the children are stranded on the church roof because their wings have vanished. Taken into the vicarage, Jane throws her arms around the vicar's wife and asks for forgiveness. Nesbit has great fun mocking the "artless prattle" of the type in the burglary scene in *The Phoenix and the Carpet*. But Jane, although avoiding baby talk, gets the burglar to reform because she expresses an innocent optimism about his character. Jane is seldom the one to initiate ideas, but she does suggest that they earn money by exhibiting Robert when he becomes a giant. She is also the one who suggests that they solve the burglar's problems by taking him to the island so that he can be a companion to the cook. **The Lamb**, so called because his first word was "Baa," is a two-year-old boy. He functions primarily as a burden to the others, who discover how much they love him when the gypsies want him and when the magic carpet whisks him away. The episode in which he becomes an affected dandy who has no use for his siblings generates hilarious comedy out of the fact that he has at least three given names: Hilary, St. Maur, and Devereux.

The Psammead, or sand fairy, is one of the most unusual and original characters in children's fantasy. A small, furry, brown creature, it has a spider's tubby body, a monkey's arms and feet, a bat's ears, a rat's whiskers, and a snail's eyes on the end of horns that move in and out like telescopes. Thousands of years old, it lives in the sand and fears water, which can be fatal to it. The Psammead grants any wishes spoken in its presence. While doing so, it holds its breath and swells until it is twice its normal size. In *The Five Children and It*, the irascible and arrogant Psammead is something of a sly trickster. Resenting that he has no choice but to grant wishes, he seems to arrange matters so that every wish results in embarrassment or inconvenience. Furthermore, he usually refuses to give advice, even when Anthea politely asks for it, thus ensuring that the children will make further inappropriate wishes. When he does offer his opinion, he criticizes the children for their foolishness, suggests that they should be wishing for such things as good tempers and good manners, and expresses his frustration at having to deal with them. Although he is testy, the children are fond of him and humor him with flattery.

In *The Story of the Amulet*, the Psammead has a different role because he no longer has to give the children wishes. Furthermore, he feels some gratitude because they saved his life by getting him out of the shop, where he would surely have been doused with water. He still feels contempt, insisting that he is worth a thousand of them, but he acts as a wise counselor. Instead of trying to embarrass them, he gives them helpful information and advice so that they can restore the amulet and thus bring their parents safely home. In explaining time travel, he also establishes the theme of relativity, declaring that time and space are only forms of thought. Nevertheless, the Psammead still tests the patience and wit of the children because he doesn't readily volunteer information. Because they don't ask him a direct question, for instance, the children make a futile and dangerous trip to Atlantis. In addition, he maintains his comic function, granting inappropriate wishes to those who utter a wish in his presence. These wishes do, however, have a darker, satiric edge, as in the case of the Babylonian Queen, who wishes her guards would kill the people of modern London. Petulant but lovable, powerful yet dependent, the Psammead finally gets his desire for peace when the learned gentleman wishes the Psammead back into the past where he will be safe.

The Phoenix, a glorious golden bird, is a counselor, advising the children about the use of the magic carpet. He often does so, however, in long-winded stories that try the patience of the children, who have to force him back to the point at hand. The Phoenix is also a pragmatic helper who gets the children out of several predicaments by going to the Psammead and wishing them out of trouble. He even

assumes the role of wily trickster, throwing his voice to lure away a policeman who comes to investigate the noise caused by all the Persian cats. What makes him most memorable, however, is his comic vanity. Although constantly claiming modesty, the Phoenix is filled with self-admiration. He thus insists that the Phoenix Fire Office is a temple built in his honor, and he has all of the executives sing songs praising him. He even composes his own ode of praise: "For beauty and for modest worth / The Phoenix has not its equal on earth." His vanity becomes destructive when he visits the theater and, thinking it is a temple in which songs are sung in his praise, sets it on fire. (In his defense, it must be noted that he magically undoes the damage the next day.) The Phoenix stays only a short while in London, declaring that in two months he has lived at a pace that balances five hundred years spent in the desert. He therefore arranges his fiery end after ensuring that his egg is sent where it will not hatch for another two thousand years. Grateful to the children for helping him, he arranges with the Psammead for a last wish and thus provides gifts for the children and their parents.

Few of the many characters who appear in the series are more than devices for generating comedy or, in the last volume, social criticism. Some do bear mention, however. **Mother**, although conveniently absent for most of the series, is morally uncompromising. She tests Anthea's wit in the first book with her stern insistence on going to the police about the jewels and with her anger over Martha's fiancé. In the second book, she insists that the children try to return the Phoenix's egg to the carpet seller. **Martha**, the housekeeper in the first volume, cares for the children while their mother is absent. She is central to comic episodes when she locks out the beautifully transformed children, when she picks up the full-sized Lamb because he appears as an infant to her, and when she ends up with water on her head because she is in the same place as the army besieging the castle. **The cook** in *The Phoenix and the Carpet* is hot-tempered and annoys the children. Ironically, she receives her greatest wish of becoming a queen who doesn't have to work when the children remove her from their lives by taking her to a tropical island. **The burglar** turns to crime only because he has been a victim of theft himself. He is reformed, however, by Jane's innocent talk and by the presence of the cow, which brings back memories of his childhood. He gratefully marries the cook. **Reverend Septimus Blenkinsop**, the young minister who marries them, is comical because, like most adults in the series, he can't accept magic. He also believes that he is suffering from fits of insanity.

Some characters in *The Story of the Amulet* generate social criticism. The **Queen of Babylon**, a wily despot, brings her arrogant contempt when she journeys into the children's London. She is comical when she wishes that the Babylonian artifacts would come out of the museum and that Londoners were dressed like Babylonians. She seems evil, though, when she orders her guards to kill those who protest her actions. Her most important function is to draw a parallel between the slaves of her era and the British workers of the children's time. **The mother of the boy who was expelled** from school provides a similar function by explaining the basis of the utopian future and by expressing sorrow and horror at the barbarity she sees in the London of the children's time. **Imogen**, the dirty, eight-year-old orphan whom Anthea befriends, contrasts with the woman's son, who cries because he is expelled but knows that he has a place in a loving society. Imogen cries because she is a victim of social brutality, her society having no meaningful place for the poor. She finds happiness only in a past that treasures children.

Rekh-mara, an Egyptian priest in the temple of Amen Ra, is morally ambiguous until the end. Desirous of knowledge, he seems willing to trick the children until the Psammead threatens him into cooperating. After they acquire the amulet, he undergoes a moral transformation, the bad part of his soul becomes a centipede that Robert squashes, while the noble part becomes the historically inspiring element of the learned gentleman's soul. The **learned gentleman**, who reveals that he was called **Jimmy** in his youth, is a long, thin man. Obviously an archeologist or antiquarian, he treats children as grownups. He undergoes a transformation as a result of his contact with the children, particularly

Anthea. As she feeds and talks to him, he gradually learns to smile again. He seems comically absurd because he can't accept the children's adventures, even when he accompanies them, as anything other than a dream. He receives his heart's desire at the end. Symbolically reborn as an inspired antiquarian when his soul merges with that of Rekh-mara, he is given the ability to write about the past in vivid detail.

The Railway Children
(novel, 1906)

PLOT: Although it comes perilously close to sentimentality, *The Railway Children* successfully combines scenes of domestic relationships, exceptional generosity, and romantic adventure to advance a theme about the value of "loving-kindness." When Father suddenly leaves, Mother moves with Bobbie (Roberta), Peter, and Phyllis to the country. Made aware of their new poverty, Peter "mines" coal at the railway station, but the Station Master catches him. Because Bobbie and Phyllis intercede, Peter escapes with a warning not to steal again. Fascinated by the railway, the children begin waving to an old gentlemen who passes by on a train every day. The children send a note to him when Doctor Forrest says that their mother needs expensive items to cure an illness, and the old gentleman supplies everything. Shortly afterwards, Bobbie accidentally ends up riding in a locomotive when she seeks out someone to fix Peter's damaged model train, which he has let her share as a birthday gift.

The family also helps others. When Mr. Szczepansky, a Russian writer, becomes stranded after losing his railway ticket, the children take him home. Bobbie then asks the old gentleman for help, and he eventually finds the Russian's family. Before he does so, however, the children mend fences with Albert Perks the Porter, who mistakenly feels slighted because they did not tell him the Russian's story.

Shortly afterwards, the children become heroes, flagging down a train before it crashes into a landslide covering the tracks. The children next save a dog and a baby from a burning barge, even though the bargee was mean to Peter. Another temporary misunderstanding occurs when Perks regards the birthday gifts that they give him as insulting charity. Ironically, Perks unintentionally causes Bobbie sorrow by giving her some old papers in which she discovers that her father has been imprisoned for stealing state secrets. Bobbie therefore asks the old gentleman for more help. Before she hears from him, the children aid two people during a single adventure. They rescue a boy with a broken leg from the railway tunnel and then wake up a switchman who has fallen asleep at his post. The injured boy is taken to their home, and his grandfather, the old gentleman, pays Mother to care for him. The old gentleman then succeeds in proving that Bobbie's father is innocent. In the final scene, Father rejoins his family.

CHARACTERS: The children display kindness themselves and bring it out in nearly every adult they meet. **Bobbie** (short for **Roberta**) is the favorite of both Mother and the narrator, who states, "The more I observe her the more I love her." A twelve-year-old who is "oddly anxious to make other people happy," Bobbie is central to the theme of "loving-kindness." Sensitive, she is the only child who realizes that Mother is sorrowful and worries about why this is. After she finds out about her father, she considerately protects the others by maintaining the secret. Her sensitivity is also evident when she faints after saving the train and when she rebels against Peter's talk about the injured boy's broken bones. Bobbie has a highly developed sense of propriety that leads Peter to call her priggish, a charge she resents. Nevertheless, Bobbie insists that they not ask the servants for information about their father, and she suggests getting Mother's permission before arranging for birthday gifts for Perks. When Peter is "mining" coal, she humors him by

pretending that she doesn't know what he is doing. But she freely admits her share of the guilt when the Station Master catches him. Bobbie is also frequently a peacemaker, calming the volatile Peter.

Bobbie consistently shows charitable kindness. When Peter gives her a share in his damaged model train, Bobbie realizes that she has embarrassed him into doing so and therefore gets it repaired so that she can return it to him. She is also the one who suggests that they give gifts to Perks. More significantly, Bobbie nurses her mother during her illness; and she overcomes fears of the dark railway tunnel to stay with the injured boy while Peter and Phyllis go for help. Bobbie shows moral courage by seeking help in spite of her mother's injunctions against discussing family business with outsiders. Certain she is correct, Bobbie speaks to the doctor about the family's inability to pay for his services, and she secretly asks the old gentleman to help in establishing her father's innocence. Bobbie even seeks help for others, getting the old gentleman to help find the Russian's family.

Ten-year-old **Peter** is impetuous, dismissing Bobbie's qualms as Sunday-school priggishness. Willfully naive, he convinces himself that taking coal from the middle of a pile is mining, not stealing. Nevertheless, he gallantly conceals his plan from his sisters so that they won't share the guilt if his actions are wrong. Peter has integrity, however, and he ensures that the Station Master recognizes him as the one who stole coal before he resumes friendly relations with him. Peter can be spirited. He insists on taking the lead in stopping the train and in rescuing the infant from the barge. This spirit causes quarrels with his sisters, whom he loves to tease. For example, although she asks him to stop, he deliberately makes Bobbie squeamish by describing in graphic detail how the doctor is fixing the boy's broken leg. It also leads to an unnecessary confrontation with the bargeman, whom he resents for chasing him away from a fishing spot. On a more positive note, his spirit supports his honor and integrity. Thus, he contemptuously knocks the coins away when the switchman tries to bribe him into remaining silent about being asleep on duty.

Phyllis is the least well-defined of the children. Her habit of repeatedly stopping to tie up her boot laces and her expressions of fear when they enter the railway tunnel suggest that she is a stereotypically incompetent youngest child. Phyllis has an innate sweetness, and she speaks openly and honestly to everyone. When Perks is upset with them about the birthday gifts, she softens his resentment by declaring that the children will continue to be his friends no matter how unpleasant he is to them. Similarly, although she tells the switchman that he is nasty for trying to bribe Peter, she says that she will forgive him even if Peter won't.

Mother, often identified as a projection of Nesbit because she too supported her family by writing, is the long-suffering, impossibly idealized center of the family. Before their financial reverses, she is always present and attentive to her children. Afterwards, she tries to protect them by keeping from them knowledge of their father's arrest and by concealing her own sorrow. Her need to earn money, however, keeps her from them, giving them the freedom for their adventures. Mother is proudly class conscious, insisting that the children not speak of family matters outside the house and not ask for charity, which she apparently finds demeaning. Nevertheless, she herself is charitable, showing a good heart and deep maternal instincts by taking in the Russian and the injured boy. **Father** is equally idealized, being always in good temper and always ready for a game. A telling sign that he represents an ideal comes when he tells Peter that girls can be just as clever as boys.

Thirty-two-year-old **Albert Perks** the Porter, simply called **Perks**, brings out the loving kindness in the children. A family man, Perks is the children's favorite friend because he is approachable and an easy confidant. Nevertheless, he has a touchy temperament, refusing to speak to them when he mistakenly thinks they have slighted him by keeping from him details of the Russian's life. Only Phyllis's kiss and apology melts him back into friendliness. His prickly sense of honor is evident on his birthday. A proud man who doesn't want to seem incapable of supporting his family, he first refuses the gifts until Bobbie convinces him that they indicate that the community respects him. **Doctor W. W. Forrest** is

a poor man, but he shows loving kindness by telling Bobbie not to worry about her mother's medical bills. When he finds that Peter has been teasing Bobbie about blood and bones, he fulfills the role of the absent father by giving him advice about proper conduct. Although his talk about strong males and weaker females is dated, he indicates that gentlemanly conduct is more than a matter of resisting violence when he tells Peter to watch his words as well as his fists. The narrator's refusal to divulge the name of the **old gentleman** emphasizes that he is there to serve a function instead of being a plausible person. The old gentleman shows his kindness by responding to the pleas of children he has only seen from his railway coach, sending the expensive items necessary for their mother's cure. He similarly helps by finding the Russian's family, by paying Mother to care for his grandson, and by helping to prove that the children's father is innocent.

Further Reading

Bell, Anthea. *E. Nesbit*. London: Bodley Head, 1960.

Berger, Laura Standley, ed. *Twentieth-Century Children's Writers*. 4th ed. Detroit: St. James, 1995.

Bingham, Jane M., ed. *Writers for Children: Critical Studies of Major Authors since the Seventeenth Century*. New York: Scribner's, 1988.

Briggs, Julia. *A Woman of Passion: The Life of Edith Nesbit, 1858-1924*. New York: Amsterdam Books, 1987.

Children's Literature Review. Vol. 3. Detroit: Gale Research, 1978.

Collier, Laurie, and Joyce Nakamura, eds. *Major Authors and Illustrators for Children and Young Adults*. Detroit: Gale Research, 1993.

Contemporary Authors. Vol. 137. Detroit: Gale Research, 1992.

Fuller, Muriel, ed. *More Junior Authors*. New York: H. W. Wilson, 1963.

Moore, Doris Langley-Levy. *E. Nesbit: A Biography*. Rev. ed. New York: Chilton Books, 1966.

Moss, Anita. "*The Story of the Treasure Seekers*: The Idiom of Childhood." In *Touchstones: Reflections on the Best in Children's Literature*, Vol. 1. Edited by Perry Nodelman. West Lafayette, IN: Children's Literature Association, 1985.

Nesbit, Edith. *Long Ago When I Was Young*. London: McDonald & Jane's, 1974.

Streatfield, Noel. *Magic and the Magician: E. Nesbit and Her Children's Books*. London: Ernest Benn, 1958.

Yesterday's Authors of Books for Children. Vol. 1. Detroit: Gale Research, 1977.

Zaidman, Laura M., ed. *British Children's Writers 1880-1914.* Vol. 141 of *Dictionary of Literary Biography.* Detroit: Gale Research, 1994.

Evaline Ness

1911-1986, American illustrator and author

Sam, Bangs & Moonshine

(picture book, 1966)

PLOT: This Caldecott Medal winner is a cautionary tale about the difference between using imagination and telling harmful lies. Samantha—always called Sam—lives on an island with her father. Sam has "the reckless habit of lying" which her father calls "moonshine." She claims that her deceased mother is a mermaid, that she has a baby kangaroo, and that her cat, Bangs, can talk. Ignoring her father's warning that "moonshine spells trouble," Sam tells her friend Thomas that the baby kangaroo is with her mermaid mother at Blue Rock. Thomas sets off to see them. Saying that the tide will soon cover Blue Rock, Bangs follows him. When a storm develops, Sam's father rescues Thomas, but Bangs is washed away. Her father now tells Sam to think about the difference between real and moonshine. Sam accepts that the kangaroo and her mermaid mother are moonshine. Shortly afterwards, Bangs returns, and Sam realizes that moonshine almost cost Thomas and Bangs their lives. The next morning, her father brings her an African gerbil, which looks like a baby kangaroo. Naming it Moonshine, Sam gives it to Thomas.

CHARACTERS: The four characters clearly serve didactic purposes, but the central character has

Sam and her cat, Bangs, in an illustration by Ness from her book, **Sam, Bangs and Moonshine.**

psychological depth. **Sam** (short for Samantha) is a dreamy, lonely, self-centered child who uses her imagination to escape from painful reality. As her story about her mermaid mother indicates, Sam has not accepted her mother's death. She therefore dreams that a chariot pulled by dragons takes her to distant worlds. Sam does not realize that she is cruel to Thomas when she repeatedly sends him on futile searches for the baby kangaroo. She is simply so absorbed by her stories and her own pain that she is callous about his feelings. After she sends Thomas to Blue Rock, Sam changes. She loses interest in escaping to other places and thinks about what she has done to Thomas and Bangs. Consequently, she tearfully confesses everything to her father. Afterwards, Sam grows psychologically and morally. Showing maturity by distinguishing between moonshine and reality, she accepts that her mother is dead, that Bangs can't talk, and that her world consists of her father, Bangs, and Thomas. What makes Sam engaging and realistic, however, is that her understanding of bad moonshine—harmful lies—does not make her reject good moonshine—enriching imagination. She thus decides that she may keep her imaginary chariot. She shows her greatest growth, though, when she acknowledges Thomas's feelings by giving him the gerbil. Her father has warned her that it is not a kangaroo and that she should call it by its real name, so Sam names it Moonshine. By doing so, she obeys her father, yet she simultaneously allows good moonshine to connect her to Thomas.

Sam's **father**, a fisherman, expresses the didactic messages. Frustrated by Sam's lying, he foreshadows disaster when he warns her that "moonshine is trouble." A good teacher, he contributes to Sam's psychological growth by urging her to distinguish between moonshine and reality. He also announces the theme by declaring that Sam must learn the difference between bad and good moonshine. **Bangs**, Sam's cat, is real, but Sam's imagination turns him into a talking animal. His primary role is to make Sam more aware by expressing ideas that she is ignoring. He thus explains that moonshine is "flummadiddle" and that real is the opposite. He also alerts her to the danger of sending Thomas to Blue Rock. His disappearance makes Sam acutely aware that her lies can cause harm. **Thomas**, Sam's friend, is a victim who suggests that reckless lies may have disastrous consequences. Thomas, the only person who believes Sam's lies, is naive. Persistent, he is undeterred by his repeated failures to see the baby kangaroo. Although his numerous futile quests may make us question his ability to learn from experience, his innocent enthusiasm is important for emphasizing Sam's lack of concern for others.

Further Reading

Berger, Laura Standley, ed. *Twentieth-Century Children's Writers*. 4th ed. Detroit: St. James, 1995.

Children's Literature Review. Vol. 6. Detroit: Gale Research, 1984.

Collier, Laurie, and Joyce Nakamura, eds. *Major Authors and Illustrators for Children and Young Adults*. Detroit: Gale Research, 1993.

Contemporary Authors New Revision Series. Vol. 37. Detroit: Gale Research, 1992.

De Montreville, Doris, and Donna Hill, eds. *Third Book of Junior Authors*. New York: H. W. Wilson, 1972.

Estes, Glenn E., ed. *American Writers for Children since 1960: Poets, Illustrators, and Nonfiction Authors*. Vol. 61 of *Dictionary of Literary Biography*. Detroit: Gale Research, 1987.

Something about the Author. Vols. 1, 26. Detroit: Gale Research, 1971, 1982.

Something about the Author Autobiography Series. Vol. 1. Detroit: Gale Research, 1986.

Mary Norton

1903-1992, English novelist

The Magic Bed-Knob

(fantasy, 1943)

PLOT: Although it involves magic journeys, the plot of *The Magic Bed-Knob* is relatively unexciting until near the end. During the bombing raids of World War II, Carey, Charles, and Paul Wilson are sent from London to Bedfordshire, where they live with elderly Aunt Beatrice. One day, they aid a peculiar woman named Miss Eglantine Price, a spinster who has injured her ankle. Paul reveals he has seen her flying on a broom. When they visit her, Miss Price admits that she is studying to be a witch. Although she is sometimes inept, she demonstrates her power by briefly transforming Paul into a frog. She then strikes a deal with the children. In return for keeping her secret, she puts a spell on a bed knob that Paul carries. If twisted in one direction, it will take his bed anywhere they wish; if twisted the other way, it will take them back in time. The children complain the next day that the spell does not work. Miss Price tests it and informs them that only Paul can twist the knob. The delighted Paul insists they try it by visiting their mother. The bed takes them to London, but their house is locked and their mother is away. A police sergeant finds them in the street with their bed and takes them to the station. The next day, the police inspector learns the children and the bed mysteriously disappeared while in the charge of the sergeant and a kindly matron.

The next adventures involve Miss Price directly. After Carey questions Miss Price's fairness in using magic on the plants she wants to enter in a flower show, Carey invites Miss Price to accompany the children on their next trip. Miss Price agrees. She packs supplies for a pleasant day on Ueepe, a supposedly deserted South Sea island. Cannibals capture them, however, and Miss Price must defeat a witch doctor in an elaborate magic duel for possession of her broom. Turning the witch doctor into a frog, she carries the children to the bed, which they use to escape. Once home, the children conceal Miss Price. Aunt Beatrice decides to send the children back to London. While saying farewell to Carey, Miss Price says that she might give up magic. On the trip home, Paul reveals that he has kept the bed knob.

See below for character descriptions.

Bonfires and Broomsticks

(fantasy, 1947)

PLOT: This sequel involves magical journeys back in time. Two years after their adventures in *The Magic Bed-Knob*, Carey, Charles, and Paul convince their mother to let them spend the summer with Miss Eglantine Price, who has advertised for borders. They are disappointed, however, when they learn that Miss Price has given up magic. They are further disappointed when they discover that, although Miss Price has bought Aunt Beatrice's bed at an estate sale, she has hidden Paul's magic bed knob. Shortly afterwards, Carey discovers that Miss Price and Paul have secretly made a journey on the bed. Faced with Carey's sense of betrayal, Miss Price agrees to permit the children to make one trip into the past. The children find themselves in London one week before the outbreak of the Great Fire of 1666. Seeking directions, they meet the perpetually nervous Emelius Jones, a failed necromancer. They transport him back to the twentieth century, and Emelius wins over the reluctant Miss Price by his genuine praise of her skill with magic.

In spite of her fondness for him, Miss Price points out that Emelius is actually dead in the twentieth century. The children therefore return him to his own time, where Emelius is condemned to the stake for witchcraft. Miss Price, seeking reassur-

ance that Emelius arrived safely, goes back and discovers him in his prison cell. She promises to save him. The next day, however, the children witness Emelius tied to the stake and the fire started. Suddenly, a swooping figure riding a broomstick appears. When soldiers shoot and apparently kill the rider, who crashes to the ground, Charles releases Emelius. He leads the necromancer, Paul, and Carey back to the bed, where they discover Miss Price, who is angry they disobeyed her orders to remain at the bed. She is unharmed, having made her clothes fly in order to fool the troops. Although the group returns to the twentieth century, Miss Price does not remain there long. Announcing that she has accepted Emelius's proposal of marriage, she sells her house and those possessions she can't carry back to the seventeenth century. With Paul's help, the couple uses the bed to make an irreversible journey to the seventeenth century. After the couple leaves, the children walk amid the ruins of Emelius's ancestral home. Carey pretends that she hears the happy lovers going into the house in the past. She is shocked, however, when she actually hears Miss Price tell her to get out of the lettuces.

Bedknob and Broomstick *(fantasy, 1957) is a combined edition of* The Magic Bed-Knob *and* Bonfires and Broomsticks. *This book revises the earlier novels chiefly by toning down references to World War II.*

CHARACTERS: Although the thin plot in *The Magic Bed-Knob* does not permit full development of the characters, it creates interesting relationships. It also hints at the theme that unusual circumstances bring out hidden characteristics. In *Bonfires and Broomsticks*, the characters display traits consistent with those they have shown in *The Magic Bed-Knob*, but they also demonstrate some personal growth.

Miss Eglantine Price possesses two personalities. On the surface, she seems a stereotypical spinster. She wears gray coats and skirts, sports a Paisley-patterned Liberty silk scarf around her thin neck, rides a bicycle, visits the sick, and teaches piano. She is, in fact, the most "ladylike" person in the village. Her physical features, however, provide a clue to the remarkable person beneath the conventional surface. She has a sharply pointed nose and long yellow teeth, traditional physical signs of a witch. Nevertheless, Miss Price is no more the conventional witch than the conventional spinster. For example, she laments that she started too late in life to be a wicked witch. Although she once glares angrily at the children and says she should cast spells to keep them from talking, Miss Price is clearly a kind person. Her witchcraft is not a matter of ethics: it is a symbol for the development of hidden talents.

Miss Price is methodical in developing her talent, carefully labeling both her notes and her supplies. Still, she is not entirely competent. She has trouble flying on her broom and injures her ankle in a fall. Also, she is unable to recall spells when they are most needed—when she is "fussed" or bothered, she is completely incapable of performing magic. It is a notable sign of her development, then, when she confidently laughs during her contest with the witch doctor. Although it is certainly possible to criticize this scene as a racist representation of the British colonists' superiority over savages, such criticism ignores the main point: her laughter indicates that she is no longer fussed in stressful situations, and her newfound self-control permits her heroic rescue of the children. Perhaps as a result of this episode, Miss Price also develops ethically, deciding that she will not enter magically grown plants in the flower show. This decision indicates that she will not use her gifts to satisfy her vanity. She becomes a teacher of morality when she communicates her newly developed values to the children. She tells them that warm hearts, gentleness, and courage will do for them "just as well as magic."

In *Bonfires and Broomsticks*, Miss Price changes from a retiring, lonely spinster into a heroic, loving woman. The transformation occurs because she takes increasingly greater interest in others and their feelings. When the children go on their first trip to the past, for example, she worries about their safety and frets that she did not provide them with a weapon. Moreover, she worries that in being fair to the children, she has become unfair to their parents. When Emelius arrives at her house, the transformation becomes more dramatic. Although somewhat flustered by the presence of a man, she is interested in him. She signals this at first by wearing her best pink blouse to meet him. Later, she becomes almost maternal, ordering him to have a bath, cutting his hair and nails, and providing him with modern clothing. Although she is pleased by his abundant praise for her magical talents, vanity does not motivate her interest. She is happy in the discovery of a friend with whom she can share the interests of her life, and his absence saddens her. Furthermore, although she believes that she must give up contact with him, she has a genuine concern for his well-being. This concern compels her to go back to the past to check up on him. Miss Price is not yet aware of her love, but its power is evident. In spite of her tendency to forget spells, she is self-composed enough to cast one that is instrumental in freeing Emelius. Once back in her own time, she comes to realize her true feelings, and she changes. A brusque woman when Emelius first left, she becomes kind and gentle. With her typical efficiency, she disposes of her belongings and packs for her trip to the past. Her decision to go with Emelius shows that she has discovered the ability to love. No reader can doubt Miss Price's statement that these once lonely people "shall be better together." Still, one must also admire her pragmatism. Her last words, warning Carey out of the lettuces, are an admonition to stop being sentimental and to consider practical matters.

Carey Wilson, the oldest child, is a leader who takes charge when Miss Price is hurt. She reveals her bravery by asking Miss Price if she is a witch and shows cleverness in proposing the bargain of the magic spell to assure their silence. Carey has a firm idea of how people should behave. She criticizes Paul as mean because he did not tell her Miss Price could fly, and she suggests to Miss Price that using magic to win at the flower show might be unfair. At times Carey seems to keep Miss Price's secret only out of a selfish desire to preserve her own chances for magical adventures. By the time they return from the cannibal island, however, she respects Miss Price as a friend and keeps the secret to protect her.

In the second book, Carey maintains the forceful concern for fair play she exhibited in *The Magic Bed-Knob*. She is outraged at the unfairness of Paul and Miss Price traveling alone in the bed, and she is the one who suggests that Miss Price honor her promise of allowing a proper return visit to check up on Emelius. More significantly, Carey shows increasing sensitivity and emotional maturity. When she discovers that Emelius is only thirty-five years old, for instance, she immediately asks if he has had a sad life. Later, she worries about him making the right impression on Miss Price. Carey likes Emelius and Miss Price, and she does all she can to see that they like each other. Her ability to imagine their happiness in the past suggests that she herself is on the verge of womanhood.

Six-year-old **Paul Wilson** is frequently annoyed at being treated as the baby of the family. Consequently, he treasures his secret knowledge of Miss Price's witchcraft. Furthermore, he delights in the power and prestige he gains when his siblings learn that only he can make the bed fly. A stubborn and determined child, he insists that they visit their mother, an indication that he is homesick and lonely. During their adventures, Paul is comically naive. He expresses joy when he thinks the police station is a prison, and he is excited when he tells his brother and sister that the cannibals are planning to eat them. Nevertheless, Paul is the one who reminds Miss Price that she can turn people into frogs and thereby helps her to defeat the witch doctor. Fittingly, he keeps the bed knob, showing faith that magic can again enter his life.

Paul at first seems as selfishly devoted to secrets in *Bonfires and Broomsticks* as he was in the previous book. He conspires to test the bed with Miss Price, and he refrains from letting his sister and brother know Miss Price is again interested in magic. The one sign of his development is subtle: he agrees to twist the bed knob that will send Emelius and Miss Jones to the past. By doing so, he places the bed knob forever out of his reach. In giving up all possibility of further magical adventures, as well as the respect his power over the bed knob commanded with his siblings, Paul shows that he has at last put the welfare of others ahead of his own desires.

Charles Wilson, the middle child, does not seem to develop at all in *The Magic Bed-Knob*. He is "by nature extremely retiring" and says very little. He does kick Paul to stop him from accidentally revealing Miss Price's secret, and he remains calm when the cannibals capture him. Whereas Carey develops inwardly, in *Bonfires and Broomsticks*, Charles develops outwardly, especially in their final journey to the past. The boy who showed he was "by nature extremely retiring" in the earlier novel, now becomes decisively active. He leads the children to disobey Miss Price's instructions by going to the execution. When the figure on the broom crashes, he becomes a hero. He has the presence of mind to grab the sword and to free Emelius, removing Emelius's cloak so he will not be easily recognized. Finally, he asserts full control by silencing Carey, whose distress over the apparent death of Miss Price threatens them all.   When the children discover him in *Bonfires and Broomsticks*, **Emelius Jones** is a disillusioned and nervous thirty-five-year-old necromancer who looks aged beyond his years. Having devoted himself to the study of his craft, he lost hope when his master told him magic did not exist. Because necromancy was a capital offense, he spent most of his time dreading every knock on the door and avoiding daylight. His encounter with Miss Price restores him. Although he has never cast a spell, he deeply admires her ability. Furthermore, in spite of his messiness and incompetence, he possesses a knowledge of plants that delights and fascinates the orderly Miss Price. He literally owes his life to Miss Price, who rescues him and encourages him to take up residence in the country. In turn, he also saves her. His graceful attentions and respect for Miss Price awaken her dormant feelings and make her able to express love for another.

The Borrowers

(fantasy, 1952)

PLOT: *The Borrowers* is a frame tale: one story frames, or contains, another. In the outer tale, Mrs.

Arrietty Clock and the boy who helps her in an illustration by Beth and Joe Krush from Norton's **The Borrowers.**

May tells the main story while she and her niece, Kate, make a patchwork quilt. Her story is about the Clocks, a family of Borrowers. These six-inch-tall people live under the floorboards of a house and survive by taking things—they call it borrowing—from "human beans."

Mrs. May's story begins in spring. Pod returns from a borrowing expedition and informs Homily, his wife, that he has been seen by a human boy. Because it can endanger the Borrowers, being seen requires immediate emigration. Homily, however, protests. She fears they will end up living in a badger's set like her relatives, the Hendrearys. In contrast, their daughter, Arrietty, is overjoyed at the idea of emigrating. Having no one to play with and being forbidden to leave the dark family home under the floorboards, she is bored and lonely. Homily decides that if they are to stay in their home they must break another rule and let a girl learn to borrow. Arrietty thus achieves one notable wish and accompanies her father to the bright upper world of the house. While he gathers brush from a doormat, her father sends her alone into the garden. There, the boy who saw her father sees her. Arrietty talks to the boy and is amazed to learn the world contains thousands of humans. She is also distressed when the boy suggests that the Borrowers might be dying out. Concerned about the survival of her race,

Arrietty strikes a bargain with him: she will read to him, if he will deliver a letter to the Hendrearys.

One night, after Pod visits Great-Aunt Sophy, the owner of the house—he is not afraid to visit her because she thinks that Pod is an hallucination brought on by drinking sherry—he sees Arrietty with the boy. Although she protests that she is trying to save the race, her parents are angry. Nevertheless, Homily still refuses to emigrate. Later that night, the boy lifts up the floorboard and brings them doll furniture. This begins a "golden age," in which the boy lavishes presents on them. Eventually, Mrs. Driver, the housekeeper, notices things missing from the morning room and sets out to discover the thief. Believing the boy has hidden stolen items beneath the floorboards, she rips them up and discovers the three Borrowers. Although Crampfurl, the gardener, scoffs at her story of thousands of mice wearing clothes, he does bring in the police. Mrs. Driver finds the boy in the kitchen trying to help the Borrowers escape. She locks him in his bedroom for three days and calls in an exterminator. On the day that he is to take a taxi to begin his return journey to India, the boy is released by Mrs. Driver, who then forces him to watch the extermination. Left unguarded for a moment, he goes to the clock to open a sealed hole, the Borrower's only route into the house. Failing this attempt, he rushes outside and pries open a grate leading to the Clocks' home, but he is forced into a taxi without ever knowing whether he saved the Borrowers. Mrs. May reveals, however, that the boy was her brother, and she left food and doll furniture near a badger set a year later. When she returned, the gifts were gone. Mrs. May and Kate imagine how the Clock family would live in this new home. At the end, however, Mrs. May calls into question the entire story, noting that Arrietty and her brother had the same handwriting.

CHARACTERS: In accepting the Carnegie Medal for *The Borrowers*, Mary Norton said it "has something of the whole human dilemma—a microcosm of our world and the powers that rule us." She also said "only youth is restless and brave enough to try to get out from 'under the floorboards.'" *The Borrowers* depicts this bravery in both Arrietty and the boy, who struggle against adult oppression. In addition, it uses characters in the frame and the framed story to develop themes about knowledge and the growth of sympathy.

As a race, **Borrowers** live by taking things, even their names, from human beings and adapting them to their own needs. They are like characters in some folk tales because their existence explains the disappearance of household articles. Indeed, Mrs. May connects them to stories of the "little people," who were once well known in England, and notes that her brother suggested each generation became smaller and more hidden because they were frightened by the world.

Arrietty Clock does not display this fear and grows in mature insight as a result. In the beginning, she is a thirteen-year-old female child who finds her home life limited and lonely. As a female, she has no freedom. She is confined to the home, where she must help her mother with domestic tasks. Consequently, she spends free time staring through a grate at the world outside that she longs to visit. As a child, she has no playmates because the Clocks are the last Borrowers living in the house. Because her opportunities are so restricted, she is openly rebellious, firmly believing that she could perform the male task of borrowing. Arrietty's visit to the garden is a literal and symbolic crossing of thresholds. Her journey from the dark world beneath the floorboards to the bright sunshine symbolizes a progression from ignorance to knowledge.

Arrietty's encounter with the boy forces her to question her ethnocentrism. At first she sees Borrowers as the center of the universe, insisting that "Human beans are *for* Borrowers—like bread's for butter!" Gradually, however, she learns from the boy that humans are greater in number than Borrowers and that she may be one of the last of her race. Whereas Borrowers normally regard being seen as frightening and dangerous, Arrietty finds this experience liberating. She develops insight, seeing her family and herself as they are. She is, of course, frightened that her race might be dying out, but she turns her cleverness to advantage. Arrietty taught herself to read and to write by examining the miniature books and the scraps of paper with writing that her father borrowed. She reveals her resourcefulness by getting the boy to agree to deliver a note to the Hendrearys in return for her reading to him. Ironically, in reading and talking to the boy, she gains the knowledge that the Borrowers are not the center of the universe. Arrietty's story is inconclusive because readers do not find out what happened to her. What we do know of her story, however, makes it a triumph of female development. Arrietty comes to realize that, although she loves home, she can't stay there and have the adventures she craves. In insisting on adventure, in being so happy they are finally emigrating, she shows that she is not an overly protected child but is ready to face the world.

Pod, Arrietty's father, is a skillful borrower who takes pride in his ability to reach and borrow items of value. He is also a clever craftsman who can transform what he borrows into useful or decorative items that improve life beneath the floor. Although he was dashing and daring in his younger days, Pod is now a deeply conservative man. He believes in the division of duties by gender and in invariable rules governing all phases of life. Nevertheless, Pod is not the actual head of his home. Because he is unable to understand his wife's shifting moods, she manipulates him into going on unnecessary borrowing expeditions. Pod also breaks the rule about emigrating when the boy sees him because he is unable to oppose his wife's strong will. With Arrietty, however, Pod is overly protective and confines her to their home. Only he knows the way to the upper world, and only he knows how to open the elaborate gates he has erected to keep Arrietty from wandering away. In some sense, Pod is the parent who can't accept that his daughter is growing up and tries to keep her innocent and ignorant of the world. He lets his daughter accompany him to the upper world only after his wife forces him to do so. Once there, she loses her childhood innocence, even to the point of seeing Pod for the first time as "small," but she never ceases to love her family or to work for its well-being. Pod finally asserts himself after Mrs. Driver sees the family, but by then it is nearly too late.

As Arrietty's diary entries indicate, her mother, **Homily**, is frequently angry. A selfish woman, she places her own fears and desires above the safety of her family. Afraid of having to live in dirty and primitive conditions, she vehemently resists the duty to emigrate. Homily is also a snob. An ignorant, illiterate woman, she takes great pride in her daughter's ability to read and write. Although she mocks the pretensions of other Borrower families, Homily is no different. When the boy initiates the "golden age" that gives her every material possession she could desire, her only regret is that no one can see her in the new luxurious surroundings. But even though she is predominantly a negative character, Homily loves her family, worries about her husband's safety, and spends hours telling stories to Arrietty. Homily represents the repressed woman, the woman confined by her role as housewife and kept in literal and symbolic darkness. Homily does, however, play a vital and positive role in the plot. Because she does not want to emigrate, she nags Pod into taking Arrietty borrowing. Ironically, this selfish act begins her daughter's liberation.

The **boy**, Mrs. May's unnamed brother, is the actual hero in the Clocks' adventure. Born in India but educated in England, he feels somewhat inferior to his sisters because he is unable to read well. A sickly child who is at the house to recover from rheumatic fever, he is as lonely as Arrietty because he has no one to play with. His Great-Aunt Sophy sees him only in the morning, when she is always in a cross mood, to give him lessons, and Mrs. Driver treats him roughly, too. When he meets Arrietty, he is at first frightened, but they soon become friends. Although he knows much more about the world than Arrietty and teaches her many things, this meeting is educational for him. He learns that she is not a fairy, and he eventually realizes that, though there are more humans than Borrowers, humans are no more the center of the world than are Borrowers. His friendship with Arrietty brings out the best in the boy. He proved his kindness by helping Pod borrow a teacup, but now he lavishes gifts on the Clocks, who become a substitute for his absent family. Furthermore, he keeps his word and delivers a letter to the Hendrearys, cleverly making sure no one discovers the existence of his miniature friends. When Mrs. Driver accuses him of stealing things, he shows courage and an ability to identify with others' feelings: He declares that he is not a thief but a Borrower. Finally, the boy becomes heroic by attempting to save the Clock family. His actions show that he is brave and that he can think clearly under pressure, for he immediately pries open the grate when he can't open the sealed hole behind the clock. Although the boy disappears from the novel at this point, Mrs. May says he became a colonel and died "a hero's death." She also indicates that he was a great tease and implies that he might have invented the entire story. Nevertheless, the boy's experience in overcoming fear and in trying to rescue the Borrowers seems to be the source of his later courage.

In the main story, two women play minor roles. **Great-Aunt Sophy** has been an invalid since a hunting accident twenty years earlier. A lonely woman whose children are either dead or living far away, she drinks a decanter of Fine Old Pale Madeira every night. She is fond of talking to Pod about the old days, but she thinks he is the product of her drinking. **Mrs. Driver**, a fat woman with a visible mustache, is the housekeeper who likes to control everything. She is an arrogant thief who believes she is entitled to the madeira and other items she steals from her employer. She thereby contrasts with the Borrowers, who take out of necessity, and the boy, who borrows out of friendship. Her limited sympathies and insight are evident in her inability to accept the idea of the Borrowers after she sees them. In fact, she is a vicious woman. Mrs. Driver first imprisons the boy so that he can't interfere with her plans to exterminate the Borrowers and then delights in trying to make him watch the actual extermination.

As the English edition of the novel makes clear, **Kate** was a wild and self-willed child when she first heard the story of the Borrowers, but she later changed. In some respects, she resembles Arrietty. Both are lonely and confined to houses in which they associate only with another woman. Kate, however, learns to develop imaginative insight and sympathy for others by hearing about trouble, rather than by experiencing it. In helping Kate to think about stories, life, and the problems of others, **Mrs. May** is the ideal teacher. The elderly sister of the boy, she develops Kate's insight by helping her see the invisible Borrowers in the same way the boy helped Arrietty see absent humans. Her gentle instruction is symbolized by the patchwork quilt. Just as she and Kate work together on the quilt, they must cooperate to construct a satisfying conclusion to the tale. Their success is a sign that the once willful Kate has developed concern for others.

Further Reading

Berger, Laura Standley, ed. *Twentieth-Century Children's Writers*. 4th ed. Detroit: St. James, 1995.

Children's Literature Review. Vol. 6. Detroit: Gale Research, 1984.

Collier, Laurie, and Joyce Nakamura, eds. *Major Authors and Illustrators for Children and Young Adults*. Detroit: Gale Research, 1993.

De Montreville, Doris, and Donna Hill, eds. *Third Book of Junior Authors*. New York: H. W. Wilson, 1972.

Rees, David. "Freedom and Imprisonment—Mary Norton." In *What Do Draculas Do? Essays on Contemporary Writers of Fiction for Children and Young Adults*. Metuchen, NJ: Scarecrow Press, 1990.

Something about the Author. Vols. 18, 72. Detroit: Gale Research, 1980, 1993.

Stott, Jon C. *Mary Norton*. New York: Twayne, 1994.

Robert C. O'Brien
(pen name for Robert Leslie Conly)
1918-1973, American author and editor

Mrs. Frisby and the Rats of NIMH
(science fiction/animal fantasy, 1971)

PLOT: A blend of animal fantasy and science fiction, this Newbery Medal winner explores issues of identity. Mrs. Frisby, a widowed field mouse, lives in Mr. Fitzgibbon's garden with her children, Teresa, Martin, Timothy, and Cynthia. When Timothy becomes seriously ill, she gets medicine from Mr. Ages, a mouse who warns her that Timothy must rest and keep warm. On the way home, Mrs. Frisby rescues Jeremy, a crow she finds entangled in string, and they narrowly escape Dragon, the Fitzgibbons' cat. Later, Mrs. Frisby overhears Mr. Fitzgibbon and his sons, Paul and Billy, talk about how the plowing will begin in five days. Knowing that plowing will destroy her home and that Timothy is too frail to survive a move, Mrs. Frisby asks Jeremy for help. He flies her to a wise owl, who, after learning that she is Mrs. Jonathan Frisby, advises her to seek help from the rats.

The rats live under a rosebush on the Fitzgibbon farm. Although young Brutus turns her away, Mrs. Frisby gains admission after Mr. Ages identifies her. The rats impress Mrs. Frisby: they are bigger and smarter than normal rats, have electricity and running water, and know how to read and write. She is amused by Isabella, a girl rat in love with the handsome Justin, and impressed by Arthur, the head engineer. She remains puzzled by the rats' respect for her late husband. After promising to move her house to safety, Nicodemus, their leader, tells Mrs. Frisby about the origin of the rats of NIMH. They were once normal rats who were captured and

Mrs. Frisby consults the wise Mr. Ages in Zena Bernstein's illustration for O'Brien's Mrs. Frisby and the Rats of NIMH.

transformed into intelligent rats by Doctor Schultz, a scientist at NIMH (the National Institute for Mental Health). One rat, Justin, organized an escape, taking along two transformed mice, Jonathan Frisby and Mr. Ages, with the rest of the rats. The group eventually reached Mr. Fitzgibbon's farm. Nicodemus convinced the rats to establish themselves as a civilization by following "the Plan" to go to a remote valley, give up stealing, and grow their own food. However, a group of seven dissenting rats, headed by Jenner, rejected the plan and left the colony.

To enable the rats to move her house safely, Mrs. Frisby agrees to put a sleeping potion into Dragon's food. She succeeds, but Billy captures her. Confined in a bird cage, she learns that a scientist from NIMH is coming to gas the rats. When Justin rescues her, she warns him of the danger they are in. She then rushes home, where she convinces a lady shrew attacking Arthur to let him move her house. Once

her family is safe, she witnesses the rats' escape. During the gassing of the colony, ten rats stay behind and create the illusion of a horde of ordinary rats to distract the humans and allow the others time to flee. Mr. Ages and Mrs. Frisby revive Brutus, but two other rats succumb to the gas. Mrs. Frisby never sees the rats again, but her son Martin vows to visit them one day. When Timothy is recovered and the weather turns warm, Mrs. Frisby leads her family to summer quarters.

CHARACTERS: Bridging fantasy and science fiction, the characters not only explore conventional issues of personal identity but also generate questions about the nature of civilization and morality. **Mrs. Frisby**, a widowed field mouse with four children, develops an identity as a compassionate hero. Mrs. Frisby begins as a devoted mother. Even when times are tough, she works hard and keeps her family happy. When Timothy is ill, she takes a dangerous journey to Mr. Ages's home and an even more perilous path home to save time in getting Timothy his medicine. Later, when seeking a way to avoid the move that would likely kill Timothy, she bravely flies on Jeremy's back and enters the owl's home. Always trying to protect her children from worry, she does not tell them about her adventures or their father's history until all dangers are past. Although she has not been genetically altered, as her husband was, Mrs. Frisby is intelligent and has learned to read simple words. She is also observant, noticing such things as Jeremy's attachment to a female and the way into the rosebush.

Mrs. Frisby begins to question her identity when she realizes that the owl and the rats are helping her only because she is Mrs. Jonathan Frisby. Even before learning of her husband's reputation, however, she begins developing her own identity as a hero. Thus, although she is in a hurry to return to Timothy, she displays compassion by saving Jeremy from Dragon. Later, she shows that she is her husband's equal by undertaking the same task that had cost him his life: putting a sleeping draught in

Dragon's food. After Billy captures her, Mrs. Frisby becomes involved in a new quest: warning the rats about NIMH's plans to gas them. After Justin rescues her, she saves the rats by warning them they are in danger. Her excellent memory, which enables her to repeat conversations precisely, gives the rats the information necessary to plan their escape. During that escape, Mrs. Frisby again shows bravery and compassion by helping Mr. Ages to revive Brutus. Although she returns to being the proud and devoted mother, her adventures provide her and her children with a greater understanding of themselves and their history.

Jonathan Frisby, Mrs. Frisby's husband, is present only in flashback and by reputation. He is a brave and kind mouse who has been genetically altered at NIMH into a highly intelligent mouse. Mrs. Frisby's children play minor roles. **Teresa**, the oldest, takes on Mrs. Frisby's duties and watches over Timothy during her mother's absences. **Martin**, the biggest, is strong, dark-haired, and handsome. He shows that the next generation is willing to develop its own identity when he declares that he will make an unprecedented visit to the rats in their remote valley. **Timothy**, the younger of the boys, is dark and thin, with a narrow face and large, bright eyes. Possibly because of a poisonous spider bite when he was younger, he is a frail hypochondriac. Timothy is the smartest and most thoughtful of the children. He has a sense of humor, but he does not tease his little sister as the others do. He is imaginative, having entertained Cynthia with a seemingly inexhaustible supply of stories when she was ill. **Cynthia**, the youngest child, is a timid, light-haired mouse who is scatterbrained and always loses things. Because Timothy is kind to her, he proves himself even more worthy of being saved by his mother and the rats.

The rats of NIMH have been genetically altered to be bigger and smarter than ordinary rats. **Nicodemus**, the leader, is a philosopher. He has a scar that runs across his face and over his left eye, which is covered by a patch. He speaks graciously and has a dignified air; his dream of establishing a true civilization is the basis of the Plan. In order for the rats to become independent, he encourages them to abandon human technology, to cease steal-

ing from humans, and to start growing their own food. A brave and clever leader, he designs the escape so that the men will not continue searching for the mutated rats. **Jenner**, who only appears in the flashback narrated by Nicodemus, connects the identity theme to the rats. He notes, that is, that they don't know where to go when they leave NIMH because they don't know who they are. Nevertheless, the cynical Jenner, once Nicodemus's best friend, contrasts with him. He is content with stealing, thinking of humans as "cows" to be used by rats. He rejects the Plan and strikes out with six followers. Ironically, it is human technology that kills him, for he apparently dies while trying to steal an electric motor. **Justin**, a handsome rat, is the first to become clever enough to figure out how to escape from NIMH. He does not become leader, however, because he is younger than Nicodemus. Justin is warm and friendly. He is even able to reassure Mrs. Frisby's children after she is captured. Although his fate is unknown, the suggestion lingers that he may have died a hero's death by trying to save another rat during the gassing. **Brutus** is a young, muscular rat who is unaware of Jonathan Frisby's reputation. He brings out the compassionate side in Mrs. Frisby and Mr. Ages when they revive him from the gas's effects. **Arthur** is the confident and efficient head engineer. He successfully designs amenities for the rats and plans the moving of Mrs. Frisby's home. **Isabella** adds comedy to the portrayal of the rats. A pretty, young rat, she is eager to grow up because she is in love with Justin and wants to marry him. Although she resents it when her brother calls her Izzy, she is flattered when Justin does so.

Mrs. Frisby has several other helpers. **Jeremy** the crow is a young and foolish creature. He becomes entangled in the shiny string that he has been collecting to give to his mate for a nest. Although he is not particularly bright, as his noisy and inept attempt at escape shows, he is grateful and kind. He expresses gratitude to Mrs. Frisby and offers to help her. By flying her to the owl, he gives her a broader understanding of her environment and provides the key to her later success in saving Timothy. **The owl**, who lives in a dying tree, is reputed to be one of the oldest and wisest creatures in the woods. He is impatient and bluntly unsympathetic to Mrs. Frisby until he learns her identity. Then he becomes helpful, directing her to the rats and giving her information about the safe placement of her house. **Mr. Ages**, the other mouse who was genetically altered at NIMH, is a healer and a wise adviser. Possibly because he has glossy, gray-white fur, Mr. Ages seems old. He lives alone in a bare home and concocts medicines from herbs and plants. He issues the warning about Timothy's health that provokes Mrs. Frisby's desperate quest to save her son.

Several antagonists threaten Mrs. Frisby and the rats. **Dragon**, an enormous orange and white cat with glaring yellow eyes, presents the most immediate danger. He has seven claws on each foot and has a strangled scream that freezes his victims with terror. Dragon's presence gives Mrs. Frisby two opportunities to display courage: when she rescues Jeremy and when she puts powder in the cat food. **Mr. Fitzgibbon**, the farmer, is an antagonist at first only because his yearly plowing comes at a bad time for Mrs. Frisby. His joking reference to rats brings the men to exterminate them, but his discussion of the episode allows Mrs. Frisby to warn the rats. His son **Paul** is a quiet, hard-working fifteen-year-old whose suggestion that the rats might have rabies provides a reason for their extermination. His son **Billy** is a noisy twelve-year-old who captures Mrs. Frisby and thereby allows her to learn of the impending extermination. The only physical description of **Dr. Schultz**, the neurologist from NIMH, is that he wears heavy, horn-rimmed glasses. The absence of description makes him more mysterious and ominous. He represents human arrogance because he obviously defines rats as inferior creatures he can use and kill when he wants. He seems driven by an ambition to publish a scientific paper, but he is so cautious about testing the success of his experiment that he gives the rats a chance to escape.

Further Reading

Authors and Artists for Young Adults. Vol. 6. Detroit: Gale Research, 1991.

Berger, Laura Standley, ed. *Twentieth-Century Young Adult Writers.* 1st ed. Detroit: St. James, 1994.

Children's Literature Review. Vol. 2. Detroit: Gale Research, 1976.

Collier, Laurie, and Joyce Nakamura, eds. *Major Authors and Illustrators for Children and Young Adults.* Detroit: Gale Research, 1993.

Contemporary Authors. Vols. 73-76. Detroit: Gale Research, 1978.

De Montreville, Doris, and Elizabeth D. Crawford, eds. *Fourth Book of Junior Authors.* New York: H. W. Wilson, 1978.

Helbig, Alethea K. "Robert C. O'Brien's *Mrs. Frisby and the Rats of NIMH:* Through The Eyes of Small Animals." In *Touchstones: Reflections on the Best in Children's Literature,* Vol. 1. Edited by Perry Nodelman, pp. 204-12. West Lafayette, IN: Children's Literature Association, 1985.

Something about the Author. Vol. 23. Detroit: Gale Research, 1981.

Scott O'Dell

1898-1989, American author

Island of the Blue Dolphins

(historical novel, 1960)

PLOT: This Newbery-winning Robinsonade, or island survival story, advances an ecological theme by presenting the psychological development of a girl who endures extreme isolation. Karana, the narrator, witnesses a Russian, Captain Orlov, and his Aleut otter hunters cheat and then kill her father, Chief Chowig, and many of her tribe. Later, when a ship removes the tribe from their island, Karana notices that her brother, Ramo, is still on shore. Karana swims back to the island to care for Ramo, but wild dogs kill him.

Karana then vows to kill the wild dogs. She also decides to violate the taboo forbidding women to make weapons. First, though, Karana burns her deserted village and then flings into the sea beads that Captain Orlov had brought. After a year, Karana leaves the island in a repaired canoe. It leaks, however, forcing her return. Karana now makes a home on the island, protecting it from wild dogs with a fence made from the bones of beached whales. In need of spear points, but unable to kill a bull sea elephant, Karana eventually uses the tusks from one that was killed fighting a rival. Having made weapons, Karana then attacks the wild dogs. She wounds their leader, but she can't bring herself to kill it. After nursing and taming Rontu, as she names it, Karana finds life less lonely. Later, she captures and tames two birds, Tainor and Lurai.

Significant adventures punctuate Karana's endless routine of gathering and preserving food. She is nearly killed while rescuing Rontu from the tentacles of a giant devilfish (octopus). On another occasion, the rising tide traps her inside Black Cave, where she sees the skeleton of one of her ancestors. She vows never to go there again. When Aleut hunters return to the island, Karana hides, but a girl named Tutok discovers her. Karana can't bring herself to kill Tutok, and they become friends. Eventually, Karana accepts a necklace from Tutok; in return, Karana gives Tutok hair ornaments and reveals her own secret name. After the Aleuts leave, Karana nurses a wounded otter, Won-a-nee. Realizing her loneliness, Karana then determines never to kill another animal. Nevertheless, Karana's loneliness increases. Rontu dies; she tames one of his children, but she gives up counting the days. She survives a tidal wave and an earthquake. She also survives disappointment when some men land but leave before she contacts them. Two years later, their ship returns. Karana dons a cormorant dress and marks her face with the tribal signs of an unmarried girl. After eighteen years alone, she leaves the island.

Zia (1976) is a sequel.

CHARACTERS: Minor characters and animals reveal the changes in Karana, whose attitudes are the focus. **Karana** (known in public as Won-a-pa-lei, "The Girl with the Long Black Hair") is based on "The Lost Woman of San Nicolas," who lived alone on an island from 1835 to 1853. According to O'Dell, Karana's story indicates that "The human heart, lonely and in need of love, is a vessel which needs

replenishing." Karana replenishes her heart by forming new attitudes to animals and human society. Twelve-year-old Karana is a responsible and dutiful member of her tribe. When the Aleut ship arrives, she suppresses her curiosity and continues to dig roots that her people need for food. A loving family member, Karana always watches and protects her little brother. Because she knows that he can't survive alone, she swims back to the island. Ramo's death, however, makes her desperate act of heroism futile.

In some ways, Karana is typical of survival story heroes. Tough-minded, she passes the physical and emotional tests of isolation. Thus, by burning her village, she symbolically erases thoughts about the past that would make it difficult to continue. Her later vow never to return to Black Cave parallels this act, showing her determination to dwell on the present and to avoid debilitating thoughts about death. Of course, burning the village also makes total self-reliance necessary. Karana succeeds alone because she is energetic, patient, observant, clever, and resourceful. These qualities come to the fore after Karana fails in her brave attempt to leave the island. Filled with joy at the good omen of seeing dolphins and at the sight of playful otters, she stops behaving like a stranded person awaiting rescue; instead, she becomes intent on establishing a true home. Karana therefore patiently and carefully evaluates the sites where she can build a house. She then shows resourcefulness by erecting the protective fence of whale bones. She also shows an ability to adapt. After she fails to kill the sea elephant, she understands that she must sometimes let nature take its course and provide solutions to her problems. Furthermore, when she patiently fashions its tusks into spear points, she shows her independent spirit. By breaking the taboos forbidding women to make weapons, that is, she frees herself from all social restrictions.

Parallel scenes reveal changes in character that make Karana more than a typical hero. In the first, Karana is unwilling to kill Rontu after wounding him. By showing compassion, Karana frees herself from the hatred that has dominated her. In doing so, she learns that friendship with an animal can also free her from oppressive loneliness. In the second scene, Karana is similarly unable to kill Tutok. The scenes are further connected because Tutok obviously was Rontu's previous owner. As she did with Rontu, Karana sets aside her hatred because of her need for companionship. By then accepting Tutok's gift of the necklace, she shows that she has overcome the bitterness that earlier led her to throw jewelry into the sea and that she has forgiven an enemy. Furthermore, by revealing her secret name, Karana, who felt that her father made himself vulnerable when he told Orlov his name, shows that she trusts Tutok.

Karana's relationships with Rontu and Tutok have profound consequences. Her friendship with Rontu leads her to display love and bravery when she rescues Rontu from the devilfish. More importantly, it leads her to create a society of animal friends. Eventually, she nurses and befriends Mon-a-nee, a wounded otter, a compassionate act that also grows out of her earlier worries that the Aleuts were slaughtering all the otters. She goes beyond simple compassion, however, and decides that she will never again kill an animal because doing so would make the earth unhappy. By thus showing reverence for life, Karana establishes the novel's ecological theme. Because her decision runs counter to the teachings of her tribe, it is the ultimate sign of her independence. At the same time, however, Karana's thoughts of Tutok and her own sister make her realize that she needs human society. This need becomes acute after Rontu dies. Karana gives up counting the days, thus showing the emptiness and loneliness she feels. Nevertheless, she does not plunge into complete despair. When the tidal wave that precedes the earthquake destroys her canoes, she patiently sets about to reconstruct one. When she fails to contact the men who come to the island, she spends the next two years ensuring that she is prepared for their return. When the ship returns, Karana puts on her finest clothes and marks her face with the signs of a maiden. Her concern for her appearance, part of her earlier social attitudes, signals her desire to rejoin society. Bravery, persistence, and psychological strength enabled her to endure; loneliness, however, matured Karana, ena-

bling her to feel deep love for both animals and human society.

Chief Chowig, Karana's father, is wisely suspicious of intruders and brave in defending his people's rights. He becomes, however, a victim of his own and Captain Orlov's greed. As well, his lack of concern for the otters is thematically significant because it highlights his daughter's attachment to animals. **Captain Orlov**, the Russian who brings the Aleut hunters, represents imperialist greed and deception, but he, too, adds to the ecological theme. Driven by a desire for profit, he cheats the native population and engages in a wholesale slaughter of animals that sickens Karana. **Ramo**, Karana's six-year-old brother, is mischievous. His disobedience in going home for a fishing spear strands him on the island and leads to Karana's tribulations. His proud assumption of independence leads to his death, which makes Karana hate the dogs. **Tutok**, an Aleut girl, twice accompanies hunters to the island. Bright and friendly, she contributes to Karana's maturity by making Karana see her as an individual instead of a member of an enemy tribe. Karana's acceptance of **Rontu**, the Aleut dog who killed her brother, foreshadows her acceptance of Tutok, once Rontu's owner and a member of the tribe that killed her father. Rontu is fierce and brave as leader of the wild pack. Once he becomes a pet, he establishes that harmony between animals and people enriches life.

Further Reading

Authors and Artists for Young Adults. Vol. 3. Detroit: Gale Research, 1990.

Berger, Laura Standley, ed. *Twentieth-Century Young Adult Writers*. 1st ed. Detroit: St. James, 1994.

Children's Literature Review. Vols. 1, 16. Detroit: Gale Research, 1976, 1989.

Collier, Laurie, and Joyce Nakamura, eds. *Major Authors and Illustrators for Children and Young Adults*. Detroit: Gale Research, 1993.

Contemporary Authors New Revision Series. Vol. 30. Detroit: Gale Research, 1990.

Contemporary Literary Criticism. Vol. 30. Detroit: Gale Research, 1984.

Estes, Glenn E., ed. *American Writers for Children since 1960: Fiction*. Vol. 52 of *Dictionary of Literary Biography*. Detroit: Gale Research, 1986.

Fuller, Muriel, ed. *More Junior Authors*. New York: H. W. Wilson, 1963.

Something about the Author. Vols. 12, 60. Detroit: Gale Research, 1977, 1990.

Peggy Parish

(pen name for Margaret Cecile Parish)

1927-1988, American teacher and author

Amelia Bedelia

(picture book, 1963; illustrated by Fritz Siebel)

PLOT: Mrs. Rogers leaves a note for Amelia Bedelia telling her what to do on her first day as a maid. After making a lemon meringue pie as a surprise for her employers, Amelia Bedelia begins to follow the listed instructions. She cuts up the towels to change them, scatters dusting powder over the furniture to dust it, sketches the window in order to draw the drapes, puts the lightbulbs on the clothesline because she has been told to put them out, measures the height of two cups of rice, puts lace around a steak to trim its fat, and puts trousers and socks on a chicken to dress it. Mrs. Rogers is furious. She opens her mouth to fire Amelia Bedelia, but Mr. Rogers sticks in a piece of lemon meringue pie. It is so good that Mrs. Rogers decides that Amelia Bedelia can stay. Afterwards, Mrs. Rogers learns to give instructions more carefully so that Amelia can understand them.

The sequels had three illustrators. Fritz Siebel illustrated Thank You, Amelia Bedelia *(1965) and* Amelia Bedelia and the Surprise Shower *(1966). Wallace Tripp illustrated* Come Back, Amelia Bedelia *(1971) and* Play Ball, Amelia Bedelia *(1972). Lynn Sweat illustrated* Teach Us, Amelia Bedelia *(1977);* Amelia Bedelia Helps Out *(1979);* Amelia Bedelia and the Baby *(1981);* Amelia Bedelia Goes Camping *(1985);* Merry Christmas, Amelia Bedelia *(1986); and* Amelia Bedelia's Family Album *(1988).*

CHARACTERS: Commenting on the popularity of her creation, Parish suggested that "perhaps in Amelia Bedelia children have the opportunity to laugh at adults." **Amelia Bedelia** (she is always

The silly, befuddled maid Amelia Bedelia, as illustrated by Fritz Siebel for Parish's comical book.

called by both names) is a simpleminded maid who parodies the superbly competent nannies in such British works as *Mary Poppins*. In fact, like Mary Poppins, Amelia Bedelia arrives carrying an umbrella. Furthermore, although the three illustrators of the series portray her differently, all show her appropriately attired for her role as a maid. Amelia Bedelia's primary function, however, is to generate humor by showing the vagaries of the English language. Amelia Bedelia is both obedient and energetic, traits that inevitably create disasters because she is so literal-minded. Thus, she sketches the drapes to draw them and puts clothes on a chicken to dress it. When left to her own resources, however, as when she bakes the pie, she shows that she can be competent and generous.

Mrs. Rogers, Amelia Bedelia's employer, is a large, wealthy woman pictured wearing a fox stole. She understands that Amelia Bedelia will not change, so she wisely learns to speak in a way that Amelia Bedelia understands. **Mr. Rogers** is a caricature of the easygoing husband. He does not care about domestic chaos as long as Amelia Bedelia makes her delicious pie.

Further Reading

Berger, Laura Standley, ed. *Twentieth-Century Children's Writers*. 4th ed. Detroit: St. James, 1995.

Children's Literature Review. Vol. 22. Detroit: Gale Research, 1991.

Collier, Laurie, and Joyce Nakamura, eds. *Major Authors and Illustrators for Children and Young Adults*. Detroit: Gale Research, 1993.

Contemporary Authors. Vols. 73-76. Detroit: Gale Research, 1978.

Contemporary Authors New Revision Series. Vols. 18, 38. Detroit: Gale Research, 1986, 1993.

De Montreville, Doris, and Elizabeth D. Crawford, eds. *Fourth Book of Junior Authors*. New York: H. W. Wilson, 1978.

Something about the Author. Vol. 73. Detroit: Gale Research, 1993.

Katherine Paterson

1932-, American teacher, missionary, and author

Bridge to Terabithia

(novel, 1977)

PLOT: Inspired by the death of a close friend of Paterson's son, *Bridge to Terabithia* deals honestly with the grief and confusion caused by an accidental death. The focus, however, is on friendship. Jess Aarons lives in rural Virginia with two older sisters, Ellie and Brenda, two younger ones, May Belle and Joyce Ann, his mother, and his father, who is contemptuous of his interest in art. On the first day of school, Jess loses his dream of being the fastest runner. He forces Gary Fulcher to let Leslie Burke, his new neighbor, enter their races, and Leslie easily beats all the boys. Nevertheless, Jess befriends Leslie. When Leslie, angry after being teased for revealing that her parents don't have a television, sits in Janice Avery's bus seat, Jess even rescues her from the bully. (Later, Janice gets Jess thrown off the bus by pretending that he tripped her.)

Jess and Leslie then become fast friends. Leslie invents the imaginary country of Terabithia, which they enter by swinging on a rope across a gully. Jess builds a castle from scrap wood, Leslie entertains him with stories, and both conduct ceremonies and wage battles. Leslie and Jess also exact revenge when Janice Avery steals May Belle's Twinkie. Excited by a phony love note they send, Janice humiliates herself by waiting for a boy who never appears. (They later take pity when Janice cries after breaking an unwritten rule against revealing family secrets.) At Christmas, Jess spends all his money on a Barbie for May Belle, so he obtains a free dog for Leslie; she gives him paints, brushes, and paper. Jess meets Bill and Judy Burke, Leslie's parents, and he helps Bill and Leslie renovate their house. At Easter, Leslie accompanies the Aarons family to church. She enjoys the service, but May Belle says that Leslie will go to hell unless she believes in the Bible.

On the day that Jess decides to admit his fear of swinging over the rain-swollen creek into Terabithia, his music teacher, Miss Edmunds, takes him to the National Gallery in Washington. Upon returning, he learns that Leslie was killed when the rope swing snapped. Grief-filled, Jess runs away, but his father carries him back. Later, after attending Leslie's wake with his parents, he angrily throws away her Christmas gifts. His father then talks to Jess like a man, reassuring him that God doesn't send little girls to hell. When Jess later revisits Terabithia to hold a funeral ceremony, May Belle follows. She becomes so frightened while crossing a log over the creek that he must rescue her. Shortly afterwards, when Mrs. Myers, a teacher, shows that she shares his grief, Jess decides to pass on Leslie's gift of imaginative vision. He therefore builds a bridge into Terabithia and leads May Belle into a kingdom awaiting a new queen.

CHARACTERS: The important characters build bridges to new relationships and understandings. **Jess Aarons (Jesse Oliver Aarons, Jr.)** is a ten-year-old with long legs and straw-colored hair. His artistic talent isolates him. At school, only Miss Edmunds encourages his drawing, and he therefore has a crush on her. At home, his father regards artistic interests as effeminate. To bridge the gulf between himself and his father, Jess practices running diligently until Leslie destroys his dream of being the fastest at school. Jess has another problem: he worries that he is a coward. He is, however, brave in his own way. He taunts Gary Fulcher into letting Leslie enter the boys' races, he overcomes his fear of befriending Leslie, and he cleverly hides his fear when he confronts Janice Avery on the bus. Still, he is reluctant to admit his justified fear of swinging into Terabithia.

Sensitive, Jess cringes when Leslie reveals that her parents don't have a television because he knows that her admission opens her to teasing. More tellingly, he feels sorry for Janice Avery after he and Leslie humiliate her, and he urges Leslie to find out what is wrong when Janice cries in the girls' washroom. Aware that May Belle needs something special for Christmas, Jess generously spends all of his money on a Barbie. By then giving a dog to Leslie, he partially fulfills her need for companionship. Jess deepens through Leslie's stories, which make him value imagination. Their imaginative play enhances his self-esteem so that he feels "taller and stronger and wiser" in Terabithia. Jess is not perfect, however. When Miss Edmunds invites him to Washington, he cunningly asks for permission while his mother is sleepy, and he does not immediately think of asking his teacher to invite Leslie. He becomes absorbed in the pleasure of being alone with an admired teacher and of seeing great art, but he looks forward to telling Leslie about his experiences.

Following Leslie's death, Jess plunges into grief. He goes through denial, trying to run away from reality, and anger, blaming Leslie for deserting him. He becomes full of self-pity, imagining that he's the only one genuinely suffering and reveling in the thought of being pitied at school. He feels guilt for deserting her, and he becomes numb. Jess begins to change when he rescues May Belle, an act requiring brave consideration of another. After learning that Mrs. Myers also feels Leslie's loss, Jess fully matures. Appreciating that Leslie gave him vision and strength, he determines to repay her gift by adding beauty and caring to the world. In what Paterson calls "an act of grace," he builds May Belle a bridge into Terabithia, offering her a chance to enrich her imagination. Jess thus keeps alive Leslie's legacy of friendship.

Jess Aarons and Leslie Burke, portrayed here by Donna Diamond, in a scene from Paterson's **Bridge to Terabithia.**

Leslie Burke, an athletic, talented, and imaginative outsider, arouses antagonism because she doesn't know the unwritten rules or her place in her new school. On the first day, she dresses in faded cutoffs, a blue undershirt, and sneakers without socks, whereas the other children wear their best clothes. Furthermore, she soundly trounces the boys in their races. When she reveals that she has no television, she emphasizes her difference and unwittingly invites teasing. Finally, the lonely Leslie doesn't realize that she alienates Jess by forcing herself on him.

Leslie is sensitive with Jess, expressing faith in his artistic talent and giving him good art materials. Although Leslie understands other people, she lacks similar sensitivity. She realizes, for example, that Janice Avery fears looking foolish. She therefore composes a love letter that prompts Janice into talking about it. Pleased with her success, Leslie is surprised that Jess has sympathy for the humiliated Janice. Through Jess, however, Leslie develops pity.

Identifying with the crying Janice, she builds a bridge by teaching her how to overcome taunts.

Leslie has read widely and is a gifted storyteller who stirs Jess's imagination. She is also a skillful writer. Most importantly, Leslie is vigorously imaginative. She turns the woods into a magical kingdom and populates it with allies and villains. She also creates ceremonies that evoke genuine religious feelings. Improbably, Leslie knows nothing of Jesus, but she enjoys the beauty of the Christian story of salvation. Leslie is more self-sufficient than Jess, for, unlike him, she can make Terabithia magically alive when she is alone. Her death illustrates that life is unpredictable, but it also reveals that friendship is a legacy that gives lasting beauty to life.

Mr. (Jesse) Aarons at first seems to be an ignorant and embittered man whose financial struggles sap his patience. A philistine who is seldom around his family, he suggests that Jesse is effeminate for wanting to be an artist. Nevertheless, Mr. Aarons builds a bridge after Leslie's death. When his son runs away, he becomes a compassionate father, carrying him back like a baby. He gets Jess to face reality: he has him attend the wake, he tells him that he is foolish to throw away Leslie's gifts, and he comforts him by talking to him like a man and by insisting that Leslie is not going to hell. The inarticulate, weary **Mrs. Aarons** demonstrates the intolerance of the rural community. She criticizes the Burkes as hippies because they are different, and she worries that Leslie will embarrass the Aarons family by dressing inappropriately for church. She places excessive demands on her son, but she is concerned after Leslie's death. Jess's older sisters, **Ellie** and **Brenda**, are materialists who manipulate their mother to get things or to avoid chores. Brenda, whom Paterson has called "graceless," is a chubby eighth grader who incessantly teases Jess about Leslie. **May Belle**, who is going on seven, is skinny and homely. She annoys Jess because she follows him around when he is with Leslie. At the same time, May Belle, who worships him, brings out his compassion. He therefore builds a bridge from her loneliness to a world rich with imaginative possibilities. The youngest child, **Joyce Ann**, is a four-year-old who tries Jess's patience.

Leslie's family is closer and more cultured than Jess's. **Bill Burke**, Leslie's father, is a political writer. He talks to his daughter on an adult level about music and literature, but he is so absorbed by his work that he sometimes ignores her. After finishing his book, however, he makes Leslie happy by involving her in the house renovations, and he builds a bridge that enables Jess to experience culture and family warmth. **Judy Burke**, a novelist who writes under the name of Judith Hancock, is more famous than her husband. She remains remote from her daughter much of the time, but she provides a more stimulating and nurturing environment than Jess's mother does.

Mrs. Myers, a fat teacher derisively called "Monster-Mouth Myers," is reputed to smile only on the first and last days of school. Although she lacks appreciation for Jess's art, she responds to Leslie's writing with first-day smiles. After Leslie's death, she bridges the generations, suggesting that she and Jess comfort each other. By so doing, she provokes Jess into a mature concern for the feelings of others. **Miss (Julia) Edmunds**, the young guitar-playing music teacher, arouses hostility in Mrs. Aarons, who calls Miss Edmunds a hippie because she has long black hair and wears makeup only around her eyes. Miss Edmunds is unconventional, but she inspires students. She builds a bridge by encouraging Jess in his drawing and by introducing him to great works of art. **Gary Fulcher**, Jess's main racing rival, is an arrogant and sexist boy who represents the close-minded, intolerant attitudes of the students. He tries to keep Leslie from running when he realizes that she can beat him, and he later teases Jess about Leslie. **Janice Avery**, an overweight seventh-grade bully with frizzed blonde hair, is mean and deceitful. She steals May Belle's Twinkie, and she lies to get Jess kicked off the bus. Metaphorically, she is the giant whom the heroes from Terabithia must slay. Her eagerness to meet the boy who wrote the phony love note and her distress when she reveals that her father has beaten her, however, suggest that she is actually a lonely girl whose aggression conceals pain and a longing for love. Sympathetic understanding of Janice's pain enables Leslie to build a bridge that gives Janice at least a glimpse of compassion.

The Great Gilly Hopkins

(novel, 1978)

PLOT: A girl's successful quest for a reunion with her mother ironically teaches her that fairy-tale endings are lies. Driving to another foster home, Gilly (Galadriel) Hopkins annoys her social worker, Miss Ellis, by blowing a bubble that bursts and sticks to Gilly's hair. Gilly's new foster mother, the enormously fat Maime Trotter, lives in a dusty house with William Ernest (W. E.) Teague, whom Gilly thinks is retarded. At dinner time, Gilly is horrified to learn that blind Mr. Randolph, a black man, eats there every night. The next day, when Trotter makes no comment about her messy hair, Gilly angrily cuts the gum from it. At school, Gilly is unpleasantly surprised to find that her teacher, Miss Harris, is black. Gilly soon fights with six boys, earning the admiration of Agnes Stokes, who follows her everywhere.

A two-line postcard from her mother, Courtney, whom Gilly hasn't seen in eight years, convinces Gilly that her mother wants them to be together. After Gilly discovers ten dollars behind some books in Mr. Randolph's house, she decides to steal more money for a bus ticket to California. Believing that she will need W. E.'s help, she begins to treat him kindly, earning a loving look from Trotter. At school, however, Gilly shows characteristic anger by sending a racist card to Miss Harris. Helped by Agnes Stokes and W. E., Gilly steals Mr. Randolph's money, but it is not enough for a bus ticket. In desperation, she writes to her mother, exaggerating her living conditions.

Gilly leaves when she gets the opportunity to steal money from Trotter's purse. Gilly is arrested, but Trotter and W. E. bring her back home. The next day, Gilly overhears Trotter telling Miss Ellis that she will never give up Gilly. Gilly now feels comfortable at Trotter's. At Thanksgiving, Mr. Randolph, W. E., and Trotter become sick. While Gilly is nursing them, she receives a visit from her grandmother, Nonnie (Mrs. Rutherford Hopkins), whom Courtney has contacted because of Gilly's letter. Shocked by the conditions of Trotter's home, Nonnie arranges to become Gilly's guardian. Although Gilly thinks of Trotter and the others as her family and no longer wants to leave, she is forced to live with Nonnie. At Christmas, when Gilly finally meets Courtney, she learns that her mother, who has come only because Nonnie paid for the ticket, does not really want her. In tears, Gilly calls Trotter. She expresses love for Trotter and the desire to return home, but Trotter makes her accept that her home is with Nonnie.

CHARACTERS: Most of the characters have handicaps or significant limitations. Eleven-year-old **Gilly Hopkins** (Gilly is short for Galadriel) hardens herself and refuses to face reality, a trait symbolized by the bubble she blows to blot out sight of Miss Ellis. Gilly eventually gains mature understanding and the capacity to love. She was abandoned when she was three and is angry at everyone except her mother. Insecure and needing to feel in charge, she controls others by being obnoxious. At previous schools, for example, she made the teachers admire her intelligence and then failed everything. More significantly, Gilly forces those who want to call her Gilly to call her Galadriel, and vice versa. This contrariness indicates anxiety about her identity. Gilly generally thinks of herself as either gruesome Gilly, a brilliant child who needs no one's help, or gorgeous Galadriel, daughter of a beautiful, loving mother. Gruesome Gilly protects herself from pain by ensuring that no one can love her. Perceptive and manipulative, she controls others by flashing a range of smiles, from an old lady's to a barracuda's. Galadriel, her identity in fairy-tale daydreams, desires a reunion with her loving mother.

Gilly is narrow-minded and bigoted, but she changes. She initially rejects Maime Trotter because her house is run-down and she is fat, uneducated, and religious. When Trotter comes to take her home from the police station and then tells Miss Ellis that she will never give Gilly up, Gilly begins to love Trotter as a mother. Similarly, Gilly at first judges W. E. to be retarded. She delights in intimidating him, turning kind only to use him. Extended contact, however, makes her appreciate him. She therefore tells Agnes that he is her brother, and, because

Trotter is unable to do so, she teaches him to protect himself. When she first meets Mr. Randolph, the racist Gilly feels revulsion, guiding him by his elbow, not the hand he offers. After Mr. Randolph forgives her for stealing, she takes his hand. She later tells Agnes Stokes that he is her uncle. Gilly is also a racist with Miss Harris, abusing her because she can't control her teacher. Gilly is unable to express a change of attitude to Miss Harris, but she shows her love for her adopted "family" by making them a belated Thanksgiving dinner. Gilly, who remained aloof by eating less than she wanted when she first arrived, thus promotes genuine communion.

Through disillusionment, Gilly matures. In a scene contrasting with her arrival, Gilly is polite when Nonnie takes her away from Trotter's. Subsequently, Gilly lies to please, not hurt. For example, she entertains W. E. by writing that she owns racing horses, and she tells Nonnie that she looks nice after a trip to the beauty parlor. Gilly stops lying to herself, however. She unconsciously acknowledges that her mother is not a loving fairy-tale queen when she can't find a place in her room to put Courtney's picture. When she meets her mother, Gilly consciously recognizes that she has made Courtney into something she is not and that Courtney doesn't want her. Gilly then admits for the first time that she loves Trotter. Realizing that she has lost a true mother and a real home, the mature Gilly abandons her fairy-tale dreams and bravely accepts that happy endings are lies, that life is tough, and that Nonnie's house must be home. Whereas she initially thought she was great because she terrorized others, Gilly becomes truly great by accepting her lot with grace.

Paterson said that Gilly "had to learn how to reckon with a force greater than her own anger," the "immense loving energy" of **Mrs. Maime M. Trotter**, a character larger than life. Enormously fat and poorly educated, Trotter is a bad housekeeper who possesses a genius for love. Refusing to display anger or to argue, even when Gilly has gum in her hair, Trotter is beyond Gilly's control. Trotter herself extends unqualified love, reaching out with kindness, understanding, and abundant food. Trotter is protective of W. E., ensuring that no one hurts him. She thus gives Gilly looks of motherly love when Gilly treats W. E. kindly. Later, she kisses Gilly for teaching W. E. how to fight. When hurt, Trotter responds with loving sympathy. Even after Gilly steals her money, Trotter brings Gilly "home." Trotter appears soft and lenient, but she is determined and wise. When Miss Ellis tries to remove Gilly, Trotter resists, declaring that Gilly needs someone to favor her and that she is a mother who deeply needs Gilly. Furthermore, Trotter is the one who forces Gilly to face the hard truth, both when Nonnie takes her away and when Courtney visits. Knowing that life is hard, she teaches that one finds happiness by accepting duty. She thereby inspires Gilly, who wants to make Trotter proud.

William Ernest Teague (**W. E.** for short), a shy seven-year-old with muddy brown hair and thick steel-rimmed glasses, seems slow because he hides behind Trotter and watches *Sesame Street*. Nevertheless, Gilly soon realizes that he is fearful, not stupid, and that he is likable. Because he is incapable of manipulating people, W. E. breaks through Gilly's shell. His heartfelt plea for her to come home after her arrest melts her frozen heart: it marks the point at which she recognizes that she has a home. Thereafter, W. E. provides a means for Gilly to display her changed character. By teaching him to defend himself, she shows unselfish concern, giving him pride and independence; by nursing him during his illness, she shows sisterly love; and by writing that she owns horses, she shows that she is now concerned with pleasing, not controlling, others.

Mr. Randolph, Trotter's elderly, blind African American neighbor, is not only a vehicle for showing Gilly's movement away from racial prejudice but also the voice of wisdom and culture. Mr. Randolph, an independent man who scorns his son's efforts to move him out of his home, relishes and elaborately praises Trotter's meals. A sympathetic man, he quietly accepts Gilly's apology for the theft, allowing her to maintain dignity. Thereafter, Gilly shows that she has overcome her bigotry by holding his hand and by calling him her uncle. Mr. Randolph fulfills his most important role, however, when he has Gilly read Wordsworth's "Ode: Intimations of Immortality." Although she doesn't fully understand the poem, she later enacts its message by valuing the hearts of those around her and by bringing some "clouds of glory" to her earthly home.

Nonnie (Mrs. Rutherford Hopkins), Gilly's widowed grandmother, is awkward, uncertain, and talkative around Gilly, but she does her duty by taking Gilly in and by arranging Courtney's visit. **Courtney Rutherford Hopkins**, Gilly's selfish, loveless mother, contrasts with Trotter, who loves indiscriminately. The unmarried Courtney gave up Gilly when she was three and never tried to see her again. Courtney appears in two guises. In Gilly's daydreams, which are inspired by a glamorous photograph, Courtney is a fairy-tale queen, tall, willowy, beautiful, and loving. In reality, Courtney is a short, stringy-haired, dumpy woman, "a flower child gone to seed." Unlike the "mean flowers" mentioned in Wordsworth's Ode and represented by W. E., Mr. Randolph, and Trotter, and unlike Gilly herself (a gilly is a flower), Courtney can't touch souls because she lacks spiritual beauty. **Miss Ellis**, a social worker with long blond hair and a professional smile, genuinely cares about Gilly. She tries to tell her the truth about Courtney and forces her to accept the consequences of the anger that made her write her exaggerating letter. Gilly resents her sixth grade teacher, **Miss Harris**, because she is black and can't be controlled. Miss Harris is clever, acting calm after receiving Gilly's card. By pointing out that they are alike in their anger, however, Miss Harris undermines Gilly's racism and teaches her that she must channel her emotions to avoid destroying herself. **Agnes Stokes**, a shriveled sixth grader with long, greasy red hair, is a cautionary figure. Abandoned to the care of a grandmother, she illustrates the desperate longing and the selfish sneakiness that can develop when no Trotter is there to provide love.

Park's Quest

(novel, 1988)

PLOT: *Park's Quest* fuses together Arthurian legend with the story of a contemporary adolescent's struggle to understand his family background. Parkington Waddell Broughton the Fifth, known as Park, lives in Washington with his mother, Randy. Randy refuses to talk about his father, who was killed in the Vietnam war. Anxious to know about him, Park secretly reads the books his father owned. Park, who daydreams about knights, then embarks on a quest, likened to the quest for the Holy Grail, to discover the truth about his father. He begins by going to the Vietnam Memorial, where he touches his father's name. After he tells his mother, she arranges for Park to visit his grandfather, Colonel Broughton, in Virginia.

The next stage of Park's quest for knowledge begins poorly. He mistakes his Uncle Frank for a servant, and he is not permitted to see his grandfather, who has suffered two strokes and is upset by Park's arrival. The unpalatable meals prepared by Mrs. Sada Davenport and the rude teasing of Thanh, the daughter of Frank's Vietnamese wife, also make Park regret coming. One night, Park hears crying and discovers his grandfather, whose paralyzed features and inarticulate sounds horrify him. Park thinks of leaving but continues to help on the farm. He also gets Frank to teach him to shoot a rifle. Frank, having accidentally revealed that Park's mother divorced her husband, then has Park watch over the Colonel. Park falls asleep and awakens to see Thanh pushing the Colonel's wheelchair toward the spring house. After Thanh gives the old man a drink, Park is amazed to see him smile.

When Frank takes his wife to the hospital to deliver her baby, Park sneaks the rifle to practice shooting. Thanh attacks him, and he accidentally shoots and injures a crow. She then rails at him as a "nothing." When he goes to Thanh's house to tell her that the crow is alive, he discovers a picture of Thanh with her mother and his own father. He then realizes that Thanh is his sister. He also understands that Thanh fears that Frank will reject her if her mother delivers a boy. In a telephone conversation, Park tells his mother what he has discovered and learns that she feels guilty because she could not forgive her husband. That night, Park and Thanh bring the Colonel when they go to feed the wounded crow. Briefly alone with his grandfather, Park realizes that the Colonel is saying his name and that he feels guilty about his son's death. As they tearfully hug each other, Thanh returns with the news that the crow has flown away. She also brings water in a coconut shell. In the final image, the shell is the Grail, and the three are united as they drink Holy Wine from it.

CHARACTERS: As several critics have shown, parallels with the Arthurian and Grail legends give the central character archetypal significance. **Parkington Waddell Broughton the Fifth** calls himself **Park**, but his mother calls him **Pork**, the hated nickname his father gave him in infancy because he looked like Porky Pig. Park is an eleven-year-old who wears glasses and has pale-blue eyes, hair that is almost white, and a short nose. Park habitually transforms the mundane events of his life into imaginary chivalric episodes. By doing so, he gives himself a noble identity, and he casts his problems into a comprehensible form. Knowing little about his father, except that he was killed in Vietnam, Park feels a void in his life. By identifying with Sir Gareth, who disguised his nobility, and Sir Percival, whose bitter mother took him far from the courtly world after his father died in battle, he maintains the belief that his impoverished circumstances do not indicate his true identity or future greatness. Park is descended from a kind of nobility, wealthy Virginians who have always been military men. His archetypal quest teaches him, however, that his father was not the gallant warrior he imagined, but a flawed man who hurt his wife and family.

Park's great need makes him determined. He learns about his father by secretly reading his books, and then he goes without permission to the Vietnam Memorial, a trip he imagines as a quest for the Grail. His naivete, however, causes frustration. In Virginia, he is so absorbed by an Arthurian daydream in which he is the young heir who restores the family's happiness that he does not realize that Frank is not a servant. Park is also bitterly disappointed when his infirm grandfather fails to fit the Arthurian image of kingship. Furthermore, because he obeys his mother's injunctions against asking too many questions,

Park fails to learn that the Colonel is upset with himself. Consequently, Park fears the Colonel and sees himself as somehow responsible for his father's death and his mother's pain.

Park's increasing bitterness makes him see Thanh as a "geek" responsible for killing his father and debilitating his grandfather. When Thanh pushes the Colonel to the spring house, a sacred place in the symbolic Arthurian overlay, Park finally glimpses their humanity. Subsequently, Park becomes sensitive, appreciating that Thanh attacks him when he has the rifle because she was shot at in Vietnam. After she humbles him by calling him a nothing, he finally develops a noble identity. When he discovers that Thanh is his half-sister, he loses his bigotry and literally accepts the kinship of other races. He also reassures her when she is anxious about being displaced by the baby. Park shows similar maturity by understanding his mother's lonely struggle with grief and guilt. He rises to his highest point, however, with his grandfather. By accepting that his grandfather is calling out their mutual name, he overcomes his fear and completes his quest for an identity and a place in his father's family. By verbalizing his grandfather's guilt, he heals the old man's pain. In terms of the Arthurian symbolism, he thus heals the wounded and impotent Fisher King, renewing the kingdom suffering under a curse. By feeling one with Thanh and his grandfather as though they were with the Holy Grail, Park overcomes their years of solitude and pain in a moment of mystical unity.

Randy Broughton, Park's mother, is a thin woman with curly blond hair and clear blue eyes. A Texan who obviously felt inferior to her husband's aristocratic family, she has a coldness and a darkness that Park can't understand. This darkness is evident in her silence about her husband, even though it causes Park immense pain. Wounded deeply when her husband betrayed her, she was unable to forgive and therefore divorced him. After his death, however, she endured guilt because she lacked a second chance to grant forgiveness. Her son's quest, in which he learns the truth, relieves her of her burden and allows her to establish a new relationship with him, which she does by calling him

Park for the first time. **Frank Broughton**, Park's uncle, is a short, lean, muscular man with a dark-red face, neck, and hands. He is friendly, but slightly shy, and he displays immense patience with both Thanh and Park. An honorable man who married the Vietnamese woman with whom his brother had had an affair, he is a counselor. After unwittingly revealing that Park's mother is divorced, he thus assures Park that he is still part of the family. He also sets up the meeting that allows both Park and the Colonel to be healed of their grief and loneliness. **Thanh**, Park's Vietnamese half-sister, is so insecure that she protects herself with rudeness and mockery. Fearing that she will have no legitimate call on Frank after her mother gives him a child of his own, Thanh is surly with Frank and sarcastic with Park. In an attempt to keep her world intact, she insists that the spring house is hers, not Park's. Thanh despises guns because she was shot at in Vietnam, and so she attacks Park when he uses one. Like Park, Thanh needs knowledge of her father. When she learns that she and Park share the same father and that he is dead, she matures, accepting Park and her own situation. When she brings the water in the coconut cup Grail, Thanh unites herself with the other members of the family who have suffered because of her father. **Colonel Parkington Waddell Broughton the Third**, Park's grandfather, is the wounded Fisher King within the Arthurian legend. A sixty-three-year-old man with a beaked nose and balding head, he is paralyzed because of two strokes. He is a proud man, who secretly practices with a walker at night, all the time crying with inarticulate grief. His guilt about his son's death may be because the family's military tradition encouraged a love of war or because he harshly judged his son for marrying beneath his station and then for fathering a Vietnamese child. In any case, by calling out their name, he gives Park the acceptance for which he longed, and he reestablishes the noble family line that had been broken by lonely guilt and grief. **Mrs. Sada Davenport**, a plump, talkative woman of about fifty, is the Colonel's housekeeper. Her inability to make palatable food symbolizes her failure to provide proper emotional sustenance. Her unsympathetic treatment of the Colonel emphasizes the humane feelings Thanh and, later, Park have for him.

Further Reading

Authors and Artists for Young Adults. Vol. 1. Detroit: Gale Research, 1990.

Berger, Laura Standley, ed. *Twentieth-Century Children's Writers.* 4th ed. Detroit: St. James, 1995.

———, ed. *Twentieth-Century Young Adult Writers.* 1st ed. Detroit: St. James, 1994.

Children's Literature Review. Vol. 7. Detroit: Gale Research, 1984.

Collier, Laurie, and Joyce Nakamura, eds. *Major Authors and Illustrators for Children and Young Adults.* Detroit: Gale Research, 1993.

Contemporary Authors New Revision Series. Vol. 28. Detroit: Gale Research, 1990.

Contemporary Literary Criticism. Vols. 12, 30. Detroit: Gale Research, 1980, 1984.

Estes, Glenn E., ed. *American Writers for Children since 1960: Fiction.* Vol. 52 of *Dictionary of Literary Biography.* Detroit: Gale Research, 1986.

Holtze, Sally Holmes, ed. *Fifth Book of Junior Authors and Illustrators.* New York: H. W. Wilson, 1983.

Paterson, Katherine. *Gates of Excellence: On Reading and Writing Books for Children.* New York: Elsevier/Nelson Books, 1981.

———. *The Spying Heart: More Thoughts on Reading and Writing Books for Children.* New York: Lodestar Books, 1989.

Rees, David. "Medals and Awards: Katherine Paterson." In *Painted Desert, Green Shade: Essays on Contemporary Writers of Fiction for Children and Young Adults.* Boston: Horn Book, 1984.

Schmidt, Gary D. *Katherine Paterson.* New York: Twayne, 1994.

Something about the Author. Vols. 13, 53. Detroit: Gale Research, 1978, 1988.

Jill Paton Walsh

1937-, English author

The Green Book

(science fiction, 1981)

PLOT: This outer-space adventure celebrates the wisdom and perception of childhood. When Earth succumbs to disaster, Father, Joe, Sarah, and Pattie are among those hand-picked to settle a distant planet. During the voyage, Joe and Sarah, having read the one book each is permitted to bring, demand a chance to read Pattie's. When Pattie produces a blank, green-covered commonplace book, everyone laughs at her foolish choice. After the colonists land, Pattie is allowed to name the new community; she calls it Shine. Father, who intends to become important as a maker of gadgets, then figures out how to use fire to soften the trees so that the settlers can fell them and build houses. He also develops a seed drill for planting wheat. Because he values literature and his family longs for stories, Father trades work for a reading of Grimms' tales.

The adults worry when their vegetables prove to be inedible, their rabbits die of starvation, and their wheat seems crystalline. Pattie and her friends, however, happily explore Shine, finding "candy trees," trees with a sweet sap that the settlers harvest. Later, Pattie and her friends witness the hatching of a race of moth people. She feeds them tree candy, and the moths soon play games with the children. After a mating ritual, however, the moth people fly away. Those that return die immediately upon laying their rocklike eggs.

The settlers then harvest their wheat. Because they have enough seeds for only one planting and the wheat kernels resemble glass beads, everyone despairs, thinking that they will soon have to take suicide tablets. Sarah, however, discovers that she can grind the kernels into flour and bake it into edible bread. Now that the colony will survive, Father asks for Pattie's blank book so that he can record everyone's share of the food. When she produces it, however, it is filled with a story about Shine. The settlers eagerly demand Pattie's story, the same one the reader has just finished.

CHARACTERS: Only Father and his youngest daughter are fully characterized. Other characters are mentioned merely to establish different value systems among the settlers and to contrast the perceptions of the adults and the children. **Pattie**, the youngest in her family, is an innocent child. Like the book she takes, her character is a blank page that will be written in a new world. She shows her optimism, which contrasts with the pessimism of many of the adults, when she names the settlement Shine. Pattie has no memory of Earth, so her attitudes are developed from experiences on Shine. She shows great powers of observation and a willingness to experiment when she finds the candy trees. She is a brave girl. When the large objects they thought were boulders prove to be moth eggs, she guides the young people away. She then shows openness to her new world by befriending the moths, feeding them the sweet tree candy and playing games along with them. Pattie's greatest role, however, is in giving the story-starved community a record of its own history.

Just as Pattie learns to feed the spirits of the settlers, **Sarah**, her older sister, learns to feed their bodies. In the beginning, she is immature, choosing *The Pony Club Rides Again* as her book. Once on Shine, however, she grows up. Unlike the adults, she doesn't immediately despair when the wheat looks unusual. Furthermore, she doesn't jump to the conclusion that it is necessarily fatal, and she therefore makes the discovery that saves the community. **Joe**, the oldest of the three children, is a practical person who does an adult's work but is close enough to the children to learn about their discovery of the candy trees. Joe may lack imagination—like several other settlers, he brings along *Robinson Crusoe*—but he speaks for the idealism of youth, insisting to his father that everyone will be equal on the new planet.

Father is central to themes about class and culture. Bitter that he was insignificant in Earth's class system because he was only a mechanic, Father is determined to be more than the "population fodder" and muscle for which he was chosen as a space traveler. He believes that he can become a respectable and important citizen by providing mechanisms that solve practical problems. Father moves toward his goal of proving that he is as good as anyone in the group by cleverly solving the problems of felling trees and planting wheat. In spite of his humble social origins, Father is culturally superior to most of the settlers. He loves literature and believes that it should be preserved, but he sacrifices his desires for the sake of the community and his social ambitions. He therefore takes along a book on technology instead of the complete works of Shakespeare that he desires. Father is later a vehicle for criticizing the failure to appreciate culture because he notes that very few people brought worthwhile books. Regretting that he is forgetting so much, such as Wordsworth's poems, he tries to give his children culture by trading his labor for a chance to read Grimms' tales and by tricking another settler into letting him read Homer. Significantly, he satisfies the settlers' hunger for stories, which develops when their physical security is assured, by reading them Pattie's history of Shine.

Further Reading

Berger, Laura Standley, ed. *Twentieth-Century Young Adult Writers*. 1st ed. Detroit: St. James, 1994.

Collier, Laurie, and Joyce Nakamura, eds. *Major Authors and Illustrators for Children and Young Adults*. Detroit: Gale Research, 1993.

Contemporary Authors New Revision Series. Vol. 38. Detroit: Gale Research, 1993.

Hunt, Caroline C., ed. *British Children's Writers since 1960: First Series*. Vol. 161 of *Dictionary of Literary Biography*. Detroit: Gale Research, 1996.

Something about the Author. Vols. 4, 72. Detroit: Gale Research, 1973, 1993.

Something about the Author Autobiography Series. Vol. 3. Detroit: Gale Research, 1986.

Gary Paulsen

1939-, American juvenile novelist and poet

Hatchet

(novel, 1987)

PLOT: As with most contemporary Robinsonades—survival stories following the patterns of *Robinson Crusoe*—*Hatchet* portrays both physical and psychological struggles. Brian Robeson is flying in a small plane to the Canadian woods to spend the summer with his recently divorced father. Flashbacks indicate that Brian is still upset about his earlier discovery—which he calls the "Secret"—that his mother was having an affair that led to the divorce. When his pilot has a fatal heart attack, Brian crash lands the plane in a Canadian lake. He

swims ashore, and, equipped only with a small hatchet his mother had given him as a parting gift, which he originally considered useless, he begins a lonely struggle for survival. At first, the despairing Brian suffers from mosquitoes, whose stings cause his eyes to swell shut, and from sickness after he drinks water too rapidly. Memories of Mr. Perpich, an English teacher who taught him positive thinking, make Brian realize, however, that he is his own most valuable asset. Brian subsequently has luck in finding a cave for shelter. By following birds, he locates berries, but he eats so many that he becomes violently ill. Shortly afterwards, seeing a reflection of his swollen and bloodied face in the water, he destroys this "mirror" in disgust. Brian soon builds a home in the cave and learns to eat carefully. He even regards himself as rich when he finds raspberries. After he panics when he meets a bear, he realizes that he must consider his actions and their results more carefully.

The turning point in Brian's fortunes comes when he smells something foul in his cave one night. Unable to see in the dark, he throws his hatchet, which sends a shower of sparks when it harmlessly strikes the cave wall. His intruder is a porcupine that shoots quills into his leg. Brian cries with self-pity, but he realizes that crying will not solve his problems. That night, his father and his best friend appear in his dreams with a message. The next morning he understands: he can use the hatchet to make fire, his most pressing physical need. Patiently, Brian learns to use the hatchet to build a fire, which drives away the mosquitoes, and Brian begins to feel in control. Observing turtle tracks, he realizes that he is a "city boy" who must understand nature to survive. He then suddenly realizes that the turtle was not playing on the sand but was burying eggs, which he digs up for food.

When Brian misses signaling a passing plane, he plunges into a period of profound depression during which he lets the fire go out and wishes he were dead. He is "reborn," however, as a self-reliant person who can rely on "tough hope." Thereafter, Brian patiently learns to fish and hunt birds. When a bull moose attacks him, Brian plays dead and survives. Even after a tornado destroys his home and

garden, a place of beauty, constant good weather, varied activities, and sympathetic companionship, symbolizes childhood. It compensates Tom for lost opportunities at home by enabling him to help with the building of a tree house. Because it is more intricate than the garden at home, the garden suggests that Tom's childhood becomes richer and more varied. The garden also affects Tom's character. Tom initially dismisses Hatty as "only" a girl. Her knowledge of the garden, however, makes him appreciate her as the perfect playmate. Sensitive to her feelings, he comforts her when she mourns the death of her parents and when she cries after he suggests that she is a ghost. He also plays with her, acting as a substitute for her cousins.

Although Tom shows sympathetic understanding in the garden, he suffers failures of understanding during the day. Tom insists that he has not been imagining his experiences. Ironically, his attempts to apply the logic that Uncle Alan advocates leads to errors. After he learns that Mrs. Bartholomew bought the house a few years ago, Tom rejects the idea of consulting her, yet she is the one person who could give him answers. He also concludes that Hatty's clothes indicate that she is an early Victorian ghost. Most seriously, once he has understood the difference between time in the flat and time in the garden, Tom assumes that he can remain perpetually in the garden of childhood. Significantly, when he goes to tell Hatty his intentions, she takes him out of the garden to the cathedral at Ely. In winter, the symbolic season of death, Tom loses his naivete because Peter appears and makes him understand that Hatty has become a woman.

Afterwards, Tom grows to understand his own world better. Instead of seeing a threatening old landlady when he visits Mrs. Bartholomew, he sees Hatty. By accepting that Mrs. Bartholomew was and is Hatty, Tom comprehends that past and present coexist. Furthermore, he recognizes that his feelings of loneliness and longing were not unique because Hatty the girl had precisely the same feelings. Sympathy and imagination thus provide meaning where logic has failed. By appreciating that time changes everything but is also a continuing imaginative reality, Tom shows that he has matured. No longer

bitter, he looks forward to seeing his parents and to sharing his adventures with his brother.

During Tom's midnight excursions, **Hatty Melbourne** (Hatty is short for Harriet) is a young orphan, and during the day she is an elderly, reputedly crotchety, landlady called **Mrs. Bartholomew**. A lonely orphan, Hatty needs a meaningful identity, so she convinces herself that she is a princess being held prisoner by the Melbournes. She also retreats into her romantic imagination. Glimpsing Tom, she leaves a note addressed to Oberon, king of fairies. Later, she coyly suggests that she did not leave it. On another occasion, she makes the gardener into a biblical character, telling Tom that Abel killed his brother. Hatty is intelligent, understanding that her cousins will play only when they can be in charge. She also knows the garden so well that she can spy on everyone without detection. Because her aunt despises her and keeps her physically and emotionally isolated in the garden, Tom is a psychological necessity, a symbolical projection of her desires. Tom thus provides companionship by playing with her and knowledge by describing the world beyond the garden wall.

Hatty naively believes that the garden will always be there and that she and Tom have plenty of time for each other. As she grows older, however, she loses the need for Tom's companionship. She thus sees him as transparent and insubstantial. When she goes out of the childhood garden with Tom, during the expedition to Ely, their relationship ends. On the way home, she falls in love. Having eyes only for Barty now, she no longer sees Tom. Fittingly, on the eve of her wedding, during what is an earlier trip for Tom, a storm destroys the fir tree. This event marks her entry into adulthood. Afterwards, she forgets both the garden and Tom. As a shrunken old lady remembering her childhood, she drags Tom into it. Although she thereby serves the needs of her childhood self, she also helps to restore Tom to psychological health. In addition, Mrs. Bartholomew is the archetypal wise old woman, interpreting events for both Tom and the reader. She thus makes explicit the theme that all things change, but her experiences indicate that time is also an emotional construct that is always present.

In this novel, only those sensitive to others see someone from a different period. At the Melbourne house, **Abel**, the rustic gardener, is the only one besides Hatty who sees Tom. A large-framed young man with a weathered face, Abel is attentive to Hatty and sympathetic to her plight. His ability to see what she sees thus demonstrates his concern. Because he is deeply religious, however, Abel regards Tom as a devil threatening Hatty. He therefore prays whenever Tom is around and warns Hatty to be careful. Abel is protective, destroying Hatty's arrows and giving her a blunt knife for carving. When he believes that Hatty is in physical danger, he grabs her and makes her promise that she will not climb on the garden wall. He also blames Tom, telling him to go back to hell, when Hatty injures herself by falling out of the tree house. Although he is a caring man, Abel is intellectually limited. Predisposed to see Tom as a devil in spite of his innocent actions, Abel accepts Tom only after he sees the boy looking up a biblical passage. **Peter Long**, Tom's brother, is the only other character from the present who sees a person from the past. Longing for the same things that Tom wants, he begins dreaming of Tom's experiences. His desire and concern for Tom pulls him into Hatty's world. When he sees Hatty, Peter becomes the voice of innocent vision, helping Tom to see that Hatty has changed.

Hatty's aunt, **Mrs. Melbourne**, is a tyrannical woman who is extremely cold to Hatty. She openly expresses contempt for the girl, and she tells her son James that she will disinherit him if he marries her. **Hubert Melbourne**, her oldest son, is almost a grown man when Tom first sees him. He generally ignores Hatty. **James Melbourne**, her middle son, first appears as a boy whose soft voice is constantly breaking. The only one whom Tom likes, James alone shows compassion. He expresses pity for Hatty and suggests allowing her to make friends. As a man, he falls on hard times, and Hatty's husband buys the Melbourne household and the clock from him. **Edgar Melbourne**, the youngest son, is closest to Tom in age. A boy with brindled hair and brindled brown eyes, Edgar is nasty. He is reluctant to give Hatty an apple, he laughs unpleasantly and calls her queer when she tells him the she is talking to an invisible friend, he throws a stick that trips her during a chase, and he suggests to his mother that Hatty is to blame for the geese invading the garden.

In contrast to the Melbournes, the Kitsons are comical in their oppression. **Uncle Alan Kitson** is a pompous intellectual bully. He insists on rationality, but he constantly explodes with anger because Tom can't understand or will not accept what he is saying. Uncle Alan takes a coldly logical approach to Tom's questions, providing mathematical and scientific analyses that Tom can't understand and can't accept because they deny the reality of his experiences. **Aunt Gwen Kitson** is kinder. An overly attentive woman who feeds Tom so much that he is unable to sleep, she fears her husband's explosions of temper. Therefore she constantly suggests that Tom's questions are the result of reading too many fairy stories. Because she is kind at heart, however, Aunt Gwen glimpses the truth when she tells her husband that Tom hugged Mrs. Bartholomew as if she were a little girl.

Further Reading

Berger, Laura Standley, ed. *Twentieth-Century Children's Writers*. 4th ed. Detroit: St. James, 1995.

Children's Literature Review. Vol. 9. Detroit: Gale Research, 1985.

Collier, Laurie, and Joyce Nakamura, eds. *Major Authors and Illustrators for Children and Young Adults*. Detroit: Gale Research, 1993.

Contemporary Literary Criticism. Vol. 21. Detroit: Gale Research, 1982.

De Montreville, Doris, and Donna Hill, eds. *Third Book of Junior Authors*. New York: H. W. Wilson, 1972.

Hunt, Caroline C., ed. *British Children's Writers since 1960: First Series*. Vol. 161 of *Dictionary of Literary Biography*. Detroit: Gale Research, 1996.

Jones, Raymond E. "Philippa Pearce's *Tom's Midnight Garden*: Finding and Losing Eden." In *Touchstones: Reflections on the Best in Children's Literature*. Vol. 1. Edited by Perry Nodelman. West Lafayette, IN: Children's Literature Association, 1985.

Rees, David. "Achieving One's Heart's Desires: Philippa Pearce." In *The Marble in the Water: Essays on Contemporary Writers of Fiction for Children and Young Adults*. Boston: Horn Book, 1980.

Something about the Author. Vols. 1, 67. Detroit: Gale Research, 1971, 1992.

Townsend, John Rowe. "Philippa Pearce." In *A Sense of Story: Essays on Contemporary Writers for Children*. Philadelphia: J. B. Lippincott, 1971.

Robert Newton Peck

1928-, American author

Soup

(autobiographical short stories, 1974)

PLOT: Set in 1930s rural Vermont, this book of unconnected "good bad boy" tales describes the escapades of the narrator, Rob (Robert) Peck, and his best friend, Soup (Luther Wesley Vinson). Half of the chapters are amusing anecdotes: Rob tries to talk himself out a punishment after he is rude at school, but he finally tells the truth; Rob plays a game with Aunt Carrie, refusing to untie her from a tree until a storm strikes; Rob vomits after he and Soup make acorn pipes and smoke corn silk; Rob gets his mother to help him find his silver valve, which is always missing when he wants to inflate a football; and Rob, trying to look like his favorite movie star, borrows Aunt Carrie's best brush to comb his goop-smeared hair.

Other chapters are more substantial. In a farcical tale of poetic justice, Rob and Soup stick branches through apples, which they whip into the distance. When Soup whips one through a church window, he disappears. To prove that Rob could whip an apple as far as the church, Mrs. Stetson tries her hand at whipping one. It sails in the wrong direction, breaking a window in the house owned by Mr. Haskins, who chases them into a garage. Soup, who is also hiding in the garage, thinks that Mrs. Stetson is after him, so he rushes out, crashing into Mr. Haskins, who whips him. In another slapstick tale, Soup makes Rob roll down a hill in an apple barrel. When the barrel crashes through a chicken coop, Soup again disappears. Although his sweater unraveled during his harrowing trip, Rob is happy with his own bravery.

Rob and Soup resort to cheating when they need money to see a movie. They hide a stone inside the tinfoil they sell to Mr. Diskin, the Jewish junk dealer. He pays them what they need, silently returning the stone. In another tale, Rob accidentally earns the

enmity of Eddy Tacker, the school bully. Fleeing in terror from Eddy, Rob sees his mother coming toward him. Realizing that she offers protection, Rob seizes the opportunity for revenge by suddenly stopping and punching Eddy. Afterwards, Mama buys them ice cream and makes them shake hands. She then takes Rob shopping, forcing him to try on numerous pairs of knickerbockers. While he is standing in his underwear, the girl he likes best enters the store. Embarrassed, Rob grabs an enormously large pair of knickerbockers and says that they are perfect, so his mother buys them. The last tale is a touching display of friendship. Soup is anxious to show off his new pair of squeaky orange shoes. He and Rob race, but Rob trips, tearing his shoes. When Rob cries, saying that he hates Soup and will not go to school with ripped shoes, Soup trades shoes, allowing Rob to feel proud and important.

Sequels include Soup and Me *(1975),* Soup for President *(1978),* Soup's Drum *(1980),* Soup on Wheels *(1981),* Soup in the Saddle *(1983),* Soup's Goat *(1984),* Soup on Ice *(1985),* Soup on Fire *(1987),* Soup's Uncle *(1988),* Soup's Hoop *(1990)* Soup in Love *(1992), and* Soup Ahoy *(1994).*

CHARACTERS: Robert Peck, the narrator who goes by the name **Rob**, is a third grader with sandy curls. Afflicted with hero worship, he regards his friend Soup as the authority on most subjects. Because Soup also intimidates him, Rob repeatedly defers to Soup. Although Rob often betrays a comic naivete, he can be artful. After bringing home the note about his rudeness, for example, he cleverly deflects blame, getting his mother to resent the nurse to whom he was impolite. When his mother directly asks whether he intended to be rude, however, Rob confesses. On another occasion, he demonstrates a quick wit, seizing the opportunity of his mother's presence to deliver a surprise blow to Eddy Tacker. In some escapades, Rob appears ridiculous. For instance, he bears the blame for breaking both the church window and the chicken coop because Soup has run away, and he buys an extraordinarily large pair of knickerbockers when a girl sees him in his underwear. In other episodes, he is proud despite the disasters that befall him. When he gets sick after smoking, he nevertheless feels that he has passed a test of manhood; after being covered with rotten apples and chicken manure during his barrel ride, he is proud to have passed a test of bravery. Although Rob does things, such as smoking, that he knows his mother would forbid, he is truly dishonest only once. He knows that it is wrong to cheat Mr. Diskin, even though he has heard others claim that it is okay to cheat Jews. But Rob's desire to go to the movies overcomes his pangs of conscience. He is, however, sensitive enough to feel bad afterwards. In spite of this lapse, Rob emerges as a naive, exuberant, clever boy with an engaging but childish sense of humor and a strong attachment to his friends.

Rob's friend **Luther Wesley Vinson** became known as **Soup** because he refused to answer to his given name, coming to meals only when his mother called, "Soup's on." Soup teaches Rob to use his nickname after hitting him when he calls him Luther. Rob describes Soup as a "regular genius" for getting the two of them into trouble. Soup is always coming up with ideas—such as whipping the apples, smoking, and rolling in the barrel—that end in disaster. Unlike Rob, Soup is alert enough to run from disaster. Ironically, Soup suffers once for his transgressions. While avoiding Mrs. Stetson, he runs into Mr. Haskins, who punishes him for breaking the window that Mrs. Stetson broke. Soup sometimes seems comically naive, delighting, for instance, in the music of his squeaky orange shoes. But, because he is older than Rob, Soup is an authority on the ways of boyhood. Sometimes he exerts his authority through intimidation, but he is also willing to share his wisdom. He thus teaches Rob that silence conceals transgressions by keeping adults ignorant of what their children are doing. In spite of such cynicism and his tough exterior, Soup is a caring friend. When Rob cries and expresses frustration because he is always the one hurt, Soup is surprisingly mature and generous. He tenderly cleans Rob's face and bleeding hands. Seeing Rob's humiliation, Soup then sacrifices the joy of bragging about his new shoes, allowing Rob to be the center of atten-

Rob Peck and his good-hearted, troublemaker friend, Soup, in a scene illustrated by Charles C. Gehm from Peck's Soup.

tion. In this final act, Soup shows that his genius for trouble is matched by a genius for friendship.

Minor characters receive cursory treatment. **Mama (Mrs. Peck)** seldom sees matters from her son's perspective. She thus forces him to strip down to his underwear in the store when they are buying knickerbockers, and she insists on buying a pair into which he can grow. **Aunt Carrie** is characterized by a repeated utterance: her belief that Rob needs a good thrashing. She becomes absurd when she panics while tied to the tree. **Mr. Diskin** the Jewish junk dealer, is a kind man who likes children. When children sell him tinfoil, he always manages to pay them a dime, the price of admission to the movies. His kindness is evident after Rob and Soup try to cheat him: he remains silent, giving them both dimes and returning the stone, a symbol of their betrayal of a trust. **Eddy Tacker**, the school bully, is a vicious, vengeful boy who delights in torturing his victims by announcing what he will later do to them. He becomes a victim of Rob's surprise counterattack, but the unnecessary pressure he exerts when shaking hands afterwards implies that he has not really changed.

Further Reading

Authors and Artists for Young Adults. Vol. 3. Detroit: Gale Research, 1991.

Berger, Laura Standley, ed. *Twentieth-Century Young Adult Writers.* 1st ed. Detroit: St. James, 1994.

Collier, Laurie, and Joyce Nakamura, eds. *Major Authors and Illustrators for Children and Young Adults.* Detroit: Gale Research, 1993.

Contemporary Authors New Revision Series. Vol. 31. Detroit: Gale Research, 1991.

Contemporary Literary Criticism. Vol. 17. Detroit: Gale Research, 1981.

Holtze, Sally Holmes, ed. *Fifth Book of Junior Authors and Illustrators.* New York: H. W. Wilson, 1983.

Something about the Author. Vols. 21, 62. Detroit: Gale Research, 1980, 1991.

Something about the Author Autobiography Series. Vol. 1. Detroit: Gale Research, 1986.

Eleanor H. Porter

(pen name for Eleanor Stuart)

1868-1920, American singer, teacher, and author

Pollyanna

(novel, 1913)

PLOT: Like *Rebecca of Sunnybrook Farm* and *Anne of Green Gables*, Pollyanna is about an irrepressible child who transforms everyone she meets. After the death of her father, Pollyanna Whittier is sent to Beldingsville, Vermont, where she is to live with Miss Polly Harrington, a stern aunt who takes her in only out of a sense of duty. Nancy, the hired girl, therefore befriends the poor orphan. Pollyanna, however, overwhelms Aunt Polly with affection, turns attempts at discipline into pleasures, and gets Aunt Polly to move her out of the attic into a pleasant room. Pollyanna succeeds because of what she calls the "just being glad game," in which she finds something good in every situation. Pollyanna soon affects others. For example, she cheers Mrs.

Snow, a cantankerous invalid, by teaching her the game. Pollyanna fails, however, to get either Aunt Polly or the Ladies' Aid group to give a home to Jimmy Bean, an orphan she meets on the street.

A romance plot develops after Pollyanna discovers John Pendleton lying on the ground with a broken leg and calls Dr. (Thomas) Chilton to help. Nancy, who heard from Old Tom Durgin, the gardener, that Aunt Polly once quarrelled with a lover, convinces Pollyanna that Pendleton is that lover. To cheer him, Pollyanna teaches the bedridden Mr. Pendleton the Glad Game, and he asks Pollyanna to live in his house. Convinced that Aunt Polly wants her, she refuses, and Mr. Pendleton then reveals that he loved Pollyanna's mother. Pollyanna continues to teach the game to such people as Reverend Paul Ford, but she soon fails in it herself. Struck by an automobile, she overhears a specialist say that she will never walk again and she becomes despondent. After the people she has influenced send messages saying how she has brightened their lives and after Aunt Polly learns the game, Pollyanna is glad that she once had legs because they helped her to make others happy. Eventually, Jimmy Bean, now living with Mr. Pendleton, overhears Dr. Chilton say that Pollyanna can walk again but that Aunt Polly won't let him examine her. Jimmy reports the news to Aunt Polly, who has not allowed Chilton in the house since their lovers' quarrel fifteen years earlier. Polly then summons Chilton. Aunt Polly and Chilton reconcile and later marry; Pollyanna is sent to a specialist who helps her to walk again.

Pollyanna Grows Up (1915) is a sequel.

CHARACTERS: Critics deride *Pollyanna* as saccharine and use the name of its heroine as a synonym for vacuous optimism. Unlike others of her ilk, such as Rebecca Randall and Anne Shirley, **Pollyanna Whittier** is tiresome because she is limited to one major trait, her indefatigable optimism. She simply talks so much about being glad that she becomes unbearable. These speeches match the breathless pace of those her rivals deliver, but they lack the spontaneity and unforced humor. Furthermore, the speeches about her angelic mother are cloyingly sentimental and improbable for an eleven-year-old. Nevertheless, in the first part of the story, in which her antics are relatively fresh and varied, Pollyanna, who has two thick flaxen braids and freckles, is likeable and charming. She is a talkative girl who pours out her feelings without pause for breath. She naively assumes that Aunt Polly is kind and generous, and she refuses to let obvious facts change her mind. She learned her notorious optimism from her father, a minister in the West. When she found a pair of crutches instead of the doll she expected in a missionary barrel, her father told her to be glad that she didn't need them. Since then, she has responded to adversity by consciously finding something to make her glad. She thus overcomes disappointment at her spartan attic room by being glad that it lacks a mirror that would remind her of her freckles. Pollyanna particularly enjoys the game, however, when a situation is challenging. She thus tells Mrs. Snow, an invalid, to be glad that everyone is not like her, a statement that first angers and then transforms the woman.

Although Pollyanna can be naive to the point of insensitivity and optimistic beyond the bounds of credibility, she shows flashes of complexity. At times, she seems a clever manipulator. For example, she welcomes Aunt Polly into her room as a visitor, even though Aunt Polly was not coming to see her, and then she reveals that she had hoped for a room with carpets and curtains, all the time declaring that she had not meant to reveal her desires. Subsequently, Aunt Polly moves her into a better room. When she goes to Mrs. Snow, she cleverly asks her what she wants before revealing that she has brought three kinds of food so that Mrs. Snow can't be disappointed. Pollyanna even generates social criticism, coming to far more rational conclusions than those of the adults. After her failure to convince the Ladies' Aid group to adopt Jimmy Bean, she declares to herself that they are wrong to be concerned about raising money for foreign missions when they could help someone in the immediate community. The final sign that Pollyanna is not completely shallow is her plausible inability to find anything to be happy

about when she is paralyzed. The focus on her improbable efforts to be glad overwhelms the other elements in the story, making Pollyanna one of the most taxing characters in children's literature.

Miss Polly Harrington, Pollyanna's aunt, is a stern forty-year-old woman who seems older because she is joyless. Proud and hard-hearted, she accepts Pollyanna into her home out of a sense of duty. Her lack of family love is symbolized by the painfully bare attic room that she assigns to Pollyanna. Aunt Polly's emotional sterility is the product of stubborn pride. She is alone because she quarreled with Dr. Chilton over some trivial matter. She also disapproved of her sister's marriage to pastor Whittier, and still refuses to allow Pollyanna to mention his name. As a consequence, she remains ignorant of the Glad Game and thus of Pollyanna's character. As she associates with Pollyanna, however, Aunt Polly frequently experiences a choking feeling, a sign of long suppressed tender emotions rising to the surface. She also begins to take an interest in her appearance, letting Pollyanna release her curls from her tight bun. Pollyanna's charming ways ease her out of her isolation, making her feel an attachment for the first time in years. After Pollyanna is injured, she becomes so devoted to her that she plays the Glad Game and then swallows her pride by summoning Dr. Chilton. This act leads to Pollyanna's cure, but it is also a plea for forgiveness from the man she wronged years earlier and therefore earns her the reward of marriage.

John Pendleton, a wealthy man who is not quite sixty, became sullen and lonely after he failed to win the hand of Pollyanna's mother. Mr. Pendleton has a reputation as a miser and does not retain a staff in his house, which he does not regard as a true home because it lacks the presence of a woman or a child. After he breaks his leg, he becomes so dependent on Pollyanna that he begs her to move in with him. After Pollyanna's accident, he adopts Jimmy Beam to please her, and he himself gains the happiness of a home. **Dr. (Thomas) Chilton** is also lonely and desires a true home that is only possible with the presence of a loving woman. He is a kind man who wants to help Pollyanna, but he is constrained by professional pride and etiquette, which demands that he be asked to consult in her case. His swift reconciliation with Polly shows that he has maintained his devotion to her.

Mrs. Snow, an invalid who has given up on life, is unkempt and cantankerous. When people bring her food, she always complains that she wanted something else. Pollyanna lets light into her darkened room and fixes her hair, thereby restoring Mrs. Snow's interest in her appearance. Pollyanna also cheers her up, giving her a renewed interest in life. **Jimmy Bean**, a dirty ten-year-old orphan, longs for a place with a mother and not a matron. He says that he doesn't want charity and is willing to work for his board. He brings out Pollyanna's unselfish concern for others, illuminates the narrow and selfish attitudes of the Ladies' Aid, and brings out the paternal feelings in Mr. Pendleton. **Reverend Paul Ford** appears in a set piece that gives religious significance to Pollyanna's primarily secular optimism. By telling the minister that her father emphasized the Bible's eight hundred "rejoicing texts," those passages of joy and praise, she inspires him to see that calling out the best in humanity, rather than resorting to the religion of fear and condemnation, is the best approach to motivating his congregation. **Nancy**, Polly's housemaid, is a foil to her mistress because she has an immediate concern for and attachment to Pollyanna. A naive woman, she sees the elements of a romance novel in John Pendleton and therefore jumps to the false conclusion that he once courted Aunt Polly. Her conversations with **Old Tom Durgin**, the elderly and bent gardener, functions as a choric device by providing family histories essential for the plot. He is also the recipient of Pollyanna's most startling piece of advice: she tells him that he can be glad his spine is crooked because he doesn't have far to bend over for his work.

Further Reading

Berger, Laura Standley, ed. *Twentieth-Century Children's Writers*. 4th ed. Detroit: St. James, 1995.

Contemporary Authors. Vol. 109. Detroit: Gale Research, 1983.

Griswold, Jerry. "Radical Innocence: *Pollyanna*." In *Audacious Kids: Coming of Age in America's Classic Children's Books*. New York: Oxford University Press, 1992.

Martine, James J., ed. *American Novelists, 1910-1945*. Vol. 9 of *Dictionary of Literary Biography*. Detroit: Gale Research, 1981.

Beatrix Potter

1866-1943, English artist and picture book author and illustrator

The Tale of Peter Rabbit

(picture book, private edition, 1901; revised edition, 1902)

PLOT: Based on letters Potter sent to Noel Moore, the son of her last governess, *The Tale of Peter Rabbit* was the first of the author's tiny animal fantasies. A cautionary tale about obeying one's mother, it traces the title character's journey from the safety of home to a perilous, forbidden place and back home again.

Before Mrs. Rabbit goes shopping for supper, she warns her four children to stay out of Mr. McGregor's garden: their father had an accident there and ended up in a pie. The three girls, Flopsy, Mopsy, and Cotton-tail, obediently go to gather blackberries, but her son, Peter, immediately crawls under Mr. McGregor's gate. Wandering about the garden, he eats so much that he gets sick. Peter's naughtiness nearly costs him his life when Mr. McGregor sees him and gives chase. Frightened, Peter rushes about and soon loses both shoes. Caught in a gooseberry net, Peter nearly gives up hope of escape. Encouraged by sparrows, he wiggles out of his jacket and narrowly escapes a sieve that Mr. McGregor tries to put over him. Peter, now without clothes, hides in a watering can in the tool shed. Mr. McGregor finds Peter when he sneezes, but Peter escapes out a window. Peter cries when he is unable to find the gate. Resuming his search for the exit, he carefully avoids a cat at the goldfish pond. Finally, he sees both Mr. McGregor and the gate beyond. He dashes for it and escapes. Mr. McGregor uses Peter's clothing to make a scarecrow. When Peter's mother sees that her son has lost his second jacket and pair of shoes in two weeks, she puts the exhausted Peter to bed and gives him a dose of camomile tea. His sisters, however, enjoy a supper of bread, milk, and blackberries.

CHARACTERS: This simple tale keeps a tight focus on the central character and provides no description of the thoughts or feelings of the minor characters. Dressed in his blue jacket with brass buttons, **Peter Rabbit** is one of the most familiar of all characters in children's literature. As the first three pictures indicate, Peter literally stands apart from his sisters. One reason may be that he is the only boy in the family. A more likely reason, however, is that he is not as well-behaved or as socialized as they are. Thus, when his mother issues warnings about the dangers of Mr. McGregor's garden and hands his sisters baskets, Peter stands with his back to her. Quite evidently he has no interest in doing boring work or in listening to restrictions on his freedom. Peter shows that he is both naughty and daring when he immediately enters the garden. His first actions inside show that he is also selfish and greedy. While his sisters and mother are gathering food for the family, he becomes sick by stuffing himself.

Once Mr. McGregor sees him, Peter's subsequent adventures test his character. At first, he displays a dangerous immaturity when, in a panic, he forgets the way back to the gate. Later, he almost gives into despair when he is caught in the gooseberry net. Only the encouragement of the sparrows (birds are archetypal symbols of spiritual or psychological powers) enables him to escape. Peter's panic strips him of his clothes and his foolish bravado. He becomes completely an animal and even runs on four feet. After hiding in the can of water, Peter begins to change. At first, he shows signs of despair, crying when a mouse will not give him directions, but Peter quickly assumes responsibility for his own survival and resumes his search for the gate. When he becomes confused during his search, he shows some wisdom in cautiously avoiding the cat and going back to the tool shed. By the story's end, he shows more self-control. Instead of panicking when he sees Mr. McGregor a second time, he quietly but swiftly makes his way to the gate. Even though his

mother punishes him, Peter is successful in passing a kind of initiation: he has survived in the very place where his father failed.

Flopsy, Mopsy, and **Cotton-tail**, Peter's sisters, wear red cloaks that distinguish them from Peter. As "good little bunnies" who pay attention to their mother and gather food for supper, they serve as foils. Through their obedience and consideration, they emphasize Peter's dangerously selfish naughtiness. **Mrs. Rabbit**, Peter's widowed mother, obviously understands her son. In the third picture, her daughters are already past the landing when she grasps Peter firmly by the collar, compelling his attention while issuing her warning not to get into mischief. In the end, she shows both her love and exasperation. She treats the sick Peter with camomile tea, and she punishes him by sending him to bed without supper.

The Tailor of Gloucester

(picture book, private edition, 1902; revised edition, 1903)

PLOT: Inspired by a legend Potter heard about an actual tailor in Gloucester, this story is a fairy tale reminiscent of "The Shoemaker and the Elves" collected by the Brothers Grimm. Both stories tell how magic intervenes to save impoverished but worthy craftsmen from ruin. The old Tailor of Gloucester has a commission for a coat and waistcoat for the mayor's wedding on Christmas day. Knowing that he does not have enough thread to finish his projects, he sends his cat, Simpkin, with the last of his money to buy food and twist. While the cat is away, the Tailor hears sounds and frees the mice that Simpkin has trapped under overturned teacups. When Simpkin returns and discovers that the Tailor has freed his supper, he hides the thread. The old man, fatigued and worried to the point of illness, goes to bed. Over the next three days, the mice go to work to finish the coat and waistcoat. On Christmas Eve, when animals can talk, Simpkin goes out and hears the mice joyfully at work in the shop. They close the shutters on him. The next morning, Simpkin feels repentant and presents the Tailor with the thread. They go to his shop to find that the commission has been completed, except for one button hole. A tiny note on the coat says, "No more twist." The Tailor uses his thread to finish the coat. He then becomes prosperous and is noted for button-hole stitches that are so small "they looked as if they had been made by little mice!"

CHARACTERS: This story is unusual in that its animal characters fit uneasily somewhere between those in realistic and conventional talking animal fantasies. The unnamed **Tailor of Gloucester** was inspired by an actual tailor named Prichard, who advertised that his waistcoats were made at night by fairies. A little old man in spectacles, he has a pinched face and crooked fingers, both of which signal years of hard work and poverty. He is obsessed with his commission, which he knows can be the making of his fortune, and talks about it constantly to himself. Although he worries about being fair to Simpkin, it is clear that he is a kind man who does the right thing when he frees the mice. By doing so, he earns the reward of their help. His kindness leads to the fulfilling of his dreams, and he becomes stout and wealthy.

Simpkin the cat is a strange character. He can't talk and doesn't wear clothes about the house, yet the Tailor gives him money to go shopping. He is clearly both a pet and a domestic helper who can serve tea. In any case, Simpkin is foolishly vindictive when he discovers that the Tailor freed the mice. By hiding the thread, he risks ruining the Tailor, and himself in the bargain. He does have good qualities, however, and he becomes ashamed of himself when he thinks about how kind the mice are to his master. The **mice** also fit somewhere between human and animal characters. They can't talk, except on Christmas, yet they wear old-fashioned clothing at all times. They are generous in rewarding the Tailor for freeing them. As in many folk tales, they represent

goodness, bringing success to those who have been kind to the world's creatures.

The Tale of Squirrel Nutkin
(picture book, 1903)

PLOT: Like a typical folk tale, this story consists of repeated episodes that build in intensity to a violent resolution. Nutkin and his brother, Twinkleberry, are red squirrels who live with their cousins on the edge of a lake. In the autumn, all the squirrels sail to an island in the middle of the lake. Twinkleberry and the other squirrels give Old Brown, the owl who rules the island, a gift of three fat mice and politely ask him for permission to gather nuts. Nutkin, however, impertinently bobs about asking an old riddle. The owl pays no attention. Similar events occur on each of the following days, with Twinkleberry and his cousins bringing gifts and Nutkin being progressively more impertinent. On their sixth visit, Nutkin tells three riddles that taunt the owl by implying that he is powerless. He concludes by jumping on Old Brown's head. Outraged, the owl intends to skin Nutkin, but Nutkin pulls away so hard that he snaps off his tail and escapes. Now, when Nutkin is asked to tell a riddle, he becomes angry and makes a chattering squirrel sound.

CHARACTERS: Although this is in some ways a *pourquoi* tale that explains the chattering of red squirrels, as well as a simple narrative device for introducing children of the day to a series of familiar riddles, its characters are symbolically suggestive.

Nutkin, the impertinent red squirrel, represents a youthful mocking of authority and tradition. In traditional stories, a riddling contest tested the wit of the opponents and symbolically functioned as a ceremonial initiation. Knowing answers, that is, suggested that one deserved full membership, especially in an adult religious group. In this case, Nutkin is arrogant in riddling the owl. For one thing, all of his riddles are well known, so he is not particularly witty in devising them. (Incidentally, contrary to what some commentators have said, the riddles should not be obscure to Americans. Potter places the answer in italics near the riddle. Furthermore, Nutkin often pantomimes the answer. On the first trip, for instance, he bobs like a *cherry*, acting out the answer to his riddle.) Nutkin becomes so obsessed with taunting the owl that he neglects work. He demonstrates both naivete and foolishness when he jumps on the owl. Quite clearly, he has mistaken inaction for the inability to act. Only luck allows him to survive. Obviously marked by his experiences for the rest of his days, he seems to gain some maturity because afterwards he angrily rejects invitations to riddle.

Twinkleberry, Nutkin's brother, is more of a named representative of the obedient squirrels than an individual. He displays due respect for authority, wariness of offending those in power, and dedication to the practical tasks of gathering food. **Old Brown**, the owl, is a god figure who represents authority and power. He is tolerant of the disrespect and foolishness of youth. Repeatedly, he ignores Nutkin or moves out of range of his taunting, rather than exert his power against him. But when he is provoked to the point of being humiliated, he shows that inaction does not necessarily mean inability. He may not, as Nutkin riddles, have the power to catch the wind, but he does have the power to catch Nutkin.

The Tale of Benjamin Bunny

(picture book, 1904)

PLOT: In this sequel to *The Tale of Peter Rabbit*, Peter accompanies Benjamin Bunny, his cousin, on another trip to Mr. McGregor's garden. Having lost his clothes in his earlier adventure, Peter wears a red pocket handkerchief. Benjamin has seen Mr. and Mrs. McGregor driving away for the day, so the two of them climb to the top of the wall and down a pear tree to get Peter's clothes from the scarecrow. After retrieving the clothes, Benjamin munches on lettuces and gathers onions as a present for his aunt. Nervous throughout his stay in the garden, Peter twice drops the parcel of onions. On their way to the gate, they discover the cat blocking their way. They hide under a basket, but the cat gets on top and sits there for five hours. Eventually, old Mr. Benjamin Bunny passes along the garden wall. He jumps down and chases the surprised cat into the greenhouse. He frees the boys, whips them, and marches them out of the garden. Peter's mother readily forgives him, however, because she is pleased that he recovered his clothes.

Both Benjamin Bunny and Peter Rabbit appear as adults in The Tale of the Flopsy Bunnies *(1909) and* The Tale of Mr. Tod *(1912).*

CHARACTERS: Full appreciation of the contrast between the two central characters requires knowledge of events in *The Tale of Peter Rabbit*. **Benjamin Bunny**, Peter's cousin, seems more mature and competent than Peter. As the one who initiates the quest for Peter's clothes, he is Peter's mentor. He points out that squeezing under gates, as Peter did in the earlier volume, spoils a person's clothing. Therefore, he teaches Peter the "proper" way of getting into gardens. Later, he explains to Peter that they must exit a different way because they are loaded down with onions. Unlike Peter, he knows his way about the garden. Accustomed to accompanying his father there to gather lettuces for Sunday dinner, Benjamin remains calm throughout the initial stages of their adventure. He even suggests that they gather onions for Peter's mother, turning their adventure in a forbidden place into a productive quest for food. Benjamin thus shows both generosity and a cunning understanding of how to avoid trouble with adults. Benjamin's only sign of immaturity, one that requires adult intervention, comes when he hastily hides under the basket. Doing so makes adult intervention necessary if his quest in the garden is to end successfully.

Peter Rabbit begins feeling poorly, sitting by himself. Dressed only in a pocket handkerchief, Peter lacks a sense of dignity that he can restore only by retrieving his clothing. Throughout his stay in the garden, Peter shows that he now recognizes the danger of the place. Unlike Benjamin, he is nervous. He drops the onions twice, suggesting that he is not yet a competent food gatherer. Although old Benjamin Bunny punishes him, Peter achieves a reward for this journey into the garden: his mother forgives him because he recovered his clothes. In the book's last picture, Peter is once again a happy part of the family as he helps his sister Cotton-tail fold the handkerchief. Old **Mr. Benjamin Bunny** serves as a *deus ex machina*, a convenient device for extricating the boys from their dangerous adventure. Nevertheless, he demonstrates adult competence and bravery by imprisoning the cat that frightened the boys. He also shows loving anger by whipping the boys for foolishly imperiling themselves.

The Tale of Two Bad Mice

(picture book, 1904)

PLOT: This story is unusual for two reasons. First, it is a doll story that moves away from the expected animation of the dolls to consider the imagination of the girl who owns them. Second, it proceeds beyond an announced conclusion to provide details that add significant character traits. The story begins when the dolls Lucinda and her cook, Jane, go out for a ride in a perambulator. Two mice, Tom Thumb and his wife, Hunca Munca, enter their house while they are gone. When they discover that all the beautiful food is only plaster, they become angry and begin to destroy everything. Hunca Munca, however, soon realizes she could use many of the things in the doll

house. Therefore, they carry off whatever fits through their mouse hole. Upon returning to their vandalized home, Lucinda and Jane, being dolls, can say nothing. Their owner, however, decides to get a doll dressed like a policeman, and the nurse sets out mouse traps. The story continues past its announced ending to indicate that the two Bad Mice place a crooked sixpence in the stockings of Lucinda and Jane and that Hunca Munca comes early every morning to sweep out the house.

CHARACTERS: This story makes unusual use of three groups of characters. The mice are active, and the reader is given insight into their characters. The dolls are described as if they are alive, but the pictures clearly indicate that they never become human. The humans are never seen, but we hear them and can judge the consequences of their actions.

The two bad mice of the title actually become lovable during the course of the story. **Tom Thumb** is especially violent when he is frustrated in his quest for food. He is the leader in the destruction of the doll house. **Hunca Munca**, his wife, shares his anger, but she quickly brings it under control because she has "a frugal mind." Thus she realizes that many of the things in the house can serve useful purposes in their own home. Both seem to be good parents who lead a comfortably domestic life beneath the floorboards. Hunca Munca is pictured showing one of her children the policeman, and the two parents are shown together while Tom Thumb lectures his offspring on the dangers of the mousetrap.

Lucinda and **Jane**, the dolls, are only characters in a limited sense. The narrator talks about them as if they were alive, but it becomes clear near the end of the story that they are alive only because their owner imagines them to be. Their stiff inability to use the items in the doll house makes the mice's theft of these items charming and acceptable. So does their inability to express any reaction to the theft. At the same time, their silence highlights the differing reactions of the humans. The **girl** naively imagines that a policeman doll will reestablish order. The picture of Hunca Munca holding a baby up to see the policeman shows, however, that such a device cannot keep the mice away from the doll house. The **nurse** resorts to the pragmatic approach of a trap, but the picture of Tom Thumb pointing to the trap while lecturing his children indicates that she, too, will fail to drive away the mice. The failures of the humans thus highlight the bravery and wit of the mice.

The Tale of Jemima Puddle-Duck

(picture book, 1908)

PLOT: *The Tale of Jemima Puddle-Duck* alternates between realistic scenes of Potter's own Hill Top Farm at Near Sawrey and the fairy tale world of "Little Red Riding Hood." The story begins with Jemima Puddle-duck determined to hatch her own eggs, in spite of the warning of Rebeccah Puddle-duck, her sister-in-law, that she wouldn't be able to keep them warm. Jemima hides them, but they are always found and removed. One spring day, therefore, Jemima puts on her poke bonnet and shawl and flies away. Entering the fairy tale world, she meets the elegantly dressed "gentleman with sandy whiskers." Impressed by his appearance and not realizing that he is obviously a fox, she explains that she is searching for a place to lay her eggs. He offers to let her use a shed at his house. Jemima finds it so full of feathers that she almost suffocates, but she decides to make her nest there anyway. Jemima returns every day and lays nine eggs in her nest. When she tells the gentleman that she is going to begin the serious business of sitting on them until they hatch, he suggests that they have a dinner party first. He says he will make an omelet and instructs her to bring onions, sage, and other herbs. Jemima gathers the herbs, but while she is bringing onions to the kitchen, Kep, the collie, questions her about her absences and her reasons for taking the onions.

A foolish duck is outwitted by the "gentleman with the sandy whiskers" in Potter's self-illustrated The Tale of Jemima Puddle-Duck.

Jemima returns to the gentleman's house, where she soon hears sounds outside. Kep and two fox-hound puppies chase away the gentleman, who is never again seen. Unfortunately, Kep is not fast enough to stop the puppies from eating Jemima's eggs. They then lead the tearful Jemima home. In June, she is permitted to keep a new batch of eggs, but she manages to hatch only four. She blames her failure on nerves, but the narrator concludes that she has always been a bad sitter.

CHARACTERS: Jemima Puddle-duck is based on one of Potter's own ducks, which always tried to hide its eggs. Jemima exists in two worlds. In the farm scenes, she is represented fairly realistically without clothes. In the beginning, she seems natural and even noble in her desire to hatch her own eggs. Once she puts on clothes and enters the fairy tale world, however, she becomes demonstrably foolish and incompetent. She does not, for example, recognize that the polite and handsome gentleman is a fox. Later, she can't figure out why the gentleman has so many feathers in his house. Most ominously, she proves she is, as the narrator says, "a simpleton": she does not understand that the gentleman requires eggs for the omelet he promises to make, and she does not understand that the onions and herbs he requests are the ingredients typically used for stuffing roast duck. When she returns to the realistic world of the farm, she gets her wish to sit on her eggs, but in spite of her claim of nerves, proves that Rebeccah Puddle-duck was correct about her lacking patience to sit on them properly.

The **"gentleman with the sandy whiskers"** is a classic trickster. He is never called a fox, although illustrations clearly indicate that he is one. Elegantly dressed, handsome, and civil, he is like the wolf in "Little Red Riding Hood": he carefully questions his naive victim in order to develop a plan that will reap the greatest reward. He drops his civil facade only after Jemima returns with the herbs and onions. Although the nervous Jemima does not understand the reason for his change of character, the picture, which shows the hounds nearby, and the text, which reports that the fox is sniffing the air, suggest that he has detected enemies and is eager to conclude his nasty business. Unlike the wolf in "Little Red Riding Hood," he suffers only in being deprived of his carefully planned meal and in being driven from the neighborhood.

Kep, the wise collie, protects Jemima by serving as the *deus ex machina*. He shows intelligence in questioning Jemima and resourcefulness in recruiting fox-hounds to help him rescue the duck. Although he is a hero who suffers wounds in the rescue, he is not perfect: he forgets that puppies are as likely as foxes to eat eggs.

Further Reading

Aldis, Dorothy Keeley. *Nothing Is Impossible: The Story of Beatrix Potter.* New York: Atheneum, 1969.

Berger, Laura Standley, ed. *Twentieth-Century Children's Writers.* 4th ed. Detroit: St. James, 1995.

Buchan, Elizabeth. *Beatrix Potter.* London: Hamish Hamilton, 1987.

Children's Literature Review. Vols. 1, 19. Detroit: Gale Research, 1976, 1990.

Collins, David R. *The Country Artist: A Story about Beatrix Potter.* Minneapolis: Carolrhoda Books, 1989.

Crouch, Marcus. *Beatrix Potter.* London: Bodley Head, 1960.

Eastman, Jackie F. "Beatrix Potter's *The Tale of Peter Rabbit:* A Small Masterpiece." In *Touchstones: Reflections on the Best in Children's Literature.* Vol. 3: *Picture Books.* Edited by Perry Nodelman, pp. 100-107. West Lafayette, IN: Children's Literature Association, 1989.

Haycraft, Howard, and Stanley J. Kunitz, eds. *The Junior Book of Authors.* 2nd ed. New York: H. W. Wilson, 1951.

Lane, Margaret. *The Magic Years of Beatrix Potter.* London: F. Warne, 1978.

———. *The Tale of Beatrix Potter: A Biography.* London: F. Warne, 1968.

Linder, Leslie. *A History of the Writings of Beatrix Potter.* London: F. Warne, 1971.

MacDonald, Ruth K. *Beatrix Potter.* Boston: Twayne, 1986.

Mayer, Ann Margaret. *The Two Worlds of Beatrix Potter.* Mankato, MN: Creative Education, 1974.

Sale, Roger. "Beatrix Potter." In *Fairy Tales and After: From Snow White to E. B. White.* Cambridge, MA: Harvard University Press, 1978.

Taylor, Judy. *Beatrix Potter: Artist, Storyteller, and Countrywoman.* London: F. Warne, 1986.

Yesterday's Authors of Books for Children. Vol. 1. Detroit: Gale Research, 1977.

Zaidman, Laura M., ed. *British Children's Writers, 1880-1914.* Vol. 141 of *Dictionary of Literary Biography.* Detroit: Gale Research, 1994.

Arthur Ransome

1884-1967, English journalist and author

Swallows and Amazons

(novel, 1930)

PLOT: Set in August 1929, *Swallows and Amazons* describes the adventures of children vacationing in England's Lake District. Part of its appeal lies in detailed descriptions of sailing, camping, and fishing. What makes it superior to other "holiday-

Ransom created this illustration of the Walker family for his book, Swallows and Amazons.

adventure" novels, however, is that it manages to be true to both the external and the imaginative lives of its protagonists. The adventures begin when Commander Walker, a naval officer, sends a telegram giving his children permission to camp alone on a small island: "BETTER DROWNED THAN DUFFERS IF NOT DUFFERS WONT DROWN." Leaving behind their baby sister, Vicky, and their mother, John, Susan, Titty, and Roger Walker sail away in their borrowed boat, the *Swallow*, and set up camp. Their mother brings additional supplies, but the children are basically left alone. When Nancy (Ruth) and Peggy Blackett sail by in the *Amazon*, the Walkers hear an explosion on a nearby houseboat. Later, naming themselves after their boats, the

"Swallows" form an alliance with the "Amazons": each will try to capture the other's boat. Then they will jointly wage war on the houseboat's owner, the girls' uncle, Jim Turner, whom they call Captain Flint.

Before beginning battle, the Swallows visit two charcoal burners, who ask them to warn Mr. Turner that some people may rob his boat. Returning to camp, the Swallows find a letter from Mr. Turner telling them to stay away from his boat. When John tries to deliver the warning, Mr. Turner refuses to believe that John didn't throw the firecracker that exploded on his boat, calls him a liar, and refuses to listen to his warning. The next day, the Swallows leave Titty behind and set out to capture the *Amazon* after dark. Mother visits Titty and plays Man Friday with her. That night, the Swallows fail to find the boat because the Amazons have sailed it to the island. Titty captures it and sails it away. Anchored in the dark, she overhears some men burying something that they stole from Mr. Turner's houseboat.

The Swallows now join the Amazons in their war against Captain Flint. When the girls, who have also set up camp on the island, tell Captain Flint that they threw the firecracker, he apologizes to John and agrees to a "war." The next afternoon, the children attack the houseboat, capture Captain Flint, make him walk the plank, and then join him for a feast. Implausibly, with one day left of their vacation, Titty finds the "treasure" stolen from the houseboat: the memoirs Mr. Turner was writing. On their final night, a storm knocks down the tents of the Swallows. The next morning, after promising to have more adventures next year, the children leave.

The series continues with Swallowdale *(1931),* Winter Holiday *(1933),* Pigeon Post *(1936),* We Didn't Mean to Go to Sea *(1937),* Secret Water *(1939),* The Picts and the Martyrs *(1943), and* Great Northern? *(1947).*

CHARACTERS: Although Ransome based the Walkers on the five children of Dora and Ernest Altounyan, grandchildren of his friend, W. G. Collingwood, they display Ransome's own characteristics and enthusiasms. **John Walker**, the oldest of the Swallows, is serious, resolute in fulfilling duties, responsible in watching over his siblings, and thoroughly ethical. John obviously admires his father and tries to be worthy of his respect. Intent on proving that he is not inept (a duffer), John takes his father's books to the island to study nautical skills. He also takes pride in doing properly such things as rowing the "navy stroke" without splashing the oars. Because John has a highly developed sense of gentlemanly honor, he is deeply hurt when Mr. Turner calls him a liar, and he immediately confesses to his mother his

foolishness in taking the boat out at night. **Susan Walker**, the next oldest, is a conventional, pragmatic girl who delights in displaying domestic skills. Acting like a mother, she reminds the others of bedtime and does the cooking and cleaning. She shares John's moral rectitude: until John confesses to their mother about being out all night, she acts like a "native," the term the children assign to adults, and is unable to play at her role as *Swallow*'s mate.

The viewpoint and feelings of **Titty Walker** (Titty was the nickname of Mavis Altounyan) fuse the inner world of pirate adventure with the outer world of a holiday adventure. Romantically imaginative, Titty delights in acting out scenes from the adventure novels she takes to the island. She thus plays Robinson Crusoe to her mother's Man Friday. At times, Titty confuses fiction and life. Thoroughly believing, for instance, that Mr. Turner is a retired pirate who has treasure, she repeatedly suggests that they sink his boat. Titty enjoys being alone to indulge her fantasies and therefore responsibly fulfills her duties as lighthouse keeper when the others sail off. She also remains true to her own vision and understanding, searching for the stolen memoirs even after everyone else assumes that she is mistaken about hearing some men bury it. **Roger Walker**, who is seven, develops the least. He is eager to join the others on the island to prove that he is not a baby, and he obediently learns how to swim so that he will not be a duffer. For the most part, he mimics the responsible behavior of John, whom he admires. Chubby **Vicky Walker** (her name is **Bridget Walker**, as the reader learns in later books) received her nickname because she looks like the elderly Queen Victoria. She celebrates her second birthday on the island.

The two Amazons are only sketched. Showing a comical literal-mindedness, **Ruth Blackett** changed her name to **Nancy Blackett** after her uncle told her that Amazons were "ruthless." She is indeed ruthless in her hostility to Uncle Jim when he wants to be left alone to write his book. Resentful that he does not play with her as he once did, she bombs his boat with a firecracker and decides to raid and loot it whenever she can. A skilled sailor with the reputation of being a tomboy, she is daring and wily, sneaking away from home to attempt a nighttime capture of the *Swallow*. Nancy tries to act like a veteran sailor by using the bombastic nautical expressions of romance novels and by calling her sister colorful names. **Peggy Blackett**, her younger sister, chatters when she first meets the Swallows, but she has little individuality or personality in later scenes. She acts simply as Nancy's loyal subordinate.

Only two adults are important. **Mrs. Walker** is an exceptionally understanding mother, allowing her children independence but knowing when to draw a firm line. Thus, she forbids them to take medicines to the island, insists that the children watch Roger carefully, and ensures their safety by checking up on them. Mrs. Walker never talks down to her children and has a rare ability to teach without being preachy. Furthermore, because she appreciates the importance of play, she lovingly assumes the role of "native" in their imaginative world, even inventing native words to intensify their pleasure. Fat, balding **Jim Turner**, the Blackett girls' uncle, is called **Captain Flint** because he has a parrot and has traveled around the world. Because he is writing his memoirs and repeatedly claims that writing is the hardest work he has ever done, many critics maintain that he portrays Ransome himself. Regardless, Uncle Jim is an exuberant, colorful man of extremes. While working on his book, he becomes surly, completely shutting his nieces out of his life. Intemperate, he is overly hasty in blaming the Walkers for the firecracker and thoroughly rude in calling John a liar. Having learned the truth and having apologized for his error, however, he shows another side of his personality. Childish himself, he is aware of precisely what children desire. He therefore stages an elaborate battle, reconciling himself with the children by allowing them to gain victory, seize his boat, and punish him by making him walk the plank. Furthermore, he gives his parrot to Titty as her reward for finding his manuscript because he knows how hard it is to wait for something.

Further Reading

Berger, Laura Standley, ed. *Twentieth-Century Children's Writers*. 4th ed. Detroit: St. James, 1995.

Bingham, Jane M., ed. *Writers for Children: Critical Studies of Major Authors since the Seventeenth Century*. New York: Scribner's, 1988.

Brogan, Hugh. *The Life of Arthur Ransome*. London: J. Cape, 1984.

Children's Literature Review. Vol. 8. Detroit: Gale Research, 1985.

Collier, Laurie, and Joyce Nakamura, eds. *Major Authors and Illustrators for Children and Young Adults*. Detroit: Gale Research, 1993.

Contemporary Authors. Vols. 73-76. Detroit: Gale Research, 1978.

Hardyment, Christina. *Arthur Ransome and Captain Flint's Trunk*. London: J. Cape, 1984.

Hunt, Peter. *Arthur Ransome*. Boston: Twayne, 1991.

Kunitz, Stanley J., and Howard Haycraft, eds. *The Junior Book of Authors*. 2nd ed. New York: H. W. Wilson, 1951.

Ransome, Arthur. *The Autobiography of Arthur Ransome*. London: J. Cape, 1976.

Shelley, Hugh. *Arthur Ransome*. New York: H. Z. Walck, 1964.

Something about the Author. Vol. 22. Detroit: Gale Research, 1981.

Ellen Raskin

1924-1984, American artist, designer, illustrator, and author

The Westing Game

(novel, 1978)

PLOT: This Newbery Medal-winning "puzzle mystery" is based on an elaborate game in which sixteen people are assembled to find the name of a murderer, with the winner to become heir to a fortune. The real purpose of the game, and the theme of the novel, however, is self-discovery: the characters all change for the better.

The first part of the novel introduces the large cast of characters. All are selected by Barney Northrup to live in Sunset Towers. After the move, Tabitha-Ruth "Turtle" Wexler hears the doorman, Sandy McSouthers, tell a frightening story about someone who entered the Westing mansion. She bets that she can stay in the supposedly deserted house on Halloween. When she enters, she discovers the body of millionaire Samuel W. Westing and runs away in fear. Once the death is announced, all but two of the tenants receive notice that they are heirs and must come to the reading of Westing's will. Edgar Jennings Plum, a bumbling lawyer, reads the will, in which Sam Westing says that he was killed by one of the heirs. It also sets up the Westing game by grouping the heirs into pairs, each of which is given $10,000 and a set of clues. The parings are: Dr. Jake Wexler and Madame Sun Lin Hoo, Turtle Wexler and Flora Baumbach, Christos Theodorakis and Dr. D. Denton Deere, Sandy (Alexander) McSouthers and Judge Josie-Jo Ford, Grace Windsor Wexler and James Shin Hoo, Berthe Erica Crow and Otis Amber, Theo Theodorakis and Doug Hoo, and Sydelle Pulaski and Angela Wexler.

The major portion of the novel records the intricate efforts of the players to solve their clues. During this process, they learn more about each other and their connections to Westing. On three occasions when the players meet, bombs go off; the third explosion scars the beautiful Angela. Turtle, her younger sister, knows that Angela resents being pushed into a marriage with Dr. Deere. Angela has therefore become a mad bomber as a protest against her domineering mother. To protect Angela, Turtle sets off a bomb in the elevator. When she is caught, she confesses to all the bombings. The climax of the novel comes when the players are assembled to give their solution to the game. When the players are told that all their answers are wrong, Judge Ford realizes that Sandy McSouthers is actually Westing. Sandy dies, however, and Berthe Erica Crow, who was once married to Westing and drove their daughter to suicide by pushing her toward an inappropriate marriage, confesses and claims the prize. Turtle continues the game, however, by holding a court session in which she interrogates the other players. As a result, she solves the mystery, but doesn't tell

anyone about it. The next day, she rides out to the home of the president of Westing Paper, Julian R. Eastman. Turtle has realized that Eastman is the fourth and final identity of Windy Windkloppel, who became Samuel W. Westing, Barney Northrup, and Sandy (Alexander) McSouthers. The last two chapters trace the fates of the various players over the next decade, concluding with Turtle at Eastman's bedside when he really dies.

CHARACTERS: The sixteen major characters (the number on one side in a chess game) are varied in age, gender, class, and race. Raskin said they are "imperfect, each handicapped by some physical, emotional, or moral defect."

Samuel W. Westing, born **Sam "Windy" Windkloppel**, is an immigrant's son who achieved the American dream of financial success. Consequently, he is very patriotic. He loves the Fourth of July, for example, and he disguises himself in patriotic costumes. He also uses words from "America the Beautiful" as clues in the game. Nevertheless, Sam has a darker side. He lost interest in his daughter, Violet, when he learned she didn't want to take over his business. As a result, Violet was dominated by her mother and committed suicide rather than marry the man her mother chose for her. Westing disappeared after a car accident. His photographs show a man with a nose beaked like a turtle's (a clue to his relationship to Turtle Wexler). He also was a gamesman who used chess to teach lessons about life. As **Barney Northrup**, he appears as a salesman with slicked black hair, a black mustache, and buck teeth. Ironically, Northrop, who lies to get his tenants into Sunset Towers, benefits each. Westing thus uses this identity to undo the harm he did as an entrepreneur. As **Sandy (Alexander) McSouthers**, a sixty-five-year-old doorman, he attributes his broken nose and chipped tooth to his years as a boxer. Sandy pretends to be a drinker, but he actually has medicine in his flask. Sandy represents the victims of Westing's climb up the ladder, complaining that Westing fired him for organizing a union. He thereby keeps the negative side of success prominent. As **Julian R. Eastman**, the current chairman of his company, Westing gives himself another chance at being successful in both business and personal relationships, welcoming Turtle as his heir.

Jake Wexler, a forty-five-year old Jewish podiatrist with thinning, light brown hair, is actually a small-time bookie. He seems unable to control his domineering wife, but his encouragement allows Angela to make the final break from her mother's influence. Jake is the only one to take an interest in Madame Hoo and begins to teach her English. Because of the game, he regains the respect of his wife, and he becomes an official with the State Gambling Commission. His partner, twenty-eight-year-old **Sun Lin Hoo**, becomes an individual because of the game. Initially, she did not speak English and stole things so that she could earn money to go to China. She comes alive after Jake treats her like an individual. She does go to China after her husband dies, but she returns to America to run their business.

Turtle Wexler, whose given name is Tabitha-Ruth, first appears as a thirteen-year-old brat who kicks anyone who touches her long braid. She is not pretty like Angela, her sister, and is therefore neglected by her mother. She fills the emotional void by adopting the name "Alice" and by calling Mrs. Baumbach "Baba" (grandmother). Turtle is interested in finances. She uses the dare about entering the Westing mansion to earn money for a subscription to the *Wall Street Journal*, and she uses the money given to her for entering the game to buy stocks. Turtle becomes heroic when she takes the blame for the bombings. She has a fierce desire to win the game, and she shows her intelligence by solving the puzzle. In later years, she earns a master's degree in business administration and an advanced degree in corporate law. She remains friends with Westing (as Eastman) until his death. Significantly, she finally beats him in chess on the night before he dies, a symbol that she is ready to take his place. Turtle's partner, sixty-year-old **Flora Baumbach**, is a short, rotund dressmaker who always has a peculiar smile. She devoted herself to her retarded daughter and thereby teaches Turtle that she doesn't have to be

beautiful to be loved. Flora later moves in with Turtle, who fills the empty space left by her dead daughter.

Fifteen-year-old **Christos Theodorakis** was afflicted four years earlier with a disease that confines him to a wheelchair. Unable to communicate easily, he is delighted by the game because it gives him contact with other people. Thus, he initially refuses to sign his check so that Dr. Deere will have to visit him again. Chris is intelligent, and his understanding of events focuses the theme of the game. For example, he points out that Westing gave everybody the perfect partner for making friends. A bird watcher as a boy, Chris grows up to be a professor of ornithology. His partner, **Dr. D. Denton Deere**, is a twenty-five-year-old plastic surgery intern. His medical specialty symbolizes his superficiality. He is always in a hurry and tries to impress others by making up diagnoses. Although he initially resents being paired with Chris, he becomes humanized by the contact and arranges for Chris to receive treatment that controls his seizures. After Angela Wexler breaks off their engagement, he becomes a neurologist. He eventually marries Angela.

Judge Josie-Jo Ford is a tall forty-two-year-old black woman whose short-clipped hair shows a touch of gray. Her mother and father were servants at the Westing mansion. Westing taught her to play chess, saw her intelligence, and financed her way through university. She became distrustful, however, assuming that Westing would try to use her position to benefit himself. As a result, she is a severe, pitiless woman, who considers smiling to be demeaning. Once in the game, she unwittingly pays her financial debt to Westing by signing her checks over to her partner, Sandy McSouthers. She shows moral growth by financing Chris's education. She eventually becomes a justice of the Supreme Court.

Theo Theodorakis is a dark, broad-shouldered, slim-wasted seventeen-year-old high school senior. He defines himself as a brother because he spends his spare time caring for Chris. He has a gift for telling stories and eventually becomes a novelist after he marries Turtle. His eighteen-year-old partner, **Doug Hoo**, is a runner who goes on to win two Olympic medals and becomes a sports broadcaster.

Grace Windsor Wexler is a forty-two-year-old honey blond whose real maiden name was Grace Windkloppel. She is pretentious, claiming to be an interior decorator but never actually working at it. She is also bigoted, something both Judge Ford and Mr. Hoo sense. A domineering social climber, she bullies Angela into an engagement with Dr. Deere. The Westing Game, however, transforms her. She learns that she has genuine talent in running a restaurant, and she rediscovers her love for her husband. She eventually buys a chain of Chinese restaurants. **James Shin Hoo**, Grace's partner, is a fifty-year-old owner of a failing restaurant. He constantly eats chocolate bars and therefore has a protruding stomach. Mr. Hoo is bitter because Westing stole his idea for paper diapers. The game restores his image of himself because Sandy inspires him to invent paper inner soles. He becomes a successful businessman before his death.

Berthe Erica Crow, a fifty-seven-year-old cleaning woman, is actually Westing's divorced wife, the woman who drove her daughter to suicide. Crow, who has dead-white skin and dresses in black, looks like she has had a hard life. She has apparently sought atonement for her treatment of her daughter by founding a soup kitchen for the poor, but she has also become a religious fanatic. Perceiving Angela's resemblance to her daughter, she comes close to exacting revenge on Mr. Hoo, whom she at first blames for the bombings that resulted in Angela's injury. Because she drove their daughter to her death, she also symbolically killed Westing. The game forces her to admit her guilt, although her confession becomes merely one of Westing's ploys to mislead the players in the game. Crow soon marries her partner, **Otis Amber**. Otis, who has a long, thin face, pointed chin, and gray stubble, pretends to be a simple-minded sixty-two-year-old delivery boy. As part of his ruse, he wears a leather aviator's helmet and scares other players by shouting "Boom." In fact, Otis is a private detective hired by Westing to watch Crow. Having come to love her, he decides to work in the soup kitchen with her.

Fifty-year-old **Sydelle Pulaski** enters the game by mistake. She is a wide-hipped, unattractive secretary with a garish sense of style. She is so desperately lonely and eager to be noticed that she begins using gaudily painted crutches and claims to have a disease. Ironically, people think that she is wealthy when the game ends, and she marries her boss. She also becomes the lifelong friend of her partner, twenty-year-old **Angela Wexler**. Angela is a beautiful, fair-skinned blond who is timidly obedient to her mother. She is engaged to Dr. Deere, but the rash on her finger and her habit of leaving her ring in the bathroom suggest that she does not want to get married. She becomes so upset at being treated as only a face, a thing defined only by her relationship to Dr. Deere, that she becomes the mad bomber. When Turtle gets too close to an explosive hidden in a shower gift, Angela tilts the package and is thus scarred herself. She refuses to have plastic surgery afterwards because the scar signals that she has become a fallible human instead of an impossibly perfect angel. Angela becomes a lifelong friend to Sydelle. She even tells her that the doctors have said that Sydelle has a disease so that the attention-starved secretary won't be embarrassed by her previous attempts to be noticed. Because she gains an independent identity, Angela gives back Dr. Deere's ring and returns to school. She becomes an orthopedic surgeon, marries Dr. Deere, and has a daughter named Alice (the name Turtle used with Mrs. Baumbach).

Further Reading

Berger, Laura Standley, ed. *Twentieth-Century Young Adult Writers.* 1st ed. Detroit: St. James, 1994.

Children's Literature Review. Vols. 1, 12. Detroit: Gale Research, 1976, 1987.

Collier, Laurie, and Joyce Nakamura, eds. *Major Authors and Illustrators for Children and Young Adults.* Detroit: Gale Research, 1993.

Contemporary Authors New Revision Series. Vol. 37. Detroit: Gale Research, 1992.

De Montreville, Doris, and Donna Hill, eds. *Third Book of Junior Authors.* New York: H. W. Wilson, 1972.

Estes, Glenn E., ed. *American Writers for Children since 1960: Fiction.* Vol. 52 of *Dictionary of Literary Biography.* Detroit: Gale Research, 1986.

Olson, Marilynn Strasser. *Ellen Raskin*. Boston: Twayne, 1991.

Something about the Author. Vols. 2, 38. Detroit: Gale Research, 1971, 1985.

Lynne Reid Banks

1929-, English author

The Indian in the Cupboard

(fantasy, 1980)

PLOT: The theme of this toy fantasy is the need to respect the humanity of others. Many critics complain, however, that its plot subverts this theme by reinforcing racial stereotypes and imperialistic attitudes. On his birthday, Omri receives a plastic figure of an American Indian from his friend Patrick and a discarded medicine cupboard from his brother Gillon. When Omri puts the Indian in the cupboard and locks it with an old key given to him by his mother, the toy is transformed into a three-inch high Indian named Little Bear. Using the magic cupboard, Omri provides a horse and then a World War I medic, Tommy Atkins, to treat a wound caused by the horse. The next toy transforms into an old Indian chief. When he dies, Little Bear takes his headdress and proclaims himself chief. When he learns Omri's secret, Patrick demands that he put a toy cowboy in the cupboard; it comes to life as an Indian-hater named Boone.

Patrick's next demand, that Omri bring Boone and Little Bear to school, nearly causes disaster, especially when Patrick shows them to Mr. Johnson, the headmaster. Fortunately, the headmaster doesn't believe his eyes. Omri then lets Boone draw a minuscule picture that he passes off as his own. After school, Omri is accused of shoplifting a toy Indian woman, but Patrick vouches for his honesty. Patrick also helps Omri when his brother Adiel hides the cupboard. After retrieving the cupboard, Omri is unable to transform the Indian woman because the key is lost. That evening while the boys, Little Bear, and Boone watch a television western, Boone's racist comments anger Little Bear, who shoots him

Omri makes an amazing discovery in Reid Banks's **The Indian in the Cupboard,** *illustrated by Brock Cole.*

with an arrow. To save Boone, Little Bear goes beneath the floorboards to find the key, narrowly escaping Gillon's pet rat. Omri then brings Tommy back to treat Boone and transforms the toy woman into Bright Stars, a wife for Little Bear. Boone and Little Bear now become blood brothers. After also becoming Little Bear's blood brother, Omri sends the little people back home and gives the key to his mother for safekeeping.

The Return of the Indian *(1987) and* The Secret of the Indian *(1989) are sequels.*

CHARACTERS: Omri is kind and sensitive. He spares Patrick's feelings by concealing his disappointment at the gift of a second-hand toy Indian. Furthermore, although he enjoys keeping secrets, he tells Patrick about the magic cupboard so that they can continue as friends. Omri is a good judge of character. His recognition that Patrick is unfit to care for the little people because he uses them illustrates the theme of respecting others in spite of differences. Omri also knows that Patrick will tell their secret if he doesn't get his way, so he gives in and brings Little Bear and Boone to school. Although Omri himself uses Boone to create fun during art class, he respects the cowboy and the Indian, and he understands their feelings. In addition, he tries to promote respect by pointing out that Boone is dirtier than the "dirty savages" he detests.

Because he is a gigantic child with authority over an adult from another culture, Omri symbolizes an imperial power that feeds, shelters, and protects the Indian. Tones of adult authority establish Omri's superiority: like his mother, Omri warns Little Bear not to wander off and tells him to eat his dinner; in his father's voice, he demands an end to a fight with Boone; like the headmaster, he compels Little Bear to obey his command to see if Boone has been killed. Such imperial and paternalistic overtones may water down the theme of acceptance, but they do not negate Omri's significant qualities as an individual. He is kind, generous, and clever. He shows such qualities by sending the little people back to their own times and by ensuring that Little Bear and Bright Stars will remain together during their magic journey. Finally, Omri shows responsibility and maturity by giving the key to his mother so that he won't be easily tempted into magically asserting authority over others again.

Unlike Omri, **Patrick** changes. Initially selfish and insensitive, he foreshadows his lack of respect for others by admitting that he is giving Omri the toy Indian only because he has no use for it. Patrick becomes a major source of conflict because he places his own desires ahead of everything. Thus, he is willing to end their friendship if Omri doesn't share his secret. Worse, overcome with the desire of controlling the transformed toys, he recklessly threatens to tell the secret, thereby blackmailing Omri into bringing them to school. Patrick betrays Omri by showing the little people to the headmaster, but he does so because he fears that the headmaster will call his father. Patrick's transformation begins after

this betrayal, when he vouches that Omri is not a shoplifter. Shortly afterwards, Patrick again helps Omri by finding Adiel's shorts, thus regaining Omri's hidden cupboard. Patrick subsequently becomes more sensitive, even seeing things as the little people do. Although saddened by the necessity, the once possessive Patrick shows maturity and understanding by agreeing that the little people must go back to their homes.

Three-inch-high **Little Bear**, transported from the eighteenth century, has blue-black plaited hair and fierce, dark eyes. He wears a single feather in a headband, buckskin leggings, and a bandolier across his chest. His role is paradoxical. On one hand, by insisting that he is an Iroquois and lives in a longhouse, not a teepee, he escapes the generic stereotypes of Indians. Furthermore, he teaches Omri lessons about Indians by pointing out that whites introduced both scalping and the blood brother ceremony. Finally, he speaks of Indian victimization, blaming the white man for moving onto the land, using the water, and killing the animals. (There has been criticism that Little Bear speaks as if he were from the nineteenth century.) On the other hand, as an individual, Little Bear conforms to the stereotype. He barks, grunts, growls, or shouts in halting English. When upset, he becomes childishly petulant and adopts the stereotypical posture of a movie Indian, folding his arms across his chest and glowering silently. Full of self-importance, he callously grabs the dead chief's headdress to proclaim himself a chief. Little Bear also conforms to the stereotype of the savage because he is violent, twice stabbing Omri and nearly fatally shooting Boone. Furthermore, he superstitiously regards Omri as the Great White Spirit. Finally, although he constantly demands food and supplies, he is too rude to thank Omri for them.

As a diminutive native dependent on a powerful white person, Little Bear may symbolize the imperial subject. After he stomps on his headdress, thereby indicating that he is unworthy of being a chief, Little Bear performs generous acts and regains his status. First, he descends into the underworld beneath the floor to retrieve the key, a magic object necessary to save Boone. Although Little Bear's ignorance of the rat's presence limits his heroism, his act resembles the quests of mythic heroes, for it is a perilous journey undertaken to benefit another. Second, after he returns with the key, Little Bear becomes blood brother to both Boone and Omri. He thus makes peace with his former enemy, Boone, and finally signals his gratitude to and acceptance of Omri as his benefactor.

In his plaid shirt, buckskin trousers, high-heeled boots, and big hat, **Boone** is a stereotypical, late nineteenth-century cowboy. In keeping with this image, he is an alcoholic, speaks in a Texas drawl, and never bathes. Furthermore, he hates Indians, regarding them as dirty savages. Nevertheless, Boone has redeeming features. He claims to have tender feelings that make him cry at the slightest provocation, a tendency that has earned him the nickname Boohoo. Although alcoholism may be partially responsible for his tears, his artistic talent, which he shows by drawing in Omri's art class, suggests that he is sensitive beneath his coarse exterior. Still, Boone lacks tact, and he is foolishly provocative during the television western. After he is shot, he doesn't hold a grudge, declaring that violence is natural to an Indian. This bigoted statement shows that Boone believes that Indians are fundamentally different. Boone never acknowledges that cowboys and Indians share a common humanity, but after he becomes Little Bear's blood brother, he declares that he himself is now part Indian and that he will no longer say anything against Indians.

Tommy Atkins, a World War I medic, is a helper who treats both Little Bear and Boone. He is comical in believing his experiences are part of a battlefield dream, but he is also dedicated to duty, insisting that he doesn't want such dreams during an attack. **Adiel**, Omri's older brother, creates domestic conflict by blaming Omri for taking the soccer shorts that he himself mislaid. By losing the key when he vengefully hides the cupboard, he tests Omri's cleverness and Little Bear's compassion and courage. **Gillon**, Omri's other brother, gives him the medicine cupboard, which he found in the alley, because he has no money to buy a present. Careless about keeping his white rat caged, he unintentionally endangers Little Bear's life.

Further Reading

Authors and Artists for Young Adults. Vol. 6. Detroit: Gale Research, 1991.

Berger, Laura Standley, ed. *Twentieth-Century Young Adult Writers*. 1st ed. Detroit: St. James, 1994.

Children's Literature Review. Vol. 24. Detroit: Gale Research, 1991.

Collier, Laurie, and Joyce Nakamura, eds. *Major Authors and Illustrators for Children and Young Adults*. Detroit: Gale Research, 1993.

Contemporary Authors New Revision Series. Vol. 38. Detroit: Gale Research, 1993.

Contemporary Literary Criticism. Vol. 23. Detroit: Gale Research, 1983.

Holtze, Sally Holmes, ed *Sixth Book of Junior Authors and Illustrators*. New York: H. W. Wilson, 1989.

Something about the Author. Vols. 22, 75. Detroit: Gale Research, 1981, 1994.

H. A. Rey

(pen name for Hans Augusto Ryersbach)

1898-1977, American author and illustrator

Curious George

(picture book, 1941; published in England as Zozo)

PLOT: In this perennial favorite, the curiosity of George the monkey produces a series of fast-paced slapstick adventures. George's troubles begin when he sees a man place a big yellow hat on the ground. When George plays with the hat, he is captured. On the ship taking him from Africa, George tries to fly like the gulls. He falls overboard, and the sailors must rescue him. In the man's apartment, George plays with the telephone and accidentally dials the fire department. Discovering that they have responded to a false alarm, the angry firemen put George in jail. Because of a clumsy guard, George gets out of his cell and escapes from prison by walking along the telephone wires. When he then tries to snatch a balloon from a balloon vendor, he accidentally grabs the bunch. The balloons carry him high into the sky.

The lovable, ever-mischievous Curious George, as illustrated by the author, H. A. Rey.

He finally comes down on a traffic light, and the man with the yellow hat rescues him. After paying for the balloons, the man takes George to live at the zoo.

Sequels are Curious George Takes a Job *(1947),* Curious George Rides a Bike *(1952),* Curious George Gets a Medal *(1957),* Curious George Flies a Kite *(1958),* Curious George Learns the Alphabet *(1963), and* Curious George Goes to the Hospital *(1966).*

CHARACTERS: In this and the rest of the series, George dominates; other characters exist merely to incite his curiosity, to respond to his mischief, or to rescue him from trouble. **Curious George (Zozo** in Britain) is a young African monkey. Because he has an expressive face but lacks a tail, George is essentially a high-spirited child. The drawings in which he eats at a table, smokes a pipe after dinner, and wears pajamas reinforce the idea that he is a substitute human. Although he repeatedly gets into trouble, George is not deliberately mischievous. Like a child, he is perpetually curious. Curiosity leads to trouble because George lacks the knowledge and the self-

control that come from education and experience. George is unaware, for example, that monkeys can't fly, and he therefore falls off the boat while imitating the gulls. Similarly, he imitates the man's gestures with the telephone without understanding what he is doing and accidentally dials the fire department. Finally, like the little boy pictured with the balloon man, George reaches out for the brightly colored balloon he desires. (As an animal, he does not understand property rights or the necessity of paying for what he wants.) He releases the bunch by accident, probably because he doesn't understand how they are fastened. Much of George's appeal lies in the fact that his rule-breaking antics provide adventures, but his innocence ensures that adults, like the man in the big yellow hat, find him worthy of love, protection, and happiness.

As the illustrations show, **the man with the big yellow hat** dresses entirely in yellow. Throughout the series, his distinctive attire makes it possible to locate him at the climactic moment. When George is hanging on to the balloons and looking down on the city, for example, he appears in his car in the bottom right corner. The man is important because he functions as a surrogate parent. Thus, when the man is absent, George has the opportunity for trouble. Like a protective parent, however, the man always shows up to set things right for George. Thus, the man pays for the balloons, ensuring that George is not a thief, and then takes George to the zoo, where he will be safe and happy.

Further Reading

Berger, Laura Standley, ed. *Twentieth-Century Children's Writers.* 4th ed. Detroit: St. James, 1995.

Cech, John, ed. *American Writers for Children 1900-1960.* Vol. 22 of *Dictionary of Literary Biography.* Detroit: Gale Research, 1983.

Children's Literature Review. Vol. 5. Detroit: Gale Research, 1983.

Collier, Laurie, and Joyce Nakamura, eds. *Major Authors and Illustrators for Children and Young Adults.* Detroit: Gale Research, 1993.

Contemporary Authors New Revision Series. Vol. 6. Detroit: Gale Research, 1982.

Kunitz, Stanley J., and Howard Haycraft, eds. *The Junior Book of Authors.* 2nd ed. New York: H. W. Wilson, 1951.

Something about the Author. Vols. 1, 26, 69. Detroit: Gale Research, 1971, 1982, 1992.

Mordecai Richler

1931-, Canadian author

Jacob Two-Two Meets the Hooded Fang

(dream fantasy, 1975)

PLOT: The circular journey pattern of this satirical dream fantasy develops a theme about self-worth. Jacob Two-Two, the youngest of five children, is teased because he is incapable of doing some things well. Because Jacob feels rejected by everyone, his father sends him on an errand that will enable Jacob to prove that he is not too little to be useful. When Jacob, who has the habit of saying everything twice to gain attention, asks the greengrocer for tomatoes, Mr. Cooper threatens to have him arrested for insulting an adult. Jacob runs away, falls asleep, and has a dreams that he is on trial. His lawyer is the incompetent Louis Loser and the judge is Justice Rough, who gleefully sentences him to Children's Prison. Before Jacob is taken away, however, the superheroes of Child Power give him a supersonic bleeper. The intrepid Shapiro and the fearless O'Toole (roles his sister Emma and his brother Noah played when Jacob was awake) will use the bleeper to locate the prison and free the children.

At the prison on Slimer's Isle, however, Jacob faces two problems. First, a guard named Mr. Fox takes the bleeper, making Jacob feel that he is a failure. Later, Shapiro and O'Toole capture Mr. Fox while he is sabotaging a toy store. Because he tells them that Jacob is dead, Jacob must depend on himself if he is to be saved. Jacob's second problem is the warden, the Hooded Fang, who tries to make Jacob fear him. Jacob sees that the Fang is not really cruel, however. By resisting the Fang's efforts to make him give up his identity as a Two-Two who

Jacob Two-Two slaves away in the children's prison in a scene from Richler's Jacob Two-Two Meets the Hooded Fang, *illustrated by Fritz Wegner.*

says everything twice, Jacob gains confidence. He bribes the Fang into sending a letter to Shapiro and O'Toole, which gives them the information they need to capture Mr. Fox and force him to lead them to the prison. For his part, Jacob organizes the prisoners into a revolt. They turn off the fog machines, which protect the child-hating adults from the sun. With the help of Shapiro and O'Toole, the children defeat the guards. Jacob then exposes the Fang as a childish adult. At this point, Jacob is awakened by his father. That night, in an act that signals acceptance of his identity, Jacob Two-Two receives a uniform with two Child Power logos on it.

Jacob Two-Two and the Dinosaur *(1987) and* Jacob Two-Two's First Spy Case *(1995) are sequels.*

CHARACTERS: The characters are satiric caricatures who expose a child's feelings that adult attitudes to children are unfair. **Jacob Two-Two** has received his name because he repeats everything in order to be noticed. He is only six years old, so he can't do some of the things that his brothers and sisters do, such as ride a bicycle or slice bread properly. Because they tease him and insist that he is too little to be with them, Jacob Two-Two feels inadequate. He tries to overcome this feeling by asking for an errand, an age-appropriate version of the heroic quest. When he runs away from Mr. Cooper's teasing, however, he fails this test. His dream therefore provides him with another opportunity to display competence. In the dream, Jacob transforms the things that frightened him in the waking world and overcomes them. The Children's Prison, for example, is based on the stories Noah told him about punishment cells at school, and the Hooded Fang is based on a scary wrestler he saw on television. Jacob proves his independence and competence by devising the rescue plan. Furthermore, his identity as a Two-Two, which led to his trouble with Mr. Cooper in the waking world, becomes a source of strength. By refusing to use a number other than two in spite of the Fang's threats to feed him to the sharks, Jacob proves that he is stronger than the Fang. Jacob also shows that he is smarter by recognizing that the Fang is not so scary and by forcing the Fang to help him. Jacob apparently carries his newfound confidence into his waking life. He may, however, only be dreaming that his brother and sister accept him: the unique Child Power uniform he receives has a real cape, not the towel that Noah and Emma wore in the waking world.

Jacob's enemies are satirical portraits of adults. **Mr. Cooper**, the greengrocer, reveals two sides to his personality, as do most adults in the novel. He is pleasant to children when their parents are around, but he bullies them when they are alone. He delights in showing the superiority of adults by teasing Jacob. Jacob overcomes his fear of the grocer by projecting Mr. Cooper's teasing ways onto the Hooded Fang. **The Hooded Fang** is based on a television wrestler who frightened Jacob when he was awake. The Fang claims to resent children because one laughed at him during a match. He says things to frighten Jacob, but he is actually kind and secretly

gives him chocolate. The Fang's character contains one glaring inconsistency: his threat to feed Jacob to the sharks is not presented as a bluff. Jacob exposes the Fang by showing that he does not really hate the sun, as all child-hating adults in the dream do. Symbolically, the Fang suggests that adults fear their own childish side and therefore suppress it. **Justice Rough** satirizes the hypocrisy of adults who discipline children. He mouths the clichés about punishment hurting the adult more than the child, but he clearly delights in handing out sentences himself. Like the other villains, he is a coward who fears the vitality children represent. **Mr. Fox**, the guard who takes Jacob's supersonic bleeper, is a truly nasty man. He adds a *pourquoi* element to the tale. He mixes up parts in plastic kits, thus explaining why little children have difficulty assembling models.

The superheroes of Child Power, the intrepid **Shapiro** (Jacob's sister **Emma**) and the fearless **O'Toole** (his brother **Noah**) are playtime versions of comic book superheroes. They provide Jacob with a way of establishing his worth. In the waking world, Emma and Noah dismiss Jacob as too little to understand their complicated game. In the dream world, however, they depend upon his complex plan to liberate the imprisoned children. **Louis Loser**, Jacob's lawyer, adds another dimension to the theme of competence. Because he has never won a case, he demonstrates that adults can also be incompetent.

Further Reading

Children's Literature Review. Vol. 17. Detroit: Gale Research, 1989.

Collier, Laurie, and Joyce Nakamura, eds. *Major Authors and Illustrators for Children and Young Adults.* Detroit: Gale Research, 1993.

Contemporary Authors New Revision Series. Vol. 31. Detroit: Gale Research, 1991.

Contemporary Literary Criticism. Vols. 3, 5, 9, 13, 18, 46, 70. Detroit: Gale Research, 1975, 1976, 1978, 1980, 1981, 1988, 1992.

New, W. H., ed. *Canadian Writers since 1960, First Series.* Vol. 53 of *Dictionary of Literary Biography.* Detroit: Gale Research, 1986.

Ramraj, Victor J. *Mordecai Richler.* Boston: Twayne, 1983.

Something about the Author. Vols. 27, 44. Detroit: Gale Research, 1982, 1986.

Mary Rodgers

1931-, American script editor, composer, and author

Freaky Friday

(fantasy, 1972)

PLOT: Like F. Anstey's classic *Vice Versa; or, A Lesson to Fathers* (1882), this comic novel uses the idea of a parent and child gaining understanding of each other by switching bodies. Thirteen-year-old Annabel Andrews is miserable: she hates her brother, Ben, whom she calls Ape Face; she feels oppressed by her mother, Ellen; and she considers herself ugly. On Friday, when Annabel wakes up in her mother's body, she is pleased to be attractive and to have adult freedom. At first things go relatively smoothly. She makes breakfast, borrows housekeeping money from her father, William (Bill), and sends Ben and Annabel to school. When fourteen-year-old Boris Harris returns a colander, she plays Nok Hockey with him. Afterwards, however, things become complicated. The washing machine overflows, and the repairman insists that no one can come for a week. Rose Schmauss, the cleaning lady, blames teenage Annabel for stealing gin, so the real Annabel fires her. Forgetting that her mother always meets Ben at his bus, she is late and encounters a rude policeman.

At lunch, Annabel learns that Ben genuinely likes his sister and is proud to be called Ape Face. When Bill then telephones to tell her that they will have important clients for dinner and reminds her that she has to see Annabel's teachers, she arranges for Boris to baby-sit Ben and to make dinner. At Annabel's school, she has a stormy meeting with the principal, Arnold Dilk, the English teacher, Felicia McGuirk, and the psychologist, Dr. Cassandra Arturian. Returning home, she discovers that Ben is missing. When Boris tells her that Ben went away with a "beautiful chick," she makes a confused call to the police, who think that she is crazy. Meanwhile her husband's clients arrive, smell Boris's "beetloaf" dinner, and decide to return the next night. Finally,

Annabel Andrews switches bodies with her mother, and learns a lot about herself, in Rodgers's hilarious 1972 story.

after breaking down in tears, Annabel reenters her own body. She then learns that she is the beautiful girl who took away Ben: while in Annabel's body, Ellen bought attractive clothes, went to the beauty parlor, and had her braces removed. All the minor problems are now resolved, as Annabel meets Boris, whom she has secretly admired. At the end, Annabel reveals that the novel is actually her English report.

Sequels are A Billion for Boris *(1974) and* Summer Switch *(1982).*

CHARACTERS: Annabel Andrews, the narrator, is a bright, witty, loud thirteen-year-old. She demands more freedom, but she is irresponsible and uncooperative. Extraordinarily messy, she refuses to tidy her room, even though she is never able to find what she wants in it. She feels ugly because she has stringy brown hair, brown eyes, and braces. She hates her little brother, especially because he is cute, and she is an underachiever at school. When she becomes her mother, Annabel learns responsibility through comical errors, such as overloading the washing machine and forgetting to pick up Ben. More importantly, she learns how others see her. She is not startled to see that Rose Schmauss considers her a disgraceful pig and that Boris (Morris) Harris thinks that she is violent and ugly (she hit him several years earlier), but she is startled that Ben truly loves and admires her. At school, she is surprised to learn that Miss McGuirk feels that she has failed as a teacher because Annabel is so uncooperative.

Another transformation resolves Annabel's problems and emphasizes the theme that self-worth often depends on one's sense of personal appearance. Her mother, while in Annabel's body, has dressed in attractive clothes, groomed her hair, and removed her braces. This fairy-tale outward change precipitates and symbolizes an internal change. Looking in the mirror, Annabel accepts herself as beautiful and then becomes an attractive, loving, generous, understanding, and responsible person. She shows generosity, for example, by giving up the trip to an expensive summer camp (which she earlier wheedled her mother into granting) so that the family can vacation together. Furthermore, she becomes responsible, turning her adventures into an overdue English assignment that enables her to pass the class.

The minor characters have limited roles. **William (Bill) Waring Andrews**, Annabel's thirty-eight-year-old father, is an advertising executive. He seems sexist and patronizing when he accuses the transformed Annabel of being a wasteful wife when she borrows housekeeping money. Otherwise, he is a stereotypical father. **Ellen Jean Benjamin Andrews**, Annabel's thirty-five-year-old mother, is a pretty woman with a good figure. She shows exceptional understanding of her daughter's troubled life, shaking her out of her self-absorption by mysteriously causing their body switch and then transforming Annabel's body so that she can accept herself. **Ben Andrews**, whom Annabel calls **Ape Face**, contrasts with his sister. He is an attractive six-year-old who has his father's blue eyes, long eyelashes, and curly hair. Unlike Annabel, he is pleasant and neat. Ben is a bright and loving boy. He admires his sister and never tells her that he likes his nickname because he knows that she would then abandon it.

Because fourteen-year-old **Boris Harris** is afflicted with adenoids and speaks through a stuffed nose, no one realizes that his real name is **Morris**. He is a good cook, but he surprises everyone when his "meatloaf" actually is "beetloaf." Annabel secretly admires him, but Boris remembers her only as an ugly child who hit him several years earlier. The fact that he doesn't recognize Annabel as the "beautiful chick" who takes Ben away underlines her change from ugly duckling to beautiful young woman. **Rose Schmauss**, the cleaning lady, views Annabel as a disgraceful pig who has not received proper discipline. A gin-stealing bigot, she brings out Annabel's racial tolerance. Mrs. Schmauss is fired for blaming the liquor thefts on Annabel. The three school officials allow Annabel to see herself as an intelligent underachiever. **Mr. Arnold Dilk**, the principal of the Barden School, is a slick Jekyll and Hyde figure who changes from casual pleasantry and flattery to forceful strictness when he vows to expel Annabel unless she matures. **Miss Felicia McGuirk**, Annabel's English teacher, considers Annabel one of the brightest students she has ever taught. A genuinely caring teacher, she breaks down in tears because she believes that she is a failure for not motivating Annabel. **Dr. Cassandra Arturian**, the school psychologist, generates comedy with her psychological analysis, especially after Annabel forgets that she is her mother and refers to Bill as her father instead of her husband.

Further Reading

Berger, Laura Standley, ed. *Twentieth-Century Children's Writers.* 4th ed. Detroit: St. James, 1995.

Children's Literature Review. Vol. 20. Detroit: Gale Research, 1990.

Collier, Laurie, and Joyce Nakamura, eds. *Major Authors and Illustrators for Children and Young Adults.* Detroit: Gale Research, 1993.

Contemporary Authors New Revision Series. Vol. 8. Detroit: Gale Research, 1983.

Contemporary Literary Criticism. Vol. 12. Detroit: Gale Research, 1980.

Holtze, Sally Holmes, ed. *Fifth Book of Junior Authors and Illustrators.* New York: H. W. Wilson, 1983.

Something about the Author. Vol. 8. Detroit: Gale Research, 1976.

John Ruskin

1819-1900, English art critic and author

The King of the Golden River; or, The Black Brothers

(fairy tale, 1851)

PLOT: Modeled after the Grimms' tales, Ruskin's fairy tale uses conventional elements, such as three main characters, three journeys, and three tests, to warn against the greedy exploitation of nature and the callous neglect of people in need. The main characters, three brothers, own a prosperous farm in fertile Treasure Valley. The older brothers, Schwartz and Hans, are called the Black Brothers because they are stingy and cruel. One day, the youngest brother, Gluck, gives shelter to a peculiar-looking man. Hans and Schwartz, however, attack the man. That night, a storm destroys everything the brothers own. The man appears, identifies himself as Southwest Wind, Esquire, and then leaves, turning Treasure Valley into a desert. The impoverished brothers now go to the city to work as goldsmiths. Failing in their trade, the older brothers order Gluck to melt his gold drinking mug. The mug transforms into the King of the Golden River, who tells Gluck that anyone pouring three drops of holy water into the source of the Golden River will turn it into gold, but anyone pouring unholy drops will be turned into a black stone.

The older brothers fail when they undertake the quest. Hans steals some holy water. Thirsty himself, he refuses to share his water with a dying dog, a fair child, and an old man. When he throws the remaining drops into the river, he is turned into a black stone. Schwartz, who buys holy water from a bad priest, refuses to share his water with the fair child, the old man, and an apparition of Hans. He, too, is turned into a black stone. The youngest brother, however, succeeds. Gluck asks a priest for holy water, and he shares it with the old man, the child, and the dog. The King of the Golden River then presents him with a lily containing three drops of water. When Gluck throws these into the river, it begins flowing into Treasure Valley, which becomes fertile. Gluck becomes wealthy and happy.

CHARACTERS: The physical ugliness of **Schwartz** (German for "black") and **Hans**, two stock villains, is in keeping with their evil natures. Symbolically called **the Black Brothers**, they are stingy, cruel, and materialistic. They kill everything that does not pay for its keep, cheat their laborers of their wages, overcharge their drought-stricken neighbors for food, and frequently beat Gluck to teach him obedience. Although their failure to show charity to Southwest Wind, Esquire, costs them their material possessions, the Black Brothers are too dense to learn from experience. They become goldsmiths because, as Schwartz declares, it is "a good knave's trade." They fail at it because people detect their deceptions and because they are so self-indulgent that they drink away their earnings. Their selfishness in placing themselves above nature (the dying dog), needy and vulnerable members of society (the child and old man), and even family members (the apparition of Hans), ensures that they fail in their quests. Appropriately, these hard-hearted brothers are transformed into stones, a conventional punishment for those lacking humane feelings. In contrast, their twelve-year-old brother, the blonde, blue-eyed **Gluck** (German for "luck" or "happiness"), is as fair in character as he is in features. Naturally kind, Gluck gives shelter to the peculiar old man, and he even decides to give him his portion of mutton. Gluck displays similar pity when he gives water to the old man, gives the fair child a drink instead of taking one himself, and gives the last of his holy water to the dog, even though he believes that doing

The kind Gluck shelters a rain-drenched stranger in Ruskin's fairy tale, The King of the Golden River, *illustrated by Richard Doyle.*

so will prevent him from turning the river into gold. His charitable feelings and his respect for nature earn the reward of wealth and happiness.

The magical characters are agents of fate. **Southwest Wind, Esquire**, appears as a comically peculiar old man with a large nose, red cheeks, twinkling eyes, long eyelashes, shoulder-length hair, and corkscrew mustaches. Four-and-a-half feet tall, he wears a conical pointed hat of nearly his own height that is decorated with a three-foot-long feather and a cloak four times his length. Nevertheless, he has a serious function: he reveals the kindness of Gluck and the evil natures of the miserly Black Brothers. Beyond their control, as he illustrates by tumbling the older brothers into the corner when they try to eject him from their house, Southwest Wind, Esquire, represents the forces of nature that the brothers ruthlessly exploit. By turning the fertile Treasure Valley into a desert, he symbolically teaches that greed destroys nature's wealth. **The King of the Golden River** rewards and punishes social conduct. He emerges from Gluck's mug, which is shaped like a fierce little face. He is a foot-and-a-half tall dwarf dressed in spun gold and having a wavy beard and hair that fall halfway to the ground. He has a coarse face and a stubborn, unyielding appearance, but he is the voice of moral wisdom. He explains that the Black Brothers failed because water refused to the thirsty, no matter who has blessed it, is unholy, but water, even that defiled by corpses, is holy when in a vessel of mercy. By turning the Black Brothers into stone, the King symbolically indicates that, without charity, people are insensitive things. By making the river fertilize Treasure Valley, thus undoing the damage the Black Brothers caused by driving away Southwest Wind, Esquire, he suggests that true wealth is not found in minerals but in a respect for living nature.

Further Reading

Bingham, Jane M., ed. *Writers for Children: Critical Studies of Major Authors since the Seventeenth Century.* New York: Scribner's, 1988.

Contemporary Authors. Vol. 129. Detroit: Gale Research, 1990.

Something about the Author. Vol. 24. Detroit: Gale Research, 1981.

Thesing, William B., ed. *Victorian Prose Writers before 1867*. Vol. 55 of *Dictionary of Literary Biography*. Detroit: Gale Research, 1987.

Cynthia Rylant

1954-, American librarian, college lecturer, and writer

Henry and Mudge

(picture book, 1987; illustrated by Suçie Stevenson)

PLOT: The short episodes in this warmhearted early reader demonstrate the love and companionship that a big dog brings to a boy. Henry is lonely because he has no brothers or sisters and because he lives on a street without other children. His parents refuse to give him a sibling or to move, but they do allow him to get a dog. Henry chooses a tiny puppy named Mudge, who quickly grows into an enormous dog. Henry and Mudge become inseparable. Mudge walks to school with Henry and sleeps in his bed at night. The only drama occurs when Mudge becomes lost. Henry at first cries, but then he searches for and finds his dog. Afterwards, Henry and Mudge have the same dream about being alone and therefore draw closer to each other when they awaken.

Rylant and Stevenson have collaborated on twelve sequels: Henry and Mudge in Puddle Trouble *(1987),* Henry and Mudge in the Green Time *(1987),* Henry and Mudge under the Yellow Moon *(1987),* Henry and Mudge in the Sparkle Days *(1988),* Henry and Mudge and the Forever Sea *(1989),* Henry and the Mudge Get the Cold Shivers *(1989),* Henry and Mudge and the Happy Cat *(1990),* Henry and Mudge and the Bedtime Thumps *(1991),* Henry and Mudge Take the Big Test *(1991),* Henry and Mudge and the Long Weekend *(1992),* Henry and Mudge and the Wild Wind *(1992), and* Henry and Mudge and the Careful Cousin *(1994).*

CHARACTERS: Although Henry's young parents contribute to the theme of loving relationships,

Henry and Mudge are decidedly central. The text describes Mudge, but the drawings only portray Henry. **Henry**, illustrated as a small, red-cheeked boy with unruly orange hair, is lonely until he acquires Mudge. Having a companion makes Henry happier and more confident. On his walks to school, for example, he no longer worries about tornadoes or bullies. Instead, reassured by Mudge's huge presence, he thinks about the good things in life. Although Henry cries for an hour when Mudge is missing, he then shows intelligence, loyalty, and courage. Realizing that Mudge wouldn't deliberately leave him, Henry concludes that Mudge is lost and, therefore, searches for him. His dream at the end shows that he understands loneliness and that he deeply loves his dog.

Mudge is a straight-haired, floppy-eared, drooling dog who weighs one hundred and eighty pounds and stands three feet tall. In spite of his enormous size, he is gentle and affectionate. For example, he loves to get into Henry's bed and lick him all over before falling asleep. Mudge is as attached to Henry as Henry is to Mudge. He therefore eats and sleeps with Henry. Furthermore, he has the same dream as Henry. Remembering what it felt like to be lonely, Mudge therefore stays close to Henry when he awakens.

Missing May

(novel, 1992)

PLOT: This spare Newbery Medal winner about coping with grief focuses on twelve-year-old Summer, an orphan who has lived with Aunt May and Uncle Ob since she was six. Six months after May's death, Summer and Ob still deeply miss May. Summer also fears that Ob will die of a broken heart. One day, Ob tells her that May has visited him. Ob then becomes convinced that Summer's schoolmate, Cletus Underwood, who believes that he once visited the afterlife, can help him contact May. After they fail to contact May, Ob gives up on life. Cletus, however,

Cletus Underwood, Summer, and Uncle Ob, from the cover of Rylant's Newbery Medal-winning book.

suggests a trip to seek help from a spiritualist minister. Ob and Summer therefore visit Mr. and Mrs. Underwood to get permission for Cletus to come with them. During the visit, Summer gains insight into Cletus, realizing that the boy whom she hates is beloved at home.

Ob promises that, after visiting the minister, they will go to the West Virginia State Capitol, which Cletus longs to see. Ironically, when they arrive at the church they learn that the spiritualist is dead. The despondent Ob then drives past the Capitol, intending to go home. Suddenly, in a moment that marks his renewed acceptance of life, he turns the car around and takes Cletus and Summer to spend the day at the Capitol. When they get home, an owl brushes past Summer; she cries, letting out her grief. That night, May speaks to her in a dream, talking about a similar encounter with an owl when Summer first came to live with her. The next morning, Ob shows his changed spirits, filling May's dead garden

with whirligigs. The wind sets these whirligigs in motion, symbolizing Ob and Summer's freedom from grief.

CHARACTERS: Rylant has said that her aim is to "put words to feelings" and that "It is the interior I'm most interested in." *Missing May* is intensely emotional, but the eccentric characters are novel enough to prevent mawkishness and to add freshness to well-worn themes.

Summer, the twelve-year-old narrator, develops by coping with her grief. An orphan treated "like a homework assignment somebody was always having to do," Summer became magical, a chosen child, with Ob and May, who gave her the heaven of a loving home. After May dies, Summer needs to understand death in terms other than of loss and regret. Summer's pessimism and fear compound her pain. She feels that Ob's loss of his will to live indicates that she is not important enough to keep him interested in life. She further believes that she will never have another chance at happiness. Although Summer begins as gloomy as the February weather, she changes because she is observant and intelligent. When she meets Cletus's parents, she sees that they love him and that Cletus is therefore free to be himself with them. Furthermore, she sees herself through his eyes, realizing that her hostility made him ashamed.

Although Summer does not know what makes Ob turn around at the Capitol, his decision gives Summer a sense of worth. That is, she believes that Ob chooses life rather than having to say good-bye to her. Once free from worry about Ob, Summer is able to express her own pain. The owl brushing past her symbolizes the presence of the spiritual world. It sets off memories of a similar event with May, enabling Summer to cry the tears repressed during the funeral. Her dream of May, who recounts the owl episode, thus marks a point of understanding and freedom. Earlier, Cletus claimed that Summer fought her visions. By accepting this vision, Summer is purged of pain. She feels renewed, optimistically sensing the approach of spring. Knowing that May will be with her always, Summer experiences the joyous freedom symbolized by the twirling whirligigs.

Although she appears only in a dream and memories, **Aunt May** is a vital character. Summer correctly regards May, who was a huge woman with long yellow hair, as "a big barrel of nothing but love." May turned a rusty trailer in West Virginia into a paradise for Summer, making her happy and constantly praising her. May represents the triumph of the human spirit. Although she has known sorrow—she lost her parents in a flood, and she was unable to have a child—May remained optimistic, appreciating what she had and saying that better times would follow in the next world if we fail here. Her appearance in Summer's dream parallels her own experience of her parents' continued presence in her life and establishes the idea that loved ones live on in memory.

Uncle Ob is a scrawny Ichabod Crane type with only a few strands of hair. Wounded in World War II, he has been unable to work. Instead, he spends his time making whirligigs representing what he calls "The Mysteries," such as thunder, heaven, and May's spirit. A kind, observant man, Ob took Summer home after noticing that she was too afraid to ask for more milk. Although his behavior generally seems odd, he has a slick understanding of others, as he shows by withholding the true purpose of the journey from Cletus's parents. His need to contact May and his subsequent depression suggest his inability to accept change. The reason he suddenly decides to live is conjectural. Probably, however, Ob's sensitivity and powers of observation are responsible. Knowing that Cletus longs to visit the Capitol and that Summer depends on him, Ob satisfies their needs. By reconnecting himself to life, he frees Summer to grieve. He also frees himself, setting his whirligigs outside for the first time, where the wind that sets them in motion symbolizes a freed spirit.

Cletus Underwood disgusts Summer because he has long, straight, greasy black hair and behaves strangely. She thinks that Cletus is crazy because he carries around a suitcase full of pictures and imagines stories about them. Cletus also displays annoying patience, talking with Ob for hours. Although Cletus is strange—he believes that he visited the afterlife when he nearly drowned—he is sympathetic and accepting. He has the gift of knowing when to talk and when to be quiet. Thus, he remains silent while letting Ob express his grief. At home, however, Cletus behaves more normally because his loving parents free him from the need to be eccentric. Unlike Summer, Cletus is optimistic and enthusiastic. He admires accomplishments, especially the political greatness symbolized for him by the golden Capitol, and is studying to be a Renaissance Man. Cletus plays his most important role at the end of the story. By reading a passage about spirit messages providing consolations for life's sorrows, he overtly establishes the symbolism of the whirligigs. Like May and Ob, Cletus's elderly parents represent unconditional love. **Mr. Underwood** is a stooped, elflike man with a long gray beard. **Mrs. Margradel Underwood** is a small, withered woman, whose right eye is nearly blind. Through them, Summer appreciates that Cletus is can be sensitive and loving.

Further Reading

Authors and Artists for Young Adults. Vol. 10. Detroit: Gale Research, 1993.

Berger, Laura Standley, ed. *Twentieth-Century Children's Writers.* 4th ed. Detroit: St. James, 1995.

Berger, Laura Standley, ed. *Twentieth-Century Young Adult Writers.* 1st ed. Detroit: St. James, 1994.

Children's Literature Review. Vol. 15. Detroit: Gale Research, 1988.

Collier, Laurie, and Joyce Nakamura, eds. *Major Authors and Illustrators for Children and Young Adults.* Detroit: Gale Research, 1993.

Contemporary Authors. Vol. 136. Detroit: Gale Research, 1992.

Holtze, Sally Holmes, ed *Sixth Book of Junior Authors and Illustrators.* New York: H. W. Wilson, 1989.

Something about the Author. Vols. 44, 50, 76. Detroit: Gale Research, 1986, 1988, 1994.

Something about the Author Autobiography Series. Vol. 13. Detroit: Gale Research, 1992.

Antoine de Saint-Exupéry

1900-1944, French aviator and author

The Little Prince

(fantasy, 1943; published in France as Le petit prince*)*

PLOT: Critics argue about whether *The Little Prince* is truly a children's book and about its symbolic meaning. *The Little Prince* obviously celebrates childhood innocence, criticizes adult values, and affirms loving relationships as the source of life's meaning. The narrator, an aviator repairing his plane after a crash in the Sahara Desert, meets the little prince, who asks him for a drawing of a sheep. The little prince then recounts his travels. Having come to distrust the only flower on his asteroid, the little prince journeyed to six asteroids, each inhabited by a single person: a king, a conceited man, a drunk, a businessman, a lamplighter, and a geographer. On Earth, he discovered a garden containing roses exactly like his flower, and he met a poisonous snake, a fox who asks to be tamed, a railway switchman, a merchant who sells pills against thirst, and then the aviator. The aviator gives the little prince some drawings. Having run out of water, he and the little prince find a well, where the aviator helps the boy to drink. The little prince, implying that it is the only way that he can return to his beloved flower, has the snake bite him. He dies, but the aviator can't find his body the next morning. Six years later, the aviator tells the story.

CHARACTERS: The little prince, a small, golden-haired boy who wears a golden muffler, is the sole inhabitant of Asteroid B-612. He symbolizes childhood innocence. He finds, for example, a picture of a sheep to be as valuable as the actual animal. Curious, he is a tenacious questioner. At the same time, he is mysterious and unknowable because he never answers questions. The little prince is exceptionally disciplined in caring for his tiny home; every day he uproots the baobabs that threaten to overrun it. His

naivete, however, leads him to leave. Having believed his flower's claims that she is unique, he does not know how to maintain a relationship once her lies make him doubt her. His departure thus symbolizes an escape from the demands of loving others in spite of their faults. At the same time, it is an unconscious quest to learn what is important.

The little prince succeeds in his quest for knowledge. His journeys to the asteroids teach him to recognize the foolishness of adults, who think that only material facts are matters of consequence. His discovery of the garden of roses, where he learns that his flower is not physically unique, plunges him to his lowest point. Feeling that he has been deceived, the little prince has a crisis of identity and no longer feels special. He learns from the fox, however, that he must value that which is unseen and that he will find uniqueness through loving another. By taming this fox, he shows himself again capable of loving and reestablishes his identity.

The little prince gains wisdom, but he rejects adult values. Instead, he acquires a higher form of innocence that renews his love for the flower and makes him accept responsibility for it. Because the little prince expresses a message of love, some critics see him as symbolizing Christ. He appears, for example, in the desert, where Christ endured spiritual testing and, like Christ the Good Shepherd, he is concerned with sheep. Furthermore, the little prince saves the aviator by mysteriously finding water that the aviator calls good for the heart and may symbolize Christ's thirst-ending water of life, the message of salvation. The little prince's own statement that he is thirsty also reminds the reader of Christ's statement of thirst on the cross. Finally, the little prince's willing death and the disappearance of his body suggests Christ's sacrificial death and resurrection.

The narrator, an aviator, is an adult with an admirably childish vision and childish values. He repeatedly points out adult failures to recognize his childhood pictures of the inside and outside of a boa constrictor as examples of adult failures to see important things in life. He is guilty of shallow adult behavior when he claims that fixing his plane is a matter of consequence more important than the little prince's questions about the flower. On most occasions, however, he shows loving concern. Seeing that the little prince is weak, for example, he draws the water from the well. Like the little prince, the narrator is transformed by his journey to the desert. He also learns to love things invisible, worrying about the survival of love in a dangerous universe. Because he forgot to draw the strap on the muzzle he gave the little prince, that is, he worries about whether the little prince can protect the rose from being eaten by a sheep.

The fox represents instinctual values, not the artificial ones represented by the men on the asteroids. A helper, he is the only one who gives wise advice. Bored because all men are the same to him, the fox points out that relationships create individuality. He has the little prince tame him so that he becomes unique to the little prince and the little prince becomes unique to him. The fox then states the major theme: one must see with the heart, not the eyes. The little prince's **flower**, a rose, illustrates this point while showing that flaws do not disqualify one from being worthy of love. Because she is vain and given to telling lies, she tests his worthiness. After he learns to see beyond her physical similarity to the roses on Earth, the little prince learns that she is, as she claimed, unique in the universe.

The other characters are simple, if puzzling, types. **The King**, whose royal purple and ermine robe crams every part of his planet, represents the illusions of adult authority. Viewing everyone as a subject, he maintains his illusion of absolute power by giving orders for actions that would have occurred without them anyway. **The conceited man** represents those who can't form relationships because they insist on their own superiority. Viewing others only as admirers, he wears a hat so that he can raise it when they acclaim him. Absurdly, he is pleased to be admired as the best-looking and richest person on his planet, even though he is the only one on it. **The tippler**, who drinks because he is ashamed of his drinking, represents those who escape from responsibilities. **The businessman**, who is obsessed with counting and owning things, represents those who think that only material values are of consequence. **The lamplighter**, unlike the other

The Little Prince tends to his little planet in this illustration by Saint-Exupéry.

men, does useful work, but he blindly follows orders and is therefore so consumed by his adult work that he has no time for enjoyment. **The geographer**, an old man who depends on others for his knowledge, confuses magnitude with value. He treasures mountains, but he dismisses the flower (and thus the love she represents) as ephemeral. **The railway switchman** interprets the movement of people on railways as a symbol of the purposelessness and dissatisfaction of adults. **The merchant** who sells pills to quench thirst represents those who value the artificial at the expense of the genuine experiences of life.

Further Reading

Brosman, Catharine Savage, ed. *French Novelists, 1930-1960.* Vol. 72 of *Dictionary of Literary Biography.* Detroit: Gale Research, 1988.

Children's Literature Review. Vol. 10. Detroit: Gale Research, 1986.

Collier, Laurie, and Joyce Nakamura, eds. *Major Authors and Illustrators for Children and Young Adults.* Detroit: Gale Research, 1993.

Contemporary Authors. Vol. 132. Detroit: Gale Research, 1991.

De Montreville, Doris, and Elizabeth D. Crawford, eds. *Fourth Book of Junior Authors.* New York: H. W. Wilson, 1978.

Something about the Author. Vol. 20. Detroit: Gale Research, 1980.

George Selden

(pen name for George Selden Thompson)

1929-1989, American author

The Cricket in Times Square

(animal fantasy, 1960)

PLOT: This animal fantasy celebrates the beauty and power of music while developing a theme about friendship. Chester Cricket finds himself in New York after being trapped in a picnic basket in Connecticut. Mario, who works at his parents' news-stand in the subway station at Times Square, finds Chester. Mama Bellini doesn't want him to keep Chester as a pet, but Papa Bellini says that Mario can keep the cricket at the newsstand. After the Bellinis go home, Chester is befriended by Tucker Mouse and Harry Cat, who live together in a drain pipe in the station. A few days later, Mario goes to Chinatown, where Sai Fong, an elderly storekeeper, tells him the story of the origin of crickets, sells him a pagoda-shaped cage, and gives Mario a tiny bell for the cage.

Although crickets are supposed to be lucky, Chester soon brings misfortune to the Bellinis. First, he chews on a two-dollar bill in his sleep. Mama Bellini insists that Mario get rid of Chester. She changes her mind after Tucker puts two dollars in coins that he has scavenged into Chester's cage. A little later, Chester plays some music that he hears on the radio. Tucker dances to it, spills some matches, and starts a fire. Mama Bellini again demands that Mario get rid of the cricket. At the urging of Tucker, Chester immediately begins playing an Italian folk song. Mama Bellini is so moved that she allows Mario to keep the cricket. Soon, Mr. Smedley, a music teacher, hears the cricket and writes a letter to the newspaper. Hundreds of people begin showing up to hear Chester's concerts, and the Bellinis' failing newsstand prospers. Chester is, however, unhappy. He gives one final concert, which brings Times Square to a halt, takes his bell as a memento, and, with the help of Tucker and Harry, boards a train for the country. Mario, seeing that Chester has taken the bell, is happy in the knowledge that his pet has gone home.

Sequels are Tucker's Countryside *(1969),* Harry Cat's Pet Puppy *(1974),* Chester Cricket's Pigeon Ride *(1981),* Chester Cricket's New Home *(1983),* Harry Kitten and Tucker Mouse *(1986), and* The Old Meadow *(1987).*

CHARACTERS: The novel keeps a strict division between animal and human characters. The animals talk only to each other, but they show concern for the feelings and well-being of the humans. **Chester Cricket** is honorable, loyal, and talented. After he eats the two-dollar bill, he refuses to destroy the evidence of his guilt or to let Tucker frame the janitor as a thief. He also refuses to run away because he doesn't want to be unfair to Mario. When the fire destroys the newsstand, Chester's compas-sion and honor lead him to devote his exceptional musical talent to saving the Bellinis from financial ruin. Although he thereby brings people happiness, Chester himself is unhappy. He values his freedom and therefore does not like sleeping in his elegant cage. A shy creature, he also dislikes the stares of the crowds who come to hear him. Most of all, Chester, the self-proclaimed country cricket, misses contact with nature in his native Connecticut. In New York, Chester must play human musical compositions; he much prefers his own natural ones. Chester loyally persists in his wearying round of concerts, however, until Mario indicates that he wants him to be happy. Chester's musical greatness appears in his final concert, when, like the mythical Orpheus, he makes the world pause. By taking the bell as a memento of his city friends, Chester leaves a final sign for his friends to remember the heart that created such beautiful music.

Chester has two animal friends. **Tucker Mouse** is a messy scavenger who lives in a drain pipe. Tucker loves money and even wants to sleep on dollar bills in Chester's pagoda. He is also a miser. He gives up his coins to save Mario from having to earn extra money only when Chester's integrity embarrasses him into doing so. Tucker lacks Ches-ter's ethical sensitivity, as is evident in his sugges-tion that they frame the janitor, but he is a shrewd judge of human and animal character. He makes Chester play after the fire, for example, because he realizes that music will soften the angry Mama Bellini. As Chester's flashy-talking manager, he seems to be an opportunist who is interested more in money than displaying Chester's talent. Nevertheless, as the dance that started the fire indicates, he is sensitive to music, a sign of his inner goodness. Furthermore, from the beginning he shows his friendship to Chester by offering to help him escape. As a city dweller, Tucker has given up the animosities found in nature. His best friend, therefore, is **Harry Cat**, a huge tiger cat with gray-green and black stripes. Harry is quiet and intelligent. He respects Chester's longing for freedom and is the one who first lets him out of the cage. Whereas the flamboyant Tucker is primarily concerned with Chester's retirement as an exciting gesture, the calm and sensible Harry considers Chester's emotional state. He voices one major theme, therefore, when he wisely asks about the value of fame if it makes a person unhappy.

As his concern for Chester suggests, **Mario Bellini** is a good, sensitive boy. He is always concerned with the welfare of the cricket. He goes to Chinatown to get a special cage for Chester and later goes back to ask Sai Fong about how to feed his pet properly. Mario defends the cricket when his mother wants to get rid of it. He shows his love and determination by sacrificing his own pleasures and by taking on extra jobs so that he can replace the money Chester ate. Because he is able to imagine himself in the cricket's position, he understands when Chester becomes sad. A true friend, he almost wishes that the cricket had not come. He thereby gives Chester the moral right to leave. After Chester leaves, Mario again shows that he is a true and sensitive friend: he sees that the bell is gone and is happy knowing that Chester has returned home. **Mama Bellini**, a short, stout woman who wheezes and becomes red when she climbs stairs, is initially an antagonist. Declaring that crickets are dirty bugs, she refuses to allow Chester to live in her home. Later, she tries to get rid of the cricket because it eats money and because it is responsible for the fire. Mama is a practical woman, however, who shares Tucker's concern with money. Therefore, she allows Mario to keep Chester once the damaged money is

Garth Williams's illustration of Tucker Mouse and Harry Cat in Selden's A Cricket in Times Square.

replaced. Furthermore, although music makes her sentimental and causes her to change her mind about getting rid of Chester, she insists on turning Chester's concerts into economic opportunities. **Papa Bellini** is far more sensitive to Mario's feelings than his wife is. He understands her moods and how to deal with them. Although he can be forceful, he suggests compromises, such as having the cricket stay in the newsstand, to prevent bitterness and fighting in the family. Like the other members of the family, he loves music, especially Italian opera.

Two humans serve as important teachers in the story. **Sai Fong**, the kind, elderly Chinese storekeeper, generously sells the cage at far less than its value when he finds that Mario loves his cricket. He instructs Mario in the care of the cricket. He also tells a story about the origin of crickets that establishes their importance. To Sai Fong, the cricket's music is the sound of truth and ancient wisdom. Hearing him, Chester feels good about himself. **Mr.**

H. P. Smedley, the music teacher, contributes to both plot and theme. An eccentric man who always carries a furled umbrella, he becomes a device for saving the Bellinis from bankruptcy when he writes the letter to the newspaper and thereby brings crowds to their newsstand. He is knowledgeable and establishes the extraordinary quality of Chester's talent by pointing out that the cricket has perfect pitch. Thematically, Mr. Smedley testifies to the power and beauty of music by introducing the myth of Orpheus.

Further Reading

Berger, Laura Standley, ed. *Twentieth-Century Children's Writers*. 4th ed. Detroit: St. James, 1995.

Children's Literature Review. Vol. 8. Detroit: Gale Research, 1985.

Collier, Laurie, and Joyce Nakamura, eds. *Major Authors and Illustrators for Children and Young Adults*. Detroit: Gale Research, 1993.

Contemporary Authors New Revision Series. Vol. 37. Detroit: Gale Research, 1992.

De Montreville, Doris, and Elizabeth D. Crawford, eds. *Fourth Book of Junior Authors*. New York: H. W. Wilson, 1978.

Estes, Glenn E., ed. *American Writers for Children since 1960: Fiction*. Vol. 52 of *Dictionary of Literary Biography*. Detroit: Gale Research, 1986.

Something about the Author. Vols. 4, 73. Detroit: Gale Research, 1973, 1993.

Maurice Sendak

1928-, American illustrator and author

Where the Wild Things Are

(picture book, 1963)

PLOT: This Caldecott Medal winner depicts a circular dream journey: a boy runs away from home, has experiences that change him, and therefore happily returns. The boy, Max, puts on his wolf suit one night and causes mischief, damaging the house, hanging his toy dog, chasing his real dog with a fork, and threatening to eat his mother. Sent to his bedroom without any dinner, Max discovers a forest growing there. He takes a boat and sails away to the land of the Wild Things, who make him their king. Max orders a wild rumpus, but he soon longs for someone to love him. Smelling good things to eat, he ignores the threats of the Wild Things and returns to his own room, where a warm supper awaits him.

CHARACTERS: *Where the Wild Things Are* develops its story from the viewpoint of Max, the only important character. The reader never sees Max's mother, and the Wild Things whom he visits are merely projections of the inner world of his emotions.

In the initial part of the story, **Max** demonstrates that clothes do indeed make the boy: by wearing a wolf suit, he transforms himself into the very image of an antisocial fairy-tale monster. His growing hostility is evident in the increased violence of his attacks: he moves from a toy dog, to a real dog, to his mother. Max is, however, both intelligent and sympathetic. He tames the Wild Things by staring into their eyes without blinking, a "magic trick" that he has obviously learned from his mother. Furthermore, he comes to sympathize with the frustration his mother feels, for he subjects the Wild Things to the very punishment she used on him by sending them to bed without supper. His decision to return home shows that he has come to value, at least for now, the sharing of love rather than the independence of power.

The **Wild Things** are fanciful monsters. Although each has "terrible" claws, teeth, and yellow eyes, no two are alike in appearance. Each is pictured as being formed from a different inappropriate combination of parts from a variety of animals or mythical beasts. As a picture Max has drawn before he begins his adventure suggests, the Wild Things are products of his imagination and act out his aggressions, even threatening to eat him, just as he threatened to eat his mother. By controlling them, Max controls his own emotions.

Max's **mother** speaks, but is never seen. Although she seems severe when she punishes Max by sending him to bed without food, the symbol of love in this story, she reveals her nurturing love by leaving a hot meal for him to eat when he returns from his dream voyage.

In the Night Kitchen

(picture book, 1970)

Max at his monstrous worst in an illustration from
Sendak's **Where the Wild Things Are.**

PLOT: Sendak has said that *In the Night Kitchen* is the second volume of a trilogy about children mastering strong emotions. Like the first volume, *Where the Wild Things Are*, it is a dream-fantasy, but it has proved to be far more controversial. When it was published, some people objected to its depiction of a naked boy, and a few librarians even painted diapers on its hero. Whereas some critics dismissed the book as trite, others felt it symbolizes psycho-sexual anxieties. For such critics, the book is a psychological story about masturbation, concern about the origin of babies, or jealousy about the coming of a sibling.

Presented as a tongue-in-cheek legend or a satire of *pourquoi* tales, the plot explains why young Mickey is responsible for the cake we have every morning. Lying in his bed at night, Mickey is disturbed by noises. Angrily shouting for quiet, he falls out of both his bed and his pajamas into the Night Kitchen. Three identical bakers mistake him for milk and mix him into their cake batter. They place the batter in the oven, but Mickey soon bursts free. He fashions an airplane from rising bread dough and flies up to a milk bottle, where he gets the milk the bakers need. Having restored order to the Night Kitchen, Mickey again falls, this time into his bed and his pajamas.

CHARACTERS: Because Mickey is dreaming, the bakers and the comic book presentation reflect his concerns. Sendak has said that as a child he was bothered by advertisements for a bakery. It seemed unfair to him that bakers would bake all night while he had to go to bed. The anger that **Mickey** expresses at the beginning of the story reflects a similar sense of being unfairly excluded from secret adult activities. When he falls into the kitchen, Mickey is not recognized as someone important, but Mickey is unwilling to let adults shape him or confine him. When he bursts forth from the cake, he boldly asserts his identity. He next proves the value of his individuality by ingeniously solving the bakers' problems. Skillfully shaping dough into a plane (foreshadowed by the plane hanging over his bed), Mickey flies to get the milk that the bakers need. He thereby proves himself vital to the activities from which he was formerly excluded. He returns to his bed delighted with the fact that he now has a secret that his mother and father do not share.

The **bakers** are foils to Mickey. Because they are identical in appearance, they suggest that adults are alike, whereas Mickey is an individual. The bakers resemble the early film comic Oliver Hardy, making them humorous stereotypes of incompetent adults. Their appearance suggests that Mickey forms his dream of heroic individualism from elements from the real world, such as the movies he has watched. The bakers' frustrated demands for milk establish that Mickey, who knows how to get it, is more resourceful and more competent. Significantly, the bakers howl when they are upset, showing a lack of control that contrasts with Mickey's calm self-assurance during his dream.

Outside Over There

(picture book, 1981)

PLOT: Sendak has identified "The Goblins," a tale he illustrated for a collection of stories by the Brothers Grimm, as "the seed" for *Outside Over There*. He has also said that the book "isn't about a plot" but "is a metaphor for something else." Critics have severely criticized this third volume of Sendak's picture book trilogy, however, because that "something else" is obscure. In spite of its elusive symbol-

ism, though, *Outside Over There* is clearly a fairy tale with a theme about neglected responsibility and the ultimate acceptance of duty.

Ida's neglect of responsibility is clear. Her father is away at sea, and her mother is in the arbor, apparently sad because of her husband's departure. Ida must tend to her baby sister, but she turns her back on the infant to play her wonder horn. Because of her negligence, goblins exchange the baby for one of ice. When the ice baby begins melting, Ida realizes that the goblins have stolen her sister to be a bride. Putting on her mother's rain cloak, Ida sets off to rescue her sister. She immediately makes "a serious mistake," going backwards out the window. Consequently, Ida floats over the countryside, unable to locate the goblins. After she hears words of advice in a song her absent father sings, she turns around and quickly locates them. The goblins look like babies, and Ida charms them by playing her horn. The goblins dance until they dissolve into a stream. Ida then takes her sister home, where her mother reads a letter from Ida's father. It asks Ida to care for both her mother and her sister. The story closes with Ida accepting this double responsibility.

CHARACTERS: Although the father plays a role through song and a letter, all of the illustrated characters are female. Several critics see them as embodying attitudes to the duties society traditionally imposes on females.

Ida is a young girl who is torn between duty and personal pleasure. She, not her mother, is pictured holding the baby. Clearly, she finds the crying child a tedious burden. By literally turning her back on the child and playing her horn, Ida chooses personal pleasure over imposed duty. Nevertheless, once Ida realizes her neglect, she wants to correct it. Ida thus tries to assume a more mature role, symbolized by her wearing of her mother's rain cloak. By backing out of the window, however, Ida shows that she is not mature. Instead, she has plunged into action without understanding the proper way to proceed. But Ida is able to learn from her mistakes, and her father's song may symbolize intuitive wisdom. By turning physically in the right direction, Ida demonstrates that she will no longer turn her back on her duties. She then displays wit by using her horn to discover which of the infants facing her is her baby sister. Ida's successful journey home with her sister establishes her competence as a caregiver. Knowing her powers, she willingly accepts the additional duty of caring for her mother.

Sendak has said that **Ida's baby sister** has her own story in the book. Her role, however, is passive and symbolic. She teaches Ida that infants may sometimes be as cold as ice or as mischievous as goblins. The **goblins** personify the darker side of Ida's selfishness. They give Ida what she secretly desires, a life free from responsibility for the baby. But they also represent uncontrolled desire because they simply take whatever they want. In both cases, they test Ida's understanding and intelligence by appearing to be only infants. Ida's **mother** illustrates that parents may become so involved with their own lives and feelings that they are unaware of their children. Ida's **father**, who is a presence through his song and his letter, suggests that parental lessons and wisdom may influence children even when the parents are absent.

Further Reading

Berger, Laura Standley, ed. *Twentieth-Century Children's Writers*. 4th ed. Detroit: St. James, 1995.

Children's Literature Review. Vols. 1, 17. Detroit: Gale Research, 1976, 1989.

Collier, Laurie, and Joyce Nakamura, eds. *Major Authors and Illustrators for Children and Young Adults*. Detroit: Gale Research, 1993.

Estes, Glenn E., ed. *American Writers for Children since 1960: Poets, Illustrators, and Nonfiction Authors*. Vol. 61 of *Dictionary of Literary Biography*. Detroit: Gale Research, 1987.

Fuller, Muriel, ed. *More Junior Authors*. New York: H. W. Wilson, 1963.

Jones, Raymond E. "Maurice Sendak's *Where the Wild Things Are*: Picture Book Poetry." In *Touchstones: Reflections on the Best in Children's Literature*. Vol. 3: *Picture Books*. Edited by Perry Nodelman, pp. 122-31. West Lafayette, IN: Children's Literature Association, 1989.

Lanes, Selma G. *The Art of Maurice Sendak*. New York: Harry N. Abrams, 1980.

Something about the Author. Vols. 1, 27. Detroit: Gale Research, 1971, 1982.

Sonheim, Amy. *Maurice Sendak*. New York: Twayne, 1991.

Dr. Seuss

(pen name for Theodor Seuss Geisel)

1904-1991, American picture book author and illustrator

Horton Hatches the Egg

(picture book, 1940)

PLOT: After a breeze in his workroom blew a picture of an elephant on top of a picture of a tree, Dr. Seuss devised a plot to account for the elephant's predicament. The resulting story, *Horton Hatches the Egg*, written in anapestic couplets, celebrates the absurdly positioned elephant's determination to keep his word. Mayzie, a lazy bird hatching an egg, becomes bored with her inactivity. When Horton the elephant passes by, Mayzie asks him to take over. Horton first laughs at the idea, but Mayzie persists, and he agrees to sit on the egg. Horton then props up the tree to withstand his weight and climbs to his precarious perch. Now unburdened of her responsibility, Mayzie goes to Palm Beach and decides never to return. Although hardships test his resolve, Horton remains faithful to his promise, constantly repeating the refrain, "I meant what I said, and I said what I meant. . ./ An elephant's faithful—one hundred per cent!" He endures a rainstorm that night and withstands the ice and cold of winter; he tolerates the ridicule of other animals in the spring; and when hunters arrive, Horton defiantly faces their guns. Instead of killing him, however, the hunters transport him and his tree to New York, where they sell him to a circus. Throughout his humiliating tour as a sideshow spectacle, Horton faithfully remains on the egg. One day, when the circus nears Palm Beach, Mayzie drops in to amuse herself. When the egg subsequently begins to hatch, Mayzie accuses Horton of stealing it and claims it as her own. What emerges from the egg, however, is a creature with the ears, trunk, and tail of an elephant. Everyone declares that it *should* be an elephant-bird that came from the egg. As a reward for his steadfast dedication to duty, the people send Horton and the elephant-bird home to the jungle, where he is "Happy,/ One hundred per cent!"

CHARACTERS: The two main characters serve as foils who bring a serious message to an absurd story. The memorable pictures of **Horton** the elephant sitting on a nest in a tiny tree make him comically absurd. In one sense, Horton becomes a victim through his naive and trusting nature. Although he himself laughs at the ridiculous notion of an elephant sitting on an egg, he does not know how to resist the bird's insistent pleas for help. A kind-hearted creature, Horton innocently believes everything Mayzie tells him. Nevertheless, he is also practical, reinforcing the tree to support his weight. Ironically, although Horton allows himself to be swayed in his belief that elephants should not sit on eggs, he becomes a hero by remaining firm to his word once he has given it. His integrity forces him to endure miserable weather, social isolation, and humiliation. Through it all he never once considers abandoning his duty. Although Horton temporarily loses trust in himself and capitulates to Mayzie's demand that he leave the nest, circumstances prevent him from again becoming a victim. The hatching of the elephant-bird, which clearly loves him, proves the value of loyalty and responsibility. In a world dominated by opportunists such as Mayzie, the hunters, and the circus owner, the birth of the elephant-bird and Horton's joyful return to the jungle illustrate that honesty and integrity do bring rewards.

Mayzie the bird is described as lazy, but she has more serious faults. A fast-talking bird, she lacks any semblance of honor. Although she wants a vacation because sitting on the egg is physically uncomfortable and boring, she blatantly lies to Horton, assuring him that he will easily accomplish the task. Furthermore, unlike Horton, she does not value her word. She tells Horton that she won't be long, but

she soon decides to abandon her nest completely. The major contrast between the devoted Horton and the self-indulgent Mayzie is presented in pictures. Between the illustrations of Horton miserably but heroically enduring the rain and snow in his small tree is one of Mayzie stretched out and resting on the top of a big tree. Always an opportunist, Mayzie claims the hatching egg as her own when the tedious work of sitting is finished. Of course, the truth literally emerges from the egg, and Mayzie is last seen isolated and angry in one corner of the circus tent.

Horton Hears a Who!

(picture book, 1954)

PLOT: Inspired by a post–World War II visit to Japan, *Horton Hears a Who!* is, as Seuss admitted, a political allegory seeking tolerance for the defeated Japanese. Although few readers are now aware of its original intention, the story is still an effective plea to respect those who are different. The story begins with Horton hearing a faint cry for help from someone floating on a dust speck. When Horton places the speck safely on a flower, a kangaroo and her child ridicule him for being a fool. Horton insists that a small family could be living on the speck. They deserve safety, he repeatedly insists, because "A person's a person. No matter how small." He therefore searches for a safer place for the speck on the flower. When a group of monkeys, the Wickersham Brothers, fail to hear what Horton hears, they steal the flower. They give it to a black-bottomed eagle named Vlad Vlad-i-koff. The eagle drops the flower into a huge field of clover, but the persistent Horton eventually finds it. The kangaroo and the Wickersham Brothers, along with their relatives, suddenly appear, intending to cage Horton and to boil the dust speck. Frantically, Horton calls for the Whos on the speck to make themselves known. The Mayor of Who-ville gets everyone to shout, but the kangaroo and monkeys can't hear anything. Frantic, Horton tells the Mayor to make certain that everyone is helping. The Mayor searches and discovers that little Jo-Jo is not making a sound. When Jo-Jo finally adds his "Yopp" to everyone else's, the kangaroo and monkeys hear the Whos. The kangaroo and her child then pledge to help Horton to protect the small beings.

CHARACTERS: Through their conflicts, the characters convey the theme that both the powerful and the powerless have responsibilities. In Seuss's political allegory, **Horton** the elephant represents the United States, an immense power with a duty to recognize and protect lesser nations. In its widest application, however, Horton symbolizes the hero who stands up for the weak, regardless of their appearance or background. His refrain, "A person's a person. No matter how small," expresses his moral code. He is as committed to his word as he was in *Horton Hatches the Egg*, doing his best to protect the nearly invisible Whos. Horton maintains his belief in himself, insisting that he has heard the Whos even when the others want to imprison him for his belief. In addition to his characteristic faithfulness, Horton demonstrates sympathy and creativity. His sensitivity, as well as his large ears, enables him to hear what others can't. In addition, Horton's imagination provides him with insight. Whereas he at first imagines one family living on the speck of dust, his conversation with the Mayor enables him to realize that a whole world exists on it.

Horton also possesses other qualities that ensure his success. He has the determination of the questing hero when he follows the eagle who has stolen the flower; his tenacity prevents him from despairing while searching in the clover. Horton is also intelligent. He realizes that the Whos must make people notice them if they are to survive, so he suggests that they make loud noises and, when that tactic fails, asks them to make certain that *everyone* is yelling.

Although they clearly represent the Japanese in the political allegory, the **Whos** and the **Mayor of Who-ville** also symbolize any group without power or prestige. The insignificance of these insectlike creatures is suggested by typography: all their words appear in a tiny type that indicates soft speech. In

Horton protects his dust speck from the disapproving kangaroo in Seuss's beloved Horton Hears a Who!

spite of their size and appearance, however, the Whos have a fully developed civilization on their speck of dust (only the readers actually see it; Horton hears about it and believes in it). Although the plot indicates that their diminutive size subjects the Whos to forces beyond their control, it does not prevent them from helping themselves. Thus, **Jo-Jo**, the Who lad who does not make a sound at first, illustrates that even the least significant being can play a major role. Jo-Jo represents a cautionary figure, an allegorical testimony to the importance of voting, in which citizens influence both the administration *and* administrators of governments.

The **kangaroo** is initially described as sour. She depicts the person of limited imagination, prejudiced against new experiences. She becomes a cruel bigot who tries to destroy the dust speck and to imprison Horton because he insists on believing in the Whos. Once she realizes that the Whos do exist, however, she is the first to join Horton in protecting them. In this way, she illustrates the possibility that people can change their attitudes. The **young kangaroo in her pouch** emphasizes this lesson. Until the last page, it says what its mother says and looks exactly like its mother. On the final page, however, the young kangaroo has an expression different from its mother's. It offers an umbrella to protect the Whos, an act that individualizes it and echoes the lesson illustrated by Jo-Jo: even the smallest person can make a difference.

The Cat in the Hat

(picture book, 1957)

PLOT: Deliberately designed to prove that a book with a limited vocabulary need not be as stilted as the stories about Dick and Jane included in the basal readers of the day, *The Cat in the Hat* revolutionized books for beginning readers. Pictures narrate the story and illustrate elements beyond the simple vocabulary, but the text also sets up intriguing problems. On a rainy day, the unnamed narrator and his sister, Sally, sit bored while their mother is away. The Cat in the Hat brazenly enters the house, offering to show them some tricks. The children's fish protests, advising them to send the Cat in the Hat away. The Cat, however, begins a trick called "Up-Up-Up with a fish." Holding the fishbowl on the end of his umbrella, he bounces on a ball while balancing an array of objects. When he falls, he creates a mess. The fish, landing in a teapot, orders the Cat out of the house, but he refuses to leave. Instead, he brings in a large box containing two creatures called Thing One and Thing Two. The fish insists that the children send the Things away, but the Cat waves aside the objection, contending that they are tame. Contrary to the Cat's assertion, the Things then begin a wild game of kite-flying in the house, knocking over everything in sight. The fish sees the children's mother returning, so he calls on the children to act quickly. The narrator captures the Things in a butterfly net. The disappointed Cat then packs them up and leaves. The children stare in dismay at the mess he has left behind. The Cat in the Hat returns, however, with a strange machine that restores perfect order. The story ends with the question of whether the children should tell their mother about what has happened.

The Cat in the Hat Comes Back! (1958) is a sequel.

CHARACTERS: Dr. Seuss told critic Jonathan Cott that *"The Cat in the Hat* is a revolt against authority, but it's alleviated by the fact that the Cat cleans everything up at the end." What remains unresolved, however, is whether the characters who enact the revolt exist outside the children's imagination.

The Cat in the Hat is a classic trickster who challenges the rules and initiates comical chaos. As depicted, he is a parody of the dapper gentleman: he carries an umbrella, wears a large red bow tie and a somewhat misshapen red-and-white-striped top hat, and speaks in a highly formal manner. Whether he is a real character or only a creature of the children's imagination, the Cat represents anarchy. He sets out to enjoy activities that the mother, if present, would forbid, and the children recognize the inherently naughty behavior as completely inappropriate. The Cat is, however, somewhat incompetent. He falls during his first trick, creating a mess. He is not quite truthful when he describes the Things as tame, and they create even more of a mess. Although the Cat's childish fun gets out of hand, he assumes the role of model child when he returns to pick up his "playthings." By so doing, he suggests both that the revolt against authority need not be harmful, and that "cleaning up" after one's activities is proper.

Because they are a pair, **Thing One** and **Thing Two** more directly represent the brother and sister. Even their appearance suggests that they are their dream projections: they wear the red sleepers of very young children. Although the Things politely shake hands when the Cat introduces them, they are not, as he insists, tame. In fact, their boisterous and unrestrained behavior exceeds that of the Cat, and they nearly destroy the home with their kite flying. The narrator's capture of them signifies a regaining of self-control. Furthermore, the Cat's packing of the Things into a crate may symbolize confining the chaotic rebellion they represent to the subconscious.

Whereas the Cat in the Hat represents the children's anarchic desires, the **fish** represents their well-schooled consciences. Its protests against letting the strange visitor into the house and against playing frenzied games obviously repeat the mother's regular warnings. As a fish, however, it lives a confined life in a bowl; it lacks the mobility, the power, and the persuasiveness of the anarchic Cat. The fish gains control only by bringing up the issue of consequences, which rouses the narrator to action for the first time. Significantly, the fish asks what the mother will do to "us." This question indicates that the fish identifies with the children and suggests that it will not tell the mother about what happened.

Their passive role as observers during much of the chaos suggests that the unnamed **narrator** and his sister, **Sally**, are so bored that even an imaginary rebellion against the rules will constitute a form of amusement and entertainment. Although they allow chaos to reign, the boy asserts control when he realizes that he must act to avoid punishment. His question at the end lightly raises an ethical issue, but most commentators have suggested that the children and the fish will remain silent: because they can't produce evidence of their disobedience, their mother is not likely to believe their story anyway.

How the Grinch Stole Christmas

(picture book, 1957)

PLOT: Without making any religious references, this book celebrates Christmas as a season of joy and camaraderie. A creature who hates the joyous celebrations of the Whos, the Grinch decides to prevent Christmas from coming to Who-ville by stealing all of their decorations, presents, and food. Disguising himself as Santa Claus and his dog, Max, as a reindeer, he descends from his mountain home to Who-ville. "Grinchy Claus" descends a chimney with an empty sack and begins stripping a house bare of all festive trappings. While he is shoving the

tree up the chimney, little Cindy-Lou Who gets up for a drink, sees him, and asks why he is taking the tree. The Grinch lies, saying that he is taking it away to fix a broken light. He then gives her a drink and sends her off to bed. The Grinch subsequently robs all the other houses in Who-ville and absconds with their possessions to the top of Mount Crumpit to hurl them over the edge. Before he can do so, however, he hears a noise that he gleefully thinks must be the Whos crying. Instead, the Whos are singing joyfully, and the Grinch realizes both that he can't destroy the spirit of Christmas and that Christmas "*doesn't* come from a store." As a result of his insight, his heart grows three sizes, and he returns to the Whos all the things that he stole. At the Christmas feast, the Grinch smilingly carves the roast beast.

CHARACTERS: The story focuses on only one individual character, the Grinch. The **Grinch** begins as a grouch, but undergoes a transformation. Initially, as suggested by his malevolent pink eyes in the pictures, the Grinch is dominated by hatred. Because he has a heart "two sizes too small," the Grinch is not a charitable person. Living in isolation in his mountain cave, he feels excluded from the community. He particularly resents the sounds of communal merriment that pervade Who-ville on Christmas. The Grinch then becomes a perversely clever villain. By donning a Santa disguise, he turns a symbol of generosity into one of selfishness. Furthermore, when **Cindy-Lou Who** sees him, he quickly tells a lie to fool the innocent child. His cleverness is, however, also responsible for his transformation. When he realizes that the Whos sing carols on Christmas as if nothing had happened, the shocked Grinch ponders "until his puzzler was sore." When he finally understands the Christmas spirit, his two-sizes-too-small heart grows three sizes, becoming bigger than normal to indicate the great increase in his spirit. He therefore returns what he stole. Once lonely and filled with hatred, the Grinch becomes central to the Whos' feast, for he is given the place of honor in carving the roast beast. In the final illustration, two details underscore his transformation.

First, the Grinch's eyes, closed in joy, prevent the reader from seeing the previously-spiteful shade of pink. Second, a wreath, like a halo, hangs above the smiling Grinch.

As foils, the **Whos** demonstrate the true spirit of Christmas by singing together even after they lose their material possessions. They also exhibit their loving natures by forgiving the Grinch and by honoring him as a special guest at their feast.

Further Reading

Berger, Laura Standley, ed. *Twentieth-Century Children's Writers.* 4th ed. Detroit: St. James, 1995.

Children's Literature Review. Vols. 1, 9. Detroit: Gale Research, 1976, 1985.

Collier, Laurie, and Joyce Nakamura, eds. *Major Authors and Illustrators for Children and Young Adults.* Detroit: Gale Research, 1993.

Cott, Jonathan. "The Good Dr. Seuss." In *Pipers at the Gates of Dawn: The Wisdom of Children's Literature.* New York: Random House, 1983.

Estes, Glenn E., ed. *American Writers for Children since 1960: Poets, Illustrators, and Nonfiction Authors.* Vol. 61 of *Dictionary of Literary Biography.* Detroit: Gale Research, 1987.

Fuller, Muriel, ed. *More Junior Authors.* New York: H. W. Wilson, 1963.

Lanes, Selma G. "Seuss for the Goose Is Seuss for the Gander." In *Down the Rabbit Hole: Adventures & Misadventures in the Realm of Children's Literature.* New York: Atheneum, 1971.

MacDonald, Ruth K. *Dr. Seuss.* Boston: Twayne, 1988.

Morgan, Judith, and Neil Morgan. *Dr. Seuss & Mr. Geisel: A Biography.* New York: Random House, 1995.

Something about the Author. Vols. 1, 28, 75. Detroit: Gale Research, 1971, 1982, 1994.

Anna Sewell

1820-1878, English teacher and author

Black Beauty

(novel, 1877)

PLOT: Shortly before her death, Anna Sewell wrote that the "special aim" of her only novel was "to induce kindness, sympathy, and an understanding treatment of horses." She achieved this didactic aim by creating a plot in which a horse, who narrates the tale, is sold to various masters and thereby endures, witnesses, or hears about nearly every kind of treatment a horse can receive. Originally called Darkie, the horse begins life on a farm, where he is well treated. At age four, he is sold to Squire Gordon of Birtwick Park and becomes a riding and carriage horse called Black Beauty. He meets and learns about other horses: Sir Oliver, who has a docked tail; Ginger, who was abused by Samson Ryder; and Merrylegs, who is a cheerful pony. He is well tended by John Manly, the coachman, and James Howard, the stable boy, who rescues the horses from a barn fire. Black Beauty proves his worth one stormy night by refusing to cross a broken bridge. Later, he saves the life of his mistress, running as hard as he can when fetching the doctor. Afterwards, little Joe Green, the new stable boy, tries to care for him but does not warm and feed him properly.

Black Beauty suffers after he and Ginger are sold to the Earl of W—, whose fashion-conscious wife insists that carriage horses wear bearing reins, which lift their heads unnaturally high. In addition, both horses are ruined. Ginger is physically broken by the hard riding of the earl's son; Black Beauty, renamed Black Auster, suffers injuries when Reuben Smith, a drunken groom, neglects a loose shoe, rides him, and causes him to hurt his knees in a fall. Black Beauty now descends the social scale, being sold first as a job-horse and then as a riding horse for Mr. Barry. Because Mr. Filcher cheats the horse out of food and Alfred Smirk neglects it, the horse becomes less valuable to Mr. Barry, who decides to sell it. Black Beauty thus becomes Jack, the cab horse of Jerry (Jeremiah) Barker. Although treated well, Jack witnesses hardships: Captain, his companion, is shot after being injured by a drunken wagon driver, and Ginger, now a worn-out cab horse, is so miserable that she longs for death. Because Jerry moves to the country after an illness, Jack is sold to a corn dealer and then to Nicholas Skinner, a cab owner who overworks both cab drivers, like Seedy Sam, and his horses. One day, while pulling an over-loaded carriage, Jack collapses. He is then sold to Mr. Thoroughgood, a farmer, whose grandson, Willie, names him Old Crony and restores him to health.

The horse's travels end happily: sold to three kind ladies, he discovers that their groom is little Joe Green, now a knowledgeable horseman, who again names him Black Beauty.

CHARACTERS: Although the first edition's claim that *Black Beauty* was "translated from the original equine" now seems quaint or absurd, the first-person viewpoint forces humans to consider animals' feelings. The narrator is a handsome horse who has a shiny black coat, one white foot, and a white star on his forehead. As his role changes from spirited colt to carriage horse, saddle horse, job-horse, and cab horse, so his name also changes: **Darkie** becomes **Black Beauty**, **Black Auster**, **Jack**, and **Old Crony**. In spite of these shifting roles and names, Black Beauty does not change. Human in personality, he is sociable, observant, pleasant to animals and people, and always willing to do his best. His character depends partly on nature: good breeding is evident in both his descent from race horses and in his mother's wise advice about watching his manners. As he himself stresses, however, he is also the product of humane treatment: his master ensures good temper by refusing to break him or work him too soon. He repeatedly proves his worth by saving lives and by doing his best in every job.

By explaining his physical sensations, Black Beauty provides what amounts to a course in the proper care of horses. Sometimes he accentuates the positive, noting how comfortable he feels when he can move about in a stall and has adequate food and water. Most often, however, he is a victim who suffers the wanton cruelty of stone-throwing boys, the ignorance of those who do not know how to groom or to drive horses properly, the insensitivity of those who abuse horses for the sake of fashion, and the callousness of those who overwork horses for economic reasons. Sewell's moving descriptions led to reforms, such as the banning of bearing reins. Horses are no longer a part of daily life, but Black Beauty still engages readers because he endures suffering with quiet dignity and never becomes maudlin.

Ginger, a tall chestnut mare with a long, handsome neck, contrasts with Black Beauty. She, too, has good breeding, but she is ill-tempered because she was broken young, abused by a trainer, and suffered bearing reins. Ginger prospers under kind treatment and becomes a good worker, but she never entirely trusts humans. Her descent into misery is more profound than Black Beauty's. She becomes a miserable, worn-out cab horse who receives her wish of escape through death. **Merrylegs**, a fat little twelve-year-old gray pony with a pretty head and pert nose, is cheerful and good-tempered because he has been treated humanely all of his life. He is comically vain about his appearance and work, yet he is wise. He thus recognizes that Birtwick Park is a good place for horses, and he foretells disaster unless Ginger changes. Like Ginger, Merrylegs rebels at abuse. When some boys whip him hard while riding, he dumps them to the ground. By doing so gently so that he doesn't hurt them, however, he teaches them a lesson while retaining the respect of his master. **Sir Oliver**, an old brown hunter, says horses should be content if kindly treated, but he also describes the misery that horses endure in the name of fashion when he explains that flies have tormented him ever since his tail was docked. **Captain**, a tall, white, old cavalry horse once called Bayard, describes the horrors that horses face in war. He becomes a device to promote temperance when a drunken wagon driver injures him and he must be destroyed.

Several humans are kind. The surname of **John Manly**, the coachman at Birtwick Park, suggests that he embodies noble male virtues. Like the horses, John has a kind and gentle nature because of his youth: he received kindness after being orphaned. Manly acts as an authorial voice, condemning ignorance, such as that of little Joe Green, because its results are as devastating as those of deliberate cruelty. Furthermore, his insistence that people must interfere when they see animals being abused announces a theme that is illustrated in several episodes. **Jerry (Jeremiah) Barker**, the London cab driver, is the urban counterpart of John Manly. A devoted father and husband, he is gentle and merry, passing time by composing songs. Jerry is the ideal horse owner: he makes his horses feel good by talking to them, by giving them adequate food, and by grooming and stabling them properly. He is also important in developing three issues. First, he supports the temperance theme, having given up drink to preserve his job, marriage, and soul. Second, he criticizes those who prevent the cab drivers from honoring the Sabbath: Jerry himself steadfastly refuses to work on Sunday because doing so would rob him of his home life and would overwork his horses. Third, Jerry illustrates the hardships cab drivers endured, becoming seriously ill and having to retire after some rich men keep him waiting in the cold. **James Howard**, the nineteen-year-old stable boy, pleases the horses by skillful and kind grooming that never arouses ill temper. He bravely rescues the horses from the barn fire. Fourteen-year-old little **Joe Green** shows that knowledge as well as good intentions are necessary when dealing with horses. Although Joe tries to be kind, he causes Black Beauty distress by failing to warm him or to feed him properly. Joe Green learns, however, and grows up to be a good groom. **Mr. Thoroughgood**, an appropriately named gentleman farmer, and **Willie**, his grandson, love horses. Their kind and intelligent treatment restores Black Beauty's youthful beauty and vigor.

Among the humans who abuse horses through ignorance, callousness, concern for fashion, or greed, several are notable. **Samson Ryder** is a hard man who boasts of his power over horses. His brutal force ruins Ginger for life. **Reuben Smith** illustrates the temperance theme. Skillful when sober, he becomes negligent when drunk, causing the accident that destroys Black Beauty's knees and costs him his own life. **Mr. Filcher**, who tends Black Beauty for Mr. Barry, is a thief. He abuses the horse by substituting inadequate food for the proper diet he has been paid to provide. **Alfred Smirk**, a groom with a suggestive surname, is polite and servile, but he is also conceited and lazy, admiring himself instead of cleaning the horse and its stall. His neglect causes Black Beauty to suffer hoof problems. **Nicholas Skinner** places profit above social and moral considerations. A man with a harsh, grinding voice, he victimizes cab drivers by charging exorbitant rates

for equipment. Skinner is thus responsible for the death of Seedy Sam, who becomes ill because he can survive only by working long hours seven days a week. Skinner also overworks horses, driving them as hard as possible and selling them when he can no longer exploit them.

Further Reading

Baker, Margaret Joyce. *Anna Sewell and Black Beauty*. London: Harrap, 1956.

Berger, Laura Standley, ed. *Twentieth-Century Children's Writers*. 4th ed. Detroit: St. James, 1995.

Bingham, Jane M., ed. *Writers for Children: Critical Studies of Major Authors since the Seventeenth Century*. New York: Scribner's, 1988.

Children's Literature Review. Vol. 17. Detroit: Gale Research, 1989.

Chitty, Susan. *The Woman Who Wrote Black Beauty*. London: Hodder & Stoughton, 1971.

Collier, Laurie, and Joyce Nakamura, eds. *Major Authors and Illustrators for Children and Young Adults*. Detroit: Gale Research, 1993.

Something about the Author. Vol. 24. Detroit: Gale Research, 1981.

Margery Sharp

1905-1991, English author

The Rescuers

(animal fantasy, 1959)

PLOT: The Mouse Prisoners' Aid Society (MPSA) comforts prisoners. Members are therefore startled when the Chairwoman proposes that they free a Norwegian poet held in the notorious Black Castle. Her plan requires a mouse who can speak Norwegian. Fortunately, the Ambassador is moving to Norway, and his Boy has a pet mouse, Miss Bianca. Bernard, a pantry mouse, visits Miss Bianca in her elegant porcelain pagoda. Miss Bianca faints upon hearing the mission, but agrees to help. Flying to Norway in the Boy's diplomatic bag, Miss Bianca enlists the aid of Nils, a seafaring mouse. Eager to see Bernard again and having failed to draw a useful map (she has actually drawn a picture of a hat), Miss Bianca decides that she must return with Nils.

Traveling by ship and by toy boat, they arrive at the MPSA meeting, where Bernard volunteers to join Nils, and Miss Bianca declares that she will accompany them.

Sneaking a ride on supply wagons, they enter the Black Castle and make quarters in the Head Jailer's filthy room. They are unable, however, to devise a rescue. Complications arise when Mamelouk, a vicious cat, captures Miss Bianca, who has not learned to fear cats. But she manages to tire him out and escape. She carries away a bit of cloth that was stuck in Mamelouk's fur: written on it in blood are Norwegian words. Rededicated to their mission, the male mice explore the castle, while Miss Bianca charms information out of Mamelouk. She thus learns that they can stage an escape when the cat and the guards are incapacitated following their New Year's Eve feast. Nils and Bernard, returning to report their discovery of a way into the dungeons, walk into Mamelouk's paws. Miss Bianca then tricks Mamelouk into relaxing his guard, permitting them to escape. On New Year's, Bernard climbs upon a sleeping guard to take the keys for the door. The mice enter the dungeons and release the poet. Outside the castle, the poet nearly drowns, but people on a raft rescue him and take him to the capital. He then returns to Norway. Nils sails away in the toy boat. Miss Bianca is captured by palace servants and sent back for a joyful reunion with the Boy. Bernard becomes Secretary of the society.

The "Miss Bianca Series" continues with Miss Bianca *(1962),* The Turret *(1963),* Miss Bianca in the Salt Mines *(1966),* Miss Bianca in the Orient *(1970),* Miss Bianca in the Antarctic *(1979),* Miss Bianca and the Bridesmaid *(1972),* Bernard the Brave *(1976), and* Bernard into Battle *(1978).*

CHARACTERS: Miss Bianca engagingly blends sophistication and naivete, romantic sentiment and snobbish aloofness. She is a small mouse whose soft, silver-white coat and deep brown eyes give her the appearance of a powdered beauty in the court of Louis XV. She leads a life of elegance, living in a porcelain pagoda, eating cream cheese from a silver bon-bon dish, and wearing a fine silver chain about her neck. Intelligent and refined, Miss Bianca writes poetry. Although she has never been with other mice, she is not lonely, insisting that she has a duty to the Boy because she is his only friend. In fact, Miss Bianca refuses the demands of the world beyond her home, fainting when Bernard tells her about the mission to save the poet. As in many hero stories, this loss of consciousness symbolizes the death of one phase of her life. After being revived, Miss Bianca leaves the splendor of selfish isolation and enters the dangerous world of heroic action. Of course, she agrees to the mission only because Bernard assures her that her task is relatively easy and because Bernard's praise of her beauty awakens feelings of love. Furthermore, she does not change completely. She remains acutely class conscious. Thus, although she hides her feelings, she is not grateful when Nils makes her wear shabby galoshes. During the journey to the castle, she doesn't associate with the field mice who come to their camps, feeling that they lack education and sophistication. More significantly, she worries about her feelings for Bernard because he is socially undistinguished.

Ironically, at least some of Miss Bianca's flaws are crucial to her growth. In Norway, when she fails to draw a map for Nils, vanity compels her prove that she can draw. Subsequently embarrassed because Nils accepts her drawing of a hat as a chart, she volunteers to guide him. She then realizes that she also wants to see Bernard again. Her vanity also leads her to continue the mission. Thus, eager to bask in the glory of success, she accompanies Nils to the MPSA meeting, and her desire to see more of Bernard impels her to go to the castle. At this point, Miss Bianca is comically naive, carrying toilet articles and a small fan instead of practical tools. Once inside the Castle, her naivete is nearly fatal: having been friends with a Persian cat, she does not properly fear Mamelouk. Unaware that Mamelouk is trying to torture her, she shows such wild exuberance that she confuses and tires the cat, therefore avoiding harm.

Once Miss Bianca accepts that Mamelouk is dangerous, her virtues of wit and resourcefulness transform her into a trickster hero. Wisely seeing that she fascinates Mamelouk, she charms useful information out of him. While doing so, she proves herself a good judge of character, recognizing that vanity makes Mamelouk lie about never becoming cranky. She shows her greatest courage and self-control, however, when Mamelouk captures Nils and Bernard. Instead of fainting, as she once would have, she calmly plays on his appetite, vanity, and sense of identity, confusing the cat into relaxing his guard before directing Nils and Bernard to escape. As the pressure of heroic necessity diminishes, Miss Bianca returns to her former identity. Fate, in the form of the servants who send her back to the Boy, prevents her from indicating whether she wants to stay with Bernard. Nevertheless, the fact that she is happy and decides that life in the porcelain pagoda suits her best indicates that she remains too status conscious to give herself to someone who is socially inferior.

Bernard, the rough but decent pantry mouse, is brave but modest. He is motivated by an unrequited love for Miss Bianca. Having seen her faint and feel fearful earlier, he gallantly tries to keep her ignorant of Mamelouk's existence, an overly protective gesture that proves nearly fatal. His brave resourcefulness is most evident when he recognizes that a sleeping guard is like a mountain and that, consequently, he can climb him to reach the keys. Bernard seems comically pathetic when the servants who snatch Miss Bianca away cut off his humble proposal. He goes on to achieve a significant position and a good career. **Nils**, the sea-faring Norwegian, contrasts with the serious Bernard because he is a comical character. Wearing tar-smelling sea boots and a dirty stocking cap, he is a rough and ready character who is unperturbed by danger. He laughs about not being a family man, but he can be sentimental, reciting a patriotic motto before going into action. Although he seems foolish in his insistence that the drawing of the hat is the best chart he has ever had (a claim remarkably substantiated when he uses it to sail directly to the capital), he becomes a serious, observant, and resourceful hero at Black Castle. He discovers the entrance into the dungeons, making the escape possible. **Mamelouk**, an enormous, black, half-Persian cat with eyes like dirty emeralds, is demonically cruel. He delights in torturing prisoners by spitting on them. He also

enjoys the idea of torturing mice. He is vain, boasting that he never gets sick because of his iron stomach. Like most seemingly invincible villains, he has a weakness: his stupidity. He is not clever enough to fool Miss Bianca, who recognizes that he is a chronic liar. His stupidity, intensified by his greed and vanity, is his undoing. Made to feel that he will be too sated to enjoy the New Year's feast if he eats Nils and Bernard and that he will be no better than a goldfish if he kills them to eat later, he becomes so confused that the mice escape.

Further Reading

Berger, Laura Standley, ed. *Twentieth-Century Children's Writers*. 4th ed. Detroit: St. James, 1995.

Children's Literature Review. Vol. 27. Detroit: Gale Research, 1992.

Collier, Laurie, and Joyce Nakamura, eds. *Major Authors and Illustrators for Children and Young Adults*. Detroit: Gale Research, 1993.

Contemporary Authors New Revision Series. Vol. 18. Detroit: Gale Research, 1986.

De Montreville, Doris, and Donna Hill, eds. *Third Book of Junior Authors*. New York: H. W. Wilson, 1972.

Hunt, Caroline C., ed. *British Children's Writers since 1960: First Series*. Vol. 161 of *Dictionary of Literary Biography*. Detroit: Gale Research, 1996.

Something about the Author. Vols. 1, 29. Detroit: Gale Research, 1971, 1982.

Zylpha Keatley Snyder

1927-, American author

The Egypt Game

(novel, 1967)

PLOT: By mixing a personal problem story and a murder mystery, this popular novel advances themes about maturity, friendship, false appearances, and imagination. April Hall has been sent to live with Caroline, her grandmother, while her mother, Dorothea Dawn, goes on tour as a singer. April meets Melanie Ross, an African American her age. In spite of April's outlandish attire and ill-fitting false eyelashes, the girls become friends because both

love imaginative play. One day, the girls and Marshall, Melanie's four-year-old brother, enter a deserted yard behind an antique shop run by an old man known as the Professor. Finding a bust of Nefertiti, the girls convert the yard into an Egyptian temple and begin an elaborate game about ancient Egypt. Soon, they include nine-year-old Elizabeth Chung in their game.

When a child is murdered one evening, the ensuing panic forces the girls to suspend the game. On Halloween, however, they escape from the adults escorting them so that they can perform a ceremony. While they are doing so, two boys, Toby Alvillar and Ken Kamata, invade "Egypt." Allowed to join the game, they promise not to reveal the girls' secret. Although April becomes sullen after she learns that her mother has married and that she will have to stay longer with Caroline, the game resumes. The children perform a ceremony for Elizabeth's dead parakeet and begin asking questions of and receiving written answers from the oracle Thoth. When Marshall asks Thoth the whereabouts of his missing stuffed octopus, Security, Toby confesses to the others that he has written the oracle's answers. Toby insists, however, that he is not the author of the message revealing the location of Security. Later, while babysitting Marshall, April realizes that she has left a school book in "Egypt" and goes with Marshall to retrieve it. While there, April is attacked. Someone shouts for help, however, and her assailant flees. Although the police suspect the Professor,

April Hall, Melanie Ross, and their friends play an imaginative game that is spoiled by a real murder in Snyder's The Egypt Game, *illustrated by Alton Raible.*

Marshall identifies the attacker as a mentally unstable man who works nearby.

April's mother now invites her to come for Christmas, but April decides to spend the holidays with Caroline. On Christmas Eve, the Professor, Dr. Julian Huddleston, reveals that he watched the children, wrote the message about the octopus, and called for help when April was attacked. He presents each of the Egyptians with a personalized key to the yard. Melanie and April realize that the Egypt Game can never be the same, but April suggests playing gypsies.

CHARACTERS: *The Egypt Game* was one of the first novels to present—without didactic comment—central characters representing a variety of racial backgrounds. Eleven-year-old **April Hall** is a thin, pale blond who has freckles spattered over her high cheek bones and short nose. April is intensely lonely. Her father, whom she hardly knew, died in the Korean War, and her mother neglects her to pursue a singing career. Feeling rejected, April disguises her pain by creating a new identity. She frequently introduces herself as April Dawn, thus employing her mother's surname. Although she tries to look sophisticated, April is unintentionally comical. Her clothes are outlandish, her false eyelashes are crooked, and her hair is a straggly pile because she can't create the upswept hairdo that her mother wears. April also constantly brags about having lived in Hollywood. Consequently, few children have liked her, and she has never really had any playmates.

April gains friends and matures because of her powerful imagination. She and Melanie come to like each other because they both love to use their imaginations. Games of imagination provide April with a world in which she is powerful and special, but they also force her to compromise and cooperate. As a result, she gains additional friends and matures enough to abandon her outlandish wardrobe. April also matures in her relationships with adults. She believes that she understands adults, which she demonstrates by insisting that the Professor could not be the murderer. She is, however, reluctant to recognize that her mother does not really want her. Furthermore, she tries to maintain an emotional distance from her grandmother, pointedly insisting on calling her Caroline. Later, however, April shows that she is growing when she allows Caroline to cut her hair and to apply her false eyelashes. By doing so, she moves away from the mother who rejected her and toward the grandmother who loves her. April's final moment of maturity comes when she rejects her mother's invitation. She shows that she has found a loving home and good friends by deciding to spend Christmas with Caroline.

Melanie Ross is a well-rounded character in her own right, but her main function is to interpret April's conduct. She realizes and thus explains to the reader, for example, that April's bragging is a way of coping with homesickness. Melanie is a thin, eleven-year-old African American who loves reading and what she calls "imagining games," creating stories with paper dolls. April's arrival tests Melanie, who wants a friend in her own building. Melanie sees beneath April's outrageous appearance, but she knows the importance of first impressions. To prevent other children from immediately rejecting April on the first day of school, Melanie therefore hides April's false eyelashes. By doing so, she shows the depth of her friendship and becomes instrumental in widening April's circle of friends.

Four-year-old **Marshall Ross**, Melanie's brother, is deeply attached to Security, his stuffed octopus. Marshall is secretive. He knows that the Professor watches the children, but he never tells anyone. He is also stubborn, a trait that annoys the children but proves a blessing for April and the Professor. Marshall refuses to be left alone when April goes to get the school book she has left behind in "Egypt." Marshall is thus in a position to signal the Professor for help, thereby saving April, and to identify the attacker, saving the Professor. Tiny **Elizabeth Chung** is only nine years old, but April and Melanie invite her into the game because they think that she looks like Nefertiti. Although Elizabeth is valuable to the Egypt Game primarily because she admires the inventions of the others, she adds one important element: artistic and clever with her hands, Elizabeth originates the idea of wearing costumes. Elizabeth also saves the game when she makes a heartfelt plea to the boys not to expose their secret and openly invites them to join the game. **Toby Alvillar** supposedly has a talent for making people laugh, but none of his statements or actions is particularly funny. Toby is a skillful actor who throws himself fully into the game. He is also a prankster: he secretly answers messages to the oracle in order to inject more mystery and excitement into the game. **Ken Kamata**, Toby's friend, does not share Toby's delight in games of imagination. He finds pretending to be awkward and embarrassing.

Several adults play important roles in the story. Like April, **the Professor, Dr. Julian Huddleston**, is linked to a theme about false appearances. He also moves from bitter isolation to active involvement in life. A tall, bent man with a thin beard and eyes set so deep that they look like empty holes, he has become a figure of fear to most of the children. Consequently, many in the neighborhood immediately suspect him of the murder. Actually, the Professor is a lonely man who withdrew from life after his anthropologist wife was killed by the very people she was trying to help. Watching the imaginative games of the children brings him back into life. He enters more fully into their lives by saving Security from the rain and then writing the note that enables Marshall to find it. He finally breaks free of his self-imposed prison when he responds to Marshall's look and silent plea for help when April is attacked. **Caroline**, April's grandmother, is a kind, nonjudgmental woman. Caroline never utters critical comments, even when April rejects her request to be called grandmother. Nevertheless, she provides the love and stability that April needs. **Dorothea Dawn**, April's mother, appears only in letters and through April's thoughts about her. A singer and aspiring bit player in Hollywood, Dorothea is self-indulgent and negligent. She does not write often, and she does not realize that April expects to be with her grandmother only a short time. When April rejects Dorothea's invitation to visit with her and her new husband at Christmas, April shows awareness of her mother's shallowness and of Caroline's love and acceptance.

Further Reading

Berger, Laura Standley, ed. *Twentieth-Century Young Adult Writers*. 1st ed. Detroit: St. James, 1994.

Children's Literature Review. Vol. 31. Detroit: Gale Research, 1994.

Collier, Laurie, and Joyce Nakamura, eds. *Major Authors and Illustrators for Children and Young Adults*. Detroit: Gale Research, 1993.

Contemporary Authors New Revision Series. Vol. 38. Detroit: Gale Research, 1993.

Contemporary Literary Criticism. Vol. 17. Detroit: Gale Research, 1981.

De Montreville, Doris, and Donna Hill, eds. *Third Book of Junior Authors*. New York: H. W. Wilson, 1972.

Something about the Author. Vols. 1, 28, 75. Detroit: Gale Research, 1971, 1982, 1994.

Something about the Author Autobiography Series. Vol. 2. Detroit: Gale Research, 1986.

Donald J. Sobol

1924-, American author

Encyclopedia Brown, Boy Detective

(mystery, 1963)

PLOT: This book, which sets the pattern for the series that followed, consists of ten brief, independent mysteries that Encyclopedia (Leroy) Brown solves through deduction. Encyclopedia begins his career one night at the dinner table. While Mrs. Brown serves dessert, his father, the Idaville police chief, reads aloud a statement about a robbery in a clothing store. Spotting a discrepancy in the evidence, Encyclopedia immediately proves that the store owner staged the robbery to fool his partner. Because of his success, Encyclopedia opens a detective agency, solving crimes for the fee of twenty-five cents. (The solution to each of the subsequent cases is printed at the back of the book.) His first two cases involve Bugs Meany, the leader of the Tigers. Encyclopedia proves that Bugs took a tent that doesn't belong to the Tigers and then exposes his attempt to sell a fake Civil War sword. After defeating tough Sally Kimball in a contest that requires solving a mystery that she poses, Encyclopedia makes her his junior partner and bodyguard. Sally accompanies Encyclopedia on some cases, but he actually solves them.

The series continues with twenty-one more titles.

CHARACTERS: This formulaic series depends on snappy dialogue and simple plots; characterization is of the most basic kind. Ten-year-old **Leroy Brown** is called **Encyclopedia Brown** by everyone in Idaville because he has filled his head with the facts gleaned from his reading. Encyclopedia seems like any other fifth-grader, except that he never talks about himself. Because he wants people to like him, he tries not to appear too smart. Therefore, he always pauses before answering questions. This sneaker-wearing detective has one other idiosyncrasy: he always closes his eyes when he thinks hard. Encyclopedia solves all his cases by paying close attention to details and by noticing inconsistencies. Young readers trying to solve the mysteries must therefore pay close attention to the text.

Encyclopedia's father, **Chief Brown**, is no fool, but he is not as observant as his son. He discusses cases with Encyclopedia and lets his son accompany him, but he protectively makes him wait in the police cruiser when he interrogates suspects. **Mrs. Brown**, Encyclopedia's mother, adds a comic touch. She is proud that her son has learned deduction from books, not television. Once an English teacher, she constantly corrects his grammar, making him say *may* instead of *can*. Encyclopedia's friend, fifth-grader **Sally Kimball**, is pretty and athletic. She is also tough. When she sees Bugs Meany bullying a little boy, she orders him to stop. When he refuses, she repeatedly knocks him to the ground. Sally is a bit arrogant, trying unsuccessfully to prove in a contest that she is smarter than Encyclopedia Brown. (Unfortunately, the contest is lopsided, requiring Sally to set a puzzle for Encyclopedia but not requiring him to set one for her.) In this volume, **Bugs Meany**, the toughest member and the leader of the Tigers, is the major villain. He is a liar who steals a tent belonging to another boy and a cheat who tries to pass off an old sword as one owned by Stonewall Jackson. Not surprisingly, he is a bully who picks on little kids.

Further Reading

Berger, Laura Standley, ed. *Twentieth-Century Children's Writers*. 4th ed. Detroit: St. James, 1995.

Children's Literature Review. Vol. 4. Detroit: Gale Research, 1982.

Collier, Laurie, and Joyce Nakamura, eds. *Major Authors and Illustrators for Children and Young Adults*. Detroit: Gale Research, 1993.

Contemporary Authors New Revision Series. Vol. 38. Detroit: Gale Research, 1993.

De Montreville, Doris, and Elizabeth D. Crawford, eds. *Fourth Book of Junior Authors*. New York: H. W. Wilson, 1978.

Something about the Author. Vols. 1, 31, 73. Detroit: Gale Research, 1971, 1983, 1993.

Elizabeth George Speare

1908-, American writer

The Witch of Blackbird Pond

(historical novel, 1958)

PLOT: This Newbery Medal-winning romance examines a Puritan society in colonial America that is oppressive in manners but fiercely independent in its political ideals. Impoverished after her grandfather's death, Kit Tyler sails from Barbados to America without informing her relatives that she is coming. At the first port, Kit's manners create conflict when she impulsively dives into the water to retrieve Prudence Cruff's doll, and Goodwife Cruff suggests that Kit is a witch because she floats. When Kit arrives in Wethersfield, Connecticut, Uncle Matthew Wood, a stern Puritan, disapproves of her attire and ways but allows her to stay. Kit likes Aunt Rachel and her cousins, Judith and the lame Mercy, but she finds Matthew intolerant and Puritan life dreary. That summer, Kit teaches school, but Eleazer Kimberley dismisses her for having her students act out a biblical scene. Distraught, Kit runs to a meadow, where she meets Hannah Tupper, an old Quaker reputed to be a witch. Hannah reintroduces her to Nathaniel Eaton, whom Kit met earlier on the ship. Hannah also advises Kit, who subsequently gets Mr. Kimberley to reinstate her. Although forbidden to do so, Kit continues to visit Hannah. She also secretly teaches abused Prudence Cruff to read.

For most of the novel, mismatched courtships, political arguments, and social resentments dominate. The romantic mismatches begin when wealthy William Ashby courts Kit, who sees him mostly as a means for escaping her oppressive home. Superficial Judith eyes John Holbrook, the serious student of Reverend Gersholm Bulkeley. Although Mercy and John love each other, John is trapped into courting Judith. At this point, political events interrupt. Matthew and the Connecticut freemen resist the royal governor's efforts to revoke their charter. Kit then weakens her social standing by publicly talking to Nat Eaton, who has been put in the stocks for setting jack-o-lanterns in William's house.

John Holbrook then breaks from the royalist Bulkeley by leaving with the militia. Soon afterwards, a fever sweeps the community. Judith and Mercy become ill and three children die. Reverend Bulkeley sets aside political disagreements to tend to Mercy. Others, however, blame the illness on the witchcraft of Hannah. They burn Hannah's cabin, but Kit gets her to the safety of Nat's ship. Kit is then charged with witchcraft. At her trial, Goodwife Cruff and her husband, Adam, are the chief accusers. Matthew defends Kit, but evidence that she disobeyed him seems to doom her. When Nat brings Prudence Cruff to court, however, her ability to read and write fills Adam Cruff with pride, and he renounces his charges. Kit is thus acquitted. Afterwards, Kit ends her courtship with William because he did not support her during the trial. When John Holbrook returns after being held captive by Indians, he proposes to Mercy, and William proposes to Judith. Kit, realizing that she belongs in New England, accepts a proposal from Nat Eaton, now the owner of his own sloop.

CHARACTERS: As representative social types, the characters demonstrate that Puritan society was far from homogeneous. Several are based on actual people, but only one of these plays a notable role. Sixteen-year-old **Kit Tyler** (Kit is short for Katherine) enlists sympathy because her cheerfulness, independence, and impulsiveness make her an outsider. Her enlightened attitudes toward witchcraft, her appreciation of imaginative literature, and her love of natural beauty also make her seem more sensitive than the dour Puritans. Furthermore, Kit shows admirable resourcefulness by sailing for America after her grandfather's death. Nevertheless, she has flaws. Kit is sometimes proud and unsympathetic with the Puritans. She also lacks restraint, although her characteristic impulsiveness is often motivated by good intentions. Sympathy causes her to dive into the water to retrieve Prudence's doll, a delight in beauty leads her to offer her aunt and cousins fine clothing, and a genuine desire to interest her students prompts her to have them act out biblical scenes. She fails to consider, however, that the colonists perceive such actions to be frivolous, unseemly, or irreligious. At other times, her impulsiveness is unquestionably negative. For example, resentful of the tedious work, Kit becomes impatient when preparing corn pudding, consequently ruining the family's meal.

Detesting Puritan restrictions, Kit secretly rebels. Although Matthew forbids it, Kit visits Hannah because the old woman is lonely. Furthermore, because she perceives a spark of interest in Prudence, Kit secretly teaches her to read and write. Even during her trial, Kit maintains this secret, showing both foolish disregard for her own safety and a heroic regard for Prudence's welfare. Kit learns her greatest lessons in different ways. By witnessing Matthew's independence and his love of the land, Kit learns to respect him and other New Englanders; by being sensitive to the changing seasons, she learns that she belongs in New England; and by heeding Hannah's advice, she understands that she needs love, not escape from oppression. No longer feeling proudly superior, Kit finally understands that she loves both New England and Nat.

At first, **Uncle Matthew Wood** seems like a stereotypically stern and uncompromising religious zealot. Tall and angular, with dark, fiercely glowering eyes and heavy eyebrows, he is cold and frequently angry. His harsh condemnation of Kit's gift of dresses as "frippery" is a typical expression of his moral certainty. Matthew's fierce defense of freemen's rights, however, deepens his portrait by suggesting he possesses the same spirit that ultimately inspired the Revolution. Furthermore, Matthew occasionally shows a human side. He is a caring father when he forgets political squabbles so that Bulkeley can treat Mercy. He also humbles himself when he tells Kit that her efforts during the illness proved that he had misjudged her. Although Matthew is callously unconcerned about Hannah's safety because she is a Quaker, he firmly and intelligently denies that she is a witch. Finally, he shows that he is above ignorant bigotry and petty resentments when he bravely defends Kit. **Aunt Rachel Wood**, who ran away from England and married without her family's blessing, has become a thin, gray-haired woman whose harsh life has robbed her of beauty. Usually timid and deferential with her husband, Rachel is kind, understanding, and accepting of others. She takes Kit in, insists that she would be proud to accompany Kit to Meeting in spite of her husband's objections to Kit's fine apparel, and keeps secret Kit's visits to Hannah.

Kit's cousins are Judith and Mercy. Sixteen-year-old **Judith**, who has blue eyes and curly black hair, possesses the beauty her mother lost. Judith is superficial, but she is also blunt and outspoken. Anxious to marry, she is attracted to John Holbrook because he is handsome and to William Ashby because he is wealthy and shares her concern for material possessions. **Mercy**, the novel's most improbable character, is a model of patience and self-renunciation. Crippled by a childhood disease, she is the calm center of the household and exemplifies the patience that Kit lacks. She never demands anything and never criticizes others. Mercy is so accustomed to being a self-effacing saint that she hides her feelings for John Holbrook, who is therefore trapped into courting Judith.

Markedly different suitors provide the conventional love interest to the novel. **Nat Eaton** (Nat is short for Nathaniel), the thin and wiry son of a ship's captain, has sun-bleached, sandy hair. Independent, proud, and witty, Nat frequently mocks Kit's pretensions. He is also kind and protective. He warns Kit that others find her conduct offensive and provides Hannah Tupper with gifts and labor. Although he demonstrates immature jealousy when he puts lighted pumpkins in William's house, Nat is brave and resourceful, saving Kit by bringing Prudence to the trial even though he has been banished from the settlement. In contrast, nineteen-year-old **William Ashby** seldom speaks in Kit's presence and never jeopardizes his social standing. Holding the important position of Viewer of Fences, he is obsessed with wealth and status, talking only about the house he is building. His conversion to the freemen's position earns Kit's respect, but his shallowness is painfully evident when he fails to support her or to attend her trial. **John Holbrook**, a tall, angular man with a pale face and fair, shoulder-length hair, is the only suitor who changes significantly. Too poor to attend Harvard, he studies medicine and theology with Reverend Bulkeley. A serious, dedicated student in both fields, John is overly impressed with Bulkeley and echoes even his royalist sentiments. Eventually, John matures and realizes that loyalty to Bulkeley as a teacher does not require that he abandon his own opinions. John adds comedy to the love story because he is timid in his romantic affairs. Although he loves Mercy, he is so shocked by

Judith's assumption that he is courting her that he fails to correct her. Only after he has escaped from Indian captivity, thereby proving his manhood, does he express his true feelings.

There are several minor but important characters in the novel. **Hannah Tupper**, an elderly, toothless Quaker widow living beside swampy Blackbird Pond, is important as a device for revealing character. Dogmatic Matthew considers her to be a heretic unworthy of help until she repents. The ignorant settlers consider her a witch who curses their village with a disease. To the tender-hearted Nat and Kit, however, she is a lonely woman, an outsider, as both of them are, who is kind, loving, and wise. **Goodwife Cruff** is an ignorant shrew who expresses the community's most negative and insular feelings. She seems particularly villainous because she physically and mentally abuses her daughter, Prudence. **Adam Cruff** rises from cowed husband to independent man when parental pride shows him that his wife has wrongfully claimed that Prudence was slow-witted. Scrawny **Prudence Cruff** represents hope for the future. Abused at home, she becomes a brighter, better person after she overcomes her fear of Hannah and after she learns to read and write. She shows great courage by testifying in Kit's defense. Of the actual historical personages in the novel, **Reverend Dr. Gersholm Bulkeley**, the learned theologian and physician, is the most important. He represents the royalist, conservative element of society. He angers Matthew when he comes to dinner by enlisting the Bible to support the royalist cause. Bulkeley establishes that good men can be on opposing sides, however, when he comes unbidden to treat Mercy.

The Bronze Bow

(historical novel, 1961)

PLOT: Speare's second Newbery Medal winner develops themes of faith and love. Daniel bar Jamin, a blacksmith who fled from an abusive master, belongs to Rosh's gang of outlaws. Although Daniel believes that Rosh will lead the Jews against the hated Romans, Rosh plunders and robs only for his own benefit. On one raid, the outlaws steal Samson, an enormous black slave who becomes devoted to Daniel. Later, Daniel visits his grandmother and his sister, Leah, who has not left the house since her father's crucifixion. He also accompanies Simon the Zealot to hear Jesus. Rosh then sends Daniel to enlist Daniel's friend Joel bar Hezron into their cause. Before he can recruit Joel, Daniel argues with Joel's father about how to deal with the Romans, and the elder Hezron orders him never to return. Shortly afterwards, Daniel shows defiance to a Roman soldier, who wounds him. Daniel escapes to Joel's house, where Joel and his twin sister, Malthace, secretly nurse him. Taking the bronze bow mentioned in Psalms 18:34 as their emblem, all three vow to fight for God's victory.

After Daniel rejoins the outlaws, he robs a miser, but Rosh denounces him as soft because he spares the miser's life. Shortly afterwards, when his grandmother dies, Daniel goes to live with Leah in the home and shop of Simon the Zealot, who has left to follow Jesus. Nevertheless, Daniel still works for Rosh, recruiting villagers to the Jewish cause and getting Joel to spy for him. Daniel soon learns, however, that he has misplaced his faith. Rosh, who used Joel's information to plunder wealthy homes, refuses to rescue Joel when the Romans arrest him. Finally seeing Rosh for what he truly is, Daniel and Joktan, a young outlaw, quit the band. Daniel then organizes a rescue attempt, which succeeds only because Samson suddenly appears and saves both Joel and Daniel. Captured himself, Samson is taken away to be executed. Later, Daniel goes to Jesus, who tells him to give up his hatred. Unable to do so, Daniel rejects Malthace's love. His hatred then sends Leah into her shell because Daniel denounces her for talking to Marcus, a Roman soldier. Not long after that, Leah becomes seriously ill. Malthace brings Jesus, who heals Leah. Daniel sees that he wants to follow Jesus and that he and Malthace are in love. Now understanding that love can bend a bronze bow in God's service, Daniel invites Marcus into his home to see Leah.

CHARACTERS: Speare said that her aim was to "show the change wrought in just one boy who came to know the teacher in Galilee." The secondary characters illuminate the political, social, and religious contexts of the protagonist's transformation.

Daniel bar Jamin changes from a boy filled with "black hatred" to a man practicing the Christian message of love. A tall eighteen-year-old with a lean, hard body, Daniel lives only for vengeance. Ten years earlier, he saw the Romans crucify his father and his uncle. Shortly thereafter, Daniel's mother died. Blaming the Romans for making him an orphan, Daniel vowed to hate, fight, and kill them. Because Daniel is naive, however, he unwittingly works against his people. Thus, his hero worship of Rosh, who rescued and raised him, leads Daniel to believe Rosh's claims that robbing Jews will advance the campaign against the Romans. His childish jealousy also makes Daniel an eager victim of Rosh's deceptions. More seriously, Daniel's hatred makes him lose self-control. Thus, he throws water on one soldier, who subsequently wounds him; he spits when a soldier orders him to carry his pack, thereby endangering the disguised Malthace; and he orders Marcus out of his shop, declaring that he would let Leah die before permitting him to say farewell to her. Similarly, his hatred makes him lose patience with those, like Hezron, who do not accept violence. Daniel's hatred also isolates him, preventing him from recognizing that Samson is a friend and causing him to reject Malthace's love.

Although he is rash and foolish, Daniel has virtues. Ironically, the softness that Rosh denounces as a flaw is actually the virtue of compassion. It indicates that Daniel is able to love. Daniel displays this compassion when he spares the miser and when he tells Rosh that his plundering makes poor farmers suffer. Daniel's idealism is also a virtue. Initially, it takes the form of revolutionary nationalism. Later, it becomes a spiritual dedication to the kingdom of God, which is established by love, especially love of one's enemies. Daniel is transformed because he gains spiritual insight. Thus, he sees that Rosh is a manipulative outlaw, Jesus is his real leader, Malthace is offering the gift of her love, and Marcus is capable of the same feelings he has. By inviting Marcus into his home, Daniel shows that he has placed his faith in Jesus, has gained control of himself, has banished his hatred, and has truly become a man.

Leah, Daniel's fifteen-year-old sister, is a touchstone who reveals the true nature of those around her. A beautiful, blue-eyed, blond-haired girl (her grandmother was a Greek slave), she has been a fearful recluse ever since she saw her father crucified. The villagers thus superstitiously fear her as one possessed by demons. Leah's delight in clothing and stories brings out the kindness in Daniel. Her girlish enthusiasm for their friendship shows Malthace's loving nature, and her ability to share feelings with Marcus establishes that he is sensitive and humane even though he is a Roman. Because she has been cut off from the world for so long, Leah is naive and fragile. Consequently, Daniel's anger that she has talked to Marcus plunges her into her former darkness, thereby supporting the theme that hatred is the real enemy. Leah is restored through the love of Malthace, who brings Jesus to her, and the faith of Daniel, who gives up his hatred to follow Jesus.

Joel bar Hezron, a wealthy, intelligent, polite, and self-controlled student, represents the idealists who long for the end of the Roman occupation. Youthfully impatient, he dismisses his father's passive approach of leaving the future to God. As a result, he suggests that Rosh may be the messiah. After he is saved from the Romans, Joel shows maturity and patience, deciding to do something worthy and to make his father proud of him. He thus resumes his studies so that he can be persuasive when a true leader arises. Joel's twin sister, **Malthace**, who is also called **Thace** and **Thacia**, contrasts with Daniel because love motivates her. Sensitive, spiritual, and intelligent, Malthace interprets the bronze bow as a sign that people can accomplish seemingly impossible deeds when God strengthens them. Malthace is most notable for her characteristic compassion, displayed when she nurses Daniel, when she befriends Leah, and when she brings Jesus to her. She also provides a conventional love interest,

accepting Daniel in spite of class differences. **Hezron**, Joel's father, is a tall, narrow-faced Pharisee. He primarily represents the established Jewish community, displaying a cold dedication to the letter of the Law. He also suggests to Joel that Jesus is not a true rabbi because he advocates breaking the Law. The pragmatic Hezron opposes armed revolution as futile; he resigns himself to waiting for God to end the suffering of the Jews.

Two contrasting leaders attract faithful followers. **Jesus** voices the theme of the novel when he tells Daniel that hate is the true enemy and that those who follow him must learn to love. He is a charismatic speaker whose voice thrills Daniel and whose eyes seem to penetrate his thoughts. Although some followers want him to be a military leader, the kingdom he talks about is spiritual. Throughout, Jesus is characterized by weariness, the result of caring for the afflicted and the poor. Nevertheless, he shows humor and understanding, healing Leah when he sees into her brother's changed heart. The outlaw leader **Rosh**, a false messiah, is a foil to Jesus. A squat, thick, muscular man with a matted beard, grizzled eyebrows, and small black eyes, he pretends to fight for the Jewish cause. Actually, he is self-centered and manipulative, engaging in criminal activities designed to enrich himself. What good he does—such as saving Daniel when he ran away from his master or freeing slaves like Samson—he does for his own benefit. He most clearly places himself in opposition to Jesus, however, when he condemns Daniel's compassion as a flaw and vows to drive all softness out of him. **Joktan**, a skinny, jagged-toothed, stuttering boy, leaves Rosh's band when he sees that Rosh is a callous hypocrite. Joktan finds contentment because, unlike Daniel, he has a pleasing disposition and willingly undertakes tasks considered to be women's work.

Simon the Zealot, a blacksmith, rejects Rosh, telling Daniel that he prefers to earn, not steal, his bread. Simon is a man of perfect faith who gives up his possessions in order to follow Jesus. **Samson**, a huge black slave who never speaks, illustrates that friendship can cross the boundaries of race and class. Grateful to Daniel for breaking his manacles, Samson sacrifices himself to save Daniel. **Marcus**, the blond German serving in the Roman army, establishes a similar idea: the humanity of one's enemies. A homesick, kind, sensitive young man, Marcus has strong feelings for Leah. His sigh of relief when told that she is cured shows Daniel that Romans have the same feelings that he does.

Further Reading

Berger, Laura Standley, ed. *Twentieth-Century Young Adult Writers*. 1st ed. Detroit: St. James, 1994.

Children's Literature Review. Vol. 8. Detroit: Gale Research, 1985.

Collier, Laurie, and Joyce Nakamura, eds. *Major Authors and Illustrators for Children and Young Adults*. Detroit: Gale Research, 1993.

Contemporary Authors. Vols. 1-4. Detroit: Gale Research, 1967.

Fuller, Muriel, ed. *More Junior Authors*. New York: H. W. Wilson, 1963.

Something about the Author. Vols. 5, 62. Detroit: Gale Research, 1973, 1991.

Armstrong Sperry

1897-1976, American novelist and nonfiction writer

Call It Courage

(novel, 1940; published in England as The Boy Who Was Afraid, *1942)*

PLOT: Identical opening and closing paragraphs frame the narrative of this Newbery Medal winner, emphasizing that it is an account of legendary heroism. Set in the days before missionaries and traders came to Polynesia, the story follows the adventures of Mafatu, son of the Great Chief of the island of Hikueru. When he was three, Mafatu and his mother were caught by a sudden storm that pushed their canoe out to sea and capsized it. Mafatu's mother saved him before dying. Now Mafatu, because he fears the sea upon which his people depend for food, is an outcast forced to do the work of girls and women. His only companions are Kivi, a

Young Mafatu overcomes his fear of the sea in Sperry's award-winning, self-illustrated book, Call It Courage.

wounded albatross he has healed, and Uri, a mongrel dog. After Mafatu overhears Kana, the only boy still friendly to him, ridicule him as a coward, Mafatu determines to leave Hikueru and never return until he can make his father proud of him.

Mafatu's adventures help him to achieve his desire. Accompanied by Uri and led through the reefs by Kivi, Mafatu sets out for unknown islands. Far out at sea, a mighty storm swamps his canoe, causing him to lose his drinking water, his weapons, and even his clothing. After great suffering, he arrives on a mountainous island, where the once hateful female tasks, such as net mending, prove essential to his survival. Circumstances also give him the chance to develop his courage. First, in spite of his fear of violating taboos, he takes a spearhead from an altar set up by cannibals. Later, he makes three kills that show his courage and skill as a hunter: first, he dives into the water and kills a shark attacking his dog; second, he kills a wild boar, something no one on his island has done; third, he kills an octopus that attacks him when he is diving to recover a knife he dropped. When the cannibals suddenly arrive, Mafatu flees the island. His journey home allows one more test of his courage. Believing that he is going to die, he shouts defiance at Moana, the Sea God, showing at last that he does not fear the sea. At that moment, he notices Kivi and, watching the bird's flight, realizes that he has safely returned to Hikueru. When he arrives, his father praises his bravery, just as Mafatu had dreamed he would.

CHARACTERS: As a Robinsonade—a survival story set, as is Daniel Defoe's *Robinson Crusoe* (1719), on a tropical island—*Call It Courage* essentially focuses on one character, whose physical actions reveal his psychological development.

Mafatu, whose name means "**Stout Heart**," is fifteen, the age at which boys are supposed to kill bonitos (a type of fish) as the first stage in their initiation into manhood. But Mafatu has feared the sea ever since he was three, when his mother drowned during a storm. He is so terrified of the sea that he can't speak when Kana tries to talk to him about bonito fishing. Kana mocks him, an act that represents Mafatu's loss of meaningful identity, for it signals that instead of being Stout Heart he is now the Boy Who Was Afraid. Throughout the novel, references to Mafatu's heart point to his failure and then his success in living up to his original name, but most of his development is visible from his actions. His decision to run away and prove his courage on a different island marks the first positive step in this development. The loss of his water, weapons, and clothing at sea not only tests his determination to survive but also symbolically establishes his adventures on the cannibal island as a rebirth, a chance to recreate his identity.

Mafatu's new identity develops slowly, beginning with thoughts of killing a boar, something requiring "a strong arm, and a stouter heart." He knows that this is a deed he had not even dreamed about on Hikueru. His personal growth continues when he overcomes his fear of invisible enemies, the unknown spirits, by taking the spearhead from the cannibal altar. This marks his first challenge of the gods and foreshadows his final challenge to Moana,

the Sea God, who has terrified him all his life. When Mafatu kills the shark, he overcomes his first visible enemy, but he does it more out of rage than courage. (He jumps in after the shark because he does not want it to kill his dog, which has fallen from the canoe.) His killing of the wild boar is a different matter. This time he carefully plans the deed, acquiring the tusks that are status symbols that show he is "charged with the ancient fierceness of his race." Mafatu demonstrates more courage when he dives into the sea, which he still fears, to recover a knife. He has to kill an octopus to survive, and his victory chant afterwards makes him an ideal representative of the courage his people worship. At sea Mafatu demonstrates the final signs of his new, courageous identity. He escapes from the cannibals, who arrive on the one day he has not been on the lookout for them, showing courage because he does not give in to fear, even though the sight of sixty cannibals is enough "to quake the stoutest heart." Finally, Mafatu signals that he belongs among his people when he shouts defiance at Moana, showing that he is no longer afraid of the sea.

Mafatu has two friends that accompany him but play only minor roles in the adventure. **Uri** is a nondescript yellow dog who inspires Mafatu to face death bravely when they are overcome by thirst. Love for Uri also causes Mafatu to display his first physical sign of bravery. **Kivi** is much more important. This albatross, which has one foot shorter than the other, is like Mafatu, for all of his companions torment him because of his differences. Kivi flies ahead of the canoe, acting as a kind of guide. Repeatedly described as gleaming with sunlight or moonlight, Kivi is a symbol of the spirit because he appears only during the voyage to and from Hikueru and makes his presence especially known when Mafatu is on the point of giving up hope.

Other humans play an even smaller role in Mafatu's adventures. **Kana** is the only boy Mafatu's age who has been friendly to him. He tries to make Mafatu feel his excitement about fishing for bonitos, and his subsequent scorn shows that Mafatu has lost all identity among his people. **Tava Nui**, the Great Chief of Hikueru and father of Mafatu, helps explain the extent of Mafatu's achievement. At first he is silent about his cowardly son, but at the end he loudly proclaims his pride and indicates that Mafatu has indeed lived up to the name Stout Heart.

Further Reading

Berger, Laura Standley, ed. *Twentieth-Century Children's Writers*. 4th ed. Detroit: St. James, 1995.

Collier, Laurie, and Joyce Nakamura, eds. *Major Authors and Illustrators for Children and Young Adults*. Detroit: Gale Research, 1993.

Haycraft, Howard, and Stanley J. Kunitz, eds. *The Junior Book of Authors*. 2nd ed. New York: H. W. Wilson, 1951.

Something about the Author. Vol. 1. Detroit: Gale Research, 1971.

Jerry Spinelli

1941-, American author

Maniac Magee

(novel, 1990)

PLOT: *Maniac Magee*, which won a Newbery Medal, turns a runaway orphan's experiences into legendary adventures. When he was three, Jeffrey Lionel Magee's parents were killed on a high-speed trolley that plunged from a bridge. For the next eight years, Jeffrey lived with Aunt Dot and Uncle Dan, who hated each other. Unable to stand the constant tension, Jeffrey suddenly screams at them one day during a school concert, begging them to talk to each other. He then runs away.

Jeffrey's subsequent adventures develop themes about the truth of fiction, the need for home, and the folly of racial prejudice. A year after he disappears, Jeffrey reappears in Twin Mills, Pennsylvania. His arrival in town draws attention when he performs feats of daring and prowess previously unknown to the local residents; his exploits elevate him to near-heroic status among the neighborhood children. On the school football field, he intercepts a pass with one hand, outruns the fastest player, and kicks a perfect spiral. He then rescues a child thrown, as a prank, into the backyard of the universally feared recluse Finsterwald. He shows up uninvited for dinner at the home of Mrs. Valerie Pickwell before going to the ball field and ruining Giant John McNab's strikeout record. When the frustrated McNab pitches a frog at him, Jeffrey bunts it and scores an in-the-park home run. Because only Amanda Beale—with whom he became friends on his first day in town when she loaned him a book from the suitcase she carries to school—knows his real name, Jeffrey's stunts earn him the moniker "Maniac."

When Mr. and Mrs. Beale insist that he live with them, Maniac is proud to have an address, his symbol of "home." He gets along well with this black family and keeps their children, Hester and Lester, out of mischief. Although he tries to fit in, some people in the segregated black community refuse to accept him. Eventually, Mars Bar Thompson defaces the Beale home with signs telling the "fishbelly" to go home. Maniac remains, however, until he completes his next major exploit, becoming the first person to succeed at untying the famous Cobble's Corner Store Knot. Afterwards, he learns that someone has destroyed Amanda's prized encyclopedia and again runs away from a home.

The second section of the novel is set in the West End, the white area of Two Mills. Maniac lives in the buffalo pen at the zoo and injures himself in a fall from a fence. Earl Grayson, an illiterate, lonely parks worker, saves him and gives him a place to stay. In turn, Maniac becomes Grayson's savior by befriending him. He encourages the old man to relate stories about his years as a minor league baseball player, he teaches him that the blacks who live on the East End are the same as the whites on Grayson's side, and he teaches him to read. When Grayson moves into the band shell where Maniac has been living, Maniac paints an address over its door to signify that it is now a home. At Christmas, Grayson gives Maniac his old ball glove, and Maniac writes him a book about Grayson striking out Willie Mays. Grayson dies shortly after Christmas, and Maniac moves on.

In the last section, Maniac stops Russell and Piper, John McNab's brothers, from running away. When Maniac helps John to save face with them, he invites Maniac to live with the McNabs. Unlike previous homes, however, the messy McNab house has no visible address, and the McNabs are racists who fear an uprising of the blacks. They even make part of their house a fortified pillbox. While staying there, Maniac performs legendary actions to bribe Russell and Piper into going to school. Eventually, the boys kick Maniac out, but Piper later invites Maniac to his birthday party. Maniac brings Mars Bar with him, nearly causing a fight.

Maniac then begins living in peoples' backyards. Every morning, he goes jogging, and Mars Bar Thompson ends up running silently beside him. One morning, the two are called on to rescue Russell from a train trestle. Remembering the death of his parents, Maniac walks away, and Mars Bar rescues the little racist. Later, Mars Bar invites Maniac to his house. When Maniac refuses, Mars Bar brings Amanda, who orders Maniac to live with the Beales. Maniac agrees, knowing that he finally has a home.

CHARACTERS: The absence of detailed physical description permits the characters to take on the larger-than-life quality of figures in a tall tale or legend. **Maniac Magee** is the legendary and heroic identity of **Jeffrey Lionel Magee**. Spinelli has indicated that Maniac represents universal childhood: "He is us and ours, was and is." Maniac demonstrates the athletic prowess typical of idealized boy heroes. He catches a football with one hand, hits home runs off the toughest pitcher, runs on top of the rails, and sprints backwards at the finish line when winning a race. Maniac also exhibits exceptional wit and patience, being the only one able to untie the challenging and baffling Cobble's Knot. Unlike most boy heroes, however, he is equally adept at being caring and nurturing. When he moves in with the Beales, for example, he becomes the perfect baby-sitter for Hester and Lester.

Maniac's development occurs in stages. When he screams at Aunt Dot and Uncle Dan to start communicating with each other, he utters "the birth scream of a legend." At the age of twelve, however, Maniac's ignorance of social rules keeps him blind to prejudice. When he discovers that people hate him because of his white skin, he leaves the Beales's home. In the next stage of his development, by talking with Earl Grayson, Maniac learns that perception is the basis of racial intolerance. He also learns about giving and sharing when Grayson teaches him baseball and he in turn teaches Grayson to read. When he writes a book about Grayson and gives it to him for Christmas, he indicates that he understands the feelings of others and the importance of their self-worth. Grayson's death also teaches Maniac about grief.

Maniac's growing strength of character reveals itself when he refuses to see John McNab disgraced in front of his brothers. Although he understands that Piper and Russell use him to increase their own prestige, he believes his actions can benefit them. Maniac applies the lessons about perception he learned with Grayson to the situation. He lets Mars Bar see the best and worst of white people, taking him to the homes of both the Pickwells and the McNabs. Simultaneously, he lets Piper and Russell see that blacks are not "wild rebels."

In the beginning of the story, the narrator warns readers not to let the "facts get mixed up with the truth." The facts of Maniac's story suggest that he is a naturally good person who heroically takes responsibility for the well-being of others; the truth is that he is still a vulnerable child who needs the permanent home that an address over a door symbolizes. The reality of Maniac's circumstances converge when he is incapable of rescuing Russell from the bridge. His failure makes it possible for others to look past his bigger-than-life exploits and see the child within. In the end, Maniac again becomes Jeffrey when the legend willingly becomes an innocent boy in order to gain a loving home.

Aunt Dot and **Uncle Dan**, with whom Jeffrey lives after the death of his parents, are eccentric in their mutual hatred, but because they are strict Catholics they can't get a divorce. They refuse to speak to each other, and they do not share any part of their respective lives: They own two toasters, two televisions, two of everything. Their dichotomy symbolizes the divisions that also separate Twin Mills. The solution that Jeffrey offers—that of talking to each other—turns out to be one of the keys to ending racial strife in Twin Mills.

The other secondary characters may be identified as either East Enders or West Enders. The members of the East End Beale family represent the ideal of African American family life. **Amanda Beale** has a deep love of knowledge, symbolized by the suitcase of books she carries daily to school. A tough-minded girl, she berates Mars Bar for tearing her book and stops him from fighting with Maniac. Eventually, she renames him Snickers, insisting that he will not misbehave if he has a comical name. She also insists that Maniac make the Beale house his home. **Hester**, Amanda's four-year-old sister, and **Lester**, her three-year-old brother, are mischievous, energetic children. Their immediate attraction to Maniac shows both how willingly they accept a person of another color and how well Maniac adapts to their needs. **Mr. Beale** and, more obviously, **Mrs. Beale** are concerned and loving parents. They immediately take Maniac into their home when they see that he is homeless. Mrs. Beale is an extraordinarily clean and conscientious housekeeper. Although she disciplines Maniac when he indulges in unacceptable "trash talk," Maniac loves her like a mother.

Whereas the Beale family represent middle-class African Americans, **Mars Bar Thompson** at first represents the stereotypical ghetto hoodlum. Always carrying a chocolate bar, he uses a showy jive walk to stop traffic. Racially intolerant, he resents a white boy entering his territory and tries to fight him. Nevertheless, Mars Bar has many redeeming qualities beneath his tough exterior. After dining with the Pickwells, he recognizes that whites can be generous. He suffers verbal abuse from the racist McNabs when he courageously attends Piper's party, but he shows his moral strength by rescuing Russell. His daily jogging sessions with Maniac suggest that he admires Maniac's tenacity and persistence. The once-hostile Mars Bar changes when he makes friends with the racist Piper and Russell and reaches out to Maniac, his former rival.

The West Enders fall into three groups. **Mrs. Valerie Pickwell** and her family represent the "ideal" white family. The Pickwells display exceptional charity, inviting so many people over for dinner that Mrs. Pickwell thinks of her home as a "small nation." Less fortunate is **Earl Grayson**, a grizzled and gray former baseball player who is a more worthy person than he realizes. An ignorant yet kind man, Grayson has no personal experience with blacks, so he is surprised when Maniac explains that their family lives are exactly like those of whites. Grayson insists that he has no stories to tell, yet when Maniac urges him to talk about his career as a minor league ballplayer, it is evident that his present state doesn't reflect his rich and interesting past. By writing a book about Grayson, Maniac reveals the legendary qualities in even the most ordinary lives. His teaching Grayson to read also suggests that knowledge improves lives, and by symbolically becoming Grayson's son, Maniac shows that caring relationships make life meaningful.

The third group of West Enders represents the worst side of white society. The McNabs live in a filthy, dilapidated house, which illustrates that they do not, like the Beales, have a true home. **Giant John McNab**, who becomes a tall-tale villain, is an arrogant bully. He gloats over the Little League strikeout record he has set and forces people to stay after the game to face more pitches. When he can't strike out Maniac, he displays cruelty and rage by pitching a frog. A racist like his father, Giant John McNab leads a beer-drinking group of toughs called the Cobras. John is not particularly intelligent and seems permanently set in his racism. Superficially, **Piper** and **Russell** resemble the mischievous Hester and Lester Beale. They are rambunctious, repeatedly try to run away, and seldom attend school. Unlike Hester and Lester, however, their naughtiness stems from neglect. Furthermore, they are selfish and lack the intellectual curiosity of the Beale children, who love books and stories. Piper and Russell are racists because they have grown up in a racist house. Because of their young age, however, they offer at least limited hope for the future. After Mars Bar rescues Russell, the two boys refuse to let him go. They let his mother fuss over them, and they plead with Mars Bar to play Rebels with them. It is clear that they do not hate individual blacks and that more experience might change their attitudes.

Further Reading

Authors and Artists for Young Adults. Vol. 11. Detroit: Gale Research, 1993.

Berger, Laura Standley, ed. *Twentieth-Century Young Adult Writers*. 1st ed. Detroit: St. James, 1994.

Children's Literature Review. Vol. 26. Detroit: Gale Research, 1992.

Collier, Laurie, and Joyce Nakamura, eds. *Major Authors and Illustrators for Children and Young Adults*. Detroit: Gale Research, 1993.

Something about the Author. Vols. 39, 71. Detroit: Gale Research, 1985, 1993.

Johanna Spyri

1827-1901, Swiss author

Heidi

(novel, 1880; first English translation, 1884)

PLOT: *Heidi* is a story of education, reformation, and healing. When Aunt Dete decides that she can no longer care for five-year-old Heidi, she takes the orphan to live with her grandfather, an embittered recluse. Heidi loves the Alm-Uncle, as he is called, and he is affectionate with her. She also becomes friends with Peter the goatherd and his blind grandmother. After a couple of years, Aunt Dete returns to take Heidi to Frankfurt to be the companion of Clara Sesemann, an invalid. Heidi and Clara get along, but Heidi is unhappy in the city. Sebastian, the butler, is kind, but Fraulein Rottenmeir, the housekeeper, dislikes her, especially after Heidi brings kittens into the house. Fraulein Rottenmeir asks Clara's father to send her away, but Herr Sesemann, unaware that Heidi is homesick, refuses. Heidi becomes happier when Grandmother Sesemann visits. She teaches Heidi, who could not learn the alphabet from the tutor, to read. She also teaches Heidi to understand the importance of prayer. After the visit, however, Heidi physically deteriorates. She is saved when Herr Sesemann discovers that the ghost that is frightening the household is Heidi, who has been sleepwalking because of homesickness. On the advice of Dr. Classen, he immediately sends Heidi home.

Restored to home and health, Heidi then helps others. She purchases soft rolls for Peter's grand-

mother and comforts her by reading hymns. Because of Heidi's faith, her grandfather finally prays to God for forgiveness, attends church for the first time in years, and agrees to spend winters in the village to have Heidi educated. When Dr. Classen, depressed by his daughter's death, visits, he is restored by the Alpine air, his conversations with Heidi, and the friendship of the Alm-Uncle. During the winter, Heidi amazes everyone by teaching slow-witted Peter to read. In the spring, Clara Sesemann makes a long-promised visit. Jealous of their friendship, Peter pushes Clara's wheelchair off a mountain. Nevertheless, Heidi has Clara taken to the goat pasture, where she convinces Clara to try to walk. Strengthened by mountain air and simple food, Clara succeeds. Herr Sesemann then unexpectedly arrives and declares that his happiness has been restored. Grandmother Sesemann distributes rewards. Characteristically, Heidi asks for a bed for Peter's grandmother. That winter, the retired Dr. Classen moves next to Heidi and her grandfather in the village. He assures her grandfather that he will provide for Heidi's future financial needs.

CHARACTERS: Heidi is the first major presentation of the orphaned Romantic Child. Other characters reveal her innate qualities, contribute to her education, or show how she uses her education. **Heidi** (her real name is **Adelheid**) is a thin, loquacious, five-year-old Swiss girl with the dark eyes and short, curly black hair. As a Romantic Child, Heidi has a deep love of nature and innate goodness. Heidi reveals her character when she first comes to her grandfather's cabin. Symbolically rejecting artificial constraints, she sheds two frocks and her boots in order to be as free as the goats. Thereafter, her beloved mountain-top home becomes so spiritually essential that Heidi physically wilts when Dete takes her to Frankfurt. Desperately longing to hear the wind in the pines—the wind conventionally symbolizes spirit or godhood—Heidi sleepwalks while dreaming that she is home. Significantly, in a scene paralleling her first visit to the mountain, she gives away her fine clothes before she returns to her grandfather, thereby showing humility and pastoral simplicity.

From the beginning, Heidi shows another central trait of the Romantic Child, an ability to make others better and happier people. Her frankness and innocence stimulate her grandfather's affection, and her constant chatter brightens the grim life of Peter's grandmother. Naturally charitable, Heidi constantly thinks of others. Thus, she has her grandfather repair the drafty cabin where Peter's grandmother lives. Heidi develops beyond her natural innocence because of her education in Frankfurt. Before meeting Grandmother Sesemann, Heidi naively believed Peter's assertions that reading was too difficult. Once Grandmother Sesemann teaches Heidi to have faith in herself, however, Heidi quickly learns to read. Grandmother Sesemann also teaches Heidi to have faith that God does everything for the best. Heidi subsequently accepts the delay in answering her repeated prayers to go home because it permits her to acquire knowledge and gifts of money, both of which benefit others. Heidi thus uses her education unselfishly. She reads to Peter's grandmother and she teaches Peter to read. Although unaware that she has done so, Heidi reforms her grandfather when she speaks about faith in God and then reads the story of the prodigal son. Throughout, Heidi remains unspoiled and unselfish, as she shows by using her money to purchase soft rolls for Peter's grandmother and by asking for a comfortable bed for the old woman instead of a reward for herself. Heidi's unaffected honesty, her delight in natural beauty, her optimism, her charity, her determination, and her religious faith affect nearly everyone she meets, making her an endearing and powerful example of romantic childhood.

Heidi's **grandfather**, called **the Alm-Uncle** because he lives alone on the Alm, demonstrates the spiritual influence of the Romantic Child. At first, he is bitterly at odds with his community and with God. According to Dete, he left home and wasted his inheritance when he was young. When he returned, the villagers, believing rumors that he had killed a man, shut their doors to him. He, in turn, rejected them by moving to the mountain top. Although this

Heidi and the begrudging Peter help Clara to walk in this scene from Spyri's Heidi, illustrated by Jessie Willcox Smith.

seventy-year-old man with heavy gray eyebrows and a huge beard frightens the villagers with his fierce appearance and gruff manners, he is kind and gentle with Heidi. Only his stubborn refusal to move to the village so that Heidi can be educated prevents him from being an ideal, loving grandfather. Although his conduct with Heidi implies that the village gossips exaggerated his sins, the Alm-Uncle has truly cut himself off from God. Heidi's faith, her reading of the story of the prodigal son, and her peaceful expression while she sleeps reform him. He prays for forgiveness, attends church, and resumes his fellowship with the villagers, thus illustrating the theme that bringing God into one's life can set things right.

Heidi has two young friends who have important roles. **Clara Sesemann**, a thin, twelve-year-old invalid whom Heidi takes care of in Frankfurt, has a pale face, mild, blue eyes, and is very patient. Although older, she is kind to Heidi. Clara's major function is to establish the benefits of the pastoral life and positive thinking. Appropriately, she visits Heidi in spring, the season of rebirth. Fed simple food and exposed to fresh mountain air, Clara grows physically stronger. Because she wants to see beautiful flowers, she responds to Heidi's encouragement and, improbably, she walks. **Peter the goatherd** contrasts with Heidi because he is somewhat simpleminded and intellectually lazy. Given to skipping school regularly, he stubbornly refuses to believe that he can learn to read. He eventually learns only because Heidi is forceful and understanding. Peter's cowardice, apparent in his fear that the Alm-Uncle will beat him if he skips school and in his worry that Herr Sesemann is a policeman coming to arrest him, provides comic relief. Furthermore, his foolish materialism in asking Grandmother Seseman for a penny a week as a reward for his role in helping Clara amusingly accents Heidi's charity. Peter also contributes to the serious religious themes. His jealous destruction of Clara's wheelchair enables Grandmother Sesemann to teach that anger makes people foolish, that a guilty conscience can't be hidden, and that God always forgives. Moreover, because this destruction leads directly to Clara walking, Heidi points to Peter's deed as another example of the way in which God turns evil into good.

Peter's grandmother provides evidence of Heidi's natural goodness and the love that she inspires in those who meet her. Blind and too poor to eat properly or to keep warm, she benefits from Heidi's gifts of food, clothing, and a bed. What Peter's grandmother treasures most, however, is Heidi's presence because her chatter acts as a restorative tonic. A second function of Peter's grandmother is to suggest that the Alm-Uncle is not as evil as the villagers believe: having direct knowledge of the kindness he displayed when he repaired her cabin, she defends him when others ignorantly accuse him of hardness. **Aunt Dete**, a sturdy twentysix-year old woman whose sister was Heidi's mother, places her own interests ahead of Heidi's. She therefore leaves Heidi with the Alm-Uncle when Heidi becomes a burden and removes Heidi when she sees a personal benefit in doing so. Her fashionable attire suggests her artificiality and makes her as

socially out of place on the mountain as her selfish treatment of Heidi makes her morally out of place.

Herr Sesemann, Clara's father, is a compassionate and loving man who makes sporadic appearances because he is frequently away on business. Consequently, although he kindly indulges Clara and demands that Heidi be treated as an equal, he makes Clara almost as much of an orphan as Heidi is. Herr Sesemann is profoundly unhappy because his wealth doesn't help Clara. Because of Heidi's friendship with his daughter, however, he rediscovers happiness when Clara is restored to health, and he then devotes time to her. **Grandmother Sesemann**, his mother, is an archetypal wise woman. Unlike Fraulein Rottenmeir and the tutor, she has great sympathy for children. Consequently, she gives Heidi the self-confidence to learn to read. She also articulates the major religious themes when she teaches Heidi about the need for prayer and when she offers Peter forgiveness.

Through contact with nature, **Dr. Classen** undergoes a spiritual recovery that foreshadows Clara's physical recovery. Deeply depressed by the death of his daughter, Dr. Classen is psychologically restored by the spiritual grandeur of the mountains, by the warm friendship of the Alm-Uncle, and by his love for Heidi, who symbolically becomes his new daughter when he offers to secure her future. **Fraulein Rottenmeir**, Herr Sesemann's stern housekeeper, shows a similar concern for fashion when she tries to throw away the rustic apparel that Heidi favors and when she insists, unlike Grandmother Sesemann, on calling Heidi by her real name. A disagreeable woman, Fraulein Rottenmeir lacks sympathy and understanding. She becomes contemptibly comic when, like many bullies, she proves to be a coward. Her fear of kittens seems improbable, but it clearly puts her at odds with nature. **Sebastian**, the Sesemanns' butler, is kind to Heidi, partly because he detests the housekeeper. He is a foil to Herr Sesemann because he fears the ghost and dislikes the mountains. **The tutor** (in the German text he is addressed as **Herr Kandidat**, a generic term for a candidate for an advanced degree) is a foil to Grandmother Sesemann. Given to pompous speeches, he fails to educate Heidi because he lacks understanding and does not inspire confidence. Nevertheless, he is a cautious man whose refusal to support Fraulein Rottenmeir's claim that Heidi is out of her mind makes the housekeeper seem even more extreme and bigoted.

Further Reading

Bingham, Jane M., ed. *Writers for Children: Critical Studies of Major Authors since the Seventeenth Century.* New York: Scribner's, 1988.

Children's Literature Review. Vol. 13. Detroit: Gale Research, 1987.

Collier, Laurie, and Joyce Nakamura, eds. *Major Authors and Illustrators for Children and Young Adults.* Detroit: Gale Research, 1993.

Contemporary Authors. Vol. 137. Detroit: Gale Research, 1992.

Something about the Author. Vol. 19. Detroit: Gale Research, 1980.

Usrey, Malcolm. "Johanna Spyri's *Heidi:* The Conversion of a Byronic Hero." In *Touchstones: Reflections on the Best in Children's Literature.* Vol. 1. Edited by Perry Nodelman. West Lafayette, IN: Children's Literature Association, 1985.

William Steig

1907-, American cartoonist, artist, and author

Sylvester and the Magic Pebble

(picture book, 1969)

PLOT: William Steig has explained why he writes animal fantasies: "I think using animals emphasizes the fact that the story is symbolical—about human behavior. And kids get the idea right way that this is not just a story, but that it's a way of saying something about life on earth." In *Sylvester and the Magic Pebble,* winner of the 1970 Caldecott Medal, the misadventures of a donkey symbolically convey themes about personal transformation and the power of love.

Sylvester Duncan, a young donkey from Oatsdale, collects unusual pebbles. One day, he discovers a magic pebble that grants any wish. While hurrying to show it to his parents, he encounters a lion. Frightened, he wishes he were a rock. He receives his wish, but because he is no longer holding the pebble, Sylvester cannot change himself back to a donkey after the puzzled lion leaves. When he does not return home, his worried parents unsuccessfully search for him. Sylvester remains a rock through autumn, winter, and into spring. His parents, Mr. and Mrs. Duncan, then decide to picnic at this rock, where Mr. Duncan finds the pebble and places it on the rock. Hearing his parents express their desire for him to be with them, Sylvester wishes to be himself again. Quickly transformed into his own body, Sylvester joyfully reunites with his parents. They carefully put away the pebble because they know that their mutual love is all they really want.

CHARACTERS: Although pictures depict an entire community, the text of this transformation tale focuses on Sylvester and his parents to establish the importance of love. **Sylvester Duncan** is a donkey who must learn the value of love. When he finds the pebble, he tests it thoroughly to establish how it works. He believes that the pebble will ensure happiness, for he declares that by using it, "anybody at all can have everything anybody wants!" His subsequent actions symbolically establish that he does not adequately understand the value of life. They also reveal that he lacks both emotional control and security in his identity. Sylvester thus panics when he sees the lion and, instead of making a clever magical escape, he utters a foolish wish to be a stone. His existence as a stone serves as a classic fairy tale symbol for emotional numbness. It also indicates a rejection of his role as a family member. Quite literally, Sylvester cuts himself off from others and enters an "endless sleep" as a stone. As the seasons pass, he goes through a symbolic death in winter and a resurrection from this emotional death in spring, the season of rebirth. What finally unlocks Sylvester from the isolation and emotional coldness of stone is the love of his parents. Understanding how much they miss him, Sylvester wishes to be his "real self" again. Upon his transformation back into his original shape, the picture in which he lovingly embraces his parents clearly illustrates that he is not the same donkey. He has learned that he is loved, and that connecting to others through love is the most valuable achievement in the world. Now satisfied with himself and his life, Sylvester has no need for magic.

Mr. and **Mrs. Duncan** are model loving parents. They desperately search for their child when he disappears, and they grieve over his loss long after he is gone. Symbolically, they are crucial in restoring Sylvester both physically and emotionally. By voicing their desire that Sylvester be present with them, they express the love that Sylvester needs. They thus prod him into accepting himself and his emotions. With their loving child returned to them, Mr. Duncan shows himself to be a wise parent. He simultaneously protects his child and affirms the central role of love by putting the stone safely away.

Abel's Island
(novel, 1976)

PLOT: Like *Sylvester and the Magic Pebble*, *Abel's Island* is the story of a character transformation. While lost in the wilderness, its central character undergoes a symbolic death and rebirth. As a result, he gains a better appreciation of nature and subsequently discovers his true identity.

Abelard Hassam di Chirico Flint—commonly known as Abel—of the upper crust Mossville Flints, is a wealthy and somewhat snobbish mouse who has been married to Amanda for less than a year. While they are having a picnic in August, 1907, a storm arises, and a stiff breeze snatches away Amanda's scarf. Abel chases after it but falls victim to violent winds. He clings desperately to a board, riding down a flooding river. His journey ends in a birch tree on an island. As a Robinsonade (a survival story reminiscent of *Robinson Crusoe*), the novel then details Abel's physical and psychological struggles. Abel fails in his repeated attempts to escape the island by building stone bridges, rope lines, and boats, so he makes a home in a rotted log. Finding comfort in the appearance of his personal star, Abel believes that he is able to visit Amanda in his dreams. He later finds two other items to sustain him in his isolation:

a watch and a book about a civilization of bears. Abel's most important discovery, however, lies in his recognition of his artistic talent, which surfaces after he creates life-sized statues of Amanda and his relatives.

On the island, Abel heroically endures both physical and psychological troubles. When an owl grabs him, he frees himself from its grasp by slashing it with his knife. Abel maintains constant vigilance afterwards, however, because the owl continues to stalk him. During the long winter, he enters a period of profound depression during which he succumbs to a mental torpor. With the return of spring, his spirits revive. He also learns to appreciate company when Gower Glacken, an elderly frog who has had an experience similar to Abel's, is washed up on the island. No longer class-conscious, Abel becomes friends with Gower and sculpts an exquisite artistic representation of him. Gazing at his own handiwork after Gower leaves the island, Abel gains insight into his friend and realizes that, despite his intentions, Gower will forget to send help. Rather than wait, he takes advantage of a temporary drought, which lowers the surrounding waters and provides his one opportunity for escape. He again shows heroic endurance in an arduous swim to the other shore. Just when he thinks he is safe, however, a cat captures him. After escaping its clutches, he makes his way home, washes, and changes into his rich clothing. When the ecstatic Amanda stops kissing him, the now-modest Abel says simply, "I've brought you back your scarf."

CHARACTERS: As a story of wilderness isolation, *Abel's Island* is almost exclusively focused on Abel to illustrate how his solitude forces self-reflection and self-improvement. **Abel**, whose full name is **Abelard Hassam di Chirico Flint**, emerges from his symbolic death and rebirth on the island changed for the better. Initially a wealthy, foppish mouse, his foolish attempt to retrieve Amanda's scarf exposes him as a parody of the questing hero. Nevertheless, Abel harbors serious feelings. Deeply in love with his wife, he preserves that love, just as he preserves the scarf, during all of his hardships. A smug show-off in

Abel and his friend, Gower Glacken the frog, in a scene from Abel's Island, *illustrated by Steig.*

society, Abel learns humility on the island after sighting his personal star. As a child, he had talked to this star when he was being "his most serious, real self." Its reappearance indicates a return to his true identity and a recovered spiritual integrity.

Abel questions whether his experiences are truly accidental or some sort of personal test. His questions, subtle signs of egotism, indicate that he sees himself as central in all events. Nevertheless, although nature does not conspire against him specifically, Abel's experiences prove his mettle. His repeated attempts to escape try his tenacity and resourcefulness, and his encounters with the owl challenge his wit and courage. More significantly, his experiences transform him. Because Abel thinks deeply, he comes to appreciate both nature and civilization. During much of the story, for example, he hates the owl as a fiend. Eventually, he realizes that the owl, like the cat that later torments him, simply acts according to its nature, even as Abel must. No longer obsessed with appearances, Abel learns to appreci-

ate the wonders of the natural world. By the time he leaves, he even thinks lovingly of the island as his parent. But although Abel now values nature, he does not reject civilization. His attachment to the watch indicates an appreciation of civilized order and regulation, just as his love of the book suggests an appreciation of art, especially when it leads to an understanding of others. Abel's own art reveals hidden truths, enabling him to understand Gower's character.

Although Abel's success in overcoming physical dangers provides drama, his victory over psychological hazards emerges as more thematically significant. Abel arises from the symbolic death of his winter of doubt feeling a reborn attachment to others. This new emotional connection appears when he resumes mental communication with his beloved Amanda. As well, he strikes up a genuine friendship with Gower, a creature with whom he once would have been reluctant to shake hands. Alone, Abel has discovered his true self. His return to society, however, illustrates that he has become a better person, an artist who knows the central place in life of love and friendship.

Gower Glacken, an elderly country-and-western musician, provides a foil to Abel. Abel's attachment to this common frog shows how far he has progressed from his earlier snobbery. Gower's habit of descending into "reptilian torpors," during which he seems oblivious to the world, highlights Abel's pensiveness, which leads him to greater understanding. Similarly, Gower's inability to remember his promises to send rescuers emphasizes the importance of Abel's unflagging memory of Amanda and his friends.

Further Reading

Berger, Laura Standley, ed. *Twentieth-Century Children's Writers*. 4th ed. Detroit: St. James, 1995.

Children's Literature Review. Vols. 2, 15. Detroit: Gale Research, 1976, 1988.

Cott, Jonathan. "William Steig and His Path." In *Pipers at the Gates of Dawn: The Wisdom of Children's Literature*. New York: Random House, 1983.

De Montreville, Doris, and Donna Hill, eds. *Third Book of Junior Authors*. New York: H. W. Wilson, 1972.

Estes, Glenn E., ed. *American Writers for Children since 1960: Poets, Illustrators and Nonfiction Authors*. Vol. 61 of *Dictionary of Literary Biography*. Detroit: Gale Research, 1987.

Something about the Author. Vols. 18, 70. Detroit: Gale Research, 1980, 1993.

Robert Louis Stevenson

1850-1894, Scottish novelist, poet, and essayist

Treasure Island

(novel, 1882)

PLOT: Gripping action and memorable characters make *Treasure Island* the quintessential romantic adventure. Set in the 1700s, this quest for buried pirate treasure is a coming-of-age story that ex-

plores the destructiveness of greed and the ambiguity of moral codes.

The first part of the novel introduces the deadly consequences of greed. When an old seaman who calls himself Billy Bones takes lodging at the Admiral Benbow Inn, the innkeeper's son, Jim Hawkins, is both frightened and fascinated by the man. Bones gets drunk every night, sings about a dead man's chest, tells dreadful stories that give Jim nightmares, and even threatens Dr. Livesey with a knife. Bones is terrified of encountering a man with one leg, so he hires Jim as a lookout. After the evil-looking Black Dog visits the Inn, Bones has a stroke. He then reveals to Jim that he has a map to buried treasure. Shortly afterward, Jim's sickly father dies, followed quickly by Bones, who succumbs to another stroke after a visit from the pirate Blind Pew. Pew and a gang of pirates then come to the Inn seeking the treasure map. Because Jim's mother insists on searching through Bones' room for money to pay what he owed for his lodging, she and Jim barely escape. However, Jim manages to take the map, which he shows to Dr. Livesey and Squire Trelawney. Filled with dreams of easy money, the squire hires the *Hispaniola*, along with a captain and crew. Jim becomes suspicious when he sees Black Dog in the tavern owned by Long John Silver, the ship's one-legged cook. The charming Silver soon puts Jim's doubts to rest, however, and becomes the best of friends with him.

During the voyage out, Jim and his companions lose their naivete. Jim, hiding in an apple barrel, overhears Silver plotting mutiny once the treasure is located. Captain Smollett and his companions decide that, because they are outnumbered, they must delay moving against the mutineers. Once on the island, Jim's romantic dream of an easy treasure hunt turns into a nightmare. He witnesses Silver killing a crew member who refuses to join in the mutiny. Then he encounters Ben Gunn, who has been marooned on the island. Ben agrees to help Jim fight against the pirates, but he refuses to join Smollett, Trelawney, Livesey, and Jim in the island stockade, where they have taken refuge with a few loyal crew members. After a battle in which Smollett is wounded, Jim deserts his post and sets out for the

Hispaniola. Once on board, he is forced to kill a mutineer, the treacherous Israel Hands. He then hides the ship and returns to boast of his accomplishments. Unfortunately, Silver and the pirates have taken over the stockade during his absence, and Jim becomes their prisoner.

Silver's men begin turning against him, however, and they give him the black spot as a sign of their revolt. Silver responds by secretly striking a deal with Dr. Livesey. Silver promises to protect Jim, while the doctor promises to do his best for Silver at a later trial. The disgruntled buccaneers then set out to recover the treasure. During their search, the hidden Ben Gunn plays tricks to arouse their superstitious fears. When they reach the treasure pit, they discover that the money has vanished, and a deadly battle ensues. Eventually, Jim and his companions recover the treasure, which Ben Gunn has hidden. They leave the island and maroon three buccaneers, but they take Silver with them. At the first port, however, Silver—aided by Ben Gunn—takes some of the treasure and escapes, never to be heard from again.

CHARACTERS: Stevenson once declared, "Character to the boy is a sealed book; for him, a pirate is a beard, a pair of wide trousers and a liberal complement of pistols." In keeping with this view, some of his characters are colorful and one-dimensional. Others, however, are more than stereotypical villains or heroes—they display a mixture of admirable and base qualities that lends thematic depth to an otherwise conventional plot.

Jim Hawkins is fourteen years old when his adventure begins, but he tells the story after it is over. Jim is a sensitive boy who tends to attach himself to strong male figures, probably because his father is a weak and sickly man. His first attachment is to Billy Bones. Jim does not cry when his father dies, but he does cry when the pirate has a fatal stroke. Although Jim later rationalizes his behavior as the result of shock, it seems clear that the domineering Bones affects him more powerfully than does his father. Bones sparks Jim's curiosity, sets him dreaming about adventure, provokes deep

fears and nightmares, and eventually arouses pity. More significant in Jim's life is Long John Silver, who becomes almost a substitute father. Their relationship depends upon Jim's innocence. When Jim first encounters Silver, he suspects him of being the one-legged pirate Bones feared. Jim changes his mind because he bases his judgment on superficial characteristics. To Jim, who believes that evil must appear dirty, no one as neat and clean as Silver can be a pirate. Furthermore, Jim is eager to be accepted, and the charming Silver makes Jim feel like a confidant. Jim thus laughs along with Silver even when he does not understand the joke. Because Silver treats him as a special friend, Jim likes and respects him. Conversely, Jim deeply dislikes Captain Smollett because the upright captain does not permit favoritism on his ship. Jim gains a deeper understanding of his shipmates only after he luckily overhears Silver reveal his plans for mutiny. Hiding in the apple barrel, a location suggesting that he is tasting the proverbial fruit of knowledge, Jim falls from innocence and into a deeper knowledge of human duplicity.

Like the typical boy heroes of nineteenth-century romances, Jim succeeds in his adventures because of exceptional luck, resourcefulness, and bravery. At times, however, his attempts to play the role of hero are foolish and dangerous. For one thing, Jim is prone to "mad notions," impulses that cause him to disobey his superiors. He first disobeys when he sneaks ashore to spy on Silver, whom he sees murdering a sailor for refusing to join his mutiny. Jim disobeys again when he deserts his post at the stockade, takes Gunn's coracle, and recaptures the *Hispaniola.* Ironically, because Jim is lucky, good comes from his disobedience in both instances. Dr. Livesey and Captain Smollett severely criticize him for his desertion, but the positive results of Jim's actions bring into question their rigid adherence to moral codes. On other occasions, Jim's youthful arrogance makes him seem foolish. Romantic ideas of adventure lead him to board the captured *Hispaniola.* Once he recaptures it, however, he becomes so vain about his role as captain that he leaves himself vulnerable to attack by Israel Hands. Again, he survives mostly because of luck. Nevertheless, the conceited Jim returns to the others intending to brag about his exploits. He is so absorbed by his adventures, though, that he does not realize that the pirates occupy the stockade he deserted.

Ironically, once captured, Jim becomes the model of the conventional British hero and adheres rigidly to the code of gentlemanly behavior he had violated. Jim resists Livesey's suggestion to escape, for example, because he has given his word to Silver that he will not. During this time, Jim's major concern is that he act bravely if he should be tortured. In another of the novel's twists on ordinary moral codes, Jim earns the respect and protection of Silver by freely admitting this fear. At the end, when he looks back over his adventures, Jim shows that he has gained more than gold from his search for treasure. He has gained a more mature understanding of his youthful foolishness and of the mixed qualities that reside within human nature. His youthful dreams have become his adult nightmare; his decision never to return to the dragon-shaped Treasure Island indicates that he has put behind him both his naive view of adventure and the inordinate greed that cost so many lives.

Long John Silver is an extreme mixture of contradictory qualities. He is the most charming character in the novel, but he is also its supreme villain. Stevenson said that he based Silver on his friend William Ernest Henley but removed Henley's finer qualities, leaving "his strength, his courage, his quickness, and his magnificent geniality." Indeed, the genial Silver fools Jim because he is the only person whose appearance is not an accurate sign of his moral character. Tall, strong, neat, clean, and pleasant-tempered, the smiling, blonde-haired Silver violates Jim's stereotype of dark and dirty pirates. He also fools Jim's companions, who see him only as **Barbecue**, the agreeable and dutiful ship's cook. Silver does, however, have one physical sign of his true character: his left leg has been cut off near the hip. In this novel, physical mutilation symbolizes moral depravity: several of the novel's pirates have physical infirmities that are both the result and sign of unlawful activities. A skillful liar, Silver says that he was wounded serving his country, but the truth is that the only England he served was a pirate by that

name. Silver copes well with his infirmity. He is nimble on his crutch, which he readily turns into a deadly weapon. Subtler signs of Silver's depravity are also evident. He carries on his shoulder a parrot called Cap'n Flint, who is named after the notorious pirate captain he once served. The ancient bird, witness to a hundred years of bloodshed, serves as a reminder of the evil traditions that Silver upholds. Silver has also married a "colored" woman. In the racist symbolism of the times, this fact suggests that he is attracted to the exotic and is unafraid of violating conventional standards of respectability.

The contradictions in Silver's character appear throughout the novel. He is an educated man whose use of the pirates' slang belies his intelligence. An engaging conversationalist, he is able to manipulate not only Jim and his companions, but also the crew. As the central villain, he is both brutal and brave. Thus he coldly murders a sailor who refuses to join the mutiny, and he laughs down the men's superstition when they give him the dreaded black spot. He can also be affectionate and noble, however. He develops a genuine liking for Jim, even calling him "son." His admiration for Jim's display of bravery and honor is partially responsible for Silver's decision to protect him. Of course, Silver is never absolutely noble because he is always searching for ways to help himself. He switches sides when he sees that the mutineers cannot succeed, and he protects Jim to receive favorable testimony at a later trial. Probably the most powerful force in his character, however, is greed. As his surname suggests, Silver is driven by the desire for money. Even though he is frightened when Ben Gunn begins playing his tricks on the superstitious sailors, he remains firmly determined to pursue the treasure. Jim's conclusion that Silver will not find happiness in the afterlife compounds the novel's moral ambiguity by emphasizing that the vicious yet likable pirate thrives in this life.

Even the "good" characters in the novel are not entirely admirable. **Mrs. Hawkins,** Jim's mother, is both honest and greedy. She is willing to take only what is due to her, but she is so obsessed with money that she imperils herself and her son. **Squire Trelawney,** a tall man whose face has been roughened and reddened by travels at sea, appears at first to be a buffoon. He is so talkative, even after promising secrecy, that Silver easily learns the purpose of the voyage. Trelawney, whose dark eyebrows suggest his quick temper, is not a good judge of character. He falls for Silver's charms and considers him the best of men because he has a bank account. Conversely, he takes an instant dislike to Smollett when the captain criticizes his preparations for the voyage. Somewhat childish in his enthusiasm for adventure, Trelawney dresses up in nautical finery before they set sail. However, he does have the courage to admit freely his errors of judgment when Jim reveals the mutiny plot. Calling himself an ass, he submits completely to the captain's orders and shows that he is a competent soldier.

As a doctor and a magistrate, the neatly attired **Dr. Livesey** represents the health and order of lawful life. The doctor laughs at the fever-stricken pirates, however, and delights in the fact that he has given them rule of the stockade, where sickness is sure to seize them. In defending the rule of law, he is uncompromising. A brave man himself, as is evident when he faces down the knife-wielding Bones, he condemns Jim as a coward for deserting his post. Nevertheless, he admits that Jim's discovery of Ben Gunn, which resulted from disobedience, was the best thing Jim did. Furthermore, neither he nor any of his companions ever questions his own right to the treasure.

Even more stern and inflexible is **Captain Smollett**. A sharp-looking man who speaks bluntly to the point of offending others, he is a shrewd judge of situations. He realizes before they sail, for example, that the ship may be headed for mutiny. A stickler for rules, he insists on flying the flag at the stockade. Ironically, this gesture endangers his men because it allows the pirates on the *Hispaniola* to find the range with their cannons. Smollett's moral rigidity is especially evident in his treatment of Silver. When Silver calls himself the new captain, Smollett sternly insists that Silver can be only a loyal cook or a pirate. Smollett is a good military leader who also reveals a strong understanding of people. For example, he deliberately and contemptuously refuses to help Silver stand up in order to anger him. Smollett thus provokes the pirates into a disas-

trous premature attack. The wisdom of Smollett's inflexibility, though, is brought into question by his condemnation of Jim's desertion, an act that saves the very ship that Smollett lost.

The song "Fifteen Men on a Dead Man's Chest," which is repeated a number of times in the novel, links "drink and the devil" and thus suggests that the rum-swilling pirates are damned. Furthermore, the pirates reveal their characters by their appearance and by their somewhat symbolic names. Each pirate who is introduced is dirtier and more mutilated than the last, signaling his increased viciousness. The first pirate calls himself **Billy Bones**, a name that suggests death, as does the song he sings about the dead man's chest. A tall, strong, heavy, dark man, he has dirty hands with broken nails and a scar from a saber cut across one cheek. His clothes are heavily soiled and he has a tarry pigtail. Bones is a vulgar man who sings and swears loudly when he drinks. He also has the habit of blowing loudly through his nose. Like all of the pirates, Bones hides his true identity, and he tries to increase his status by calling himself a captain, when in truth he was the pirate Flint's first mate. A greedy man, Bones cheats Jim's father out of his rent and seldom pays Jim for acting as his lookout.

Black Dog, another pirate whose name symbolizes death, is a pale, tallowy man who is missing two fingers on his left hand. His half-sneering, half-fawning way of talking suggests that he does not really understand how to control people. Billy Bones easily drives him away. Blind **Pew**, whose name suggests that he cannot see the moral values of the church, claims to have lost his sight while defending England. His physical posture further suggests his moral qualities, because he hunches over and appears deformed. Nevertheless, he has a vice-like grip, and his cold, cruel, and ugly voice commands instant obedience from the frightened Jim. Pew's viciousness is most apparent when he expresses a desire to put out Jim's eyes.

Israel Hands is not physically mutilated, but he is as vicious as any of the mutineers. An old brandy-faced seaman, he is the coxswain on the *Hispaniola* and one of the squire's own men. Even Smollett trusts him. Hands, however, was once Flint's gunner. As his name suggests, he does not serve Christian masters. Indeed, when he murders one of his fellow pirates, he leaves the body "with arms stretched out like those of a crucifix." Hands is thus the character who most openly represents the godlessness of the pirates. He even presents his views in a mockery of conventional prayer: "I never seen good come o' goodness yet. Him as strikes first is my fancy; dead men don't bite; them's my views—amen, so be it."

Fitting somewhere between Jim's upright companions and the blood-thirsty pirates is **Ben Gunn**. Once a pirate himself, he has spent three years marooned on Treasure Island. Severely sunburned and with blackened lips, he has a voice that is rusty from lack of use. Ben wears remnants of ship's canvas and sea cloth held together with assorted fasteners and a brass-buckled leather belt. Although he seems mad from isolation, especially in his frequent desire for what he calls a Christian diet of cheese, Ben is also shrewd. He has hidden the treasure, he kills one of Silver's men while the pirates are in a drunken stupor, and he pretends to be a ghost to scare the superstitious treasure hunters. Stevenson uses Ben to satirize conventional stories of reformation. Ben claims that Providence placed him on the island as punishment for his sinful ways, which began with youthful gambling. He swears that he will return to piety, but he also says that he will drink rum the first chance he gets. When he returns to England, he fulfills his own prophecy, falling prey to drink and quickly squandering his fortune.

Kidnapped

(novel, 1886)

PLOT: *Kidnapped* combines romance and history through two stories of dispossession. In the main story, a young boy is robbed of his family inheritance and must endure a number of adventures to restore it. In the secondary story, a Scots Highlander's efforts to avoid capture by the English highlight an entire people's loss of home and culture. Set in 1751, six years after the rebellion led by the Young Pretender, Bonnie Prince Charles (Charles Edward Stuart), was crushed at Culloden Moor, the novel forms these stories into a coming-of-age tale.

The novel begins as a conventional adventure. After his father dies, the narrator, David Balfour, goes to meet his uncle Ebeneezer at Shaws, his ancestral home. Ebeneezer tries to kill David by sending him out into the dark to climb up the uncompleted staircase of a tower. When this plot fails, Ebeneezer makes an arrangement with Captain Hoseason to kidnap David and sell him into slavery in the Carolinas. After David is lured on board the brig *Covenant* and knocked out, Mr. Riach, the second officer, kindly tends to him. Meanwhile the other officer, Mr. Shaun, kills Ransome, the cabin boy, in a drunken fury, so David must take over Ransome's duties. Shortly afterward, the captain takes on board the sole survivor of a boat the *Covenant* crashed into in the fog. When David overhears the captain and his two mates plotting to kill the Jacobite stranger, Alan Breck Stuart, David warns him. Ensconced in the brig's roundhouse, the two hold off an assault by the entire ship's company.

After the ship hits a reef and David is swept overboard, he sees firsthand the dispossession suffered by the Highlanders. David first spends several days trapped on an island, unaware that he could walk off it at low tide. When he eventually gets to the mainland, he finds that Alan has left a message for him to follow. After encounters with a number of guides—some of whom help and some of whom try to cheat or harm him—David impulsively asks directions of some official-looking men. Unwittingly, David has stopped Colin Roy Campbell of Glenure, a man called the Red Fox, who is driving the Highlanders from their homesteads. While David addresses him, the Red Fox is shot and killed. David is considered an accomplice and must flee for his life. Alan suddenly appears to help David escape. Their flight leads to encounters with several men who teach the Lowlander David something of the wildness, dignity, and pathos of the Highlanders. After several narrow escapes, Alan plays on the sympathies of a barmaid, who procures a boat for them so that they can cross to a place of relative safety.

Having completed this colorful excursion into Highland life, the novel now concludes the dispossessed orphan plot. Alan tricks Ebeneezer into confessing his role in the plot against David while Mr. Rankeillor, his lawyer, secretly listens. The lawyer then arranges for David to receive money and, in due time, the House of Shaws. For his part, David decides to help Alan escape to France and to do his best to save the impoverished clan head, James Stewart, who has been falsely accused of murdering the Red Fox. David's efforts to help both men are important elements in the sequel, *David Balfour* (titled *Catriona* in England), which was published in 1893.

CHARACTERS: Many of the characters who add color to *Kidnapped* make only brief appearances in set pieces. Those who have more substantial roles tend to display the contradictory qualities typical of Stevenson's best characterizations.

David Balfour is seventeen in 1751, the year of his adventures (he says he is sixteen in the opening chapter, but he later gives his birth date as March 12, 1734). Although he is filled with a conceited sense of his own shrewdness, David is basically naive. He survives his uncle's first plot only because of a romance hero's typical luck: lightning flashes to reveal the end of the tower's staircase. Lacking a similar flash of inspiration, he succumbs to his uncle's second effort to be rid of him. Even though he is shrewd enough to determine that boarding a ship would be dangerous, he is not mature enough to maintain his determination. Because of his boyish curiosity about boats and his vanity, which Captain Hoseason exploits by treating him as an adult, David aids in his own kidnapping by boarding the *Covenant.*

David often acts like a stiff, priggish Lowland Protestant. For example, he sternly refuses to play cards with Alan and a Highland outlaw. Afterwards he refuses to talk to Alan because Alan gambled away David's money. Even when their lives are in jeopardy, David insists on following the letter of his moral code. He can't, for instance, endure the idea that people might think he is a Jacobite. Consequent-

David Balfour, as illustrated by Lynd Ward for Stevenson's **Kidnapped.**

ly, he tells the barmaid that he is loyal to England's king. Ironically, his impulsive rectitude serves him well because it convinces the barmaid to sneak a boat for him. This stern adherence to principles becomes admirable when David decides that it would be shameful to abandon Alan, even though he exposes himself to danger by staying with the Highlander. In the end, David's journey gives him a more mature understanding of morality. He understands the evil in Ebeneezer, a member of his own family, and the good in the Highlanders, people opposed to his own religious and political beliefs. Instead of safely thinking only of his own interests, he decides that he will do his best to help James Stewart and Alan Breck Stuart, Highlanders whom he has learned to like and respect.

Alan Breck Stuart does not have the appearance of a conventional romantic hero. A short man who refuses to admit that he is small, he has a sunburned, freckled face that is pitted with smallpox scars. He does, however, have a hero's dancing, roguish eyes and elegant and sometimes flamboyant manner. Alan is also heroic in deed. A strong and brave fighter, he thinks clearly under pressure, is nimble when fighting or fleeing, and is both resourceful and sly when evading capture. Alan is also notably proud. Forever pointing out that he bears a king's name, he is quick to take offense at any perceived slight of the Highlands or its people. He does, though, freely declare that his opponent in a bagpiping contest is a far better musician. Perhaps his most significant trait is loyalty. He risks his life out of loyalty to the Jacobite cause, but at the same time, this Highland Catholic remains almost paternally loyal to David, a Lowland Protestant who supports the English king. Ultimately, Alan is a mentor who teaches David to be brave and to be more tolerant of others.

Although **Ebeneezer Balfour**, David's uncle, was dashing and even handsome in his youth, he has become as ugly in appearance as he is in character. A stooping, unshaven, clay-faced man, he is a miser who eats porridge for every meal and begrudgingly shares his small pint of beer rather than granting David a full measure. A shifty-eyed plotter, Ebeneezer can't look David straight in the eye. In fact, Ebeneezer follows a strange and cowardly code. He tries to kill David by tricking him into ascending the uncompleted staircase. He recoils, however, when it is suggested that he have David murdered, because David is family. Nevertheless, he is willing to have David sold into slavery or imprisoned for life. Significantly, the House of Shaws where Ebeneezer lives is always dark inside, reflecting his self-imposed ignorance and evil disposition. His decision to halt construction on the house in order to save money is also a metaphor for the old bachelor's failure to complete and maintain the family, the real House of Shaws. Ebeneezer's failings are attributable to one moral flaw that is symbolized by a physical imperfection. As he explains to David, Ebeneezer has a bad heart.

The sailors are studies in contrasts, and **Captain Hoseason** shows more contradictions than any. According to David, this tall, dark, sober-looking sailor was two men, "and left the better one behind as soon as he set foot on board his vessel." On shore, Hoseason is noted for his religious devotion. He charms David by acting like a fatherly confidant; he is devoted to his mother and fires a salute to her whenever he sails past her house. In all other instances, however, he is a man of iron. Hoseason likes overly hot rooms because, as he states without being conscious of the symbolism, he has cold blood. A cool, calculating, self-possessed man, Hoseason has no honor. Shortly after he agrees to deliver Alan Breck Stuart ashore, he forms a plot to kill him.

Hoseason's officers also have complex personalities. The small, red-headed **Mr. Riach** knocks David out, yet saves his life by tenderly caring for him. He is harsh and sullen during the rare instances when he is sober, but he is kind and considerate when he is drunk. He is also the only sailor with moral scruples. After the shipwreck he sides with Alan against his own captain and shipmates. **Mr. Shaun** is the exact opposite of Mr. Riach, being kind when he is sober but extremely brutal when he is drunk. His cruelty is most notable in his murder of Ransome. **Ransome**, the friendly cabin boy, combines childish innocence with a desire for adult depravity. A heavy-drinking and tattooed child who views the land as a prison, Ransome swears profusely and boasts constantly of wild deeds in his attempts to belong to the company of sailors. Somewhat simpleminded, he can't see that the beatings he endures aboard the ship are worse than anything the shore would inflict.

Mr. Rankeillor, the lawyer, is both comical and shrewd. A ruddy, kind-looking man who wears a well-powdered wig and spectacles, he pretentiously sprinkles his speech with Latin phrases. David pities him because he seems foolish in repeatedly telling stories about how blind he is without his glasses. As David eventually finds out, Rankeillor knows how to balance his duty as an officer of the court with his compassionate concern for others. By refusing to let David use Alan's name, and by making a point of leaving his glasses behind when he meets Alan, Rankeillor manages to help the Jacobite without compromising his legal obligations. For this reason, he is the last and most successful of David's paternalistic mentors.

Further Reading

Children's Literature Review. Vols. 10, 11. Detroit: Gale Research, 1986.

Collier, Laurie, and Joyce Nakamura, eds. *Major Authors and Illustrators for Children and Young Adults.* Detroit: Gale Research, 1993.

Fredeman, William E., and Ira B. Nadel, eds. *Victorian Novelists after 1885.* Vol. 18 of *Dictionary of Literary Biography.* Detroit: Gale Research, 1983.

Saposnik, Irving S. *Robert Louis Stevenson.* New York: Twayne, 1974.

Thesing, William B., ed. *Victorian Prose Writers after 1867.* Vol. 57 of *Dictionary of Literary Biography.* Detroit: Gale Research, 1987.

Yesterday's Authors of Books for Children. Vol. 2. Detroit: Gale Research, 1978.

Zaidman, Laura M., ed. *British Children's Writers 1880-1914.* Vol. 141 of *Dictionary of Literary Biography.* Detroit: Gale Research, 1994.

Sydney Taylor

1904-1978, American dancer, actress, and writer

All-of-a-Kind Family

(novel, 1951)

PLOT: Set on the East Side of New York City in 1912-13, this episodic novel develops many incidents around Jewish holidays. It focuses on the relationships of the poor All-of-a-Kind Family, so called because the children are all girls who dress the same: Ella is twelve years old, Henny is ten, Sarah is eight, Charlotte is six, and Gertie is four. The initial episodes involve secular situations. In the first, Sarah arranges to pay Miss Allen, the librarian, for a lost book. Later, Mama turns dusting into an enjoyable game by having the children search for hidden buttons. One rainy day, Papa, a junk dealer, delights his children by letting them choose books from a pile he has purchased. When bachelor Uncle Hyman gives the children some money in another episode, Charlotte and Gertie buy candy and crackers for a late-night feast in bed.

Religious celebrations become more prominent with the fifth chapter, which describes a shopping trip and Sabbath dinner. In the sixth, Papa is shocked at the waste of money when the girls give him a cup for his birthday, but he realizes that he must not spoil their pleasure. At Purim, the children dress in outlandish clothes to deliver baskets. Domestic tribulations come to the fore in the next two episodes. First, Sarah refuses to eat her rice soup, so her parents won't let her eat anything else until she gives in. Next, four of the children become ill with scarlet fever at Passover. In the Fourth of July episode, Papa's helper, Charlie, entertains the children with fireworks. Later, Charlie tells Papa that he is Herbert Charles Graham and is estranged from his wealthy family because they disapproved of the girl he wanted to marry. His beloved disappeared and the lonely Charlie has spent years searching for her. A visit to the beach, during which Henny becomes lost, interrupts Charlie's story. Miss Allen, invited to see the Succah, is discovered to be Kathy, Charlie's beloved, and is reunited with him. In the final episode, Mama gives birth to a boy, who is named Chaim but referred to as Little Charlie.

Sequels are More All-of-a-Kind Family *(1954),* All-of-a-Kind Family Uptown *(1958),* All-of-a-Kind Family Downtown *(1972), and* Ella of All-of-a-Kind Family *(1978).*

CHARACTERS: Although the girls dress alike and act as a close-knit and loving group—all of them, for example, contribute money to pay Sarah's library fine—they are characterized by distinctive touches. The adults are idealized stock types. Twelve-year-old **Ella** is serious and talented. She is a good actress who can entertain others by imitating the voices and gestures of the peddlers she saw on the shopping trip. She also possesses a beautiful singing voice. Ella has a crush on Charlie. She is generally stiff and awkward around him, but is ecstatic when he holds her hand and praises her singing. Ella is hurt when she discovers that Charlie loves someone else, but she wants him to be happy. **Henny** (short for **Henrietta**) is a ten year old with blond curls. She is the only girl who doesn't like sharing a bed, so she sleeps alone. The mischievous Henny likes to jump on the bed. She also has a sweet tooth; she tries to sneak a Haman taschen (a Purim cake), she is doubtful about going a week without candy in order to buy Papa's birthday present, and she enjoys being lost because the police buy her ice cream. Eight-year-old **Sarah** has integrity. Having taken responsibility for paying for the lost library book, she refuses to miss a payment, even though she wants to buy a present for Papa. Instead, she shows her practical side by making a payment from her savings so that all the girls can chip in for the present. Nevertheless, she can be a "contrary imp," as she shows when she suddenly decides that she won't eat her rice soup. **Charlotte**, the six year old, is imaginative. She directs the late-night eating games and makes up stories and games for Gertie, her bedmate. Four-year-old **Gertie** does help her sisters when she spots the cup that they buy for Papa's birthday, but she is usually just the baby of the family. She is scared of the noise of a fire engine, and she feels threatened by the arrival of the new baby, declaring, "I'm the baby." Her sisters, however, convince her that being older than a sibling has advantages, especially when the baby is a boy.

    Mama is the loving center of the family. Instead of being round and dumpy, like most of the other mothers in her neighborhood, she is tall and slim. A proud woman whose children feel proud of her in return. Mama is a stern but loving parent. Even though enforcing the rules makes her anxious, she insists that Sarah eat her soup before receiving other food. Wise and compassionate, she ensures that she will have no further resistance, however, by making sure that she doesn't serve vegetables once Sarah gives in. Mama is also clever in devising the button game that tricks the girls into dusting. She is considerate in taking them on shopping expeditions and a trip to the beach; she shows loving dedication by nursing them through the scarlet fever. Finally, Mama points to the essence of family life when, after the arrival of the baby, she insists that the term all-of-a-kind family now means that they are close, loving, and loyal. **Papa** is a gentle, kind, and deeply religious man. The gentile peddlers who supply his junk shop obviously like and respect him. Charlie even confides in him. Papa does what he can to please his family. He thus involves his daughters in the building of the Succah. Although he considers the cup that his daughters give him to be an extravagance, he values their happiness and praises it as a gift he has always wanted. One other adult member of the family is worth mentioning because he is prominent in the first sequel. **Uncle Hyman**, Mama's youngest brother, is a short and stocky bachelor who loves to eat dinner at his sister's home. His red face literally glows as if he had scrubbed it hard. Hyman is jolly and generous, insisting on paying for his food and on giving the children money.

    Relationships with the All-of-a-Kind Family reveal the basic goodness of the two lovers and are instrumental in reuniting them. **Charlie**, who is actually **Herbert Charles Graham**, is a handsome blue-eyed, blond gentile. His grace and charming manner are evidence of his wealthy background. Nevertheless, Charlie is at home with the poor Jewish family, and he brings gifts to the children when they are ill. His affection for the family shows that he values character above wealth. In spite of occasional merriment, Charlie is generally sad because his beloved left after his family objected to her. He therefore cut himself off from his domineering family and adopted a new identity while searching for her. **Miss Kathy Allen** is a librarian who has blue eyes and dimples on her obviously compassionate face. She takes an interest in the children, kindly arranging for Sarah to pay for the lost book and save for a doll at the same time. She also sends them a magazine when they are ill. Once reunited with Charlie, she again shows her moral worth by insisting on an immediate reconciliation with his family.

Further Reading

Berger, Laura Standley, ed. *Twentieth-Century Children's Writers*. 4th ed. Detroit: St. James, 1995.

Collier, Laurie, and Joyce Nakamura, eds. *Major Authors and Illustrators for Children and Young Adults*. Detroit: Gale Research, 1993.

Contemporary Authors New Revision Series. Vol. 4. Detroit: Gale Research, 1981.

Fuller, Muriel, ed. *More Junior Authors*. New York: H. W. Wilson, 1963.

Something about the Author. Vols. 1, 28. Detroit: Gale Research, 1971, 1982.

Theodore Taylor

1921-, American seaman, journalist, public relations
director, filmmaker, and author

The Cay

(novel, 1969)

PLOT: This Robinsonade, or survival story patterned after Daniel Defoe's *Robinson Crusoe* (1719), is about overcoming racial prejudice and discovering true friendship. The narrator, eleven-year-old Phillip Enright, Jr., is a white American living with his parents in Willemstad, Curaçao, during World War II. As the novel opens, Phillip thinks of war as only a game or adventure. After a German submarine is spotted off the coast, Grace, Phillip's mother, overcomes the objections of Phillip, Sr., and embarks with her son for Virginia. Their freighter is torpedoed, and during the evacuation Phillip is hit on the head. Phillip, whose mother has taught him to despise blacks, awakens on a raft with Timothy, an elderly West Indian sailor, and Stew Cat, the cook's cat. Shortly afterward, Phillip goes blind. He becomes dependent on Timothy, who rations their water, pulls him out of the shark-infested waters when he falls from the raft, and gets them ashore on a cay in the Devil's Mouth.

Timothy builds a shelter and finds food for them. Nevertheless, Phillip feels superior because Timothy doesn't know how to write a help sign in the sand. Their relationship changes when Phillip, after refusing to weave mats, insults Timothy and the black man slaps him. Phillip thereafter treats Timothy as a friend and with more respect. He even rescues Timothy from a possible drowning when the old man becomes delirious from malaria and plunges himself into the water. Timothy, in turn, gives the boy lessons in independence, teaching Phillip how to fish and encouraging him to climb a tree for coconuts. When a hurricane strikes, Timothy dies shielding Phillip from its fury. Naked because the storm has ripped the rags from his body, Phillip puts Timothy's lessons to use. He despairs after an airplane misses his signal flare, but he figures out how to create black smoke that will be visible for a long distance. Eventually, a boat, alerted by an airplane, rescues Phillip from the cay. Reunited with his parents, he undergoes three operations to restore his vision. By the time he returns to Willemstad, he has matured considerably and realizes that both he and his mother have changed for the better.

Timothy of the Cay (1993) is a "prequel-sequel," covering Timothy's life before he meets Phillip and Phillip's life after he is rescued from the cay.

CHARACTERS: Taylor has said that in writing *The Cay* he "hoped to achieve a subtle plea for better race relations and more understanding." Although his novel won a number of awards, critics later charged him with perpetuating racial stereotypes. Defenders of the novel point out, however, that such stereotypes are the products of a first-person narrator who actually modifies them as he becomes more tolerant.

Taylor patterned eleven-year-old **Phillip Enright, Jr.**, after a boyhood friend whose mother taught him to hate black people. Phillip's bigotry is apparent in his initial reaction to Timothy, whom he considers to be ugly. Furthermore, although his parents have taught him to call all adults "mister," Phillip can't bring himself to address a black man that way. Phillip's naivete and self-centeredness intensify his bigotry. On shore he had thought of war as merely an exciting adventure, and on the raft he assumes that his parents will send out planes and quickly rescue him. Thus, when Timothy refuses to increase his meager ration of water, Phillip interprets this wise precaution to be merely foolish stubbornness. Filled with self-pity, the tearful Phillip even charges Timothy with saving the water for himself.

The physical blindness that Phillip suffers serves as a metaphor. As Taylor has said, Phillip is already blind because he is biased. Phillip develops insight while on the cay, however. At first, resenting Timothy's refusal to take him to the reef until he has explored it, Phillip accepts his mother's hateful view of blacks. Phillip also feels superior because Timothy is illiterate. Nevertheless, he lets Timothy pretend that he can read, thereby protecting the old man's dignity and foreshadowing his own change.

This change begins with rebellion. Frustrated by his inability to weave a mat, Phillip calls Timothy ugly and stupid. Timothy strikes him, and the shock of this action knocks some sense into Phillip. Soon after, Phillip openly declares that he wants to be Timothy's friend, asking him to call him Phillip instead of "young bahss." When he snuggles up to Timothy for warmth during a rainfall, Phillip realizes that Timothy does not feel black or white. Furthermore, after he rescues the delirious Timothy, the once timid Phillip develops the courage to climb a coconut tree. For Phillip this is graduation from a survival course, but it is also a moment of profound internal change. Phillip no longer thinks of Timothy as being ugly: he has the insight to envision Timothy's face as kind and strong.

The final stage of Phillip's development begins with symbols suggestive of the archetypal hero's death and rebirth. Just as unconsciousness marked the end of his naive life with his mother when he awoke on the raft, it also ends his dependence on Timothy. During the hurricane, he becomes unconscious, thereby symbolically dying as a dependent youth, and the wind strips him of all his clothes, suggesting his rebirth as a new and self-reliant person. Left alone after Timothy's death, he shows courage by managing to survive on his own. Phillip nearly succumbs to despair, however, when the first airplane misses his signal, but he has the psychological strength to figure out a more effective means for signalling. The restoration of his physical eyesight complements his development. Upon his return to Willemstad, Phillip shows that he has developed a mature insight into the horror of war and the humanity of black people.

Timothy (the sequel indicates that late in life he used the surname of Hannah Gumbs, his foster mother) is a helper figure. He enables Phillip to survive physically and to develop morally. Timothy is a huge, heavily-muscled black man from St. Thomas in the Virgin Islands. At least seventy years old, he has wiry gray hair and a welt across his left cheek. He also has a soft, musical voice. Timothy does exhibit some traits of the stereotypical ignorant black servant: he speaks in a dialect, calling Phillip "young bahss"; he tries to cover his illiteracy by

pretending that he is approving Phillip's spelling; and he is superstitious, making a statue of Stew Cat to drive away bad luck. Nevertheless, Timothy is not a stereotype or a comical fool. He is heroic, for example, when he enters the shark-infested waters to save Phillip when he falls off the raft. He is resourceful in ensuring their survival and properly stern when rationing precious water. Timothy proves himself a capable provider by building a shelter, making a guide rope so that Phillip can find his way, staking out the reef so that he can fish safely, and stowing away supplies during the hurricane.

Patient and kind, Timothy teaches Phillip to survive on his own. He is gently persistent in getting Phillip to weave a mat and to climb the coconut tree. Timothy controls his temper, resorting to silence when Phillip offends him. Nevertheless, Timothy does strike the boy when Phillip refuses to weave and insults him. That blow establishes Timothy's dignity and earns Phillip's respect. Timothy does not, however, hold a grudge. When Phillip indicates that he wants to be a friend, Timothy quietly notes that he has always been his friend, and he begins to call him Phillip. Later, Timothy teaches a lesson in race relations by noting that although he himself doesn't like some whites, he would be foolish to hate all of them. Because he is the ideal friend, Timothy transforms Phillip into a mature and tolerant young adult.

Grace Enright, Phillip's mother, is a bigot who teaches Phillip that whites and blacks belong to separate spheres. A nervous woman, Grace dislikes Curaçao and has consequently become distant from her husband. When Phillip suggests that he stay with his father after Grace has determined that she will leave with him, she wins her way by bursting into tears and proclaiming that her husband and son do not love her. Ironically, Grace is calm when their ship sinks. Afterwards, she returns to her husband and indicates that she has no intention of leaving the islands. Although this act suggests that she is no longer so self-absorbed, the novel provides no evidence that she has lost the prejudice that poisoned her son. **Phillip Enright, Sr.**, her husband, is an expert on refineries. He has a sensible, clear-sighted understanding of their situation. Nevertheless, he can't withstand his wife's histrionic appeals to let her leave with their son.

Further Reading

Authors and Artists for Young Adults. Vol. 2. Detroit: Gale Research, 1989.

Berger, Laura Standley, ed. *Twentieth-Century Young Adult Writers.* 1st ed. Detroit: St. James, 1994.

Children's Literature Review. Vol. 30. Detroit: Gale Research, 1993.

Collier, Laurie, and Joyce Nakamura, eds. *Major Authors and Illustrators for Children and Young Adults.* Detroit: Gale Research, 1993.

Contemporary Authors New Revision Series. Vol. 38. Detroit: Gale Research, 1993.

De Montreville, Doris, and Elizabeth D. Crawford, eds. *Fourth Book of Junior Authors.* New York: H. W. Wilson, 1978.

Something about the Author. Vols. 5, 54, 83. Detroit: Gale Research, 1973, 1989, 1996.

Something about the Author Autobiography Series. Vol. 4. Detroit: Gale Research, 1987.

J. R. R. Tolkien

1892-1973, English academic and author

The Hobbit; or, There and Back Again

(fantasy, 1937; revised, 1951)

PLOT: Its archetypal quest plot, in which treasure seekers confront evil monsters, has made *The Hobbit* the model for many "sword-and-sorcery" high fantasies. Its true subject, however, is the central character's discovery of heroic inner resources. Bilbo Baggins, a hobbit, finds himself entertaining the wizard Gandalf and thirteen dwarves: Dwalin, Balin, Kili, Fili, Dori, Nori, Ori, Oin, Gloin, Bifur, Bofur, Bombur, and their leader, Thorin Oakenshield. Hurt when Gloin ridicules him, Bilbo agrees to become the burglar who will recover a treasure stolen a hundred years earlier by Smaug the dragon.

Bilbo has little success in establishing his new identity in his early adventures. When he discovers three trolls, Bill, Bert, and Tom, and tries to be a burglar by picking Bill's pocket, the trolls capture him and put the dwarves into sacks. It is then left to Gandalf to rescue everyone. Hiding nearby, Gandalf imitates the voices of the trolls and provokes them into arguing until sunrise turns them into stone. After obtaining magical weapons from a cave, the questers proceed to the Last Homely House, where the elf Elrond explains the runes on their treasure map.

In the second phase of his adventure, Bilbo encounters enemies three times. First, goblins capture the party. Gandalf kills the Great Goblin and leads their escape. Bilbo, however, is knocked unconscious. Waking up alone in a cave, Bilbo finds a ring and then encounters Gollum, the creature who lost it. Through luck, Bilbo defeats Gollum in a riddling contest. He then puts on the ring, which makes him invisible, follows Gollum to the cave's exit, squeezes between the doors, and rejoins his companions. The third encounter with enemies occurs when wargs (wild wolves) force the group to seek safety in the trees. Goblins set fire to the trees, but eagles rescue the party. Gandalf then uses wit to gain admittance to the house of Beorn, a skin-changer who can turn himself into a bear, who equips them for the next stage of their journey.

Gandalf leaves the party as it enters Mirkwood, the setting of the third stage of the story. After Bombur awakens from an enchanted sleep, he maddens his tired and hungry companions by telling them about his dreams of feasting. Ignoring Gandalf's earlier warnings, the party leaves the path to chase elf fires, which go out at their approach. Bilbo goes to sleep and wakens to discover that he is being wrapped by a giant spider. Bilbo kills it, slips on his ring, taunts the other spiders into chasing him, and rescues the dwarves, whom the spiders have encased in cocoons. Shortly afterwards, wood elves capture everyone, except the invisible Bilbo. Bilbo follows, releases the dwarves from the Elvenking's dungeons, puts them in barrels, and floats them downriver to the lake town of Esgaroth, where the greedy Master shelters them.

The final adventures occur at Lonely Mountain, home of Smaug. Discovering the cave's back door, Bilbo enters alone and steals a cup from the sleeping dragon. On his second trip, Bilbo tricks Smaug into revealing a vulnerable spot in his armor. An old thrush reports this news to Bard, who kills Smaug when he attacks Esgaroth. Meanwhile, Bilbo enters the cave and takes the Arkenstone, the greatest of the treasures. Thorin, now proclaiming himself King Under the Mountain, comes under siege when he refuses to give Bard and the wood elves a fair share of the treasure. To make peace, Bilbo gives Bard the Arkenstone to use in negotiations. When goblins and wargs attack, the feuding parties unite and, aided by the eagles, defeat them. Mortally wounded, Thorin reconciles with Bilbo. Bilbo then returns home only to find that his goods are being auctioned because he has been presumed dead. Although he has lost his former comfortable lifestyle, Bilbo lives happily to an old age.

The Hobbit *forms an introduction to* The Lord of the Rings *trilogy:* The Fellowship of the Ring *(1954),* The Two Towers *(1954), and* The Return of the King *(1955).*

CHARACTERS: Many of the characters are common folktale types, but the central character belongs to a race Tolkien invented. **Bilbo Baggins** is a hobbit, a small, plump, and beardless being whose feet have leathery soles and a thick covering of hair. Although he can move quickly and quietly, abilities essential to a burglar, Bilbo is an unlikely hero. Descended from a respectable, well-to-do family that loves food and comfort, he claims to despise adventures as inconveniences. Bilbo has, however, a split identity: on his mother's side, he is descended from the adventure-loving Tooks. Bilbo's Tookish identity, symbol of suppressed or unacknowledged powers, surfaces when Gloin says that he looks more like a grocer than a burglar. Determined to prove his worth, Bilbo agrees to be a burglar. Significantly, he leaves in such a hurry the next day that he leaves behind his hat and handkerchief, symbols of his comfort-loving identity, and must don Dwalin's spare hood and cloak, symbols of the adventurous side of his identity.

Bilbo's adventures, which repeatedly occur while he is separated from the party, test and define his identity. In the first, Bilbo foolishly tries to become a "first-class and legendary burglar" by picking the troll's pocket. Captured, the terrified Bilbo absurdly defines himself as a "burrahobbit." Bilbo develops a

better public identity in the second stage. He is knocked unconscious while escaping from the goblins (unconsciousness symbolizes the death of an identity). When he awakens, he is unaware that he possesses a ring of power. He is therefore so frightened while riddling with Gollum that he survives only because he has a hero's share of luck. Bilbo does, however, show some deeper qualities. Filled with pity when he thinks of Gollum's miserable lot, Bilbo refrains from stabbing Gollum and leaps over him to escape. Gollum calls Bilbo a thief, but his leap makes him more of a saint. After Bilbo squeezes through the cave doors, marking the symbolic birth prepared by his earlier unconsciousness, he attains a new, unmerited public identity. Wisely keeping the ring a secret, he sneaks up on the dwarves, who praise him as a burglar.

Subsequent scenes parallel earlier failures to establish that Bilbo is genuinely heroic. In Mirkwood, Bilbo makes up for his failure with the trolls by assuming Gandalf's role as helper. First, he kills a giant spider, an act that makes him feel heroic: like legendary heroes, he even names his weapon. He then shows wit and bravery. Throwing his voice to enrage the spiders, just as Gandalf did with the trolls, Bilbo rescues the dwarves, who have been wrapped by the spiders, much as they were put in bags by the trolls. Bilbo again shows ingenuity in rescuing the dwarves from the elves' dungeons and floating them to safety in barrels. Bilbo's greatest heroism, however, occurs during his three visits to Smaug's cave, a setting that parallels Gollum's cave. After proving his luck and wit by discovering the secret entrance, Bilbo fights his greatest battle. Overcoming fear, he proceeds alone into the cave. Bilbo's deliberate theft of a cup from the sleeping dragon now makes him a thief in Smaug's eyes, just as his accidental discovery of the ring made him one in Gollum's. On his second trip, Bilbo shows that he has developed the self-control he lacked with Gollum. To conceal his identity so that the dragon can't gain power over him, he wisely riddles with Smaug. Bilbo also becomes a trickster, playing on Smaug's vanity to discover the dragon's vulnerable spot. On his third trip, Bilbo ironically becomes a true burglar by concealing the Arkenstone from those who hired him to find it. Unlike the dwarves, however, the generous Bilbo is not overcome with lust for wealth. Defining himself as an honest burglar, he gives the Arkenstone to Bard in order to hasten peace with Thorin. Although Bilbo plays no role in the final battle because he is knocked unconscious—a symbol that his peace-loving Baggins identity is reemerging—others recognize his heroic identity. Thorin calls him a "good thief," and the Elvenking praises him as "Bilbo the Magnificent!"

Bilbo's discovery that his neighbors have presumed him dead symbolically underscores his status as an archetypal hero: only heroes return from death. In one of the book's notable ironies, however, Bilbo finds that his heroism has cost him his respectability. Nevertheless, having discovered his inner powers, Bilbo gratefully accepts that he is only a little fellow in a big world. Bilbo thereby represents the ordinary person who responds heroically when circumstances demand and afterwards resumes his ordinary life.

Gandalf, with his long white beard that hangs below his waist, is an archetypal wise old man. A powerful wizard who delights in blowing colored rings of smoke from his pipe, Gandalf carries a staff and dresses in a tall, pointed blue hat, a long gray cloak, a silver scarf, and black boots. By insisting that Bilbo will be a burglar when the time comes and that Bilbo has more in him than either the dwarves or Bilbo himself have guessed, Gandalf establishes the theme that circumstances reveal hidden identities. As a guide, Gandalf leads the party to the havens offered by Elrond and Beorn. As a helper, he physically rescues Bilbo until Bilbo acquires the skill, courage, and confidence to manage by himself. Gandalf's departure at Mirkwood is a thematic necessity: it allows Bilbo to pass tests on his own. After the adventure, Gandalf adds to the theme. By indicating that Bilbo is only a little fellow in a wide world, he stresses that the common good is more important than even heroic individuals.

The thirteen dwarves, members of a short, stout, bearded race, wear heavy hoods of various colors. **Thorin Oakenshield**, the descendant of the king driven out by Smaug, wears a sky-blue hood with a long silver tassel. Aware of his importance, Thorin speaks in a pompous, formal manner. After Thorin establishes himself as King Under the Mountain, he becomes the new dragon. Filled with lust for the treasure, he refuses to share his hoard with those who have suffered from Smaug's raids. Although Thorin is devious and tries to think of ways to cheat the men and elves, his heroic goodness asserts itself when he joins the battle against the wargs and goblins. Mortally wounded, he reconciles with Bilbo, praising Bilbo's values because they contribute to the common good. **Balin**, who has a white beard and wears a scarlet hood, is the eldest after Thorin. The kindest dwarf, he befriends Bilbo, even accompanying him a little way into Smaug's tunnel. **Dwalin**, his brother, wears a dark-green hood and has a blue beard. He lends Bilbo a hood and cloak, thereby signalling the beginning of Bilbo's career as an adventurer. **Kili** and his younger brother, **Fili**, who wear blue hoods and have yellow beards, are the youngest by fifty years. Both are sharp-eyed and strong. Nephews of Thorin, they die defending him in the Battle of the Five Armies. When he declares that Bilbo looks more like a grocer than a burglar, the white-hooded **Gloin** simultaneously introduces the appearance theme and inspires Bilbo to join the quest. **Dori**, who wears a purple hood, is the strongest of the dwarves. He carries Bilbo during the escape from the goblins. Like Dori, **Nori** dresses in purple and values regular, abundant meals. **Bombur**, a fat, lazy, and somewhat comical dwarf, wears pale green. By talking about feasting after he awakens from his enchanted sleep, he drives the hungry dwarves into foolishly abandoning the path through Mirkwood. His brother, **Bofur** (yellow hood), his cousin, **Bifur** (yellow hood), **Ori** (gray hood), and **Oin** (brown hood) fill out the party.

Notable figures appear at each of the havens that divide Bilbo's adventure into stages. **Elrond**, the master of the Last Homely House at Rivendell, is descended from elves and heroes. Noble, fair in face, strong, wise, and kind, Elrond is the perfect host. He also is a helper. By reading the runes on the treasure map, he gives Bilbo the clue that lets him discover the hidden entrance to Smaug's cave. **Beorn** is a skin-changer: sometimes he is a huge, muscular man with a thick, black beard and hair, and sometimes he is a great black bear. Beorn is able to talk with the marvelous animals who serve him. Because Beorn angers quickly and can be dangerous, Gandalf orders the dwarves to arrive in groups, just as they did at Bilbo's house. Symbolically, this parallel situation marks Beorn's house as a new start for the adventure. Bilbo becomes the true leader when he leaves. The distrustful Beorn checks out the dwarves' story, but, satisfied that they are truthful, he becomes a helper. After providing them with supplies, he follows in the shape of a bear until they reach Mirkwood. **The Master**, a merchant who was elected leader of the lake town of Esgaroth, represents debased leadership. He is a coward who thinks only of saving himself when Smaug attacks. After the battle, he shows his greed by fleeing with the town's share of the treasure. Fittingly, he dies alone in the wastelands. By way of contrast, **Bard**, a descendent of Girion of Dale, is brave and noble by birth. An excellent archer, the grim and dark Bard faces and slays Smaug. Bard temporarily comes under the treasure's spell, but he uses his share to rebuild his ancestral home of Dale.

Various monsters test Bilbo and contribute to the identity theme. **Bill** (whose full name is **William Huggin**), **Bert**, and **Tom**, the three trolls who capture him, define Bilbo as a "little rabbit" when he calls himself a "burrahobbit." Because they are coarse and stupid, traits suggested by their lower-class or Cockney accents, Gandalf easily tricks them into arguing with each other until the sun turns them to stone. They thus enable Gandalf to demonstrate to Bilbo that wit may defeat evil. **The Great Goblin**, an evil orc with a huge head, identifies Bilbo and the dwarves as thieves, murderers, and elf-friends. Cruel and easily enraged, the Great Goblin rushes to kill Thorin, but Gandalf slays him with a magic sword, thus indirectly showing Bilbo that force is also necessary against evil.

Gollum, a small, slimy creature with long fingers, large feet, and large, round, pale eyes set in a thin face, is a pathetic case of evil. Named after the horrible swallowing sound he makes, Gollum calls himself "my precious." He also frequently calls the magic ring "my precious," however, suggesting that its loss becomes the loss of his essential identity. *The*

Lord of the Rings indicates that Gollum was once a hobbit named Sméagol (originally called Trahald) who murdered his cousin for this ring and changed in appearance because of his years of living underground alone. In the 1951 revision of *The Hobbit*, Tolkien therefore intensified Gollum's evil qualities. Gollum, defining Bilbo as a "tasty morsel" but fearing Bilbo's magic weapon, is sneaky and resorts to the riddling game to capture his prey. Gollum outwits himself, though, by foolishly permitting the contest to become a guessing game about the contents of Bilbo's pocket. After he loses, Gollum shows complete depravity. Instead of leading Bilbo from the cave, as he promised he would, he tries to become an evil trickster, leaving to get the ring so that he can kill Bilbo. Ironically, Gollum's deceitful attempt to capture Bilbo actually fulfills his promise because Gollum unwittingly leads the invisible Bilbo straight to the exit. **Smaug**, a red-golden, fire-breathing, flying dragon, presents Bilbo with his greatest challenge. Smaug is greed personified: Bilbo's theft of a single cup sends him into a rage-filled flight of destruction. Intelligent and subtle, Smaug defines Bilbo as a thief and tries to trick him into revealing his name so that he can gain power over him. Smaug does not realize, however, that Bilbo is adopting the identity of trickster. The exceedingly vain Smaug enjoys Bilbo's lavish praise, even though he recognizes its insincerity and can't resist showing off his protective coating of jewels. Overconfident, Smaug does not know himself truly because he does not know that he has a vulnerable spot. Vanity and lack of self-knowledge thus become instrumental in his destruction, for Bard kills him by shooting an arrow into Smaug's unprotected spot.

Further Reading

Authors and Artists for Young Adults. Vol. 10. Detroit: Gale Research, 1986.

Berger, Laura Standley, ed. *Twentieth-Century Children's Writers.* 4th ed. Detroit: St. James, 1995.

———. *Twentieth-Century Young Adult Writers.* 1st ed. Detroit: St. James, 1994.

Bingham, Jane M., ed. *Writers for Children: Critical Studies of Major Authors since the Seventeenth Century.* New York: Scribner's, 1988.

Carpenter, Humphrey. *J. R. R. Tolkien: A Biography.* Boston: Houghton Mifflin, 1977.

Collier, Laurie, and Joyce Nakamura, eds. *Major Authors and Illustrators for Children and Young Adults.* Detroit: Gale Research, 1993.

Contemporary Authors New Revision Series. Vol. 36. Detroit: Gale Research, 1992.

Contemporary Literary Criticism. Vols. 1, 2, 3, 8, 12, 38. Detroit: Gale Research, 1973, 1974, 1975, 1978, 1980, 1986.

Crabbe, Katharyn. *J. R. R. Tolkien.* New York: Ungar, 1981.

Foster, Robert. *The Complete Guide to Middle-Earth.* New York: Ballantine, 1978.

Fuller, Muriel, ed. *More Junior Authors.* New York: H. W. Wilson, 1963.

Kocher, Paul. *Master of Middle-Earth: The Achievement of J. R. R. Tolkien.* Boston: Houghton Mifflin, 1972.

Oldsey, Bernard, ed. *British Novelists, 1930-1959: Part Two.* Vol. 15 of *Dictionary of Literary Biography.* Detroit: Gale Research, 1983.

Something about the Author. Vols. 2, 32. Detroit: Gale Research, 1971, 1983.

Sullivan, C. W., III. "J. R. R. Tolkien's *The Hobbit:* The Magic of Words." In *Touchstones: Reflections on the Best in Children's Literature.* Vol. 1. Edited by Perry Nodelman. West Lafayette, IN: Children's Literature Association, 1985.

Tyler, J. E. A. *The New Tolkien Companion.* London: Macmillan, 1979.

P. L. Travers

1906-1996, English novelist

Mary Poppins

(fantasy, 1934; revised edition, 1981)

PLOT: In addition to the title character's strange arrival and departure, *Mary Poppins* recounts ten independent stories. Each of these adventures in some way blurs the boundaries between reality and fantasy. An east wind mysteriously blows Mary Poppins out of the sky to Number Seventeen Cherry-Tree Lane, the home of Mr. and Mrs. Banks and their four children, Jane, Michael, and the infant twins, John and Barbara. Although Mary Poppins refuses to provide references, Mrs. Banks immediately hires her as a nanny. Jane and Michael soon realize that this nanny is special. They see Mary Poppins slide up the banisters, remove oversized possessions from a

The ever-proper and intriguingly mysterious Mary Poppins, as illustrated by Mary Shepard.

small, seemingly empty carpetbag, and dispense different flavors of medicine from the same bottle. The children come to love her and ask her to remain always, but Mary Poppins promises to stay only until the wind changes.

In the episodes that follow, Mary Poppins is the center of magical action. On her day out, she and Bert, the impoverished Match-Man who draws clever chalk pictures on the pavement, mystically step into the world of one of Bert's pictures to enjoy tea and a merry-go-round ride. Later, Mary Poppins takes Michael and Jane to visit her Uncle Albert Wigg. They find him literally floating near the ceiling and join him in the air for a tea party. Afterwards, however, Mary Poppins angrily denies that anything unusual occurred. In the next two episodes, Mary Poppins helps Andrew, Miss Lark's dog, rebel against his owner's pampering, and she tells Jane and Michael the story of the Red Cow, which once had a star caught on her horn and now searches for another. The sixth chapter, "Bad Tuesday," recounts a day during which Michael simply felt like being deliberately naughty. In another exploit, Mary

Poppins uses an enchanted compass to take the children around the world. (In the original version of this chapter, they visit an Eskimo, a Black Woman, a Mandarin, and a Red Indian. Following charges that the portraits of ethnic groups constituted offensive racial stereotypes, Travers revised the chapter to have the children visit a Polar Bear, a Hyacinth Macaw, a Panda, and a Dolphin. In both versions, those they visit know and honor Mary Poppins.) Upon their return, Michael tries to use the compass himself, but the people he visited come after him seeking vengeance for his meddling, prompting him to call Mary Poppins for help. In the following episodes, Mary Poppins takes Jane and Michael to visit the Bird Woman at St. Paul's Cathedral and then to a shop to buy gingerbread from elderly Mrs. Corry and her gigantic daughters, Annie and Fannie. That night, Jane and Michael realize that Mary Poppins has removed the decorative stars from their gingerbread. They watch in amazement as Mary Poppins and Mrs. Corry replace them in the sky with glue.

The ninth chapter provides a kind of Wordsworthian interlude before the more dramatic final adventures. In this chapter, the infant twins cry when Mary Poppins says that they will forget how to talk to starlings and sunshine as they get older. Once they have their first birthday, John and Barbara lose their ability to communicate with nature. The most intense and mystical adventure in the book then follows. Answering a mysterious call one night, Jane and Michael go to the zoo, where they find everything inverted: the animals run the place, and humans, such as their neighbor, Admiral Boom, are in cages. The serpent lord of the animals, the Hamadryad, calls for the Grand Chain. The animals then dance around Mary Poppins (whose birthday has fallen on a full moon), celebrating the unity of all life. Although Mary Poppins characteristically denies the events the next day, the children see that she wears a snakeskin belt that the Hamadryad gave her. In the final episode, Mary Poppins, Jane, and Michael help Maia, one of the stars forming the constellation of the Pleiades, to shop for Christmas presents for her six sisters. In a gesture of grudging generosity, Mary Poppins gruffly gives Maia her gloves so that she

herself may also receive a gift. On the first day of spring, the only day on which Mr. Banks sings in the tub, a west wind blows, and Mary Poppins opens her umbrella and flies away as she said she would. Jane then tucks Michael into bed, just as Mary Poppins used to do.

The five sequels are Mary Poppins Comes Back *(1935),* Mary Poppins Opens the Door *(1943),* Mary Poppins in the Park *(1952),* Mary Poppins in Cherry Tree Lane *(1982), and* Mary Poppins and the House Next Door *(1988).*

CHARACTERS: Mary Poppins dominates this book. Its minor characters, such as Mr. and Mrs. Banks, are only lightly sketched. Accumulated details make the minor characters more substantial over the series as a whole. **Mary Poppins** is a puzzling, contradictory character. Described as a thin woman with shiny black hair that makes her look like a wooden doll, she has large feet and hands and small, peering blue eyes. Inordinately proud of her neat, prim clothing and her umbrella with a parrot's head for a handle, she never passes by a store window without pausing to admire her reflection. On one occasion, she sighs with pleasure when she sees three reflections of herself, thinking, "The more Mary Poppins the better." Although the children find Mary Poppins somewhat frightening because her gaze makes it impossible to disobey her, they also find her fascinating. A highly competent nanny, she smells of fresh toast and speedily and easily performs her domestic tasks. Yet she refuses to provide Mrs. Banks with references, claiming that it is an old-fashioned practice. She often presents a haughty, brusque demeanor with others. When merchants try to engage her in banter, she indignantly stares them down. She becomes cross whenever she is in a hurry, and the children soon discover that it is easy to offend her. She is frequently rude to her charges, especially Michael, mocking their understanding of things. Mary Poppins snaps at Jane for pointing out that Maia has no gift for herself. Although Mary Poppins then gives her new gloves to Maia, she does so ungraciously. Mary Poppins's temper is usually evident, however, when making her customary denials that she and her relatives have in any way participated in magical events. Still, although Mary Poppins never seems to waste time being nice to the children, she does repeatedly offer them magical adventures that enrich their understanding of the world and of themselves.

Mary Poppins, who is always called by her full name—and therefore remains somewhat distanced from the reader—possesses so many unusual qualities that critics have described her as mythic. Although she seems to know everything about everybody, she never reveals information about herself. While her origins remain an enigma, she mentions that her mother conversed with the Red Cow, and the Brown Bear at the zoo tells Michael that Mary Poppins is related to the Hamadryad, being a first cousin once removed, on her mother's side. Her strange entrance and departure add to her mythic status. Traveling on the wind and by the will of the wind, an ancient symbol of spirit, Mary Poppins is connected to the sky, realm of the gods. At one point, she does the work of mythological beings, pasting stars in the sky. When she travels around the world, the people or animals that she meets honor her. Mary Poppins is, in fact, the "Great Exception": she is the only adult who has retained the ability to talk to animals and communicate with natural elements. Her mythic status is confirmed when the animals make her the center of the Grand Chain that celebrates the unity of life.

Mary Poppins combines everyday realities with fanciful elements and petty flaws with grand insights. Although she habitually rejects any connection to the fantastic, she tells the children after her trip with Bert that she has visited Fairyland. She then insists that "everybody's got a Fairyland of their own"; her special gift is to provide a way for children and adults to enter a fantasy world everyone can share.

Most of the decidedly underdeveloped minor characters add humorous color and reveal more of Mary Poppins's facets. The fashion-conscious **Mrs. Banks** is a somewhat silly woman, easily bullied by Mary Poppins's claims to superior knowledge of how the best families act. She is a loving mother, but her ignorance of the real reason that her twins are crying highlights Mary Poppins's deeper under-

standing of life. **Mr. Banks** is comically materialistic, offering his wife a choice of a comfortable home or four children. Essentially a silly, boyish man, he wears two coats on cold days, and he periodically feels the need for treats. The Banks's children are more substantial creations. **Jane Banks**, the eldest, is sensitive and observant. She is not only acutely aware of Mary Poppins's prickly moods, but she is the one who points out that Maia has no present for herself. Significantly, she shows her maturity after their nanny leaves by letting Michael hold a picture of Mary Poppins and by tucking him in. **Michael Banks** is impetuous, readily asking questions and openly expressing doubts. He is not fully in control of his emotions, as his Bad Tuesday episode indicates. His meddling with the compass reveals a measure of his own antisocial actions and enables him to value the reassuring love that Mary Poppins represents. The infant twins, **John** and **Barbara Banks**, embody the Romantic notion of infants being closer to nature than adults, suggesting that their very innocence allows them to communicate with animals and the natural elements. They establish Mary Poppins as the Great Exception and comically suggest the limitations of their mother: they stop crying when she holds them only because they are too polite to blame her for the impending loss, due to age, of their ability to talk to nature.

Two of Mary Poppins's relatives make notable appearances. **Uncle Albert Wigg** is a fat man whose merriment contrasts with Mary Poppins's usually stern demeanor. When his birthday falls on Friday, laughter fills him with gaseous bubbles, causing him to float freely in the air. His situation symbolically points to laughter as a magical escape from human limitations. **The Hamadryad**, the serpent lord of the animals, voices the novel's most profound theme. He insists on the unity of nature: "we are all one, all moving to the same end." As the center of the Grand Chain, Mary Poppins confirms his statement by swaying in unison with the animals.

Further Reading

Berger, Laura Standley, ed. *Twentieth-Century Children's Writers*. 4th ed. Detroit: St. James, 1995.

Children's Literature Review. Vol. 2. Detroit: Gale Research, 1976.

Cott, Jonathan. "The Wisdom of Mary Poppins: Afternoon Tea with P. L. Travers." In *Pipers at the Gates of Dawn: The Wisdom of Children's Literature*. New York: Random House, 1983.

Demers, Patricia. *P. L. Travers*. Boston: Twayne, 1991.

Haycraft, Howard, and Stanley J. Kunitz, eds. *The Junior Book of Authors*. 2nd ed. New York: H. W. Wilson, 1951.

Something about the Author. Vols. 4, 54. Detroit: Gale Research, 1973, 1989.

Something about the Author Autobiography Series. Vol. 2. Detroit: Gale Research, 1986.

Brinton Turkle

1915-, American commercial illustrator and children's author and illustrator

The Adventures of Obadiah

(picture book, 1972)

PLOT: A combination of tall tale and cautionary tale, this ironic story suggests that people who lie may not be believed when they tell the truth. Obadiah Starbuck, a young Quaker living on Nantucket Island during the early nineteenth century, tells falsehoods. When Father reads a biblical passage about a wolf, Obadiah claims that a wolf chased him. His little sister, Rachel, is frightened, but the older children, Rebecca, Moses, and Asa, laugh. Mother and Father scold Obadiah. At school, Obadiah tells the teacher that he pulled a lion's tail. Mother punishes him. When the annual sheepshearing comes, Levi Bunker jokingly tells Father that he will see him at the sideshow. Obadiah thinks that Levi Bunker needs help telling the truth. When it is time to leave the shearing festivities, Obadiah turns up dirty and without his hat. He tells his parents that he rode a sheep, which threw him into one of the sideshows, where a pig and man were dressed alike; that he then entered a tent, where a lady taught him to dance; and that afterwards some sailors took him to see an Indian swallowing fire and to a gypsy to have his fortune read. He says that he lost his hat during these adventures. No one believes Obadiah. Levi Bunker, however, brings back Obadiah's hat

and confirms his story. Obadiah, having had a real adventure, retells the story on the way home.

Earlier volumes are Obadiah the Bold *(1965) and* Thy Friend, Obadiah *(1969).* Rachel and Obadiah *(1978) focuses on Obadiah's little sister.*

CHARACTERS: As in the earlier volumes in the series, the focus on Obadiah leaves his family with only minor roles. Primarily, they add to the realism by providing a historical context. **Obadiah Starbuck** is a small, red-haired Quaker boy. The fourth of five children, he has an active imagination and a desire for adventure. In *Obadiah the Bold* these qualities are evident in his daydreams about becoming a pirate. In this volume, he expresses them by lying. Why Obadiah lies is not clear, but he is probably going through a common childhood stage in which he lies to gain attention and to feel excitement. Obadiah is naive in thinking that others will believe his fantastic stories. He also shows naivete in being unable to distinguish between jokes, such as those Levi Bunker tells, and the lies he himself tells. Like his lies, his true story begins with an encounter with an animal. Ironically, his adventures have the hallmarks of a tall tale, so no one believes him. Once his family learns the truth, Obadiah delights in retelling his adventures, which provided him with experiences that would normally be forbidden to a good Quaker boy.

Father Starbuck was gentle and understanding when his son wanted to be a pirate in *Obadiah the Bold*. When Obadiah uses a biblical story as the basis for a lie, however, Father shows a stern and uncompromising sense of propriety. **Mother Starbuck** is less severe, first calling Obadiah's stories "fancying," not falsehoods. Nevertheless, she firmly opposes falsehoods and punishes Obadiah by making him write "God help me to be truthful" ten times. **Rachel Starbuck**, the youngest child, is the only one who takes Obadiah seriously. From the beginning, she is in awe of him, and she even shares her candy so that he will retell his adventures.

Moses, **Asa**, and **Rebecca**, the older children, constantly tease Obadiah, especially after he tells his fantastic but true story. **Levi Bunker**, pictured as a fat, jolly Quaker, adds complexity to the theme. His joking about seeing the Starbucks at the sideshow, which good Quakers avoid, establishes that truthfulness is a complicated issue. Levi Bunker is also a helper figure: by returning the hat and confirming Obadiah's story, he restores Obadiah to favor with his whole family.

Further Reading

Berger, Laura Standley, ed. *Twentieth-Century Children's Writers.* 4th ed. Detroit: St. James, 1995.

Contemporary Authors. Vols. 25-28. Detroit: Gale Research, 1977.

De Montreville, Doris, and Donna Hill, eds. *Third Book of Junior Authors.* New York: H. W. Wilson, 1972.

Something about the Author. Vols. 2, 79. Detroit: Gale Research, 1971, 1995.

Mark Twain

(pen name for Samuel Langhorne Clemens)

1835-1910, American humorist, short story writer, and novelist

The Adventures of Tom Sawyer

(novel, 1876)

PLOT: The story is set in the spring and summer, sometime between 1836 and 1846, in the Mississippi River town of St. Petersburg, a fictionalized version of Twain's own boyhood home of Hannibal, Missouri. Each of the three major plot lines contributes to at least one of the novel's satiric targets: the stereotypical good boy of juvenile fiction, the oppressive and sentimental moral codes of small Southern towns, and literary romances. The part that forms a nostalgic portrait of boyhood manners and morals is undoubtedly what inspired Twain to say that his novel "is simply a hymn, put into prose form to give it a worldly air." Tom Sawyer is always at odds with authority figures and the village institutions of school and church. In the opening chapter, he fights a new boy in town and lies about playing hooky from school. In an episode well known even to those who have never read the book, he turns his subsequent punishment into a triumph by tricking his friends into paying him for the privilege of whitewashing a fence. Tom also gets into trouble at Sunday School when he trades trinkets for the tickets that indicate that he has memorized enough Scripture to be awarded a free bible; he embarrassingly reveals his true ignorance when questioned during the presentation ceremony. Later, Tom runs away with Joe Harper and Huck Finn to become a pirate on nearby Jackson's Island. When he learns that he and his companions are presumed to have drowned, Tom delays going home so that he can stage a dramatic return during his own funeral.

The second subplot, a comical "love story," is divided into two widely separated parts. The first mocks the sentimentality of youth (and the romantic fiction that shapes their attitudes) by having Tom become "engaged" to Becky Thatcher and then become estranged from her. Tom tries to show off to win her back. After the Jackson's Island episode, the pattern reverses: she desperately shows off to win him. They are reconciled when Tom, displaying chivalric nobility, takes a severe whipping from the schoolmaster for ripping a book that Becky had actually torn. In the last part of the novel, he again displays chivalric courage by rescuing her when she romantically resigns herself to death after they become trapped in a cave.

The third plot line is a romantic adventure of revenge and murder that also satirizes Tom's adulation of pirates and robbers by picturing real outlaws as vicious and unromantic. It begins when Tom and Huck see Injun Joe murder Dr. Robinson in the graveyard and then frame the alcoholic Muff Potter for the crime. Although terrified of Injun Joe, Tom dramatically reveals the truth at Muff's trial. But Injun Joe, who was once horsewhipped by the Widow Douglas's husband and is plotting revenge,

Tom Sawyer presents his undeserved tickets to win a Bible in this C. Walter Hodges illustration from Twain's **The Adventures of Tom Sawyer.**

escapes from the courthouse. While searching for Injun Joe's treasure, Huck discovers and prevents Injun Joe's plan to mutilate the Widow. Tom, who is lost in the cave with Becky, discovers the hidden treasure, and, after Injun Joe dies when the cave is sealed shut, he and Huck recover the money and become wealthy. The Widow Douglas takes in Huck, but he is unable to tolerate the rules of civilization and tries to run away. Tom, however, convinces him that he has to return and be "respectable" if he wants to join Tom's new gang of robbers.

CHARACTERS: The loose, episodic structure of *Tom Sawyer* allows it to be a nostalgic examination of antebellum boyhood, a satire of moralistic fiction, and an adventure story that spoofs romantic clichés of characterization. Twain's use of contrasting char-

acters is particularly effective in giving both comic and serious expression to his themes.

According to Twain's preface, **Tom Sawyer**, an orphan of unstated age (he is probably about ten years old), "belongs to the composite order of architecture" because he is based on three of his own childhood schoolmates. Although scholars have identified these three as Will Bowen, John Briggs, and John Garth, most feel that Tom owes much to young Twain himself. More important than this autobiographical element, however, is Tom's connection to literary history. He is the most outstanding example of the "Good Bad Boy," a character type developed in such earlier books as Thomas Bailey Aldrich's *The Story of a Bad Boy* (1869). This superficially mischievous but morally sound type arose in satiric reaction to the model boys presented in the cautionary and didactic tales of the early nineteenth century. The narrator points to the tradition, noting that Tom "was not the model boy of the village." Tom's "badness" is certainly evident: he fights, he plays hooky from school, he lies, he evades chores, he cheats his friends, he sneaks a doughnut while his aunt lectures him, he tortures the family cat by feeding it medicine, and he commits fraud at Sunday school by trading for prize tickets.

Much of Tom's badness, however, is simply exuberant rebellion against boredom and the oppressive restrictions of home, school, and church. Tom, for example, finds romantic fiction about such social outcasts as robbers and pirates more interesting and meaningful than any lessons he learns in these places. Incapable of reciting even a short passage of scripture, he readily memorizes entire speeches from adventure novels; unable to obey the rules adults establish, he insists that his friends conform to the "rules" of robber and pirate behavior gleaned from novels. Furthermore, although raised by a pious aunt, Tom blandly talks about robbing and killing people, never once considering the actual nature of such deeds. Tom's badness also has roots in what the narrator calls "vicious vanity." His theatrical nature, evident in his games, drives him to be noticed and admired, as when he goes before the Sunday school to claim a prize he has not earned, or when he rehearses how he will casually let other boys know that he has taken up smoking. It is most evident, however, in two climactic scenes: his dramatic return to town during his own funeral and his startling disclosure that he and Huck are rich. On both occasions, he revels in the attention and extends it by fancifully embellishing his retelling of his adventures.

In spite of his vanity and frequent violations of the rules of village life, Tom is basically good. The Jackson's Island episode makes it comically clear that he even has a conventional conscience: he secretly says bedtime prayers and worries about having stolen some meat, an object of such value that he can't dismiss his act as merely "hooking." His conscience also impels him to expose Injun Joe's guilt at Muff Potter's trial. On one occasion, Tom's desire for drama does mute his conscience. He prolongs his aunt's agony over his supposed drowning merely so that he can return during his funeral. Ironically, Judge Thatcher praises Tom for violating conventional morality, proclaiming that when Tom saved Becky from a whipping for tearing the book he uttered "a noble, a generous, a magnanimous lie."

Tom does not mature during the novel. Although he becomes the spokesman for conventional respectability when he convinces Huck to return to the Widow, he offers an immature reason: membership in a gang of robbers.

Sid Sawyer, Tom's younger half-brother (he is loosely based on Twain's own younger brother Henry), contrasts with and thus reveals Tom's true character. A "quiet boy" who, unlike Tom, has "no adventurous, troublesome ways," Sid appears to adults to be the model boy. In fact, he is a hypocrite who steals sugar and delights in getting Tom in trouble by tattling when Tom omits bedtime prayers or lies about having gone swimming. Sid is, as Tom perceptively says, truly "mean": he deliberately spoils an attempt by the Welshman, Mr. Jones, to surprise everyone with an announcement about Huck's role in saving the Widow. He receives a suitable punishment when Tom cuffs and kicks him because he is unable to retaliate without revealing his own despicable behavior.

Huckleberry Finn, a character inspired by Tom Blankenship, the son of one of Hannibal's drunkards, is described as the "juvenile pariah of the village," a boy hated by mothers and fiercely admired by their sons. The reason for both attitudes is clear: Huck, completely devoid of both conventional moral ideals and ambition, does exactly what he pleases. Neglected by his father, Pap Finn, a notorious and mean drunk, Huck goes about without shoes and wears ill-fitting rags and a hat with a huge crescent torn from the rim. He smokes a pipe, sleeps in hogsheads or any other available shelter, and never attends school. Naive almost to the point of simplemindedness, Huck is the natural boy unfettered by social rules. Untutored in morality, he acts out of loyalty to those who have been kind to him. Thus, although he wants to run away when he comes across Injun Joe near the Widow's, he recalls that she was good to him, and he therefore seeks out help for her. Unlike Tom, however, he shuns attention and does not want recognition for his deeds. Once the Widow learns of his kindness to her and takes charge of his upbringing, Huck becomes aware of "the bars and shackles of civilization," so he tries to return to his previous freedom. Huck, a loner who often desires companionship, is talked into going back to the Widow's by Tom's statement that he must be respectable to join his new gang of robbers.

The representative of true evil in the novel is **Injun Joe**, a dirty, murderous, drunken half-breed who kills Dr. Robinson, frames Muff Potter for the crime, and plans to mutilate the Widow. Modern readers will object to the racism inherent in this portrait. Injun Joe is, for example, motivated by a long-held desire for revenge, which he himself attributes to his ancestry: "The Injun blood ain't in me for nothing." Nevertheless, Injun Joe contributes to more than melodramatic adventure. His viciousness points out the absurdities of Tom's naive adulation of the noble robbers of fiction, who exact revenge on those who betray them, wantonly murder men, and yet never hurt the women they abduct.

Becky Thatcher is based on Laura Hawkins, who lived near young Mark Twain. She provides the love interest and a means for gently mocking the sentimentality of popular fiction. The daughter of a wealthy judge recently moved from Constantinople, Missouri, she is "a lovely little blue eyed creature with yellow hair plaited into two long tails." She accepts Tom's "proposal" shortly after meeting him, but tries to wreak her revenge when she discovers his previous engagement to Amy Lawrence. She displays all of the traits of the stereotypical sentimental female. When Tom protects her by taking a whipping in her place, she admires his nobility; when she and Tom are lost in the cave, she becomes spiritless and resigns herself to death.

Two women show slightly different sides of adult concern for children. Critics have suggested that **Aunt Polly**, with whom Tom lives, is based on Twain's mother, Jane Clemens, and on the aunt of Ike, a "bad boy" in Benjamin Penhallow Shillaber's *Life and Sayings of Mrs. Partington* (1854). A "simple hearted" woman who is not quick witted enough to avoid repeatedly falling victim to Tom's tricks, she represents orthodox attitudes to childrearing. She constantly worries that she will ruin Tom by failing to punish him harshly enough

for his transgressions. Although Tom causes her anxiety, she immediately douses him with one of her quack patent medicines when he suddenly fails to show his typical high spirits. The wealthy, forty-year-old **Widow Douglas**, who is modeled after Mrs. Richard T. Holliday, represents true Christian charity. Unlike other people who reject or avoid Huck, she takes care of him when he catches fever and eventually brings him into her house to raise him properly.

A number of young people play minor roles in the story. **Amy Lawrence** serves as Tom's first love interest and the cause of his separation from Becky. **Mary**, Tom's cousin, who is based on Twain's sister Pamela, represents true kindness. She herself has earned two bibles by memorizing scripture, and she patiently tutors Tom. **Joe Harper**, Tom's "bosom friend" during the week, but his enemy on Saturdays when they lead rival armies, shows that Tom is not alone in being a Good Bad Boy. Joe runs away with Tom to Jackson's Island, but he is the first to get homesick. In contrast, **Alfred Temple**, a dandy from St. Louis whom Tom fights when he first arrives in town, is, like Sid, an example of the duplicitous good boy. Angry that Becky has used him to make Tom jealous, he pours ink on Tom's spelling book to get him in trouble.

Among the adults, **Muff Potter**, a drunk known for his kindness to children, including Huck, plays a minor but important role. His plight as a man falsely accused of murder leads Tom to overcome his fear of Injun Joe and to do the morally right thing by testifying truthfully. The schoolmaster, **Mr. Dobbins**, based on Hannibal schoolmaster J. D. Dawson, illustrates why Tom finds education so tedious. Frustrated that he could not become a doctor, Mr. Dobbins takes vindictive pleasure in punishing children for infractions. He is the center of a revenge plot that contrasts with the more serious episodes of revenge in the book. Drunkenly napping during the examination ceremonies, he is publicly humiliated when his wig is yanked off to expose a bald pate that the signpainter's boy had previously painted gold.

Further Reading

Blair, Walter. *Mark Twain and Huck Finn*. Berkeley: University of California Press, 1960.

De Voto, Bernard. *Mark Twain at Work*. Cambridge, MA: Harvard University Press, 1942.

Gerber, John C. *Mark Twain*. Boston: Twayne, 1988.

Harbert, Earl N., and Donald Pizer, eds. *American Realists and Naturalists*. Vol. 12 of *Dictionary of Literary Biography*. Detroit: Gale Research, 1982.

Molson, Francis. "Twain's *The Adventures of Tom Sawyer*: More Than a Warm-Up." In *Touchstones: Reflections on the Best in Children's Literature*. Vol. 1. Edited by Perry Nodelman, pp. 262-69. West Lafayette, IN: Children's Literature Association, 1985.

Rubin, Louis D., Jr. "Mark Twain: *The Adventures of Tom Sawyer*." In *Landmarks of American Writing*. Edited by Hennig Cohen, pp. 157-71. New York: Basic Books, 1969.

Smith, Henry Nash. *Mark Twain: The Development of a Writer*. Cambridge, MA: Harvard University Press, 1962.

Trachenberg, Stanley, ed. *American Humorists, 1800-1950*. Vol. 11, part 2 of *Dictionary of Literary Biography*. Detroit: Gale Research, 1982.

Chris Van Allsburg

1949-, American artist, teacher, children's author and illustrator

Jumanji

(picture book, 1981)

PLOT: Winner of the Caldecott Medal, *Jumanji* is a more serious and mysterious variation of the plot of Dr. Seuss's *The Cat in the Hat*: while their parents are away, two bored children have house-destroying adventures that may be dreams or products of magic. They learn, though, the importance of following instructions, both those of their parents and those of the fantastic game they enter. Before she and Father go to the opera, Mother reminds Peter and Judy to keep the house neat because they will be bringing guests home. As soon as their parents leave, however, the children make a mess with their

toys. When they become bored, they go to the park, where Peter discovers a box containing "Jumanji, a Jungle Adventure Game." At home, Judy prevents Peter from playing until she reads the instructions. She reads that the purpose of the game is to follow a path through the jungle and that the game ends only when one player reaches the city of Jumanji.

As the children move their game pieces, the situations described on the squares of the board become real: they encounter a lion and monkeys; a monsoon pours rain into the living room; they see a lost guide pondering a map; a tsetse fly bites Peter, giving him sleeping sickness; a rhinoceros stampede destroys the furniture; a python appears on the mantle; and molten lava flows out of the fireplace. While the python slithers toward the children, the desperate Judy ends the game by reaching Jumanji. Everything returns to normal; the animals and the damage to the house disappear. Peter and Judy take the game back to the park, tidy the house by putting away their toys, and fall asleep while doing a puzzle. When Mother wakes them, Peter tells her about their adventures, but she laughs. Later, Mrs. Budwing, one of Mother's guests, notices the children doing the puzzle and laments that her children, Danny and Walter, never finish anything and never read instructions. While she is talking, Peter and Judy look out the window and see Danny and Walter leaving the park with the Jumanji game.

CHARACTERS: The instructions to the "board" game indicate that it is for "bored" people, a pun underlining the idea that the game's adventures offer escape from a dull and tidy routine. Taller and older than Peter, **Judy** is the leader in their adventures. She suggests that they go to the park when they become bored, and she cajoles the reluctant Peter into bringing the game home. The cautious Judy likes to maintain control. She therefore insists that Peter not begin play until she has read the instructions. Judy has wit, self-control, and determination. Realizing that their messy adventures can't

Peter gets a lion-sized surprise while playing "Jumanji" in this illustration by Van Allsburg.

end until they complete the game, she tells the alarmed Peter to continue playing when the lion appears, and she continues alone when Peter contracts sleeping sickness. She also displays courage, playing on when the dangerous python approaches. **Peter**, her younger brother, is easily bored and quickly tires of their toys. He is pessimistic and jumps to hasty conclusions. Peter thus believes that any game left in the park must be boring, and he feels disappointed by the unpromising description of the game. At the same time, he is restless and impatient, beginning to play with the pieces before Judy reads the instructions. Once play begins, he follows Judy's instructions and becomes supportive, urging her to shake the dice as the python approach-

es. He also cooperates by helping her to clean up the mess they made with their toys. As he shows when he tells Mother about their adventures, he changes from a bored child into an open and excited boy.

Although mentioned only briefly, minor characters establish a meaningful context for understanding Judy and Peter. **Father**, who tucks his scarf into his coat, and **Mother**, who looks into the mirror to pin her hat and who reminds the children to be neat, may be overly concerned with tidiness. They create a dull and stifling environment that invites their children's messy rebellion and their fantastic adventures. Mother also lacks interest in her children's imaginations, merely laughing at Peter's description of his adventures. **Danny** and **Walter Budwing** are foils who effectively underline the didactic theme. These boys, who never complete anything and never pay attention to instructions, are pictured walking one behind the other in an ominously dark and tree-filled park. These details suggest that they will not be as successful in the game because they will not be as cooperative as Peter and Judy were.

Further Reading

Berger, Laura Standley, ed. *Twentieth-Century Children's Writers.* 4th ed. Detroit: St. James, 1995.

Children's Literature Review. Vols. 5, 13. Detroit: Gale Research, 1983, 1987.

Collier, Laurie, and Joyce Nakamura, eds. *Major Authors and Illustrators for Children and Young Adults.* Detroit: Gale Research, 1993.

Contemporary Authors New Revision Series. Vol. 38. Detroit: Gale Research, 1993.

Estes, Glenn E., ed. *American Writers for Children since 1960: Poets, Illustrators, and Nonfiction Authors.* Vol. 61 of *Dictionary of Literary Biography.* Detroit: Gale Research, 1987.

Holtze, Sally Holmes, ed. *Fifth Book of Junior Authors and Illustrators.* New York: H. W. Wilson, 1983.

Something about the Author. Vols. 37, 53. Detroit: Gale Research, 1985, 1988.

Bernard Waber

1924-, American graphic designer and children's author and illustrator

The House on East 88th Street

(picture book, 1962; published in England as Welcome, Lyle*)*

PLOT: When Mr. and Mrs. Joseph F. Primm and their son, Joshua, move into a house on East 88th Street they are frightened to find a crocodile in the bathtub. Hector P. Valenti gives Joshua a note explaining that Lyle the crocodile is friendly, performs tricks, and eats only Turkish caviar. The note also promises that Signor Valenti will return for Lyle. Lyle wins over the Primms, becoming a beloved member of the family and a popular figure outside the house. When Lyle performs tricks in a parade he becomes famous. Hector P. Valenti then reclaims Lyle and takes him on tour. Lyle is sad, however, and makes a Parisian audience cry. Because the angry manager fires them, Signor Valenti

returns Lyle to the Primms, who are happy to have him back.

Sequels are Lyle, Lyle, Crocodile *(1965);* Lyle and the Birthday Party *(1966);* Lovable Lyle *(1969);* Lyle Finds His Mother *(1974); and* Funny, Funny Lyle *(1987).*

CHARACTERS: Waber's drawings give the characters personality and make their behavior absurdly humorous. Many drawings show **Lyle the crocodile** on his hind legs, an absurd posture that makes him appear almost human. Actually, Lyle is appealing because he combines the friendliness of a puppy, the dedication of a loyal domestic servant, the social charm of a good-natured adult, and the loving attachment of a child. As the pictures show, he is a talented circus performer and a friendly companion who delights everyone he meets. Lyle is also an industrious family member, insisting on doing chores and even displaying good taste when setting the table. Most importantly, Lyle is sensitive and loving. He deeply misses the Primms. Even when Signor Valenti tickles his toes, an action that once doubled him over in childish laughter, Lyle remains sad. Lyle thus exhibits every child's pressing need for a home where he is wanted and loved.

Hector P. Valenti, a self-proclaimed star of stage and screen, is an insensitive opportunist. As he indicates by writing that he is sick of crocodiles and crocodile tears, he is not emotionally attached to Lyle. As a contrasting character to the loving Primms, Signor Valenti's selfishness is made obvious. He abandons Lyle to strangers because Lyle is expensive to feed, reclaims Lyle to exploit him in order to become rich, and again abandons the crocodile when Lyle's sadness ruins his plans. Nevertheless, Signor Valenti's odd behavior and appearance add comedy. Pictured as a bald man with mustaches, he dresses in an odd theatrical style, wearing a long coat and an overly large, pointed crown. Signor Valenti is also amusing because he communicates with idiosyncratic notes that express their most significant message in two terse postscripts.

In comparison, **Joseph P. Primm**, **Mrs. Primm**, and their son, **Joshua**, display unselfish love. The adults are comical because they panic when they first see Lyle, but they show their goodness by loving and valuing him as a family member. Their unselfish behavior is most apparent when Mrs. Primm sadly admits Signor Valenti's claim to ownership of Lyle. Joshua displays the family's unwavering love by anxiously waiting each day for the mail to bring word of Lyle.

Ira Sleeps Over

(picture book, 1972; published in England as Good Night Ben*)*

PLOT: Sibling rivalry and fear of embarrassment create the conflict in this humorous story. When Reggie invites Ira to sleep over, Ira is happy until his sister mentions his teddy bear. Ira then debates whether to take the bear. His mother and father reassure him that Reggie won't laugh at him, but his sister says that he will. Later, Ira asks Reggie about teddy bears, but Reggie ignores him. Nevertheless, Ira is ready to bring his teddy bear until his sister notes that it has a baby name, Tah Tah. Ira therefore goes next door to Reggie's without his teddy bear. After they are sent to bed, Reggie tells a ghost story that scares both boys. Reggie then gets up and brings something into bed. He finally admits that he has a teddy bear named Foo Foo. Hearing this, Ira goes home, where he tells his mocking sister that Reggie won't laugh when he brings his teddy bear. Unable to wake Reggie to show him his own teddy bear, Ira contentedly falls asleep hugging Tah Tah.

CHARACTERS: The central characters are ordinary children who experience common feelings of self-consciousness and anxiety. **Ira**, pictured as a small boy with shaggy black hair, is torn between his need for security and his need to be accepted. Like many children, he values what his sister says more than what his parents tell him. Thus, he becomes self-

conscious after his sister teases him about his teddy bear. Ira does raise the subject with Reggie, but he is too worried about embarrassing himself to press the issue. When he sees Reggie taking his teddy bear from a drawer, however, Ira gains courage and insists that Reggie admit that he has a teddy bear. Reggie's answers obviously reassure Ira that he is not foolish or babyish. He therefore retrieves his own bear. Furthermore, he achieves at least a temporary triumph over his sister when he insists that Reggie won't laugh but doesn't explain why.

Red-headed **Reggie** has difficulty discussing emotions. He thus pretends not to hear when Ira asks him about teddy bears. That night, when he needs reassurance because he is frightened by a ghost story, the apparently embarrassed Reggie doesn't tell Ira what he is taking from the drawer. He is also reluctant to answer questions about the teddy bear. Nevertheless, Reggie teaches Ira that it is normal to feel attachment to teddy bears and to want the comfort of a bedtime routine. **Ira's sister** demonstrates the smug cockiness older children exhibit, especially with their siblings. A nameless curly-haired blond, she delights in questioning Ira in order to make him doubt himself. **Ira's mother and father**, on the other hand, are ideal parents. Both are cultured: the father is shown playing the cello and holding a classical recording, and the mother is pictured reading a paper and holding a book. They also share a warm family life, preparing meals together. Throughout, they offer loving support. They do not discipline their daughter for teasing Ira; instead, they calmly reassure him that it is acceptable to take a teddy bear.

Further Reading

Berger, Laura Standley, ed. *Twentieth-Century Children's Writers.* 4th ed. Detroit: St. James, 1995.

Collier, Laurie, and Joyce Nakamura, eds. *Major Authors and Illustrators for Children and Young Adults.* Detroit: Gale Research, 1993.

Contemporary Authors New Revision Series. Vol. 38. Detroit: Gale Research, 1993.

De Montreville, Doris, and Donna Hill, eds. *Third Book of Junior Authors.* New York: H. W. Wilson, 1972.

Something about the Author. Vols. 40, 47. Detroit: Gale Research, 1985, 1987.

Reggie and Ira, from Waber's self-illustrated **Ira Sleeps Over.**

Lynd Ward

1905-1985, American illustrator and author

The Biggest Bear

(picture book, 1952)

PLOT: Comic irony abounds in this Caldecott Medal winner about a young boy's attempts to establish his

manhood. Johnny Orchard is humiliated because his family's barn is the only one without a bearskin nailed to it. The neighbors shoot bears every year, but Johnny's grandfather ran when he met one. Determined to get the biggest bearskin in the valley, Johnny goes to the woods, where he encounters a bear cub. Instead of shooting it, he takes it home as a pet. The bear grows and creates havoc by ruining a cornfield, raiding a smokehouse, and drinking the maple syrup stored in a shed. After the angry neighbors complain, Johnny's father tells him to abandon the bear in the woods. Three times, Johnny

Johnny Orchard with his troublesome, lovable pet bear in an illustration by Ward from his **The Biggest Bear.**

leads it away, but it returns. Finally, Johnny's father tells him that they must shoot the bear. While Johnny loads his gun, the bear suddenly runs, pulling Johnny along into a trap baited with maple sugar. Some men take the bear to a zoo, but they tell Johnny that he can visit whenever he wishes.

CHARACTERS: Ward, who said that he was "an artist whose stories sometimes need some words," uses the sequence of pictures to create comic reversals and details to convey emotions. **Johnny Orchard** learns to handle setbacks and to accept responsibility. Johnny is a north woods farm boy who wears overalls and a billed cap over a mop of hair. As the picture of a neighbor carrying a bear on his shoulder indicates, Johnny views bear hunting as evidence of heroic manhood. Just as clearly, he regards his grandfather as a coward. His wish to hang the biggest bearskin of all on his family's barn thus indicates a desire to prove his manhood and to redeem his family's reputation by conforming to community habits. When Johnny encounters a very small bear, instead of the big one he hoped to shoot, his kindness and affection become prominent. Ironi-

cally, by making the bear a pet, Johnny creates hostility, instead of filling the neighbors with admiration. But Johnny acts responsibly, protecting the neighbors' property by freeing the bear. He also shows determination each time the bear returns by taking it to more inaccessible places. Although Johnny originally was eager to shoot a bear, he is saddened when shooting becomes necessary. Nevertheless, by deciding to shoot the bear himself, he shows maturity, acting as a responsible and considerate neighbor. Johnny's second failure to shoot a bear ironically makes him happy, giving him a new goal of visiting the bear at the zoo.

The bear initially appears as a cuddly, mischievous pet. Four illustrations, however, show only the great damage it causes. The fifth picture, which shows that the bear is now enormous, shockingly contrasts with earlier pictures of it as a cub. The sequence thus emphasizes its rapid growth and suggests that it can't be domesticated. Nevertheless, the comical repetition of scenes in which the bear returns after being abandoned indicates that it is gentle and friendly. It is pictured as happy in the zoo, where it brings joy to Johnny and those who see it. **Grandfather Orchard** is a foil to the seemingly heroic neighbors. By joking about running away from a bear, he humiliates Johnny and inspires the boy's desire for the biggest bearskin in the valley. **Mr. Orchard**, Johnny's father, is patient and understanding. He carefully explains situations to Johnny and offers moral support when Johnny must shoot the bear.

Further Reading

Cech, John, ed. *American Writers for Children 1900-1960*. Vol. 22 of *Dictionary of Literary Biography*. Detroit: Gale Research, 1983.

Collier, Laurie, and Joyce Nakamura, eds. *Major Authors and Illustrators for Children and Young Adults*. Detroit: Gale Research, 1993.

Contemporary Authors. Vols. 17-20. Detroit: Gale Research, 1976.

De Montreville, Doris, and Elizabeth D. Crawford, eds. *Fourth Book of Junior Authors*. New York: H. W. Wilson, 1978.

Something about the Author. Vols. 2, 36. Detroit: Gale Research, 1971, 1984.

E. B. White

1899-1985, American novelist and essayist

Stuart Little

(novel, 1945)

PLOT: An episodic novel, *Stuart Little* does not develop anything resembling a plot until the eighth of its fifteen chapters. The first seven chapters comically show the efforts of a misfit to cope with the world. Stuart Little is only about two inches tall at birth, and he looks like a mouse. Stuart and his family often take advantage of his size: he descends into a drain to retrieve a ring his mother lost, he recovers lost ping-pong balls, and he goes inside the piano to make sure a key doesn't stick. Nevertheless his size creates problems, such as when he swings on the cord of a window shade that rolls up and traps him inside. In the major episode of these chapters, Stuart takes a bus to Central Park, where he commands Dr. Paul Carey's model sailboat in a race. Although caught in a squall and nearly capsized by a paper bag, Stuart sails to victory.

The eighth chapter, which begins the second section of the story, presents parallel episodes. At age seven, Stuart becomes sick after being accidentally locked in the refrigerator. Later, his mother saves the life of a nearly frozen bird that she finds on the windowsill. Stuart falls in love with the bird, whose name is Margalo, and soon saves her from Snowbell by shooting an arrow into the cat's ear. In another episode, Stuart hides from a dog in a garbage can, becomes trapped, and is dumped onto a garbage scow headed out to sea. Margalo saves him and flies him home. But Margalo leaves Stuart's home when she discovers that Snowbell and an Angora cat are plotting against her.

Beginning with the eleventh chapter, the novel becomes a quest story. Determined to find Margalo and to seek his fortune at the same time, Stuart leaves home and obtains a model car from Dr. Carey. Two episodes interrupt his quest. In the first, Stuart becomes a substitute teacher for a day; in the second, he invites the miniature Harriet Ames to go boating. The encounter turns into a disaster because someone ruins Stuart's souvenir toy canoe and rain begins to fall. Disappointed, Stuart leaves Harriet and resumes the search for Margalo. The story concludes with Stuart driving north, certain that he is "headed in the right direction." The ending is inconclusive because, as White once wrote to a young reader, "life is essentially inconclusive."

CHARACTERS: With the exception of the title character, none of the characters in *Stuart Little* is portrayed at great length. Whether human or animal, however, each plays a role in shedding light on Stuart's personality or in satirizing human nature.

Stuart Little, the second son of the Littles, has an appropriate surname: at birth he is only about two inches high, and he doesn't grow much afterwards. In addition to being tiny, Stuart looks like—and even begins to act like—a mouse. Some adult readers have been upset by the idea that human parents would have a mouse for a child, but, in spite of a bit of confusion early in the novel, such as when the doctor examining the infant Stuart finds him perfectly normal for a mouse, Stuart is not a mouse. His parents may sometimes think of him as a mouse, but Stuart himself writes to Harriet Ames that he has "a somewhat mouselike appearance," and White declared in his letters that Stuart was not a mouse but a "second son." In any case, after the fifth chapter the mouselike qualities play no role.

Stuart is also unusual in that he was able to walk at birth, and he develops a knowledge of sailing and driving without the benefit of being taught. He also has an inborn sense of proper attire and behavior. Initially, he wears a gray hat and carries a cane, but he wears a sailor suit and carries a telescope when he goes sailing in Central Park. Although he has problems that require help from others, such as when he becomes trapped in the window shade and the refrigerator, he never feels sorry for himself and is remarkably self-reliant. He realizes, for example, that he can wash himself if he has a tool with which to pound the faucets, and, although he is too small for many people to notice him, he manages to get on a bus and go to Central Park by himself. Stuart demonstrates his adventurous spirit both in sailing Dr. Carey's model boat and in setting out from home to seek Margalo and his own fortune. His intelligence shows through when he foils Snowbell's attempt to capture Margalo, and he demonstrates a brave spirit when he thinks he is facing death on the garbage scow but determines to accept his fate in a dignified manner. Stuart reveals his sense of values when he sets out on his quest for Margalo. Playing the role of Chairman of the World in the schoolroom, he teaches children that they must appreciate the ordinary joys of daily living and must never be mean to anyone. Here, as elsewhere, Stuart's actions in refusing to see his size as a liability confirm what he tells the children who think he is too small to be Chairman of the World: it is not size that is important, "It's temperament and ability that count."

Not all of Stuart's qualities are positive. He loses his self-control, for example, when his plans for an outing with Harriet Ames go wrong. In subsequently refusing Harriet's offer of dinner and dancing, he shows immaturity in his inability to adapt to changing circumstances, to make the best of situations, and to accept what life offers. At the same time, however, he shows romantic idealism by refusing to settle for anything less than the fulfillment of his dreams. Although he is a misfit in a world too large for him, Stuart's life is not pathetic: he finds meaning in his quest for the ideal beauty that Margalo represents, and he maintains hope that he is headed in the right direction, both physically and emotionally.

Margalo, a pretty, brown female bird with a yellow streak on her breast, is Stuart's love interest. Symbolically born again after Mrs. Little revives her from apparent death, this country bird takes up residence in New York City. When she rescues Stuart from the garbage scow, she represents the reborn spirit. Finding Stuart seemingly dead on the scow, she carries him into the air—literally raising him from the garbage and into the heavens—and returns him to a new life at home. Symbolically twice born like Margalo, Stuart finds new joy and purpose in life through his love for her. Margalo is more important as a symbol of human desire than as a character. Associated with pastoral nature—she comes from fields, pastures, and vales—she represents ideal beauty, the quest for which gives purpose to Stuart's life.

Mrs. Little's white cat, **Snowbell**, is an antagonist to both Stuart and Margalo, and is the only other animal character of consequence. Malicious and sneaky, Snowbell places Stuart's hat and gloves next to a mousehole so that his family will think he has gone down it after Stuart becomes trapped in the windowshade. Furthermore, although he admits that it is wrong for him to eat his family's pet bird, he sees nothing wrong with telling the Angora cat how to attack Margalo.

Stuart's father, **Frederick C. Little**, is a concerned, overly protective parent. After the initial shock of having what he thinks is a mouse for a son, Frederick resolves that he and his wife will never talk about mice in front of Stuart and that they will change nursery rhymes so that the boy will not grow up fearful. He also worries about Stuart being attracted to a mousehole, but he does not go so far in his protectiveness as to stop it up. **Mrs. Little** mostly echoes her husband's sentiments, but she does show love for her child after both the windowshade and refrigerator episodes, and she shows her kindness by reviving Margalo. **George**, their normal-sized first son, is a comical character. He repeatedly develops overly elaborate plans that he never completes, such as when he abandons efforts to remodel the bathroom. His short attention span and impracticality contrast with Stuart's ability to see things through to completion.

Two other human characters have minor roles of note. The first, surgeon-dentist **Dr. Paul Carey**, is both the childish adult obsessed with toys and a comically eccentric inventor. The owner of the model racing sloop *Wasp*, Dr. Carey takes rivalry with the fat, lazy, sulky twelve-year-old **LeRoy**, owner of another boat, as seriously as if they were competing in a real trans-Atlantic race. After quizzing Stuart to be sure that he is both sober and energetic, Dr. Carey hires him to race the toy sloop. In a scene that satirizes modern inventions, the doctor also helps Stuart in his quest for Margalo, providing him with a noiseless model car that can become invisible. This remarkable feature proves more troublesome to Stuart than it is helpful. The second notable minor character is **Harriet Ames**, the daughter of a wealthy family in the town of Ames Corners. Slightly smaller than Stuart but entirely human in appearance, she demonstrates that Stuart is not alone as a misfit. Harriet is lovely, kind, and understanding. She is also practical, offering Stuart the opportunity of both dinner and dancing after his own plans for entertaining her are ruined. Harriet represents conventional, attainable happiness, and in rejecting her Stuart demonstrates that he is unable to accept the conventional, that he must pursue the ideal that Margalo represents.

Charlotte's Web
(novel, 1952)

PLOT: When Fern Arable discovers that her father is about to kill the runt in a litter of pigs, she protests and is given care of it. Naming the pig Wilbur, she treats him like a baby. Eventually, however, Wilbur must be sold to Fern's uncle, Homer Zuckerman. Fern visits Wilbur at Zuckerman's barn, listening for hours to conversations between him and the other animals. Wilbur finds love and friendship in the form of Charlotte, a spider, who promises to save him after Wilbur learns that Zuckerman is fattening him up for slaughter. Wilbur learns to appreciate Charlotte, in spite of her taste for blood. Charlotte in turn grows to love Wilbur, in many ways acting like his mother by teaching and comforting him.

Realizing that she lives by her wits in fooling insects, Charlotte determines to save Wilbur by fooling humans. She spins the words "SOME PIG!" into her web, making Wilbur instantly famous. Charlotte continues her campaign by spinning the words "TERRIFIC" and "RADIANT," and Wilbur tries to live up to these words. Although Charlotte's efforts make Zuckerman appreciate Wilbur more, he still sees Wilbur as a source of good ham and bacon.

Charlotte the spider and Wilbur as illustrated by Garth Williams for White's Charlotte's Web.

Charlotte thus makes one final effort to save Wilbur. She accompanies him to the County Fair, where she spins her final word, "HUMBLE." This word saves Wilbur, for he is given a special prize for attracting tourists, a prize that indicates that he is more valuable alive than dead. Ironically, while Wilbur is receiving the award that ensures he will live, Fern, who first saved him, forgets all about her pig to ride a ferris wheel with Henry Fussy; Charlotte, who has laid her eggs during the same night she wrote her final word, is preparing to die. Saddened, Wilbur bribes Templeton the rat to bring Charlotte's egg sac so that it can be with him in Zuckerman's barn. When the eggs hatch the next spring, several of Charlotte's children remain in the barn, as do some of each new generation, but Wilbur never forgets Charlotte, "a true friend and a good writer."

CHARACTERS: *Charlotte's Web* combines a brief realistic story about humans with a talking animal fantasy. Both stories are about growth and change, and both involve characters making significant judgments about Wilbur and the value of life. E. B. White called the novel "a hymn to the barn," and he uses its characters to establish what he also said was "a story of friendship, life, death, salvation."

Although eight-year-old **Fern Arable** has been raised on a farm, she does not share her family's judgment that a runt pig must be killed because it will not develop into a valuable animal. Fern, protesting that such a killing is unfair, asks if they would have killed her if she had been born small. Whereas her physical attempt to save the pig by pulling the ax from her father fails, her argument moves him to give her care of the newborn white pig, whom she judges to be "absolutely perfect." Setting up a contrast in judgments, Fern establishes an important element of White's theme: that life has more than economic value. Initially, Fern seems naive, treating the pig as if it were a human baby. After she gives up the pig, Fern illustrates the romantic notion that childhood enjoys a special relationship to nature, for she is the only human who hears the animals talking. Fern begins the novel as a solitary child, but she ends up riding the ferris wheel with Henry Fussy when Wilbur receives his prize, thus adding another dimension to the novel's presentation of change. Although she declares that she has had the best time of her life with Henry Fussy, readers see that Fern's growth also brings an unacknowledged loss of her wondrous contact with nature.

Wilbur, the white runt of a spring litter, does not change as dramatically as Fern, but he does mature. Having been happy as the inseparable companion of Fern, Wilbur finds himself alone at Zuckerman's barn and becomes bored and tired of living at the early age of two months. He makes a temporary escape through a loose board, but he discovers that what he really needs to make his life bearable is love and a friend. Charlotte the spider volunteers to be this needed friend, and she replaces Fern as Wilbur's companion, providing both interesting conversation and emotional comfort. At this stage, Wilbur is innocent. He does not realize that Zuckerman and Lurvy the farmhand praise him because of his economic value, not his character. He is also childishly unable to control his emotions. When a sheep finally tells him that he is being

fattened for slaughter, he panics and becomes calm only after Charlotte assures him that she will save his life.

Another sign of Wilbur's immaturity is his lack of self-knowledge. He boasts that he, like Charlotte, can spin a web. Tying a string to his tail, but not to anything else, he throws himself from a manure pile and crashes to the ground. Wilbur, who boasted only because Charlotte seems smarter and more competent, must overcome feelings of insignificance. When Charlotte proposes her second word, for example, Wilbur denies being terrific, but he does begin to feel terrific when people come to stare at him. With the third word, Wilbur says that he feels "radiant" even before it is spun into the web. Finally, Wilbur lives up to the word "humble," being both low to the ground and aware of how much he depends on others. Even though Wilbur is never able to accept the fact that he will die one day, he approaches maturity after accepting the inevitability of Charlotte's death. In getting Templeton to retrieve Charlotte's eggs, he not only demonstrates his great love for Charlotte but also his increased competence and understanding. In order to get Templeton to help him, he offers to let the rat eat first from the slops, a gesture that indicates that he understands the rat's greed and that he is able to restrain his own appetites. Wilbur's touching act of bringing Charlotte's offspring to the barn shows a capacity to return love that makes him worthy of the efforts both Fern and Charlotte made to save his life.

The most important character in *Charlotte's Web* is the least physically imposing and the least noticed by the humans. **Charlotte A. Cavatica**, a large gray spider "about the size of a gumdrop," seems to have been born with encyclopedic knowledge. She is fond of using pompous words, such as "salutations," but she is not foolish or comical. Charlotte is a counselor who offers maternal advice to Wilbur and a trickster who fools the humans who want to kill him. She shows both wisdom and compassion: after observing Wilbur, she knows that he needs friendship and that he is worthy of it. Charlotte plays an important role in developing the novel's themes of judgment, friendship, and death. Her first contribution to the judgment theme—her claim that the plan to kill Wilbur is "the dirtiest trick I ever heard of"—echoes Fern's earlier statement to her father that killing a runt is "the most terrible case of injustice I ever heard of." Charlotte also develops the judgment theme through her role as a trickster who plays on human gullibility. She spins into her web advertising slogans designed to make people appreciate Wilbur's personality and character, not his economic value. Through her friendship, Charlotte also affectionately promotes Wilbur's own self-esteem. Charlotte herself benefits from this friendship. She tells Wilbur that a life that depends on killing flies is necessarily "something of a mess," but that his friendship has lifted it a little.

Charlotte's most important contribution, however, is to the theme of death. Her justification of fly catching points out the necessity of death in nature (while avoiding the whole question of people needing to kill animals to live). Furthermore, although she understands that Wilbur can't face the idea of his own death and even reassures him that "Maybe you'll live forever," her dignified acceptance of her own mortality emphasizes the role of death in the natural cycle. From her death comes the new life of her offspring, and this cycle of rebirth is part of "the glory of everything" that the novel celebrates.

Although most of the novel is set in the barn, the animals other than Charlotte and Wilbur have distinctly minor roles and, with one exception, do not even have names. **Templeton** the rat's complete selfishness serves as a contrast to the goodness of both Charlotte and Wilbur. He accidentally saves Charlotte's life when the smell of a hoarded rotten goose egg drives away Avery, who steps on it when he tries to capture the spider. He is only deliberately good, however, when he can profit from it, such as when he retrieves Charlotte's eggs after Wilbur offers him slops. Unlike Wilbur, Templeton, who says of himself, "I am a glutton but not a merry-maker," neither sees nor appreciates the glories of life.

Most of the minor human characters contribute to the theme of judgment. **Lurvy**, the farmhand, and **Homer Zuckerman**, Fern's uncle, value Wilbur only for the money he will bring. Zuckerman, who has actually done nothing to merit it, seems foolish

for reveling in the attention that Wilbur's fame brings. Lurvy and Zuckerman also advance White's satire by being the most gullible of those who believe whatever Charlotte writes. In contrast, **Mrs. Zuckerman** at least suggests that the spider is the special one, and **Doctor Dorian**, the conventionally bearded wise old man, tells Fern's mother that the real miracle is an ordinary spider's web, for no one teaches a spider how to spin. Doctor Dorian also makes an important foreshadowing contribution to the theme of change when he assures the worried mother that Fern is normal in spending time alone with the animals—his wisdom is such that he does not deny that animals may talk—and then predicts that Fern will one day be more attracted to boys than animals. Throughout, **Mrs. Arable** represents the person who appreciates only the normal and predictable in life, being quite happy when Fern turns her attention to Henry Fussy. **Mr. Arable** is the one who first threatens Wilbur's life, but he does show some tenderness in giving over Wilbur to Fern's care. On the other hand, his son, **Avery Arable**, never shows sentiment and rejects the runt pig. This "heavily armed" ten-year-old boy adds comical chaos to the plot, especially when he tries to catch Charlotte.

The Trumpet of the Swan
(novel, 1970)

PLOT: While on a camping trip in Ontario with his father, Sam Beaver observes a pair of mating trumpeter swans and saves the female from a stalking fox. When the swans' cygnets hatch, one of them, Louis, lacks a voice. After the swans migrate to an area near Sam's house, Louis seeks Sam's help. Sam takes Louis to school, where the young swan learns to read and write. Although he now can write messages using a slate and chalk that he carries around his neck, Louis can't communicate with other swans or make the "ko-hoh" sound that will win the love of a mate. To help his son, Louis's father steals a trumpet, which Louis learns to blow.

Louis has two quests: he wants to win the love of Serena, who ignored him because of his silence, but first he wants to restore his father's honor by paying for the stolen trumpet. Louis earns money at Camp Kookooskoos in Ontario, where he is a bugler and where he also receives a medal for saving a boy from drowning. In Boston, he floats ahead of the Swan Boats in the Public Garden, playing his trumpet, and in Philadelphia he plays in a night club. In return for free Sunday concerts, the Philadelphia Zoo allows him to stay in its Bird Lake. One night a storm drives Serena to the zoo, and Louis wins her love by playing his trumpet. The Head Man in Charge of Birds wants to keep Serena, but Louis beats off the men trying to clip her wings and telegraphs Sam. Sam strikes a deal: Louis agrees to give to the zoo any future offspring who need special care, and the Head Man promises not to pinion Serena. Louis returns home, and his father pays his debt, although he is slightly wounded in the attempt by the frightened music store owner. The novel concludes with accounts of Louis repeatedly returning to the Ontario lake where he was born for the hatching of his own cygnets and of his visits to all the scenes of his earlier fame with each succeeding generation.

CHARACTERS: In presenting its animal characters, *The Trumpet of the Swan* blends animal and human traits far more than White's earlier books do. Possibly as a result, it has not earned the critical respect enjoyed by his two previous novels.

Louis the Swan has a defective voice but is blessed with an abundance of other qualities. He is very intelligent, learning to read and write easily so that he can communicate with humans, and he has exceptional musical talent. Determined to play more complex music, he has his webbed toes split so that he can press his trumpet's valves. His subsequent playing moves both humans and animals and even wins him his bride. Most of all, Louis has great determination. He puts aside his own quest for Serena to earn money to redeem his father's honor, which he feels has been stained. Louis also proves to be noble—he saves a drowning boy who dislikes him—and brave, for he beats off the men who try to pinion Serena. Louis is comical in appearance, especially when he carries a slate, chalk, trumpet, life-saving medal, and money bag around his neck, but in the end he becomes the model of the loving husband and doting father.

Louis's **father**, the cob, is comical in his use of pompous, long-winded, self-glorifying speeches. Nevertheless, he is a devoted father. He may later worry about his honor, but he daringly dives through a music store window in order to get a trumpet for his voiceless son. The cob's speeches also provide much of the information about swans and thereby suggest the wonder of the cycle of life. Louis's **mother** is a devoted parent who is the first to notice her son's defect and worry about him. She is foolish in thinking that Serena is not good enough for her son but level-headed in stopping her husband's speeches and getting him to act. **Serena**, a beautiful young female, is primarily a love interest and has little individuality. The fact that she completely ignores Louis at first emphasizes the importance of a Trumpeter Swan's call.

The most important human character is **Sam Beaver**. Eleven when the novel opens, Sam has a Native American's dark hair and eyes, and he walks silently like a Native American, comparisons that suggest his closeness to nature. Although he likes his father, Sam prefers exploring nature alone and keeps secret his sighting of the swans out of fear that his father will come and spoil the experience. Sam's odd habit of ending daily diary entries with a question shows his inquisitive mind. He displays resourcefulness in arranging schooling for Louis and in negotiating Serena's freedom. This last act helps him answer an important question about his future: he learns that he wants to work in a zoo when he grows up.

Although a number of human characters play minor roles, only two are notable in developing plot and theme. In his relationship with his son, **Mr. Beaver**, Sam's father, presents a contrast with the ideal relationship between Louis and the cob, who communicate openly and understand each other. **The Head Man in Charge of Birds** displays the arrogance of humans toward nature. He thinks of Serena only as the property of the zoo. He does not value emotions, dismissing the heartbreak that Serena and Louis would feel if she were not free. Concerned with property rights alone, he gives up his claim only after a promise that he will receive cygnets in the future.

Further Reading

Anderson, A. J. *E. B. White: A Bibliography*. Metuchen, NJ: Scarecrow Press, 1978.

Cech, John, ed. *American Writers for Children 1900-1960*. Vol. 22 of *Dictionary of Literary Biography*. Detroit: Gale Research, 1983.

Children's Literature Review. Vol. 21. Detroit: Gale Research, 1990.

Elledge, Scott. *E. B. White: A Biography*. New York: Norton, 1984.

Griffith, John. Charlotte's Web: *A Pig's Salvation*. Boston: Twayne, 1993.

Landes, Sonia. *"Charlotte's Web:* Caught in the Web." In *Touchstones: Reflections on the Best in Children's Literature*, Vol. 1. Edited by Perry Nodelman, pp. 270-80. West Lafayette, IN: Children's Literature Association, 1985.

Sale, Roger. "Two Pigs." In *Fairy Tales and After: From Snow White to E. B. White*. Cambridge, MA: Harvard University Press, 1978.

Sampson, Edward C. *E. B. White*. New York: Twayne, 1974.

Something about the Author. Vols. 2, 44, Detroit: Gale Research, 1971, 1986.

Weales, Gerald. "The Designs of E. B. White." In *Authors and Illustrators of Children's Books: Writings on Their Lives and Works*. Edited by Miriam Hoffman and Eva Samuels, pp. 407-11. New York: Bowker, 1972.

White, E. B. *The Annotated Charlotte's Web*. Introduction and notes by Peter F. Neumeyer. New York: HarperCollins, 1994.

T. H. White

1906-1964, English author

The Sword in the Stone

(fantasy, 1938)

PLOT: Filled with puns, wordplay, anachronisms, and slapstick humor, *The Sword in the Stone* parodies medieval romances yet supports a serious theme, the education of a king. Wart, a young orphan being raised by Sir Ector, begins his educational adventures when Kay, Ector's son, foolishly releases Cully the hawk. Trying to recapture Cully, Wart meets Sir Pellinore, a knight chasing the Questing Beast. He also finds Merlyn, a magician who recaptures the hawk and then becomes Wart's tutor. To educate Wart, Merlyn transforms him into various animals: as a fish, he meets a Pike; as a merlin, he encounters the mad Cully; as a snake, he converses with a snake of the T. natrix species; as an owl, he accompanies Merlyn's owl, Archimedes, and receives visions from the goddess Athene; and as a badger, he visits another badger for his final lesson.

Wart also has adventures in his human shape. The first is a "Hansel and Gretel" variation that begins when a crow steals Wart's arrow, thereby luring Wart and Kay to the cottage of Madame Mim, who captures and prepares to eat them. Wart frees an imprisoned goat and sends it to Merlyn. In a battle of magical transformations, Merlyn kills Madam Mim by becoming disease-causing microbes. Merlyn then shows Wart a joust between King Pellinore and Sir Grummore Grummursum, whose heavy armor makes them ungainly and ludicrous. When Kay becomes jealous and also wants an adventure, Merlyn sends the boys with Little John, Marian, and Robin Wood to assault Morgan the Fay's castle. Morgan disappears, but Wart rescues Wat, the Dog Boy, and Friar Tuck, whom Morgan transformed into ornaments, and Kay kills one of her griffins. The Questing Beast is prominent in the next adventures. First, after a boar hunt led by William Twyti in which Wart sees the attachment men have to dogs, Sir Pellinore discovers the Beast. The Beast is pining away because the knight no longer seeks it. Next, the Beast comes to the rescue when the giant Galapas, who has imprisoned Sir Pellinore, goes to kill Merlyn and Wart, who have entered his castle by becoming invisible.

Seven years after Merlyn's arrival, Kay becomes a knight and Wart his squire. In London for a tournament, Kay sends Wart to fetch his sword. Unable to enter the locked inn, Wart removes a sword stuck through an anvil and into a stone. Not realizing that only the rightful king could remove the sword, Wart presents it to Kay, who claims that he drew it from the stone. When Sir Ector asks him to replace the sword and draw it out again, Kay confesses his lie. At the coronation, Merlyn magically appears to announce that Wart faces a "glorious doom" as King Arthur.

A revised version of The Sword in the Stone *forms the opening of* The Once and Future King *(1958), which also contains* The Queen of Air and Darkness *(revised version of* The Witch in the Wood, *1939),* The Ill-Made Knight *(1940), and* The Candle in the Wind *(previously unpublished). A final volume,* The Book of Merlyn, *was published posthumously in 1977.*

CHARACTERS: Human characters mock traditional heroic figures; animal characters convey lessons about violence, antiwar sentiments that were intensified in the 1958 revision. **Wart**, who becomes **King Arthur**, seems insignificant because he is an orphan with a low, ugly nickname (given to him by Kay). Feeling inferior, Wart is "a born follower" and "a hero-worshipper": he admires Kay and naively thinks that knights and jousts are glorious. Wart therefore must learn to judge for himself, to lead, and to become truly heroic. His development begins with an unwitting quest: searching for the crow, he finds his tutor, Merlyn, who knows his true identity. Wart subsequently develops a kingly character because of both magical transformations and human adventures. The transformations test him: as a fish, he must keep his wit to avoid being eaten by the pike, and as a merlin he must pass a formal test of courage by standing near a mad, bloodthirsty hawk. During his transformations he also hears stories or receives visions that teach him lessons about power, fear, and cruelty. In particular, they teach him that might is not right and that humans have a history of wanton cruelty.

Wart's human adventures are less overtly didactic: they test and reveal his latent nobility. Wart repeatedly displays concern for others, showing that he can be a compassionate leader. When Kay walks away after releasing the hawk, Wart remembers the trainer's efforts, so he persists in his quest to find the hawk. When the boys are captured, Wart realizes that Madame Mim will kill Kay if he escapes, so he releases a goat and sends it for help. Wart even shows concern for Kay, begging Merlyn to give him

his own adventure. During that adventure, Wart shows persistence, refusing to quit until he finds the prisoners, whom Morgan has transformed into knickknacks.

Although Wart sees the foolishness of the joust between King Pellinore and Sir Grummore, he remains naively romantic. Even when disappointed, as he is when Galapas turns out to be shorter than Wart thought, he clings to the romantic thrill of adventure. Understandably, Wart feels sorry for himself when Kay is made a knight. Longing to oppose the world's evils, Wart is jealous and resents being subservient to Kay merely because he lacks noble birth. Nevertheless, Wart shows how big his heart is by doing his best as a squire. Consequently, he unwittingly passes the final test, establishing his nobility by removing the sword from the stone. Notably, however, he succeeds only because a vision of all the creatures he encountered during his transformations inspires him to display strength, persistence, and coordination. Wart completes his development from boy to man and from insignificant orphan to king by receiving his proper title and name, King Arthur.

Both education and personality make Sir Ector's son, **Kay**, a foil. Two years older than Wart, Kay receives the conventional education of a knight, which does nothing to develop his character. Unlike the compassionate Wart, Kay becomes more arrogant and status conscious. From the beginning, Kay has disdain for those beneath him in station. Basically ineducable, as he shows by ignoring the warnings against flying the hawk, he contemptuously refuses to search for the hawk because its trainer is a mere villein, or peasant. He enters Madame Mim's cottage, thus endangering the boys, only to show his good form in condescending to his social inferiors. As he moves closer to knighthood, Kay also distances himself from the untitled Wart, ignoring their past friendship. At the tournament, Kay even insultingly reduces Wart to the level of an anonymous servant by offering him a shilling to fetch his sword.

Kay's personality is notably different from Wart's. Selfish and ill-tempered, he is mean spirited. He thus gives Wart his nickname (he himself is too dignified for one) and demeans him by insisting that being different, as Wart is because he has no parents, is wrong. Jealous, Kay casts aspersions on Wart's successful quests for the hawk and the tutor. Furthermore, Kay is neither as heroic nor as self-controlled as Wart. When Madame Mim captures them, he cries, leaving Wart to save them. He is also insensitive to nature, as he shows when he bursts in on Merlyn and Wart, who are praising birds, to show them a thrush he has killed. But Kay is not entirely bad. He is brave during the assault on Morgan the Fay's castle and the attack on the griffins. The narrator also claims that Kay is not unpleasant, that he is "clever, quick, proud, passionate and ambitious," and that he is an "aspiring heart" impatient with his own limitations. In the dramatized action, however, Kay is seldom pleasant. Fulfilling Merlyn's prediction that he will bring sorrow on himself from his mouth, Kay claims to have withdrawn the sword from the stone. Ironically, Kay then performs his most noble deed, confessing that he is a liar. The new king demonstrates his own goodness by forgiving Kay and generously making him his seneschal, or chief steward.

Merlyn the wizard is a comic version of the archetypal wise old man and helper. Merlyn has a long white beard and mustaches, looks as if a bird has nested in his hair, and wears a gown smeared with bird droppings. Because he lives time in reverse, Merlyn introduces numerous comic anachronisms. For the same reason, Merlyn knows what will happen in the future. Unfortunately, he becomes bewildered and can't communicate his knowledge. He is therefore unable to provide Wart with protective knowledge about his future. Furthermore, Merlyn frequently seems a bumbler. He becomes confused during his battle with Madame Mim, for example, and defeats her only when he remembers that he can give her an incurable disease by turning into microbes. While invisible in the castle of Galapas, he speaks so loudly that Galapas notices and nearly kills him. Merlyn is, however, central to the theme of education. Ridiculing Kay's conventional education, he claims that true education depends on experiences that develop self-reliance. He therefore transforms Wart into various animals to broaden the boy's understanding and his sympathy by teaching

him that might does not make right and that man should not engage in senseless killing. Like conventional wise helpers, Merlyn withdraws to enable Wart to face the final test alone. He then returns, promising to be with Arthur through the rest of his tragic career.

For much of the novel, **Sir Ector**, Kay's father, comically supports the education theme by insisting that the boys need "a first-rate eddication." Although he seems boorish and poorly educated himself, Sir Ector is good-hearted. He cares for and is proud of his farm workers, and he feels as close to Wart as he does to his son. Knowing Kay, he forces him to reveal the truth about his deception and then begs Arthur to make the boy his seneschal.

Although he appears magnificent from a distance, **King Pellinore** is farcical. A clumsy man who wears horn-rimmed spectacles, he can't keep his visor up, can't stay on his horse, and can't prevent his hound from becoming tangled in his lead. Inept in his pursuit of the Questing Beast, whose fewmets, or droppings, are his proudest possession, he longs for the comfort of a feather bed. Nevertheless, he shows compassion when he resumes his quest so that the Beast can have a reason for living. In a sense, **the Questing Beast**, also called the Beast Glatisant, is the romantic spirit of Sir Pellinore. It needs him to make its life worthwhile, and it begins pining away when Pellinore temporarily adopts a sedentary life. The Beast, which has the head of a serpent, the body of a leopard, the haunches of a lion, and the feet of a hart, shows its loyalty by rescuing Pellinore when Galapas captures him. **Sir Grummore Grummursum** contributes to two elements of the satire. Engaging in a drunken conversation with Sir Ector, he comes off as an uneducated boor, thus adding to the satire about education. In his most memorable scene, he engages in a lumbering and ludicrous joust with King Pellinore, thereby undermining Wart's romantic notions about the rituals of knighthood. **Robin Wood**, whose name Wart had heard was Robin Hood, is not conventionally romantic, being a clean-shaven, gnarled man of thirty years. He does, however, display the competitive spirit associated with the conventional Robin Hood, engaging in an archery contest with Little

John. His major function is to give Kay a traditional romantic adventure. **Little John**, who claims that he was John Naylor before he became an outlaw, is Robin's companion. He contributes to the satire by mocking the "book-learning chaps" who have confused Robin's name. **Marian**, Robin's beloved, constantly mocks his boyish need for competition. During the adventure, she proves as brave and adept as any male.

William Twyti, King Uthor Pendragon's hunt master, contributes to Wart's education by crying when he must kill a wounded dog, thus showing that men may feel sympathy for animals. **Wat**, a simple-minded old man who has no nose, brings out Wart's compassion. Wart has Merlyn restore the poor man's wits. **The Dog Boy**, a child who teased and threw stones at Wat, learned a painful lesson when Wat bit off his nose and the villagers then threw stones at him. Both Wat and the Dog Boy remove the artificial noses that Merlyn makes for them, finding them unnecessary for living among the dogs, whom they value more than human society.

Madame Mim is a comical but deadly villain. A cannibalistic witch, she tests Wart's wit and courage by capturing him and announcing her intentions to eat him. Her magical duel with Merlyn connects to the education theme because Merlyn sees it as a contest between his own private, and thus unconventional, education and her formal, institutional training at Dom-Daniel. **Galapas** the ten-foot giant is another comical but dangerous enemy. He contributes to Wart's education by undermining his romantic notions that giants are all sixty feet tall. He also brings out Wart's idealism and heroism because Wart tries to convince Merlyn that the prisoners, no matter how foolish, should be rescued. Galapas himself seems ridiculous because these prisoners defy him, refusing, for instance, to return his elastic stays. At the same time, he is genuinely cruel and tries to kill Merlyn and Wart.

Several animals (and a goddess) teach Wart lessons about what is good and what is bad. **The Pike**, known as the King of the Moat, Old Jack, or Black Peter, is a negative example of kingship. Proud, cruel, selfish, and lonely, this absolute monarch insists that might makes right and that love is

merely a trick of evolution. **Cully**, the hawk released by Kay is a mad, bloodthirsty creature who is a colonel in the army of the birds. His ominous threats, echoing lines from Shakespeare's *Macbeth*, test the transformed Wart, showing that Wart has the courage of a king. **T. natrix** (the initial stands for Tropidonotus), is a male garden snake with a fondness for precise classification. He tells a story about a battle between two dinosaurs in which greed destroyed the evil one. The point of the story, however, comes when Saint George wantonly slays the peaceful, vegetarian survivor, thus illustrating man's wanton violence. **Archimedes**, Merlyn's pet owl, becomes so confused around strangers that he tries to deny the reality of patently obvious facts. He takes Wart to see **Athene**, goddess of wisdom, an invisible presence who teaches Wart by giving him two dreams. In the Dream of Trees, Wart learns about the various attributes of each tree, especially the strength of the oak. In the Dream of Stones, he sees the slow development of Earth, the brief span during which man has been on the planet, and Cain's murder of Abel. **The badger** insists that the end of philosophy is contained in two lessons: to dig and to love one's home. He offers hope for mankind by telling Wart a story about embryos: only the human embryo was satisfied with what God gave it. God therefore blessed mankind and made humans masters over the animals.

Further Reading

Berger, Laura Standley, ed. *Twentieth-Century Young Adult Writers.* 1st ed. Detroit: St. James, 1994.

Collier, Laurie, and Joyce Nakamura, eds. *Major Authors and Illustrators for Children and Young Adults.* Detroit: Gale Research, 1993.

Contemporary Authors New Revision Series. Vol. 37. Detroit: Gale Research, 1992.

Contemporary Literary Criticism. Vol. 30. Detroit: Gale Research, 1984.

Crane, John K. *T. H. White.* New York: Twayne, 1974.

Hettinga, Donald R., and Gary D. Schmidt, eds. *British Children's Writers, 1914-1960.* Vol. 160 of *Dictionary of Literary Biography.* Detroit: Gale Research, 1996.

Kertzer, Adrienne. "T. H. White's *The Sword in the Stone:* Education and the Child Reader." In *Touchstones: Reflections on the Best in Children's Literature.* Vol. 1. Edited by Perry Nodelman. West Lafayette, IN: Children's Literature Association, 1985.

Something about the Author. Vol. 12. Detroit: Gale Research, 1977.

Kate Douglas Wiggin

1856-1923, American educator and author

Rebecca of Sunnybrook Farm

(novel, 1903)

PLOT: This episodic novel celebrates a New England girl's youthful innocence and imagination. At ten, Rebecca Rowena Randall is sent from her poor farm to Riverboro, Maine, to live with her maiden aunts. Rebecca's lively talk charms Jeremiah Cobb, the stagecoach driver. (He later calls himself Uncle Jerry and, with his wife "Aunt Sarah" Cobb, becomes her closest friend.) Rebecca's liveliness also attracts Aunt Jane Sawyer, but stern Aunt Miranda is frequently annoyed that Rebecca forgets or ignores her rules. At school, Rebecca is embarrassed when her teacher, Miss Dearborn, punishes her for drinking too much water, but she is otherwise happy and popular. Her only enemy is Minnie Smellie, whom she stops from taunting the Simpson children about their frequently jailed father, Abner Simpson. Rebecca also stands up to Aunt Miranda, who, while criticizing Rebecca for wearing a good dress to a school recitation, insults Rebecca's late father, Lorenzo de Medici Randall. Aunt Jane quietly supports her, but the miserable Rebecca runs away. She immediately returns, however, when Mr. Cobb convinces her that doing so is best. Still, Rebecca continues to make mistakes: she gets paint on her dress from leaning on a bridge, and she jams the chain when she tries to punish herself by throwing her parasol down the well. The most significant episode of her childhood occurs when Rebecca and Emma Jane Perkins sell soap to help the Simpson children win a banquet lamp. Adam Ladd, whom Rebecca calls Mr. Alladin, is so charmed by Rebecca that he buys three hundred cakes of soap and later gives both girls annual Christmas presents. Miranda continues to be stern, but she softens somewhat when Rebecca, representing the family at a meeting,

Rebecca with her Aunts Miranda and Jane Sawyer in Wiggin's Rebecca of Sunnybrook Farm, *illustrated by Helen Mason Grose.*

shows signs of her Sawyer ancestry by inviting some missionaries to spend the night.

Rebecca grows from a little child into a young lady when she and Emma Jane go to school at Wareham. Miss Emily Maxwell, an English teacher, befriends Rebecca, who becomes the first female voted to be editor of the student paper. Although Rebecca is not interested in boys, she is jealous when she sees the coquettish Huldah Meserve walking with Adam Ladd. Mr. Ladd, however, maintains his interest in Rebecca, giving financial aid to Miss Maxwell so that she can take Rebecca for a vacation. Later, Rebecca wins an essay contest Mr. Ladd sponsors, becomes president of the graduating class, and receives two offers of employment. Immediately after her graduation, however, Rebecca leaves to care for Miranda, who has had a stroke. When her mother falls from a hay mow, Rebecca returns to the farm to nurse her, thereby losing her employment opportunities. Miranda soon dies and bequeaths her house to Rebecca, now a young woman with the means to move her family to Riverboro and to care for them.

New Chronicles of Rebecca (1907) contains episodes set during the same period as this book.

CHARACTERS: At the center of the novel is the Romantic Child, an imaginative character filled with a love of Nature. She affects all the other characters, who are defined by their responses to her. **Rebecca Rowena Randall** develops from child, to young lady, to woman. Named after the contrasting heroines in Sir Walter Scott's *Ivanhoe*, she combines the artistic sensitivity of her father, the late Lorenzo de Medici Randall, and the New England pragmatism of the Sawyers, her mother's family. Rebecca begins as a ten-year-old ugly duckling, with a colorless face, dark braids that make her head seem small, and overly large eyes. These eyes attract attention and testify to her imaginative depth. Her imagination is also evident in her rapid stream of lively talk, her habit of acting out scenes from poems and stories, her artistic and musical talent, and her comical attempts to write poetry. Furthermore, Rebecca is sensitive to nature, a conventional romantic sign of spirituality and goodness. Although generally a positive quality, this sensitivity causes some trouble when Rebecca becomes so absorbed in the beauty of the river that she leans on a freshly painted bridge.

Rebecca is a good girl who gets into trouble because she is forgetful, careless, or unlucky. When her mind is preoccupied, for example, she forgets that she is not allowed to use the front stairs. When she tries to please Miranda by throwing her parasol into the well, to cite another instance, she has bad luck because it jams the mechanism. Rebecca's innate goodness is, however, readily apparent. She stops Minnie Smellie from taunting the Simpsons, she sells soap for them, and she refuses to engage in gossip. Sensitive and loyal to her family, she even insists that Miranda not insult her father. Indeed, Rebecca is so sensitive to what is proper that she invites the missionaries home when she learns that Miranda's father, Deacon Sawyer, did so in the old days. Furthermore, she convinces Miranda that she

possesses Sawyer practicality, not just Randall dreaminess, by competently performing all the domestic chores during the visit.

As she grows from a child to a girl of thirteen who attends Wareham, Rebecca stops being so troublesome. Increasingly thinking of others, she devotes herself to completing her education in three years instead of four so that she can help support her family. She also shows increased maturity by accepting criticism of her earlier writing. As more people recognize her talent and goodness, they begin to see her as a handsome young woman. Her increased physical beauty is matched by her moral qualities. Rebecca unhesitatingly rushes from her graduation to attend to Miranda, who has never once displayed affection, and she rushes to tend her mother, sacrificing her own employment prospects by nursing her. In one area, however, she does not mature. Rebecca remains uninterested in the opposite sex. She becomes momentarily jealous when she sees Huldah walking with Mr. Ladd, but any overt romantic interest in Mr. Ladd ends when he tells her not to become like Huldah. Although it is readily apparent that she and Mr. Ladd love each other, she is not conscious of her feelings. The novel ends with Rebecca making the kind of sacrifices expected of female adults of the era. Seventeen-year-old Rebecca, that is, sets aside her own feelings and puts on the "inevitable yoke" of duty, caring for her mother and planning for the her family to move into the brick house.

Miranda Sawyer, Rebecca's aunt, is a conscientious, frugal, industrious, and pragmatic New Englander. A woman somewhere between fifty and sixty years of age with limited education and narrow interests, she attends church regularly but is completely lacking in charity. Her "chilly virtues" and forbidding demeanor make her unappealing to Rebecca. Indeed, Miranda, who resents Rebecca's flamboyant father—possibly because she once expected to be the object of his attentions—expects and looks for only the worst in Rebecca. Furthermore, Miranda has no understanding of childhood and no love of beauty. She is thus against Rebecca having dresses of various bright colors, and she forbids Rebecca to take lessons in either art or music. Stern, rule-bound, and uncompromising, Miranda is a pessimist who expects the worst of Rebecca. She believes that she knows how to raise children, even though her goal seems to be to raise a child devoid of originality and spirit. Consequently, she regards Jane's empathetic treatment of Rebecca as a sign of weakness. Nevertheless, having given her word to educate Rebecca, she makes personal sacrifices when times become tough and never informs Rebecca of her troubles. In fact, although she softens somewhat after she detects in Rebecca a resemblance to Deacon Sawyer, Miranda is so distrustful of emotions that she never once shows affection or pride in Rebecca's accomplishments. In the end, however, Miranda bequeaths the house to Rebecca, a gesture that Jane interprets as an apology for her harshness.

In contrast to the harsh Miranda, **Jane Sawyer**, her younger sister, is a gentle, sympathetic woman. Whereas Miranda expects the worst of Rebecca, Jane, although puzzled by her, is ready to believe the best. Jane, who is better educated, has lost her fiancé during the Civil War; since she has known both love and sorrow she is better able to accept Rebecca. For years Jane has submitted to Miranda's iron rule, but she begins to change under the influence of Rebecca's lively presence. Finding life now more interesting because of the child, she quietly sides with Rebecca. For example, she convinces Miranda to give in to Rebecca's desire for dresses of different colors, and she praises Rebecca when Mrs. Perkins becomes demonstrative about Emma Jane. Jane also stands up to Miranda more often, as when she says Miranda's attacks on Rebecca's father are neither good manners nor good religion. Still, the charitable Jane never criticizes Miranda in front of Rebecca and, after Miranda's death, defends her as a good woman who didn't mean any harm to Rebecca. **Aurelia Randall**, Rebecca's mother, shows a similar charity. Aurelia tells her daughter that Miranda's support of her education has made up for the harsh way she treated Aurelia and her flamboyantly improvident husband, Lorenzo de Medici Randall. She even provides a partial explanation for Miranda's bitterness by suggesting that Miranda may have had her own eye on Lorenzo. Nevertheless, prior to Miranda's death, Aurelia is completely pragmatic

and totally unsentimental. When her sisters offer to educate Aurelia's oldest child, for instance, she decides, without consulting them, to send a substitute. Knowing that Hannah, the oldest girl, is more help to her around the farm, Aurelia, who places little stock in imagination and artistic talent, sends Rebecca in her place.

Among the others who befriend Rebecca, **Adam Ladd**, whom Rebecca calls **Mr. Alladin**, is the most influential. A wealthy bachelor eighteen years her senior, the sad, lonely Mr. Ladd is a benefactor who provides gifts, advice, and secret financial support. Charmed during his first encounter with Rebecca, he kindly purchases all the soap that she is selling. Although he later sends both Rebecca and Emma Jane annual presents, his inability to remember Emma Jane's name indicates that Rebecca is the true object of his concern. He therefore arranges for Rebecca to have a vacation with Miss Maxwell and sponsors an essay contest that she wins. Although Mr. Ladd suggests that he can be interested in Rebecca only while she is a child, he exhibits jealousy when he sees her innocently talking to the male editor of the student newspaper, therefore signalling his romantic involvement. A similar hint appears when Mr. Ladd, having just seen Rebecca, dreamily reads the story of Alladin's love for the Princess Badroulboudour. Given that Rebecca earlier named him Alladin, this story seems to express his own feelings and hopes.

More unlikely helpers are **Jeremiah Cobb** and his wife, **Sarah Cobb**, who call themselves **Uncle Jerry** and **Aunt Sarah**. The intellectually slow Uncle Jerry is immediately attracted to Rebecca and becomes one of her most steadfast supporters. He takes her for an outing to a larger town and cunningly convinces her to return when she runs away. His enthusiastic appreciation of Rebecca becomes comical when it leads to inappropriate outbursts at public events, such as her graduation. Aunt Sarah has a lesser role, but she tries to save Rebecca's dress after she gets paint on it from the bridge, provides motherly comfort, and praises Rebecca when the women gossip.

The portrait of **Miss Emily Maxwell**, the Wareham English teacher, emphasizes the importance of skillful teachers in developing even talented individuals. Based on Mary Smith, who taught the author, Miss Maxwell is an ideal educator. Bright, honest, considerate, and dedicated, she recognizes Rebecca's talents and deficiencies. Miss Maxwell gives Rebecca honest criticism of her writing, provides additional lessons, and conspires with Mr. Ladd to give her a needed vacation.

The various girls whom Rebecca encounters reveal her virtues. **Emma Jane Perkins**, Rebecca's best friend, is a pretty blonde who, by contrast, emphasizes Rebecca's intelligence, imagination, and drive. Emma Jane becomes embarrassed when playing the imaginative games that delight Rebecca. She also has no genuine interest in education and attends Wareham only to be near her friend. Indeed, her major function is to demonstrate Rebecca's ability to attract lifelong admirers. **Minnie Smellie**, who is described as a ferret-eyed, blonde-haired, spindle-legged creature, possesses a moral character that matches her unattractive physical appearance. Suspected of being a cheater at school, Minnie is completely insensitive to the feelings of others and therefore humiliates the Simpson children by calling them jailbirds. She therefore contrasts with the noble Rebecca, who does not judge people by their parents or their social station. **Huldah Meserve**, a pretty girl with auburn hair, tiny freckles, porcelain skin, and curling lashes over her merry eyes, contrasts with Rebecca because she is vain and trivial. Huldah constantly talks about her appearance and about the boys who admire her. Her actions emphasize that Rebecca, who has no interest in boys, is innocent, modest, and serious-minded.

Further Reading

Berger, Laura Standley, ed. *Twentieth-Century Children's Writers.* 4th ed. Detroit: St. James, 1995.

Bingham, Jane M., ed. *Writers for Children: Critical Studies of Major Authors since the Seventeenth Century.* New York: Charles Scribner's Sons, 1988.

Contemporary Authors. Vol. 111. Detroit: Gale Research, 1984.

Estes, Glenn E., ed. *American Writers for Children before 1900.* Vol. 42 of *Dictionary of Literary Biography.* Detroit: Gale Research, 1985.

Griswold, Jerry. "Spinster Aunt, Sugar Daddy, and Child-Woman: *Rebecca of Sunnybrook Farm.*" In *Audacious Kids: Coming of Age in America's Classic*

Children's Books. New York: Oxford University Press, 1992.

Yesterday's Authors of Books for Children. Vol. 1. Detroit: Gale Research, 1977.

Laura Ingalls Wilder

1867-1957, American teacher, farmer, loan association officer, columnist, and author

The Little House Series

(autobiographical fiction, 1932-1943)

PLOT: Laura Ingalls Wilder, who wrote "The Little House Series" with the editorial help of her daughter, Rose Wilder Lane, said that she "wanted the children now to understand more about the beginnings of things, to know what is behind the things they see—what it is that made America as they know it." Although the series is primarily a vivid social history of pioneer America, it is cast as an autobiography, giving it more immediacy and dramatic interest.

Little House in the Big Woods (1932), the first volume, is a detailed account of pioneer life. It describes one year, probably 1872, in the life of Pa (Charles) and Ma (Caroline) Ingalls and their three daughters, Mary, Laura, and baby Carrie, who live in a log house in the Big Woods near Pepin, Wisconsin. With winter approaching, Pa smokes venison and butchers a pig. When the snow comes, he sets traps and shoots a bear. The girls help Ma with churning and baking and Pa with making bullets. The best times, however, are the evenings, when Pa plays games, tells stories, and plays the fiddle. At Christmas, relatives visit. Laura makes snow pictures with their children, treasures a rag doll that she receives, and enjoys the feasting. On her fifth birthday, Laura receives a ceremonial spanking and some presents. The winter passes happily, except for boring Sundays.

As spring approaches, the Ingalls have two amusing encounters. In the dark, Ma swats what she thinks is the cow, only to discover that it is a bear. Returning home that night, Pa attacks a bear blocking his path, but it turns out to be a stump. During maple sugar time, the family goes to a dance at

Pa, Laura, and Mary Ingalls in a scene from **Little House on the Prairie,** *illustrated by Garth Williams.*

Grandpa's, where "wild" Uncle George loses a jigging contest to Grandma and Laura defends Carrie as the best-looking baby. When Laura goes to town for the first time, she behaves shyly with a storekeeper who praises Mary's looks. At a lake, she tears her pocket by filling it with too many pretty stones. Throughout the summer, Laura is jealous of Mary's golden curls, so she slaps Mary when Mary taunts her. During the fall oat harvest, Cousin Charley, who avoids work by playing tricks on Uncle Henry and Pa, is stung by yellow jackets. Pa, an advocate of progress, brings in a threshing machine to separate the grain. As winter approaches, Pa tells how he was too involved in watching some deer and a bear to shoot them for meat. Pleased with him and happy with her life, Laura goes to sleep in her cozy house.

Farmer Boy (1933) complements the first book by telling about the boyhood of Almanzo Wilder, Laura's future husband. It is set in the late 1860s on a prosperous farm near Malone, New York. James Wilder and his wife have four children: Royal, Eliza

Jane, Alice, and Almanzo, who is nearly nine when the novel opens. *Farmer Boy* is filled with detailed descriptions of such pioneer work as chopping ice, planting potatoes, saving corn from an early frost, training cattle to haul logs, shearing sheep, and baling hay. The book also contains scenes of commercial activity: Mother bargains with a tin peddler and sells her butter; Father sells potatoes and bargains with a slick horse dealer; a visiting cobbler makes boots; and Almanzo handles the sale of their hay. As far as the story concerns Almanzo, however, it is a tale of wish fulfillment. Almanzo loves horses and wants to break them, but Father says that he is too young and will spoil them.

A few events contain dramatic interest. The new school teacher, Mr. Corse, bullwhips a gang of boys when they try to thrash him. Almanzo falls into the water during ice chopping. At the Fourth of July festivities, cousin Frank dares Almanzo to ask his father for a nickel for lemonade. Father gives Almanzo a half dollar and a lecture about the value of money, inspiring him to buy a suckling pig. During the summer, Mr. and Mrs. Wilder go away for a week. Left in charge of the house, their children make ice cream, cake, and candy, but neglect the chores. When they desperately clean up on the eve of their parents' return, bossy Eliza Jane provokes Almanzo, who throws a stove-blacking brush at her. It stains the parlor wallpaper, but Eliza Jane surprises Almanzo by secretly patching the wallpaper. At the county fair, Almanzo wins first prize for his milk-fed pumpkin. At Christmas, Frank dares Almanzo to touch the colts, and Royal stops Frank from bothering them and pulls Almanzo by the ear. In the final episode, Almanzo finds a wallet containing fifteen hundred dollars. He returns it to Mr. Thompson, who counts the money and then offers a nickel reward. Doubly insulted, Almanzo refuses the nickel; a merchant, Mr. Paddock, threatens the miser into giving Almanzo two hundred dollars. Mr. Paddock then offers to take Almanzo as an apprentice. When Almanzo lets his father know that he would rather train horses, however, his proud father gives him a colt to train.

The series returns to Laura's story in *Little House on the Prairie* (1935). Feeling crowded by the growing population, Pa sells the house in the Big Woods, loads his family into a wagon, and heads for Indian Territory. They cross the Mississippi just before the ice breaks and later make a harrowing crossing of a swollen stream. In Kansas, about forty miles from Independence, Pa finds a place for a home. Detailed descriptions of Pa building the house and barn dominate, but the novel contains dramatic moments, such as when Ma is injured by a log rolling onto her foot. Shortly afterwards, Pa visits neighbors, helps a sick family stranded in their wagon, and encounters a pack of wolves, who trot beside him but do not attack. Later, the family spends a frightening night when howling wolves surround the house.

Episodes increasingly involve Indians and other settlers. While Pa is away, for example, two Indians enter the house; Laura and Mary decide against releasing their dog to attack them, and the Indians leave after Ma feeds them. Much later, an Indian threatens to shoot the dog, which is blocking his way on the trail, and Pa afterwards keeps the animal chained. In one of the pleasant times, Pa takes Laura and Mary to a deserted Indian camp, where the girls find beads. Episodes with the settlers are also dramatic. Pa must rescue Mr. Scott, a neighbor who is helping them dig a well, when he is overcome by gas. During the summer, the family contracts malaria and is saved by Dr. Tan, the first black man Laura has seen, and Mrs. Scott. At Christmas, Mr. Edwards, a bachelor who helped Pa build the cabin, crosses a raging stream to ensure that Mary and Laura receive gifts. The last part of the novel is tensely exciting. First, Ma and Pa defend the house against a prairie fire. Then angry Indians fill the night air with war whoops. After the Osage Indians stop the gathered tribes from massacring the settlers, the Indians leave. Pa learns, however, that the army will be removing the settlers from Indian land. He therefore packs up everything, and the family leaves the house and plowed fields.

At the beginning of **On the Banks of Plum Creek** (1937), the family arrives in Minnesota, where Pa buys a homestead with a dugout. At the new home, Laura is sometimes naughty: she goes to a swimming hole without permission, she slides down straw stacks, and later she foolishly enters the swollen stream. Pleased with his prospects, Pa builds a new house on credit. Laura enjoys playing outside at their home, but Ma now insists that her girls attend school in town. Mary and Laura soon come to like it, but Laura develops a feud with Nellie Oleson, a storekeeper's daughter, who bullies the other children and has contempt for "country girls." Nevertheless, Nellie invites Mary and Laura to a party. During the party, she insultingly forbids Laura to touch a doll. Laura exacts revenge the following week at her own party, tricking Nellie into wading in a stream full of leeches. Shortly afterwards, the girls attend church for the first time, meeting the kindly missionary, Reverend Alden.

When clouds of grasshoppers destroy his wheat crop, Pa walks three hundred miles to work on the eastern harvests. The family misses him and Laura is particularly upset when she is forced to give up her rag doll to Mrs. Nelson's baby, a doll she later finds thrown out in a puddle. That year, Christmas is particularly joyful for Laura. Reverend Alden's eastern parishioners send presents for his congregation, and Laura receives a fur cape and muff prettier than anything Nellie Oleson owns. The next summer, Pa is downhearted to see grasshopper eggs throughout his fields. The hatching grasshoppers again destroy the crops, forcing Pa to go east again for work. After he returns, storms become a problem. He and Ma go to town when one comes, and the girls fill the house with firewood. Shortly afterwards, Pa goes to town alone and is caught in a blizzard while returning. He survives three days buried beneath the snow in a gully. Digging himself out on the fourth day, he sees that he is in sight of his home. Although there are no Christmas presents this year because he ate the candy to help him survive, the family is happy to have him safe. He is also happy because the heavy snow promises a growing season without a grasshopper infestation.

By the Shores of Silver Lake (1939) begins two years later. Crops have been poor, and Mary is blind because of the scarlet fever that also attacked Ma, Carrie, and the new baby, Grace. When Aunt Docia offers Pa a job working on the railroad for her husband, Uncle Hi, Ma agrees to another move. Pa leaves immediately and the family follows by train. At the railway camp at Silver Lake, Dakota Territory, Laura becomes friends with Lena, Aunt Docia's wild daughter, and watches the work on the railway. Ma warns her, however, to be wary of the men and to act like a lady. Indeed, the camp is rough: only the intervention of a half-breed gambler named Big Jerry saves Pa when the workers threaten to riot to receive their full pay. After the camp breaks up, the family moves into a surveyor's house for the winter. One day, while hunting for wolves Laura and Carrie encountered while sliding on the ice, Pa discovers the perfect homestead site. On Christmas Eve, Mr. (Robert) Boast and his bride, Nell (Ella), arrive and warn Pa about an impending land rush. Winter storms prevent Pa from filing his claim, however, and then travelers begin to seek shelter in their house. Among them is Reverend Alden, who tells the family about a school for the blind in Iowa.

While Ma and Laura earn money sheltering and feeding the daily stream of settlers, Pa goes to file his claim. At the land agent's door, a man tries to pick a fight with him so that his friend can file on Pa's land, but Mr. Edwards comes to Pa's aid. When he returns, Pa moves the family to the growing town of De Smet, where he has erected a building he hopes to sell. Laura, burdened with Ma's insistence that she become a teacher, begins a school for Carrie and her friends. With news that a claim jumper has murdered a settler, however, Pa moves the family into a shanty on their homestead. The family has a scare when Grace wanders off and is lost in a buffalo wallow, but she is found again. The book ends as the Ingalls plant trees for a windbreak and settle into what Ma says is their last home.

The Long Winter (1940) tells of the harsh winter of 1880-81, during which blizzard after blizzard strikes De Smet, supplies run out, and people begin to starve. In the fall, Laura helps Pa harvest the hay. Pa feels uneasy—the muskrats have made thick walls for their homes, an early blizzard has struck, and an old Indian has predicted seven months of winter—so he moves the family into the store he built in town. Laura and Carrie briefly go to school. One day during a blinding blizzard, the teacher and children become lost on the open prairie until Laura bumps into a building. Pa and some men from town then dig out a train, which is carrying supplies. More storms, however, make it necessary for the railroad company to announce that no more trains will run until spring. Whenever the weather lets up, Pa makes dangerous trips to the homestead for hay. After Christmas, when their coal runs out, Pa and Laura twist the hay into sticks for fuel. Pa also accompanies the other townsmen on an antelope hunt, but an excited hunter scares off the herd.

When the last of their wheat runs out, Ma refuses to let Pa search for a homestead where a settler is rumored to have wheat. Pa therefore forcefully insists on buying some of the seed wheat that Almanzo Wilder has hidden in the walls so that his brother, Royal, won't sell it. Afterwards, Almanzo and Cap Garland, one of Laura's schoolmates, set out to find the settler with the wheat. They locate the settler, Anderson, convince him to sell some wheat, and return just as another blizzard begins. Mr. Loftus, the storekeeper who bankrolled the trip, then tries to make an exorbitant profit, until Pa and the other townsmen convince him that he will suffer later from the loss of goodwill. April brings a thaw, but trains don't get through until May. When the trains do arrive, the Ingalls family receives a still-frozen turkey among supplies sent by Reverend Alden. Mr. and Mrs. Boast join them for a Christmas feast in May.

Little Town on the Prairie (1941) focuses on Laura's social experiences in town. The novel begins, however, on the homestead claim, where Pa enlarges the house and plants crops. To earn money for Mary's college education, Pa and Laura work in town: he does carpentry, and she sews shirts. Work dominates the summer, but Pa treats Laura and Carrie to a Fourth of July outing in town. Blackbirds then destroy the crops, forcing Pa to sell the calf so that Mary can still go to college. After Mary leaves, the family moves to town for the winter. Laura and Carrie go to school, where Laura is friends with Mary Power, Minnie Johnson, and Ida Wright Brown. Nellie Oleson, who is now living on a claim, turns the teacher, Miss Eliza Jane Wilder, against Carrie and Laura by claiming that they believe that they can do what they want because Pa is on the school board. Miss Wilder becomes so unfair to them that the other students rebel. Pa and two other school board members restore discipline, and Miss Wilder leaves at the end of the term. In the new term, the pretentious Nellie starts a craze for name cards, and Pa allows Laura to have some printed. More seriously, Nellie repeatedly grabs the candy that Cap Garland brings for Mary Power, pretending that Cap is bringing it for her. Laura stops Nellie by grabbing the candy and giving it to Mary. Nellie also brags that she will ride in Almanzo's buggy, but Almanzo offers Laura a ride first.

Outside of school, Laura has new social experiences: a boring Ladies' Aid sociable, an enjoyable New England church supper, Friday night literary society meetings—including a spelling bee that Pa wins, a musical evening, a pantomimed wax museum display, and a minstrel show—and Ben Woodworth's birthday party. The next fall, after another poor harvest, the family returns to town. Almanzo shows interest in Laura, asking to walk her home after Reverend Brown's revival meeting and taking her for a ride in his cutter after Laura's impressive performance at the school exhibition. The day after the exhibition brings a dramatic change. Mr. Brewster offers to hire Laura as a teacher for a neighboring settlement. The school superintendent examines her, and Laura, although only fifteen, receives a teaching certificate.

These Happy Golden Years (1943) is the story of Laura's maturation. Laura takes up her teaching position, boarding with Mr. (Lewis) and Mrs. (Lib) Brewster. Laura is miserable. Mrs. Brewster, sullen and depressed, wants to go east. One night, she even threatens her husband with a knife. The five students in Laura's school—Ruby, Tommy, and Clarence Brewster, and Charles and Martha Harrison—become discipline problems, not even attempting to do their lessons. At night, Laura studies to keep up with her class in town. Almanzo takes her home every Friday and drives her back to the Brewsters' on Sunday. When her students tease her that she has a beau, Laura somewhat rudely tells Almanzo that she won't ride with him once she moves back to town. Nevertheless, Almanzo continues to make the cold and dangerous journeys every week. After Ma and Pa give her advice, Laura takes command of the school, inspiring Martha with confidence and Clarence with a desire to keep up in his studies.

When she moves back to town, Laura returns to school and finds herself accepting rides in Almanzo's cutter. In the spring, Laura keeps Mrs. McKee company on her claim until Mary visits. The next year, she again passes the teacher's examination and takes a position teaching three students in a nearby settlement school. She uses the money to buy an organ for Mary, but Mary decides not to visit that year. Almanzo takes her for rides every Sunday, but one day shows up with Nellie Oleson. Nellie accompanies them each week until Laura makes it clear that she will not go out again if Nellie is with them. That fall, Almanzo and Laura become engaged. He goes to Minnesota for the winter but returns unexpectedly on Christmas Eve. In the spring, one of Laura's friends fails the teacher's examination and offers the teaching position she was going to take to Laura, who passed the test. The next fall, to avoid the expensive church wedding Almanzo's mother and sister want, eighteen-year-old Laura and Almanzo quickly marry. After a supper with the Ingalls family, Laura and Almanzo go to their own "little gray home in the west."

CHARACTERS: Laura Ingalls Wilder devotes most of her attention to describing pioneer activities, but the major characters gain substance through these activities. Minor characters are often little more than names who fulfill roles necessary for full descriptions of farm or town life.

A rugged man with wild brown hair, a long beard, and merry blue eyes, **Pa (Charles) Ingalls** is a true patriarch, protecting and providing for his family, lifting their spirits in times of trouble, and filling them with a love of home. As the one who controls the family's destiny, he is the central figure in the earlier volumes, performing as an ideal father, husband, and pioneer. As a father, Pa demands that the children be seen and not heard until he is ready to listen. Although he whips the children for disobedience, he is loving and tender. He shows affection for his children by letting them help him, by playing with them, by hugging them, and by entertaining them with his stories and with his fiddle. He also has a good sense of humor, telling jokes and making puns. No matter how poor the family is, he makes Christmas and family gatherings pleasant. After Mary becomes blind, he makes sacrifices to ensure that she can go away to college, and he later buys an organ so that she can practice music on the homestead. As a husband, he is devoted to his wife, suppressing his own wanderlust—he finds even the area around De Smet too crowded for his tastes—because she wants the children to receive an education. He also shows his love by making her articles, such as a shelf for her one ornament, and by buying luxuries, such as a sewing machine. As a pioneer, Pa is extraordinarily competent. He is a skilled carpenter and can build a house without nails. He is a knowledgeable trapper and hunter, obtaining food and furs to trade. He is an industrious farmer,

breaking land, sowing seeds, and harvesting. Pa is energetic and resourceful. He trades work with Mr. Edwards so the house walls may be built safely. When the long winter strikes, he makes perilous journeys to the claim for hay and then spends agonizing hours twisting it into sticks that will burn and keep his family warm. When the family runs out of wheat, he becomes forceful, denying Almanzo the right to withhold seed wheat from sale. Throughout, however, he is a good neighbor and citizen, aiding various people in distress.

Pa is surprisingly well educated, as he shows when he defeats the town in the spelling bee, but more importantly, he has wisdom. He is the voice of progress, praising machines that cut the labor involved in harvesting. At the same time, he is pragmatic, speaking against mortgaging the future to acquire such machinery. He is also fair minded, speaking against his wife's intolerance by recognizing that Indians are not bad. Finally, he is a shrewd judge of character, as he shows in his relationships with Miss Wilder, Almanzo, the railroad workers, and numerous pioneers. Such understanding helps him to advise Laura, obviously his favorite, to think before acting if she wants to succeed as a teacher.

Whereas Pa represents the American pioneering spirit, **Ma (Caroline) Ingalls** embodies domestic desires. As a dutiful nineteenth-century wife, Ma seems patient and submissive to her husband, but she does get her way in important things. For instance, she exacts from Charles, who prefers to live in the wilderness, a promise that they will live where the children can receive schooling. Ma's major preoccupation is raising her children to be ladies. She insists that they speak only after they have been spoken to, that they observe the rules of etiquette, and that they share even their favorite toys with others. A former teacher, she constantly corrects her daughters' speech, often frustrating them when they are trying to say something. She insists that they apply themselves to their school work. She also protects them, frequently sending warning glances to her husband and others when she thinks that they might say something to upset the children. Ma is as resourceful as Pa: she makes her children's clothes, she uses a coffee grinder to grind wheat into flour, she manages to have Christmas gifts and a good meal each year, and she can turn green pumpkins into mock apple pie. Ma likes things to be pretty, so she colors the butter, puts up curtains, and displays a china statue, an object signaling that the house is a home.

Ma has great self-control most of the time. When she mistakenly swats the bear in *Little House in the Big Woods*, for example, she calmly ensures that Laura gets to safety. She does, however, lose control under the endless confinement during the long winter, thereby suggesting how unbearable conditions are. She is also given to worrying when her husband is away, although she hides her emotions from the children. Finally, she expresses concern about Laura driving with Almanzo's wild horses, reluctantly submitting to her husband's assurances. Ma has one glaring flaw: she hates Indians. She also expresses an intolerance for foreigners. Nevertheless, like Pa, she gives wise advice. Although she prides herself on her own thin waist and was a fashionable woman before her marriage, she warns her daughters against vanity by insisting that true beauty lies in deeds, not appearances. Moreover, she often helps them handle problems. When Laura has trouble with Clarence Brewster at her first school, Ma is thus able to suggest that Laura ignore him because he is just seeking attention.

Laura Ingalls grows from a jealous four-year-old child to a responsible, married, eighteen-year-old woman. In the early volumes, brown-haired Laura is jealous of Mary, who has golden curls. When Mary spitefully says that golden hair is prettier than brown hair, Laura slaps her because she feels both the truth of the statement and the unfairness of life. Laura is also upset because Mary finds it easy to be good, whereas she is always in trouble. Laura, for instance, rips her pocket by filling it with pretty pebbles, something that she knows Mary would never do. Much later, Laura, who wants to keep the beads she found in the deserted Indian camp, resents Mary for suggesting that they give them to Carrie. At Plum Creek, Laura shows her willfulness by disobeying her father's injunction against going near the swimming hole and her wildness by swinging from the bridge into the raging

water. Laura also takes malicious delight in getting even with Nellie Oleson by leading her into a pool filled with bloodsuckers and, years later, by deliberately scaring Almanzo's horses to frighten her during a buggy ride. Nevertheless, Laura shows both her essential goodness and the excellence of her upbringing because she confesses her girlish transgressions and never lies to Ma or Pa. Furthermore, after Mary becomes blind, Laura is considerate, acting as her eyes by describing everything that she sees.

Laura shares her father's pioneering spirit, loving the outdoors more than the house and the country more than the settlements. Indeed, she prefers to be with her father, rather than with her mother. She thus helps him to make bullets in the Big Woods, to make a door in Indian Territory, and to harvest the hay and twist it into sticks in De Smet. In spite of her love for the homestead, however, Laura has a greater devotion to her family. The five-year-old Laura expresses this devotion by insisting that Carrie is the most beautiful baby in the world; the teenage Laura does so by taking a sewing job in town to earn money for Mary's college fund. Furthermore, although she hates the idea of teaching, Laura places duty ahead of personal preference, studying hard so that she can become a teacher and thereby earn money for Mary. This same devotion makes her endure life with the Brewsters during her first teaching job because she knows that quitting would disqualify her from further positions. Later, she insists on giving money from her last position to Pa as a final sign of her appreciation for the life that her parents gave her.

Laura's maturation is inextricably tied to her primary role of providing an illustration of the lives of pioneer children and adolescents both on farms and in towns. Laura thus learns to curb her unladylike ways, resisting the urge to play with the boys at school and doing the sedate things left for girls. She begins to take delight in fashion, obtaining name cards, cutting her bangs, and wearing hooped skirts. She also learns to appreciate social life in town and gains enough confidence in herself to perform well at the school exhibition. Her most dramatic change comes when she conducts herself as an adult by performing commendably in her first teaching position while simultaneously keeping up with her own studies. At the same time, Laura goes through the courtship rituals characteristic of an earlier time. At first, she does not even recognize them as such, being puzzled by Almanzo's desire to walk her home and to bring her back from the Brewsters'. She is even rude to him, insisting that she is only using him for the rides and will not be riding with him after she returns to town. Nevertheless, after she slides into a routine of weekly rides, she realizes that she looks forward to seeing him. She nowhere expresses the passionate emotion of twentieth-century love, but her declaration that Almanzo can kiss her after they have become engaged stands as a sign of her emotional maturity. Her later insistence that she will not promise to obey him indicates characteristic honesty, an independence of mind, and a confidence in her identity. Laura enters marriage with a firm understanding of hardships and the skills and attitudes necessary to survive them.

Mary Ingalls, who is about a year older than Laura, is a foil who contrasts with her sister in almost every respect. She has golden curls and attracts comments about her looks from everyone. Although she occasionally slips, as she does when she provokes Laura into slapping her, she is usually obedient and passive. Unlike Laura, she loves to stay indoors with Ma. Whereas Laura bursts into action when frightened, Mary freezes. Before she becomes blind, Mary loves to study and dreams of fulfilling Ma's wish that she become a teacher, a job that Laura dreads. After she becomes blind, Mary accepts her lot with saintly grace. Mary tells Laura, though, that Laura must struggle to be good and that her own early goodness was merely a form of vanity and pride, a way of showing off. Laura has mixed feelings about this revelation. On one hand, she is shocked to realize that she is hearing something that she has suspected all along. On the other, she knows that Mary is truly good. Laura also sees that blindness has strengthened Mary's faith in God and made her more certain of goodness. Mary does, however, have one flaw. She is prosaic: when Laura acts as her eyes, Mary constantly criticizes Laura's lively descriptions as too fanciful.

The other sisters have small roles. **Carrie Ingalls**, who is about four years younger than Laura, is at first a duty and a worry, becoming lost in the tall grass around their home in Indian Territory. She becomes more distinctive when she is ten and goes to school with Laura. Thin, pale, and spindly, with eyes that seem too large for her face, she is small for her age. She is also sickly, being prone to headaches that make her fail school lessons. As a consequence, she becomes a victim of Miss Wilder's pettiness. In doing so, Carrie establishes Laura's fierce family loyalty and sense of justice because Laura leaps to her sister's defense and takes the punishments directed at Carrie. **Grace Ingalls**, who is too young to be involved in Laura's social activities or the hardships of establishing the homestead, is little more than a name periodically mentioned.

Although their relatives make visits throughout the series, only a few warrant attention. In the first book, **Grandma Ingalls** is a model pioneer woman. Fun-loving and vigorous, she defeats Uncle George in the jigging contest, but she is still concerned about her duties and rushes into the kitchen to make sure that the syrup for the snow candy is ready to be served. **Uncle George Ingalls**, who ran away at fourteen to be a drummer boy in the army, has the reputation for being "wild." A big, broad, swaggering man with merry blue eyes, he dances with Laura, which makes her like him. His love of fun is evident when he starts the jigging contest with Grandma. **Cousin Charley**, the eleven-year-old son of Uncle Henry and Aunt Polly, contrasts with the obedient Ingalls sisters. Spoiled by his parents, he is unwilling to work. He therefore makes such a nuisance of himself that his father sends him away. He then maliciously pretends to be in trouble, bringing the men rushing to his aid. Ironically, the fourth time he cries for help, he needs it, having stepped on a nest of yellow jackets, but the men do not come. He turns out better than expected when he reappears briefly in *By the Shores of Silver Lake*, in which he helps Uncle Henry by cooking at the railroad camp. That novel also introduces fourteen-year-old **Lena**, daughter of Aunt Docia and Uncle Hi, a girl with curly black hair and snappy black eyes. Lena is a hard worker, but she is boisterous and loves wild rides on the ponies. Consequently, Ma uses her as a negative example and warns Laura to behave in a more ladylike manner. **Aunt Docia**, a pretty woman who married a widower, shows concern for family by offering Pa a job. **Uncle Hi**, her husband, is a fat, good-natured, easy-going railroad contractor. Cheated by the company, he exacts revenge by carting off the store's goods, an act Pa finds just and amusing.

Portraits of other pioneers provide a context for understanding the Ingalls family, Pa in particular. In *Little House on the Prairie*, **Mr. Edwards**, a tall, lean, tanned bachelor who calls himself a wildcat from Tennessee, impresses Laura with his accurate aim in spitting tobacco juice. He shows the frontier spirit of cooperation by trading work with Mr. Ingalls and by lending him nails for his roof. He is a kind man: he walks forty miles to town and risks his life in a raging stream so that Mary and Laura can have gifts for Christmas. He shows his sense of humor and understanding of children by telling them that Santa Claus, whom he met in Independence, asked him to deliver the gifts because he himself was too fat to cross the stream. His tale is one of the most memorable in the entire series. Like Pa, he leaves his prairie home when he hears that the army is coming. In *By the Shores of Silver Lake*, he fights the man who is trying to stop Pa from filing his claim. In *The Long Winter*, he passes by on the last train, leaving twenty dollars for Mary's college fund.

Mr. Scott is a short, stout man whose skin is red and scaly because he peels instead of tanning. Careless and excitable, he is a foil to Pa in *Little House on the Prairie*. He thus neglects to use a candle to check for gas during the digging of the well and is overcome by fumes. Incited by his wife's fears, he exhibits the racism of many of the settlers, declaring that the only good Indian is a dead one. Unlike Pa, he apparently doesn't believe that the army will drive away the white settlers and therefore decides to stay. **Mrs. Scott**, his overweight wife, exhibits both the charity and intolerance of the pioneers. She is friendly and considerate in caring for the Ingalls family when they are overcome by malaria. Because she has memories of a massacre in Minnesota, however, she despises Indians. She thus

declares that common sense and justice demand that the land should belong to those that farm it and that Indians are only good when they are dead. **Mr. (Robert) Boast**, who has a homestead claim in the region of Silver Lake, is a good-natured man with a contagious laugh. Kind and considerate, he repeatedly warns Pa that settlers are flooding the area and that Pa should file a claim soon. He also tells Laura before he brings the superintendent to examine her that she need not reveal that she is only fifteen unless she is asked her age. **Mrs. (Ella) Boast** (her husband calls her **Nell**) is a pretty woman who is the perfect companion to her husband because she is also merry and fun-loving. She shows consideration at various times, as when she secretly brings popcorn for their first Christmas in the west and when she sends chicks to them so that the Ingalls family can begin raising poultry. The couple with whom Laura boards while teaching her first school are foils to the Boasts. **Mr. (Lewis) Brewster**, who knew Mr. Boast back east, seldom talks or smiles. He endures his wife's bitterness by staying away or by reading the paper. He offers Laura no support, but his physically and emotionally cold home helps her to appreciate what Pa and Ma have provided. **Mrs. (Lib) Brewster**, his wife, resents having to endure pioneer hardships. Sullen, mean, and bitter, she takes her resentment out on Laura by ignoring her when she is present and by audibly arguing about wanting to leave the homestead as soon as Laura is in bed. She even threatens her husband with a knife, making Laura terrified for the rest of her stay.

Mrs. McKee, the tall, slender dressmaker in De Smet, represents the fearful newcomers to the frontier. She convinces her husband that he will have to give up the claim if she must stay alone on it while he works in town. She is not, however, selfish and mean like Mrs. Brewster, so she compromises, hiring Laura to stay with her. After Laura leaves, she decides that she doesn't need anyone else to help her. **Reverend Alden**, a minister who divides his time between an eastern parish and his missionary church in Minnesota, is a tall, thin man with a dark beard and warm blue eyes. Kind and considerate, he takes a genuine liking to Laura and Mary. Perhaps because of Nellie's teasing, he sees that Laura gets a fur cape and muff when he distributes Christmas presents. In *By the Shores of Silver Lake*, he stays a night with the family, telling them about a school for the blind in Iowa. Laura does not really like **Reverend Brown**, the Congregationalist minister in De Smet. He claims to be a cousin of John Brown of Ossawatomie and has the same fierce eyes beneath his shaggy white eyebrows. Reverend Brown is untidy, and his long white beard has a yellow stain. Laura amuses herself by correcting the grammar in his sermons. Surprisingly, Reverend Brown agrees with her about wedding vows and performs the wedding ceremony for her without requiring the vow of obedience to her husband.

Nine-year-old **Almanzo Wilder** is eager to grow up because he loves horses and wants to train them. Desperate to show his father that he is not too little, he unwittingly appears immature and incompetent. For example, he falls into the water during the ice chopping. While loading logs, he proves too weak to prevent one from rolling onto him. Afterwards, trying to do as much work as the men, he overloads his sled, leading his father to lecture him about the proper way to handle animals. He then makes mistakes while driving the calves, getting them stuck in the snow and failing to keep them on the road. Almanzo is comically naive when he overeats in order to grow more quickly, but he is generally serious and purposeful. He is responsible in buying and raising his pig. He shows patience in training the calves and in producing a prize-winning, milk-fed pumpkin. He also shows a maturing ethical understanding. He is tempted to lie to his father to get lemonade and to the judges when he thinks that they may take the ribbon away if he reveals the method he used to grow his pumpkin, but on both occasions he tells the truth. Indeed, in the latter instance, he realizes that his father would never have permitted him to enter the contest if the method were unethical. Under his father's tutelage, then, Almanzo, who hates formal schooling, learns the value of money and the way to bargain like a man, successfully getting his father's desired price for his hay. Almanzo shows his full maturity, pride, and integrity, however, when he returns Mr. Thompson's wallet. Insulted by both the puny reward of one

nickel and by the miser's insinuation that he might steal, Almanzo shows wit and courage by announcing that, since he has no change, he can't take the nickel. Afterwards, his father shows respect for his maturity by allowing him to choose his own future and by granting him his wish to train horses.

In *The Long Winter*, Almanzo is still trying to show that he is a man. Feeling that the law is unjust because it denies him independence and freedom, nineteen-year-old Almanzo lies about his age to file a homestead claim. He continues to show his skill with horses, breaking and selling them. He also shows his understanding of Royal's mercenary nature by hiding the seed wheat in the wall. Once Pa Ingalls forcibly buys some, however, Almanzo, who thinks deeply before making a statement or taking action, decides that he has a duty to help the town. He therefore heroically obtains grain and magnanimously does not charge for his efforts. As he tells Laura, he does not do things merely to achieve a personal advantage. He thus drives her back and forth to her teaching position because he recognizes that she is miserable living with the Brewsters. Although Almanzo's hardworking nature and common sense immediately impress Pa, Laura thinks of Almanzo as only an old bachelor with magnificent horses. Almanzo doesn't talk much, but Laura eventually sees that they share a love of nature. His willingness to omit the word "obey" from their wedding vows signals that he respects her as an independent person and therefore is her perfect mate.

Like Pa Ingalls, **James Wilder**, Almanzo's father, is a patriarch who possesses a wide number of skills that benefit his family. His hard work, careful management, and shrewd business decisions, such as planting a bumper crop of potatoes because he anticipates high prices after a year of low ones, have made him prosperous. He is most notable as a spokesman for the wise management of money. He thus tries to teach Almanzo prudence by giving him a half dollar to spend as he sees fit, by telling him that he should think of money in terms of the labor it costs to earn it, and by advocating a bank account as a wise way of earning money. Although Mr. Wilder at first refuses to grant his son's desire to work with horses, he shows that he is a wise and proud father by letting his son choose his own destiny and by giving him a horse when he sees that the boy wants to be an independent farmer. **Mrs. Wilder**, his spouse, is a skillful pioneer wife, but she is also a shrewd businesswoman, cleverly out-bargaining the tin peddler and obtaining a good price for her butter. Like her husband, she views farmers as independent people and is against the idea of Almanzo working in town, where the merchants make their living only by serving others. **Royal Wilder**, who is thirteen at the beginning of *Farmer Boy*, is a competent farmhand, but he longs for an easier life—that of a merchant—a dream he partly fulfills by opening a store in De Smet. Alice Wilder, who is ten, is not a well-realized character. Because she is next to him in age, she shares a special feeling with Almanzo. Her most notable role comes when she expresses mixed feelings: she longs for the freedom given to boys, yet she loves typically feminine things.

Eliza Jane Wilder is a bossy twelve-year-old in *Farmer Boy*. Although she is often a tattle-tale, she shows surprising generosity and consideration: after she provokes Almanzo into throwing the stove-backing brush, she patches the wallpaper so that he will not be whipped. In *Little Town on the Prairie* she is an inept teacher. Wanting to rule by love rather than fear, she loses control of the school because she is a bad judge of character and a poor disciplinarian. On the first day of school, for example, she asks Minnie Johnson to give up the seat that she was promised because Nellie demands it. Afterwards, Miss Wilder confides in Nellie and believes Nellie's claim that the Ingalls sisters are bragging that they can run the school. Consequently, she becomes nearly mad with resentment, conducting a nasty vendetta against Laura and Carrie. Ultimately she loses everyone's respect, and her students, who refuse to be quiet or study, openly mock her. She doesn't appear in the final volume, but the news that she is coming to take over wedding arrangements prompts Almanzo to ask Laura to marry him immediately.

Three minor characters are notable in *Farmer Boy*. **Frank**, Almanzo's cousin, is a braggart who constantly dares Almanzo to do unwise or forbidden things. When he dares Almanzo to ask for a nickel,

Almanzo shows his honesty by correcting his father's statement that Frank has already treated him to lemonade. When Frank willfully disturbs the horses during his Christmas visit, Almanzo proves that he is responsible by trying to stop him. Almanzo gets even with Frank by soundly beating him in a game of snow forts. **Mr. Corse**, a slim, pale young teacher, shows that wit and courage were necessary to survive in pioneer schools. Following Mr. Wilder's suggestion, he uses a bullwhip to beat the ruffians who try to attack him and to wreck the school. **Mr. Paddock**, the big, jolly wagon-maker, stands up for Almanzo against miserly Mr. Thompson. He suggests Almanzo's worth by thinking of him as a son, promising to take him as an apprentice and eventually giving his business to the boy. This handsome offer precipitates the climax, in which Father and Mother express appreciation for the life of a farmer and Almanzo is finally able to achieve his dream of having a horse.

Nellie Oleson, a pretty girl with long curls of yellow hair, is completely unlikable. The daughter of a Plum Creek storekeeper, she is arrogant and rude, contemptuously wrinkling her nose at Laura and Mary as "country girls" because of their short skirts. When the girls go to her father's store, she grabs candy and sticks her tongue out at them instead of sharing it. She is also vain and ill-mannered, bragging that her fur cape is something Laura's father could not afford, claiming at Laura's party that she did not wear her best clothes to a country party, and failing to thank Mrs. Ingalls for her hospitality. Furthermore, she is a bully who forces the other girls to play what she wants at recess and who shouts a warning to Laura that she must not touch her doll. Nellie brings out Laura's vengeful nature. Laura gets even at her party when she deliberately leads Nellie into the bloodsuckers, but her most satisfying vengeance is accidental: Laura receives a fur cape and muff far more elegant than the cape that Nellie owns.

When Nellie reappears in *Little Town on the Prairie*, she has not changed at all. She viciously turns the young teacher against the Ingalls sisters by misrepresenting what Laura said about her father. She puts on airs, always talking about New York

State and pretending that she has name cards, a far more fashionable item than the autograph book Laura receives for Christmas. (Laura discovers that Nellie purchased her cards in town after the other girls did.) Arrogantly certain of her ability to manipulate males, she takes the candy that Cap Garland brings for Mary Power and annoys Laura by saying that she will ride with Almanzo. When she does so, in *These Happy Golden Years*, Nellie is as talkative and domineering as when she bullied Cap. As in the candy episode, Laura stops Nellie's interference. Laura deliberately scares the horses to reveal to Almanzo that Nellie is afraid of them, and then she firmly tells Almanzo that she will not ride again with Nellie. The last word about Nellie is that she has gone to live with relatives in New York.

Laura's other schoolmates are kinder. **Ida Wright Brown**, adopted daughter of Reverend Brown, is modest, good-natured, and hard-working. Because her father is a tailor, **Mary Power** wears stylish clothes. She is too proud to say anything when Nellie grabs the candy that Cap Garland brings for her. **Cap Garland** is fun-loving, but he is also hardworking and enterprising. He is truly heroic when he accompanies Almanzo on the dangerous winter journey to find wheat for the starving town. Although he is spunky and enjoys teasing Laura, he does not understand how to deal with an aggressive, manipulative girl like Nellie Oleson. He thus stands silent and helpless every day when she takes the candy he wants to give to Mary Power.

Two of Laura's students bear mentioning. Sixteen-year-old **Martha Harrison** brings out Laura's considerate nature. By studying with Martha, who has trouble understanding grammar, Laura gives her the confidence to learn on her own. **Clarence Brewster**, a big, tough, hardy boy who is older than Laura, tests the ability of Laura, who is small for her age, to manage a school through wit, not strength. Following her parents' advice, Laura cleverly avoids a confrontation with Clarence and, through a combination of subtle shaming and her own example of diligence, motivates him into keeping up with his studies. Like all of Laura's students, Clarence respects her at the end.

Further Reading

Berger, Laura Standley, ed. *Twentieth-Century Children's Writers*. 4th ed. Detroit: St. James, 1995.

Bingham, Jane M., ed. *Writers for Children: Critical Studies of Major Authors since the Seventeenth Century*. New York: Scribner's, 1988.

Cech, John, ed. *American Writers for Children, 1900-1960*. Vol. 22 of *Dictionary of Literary Biography*. Detroit: Gale Research, 1983.

Children's Literature Review. Vol. 2. Detroit: Gale Research, 1976.

Collier, Laurie, and Joyce Nakamura, eds. *Major Authors and Illustrators for Children and Young Adults*. Detroit: Gale Research, 1993.

Contemporary Authors. Vol. 137. Detroit: Gale Research, 1992.

Kunitz, Stanley J., and Howard Haycraft, eds. *The Junior Book of Authors*. 2nd ed. New York: H. W. Wilson, 1951.

Something about the Author. Vols. 15, 29. Detroit: Gale Research, 1979, 1982.

Spaeth, Janet. *Laura Ingalls Wilder*. Boston: Twayne, 1987.

Maia Wojciechowska

1927-, American tennis professional, editor, translator, and author

Shadow of a Bull

(novel, 1975)

PLOT: Wojciechowska has said that this Newbery Medal winner is "mostly about pride and being locked in." Young Manolo Olivar must maintain his self-esteem while gaining independence. Manolo lives in the shadow of his father, Juan Olivar, a great bullfighter who was killed in the ring. The Andalusian town of Arcangel expects Manolo to do precisely as his father did, and he doesn't want to disappoint the town. By the time he is nine years old, however, he believes that he is a coward because he is afraid to jump from a high hay wagon. When six *aficionados*, men who love bullfighting, see Manolo jump away from a speeding car one day, they decide to prepare him for his destiny by taking him to bullfights. Count de la Casa, the man who launched Juan Olivar's career, soon decides that Manolo should meet a bull

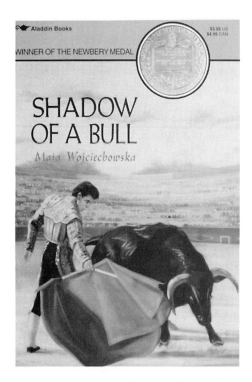

Young Manola Olivar tries to live up to his father's legacy in Wojciechowska's Newbery Medal-winning novel.

at the next *tienta*, or testing. Meanwhile, Manolo's best friend, Jaime García, is worried about his brother, Juan, who practices at night with bulls in nearby pastures. When Manolo goes to ask Juan about fear, Juan's embittered father, Señor García, tells about his own lack of opportunity to become a successful bullfighter. Manolo then promises to get Juan a chance to show his skills. That night, Juan and Manolo practice passes with a bull. It knocks Juan down, but the frightened Manolo saves him. The next day, the same bull gores "El Magnifico," a young matador. Manolo helps the attending doctor and decides that he wants to be a doctor himself.

The night before the *tienta*, Manolo's mother tells him that his father was proud and did things for himself. In the morning, the *aficionados* tell him that even his father felt fear. Manolo then meets Alfonso Castillo, the greatest of bullfight critics, who tells him that, instead of trying to be like his father, Manolo must be himself. Looking at a painting of his

father meeting his first bull, Manolo decides that this may be his day to become a man. He then faces his first bull. Although he shows some grace, he soon becomes awkward. After announcing that he does not want to be a bullfighter, Manolo turns the bull over to Juan García, who delights the spectators. Manolo sits in the stands with the doctor, who tells Manolo that he will become a fine doctor.

CHARACTERS: In Manolo's struggle to choose between public expectation and private desire, secondary characters have a choric role in voicing key elements of his debate. **Manolo Olivar** demonstrates that courage takes different forms. At first, Manolo feels trapped by fate, believing that he can make no honorable choice about the direction of his life. Manolo resembles his famous father: he is thin and has the same sad eyes and long nose, a conventional sign of bravery. His fear of jumping from a hay cart or of being hit by a speeding car, however, leads Manolo to believe that he is a coward. Nevertheless, Manolo has pride. He does not want to disappoint the town, which financially provided for him and his mother after his father's death, and he does not want to shame himself, his family, or the town. Consequently, he allows the six *aficionados* to teach him about bullfighting, and he secretly practices cape moves so that he will not be embarrassed when he meets his first bull. Although Manolo appreciates the art in bullfighting, he fervently prays that he will never have to kill a bull. A sensitive boy, he believes that becoming a doctor is the noblest of callings.

At the age of eleven, Manolo undergoes a coming of age in which he ironically follows his father's footsteps but establishes his independence. Manolo frees himself from the town's expectations while maintaining his pride and self-worth because he learns from others. His mother tells him that his father always determined for himself what he would do. The *aficionados* tell him that even his father felt fear, making Manolo realize that he has confused natural fear with cowardice. Finally, Alfonso Castillo insists that Manolo is not like his father and must be himself to be honorable. Inspired by these lessons and a portrait of his father's ceremonial coming of age, Manolo displays physical courage by facing the bull. Most importantly, he displays the moral courage to be true to himself by declaring that he does not want to be a bullfighter. Generously and without envy, he points out that Juan García is the great bullfighter that the town desires. By then joining the doctor in the stands, Manolo refuses to be a victim of fate; instead, he comes of age as a man who, like his father, chooses his own course.

The choric figures represent community pressure or advocate free will. **Count de la Casa** represents the power of the community. A wealthy man of nearly seventy years who spends most of his time in France, the Count is a straight, thin man with close-set, black eyes and a harsh voice. Because he was instrumental in starting Juan Olivar's career, he assumes the right to determine Manolo's life. Thus, whenever he meets Manolo, the conversations are ritualistic and identical, never allowing Manolo to emerge as an individual. The **six aficionados** function as a single character. Always together, they look identical in black suits and white shirts, and they talk and think alike. These devoted followers of Juan Olivar's career actively express the community's desires. Passionately in love with bullfighting, they refuse to acknowledge Manolo's individuality, insisting that he do everything exactly as his father did. Ironically, their admission that Juan Olivar felt fear starts Manolo on his way to freeing himself from their power.

The primary advocate of free will is **Alfonso Castillo**, the most famous of bullfight critics. A gaunt man with deep-set eyes who is confined to a wheelchair because of an auto accident, he is the voice of wise experience. He sees immediately that Juan García is a born bullfighter and that Manolo is not like his father. More importantly, Castillo understands fear, which may have contributed to his accident because he was on his way to fight a bull when it occurred. He thus teaches Manolo that courage is the ability to act in spite of fear. He also articulates the central theme, noting that a man has a choice between being true or untrue to himself. **The doctor** is another example of the wise old man archetype. An old, white-haired man who shuffles tiredly, except when tending a patient, he, like

Castillo, sees immediately that Manolo is not a born bullfighter. The doctor also offers advice indirectly, pointing out that the tragedy of bullfighting is that it wastes lives because many boys know of nothing else to do. By forcing Manolo to help him to tend "El Magnifico's" wounds, the doctor gives Manolo wider knowledge and inspires him to want to become a doctor himself. Manolo's mother, **Señora Olivar**, a quiet, pale woman, who claims to have prayed for a daughter so that her child would not have to be a bullfighter, seems resigned to her son's fate. Nevertheless, she influences his decision to reject bullfighting when she tells Manolo that his father was a noble and honorable man because he never let others dictate his actions.

The members of the García family act as foils. Fourteen-year-old **Juan García** has the *aficinç*, or passionate love of bullfighting, that Manolo lacks. In spite of the danger, Juan goes out at night to practice with the bulls in the pastures. Juan's obvious bravery and confidence contrast with Manolo's constant fear and sense of cowardice. Cheerful and good-natured, Juan understands that Manolo was afraid when he saved him from the bull. Later, he cheerfully admits that he is both afraid and excited when he challenges bulls. Juan thus voices a lesson about courage and the deceptive nature of appearances. **Señor García**, a short, unkempt man, is a bitter recluse whose spirit has been broken by his failure to be a successful bullfighter. Because he fought bulls that had already been in the ring, he was gored many times and blinded in one eye. When he worked as a *banderillero*, Juan Olivar mistakenly fired him for drinking. Señor García's feeling that his family is ill-fated because they do not have an opportunity to be successful bullfighters ironically emphasizes Manolo's sense that he is unlucky precisely because he is destined to be a bullfighter. **Jaime García**, Manolo's best friend, unintentionally makes Manolo lose self-confidence. Jaime seems so delighted to jump from the hay wagon that he makes the fearful Manolo think of himself as a coward.

Further Reading

Authors and Artists for Young Adults. Vol. 8. Detroit: Gale Research, 1992.

Berger, Laura Standley, ed. *Twentieth-Century Young Adult Writers*. 1st ed. Detroit: St. James, 1994.

Collier, Laurie, and Joyce Nakamura, eds. *Major Authors and Illustrators for Children and Young Adults*. Detroit: Gale Research, 1993.

Contemporary Authors New Revision Series. Vol. 41. Detroit: Gale Research, 1993.

Contemporary Literary Criticism. Vol. 26. Detroit: Gale Research, 1983.

Children's Literature Review. Vol. 1. Detroit: Gale Research, 1976.

De Montreville, Doris, and Donna Hill, eds. *Third Book of Junior Authors*. New York: H. W. Wilson, 1972.

Something about the Author. Vols. 1, 28. Detroit: Gale Research, 1971, 1982.

Something about the Author Autobiography Series. Vol. 1. Detroit: Gale Research, 1986.

Wintle, Justin, and Emma Fisher. *The Pied Pipers: Interviews with the Influential Creators of Children's Literature*. New York: Paddington Press, 1974.

Patricia Wrightson

1921-, Australian novelist

The Nargun and the Stars

(fantasy, 1973)

PLOT: This Australian fantasy explores themes of personal identity and environmental sensitivity. After his parents are killed, Simon Brent goes to Wongadilla, a sheep station owned by distant relatives—Charlie Waters and his sister, Edie. Simon misses the sounds of the city. Hating that Charlie calls him Simey, he refuses to call Charlie and Edie anything at all. While exploring one day, Simon scratches his name in the lichen on a boulder, which he later discovers is the Nargun, a stone monster that has wandered into Wongadilla. After Simon places a frog killed by a road grader in the swamp, the Potkoorok, a frog-like trickster, befriends him. During a fierce storm that night, Simon sees the Turongs, spirits of the trees, carry away the grader.

He also notices the Nargun near the house. After the Potkoorok tells him about the Nargun, Simon tells Charlie and Edie. He then realizes that Edie has been giving him two apples so that he can share with the Potkoorok; he therefore calls her by name for the first time.

After they discover that they can't move the sheep-killing Nargun, Charlie seeks the Potkoorok's advice. It sends him to the Turongs, who send him to the Nyols, spirits living in the mountain. Simon, Charlie's messenger, can't get the Nyols to help, but he sees that they have carried inside the mountain a bulldozer that had been used for clearing trees. He further learns that noise bothers the Nargun. Finally, angered because Simon doesn't recognize his abilities, the Potkoorok decides to prove his powers. It takes Simon underwater, through a frighteningly narrow opening, and into the Nyols' caves. There it creates an illusion of a flood on which the Rainbow snake is swimming. The trick drives the Nyols from their caves, allowing Charlie to start the noisy bulldozer. Meanwhile Simon and Edie drive around in the tractor, making noise to keep the Nargun away from the house. They narrowly escape when the angry Nargun destroys their tractor. The Nargun then heads after the bulldozer. The machine's vibrations cause a rock slide, sealing the Nargun in the cave, where the Nyols reverently tend it.

CHARACTERS: To create a fantasy appropriate to the Australian landscape, Wrightson bases the fantastic characters on figures from Aboriginal myths and tales instead of European stereotypes. **Simon Brent** comes to terms with his identity and learns to appreciate the land. A thin-faced boy with heavy brown hair and sullen brown eyes, Simon is filled with rage after his parents are killed in an automobile accident. Gruff, withdrawn, and lonely, he resents that Charlie calls him Simey, a nickname that challenges his sense of identity. He signals his resentment by refusing to call Charlie and Edie by name. He further indicates a need to assert his identity by scratching his name on a boulder (actually the Nargun). Simon is also at odds with nature, preferring the noise of machines to nature's silence. But Simon changes, ultimately seeing that the bulldozer is as much a monster as the Nargun, because he is remarkably sensitive. Simon has reverence for all life, as he shows by placing the dead frog in the swamp. The very fact that Simon sees the Potkoorok and other "old ones" also shows his sensitivity and growing understanding of the land. In turn, Simon's appreciation of the land helps him to feel at home. He thus calls Edie by name, accepting her because she has quietly fostered his friendship with the Potkoorok. He later also accepts Charlie, who teaches him how to communicate with nature's spirits. Through contact with nature, Simon acquires profound knowledge. He accepts that people live for a relatively brief time and can't truly own the land. Simon also learns that the Nargun, and nature in general, is neither good nor evil. Consequently, Simon can both fear and pity the Nargun.

Simon's actions follow the symbolic pattern of mythical heroism. His brave journey beneath the water and into the caves indicates a plunge into the unconscious. By squeezing through the narrow entrance to the Nyols' cavern, Simon is symbolically reborn. Subsequently, he helps to confine the Nargun, which bears his name and thus represents his own previous stonelike existence. Because the lichen in which Simon scratched his name withers, the Nargun's confinement suggests that Simon has come to terms with the loneliness, fear, and hostility that the Nargun represents.

Charlie Waters, who runs a sheep station, is an example of the elderly mentor common in pastoral romances. Taller and thinner than anyone Simon has ever seen, and with gray streaking his black hair and lines throughout his brown face, Charlie is a stereotypical country man. He is relatively inarticulate, punctuating his observations with "There you are, then" or a grunted "M'p." Nevertheless, he is patient, humble, and wise. He understands Simon's resentment and never criticizes him. He teaches him about stewardship of the land, calling himself "the man in charge" instead of "the owner." He shows trust in Simon by bequeathing him the land and teaches him the etiquette involved in communicat-

ing with the old ones. Charlie can, however, be wily. He is patient with the Potkoorok but uses veiled threats to coerce its cooperation. When the final confrontation with the Nargun comes, Charlie is brave and resourceful. **Edie Waters**, his sister, is a second cousin of Simon's mother. Stout but with skinny legs, she has a face like wilting petals and gray eyes. She is compared to the swamp because of her profound stillness. Edie is kind and understanding, silently promoting Simon's closeness with nature by giving him apples to share with the Potkoorok. Edie is not skillful when driving the tractor, but she is brave.

The "old ones" are spirits associated with specific features of the land. **The Nargun** is both a primeval monster and a symbol. As a physical entity, the Nargun is a squat, solid creature of stone with a blunt-muzzled head, indentations for eyes, and rough arms and legs. Sometimes standing erect and sometimes on all fours, it moves at night because light makes it uneasy. Its cry is a savage "Nga-a-a!" As old as the earth itself, the Nargun is psychologically primitive. Lonely and filled with longing, it feels love for the earth and anger when it sees changes in nature or when it is hungry. It eats at intervals from ten to fifty years. Although it is monstrous because it kills humans, the Nargun is not evil. It violates only one Aboriginal law, moving from its home territory to a place where it does not belong because technology disturbed it. As a symbol, the Nargun is a projection of Simon's psychological condition. Like Simon, it is a stranger in Wongadilla. By bearing his name, it suggests that his grief and hatred have turned him to stone. After the Nargun is confined to the cave, the withering of the lichen with Simon's name suggests that Simon has successfully confined his grief, anger, and sorrow.

The Potkoorok is a trickster, mentor, and helper who is both silly and profound. A water spirit living in the swamp, the Potkoorok is about two feet tall. He has yellow-green skin, webbed feet and fingers, and a froglike face with golden eyes. The Potkoorok delights in tricking humans. Some tricks, such as tripping Simon, are childish; some, such as hiding the grader in the swamp, represent living nature's war with technology. Regardless, the

Potkoorok marks each of its triumphs with a watery chuckle. The Potkoorok is notably pompous and self-important. Annoyingly, it expresses superiority by responding to Simon's queries with its own questions. Nevertheless, it possesses ancient wisdom and imparts thematically important messages. It teaches Simon that the Nargun is neither good nor evil, thus suggesting that Simon must take nature on its own terms. It also points out that men can't own the land because their stay on earth is relatively brief. The Potkoorok is itself neither good nor bad. It helps in the battle against the Nargun only because Simon innocently wounds its pride by suggesting that it could not go as far as the mountain. Although it helps only to boast about its own power, it fulfills the role of the animal-helper of folklore. Thus, it gives Simon magical powers to breathe underwater and it leads him through the passage that marks his symbolic rebirth. **The Turongs**, sticklike tree spirits with scraggly beards, are also tricksters. Their presence emphasizes that nature is alive but is vulnerable to destruction by technology. **The Nyols**, the spirits of rock, are strong creatures who love to wrestle. They honor the Nargun as their "dreaming," or point of origin. They add ironic pathos to its fate, treating is as a god by softly crooning to it and offering it meals of dead lizards while it wanders in their caves.

Further Reading

Authors and Artists for Young Adults. Vol. 5. Detroit: Gale Research, 1991.

Berger, Laura Standley, ed. *Twentieth-Century Young Adult Writers.* 1st ed. Detroit: St. James, 1994.

Children's Literature Review. Vols. 4, 14. Detroit: Gale Research, 1982, 1988.

Collier, Laurie, and Joyce Nakamura, eds. *Major Authors and Illustrators for Children and Young Adults.* Detroit: Gale Research, 1993.

Contemporary Authors New Revision Series. Vol. 36. Detroit: Gale Research, 1992.

Rees, David. "Aboriginals and Happy Folk." In *What Do Draculas Do?: Essays on Contemporary Writers of Fiction for Children and Young Adults.* Metuchen, N.J.: Scarecrow Press, 1990.

Something about the Author. Vols. 8, 66. Detroit: Gale Research, 1976, 1992.

Something about the Author Autobiography Series. Vol. 4. Detroit: Gale Research, 1987.

Johann David Wyss
1743-1818, Swiss army chaplain and pastor

The Swiss Family Robinson
(novel, 1812-1813; published in German as Der schweizerishche Robinson*)*

PLOT: Written by Johann David Wyss and published under the name of his son, Johann Rudolf Wyss (1781-1830), who edited the manuscript, this novel has been expanded and altered by various writers, notably Baroness Isabelle de Montolieu. Designed to illustrate Rousseau's theories of education, *The Swiss Family Robinson* is filled with long discourses and often inaccurate descriptions of natural life. As fiction, it lacks notable conflict: living in a tropical paradise, the family easily overcomes even the gravest of dangers. Nevertheless, some adventures, such as the one in which a boa swallows a donkey, are memorable.

When the ship on which they are emigrating wrecks on a reef, the Robinson family is abandoned by the sailors. After spending a night on board, pastor Robinson builds a vessel out of tubs. Filling it with supplies, he and his family—his wife, Elizabeth, and their four sons, Fritz, Ernest, Jack, and Franz (Francis)—safely paddle to a deserted island. They thank God for deliverance and then make camp, using sails for a tent. They obtain their first food when a lobster bites Jack and they catch it. While Elizabeth and the boys work on domestic arrangements, the father and Fritz explore the island, bringing back gourds to use as bowls, coconuts, and sugar cane. Trouble comes when they must defend their camp against jackals. Over the next weeks, the father and Fritz make several trips back to the ship, towing back domesticated animals and other supplies. After stripping every useful item from it, they explode the ship.

The ship's supplies, as well as its doors and windows, become useful when the Robinsons erect a tree house that gives them security from animals. Later, Pastor Robinson even builds a spiral staircase inside the giant tree's trunk. They plant crops, raise animals, hunt, fight off predators such as monkeys and jackals, and explore their new home. They make everything from pottery to clothing; they encounter an impossible array of animals, including penguins, kangaroos, and lions. They also tame buffaloes and ostriches for use as steeds. The family then moves into a cave, converting it into an elegant home, and they erect a barrier to prevent the most dangerous animals from entering their realm. Ten years later, Fritz finds a message attached to the leg of an albatross. Setting off in his kayak, he rescues Emily Montrose, a shipwrecked English girl. Emily joins the family. Eventually, an English ship arrives. Three members of the Wolston family ask to live with the Robinsons, and Emily, Fritz, and Franz board the ship to sail to England.

CHARACTERS: The characters are wooden and static, undergoing no significant development. **Pastor Robinson** is a benign, impossibly learned patriarch. Following the methods of Rousseau, he believes that he can educate his children by exciting their curiosity, allowing them time to figure things out, and then correcting their errors. However admirable as pedagogy, the author's methods are absurd dramatically. For example, Pastor Robinson actually takes the time to deliver a discourse on the principle of the lever when they are trying to build a craft to leave the abandoned ship. Mr. Robinson himself has an incredible store of knowledge about every plant and animal they encounter. He also possesses exceptional manual skills. He is a superb carpenter, and he has the patience to become adept at other crafts, such as candle making and pottery. He is kind, protecting his wife and the younger children from distressing news. He is also cautious, dressing as a native until he is assured that the rescue ship is not manned by pirates. **Mrs. Elizabeth Robinson**, his wife, is an idealized homemaker, ever ready with her handy sewing basket to repair or stitch some needed item. She is adaptable, learning to make food out of new substances and contriving to decorate her cave home to make the family both comfortable and civilized. She is a hard worker, tending the animals and crops. On a few occasions, she is a stereotypically

Lynd Ward's illustration of Wyss's Robinson family.

worried female, but she is generally brave. An observant and creative woman, she is the one who suggests building a tree house.

Fritz Robinson, a handsome, curly-haired boy, is not yet fifteen years of age when he arrives on the island. His father's favorite, Fritz is a brave and able boy. Early in the adventure, he displays a bad temper, striking out with his gun at some fighting dogs. He is also jealous of his brothers' adventures, wanting to be the first to achieve each accomplishment. As he matures, he controls these traits. Fritz is clever in training an eagle to hunt. He is knowledgeable and resourceful, remembering how to roast a wild pig in the Tahitian manner. He is a brave explorer and sets out in his kayak to rescue Emily. He is also a gentleman, protecting Emily by first presenting her as a boy. Obviously restless, he decides to return to Europe. **Ernest**, who is twelve when he reaches the island, is a lazy, pleasure-loving child. But he is also extremely clever, coming up with solutions to numerous problems. Somewhat selfish at first, he obtains shells for the family to use as spoons in the soup pot, but he reserves a mussel shell for himself that is large enough to be a soup bowl. As he matures, Ernest devotes himself to study, learning so much about nature that his father calls him the doctor and the philosopher. Ernest is not as adventurous as the others, preferring to stay at camp with his mother, a preference he worries about but accepts after his father explains how useful he is. Ernest decides to stay on the island because it offers opportunities for study.

Jack Robinson, who is ten years old when he arrives on the island, is the only one whose character undergoes a transformation. A light-hearted and audacious child, he is the least intellectual and least knowledgeable family member. Ernest even fools him into thinking that the bones of a whale that he earlier saw beached are those of a mammoth. Nevertheless, Jack has abilities. He is a skilled marksman, and he is the most adept at riding wild animals, especially the ostrich. He even makes a jackal into a pet. Jack is rash (he foolishly strikes at a beehive) and he is boastful, bragging about his riding and his other accomplishments. In the second half of the novel, which Wyss did not write, Jack becomes a coward. Even his father joins in the mockery when Jack, fooled into believing that a jaguar is approaching, flees in terror. **Franz**, called **Francis** in most translations, is a sweet and happy six-year-old at the time of the shipwreck. The family dotes on him. Perhaps because he is so young and must remain with his mother during many adventures, his character is hardly developed. When the opportunity arises, he leaves for Europe. **Emily Montrose**, a young English girl who spent three solitary years on an island after being shipwrecked, is obviously brave and resourceful. Cautious of her virtue, she at first appears among the Robinsons disguised as a boy. They readily accept her as a sister, however, and she becomes part of the family. She even calls Pastor Robinson "Papa."

Further Reading

Collier, Laurie, and Joyce Nakamura, eds. *Major Authors and Illustrators for Children and Young Adults.* Detroit: Gale Research, 1993.

Something about the Author. Vols. 27, 29. Detroit: Gale Research, 1982, 1982.

Taro Yashima

(pen name for Jun Atsushi Iwamatsu)

1908-1994, American artist, illustrator, and author

Crow Boy

(picture book, 1955)

PLOT: Set in a Japanese village, this simple story traces a lonely boy's growth in self-esteem and shows how a community comes to understand and accept those who are different. On the first day of classes, a boy is found hiding under the school. Nicknamed Chibi, or "tiny boy," he is so frightened that he doesn't learn anything or make friends with the other children. Always left to himself, he draws inward, amusing himself by looking at and listening to everything around him. Consequently, everyone calls him stupid.

Five years pass. A new teacher, Mr. Isobe, is amazed at Chibi's knowledge of nature. He displays Chibi's drawings and writing, and he talks to him in private. At the talent show, Mr. Isobe announces that Chibi will imitate the voices of crows. The children are scornful at first, but Chibi's remarkable crow sounds touch them, and they become sorry that they were cruel to him. After graduation, Chibi receives a new name. When he comes to the village to sell charcoal, everyone greets him as Crow Boy, a name he likes.

CHARACTERS: The impressionistic drawings communicate Chibi's inner world. White spaces suggest his initial isolation, whereas his dominant position as the object of everyone's attention in the later pictures conveys the change in his status. **Chibi**, or **tiny boy**, earns a new identity as **Crow Boy**. At first, Chibi is named and judged according to his appearance. He is a very small boy who is afraid of the teacher and the other children. To avoid the pain of rejection and loneliness, Chibi retreats into an inner world. He crosses his eyes so that he won't see the taunting faces of his classmates. He also studies the patterns of the world that surrounds him and listens

Taro Yashima's Chibi earns the respect of the other children in the author's self-illustrated **Crow Boy.**

carefully to its sounds. Because he is silent and different, the children mock him as stupid. Chibi reveals his true identity because Mr. Isobe treats him with kindness and sympathy. In the talent show, Chibi displays his great sensitivity to nature and a remarkable ability to mimic all phases of the life of crows. Chibi thus shows that he is at heart an artist who can move others by imitating nature. He also reveals his courage and determination. He has developed his skill during the long walks from his remote home to the school. In spite of the length of the journey and the abuse he endured when he arrived, Chibi is the only student to have perfect attendance through all six years. By renaming him Crow Boy, then, the other students no longer focus on his appearance. Instead, they publicly acknowledge that he is a boy with a unique identity, a boy sensitive to his environment and talented in helping others to imagine it.

Mr. Isobe, the sixth grade teacher, transforms Chibi, thereby demonstrating the power of acceptance and understanding. A kind and friendly man, Mr. Isobe shows that Chibi is not stupid, as the others think, by letting him share his great knowledge of nature on school outings and in the school garden. He gives Chibi a sense of self-worth and makes him feel that he belongs by displaying his work, even though no one else is able to read Chibi's writing. He also takes the time to talk to Chibi, thus learning about his life. He puts his knowledge to use having Chibi perform his crow calls. By giving Chibi the chance to move others and by following Chibi's performance with an explanation of his lonely life, Mr. Isobe becomes the ideal teacher. He draws out the talents of his student, teaching the poor, lonely boy to have confidence. Just as significantly, he teaches an entire community to be tolerant and to avoid hasty judgments.

Further Reading

Berger, Laura Standley, ed. *Twentieth-Century Children's Writers.* 4th ed. Detroit: St. James, 1995.

Children's Literature Review. Vol. 4. Detroit: Gale Research, 1982.

Collier, Laurie, and Joyce Nakamura, eds. *Major Authors and Illustrators for Children and Young Adults.* Detroit: Gale Research, 1993.

Contemporary Authors New Revision Series. Vol. 45. Detroit: Gale Research, 1995.

Fuller, Muriel, ed. *More Junior Authors.* New York: H. W. Wilson, 1963.

Something about the Author. Vols. 14, 81. Detroit: Gale Research, 1978, 1995.

Jane Yolen

1939-, American author and editor

Commander Toad in Space

(animal science fiction fantasy, 1980; illustrated by Bruce Degen)

PLOT: The Commander Toad series of early readers satirizes *Star Wars* and other space adventures. Commander Toad is captain of The *Star Warts*, a long, green spaceship that resembles a tadpole in Degen's pictures. In the first adventure, Commander Toad, Mr. Hop, and Lieutenant Lily prepare to land on a new planet. Jake Skyjumper informs them, however, that the planet is entirely covered by water. Commander Toad therefore takes along a rubber lily pad, which becomes a floating landing site for his space skimmer. While the crew is on the lily pad, the angry monster Deep Wader jumps out of the sea. Lieutenant Lily shoots him, but Deep Wader laughs as if tickled. The waves created by the monster's jumps shake the space skimmer off the lily pad. Although it seems as if the crew can't return to their ship, Commander Toad saves the day. While Mr. Hop tells riddles and Lieutenant Lily sings in order to distract the monster, he uses lighted candles to fill the lily pad with hot air. Just when the monster decides to eat them, the lily pad, now a hot air balloon, rises. While they sail toward the *Star*

Warts, Lieutenant Lily asks how they can consider themselves brave when all they did was run away. Commander Toad replies that one needs to be afraid before being brave. Since she was afraid, Lieutenant Lily agrees with Commander Toad that they were all brave. They then resume their mission of finding new planets, where, Mr. Hop says, they won't have to be so brave.

Sequels are Commander Toad and the Planet of the Grapes *(1982),* Commander Toad and the Big Black Hole *(1983),* Commander Toad and the Dis-Asteroid *(1985),* Commander Toad and the Intergalactic Spy *(1986), and* Commander Toad and the Space Pirates *(1987).*

CHARACTERS: Bruce Degen's drawings, which are reminiscent of Arnold Lobel's pictures of Frog and Toad, provide the physical descriptions of the crew. Their actions and conversations, however, give them distinct personalities.

Throughout the series, **Commander Toad** is called "brave and bright, bright and brave." He repeatedly lives up to this description. He shows his ingenuity by using the rubber lily pad as a landing site and by later converting it into a balloon. Commander Toad is dedicated; although the others relax after they land, he listens attentively and is the first to hear the monster. Commander Toad shows bravery during the confrontation with Deep Wader because he does not panic. He also shows that he is a good leader when he reassures Lieutenant Lily that she has been brave in spite of her great fear. As the pictures indicate, Commander Toad's companions are frogs. **Mr. Hop**, the copilot, is described as one who thinks deep thoughts. He frequently closes his eyes to concentrate. Significantly, Commander Toad always comes up with a solution before Mr. Hop can. In fact, when the monster attacks, Mr. Hop can't offer a plan because he is "thought out" and seasick. Nevertheless, Mr. Hop understands Commander Toad's intentions before Lieutenant Lily does, and he has wit enough to give the monster a riddle. He is also pragmatic about bravery, pointing out to Lieu-

Two of Yolen's comical amphibian heroes from
Commander Toad in Space.

tenant Lily that one can't be brave in a monster's stomach. **Lieutenant Lily** is the only female crew member, and her portrait breaks sexual stereotypes. Lieutenant Lily, that is, is the most physically accomplished of the crew. She loves machines and fixes the spaceship's engines. She smiles when ordered to bring a gun because she is the best shot of them all. She also does dangerous and strenuous things. She is lowered by rope to inflate the lily pad and to test its safety. The only weakness in her portrait occurs when she seems to panic after the skimmer falls into the sea. Nevertheless, she proves brave afterwards. Having once been in a musical called *Warts and Peace*, she even sings to distract the monster. **Jake Skyjumper**, the navigator, is the youngest crew member. Jake always stays behind when the crew lands on a planet, so he does not play a major role. Jake draws the maps for the ship's journeys, and he

ensures their safety by informing the landing party that the new world is covered in water. (Beginning with the second book of the series, **Doc Peep**, a doctor who wears a grass-green wig, becomes a crew member.)

Yolen describes herself as an "incorrigible punster." Thus, she mocks Darth Vader, the villain of *Star Wars*, by naming the monster **Deep Wader**. He is pictured as a fanciful beast with a chubby body, webbed feet, a tail tipped with an arrow head, wings, and a large head filled with teeth. The text indicates that his spotted body is black, white, all colors, and no color. His terrible roar is frightening, but his singing is worse. He is slightly silly when he is distracted by the riddle and song. Nevertheless, he is clearly dangerous and nasty, for he puns on Commander Toad's statement that they have come in peace, saying that he likes them in chewy pieces. Because the crew cannot physically defeat him—their ray guns merely tickle him—his function is to test their wit.

Further Reading

Authors and Artists for Young Adults. Vol. 4. Detroit: Gale Research, 1990.

Berger, Laura Standley, ed. *Twentieth-Century Young Adult Writers.* Detroit: St. James, 1994.

Children's Literature Review. Vol. 4. Detroit: Gale Research, 1982.

Collier, Laurie, and Joyce Nakamura, eds. *Major Authors and Illustrators for Children and Young Adults.* Detroit: Gale Research, 1993.

Contemporary Authors New Revision Series. Vol. 29. Detroit: Gale Research, 1990.

De Montreville, Doris, and Elizabeth D. Crawford, eds. *Fourth Book of Junior Authors.* New York: H. W. Wilson, 1978.

Estes, Glenn E., ed. *American Writers for Children since 1960: Fiction.* Vol. 52 of *Dictionary of Literary Biography.* Detroit: Gale Research, 1986.

Something about the Author. Vols. 4, 40, 75. Detroit: Gale Research, 1973, 1985, 1994.

Something about the Author Autobiography Series. Vol. 1. Detroit: Gale Research, 1986.

Character and Title Index

C

E

H